CCH®

2009 U.S. MASTER™

Human Resources Guide

Donald W. Myers, D.B.A.

Wolters Kluwer
Law & Business

Publisher: Paul Gibson

Executive Editor: Joy Waltemath

Coordinating Editor: David L. Stephanides

Production Editor: Amy M. Mathews

ISBN 978-0-8080-2037-0

4025 W. Peterson Ave., Chicago, IL 60645-6085

1-800-248-3248

hr.cch.com

A WoltersKluwer Company

PREFACE

Things have changed during the past year, but one enduring fact remains—human resources management continues to be one of the most challenging fields of work that exists. Tantamount among the challenges are an enlarging and changing body of knowledge, an expanding role in both strategic and tactical management, and an increasing obligation for organizational success. When today's typical practitioner commenced a career in human resources, the field was long on art and relatively short in science. Today, things have changed. Skill in practicing human resources is still important, but the body of knowledge has burgeoned to the point that even the most accomplished individuals are challenged to master it. Mastery, however, is the crucial first step for a practitioner's credentials. Just like the adage that guides decisionmaking in job evaluation, "One thinks and does with what one knows," comprehending the body of knowledge in human resources is fundamental to effectively perform work within the field. Furthermore, unlike other disciplines, the body of human resources knowledge frequently changes, requiring continuing career development and life-long learning. Some changes are revolutionary; thus, what may be true today is false tomorrow. Other changes are evolutionary; the benchmark of techniques or procedures for today may be outmoded by next year. One purpose of this *Guide* is to significantly aid practitioners in maintaining a state-of-the art knowledge of human resources.

The attainment of a professional designation is evidence that one has successfully demonstrated mastery of the body of knowledge within a discipline. There are various designations available within human resources, depending upon one's personal and career inclinations. The *Professional in Human Resources* and the *Senior Professional in Human Resources* are two designations frequently sought by practitioners. The material in this *Guide* includes those subjects in the subject matter content outline of the test specifications, as defined by the Human Resources Certification Institute, which is used in preparing the examinations for those two designations. Consequently, the *Guide* is an excellent resource to use either alone in preparing for the certification examinations or to supplement other study materials. The *Guide's* index contains all of the subjects in the body of knowledge either separately or under the appropriate general heading.

Staffing firms continue to perform essential human resources roles to employers. In 2004, 3.5 million jobs were handled by staffing firms. During the period 2004 – 2014 staffing firm employment is expected to increase by 45 percent. This revision of the *Guide* includes an analysis of the expected growth of staffing firms' employment by major occupational groups.

The Fair Labor Standards Act poses difficulties for some employers; even those in very large firms. The most frequent problems involve misclassifying workers as supervisors, failing to pay overtime, and violating child labor provisions. The *Guide* contains a full discussion of the latest provisions (including those in the Genetic Information Nondiscrimination Act of 2008) in the Act in these and other areas.

The Iraq war caused a number of challenges for employers, such as filling vacancies in critical jobs created by employees in National Guard units activated for extensive tours of duty. Employers of active duty personnel must follow the provisions of the Uniformed Services Employment and Reemployment Rights Act of 1994, such as ensuring these employees continue to receive the benefits of employment while on active duty and reemployment rights are extended to them when they return. The *Guide* contains extensive material on the latest provisions of this law.

This edition of the *Guide* contains a new and full explanation of the Family and Medical Leave Act of 1993, as amended, that seamlessly incorporates the comprehensive new material in the "Final FMLA Rule." The new rule took effect January 16, 2009. This explanation was organized to facilitate HR professional's understanding of, and compliance with, the FMLA, as amended. Among many changes are provisions for leave requests for "qualifying exigencies" due to National Guard and Reserve unit deployments and up to 26-weeks of leave to care for a "covered servicemember" with a serious injury or illness. In addition to these subjects this edition of the *Guide* includes all the other changes, such as provisions to address employer and employee notice requirements, medical certification, fitness-for-duty certification, intermittent and reduced schedule leave, substitution of paid leave, light duty assignments, breaks in service, employee's worksite definitions, joint employer coverage and provisions that conform with the 2002 U.S. Supreme Court's decision in *Ragsdale v. Wolverine World Wide Inc.* Special rules apply to school employees and these were included in this edition. Terms are fully defined both as they appear in the material and at the end of the law's discussion. Finally, Appendix 4 was added to the *Guide* for the inclusion of copies of all the new and revised forms for employer use to meet notice requirements, to obtain health care provider certifications of employee's and family member's serious health conditions, for certifications of serious injury or illness of covered servicemembers and for certifications of qualifying exigencies for military family leave. Material in the *Guide* references each form at the appropriate provision of the FMLA, so Appendix 4 should aid understanding by relating the forms to provisions.

Many employers have used the occasion of the large influx of veterans being separated from active military service to offer incentives to these individuals to retain their coverage in the Department of Defense healthcare program (Tricare) in lieu of enrollment in the employer's health plan. This practice shifted health-care costs from employers to the U. S. Government, according to legislators who supported the law. To prevent the practice, a new law which was effective January 1, 2008, the John Warner National Defense Authorization Act, prohibits this practice for public and private employers with 20 or more employees. Each violation of the Act subjects the employer to a $5,000 fine.

Employee access to workplace computers has dramatically increased productivity but not without some serious issues for employers resulting from improper computer use, such as security breaches, computer misuse and even criminal activity. These issues raise the prospect of legal liabilities for employers and are costly in other ways including lost productivity when computers are used for non-business purposes and the loss of business resulting from security breaches. Last year's edition of the *Guide* had an extensive review of this topic. This edition contains new information related to the *Quon* case involving communications disclosures by employers, supervisors, and internet service providers or electronic communications facilities. This is an emerging area in which HR professionals should seek legal counsel before developing and implementing policy on the topic. In a somewhat related area, this edition reorganizes and cross-references material in which employers have responsibilities to maintain employee privacy and/or confidentiality of information.

HR professionals should get ready for the Genetic Information Nondiscrimination Act (GINA) which is effective November 21, 2009. This edition explains actions prohibited by this act. What is *genetic information*? Five of the basic areas of the definition are covered. Also discussed are the groups of employers covered by GINA. Most importantly, some suggestions are offered to help HR professionals get ready to comply with the law[1].

The ADA Amendments Act of 2008, which is effective January 1, 2009, is another important law that was enacted so courts would interpret the definition of a "person with a disability" in a manner consistent with how they defined a "handicapped person" under the Rehabilitation Act of 1973. The amendment specifically made reference to two U.S. Supreme Court cases, *Sutton v. United Air Lines* (1999) and *Toyota Motor Manufacturing, Kentucky, Inc. v. Williams* (2002), which narrowed the definition of a "person with a disability" beyond what Congress intended in the Americans with Disabilities Act of 1990. The amendment further states the EEOC's current regulations for the term "substantially limits" in the definition of a "person with a disability" are not consistent with Congress's intent since the standard is too high. These decisions of the court and the EEOC's definition are covered in the appropriate sections of this edition. The EEOC material will be revised in a future edition of the *Guide* when it issues new regulations mandated by the ADA Amendment.

This edition of the *Guide* contains an extensive revision of material pertaining to the I-9, including a section-by-section discussion of the responsibilities of both employees and employers and record retention/production provisions. The List A Documents has been changed and a summary of the new documents are in this revision. Also covered are the new penalties for each unauthorized alien that is employed and instances of knowingly employing undocumented workers and committing document fraud. The E-Verify Program is briefly discussed along with steps employers can follow to become IMAGE Certified, including the Best Employment Practices related to being certified. Finally, employers may not discriminate against aliens who are legally employable. This edition of the *Guide* contains the corrective actions and penalties for such discrimination.

A number of employers provide participants in wellness programs with health plan incentives, such as premium reductions and lower deductibles contingent upon the attainment of goals in these programs. Federal agencies esti-

---

[1] CCH, *Human Resources Management: Ideas & Trends* (July 16, 2008), p. 111.

mate about 30,000 plans with 1.1 million participants vary premiums among similarly situated participants based upon attainment of goals related to a health factor. The agencies estimate that about 13,000 plans with 460,000 participants vary benefits or offer lowered deductibles, among similarly situated employees based upon goal attainment. On their face, incentives appear health factor neutral, but conditions like heredity, may stymie the most diligent efforts, for example, to reduce low density lipoprotein cholesterol levels. To level the playing field, HIPAA nondiscrimination provisions, which were generally effective January 1, 2008, must be observed; this edition of the *Guide* discussions these provisions.

As noted above, GINA made extensive modifications in the child labor provisions of the FLSA. This edition of the Guide fully discusses child labor restrictions, including the definition of "serious injury" of a child. Also covered are the subjects of certificates of age and safe work acts/conditions/job training. This edition also covers violations of minimum wage and overtime pay.

Unions use various means to communicate with members. Email is a more technologically advanced method of communication and unions are increasingly resorting to its use, but legal issues arise when the email system used belongs to the employer. In one ruling, a majority of the National Labor Relations Board ruled that employers may prohibit employees from using the employer's email system to engage in union-related activities. In the case, the employer had permitted employees to use its email system for personal communications, but not with outside organizations. The Board ruled the union was an outside organization so the employer was consistent in denying it access to its email system. Subsequent to the Board's decision the NLRB's Office of the General Counsel issued five decisions in other cases to ensure consistency. This edition of the *Guide* contains a summary of these five decisions.

This edition of the Guide updates information on several other subjects. For example, on the topic of employment-at-will, estimates are made of the groups and numbers of employees who are not employed-at-will. Revised material on nonimmigrant visas for those seeking temporary employment in the U. S. is covered in this edition of the *Guide*. This material includes H-1B employer exemptions, H-1B advanced degree exemptions, and H-1B1 exemptions for non-immigrants from Chile and Singapore.

Six important decisions of the U. S. Supreme Court were made in 2008 that impacted HR. In *Chamber of Commerce of the United States of America et al. v. Brown, Attorney General of California, et al.* (2008), the Court ruled the provisions of California Govt. Code Ann. §§ 16645.2(a), 16645.7(a) prohibiting "employers that receive state grants or more than $10,000 in state program funds per year from using the funds 'to assist, promote, or deter union organizing'" are pre-empted by the NLRA.

In what the Court found to be an employment-at-will case [*Engquist v. Oregon Department of Agriculture et al.* (2008)] an employee alleged she was laid-off for "arbitrary, vindictive, and malicious reasons." In response to the suit, an appeals court ruled against her. In affirming the decision of the appeals court, the

U. S. Supreme Court ruled that treating ". . . an employee differently from others for a bad reason, or for no reason at all, is simply consistent with the at-will concept. The Constitution does not require repudiating that familiar doctrine."

In a defined contribution plan case, [*LaRue v. DeWolff, Boberg & Associates, Inc.* (2008)], an employee who was a participant in a defined contribution plan, alleged the plan administrator failed to exercise fiduciary responsibility by not following investment instructions resulting in a $150,000 loss. While the District and the Appellant Court ruled the individual was not entitled to recovery, the U. S. Supreme Court ruled that remedies are available in a defined contribution plan under the ERISA if an administrator's actions adversely affected an individual employee.

In *Meacham et al., v. Knolls Atomic Power Laboratory* (2008), a contractor for the federal government, who was ordered to reduce its number of employees, used a plan to appraise employees on their "performance," "flexibility," "critical skills," and gave points for years of service. Thirty of the 31 employees who were laid-off were at least 40 years old and some of them filed a disparate impact suit under the Age Discrimination in Employment Act. They used the results of an analysis conducted by a statistics expert to show that there was a statistically significant inverse relationship between the appraisals and age. The U.S. Supreme Court ruled that the contractor had the burden of production and persuasion for its "reasonable factors other than age" (RFOA) affirmative defense to the disparate impact suit.

In *Metropolitan Life Insurance Co. et al. v. Glenn* (2008), Metropolitan Life Insurance Company (MetLife) is the administrator and insurer for Sear, Roebuck and Company's long-term disability insurance plan. In fulfilling the dual roles of administrator and insurer, respectively, MetLife determines the validity of employee' claims and then pays benefits to employees with valid claims. An employee who was denied benefits from the plan filed suit. The U.S. Supreme Court said a potential conflict of interest exists when a benefits administrator both determines the validity of a claim and pays benefits on it. Whether the conflict is fairly resolved depends upon the administrator's actions, which in this case were unreasonable.

In a case involving the Fourth Amendment, the Stored Communications Act and California privacy rights [*Quon v. Arch Wireless Operating Co., Incorporated, a Delaware corporation; City of Ontario, a municipal corporation; Lloyd Scharf, individually and as Chief of Ontario Police Department; Ontario Police Department; Debbie Glenn, individually and as a Sergeant of Ontario Police Department* (2008)] the Court unanimously ruled that a page message search was a violation of the Fourth Amendment and "California constitutional privacy rights because (the plaintiffs-appellants) had a reasonable expectation of privacy in the content of the text messages and the search was unreasonable in scope." The Court ruled that based on the facts in the case only one defendant had qualified immunity, but "the Appellants' Stored Communications Act claim against Arch Wireless and the claims against the City, the Police Department and a sergeant under the Fourth Amendment and the California Constitution" could proceed.

In sum, this *Guide* was developed to provide a comprehensive and complete resource book to assist today's human resources practitioner with state-of-the art practices.

PERSONAL DEDICATION

To Phyllis Schiller Myers and Libby.

ACKNOWLEDGMENTS

Dr. Joseph Blacow of Monterey Peninsula College suggested human resources as a career for me many years ago, and it turned out that he was right. Before his death, I personally thanked him for his wise counsel, but I now do so in writing. Over the years, many persons have influenced my inclinations and development in this engrossing field. An important person was Lynn Taylor, an editor at Greenwood Press, who encouraged me to write my first book. I am also indebted to Tony Citera, who is now retired from CCH, Incorporated, for his encouragement to write for CCH. Others at CCH that I wish to acknowledge are Paul Gibson and Larry Norris. In conjunction with the development of this *Guide*, I wish to acknowledge the fine editorial work of Joy Waltemath.

I am fortunate in working at a university, where interaction among colleagues is encouraged. I particularly express appreciation to my colleague, Dr. George Gray, and to Dr. Phyllis Schiller Myers, my wife and colleague. I also acknowledge my friendship and professional association with Dr. Thomas H. Patten Jr., Professor of Human Resources and Director of Research, College of Business Administration, California Polytechnic University—Pomona, with whom I co-authored *Exercises for Developing Human Resources Management Skills*, also published by CCH.

Part of the joy of research and writing is sharing it with close friends and relatives. In the former category I cherish the friendship of Hank and Phyl Smith and Jim and Nancy Kopnisky. Family includes Drew and Barbara Cervasio, Beth, William, Ballard, Ralph, Mom Schiller, Sharon, Scott, Charles Myers and Carolee Western. Twenty years ago my brother, Charles Myers, a retired English instructor, gave me a two-hour tutorial in writing composition that has been invaluable to me. Over the years he helped me in other ways father-figure, protector, and above all, a friend.

International human resources management is a complex subsystem within human resources. While some activities are similar to those performed in a domestic environment, others, such as compensation systems and selection methods, differ. For over 18 years, I have received guidance in this fascinating area of human resources from Mr. Richard B. Jackson, the former Senior Vice President of Administration at Reynolds International, who is currently consulting in the field and teaching a course in International Human Resources Management at Virginia Commonwealth University.

One of the greatest pleasures in teaching is having the opportunity to participate in the education of the future leaders of business. I have witnessed many former students progress within human resources and other disciplines. Furthermore, I maintain contact with some former students and am pleased to interact with them regarding both personal and professional matters. There are too many names to formally acknowledge each one without the risk of omitting someone, so I hope it will suffice to simply acknowledge them all en masse. To my past and present students, one and all, I express my deepest gratitude for having the opportunity of sharing in your learning experience.

For ten years, I conducted two-day, semi-annual review sessions for human resources professionals preparing to take the *Professional in Human Resources* and the *Senior Professional in Human Resources* examinations. I especially looked forward to these opportunities to interact with practitioners who are motivated to test their mastery of the body of knowledge in their chosen profession. This is not an easy undertaking for them, since it requires hard work, motivation and discipline. I formally acknowledge the example these individuals have set for their peers in increasing the professionalism of human resources management.

Finally, I accept sole responsibility for any errors or omissions.

Donald W. Myers

December 2008

ABOUT THE AUTHOR

Donald W. Myers received a Bachelor of Arts degree from California State University-Sacramento and Master of Business Administration and Doctor of Business Administration degrees from Georgia State University.

Dr. Myers is Professor Emeritus of Human Resources Management in the School of Business at Virginia Commonwealth University, where he taught courses in basic and advanced HR management subjects. Two-time recipient of the Distinguished Teacher Award in the School of Business, as well as the Distinguished Professor in the School of Business, Dr. Myers is a prolific author, editor and respected researcher.

Contents

CHAPTER 1

THE HUMAN RESOURCES MANAGEMENT FUNCTION

Chapter Highlights
- Introduce the HRM/personnel function
- Briefly explain the major activities in HRM
- Explain the three types of authority of HR managers and specialists
- Understand the growing professionalism in HRM

Introduction

Few professions are more interesting and challenging for the practitioner than human resources management (HRM). HRM is interesting because it deals with the most important part of any private or public organization—its people—and how they are selected, developed and rewarded for the organization's mission to be accomplished. Organizational success depends upon qualified employees who are committed to performing their work at the optimum level of performance. Employees—people—do make the difference in an organization's success. For example, in a large metropolitan community, one chain of grocery stores was magnificently successful, while another one failed. They both offered basically the same products with no significant difference in prices. Other factors that are important in the grocery business were essentially the same for both stores, such as customer parking, location and convenience. In one category, however, the two chains were decidedly different—their employees. The successful business had employees who were obviously well-trained, friendly, neat in appearance and courteous. The employees in the other store were generally lacking in one or more of those qualities. The employees in the successful store did not acquire those qualities by accident or fate. On the contrary, the attitude and professionalism of those employees were the result of a well-defined goal that, simply stated, expressed the firm's commitment to employing, developing, and rewarding a workforce of the highest caliber. Being a part of an effort towards achieving that type of goal is what makes HRM so interesting and rewarding.

HRM: A Challenging Career

In addition to being an interesting and rewarding career, HRM challenges the practitioner to a degree seldom experienced by those employed in other fields of work. Practitioners in HRM must learn a comprehensive body of knowledge. Furthermore, that body of knowledge varies in both depth and scope among the diverse specialties within the field. For example, a specialist in employee benefits must possess detailed knowledge of the provisions of the Employee Retirement Income Security Act, must understand the methods of providing medical expense benefits and must be able to structure benefit programs to achieve organizational objectives. Furthermore, the specialist must be creative in responding to the ever-changing need to contain the costs of benefit plans, while providing programs that will aid in the recruitment and retention of quality employees. Similar challenges face specialists in other areas of HRM, such as human resource development, pay administration, safety management, and labor relations.

HR is a constantly changing field of work. Maintaining a working comprehension of the current body of knowledge is a continual challenge, since new products are being offered, new methods are being developed, new laws are being implemented and old ones are being amended, and public policy is being shaped and refined by judicial decisions and government agency regulation. Due to these and related changes, the challenge for practitioners is to stay abreast of the body of knowledge and the science of sound practice in HRM. Finally, there are significant social and economic costs of failing to know and apply the latest developments in the science of HRM. Lost productivity, poor work quality, and monetary penalties for noncompliance with regulatory requirements are examples of those costs. In sum, the challenge of HRM makes the profession a rewarding one to enter and practice, but it also poses significant risks to practitioners who do not make the necessary investment in continuing self-development and renewal.

Human Resources Management

Human resources management is the organization function consisting of the activities involved in obtaining and maintaining an effective team of employees who make it possible for organizations to accomplish desired goals. Organizations accomplish results through the combined work products of employees. The purpose of HRM is to ensure the optimum number of competent and committed employees are employed to achieve the desired goals. A number of distinctly different types of work, such as recruiting and selecting employees, constitute HRM. These activities are performed in all organizations regardless of their size.

In the smallest organizations, the activities are typically performed by the owner. Organizations with 100 or more employees usually have individuals with such titles as *Human Resource Manager* or *Personnel Manager*, who are authorized to perform all HR activities, including recruitment, selection and pay administration. Other titles include *Personnel Director* or *Personnel Officer*. In some organizations with unions, the title of the job might be *Director of Personnel and Industrial Relations* or *Director of Human Resources and Labor Relations*. Since the duties in these jobs consist of a variety of HRM tasks, they are *generalist* jobs.

HRM *specialist* jobs are those restricted to a smaller number of tasks, such as recruitment or compensation. Some titles of specialist jobs are *Human Resources Assistant, Human Resources Coordinator,* or *Personnel Analyst.* Sometimes, a specialist job includes only one activity, for example, recruitment or compensation. In these situations, the respective job titles might be *Recruiter* or *Compensation Analyst.* Specialist positions usually exist in large organizations. In some organizations, various activities, such as the recruitment of new employees or the administration of medical expense benefits, may be outsourced to consultants or contractors.

Human Resources Management Roles and Authority

The discipline of HRM began in the early 20th century, perhaps as early as 1900. The reputed father of "modern personnel administration" was Ordway Tead, a social worker who redefined himself and converted to what was then referred to as *personnel administration*. Over time, the title of the discipline changed to *personnel management*, and, finally, to *human resources management*. The changes in the title of the discipline of HRM were accompanied by significant changes in the roles of HRM.

HRM Roles

In the early period of HRM, the role of practitioners was largely confined to performing basic but essential services to facilitate the accomplishment of organizational goals. This role has expanded as both the external and internal environments of business changed. Today, in addition to providing services, the contemporary HRM practitioner fulfills advisory, control, change agent, managerial and strategic roles.

Service Role

The fledgling field of HRM evolved from the need of employers to functionalize work as organizations grew larger and the processes of producing and distributing goods and services became more complex. Instead of supervisors individually performing the activities involved in recruiting and screening new employees, typically done in many businesses, the work was delegated to *personnel departments*, which were established for those and related purposes. Another duty assigned to the early personnel departments was training new employees, particularly orientation and basic skills training. Other services the personnel department either performed for line managers or assisted them in performing, included the administration of pay systems, the preparation and maintenance of personnel paperwork and records, and the administration of performance evaluations. These service activities were so paramount among work performed in the personnel department that Tead and a colleague, Henry Metcalf, emphasized that they viewed "personnel work as a service function."[1]

This service role has continued to expand significantly. In addition, the core services, such as recruitment, selection, personnel record maintenance, pay administration, performance appraisal, and training, which are fundamental in the contemporary HRM world, have changed. For example, many recruitment and selection activities have been outsourced to employee search firms. Likewise, other service activities, such as employee benefits administration, and even services of relatively recent origin, including employee assistance plans, outplacement, and human resource information systems, have been outsourced in many firms. Whether the services are provided in-house or outsourced, HR

---

[1] Tead, O. and Metcalf, H.C., *Personnel Administration* (New York: McGraw-Hill Book Company, Inc. 1933), p. 4.

practitioners are responsible for a large, diverse, and always changing body of services necessary to help management efficiently achieve organizational goals.

Advisory Role

Due to the extensive knowledge that HRM practitioners possess, it is only natural that their advice is sought on a range of topics by personnel at all organizational levels. Employees ask for assistance in diverse areas ranging from advice about how to handle personal problems to which medical expense benefit plan to select from several options available to them. While the advisory role appears innocuous among the other roles performed in HRM, it frequently involves fundamental issues about employees' lives, including their personal adjustment and happiness and their future economic security. Consequently, the environment in which advice is sought, and given, is typically a somber and thoughtful one. Furthermore, giving advice to employees requires the utmost of personal ethics and responsibility. Personal information that employees disclose about themselves must be treated confidentially. HRM practitioners must be able to discern when it is appropriate for them to offer assistance and when and to whom employees should be referred for issues beyond the practitioners' competence.

HRM practitioners also offer counsel and assistance to supervisors on topics ranging from employee recognition and rewards to the administration of discipline for performance deficiencies. Many of these scenarios require specific personal attributes, such as a balanced sense of equity. Furthermore, experience is generally required for giving any advice affecting an employee's career. For example, giving advice about discipline requires experience in dealing with different job deficiencies, administering progressive discipline, and discovering viable alternatives to pursue. Supervisors also often seek advice from HRM practitioners on other topics, including how to deal with troubled employees, how to conduct performance appraisals, and how to train employees.

Control Role

Starting in the mid-1930s, the role of HRM practitioners was significantly expanded by the passage of the National Labor Relations Act (NLRA) in 1935 and the Fair Labor Standards Act (FLSA) of 1938. The NLRA gave employees the right to self-organize, form or assist labor organizations, bargain collectively through representatives of their own choosing, and engage in other concerted activities. The FLSA established minimum rates of pay, set maximum hours of work before overtime pay was required, and established working conditions governing the employment of children under the age of 18. Somewhat earlier, other laws, such as the Railway Labor Act (1926) and the Davis-Bacon Act (1931), also changed the legal environment affecting the employment of workers.

Also occurring during this period were dramatic changes in the techniques of HRM work, such as the introduction of job evaluation and more refined methods of selecting employees. These changes translated into more responsibilities, and, more importantly, legal responsibilities affecting HRM. Prior to this period, the legal environment affecting HRM was confined to state laws, which typically had a relatively minor impact upon management decision-making. The new laws were different because they involved newly established federal agencies, federal courts, and the prospect of expensive penalties for violations. Furthermore, and more directly related to the topic of roles, authority was delegated to HRM practitioners to ensure that the control responsibilities assigned to them were supported by sufficient functional authority to see that work was properly done. Over time, the control role of HRM has greatly expanded, due to additional laws dramatically affecting the function.

Change Agent

As noted above, the science of HRM has changed dramatically since the fledgling function of personnel administration emerged many years ago. Implementing the changes in this science required HRM practitioners to assume the role of change agent. Through experience, management found that simply introducing changes was not sufficient since change agents, which typically were HRM practitioners, were needed to facilitate the process of fully integrating the new science into the fabric of the organization. More recently, management has embarked on the journey of reinventing their organizations, and HRM practitioners have been assigned the responsibility for facilitating this process. As key players in managing the challenges of an ever-changing environment, HRM practitioners are involved in both the *process* and *content* of change.

Process of Change

HRM practitioners serve as change agents through motivating and suggesting methods through which change can occur, such as using techniques like benchmarking to identify which dimensions of the organization might require reengineering or change.

Content of Change

HRM practitioners also serve as change agents in implementing the content of changes that are needed. For example, HRM practitioners are fundamentally involved in designing jobs that are identified through reengineering and in facilitating any necessary training or retraining.

Managerial Role

HRM practitioners also fulfill a managerial role, if they supervise the work of at least one employee. As HRM work has become broader in scope and more important, the size of the HRM department has enlarged, creating a managerial role for some individuals. Individuals in the positions of Vice President, Human Resources or Human Resources Manager typically have such authority. Sometimes, specialist positions, such as Compensation Specialist or Training Specialist, may also have managerial responsibilities.

Strategic Role

For most firms, HRM is a partner in the strategic planning process. For example, 93 percent of 456 respondents in a national survey indicated strategic planning was conducted in their organizations in the area of human resource forecasting/planning. In 96 percent of those firms, the respondents stated that HR was involved either solely (69 percent of firms) or in conjunction with other departments (27 percent of firms) in this strategic planning activity.[2] Other dimnensions of HR's role in strategic planning are discussed in Chapter 3.

Consultant Role

HR frequently serves as an intra-organizational consultant in improving organizational efficiency. This role is similar to but quite different from the role of change agent. In facilitating change, HR is involved in strategies that remake, remold, or make fundamental changes in the organization itself or within a component of the organization. In the consultant role, HR is involved in making the existing organization more efficient. Among the techniques used in this role are various organizational development (OD) interventions, including team-building. Other techniques used in the consultant role involve problem identification and group problem-solving through the nominal group method and the Delphi technique.

Since many initiatives to improve organizational efficiency involve people, HR is ideally qualified to render important consultant services. Eighty-seven percent of the firms in the national survey discussed above conduct OD activities in relation to strategic planning. HR is solely responsible for the OD work in 37 percent of the firms that conduct it and is responsible together with other departments in 55 percent of the firms.[3]

Consulting services are also offered by external consultants who possess the requisite HR knowledge.

Roles and Authority

The various roles HRM practitioners perform require the delegation of the appropriate types of authority. Exhibit 1-1 shows the five roles performed in HRM, an example of how each one is fulfilled and the authority that is delegated to accomplish the respective role.

Exhibit 1-1
Roles of Human Resource Management Practitioners

Role	Example of how role is fulfilled	Type of authority
Service	Assisting an employee who was injured on the job to file a Workers' Compensation claim	Staff
Advisory	Advising a manager how to conduct a performance appraisal interview	Staff
Control	Conducting a job evaluation, using the organization's job evaluation system	Functional
Change agent	Serving as a facilitator in designing and implementing a team self-management structure replacing a traditional hierarchical structure	Staff/Functional

[2] SHRM-BNA Survey No. 65: Human Resources Activities, Budgets, and Staffs: 1999-2000. *Bulletin to* *Management*, The Bureau of National Affairs (June 29, 2000), p. S-7.
[3] Ibid.

Role	Example of how role is fulfilled	Type of authority
Managerial	Managing other HRM personnel. Assumes the job incumbent has responsibility for the work of at least one person.	Line
Strategic	Participating in strategic planning, such as the effects of human resource needs on decision-making to enter a new market.	Staff/Functional
Consultant	Defining strategies and tactics to improve organizational efficiency.	Staff/Functional

Authority

Authority is the right to use an organization's resources to accomplish its goals. In a private organization, authority is delegated from the owners, such as the stockholders in a corporation. In a public organization, authority is delegated from the voters or some other constituency the organization serves. The three types of authority are *line, staff,* and *functional.* The context in which the authority is used, that is, the work activity or activities for which the authority is delegated to HRM practitioners, may vary in different organizations. For example, in one organization, functional authority may be delegated to the HRM department for the administration of all the traditional HRM activities, including recruitment and performance appraisal. In another, the functional authority delegation may be limited to only selected activities. Also, the extent of the authority delegation may differ among organizations. For example, the HRM departments in two different organizations have functional authority for the administration of the job evaluation plan. In one organization, the HRM department has the final authority in deciding what pay grade will be assigned to jobs but, in the other organization, the HRM department only recommends which pay grade will be assigned.

Line Authority

Line authority is delegated to employees who manage the work of other employees. This authority includes the right to select employees, set performance standards, and direct and appraise the work of these employees. HRM practitioners who have least one employee reporting to them have line authority, which is also called supervisory or managerial authority.

Staff Authority

Staff authority is the right given to HRM professionals to render advisory or expert opinions or to serve as internal human resources subject matter consultants to others within the organization. This expertise is recognized and utilized within the organization through several means. For example, standing committees, such as promotion panels and safety and health committees, are formal situations in which HRM practitioners give expert advice. Informal situations in which advice is given include assisting a supervisor who requests advice about how to approach an employee who is having attendance problems.

Functional Authority

Functional authority, which can also be thought of as programmatic authority, is the right to direct designated work activities (or programs) of a particular function, like human resources or purchasing throughout the entire organization. Purchasing managers, for example, have functional authority over the manner in which items are purchased for use in the organization. A production supervisor who wants to purchase a new piece of equipment follows the purchasing procedures defined by the purchasing manager. HRM practitioners are delegated functional authority over various work activities within the HRM function, such as the selection of new employees. A production supervisor who wants to fill a vacant job does so by following procedures established by HRM practitioners.

HRM practitioners are delegated functional authority to define procedures and establish safeguards to ensure they are followed in a range of HRM activities. A major reason for this authority delegation is the perceived need to implement new methods and programs in various HRM activities, such as new methods of compensating employees or new approaches to containing medical expense benefits costs. Another major reason for delegating this authority to HRM practitioners is the changing legal environment of business. Laws affecting HRM, and the regulations that are promulgated to implement the laws, are complex and technical. Failure to comply with these requirements can subject an employer to significant liabilities.

Studying Human Resources Management

The 38 chapters in this *Guide* are organized into the 11 functional areas shown in Exhibit 1-2. The subject matter in these 38 chapters is briefly examined to give the reader a broad perspective of how the *Guide* is organized. This examination begins with a discussion of how HRM meets the traditional standards of a profession.

Human Resources Management—The Profession

Is HRM simply an organizational function, like finance or production, or is it a profession, thus mandating higher standards for practitioners? Traditionally, a profession was defined as a vocation requiring special training and preparation. Over time, however, that definition was expanded. For example, Mary Parker Follett, a serious contributor to management philosophies early in the 20th century, said a profession requires a foundation of science and a motive of service.[4] Is human resources management a profession? Perhaps the best way to answer that question is to the look at the six conditions which characterize the traditional professions, such as medicine, nursing, dentistry and law:

1. A gate-keeping procedure for entrance into the profession. This is to ensure that those individuals who refer to themselves as qualified practitioners of the profession are in fact qualified to make such claims;

---

[4] Metcalf, H.C. and Urwick, L., editors, *Dynamic Administration* (New York: Harper and Brothers, 1940), p. 117.

2. A uniform college curriculum required of all practitioners in the profession;

3. A recognized body of knowledge representing the science of the profession, which is derived from, and augmented by ongoing research and scholarship;

4. A standardized certification, accreditation or licensing procedure required for entry into the profession;

5. A requirement for periodic training or education to continue practicing in the profession; and

6. A code of ethical conduct and a method of monitoring performance, which is enforced through a public, quasi-public or private organization that has the authority to bar a practitioner from working in the profession.[5]

Of the six conditions, (3) through (6) exist, to some extent, in HRM. For example, several organizations have established a body of knowledge within the field of HRM. In addition, most of these same organizations have developed certification or accreditation procedures and require individuals who possess the respective designations to meet certain stipulations, such as continuing education, to retain the designations. Condition (6) exists to the extent that several organizations of practitioners in the field of HRM do have codes of ethics for their members. However, none of these organizations have the authority to prevent a practitioner from working in the field. Later in this chapter, several organizations that have certifications in the field of HRM are examined.

Ethics, Legality and Right v. Wrong

HR practitioners are often faced with issues involving ethics, legality and right and wrong. In the context of organizational behavior these are practical definitions of the terms:

- *Ethical* behavior is in accord with a set of values.[6]

- *Legal* behavior conforms to state or federal law.

- Behavior that is considered *right* is correct, proper or just, respectively, depending upon the situation.

These concepts are often confused.

EXAMPLE: Discharging a person just prior to their 40th birthday so a younger person could be hired for a lower salary is not *illegal* under the Age Discrimination in Employment Act but it may not be the *right* thing to do. In addition, if the HR person who handled the discharge believes that abiding by the spirit of a law is ethical behavior that is according to his or her set of values then that person may view the discharge as *unethical*.

---

[5] For a discussion of the conditions characterizing a profession, see R.A. Gordon and J.E. Howell, *Higher Education for Business* (New York: Columbia University Press, 1959), pps. 69-73; also see F.C. Pierson, et. al., *The Education of American Business-* *men* (New York: McGraw-Hill Book Co., 1959), pp. 27-33.

[6] Myers, Donald W., *Human Resources Management: Principles and Practice* (Chicago: Commerce Clearing House, Inc., 1986), p. 297.

Judging behavior as either ethical or unethical, absent guides, such as a professional or organizational code of ethics, is often in the eye of the beholder. For example, some opine as unethical what others might consider to be greediness, such as executives who earn extremely high salaries[7] or get large stock options or elaborate perquisites. Still, others might consider such behavior as proper.

Some ethical issues facing management are these:

- Conflicts of interest.
- Receiving gifts, favors and the related in the return for performance of normal job duties.
- Using inside information to gain an advantage.
- Proper utilization of an organization's assets, such as office equipment for personal use.
- Disclosing confidential or personal information.
- Misuse of copyrighted material.

Use of Copyright Materials

The *Copyright Statutes* are covered by the U.S. Copyright Act, 17 U.S.C. §§ 101-810 and protect the rights of ownership to such items as books, audiovisual works, and pictorial, graphic and sculptural works. Only the owners of a copyright have the exclusive rights to do or to authorize any of the following:

1. To reproduce the copyrighted work in copies or phono records.
2. To prepare derivative works based upon the copyrighted work.
3. To distribute copies or phono records of the copyrighted work to the public by sale or other transfer of ownership, or by rental, lease, or lending.
4. In the case of literary, musical, dramatic, and choreographic works, pantomimes, and motion pictures and other audiovisual works, to perform the copyrighted work publicly.
5. In the case of literary, musical, dramatic, and choreographic works, pantomimes, and pictorial, graphic, or sculptural works, including the individual images of a motion picture or other audio-visual work, and to display the copyrighted work publicly.
6. In the case of sound recordings, to perform the copyrighted work publicly by means of a digital audio transmission.

Fair Use

Copyrighted materials can be used under the concept of *Fair Use* for such purposes as criticism, comment, news reporting, teaching (including multiple copies for classroom use), scholarship, or research. In determining whether the use made of a work in any particular case is *Fair Use* is determined by such factors as these:

---

[7] Moorhead, Gregory and Griffin, Ricky W., *Organizational Behavior: Managing People and Organiza-* *tions* (Boston: Houghton Mifflin Company, 1998), p. 91.

1. The purpose and character of the use, including whether such use is of a commercial nature or is for nonprofit educational purposes.

2. The nature of the copyrighted work.

3. The amount and substantiality of the portion used in relation to the copyrighted work as a whole.

4. The effect of the use upon the potential market for or value of the copyrighted work.

Published v. Unpublished Work

The fact that a work is unpublished shall not itself bar a finding of fair use if such finding is made upon consideration of the four factors above. Also, it is not required to register a work for the copyright protection to apply.

Examples of Copyright Materials

In HR, copyrighted materials typically may consist of such items as application forms, performance appraisal forms, job evaluation materials, material in texts and reference books, and software. Before using such materials, permission should be sought from the copyrighted owner or limiting the use to *Fair Use*.

Duration of Copyright

A copyright is for 70 years beyond the life of the author.

Copyright Ownership

Usually the author is the owner of the copyright except when the work is "made for hire," which is the case when the work involved is produced as part of the duties of an employee. In that situation, the copyright belongs to the employer. Also, independent contractors may be covered by the "made for hire" rule if the work was produced under contract and the independent contractor and the person paying for the work expressly agree the work is "made for hire."[8]

Social Responsibility

Managers, including HR personnel have an obligation to act in a *socially responsible* manner. This responsibility includes obeying laws and regulations, such as securities laws, environmental protection laws, equal employment opportunity laws, and antitrust laws. As Peter Drucker says, "Management is responsible for conducting the enterprise so as not to undermine our social beliefs and cohesion."[9]

Some critics, of those who advocate for socially responsible management, are nevertheless cognizant of ethical behavior. For example, one such critic, Milton Friedman contends the basic responsibility of managers is to ". . . make as much money as possible . . ."but he adds managers must do so ". . . while

---

[8] Crews, Kenneth D., *You and Your Copyrights: Securing, Managing, and Sharing the Legal Rights*, IUPUI (December 26, 2002).

[9] Drucker, Peter, The responsibilities of management, in Nelson, Charles A. and Cavey, Charles A., *Ethics, Leadership, and the Bottom Line* (New York: North River Press, 1991), p. 243.

conforming to the basic rules of society, both those embodied in law and those embodied in ethical custom."[10]

A more enlightened contemporary approach advocates a much broader view of social responsibility to include these issues:

- Management is responsible to participate fully in state and federal initiatives, such as welfare to work and child support enforcement programs.

- Management should engage in philanthropic outreaches, such as funding college scholarships.

- Management should participate in community-based programs, such as blood drives and united appeal campaigns.

- Management has a social responsibility to protect the environment and conserve national resources. In addition, management can meet its responsibility in these areas by partnering with community action groups to eliminate pollution and protect natural resources.

Management Concepts

Chapter 2 covers the management concepts that HRM practitioners use in performing their work. For example, as change agents, HRM practitioners utilize theories in determining how employees should be involved in the processes of implementing change. HRM practitioners also understand the process of management and how managers who are also leaders are more effective in accomplishing work. These concepts, including traitist, behavioral, contingency-situational, and transactional/transformational approaches to leadership are discussed in the chapter.

Exhibit 1-2
Functional Areas and Chapter Topics

Functional Area	Chapter Topic
Human Resources Framework	Chapter 1—Human Resources Management Profession
	Chapter 2—Management Concepts
	Chapter 3—Human Resources Planning
	Chapter 4—Human Resources Function Outsourcing
	Chapter 5—Human Resources Systems
	Chapter 6—Human Resources Research and Audit
Legal Environment	Chapter 7—Federal Employment Laws and Regulations
	Chapter 8—Employment Tort Law
Job Analysis and Structuring	Chapter 9—Job Analysis
	Chapter 10—Job and Organization Structure
Fair Employment	Chapter 11—Human Resources Diversity
	Chapter 12—Employment Discrimination
	Chapter 13—Workplace Harassment

[10] Friedman, Milton, The social respnsibility of business is to increase its profits, in Nelson, Charles A. and Cavey, Charles A., *Ethics, Leadership, and the Bottom Line* (New York: North River Press, 1991), p. 246.

Functional Area	Chapter Topic
Staffing	Chapter 14—Validity and Reliability Methods
	Chapter 15—Recruitment
	Chapter 16—Selection
	Chapter 17—Employment Verification
Compensation Planning and Benefits Administration	Chapter 18—Compensation Planning
	Chapter 19—Health Benefits, Insurance, and Perquisites
	Chapter 20—Counseling
	Chapter 21—Wellness
	Chapter 22—Retirement Plans
	Chapter 23—Mandated Benefit Programs
	Chapter 24—Benefits Cost Containment
Monetary Rewards	Chapter 25—Compensation Surveys and External Equity
	Chapter 26—Job Worth and Internal Equity
	Chapter 27—Executive Compensation
	Chapter 28—Pay Structure Management
	Chapter 29—Job Performance Management
	Chapter 30—Performance Based Pay
Safety, Health, and Security	Chapter 31—Safety and Health
	Chapter 32—Security and Workplace Violence
Human Resources Utilization	Chapter 33—Human Resources Development
	Chapter 34—Career Planning
Employee and Labor Relations	Chapter 35—Labor Relations
	Chapter 36—Collective Bargaining
	Chapter 37—Employee Relations
International Human Resources	Chapter 38—International Human Resources Management

Human Resources Planning

Human resources planning is the application of the management function of planning to human resources. The human resources planning process includes determining human resource needs, comparing those needs to the human resources available, and establishing plans to fill the shortages or accomplish the necessary reductions. The planning process is preceded by an environmental scan, which includes defining the political, social, and economic environment in which the organization exists. Human resource planning is also involved in decision-making effecting the structure of the organization, such as the types of jobs needed to most effectively perform available work and the resulting reporting relationships.

Human Resources Function Outsourcing

Like other functions in businesses, some activities in HRM are being outsourced to external service providers to achieve cost reductions and to better focus organizational resources on the firms' core business units. Among the activities that are most frequently outsourced are employee staffing, drug testing, employee benefits administration, policy preparation, legal compliance, training, security, employee assistance programming, and wellness programming. Some firms have historically outsourced particular activities, such as temporary staffing, to employment agencies. Using outsource vendors for some tasks, such as job description preparation and maintenance, are newer approaches.

Human Resources Systems

Human resources systems (HRS) are software programs to aid HR planning, decision-making and reporting. These systems have dramatically improved the efficiency of HRM work. The components of a HRS may vary among organizations. In some firms, the HRS consists solely of demographic variables, sometimes called *employee record systems*. In other organizations, the HRS also includes two or more modules, such as an *applicant tracking system*, an *employee benefit system*, a *performance planning and appraisal system*, a *job analysis system*, a *job evaluation system*, a *drug testing data system*, an *employee attendance control system*, and an *employee career planning system*. Information on various human resources software systems is discussed in Chapter 5.

Human Resources Research and Audit

Human resources management research is the investigation of HRM activities to determine facts and theories and to find ways of applying them. HRM professionals conduct research, usually consisting of literature reviews, to determine state-of-the-art or current practices in a particular area, such as performance appraisal or training and development. At other times, quasi-experimental designs may be used to measure the effectiveness of an intervention, such as a training program, before embarking on more widespread implementation. Other less sophisticated forms of research include conducting evaluations of activities, including performance appraisals or incentive pay plans. *Human resources management audit* is the verification of HRM accomplishments and comparing them to goals or standards. *Benchmarking* is a technique sometimes used in audits, which involves comparing a particular process or method used in a firm with those used by the best organizations in a field.

Federal Employment Laws and Regulations

Prior to 1963, virtually all federal employment laws and regulations dealt exclusively with labor-management relations. The sole exceptions were the Fair Labor Standards Act of 1938 and wage laws that applied to federal contractors, such as the Walsh-Healey Act of 1938 and the Davis-Bacon Act of 1931. The Equal Pay Act of 1963 was the beginning of a revolution in federal law affecting virtually every function of HRM. Furthermore, the regulatory environment of HRM has also been significantly impacted by federal case law and regulatory actions by federal agencies that were created to implement and enforce the federal laws. These laws, regulations, and court decisions have profoundly expanded the body of knowledge in HRM. They also have fundamentally changed the methodologies, techniques, and practices that constitute the science of HRM.

Employment Tort Law

State laws, court decisions and regulatory policies in the employment arena have added to the science of HRM in two ways. First, legal actions in many states have supplemented federal employment law and regulation in particular HRM functions, such as the minimum number of employees an employer must have to adhere to employment discrimination requirements, which is less than those required by federal law. In addition, some states have laws in employment areas where there is no federal law, such as requiring disability insurance protection for employees who become temporarily disabled in non-occupational settings. State tort activity has also occurred in a number of employment categories, such as negligent hiring, employment at will, and defamation in employment verifications. Local ordinances have been enacted addressing various employment situations, such as workplace smoking, employment testing, and employment discrimination.

Job Analysis

Job analysis is the systematic process of obtaining, analyzing and interpreting valid information about jobs, such as the tasks performed and the working conditions in which the tasks are performed. Job analysis also involves the study of the knowledge, skills, abilities, training, education and experience needed to safely and adequately perform the job duties. Job analysis is a fundamental antecedent in many other HRM activities, such as recruitment, selection, performance appraisal, pay administration, and safety and health standards.

Job and Organization Structure

Job structuring is part of the organizing function of management concerned with the formal and informal process of assigning tasks to jobs and delegating authority to accomplish them. Job structuring includes determining how the work within an organization should be divided among different jobs and preparing job descriptions. Some job structuring strategies, such as enriching or enlarging jobs, are important in increasing the intrinsic satisfaction employees receive in performing their job tasks.

Human Resources Diversity

Diversity management is the process of motivating employees who have diverse backgrounds to increase their interpersonal communication and cooperation to unify their efforts to optimize the organization's goals. *Equal employment opportunity* (EEO) is the equal treatment of people in all HRM activities from recruitment to retirement. *Affirmative action* (AA) is planning and implementing strategies to select applicants from groups which have traditionally experienced employment discrimination. Voluntarily practicing EEO is simply the right thing for an employer to require in any organization. Furthermore, the employer's or the top manager's actions can set an example of EEO for all employees to follow. Federal, state and local laws mandate EEO. AA has traditionally included the implementation of quotas, as well as good faith efforts to correct any imbalances through more rigorous efforts to recruit applicants from those groups that are under-represented in various job categories. More recently, quota plans have been criticized as discriminatory.

Employment Discrimination

The bases for prohibited employment discrimination have gradually widened since the Civil Rights Act of 1964 became law. Originally, employers with 15 or more employees were prohibited from discriminating on the basis of national origin, race, color, religion, or gender. Since that time, other groups, such as veterans, people with disabilities, and persons 40 and over, have been extended federal protection from employment discrimination. Both intentional discrimination, as well as employment actions which appear non-discriminatory but result in adverse impact to those protected by law, are prohibited. The remedies, penalties, and compensatory financial awards to victims of discrimination can be substantial.

Workplace Harassment

Workplace harassment, which is caused by a *hostile work environment* to certain employees based upon their national origin, religion, gender, race, color, disability, and age, is prohibited. Furthermore, *quid pro quo* sexual harassment is also prohibited. Employers have the obligation to educate employees about workplace harassment to prevent it from occurring. Employers also are expected to take swift administrative action against individuals who commit workplace harassment.

Recruitment

Recruitment is the HRM activity concerned with the development of sources of qualified applicants. The recruitment process is initiated after human resource needs are determined through human resources planning. The other components of the recruitment process include identifying sources of applicants, attracting applicants for job vacancies, and conducting recruitment interviews. Evaluating the results of recruitment efforts is also important in determining the relative success of recruitment efforts and making any necessary changes in future recruiting. Recruitment is the first phase of selection, since the results of recruitment interviews are used to determine which applicants should receive additional consideration for employment. Recruiters use the information in job descriptions to make initial determinations about the relative qualifications of applicants.

Validity and Reliability Methods

Validity, as applied to an employment selection procedure, means the procedure accurately measures applicants' qualifications which are required for a job and that there is a relationship between how well applicants meet the selection procedure standards and how well they perform on the job. Employers are required to use selection methods that are either valid or justified on the basis of a bona fide occupational requirement. There are several approaches employers can use to validate their selection methods. *Reliability* means that a selection procedure yields consistent results.

Selection Methods

Selection is the HRM activity of choosing people for positions or assignments by comparing their qualifications with the job specifications. Selection processes are used to fill positions at all organizational levels, including initial entrance positions. Selection methods, such as interviews and tests, are based upon the information in job descriptions. Job description information, in turn, is derived from job analysis to ensure that the selection methods are related to successful job performance. This process of determining the relationship between selection methods and job success is called *validity* and is requisite for effective personnel management. It is also a legal requirement if selection methods have an adverse impact upon protected groups.

Employment Verification and References

Employment verification is the process of determining the accuracy of information furnished by applicants who are seeking employment. Employers have the obligation to verify information provided by applicants for jobs in which there may be possible public policy implications for the actions of employees. For example, employees who are placed in jobs affecting the security, health, or safety of persons with whom they either interact or protect, must be trustworthy and possess other qualifications to perform the tasks to which they are assigned. In addition, employers may have a legal obligation to disclose relevant information about previous employees to prospective employers who are requesting information about applicants for employment in jobs affecting the security, health, or safety of others.

Compensation and Benefits Planning

Employee benefits are the current and deferred non-monetary rewards employees receive as a condition of their employment. There are both compulsory and voluntary employee benefits. Compulsory benefits include Social Security, workers' compensation and unemployment insurance. Some states also require employers to provide disability income insurance. Voluntary benefits include medical expense benefits, life insurance, vacation days, holidays, and retirement benefits. Employee benefits are a major expense; thus, benefit planning is important in ensuring the accomplishment of the objectives that employers have for providing the benefits.

Health Benefits, Insurance, and Perquisites

Among the delivery systems for medical expense benefits are preferred provider organizations (PPOs), health maintenance organizations (HMOs), insurance companies, and health care cooperatives. In recent years, there has been a decline in the percentage of employees who have access to health care coverage through their places of employment. Since 1990, a number of laws have been enacted dealing with health care issues. The most significant of these laws are the Consolidated Omnibus Budget Reconciliation Act of 1990; the Older Worker Benefit Protection Act of 1990; the Health Insurance Portability and Accountability Act of 1996; the Mental Health Parity Act of 1996; and, the Newborns' and Mothers' Health Protection Act of 1996. Other benefit programs offered to employees are disability income, sick leave, legal services, paid lunch and rest periods, paid holidays, paid vacations, day care, educational assistance, retirement plans, wellness programs, and employee assistance programs. The latter three programs are covered in separate chapters.

Counseling

Counseling consists of giving basic, technical, and in some cases, professional human assistance by skilled and knowledgeable individuals who are professionally qualified to render such level of service. Employee assistance programs (EAPs) are a type of counseling program designed to assist employees who are troubled by alcoholism and alcohol abuse, compulsive gambling, drug abuse, emotional and mental problems, family and domestic problems, financial difficulties, legal problems, and stress. Some employers employ in-house EAP counselors; however, most employers who offer such assistance contract with external counseling services.

Wellness

Wellness is employee mental and physical well-being as a result of employer and employee commitment to complete human health in both work and non-work life. Some employers provide wellness programs to help contain employee benefit costs, particularly the costs of medical expense benefits. Wellness programs may have one or more components, such as blood pressure checks, diabetes screening, educational courses in safe driving, exercise programs, paid subscriptions to health publications, paid memberships in health clubs, and assistance with planning dietary programs, weight reduction, and smoking cessation.

Retirement Plans

A *retirement plan* is a generic term for an employee benefit that provides income for employees upon reaching an age at which they no longer desire to work for a particular employer or are unable to work for the employer. Some individuals retire from one place of employment, begin receiving retirement benefits, and seek employment elsewhere. This may be due to reaching a legal mandatory retirement age for that occupation, such as fire fighters. Organizational restructuring and downsizing plans have also contributed substantially to the numbers of persons who have retired, commenced receiving retirement benefits and resumed employment elsewhere. There are significant legal requirements for employers who establish retirement plans in order for these plans to qualify for tax benefits.

Mandated Benefits

Mandated benefits are those employee benefit programs which are required by either federal or state law. The three principal types of mandated benefits are Social Security, workers' compensation, and unemployment insurance. Several states require employers to provide disability insurance, which is typically intended to extend income protection to employees who become temporarily disabled due to non-occupational causes. Mandatory benefit plans have various funding arrangements, benefit provisions, and eligibility conditions. Some employers coordinate mandatory benefits with the voluntary ones they offer to employees.

Benefit Cost Containment

The control of benefit costs is a major concern for employers. Among the strategies employers use to control these costs are plan design, claim administration, alternatives to retrospective reimbursement for medical expenses, different funding arrangements, and cost shifting to employees through higher deductibles. Employers are also increasingly requiring employees to contribute toward the premium costs of medical expense plans.

Pay Surveys and External Equity

External equity is a characteristic of an employer's compensation program in which it is competitive with the programs of other employers in the same labor market. Employers conduct surveys to determine the pay other employers in the market are offering to employees in various jobs. The usual information collected in the surveys is the minimum, median and maximum rates of pay. The process of conducting pay surveys includes identifying the applicable market areas and the firms within the areas that are competing for the same potential employees. Obtaining cooperation from employers to participate in the survey and analyzing the results are other steps in the process. Various organizations, including the Bureau of Labor Statistics, conduct both pay and benefit surveys.

Determining Job Worth and Internal Equity

Internal equity is a characteristic of an employer's compensation program in which employees in different jobs are equitably rewarded for the tasks they perform. Internal equity is affected by the systems of monetary payments that are used, including the methods to reward performance. *Job evaluation* is one method used to achieve internal equity. The principal methods of job evaluation are ranking, classification, point, and factor.

Executive Compensation

The methods of compensating those individuals employed at the executive level of management include incentive stock options, stock appreciation rights, salaries, bonuses, and long-term payments. Compensation plans are also created to reward executives in the event of hostile takeovers. Other compensation plans are designed to prevent executives from prematurely leaving the firm. In addition to special types of payment methods, executives are given the exclusive right to certain benefits, such as financial counseling, retirement plans, the payment of country club dues, automobiles, and first-class air travel.

Pay Structure Management

Pay management is the preparation and administration of equitable methods of paying employees. Most pay systems are constructed from the process of job evaluation. *Pay equity*, which is the concept involving the equitable treatment of members of both sexes in pay administration, is a major issue in pay administration. *Comparable worth*, which is the concept involving paying members of both sexes equally for dissimilar jobs having the same relative worth to an employer, is another issue in pay administration.

Job Performance Management

Performance appraisal is the HRM activity of establishing written standards of performance, telling employees about those standards and frequently informing them how they are performing in relation to the standards. Federal regulations stipulate that performance appraisal is a selection method, since the information derived from the process is typically used in making selection decisions, such as lateral assignments and promotions. Furthermore, the decision regarding the discharge of an employee is often based upon information derived from that employee's performance appraisal. Since selection decisions are made from performance results, employers must demonstrate a valid relationship between performance appraisal methods and actual job performance, especially if the results of the performance appraisal system have an adverse impact upon protected groups.

Performance-Based Pay

Pay for performance involves the use of pay systems that are based upon some measure of job performance. These payments can either be deferred, such as profit-sharing plans which are used to fund retirement plans, or can be made on a current basis, such as annual bonus distributions made under a Rucker-type of gainsharing plan. Pay-for-performance systems are used to reward employees for a number of different performance outcomes, such as acquiring greater knowledge (pay-for-knowledge plans), performing competently (competency-based pay plans) or gaining more skills (skill-based pay systems).

Safety and Health Concerns

Safety involves providing working conditions and requiring work acts to prevent occupational accidents. *Health* is the activity of maintaining the state of physical and mental well-being and the absence of illness or disease. Employers are concerned with employee safety and health because of the pain and suffering resulting from occupational injuries and illnesses. In addition, the losses which result from such injuries and illnesses can adversely affect a firm's bottom line.

Security and Workplace Violence Issues

Security is defined as the domestic and international protection of an organization's assets, its employees, and the property of employees on the employer's premises. *Workplace violence* concerns physical acts, verbal threats or profanation, written threats, or visual threats committed against employees by a person or persons who either have an employment-related connection with the establishment or are outsiders. Workplace violence is a major cause of death at work. Various strategies are available to employers to help prevent this violence.

Human Resources Development

Human resources development is the process of preparing employees to maximize both their utility to the organization and their job satisfaction. The American Society for Training and Development is an organization composed of

70,000 members the mission of which is "to provide leadership to individuals, organizations, and society to achieve work-related competence, performance, and fulfillment."[11] Private and public sector organizations make substantial investments annually in training employees to increase their competence.

Career Planning

Career planning is the process of assisting employees in defining their career interests and preparing for career changes through human resources development. Organizational restructuring and reengineering are requiring employers to invest more in the career development of their employees. Employees are also interested in career planning in order to update their skills and learn new ones to replace those that have become obsolete due to technology changes and job restructuring.

Labor Relations

Labor relations is the HRM activity involving unions and union activity. Included in labor relations is preventing union organizing campaigns to represent employees and engaging in collective bargaining with unions that are the recognized to represent the employees in a bargaining unit. *Union recognition* is the process through which unions become certified or decertified to represent a group of employees. The union movement in the U.S. has historically experienced swings in membership and influence. Knowledge of the political, social and economic causes of those changes is necessary to understand various issues involving unions, such as strikes and collective bargaining demands of unions. Unions remain a viable force in the U.S., despite shrinking membership.

Collective Bargaining

Collective bargaining is the process through which union and management representatives negotiate an agreement on wages, hours and other terms and conditions of employment. Involved in the collective bargaining process are the preparation for collective bargaining, the bargaining process, the resolution of impasses, and contract administration.

Employee Relations

Employee relations is the process of disciplining and communicating with employees. The sources of discipline include self-discipline, group-imposed discipline, and organizational discipline. Traditionally, employers have relied upon progressive discipline to correct employee performance deficiencies. Today, however, in addition to progressive discipline, employers are attempting to influence employee behavior toward desired outcomes through such initiatives as pay incentives, establishing partnership arrangements with employees and job redesign.

---

[11] *ASTD: An Overview* (Alexandria, VA: American Society for Training and Development, 1997), p. 1.

International Human Resources Management

International human resources management involves the performance of all HRM activities in obtaining and maintaining an effective workforce in the foreign operation of a U.S. firm. Some HRM activities performed in both a domestic and an international operation are the same; but other activities may differ. For example, recruiting and selecting employees for overseas assignments involve considerations of the cross-cultural adjustment of the employee and dependents, family relocation, security concerns, income tax issues, and housing availability.

Certification/Accreditation in Human Resources Management

Earning a designation from practitioner organizations in HRM is a significant career milestone. The following organizations offer some of the major designations in the HRM field.

WorldatWork

WorldatWork, (formerly known as the *American Compensation Association*) offers three certification options, *Certified Compensation Professional*, *Certified Benefits Professional*, and *Global Remuneration Professional*.

Certified Compensation Professional (CCP)

Introduced in 1976, the CCP designation focuses on pay compensation. Applicants for this designation are required to pass nine examinations. Each examination consists of approximately 100 multiple-choice questions comprising the body of knowledge in the respective area. Six of the examinations are "core" or required examinations which must be passed by all applicants. Three of the examinations can be selected from a group of "elective" areas, depending upon applicants' interests.

Certified Benefits Professional (CBP)

The CBP designation, which was introduced in 1993, is available for practitioners who wish to have a designation that focuses on employee benefits. Like the CCP, to earn the CBP, an applicant must pass nine examinations, each consisting of 100 multiple-choice questions. Also like the CCP, the CBP has six "core" examinations required of all applicants and three examinations that may be selected from a list of "elective" areas.

Dual Certification

Practitioners who seek both the CCP and the CBP designations are required to pass 15 examinations plus an additional three examinations which are in the common core for both designations.

Global Renumeration Professional

To meet the need for international compensation expertise, the *Global Remuneration Professional* was developed. To obtain the designation requires passing scores on eight examinations.[12]

Employee Services Management Association

Employee Services Management Association (formerly known as the *National Employee Services and Recreation Association*) is a nonprofit organization of 2,000 members whose jobs involve various aspects of providing employee services designed to "improve relations between employees and management, increase overall productivity, boost morale, and reduce absenteeism and turnover."[13] Among the programs this organization offers its members is the opportunity to obtain certification as a *Certified Employee Services Professional*.

International Foundation of Employee Benefit Plans (IFEBP)

IFEBP is a nonprofit educational organization providing services to the employee benefits industry. Among the services provided is the *Certified Employee Benefits Specialist* (CEBS) designation. The CEBS designation requires the completion of eight exams in designing and administering employee benefit programs. The CEBS designation originated in 1976.

The IFEBP also offers three other designations. The *Compensation Management Specialist* requires the successful completion of three courses. The *Group Benefits Associate* requires successfully completing three required courses plus one optional course chosen from two alternatives. The *Retirement Plans Associate* also requires successfully completing three required courses plus an additional course selected from two others.

Human Resource Certification Institute (HRCI)

The HRCI is a credentialing organization that is affiliated with the Society for Human Resource Management. The HRCI offers two designations, the *Professional in Human Resources* (PHR) and the *Senior Professional in Human Resources* (SPHR). Both designations require two years professional exempt experience in HR and passing a 250-question, multiple-choice examination but the types and format of the questions differ on the two examinations. The body of knowledge for the two designations represents all the major activities of human resource management, that is, management practices, selection and placement, training and development, compensation and benefits, employee and labor relations, and health, safety and security. The HRCI certification programs began in 1976.

Board of Certified Safety Professionals (BCSP)

In 1969, the BCSP was created by the selection of nine directors who represented both the safety profession and various professional organizations. The BCSP offers the Certified Safety Professional designation to individuals who have the requisite education, who have sufficient experience in required areas,

---

[12] WorldatWork, *About Certification Requirements*, 2002.

[13] Employee Services Management Association, *About Us*, 2002.

and who successfully pass the Safety Fundamentals and/or Comprehensive Practice Examination.

Employee Involvement Association (EIA)

The EIA is a non-profit organization of private and public sector members who share a common interest in, and a dedication to, employee suggestion systems and other forms of employee involvement. This organization, which was originally known as the National Association of Suggestion Systems, was founded during World War II. In 1992, the name was changed to the Employee Involvement Association to recognize the world-wide evolution of suggestion systems in involving employees in all types of organizations. The EIA offers the *Certified Administration of Suggestion Systems* designation.

CHAPTER 2
MANAGEMENT CONCEPTS

Chapter Highlights
- Review approaches to management
- Understand theories of leadership
- Study authority and power relationships
- Review theories of human behavior

Introduction

A key reason for the economic success of the U.S. is the ability of management to get the right things done at the right time. Many other countries have sufficient natural resources, agreeable climates, and access to means of transportation but are unable to successfully deal with poverty and widespread unemployment. To be sure, the U.S. version of capitalism, that is vested self-interest, mobility of labor, an educated and trained labor force and flexibility in prices, plays a significant role in this country's economic progress. In addition, the role of government in the U.S. has a significantly less prominent presence than in most other developed countries of the world. The other important ingredient, however, is a philosophy of management that focuses on the effective accomplishment of desired objectives.

Management is the process of planning, organizing, directing, and controlling the tasks of employees toward the accomplishment of goals within an organization structure.

Management Functions

The process of management is accomplished through these functions:

- Planning;
- Organizing;
- Directing; and
- Controlling.

Some management theories also see *leadership* as playing a vital role in management. Other theorists include *delegating* as a function.

Planning

Planning includes determining what is to be done, who is to do it, and when and how it will be done. Planning includes strategic or long-term planning, intermediate planning, and operational or short-term planning. The time periods for these three types of planning are discussed below.

Operational Planning

Operational planning is short-term planning, that is, objectives which are planned for accomplishment within a period of one year. *Management by Objectives* (MBO), which is a popular form of performance appraisal, is typically used for the formulation and accomplishment of short-term plans. Usually, MBO plans also include the means for tracking progress, including what is to be achieved within specific time periods or set dates. Typically, MBO plans have financial incentives related to the accomplishment of the plans.

Operational planning also involves responding to unexpected events which demand immediate action. A late-arriving shipment of raw materials may mandate a revision of equipment utilization or staffing needs. Of necessity, some operational planning is reactive to the almost daily changing demands of the work environment.

Intermediate Planning

Intermediate planning involves work that has some aspects of short-term objectives but also involves work that may extend several years into the future. For this reason, intermediate planning involves a time period extending from one to five years. Sometimes, activities involve more than an operational period of time, that is, the work cannot be accomplished within a year but does not have strategic implications. For example, the implementation of a new plant start-up involves considerable planning for the lay-out, installation and fine-tuning of equipment. In addition, the selection, training and placement of personnel is an important part of new plant start-ups. These types of activities, which frequently demand considerable intermediate planning and are important for organizational success, do not involve major shifts of organizational resources.

Strategic Planning

Strategic planning (also called long-term planning) includes activities that have planning horizons beyond five years. Strategic planning involves focusing the resources of the organization in a manner which fundamentally affects the positioning of the business in relation to the market or markets in which it functions. Included in this process is the key role of conducting an environmental scan involving both the internal and the external environment. Within the external environment, strategic planning includes: laws and regulations, which must be considered; planned and actual responses of the competition; anticipated consumer demand for the product or service; financial institutions, which may need to be accessed for funding; any changes to existing technology or new technology; and the availability of personnel. The strategic implications of the internal environment include the organization's culture, the financial condition of the firm, and the characteristics of the labor force, that is, the training, education and skills that employees possess. Among the outputs of the strategic planning process are the organization's mission statement, strategic goals, policies and objectives. In more concrete terms, the strategic plans concern defining market strategies and developing production systems. Decisions concerning such matters as increasing or decreasing market share, entering or exiting an industry, and acquiring or divesting an operation or business, are examples of strategic planning activities.

A *mission statement* defines the basic service or good the organization is designed to provide within a generally defined market.

Example of a Mission Statement:

The mission of The Gillette Company is *"To achieve or enhance clear leadership, worldwide, in the core consumer product categories in which we hold the world leadership position."*

Goals are the long-term conditions the organization intends to achieve. Goals typically are established for: (1) profitability or commitments to stockholders, (2) customer service and product quality and price, (3) social responsibility and responses to societal conditions such as laws, and (4) commitment to employees.

Example of a Goal:

Provide employment opportunities where employees can maximize their potentialities regardless of race, color, religion, sex, national origin, veteran's status, disability and age.

Policies are broad guidelines, usually in writing. *Goals* define the direction in which organizational resources should be expended; *policies* specify the guidelines to follow in those expenditures.

Example of a Policy:

All personnel selections will be made without regard to race, color, religion, sex, national origin, veteran's status, disability, and age.

Strategies are long-term plans explaining how goals will be accomplished.

Example of a Strategy:

Establish selection procedures for employment decision-making that will be job related and will not discriminate on the basis of race, color, religion, sex, national origin, veteran's status, disability, and age.

Strategic planning techniques include SWOT analysis and PERT diagraming. *SWOT analysis* is an acronym for *S* trengths, *W* eaknesses, *O* pportunities, and *T* hreats, which is used to help in the strategic planning processes of focusing the direction of an organization. *PERT* is an acronym for *P* roject *E* valuation *R* eview *T* echnique, which is used in planning the accomplishment of major projects. Two frequent constraints in such projects are time and money, since the work is often required to be completed within a specified period of time or within an overall budget. PERT uses either time or money to chart multiple events in the accomplishment of a project. The *critical path* in a PERT diagram is the sequence which results in the lowest cost and/or the earliest time for completion.

Organizing

Organizing is the management activity involved with getting ready to do what needs to be done to accomplish the desired plans. Some of the key components of the organizing function of management are:

Organization Structure

The *organization structure* is that part of the management function concerned with the arrangement of people and resources for the accomplishment of the its goals; the ultimate goal is designing an effective *organization*.

An *organization* is two or more people united to accomplish a common purpose (or a mission).

The two most frequently used methods of organization structuring are *functional* and *divisional or product*. Organizations are also structured into *geographical* areas.

Functional organization. An *organizational function* is a component in which the tasks certain employees perform are clearly different from those that others perform. Examples of organizational functions are manufacturing, finance, marketing, and human resources.

Divisional or product organization. A *divisional organization* is split into major product lines. An example of a divisional organization would be a firm with a consumer products division and an industrial products division.

Geographical organization. A *geographical organization* decentralizes some or all of a firm's activities into different geographical areas. For example, a firm may decentralize product distribution into several areas to facilitate meeting customer needs.

In addition to these principal methods of organizational design, there are micro-organizational designs used to accommodate authority delegations. The main types of these micro designs are *matrix* and *team concept* designs. These designs are discussed further, with examples of each, in Chapter 10.

Job Structuring

Job structuring is concerned with the formal and informal process of assigning tasks to jobs and delegating the authority to accomplish them. Among the strategies used in structuring jobs are *job enlargement* and *job enrichment*. These job structuring methods are covered more extensively in Chapter 10. More contemporary strategies include structuring jobs to accommodate performance-based pay systems, such as *pay-for-knowledge, skill-based pay,* and *competency-based pay*. All of these systems allow the employee to have a major role in determining how his/her personal job will look, what tasks are performed in it, how tasks are accomplished, and even what rewards will be assigned to the tasks. Through this process of performance-based pay systems, employees are being empowered as never before in what they do at work.

Authority

Authority is the official right to use an organization's resources in accomplishing objectives. These are the types of authority:

- *Line authority* is the right to use organization resources in managing the activities of one or more other employees. Typically, this authority includes the right to select, reward, develop, assign, and ensure the proper performance of other employees.

- *Staff authority* is the right to use organization resources in giving advice and assistance involving the work performed within a function. The HR department, for example, is typically given staff authority in advising managers about compensation matters.

- *Functional authority* is the right to use organization resources in directing the activities of a function throughout an organization. The HR department is usually assigned considerable authority involving various activities in the HR function. Some of the key functional authority delegations involve staffing procedures that will be used, the methods and uses of performance appraisal systems, the development and administration of equitable systems of rewarding employees, and the establishment of employee benefit plans. In the past, many of the functional authority delegations were predicated on ensuring legal compliance and to protect the organization from adverse actions by regulatory agencies. Contemporary management in the best-managed organizations, however, views these functional delegations as a method of ensuring the strategic involvement of HR in the conduct of business.

Power

Sometimes *authority* is used synonymously with *power*; however, the two terms may mean very different things. *Authority* is always based upon formal delegations occurring through the hierarchical structure of an organization. The ultimate source of authority in a publicly held corporation is the stockholders. The stockholders elect a board of directors to meet their interests. Boards of directors, in turn, select the management team that will manage the organization. Authority delegations from the stockholders are transmitted throughout the organization as needs arise.

Power is the formal and informal means of accomplishing something. Power may be conferred upon groups or individuals. The source of the power may be from the formal organization or from peers, managers, or others within the organization. These are the types of power[1]:

- *Coercive power* is the ability to make someone do something that they may or may not want to do because they are forced to do so, through such means as threats or fear.

- *Expert power* is conferred upon someone because of their superior knowledge. Some employees are recognized as experts at particular tasks; for example, in using a particular type of software. On the other hand, a person's expertise could be in a more complex area, such as making machine tools used in the manufacturing process. Employees may be

---

[1] French, J.R.P. and Raven, B., "The Bases of Social Power," in Cartwright and Zander, A.F., *Group Dynamics* (Evanston, Ill.: Perterson, 1960), pp. 150-167.

informally recognized by their peers as the expert in an area, or the organization may make formal announcements explaining the employee's particular expertise and suggesting that employees consult that person for any assistance needed within that specific area.

- *Legitimate power* is granted to an individual because of his/her hierarchical position in an organization. This type of power is synonymous with *formal authority* because the person is recognized through delegation as having power within a specific function.

- *Referent power* is conferred on an individual because of the person's traits, such as power given to a person who is respected in the organization as being a dependable and hard-working individual. Also, a person whose judgment is recognized as being well-reasoned and sound may be given referent power in particular areas.

- *Reward power* is granted to an individual because of the person's capacity to distribute perks. Reward power may or may not be conferred upon an individual because of the person's formal hierarchical position. A clerk whose job entails the assignment of personal computers and other equipment may have significant power because of those assignments.

Authority Delegation

Delegation is the process of assigning authority to employees who have the requisite qualifications, such as the knowledge, skills, abilities, education, training, experience and other special attributes to do the work and have the motivation and physical and mental capabilities to do it. Due to an emphasis on employee empowerment, there is less need to formally delegate authority, which was the pattern in traditional management. A key concern in such an environment was to ensure that employees are held accountable for work that is delegated to them. In addition, there is the time-worn phase that while authority can be delegated, the ultimate responsibility rests on the shoulders of those who made the delegation. To some extent, this concept is being replaced. Through empowerment and performance-based compensation, employees can expand beyond the traditional domains of their jobs, and they are expected to be accountable and responsible for what they do since they are being compensated for it.

Authority and Power Combinations

Various combinations of power and authority significantly affect an individual's ability to accomplish tasks. An employee who is recognized as an expert within an area of work and who is revered for his/her personal qualities may be able to accomplish more than a person who only has formal authority within the same area. A person who has both formal authority and power conferred by peers or others within the organization may be able to more effectively accomplish work in some areas than other individuals who has power in a restricted area.

Directing

Directing is that function of management concerned with implementing the plan via the organizational design, staffing the organization with qualified personnel, and motivating and leading those personnel to goal accomplishment through effective decision-making. Some management theorists prefer the term *leading* to *directing*; however, *directing* is more than just *leading*. Other theorists prefer the term *staffing* in lieu of *directing*, but as noted in the definition, the process of *directing* involves more than simply staffing the organization with qualified personnel. The process of leadership is discussed later in this chapter.

Controlling

Controlling is the management function that establishes systems for ensuring that the plans that were formulated in the planning function are completed and monitoring activities to determine if important planning milestones are being met. Controlling mechanisms are as important in operational planning as they are in strategic planning. A well-designed plan, such as a particular activity planned through an MBO instrument, will have some feedback loops to help the individual determine if he/she is on track for goal accomplishment. More involved plans, such as those involving multiple events and dates, will require more extensive control methods, using computer tracking. Some key components of controlling include:

- *Timetables for events*. An effective plan will include the dates when events are to be completed.

- *Feedback mechanisms*. Feedback systems can be designed in the plan to aid decision-makers in determining if progress is on track or if corrective action is needed.

- *Tracking systems.* More elaborate plans, such as those involved in both intermediate and strategic plans, will require tracking systems, which provide periodic reports, such as planned versus actual sales or production rates, to determine at the earliest feasible date if the plan is being successfully met.

- *Corrective action or goal revision*. Even the best plans may require corrective action if desired events are not being achieved as planned. In some cases, this action may include revising the plan. Comprehensive plans typically include some alternative strategies for these types of contingencies.

- *Span of control*. Span of control, which is sometimes referred to as *span of management*, may involve setting a hypothetical number of employees that can be successfully managed by one person. Eight persons is the number traditionally thought as an optimum span of control. More realistically, a span of control is determined by a number of variables, such as the number of subordinates and the proximity, variety, and complexity of the work of the subordinates.

Approaches to Management

Management concepts, theories, and principles have a rich tradition in the U.S. This body of knowledge evolved over many years, but primarily began early in the 20th century. Contemporary management practices contain some remnants of this knowledge. Management history can be categorized by somewhat distinct approaches, but it is important to note that these approaches are not necessarily chronological. Indeed, some of the early practitioners of the behavioral management approach made their contributions during the same period as those who advocated the classical management approach.

Classical Management

Classical management, which is also referred to as scientific management, represented the contributions of many persons, including those who espoused scientific management. Notable among those who made contributions to this approach were Frederick Winslow Taylor, Frank Gilbreth, and Harrington Emerson. Taylor articulated four tenets of scientific management:

- A science of management to replace the old rule-of-thumb approaches to work.

- The scientific selection, training and placement of employees to do the work they are most qualified and motivated to perform.

- Cooperation between management and employees in order for the science of work to be accepted.

- An equal division of work between management and employees, in which each party does those things they are best qualified to do. For the most part, this meant that management should select the proper tools, plan the order in which work is to be done, implement incentive systems of paying employees for their work and thus stimulate and reward accomplishments.[2]

While Taylor espoused an incentive wage system to accompany his concepts, he envisioned scientific management as much more than simply a method of financial incentives. He saw scientific management as:

- Science, not rule-of-thumb.

- Harmony, in place of discord in which employees oppose management's efforts to increase efficiency.

- Cooperation, replacing individual self-interest, so that all will benefit, not just a select few.

- Maximum output, instead of restricted production, which resulted from what Taylor referred to as "soldering," where employees deliberately withheld labor for various reasons, including the unjustified management practice of unilaterally raising work requirements.

- The development of all employees so that they are able to achieve their highest possible level of prosperity.

- Taylor used the term *first-class workers* to describe high performers who could produce from two to three times more work under scientific man-

[2] Taylor, Frederick Winslow, *The Principles of Scientific Management* (New York: The Norton Company, 1967), pp. 36-37.

agement than they formerly did. Taylor conducted numerous studies in several different industries, and he concluded that every employee can be first class at some job. Taylor found that many incentive pay plans failed because management did not explain the system to employees and gradually convert them to it. Taylor called this conversion the "mental revolution," and he said it was accomplished though "object lessons." An *object lesson* was experienced by each worker when he discovered that rewards were indeed greater under the new system. A *mental revolution* is a summation of the object lessons of many employees. Taylor cautioned that incentive pay systems may take as long as several years to fully convert employee thinking. Under scientific management, workers are paid from 30 to 100 percent more. The remainder of the savings resulting from the improvement in productivity are shared with stockholders by way of dividends and with customers through lower prices.

Behavioral Management

The behavioral management direction in management theory was more diverse than that which occurred during the scientific management era. Consequently, a single individual, such as Taylor in the scientific management era, cannot be used to adequately discuss the contributions of the individuals who had key roles in the behavioral management period. At the outset, a distinction should be noted in *behavioral management* and *behavioral leadership*. The concepts and the key players differ between the two theories. *Behavioral leadership* is discussed later in this chapter.

Among the leading practitioners of behavioral management were Edward Cadbury of the Cadbury Chocolate Company, Mary Parker Follett, and Elton Mayo.

Edward Cadbury

The Cadbury Company was a leader in recognizing how management initiatives, affecting the welfare of employees, resulted in behavioral changes in employees, including improvements in attendance, productivity, and turnover. Industrial welfarism was certainly typical of some of the improvements made at Cadbury, but many of the initiatives extended beyond that. Even the title of the book (*Experiments in Industrial Organization*) that Cadbury wrote describing the experimental work being done at Cadbury suggests that many of the initiatives made at the company were innovative. Cadbury was among the first companies to recognize the importance of encouraging employees to make suggestions for the improvement of the business. In 1902, the Cadbury Company established a formal suggestion program to suggest ways of improving products, making improvements in manufacturing methods, improving the marketing of products, and improving the work life of employees. Committees were established to publicize the program, receive suggestions and evaluate ideas. Cash awards were given to ideas that were adopted. Records were maintained on the number of suggestions that were received, the number adopted, and the amount of cash awards.

Recreation programs were introduced at Cadbury as early as 1852. The company sponsored various athletic clubs for employees. Among the other efforts made toward the maximum "development" of each employee were gardening classes, special educational schooling, dance instruction, swimming classes, wage bonus systems, physical and dental examinations, and vacations. Cadbury's practices became the standard for many other companies. For example, the chief executive of the National Cash Register Company (NCR) visited the Cadbury plant in England. Upon his return to the U.S., he implemented a plan in which he gave NCR managers copies of the book, *Experiments in Industrial Organization*, which featured many of the innovations at Cadbury. He requested that the managers read the book and inform him of the five most important programs introduced at Cadbury.[3]

Mary Parker Follett

Mary Parker Follett was among the first management philosophers to receive widespread recognition for her contributions. She devoted much of her life to understanding, refining and advancing principles applicable to improving the human factor and the efficiency of business and other organizations. For example, she found that the cornerstone of business success, as well as the improvement of mankind, was the coordination of effort. She further hypothesized that the desired level of coordination was not possible without the ability of people to cooperate. This cooperation, furthermore, could not be attained unless people could effectively communicate with each other. She believed business leaders could serve as examples to others how the desired level of coordination could be attained. This quote summarizes her thoughts on this subject:

> Certain changes have been going on in *business practice* which are destined, I believe, to alter our thinking fundamentally. I think this is a contribution which business is going to make to the world, and not only to the business world, but eventually to government and international relations. Men may be making useful products, but beyond this, by helping to solve the problems of human relations, they are perhaps destined to lead the world in the solution of those great problems of coordination and control upon which our future progress must depend.[4]

Most of her observations, which led to her theories, were conducted in business, although she also had a keen interest in, and made contributions toward, the field of political science. Mary Parker Follett did not characterize herself as a theorist. In fact, she enjoyed working among business managers because of their practicality. Nevertheless, many of her ideas were theories or assumptions about the way things should be done in business. For example, in a paper advising managers how to give orders to employees, she stressed the importance of those receiving the order understanding the purpose of it and accepting the reason for the order.

[3] Cadbury, Edward, *Experiments in Industrial Organization* (London: Longmans, Green, and Co., 1912), Foreword.

[4] Metcalf, Henry C. and Urwick, L., *Dynamic Administration: The Collected Papers of Mary Parker Follett* (New York: Harper & Brothers, 1940), p. 25.

Elton Mayo

Elton Mayo was a Professor of Industrial Research at the Graduate School of Business, Harvard University. Mayo conducted experimental studies in business to test the effects of different variables on the work performance of employees. In one of his earliest published studies, Mayo analyzed work in the mule-spinning department of a textile mill in Pennsylvania. The object of the study was to reduce the turnover rate among employees. Chief among the innovations which were introduced to address the turnover problem was the use of rest periods. Four rest periods were introduced; turnover went down, while production went up. When the rest periods were withdrawn, the production dropped again. The president of the company ordered that the rest periods be reinstituted, and the production returned to the higher level. The turnover rate during the 12-month experimental period fell to five percent, which matched the turnover rate in the whole plant.[5]

A later study, which was the hallmark of Mayo's industrial research, was conducted in 1926 in the relay assembly room of the Hawthorne plant of the Western Electric Company. Mayo introduced various innovations into the work setting of a selected group of workers. Then he measured the effects of the changes on the production of the workers. Among the innovations were the introduction of rest periods and changes in the illumination in the room. Virtually every change resulted in increased production. In retrospect, Mayo and his co-researchers reached the conclusion that the workers in the experimental setting were simply responding to the what they felt the researchers wanted. So, whether the illumination was decreased or increased, production still increased. The change in the experimental conditions did not produce the change—the employee's perception of what the researchers wanted produced the change. As a result of this experiment, the term *Hawthorne error*, also known as the *Hawthorne effect*, was coined. The *Hawthorne effect* occurs when the subjects in a pilot study, particularly those in the treatment groups, attempt to produce the results desired by the researchers.

Management Science

Management science is the application of statistics, mathematical models and other quantitative methods to management and decision-making processes. Advances in mathematics and other quantitative methods have led to their increasing use in management. In addition, managers' increased awareness of how these methods can be used in business decision-making has facilitated the process. Mathematics can be used in many business decisions, ranging from the establishment of minimum economic order quantities to optimum mixes of scarce resources.

Systems Theory

As the environments in which decision-making takes place have become more complex, managers have learned to incorporate both the external and the

---

[5] Mayo, Elton, *The Human Problems of an Industrial Civilization* (Cambridge, Massachusetts: The Murray Printing Company, 1946), pp. 62-67.

internal environment in the decision-making process. An organization does not function in a vacuum but rather must react with the environment in which it exists. Depending upon the society, the mission of the organization, and other variables, an organization may not be required to interact with or be cognizant of the environment. Such a system is called a *closed system*. In other settings, and when other variables exist, the organization may be required to respond to the external environment. These systems are called *open systems*.

Contingency Approach

Contemporary management realizes that no one approach to management is right for every occasion. Indeed, the environment in which an organization functions, the type of organization, the culture of both the external and internal environment, and other variables may influence the approach.

Leadership

A *leader* is a person who accomplishes results through others by satisfying their needs or influencing their behavior. A manager receives authority from the organization; a leader receives authority from those led. Stephen Covey believes *management* emphasizes efficiency and structure and *leadership* focuses on ensuring that the right things are being done.[6]

The four evolutionary stages through which leadership theories emerged are traitist, behavioral, contingency-situational, and transactional.

Traitist

The *traitist* theory of leadership assumes that outstanding leaders have one or more common characteristics or traits. One study found that successful leaders were ethical, inspirational, effective, intelligent, and future-oriented.[7]

Behavioral

The *behavioral* theory of leadership is distinctive from the *behavioral* theory of management. This theory assumes the leader's behavioral philosophy toward subordinates influences their behavior. These are some of the pioneers of this approach:

- *MacGregor's X and Y Theory of Management.* While this is a "theory of management," it actually describes the approaches which managers take in assuming leadership of their employees. The theory supposes that managers are either:
  - *Theory X* managers, who believe that subordinates naturally abhor work and must be controlled to see that tasks are accomplished, or
  - *Theory Y* managers, who believe that subordinates do not naturally dislike work and will actually enjoy work if properly motivated and rewarded.[8]

---

[6] Covey, S.R., *The 7 Habits of Highly Effective People* (New York: Simon & Schuster, 1990), pp. 101-103.

[7] Kouzes, J.M. and Posner, B.Z., *The Leadership Challenge* (San Francisco: Jossey-Bass, 1987), p. 17.

[8] MacGregor, D. *The Human Side of Enterprise* (New York: McGraw-Hill, 1960), pp. 33-45.

- *Likert's System Theory.*[9] According to this theory, managers can be categorized according to their trust in employees:
  - System 1=no trust
  - System 2=patronizing trust
  - System 3=some trust
  - System 4=complete trust
- *Blake and Mouton.*[10] This theory involves the use of a *managerial grid* for managers to identify their concerns for *production, people,* or both *production and people.*
  - A 9,1 on the grid indicates the person has a high concern for production and a low concern for people.
  - A 1,9 is the opposite.
  - A 9,9 is a high concern for both people and production.

Contingency/Situational

The *contingency-situational* approach to leadership assumes that no single method works for all leaders but rather leadership depends upon the contingencies in the situation, such as the personnel involved, the work to be done, and the environmental factors.

- *Hersey-Blanchard leadership model.*[11] According to this model, leaders tend toward either high or low assignment of tasks to subordinates and/or either high or low relationships with subordinates. This can result in four combinations of basic leadership styles:
  - High assignment of tasks and high relationship with subordinates;
  - Low assignment of tasks and low relationship with subordinates;
  - High assignment of tasks and low relationship with subordinates; or
  - Low assignment of tasks and high relationship with subordinates.
- *Fred Fiedler's three dimensions of leadership situations* (an optimum situation is when it is high in all three situations):[12]
  - *Leader-member relations.* This dimension involves trust or loyalty to a leader; it can be either high or low.
  - *Task structure.* This dimension concerns how clear goals and tasks are defined for the manager, which also can be either high or low.
  - *Position power.* This dimension is the perceived authority the manager has to get the job done, which, like the other dimensions, can be either high or low.

---

[9] Likert, R. *New Patterns of Management* (New York: McGraw-Hill, 1961), pp. 222-236, and *The Human Organization* (New York: McGraw-Hill, 1967).

[10] Blake, R. and Mouton, J., *The Managerial Grid* (Houston: Gulf Publishing Co., 1964).

[11] Hersey, P. and Blanchard, K.H., *Management of Organizational Behavior* (Englewood Cliffs, NJ: Prentice-Hall, 1977), p. 161.

[12] Fiedler, F.E., *A Theory of Leadership Effectiveness* (New York: McGraw-Hill, 1967).

Transactional/Transformational

A relatively new approach to leadership is the *transactional* or *transformational* theories. Bernard Bass[13] and John Burns make a distinction in the terms as follows:

- *Transactional leader.*
  - Defines desired performance;
  - Knows the rewards employees seek; and
  - Provides an environment in which these rewards are contingent upon employees achieving desired performance.
- Transformational leader:
  - Has charisma;
  - Uses intellectual stimulation; and
  - Uses individualism to recognize each employee for his or her contribution.

Decision-Making

Decision-making is the act of selecting a course of action, frequently from among several alternatives. There are various theories about the styles of decision-making which can be used.

- *Kepner-Tregoe* is a decision-making process involving:
  1. Recognizing the problem and determining what it does not include;
  2. Setting a priority for this and other problems;
  3. Assessing causes and effects; and
  4. Resolving the problem.[14]
- The *Vroom-Yetton model* proposes that a decision-maker can use one of five participation approaches in making a decision:
  - *Style A:* Make the decision alone;
  - *Style B:* Receive information from subordinates and then make the decision.
  - *Style C:* Inform individual employees of the problem, get ideas, and then make the decision.
  - *Style D:* Tell all employees as a group about the problem, solicit their ideas, and then make the decision.
  - *Style E:* Allow the group to solve the problem.

The model also proposes the use of a decision-tree in aiding the decision-maker.[15]

---

[13] Bass, B., *Leadership and Performance Beyond Expectations* (New York: Free Press, 1985).

[14] Kepner, C.H. and Tregoe, B.B., *The Rational Manager* (New York: McGraw-Hill, 1985).

[15] Vroom, V.H. and Yetton, P.W., *Leadership and Decision-Making* (Pittsburgh: University of Pittsburgh Press, 1973).

Quality Management

Contemporary management is very mindful of quality. This concern is evident in the multiple measures of quality used to track customer opinions about product quality. The major approaches to *Total quality management* and their proponents are:

- *W.E. Deming.* Deming's 14 points for quality management are:
    1. Make product improvement a constant purpose;
    2. Adopt the new philosophy of quality;
    3. Stop dependence on mass inspection;
    4. Stop awarding business on price alone;
    5. Constant improvement of product or service;
    6. Train all employees from top management down;
    7. Lead employees but don't supervise them;
    8. Eliminate the fear of change;
    9. Stop communication barriers among staff;
    10. Stop slogans and targets for workers;
    11. A. Eliminate numerical quotas for workers;
    12. B. Eliminate numerical quotas for management;
    13. Remove barriers to pride in workmanship;
    14. Encourage education and self-improvement; and
    15. Take action to accomplish these changes.[16]

- *J.M. Juran.* The three processes in the Juran Trilogy are "Quality planning, Quality control, and Quality improvement." In an effort to unify different definitions of quality, Juran states some people in the field developed the term "fitness for use." But he believes it unlikely that one term will be accepted by all.[17]

- *P.B. Crosby.* Crosby's 14 points for quality management are similar to Deming's, but there are also some differences, such as the use of quality improvement teams and quality councils.[18]

Quality Awards

Several national quality awards are given for outstanding achievements in product quality. Among them are the Baldrige National Quality Award. The award is presented by the President of the U.S. to large and small businesses in manufacturing and service and to education and health care organizations. Successful applicants must be judged outstanding in these seven areas: leadership; strategic planning; customer and market focus; measurement, analysis, and knowledge management; human resource focus; process management; and, re-

---

[16] Deming, W.E., *Out of the Crisis* (Cambridge, MA.: Massachusetts Institute of Technology, 1982).

[17] Juran, J.M., *Juran on Quality by Design* (New York: The Free Press, 1992).

[18] Crosby, P.B., *Quality Without Tears* (New York: McGraw-Hill, 1984).

sults. The program is managed by the U.S. Department of Commerce's National Institute of Standards and Technology in cooperation with private sector representatives.

Benchmarking

To measure themselves in various dimensions of a firm's operations, including quality, the management in some firms compares its organization to others in the field. This practice, which is known as *benchmarking*, consists of observing and using the practices of the best organizations in a field to compare oneself to and to adopt.

Theories of Human Behavior

Two of the principal theories of human behavior are *stimulus-response* and *cognitive*.

Stimulus-Response

Among the persons who contributed to the stimulus-response theory of behavior were Ivan Pavlov, Edward L. Thorndike and John B. Watson. Advocates of this approach rejected other theories that used intuition and subjectivity to explain human behavior. In the words of John B. Watson, who was a major force in the development of stimulus-response research, the introspective psychologist is not a scientist because " . . . no other human being can make an introspective observation upon any behavior but himself."[19]

Stimulus-response psychology was a logical outgrowth of the early twentieth century preoccupation with the science of human behavior. Scientific management was also spawned in this same milieu. *Behaviorism* was that part of stimulus-response theory that had the most impact upon various HR practices. For example, several of the concepts used in HR development, such as programmed instruction, are based upon the learning and reinforcement theories of behaviorism. Also, various types of incentive reward systems are based upon these same concepts.

John B. Watson is acknowledged as the major force in what was then the "new" science of human behavior. Later, Watson's protege, Benjamin Skinner, refined his theories through additional research.[20]

Unconditioned and Conditioned Stimuli

Behaviorists believe human behavior is conditioned by the results of past behavior, that is, people learn from their past experiences, which shape their future behavior. The two categories of these experiences are:

- *Unconditioned stimuli;* and
- *Conditioned stimuli.*

Ivan Pavlov, the famous Russian physiologist, used a dog in his famous experiments with conditioned and unconditioned stimuli. Pavlov found that the

---

[19] Watson, J.B., *Psychology from the Standpoint of a Behaviorist* (Philadelphia: J.B. Lippincott Company, 1924), p. 396.

[20] Skinner, B.F., *Contingencies of Reinforcement* (New York: Appleton-Century-Crofts, 1969).

dog would salivate in response to conditioned and/or unconditioned stimuli. The dog salivated when a meat paste was placed before him. This is an example of an *unconditioned stimulus*, since hungry animals naturally salivate when food is placed before them. In this case, the food is the unconditioned stimulus that causes the saliva, which is the *unconditioned response*. Pavlov began using a tuning fork prior to giving the meat paste to the dog. Eventually, the dog started salivating upon hearing the tuning fork. The sound of the tuning fork was the *conditioned stimulus* that produced the saliva, which was the *conditioned response*.

Relevance of Stimulus/Response Theory

While no one would imply that dogs are human, this theory has considerable relevance to some HR activities, particularly in HR development and compensation. For example, one organization trains truck driver trainees to be alert in backing situations through the use of both a warning buzzer and an oral caution by a trainer. Through repeated oral warnings in each backing exercise, the trainee becomes conditioned to be alert when the buzzer sounds, even though the trainer is not present. In another organization, each employee is given a number of coupons at the beginning of each month, redeemable for merchandise at the end of the month. Employees are required to relinquish a given number of coupons each day they are late for work. A larger number of coupons must be forfeited for each unscheduled absence. A box is mounted near the time clock for employees to deposit their daily forfeitures. The coupons are intended to condition employees to be punctual and regular in attendance.

A bank uses the concept of behaviorism in 75 different incentive-pay programs covering about 339 of its 485 employees, in jobs ranging from clerks to senior vice presidents. Officials of the bank state that the incentive programs are responsible for a two to three times increase in productivity.

Reinforcement

Conditioning through reinforcement is intended to influence desired behavior by the administration of stimuli in response to behavior. For example, under a piece-rate pay system, a machine operator is rewarded for each finished piece of work that meets quality standards. The reward reinforces the behavior. *Reinforcement*, therefore, is the process of recognizing and responding to behavior so that desired acts will be learned and repeated, and undesirable ones will not.

Operant Conditioning

An *operant* is an approach that "operates" upon the environment in which behavior occurs. Thus, *operant conditioning* uses various stimuli to influence behavior.

Vicarious and Personal Experiences

Behaviorists believe employee performance is conditioned by responses to past behavior. This conditioning or learning may be reinforced through vicarious and/or personal experiences. For example, an employee may be punctual because he was counseled (personal experience) by his supervisor for not reporting for work on time. The employee's punctuality may also be influenced by observing other employees being counseled (vicarious experience) for not reporting on time. An employee's punctuality is also influenced by other variables, such as prior conditioning, which is called *reinforcement*. For example, if an employee is commended for being punctual, his behavior is positively reinforced, which increases the likelihood that it will be repeated.

Law of Effect

The *law of effect* states that people learn and repeat acts that are reinforced and rewarded and will avoid acts associated with unpleasant stimuli or punishment.

Schedules of Reinforcement

The different frequencies of reinforcing behavior are called *schedules of reinforcement*. These are the common schedules:

- *Continuous reinforcement*. The behavior is reinforced each time it occurs. For example, each time an employee is late, he/she is counseled by his/her supervisor.

- *Intermittent reinforcement*. This reinforcement is made on the basis of the instance or instances in which a behavior occurs (*ratio reinforcement*) or after a period of time has elapsed (*interval reinforcement*).

  - *Ratio reinforcement*. This reinforcement is based upon the instance that a behavior occurs. Ratio reinforcements can be either *fixed* or *variable*.

    - *Fixed ratio reinforcement* is providing reinforcement following a fixed number of responses, such as giving an employee a cash bonus for producing 500 widgets without making an error.

    - *Variable ratio reinforcement* provides reinforcement after a given number of responses, but the number varies from one reinforcement to the next. After producing 100 widgets without an error, the worker is given a cash bonus. Next, the worker gets a bonus after producing 50 widgets without an error. Payoffs from slot machines are an example of this type of reinforcement. Gambling experts believe that the variable ratio payoffs from gambling reinforce the destructive gambling behavior of compulsive gamblers.[21]

  - *Interval reinforcement*. This schedule of reinforcement is based on time. The period of time can be either *fixed* or *variable*.

    - *Fixed interval reinforcement* provides a reinforcement after a set period of time; for instance, an employee receives a paycheck every two weeks.

    - *Variable interval reinforcement* provides a reinforcement after a period of time that varies. For example, safety performance in a plant can be rewarded on an unpredictable, variable interval reinforcement schedule. After one hour of accident-free work, all the employees in the plant will receive free refreshments during their breaks. The

---

[21] Myers, D.W. and Custer, R.L., "Pathological Gambling," in *Employee Problem Prevention and* *Counseling: A Guide for Professionals* (Westport, CT: Greenwood Press, 1985), p. 90.

schedule may then vary to four hours without an accident, and workers may receive a small cash bonus.

Cognitive Psychology

The cognitive approach to human behavior stresses the importance of the needs, wants, and beliefs of people as the major causes of their behavior. Thus, people are moved to act in certain ways because of their needs or other internal characteristics. Where behaviorism searches for the external stimulus that prompted a person's response, cognitive psychology looks for the internal needs, desires, or other personal characteristics that motivated the action.

Cognition

Cognition is the process of learning that incorporates numerous personal characteristics, such as experience and judgment. People categorize their experiences and utilize them in the future. The information obtained through this cognitive process is used in other situations where it can help a person make decisions. Sometimes, these new experiences result in a rearrangement or change in old perceptions. In short, human behavior is the result of an internal thought process in which people relate their past experiences and perceptions to present events.

Content and Process Theories

Content theories attempt to explain the particular cause or causes of human behavior. *Process* theories focus on the method or *process* in which motivation occurs.

Need Hierarchy

The best known of the content theories of motivation is Abraham Maslow's *need pyramid*.[22] In this pyramid or hierarchy, human needs are arranged from the lowest level of needs, the subsistence level, up to self-actualization, which is the highest level. These are the levels of needs:

- *Subsistence level.* The subsistence or physiological needs, as Maslow called them, are basic and predominant over all others until they are satiated. Included in the basic needs are fatigue, hunger, sex and thirst.

- *Safety needs.* The context of safety includes physical and psychological well-being, as well as freedom from fear of chaos, need for strength, confidence in being protected, and the need for structure. As a general rule, people seek an environment that is predictable and secure. These needs become aroused, for example, when there is talk at work about a reorganization or a merger. As was true with the physiological needs, the safety needs will dominate higher level needs if a person's physical or mental well-being is threatened.

- *Belonging, group, or love needs.* These needs include feelings of acceptance, friendship, receiving and giving affection and simply having contact with

---

[22] Maslow, A.H., *Motivation and Personality* (New York: Harper, 1954), pp. 35-58.

other people. In an organizational environment, people will demonstrate their concern for love and belonging by such actions as forming cliques.

- *Esteem needs.* These needs are best explained by the observation that people want to be considered worthy and be respected. Maslow believed esteem needs could be divided into two groups. The first group includes characteristics more closely associated with self-esteem, such as the self-satisfaction from achievement or accomplishment and the need to be independent and self-sufficient. The second group concerns esteem or respect from other people, such as achieving fame or recognition, being treated with dignity and respect and receiving attention.

- *Self-actualization.* The pinnacle of the need hierarchy is self-actualization or the desire to become everything that one is capable of becoming. Self-fulfillment is another term that describes the need for actualizing one's life.

Maslow noted that a need did not require 100-percent satisfaction before the next one becomes an important determinant of behavior. At any point in time, most people have only partially satiated their various needs. To emphasize this fact he said, " . . . it is as if the average citizen is satisfied perhaps 85 percent in his physiological needs, 70 percent in his safety needs, 50 percent in his love needs, 40 percent in his self-esteem needs, and 10 percent in his self-actualization needs."[23]

Applying the Need Hierarchy

Exhibit 2-1 contains selected examples of various compensation methods as they relate to different need levels. Properly planned and communicated, the various methods of compensation can be effective in meeting human needs. For example, bonuses help meet employees' basic needs by providing the income necessary to maintain a subsistence standard of living. Bonuses, like other types of incentive-pay systems, may adversely affect employees' safety needs if the systems are not carefully explained so employees understand how they function. Also, bonuses paid on an infrequent basis, such as annually, cause employee concerns, such as how much the bonus will be and whether management is correctly maintaining records so that employees will be properly paid.

Exhibit 2-1
Compensation Methods and Human Needs

Compensation Method	Level of Needs Met				
	Basic	Safety	Group	Esteem	Self-Actualization
Direct					
Bonus				✓	✓
Profit-sharing/Gainsharing			✓	✓	✓
Salary/Wages	✓	✓			
Indirect					
Dependent Care		✓	✓		

---

[23] *Ibid.*, p. 54.

Compensation Method	Level of Needs Met				
	Basic	Safety	Group	Esteem	Self-Actualization
Disability Income	✓	✓			
Educational Assistance				✓	✓
Employee Assistance Programs			✓		
Legal Services	✓	✓			
Life Insurance	✓	✓			
Medical Expenses	✓	✓			
Outplacement Counseling	✓	✓			
Paid Holidays			✓		
Pension/Retirement Plan	✓	✓			
Retirement Counseling	✓	✓			
Social Security	✓	✓			
Unemployment Insurance	✓	✓			
Vacations			✓		
Wellness Plans		✓	✓	✓	✓
Workers' Compensation	✓	✓			

Compensation methods, like profit-sharing plans, help develop esteem needs. Group or love needs may also be met through such indirect compensation methods as dependent care. Pay-incentive plans are especially suited for recognizing the individual efforts of employees, which appeal to their esteem needs. Cash payments made to top performers, particularly when they are publicized, increase employee esteem and feelings of self-worth.

Pay incentives can also help fulfill employees' self-actualization needs. For example, insurance companies recognize sales personnel who achieve top sales commissions. Among the awards given are membership in elite groups, such as the President's Club. Educational assistance programs are another type of benefit that helps employees fulfill their self-actualization needs.

Expectancy Theory[24]

Expectancy theory is one of the more elaborate attempts to conceptualize the internal thought processes that cause or actuate human behavior. Obviously, since such thought patterns cannot be directly observed, they cannot be precisely measured. To overcome this significant deficiency, however, theorists attempt to describe relevant variables that people generally seem to consider in some aspects of their behavior, particularly when they have the time to do so. Victor Vroom, who developed the expectancy theory, believes that five such variables in human behavior are:

- Expectancy;
- Instrumentality;
- Valence;
- A first-level outcome; and

---

[24] Vroom, Victor, H. *Work and Motivation* (New York: Wiley, 1964).

- A second-level outcome.

Expectancy/Instrumentality

Expectancy and *instrumentality* are probabilities that people assign to outcomes.

Expectancy. The expectancy probability is +1.0 if a person is certain an outcome will occur. The probability of zero means the opposite. For example, employees make estimations about whether their increased effort on a job will result in improved performance. These estimations or probabilities can range from +1.0 to zero. This example expresses expectancy probabilities in common terms: "To what extent can I *expect* (the expectancy or first level probability) my performance to improve if I put forth more effort?" The *first-level outcome* in this situation is the level of the employee's job performance.

Instrumentality. *Instrumentality*, as noted above, is also a probability estimation but the magnitude of it differs from expectancy, since it ranges from +1.0 to −1.0. The reason for the difference is that the instrumentality probability is conditional upon the occurrence of a first-level outcome. An instrumentality of +1.0 means a specific outcome is certain if a first-level outcome occurs and −1.0 means an outcome will not occur if the first-level outcome does occur. These concepts can be applied to the example in the previous paragraph illustrating the idea of expectancy probability. Assume an organization communicates to employees the amount of merit pay increases to be awarded based upon employees' job performance. In this case, employees would make assessments of the probability (instrumentality) concerning the effects that the first-level outcome (improved job performance) would lead to a desired second-level outcome (a merit pay increase). This statement expresses the two probabilities and the two outcomes in a logical sequence: "To what extent can I *expect* (first-level probability) that my increased effort will result in improved job performance (a first-level outcome) and, should that occur, how *instrumental* (second-level probability) will it be in getting a merit pay raise (a second-level outcome)?"

Valences. *Valences* are the values people assign to different outcomes; they may be either positive, such as a pay increase, or negative, such as a warning letter.

Effort Formula. This theory assumes a person's motivation or effort can be conceptualized by this formula:

Effort = E(IV)

Where:

E = the expectancy or probability that a first-level outcome will occur.

I = the instrumentality or probability that a second-level outcome will occur.

V = valences (values) people assign to second-level outcomes.

Illustrations. The information in Exhibit 2-2 illustrates how the theory could conceivably function. Assume John Billman is a Machine Operator for Crown Manufacturing Company. Assume Crown is implementing a new pay plan. Each operator will be placed in one of three plans, depending upon their productivity. The new top pay grade, Pay Grade 3, will be 50 percent above the existing rate. Pay Grade 2 will 15 percent above the current rate, and Pay Grade 1 will be equivalent to the present pay rate.

Exhibit 2-2
Illustration of Expectancy Theory

	Expectancy	Instrumentality	Valences
Decision A	.8 = Productivity will	.6 = Pay Grade 3	+ 4
Work at	increase	.4 = Pay Grade 2	+ 2
top		−.4 = Pay Grade 1	− 3
performance			
	.2 = Productivity will	−.2 = Pay Grade 3	+ 6
	remain the same	.4 = Pay Grade 2	+ 3
		.8 = Pay Grade 1	+ 1
Decision B	.3 = Productivity will	.6 = Pay Grade 3	+ 4
Work at present	increase.	.4 = Pay Grade 2	+ 2
level of		−.4 = Pay Grade 1	+ 1
performance			
	.7 = Productivity will	−.2 = Pay Grade 3	+ 6
	remain the same	.4 = Pay Grade 2	+ 3
		.8 = Pay Grade 1	+ 1

In this situation, employees would typically consider many alternatives in deciding how they would respond to the conditions proposed by the company. For simplicity purposes, the data in Exhibit 2-2 assumes that John is considering only two alternatives. The first is to work at his top performance level (Decision A). The second is to work at his present level of performance (Decision B). John makes estimates of the probabilities (expectancies) of whether his productivity will increase or remain the same under both decisions. Furthermore, he estimates the probabilities (instrumentalities) of being placed in the each of the three pay categories, depending upon the first-level outcome. John assigns different values to the three pay grades for the two alternatives and the various first- and second-level outcomes.

Below are the calculations using the formula, Effort = E(IV). John selects Decision A, since it has a higher numerical value.

Decision A = .8 [(.6 × 4) + (.4 × 2) + (−.4 × −3)] + .2 [(−.2 × 6) + (.4 × 3) + (.8 × 1)] = 3.68
Decision B = .3 [(.6 × 4) + (.4 × 2) + (−.4 × 1)] + .7 [(−.2 × 6) + (.4× 3) + (.8 × 1)] = 1.40

Relevance of Expectancy Theory

Obviously, there are limitations to the application of expectancy theory to management. First, it is doubtful that any person makes the many intricate calculations assumed by the theory. For example, people typically do not consciously assign probabilities to even the simplest of outcomes. Also, it is evident to even the most casual observer of human behavior that people seldom engage in rational decision-making to the extent that they consider the possible outcomes of their behavior, let alone contemplate different alternatives, probabilities and valences.

In spite of these deficiencies, expectancy theory is important because it helps explain how employees' past employment experiences with various compensation methods, such as an incentive pay plan, will affect their reactions to a management initiative to install one. If these past experiences were negative, such as the plan was poorly administered or, even more important, management did not keep its commitments, even the best-designed plan will be opposed by employees.

The theory also makes a major contribution by describing how people have different values. Management would be wise to measure these values before proceeding too far with initiatives designed to influence employee effort and motivation.

Reward Theory

Employees receive varying amounts of both extrinsic and intrinsic rewards from work. Examples of both types of rewards are shown in Exhibit 2-3.

Exhibit 2-3
Examples of Extrinsic and Intrinsic Rewards

	Extrinsic		
Intrinsic	Compensation		
	Direct	*Indirect*	*Noncompensation*
Challenge	Base pay	Dependent care	Certificates
Creativity	Bonuses	Disability income	Commendations
Feedback	Gainsharing	Paid holidays	Peer recognition
Fulfillment		Pension	Praise
Task autonomy		Vacation	Prizes
Task identity		Wellness plans	
Task significance			
Task variety			

Extrinsic Rewards

As the term suggests, *extrinsic rewards* are those compensatory and noncompensatory rewards from work that are external to the job and are granted as a condition of employment and in recognition of task performance.

Compensatory Rewards. Compensatory extrinsic rewards include both direct compensation, such as wages and salaries, and indirect compensation, such as medical expense benefit plans.

Noncompensatory Rewards. As most employers know, employees are motivated to varying degrees by the noncompensatory types of extrinsic rewards. For example, a trophy or plaque awarded for outstanding performance is a permanent testimony of an individual's worth and accomplishment. Some employees typically place such awards in prominent places in their homes and offices.

Often, the motivational impact of compensatory rewards upon employees is less apparent than noncompensatory ones because of the failure to properly inform employees about them. For example, employees often take for granted employee benefit programs, such as retirement plans, that may be a major expense item for an employer. Even a cash bonus is rather quickly forgotten once the funds are spent. Sometimes, the reason compensatory programs, even ones directly related to performance, do not have the intended motivational appeal is because the provisions are too complex and employees do not understand them.

Intrinsic Rewards

Intrinsic rewards are those rewards employees personally experience from within their psyche as a result of performing their job tasks. Some examples of intrinsic rewards are shown in Exhibit 2-3. While all jobs have extrinsic rewards, not all of them have intrinsic rewards. This is not necessarily bad, unless an employee wants such rewards. Studies have demonstrated that, for some employees, monotonous and unchallenging jobs can result in expressions of job dissatisfaction, absenteeism, product defects, excessive errors, lower production and turnover.

There is evidence that job dissatisfaction may result in various acts of vandalism by employees. For example, an unhappy computer operator removed the labels from a number of computer tape reels. Many hours of time were expended to re-label the tapes. Dissatisfied employees also may commit criminal acts. For example, one-third of the employees responding to a survey of 47 firms said they stole company property. The theft was more common among those employees who were more dissatisfied with their supervisors and their organization's " . . . attitude toward the work force."[25] Disturbed employees have also committed more heinous crimes, such as murdering their peers and supervisors.

Equity Theory

Equity is the perceived fairness of the intrinsic and extrinsic rewards that employees receive in exchange for their performance of job tasks.

Job Inputs/Rewards

The input portions of employees' equity assessment are their personal qualifications and the level of their job performance. The outputs are the intrinsic and extrinsic rewards the employees receive. The theory suggests that employees view the equity exchange from these three perspectives:

- First, employees view their personal exchange, that is, what they bring to a job and what they get from it.

- Next, employees enlarge the scope and compare their personal exchange with the exchange of their peers within the organization. To some extent, this assessment may be inhibited by a company's policy prohibiting employees from discussing personal pay matters with their peers.

- Finally, in the third analysis, employees compare the exchanges (both personal and with peers) within the organization with the exchanges of employees in other organizations in the labor market.

---

[25] "Survey finds pilferage by workers widespread," *Richmond Times-Dispatch* (June 11, 1983), p. A-11.

Exchange Assessments Outcomes

Employees may initially feel their exchanges are equitable; however, this opinion may change when they compare their personal exchange with the exchanges of their peers. For example, an employee may be happy with a five-percent pay raise until he realizes that a peer, whose work he feels is inferior, got a seven-percent raise. In the same vein, employees may be generally satisfied with their benefit plan until they learn that employees in another firm in the area have what they believe to be a better benefit plan.

Equity comparisons may cause employees to react in a number of ways. Perceptions of fair exchanges promote employee loyalty to the firm, job satisfaction, low absenteeism, and low turnover. Perceptions of inequities cause the opposite reactions. In addition, these perceptions of inequities may cause employee frustration and counterproductive behavior, such as aggression that can lead to criminal acts, like stealing or destroying company property.

Internal and External Equity

In view of the importance of employee assessments of equity, employers attempt to achieve it through compensation practices focusing on *internal equity* and *external equity*.

External equity. *External equity* is the degree to which an organization's compensation program rewards employees relative to their contributions compared to the rewards received for similar contributions by employees of other employers in the labor market.

Internal equity. *Internal equity* is the degree to which an organization's compensation program rewards employees relative to their contributions within the organization.

CHAPTER 3
HUMAN RESOURCES PLANNING

Chapter Highlights
- Introduce human resource planning
- Explain the role of strategic planning
- Describe various techniques used in human resources planning

Introduction

In recognition of the valued contribution of HR to organizational success, the top U.S. firms are incorporating human resources planning in every stage of strategic management, from the development of strategic goals to the formulation of operational plans.

Human resources planning (HRP) is the management function of planning applied to human resources management.

Planning includes determining what is to be done, who is to do it, and when and how it will be done. As shown in Exhibit 3-1, HRP is involved in all levels of planning, including strategic planning and the operational implementation of the strategic plan. In addition, HRP is incorporated in HRM activities, such as recruitment planning, planning selection procedures and planning for negotiations in the collective bargaining process. Typically, HRP involves staffing activities, which include recruitment and selection, for all levels of the organization, from entry-level jobs to top management succession planning.

Human Resources Planning Staffing Process

The typical HRP process involving staffing entails these four steps:

- *Determine human resource needs.* If a planned action will be taken, such as marketing a product in a new area, what will be the resulting effect upon human resources? This "what if" type of scenario analysis begins with determining what the human resource needs for each job will result from this action. First, all jobs affected by the proposal will be identified. Next, estimations are made of the number of positions that will be needed for each job should a particular plan be implemented. Various techniques can be used in making these estimations, including quantitative ones, such as those used in forecasting models, and qualitative ones, including personal judgments of informed individuals. Examples of both quantitative and qualitative methods of forecasting are discussed later in this chapter. Sometimes, a range of the possible needs for each job is determined. In addition, to get some idea of the criticality of the needs, jobs can be grouped into various categories, such as *basic importance, very important* and *essential.*

- *Determine human resource supply.* After estimations of personnel needs have been made, the next step is to determine the existing supply of employees for those jobs. This refers to the supply of personnel who are currently employed in the organization. These employees could be employed in either the jobs affected by the proposed plan or in other jobs, if the individuals are known to be qualified to meet the proposed need. The organization's human resource information system is typically used to identify personnel who are qualified for placement in the jobs where the need exists. Other sources of information about qualified employees are the career planning program, replacement charts, or in-house application files. Equally important is identifying those jobs for which there is an abundant, perhaps even an excess, supply of potential in-house candidates.

- *Analyze needs and supply.* A comparison between planned personnel needs and existing supply is the third step. Short-falls of personnel, particularly in those jobs determined to be essential, would be highlighted, since they could impact how efficiently and quickly a proposed plan could be implemented. Equally important is identifying the number of personnel, by job, that would exceed needs.

- *Propose actions to fill the shortages and eliminate surpluses.* A key step in deciding whether and/or when a particular plan should be implemented is based on a feasible timetable for resolving any differences in personnel needs and the supply of personnel. Estimations are often required in this step, including the probability that necessary personnel, particularly those to fill the essential jobs, can be selected and be ready to assume the job tasks as required by the plan. A delay in a proposed plan may be required until the estimated date qualified personnel will become available. Plans resulting in excess personnel, which in turn will necessitate lay-offs or terminations, also may require postponements to meet legal notice requirements.

Exhibit 3-1
Human Resources Planning and Strategic Planning

Planning Environment	
Internal	External
• Culture	• Laws and Regulations
• Financial Condition	• Competition
• Employee Characteristics	• Consumer Demand
	• Financial Institutions
	• Technology
	• Labor Market

Strategic Planning	
Human Resources Planning Input	Strategic Planning Outcomes

• Process
  ▶ Forecast Human Resources Needs
  ▶ Determine Human Resources Supply
    ▶ Analyze Needs and Supply
    ▶ Action Planning
• Decision-Making
  ▶ Acquisitions/divestitures
  ▶ Market Entrance/Egress
  ▶ Market Share
  ▶ Technology Implementation
  ▶ Organization Design
	• Mission Statement
	• Strategic Goals
	• Policies
	• Objectives

Operational Planning (Example)	
Human Resources Planning Input	Areas
• Staffing • Human Resources Utilization • Employee and Labor Relations	• Budgeting • Capital Investment • Efficiency Improvements

Planning Time Horizons

Planning outcomes can be rather conveniently categorized into three groups:

- *Short-term planning* involves plans that typically are accomplished in less than one year. For example, *management by objectives* is a performance appraisal system in which employees set the objectives they intend to accomplish within the ensuing year.

- *Intermediate planning* is focused on activities that have a time horizon ranging from one to five years.

- *Long-term planning* involves time periods of more than five years. Because of the time horizon of long-range planning, most strategic plans, that is, those activities immediately directed towards the accomplishment of the organization's mission, are long-term.

The Planning Environment

All planning is conducted within an organization's internal and external environment. The internal environment is unique to each organization; the external environment may differ among organizations, depending upon such factors as the organization's locality, size and industry. The planning environment exerts a persuasive role in both strategic and operational planning.

Internal Environment

The *internal environment* is unique in each organization because it includes the culture and characteristics of the employees in the organization.

Organization Culture

The *organization culture* is the institutionalized customs, beliefs, rules, values, and management philosophies that exist in an organization:

- *Customs* are expressions, habits, and ways of accomplishing things. In some organizations the customs may include a unique language used in communicating different situations that occur in the organization. One custom which is changing in many organizations is "the organizational dress code." Many organizations are switching from the traditional white shirt and tie to more casual attire. Even changes in customs like the dress code require a phase-in period for employees to fully accept them.[1]

- *Beliefs* are the expectations and opinions those organization members acquire as they become acclimated to the organization. Sometimes these beliefs are so accurate that employees can predict future organizational events and decisions.

- *Rules* are written and unwritten standards to which employees are expected to conform. All organizations have some rules, since, without basic ones, the result would be chaos. Rules tend to give order in organizational life. More formalized and bureaucratic organizations tend to have more extensive systems of rules' but excessive rules tend to stifle employee creativity and spontaneity. Obviously, a balance is needed between too much and too little regulation.

- *Values* are opinions based upon such judgements as the relative worth of different intrinsic and extrinsic rewards. Some organizations value timidity while others demand boldness.

- *Management philosophies* are the prevalent attitudes toward growth, human resource contributions to organizational success, profitability, customer service, and social responsibility.

Organizations have unique cultures that evolve over time and sometimes are difficult to change. Employees become acclimated to a particular "corporate culture," and changes to those customs and rules may be met with resistance by employees because they do not understand how the changes may affect them. Nevertheless, changes in an organization's culture may be necessitated by various conditions in a competitive business environment. For example, one manager in a high technology manufacturing industry stated, "You simply cannot run a high-level automated process without changing the culture in the plant."[2] Public organizations may also have to change the culture if budgetary reductions and other considerations mandate it.

Financial Conditions

The financial conditions in an organization, such as its profitability, liabilities and assets, affect the environment in which HRP is conducted. Organizations on a positive growth path in such areas as sales or market share may require

---

[1] Ziegler, B., "IBM Goes Casual, Drops White Shirts, and Plans a Woodsier Headquarters," *The Wall Street Journal* (February 3, 1995), p. A-6.

[2] "Winchester Plant Throws Light on Future," *Richmond Times-Dispatch* (May 29, 1990), p. A-10.

additional personnel or additional qualifications for existing personnel to meet current or expected needs. On the other hand, firms facing declining profits or even losses may be required to restructure, lay off personnel or take other actions which might affect the need for personnel. Firms sometimes have to face the reality of restructuring compensation, such as reducing or even abolishing employee benefit programs due to financial considerations.

Workforce Characteristics

The characteristics of the employees in an organization are another important part of the internal environment that is considered in HRP. These characteristics represent various dimensions of employees, such as human capital or demographic. The human capital dimension consists of the employees' qualifications, such as training, education, experience, knowledge, skills, and abilities. These components can be further divided into personal constructs, for example, personal work ethic, creativity, stress tolerance and leadership. Workforce characteristics also consist of demographic variables, such as race, sex, age, marital status and number of dependents. A strategic decision to expand into a new market must incorporate such workforce characteristics as whether there are a sufficient number of qualified personnel to perform the new work to be done.

External Environment

The external environment is the other part of the total environment in which HRP is conducted. The *external environment* includes laws and regulations, competition, consumer demand, financial institutions, rate of technological innovation in the market, and labor market conditions.

Laws and Regulations

Laws and regulations include those at the federal, state and local level, as well as court decisions or case law affecting the business. The general HRM activities which have a preponderance of the legal and regulatory requirements affecting HRM are:

- Staffing;
- Job Structuring;
- Labor Relations;
- Safety, Health and Security;
- Pay Administration;
- Benefits Administration;
- Employee Relations; and
- Human Resources/Career Development.

Strategic planning, which would affect any of these areas, must consider all applicable laws and regulations. For example, a decision to restructure a retirement or other employee benefits plan must take into account the Employee Retirement Income Security Act (ERISA).

Competition

In a competitive society, rivals' actions influence organizational planning. For example, a new product introduced by a competitor that has a lower price and better features will inevitably affect an organization's planning. Similarly, the HRM practices of firms may influence the planning of other firms who compete for employees in the same labor market. For example, firms that increase employee pay or benefits may necessitate similar changes by other firms competing for employees from the same labor market.

Consumer Demand

The demand for human resources is derived from the need for the good or service which the organization produces. Projections of changes in demand may affect personnel requirements, that is, an increase in demand may necessitate the recruitment of additional personnel or additional outsourcing.

Financial Institutions

Financial institutions, such as banks, insurance companies and investment bankers influence strategic planning decision-making in such areas as acquisitions and new product marketing through the availability of financing, interest rates and management control. For example, raising capital through a stock offering to finance an expansion may cause a dilution of ownership. Also, the interest rates banks charge for a commercial loan may necessitate cost savings or productivity improvements to avoid price increases.

Technological Innovation

Changes in technology may influence HRP in several ways. First, additional labor-saving devices may reduce the need for employees. In addition, changes in technology may require additional investments in personnel to both operate and maintain equipment. In some situations, the advent of new technology will necessitate the external recruitment of individuals who already possess the requisite knowledge and experience for effective utilization.

Labor Market

The labor market is, of course, the source of job applicants. There is not a single labor market, since the geographical area depends upon the type of job to be filled. For example, the labor market for a bank teller is decidedly different than one for a gravure printer or a genetic biologist. While the labor market for the job of bank teller would typically be local, such as the city in which the bank is located, the market for gravure printers might be as large as a state, and the market for recruiting a genetic biologist might include the entire U.S. Since HRM managers are knowledgeable about such conditions, they can significantly aid planning processes which involve personnel changes.

Strategic Planning

Strategic planning is the process of formulating the mission of an organization and developing goals and other strategies to accomplish it, taking into account the internal and external environment. Various planning techniques are used in strategic planning. *SWOT analysis* is a method that facilitates the process by helping the decision-makers focus on issues important to the firm. The term *SWOT* is an acronym derived from *S*trengths, *W*eaknesses, *O*pportunities, and *T*hreats.

Among the outputs of the strategic planning process are a mission statement, and goals, policies, and objectives supporting attainment of the mission.

A *mission statement* defines the basic service or good the organization is designed to provide within a generally defined market.

Example of a mission statement: General Motors Mission

> The fundamental purpose of General Motors is to provide products and services of such quality that our customers will receive superior value, our employees and business partners will share in our success, and our stockholders will receive a sustained, superior return on their investment.

A *goal* is a long-term plan specifying the generalized results to be attained to accomplish the organization's mission. For example, certain characteristics of a car, such as its quality, styling and safety, are important considerations for consumers. Failing to achieve customer expectations in those areas adversely affects consumer demand. Consequently, General Motors' management is concerned about those same characteristics in their cars and, as a result, the firm has a goal addressing those concerns.

Example of a goal: General Motors' Strategic Goal:

> Products that set standards in quality, performance, styling, safety and customer value.

A *policy* is a broad guideline that specifies the direction the organization intends to take with regard to a particular subject. For example, the Pittson Minerals Group of the Pittston Company produces and markets low-sulphur steam coal used in the production of electricity. The company also mines coal used in steel production. Consequently, environmental issues are a vital concern to the company.

Example of a policy: Pittston Company's Environmental Policy:

> The Pittston Company is dedicated to compliance with environmental laws and sound environmental practices. Pittston has accordingly developed broad environmental principles to govern its diverse operations. The management of each of Pittston's operating units is required to adopt and adhere to policies consistent with these broad principles, and to effectively address environmental concerns, including those of particular application to each group's business activities.

An *objective* is an action an organization intends to take to meet its policies or other stated obligations. Typically, objectives address such key areas as: (1) profitability or commitments to stockholders, (2) customer service and product quality and price, (3) social responsibility and responses to societal conditions such as laws, and (4) commitment to employees. Since Pittston has a policy with respect to environmental issues, it should not be surprising that the company has a number of objectives to implement such a policy. The following example is one of those objectives.

Example of an objective: Pittston Company's Management Objective Toward the Attainment of Its Environmental Policy:

> Educate, train and motivate employees to conduct their activities in an environmentally responsible manner.

HRM's Involvement in Strategic Planning

CEOs of firms are increasingly recognizing the importance of including HRM in the strategic planning for their firms. Prior to 1985, few firms included HRM in strategic planning and decision-making. In that period, HRM was expected to implement the results of the strategic plan to help ensure that desired accomplishments would occur without having a role in the development of it. Things have changed; HRM is no longer on the sidelines while the plan is being developed. On the contrary, for most firms, HRM is a partner in some, if not all, of the strategic planning process. For example, 96 percent of the respondents in a national survey who indicated strategic planning was conducted in their organizations in the area of human resource forecasting/planning stated that HR was involved either solely (69 percent of firms) or in conjunction with other departments (27 percent of firms) in this strategic planning activity.[3] The respondents in 87 percent of the firms indicating they conducted strategic planning in the activity of organization development stated HR was involved either solely (37 percent of firms) or with other departments (55 percent of firms) in the planning.

Key Areas of HRM Strategic Planning Involvement

HRM's role in strategic planning is of key importance in decisions involving acquisitions and divestitures, market entrance and egress, market share, technology implementation, and organizational restructuring and redesign.

Acquisitions and Divestitures. HRM has a valuable role in strategic planning involving acquisitions and/or divestitures. Audits conducted by the HRM department are part of the "due diligence" process completed prior to an acquisition to identify potential problems. For example, charges pending with the Equal Employment Opportunity Commission can be readily determined through the due diligence process. However, an adverse impact analysis audit of the selection procedures being used by the firm may reveal any potential liabilities for future owners. HRM can also assist in such planning by identifying other areas, such as potential recruitment problems, turnover, the external and internal equity of compensation systems, and the labor relations climate, all of which may affect the viability of an acquisition.

HRM's role also is fundamental in divestiture strategic planning. This role extends beyond being the traditional "watchdog" to measure the effects of such laws as the Worker Adjustment and Retraining Notification Act, Employee Retirement Income Security Act and the National Labor Relations Act. The watchdog role is important but equally so is the effect the divestiture may have for succession planning, particularly if some of the key players in the disgorged

---

[3] SHRM-BNA Survey No. 65: Human Resources Activities, Budgets, and Staffs: 1999-2000. *Bulletin to* *Management,* The Bureau of National Affairs (June 29, 2000), p. S-7.

organization had been groomed for essential jobs that will no longer exist. In tight labor markets, top management talent is not easily replaced.

Market Entrance and Egress. For decision planning involving market entrance and egress, HRM has a role that is both similar to and somewhat different from that in acquisition and divestiture planning. In entering a new market, one of the key contributions HRM can make to the decision-making process is in identifying the needs for critically important personnel and comparing them to the existing supply of personnel in the respective jobs. This process has been greatly facilitated in recent years by the introduction of sophisticated technology in human resource information systems. Decision-making regarding market egress, particularly timing, can be significantly benefitted through HRM inputs in both the watchdog and cost reduction roles. Legal mandates have notice and other requirements. The cost reduction contributions can be realized through such measures as outplacement assistance.

Market Share. Market share decisions, including both expansion and contraction, typically result in either more employees, in the former case, or fewer employees in the latter situation. As in decisions involving the entrance into a market, it will be necessary to identify personnel needs and compare them to the existing supply. Any short-falls must be adjusted according to the scheduling decisions for the market expansion. Input/output matrices, either maintained on computers or derived from human resource information data, can help prevent scenarios, such as selling additional products or services with an inadequate capacity to produce or provide them. Phasing in a market downsizing has consequences for HRM similar to those in a market egress, such as cost reduction considerations and notice requirements.

Technological Implementation/Expansion. Technology is of little value without people to implement, use, and service the technology. Phasing in those three stages requires HRM planning. A small computer firm did an excellent job in advertising and producing its products, but it had limited service staff and virtually no sales support. The firm's success in sales eventually led to its demise. The word got around, "Don't buy from them; they don't service what they sell." Even national firms with excellent reputations suffer customer falloff when they come up short of expectations due to back-orders and insufficient support or service to meet customer needs.

Organizational Restructuring/Redesign

Organizational change was the hallmark of the 1990s as management sought to reinvent their organizations. Such changes obviously affect personnel. Through reengineering, job redesign, and other methods of restructuring, both surpluses and shortages of personnel occur. HRM expertise is needed in both deciding the form the restructuring should take and in implementing the plan, including designing job descriptions and formulating authority delegations.

Operational Planning

Operational planning involves activities facilitating the completion of the strategic plans. Operational plans have very specific schedules for completion, typically within one year. However, intermediate planning, for time periods up to five years, may sometimes be required. HRP has an essential role in the *operational implementation* of the strategic plan.

HRP in Operational Implementation: Example

Some key areas of HRP input in operational planning for technology implementation are budgeting, capital investment, and efficiency improvements. As shown in Exhibit 3-1, all three areas involve planning for changes in staffing, human resources utilization, and employee and labor relations.

Budgeting. *Budgeting* allocates scarce resources to meet objectives. The typical operating budget includes workload projections and the human resources necessary to accomplish the work. These requirements list both the number of jobs and the employees necessary to perform the tasks in them. HRP must insure that qualified employees are available to both operate and maintain the technology when the budget dictates the need for them, including both workforce increases and declines.

Capital Investment Planning. *Capital investment planning* is developing capital investment projects that increase organizational efficiency and help accomplish goals. Technology investment plans rely upon HRP for the development of personnel or a reduction in human resources needs. For example, the decision to purchase new equipment is usually justified partially or even totally through savings realized by a reduction in personnel currently used in the production process affected by the new technology.

Efficiency Improvements. *Efficiency improvements* are changes in work methods or the implementation of cost savings ideas that improve productivity and quality and reduce costs and waste. HRP is necessary to insure personnel have been trained in the new methods.

Human Resource Information Systems

A human resource information system (HRIS) is a database system to aid HRM decision-making and reporting. The components of an HRIS may vary among organizations. In some firms, the HRIS consists solely of demographic variables, sometimes called *employee record systems*. In other organizations, the HRIS also includes two or more modules, such as an *applicant tracking system*, an *employee benefit system*, a *performance planning and appraisal system*, a *job analysis system*, a *job evaluation system*, a *drug testing data system*, an *employee attendance control system*, and an *employee career planning system*.

The various HRIS modules can be integrated or independent. Sometimes several modules are integrated and the others are independent. Two systems that are typically integrated are the *employee record system* and the *applicant tracking system*. Information on various human resources software systems is discussed in Chapter 5. An HRIS has important roles in both strategic and operational planning. In addition to the purposes denoted by the title of the various modules, HRISs have many important uses such as staffing control, reporting, turnover analysis, and budgeting.

Forecasting Techniques in Human Resources Planning

As noted above, determining human resources needs is the first step in the four-step model of human resources planning used in both strategic and operational planning. In most situations, forecasting is used to determine the future needs for human resources. Both quantitative and qualitative techniques are used in forecasting.

Quantitative Forecasting Methods

Three quantitative forecasting methods used to estimate future human resources needs are *trend projection, regression* and *transition matrix analysis.*

Trend Projection. *Trend projection* involves the use of historical data to predict future human resource needs. For example, the numbers of employees in the past can be shown on one axis of a chart and the years corresponding to those numbers of employees can be shown on another axis. Then the points corresponding to the various combinations of years and numbers of employees are plotted on a graph. A straight line is drawn through the plotted points to represent the approximate direction (or "trend") and relationship between the two variables.

Regression. *Linear regression* and *multiple regression* are used to predict relationships between variables using mathematics. In *linear regression,* one variable is used to predict another; for example, past production figures are used to estimate how many employees would be required to achieve a desired level of production in the future.

EXAMPLE: Assume ABC Production Company employed the following numbers of employees over the past 16 years, and these employees produced the number of units shown in Exhibit 3-2.

Exhibit 3-2

No. Employees	No. Units Produced
435	7200
400	6525
505	7765
470	7865
610	9500
540	7750
575	8960
715	11350
645	9600
680	10750
785	13560
750	11890
855	12980
820	13080
890	14350

Exhibit 3-3 is a plot of this data.

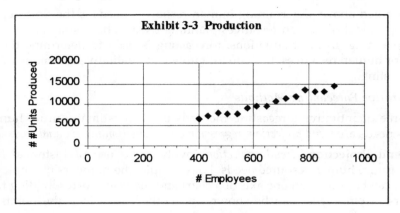

A *trend line* of this data can be developed, using *linear regression. Regression* is defined as the process or act of moving toward the *arithmetic mean* of a set of data. A *linear regression* is using a straight line to depict the mean of the values in a set of data. This is the formula for a regression line:

y=a + bx

  Where: y=the number of units produced

  a=the intersect in the y axis

  b=the slope of the line (the coefficient for x)

  x=the number of employees

The regression line is computed, using the least squares method (the math has been omitted since many spreadsheet programs, like Quatro-Pro, which is the one used in this example, can quickly provide the calculations). Following are the computed values:

  a= – 135

  b=16

The trend line or linear regression for the set of data above is:

y=–135.56 + [(16)(x)]

Exhibit 3-4 is a plot of the data using the computed regression line:

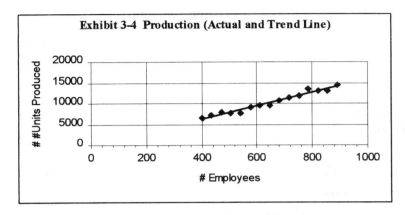

Exhibit 3-4 Production (Actual and Trend Line)

In *multiple regression* models, the mean line is the result of several variables, such as past numbers of employees, past sales volumes and the number of past sales locations. A regression equation is derived, and the future demand for employees is forecasted for various combinations of future sales volumes and sales locations.

Transition Matrix. A *transition matrix* is a type of trend analysis that depicts either actual or estimated promotions, demotions, reassignments, and exits for various jobs during selected periods. Exhibit 3-5 is a transition probability matrix calculated from an analysis of exits and past personnel flows among seven jobs. Information in the matrix is interpreted by starting with a job in the "From" column and determining what flows would occur during a forecasted period. For example, 75 percent of personnel in the Executive job remained in that job at the end of the year, and 25 percent had left the organization. During the same period, 20 percent of the Sales Manager 1 employees were promoted to Executive, 60 percent remained in the same job, five percent were assigned to Financial Manager 1, and 15 percent left the organization. Other row entries are interpreted in the same manner.

The final staffing of employees in the seven jobs can be determined by using matrix algebra to multiply the probabilities in Exhibit 3-5 by the number of persons in the jobs at the beginning of the period.

EXAMPLE: Assume this is the starting numbers of employees for each of the seven jobs:

Job	Beginning Number of Employees
Executive	20
Sales Manager 1	40
Sales Manager 2	80
Finance Manager 1	40
Finance Manager 2	80
Human Resources Manager 1	40
Human Resources Manager 2	120
Total number employees	420

These are the Transition Probabilities in Exhibit 3-5 for the seven jobs:

	(2)	(3)	(4)	(5)	(6)	(7)	(8)
Executive	.75						
Sales Manager 1	.20	.60		.05			
Sales Manager 2		.25	.60				.05
Finance Manager 1	.05	.05		.85			
Finance Manager 2			.10	.10	.70		
Human Resources Manager 1	.15			.05		.65	
Human Resources Manager 2				.05	.05	.25	.50

Exhibit 3-5
ABC Company
Transition Probability Matrix Depicting
Status Quo, Flows and Exits Among Seven Jobs

From	To							
	Executive	Sales Mgr 1	Sales Mgr 2	Finance Mgr 1	Finance Mgr 2	HR Mgr 1	HR Mgr 2	Exit
Executive	.75							.25
Sales Mgr 1	.20	.60		.05				.15
Sales Mgr 2		.25	.60				.05	.10
Finance Mgr 1	.05	.05		.85				.05
Finance Mgr 2			.10	.10	.70			.10
HR Mgr 1	.15			.05		.65		.15
HR Mgr 2				.05	.05	.25	.50	.15

The formula to compute the final staffing is this:

Staffing levels at the beginning × Transition probabilities=Ending staffing levels

Thus:

	Staff Start	Transition Probabilities								Staff End
	(1)	(2)	(3)	(4)	(5)	(6)	(7)	(8)	(9)
Executive	20	.75							31
Sales Manager 1	40	.20	.60		.05				46
Sales Manager 2	80		.25	.60				.05	56
Finance Manager 1	40	.05	.05		.85				52
Finance Manager 2	80			.10	.10	.70			62
Human Resources Manager 1	40	.15			.05		.65		56
Human Resources Manager 2	120				.05	.05	.25	.50	64
Totals	420								367

The number of staff at the end of the period (Column 9) for each of the seven jobs, as mentioned above, is derived using matrix algebra. The first number in column 9, 31, is the sum of column (1), multiplied by column (2), or:

$(20 \times .75) + (40 \times .20) + (40 \times .05) + (40 \times .15) = 31$

The next number, 46, is obtained in the same manner:

$(40 \times .60) + (80 \times .25) + (40 \times .05) = 46$

The remaining values in column 9 are derived in the same manner.

The "Exits" numbers for each of the seven jobs are calculated in the same manner:

Staffing levels at the beginning×Exit probabilities=Exit forecast

Thus:

Staff Start	Exit Probabilities		Exit Forecast
20	.25		5
40	.15		6
80	.10		8
40	.05	=	2
80	.10		8
40	.15		6
120	.15		18

Exhibit 3-6 shows the beginning and final staffing for the seven jobs.

Management staffing transition matrices can be used for several purposes, such as to determine staffing levels at future dates. Separate transition matrices can also be prepared showing race, sex, or other variable to identify areas in which members of various groups may be under-represented either now or in the future. Matrices can also be used to identify those jobs with high turnover rates and to identify those jobs in which career counseling may be required. Transition matrices are also known as *first-order Markov Models.*

Qualitative Forecasting Methods

Qualitative forecasting methods use personal judgments in making predictions. Some types of judgmental forecasting are *surveys, Delphi technique,* and the *nominal group method.*

Surveys can be conducted by polling various individuals, such as managers, for their opinions of their estimates of projected needs for human resources. Managers' opinions can be obtained for different scenarios that have different probabilities of occurring in the future.

The *Delphi technique* involves a panel of experts who independently review a number of subjects and estimate the likelihood of events occurring, such as the number of human resources that may be required in the future if a particular event occurs. Typically, the results of the panel members' initial estimations are summarized and the feedback returned to the members to make further estimates.

The *nominal group method* is a technique used in forecasting events, such as the demand for human resources, that involves a group of people who give their ideas on a subject. The persons typically are seated at a table. A subject is introduced, and the persons are asked to contribute their ideas about the subject. Each person, in turn, either makes a contribution or says "I pass." After two rounds of "I pass" by all participants, ideas on the subject are assumed to be exhausted.

Human Resources Planning in HRM Activities

Human resources planning is involved in all HRM activities. In the following sections some dimensions of that involvement are discussed.

Job Analysis

Job analysis requires extensive planning in decisions involving which methods to use, which jobs to study, and which procedures to use in implementing the results. Decision-making for job analysis studies involving recruitment, selection, performance appraisal, pay policy, job design, as well as other HRM activities, will inevitably involve planning.

Exhibit 3-6
ABC Company
Transition Matrix Illustrating Status Quo, Flows and Exits Among Seven Jobs

| From | | To | | | | | | |
	Executive	Sales Mgr 1	Sales Mgr 2	Finance Mgr 1	Finance Mgr 2	HR Mgr 1	HR Mgr 2	Exit
Executive	15							5
Sales Mgr 1	8	24		2				6
Sales Mgr 2		20	48				4	8

From	Executive	Sales Mgr 1	Sales Mgr 2	Finance Mgr 1	Finance Mgr 2	HR Mgr 1	HR Mgr 2	Exit	
				To					
Finance Mgr 1	2	2		34				2	
Finance Mgr 2			8	8	56			8	
HR Mgr 1	6			2		26		6	
HR Mgr 2				6	6	30	60	18	
Total End	31	46	56	52	62	56	64	53	367
Start	20	40	80	40	80	40	120		420

Job Structuring

Planning is necessary in job structuring strategies, such as job design. This includes determining which jobs need restructuring, what types of tasks will be added, which ones will be removed, what personnel actions will be necessary, and which employees will be affected. Job structuring also requires planning when jobs will be abolished or new ones created. Job structuring that involves reductions in personnel may require conformance with the Worker Adjustment and Retraining Notification Act that requires 60 days' advance notification of "mass layoffs" or plant closures.

Diversity Planning

Human resources planning is involved in diversity planning in several important ways, such as conducting utilization analyses to determine any under-representation of protected groups in different occupations. After flagging any under-representation, preparation for corrective action can be undertaken. Planning is also needed to determine if provisions of equal employment opportunity laws are being observed. Recruitment, human resources development, career planning, and selection activities must be designed to ensure that diversity issues are adequately addressed.

Recruitment

As noted above, planning is involved in recruitment efforts necessary to address diversity issues. More fundamentally, planning is an essential antecedent to recruitment, including identifying the sources of recruits, formulating recruitment plans, scheduling recruitment interviews, and tracking information on applicants. To facilitate the tracking process, HRIS can be used. Planning is needed in the development of these systems to decide upon the information variables to include and the type of system to select that will best meet the organization's needs.

Selection

The development of selection methods for various jobs requires extensive planning. Determinations must be made concerning what selection methods to use and how to validate them. Validation procedures must include which method to use, and decisions must be made whether concurrent or predictive validity studies will be conducted.

Performance Management

Some of the questions to consider in performance management planning include what purposes will the appraisal system serve, what method will be used, and who will administer the system. Related questions which must be given thoughtful consideration are what variables to use, what training will be given, and how much employee involvement will be entailed in the system.

Employee Benefits

Effectively managing employee benefits requires strategies for such decisions as formulating the objectives to be achieved with a benefits plan, selecting the various components of the plan to meet the objectives, and choosing providers for the components. Planning is also needed to control benefit costs. Workers' compensation costs, for example, can be reduced through designing jobs to reduce the probability of occupational disease or injury or conducting safety inspections to detect unsafe acts and conditions. Even including employee safety records in the appraisal of supervisors can help control occupational accidents and illnesses.

Counseling

Counseling programs, such as *employee assistance programs (EAP)* or *retirement planning programs,* are provided by employers to meet desired objectives. The planning phases in establishing an *EAP* include conducting a need study, preparing strategies to implement the needs the program is intended to address, designing the program's structure, and establishing a system to evaluate the program's success in meeting the stated objectives. Advance preparation is also required for other counseling programs, such as outplacement counseling and retirement planning.

Wellness

Wellness planning requires the incorporation of wellness concepts into job design, safety and health, and other HRM activities. Such programming also requires education and feedback systems, in which employees can monitor their progress against standards they have established for themselves.

Pay Administration and Rewarding Performance

Planning is necessary in designing pay systems, such as pay-for-performance plans. In such a system, performance criteria must be established, a measurement method must be developed, and personnel will require training so they understand how the system will function. Other pay matters, such as the formulation of policies involving re-evaluated jobs, promotions, demotions, and shift differentials, require preparation. Planning is also needed to ensure the firm is complying with the legal requirements of pay administration, such as the Fair Labor Standards Act. Even fundamental considerations in pay administration, such as the classification of jobs as either exempt or nonexempt, require blueprints.

Safety and Health

Organizations with exceptional safety records incorporate safety and health considerations into strategic management decisions. Planning for a safe and healthful work environment involves such issues as workplace smoking, employee and management training, emergency planning, handling of hazardous materials, safety inspections, and job structuring. The prevention of ergonomic disorders and workplace violence require strategic and operational preparations.

Human Resource Development

Human resource development (HRD), also called training and development, plays an important role in HRP, since it involves such activities as employee skills development, job orientation and training, supervisory training, and management development. After human resource needs are identified, HRD is needed to select the appropriate training methods, set training objectives and the criteria to measure them, and evaluate the training results to see if the training needs were met.

Management Succession Planning

A strategic link between HRD and HRP is the process of developing managers for top positions, since this development involves a longer lead time than other types of HRD. The steps involved in developing a *succession plan* are:

- Identify the key jobs to be included in the succession plan. Such jobs will typically be ones that are important for the continued success of the organization and will require a significant period of time to prepare applicants to qualify for promotion.

- Develop a system to assess potential candidates for those jobs. The assessment system is important because candidates who are identified will receive special work assignments and training and development through college and professional education. These work assignments and development efforts are designed to meet the organization's unique work experience and developmental needs. Typically, the pool of replacement candidates is larger than the number of anticipated vacancies because some candidates may fail to develop as planned, and others may leave the organization. In addition, some candidates may fail to perform up to expectations as they receive more responsible assignments.

- Implement a special performance appraisal system that measures candidates' work performance. This appraisal system is usually administered by someone in the corporate HRM office. This person coordinates the appraisals of candidates and discusses the results with the appraiser. In some cases, the coordinator presents the results to members of a top management succession planning committee monitoring candidates' development.

- Develop readiness lists or replacement charts of candidates for each of the key jobs in the succession plan. Exhibit 3-7 is an example of a such a chart.

Replacement or readiness decisions are based upon each candidate's work experience, assessment of potential, performance appraisal results, and learning acquired from training and development programs designed to prepare them for advancement.

Employee Relations

Employee relations consist of strategies for maintaining a productive workforce through formal communication, the equitable administration of discipline and prevention or resolution of employee dissatisfactions. Planning is necessary to develop a favorable employee relations atmosphere. Some indicators that can be tracked to measure whether action is needed include the administration of discipline and the number of grievances. Another valuable source of information is the *exit interview.* Properly conducted, these interviews can be used to determine problem areas needing attention. The validity of exit interviewing depends upon interviewer's skill and the candor of the terminating employee. Exiting employees are naturally reluctant to express their reasons for leaving an organization if they believe their opinions will prevent their reemployment with the organization or result in receiving unfavorable recommendations for employment elsewhere.

Personnel Research, Audit and Evaluation

Planning is required in *personnel research, audit,* and *evaluation.* Research studies must be designed to identify the research questions that will be studied and the methodology that will be used. Audit surveys require planning to determine the items to be included in the audit and the procedures to be followed. Evaluative studies require strategies to identify the objectives that will be evaluated and the evaluation methods to be used.

Exhibit 3-7
ABC Company
Executive Succession Plan

Key Position (Incumbent)	Candidates	Age	Length of Employment		Last Assessment	Readiness for Promotion
			Current Job	Company		
President	B. Davis	50	7	20	4	Now
I. Starr	C. Smith	45	4	7	5	1 year
	B. Egg	62	2	12	4	Now
Exec. VP	R. Russo	59	5	16	4	Now
B. Davis	B. Cooper	40	3	15	3	two years
	R. Flagg	43	3	10	4	1 year
VP GM	K. Currin	45	4	15	4	1 year
B. Cooper	F. Kennedy	39	1	11	5	Now
	P. Sloan	36	3	12	3	two years

Key Position (Incumbent)	Candidates	Age	Length of Employment		Last Assessment	Readiness for Promotion
			Current Job	Company		
VP HR	A. Arrington	37	3	7	4	Now
R. Flagg	C. Staples	32	1	10	5	Now
	F. Teadwell	41	3	11	4	Now

Union Relations

Planning is vital in several dimensions of union relations, such as preventive labor relations, opposition to union organizing strategies, preparation for contract negotiations, and strike contingency blueprints. Preventive labor relations planning includes defining strategies to prevent union organizing attempts. A preventive posture includes measuring employee opinions about wages, working conditions, and related areas to identify and correct any unfavorable situations before they become exacerbated. Conducting regularly scheduled employee opinion surveys helps track employee opinions.

In a unionized setting, planning for collective bargaining includes developing economic data on industry pay rates and comparing them to those offered by the employer. Another planning area in preparation for collective bargaining involves securing data on areas in which the union may present proposals. Special attention should be given to areas in which past grievances have occurred and to possible proposals that may limit management flexibility. Finally, contingency plans should be prepared in the event of a strike.

Evaluation of HRP

Both the operational and the strategic planning dimensions of HRP can be evaluated. As shown in Exhibit 3-8, the questions to be evaluated in operational budgeting include whether the budget was met and whether planned actions, such as forecasted expenses, were on target. In the area of capital investment planning, three subjects that should be addressed are the estimated savings, the termination of excess personnel, and whether qualified employees were available when needed to operate and maintain the new technology. The evaluation of HRP's role in efficiency improvements focuses on such variables as whether the planned improvements were realistic and whether the projects were implemented according to the planned timetable.

The evaluation of strategic planning consists of determining how effectively the steps in the human resources planning process achieved the desired results. Particularly in the area of need forecasting, the evaluation should include an assessment of how realistic were the estimated needs. A somewhat related question to be measured is how complete were the needs assessment, that is, what needs, if any, were overlooked. The evaluation should also examine how effectively the HRP resulted in tangible results for a supply of personnel to meet the projected needs. A somewhat easier estimation would involve determining the extent of the supply of employees that exceeded the need. Even here, this estimation should be evaluated to see how realistic it was. Finally, the actions taken to resolve any differences in the estimated demand and supply must be ascertained. If there was an excess supply, the evaluation should determine how effectively the HRP delineated the necessary actions to be taken. Conversely, if additional personnel were needed, the evaluation plan should assess the results of the HRP in providing a framework for action plans to meet the shortfall.

Exhibit 3-8
Evaluation of HRP in Operational and Strategic Planning
Decisions

Operational Planning	Strategic Planning
Budgeting	Need forecasting
Was the budget met?	Were estimated needs realistic?
Were forecasted expenses on target?	What needs were not planned/underplanned?
Capital investment planning	Supply estimation
Were estimated savings realized?	Did estimated sources of supply develop?
Were excess personnel terminated?	What sources were more reliable?
Were qualified employees available when needed?	Action to resolve over/under-supply
Efficiency improvement	Were excess positions abolished on schedule?
Were planned improvements realistic?	Were planned personnel available when needed?
Were projects implemented on schedule?	

CHAPTER 4
HUMAN RESOURCES OUTSOURCING FUNCTION

Chapter Highlights
- Review the activities outsourced in HR
- Examine the reasons for outsourcing HR work

Introduction

For efficiency purposes, some activities in HR are outsourced.[1]

- The activities which are *most frequently* outsourced, in descending order of frequency are employee assistance (47%), pension plan administration (31%), training (22%), outplacement services (21%), payroll (20%), and benefits (19%).

- The activities which are *least likely* outsourced are compensation planning (7%), wellness programs (7%), human resources systems (5%), and health and safety (3%).

Outsourcing, as the term is applied to HR, is the use of contractors to provide services which are part of a traditional in-house HR department.

Outsourced Activities

The major HR activities that are being outsourced are:
- Recruitment;
- Employee benefits plan administration;
- Outplacement;
- Employee assistance programs;
- Training; and
- Relocation.

Issues in Outsourcing

Some issues to be addressed in deciding what activities should be outsourced, and to whom the work should be outsourced, include:
- Conducting a needs analysis, including determining what activities can be most effectively outsourced. Typically, this is a team effort in which all

---

[1] Information on outsourcing was obtained from SHRM-BNA Survey No. 66: Human Resources Activities, Budgets, and Staffs: 2000-2001. *Bulletin to Management*, The Bureau of National Affairs (June 28, 2001).

employees in the HR department participate. In some cases, a consultant can be retained to aid in the process of determining what is feasible for outsourcing.

- Evaluating the outsourcing effort, which includes determining what evaluative criteria will be used to determine if the outsourcing is achieving the desired objectives.

- Preparing requests for proposals and identifying those firms capable of providing such services.

- Maintaining contact with employees. One reason for outsourcing is to give employees better service through a professional provider/client relationship with employees. Special attention is needed, however, to ensure that outsourcing will not alienate employees, since their contacts will be with outsiders and not in-house HR personnel.

- Ensuring that employees will accept the responsibility to become better informed about the programs that are being outsourced. Typically, employees in most organizations are dependent upon human resources for providing information in making even elementary decisions. This history of dependency will challenge outsourcing firms' efforts to teach employees to become more self-reliant.

Employee Recruitment

Employee recruitment is an area in which there has been an extensive use of outsourcing, particularly through the use of staffing firms. A *staffing firm* is a generic term that includes firms that recruit, screen, and refer applicants to employers. There are several distinctive types of firms; some deal solely with placing temporary help, and others are very specialized, placing managerial talent within a specific industry. These firms perform some selection functions in addition to recruiting applicants. For example, they may interview applicants and determine their employment interests and qualifications. In addition, they may administer job skills and knowledge tests and verify applicant qualifications.

Fee structures vary considerably within the industry. Some firms charge a flat rate, but, more typically, fees are based upon 10 to 30 percent of the job's annual salary. Although fees are sometimes paid by the applicant, most firms work only with employer-paid fees. In these situations, the firm normally guarantees that the applicant will perform satisfactorily for a minimum period or the fee is refunded.

Staffing firms recruit and employ individuals assigned to client firms that wholly or partially control their working conditions. Staffing firms were responsible for 3.5 million jobs in 2004, about 2.4 million of them are in temporary help services firms. It is estimated that staffing firm employment will increase 45 percent between 2004 and 2014[2]. The occupations involved are varied as shown in Table 1.

---

[2] U.S. Bureau of Labor Statistics.

Table 1
Employment by staffing firms (in thousands)

Occupation	Employment, 2004		Percent change, 2004-2014
	Number	Percent	
Total, all occupations	3,470	100.0	45.5
Management, business and financial	168	4.9	61.4
Professional and related	325	9.4	57.5
Service	337	9.7	56.2
Sales and related	92	2.7	50.5
Office and administrative support	848	24.4	43.0
Construction and extraction	200	5.8	58.8
Installation, maintenance, and repair	50	1.5	62.9
Production	562	16.2	39.5
Transportation and material moving	857	24.7	35.0

Note: may not add to totals due to rounding

Source: U. S. Bureau of Labor Statistics.

Staffing firms include *temporary employment agencies, contract employment firms, facilities staffing firms,* and *leasing or payrolling firms.*

Temporary Employment Agencies

Unlike a standard employment agency, a temporary employment agency recruits, screens, hires, and sometimes trains the individuals it places in temporary jobs at its clients' work sites. The agency also sets and pays the wages when the worker is placed in a job assignment, withholds taxes and social security, provides workers' compensation coverage, and bills the client for the services performed. While the worker is on a temporary job assignment, the client typically controls the individual's working conditions, supervises the individual, and determines the length of the assignment.

Contract Firms

Under a variety of arrangements, contract employment firms perform services for a client on a long-term basis and place its personnel, including supervisors, at the client's work site to perform the work. Examples of contract firm services include security, landscaping, janitorial, data processing, and cafeteria services. Like a temporary employment agency, a contract firm typically recruits, screens, hires, and sometimes trains its workers. It also sets and pays the wages when the worker is placed in a job assignment, withholds taxes and social security, and provides workers' compensation. The primary difference between a temporary agency and a contract firm is that a contract firm takes on full operational responsibility for performing an ongoing service and supervises its workers at the client's work site.

Facilities Staffing Firms

This type of firm provides one or more workers to staff a particular client's operation on an ongoing basis but does not manage the operation as a *contract firm* arrangement does.[3]

Payrolling or Leasing Firms

This is an employment arrangement in which the employees of a firm are hired by a leasing company and then leased back to the former employer. The concept was started in 1972.[4] The leasing company performs all administrative activities for payroll and benefits. Leasing companies charge from 126 to 136 percent of payroll costs; this includes an administrative fee (which can be from five to 10 percent of payroll or a monthly fee per employee) and the cost of employee benefits.[5]

Generally, individuals who work for a staffing firm are considered its employees even if the individuals actually perform work at a client's worksite. This relationship exists because the staffing firm hires the individuals, pays them, withholds taxes from their pay and has the right to fire them.[6]

Sometimes both the staffing firm and the client may qualify as the employer. For example, as noted above, the staffing firm typically hires the workers, pays them, and performs other employer-related functions. In addition, the client would also be the workers' employer if the client supervises the work of the workers, provides work space and equipment for them, and has the right to terminate them.

Staffing firms that have sole employer responsibility for persons who work for a client are *contract firms*. The reason is *contract firms* hires the workers, pays them, and in addition, supervises them at the client's worksite. The client thus does not perform any meaningful employer functions.

Even if a client does not qualify as a worker's employer, the client may be responsible for any acts of discrimination it commits, provided that it has the requisite number of employees.

EXAMPLE: Firm ZZZ has 15 employees and signs a contract with a staffing firm to provide a worker to repair computers. The staffing firm selects a person to do the work, pays the individual, provides the necessary equipment and supervises the individual. Assume the worker is a woman and when she arrives at work, the client calls the staffing firm and requests that a man be sent to do the work in lieu of the woman. The client is not the worker's employer, however, because the client has 15 employees the client is liable for discrimination under

---

[3] The definitions for these staffing firm arrangements were obtained from *EEOC Notice Number 915.002*, published by the EEOC (December 3, 1997).

[4] *Press Release*, "Marvin R. Selter, Chairman of the Board, National Staff Network," (Van Nuys, CA: National Staff Network, n.d.).

[5] Keaton, P.N. and Anderson, J., "Leasing Offers Benefits to Both Sides," *HR Magazine*, (July 1990), p.58.

[6] Payrolling or leasing firms are an exception to this situation because leased workers are typically hired by the staffing firm for the sole purpose of handling payroll and employee benefits.

equal employment opportunity laws for "interfering in the worker's employment opportunities with the staffing firm."[7]

In a similar manner, a staffing firm may only administer the payroll and employee benefit programs for a client and thereby would not be considered an employer. However, if the employee benefit program has a provision which is discriminatory towards women, the staffing firm could be liable for employment discrimination, if it had 15 employees in its own right, because "...administration of the insurance plan interferes in the workers' access to employee...benefits."[8]

Benefit Plan Administration

Among the compensation functions that are outsourced is benefit plan administration. The impetus for outsourcing benefit plan administration is to reduce staffing for HR departments, increase technology and specialization, minimize legal reporting needs, lower costs, and improve service. Also, outsourcing health benefits administration to insurance companies or other third-parties has a proven record.

Some employers outsource benefit plan administration completely. Other employers outsource only a portion of it, such as medical expense plans, which has taken place for many years as part of benefits self-funding. Self-funding is an alternative to insurance as a means of financing employee benefits. Benefit claims are paid directly from the employer's own assets. Such payment may come from the current cash flow, or funds may be set aside in advance for potential future claims. The decision to self-fund is a financial one. Generally, competition and consumer sophistication (relative to the individual market) keep insurers' profit margins low. Commission rates are also negotiable in the group market. However, if the employer can provide the promised benefits less expensively than an insurance provider, it should consider self-funding.

Loss Experience Predictability

The larger a group is, the more predictable is its loss experience and thus, it is more apt to self-fund. Predictability is a major factor that makes some types of benefits better candidates for self-funding than others. In a comparison of financing alternatives, consideration is given to savings realized by having the use of the funds that would otherwise go to the insurance company. Other savings include the state's premium tax. Earnings could also be made on the remaining portion of the premium until it is needed to pay claims and expenses. Self-funding also gives the employer control of the reserves that would be established by insurers and of the float on deposits and withdrawals. Other health care plan cost savings are realized because self-insurers are not subject to the various state-mandated provisions that insured plans are required to provide for covered employees.

In addition to the costs associated with changing from an insured to a self-funded plan, the employer should consider the additional ongoing costs. Execu-

---

[7] EEOC, *Enforcement Guidance: Application of EEO Laws to Contingent Workers Placed by Temporary Em-* *ployment Agencies and Other Staffing Firms,* December 3, 1997, p. 13.

[8] Ibid.

tives and other personnel will need to acquire competence in a field that is not related to the employer's business. A qualified staff is necessary. There are additional fees for actuarial guidance, medical reviews, audit reviews, legal work, internal reporting and disclosures, and paperwork necessary for regulatory compliance.

Although self-funding *may* increase cash flow, there is also greater uncertainty in predicting those cash flows. Reserves set aside by an employer to meet unforeseen contingencies are not tax deductible unless the employer divests control of the funds by establishing a trust which is audited annually by a certified public accountant.

Outsourcing Claims

Another disadvantage of self-funding concerns claim administration. If a claim is denied, the employee sees the employer rather than the insurer as the "bad guy." Often, borderline claims are decided in favor of the employee—particularly in strong union situations—to avoid employee dissatisfaction. Furthermore, claim administration is usually a function far removed from the employer's main line of business. Inexperience leaves the employer ill-prepared to handle a job formerly handled by an insurance company whose primary business is claim administration.

For these reasons, most employers who self-fund will continue to have claims administered by an insurance company or other provider. This type of contract is referred to as an *Administration Services Only*, or ASO. The employer still bears all the risk of claims with an ASO contract, except at contract termination. The insurer typically assumes the responsibility for claims filed after the contract has terminated. The premium tax is imposed on the fees paid to the insurer for the ASO contract. A fully insured plan and a self-funded plan represent the two opposite extreme approaches to financing employee benefits. Insurers have designed numerous financing alternatives that may be more suitable than these two extremes. The other alternatives attempt to lower the amount of money that the employer must pay to the insurer up front via lower premiums, delaying the premium due date, and reserve reduction arrangements.

Medical expense plans and pension plans are the two major employee benefits that are most often self-funded. Death benefits are least likely to be self-funded because the probability of death is more difficult for most employers to estimate. A firm may go many years without a death. When more than one death occurs in a particular year, the large amount of the benefit may place a strain on the employer's cash flows. In summary, an employer's funding choice should consider these points:

- The employer's willingness to assume risks;
- Cash flow improvements resulting from additional investment income and cost savings versus increased administrative costs;
- Tax and legal implications; and
- The effect on employees.

Full-scale "broad-based" benefit plan outsourcing is relatively new, so few employers have much experience with it.[9]

Outplacement Outsourcing

Outplacement is the process of ending a person's employment in one organization and assisting him or her in securing a position in another one.

Purposes

The purposes of outplacement programs are to:

- Help exiting employees secure employment;
- Reduce the stress on such employees;
- Promote goodwill;
- Prevent legal problems; and
- Aid managers.

Secure Employment

A primary purpose of outplacement is to help exiting employees find other jobs. Many separations, particularly layoffs, can be planned to allow a sufficient lead period for workers to remain employed until other jobs are found. Often, employees are unaware of labor markets and do not know the best way to begin a job search. Outplacement counselors can facilitate the process by helping the employee develop leads and arrange employment interviews.

Reduce Stress

Separations are stressful, regardless of the reason. Layoffs can be as stressful as discharges, since both situations cause loss of income and economic uncertainty. Involuntary separations, like layoffs and discharges, are ranked eighth of 43 stressful social situations. This stress can produce various reactions, ranging from substance abuse to severe depression. Involuntary separations cause employees to question their abilities and their self-esteem. Paradoxically, this is an inopportune time for these feelings to occur, since job searching and interviewing require mental discipline and self-confidence. Outplacement does not eliminate all the stress, but it helps by providing the employee with emotional and financial support and professional training in locating a suitable job.

Promote Goodwill

Outplacement assistance can promote goodwill among existing employees and those being outplaced. Layoffs and discharges, particularly when they appear to be done in a capricious and arbitrary manner, cause disquietude among employees who wonder, "Will I be next?" Also, workers who feel they have been treated unfairly may harbor grudges. Officials of internal security firms caution employers about the dangers of causing employees to feel embittered towards them. Vandalism, theft of company property, deliberate errors,

---

[9] Peterson, E. Scott, "From those who've been there . . . outsourcing leaders talk about their experiences," *Benefits Quarterly,* Vol. 13, No. 1 (First Quarter, 1997), pps. 6-13.

stolen records and other types of negative behavior have resulted from employee hostility caused by discharges.

Prevent Legal Problems

Outplacement can help prevent legal problems by dissuading workers from filing lawsuits alleging violations of implicit or explicit employment contracts. Outplacement may also prevent equal employment opportunity complaints if employees who are separated from service are members of protected groups. Where unions are involved, workers may access grievance procedures to delay the implementation of layoffs and discharges. Some state laws and state courts have imposed limitations on an employer's right to discharge employees. These constraints typically regulate wrongful discharges for such reasons as allegations of minimum wage violations or discriminatory acts. Furthermore, case law is broadening to include some instances of employer bad faith in discharging workers. Outplacement can help prevent these negative outcomes.

Aid Managers

Outplacement can reduce the pressure managers experience when they discharge employees. Undoubtedly, some managers avoid discharging employees because they cannot handle the stress and/or the worker's reactions to the discharge. These managers tolerate unacceptable performance because they are psychologically unable or unwilling to communicate a discharge decision. Outplacement does not eliminate all the stress, because the manager still must tell an employee that he or she is being discharged, but the manager is able to counter some reactions, such as tears or anger, by offering outplacement assistance.

Employee Reasons for Outplacement

Employees have various reasons for leaving a job. Initially, one might question the wisdom of giving outplacement assistance to an employee who is voluntarily seeking another job. Some employers even have a policy of immediately discharging any employee who is suspected of looking for another job. Such a policy is a bad practice; it causes employees to use secrecy in their job search and generates retribution motives in discharged employees.

There are valid reasons for employees to seek change of employment and for employers to give those employees outplacement assistance in their job searches. First, an employee may have career reasons for getting in the job market, including seeking job opportunities that may not exist with the present employer. For example, an employee may have recently earned a college degree and wants a job that will permit him or her to use that education. An employer would be foolish to impede such an employee's job search if they were unable to offer a suitable job opportunity. An employee may also simply want to change careers or enter a new field of work. Such worker may feel burnt-out or need rejuvenation in a different employment setting. Other career reasons are dissatisfaction with a current field of work or failure to adapt to new developments. Regardless of the reason, employers would be advised to offer some basic form of outplacement assistance.

Family considerations can also motivate an employee to seek a job with another employer. The reason may be to live near an elderly parent or to move after a traumatic family event, such as a divorce. Economic reasons, such as assuming a financial burden due to medical expenses or even an inheritance, may motivate a desire for a job change. Sometimes, financial counseling can help, but, in the final analysis, the individual must decide whether a job change is needed.

As the population gets older and as more elderly employees remain in the workforce, employers can expect an increase in job changes due to health and other related reasons. Often, the decision is to relocate to a warmer climate.

Employees may also have transitional reasons for seeking jobs with other employers. For example, an employee approaching retirement may want to reduce his or her employment obligations through either a reduction in work hours or a reversion to a less demanding job.

Employer Reasons for Outplacement

Employers may be compelled to outplace employees due to a change in employment need caused by declines in product/service demand, a downswing in the business cycle, or a plant relocation. In some industries, changing technology is a major reason for a decline in employment levels. Robotics and new production methods have also increased the need for outplacement as employment opportunities decline. Some experts believe the rate of technological displacement will substantially increase in the future.

Human resource planning will reduce, but not eliminate, the problem of excess employees. For example, market surveys and other demand projections can help anticipate reductions in employment levels. Where these trends are observed, various strategies, such as using temporary or part-time help and allowing normal attrition to reduce the excess in the workforce, can preclude some of the need for outplacement.

Typically, job deficiencies are considered the major cause of outplacement. Where possible, job reassignment, additional training, or even a job restructuring could be considered before a decision is made to outplace a deficient employee. This recognizes that performance deficiencies may result from employee-job incompatibility. A reassignment may eliminate the problem by moving the employee to a job he or she can perform. In addition, the environment or requirements of the job, such as regular overnight travel, may cause family problems that spill over into the employee's work performance. In some cases, the deficiencies may be due to unrealistic job expectations or inadequate training.

Finally, job deficiencies can result when job demands change but the employee is not capable of adapting to them. This problem occurs with greater frequency in high technology fields, where change is incessant. In this situation, employees constantly face challenges that increase in intensity. An employee may have been well qualified for the job when initially hired, but, due to rapid changes, the job eventually outdistances him or her. A similar situation occurs when employees are promoted, based upon their present job performance rather than an assessment of their potential for a new job. The humane way to handle these mismatches is through reassignment or job restructuring; outplacement should be the final alternative.

When top management is replaced, the newcomers often start to work on recruiting a "new team." Inevitably, this means outplacement for some managers. Also, poor performance or a major problem within a plant or division often means that "Some heads will roll," and outplacement counselors start to work. Sometimes a "lack of confidence" in a manager or simply a felt need for "new blood" results in outplacement for someone. Many of these reasons lack validity, but they do occur.

Employment During Outplacement

While an employee is involved in outplacement, the employment arrangements with the existing employer differ among firms. Non-managerial employees, who receive advance notices of pending layoffs, remain on the job until they either find another position or the layoff date is reached. Typically, managerial employees continue receiving their existing salary until they are outplaced. Normally, they do not remain in their old jobs, however, because the outplacement activities require their full energies.

Performing Outplacement

Outplacement is performed internally or externally by outplacement and consulting firms. Some assistance is also offered solely by unions or jointly by unions and management. The two types of internal outplacement are *individual outplacement* and *group outplacement*.

Individual Outplacement

Individualized outplacement varies considerably, depending upon the size of the organization. Some of the very largest organizations have in-house specialists who work full time outplacing employees. Smaller organizations either use functional specialists to assist in certain outplacement activities or assign all outplacement tasks to one job. Using functional specialists has some advantages because they have expertise within specific areas. For example, placement and recruiting personnel usually know which organizations have vacancies. These specialists also know their counterparts in other organizations and/or they belong to groups, like the Employment Management Association, that focus on employment-related activities. These contacts can be beneficial in helping an outplaced employee develop job leads. Employment specialists also can give advice on various steps in the application process, such as how to prepare resumes, how to apply for different jobs, how to prepare for job interviews, and what to wear for employment interviews.

Much of this assistance, while rudimentary, is forgotten after a person has been employed for some time and is not searching for a job. Other applicant skills may also be rusty, such as how to respond to interviewer questions, what questions to ask the interviewer, and what conditions, if any, the applicant should seek if a job is offered. In-house human resource development specialists may help in these areas by conducting mock interviews and role-playing sessions.

Other internal specialists can give advice and assistance. For example, compensation and benefit specialists can explain what benefits, such as group life insurance, the outplaced employee may have. Conversion provisions that give outplaced employees the right to convert from group to individual benefit plans can also be explained. Compensation personnel can also brief the outplaced employee on current pay and benefit trends within the employee's occupation. This information can help the employee formulate realistic compensation expectations and can help him or her determine any changes that may be needed in the family budget.

Finally, EAP counselors can help the employee with any personal problems precipitated by the outplacement. Employees can ventilate their feelings to the counselor and receive assistance in such areas as financial counseling and stress reduction. Professional assistance, such as mental health therapy, can be provided or appropriate referrals can be made. Moderately severe reactions, like substance abuse and emotional problems, often accompany job loss. Personal problem counseling can treat this suffering and may prevent the tragic consequences it may precipitate.

General Outplacement Services

Generalized outplacement services are not necessarily less effective simply because they are specifically or individually designed for each outplaced employee. For example, a consumer products manufacturer abolished a manufacturing facility. Employees were given almost a full-year's notice of the planned action. During the interim, the company placed announcements in the help-wanted section of the local newspaper. The ads explained the reason for the job abolishment, described the types of employees involved, and encouraged prospective employers to inquire.

Some companies also provide on-premises interviewing space for prospective employers' convenience. General assistance also typically includes group meetings where outplaced employees are advised of their rights to benefits. Workshops are conducted addressing basic job-seeking skills, such as interviewing and preparing applications. Sometimes general assistance also includes job clearinghouse functions, including posting notices of job vacancies in the community.

Outplacement Firms

Several points should be considered in selecting an outplacement firm. First, there may be advantages to selecting a local firm over a national one, provided the local job market contains sufficient employment opportunities for the employees targeted for outplacement. If the local job market is too small or if the jobs involved require searching in a larger geographical areas, a regional or national firm may be best. Second, some experts feel a firm that only deals in outplacement is preferable to one that offers a variety of management consulting services. The rationale is that consulting firms may have a conflict of interest if they are providing both outplacement and employee search services. A few associations of recruiting firms have ethical codes prohibiting members from providing outplacement services. It is also advisable to check the track record of an outplacement firm before giving it an assignment. Reference information might include the percentage of individuals who received job offers, the number of those who were placed, the starting salaries, and an opinion survey of employees who received the firm's services.

These are the typical services provided by outplacement firms (not every firm provides all the services):

- Meet the client and provide an orientation of outplacement, including the procedures and role responsibilities of both the client and the outplacement firm;

- Administer diagnostic instruments including vocational interest questionnaires and self-assessment profiles;

- Discuss the diagnostic test results with the client and select the jobs that best match the client's income needs, interests, and qualifications;

- Help the client prepare resumes;

- Give the client advice on proper attire and commence interview role playing to prepare the client for employment interviews;

- Help the client develop employment leads through former business associates, professional associations, and known job vacancies;

- Educate the client in on-line recruiting networks, including *Monster.com,* the *Nation's Job Bank,* and the *Nation's Talent Bank;*

- Review the client's progress in mailing resumes, making follow-up telephone calls, and continuing to develop a network of employment leads;

- Conduct additional role playing specially designed for particular job interviews or negotiating employment conditions;

- Review the clients' efforts in securing leads and arranging interviews and positively reinforcing progress; and

- End relationship when the client obtains a job.

Outplacement firms also offer a range of other services for both employers and clients. Some of the employer services include reviewing the adequacy of severance arrangements and advising management on the optimum methods of conducting termination interviews. Care should be taken to avoid any conflict of interest between services provided to employees and commitments made to employers. For example, one outplacement firm was accused of acquiescing to an employer's demand to steer ex-employees away from employment opportunities with competitors.[10] Employee services include financial counseling, administrative and clerical assistance for resume preparation, a place for prospective employers to leave telephone messages, and office space and telephone service. Some outplacement firms maintain job banks to aid client' job search activities.

---

[10] Lublin, J. S., "Memo Reveals Dual Allegiances of Outplacement Firm," *The Wall Street Journal* (January 27, 1995), p. B-1.

Employee Assistance Programs

Employee assistance programs (EAPs) can be operated either internally or they can be outsourced.

Employer Models

There are three common versions of in-house programs.

Employer 1 Model

In the first model, the EAP office is located on the employer's premises. The counselor is either a full-or part-time employee, depending upon the size of the organization. Counselor qualifications vary considerably: some are recovered alcoholics, and others have special training and education, such as a Master of Social Work.

The counselor assists management in the planning and organizing functions. Typically, the counselor interviews the employee, makes an assessment, and refers the employee to various public and private community resources that have been previously designated by the employer. The counselor may also perform other functions, such as problem diagnosis, case planning, service delivery, and case closure, if the counselor has the expertise and the time to perform them.

The counselor performs some case monitoring to see how the employee is progressing. Later, some aftercare and job reentry services are performed, followed by a case evaluation. Usually, the counselor realizes that some cost/benefit and other evaluative data may be needed at some date in the future to justify the EAP. With this in mind, the counselor maintains some record systems to measure activity and performance.

Counseling assistance is customarily very accessible to employees. Accessibility is an often-touted advantage of internal EAPs that have an on-site counseling office. For multipurpose operations within the same area, however, this advantage is perhaps not as great as it seems. For example, one governmental organization has counselors located in the principal office in major cities. Many of their employees, perhaps as many as 50 percent of the local workforce, work in locations away from the central facility. Those employees have two disadvantages: they must travel to see the counselor, and when they get there, they risk being seen by peers who may question their presence in the building.

Confidentiality and anonymity risks are two principal disadvantages to an internal program. These risks can have a profound impact upon problem managers who may fear disclosure. To allay these fears, it is necessary to develop special procedures for assisting problem managers. As an example, one organization sends counselors from plants in distant cities to counsel problem managers. This approach works well, since such managers are less apprehensive of being seen with a counselor who is unknown to the rest of the workforce.

Privacy is also a problem for internal programs, but steps can be taken to control it. For example, one counselor in an in-house program conducts counseling sessions wherever employees prefer them, even at the home of the employee or even the counselor. Internal program counselors can fulfill an advocacy role by protecting problem employees from supervisors' arbitrary actions. The counselors can conduct independent investigations, maintain informal records of trouble spots, and ensure that clients are treated fairly. These advocacy duties can offset any problem with employee acceptance caused by fears about lack of anonymity, confidentiality, and privacy.

Some researchers believe internal programs have more credibility if supervision is provided. While the observation may be true, this advantage may be more than offset by considerable evidence that operating supervisors are generally skeptical of all EAPS. This acceptance problem may cause the counselor to abandon the role as an advocate for problem employees. In-house counselors want to be accepted by supervisors. In contrast, counselors in external programs probably are less concerned with supervisory acceptance in a particular client organization because they usually do counseling for a number of organizations. For these counselors, the more serious acceptance concern is whether the employees in their contractor or agency organization accept them.

As time progresses, employee and managerial acceptance should develop, as the counselor becomes better known through articles in organizational newsletters and other internal communications. Acceptance can also be developed through such things as continual interviewing programs and counselor work area visits.

Unions generally want to cooperate with EAPs but, in this model, it is assumed that they are excluded. The model gives supervisors support in confrontation interviews with deficient employees; this is normally accomplished through training and consultation. Since the program is internal, it can be redesigned or changed to fit any discerned need.

Internal programs can be expensive when costs are considered for counselors' salaries, office space, and clerical support. These costs can be minimized, however, if the workload only justifies employing a part-time counselor.

Building internal and external communications is a major duty of internal counselors. A primary responsibility is making contacts with service providers. The counselor also communicates with a number of other personnel, such as first-line supervisors, top management, the personnel manager, medical or health unit personnel, and union representatives. One of the major advantages of the internal EAP is this greater opportunity for sharing information on a range of topics, from individual employee problems to general EAP concerns and needs. Liability is a problem for internal programs, since the employer may be liable for delivering services promised in policy and procedural statements. Employers also are responsible for insuring that service providers and counselors are professionally qualified. Client counseling records may also involve legal problems such as honoring subpoenas to furnish client information.

One advantage of this model is that program control is entirely internal; thus, changes in EAP procedures can be made with minimal effort. The program can be molded to fit the unique needs that may exist in an entire organization or even in one site. Changes can be made without having to consider if a contract should be renegotiated. Another advantage is the organizational knowledge that the counselor gains by being employed in the firm, which helps the counselor function better. The counselor is thus able to get more done and help insure that the EAP will accomplish its objectives.

Since internal programs are completely under management's control, any EAP aspect can be emphasized, including a preventive approach through Wellness Programs, Smoking Cessation Campaigns, Substance Abuse Seminars, and the like. Personnel procedures can be interrelated with the EAP so maximum results are attained. Professional counseling is insured, since management analyzes the job to be done and selects the applicant that best meets the job specifications. Counselors' career planning and development is another advantage of the internal programs. Since the counselor is an employee, the organization is more likely to invest in his or her growth and development.

Terminating EAP services is more difficult in the internal model than in any of the others. The main difference is that EAP personnel must be either reassigned or outplaced.

Employer 2 Model

The Employer 2 Model differs only slightly from the Employer 1 by offering counseling services on-site for some problems only. Most referrals are made to outside service providers but where possible, it is done within the counseling unit. The Employer 2 Model has more internal procedural linkages than the Employer 1 due to the service delivery that is performed. For example, when an employee agrees to accept counseling in lieu of discipline, there are internal procedures to insure that the employee's commitments are met.

Employer 3 Model

The Employer 3 Model has a management structure which may be headed by an EAP director or administrator. In addition, there may be other support personnel, such as EAP coordinators, who regulate the work of counselors. This additional structure results in more thorough planning and organizing functions. While some referrals are made to external providers, more services are provided internally. This model usually has a strong preventive component, which includes wellness, exercise, proper diet, stress reduction, and educational programs in alcohol and drug abuse. The Employer 3 Model is more expensive and more difficult to terminate than the other Employer Models.

Union Model

Some union programs are totally union-operated, while others are management-initiated with various degrees of involvement. The exclusive union model is unique because it is typically originated, administered, and maintained by union members who usually volunteer for the assignment. Some of these programs are strongly oriented toward both alcohol treatment and using a confrontational approach. Union representatives identify problem employees through observing their attendance and job performance. Deficient employees are confronted and, instead of relying upon voluntary self-referral, attempts are made to motivate the member to seek assistance. These associations train specially selected peers to recognize both behavioral abnormalities and performance deficiencies. Peer-confrontation interviews are conducted confidentially with the problem employees. The objective of the interview is to motivate the impaired colleague to seek treatment. The success achieved by this peer approach suggests that professionals in other industries may also find it useful.

Union-based plans assist in publicity and provide some limited consultation to supervisors and management. Union representatives engage in self-develop-ment activities in dealing with troubled employees and may help in assessment decisions so employees can be referred to the proper service provider. This training also helps in crisis intervention situations. Management frequently grants union EAP volunteers access to work areas because of their demonstrated success in helping problem employees. Union representatives may do some informal case monitoring and case evaluation by observing the employee's performance between counseling sessions and when treatment is concluded. The problem employee realizes he or she is being observed; thus, there is an element of peer pressure involved. This observation also inhibits co-worker cover-up.

Most exclusive union programs have at least the tacit, if not the explicit, approval of management. Typically, the fees charged by service providers in a union program, particularly those involved with alcohol and drug abuse, are covered under the union health benefit plan. This feature is a major advantage to union programs. Union-only programs are readily accessible to employees. Ano-nymity and confidentiality may be a problem in union and other peer-adminis-tered programs. Unions historically have fulfilled an advocacy role in protecting member rights, so this would be an advantage. Another advantage is member acceptance although denial problems also occur in union programs.

One of the biggest disadvantages that may result from a union-based plan is the failure of managers to cooperate with the effort. Lack of management cooperation is a problem with all EAPs, but it is probably intensified in union programs. Employee privacy concerns are another problem with union programs because the volunteers who work with the EAP are also peers of troubled employees. Thus, troubled employees may fear that problems they reveal to the EAP may be disclosed to their co-workers.

A final advantage is that a union program operates at virtually no expense to the employer. Since the program is run by volunteers, however, there is always the potential problem that the program may terminate if the volunteers are unable to continue their work.

Union-Employer Model

A union-employer program may be internally or externally operated. Some synergistic effects may result from a joint union-management program. For example, when both union representatives and supervisors are watching for deficient employee performance, there is a reduced likelihood that a cover-up can result. Other advantages to the joint union-management model begin with fostering a communication link between the parties. In addition, problem em-ployees are less prone to play the union off against management when they know both parties are cooperating. Finally, supervisors are more likely to face their confrontation responsibilities with deficient employees when they know the union representative is cooperating in an EAP.

Preventive aspects concern whether the EAP has the capability and the motivation to render service that will help prevent some employee problems through educational campaigns, training, and the like. Preventive programs, such as fitness programs and stress reduction workshops, could be ongoing. More specialized preventive services may include consultative advice to management on job design, safety performance improvements, and organizational development.

Outsourced EAP Models

There are several models of EAPs that are externally provided.

Hotline

A *hotline* is either a local or long-distance telephone service. Troubled employees dial the publicized number and talk to a listener who is trained to assess problems. The employee is referred to an appropriate service provider selected from a directory of service providers in the employee's community. In performing EAP functions, hotlines usually offer limited procedural planning assistance to management. Publicity usually consists of notices posted on employee bulletin boards, occasional paycheck inserts, and the like. Assessment accuracy is usually a function of the employee's communicative skills and the receiver's ability to understand and classify problems communicated.

Sometimes, hotlines are operated as the crisis intervention component of a total EAP. In these latter situations, it is not uncommon for the hotline number to be connected to an answering service that gives the caller the telephone number of the staff member who responds to emergency service.

Hotlines are easily accessible to employees and assure anonymity and confidentiality. They are private, since the telephone call can be placed from any location. Long-distance calls are handled through either a collect call or an 800 number. Hotlines are economical and can easily be terminated with no effect upon the organization.

Under optimal conditions, hotlines offer only minimal problem assessment and referral assistance to employees. Some organizations present hotlines as a problem diagnosis service, but, for several reasons, that may be over-estimating the model's capability. First, diagnosis is difficult even when it is conducted in person; mistakes may be made that waste both the client's and the service provider's time. Due to these and other problems, some practitioners believe that an accurate diagnosis cannot be made via telephone.

The other difficulty with hotlines is that the person who receives the call cannot be expected to be thoroughly knowledgeable about available local resources in the client's community. Even if the hotline service maintains a list of service providers, there still is the problem of timeliness. Finally, the use of hotlines for crisis intervention is doubly difficult for the same reasons noted above. Since the communication process is usually more complicated, crisis situations require personal contact.

Consortium

Consortiums are non-profit organizations that receive funding from a number of private as well as public sources, such as local, county, state, and federal governments. Revenue is also obtained from the sale of services to private and public organizations. Normally, client organizations are charged for services on a capitation basis, which is a fixed fee per employee. The unique feature of some consortiums is that they may also serve the general population in the area in which they are located, such as a county. Service charges to the public are based upon the client's ability to pay. Typically, a consortium is governed by a Board of Directors. The Board establishes and selects a principal manager who, in turn, appoints a staff of professional and clerical personnel. Like other internal and external forms of EAP structures, there are considerable differences among consortiums, both in the number and the quality of functions performed. There are two forms of consortiums.

Consortium 1 Model. The first consortium model is a spartan form that offers limited planning capability and organizing assistance that usually consists of standard or general-purpose policies and procedures. Bulletin board notices and paycheck inserts are used to publicize the program. Sometimes, a letter from a top executive is sent to employees to formally kick off the program. Supervisory training is conducted prior to program initiation. Client services typically consist of problem assessment or diagnosis. Crisis intervention is available through both a hotline and a professional staff.

Since consortium offices are located outside the worksite, they are less accessible. The beneficial side of an off-site location is that it insures client anonymity, confidentiality, and privacy. For these reasons employees are more likely to accept a consortium. Some experts feel that the element of confidentiality is a big advantage for external programs. First, when counseling and service delivery are conducted off-site, there is less likelihood that the client will be seen by peers and supervisors. In addition, employee records are considered more secure in an external counseling site. Finally, there is no risk that employees' records will be seen by internal office, computer, and administrative personnel because the external organization would be responsible for providing data analyses and reports. Since consortium counselors usually are assigned to service several contracts, they will learn general information about different management philosophies, but they will not fully understand each customer's personnel and procedures. In addition, if the counselor has a difficult time establishing a rapport with managers, the counselor may be viewed as an outsider.

Unions are inclined to cooperate with a consortium because they may feel that an external program will guard against management attempts to use it as a means of winning employee loyalty away from the union. Consortiums can offer limited customer designs, but usually there are some constraints, particularly if the service is offered by a public agency.

A major advantage of a consortium is that it permits virtually any employer to offer some degree of employee assistance. This is particularly important, since there are estimates that as many as 80 percent of all employees in the private sector are employed by firms having fewer than 100 employees. Firms of this size are obviously too small to support even a part-time internal program. Practitioners appear to have mixed opinions on the effects of consortiums upon employer liability. As one precaution, the employer could require the consortium to sign a contract provision that would hold the employer harmless from any potential liability.

Two final advantages of a consortium are a highly professional level of counseling assistance and the relative ease with which the contract could be terminated.

Consortium 2 Model. The second consortium type differs from the first in that professional services are available within the sponsoring agency to treat some problems. The services rendered usually depend upon the client population the agency was originally designed to serve.

The second consortium model performs functions in addition to those performed by the Consortium 1 model. Since the counselor is more involved in EAP activities, efforts are made to consult with first-level supervisors and middle- and top-level managers. In client service functions, this consortium renders services in one or two problem areas; those clients who are diagnosed with other problems are referred to the proper service provider. Aftercare assistance is given to recovering clients to help them readjust when they resume normal living. The Consortium 2 model has some additional advantages beyond those of the Consortium 1. Counselors are able to give some limited support to supervisors in confronting deficient employees. This support is given through supervisory requests for consultation, assistance, and training. Even though the Consortium 2 model offers some client services, the cost is still minimal. The economy of consortium services is a big advantage. There is some opportunity for custom designing a Consortium 2 program, depending upon an employer's needs. The programs are flexible. Devoting full-time service to EAPs helps the counselor gain both in-depth knowledge of the organization and more professional employee counseling skills. Potential interest conflicts surface in the Consortium 2 model, since the EAP may be referring clients to its in-house service providers. Problem prevention is a customary service offered by this model. Normally, the agency specializes in treating clients in one or two problems. This specialization increases the professionalism and service quality offered to EAP clients. Consortium 2 models can be terminated without much difficulty.

Contractor

There are three versions of for-profit private contractor models.

Contractor 1 Model. The first model provides EAP services for one or two problems, such as alcohol or drug abuse. The name of the assistance program usually denotes the problem or concern, such as Alcohol Awareness Program, Program for Alcoholic Recovery, and Drug Awareness Program. Usually, the employer has an internal program coordinator who is assigned either full- or part-time to the job, depending upon the size of the organization. The coordinator establishes the communication and procedural links between the various departments and the contractor. The contractor provides some policy and procedural guidance to the employer. Training, publicity and consultative assistance, and problem assessment are restricted to the one or two problems handled by the contractor.

If the organization has a union, union representatives are encouraged to support the program. Union assistance may also be obtained in formulating procedures and publicizing the program. Employees are informed that they may contact the contractor directly or go through either their supervisor or the coordinator. An appointment is made for the employee at the contractor's office, which is offsite. Usually, the procedures involve a direct performance appraisal connection to the assistance program. Problem employees who are experiencing job deficiencies are encouraged to seek help. Typically, disciplinary actions are held in abeyance pending the employee's acceptance of counseling assistance. This relatively strong communication and procedural relationship between the organization and the contractor is one characteristic that distinguishes this from consortium models. These linkages represent one advantage of contractor models. This involvement occurs because their primary goal is to serve the employer-client. Consortiums, on the other hand, operate EAPs to serve multiple employers. This distinction does not mean that client service quality suffers. It does mean, however, that the Contractor I Model renders more internal assistance to the employer in policy and procedural definitions and in consultation. This assistance, however, is not without cost. Contractors are more expensive for comparable client services than are consortiums. The other features of the Contractor I Model are flexibility, internal communication between the EAP and management, organizational knowledge gained from internal communication, and procedural interfaces that relate the EAP to other organizational procedures. The other advantages are counselor expertise in the limited range of services, offsite counseling, and increased employee perceptions of confidentiality. The disadvantages are supervisory reluctance to work with "outsiders," the inconvenience of offsite counseling, and lack of management direction over contractor methods. The last disadvantage would be the problem of terminating the contract, unless a carefully defined termination provision was in the contract.

Contractor 2 Model. Contractor 2 is an extension of Contractor 1 in that additional services are provided to employees. Customarily, this service extension occurs because the contractor is affiliated with service providers, such as a residential care facility. Due to the close procedural interfaces of the EAP with various organization functions, this model also may render both aftercare and job reentry services to facilitate a problem employee's return to work. The model differs from Contractor I in that substantial confrontation support is given to supervisors. This assistance is concomitant to the internal relationships that exist between the EAP and the organization. The model may also have a strong preventive component. Professional services are rendered in several areas, representing a potential interest conflict if the EAP is affiliated with the service providers, such as a residential care facility. Where such a condition exists, the counselor must be alert to complaints that the EAP is serving as a conduit to provide business for the affiliate. One possible complaint is that counselors affiliated with a residential treatment facility may substitute more expensive specialized residential care for outpatient counseling.

Some practitioners argue that this problem exists because some service providers developed and marketed EAPs to funnel referrals to their service facilities. Thus, when clients' problems are assessed, EAP counselors may refer them to their affiliated service providers instead of to those who could most closely meet the clients' needs. The second problem is that some firms, motivated by the desire to win a contract, will agree to offer services they are not qualified to perform. To guard against both of these potentialities, the organization seeking an EAP should conduct investigations before contracts are signed, to see that adequate safeguards are in place, and after the contract is negotiated, to evaluate results to make sure no interest conflicts are occurring.

Contractor 3 Model. The Contractor 3 Model differs from Contractor 2 in several distinct ways. First, the Contractor 3 Model provides the employer with expertise in all planning phases, including EAP goal integration with organizational goals. Close coordination between the EAP and the employer aids in organizing the program. This careful attention to planning and communication creates an environment where maximum results should be obtained from the EAP. When program problems occur, the necessary communication links are established to take corrective action. A full range of client services are provided, surpassing those provided by many in-house programs. As an example, some Contractor 3 models even assist employees in outplacement, career counseling, financial counseling, and pastoral counseling. To provide a broad range of services, Contractor 3 uses a combination of public and private service providers. The major difference in the two models is that the Contractor 3 is more expensive.

Training

The training or HRD activity is another one that has had some success in outsourcing. Either the entire training function or some components of it can be outsourced. Most firms use the more modest approach and provide a lead in-house person to administer the overall training function. The roles performed by this person include identifying training needs, setting training objectives, developing criteria to evaluate whether the training programs' objectives were met, selecting the methods of training delivery, and evaluating the training effort.

The types of programs most frequently outsourced are management development training, particularly those types of programs selected to meet specific needs of individuals. In addition, employers also use college courses to help train employees.

College Courses

College courses are an essential part of most HRD activities, ranging from skilled work preparation to postgraduate courses in business, engineering, science and other fields. Colleges have generally demonstrated significant flexibility in developing courses designed to meet specific needs. Some colleges even develop special purpose courses for an employer, provided there is sufficient demand for them.

Colleges have been particularly responsive to the need for managerial and executive level development. For example, in many metropolitan areas, there are full offerings of evening courses in virtually every business subject. These evening courses are intended to make education more readily available to those students who are employed and on career tracks within their chosen fields. In addition, Master of Business Administration courses are offered in a variety of nontraditional ways to meet the needs of managers and executives. These schedules include weekend courses and full-time, one- and two-week courses.

Colleges also offer non-degree, continuing education seminars. These may either be selected subjects offered on a continuous basis, such as business communications, or specific courses offered on demand. Some colleges will assist employers in conducting a HRD needs analysis and designing special courses to meet those needs.

Conference

Conference instruction is a generic term, encompassing learning situations ranging from an organization's staff conferences, in which management trainees are invited to attend and observe, to professional conferences, such as the annual national conference of the Society for Human Resource Management. Conferences typically involve different learning methods other than training courses, such as lectures, films and videotaped presentations. One important feature of conferences is that they are usually dedicated to a specific activity or function; another is the broad range of learning purposes that conferences can fulfill.

Generally, conference instruction is restricted to cognitive learning, although some workshop sessions in skill development may be conducted in conjunction with a professional conference. Also, most professional conferences have several rooms reserved for vendors of state-of-the-art technology, procedures and techniques, which help practitioners learn about the latest developments in the field.

Correspondence Courses

Correspondence courses are available for many learning situations, from taking a required college course to learning how to repair electronic equipment. Some organizations have in-house correspondence courses. For example, many insurance companies provide correspondence courses to help agents learn both the concepts of different types of insurance and the various products the organization offers. Some organizations require employees to successfully pass correspondence courses before they will be permitted to enroll in organization-sponsored classroom courses.

Correspondence courses are an excellent way to obtain cognitive learning. Trainees can learn at their own pace and in the comfort of their residences. This is convenient, and it helps keep the cost to the trainee low, since transportation expenses and the time spent in commuting to classes are avoided. The principal problem with correspondence courses is reinforcement because considerable time can elapse between submitting lessons to be graded and receiving the results. Also, correspondence courses tend to be impersonal. Some organizations successfully address this problem by telling the trainee who the grader is and encouraging the trainee and the grader to communicate with each other. Correspondence courses are not effective in either noncognitive or psychomotor learning.

Professional/Continuing Education Courses

Professional and continuing education courses are offered by numerous suppliers, such as colleges and professional organizations. Professional and continuing education courses are quite expensive with fees from approximately $300 for a one-day workshop to $1,500 or more for programs lasting a week or more. Additional costs include transportation, lodging and meals, if the course is offered at a location outside a participant's commuting area. The value of these courses ranges from minimal to extensive, depending upon such things as their applicability. More specifically, their value is determined by the degree to which they meet a need. Employers generally do not give adequate attention to determining course content and objectives and relating them to HRD needs. Without this type of analysis, there is a risk that the time and money spent on the experience will be wasted. Large organizations can ensure getting their money's worth by doing a needs analysis, asking various suppliers to submit proposals of programs to meet those needs, the training methods that will be used and the prices of those programs.

Continuing Education Unit. To help establish standards in this area, the International Association for Continuing Education and Training publishes criteria for organizations that conduct continuing education programs. Organizations that meet the criteria may award Continuing Education Units (CEU). One CEU is defined as " . . . ten contact hours of participation in an organized continuing education experience under responsible sponsorship, capable direction, and qualified instruction."[11] The contact hour is a full 60 minutes of instruction, exclusive of breaks, meals, or business meetings. The purpose of the CEU is to provide a permanent record of a person's continuing education participation. The criteria for an organization to follow in awarding the CEU relate to program sponsorship and program content.

Programmed Instruction

Programmed instruction (PI) is a learning method in which both the speed and repetition of learning are determined by the trainee. Subject matter is usually divided into small, integrated segments, starting with more elementary or basic material. Gradually, these segments increase in difficulty but, ideally, the transition is so gradual the learning is unimpeded. At the conclusion of each small segment, the trainee is asked questions to test his or her comprehension of the material just covered. The trainee answers the questions and must turn the page (in the case of PI books or other printed materials) or hit a key (when either computers or training consoles are used) to see the correct answers. If the

[11] International Association for Continuing Education and Training, *What Is IACET?* (Washington DC: May 28, 1998), p. 1.

answers are wrong, the trainee is referred to a previous section (for printed material) or is immediately shown material (computers and training consoles) explaining the correct answer. If the trainee's responses are correct, the person receives praise and is invited to proceed with the next segment. This immediate reinforcement is a major plus for PI because it builds trainee confidence, encourages the motivation to learn and corrects any misunderstandings so time spent on subsequent material is not wasted because the trainee misunderstood some basic principles or concepts.

Limitations. With PI, trainees learn more quickly and learn better than they do with other methods. However, PI also has some limitations. First, while it is extremely effective for cognitive learning, it cannot be used for either noncognitive or psychomotor learning. Another limitation is the cost of preparing courses and buying training consoles and computer terminals. Material specifically prepared for computer-assisted PI is very expensive because of the costs of computer programming.

Relocation

For most employees employed in fast-track positions and destined for higher-level ones, relocation is a frequent requirement. Also, some employees are relocated due to the discontinuance of their current positions. Relocation assistance is given to employees for the economic, social, and psychological adjustments required by job relocations. According to the Employee Relocation Council, U.S. firms relocate about one-half million employees per year, at a cost of $18 billion.[12] About 17 percent of these employees are women.

Relocating employees and their families can involve multiple difficulties. Some firms provide relocation assistance to ease the transition. A further discussion of this subject is provided in Chapter 20. Because of the technical nature of relocation, many employers outsource the work to firms that specialize in providing such services.

---

[12] Springen, K., "All the Right Moves," *Savvy Woman* (February 1990), pp. 72-73.

CHAPTER 5

HUMAN RESOURCES SYSTEMS

Chapter Highlights
- Introduce HR software planning and implementation
- Review the major HR functions adaptable to software use
- Discuss several applications to selected HR functions

Introduction

The automation of human resources (HR) systems has been an evolutionary process. The factors affecting this evolution have been the need to control the cost of the HR function, the increased need to provide more timely information for management decisionmaking purposes, the declining prices of computer hardware, and improved software systems. The original HR systems were largely confined to personnel recordkeeping and payroll. Most of these systems, particularly those involved with payroll administration, were of limited use to HR because they were dedicated to payroll maintenance. Many of the records maintained on the early payroll systems containing information about employees, such as benefits enrollment, number of dependents, sex, marital status, and other demographic variables, were coded specifically for use by the payroll unit. Even those payroll systems that tracked employee vacation and other attendance variables, such as the number of sick days or discretionary leave days that were used, were not very useful to HR management because they could only be accessed by payroll personnel, and the data was maintained in a rigid payroll-type of format. Often, when HR needed a report, even if it was recognized as urgent, the request was subordinated to payroll needs. Because of the access problems, the rigid formatting of the databases, and reporting limitations, HR information requirements were not met.

Need for HR System

Gradually, the necessity for an independent HR system became apparent. HR input into strategic management, combined with HR needs in compensation planning and record and reporting requirements, mandated the development of systems dedicated to HR requirements. Furthermore, improvements in hardware and software technology and the decreasing costs of those systems allowed even the smallest HR department to acquire them. As a result, today, there are HR software systems available to meet virtually every HR need. With this growth, the percentage of firms in which HR systems are maintained solely by HR, or between HR and another department, has grown. For example, 96 percent of the HR respondents from 400 organizations indicated they had an HR system.[1] In 68

---

[1] Bureau of National Affairs, *SHRM-BNA Survey No. 62: Human Resource Activities, Budgets and Staffs: 1996-97.*

percent of the firms, the responsibility for the activity was assigned solely to HR; in 28 percent of the firms, the responsibility was shared with HR and other departments, and in three percent of the firms, the responsibility was assigned to a department other than HR.

A human resources system (HR system) is a system to aid HR planning, decision-making and reporting.

HR System Components

The components of HR systems may vary among organizations. In some firms, the HR system consists solely of a database of employee occupational and demographic information, sometimes called *employee record systems.* In other organizations, the HR system includes two or more modules, such as an *applicant tracking system,* an *employee benefit system,* a *performance planning and appraisal system,* a *job analysis system,* a *job evaluation system,* a *drug testing data system,* an *employee attendance control system,* and an *employee career planning system.* In some organizations each module is independent; in others, one or more systems are to some extent integrated. Complete HR systems are integrated with each module consisting of one part of the entire system.

Steps in Developing an HR System

The steps involved in developing an HR system vary by organization. Typically, however, these are the steps involved in the process:

- *Determine the need.* The need for a system can be accomplished through several ways. One is to simply diagram all the manual systems and identify those that could be handled more efficiently with an HR system. The problem with this approach is that some systems may simply be reactive ones to fill *ad hoc* needs. If this approach is used, however, a flowchart of existing systems should be made to eliminate any redundancies or excess steps.

  This process can be very helpful to HR personnel, since it gives them the opportunity to review each phase of their work and analyze the way in which it is done. Next, the methods used to accomplish the work can be reviewed to determine if they can be made more efficient. A byproduct benefit of this process is that even if one or more systems are not converted to a computer database, more efficient systems will have been identified.

- A more formal approach to identifying the need for an HR system is to designate a team composed of individuals from different functions to define the applications most suitable for conversion to computerization. Both long-term and short-term needs should be identified.

- *Identify the HR network that will be required to meet the needs.* This step is usually accomplished with flowcharts showing how the various components of the system will interface. Even if a system will be designed to meet short-term needs, the network should be designed, if possible, to accommodate the long-term needs. Sometimes, a "barebones" network is designed, which must be reconfigured as additional subsystems are added. If possible, this should be avoided since it increases the eventual cost of a system. A system design that relates all the parts will show which parts intersect with others; thus, the entire system can be purchased at a lower price than separately purchasing individual modules. Finally, a system which is continually added to without an overall plan eventually becomes a patchwork quilt with few commonalities and little database sharing.

Determine the major players in the system and their need for access to the system. An important question to consider is which modules the players need to access. A matrix showing the relationships of the individuals required to access the system and the system components will help in planning this phase of the process.

- *Select an HR consultant to assist in the design of software and hardware systems to meet the HR needs.* This consultant can also help in determining requirements and in preparing flowcharts of the HR network design. If this expertise is desired in the network design phase, then the consultant should be selected earlier in the process.

- *Identify the software to accommodate the HR needs.* There is software available to meet almost any need. Available systems range from single-purpose products to fully integrated models that include multiple applications. The consultant's expertise will be important in analyzing the software programs available. In some cases, programming modifications may need to be made to meet any unique needs.

- *Identify hardware to capably manage the software applications.* The consultant will be invaluable in assisting in the design of hardware systems.

- *Determine if the HR system will be administered in-house or by contract.* There are advantages to be both in-house as well as contract systems.

- *Prepare a request for proposals (RFP), regardless of whether the HR system will be an in-house system or an outsourced one.* For contractor models, the RFP will be used to solicit bids from qualified contractors. For systems that are operated in-house, the RFP will be used to obtain bids for both hardware and software applications.

- *Consider confidentiality requirements.* This step is to ensure the three levels of access, which are discussed in Chapter 8, are followed to prevent unauthorized releases of employee information.

HR System Applications

As noted above, there are many software applications available to meet HR management needs. Among the most common systems are these:

- Employee records;

- Applicant tracking, including resume tracking, and applicant response;

- Human resources planning, including human resources forecasting and succession planning;
- Job analysis;
- Job structuring, including job descriptions and organization charting;
- Employment testing, including drug testing;
- Performance appraisal;
- Regulatory reporting;
- Employee attendance control;
- Compensation planning;
- Job evaluation;
- Benefits management;
- Employee development;
- Safety analysis and loss control; and
- Personnel policy development;

All of these systems are designed to facilitate the management of HR. Depending upon the particular software selected, there are varying degrees of complexity in installing and maintaining the systems. Most systems do require some adaption to fit the particular organization. Systems that do not have this flexibility may waste employees' time adjusting to the system.

It is important to understand that HR systems facilitate the management of HR. However, these systems must be built on a solid foundation of practices consistent with HR law and current knowledge. With few exceptions, HR systems do not automatically include these considerations. For example, performance appraisal software is predicated on the assumption that managers and other individuals performing appraisals are trained, and the system which the software is designed to support is valid and job-related. To help emphasize some of the points discussed here, several HR systems are analyzed, and other important considerations which must be present in any system are reviewed.

Employee Record Systems

An *employee record system*, consisting of a comprehensive database of information on employees, is the nucleus of an HR system. The information in employee record systems is used for such purposes as preparing the payroll and filing reports with the EEOC, OSHA, the Department of Labor and various state and local agencies. Another purpose of employee record systems is for pay planning, including determining compa-ratios by department. Employee record systems may also be used for maintaining training records and tracking employee career planning.

These are the major components in an employee record system:

- Personal information;
- Residence/past residences;
- Next of kin;

- Demographics;
- Education;
- Experience;
- Performance appraisal;
- Career planning;
- Compensation;
- Regulatory requirements; and
- Safety and health.

Personal Information

The data fields for personal information usually include the following basics:

- Name: last, first, middle
- Social security number
- Name and date of birth of spouse (if applicable)
- Names and dates of birth of children (if any)

Residences/Past Residences

- Domestic permanent address
- Temporary address
- International assignment address

Telephone Number/Emergency Telephone Number

- E-mail
- Telephone number
- Permanent telephone number
- Work location telephone number
- Cellular telephone number
- Emergency telephone number
- International telephone number
- Pager number

Emergency/Next of Kin

- Emergency contact
  - Permanent assignment
  - Temporary assignment
  - Domestic
  - International
- Next of kin
  - Domestic
  - International

Demographics

- Sex
- Age
- Weight
- Height
- Racial classification[2]

Education

- Level
- College
  - Institution
  - Degree
  - Year
  - Major

Experience

- Employer(s)
- Job titles(s)
- Dates(s)
- Supervisor(s)
- Pay
- Principal duties (Keyword listing)

Performance Appraisal

- Last review date
- Next review date
- Performance code (last 10 reviews)
- Suspension, if improvement needed
- Assessment for potential code

Career Planning

- Career objective
- Career plan date
- Last report date
- Status
  - Ready
  - Pending

---

[2] This information is used to prepare EEO-1 and/or EEO-4. Care should be exercised in maintaining racial and ethnicity information since, according to 29 CFR 1602.13, records that are used to maintain racial or ethnic information on employees must be kept separate from employee's personnel files that are used by employers in personnel decisionmaking.

Compensation History

The components in the database for compensation include both benefits and pay information.

Benefits

Depending upon the organization and the types of benefits offered, most employee record systems will contain at least the following information on benefits enrollment:

- Medical expense benefits plan;
- Life insurance amount;
- Number of days of vacation; and
- Optional discretionary days;

Other options which may also be included are:

- Legal services enrollment;
- Tuition reimbursement;
- Health profile (as part of a wellness program); and
- Optional disability coverage;

Pay

Typical data fields pertaining to pay include:

- Existing pay
- FLSA status (exempt/non-exempt)
- Determination of FLSA status, if exempt; that is administrative, executive, outside sales, professional, or programmer/analyst;
- Person who determined exempt status;
- Last date exempt status was reviewed;
- Pay grade;
- Compa-ratio;
- Step in pay grade, if stepped grades are used; and
- History of pay increases, shown by year.

Regulatory

- I-9 confirmation and documents used for confirmation;
- Name of employee making confirmation; and
- COBRA notifications and date sent.

Safety and Health

- Dates of occupational reportable incidents;
- Classifications of accidents as preventable/nonpreventable;
- Dates of lost time injuries and illnesses;
- Dates restored to full duty;

- Classifications of accident causes (direct, indirect, and basic) for all accidents;
- Failure sources for all accidents;
- Amount of property damage for each accident; and
- Dates remedial training given, if warranted, for each accident.

Applicant Tracking System

An *applicant tracking system* (AT system) is used to record key information on job applicants. If job applicant information will also be used for calculating adverse impact, care should be taken to ensure the information includes those individuals defined as "applicants" by the *Uniform Guidelines on Employee Selection Procedures* as follows:

> "An *applicant* is a person who has indicated an interest in being considered for hiring, promotion, or other employment opportunities. This interest might be expressed by completing an application form, or might be expressed orally, depending upon the employer's practice."[3]

Persons who voluntarily either formally or informally withdraw from selection consideration are not applicants and should not be included in adverse impact calculations. However, records of all persons, including those who voluntarily withdraw should be retained.[4]

Some systems have scanning capability, which eliminates the burden of keying applicant information. The systems include basic information, including the job for which the individual applied, whether contact can made with the present employer and the interviewer assessments of the applicants' qualifications. Typically, the system is also used to send acknowledgment letters to applicants and to keep them informed about the status of their applications. Depending upon the needs of the organization, it is usually best if the AT system is integrated with the employee record system; if an applicant is selected for employment, the information in the AT system is easily copied. The typical information to be included in these systems is as follows:

- Applicant's name;
- Present address;
- Temporary address, if different from the permanent address;
- Country in which the applicant lives;
- Confirmation of applicant's legal residence and employability;
- Permanent and temporary telephone numbers;
- Date of application;
- Place where application was received;
- Type of application, such as resume or formal application;
- Recruitment source, such as newspaper, walk-in, or employee;

---

[3] *Uniform Guidelines on Employee Selection Procedures*, "Employee Selection Guidelines (Questions and Answers), Question 15," August 25, 1978.

[4] Ibid.

- Social security number;
- Gender;
- Veteran's status;
- Military experience;
- Military occupational code;
- Military job title;
- Length of military service;
- Category for EEO-1 or EEO-4 reporting;
- Race, using EEOC's groupings;
- Age status;
- Code for disability/handicap;
- Codes for other protected groups, depending upon the jurisdiction, such as sexual orientation, student status, or political affiliation;
- Job code for the position;
- Job title;
- Full-time or part-time work;
- Exempt or non-exempt status;
- Pay grade;
- Name of interviewer, if the applicant was interviewed;
- Name of person who screened the application for completeness; and
- Termination date for maintaining application.

Job Structuring Applications

Many aspects of job structuring, such as preparing job descriptions and job specifications and designing jobs to meet employee needs, depend upon information obtained through a job analysis. Job analysis studies are also important in organizational restructuring to prevent task redundancy and to ensure tasks are not omitted. Job structuring applications include job description and organization charting software. The typical components in job description software are:

- Job title;
- Occupational code, using the Standard Occupational Classification or other recognized system of coding;
- Exempt/non-exempt status code;
- Listing of essential functions/tasks, in order of importance and percentage of time required;
- Job specifications, including required knowledge, skills, abilities, training, education and experience; and
- Any special requirements, including driver's license, certification or related documents.

Usually, job description software includes fairly detailed job descriptions and some suggested job specifications. The user imports the description into a word processing software and makes any necessary modifications so that the final description reflects the actual job. These caveats should be observed:

- First, these job description applications are not a substitute for conducting a full job analysis. The user must first complete a job analysis and then modify the job description profile to fit the actual job. Not following this procedure places the user at risk of perpetuating inaccurate job descriptions for such purposes as selection, training and performance appraisal. In adverse impact situations, the *Uniform Guidelines for Employee Selection Procedures* (Guidelines) require that the offending selection procedure be validated by job criteria obtained from a job analysis.[5]

   A *partial* job analysis is required in criterion-related studies, if production or error rates or other measures like absenteeism or tardiness are obtainable and important in the employment situation, or if an overall method of determining job performance can be shown to be related and necessary for job success. If this information cannot be obtain, a *full* job analysis must be conducted. In addition, a full job analysis is required in all content or construct studies.

- Second, the Guidelines state that task descriptions should indicate all "important work behaviors" and should state both "their relative importance and their level of difficulty."[6] For example, cashing checks is one of the most important tasks in the job of Bank Teller. The Guidelines state that task descriptions should also include observable work behaviors and products and services produced and indicate the relative importance of the behaviors, products, and services in order to prepare accurate selection procedures.

   The listing of tasks should indicate which are *essential* (referred to as *"essential functions"* in the *Regulations to Implement the Equal Employment Provisions of the Americans With Disabilities Act*).[7] Employers are required to use only those tasks considered essential in making selection decisions. These are the criteria for employers to use in determining if a task is *essential*:

   - If the position exists to perform that function; for example, the job of Water Meter Reader exists to read meters.

   - If the number of employees who perform a task is limited compared to the volume of work to be done, and there is a limited opportunity to shift the task to other employees.

   - If employees who perform the task have specialized qualifications and the task cannot be shifted to other employees who do not have the requisite qualifications.

   - If the time spent performing the task is a significant portion of the workday; for example, if persons employed as Water Meter Readers

[5] Uniform Guidelines for Employee Selection Procedures, 43 FR 38295, 38314, August 25, 1978.
[6] *Ibid.*, Section 15.
[7] Technical Assistance Manual on the employment provisions of the ADA, EEOC, January 1992.

spend 60 percent of their total workday driving a vehicle, such as from one water meter to the next one.

- If the task is a part of a collective bargaining agreement.
- If past and present employees in a particular job have work experience performing certain tasks in the job.
- If a task was not performed, and the consequences of nonperformance have a serious impact on the job.

Job Specifications

Job specifications are the qualifications a person must possess to satisfactorily perform the tasks in a job. Sometimes the term job specifications is confused with *applicant qualifications*. The difference is that job specifications state the qualifications a person must possess to perform a job at a satisfactory level, while applicant qualifications consist of the experience, education and other credentials a person actually possesses.

There are various terms used in defining job specifications. The Guidelines use the terms *knowledge, skills, abilities,* and *training.* Most job specifications also designate *experience* and *education* requirements if specific levels of them are needed.

Ability

The Guidelines define *ability* as "a present competence to perform an observable behavior or a behavior which results in a observable product."[8] Thus, an ability is the capacity to perform either a required job behavior or a behavior which produces an observable product or service.

Skill

The Guidelines define *skill* as "a present, observable competence to perform a learned psychomotor act."[9] The definitions for ability and skill are very similar. *Ability* means the demonstrated capacity to do something; for example, the *ability* to make independent judgments in claim payments. Skill, however, is more than just ability, since it involves the application of learning, generally compared to some standard. Some work behaviors may involve both an ability and a skill. For example, a clerk job may involve only incidental typing, so the job specification may state, "ability to type." However, if specific levels of typing are important for success in the job, then the typing requirements may be stated more explicitly, as in, "skill in typing 40 correct words per minute."

Regardless of attempts to define skill and ability differently, it is often difficult to distinguish between them. For example, the Department of Labor method of job analysis defines the aptitude component of worker traits as "abilities required of an individual . . ."[10] However, many of the illustrative examples of various aptitudes demonstrate skills rather than abilities. For example, an illustration of verbal aptitude requires reading a written job order to accomplish this work element:

---

[8] Uniform Guidelines, Section 16.
[9] *Ibid.*

[10] U.S. Department of Labor, *Handbook*, p. 8.

Sets type by hand and machine, assembles type and cuts galleys for articles, headings, and other printed matter, determining type size, style, and compositional pattern . . . [11]

This work element obviously requires a fair amount of skill. As a rule of thumb, the word skill should be used when some standard of performance exists or the work behavior or products of work behavior obviously require the application of learning beyond the routine.

All pertinent information about a job is obtained in a job analysis. These are illustrations of the major types of information which are obtained:

- *Task information,* which includes how often the tasks are performed or what percentage of an employee's time is spent performing them, how important each task is in relation to all other tasks performed, and which tasks are deemed "essential" as required in establishing selection procedures for persons with disabilities.
- *Products and services* provided in the job.
- *Physical demands* required in the job, including walking, lifting, stooping, crawling, and sitting.
- *Physical environment* in which the job is performed, including inside/ outside work, temperature and other climatic conditions.
- *Knowledge, skills, abilities, training, education,* and *experience* required to perform the job tasks.
- *Licenses,* including craft licensure and motor vehicle license needed in the job.
- *Machines, tools, equipment* and *work aids* used in the job.
- *Relationships* developed on the job, including peers, customers, governmental employees, and supervisors.

Performance Appraisal Applications

Performance appraisal is typically a task that most supervisors dislike because of the drudgery often associated with it. Performance appraisal software systems relieve supervisors of much of this work by giving them a convenient way of recording and tracking performance immediately into appraisal files. Of course, this means the supervisor will be required to learn the software and have access to computers to keyboard the information. Most of these software programs also have some suggested text to help supervisors support their evaluations with written comments. Most software also can be used to either support an existing system or the software can be used to custom design a system. Typically, most software uses the *graphic rating scale* method of performance appraisal.

Performance appraisal systems supported by software must meet the standard requirements of appraisal systems in general; that is, they must be valid for the job, they must be standardized and objective, and they must provide a means for documenting behavior. As with other selection procedures, any adverse impact that appraisal systems may have must be supported through job-related-

[11] *Ibid.*

ness. This means a comprehensive job analysis must be conducted prior to the use of the system. Appraisal software must also control for the perceptual errors that supervisors often commit in making appraisals. These are the most common errors:

- *Central Tendency.* Central tendency is the propensity of untrained interviewers to use "the comfortable middle" in rating interviewees and avoiding either very low or very high ratings. Some supervisors commit the same error in completing formal written performance appraisals.

- *"Just Like Me" or "Similar to Me."* "Just like me" or "similar to me" is the tendency of supervisors to give higher ratings to persons who they perceive having qualities or qualifications similar to their own.

- *Halo Effect.* The halo effect is the tendency to rate a person high in all categories based upon one positive characteristic. *Horn effect* is the reverse, that is the tendency to rate a person low in all categories based upon one negative characteristic.

- *Implicit Personality Theory.* Implicit personality theory is the predisposition of raters to imply certain things about a person based upon one or more other characteristics the person has. For example, implying that a person is highly stress tolerant because he or she worked while attending college.

- *Leniency or Strictness Effect.* Lenient raters look at people through rose-colored glasses, and this causes their evaluations of people to be in error. Strict raters, who are on the opposite end of the spectrum, make such statements as "I've never interviewed (or appraised) an outstanding applicant." Both lenient and strict appraisers have unrealistic views of people.

- *First impression.* First impression is the proclivity of appraisers to base their subsequent opinions about people upon their first impression of them.

- *Contrast.* Contrast is the tendency to grossly misjudge people because those persons' characteristics differ somewhat from others. For example, if a rater interviews two candidates who are significantly under-qualified for a job, then the rater interviews a person who is marginally qualified, due to misjudging the contrast among the candidates, the marginally qualified person is given a much higher rating.

- *Stereotyping.* Stereotyping is the penchant of raters to make favorable or unfavorable conclusions about applicants based upon some particular characteristic the applicants share with others or groups to which they belong.

- *Recency Effect.* Recency effect is the predilection to make judgments based upon the most recent event. For example, if an employee had performed satisfactorily during an entire performance period but made a mistake a short time before a review, a rating error would result if the rater used only the recent error in giving the employee a poor rating.

- *Inconsistency Error.* Inconsistency is the proclivity of raters not to ask the same questions or use the same variables or standards in judging people.

Confidentiality of Employee Records

Privacy Rights

Among the rights recognized by various states on the subject of privacy include personal information that may be embarrassing to an employee, such as a person's sexual orientation, marital status, child dependencies, and financial obligations or debt payment history. Employers have obligations with regard to the following:

- Protecting employee personnel records and files.
- Protecting employee medical records.
- Avoiding intrusions into a person's personal life, such as his or her associations, alcohol use, spending habits and financial obligations, unless there is a valid job-related reason for making such intrusions.
- Preventing the public disclosure of personal information that may be embarrassing to an employee.
- Protecting the results of employment-related tests, including written tests used in making selection decisions and the results of both pre-employment and random drug tests.

Personnel Records

Personnel records, whether in hard copy form or in computer files, must remain secure at all times. There is no valid reason any person should have access to an employee's personnel file unless the individual is required to work with information in the file. Computer system access to personnel files should be coded. In the event of suits for the public disclosure of information contained in an employee personnel folder, employers will be subject to a high standard to show they have exercised due diligence in protecting confidential employee information from unauthorized individuals.

Medical Records

What is true for personnel files generally is doubly the case for medical records. Medical records should be protected by extraordinary access limitations. In hard copy form, medical records should be kept in separate sealed folders with initials across the seal. No one, even those regularly required to post information in personnel folders or files, should be permitted to review medical records. The only persons who should be permitted to see medical records are medical personnel or those individuals specifically authorized in writing by the top HR manager. Medical records should never be filed in the same manner as other information in personnel records. An important component of the Health Insurance Portability and Accountability Act is safeguards against the improper disclosure of an individual's health information. The Department of Health and Human Services (DHHS) is responsible for providing procedures to protect against any improper disclosures. As part of this responsibility, DHHS issued *Privacy Rules*(Rules) regarding disclosures. Firms and others covered (called "covered entities") by the Rules may use or disclose individuals' *Protected Health Information*(PHI) only with their written consent. PHI excludes health information in employment records maintained by an employer and education and certain other records subject to, or defined in, the Family Educational Rights and Privacy Act.[12] There are both civil and criminal penalties for violating these provisions. See Chapter 19 for a full discussion of the requirements.

Personal Life Intrusions

Generally speaking, there is no justifiable reason for employers to intrude in employees' personal lives, unless there is a valid job-related reason, such as conducting investigations of applicants for jobs in law enforcement. Questionable intrusions include investigating off-duty conduct, such as associates of the employee, his or her alcohol consumption, spending habits, financial obligations, and punctuality in paying bills. There is no valid reason for storing this type of information in an employee record system.

Disclosure of Personal Information

Special precautions must be taken to protect any investigative information that is obtained for a job-related purpose. Policies should be established concerning the length of time such information is retained. This policy should also apply to those applicants for employment who are not hired due to information disclosed in the background investigation.

Record-Keeping and Reporting Requirements

eDiscovery

HR legal issues, such as suits alleging employment discrimination or negligence in wrongful deaths occurring in the workplace inevitably involve demands for the production of HR records. To simplify record storage, reduce the cost of record retention and make records more accessible, HR makes extensive use of electronic record retention. Due to this trend, in 2006 eDiscovery procedures were added to the Federal Rules of Civil Procedures obligating employers to preserve "potentially relevant information" whether in electronic or paper form. Employees responsible for the custody of HR records need to understand their critical role in preserving and producing information and avoiding "spoliation" in legal disputes. When spoliation occurs, whether intentional or accidental, judges impose tough sanctions.[13] HR record custodians must work closely with legal counsel to ensure eDiscovery procedures are followed.

Legal Requirements

The record-keeping and reporting requirements vary with different laws. These are the major provisions:

- *Civil Rights Act of 1964, Title VII.* This law requires employers to:

    1. Keep records by race (unless one race constitutes more than 98 percent of the relevant labor area) and sex and show such data as number of persons hired, promoted and terminated.

---

[12] 20 U.S.C. § 1232g.

[13] See a $29.9 million verdict in a spoliation case and further information on eDiscovery in CCH Inc.

Human Resources Management: Ideas & Trends, "Join with in-house counsel to avoid violations," (July 2, 2008), p. 98.

2. Keep demotion/promotion records, job applications, resumes, termination records, and tests for one year from the date of the record or the date the decision was made, whichever is later. Employers also must keep records for two years on tests used, whether or not they were standardized, and validity data if adverse action exists.

3. File EEO-1 reports by September 30 every year, if there are 100 or more employees.

- The reports are submitted to the Joint Reporting Committee for the use of the EEOC and OFCCP. The reports provide the federal government with workforce profiles by ethnicity, race and gender, divided into job categories.[14]

- The EEOC uses the data to support civil rights enforcement. The EEOC also uses the data to analyze employment patterns, such as the representation of female and minority workers within companies, industries, or regions.

- OFCCP uses the data to determine which employer facilities to select for compliance evaluations. OFCCP uses a statistical assessment of the data to select facilities where the likelihood of systematic discrimination is the greatest.

- Reports must also be filed annually by employers with federal government contracts of $50,000 or more and 50 or more employees.

- In 2006 the report was revised in recognition of the shifting demographics in the contemporary workplace.

- The 2006 revision made these changes to the race and ethnic categories:

— added a new category titled "Two or more races"

— divided "Asian or Pacific Islander" into two separate categories: "Asian" and "Native Hawaiian or other Pacific Islander"

— renamed "Black" as "Black or African American"

— renamed "Hispanic" as "Hispanic or Latino"

— endorsed self-identification of race and ethnic categories, as opposed to visual identification by employers

- The 2006 revision made these changes to job categories:

— The category Officials and Managers, was divided into these two levels:

Executive/Senior Level Officials and Managers (jobs in which the incumbent plans, directs and formulates policy, sets strategy and provides overall direction within two reporting levels of the CEO).

---

[14] EEOC. *Final Revisions of the Employer Information Report (EEO-1)*, January 27, 2006. Due to the technical nature of these revisions, some full passages are verbatim from the EEOC announcement.

First/Mid-Level Officials and Managers (job tasks include the direct implementation or operations within specific guidelines set by Executive/Senior Level Officials and Managers).

— Business and financial occupations moved from the Officials and Managers category to the Professionals category. (The purpose of this change is to facilitate the analysis of trends in the mobility of minorities and women within the category).

Other groups covered by Civil Rights Act of 1964, Title VII, that must also maintain records are joint labor-management committees with apprenticeship programs, unions with 100 or more members, state and local governments with 15 or more employees, and elementary and secondary school systems or districts with 15 or more employees.

- *Age Discrimination in Employment Act.* This law requires the following:
  1. Employers must retain employee records, including name, address, and date of birth, for three years. In addition, employers must maintain other records like employment inquiries, placement actions and applicant and employee test papers for one year.
  2. Employment agencies must maintain records for one year concerning such transactions as referrals and applications.
  3. Labor organizations must maintain records on union members and applicants for membership.

- *National Apprenticeship Act of 1937.* This law requires:
  1. Employers must provide equal employment opportunity and affirmative action (AA) in recruiting, selecting, and training apprentices.
  2. Employers must keep detailed records of minority group status and gender of applicants.

  See Chapter 11 for a fuller discussion of other requirements.

- *Executive Order 11246, Vietnam Era Veterans Readjustment Assistance Act* and the *Rehabilitation Act* see Chapter 11 for a discussion of record and other requirements.

- *Equal Pay Act.* This Act is an amendment to the Fair Labor Standards Act. Extensive records, such as wage rates and job evaluation results, are required. Records are also required to document if any wage differences paid to female and male employees are due to reasons other than sex. Records must be maintained for two years from date of latest entry.

- *Fair Labor Standards Act.* Employers must keep records for three years. They must also keep supplementary records, like time cards, work schedules, and pay tables for two years. Violations include up to two years of overtime pay (three years for wilful violations) and may include doubling of overtime pay. The statue of limitations is two years (three years for wilful violations).

- *Family and Medical Leave Act (FMLA).* Employers must keep FMLA records in accordance with the record requirements of the Fair Labor

Standards Act (FLSA). Employers must produce records only when requested by a Departmental of Labor official and then no more than once during any 12-month period unless the Department believes a violation of FMLA exists or the Department is investigating a complaint.

No particular order or form of records is required. Employers must keep the records for at least three years and make them available to representatives of the Department of Labor upon request. The records may be maintained on microfilm or other basic source document provided that adequate projection equipment is available. Records kept in computer form must be made available for transcription or copying.

Records must disclose the following:

(1) Basic payroll and identifying employee data, including name, address, and occupation; rate or basis of pay and terms of compensation; daily and weekly hours worked per pay period; additions to or deductions from wages; and total compensation paid.

(2) Dates FMLA leave is taken by eligible employees. Leave must be designated in records as FMLA leave and may not include leave required under State law or an employer plan which is not covered by FMLA.

(3) If FMLA leave is taken by eligible employees in increments of less than one full day, the hours of the leave.

(4) Copies of employee notices of leave furnished to the employer under FMLA, if in writing, and copies of all written notices given to employees as required under FMLA. Copies may be maintained in employee personnel files, except for confidential records as noted below.

(5) Any documents describing employee benefits or employer policies and practices regarding the taking of paid and unpaid leaves.

(6) Premium payments of employee benefits.

(7) Records of any dispute between the employer and an eligible employee regarding designation of leave as FMLA leave, including any written statement from the employer or employee of the reasons for the designation and for the disagreement.

Covered employers with no eligible employees must maintain the records set forth in paragraph (1) above of this section.

Primary employers in a joint employment situation must keep all the records required above and secondary employees must keep records noted in (1) above.

If FMLA-eligible employees are not subject to FLSA's recordkeeping regulations for purposes of minimum wage or overtime compliance (i.e., not covered by or exempt from FLSA), an employer need not keep a record of actual hours worked, provided that:

(1) Eligibility for FMLA leave is presumed for any employee who has been employed for at least 12 months; and

(2) For employees who take FMLA leave intermittently or on a reduced leave schedule (see section titled **Employee Notice Requirements for Foreseeable FMLA Leave** Chapter 12), the employer and employee agree on the employee's normal schedule or average hours worked each week and reduce their agreement to a written record.

Confidential records. Records relating to certifications, recertifications or medical histories of employees or employees' family members, created for purposes of FMLA, shall be maintained as confidential medical records in separate files/records from the usual personnel files, and if the ADA (see Chapter 12) is also applicable, such records shall be maintained in conformance with ADA confidentiality requirements, except:

(1) Supervisors and managers may be informed regarding necessary restrictions on the work or duties of an employee and necessary accommodations;

(2) First aid and safety personnel may be informed (if appropriate) if the employee's physical or medical condition might require emergency treatment; and,

(3) Government officials investigating compliance with FMLA (or other pertinent law) shall be provided relevant information upon request.

See Chapter 19 for a discussion of the FMLA.

- *Immigration Reform and Control Act.* Employers must maintain I-9 forms for 3 years after employment date or 1 year after date of termination, whichever is later.

- *Occupational Safety and Health Act.* Employers must maintain these records:

  1. All employers with more than 10 employees must record occupational injuries and illnesses.

  2. Employers must keep records on a calendar year basis for five years.

     See Chapter 31 for a full discussion of recording and posting requirements for OSHA Forms 300, 300A and 301.

- *Federal Contractors and Subcontractors.* Employers must keep for at least two years (one year for employers with fewer than 150 employees or having a contract less that $150,000) records of applicants or employees involving but not limited to the following:

  - Hiring, assignment, promotion, demotion, transfer, lay off or termination, rates of pay and other forms of compensation;

  - Selection for training or apprenticeship programs;

  - Requests for reasonable accommodation;

  - Physical examination results;

  - Job advertisements/postings;

  - Applications and resumes submitted for employment, promotion or the related;

  - Test results; and,

- Interview results.

- Contractors and subcontractors must keep personnel records of employees terminated from employment for at least two years from the date of termination (one year for employers with fewer than 150 employees or has a contract less that $150,000).

- Contractors and subcontractors must keep records, involving any charge of discrimination, compliance evaluation or enforcement action, until the matter is resolved.

- Contractors and subcontractors must develop and implement written affirmative action programs and document good faith efforts to achieve affirmative action.

- Records for each "Internet Applicant" (see Chapter 15 for the definition of Internet Applicant) must be maintained that identify the gender, race and ethnicity of each applicant[15].

See Chapter 15 for the information that must be maintained for resumes received from internal and external applicants.

---

[15] Information in this section was obtained, and in some places directly quoted, from OFCCP, *41 CFR 60-1.12 Record retention.*

CHAPTER 6
HUMAN RESOURCES RESEARCH AND AUDIT

Chapter Highlights
- Learn the parts of HRM research
- Examine the methods of conducting research in HRM
- Learn how employee opinion surveys are conducted
- Study how research is conducted
- Understand how HRM audits are performed

Introduction

This chapter explores the various methods of HRM research. Also included in the chapter is an examination of the steps involved in conducting research. In addition, the chapter identifies the HRM activities in which research is often conducted. To better explain the ways that HRM research is conducted, the chapter includes several examples.

Research is the investigation of a subject to determine facts and theories and/or to find practical ways to apply facts and theories. *HR research* is the investigation of human resources activities to determine facts and theories and, as necessary, to define ways of effectively applying them.

HRM Research Process

HR research is conducted through these steps:

- Selecting the subject matter or cohort to be studied (see explanation below);
- Selecting variables;
- Defining and testing hypotheses; and
- Using various research methods.

Subject Matter or Cohort

Subject Matter

The *subject matter* of a HR research project could range from investigating new methods of recruitment (such as different sources of applicants found in various internet sites) to the cost/benefit results of converting to a cash balance pension plan. Numerous HR subjects are investigated through research. Typically, this research consists of literature reviews or field studies, but other types of research involving hypothesis testing are also used. More examples of typical subject matter areas of HR research are covered later in this chapter.

Cohorts

Often, HR research involves *cohorts*, such as associates of the firm and, less frequently, non-employees, such as job applicants.

A cohort, in a research study, is the group of persons who will be the subjects of the study. For example, the cohort in a validation study would be the persons who are given a selection method, such as a test, to determine whether it is a good predictor of job performance. More than one cohort may be necessary. For example, if an organization is conducting research on the efficacy of a training program, two cohorts might be used. The first cohort would consist of those individuals who are assigned to the training program, and the second would be a control group of individuals who did not receive the training. Comparisons would be made between the two groups to determine the effects, if any, of the training.

A research study of test validation could involve a cohort of job applicants or one of current employees. A *predictive validation* study is one in which the cohorts are job applicants, and the cohort in a *concurrent validation* study are present employees. Predictive and concurrent validation techniques are discussed more fully in Chapter 14.

Variables

Variables are the objects of HRM research. The variables may be such subjects as grievances, turnover, employee opinions or evaluations of various HRM programs. The three types of variables are *dependent, independent* and *moderating.*

Dependent Variable

A *dependent* variable is one that is influenced to some extent by one or more independent variables. For example, employee productivity is dependent to some degree upon an organization's pay system. Occupational illnesses and injuries are affected by training provided by the employer. The dependent variables are productivity in the first example and occupational illnesses and injuries in the second.

Independent Variable

An *independent* variable influences a dependent variable. Many HRM programs, such as employee suggestion systems, quality circles and incentive pay systems, are independent variables intended to influence employee behavior. For example, employee deficiencies, such as unscheduled and unexcused absences (dependent variables), are often caused by employee personal problems, such as alcohol abuse. Employers implement employee assistance programs (independent variable) as a strategy to help prevent and/or treat those personal problems and, thereby, control unscheduled absences.

Moderating Variable

A *moderating* variable influences or "moderates" the effect of an independent variable upon a dependent one. For example, as noted above, employee productivity (dependent variable) is influenced by an organization's pay system (independent variable). Moderating variables can effect the relationship of a pay system on employee productivity. A moderating variable in this situation might be an employee's past experience (either good or bad) with productivity-related pay systems. If the experiences were bad, the pay system would tend to have either an adverse or a reduced positive effect. Another moderating variable in this situation could be the training employees were given explaining how the system would function. Finally, the manner in which individual supervisors use the system to reinforce productivity could moderate the effects it has upon employees' production.

Presence of Moderating Variables. Most HRM systems (independent variables) designed to influence employee behavior (dependent variables) are moderated by other known and unknown events and conditions (moderating variables). For example, most managers understand that accidents are influenced by safety and health training. However, several other variables, some of which may be unknown to supervisors, such as employees' ages, employees' personal problems and even supervisors' leadership styles, also influence the number of occupational illnesses and injuries.

Importance of Moderating Variables. Recognizing the importance of moderating variables upon the relationship between independent and dependent variables causes the HRM professional to consider the following steps in designing, implementing and evaluating programs:

- What is an HRM program expected to accomplish? In short, what are the hypotheses upon which the program is based?

- What are the variables involved in the situation? Identify the dependent, independent and moderating variables.

- What programs can be designed that positively influence dependent variables?

- What evaluation system, which is part of the HRM program, measures the identified variables?

Hypotheses

Defining hypotheses is essential in HRM research. A *hypothesis* is a statement explaining a situation. For example, constructing selection methods begins with assumptions or hypotheses about the relationship among desired outcomes, such as employee productivity and work quality and various selection methods, including interviews and tests. Therefore, the simple process of defining a hypothesis causes the HRM professional to make some formal assumptions about a relationship.

Example: An HRM professional is designing a selection process for a computer sales job. A job analysis indicates interpersonal abilities, such as oral communication, sensitivity and flexibility, are among the job specifications necessary for successful job performance. The professional hypothesizes that a job simulation exercise, in which an applicant must demonstrate these abilities, is related to successful job performance.

Course of Action

Defining hypotheses also helps an HRM professional define a course of action. For example, the hypothesis regarding the selection method for the computer sales job helps guide the HRM professional to:

- Determine the job-related success criteria, such as amount of computer sales;

- Find a selection method that is content-related to the success criteria; specifically, a simulated exercise; and

- Provide the groundwork for testing to discover whether there is a relationship between applicants' performance in the simulation and subsequent sales. For concurrent validity testing, present computer sales personnel could be tested and their scores compared to their sales.

Inductive and Deductive Hypotheses

The two major types of hypotheses are *inductive* and *deductive*.

Inductive Hypothesis. An *inductive* hypothesis is a general conclusion made from independent observations. For example, a Training Assistant may observe that machine operators who attended a special 15-minute training course on error reduction methods make fewer errors than those operators who did not attend the course. Based upon this observation, the Training Assistant might want to do a more thorough evaluation of the training course using this inductive hypothesis:

> *Machine operators who attend error reduction method courses (independent variable) make fewer errors (dependent variable) than operators who do not attend.*

The Training Assistant can test this hypothesis by preparing a field experiment, using the random assignment of machine operators to treatment and control groups using this design:

R 0^2 (control group)

R X 0^2 (treatment group)

where:

R = random selection of subjects

X = the training course

0^2 = the post-test

Deductive Hypothesis. A *deductive* hypothesis is an assumed explanation of a situation derived from general theories based upon research conclusions and other factual evidence. Deductive hypotheses restate these theories in common language. For example, research studies have found that alcoholic employees have higher accident rates than nonalcoholic employees. The theory suggests that employees who receive treatment for their alcoholism will have fewer accidents than those who are not treated. A hypothesis to test this theory might be worded like this:

> *Alcoholic employees who are identified through an employee counseling program and then complete a treatment program will have fewer occupational accidents than similarly identified employees who do not complete such a training program.*

Inferential Statistics

Sometimes, inferential statistics are used to test hypotheses. In these situations, the hypotheses are either worded non-directionally or are worded in the direction of the proposed finding. An example of a directional wording of a hypothesis in the machine operator experiment might be:

> *A 15-minute error reduction training course will decrease the error rates of participants.*

A non-directional wording of a hypothesis for this same experiment might be:

> *There is a difference between the error rates of those machine operators who attend a 15-minute error reduction training course and those operators who do not attend such a course.*

Testing Hypotheses

There is a six-step procedure to test hypotheses:

1. Using either observations (inductive) or tested theories (deductive), identify an HRM topic and make a hypothesis;

2. Determine the results that should occur if the hypothesis is correct;

3. Select the appropriate research methods to obtain the data; in experimental studies, this step includes defining experimental and control groups and designing the study;

4. Obtain the data; and

5. Analyze the data, using the research methods.

6. Compare the results of the study with the hypothesis.

Testing Hypotheses Example. This is an example of an HRM research project using the six-step model:

Background: An HRD Manager reviews some research results, indicating programmed instruction is more efficient (less cost and faster trainee learning) than classroom training to teach Electronic Technician trainees basic concepts of electricity and mechanics. She decides to test the theory by randomly assigning trainees to two groups: one to receive a programmed instruction course and the other to receive the traditional classroom training course. Both groups will receive the same material on electricity and mechanics. The HRD Manager will check the effectiveness of the course by using these three *dependent* variables:

1. Score on a comprehensive test at the end of instruction;

2. Average number of days spent per trainee on the instruction; and

3. Cost of the training, including all direct costs, such as trainee salaries.

To test for differences in the two groups, the manager decides to use means-difference tests, in which the means of the three variables for the two groups will be compared. This is the process that will be followed in the research project:

• *Step 1:* The HRD Manager deduces this hypothesis from the theories she researched:

Trainees receiving programmed instruction (PI) in basic electricity and mechanics should learn the material quicker and at a reduced cost compared to trainees receiving the conventional classroom courses (CC) in the two subjects.

The Manager decides to divide this overall hypothesis into these three hypotheses so that she can check the results more accurately:

Hypothesis 1: PI trainees will use fewer days on average than CC trainees to cover the same electricity and mechanics material.

Hypothesis 2: PI trainees will, on average, score the same or higher than CC trainees will on a comprehensive examination covering both subjects at the end of the instruction period.

Hypothesis 3: PI trainees will have lower costs per trainee to complete the course than the CC trainees.

- *Step 2:* If the hypotheses are correct, the programmed instruction group, compared to a group of trainees receiving the classroom training, should: (1) require less time to learn the material, (2) make the same or better grades on a comprehensive examination at the end of the training, and (3) require less funds to be expended for the learning period.

- *Step 3:* The method used to test the hypothesis is a means-difference test. As background information, employees apply for the electricity and mechanics instruction as a prelude to acceptance for Electronic Technician trainee jobs. This pool of applicants will be used in the present study. Employees will be randomly assigned to two groups: one group will receive programmed instruction and the other one will receive the conventional course. The means-difference tests will be employed at the conclusion of the instruction, based upon the three hypotheses defined in Step 1. No pretesting will be used.

- *Step 4:* The instruction will be given, tests administered, cost data obtained, and required times computed.

- *Step 5:* Means-difference tests will be conducted, using the data obtained in Step 4.

- *Step 6:* The results in Step 5 will be used to test the three hypotheses prepared in Step 1.

HRM Research Methods

The research methods used in HRM are literature review, case studies, field studies, correlation studies, causal research and experiments.

Literature Review

A *literature review* involves investigating the research of others on a particular topic by reading relevant articles in periodicals, books, monographs, government documents, industry reports and similar works. Literature reviews may be used alone as a research method or in conjunction with other research methods, such as field studies. For example, a consultant in a management consulting firm was requested by the management of a hospital to install a Management by

Objectives (MBO) appraisal system for management personnel in the hospital. The consultant decided to investigate whether any research had been published on the use of MBO appraisal systems in hospitals in order to learn how effective they were, how they function in a hospital setting and what problems are encountered in installing them. The consultant intended to incorporate the findings of the literature review in designing a pilot MBO system for the client firm.

A secondary purpose for the literature review was to obtain the names of some hospitals using MBO systems. The consultant hoped to contact these sources to obtain copies of the MBO appraisal forms used and to receive some first-hand information on how the systems worked.

Literature reviews are indispensable in serious HRM research because they reveal what other work has been done on a subject. There may be little reason to conduct an expensive study on a topic if one or more well-documented research projects have already been done. Literature reviews can also be useful in helping an HRM professional design a research project. For example, previous studies on the same topic may describe strategies to avoid problems that may be encountered. Advantages to literature reviews are economy, speed with which results can be obtained, and simplicity.

Field Study

A *field study* or *field survey* is a research method focused on determining relationships and characteristics of social science variables in real-life settings. Field studies are an essential method of research in HRM. Typically, a field study is done *ex post facto,* but a study could also include descriptions of current events, such as the existing practices among a group of firms regarding educational expense reimbursement procedures. Field studies can also consist of subjects' intentions, such as the particular changes that a group of organizations propose to make in medical expense benefit programs. Field studies can consist of either *exploratory* studies or *hypothesis-testing* studies.[1]

Exploratory Studies. *Exploratory* studies, as the name suggests, focus on discovering what currently exists in a situation or a variable of interest.

Hypothesis-Testing Studies In *hypothesis-testing* field studies, the researcher formulates an hypothesis, which is tested from the results of the study. For example, through a literature review, a researcher may find indications that pay-for-knowledge occurs more frequently among private hospitals than among public hospitals. The researcher may formulate an hypothesis to that effect and test it from data he or she obtains through a field survey of the existence of that pay practice among private and public hospitals.

Case Study

A *case study* is a research project conducted within one organization. Some authors also refer to a case study as a field study.[2] Other authors differentiate

---

[1] Kerlinger, F. N., *Foundations of Behavioral Research* (New York: Holt, Rinehart and Winston, Inc., 1973), p. 406.

[2] Ibid, p. 406.

between a field study or survey and a case study.[3] The principal difference between the two methods is that the case study method focuses on one particular organization. Like the field study, a case study can be either exploratory or hypothesis-testing, in which an effort is made to determine the relationship between a dependent and an independent variable. For example, an HRM professional may want to investigate employees' productivity, work quality, sick day use and health benefits claims both before and after completing an eight-week physical fitness course sponsored by the company. The researcher would obtain the employees' records in these areas, compare the before and after results, and determine if the course had influenced any change.

Case study research of the hypothesis-testing variety is initiated with a hypothesis statement. For example, a researcher studying the effects of mentoring within an organization may formulate this hypothesis:

> *Mentors have a positive influence upon mentee's job adjustment.*

Correlation Study

A *correlation study* is one in which the researcher attempts to determine if there are interconnections between one or more dependent variables and an independent variable. For example, a researcher may want to determine if employee vehicle accidents are negatively correlated with the number of years of driving experience. A hypothesis for this study might be:

> *Employee vehicle accidents are negatively correlated with years of driving experience.*

To test the hypothesis, the researcher would use a simple linear regression.

Sometimes, a researcher may want to test the correlations among one dependent variable and more than one independent variable. For example, the researcher in the driving study might feel that the number of accidents is only partially attributable to years of driving experience. He may believe the age of the driver and a driver's knowledge of driving rules also influence the driver's accident rate. In this study, the researcher would hypothesize that the number of accidents a driver has is inversely correlated with these independent variables: (1) years of driving experience; (2) driver's age; and (3) driver's knowledge of driving rules, as measured by a written test. This hypothesis would be tested with a multiple regression. A multiple regression is used to measure the strength of the relationship among several variables.

Correlation studies are essential in HRM research because the results can be used to predict how a change in one or more independent variables may influence the correlated or dependent variables. Also, prediction accuracy can be determined by the magnitude of the correlation coefficient and the level of confidence.

Causal Research

Causal research is used in HRM to determine the causes of both desired and undesired events. For example, the employee turnover rate or the rate of un-

---

[3] Simon, J. *Basic Research Methods in Social Science*
(New York: Random House, 1969), p. 276.

scheduled absences may suddenly increase. Other indices might be a substantial increase in the number of grievances or a sudden drop in productivity. While these examples are all negative ones, that may not necessarily always be the case. Regardless of whether the changes are good or bad, management may want to find the cause. For example, accident investigations are conducted to find the causes, be they direct, indirect and/or contributory.

Experiments

An *experiment* is research in which the researcher has control over the variables and uses a randomization method in selecting subjects for the study. The two types of experiments are *laboratory* and *field*.

Laboratory Experiment. *Laboratory experiments* are more rigorous than field experiments, since the researcher has more control over the experimental conditions and the study variables. These conditions are not possible in HRM research because the experimenter inevitably is unable to maintain complete control over the variables. For example, a researcher testing the effects of different diets upon laboratory mice is able to isolate the mice and feed them different diets to determine the effects. A HRM researcher conducting research in the effects of a diet program for a group of employees enrolled in a company-sponsored weight reduction class is obviously not able to exercise the same degree of control.

Field Experiment. A *field experiment* is a study conducted away from a laboratory setting, and the researcher relinquishes some control over the variables. In some field experiments, such as the diet program mentioned above, the researcher may not be able to randomly select subjects for treatment and control groups. There are various reasons why subjects cannot be randomly selected. First, employees may volunteer for a program, such as the diet program. Second, ethical reasons may prevent testing the effects of various HRM programs, such as a safety training program. In this case, if the safety training program was believed to be effective in preventing accidents, the researcher would not want to limit the program to a treatment group and test the effects by comparing this group's accident rate to one for an untrained control group. A third reason that precludes the random assignment of subjects is the inability to pick employees who work in different locations. For example, if a machine operator training program is being tested, usually all operators in a particular section would receive the training rather than randomly selecting operators from different work sections. In this situation, the operators in one work location would be picked as the treatment group and the operators in another work location would be the control group.

Field experiments do have an advantage over laboratory experiments because they are conducted under actual work conditions. Consequently, the findings of field experiments can be more readily generalized to a working population, particularly if probability sampling techniques are used. Probability sampling is the process of selecting subjects from different groups within a population in proportion to their numbers as a percent of the total population. Internal and external validity questions, such as whether a study's findings can be generalized to other situations, are discussed in Chapter 33.

Scaling

A critical part of HRM research is the proper use of numbers. The four types of scales in research involving numbers are these:

- Nominal;
- Ordinal;,
- Interval; and
- Ratio.

Nominal Scale

The word *nominal* means "existing in name only," and that is a fitting description for nominal scales used in research because the numbers are simply convenient labels. For example, suppose plant accidents were being analyzed by shifts and the numbers 1, 2, and 3 are used to designate the three shifts. These numbers are only labels and they have no other properties.

Sometimes, numbers are used to designate preferences, such as a "1", for yes and a "2" for no. These numbers do not indicate magnitudes; they are just an easy way to classify responses. For example, we could not average all the 2s and 1s and get an average response.

Nominal scales also do not necessarily designate an order of something. For example, the numbers 1, 2, and 3 designating accidents by shifts do not necessarily mean that 1 is a higher order than 2, or that 2 is a higher order than 3. Scales that order subjects, data, or other properties being studied are called *ordinal scales.*

Ordinal Scale

The word *ordinal* relates to an order or a ranking. For example, the *straight ranking* method of performance appraisal involves the use of ordinal scaling, since the appraiser ranks all of his/her employees from the best to the worst performer. Ordinal scales go beyond nominal scales because the number has a property other than a simple label. For example, an employee who is ranked as the fifth best producer in a group of 25 employees is better than 20 employees but is below the top four.

Percentile ratings are ordinal scales. For example, assume a person took the General Management Aptitude Test (GMAT) and scored at the 78th percentile. This means 77 percent of the people who took the test achieved a score below that person's score, and 22 percent scored higher.

Ordinal scales cannot be arithmetically manipulated, such as summed and divided, because the intervals among the numbers are not necessarily the same. In other words, one cannot assume the difference in the productivity of two employees ranked 4 and 5 is the same as the difference in two employees ranked 1 and 2. For example, as shown in Exhibit 6-1, the difference in the number of units produced between Libby, who is the top producer, and Marjorie, who is the second best producer, is three. There is difference of eight units in the production of Herb, who is ranked fourth, and Charles, who is ranked fifth.

Exhibit 6-1
Example of Ordinal Ranking

		Production	
Employee	Ranking	Number of Units	Difference
Libby	1	42	n/a
Majorie	2	39	3
Ballard	3	27	12
Herb	4	26	1
Charles	5	18	8

Interval Scale

Sometimes, HRM researchers need a scaling method that will permit summarization and other manipulation of data. For example, a researcher may want to conduct an employee opinion survey on various aspects of the work environment. An interval scale will accommodate that need better than simply providing for a "yes" or "no" response indicating employee preferences. An *interval scale* has an equal value for each successive interval. An example is a Fahrenheit thermometer. The change in temperature from 60° to 61° is the same as a change from 92° to 93°.

There is a real need in HRM research for interval scaling. As noted above, opinion surveys better reflect employee opinions with interval scales. Also, both process and effect evaluations used to assess human resource development programs typically use interval scales, as do those that measure attitudes, values and interests. The three major kinds of interval scales are *Likert scales, Thurstone scales,* and *semantic differential scales.*

Likert Scale. A *Likert scale* is a five- to seven-point scale.

Example: (seven-point scale):

My supervisor is a fair person.

Strongly Agree	Agree	Slightly Agree	Undecided	Slightly Disagree	Disagree	Strongly Disagree
(7)	(6)	(5)	(4)	(3)	(2)	(1)

Example: (five-point scale):

My pay adequately rewards my performance.

Strongly Agree	Agree	Undecided	Strongly Disagree	Disagree
(2)	(1)	(0)	(−1)	(−2)

For practical purposes, either the five- or seven-point scales with all positive values, such as + 1 to + 7, are easier to use.

Likert scales are widely used in HRM research because they are easy to prepare, administer and score. Ideally, positive and negative statements should be randomly used, so that respondents will concentrate on them rather than simply circling all the responses in the same manner. However, this process may also cause problems if the respondents fail to note whether the statement is positively or negatively worded and thus err in making their choices. Also, as noted above, all positive values are easier to use and score.

Thurstone Scale. A *Thurstone scale* is the most difficult to construct of the three types of interval scales. The process of constructing these scales begins with the preparation of a large number of statements concerning the object to be measured. Next, a panel of from 50 to 100 judges is selected who independently review all the statements and arrange them according to the degrees of favorability. These results are summarized by determining the arithmetic means of the judges' responses. These mean values represent scales with a range of degrees in favorability. The statements are now ready for use. Respondents indicate their preferences for various statements, but they do not see the scale values. Each respondent's score is simply the mean of the values of all their selections.

The laborious process used in constructing Thurstone scales is one reason they are seldom used. Another reason is the lack of evidence demonstrating their superiority over either Likert or semantic differential scales.

Semantic Differential Scale. A *semantic differential scale* is a numerical scale represented by opposites in adjectives describing an attitude object.

Example: *In my opinion, my supervisor is:*

Fair	+3	+2	+1	0	−1	−2	−3	Unfair
Kindly	+3	+2	+1	0	−1	−2	−3	Cruel
Democratic	+3	+2	+1	0	−1	−2	−3	Autocratic
Patient	+3	+2	+1	0	−1	−2	−3	Impatient
Reasonable	+3	+2	+1	0	−1	−2	−3	Arbitrary

Semantic differential scales are more difficult to construct and administer than the Likert scales. Also, some items either cannot be readily represented on these scales or may appear awkward and, thus, may confuse the respondent. For these reasons, the Likert scale is best for clarity and conciseness in most situations.

Properties of Interval Scales. Interval scales can be summed and averaged to obtain the arithmetic mean responses for each statement. For example, these are some average Likert-scaled responses from 30 participants who completed a training course (5=Strongly Agree with the statement):

		Average
1.	The Instructor presented the course content clearly to me.	4.5
2.	The Instructor challenged me to think.	4.0
3.	The Instructor was prepared for the course.	5.0
4.	The material in the course was realistic.	4.5
5.	The refreshment breaks were too long for me.	1.5

One of the limitations of interval scales is that the distance between scale values is represented only in terms of the measurement instrument and not the variable being measured. For example, a thermometer gauges changes in temperature but is not an actual representation of temperature. Consequently, a person who is outdoors in 90° weather could not be said to be twice as warm as when the temperature is 45°. This limitation often causes problems in interpreting HRM research results where interval scales are used. For example, it was noted above that interval scales are often used in employee attitude surveys. Typically, attitude scores are associated with employee job satisfaction. However, errors in analyzing the results of such surveys can easily occur. For instance, a score of 70 on such a survey is twice as high as a score of 35, but a researcher could not conclude that an employee who scores 70 on the survey is twice as satisfied as one who scores 35. This scaling property, in which the scale values represent both the measurement instrument and the variable, exists with *ratio scales*.

Ratio Scale

A *ratio scale* is one with interval values that are equal in the measurement method used and the variable measured. For example, computing a nondisabling occupational injury incidence rate per 100 employees is a ratio-scaled measurement. The incidence rate has interval values because the interval between a rate of 2.2 and 3.2 is the same as one between 3.5 and 4.5. The interval values also are equal in the variable (the number of accidents), that is measured. Thus, a plant with a rate of 2.4 has twice the rate of another plant with a rate of 1.2. This property of ratio scales, in which the interval values are equal to the research variable, is not present in interval scales, like Likert scales. Remember, a researcher cannot conclude that an employee who scores 70 on an employee job satisfaction survey is twice as satisfied as another employee who scores 35.

Ratio scales are extensively used in HRM research. Some ratio-scaled variables are turnover rates, selectivity ratios, productivity rates, error or reject rates, customer complaint rates, grievance rates, discipline rates, and health benefits utilization rates. Ratio-scaled variables may include either physical counts or dollars.

Research—HRM Activity Relationships

Research is performed to some extent in virtually all HRM activities.

Equal Employment Opportunity/Affirmative Action

HRM research includes investigating various EEO data within the organization, such as the recruitment, selection and compensation of protected groups. Research information helps identify trends and areas where potential problems may exist. For example, selection rate data can be used to determine which selection methods may be having an adverse impact upon protected group members.

Job Analysis

The foundation of much HRM research is job analysis. Job analysis yields information about job tasks and job specifications that are used in research to test the effectiveness of various HRM activities, such as HRD programs.

Job Structuring

An analysis of quits or resignations often includes determining if jobs are properly structured or if personnel are properly assigned to jobs based upon their qualifications. Employee opinion survey results frequently hinge upon some of the critical psychological components of tasks, such as autonomy and significance. Jobs are structured to achieve employee satisfaction and organizational efficiency. HRM research provides the data necessary to accomplish these goals.

Employers also use alternative work scheduling methods to improve employee morale, reduce turnover and absenteeism and aid recruitment. Research studies can demonstrate the effectiveness of various work scheduling methods in accomplishing these objectives.

Human Resource Planning

The effectiveness of HRP depends upon the validity of forecasting and other methods used to determine human resource demand, as well as estimations of human resource supply. HRM research is used in such ways as conducting evaluation studies to determine both the accuracy of these projections and the effectiveness of plans designed to manage them. For example, management succession planning is effective to the extent that candidates receive the development necessary to qualify them for the anticipated vacancies.

Selection

HRM research is used in constructing valid and reliable selection methods. This process includes using the information obtained from job analysis to prepare job-related selection methods. Research is also necessary to design field experiments to measure the relationships among job criteria and the selection measures. Research is also needed to determine if adverse impact is present and if alternative selection methods can be developed that are equally valid and reliable without adverse effects upon protected groups.

Recruitment

HRM research is used to determine the effectiveness of various recruitment measures and to compute the costs of each one. These determinations are made by tallying the numbers of successful recruits generated from each source and calculating the cost of each method. This process results in a cost figure for each successful recruit. These comparisons help in decision-making concerning which recruitment sources to use for various jobs.

Performance Appraisal

Performance appraisal is fundamental to most HRM research projects because it is generally used as a dependent variable in determining the effects of other HRM activities. For example, the effects of some HRD programs, such as safety courses, are measured by determining their impact upon employee safety performance. The search for more effective performance appraisal systems is motivated by the objective of finding better ways of measuring performance variables. Accomplishing this objective requires HRM research.

Employee Benefits

HRM research is used to compute the costs of various benefit programs and relate them to employee preferences for various benefit provisions. Employee benefits comprise about 28 percent of total compensation costs in the average firm. Effective management of this expense involves research. For example, some employers attempt to contain health benefit costs by such tactics as requiring second opinions in nonessential surgery cases and paying employees for not using their health benefit plans. Research is necessary to accurately judge the effects of these strategies.

Counseling

Research is used in counseling programs to determine how such programs as alcohol abuse counseling are meeting objectives. For example, employees troubled by alcohol and drug abuse incur deficiencies in attendance, conduct, productivity, safety and work quality. This group of employees also cause employers to experience excessive costs due to accidents and health benefits use. Research is used to determine if counseling programs, such as employee assistance programs, are effectively controlling these costs.

Wellness

Employers implement wellness programs to increase employee health and happiness. The direct benefits from these programs include a reduction in both health benefit claims and sick leave usage. By-product benefits are improved employee morale and reduced absenteeism. HRM research is needed in such areas as employee opinion surveys to determine employee attitudes toward the programs. Utilization research data can show how extensively the programs are being used.

Pay Administration

Pay methods are under increasing scrutiny from both advocacy groups and federal and state agencies. This attention has prompted employers to use more carefully designed pay systems to ensure fairness and both intrinsic and extrinsic equity. Research studies are conducted to show wages and salaries by race, age and gender. These studies help employers identify potential problems before they become serious. Accurate market pay surveys are especially important today because of pressures prompted by comparable worth advocates. These pressures are causing employers to avoid the pitfalls of improperly conducted surveys. The research issues in these surveys include remaining current on recent court rulings and conducting literature reviews to remain current of the latest developments in this rapidly changing area of HR.

Pay Incentives

Pay incentives are intended to positively influence selected dependent variables, such as productivity, work quality or employee suggestions. Research is needed to measure whether these incentives have such an influence or if they are simply an added expense. To accurately determine the effects requires baseline historical data that can be compared to future data on the dependent variables after the incentive systems are installed.

Safety and Health

OSHA regulations require employers to maintain essential safety and health data, such as occupational injuries and illnesses, lost workdays due to such injuries and illnesses, and records of employee exposures to toxic substances. Employers can also use this data for a variety of research purposes.

Career Planning

Career planning research includes maintaining records on the number of employees enrolled in career planning programs and how they are progressing. Research is also conducted showing the effects of the programs upon the attitudes of the enrolled employees.

Career planning programs are established to accomplish multiple objectives, such as increasing employee morale, improving employee performance and preparing employees for career changes. Research is used to measure these objectives; for example, research can determine the percentage of employees who changed careers or received promotions after they completed their career development. Research can also demonstrate the cost/benefit ratio for offering career planning. Some of the costs include counselor time, career planning materials, workbooks, workshops and seminars. The benefits include improved job performance of employees enrolled in career planning programs and an increase in the number of qualified applicants, particularly for highly skilled jobs and other jobs that are difficult to fill.

Union Relations

Research is important in preparing for contract negotiations. Some of this research includes obtaining input from supervisors on various contract provisions that need to be changed and documentation concerning why a change is needed. Other contract negotiation planning research includes reviewing recently negotiated agreements involving the same union.

Preventive labor relations policies, designed to provide an environment in which employees will not be motivated to seek union representation, also involve systematic research. For example, employee attitude and opinion surveys are used to measure employee dissatisfactions with various job conditions, including pay, benefits and supervision. Some employers regularly conduct such surveys to discern any significant changes in employee opinions that may signal the initiation of a union organizing campaign.

Selected Areas for HRM Research

In addition to the HRM activities discussed above, research is conducted in many specific subjects.

Employee Opinion Surveys

An *employee opinion survey* is a formal method of measuring employee attitudes concerning selected items. An *attitude* is an individual's inclination or state of mind toward something. Such inclination may be emotional, signifying whether the person likes the object. Attitudes are learned by either direct experience with an object or from others. Two ways of discerning a person's attitude about an object are to observe his or her behavior towards it and to ask him or her for their opinion. An *opinion* is an expression of a person's attitude.

Employers are concerned about employee attitudes for several reasons. First, employers intuitively feel there is a positive relationship between employees' job satisfaction and their job performance. Research evidence supports this relationship for absenteeism, tardiness and turnover; however, no conclusive proof links productivity to job satisfaction. In spite of this lack of evidence, job satisfaction is a high priority in employee opinions about their jobs. Employers are also concerned about employee job satisfaction because of the belief that employees should be satisfied with their work. Finally, employers realize job discontent may adversely affect employees in various ways, including their physical and mental health and their adjustment in their personal lives.[4]

Purposes of Conducting Employee Opinion Surveys

Employers have these purposes for conducting employee opinion surveys:

1. Prevent employee work deficiencies;

2. Prevent employee criminal acts against the employer;

3. Increase employee work satisfaction and happiness;

4. Prevent turnover;

5. Prevent union organizing campaigns;

6. Strengthen internal communications;

7. Obtain employee opinions about compensation and employment procedures; and

8. Plan organization development interventions.

Prevent Work Deficiencies. Since employee attitudes are known to be related to attendance, employers want to correct problems that may be causing absenteeism and tardiness. Employers also intuitively feel employee dissatisfactions cause job deficiencies in conduct, such as failing to follow instructions, and in productivity, safety and work quality. For example, evidence does exist indicating that resentment against arbitrary supervision can result in employees defying safety rules and procedures.[5] These deficiencies cost employers considerable sums of money; consequently, they want to find the sources of job problems so they can be corrected.

Prevent Employee Crime. Internal security firms advise employers to treat employees fairly and find out about job problems in order to prevent employee criminal behavior.[6] Criminal acts include arson, theft, embezzlement, sabotage and murder. For example, disgruntled employees have committed arson to vent

---

[4] H.J. Reitz, *Behavior In Organizations* (Homewood, Illinois: Richard D. Irwin, Inc., 1981), p. 225.

[5] J.B. Miner and J.F. Brewster, "The Management of Ineffective Performance," *Handbook of Industrial*

and Organizational Psychology (Chicago: Rand McNally College Publishing Co., 1976), p. 1005.

[6] C.B. Gilmore, "To Catch a Corporate Thief," *Advanced Management Journal*, 47 (Winter 1982), p. 36.

their hostility against managers. Other employees have deliberately sabotaged expensive equipment or destroyed files because they felt they had been mistreated. Employees have even murdered their supervisors in retaliation for being disciplined.[7] Obviously, employers are interested in preventing such behavior, and opinion surveys are an excellent barometer of employee feelings.

Increase Job Satisfaction. Happiness in a person's nonwork life is often interdependent with happiness in his/her work life. For example, a person who has an unhappy home life or is troubled by substance abuse will often perform deficiently at work. In a similar manner, an unhappy job environment will spill over into a person's nonwork life. The cause of the unhappiness at work may vary; for example, it could be perceptions of low pay, too much responsibility, excessive stress, or an arbitrary boss. The causes of these and other sources of employee dissatisfaction will surface in a well-designed and properly implemented employee opinion survey.

Prevent Turnover. A major reason for employee resignations is job dissatisfaction. Employers are particularly concerned about the employee quit rate when it results in the loss of trained or professionally qualified talent. Some employers use *exit interviews* to identify actual and potential sources of employee dissatisfaction, but there are two problems with these interviews. First, departing employees may not disclose the real reasons for leaving because they fear reprisals in the form of bad recommendations for future jobs or discrimination should they wish to return to the firm. Most people would agree it is difficult to candidly tell an interviewer the sources of a person's job dissatisfaction. In an anonymous opinion survey, fear of reprisal is virtually nonexistent. The second problem with exit interviews is that the information is provided too late. An exit interview is like closing the barn door after the horse has run away. In sum, exit interviews provide information that is too little and too late. Opinion surveys, on the other hand, give an early reading of employees' concerns that may eventually cause resignations.

Prevent Union Organizing Campaigns. A major reason some employers use attitude surveys is to prevent union organizing campaigns. This purpose is well known to employees. For example, one employer arranged for a consulting firm to conduct an employee opinion survey whenever rumors began circulating that some employees wanted a union. In private interviews, a few employees frankly told the consultants, "I know why you are here—Management heard that some employees were talking about getting a union in here. It happens every time the union rumor starts—A few weeks later you guys show-up."

There is nothing wrong with using opinion surveys as a union prevention method. The best way to find out what is bothering employees is to ask them. Periodic opinion surveys may save management much grief in the long run. However, a survey is less effective when it is conducted only when a rumor exists of union interest among employees.

---

[7] D. W. Myers, *Establishing and Building Employee Assistance Programs* (Westport, CT: Greenwood Press, 1984), pp. 62-64.

The worse union prevention tactic is when management uses a survey to identify the employees or the particular work units responsible for the union interest and finds some pretense to discharge the suspected employee. Such a tactic is not only patently unfair but also illegal.

Strengthen Internal Communications. Employee opinion surveys are an excellent means of systematically obtaining employee input. Many communication methods, such as company newsletters and general memoranda announcing significant developments in the organization, are management-initiated. The flow in this communication is from the top down. There are relatively few communication methods, other than employee suggestion programs or organizational hotlines, that provide for a regular flow of communication from the bottom up. While these two methods are effective, they usually are used by a minority of employers and, thus, are not an accurate barometer of the opinions of all employees. Well-planned employee surveys, however, are unexcelled at providing management with conclusions that represent this cross-section.

Other Employee Perceptions. One large, nationally known organization had some serious employee problems, such as excessive turnover among highly qualified personnel. This organization's answer to the problem was simply to pour more money into salaries and benefits because management assumed it would correct the problem. If the organization had conducted an employee opinion survey, it would have learned that money was a low priority. The major problems were too little autonomy in decision-making, and an insufficient number of support personnel.

Opinion surveys also help define employee sentiments on employment conditions, such as hours of work, job structuring, the physical environment of the workplace and supervision. Finally, these surveys also reveal employee thoughts on various procedures, such as how promotions are decided.

Organization Development Strategies. Some organization development (OD) strategies, such as team-building, begin with employee opinion surveys in which employees express their thoughts and feelings about various subjects. Next, those responses are categorized, and feedback is given to employees. Then, team-building exercises, such as work groups, special projects, task forces, or even problem-solving sessions involving small groups of employees, are designed to elicit employee communication, cooperation and coordination in finding workable solutions and alternative methods.

Conducting an Employee Opinion Survey

Employee opinion surveys can be internally prepared, or commercial ones may be used. Two of the most common commercially prepared questionnaires are the Job Descriptive Index (JDI)[8] and the Minnesota Satisfaction Questionnaire (MSQ).[9] Both of these instruments are under copyright, and users must either pay a fee for use (MSQ) or secure permission from the publisher (JDI). The

---

[8] P.C. Smith, L.M. Kendall and C.L. Hulin, *The Measurement of Satisfaction in Work and Retirement* (Chicago: Rand McNally, 1969).

[9] 8 D.J. Weise, R.V. Davis, G. W. England and L.H. Lofquist, *Manual for the Minnesota Satisfaction Questionnaire* (Minneapolis: Industrial Relations Center, University of Minnesota, 1967).

Worker Opinion Survey (WOS) is a third questionnaire, and it can be used without constraint.[10] Exhibit 6-2 summarizes the subjects and number of questionnaire statements contained in these three instruments. Regardless of how well known a survey instrument is, there may be a problems if it does not adequately cover the purposes that management wants to cover. Some experts believe even the commercially available or "packaged" questionnaires cannot adequately cover the areas unique to different organizations.

Exhibit 6-2
Selected Categories in Three Employee Opinion Questionnaires

Instrument	Subject	Number Items
Job Descriptive Index	Work	
	Pay	
	Promotion	72
	Supervision	
	Co-Workers	
Minnesota Satisfaction Questionnaire	Ability utilization	
	Achievement	
	Activity	
	Advancement	
	Authority	
	Company policies & practices	
	Compensation	100
	Co-workers	
	Creativity	
	Independence	
	Moral values	
	Recognition	
	Responsibility	
	Social service	
	Social status	
	Supervision-human relations	
	Supervision-technical	
	Variety	
	Working conditions	
	General satisfaction	
Worker Opinion Survey	Promotion	
	Pay	
	Work content	
	Co-workers	48
	Supervision	
	Organization as a whole	

---

[10] 9 D. Cross, "The Worker Opinion Survey: A Measure of Shop-Floor Satisfaction," *Occupational Psychology* 47 (1973). pp. 193-208.

Internally Prepared Surveys

Internally prepared surveys may be used if there is sufficient expertise available within the organization to produce them. Some problems with internally prepared surveys include poor construction of items and improper scaling. For example, items may be imprecisely worded or fail to sufficiently cover a topical area, which result in surveys that do not represent or measure what they are supposed to cover. Many of these problems can be prevented by following the research procedures discussed in this chapter, such as defining variables and using correct scaling methods.

Steps in Preparing, Conducting, and Concluding an Employee Opinion Survey

Following are the steps in planning, constructing, and implementing an employee opinion survey:

Determine the Survey Purposes. The researcher should define, as precisely as possible, the reason(s) for the survey. Some possible purposes are mentioned in an earlier section of this chapter.

Obtain Top Management Commitment. A survey is a waste of resources if top management is not fully committed to the project. This commitment includes adequate funding to design and conduct the survey and to analyze the results. Commitment also means taking prompt corrective action in implementing those results that are feasible and explaining to employees why others cannot be implemented. Other important management assurances are to protect the confidentiality and/or anonymity of employees and to ensure all employees that no reprisals will result from any opinion an employee gives.

Select the Areas in Which Opinions Are Sought. The purposes often will dictate the areas a survey should cover. For example, if a purpose of the survey is to obtain employee opinions about personnel procedures, the areas to be included in the questionnaire should include procedures for promotions, overtime, discipline, grievances and suggestion submissions.

Prepare Questionnaire Statements and Coding Data. Coding data identifies employee categories necessary in analyzing the survey results. Some examples of coded data are: work unit, gender, length of employment, job, age, and marital status. In all such categories, precautions must be taken to protect anonymity. For example, to avoid identifying specific employees through the length of their employment, intervals can be used.

> **Example:** *How long have you worked for this company?*
>
> a. Less than a year
>
> b. One to 3 years
>
> c. Over 3 years

Also, job categories may be merged, where the number of employees in a particular category is not sufficient to ensure anonymity.

Careful thought is given to coding data to identify potential trouble spots. For example, a bank uses a survey that identifies specific branches or work units; if many employees are dissatisfied with a certain problem, such as a branch's supervision, corrective action can be taken.[11] In this same manner, respondent information for other survey items, such as specific features of employee benefit programs, need to be related to various employee categories. For example, a majority of employees may be relatively unconcerned about an organization's retirement planning program. However, if the item is categorized and analyzed by employee age groups, the results may show that most employees within a few years of the voluntary retirement age are concerned about retirement planning.

Select the Survey Method. The two principal survey methods are written questionnaires and interviews. Some organizations use both methods. These are the items of concern in preparing written questionnaires:

- Determine how many items should be prepared to adequately cover a topical area.

- Determine how long the questionnaire should be; for example, if too many specific areas are covered, the questionnaire may be too long.

- Determine what type of scaling method(s) to use.

- Decide if the responses will be tallied with computers, in which case machine scorable answer sheets can be used.

- Code each questionnaire statement.

Oral interviews are effective in surveys for several reasons. First, as noted in Chapter 33, a large portion of the adult population in the United States is illiterate. Often, these deficiencies are unknown to an employer because an illiterate or marginally literate employee will pretend to read. Consequently, even if the questionnaire is on company time, the employee will simply observe how other employees are completing the questionnaire and copy answers from a friend and/or fake reading the questionnaire and randomly mark responses. Interview opinion surveys, when used in conjunction with a written questionnaire, do not prevent this problem but they do help correct for it, if the interview results are compared with the written ones.

Interviews are also effective because some employees would prefer explaining their feelings about various items rather than writing about them. This is particularly true for sensitive items such as peer stealing or other instances of improper conduct. For example, in one organization, corporate management learned through an employee interview survey about recurrent sex parties among managers and their employees. The written questionnaires, which were also used in the survey, did not reveal any evidence of the parties. Employees who did not participate in the parties were upset about them because of the favored treatment given to those few who did participate. After learning about the parties, top management corroborated the information and took prompt corrective action.

Interviews also give interviewers the opportunity to probe further on various items. For example, in one plant, a number of employees apparently agreed

---

[11] "Listening and Responding to Employees' Concerns," *Harvard Business Review*, 58 (January-February 1980), p. 103.

among themselves to write on their written questionnaires that they were very dissatisfied with the health benefit plan. This employee concern was noticed early in the administration of the questionnaire, since the written comments on the questionnaires were read to determine if any items should be followed-up in the interviews. Interviewers were alerted about the adverse comments concerning the health benefit plan, and several follow-up questions were to be asked if employees mentioned the subject during the interviews. These were some of the questions asked when an employee expressed dissatisfaction with the health benefits plan:

1. *When did you last use the plan? And what problems did you experience with it?*

2. *What specific provision of the plan are you unhappy with?*

The interviewers found that a very small percentage of employees had *ever* used the health benefits plan. Even more astounding was the fact that virtually every employee who used the plan did not experience a single problem with it. Regarding the second question, the interviewers found employees were generally not knowledgeable about the various provisions of the plan. For example, some employees said the deductible should be lower and, when asked how much lower it should be, responded with various amounts that were either equal to or higher than the existing $50 deductible. The interviewers concluded that management needed to conduct a campaign explaining the various provisions of the health benefit plan, since it appeared the employee discontent was not well-founded.

A draft of the questionnaire and/or interview items should be prepared and timed to determine how long they would take to complete. This is also the phase in which repetitious items are removed and other fine-tuning occurs, such as correcting any ambiguities.

Select a Place to Administer the Survey. Surveys should be administered on company time and on company premises. Most companies use the cafeteria or other large room and administer the questionnaire in large groups to as many employees as can be spared from their work at one time. This reduces the probability that employees who have not been given the questionnaire will be influenced by those who have.

Interviewing should be done in private with only the interviewer and the employee present. Offices within the plant or work unit are ideal if they are available. If private space is not available, small trailers can be rented and parked on the premises.

Announce the Survey. Exhibit 6-3 is a sample letter to employees announcing the survey. Due to the costs of preparing and mailing an individual letter to each employee, a notice can be posted on all bulletin boards, or the announcement could be reproduced and copies distributed with paychecks. The announcement typically contains essential information, including:

- The name of the survey;
- The purpose(s);
- A request for employee cooperation;

- The way in which the survey will be conducted;
- The methods to be used;
- The location where the survey will be conducted.
- Assurance of confidentiality/anonymity;
- Assurance of no reprisals for information employees furnish;
- The use of coded data to analyze information by employee categories;
- The amount of time necessary to complete the various instruments;
- The date that the results will be made known to employees;
- The type of action employees can generally expect the company to take when the results are known;
- The name and telephone number of contact person for information about the survey; and
- The signature of a high-level executive, preferably the chief executive officer.

Decide When to Conduct the Survey. There are a number of logistical and timing concerns to resolve in conducting employee opinion surveys. Timing is important in employee surveys, since extremely favorable or unfavorable events prior to the administration of the survey will tend to influence the results. For example, a general pay increase will influence a survey if it is administered within a short period of time after the pay increase is granted. A serious accident or other adverse event, such as a poor performance report or an announcement of an unanticipated drop in company earnings, will similarly effect employee opinions. The problem is that these events only have a short-term effect upon employee opinions and, thus, the real long-term concerns are concealed.

The ideal period in which to conduct employee surveys is when the organizational environment is relatively stable and when "business as usual" conditions exist. This is one reason why planning is a top priority in conducting employee surveys.

Analyze Data and Prepare Results. Once the data is available in a computer database, the results can be quickly tallied and presented in numerous report formats, such as by work unit, age, gender and job classification. Survey data is much more valuable in decision-making when the results can be shown by these specific variables. In addition, the results should be compared with the results of previous surveys. These comparisons can reveal trends and determine any effects of various changes in such matters as compensation and procedures.

Normally, the tallied results are shown in percentages. These are two examples of tallied responses to survey questions:

Example: *How long have you been employed in this company?*

10% a. Less than a year

47% b. One to 3 years

43% c. Over three years

Example: *I believe our retirement planning program adequately prepares employees for retirement.*

4% Strongly agree

62% Agree

13% Slightly agree

11% Neither agree nor disagree

10% No opinion

Exhibit 6-3
Sample Letter Announcing An Employee Opinion Survey

Dear Associate:

Each year, we conduct an employee opinion survey, in which you are asked for your opinions on a variety of topics of concern. We use this information to help us decide how to most effectively meet you and your co-workers' needs. Your opinions are important.

The survey has two parts; first, you will be asked to complete a questionnaire. The questionnaire will be completed in group sessions, as it was last year. However, this year the sessions will be held in the new cafeteria to accommodate more people in order to complete the survey quickly. You will be asked for certain coded information about your work unit, job and other characteristics. This data will be combined with information for all employees in order that responses to various statements on the questionnaire can be categorized by age group, job and work unit. Your responses will be completely anonymous.

The survey also includes a private interview with each employee. The interviewing will be conducted by Grant Associates of Chicago, Illinois, a leader in the field of employee opinion interviews. The interviewers assigned to our company are Sara Brown, Mark Josselyn, Henry Smith, Phyllis Reed and Mary Neff. These individuals are well-qualified professionals, and you may be assured they will respect your anonymity. They are only interested in your opinions and will not record your name or anything else that will identify you. We use interviews because experience has shown us that some employees prefer explaining their opinions or feel they can better express their opinions by telling someone about them.

The questionnaire will require about 45 minutes to complete, and the interview will last from 15 to 30 minutes. You will be paid for the time spent for both portions.

The survey results will be summarized by Grant Associates and given to company management. No company representative will see any completed questionnaires or the results of an interview. This is another precaution to protect your anonymity. Management will prepare a memorandum to all employees explaining the survey results and the actions that will be taken on each item.

The survey will be conducted during the week of June 18-25, and the results should be available by July 1. If you have any questions about the survey at any time, do not hesitate to call Ron Mitts, Human Resources Manager, at 257-6053. Your cooperation will make this survey a success.

Sincerely,

E.W. Middlebrooks

Executive Vice-President

Take Corrective Action. One large national company conducts annual employee surveys in all its plants. The company uses an outside consulting firm to ensure employee anonymity and confidentiality and to provide greater survey validity. The consulting firm administers an anonymous written questionnaire to all employees. Employee work units are categorized, but the number of employees in each unit is large enough to protect employee anonymity. This precaution is not really necessary because employees know that no employee has ever been affected by anything he or she has written or said during a survey.

The consulting firm also conducts a private and personal interview with each employee. Employees freely speak their minds in these interviews. Employees are told that no names are taken in the interviews, and they believe it. Employees know management really wants to know any problems they have because the Executive Vice-President of the company visits the plant for a briefing as the survey is in process. The briefing usually occurs on the second or third day of the interviewing. The quantified questionnaire results have not been analyzed; however, the written comment portions have been reviewed and analyzed, and preliminary results are available from the interviews. The briefing session is attended by the consulting firm's project leader, the plant manager and the Executive Vice-President. Items are presented and, where feasible, problems are corrected immediately. Normally, the plant manager has the necessary authority to do so, but, in some cases, the Executive Vice-President's authority is needed. All corrected items are written on a special memorandum and immediately posted on all employee bulletin boards. The memorandum also explains which items were not corrected and why; the memorandum discusses the reason where action is being delayed. In most cases, 75 percent of the problems are handled within several days.

This example illustrates several important concepts in employee opinion surveys. First, if opinions are sought, then action must be taken on them. If management opposes this idea, employees should be told beforehand what will happen as a result of expressing their opinions. Second, employees will respond to a survey according to their belief about management's desire to know their opinions. Finally, anonymity and confidentiality in opinion surveys are minor concerns in environments where mutual trust exists among employees and managers.

Accidents

Research topics involving accidents might include the dollar amount of damage, rates for lost workday accidents (as discussed in Chapter 31, these are accidents which result in an employee missing work or being unable to perform his or her job tasks) or accidents in which illnesses or injuries occur, and vehicle accidents. Vehicle accident rates can be shown as the number per 100 million miles. In this case, this is the formula:

$VAR = A \div FMD \times 100$ million

where:

VAR	=	the vehicle accident rate
A	=	the number of accidents
FMD	=	the number of miles driven by all the vehicles in the fleet for the period in which the rate is computed.

Vehicle accidents are also researched on the basis of driver preventability. The National Safety Council defines a *preventable accident* as, "any occurrence involving a company owned or operated vehicle which results in property damage and/or personal injury regardless of who was injured; what property was damaged, to what extent, or where it occurred, in which the driver in question failed to do everything he reasonably could have done to prevent it."[12]

Attendance

Most employers conduct extensive research in various areas of employee attendance. *Tardiness* is reporting to work after the scheduled time, regardless of whether it is for the beginning of work or after breaks and meal periods. *Unscheduled absence* is failing to report for work as scheduled. Usually, records of these incidents are maintained for each employee. Reports can be prepared for each month or can be prepared to show employee attendance patterns. Research for these two attendance variables is aggregated for each supervisor, shift, or even an entire plant. Generally the data is reported by month or other established period. These rates usually involve a common denominator, such as the number of work days for the period involved.

Examples:

1. $TR = NT \div EWH$

where:

TR	=	the tardiness rate
NT	=	the number of tardinesses
EWH	=	the total workhours of all employees for the period

2. $UAR = NUA \div EWH$

where:

UAR	=	the unscheduled absence rate
NUA	=	the number of unscheduled absences
EWH	=	the total workhours of all employees for the period

Sick leave rates are shown for research purposes in various ways, such as the rate of sick leave use per employee. Employee rates are also aggregated and shown by supervisor, shift and plant. Individual employee rates are usually shown as sick leave used as a percent of sick leave earned or:

$ESLR = SLU \div SLE$

where:

ESLR	=	employee sick leave rate

---

[12] National Safety Council, *Safe Driver Award Rules* (Chicago: National Safety Council, 1980), p. 2.

| SLU | = | total amount of sick leave used by the employee |
| SLE | = | the total amount of sick leave earned by the employee. |

The variables in this formula can be changed to reflect the use rates during selected periods, such as a year, instead of using accumulated rates for the entire period in which an employee has been employed.

Suggestions

Employee suggestion programs research typically include the computation of suggestion submission and adoption rates.

Exaples:

$$SSR = [NSS \div NE] \times 100$$

where:

SSR	=	the suggestion submission rate
NSS	=	the number of suggestions submitted during the period
NE	=	the number of full-time equivalent employees

$$SAR = [NSA \div NE] \times 100$$

where:

SAR	=	the suggestion adoption rate
NSA	=	the number of suggestions adopted
NE	=	the number of full-time equivalent employees

Using 100 in the formulas converts the rates to the number per 100 employees. Generally, a 100-percent submission rate is considered a good one. This rate means, on average, that one suggestion is received for each employee in the organization. Naturally, some employees never submit a suggestion, while others submit many suggestions. A 25-percent adoption rate is considered to be a good one.

Suggestions are also researched for the dollar benefit value of the adopted ideas. This information is obtained by computing the tangible benefit savings and converting them to dollars. Intangible savings are used where a benefit cannot be quantified. Most suggestion systems have written procedures to help supervisors determine both intangible and tangible savings.

Turnover

Turnover analysis is a major area of HRM research. Usually, this analysis centers on voluntary separations, such as quits, because they presumably involve employees whose services are demanded by the employer. However, total separations are also used in research and for such purposes as human resource planning in estimating short- and long-term anticipated vacancies by job.

There are various methods of computing turnover. This is the basic formula:

$$TO = NS \div NE$$

where:

TO	=	turnover rate
NS	=	the total number of separations
NE	=	the total number of employees employed at the end of the period for which the rate is computed

This is a variation of the basic rate:

$$TO = NS \div [NEB + NEE]/2$$

where:

NS	=	the total number of separations
NEB	=	the number of employees at the beginning of the period for which the turnover rate is being computed
NEE	=	number of employees at the end of the period for which the turnover rate is being computed

The second turnover formula takes into consideration the effects of a planned reduction in employment levels. For example, if a company with 150 employees planned to reduce employment by 25 employees during the year, those positions would not be filled. The turnover rate would be shown as much higher under the first formula than it would be under the second one. For example, assume 25 employees did leave the company; the turnover rate in the first formula is 20 percent, or $^{25}/_{125}$. The rate under the second formula is $^{25}/_{150} \div ^{125}/_2 = 18$ percent.

Discipline

Usually, discipline rates are computed for each supervisor, shift or plant. Historical rates are maintained and used for comparison purposes with recent ones to determine trends.

Discipline, including grievances, is researched to identify the areas in which problems may exist. This data is also used in preparing for collective bargaining to anticipate union demands and/or to prepare management proposals for changes needed in the existing contract.

HRM Audits

Auditing is the process of verifying HRM accomplishments. Audits are either general or specific and are either internally or externally conducted.

Purposes of HRM Audits

The main purposes of HRM audits are to:

1. Check for legal compliance;
2. Determine if HRM plans and accomplishments are consistent with organizational goals;
3. Monitor whether HRM policies and procedures are being observed; and
4. Identify areas in which HRM plans and/or corrective actions are needed.

Legal Compliance

Legal compliance audits are conducted to determine if an employer is conforming to laws and regulations affecting HRM. Self-audits of legal compliance are conducted by employers to identify any potential problems. These audits may be internally performed by a representative from the legal or audit department. Sometimes, an HRM representative is selected to conduct the audit. A representative from HRM in the corporate office may be designated to conduct legal compliance reviews of HRM in field offices and plants. These self-audits run the gamut from Fair Labor Standards Act provisions covering such procedures as overtime pay to OSHA regulations for employee safety and health. Other legal compliance areas include Title VII and affirmative action provisions that apply to contractors who do business with the federal government. It is advisable to include attorneys on in-house audits.

The motivation behind legal compliance self-audits is simple: the cheapest and most painless way to correct mistakes is to find and resolve them before a federal or state agency becomes involved.

Plans and Accomplishments

HR activities are designed to help an organization accomplish its goals. In the Strategic Planning section of Chapter 3, it is noted that the extent of HRM involvement in strategic management varies among organizations. However, in order for an organization to accomplish its long-term strategic plans, certain HRM activities are critically important, such as selecting the best qualified personnel, developing those personnel and establishing an appraisal system that guides them toward desired objectives. Other HRM activities are also important for an organization to accomplish goals, such as pay administration and safety and health. HRM audits evaluate HRM policies and procedures to determine if they provide adequate support for the organization goals.

In HRM auditing, the auditor would review the organization goals and determine how well they are supported by HRM policies and procedures. The audit findings would include recommendations for any changes needed in either policies or procedures. This phase includes comparing policies and procedures to evaluate the way they are implemented.

Areas for Corrective Action

HRM audits are also intended to provide management with recommendations for areas in which action is needed. These recommendations may concern either corrections for omissions and errors in the way procedures are being implemented or the adoption of policies and procedures that are needed to adequately support organizational goals. For example, in reviewing an organization's affirmative action plan, a consultant may find the HRM department is not implementing certain provisions of the plan. In addition, the consultant may recommend several changes and/or additions to the plan to make it more effective.

There are various procedures used in HRM audits. For example, audits of HRM activities in federal agencies are usually conducted by in-house inspectors who arrive unannounced. The purpose of these audits is to ensure HRM activities are conducted in accordance with specific regulations. Some agencies also conduct broader audits involving areas other than compliance with regulations. These audits are usually conducted by HRM professionals who are employed in either field offices or at headquarters; the audit assignment is a temporary one; when it is completed, the employees return to their regular job.

General and Specific Audits

As noted above, HRM audits may be either general or specific.

General Audit. A *general audit* reviews the entire HRM function. The activities included in a comprehensive audit include those shown on the checklist in Exhibit 6-4.

Exhibit 6-4
Selected Items in a HRM Audit List

EEO/AA
_____ Legal compliance
_____ Utilization
_____ Goals accomplishment

JOB ANALYSIS
_____ Methods
_____ Desk audit
_____ Field audit

JOB STRUCTURING
_____ Job descriptions
_____ Job specifications
_____ Scheduling methods

HUMAN RESOURCE PLANNING
_____ Supply and demand
_____ Succession plan
_____ HR systems

RECRUITMENT
_____ Internal
_____ External
_____ Recruitment planning
_____ Checklists

HUMAN RESOURCE DEVELOPMENT
_____ Need determination
_____ Evaluation

CAREER PLANNING

SELECTION
_____ Adverse impact
_____ Validity and reliability
_____ Effectiveness

INTERNATIONAL HRM
_____ Expatriation preparation
_____ Repatriation planning
_____ Risk controls

PERFORMANCE APPRAISAL
_____ System design
_____ System implementation
_____ Purposes met

EMPLOYEE BENEFITS
_____ Administration
_____ Cost trends
_____ Cost containment
_____ Alternatives

COUNSELING
_____ Program utilization
_____ Evaluation
_____ Assessments
_____ Responsibilities
_____ Accomplishments

EMPLOYEE RELATIONS
_____ Grievances
_____ Turnover

WELLNESS
_____ Risk aspects
_____ Cost/benefits
_____ Employee utilization

PAY ADMINISTRATION
_____ Legal requirements
_____ Internal equity
_____ External equity
_____ Pay policies

PAY INCENTIVES
_____ Management attitudes
_____ Meeting purposes

SAFETY AND HEALTH
_____ Goals/accomplishments
_____ Legal compliance
_____ Commitment
_____ Inspections

SECURITY
_____ Concerns
_____ Incidents
_____ Potential risks
_____ Discipline
_____ Employee attitudes

UNION RELATIONS
_____ Negotiations planning
_____ Contract provisions

Specific Audits. *Specific audits* concentrate on one HRM activity, such as safety and health or human resource development. These audits are conducted either internally or externally. Sometimes, the external audits are conducted by regulatory agencies, such as the Office of Federal Contract Compliance Programs (OFCCP). OFCCP conducts affirmative action plan (AAP) audits of federal contractors. These AAP audits are required to determine if the contractors are meeting the requirements of laws, such as the Vocational Rehabilitation Act. OFCCP audits are very extensive for contractors with 50 or more employees and with contracts of $50,000 or more. For example, two HRM professionals in a large bank worked over two months in preparing documentation for an OFCCP AAP audit. The OFCCP audits were required under Executive Order 11357, since the bank was a depository of federal funds.

External audits may also be conducted by insurers, such as workers' compensation insurers, who assist employers identifying safety and health conditions that could result in accidents or unnecessary disease, disability or death.

Employers also engage the services of independent consultants who specialize in specific areas, such as labor relations or pay administration. These consultants conduct audits to determine if laws are being observed and if policies and procedures are appropriate. Sometimes, these specific audits are intended to prevent problems. For example, a non-union employer may hire a labor relations consulting firm to conduct an audit to determine if any changes in HRM policies and procedures are needed to prevent a union from organizing the firm's employees.

CHAPTER 7

FEDERAL EMPLOYMENT LAWS AND REGULATIONS

Chapter Highlights
- Review a brief summary of federal HR laws
- Examine summaries of federal HR regulations

Introduction

Federal laws and regulations are essential components of the external environment in which organizations must function. These laws and regulations provide the framework of basic employee rights and affect the manner in which employers make decisions about staffing, job structuring, pay, benefits, employee relations, safety and health, and labor relations. Some laws only apply to single activities, for example, the provisions of the Occupational Safety and Health Act (OSHA) are restricted to employee safety and health. Other laws apply to several HR activities. For example, the 1964 Civil Rights Acts applies to employment decisions affecting staffing, job structuring, pay, benefits, and employee relations. In this single chapter, the reader can gain a brief overall introduction in how the various laws affect different HR activities. A summary of these legal requirements is contained in Exhibit 7-1. The specific provisions of the laws are covered in more detail in the appropriate chapters.

Exhibit 7-1
Summary of Federal Employment Law

Law/Regulation	Function						
	Staffing	Job Structuring	Pay	Benefits	Employee Relations	Safety & Health	Labor Relations
Civil Rights Act of 1866	✓				✓		
Civil Rights Act of 1871	✓				✓		
Federal Arbitration Act of 1927	✓		✓		✓		✓
National Apprenticeship Act of 1937	✓						
Civil Rights Act of 1964	✓	✓	✓	✓	✓		
Civil Rights Act of 1968	✓						
Age Discrimination in Employ. Act of 1967	✓		✓	✓	✓		
Rehabilitation Act of 1973	✓	✓			✓		
Vietnam Era Veteran's Readj. Act of 1974	✓						
Executive Order 11246 of 1965, as amended	✓	✓					
Executive Order 11478	✓						
Civil Service Reform Act of 1978	✓						✓
Pregnancy Discrimination Act of 1978	✓			✓	✓	✓	
Immigration Reform and Control Act of 1986	✓						
Executive Order 13201							✓

Law/Regulation	Function						
	Staffing	Job Structuring	Pay	Benefits	Employee Relations	Safety & Health	Labor Relations
Genetic Information Nondiscrimination Act of 2008	✓	✓					
John Warner National Defense Authorization Act of 2006			✓				
Employee Polygraph Protection Act of 1988	✓				✓		
Americans with Disabilities Act of 1990	✓	✓			✓		
Civil Rights Act of 1991	✓						
Uniformed Services Employment and Reemployment Rights Act of 1994	✓		✓	✓	✓		
Personal Responsibility and Work Opportunity Reconciliation Act of 1996	✓						
Fair Credit Reporting Act of 1997	✓				✓		
Federal Bankruptcy Act	✓				✓		
Guide. on Religious Discrim. of 1966	✓				✓		
Guide. on Sex-Based Discrim. of 1972	✓				✓		
Unif. Guide. for Emp. Sel. Procedures of 1978	✓	✓			✓		
Guide. on Nat'l Origin Discrim.	✓						
Worker Adj. & Retrain. Not. Act of 1988	✓				✓		

Law/Regulation	Staffing	Job Structuring	Pay	Benefits	Employee Relations	Safety & Health	Labor Relations
				Function			
Older Worker Benefits Protection Act of 1990	✓			✓	✓		
Davis-Bacon Act of 1931			✓	✓			
Copeland Act of 1934			✓				
Walsh-Healey Act of 1936			✓				
Fair Labor Standards Act of 1938	✓		✓				
Equal Pay Act of 1963			✓				
Service Contract Act of 1965			✓	✓			
Consumer Credit Protection Act of 1970			✓		✓		
Omnibus Budget Reconciliation Act of 1993			✓				
Internal Revenue Code, Section 280G			✓				
Sec. & Exch. Com. Disclosure Reqs. of 1992			✓				
Health Maintenance Organization Act of 1973				✓			
Employee Ret. & Income Sec. Act of 1974				✓			
COBRA of 1990				✓			
Family and Medical Leave Act of 1993				✓	✓		
Health Ins. Port. and Account. Act of 1996				✓			

						Function	
Law/Regulation	Staffing	Job Structuring	Pay	Benefits	Employee Relations	Safety & Health	Labor Relations
New. & Mothers' Health Prot. Act of 1996				✓			
Mental Health Parity Act of 1996				✓			
Women's Health & Cancer Rts. Act of 1998				✓			
Pension Protection Act of 2006				✓			
Sarbanes Oxley Act of 2002				✓			
Sherman Antitrust Act of 1890							✓
Clayton Antitrust Act of 1914							✓
Railway Labor Act of 1926							✓
Norris-LaGuardia Act of 1932							✓
National Labor Relations Act of 1935							✓
Labor Management Relations Act of 1947							✓
Labor Mgt. Report. & Disclose. Act of 1959							✓
Postal Reorganization Act of 1970							✓
Occupational Safety & Health Act of 1970						✓	
Freedom of Info. Act					✓		
Privacy Act of 1974					✓		
Drug-Free Workplace Act of 1988					✓	✓	

Staffing

Staffing relates to employment decisions involving new hires, promotions, reassignments, selections for training programs, and demotions. Because of the importance of these decisions, a number of federal laws and regulations have been passed over the years governing how these decisions must be made.

Civil Rights Act of 1866

This law has been used sparingly in the past but will be used more in the future in intentional discrimination cases. Discrimination must be intentional for the Act to apply. This law permits compensatory and punitive damages (if malice or reckless indifference is present) for discrimination based upon race. There are no caps on the amount of awards for damages. The law applies to *all* employers, including those with only one employee.

Civil Rights Act of 1871

This law prohibits state laws from impacting upon individuals' rights provided by federal law. It prohibits discrimination based on age, national origin, race, religion and sex.

Federal Arbitration Act of 1927

The Federal Arbitration Act (FAA) was enacted to require judicial enforcement of arbitration agreements. In a 2001 decision, the U.S. Supreme Court held that employees who have claims, disputes, and controversies due to their employment must submit them to arbitration, if they have signed documents, such as employment applications, in which they previously agreed to such an arrangement.[1] This decision had a significant impact upon workers' rights in both unionized and non-unionized settings since any dispute, including those involving allegations of violations of federal laws, must be subjected to arbitration if workers have signed documents requiring it. The Court also held that transportation workers are exempt from the law. Some critics contend the ruling favors employers because of the belief that arbitrators are partial to them and because the law restricts employee rights to seek court action.[2]

Conceivably, if workers have signed arbitration agreements, virtually any issue in dispute arising from their employment would be subject to arbitration. Such disputes may involve staffing issues, such as allegations of discrimination under the Americans with Disabilities Act, Title VII of the Civil Rights Act, the Age Discrimination in Employment Act, and other laws. Other disputes might involve allegations of pay inequities subject to Title VII, the Equal Pay Act, the Fair Labor Standards Act, and others. Decisions affecting employee relations, such as allegations of discrimination in discipline and discharge, which otherwise might be subject to court action under Title VII, might also be affected. Finally, allegations of violations under labor relations laws, such as the National Labor Relations Act, might also be subject to arbitration.

---

[1] *Circuit City Stores, Inc. v. Adams* (2001), No. 99-1379.

[2] CCH HUMAN RESOURCES MANAGEMENT, *Ideas and Trends in Personnel* (April 4, 2001), p. 51.

Suggested wording for an arbitration agreement clause is shown in Chapter 16. See Chapter 37 for U.S. Supreme Court decisions affecting arbitration agreements.

The National Apprenticeship Act of 1937

This law prohibits discrimination based on national origin, race, color, religion, and sex in recruiting, selecting, and training apprentices. Written affirmative action plans, including goals and timetables, are required, when the percentages of individuals in the labor market area are underrepresented in the firm's apprenticeship programs.

Title VI, Civil Rights Act of 1964

This law prohibits discrimination on the basis of race, color, religion, sex and national origin in federally financed programs and activities. It was applied in the landmark case, *Bakke v. The Regents of the University of California.*

Title VII, Civil Rights Act of 1964

This law, which is often referred to as simply "Title VII," prohibits employment discrimination on the basis of race, color, religion, sex, and national origin. It applies to employers engaged in an industry affecting commerce who have 15 or more employees for each working day for at least 20 calendar weeks in the current or preceding calendar year. Employees are counted, whether or not they are actually performing work for or being paid by the employer on any particular day. Employers who have less than 15 employees and have a discrimination case in federal court cannot claim exemption from Title VII (claiming they have less than 15 employees) if they raise the issue after the close of a trial in which the merits of the case were heard.[3] "Each working day" simply means that an employee is counted as an employee for every working day, starting on the day that the employment relationship begins and ending on the last day of the employment relationship.[4] See Chapter 12 for a fuller description of this law's provisions.

Charges alleging discrimination must be filed within 180 days of the alleged unlawful practice. If the charge is initiated with an authorized state or local agency, the charge may be filed with the EEOC, 300 days from the practice or 30 days from receiving notice from the local or state agency that it is terminating its action, whichever is less. If the EEOC concludes no "reasonable cause," it sends the aggrieved a "right to sue" letter, and the EEOC concludes the case.

See the section on Title VII in Chapter 12 for a discussion of U.S. Supreme Court decisions affecting time limitations in filing charges under the law.

Title I, Civil Rights Act of 1968

This law prohibits interference with a person's application for employment or a person's actual employment.

---

[3] For a discussion of this issue see *Arbaugh v. Y&H Corp. DBA The Moonlight Café* (2006) in *Appendix 1.*

[4] See *Walters v. Metropolitan Educational Enterprises, Inc.,* 519 U.S. 202 (1997), in Appendix 1.

Age Discrimination in Employment Act of 1967, as amended

This law prohibits discrimination against persons 40 years of age and older. The law prohibits mandatory retirement ages, except in certain occupations, such as fire fighters and law enforcement. Bona fide executives entitled to an immediate nonforfeitable right to a retirement pension of $44,000 or more per year may be required to retire at age 65. The law applies to employers engaged in an industry affecting commerce who have 20 or more employees for each working day for at least 20 calendar weeks in the current or preceding calendar year. It also applies to labor unions that have 25 or more employees, employment agencies, and apprenticeship and training programs involved in interstate commerce.

The law also applies to state and local governments (including school districts). However, the U.S. Supreme Court decided that states are immune under this law for private suits brought by individuals (see *Kimel et al., v. Florida Board of Regents et al.*) in the Appendix.

Charges alleging discrimination on the basis of age must be filed with the EEOC within 180 days of the alleged unlawful practice. If the charge is initiated with a "deferral agency" (located in a state in which there is a law prohibiting age discrimination and which has an agency empowered to obtain remedies) the charge may be filed with the EEOC, 300 days from the practice or 30 days from receiving notice from the local or state agency that it is terminating its action, whichever is less. If the EEOC concludes that there is no "reasonable cause," it sends the aggrieved a "right to sue" letter, and the EEOC concludes the case.

Rehabilitation Act of 1973

This law provides rights for persons with physical or mental disabilities. The law applies to federal agencies, recipients of federal grants or federally assisted programs, and employers who have contracts with the federal government of more than $10,000. A person with a handicap (referred to as a *person with a disability* under the Americans with Disabilities Act) has a mental or physical impairment substantially limiting one or more of life's major activities *or* has a record of such an impairment *or* is considered to have such an impairment. See Chapter 11 for a fuller discussion of this law, including affirmative action requirements. See Chapter 12 for a full discussion of the definition of "handicapped" and "disabled," including important U.S. Supreme Court cases on the topic. Chapter 12 also contains a full discussion of examples of affirmative action involving persons with handicaps/disabilities.

Vietnam Era Veteran's Readjustment Assistance Act of 1974

This law applies to employers who have contracts with the federal government of $100,000 or more. It prohibits discrimination against *veterans*. A *veteran*, as the term applies to federal equal employment opportunity law, such as the Vietnam Era Veterans Readjustment Act of 1974, refers to special disabled veterans, Vietnam era veterans and "other protected" veterans.

See Chapter 11 for a full discussion of this law, including the definition of covered "veterans."

Executive Order 11246

This executive order prohibits discrimination on the basis of race, color, religion, gender, and national origin by contractors and subcontractors with federal contracts that exceed $10,000. It also requires affirmative action in the employment of the above protected groups.

Executive Order 11375

This executive order amended Executive Order 11246 by substituting "religion" for "creed" and added a prohibition on sex discrimination.

Executive Order 11478

This executive order prohibits discrimination on the basis of race, color, religion, sex, national origin, age, and disability/handicap by federal agencies. These agencies are also required to establish affirmative action programs for individuals in these groups

Civil Service Reform Act of 1978

This law contains a number of provisions, including one requiring federal agencies to establish affirmative action plans that include " . . . targeted recruitment activities wherever under-representation is found in specific occupations or grade levels." This law was the first to impose the same requirements upon federal agencies as had applied for many years to private sector firms contracting with those federal agencies.

Pregnancy Discrimination Act of 1978

This law amended the Civil Rights Act of 1964 by extending protection in hiring and discharge to pregnant women. It also bans compulsory leaves of absence for pregnancies. It gives pregnant women the right to the same employee benefits as are accorded to any other employee eligible for disability benefits.

Immigration Reform and Control Act of 1986

This law was designed to: (1) stem the flow of illegal immigrants into the U.S., (2) provide a means for certain illegal aliens to obtain legal status, and (3) to prevent discrimination against persons because of their national origin or citizenship status. The law includes the following provisions:

- It prohibits the employment of persons who are in the U.S. without authorization.

- It requires new employees, within 72 hours of hire, to provide evidence of residence and employability and to complete Form I-9. The applicant has 90 days to furnish information to support the I-9. Form I-9 must be retained for three years from date of employment or one year following termination of employment, whichever is later.

- Prohibits employers with 4 or more employees from discriminating against any person (other than an unauthorized alien) in hiring, discharging, or recruiting or referring for a fee because of a person's national origin or citizenship status. Furthermore, employers with 15 or more employees may not - in addition to discrimination based on hiring, discharging or recruiting or referring for a fee - discriminate against any person on the basis of national origin in assignment, compensation, or other terms and conditions of employment.

• Charges alleging discrimination involving employers with four to 14 employees are handled by The Office of Special Counsel for Immigration Related Unfair Employment Practices. Typically, charges involving employers with more than 14 employees are handled by the Equal Employment Opportunity Commission. See Chapter 16 for a full discussion of this law.

New hires are required to provide creditable evidence of identity and right to work or employability in the U.S. Lists of the documents that provide this creditable evidence are shown in Chapter 16.

Employee Polygraph Protection Act of 1988

A *polygraph* is an instrument that monitors respiration (rate of breathing), blood pressure, and electrical conductivity of skin surfaces (also known as galvanic responses or perspiration). The use of polygraphs among private sector employers is controlled by both federal and state law. The Employee Polygraph Protection Act of 1988 (EPPA) prohibits the use of all lie detectors except the polygraph. The law only permits certain employers to *request* applicants to take a polygraph test. Employers are also permitted, under restricted conditions, to *request* employees to take a test in the event of an economic loss. The law also stipulates requirements and qualifications for polygraph examiners. Violators of the EPPA are subject to awards of money damages, such as lost wages and benefits, court orders to stop violations and civil fines of up to $10,000.

In addition to the EPPA, many states and the District of Columbia have laws restricting the use of a polygraph in an employment setting. The EPPA does not preempt state laws that are more restrictive.

The EPPA prohibits private sector employers from administering deceptograph, voice stress analyzer, psychological stress evaluator, or any similar device to applicants or employees.[5] The Act also prohibits private sector employers from administering a polygraph, except that applicants may be *requested* to take a polygraph test if they are applying for work with either: (1) security firms (armored car, alarm, and guard), if they will be engaged in security work, or (2) manufacturers, distributors, or dispensers of controlled substances, if the applicant will have direct access to the manufacture, storage, distribution, or sale of such substances.

Neither applicant refusal to take a polygraph test nor the analysis of the results of a polygraph test can be the sole basis for denying employment. Applicants who consent to take a polygraph test may terminate the test at any time and may not be asked questions in certain areas, such as sexual behavior. Employers are required to give applicants written notice that they cannot be required to take the test as a condition of employment.

---

[5] CCH HUMAN RESOURCES MANAGEMENT, *Employment Relations*, ¶ 5686.

According to a national survey conducted by the U.S. Department of Labor, less than 2 percent of employers use polygraphs in selecting employees.[6]

Americans with Disabilities Act (ADA) of 1990

The ADA applies to employers engaged in an industry affecting commerce who have 15 or more employees for each working day for at least 20 calendar weeks in the current or preceding calendar year. This law prohibits discrimination against a person with a disability if the person is able to perform the *essential tasks* in the job. A *person with a disability* has a mental or physical impairment substantially limiting one or more of life's major activities *or* has a record of such an impairment *or* is considered to have such an impairment.

Other practices or conditions are prohibited by the ADA. For instance, employers may not segregate persons with disabilities in work areas or other areas, such as lunchrooms. Employers cannot refuse to select persons with disabilities due to administrative considerations; for example, in the case where a liability insurance policy did not cover persons with disabilities. Furthermore, it is illegal for an employer to obtain insurance or secure other employee benefits from an organization that will not extend coverage to employees who have disabilities. The law prohibits discrimination against a person because of his or her association with an organization involving persons with disabilities or because of a relationship with a person with a disability.

Employers are prohibited from conducting: (1) preemployment medical tests, (2) preemployment inquiries, (3) medical examinations of employees, or (4) inquiries about an employee's disability, *unless* such activities are job related and are necessary for business purposes. Medical examinations of applicants, conducted after a job offer but prior to their commencing work, is legal if all applicants are so examined and the medical information remains confidential.

The law requires employers to make reasonable accommodation for the employment of an otherwise qualified person with a disability, unless it can be shown that to do so would pose an undue hardship. Reasonable accommodation may include such measures as:

1. Making facilities readily accessible and usable by persons with disabilities,

2. Restructuring jobs so that persons with disabilities can perform the tasks,

3. Using various job scheduling tactics, such as arranging part-time work,

4. Making modifications to equipment,

5. Adjusting or modifying examinations, training materials or policies, and

6. Providing readers or interpreters.

See Chapter 12 for a fuller description of this law's provisions.

---

[6] Human Resource Policies and Practices in American Firms (Washington, DC: U.S. Government Printing Office, 1989), p. 13.

Civil Rights Act of 1991

The law created the Frances Perkins-Elizabeth Hanford Dole National Award for Diversity and Excellence in American Executive Management, which is awarded annually to an organization that has demonstrated leadership in developing and promoting women and minorities. The law also contains provisions for handling allegations of discrimination by these groups previously exempt from federal laws:

a. U.S. Senate employees, handled by Director, Office of Fair Employment Practices, who is a Senate employee;

b. Previously exempt state employees, handled by the EEOC;

c. Presidential appointees, handled by the EEOC or other entity designated by the President; and

d. House of Representatives employees and agencies of the U.S. Congress, which includes both the House of Representatives and the Senate, are covered by the Civil Rights Act of 1964, subject to procedures and remedies as the House of Representatives and the agencies may design.

Uniformed Services Employment and Reemployment Rights Act of 1994[7]

The Uniformed Services Employment and Reemployment Rights Act (USERRA) prohibits discrimination against a person who is a member of, applies to be a member of, performs, has performed, applies to perform, or has an obligation to perform service in a U.S. uniformed service. Such person shall not be denied initial employment, reemployment, retention in employment, promotion, or any benefit of employment by an employer on the basis of membership in the U.S. uniformed service, or application for membership, performance of service, application for service, or obligation to perform service.

Covered Employers. All employers are covered, including the federal government, states and territories, and political subdivisions of states.

Benefits of Employment. Benefits of employment include any advantage, profit, privilege, gain, status, account or interest (other than wages or salary for work performed) that accrues by reason of an employment contract or agreement or by an employer policy, plan, or practice, and includes rights and benefits under a pension plan, a health plan, an employee stock ownership plan, insurance coverage and awards, bonuses, severance pay, supplemental unemployment benefits, vacations, and the opportunity to select work hours or location of employment. A returning service member is entitled to general wage increases and pay increases due to seniority and to the current rate of pay for his/her job, if such pay is an attribute of the job. Returning service members are not entitled to any pay increases attributable to merit

Health Benefits. A person who was called into service and allows his employer's health plan to lapse, while he was away since he enrolled in military

---

[7] Most of the material in the following sections pertaining to USERRA is verbatim from the law. For a fuller description of the requirements and provisions of the law, see Title 38, United States Code, Chapter 43—Employment Rights of Members of the Uniformed Services.

health coverage, may qualify for coverage under the employer's plan upon return from the period of service. Under USERR, both the returning service member and his family should be able to resume coverage under the employer's plan. Furthermore, the plan cannot impose a waiting period or other exclusion period if health coverage would have been provided except for the military service. However, the plan can exclude from coverage any illness or injury that was caused or aggravated by the period of military service and is covered by a military health plan.

Retirement Plans. Under USERRA a period of active duty is neither considered a break in employment for retirement calculation purposes nor affects participation eligibility, vesting or benefit accruals. However, accrued benefits resulting from employee contributions are restricted to those the employee actually makes to the plan. Employers are not required to make contributions to an elective deferral plan, such as a 401(k) plan, while the employee is on duty, however, upon return to employment, the employer must make the contributions that would have been made had the employee remained employed. If employee contributions are either required or permitted under the plan, the returning service member has a period equal to the lesser of three times the period of military service or five years to make the contributions. Also, the employer must contribute any matching payments according to the plan's provisions.

Entitlement Conditions. To be entitled to rights under the law, these conditions must be met:

- The person (or an appropriate officer of the uniformed service in which such service is performed) has given advance written or verbal notice of such service to the employer. No notice is required if military necessity makes it impossible or unreasonable.

- The cumulative length of the absence and of all previous absences from a position of employment with that employer by reason of service in the uniformed services does not exceed five years. Not included in the five-year limitation is service beyond five years that is required to complete an initial period of obligated service. Also excluded is service for which the person is unable to obtain orders releasing the person from a period of service before the expiration of the five-year period, if such inability was through no fault of the person. Also excluded is service that is necessary for professional development or for completion of skill training or retraining (as certified by the Secretary of the service involved). Service is also excluded if it is due to being ordered or retained on active duty.

- The person reports for, or submits an application for, reemployment to the employer.

Covered Employees. All employees are covered including temporary, part-time, probationary and seasonal employees. Employees are not covered if they are departing from a seasonal position that is brief and non-recurrent for which there is no expectation it will continue indefinitely or for a significant period of time. All levels of employees are also covered including managerial, executive and professional.

Independent Contractors. Independent contractors are not covered.

Discharge/Layoff. A returning service member who served more than 180 days may not be discharged for one year except for just cause, such as the following:

- For a conduct deficiency for which the person had been previously informed would be grounds for dismissal.

- Other legitimate reason, such as a layoff/job abolishment which the employer can justify as legitimate.

The same provisions apply if the service member served more than 30 but less than 181 days except the protection against discharge only extends to 90 days.[8]

Work for Another Employer. A returning service member may work for another employer prior to returning to work for the pre-service employer if the work does not violate specific policies of the employer (such as if the employer had a policy prohibiting working for a competitor).[9]

Timely Application/Report for Work. These are the requirements for reemployment following a period of service:

- *Less than 31-day period of service.* Employee must report to work at the regularly scheduled work time following an eight-hour period after arriving home from a period of service unless it is impossible to do so in which case the employee must report as soon as possible after the eight-hour period.

- *More than 31 days but less than 181 days of service.* Employee must submit an application for reemployment within 14 days after the period of service ends or if it is impossible to meet this requirement, no later than one day after it is possible to submit the application.

- *More than 180-day period of service.* Employee must submit an application for employment not later than 90 days after the period of service is completed.[10]

Employees who do not meet the appropriate requirements above, do not automatically forfeit entitlement to USERRA's rights but are subject to the employer' policies regarding an unscheduled absence.

Written Notice Not to Return to Work. Employees are not entitled to non-seniority rights (such as accrual of vacation time) granted to similarly situation employees who are on furlough or leave of absence, if prior to entering service they give written notice to the employer that they do not intend to return to work after the period of service ends. However, the written notice does not waive the employees' rights to other provisions of USERRA, such as the right to reemployment.[11]

---

[8] USERRA, Section 1002.248.

[9] Ibid., Section 1002.120.

[10] Ibid., Section 1002.115.

[11] Ibid., Section 1002.152.

Escalator Position Clause. Under USERRA, the *escalator position* is the "job position that the employee would have attained if his or her continuous employment had not been interrupted due to uniformed service."[12] If not for the period of service the escalator position is one to which, ". . . the employee could have been promoted (or, alternatively, demoted), transferred, or laid off due to intervening events."[13]

- The returning employee is entitled to be returned to the escalator position and its commensurate pay, benefits, seniority and perquisites.

- In determining to which job the employee should be returned the individual's length of employment, qualifications, and any disability should be considered. The actual reemployment position may be the escalator position, the pre-service position, a comparable position to either the escalator or pre-service position or "the nearest approximation to one of these positions."[14]

- Returning employees must be "qualified" to perform the duties of the position.[15]

Nonessential tasks cannot be used to determine if the employee is qualified. Essential tasks must be used in making these determinations. These are the criteria to use in determining if tasks are "essential":

- The employer's judgment.
- Written job descriptions.
- Amount of time spent doing the task.
- Consequences if the task was not performed.
- Terms in a collective bargaining agreement.
- The work experience of past incumbents in the job.
- The current work experience of present incumbents in the job.

Prompt Reemployment. USERRA requires employers to "promptly employ" returning employees. Prompt reemployment means as soon as practicable but depends upon the circumstances. For example, "prompt reemployment" after weekend National Guard duty means the next regularly scheduled working date. Longer tours of assignment may take longer periods for the reemployment to be accomplished, however, unless there are unusual conditions, returning employees must be reemployed within two weeks after application for reemployment is made.[16]

Entitlement for Reemployment. These conditions must be met for a returning employee to be entitled to reemployment:

- The employer was given advance notice.
- The employee was gone for military service for five or less years.
- The employee timely returns to work or applies for same.

---

[12] Ibid., Section 1002.192.
[13] Ibid., Section 1002.191.
[14] Ibid., Section 1002.192.

[15] Ibid., Section 1002.198.
[16] Ibid., Section 1002.181.

- The employee was not separated from military service for a disqualifying discharge or under other than honorable conditions.[17]

Health Benefits. Employees are entitled to continuing personal and family coverage under any health benefits plan provided by the employer for the lesser of 24 months or the period commencing when the military service begins and ending when the employee fails to either return from military service or apply for reemployment.[18] These are some key provisions regarding health benefits for employees going to/returning from service:

- Cost of benefits.
- — If the period of service is less than 31 days the employee cannot be required to pay more than the regular employee's share, if any.
- — For periods of service greater than 31 days, employees can be required to pay 102 percent of the plan's full premium.
- Termination/reinstatement of coverage.
- — Coverage may be cancelled after 30 days if the employee has not elected to continue it.
- — Coverage must be reinstated to the date of departure if the employee requests it and pays back premiums.
- — Coverage must be reinstated upon reemployment.
- — Exclusions or waiting periods may only be imposed for illnesses or injuries incurred or aggravated during military service as determined by the Secretary of Veteran's Affairs.
- An employer's COBRA provisions can be followed in making health benefit decisions, provided they do not violate USERRA provisions.

Denial of Reemployment. An employer is not required to reemploy a person under the following conditions:

- The employer's circumstances have so changed as to make such reemployment impossible or unreasonable or to impose an undue hardship; or
- The employment from which the person leaves to serve in the uniformed services is for a brief, nonrecurring period, and there is no reasonable expectation that such employment will continue indefinitely or for a significant period.

Personal Responsibility and Work Opportunity Reconciliation Act of 1996

This law requires that employers report to designated state agencies the name, address, and Social Security number of each new employee hired. Employers must also report their names, addresses, and Federal Employer Identification Numbers to the same agencies. New hires must be reported to the state within 20 days of the date of hire. If an employer reports electronically or by magnetic media, such employer must report by two monthly transmissions not

---

[17] Ibid., Section 1002.32. These are the general qualifying conditions; see Sections 1002.73 through 1002.138 for exceptions.

[18] Ibid., Section 1002.164.

fewer than 12 or more than 16 days apart. Other procedures apply if an employer has employees in more than one state.

States use new-hire information in two ways. First, the states match new-hire reports against child support records to locate parents, establish an order for child support, or enforce an existing order. In addition, state agencies operating employment security and workers' compensation programs will have access to the new-hire information to detect and prevent erroneous benefit payments.

Fair Credit Reporting Act of 1997

This law requires employers to give applicants written notification on a form exclusively used for that purpose, stating that a credit report may be used in deciding employability. The employer must also obtain written approval from the applicants, authorizing the employer to obtain the credit report. Before the credit reporting agency will send a credit report, the employer is required to certify that it has complied with the law, and that the information will be used in accordance with applicable equal employment opportunity laws and regulations.

A negative employment decision, such as a denial of employment, reassignment or promotion, or a termination, resulting from information derived from a credit report, is defined in the law as an *adverse action*. Prior to taking an adverse action that was influenced, even in a minor way, by a credit report, the employer must send the individual a *pre-adverse action disclosure*. This disclosure must include a copy of the individual's consumer report and a copy of the document, *A Summary of Your Rights Under the Fair Credit Reporting Act*. The credit reporting agency is responsible for providing the employer with a copy of the document.

After the employer has taken an adverse action, the person affected by the action must be given an individual notice, orally, in writing, or electronically, that an adverse action has been taken. The notice must include:

- The name, address, and phone number of the credit reporting agency that supplied the report;

- A statement that the credit reporting agency did not make the decision to take the adverse action and cannot give specific reasons for it; and

- A notice of the individual's right to dispute the accuracy or completeness of any information the agency furnished and his or her right to an additional free consumer report from the agency upon request within 60 days.[19]

The law is enforced by the Federal Trade Commission, and there are significant legal consequences for employers who fail to comply with it.

Genetic Information Nondiscrimination Act of 2008

Genetic Information Nondiscrimination Act (GINA) prohibits discrimination based upon the possession of genetic information. See Chapter 12 for a discussion of GINA's employment discrimination provisions. See Chapter 19 for a discussion of GINA's health benefit discrimination provisions. GINA also modi-

---

[19] Federal Trade Commission, *Using Consumer Reports: What Employers Need to Know*, December 1997.

fied some Fair Labor Standards Act provisions applying to youth labor and minimum wage and overtime pay violations. See Chapter 26 for a discussion of these provisions.

Federal Bankruptcy Act

The federal Bankruptcy Act prohibits job discrimination against an individual who has filed bankruptcy, unless there is a job-related reason. It is illegal to terminate, refuse to employ, or otherwise engage in discrimination because an individual has sought protection under the Bankruptcy Act, has been financially insolvent before seeking such protection, or has not paid a debt which was dischargeable under the Act. An employer may refuse to hire a person who was bankrupt if there was verifiable evidence of financial irresponsibility because, for example, the job for which the individual is being considered requires financial responsibility.[20]

Guidelines on Discrimination Because of Religion (1966)

Employers must make reasonable efforts to accommodate employees' and prospective employees' religious practices. *Reasonable* is interpreted to mean the employer would not be expected to incur more than *de minimis* costs, such as the administrative costs in arranging shift swaps, infrequent overtime payments, or administrative costs in recording payroll record changes for employees whose assignments are changed. Employers must show that failure to accommodate employees' religious practices was due to an undue hardship on the conduct of business.

Some methods employers can use to accommodate religious practices are to actively help employees arrange assignment changes with other employees, give employees time off without pay, place employees in other jobs, make schedule changes, and provide such scheduling arrangements as flextime work scheduling, flexible breaks, staggered shift hours, and alternative off-days and holidays. Examples of undue employer hardships include arrangements that either require frequent overtime payments or violate bona fide seniority systems to the extent that other employee rights are adversely affected. Unions must also accommodate religious practices by permitting members to donate to a charity a sum equivalent to dues withholding if their religious practices prohibit them from joining a union. Efforts to accommodate employees' and prospective employees' religious practices may seem to place an undue burden on an employer; however, the actual number of employees involved in such cases is usually quite small.

Guidelines on Discrimination Because of Sex (1972)

The *Guidelines* define the circumstances in which gender is a bona fide occupational qualification, including employment conditions in which "authenticity or genuineness" is necessary, such as an actress for a female part in a play. Employers may not use state laws that conflict with Title VII as a defense in sex discrimination cases, as, for example, state laws that limit female employment in

---

[20] CCH HUMAN RESOURCES MANAGEMENT, *Personnel Practices*, ¶ 337B.

occupations where certain lifting requirements are specified or that place constraints on hours of work. These *Guidelines* also prohibit:

- Separate seniority or progression lines for males and females;

- Discrimination against married women; and

- Designation of "male" and "female" in job advertising, except where gender is a bona fide occupational qualification.

Employment agencies may not limit services to one gender, except where such service is based upon business necessity. Agencies are equally culpable with their clients if they fill vacancies on the basis of sex in the absence of a bona fide qualification requirement.

Employers may not discriminate against women in employee benefits, including benefits extended to employees' spouses and their families. Under this provision, these employer practices have been declared unlawful:

- Offering husbands of female employees benefits that are not similarly offered to the wives of male employees;

- Requiring females to pay higher contributions for pensions;

- Requiring females to take reduced pension payments; and

- Requiring pregnant employees either to commence annual leave or resign at a specified period of pregnancy, such as at the beginning of a certain month of pregnancy.

These *Guidelines* also address sexual harassment, which is defined as unwelcome sexual advances, requests for sexual favors, or other verbal or physical conduct of a sexual nature that is either an implied or an explicit condition of employment, is conveyed in a manner where acceptance or rejection of the gesture will affect the employee's status or causes an unfavorable job environment or interferes with the employee's job performance. In sexual harassment investigations, all of the conditions surrounding the complaint are investigated. Employers are responsible for the actions of employees and may be held responsible for the actions of non-employees, such as subcontractors who visit an employer's premises to deliver goods or furnish services. An employee who is denied an employment opportunity may be eligible for relief if the opportunity was given to another employee solely because the person granted sexual favors to the decision maker.

Uniform Guidelines for Employee Selection Procedures (1978)

In 1978, the EEOC released this set of *Guidelines* on selection procedures to assist employers, labor organizations, employment agencies, and licensing and certification boards in complying with the requirements of federal laws. The *Guidelines* cover a range of topics that include the forms of discrimination, methods for determining adverse impact, ways of justifying adverse impact, validation methods, technical standards for validity studies, and record-keeping and reporting requirements.

Guidelines on Discrimination Because of National Origin (1979)

These *Guidelines* prohibit requirements that may discriminate against persons on the basis of national origin because of their physical characteristics or language ability, unless the requirements are justified by a bona fide occupational qualification, business necessity or a job validation study. Examples of suspect criteria are height and weight requirements, either a requirement for or the denial of employment because of foreign training or education, a requirement for fluency in speaking the English language, and a requirement for speaking only English. Employers are also held responsible for either verbal or physical forms of harassment, such as national origin slurs, committed by employees and non-employees.

Job Structuring

Job structuring is an option used by employers to maintain an efficient and competitive position in the market. Unfortunately, in the past, some employers did not inform employees in advance about plans for downsizing, layoffs and plant closures. Also, some employers, in their haste to cut costs, have offered severance arrangements to employees, conditioned upon waiving their legal rights, without giving them sufficient opportunity to consider their options. These types of problems resulted in two federal laws protecting workers' rights.

Worker Adjustment and Retraining Notification Act of 1988 (WARNA)

WARNA applies to firms with 100 or more full-time employees (part-time workers are not included). These firms are required to give 60 days' advance notice of a *mass layoff or plant closing* to these three groups:

- Either all employees affected by a contemplated mass layoff or plant closing or to the representative of such employees, if there is one.
- The state dislocated worker unit.
- The chief elected official of the local political unit in which the layoff or closing will occur.

The 60-day notice period may be reduced if: (1) the employer was attempting to secure financing, which would have prevented either the layoff or the closing, and the advance notice would have precluded the employer from obtaining financing; (2) business conditions prevent the employer from giving the advance notice; or (3) a natural disaster occurred that caused the layoff or closure.

A plant closure is defined as the permanent or temporary closure of one employment site or one or more facilities or operating units in a single site during a 30-day period in which 50 or more full-time employees lose their employment. A *mass layoff* is defined as the loss of employment within a 30-day period at a single site of either: (1) at least 33 percent of the full-time workforce and at least 50 full-time persons, or (2) 500 full-time employees. *Loss of employment* includes layoffs exceeding six months in duration and reductions in the hours of work of more than 50 percent during each month in a six-month period; not included are: (1) employees who resign, retire or are separated for just cause, and (2) employees who are offered employment without a six-month break in an area that is either at a reasonable commuting distance or at any distance if the offer is accepted.

Employers who fail to give the required notice are liable for back pay and benefits for each day of the required notice period. Under certain circumstances, civil penalties of $500 per day of the required notification period may be assessed for failure to contact the local elected chief executive.

Older Workers Benefit Protection Act of 1990 (OWBPA)

The OWBPA places restrictions on employees who are 40 and over in their waiver of their rights under the Age Discrimination in Employment Act of 1967, such as the right to file a charge of discrimination as part of an agreement between an employee and the employer. These are the general criteria for a valid waiver:

- It is written so that the average person to whom the waiver would apply can understand it;
- It includes the specific rights a person has under the ADEA;
- The employee does not waive any rights that may exist after the date of the waiver;
- The waiver is in exchange for anything of value beyond that which the employee is already entitled;
- The employee is advised in writing to consult with an attorney prior to executing the waiver;
- The employee is given 45 days to consider the waiver and the terms of the agreement, if an incentive is offered or another termination program is offered to a class of employees; otherwise, a 21-day consideration period is required;
- The employee is given seven days to revoke the waiver agreement after he or she has signed it;
- If an incentive or other type of termination program is offered, the employer must inform the employees at the beginning of the 45-day notice period of:
  a. the class of persons covered by the program, the eligibility terms and the time limits, and
  b. the job titles and ages of those persons who are eligible or selected for the program and those who were not eligible or selected.

Employers are advised to ensure that they follow these provisions, since the U.S. Supreme Court ruled that signed waivers are illegal under the OWBPA, if the employer failed to follow the specific provisions of the law. Furthermore, the Court held that monies spent in return for signing illegal waivers did not have to be paid back, since most discharged employees probably would have spent any monies received and, thus, would be unable to repay them. This reality, the Court concluded, might tempt employers to risk noncompliance with the OWBPA's waiver provisions; knowing that it would be difficult for such employees to repay the employers, such employees would be motivated not to seek remedies under the Act.[21] This law applies to employers who have 20 or more employees as described in the Age Discrimination in Employment Act.

Pay

The manner in which employers compensate employees was an early target for federal legislation. These laws are typically some of the most difficult for employers to comprehend and comply with.

Fair Labor Standards Act of 1938

See Chapter 26 for an analysis of the Fair Labor Standards Act.

Equal Pay Act of 1963

The Equal Pay Act (EPA) requires equal pay for both sexes for performing job tasks that are substantially identical within the same establishment. The tasks need not be identical but, rather, they must be substantially the same and require substantially identical skill, effort, responsibility, and be performed under similar working conditions. Generally, the EPA applies to the same employees and employers covered under the FLSA; in addition, EPA covers executives, administrators, professionals, and outside salesmen.

The EPA provides several exceptions that allow men and women performing similar tasks to be paid differently. Differentials are permissible where pay is based upon:

- A seniority system or length of employment;
- A merit system;
- The quality or quantity of production; or
- Any factor other than sex, such as pay given to employees for adopted ideas they submit through a suggestion program.

Seniority applies in situations where pay increases, sometimes called step increases, are conditioned upon satisfactory completion of a period of employment, such as a yearly or semi-yearly step increase. Merit pay systems are typically associated with performance appraisal systems in which an employee's overall job performance is appraised, using such factors as attendance, conduct, safety, and productivity. Pay increases are granted on the basis of overall merit appraisal.

Title VII must be used for allegations of discrimination in pay for dissimilar jobs performed by males and females; for example, men who are employed as janitors and females who are employed as maids. These situations involve the concept of *comparable worth*, which is the theory that employers should provide equal pay to women and men for dissimilar jobs that have equal value to the employer.

Under the EPA, an aggrieved person is not required to file a charge with EEOC to obtain relief under the Act; that individual may take the matter directly

---

[21] See *Oubre v. Energy Operations, Inc.* (96-1291) 112 F.3d 787. A summary of the Court's decision is contained in Appendix 1.

to court. Typically, when charges are filed with the EEOC, the person is advised that compensation charges should be filed under both the EPA and Title VII.

Consumer Credit Protection Act of 1970

The Consumer Credit Protection Act provides that no employee may be discharged for a garnishment resulting from a single indebtedness. Furthermore, the maximum amount of wages that can be garnished must be the lesser of 25 percent of the employee's disposable earnings or the amount of such earnings that exceed 30 times the federal minimum.

The law protects everyone receiving personal earnings, i.e., wages, salaries, commissions, bonuses, or other income - including earnings from a pension or retirement program.[22] Tips are generally not considered earnings under this law.

"Disposable earnings," are the amount left after legally required deductions are made. Examples of such deductions include federal, state, and local taxes, the employee's share of State Unemployment Insurance and Social Security. It also includes withholdings for employee retirement systems required by law. The maximum applies regardless of the number of garnishment orders received by the employer.

EXAMPLES: The following examples illustrate the tests for determining the amounts subject to garnishment (assuming a minimum wage of $5.15 an hour).

EXAMPLE 1: An employee's gross earnings in a particular week are $235.00. After deductions required by law, the disposable earnings are $205.00. In this week 25 percent of his disposable personal income is $51.25 (25% X $205.00). The amount of earnings that exceeds 30 times the minimum wage is $50.50 [$205.00 − (30 X $5.15)]. Thus, the garnishment would be $50.50 and the employee would be paid $154.50.

EXAMPLE 2: An employee's gross earnings in a particular workweek are $240.00. After deductions required by law, the disposable earnings are $210.00. In this week 25 percent of the disposable earnings may be garnished or $52.50 ($210.00 X 25%) since this amount is less than $55.50 [$210 − (30 X $5.15)]. The employee would be paid $157.50.

The maximum amount of wages that can be withheld is higher for garnishments for child support and alimony. If the individual is supporting a second family, the limit is 50 percent; otherwise, the limit is 60 percent. An additional five percent is permitted in addition to these maximums if there are arrears over 12 weeks old.[23]

For additional information on this law, see Chapter 37.

Where Restrictions Do Not Apply

The garnishment restrictions do not apply to certain bankruptcy court orders, or to debts due for federal or state taxes. If a state wage garnishment law

---

[22] All the following information was obtained verbatim from the U.S. Department of Labor, "Fact Sheet #30: The Federal Wage Garnishment Law, Consumer Credit Protection Act's Title 3 (CCPA)," 2003.

[23] CCH HUMAN RESOURCES MANAGEMENT, *Compensation*, ¶ 4020.

differs from the Consumer Credit Protection Act of 1970, the law resulting in the smaller garnishment must be observed. Also, the Debt Collection Improvement Act authorizes federal agencies or collection agencies under contract with them to garnish up to 15% of disposable earnings to repay defaulted debts owed the U.S. government. The Higher Education Act authorizes the Department of Education's guaranty agencies to garnish up to 10% of disposable earnings to repay defaulted federal student loans. Such withholding is also subject to the provisions of the federal wage garnishment law, but not state garnishment laws. Unless the total of all garnishments exceeds 25% of disposable earnings, questions regarding such garnishments should be referred to the agency initiating the withholding action.

Omnibus Budget Reconciliation Act of 1993

This Act restricts executive compensation in publicly held corporations to $1 million, unless it is related to performance.

Internal Revenue Code, Section 280G

Organizations often grant executives special compensation called *golden parachutes*, if the control of the business changes. This compensation generally is activated when a firm is acquired by another firm, particularly in the event of hostile takeovers. Payments from these arrangements that equal or exceed 300 percent of the executive's gross income in any of the five preceding taxable years are disallowed from the firm's tax deductions. Furthermore, if the limit is exceeded, an excise tax of 20 percent is imposed on the executive. Golden parachutes are discussed more fully in Chapter 27.

Securities and Exchange Commission (SEC) Disclosure Requirements of 1992

Disclosure rules issued by the SEC require publicly traded firms to disclose all compensation, including base salary, contingent-based pay, stock options and awards for the chief executive officer (CEO) and the other four top-paid executives in the firm. The information is required to be disclosed in the annual proxy statements. Such information must also be disclosed for any individual who served as CEO during the previous year and for at least two other departing officials who, had they remained with the firm, would have been among the top four highest paid persons. The information is to be disclosed in a tabular format. Two tables are to be used for stock options and stock appreciation rights. One table must show the number of options granted and the terms of the grant. The other table must show a summary of the employees' stock actions, including the number exercised and unexercised.

The rules also require charts in the proxy statement showing the total cumulative return to shareholders during at least the previous five years. The information must be graphed. Comparative information must also be included on the same graph, which should be composed of returns to shareholders for stocks in the S&P 500 or, if the firm is not on the index, a broad index that includes the firm's stock and any nationally recognized industry index or group of peer firms.

Also required by the rules is a report by the Board of Directors or the Compensation Committee of the Board, if there is one, outlining factors of the firm's performance that were used in developing the firm's executive compensation plan. Some of the factors to be included in the report are market share, sales growth, profitability, and return on equity.

Both IRS regulations and disclosure requirements promulgated by the Securities and Exchange Commission (SEC) have impacted upon the use of base salaries to compensate executives.

Wage Laws for Federal Contractors

Employee compensation requirements apply to federal contractors who are involved in public works construction (Davis-Bacon Act), who supply materials and equipment (Walsh-Healey Act), or who supply services (McNamara-O'Hara Service Contract Act). In addition, Executive Order 11246 prohibits certain federal contractors from discriminating in matters of compensation on the basis of national origin, race, color, religion, and sex.

Davis-Bacon Act of 1931

The Davis-Bacon Act applies to all federal or federally financed contracts of more than $2,000 for construction, alteration, or repair, including painting and decoration of public buildings or public works. This law applies only to laborers and mechanics who are employed on the job site. Laborers and mechanics are generally interpreted to mean employees who work with their hands; therefore, accounting clerks, timekeepers, guards, and similar occupations are not covered. The two main provisions of the Act require employers to pay wages and fringe benefits that are prevailing in the locality. These prevailing wages and benefits are determined by the Department of Labor. In no case are wages to be below the FLSA minimum.

Copeland Act of 1934

The Copeland or "Kickback" Act prohibits the use of force, intimidation, threat of dismissal from employment, or any other means to induce an individual employed in the construction, completion or repair of any public building, public work, or building or work, financed in whole or in part by loans or grants from the U.S., from returning any part of the compensation to which that individual is entitled under the contract.

Walsh-Healey Act of 1936

The Walsh-Healey Act (W-HA) applies to all contracts with the federal government for supplies, materials, articles, and equipment that exceed $10,000. Generally, the holders of such contracts are required to pay the FLSA-mandated minimum wage and overtime pay for work over 40 hours per week. No person under 16 years of age may be employed by the contractor. The law prohibits the contractor from permitting employees to work under conditions deemed by the Occupational Safety and Health Administration to be unsanitary, dangerous, or hazardous to employee health and safety. The W-HA covers all employees of the contractor who are engaged in federal government work, except those employed in these occupations: executive, administrative, professional, office, custodial and maintenance. However, if the FLSA applies to the employer, office, custodial, and maintenance workers must be paid in accordance with those provisions.

Service Contract Act of 1965

The Service Contract Act applies to all service contracts with the federal government that exceed $2,500. This law requires the payment of locally prevailing wages and fringe benefits to all employees performing work under the contract. Employees under 16 years of age may be employed under restrictions similar to those imposed by the FLSA. As under the Davis-Bacon Act, the prevailing wages and fringe benefits are determined by the Department of Labor. All contractors, even those with contracts equal to or less than $2,500, must at least pay the FLSA minimum. The law prohibits the contractor from permitting employees to work in conditions deemed by the Occupational Safety and Health Administration to be unsanitary, dangerous, or hazardous to employee health and safety.

Executive Order 11246

Executive Order 11246 applies to all employers with contracts with the federal government exceeding $10,000. The executive order prohibits contractors from pay discrimination on the basis of race, color, national origin, religion and sex.

Benefits

Benefits, particularly medical expense benefit plans, constitute a significant portion of total compensation costs. In addition to laws mandating some benefit plans, such as Social Security, there are several key laws designed to ensure that benefit plans are provided fairly to employees and provisions are made so the plans will meet their objectives.

Civil Rights Act of 1964

This law prohibits discrimination based upon race, color, religion, sex or national origin in any aspects of retirement plans or other benefits. It is illegal to require women to make higher contributions than men in order to receive the same annuity payment upon retirement. It is also illegal for an employer to offer a choice of gender-based annuities at retirement.

Age Discrimination in Employment Act of 1967

The Age Discrimination in Employment Act (ADEA) prohibits discrimination against persons age 40 and over in the administration of retirement plans. It precludes maximum retirement ages except for bona fide executive personnel, fire fighters, law enforcement personnel, and employees in other types of jobs in which a bona fide occupational qualification can be demonstrated. Many plans provide for a reduction in some benefits, such as life insurance when employees reach a specified age—commonly, 65 years old. If a firm employs 20 or more persons, any reduction of benefits for active employees 40 years of age and older is prohibited by the ADEA. Under the provisions of "equal cost—equal benefits," either the benefits older workers receive or the expenditures made by employers to provide those benefits must be equal to those provided younger workers.

Health Maintenance Organization Act (HMO Act) of 1973

The HMO Act of 1973 was designed to encourage the formation of HMOs and consequently included financial incentives to achieve that goal. The standards under the Act are voluntary, and many HMOs have elected not to meet them. HMOs and other types of health care providers are discussed more fully in Chapter 19.

Employee Retirement Income Security Act (ERISA) of 1974

ERISA establishes basic safeguards for covered employees, requires employers to disclose essential information, and ensures that retirement plans benefit employees and their dependents and without discriminating in favor of highly compensated employees. Other provisions in the law that apply to benefit planning are:

- Age of participation for retirement plans;
- Any exclusions of classes of employees;
- Vesting schedules which will be used;
- Length of service requirement for participation;
- Reporting requirements;
- Plan termination requirements; and
- Coverage tests.

The provisions of ERISA are covered in Chapter 22.

Consolidated Omnibus Budget Reconciliation Act (COBRA) of 1985

As a result of COBRA and its subsequent amendments, group medical, dental, and vision plans must now permit employees and covered dependents to elect continuation of coverage at group rates following an event that would otherwise terminate their coverage. The Act applies to employers with 20 or more employees and excludes church and governmental plans. (Similar legislation, however, pertains to governmental plans.) The beneficiary (any employee, spouse, or dependent child who loses coverage) must be able to continue coverage identical to the employer's plan for active employees.

COBRA specifies that continued coverage must extend until the earliest of:

- 18 months for a reduction in hours or termination of employment (except for gross misconduct). A person who becomes disabled within 60 days of coverage under COBRA can receive an additional 11 months (thus having 29 months of total coverage, the same as an employee who was disabled at the time of termination of employment) of COBRA coverage (this additional 11 months of coverage is due to the Health Insurance Portability and Accountability Act of 1996).
- 29 months for disabled employees.

- 36 months for a spouse or children of an employee who dies or becomes divorced or legally separated, or for a child who becomes ineligible (typically because of age) for coverage under the parents' plan. This includes children who are born or adopted during the period of COBRA coverage (this inclusion is due to the Health Insurance Portability and Accountability Act of 1996).

- 36 months from the date that a qualifying dependent beneficiary becomes eligible for Medicare or for another group health plan (unless a preexisting condition is not covered). This includes children who are born or adopted during the period of COBRA coverage (this inclusion is due to the Health Insurance Portability and Accountability Act of 1996).

Cost for the coverage can be up to 102 percent of the entire group premium (150 percent for months 19 through 29 for persons who are eligible due to a disability). COBRA benefits stop if:

- The employee or dependent becomes eligible for another health benefits plan and does not have pre-existing conditions that are excluded under the new plan.

- The employee or spouse becomes eligible for Medicare.

- The employer discontinues the health benefits plan.

- The employee does not pay the scheduled premiums.

- The employer is required to notify the employee of the right to continue coverage on two occasions. The first time is at commencement of the plan or when an employee first enters the plan. The second notification to the employee and/or other qualifying beneficiaries is after an "event." Failure to notify can result in penalties to the employer. The extended coverage is not automatic; it must be elected by the beneficiary within 60 days of loss of coverage or upon notification by the plan administrator of the employee's option to elect, whichever occurs later.

If an employee chooses to continue group coverage as provided under COBRA regulations, he or she still has the right to convert to an individual plan when the continuation coverage terminates.

Family and Medical Leave Act (FMLA) of 1993

The FMLA applies to all employers with 50 or more employees. Leave is available to eligible employees if 50 or more employees are employed within 75 miles of their workplace. Employees can receive 12 weeks of unpaid leave during a 12-month period for these events:

- Birth of a child;

- Adoption/foster care of a child;

- Employee's own serious health condition; or

- Care of a spouse, child, or parent with a serious health condition.

- A "qualifying exigency"[24] of an employee's spouse, son, daughter or parent who is either on or has been notified/called (or impending call) to active duty.[25]

- Care for an employee's spouse, son, daughter or parent recovering from a serious illness/injury suffered in the line of duty on active military duty. Such employees are entitled to 26 weeks of all types of FMLA leave in one 12-month period to provide such care.[26][27]

To be eligible, employees must have worked 12 months, with 1,250 hours worked in the past year, and must give 30 days' advance notice, or as much notice as is possible. Employers are required to:

- Provide the leave;

- Continue providing the employee with health benefits; and

- Return the employee to the same or equivalent position.

Employees can be asked to use paid leave or vacation before receiving unpaid leave.

Leave requests by highly compensated, key employees (among the 10% highest paid employees) can be denied if holding the position open for the employee's return would cause grievous economic injury to the employer. The employer must inform the employee of his or her status as a key employee prior to the leave. The employer must tell the employee he or she will not be reinstated (if that is the case). If the employee elects not to return to work after he or she is told that reinstatement rights will not be given, reinstatement is not required. Violations of the FMLA may entitle the employee, if a lawsuit is successful, to wages, benefits, and any monetary losses plus interest. Bad faith violations may result in double damages.

The FMLA is covered more extensively in Chapter 19.

Health Insurance Portability and Accountability Act of 1996

This law provides for:

- The establishment of *Medical Savings Accounts.*

- Penalty-free withdrawals of medical expenses from Individual Retirement Accounts.

- Portability requirements that apply to medical care coverage (excluding limited-scope dental or vision, long-term care, nursing or home health care, care for a specific disease, or hospital indemnity or supplemental coverage which are offered independently of the medical care plan) for newly hired employees (and their families) in non-governmental group

---

[24] Initially, the Secretary of Labor will issue regulations defining "qualifying exigency," but in the interim the U. S. Department of Labor encourages employers to provide the leave to qualifying employees.

[25] U. S. Department of Labor, *Notice: Military Family Leave.*

[26] Ibid.

[27] "Serious illness/injury" means the Armed Forces member is "unfit to perform the duties of the member's office, grade, rank or rating." See Public Law 103-3 as amended by Section 585 of the National Defense Authorization Act for FY 2008, Public Law (110-181), enacted January 28, 2008.

health plans with two or more participants on the first day of the plan year.

- Limitations on preexisting conditions in that a medical care plan cannot exclude coverage for a preexisting condition (where medical advice, diagnosis, care or treatment was received within a six-month period ending on the enrollment date in the new employer's medical care plan) for more than 12 months (18 months for late enrollees, such as those who do not enroll at the first opportunity).

- Individuals subject to the 12 months' exclusionary clause for preexisting conditions can have this period reduced for each month of health care coverage (called "creditable coverage" in the Act) under a prior health care plan, provided there is no more than a 63-day break in coverage from the former to the new plan.

- Employers must track coverage for certification.

This law is covered more extensively in Chapter 19.

Mental Health Parity Act of 1996

This act applies to employers with more than 50 employees but such employers are exempt if the effect of the law increases the employer's health plan costs by more than one percent. The law does not require employers to provide mental health coverage, but where such coverage is provided, the plan must either:

- Include services for mental illness coverage in the lifetime of the employee, or place annual limits on what the plans will spend for medical or surgical benefits, or

- Have a separate limit for mental illness services that is not less than that provided for medical or surgical services.

The law neither requires employers to provide mental health coverage nor does it apply to the type, amount and duration of such benefits. Employers are permitted to limit the number of days of coverage and the number of office visits. Employers may also limit the scope of mental health benefits, including cost sharing and requirements regarding medical necessity. The law does not extend benefits for substance abuse or dependency.

Newborns' and Mothers' Health Protection Act of 1996

Under this law, group health plans are not permitted to restrict postpartum hospital stays to less than 48 hours for a normal delivery and 96 hours for a cesarean section. This law applies to both self-insured and insured plans only if they provide hospital stay maternity benefits for mother and child.

The Women's Health and Cancer Rights Act of 1998

This law was effective for health benefit plans for years beginning on or after October 21, 1998. The law applies to all plans that provide medical and surgical benefits with respect to a mastectomy. The Act requires that mastectomy benefits include breast reconstruction (if desired by the participant or beneficiary). Benefit coverage, in connection with the mastectomy, is extended for the following procedures:

- reconstruction of the breast on which the mastectomy has been performed;
- surgery and reconstruction of the other breast to produce a symmetrical appearance; and
- prostheses and coverage for physical complications of all stages of the mastectomy, including lymph edemas, in a manner reached through consultation with the attending physician and patient.

Deductibles and coinsurance provisions may apply but must be consistent with other benefits provided by the plan. Plan administrators are required to notify participants of the benefit.

Sarbanes-Oxley Act of 2002

In response to various types of corporate management and auditor malfeasance, such as insider trading and fraud resulting in the loss of employee investments, the Sarbanes-Oxley Act (SOX) was enacted into law in 2002. Among the provisions covered by the law include rules in such areas as:

- Attorney's conduct;
- Record retention;
- Disclosure of off-balance sheet arrangements;
- Auditor independence;
- Ownership reports and trading by officers, directors and the related;
- Corporate audit committee responsibilities; and,
- Insider trading during pension fund blackout periods.[28]

With specific reference to the last bulleted item, the SEC issued rules prohibiting, during a blackout period, any actions by a director or executive officer to directly or indirectly, "purchase, sell, or otherwise acquire or transfer any equity security...(of the firm that was)...acquired...in connection with his or her employment as a director or executive officer."[29] The SEC rule explains the reason for the prohibition is to prevent the unfairness of restricting employees from engaging in any trades of their holdings acquired as a reason of their employment with the firm, while directors and executive officers do engage in such trading.

A "blackout period" is three consecutive (business) days when no more than 50 percent of participants in the firm's plan are able to institute equity transactions, such as buying or selling securities or otherwise make changes in their 401(k) plans. Participants must be given a 30-day advance notice of the blackout period. The advance notice must contain the following:

---

[28] Securities and Exchange Commission, *Spotlight on Sarbanes-Oxley Rulemaking and Reports*(no date), pp.1-4.

[29] Securities and Exchange Commission, *Insider Trades During Pension Fund Blackout Periods*(January 26, 2003), p.1. See this rule for the definition of the terms director and executive officer.

- The reason for the blackout;

- A description of participants' rights that will be suspended during the blackout;

- The beginning and ending dates of the blackout; and,

- A statement advising participants to assess their investments with the view that they will not be able to make any changes during the blackout period.[30]

Information regarding corporate audit committee responsibilities is covered in Chapter 27.

Pension Protection Act of 2006

The Pension Protection Act of 2006 made a number of changes in pension-related issues. The changes are reflected in sections of this book to which they pertain. Briefly, the law contains these major provisions:

- Provides for pension funding modifications, particularly those involving under-funded plans.

- Requires under-funded pension plans to pay the variable rate premium ($9 per $1,000 of unfunded current vested liabilities) to the Pension Benefit Guaranty Corporation.

- Clarifies legal issues of hybrid pension plans.

- Provides for the administration of investment advice to plan participants.

- Covers changes in the distribution of pension plan documents.

- Requires the disclosure of information about plans that are "endangered or (in a) critical status."[31]

John Warner National Defense Authorization Act for Fiscal Year 2007

Former military personnel and their beneficiaries, who are covered under the Department of Defense healthcare program (Tricare) and become employed, are oftentimes offered incentives by the employer to retain this coverage in lieu of enrollment in the employer's health plan. This practice shifts healthcare costs from the employer to the U. S. Government. A provision in the John Warner National Defense Authorization Act prohibits this practice for public and private employers with 20 or more employees. Each violation of the Act subjects the employer to a $5,000 fine. These provisions were effective January 1, 2008.

Employee Relations

Employee relations concern the manner with which employers deal with employees in such areas as lay-offs, discipline, and plant closures. Decisions affecting these matters are subject to federal law.

---

[30] U.S. Department of Labor, *Labor Department Issues Final Rules on Disclosure of Pension Plan "Blackout Periods,"* (January 23, 2003), p.1.

[31] U.S. Senate Republican Policy Committee, *Legislative Notice: H.R. 4 – Pension Protection Act of 2006.*

Civil Rights Act of 1964

The Civil Rights Act prohibits an employment decision in an employee relations activity that is based upon national origin, race, color, religion, and sex. Furthermore, any selection criteria, such as performance appraisals, used as the basis for such employment decisions must be validated if adverse impact results.

Age Discrimination in Employment Act of 1967

Employers cannot use age as a basis for making an employee relations decision involving employees who are 40 years of age or older.

Privacy Act of 1974

This law prohibits federal agencies from revealing information about a federal employee without his or her permission and gives federal employees the right to examine their own records. Some states have similar laws.

Freedom of Information Act

This Act does not apply to private sector employers. Among the law's provisions are federal employees' rights to access their personnel records. The law also applies to access to government records that falls outside the scope of HR.

Drug-Free Workplace Act of 1988

This law applies to employers who have contracts of $100,000 or more with the federal government. It requires publication of a statement to employees prohibiting controlled substances in the workplace. Employers covered by the law must also establish a drug-free awareness program, publish the statement, and make other efforts to maintain a drug-free workplace. See Chapter 20 for a discussion of other provisions of this law.

Employee Polygraph Protection Act of 1988

This law involves the use of a polygraph in decisions with regard to staffing and in the event of an economic loss. See the section above on Staffing for more information about the law. Private sector employers may *request* employees to take a polygraph test in conjunction with an ongoing investigation involving economic loss or injury to the employer's business, such as theft, embezzlement, misappropriation, or industrial espionage or sabotage. The only employees that may be requested to take a polygraph are those that had access to the property that is the target of the investigation or those that the employer had reason to suspect were involved in the incident or activity under investigation. The employer is also required to give a signed statement to the employee who has been requested to take the polygraph, specifically explaining the incident or activity investigated and the basis for testing the particular employee.

No employee shall be disciplined, discharged, denied employment or promotion, or otherwise discriminated against on the basis of an analysis of a polygraph test or the refusal to take the test, without additional supporting evidence. An employee who consents to take a polygraph test may end the test at any time and may not be asked questions in specific areas, such as sexual behavior. Employers must give employees written notice that they cannot be required to take the test as a condition of employment.

Older Workers Benefit Protection Act of 1990

This law amended the Age Discrimination in Employment Act (ADEA) to clarify the circumstances under which employees may waive their rights under the ADEA. Employees may agree not to file a charge of discrimination, provided certain conditions are met, such as giving employees the right to consult an attorney prior to executing the waiver.

Stored Communications Act

See Chapter 8 for a discussion of this law.

Safety and Health

The only federal law affecting workplace safety and health is the Occupational Safety and Health Act (OSH Act) of 1970. The OSH Act covers to employers with one or more employees. The OSH Act created the Occupational Safety and Health Administration (OSHA). These are the purposes of OSHA:

- Motivating employers and employees to reduce hazards and to develop safety and health programs;

- Creating and disseminating employer and employee rights and responsibilities;

- Establishing and implementing an injury and illness reporting system;

- Preparing and enforcing safety and health standards; and

- Developing and approving state programs.

Labor Relations

Labor relations was the HR activity first subjected to federal legislation. Originally, these laws pertained to the legality of unions. As time has progressed, additional laws have been implemented affecting the unionization of employees.

Sherman Act of 1890

The Sherman Act declared illegal any activity engaged in with the intent to conspire or to monopolize or restrain trade or commerce among the states. In the *Danbury Hatters* case, the U.S. Supreme Court concluded that union threats to boycott stores that sold hats made by Danbury Hatters amounted to an attempt to restrain trade and commerce.

Clayton Act of 1914

The Clayton Act was intended to suppress the use of the Sherman Act against union activities. Specifically, the Act stated that antitrust laws were not to be construed so as to affect the existence or operations of unions. The law did not, however, preclude the use of the Sherman Act in combating strikes and other economic means unions use to gain concessions from employers.

Railway Labor Act of 1926

The Railway Labor Act (RLA) originally covered only interstate railroads, but it was amended in 1936 to include air carriers. The entire RLA applies to both railroads and air carriers, except that each has a separate board (called "Adjustment Board") to handle disputes between unions and carriers. The railroad board is the National Railroad Adjustment Board and the air carrier board is the National Air Transport Adjustment Board.

The RLA creates the rights of employees to organize and bargain collectively, permits agreements between carriers and unions to establish a union shop and dues check-off, establishes a National Mediation Board and provides a procedure for arbitrating disputes if the carrier and union involved agree to such arbitration.

The two adjustment boards (National Railroad Adjustment Board and National Air Transport Adjustment Board) are composed of an equal number of members representing the carriers and the unions (17 of each for the railroads and 2 each for air carriers). A major purpose of these boards is to provide an opportunity for each industry (rail and air, individually) to settle their disputes before resorting to outside parties. No such provision is provided by the National Labor Relations Board (NLRA).

The National Mediation Board is authorized by the RLA to designate unions to represent employees through elections and to mediate disputes between the unions and the carriers and, if those efforts fail, try to induce the parties to resolve the disputes through arbitration. If the parties agree to arbitration and choose the services of the Mediation Boards, there are specific steps in selecting a board of arbitrators to hear the dispute. The parties, however, can either decline the offer of arbitration or select their own means of arbitration.

Norris-LaGuardia Act of 1932

This law corrected those provisions of the Sherman Act that the Clayton Act had intended to correct. Federal courts were forbidden from preventing the activities of unions resulting from labor disputes.

National Labor Relations Act of 1935

The National Labor Relations Act (NLRA) of 1935 was amended by the Labor-Management Relations (Taft-Hartley) Act of 1947 (LMRA) and the Labor-Management Reporting and Disclosure (Landrum-Griffin) Act of 1959 (LMRDA). It is important to remember that both the LMRA and LMRDA contain provisions *in addition* to those amending the NLRA. The NLRA applies to most private sector employers. These are some categories of employers exempt from the law:

1. The U.S. government, including employees of private contractors employed under a federal contract and for labor relations purposes are under the federal government;

2. Federal Reserve banks;

3. State and local governments, including employees of private contractors employed under a contract to these governments, if the governments are in charge of labor relations;

4. Businesses, such as airlines and railroads, covered by the Railway Labor Act; and

5. Labor unions, except in their capacities as employers.

These groups of employees are specifically excluded from the Act:

1. Agricultural laborers;

2. Domestic workers employed in private homes;

3. Any individual employed by his parent or spouse;

4. Independent contractors;

5. Supervisors; and

6. Any person employed by an employer subject to the Railway Labor Act.

These are some principal rights the NLRA gives to employees:

1. Right to self-organize;

2. Right to form, join, or assist unions;

3. Right to bargain collectively through representatives of their own choosing;

4. Right to engage in other concerted activities for the purpose of collective bargaining or other mutual aid or protection; and

5. Right to refrain from any or all such activities, except to the extent that such right may be affected by an agreement requiring membership in a labor organization as a condition of employment.

The NLRA created the National Labor Relations Board, which has the authority to determine appropriate collective bargaining units, prevent statutorily defined unfair labor practices by employers and labor organizations or their agents, and conduct secret ballot elections among employees in *appropriate* collective-bargaining units to determine whether or not they want to be represented by a labor organization. The Board also resolves jurisdictional disputes among various groups of employees concerning which group shall be assigned work in dispute.

Labor Management Relations Act of 1947

The Labor Management Relations Act of 1947 (LMRA), also known as the Taft-Hartley Law, amended the NLRA. The LMRA contains the following provisions:

1. Establishes the Federal Mediation and Conciliation Service;

2. Provides for the establishment of fact-finding boards, called *boards of inquiry*;

3. Directs the Department of Labor to maintain copies of collective bargaining agreements and to have them available for the research and guidance of interested parties;

4. Provides for the conciliation of disputes in the health care industry;

5. Authorizes suits by and against labor organizations;

6. Permits suits against labor organizations for violations of contracts between an employer and labor organization representing employees;

7. Places restrictions on payments and loans to employee representatives or unions by employers or any persons acting for employers; and

8. Permits suits by persons who are injured by a violation of the union unfair labor practices section of the NLRA.

The Federal Mediation and Conciliation Service (FMCS) is an independent federal agency with these principal functions:

1. To facilitate the resolution of disputes between the parties in collective bargaining by encouraging them to use their own resources;

2. To encourage states to establish facilities to help labor and management in settling their disputes;

3. To offer its services in settling disputes between labor and management (except in situations covered by the RLA) when a significant interruption of commerce is threatened;

4. To offer its services in situations involving either government procurement contracting affecting the national defense or disputes in the health care industry that threaten national health and safety; and

5. To maintain a roster of labor arbitrators who meet the FMCS' established criteria and to furnish the names of arbitrators, upon request from the parties in a dispute.

The LMRA also has provisions authorizing states to enact "right-to-work" laws, which forbid union membership as a condition of employment. Twenty-two states have enacted such a law.

Labor-Management Reporting and Disclosure Act of 1959

During the period 1956-1958, several labor union leaders were found guilty of various criminal acts, such as the illegal use of union pension funds. These and other illegal or improper practices motivated Congress to pass the Labor-Management Reporting and Disclosure Act (LMRDA). The Act requires the reporting and disclosure of union financial records and administrative acts to prevent union officials from failing to fulfill their proper roles and to provide for the orderly conduct of union elections. Unlike both the NLRA and the LMRA, this Act also applies to unions covered by the RLA.

The LMRDA Bill of Rights specifies that every union member has an equal right to nominate candidates, vote and attend meetings. In addition, unions cannot increase the dues and/or initiation fees without a majority of the membership voting in a secret election. This section also makes it illegal for a union to limit some members' right to institute action either in court or in an administrative agency. Finally, unions cannot take action against a member, such as fining or expulsion from the union (except for nonpayment of dues), without giving the member written charges and a reasonable period to answer them in a hearing.

The Act imposes upon unions extensive requirements for reporting information to the Secretary of Labor. Reporting requirements include the dues, fees and other payments required of members, membership qualifications, assessments, insurance and benefit plan participation, authorizations for disbursement of union funds, financial audits, authorization of both bargaining demands and/or strikes, and terms for the ratification of contracts. Also, annual reports must be filed showing assets and liabilities, and the source and amount of receipts, salaries and other disbursements to officers and employees who earned more than $10,000 annually from the union. Unions must also report any loans of $250 or more to an officer, employee or member.

Union officers and employees are required to report to the Secretary of Labor any stock, bond, security or other interest and any income or other benefit with monetary value which the individual receives from either an employer (or the employer's consultant) of employees represented by the union or from a business that does business with such an employer. The reporting requirement also includes any such transactions involving the spouses and minor children of union officers and employees. In addition, income of union employees and union officers, or their spouses and minor children, must be reported if it were derived from a business dealing with their union.

Employers are also required to file annual reports with the Secretary of Labor for any payments of money or other things of value that they make to union officers, representatives and union employees. Employers must also report such payments made to employees to persuade them to vote for union representation or to obtain information about union activities involving a dispute with the employer. Finally, employers are required to report any arrangement and payments made to consultants employed to persuade employees during organizing campaigns or to obtain information for the employer about union activities involving a labor dispute with the employer.

The LMRDA imposes reporting obligations on the consultants mentioned in the previous paragraph. These individuals must, within 30 days of entering into an agreement with an employer, provide information, such as the terms of the agreement. These same individuals must annually report the payments received for such services, their source, and any disbursements made in rendering the services.

Executive Order 13201

Executive Order 13201 requires government contractors and subcontractors to post a poster (the Notice of *Employee Rights Concerning Payment of Union Dues* poster) informing their employees that they have certain rights related to union membership and the use of union dues and fees under Federal law. Basically, these rights are that unions can only assess members for dues and fees necessary to perform their duties as exclusive bargaining representatives in dealing with employers on labor management issues. See the section on Union Shop in Chapter 35 and *Communications Workers v. Beck*, (1988) in Appendix 1.

These contractors and subcontractors are exempt from this requirement:

- They have contracts less than $100,000.

- They have fewer than 15 employees.

- No union has been formally recognized by the prime contractor or certified as the exclusive bargaining representative of the prime contractor's employees.

- They are in states where state law forbids enforcement of union-security clauses ("right-to-work" states).

- The work to be performed under the contract is outside the U.S and does not involve the recruitment or employment of workers within the U.S.

Labor Relations in the Public Sector

Public sector labor relations law can be examined by dividing public employees into these three groups:

- All federal employees, except those in the U.S. Postal Service;

- U.S. Postal Service employees; and

- State and local public employees.

Title VII of the Civil Service Reform Act of 1978

Federal employees, other than postal employees, are covered by Title VII of the Civil Service Reform Act of 1978. This Act does not apply to agencies involved primarily in intelligence, investigative or security work, such as the Federal Bureau of Investigation. The Act also does not apply to the U.S. Postal Service. The Act excludes several other agencies, such as the Tennessee Valley Authority and the Foreign Service of the United States.

The major provisions of the act cover the recognition of unions, determination of appropriate bargaining units, national consultation rights of labor organizations, unfair labor practices, the resolution of impasses, the creation of a Federal Labor Relations Authority (FLRA), and grievance procedures.

The FLRA is responsible for administering the Act. The FLRA conducts secret ballot elections for unions that are requesting "exclusive recognition or national consultation" rights, as follows:

- *Exclusive recognition* is accorded to those unions that receive a majority vote of the employees in an appropriate bargaining unit. Unlike the NLRA, a majority vote is required of all employees in the unit, not just of those voting.

- *National consultation* is afforded to unions with memberships that constitute a substantial number of employees of the agency. National consultation is not afforded to a union if another union has exclusive recognition for the same group of employees. National consultation entitles a union to be notified of proposals involving substantial changes in personnel matters affecting its members. The union is also given the opportunity to comment on the proposals. This recognition also gives the union the right to suggest changes in personnel policies.

Unions with exclusive recognition have the same rights as those with national consultation but, in addition, they have the right to negotiate bargaining agreements with the federal agency. The issues for negotiation are restricted to personnel policies, procedures and working conditions, subject to federal law and regulations. Some of the substantive issues of collective bargaining in the private sector, such as pay and benefits, are not permitted.

There is a special procedure for settling impasses that arise during the course of negotiations. The FMCS or other third-party mediation may be used. If this effort is unsuccessful, either party may request the assistance of the Federal Service Impasses Panel. This Panel has several alternatives: it may order a settlement of the impasse; it may recommend a settlement; or it may direct the parties to use arbitration. The parties may not voluntarily use arbitration without the Panel's approval.

Postal Reorganization Act of 1970

Employees of the U.S. Postal Service may organize and bargain collectively under the Postal Reorganization Act of 1970 (PRA). The Act places postal employees and their unions under the NLRA and LMRDA. Consequently, postal unions can bargain on similar subjects that are bargainable in the private sector, such as wages, hours and working conditions.

The NLRB handles recognition elections and the FMCS is involved in labor disputes. However, should the customary FMCS efforts fail, the PRA provides settlement procedures that include compulsory and binding arbitration. The first step in the procedure is for the Director of the FMCS to name three persons to a fact-finding panel. This panel has about 45 days to investigate the dispute and make a report. The panel may, at its discretion, include recommendations for settling the impasse. If this effort fails, the matter is submitted to arbitration.

CHAPTER 8
EMPLOYMENT TORT LAW

Chapter Highlights
- Review state tort law affecting employment issues
- Examine issues of employment status
- Study state unfair labor provisions

Introduction

State tort law is an emerging area affecting the employment relationship. A *tort* is a civil wrong. In Latin, the word "tort" means "twisted." Employers, supervisors, and peers have been sued by employees for torts. Among the many actions serving as a basis for these torts include an invasion of privacy, violation of rights under drug testing policies, injury due to workplace smoking, public disclosure of confidential information, and defamation.

Privacy Rights

Among the rights recognized by various states on the subject of privacy is the protection from disclosure of personal information that may be embarrassing to an employee, such as a his or her sexual orientation, marital status, child dependencies, and financial obligations or debt payment history. In the event of suits for the public disclosure of personal information, employers will be subject to a high standard to show that they have exercised due diligence in protecting confidential employee information from disclosure to unauthorized individuals.

Following are some of the major areas in which employers have responsibilities to maintain employee privacy and/or confidentiality of information:

- Employee files related to employee assistance programs (EAPs), including visits, diagnoses, referrals, and the related (see Chapter 4);
- Employee personnel records, such as information on application forms, numbers of dependents, telephone numbers, and addresses (see Chapter 5 and other information provided later in this chapter);
- Genetic information (see Chapter 16);
- Employment-related tests, including written tests used in selection decision making, interview results, and assessment exercises (see Chapter 16);
- Results of employee opinion surveys (see Chapter 6);
- Medical records, such as the results of physical examinations, documentation of visits to health units, and illnesses (see Chapter 5);
- Drug testing results (see Chapters 17 and 20 and other information provided later in this chapter);
- Personality/behavioral test results (see Chapter 16);

- Medical and related information covered by the Health Insurance Portability and Accountability Act (see Chapter 19);

- Biometric information gathered in conjunction with an employee wellness program, such as weight, and health issues (see Chapter 21);

- Exit interview results (see Chapter 27);

- Information provided by employees through an organizational ombudsman or whistleblower hotline (Chapter 37); and,

- Electronic communications (covered in the next section).

Electronic Communications/Computer Email/Pagers/Text Messaging

Computer email and text messages sent through cell phones and pagers are potential privacy risk issues for employers. Lack of policy guidance and unsupervised use of computers, cell phones and pagers may lead to employee abuse. Another significant risk for employers may be their inadequate knowledge of the subtleties of the Electronic Communications Privacy Act of 1986 and the Stored Communications Act of 1986 and applicable state laws on privacy.[1]

Electronic Communications Privacy Act of 1986

Due to Fourth Amendment considerations governments typically have been required to obtain court orders prior to applying wire taps to telephones. The Electronic Communications Privacy Act of 1986 (ECPA) extended this requirement to government surveillance of in-transit messages by computers.

Stored Communications Act of 1986

The Stored Communications Act (SCA) is Title II of the (ECPA). As noted above, the ECPA focuses on "in-transit" communications. In contrast, the SCA applies to messages that are "in storage." Electronic communications, such as email messages sent via computers and text messages sent by cell phones and pagers are received by internet service providers (ISP) or electronic communications facilities (ECF), stored, and then sent upon demand to the recipient. While "in storage" the SCA protects the communications from disclosure by either an ISP or ECF. The sole exception to this provision is non-content records, such as telephone numbers, that can be given to private parties. This means that in response to an employer's request, it would be permissible for an ISP or ECF to furnish a listing of the websites an employee visited during working hours. For Fourth Amendment reasons, non-content records may not be disclosed to a government without subpoena.[2]

In sum, the ECPA and SCA require a court order for government access to electronic communications, but neither law inhibits employers from similar

[1] See *Quon v. Arch Wireless Operating Co., Incorporated, a Delaware corporation; City of Ontario, a municipal corporation; Lloyd Scharf, individually and as Chief of Ontario Police Depart; Ontario Police Department; Debbie Glenn, individually and as a Sergeant of Ontario Police Department* (2008) in the Appendix 1.

[2] For more information on this Act see *Quon v. Arch Wireless Operating Co., Incorporated, a Delaware corporation; City of Ontario, a municipal corporation; Lloyd Scharf, individually and as Chief of Ontario Police Depart; Ontario Police Department; Debbie Glenn, individually and as a Sergeant of Ontario Police Department* (2008) in Appendix 1.

surveillance, particularly if employees are using employer-provided equipment and networks.

Personal Computers

The advent of personal computers has dramatically changed the workplace. In a positive sense, computers have greatly facilitated employee productivity, improved customer service and increased profitability. These improvements have not been achieved without a major cost in managing employees, particularly in monitoring their computer activities.

For example, in the past, a coworker engaging in sexual harassment typically made personal advances towards the victim. The burden for the victim was to provide sufficient evidence the harassment actually occurred. In the absence of a witness, even repeated overtures, oftentimes resorted in one person's word against another's. Few perpetrators were so foolish to give victims handwritten overtures. For some reason, harassers are less cautious in their behavior when they engage in electronic communication. Some harassers, including even some at the executive level of management are so brazen they make sexual overtures using the firm's email system.[3]

Using personal computers to conduct personal matters on company time is another problem. In the past, some employees used the telephone to complete various types of personal business, such shopping and handling financial transactions. Today, such activities are greatly facilitated through personal computers. Employees use their computers to access various catalog websites, make selections and silently complete transactions within the confines of their cubicles. Even the evening meal can be ordered on line and delivered at a designated time. This convenience benefits employees but at an employer's expense in lost productivity.

Problem Areas

These are some major problems related to employee abuse of personal computers.

- *Security.* These issues include the risk of computers being lost or stolen, such as stolen notebook computers of Federal government employees containing Social Security information. Another serious security issue is hackers attaining access to datasets on hard drives. Misplaced and stolen compact and floppy discs also may contain sensitive personal or proprietary information.

- *Computer Misuse.* Misuse issues include using computers for personal reasons such as for non-business email communication, web surfing, personal shopping and improperly using copyrighted documents.

- *Criminal Activity.* Employee computer abuse includes criminal acts, such as engaging in the distribution or use of pornography and making unlawful drug purchases.

[3] Shipley, D., and Schwalbe, W., E-mail may be hazardous to your career, *Fortune* (May 3, 2007).

Addressing the Problems

To adequately address the problem of computer abuse requires a consideration of these major issues:

- **Employee Conduct.** Employee conduct issues concern whether the computer use only violated company policy or rose to the level of illegality, such as engaging in child pornography.

  (1) **Policy Violations.** Employees who are discharged for violating policy provisions may resort to filing suits for such reasons as alleging a breach of contract or violating the covenant of good faith and fair dealing.

  (2) **Violations of Law.** Employee computer use that violates laws may involve law enforcement agency intervention, including investigations, search warrants and indictments.

- **Location of Use.** Location issues include where the computer was used while a person was employed. For example, if the computer was used at work was the employee in his/her own office or was the computer in a general work area accessible to other employees. Conversely, was the computer located and used at employees' homes.

Fourth Amendment issues may be involved in an instance of employee computer abuse if the behavior triggered a law enforcement investigation. In such cases, a search warrant is typically required. However, in one federal court decision the defendant's claim of privacy was rejected because the employee visited a child pornography site through a company-provided Internet service provider using a company-owned computer. The defendant claimed the fact that the computer was in his office gave him the "legitimate expectation of privacy in his office and computer".[4] The court's decision stated the employee did have a *subjective expectation* of privacy because the computer was in his office. But, the court added he did not have an *objective expectation* of privacy since he was using a computer provided by the employer and he was using the employer's provider to access the Internet.

- **Computer Ownership.** Ownership issues include whether the computer used in employment is personally owned or employer owned. As noted in the court decision cited above, the defendant was using the company provided computer which apparently was a factor in the court ruling that the employee did not have an *objective expectation* of privacy.

In another case, a defendant brought his personal computer to work and networked it to the employer's computer. A co-worker, who was a part-time law enforcement officer and was assisting with a networking problem apparently caused by the defendant's personal computer, discovered the computer contained child pornography and alerted authorities. In this case, the court ruled the employee did not have a reasonable basis for a subjective expectation of privacy because he networked it to the employer's computer.[5]

---

[4] *United States of America v. Ziegler*, Court of Appeals, 9th Circuit, August 8, 2006.

[5] *United States of America v. Michael A. Barrows*, Court of Appeals, 10th Circuit, April 3, 2007.

- *Other Issues.* Other issues involving employee misuse of personal computers include if the computers involved were password protected, whether they were locked, and if the room in which they were used was secure.

Prevention and Control

Among the actions employers should take to prevent the misuse of computers is to insert in the employee handbook a policy statement about computer use. Controlling employee abuse of computers includes conducting surveillance of computer use. Computer abuse should be dealt with promptly. Depending upon the seriousness of the abuse, actions might include confiscating the computer and disciplining or discharging violators.

- *Legal Environment.* The Electronic Communications Privacy Act (ECPA) of 1986, provides employers with considerable discretion in monitoring electronic communications, such as email and Internet use. Many states have laws that provide somewhat more or less discretion for employers than the ECPA. Furthermore, employee suits alleging that employers' electronic monitoring activities constituted an *invasion of privacy* have made little headway since courts have found such rights do not include employer-owned computer systems.[6]

- *Policy Statement.* Employers should have comprehensive policy statements addressing employee personal computers. These are some items to consider in such statements:

   (1) Employer-provided computers are not employees' personal property and employers will reclaim them at will and without notice.

   (2) Employees have neither a subjective nor objective expectation of privacy in computer use, including any information stored on the computer or on compact or floppy discs. Employers retain the right to confiscate such information, regardless of the source.

   (3) The employer will use computer software and hardware products to monitor computer use without employees' knowledge.

   (4) Unobtrusive methods will be used to make copies of email and other communications and files without employee' knowledge.

   (5) Employees are expected to use good judgment in using personal computers.

   (6) Examples of allowable use of computer resources, including whether personal use is permitted. Extra care should be followed in drafting this provision since employees may defend their seemingly misuse under the rubric "personal use."

   (7) Examples of improper and/or illegal acts in computer use ranging from improper personal use, such as using email to harass others, to criminal behavior, such as child pornography.

---

[6] U.S. General Accounting Office, *Employee Privacy: Computer-Use Monitoring Practices and Policies of Selected Companies* (September 2002), p. 6.

(8) Employees are expected to protect all proprietary information to which they have access.

(9) Employees have the responsibility to report any violations of the policy by a co-worker or other person, such as private contractors or suppliers.

(10) Procedures for employees to follow in reporting any violations, including the name, telephone number and related information of the person responsible for implementing the policy and receiving allegations of violations.

(11) Assurance that any reports of violations will be treated anonymously and confidentially.

(12) Procedures to be followed in investigating allegations of violations.

(13) Disciplinary procedures, including discharge from employment and criminal prosecution for misuse of personal computers.

(14) Sections for employees to sign and date the policy statement acknowledging they have been informed of its contents and agree to abide by them.

- *Controlling Computer Use.*

  (1) *Computer Software.* Install software that can collect information.

  (2) *Employer Surveillance.* Conduct surveillance include collecting and retaining email, Internet communications and information stored on computers.

  (3) *Keyword Searches.* Use data mining software to scan files and emails for words or phrases associated with inappropriate behavior.

  (4) *Assign Responsibility.* Assign responsibility and authority for implementing the company policy statement.

  (5) *Policy Breaches.* Investigate policy violations discovered through data mining or reports of violations.

  (6) *Conduct Investigations.* Conduct confidential investigations of policy breaches, including interviewing the complainant and the employee involved.

  (7) *Report Illegal Activity.* Contact the proper legal authority for any apparent illegal activity.

  (8) *Take Action.* Inform employees of the outcome of the investigation, including taking disciplinary action, including employment discharge. Make recommendations to correct areas in which procedural or policy changes are needed.

  (9) *Be Consistent.* Consistency is very important in implementing the policy and taking action. This is an area of employee relations in which some legal issues have not been fully resolved. Consistency is also important in granting employee personal use of the company's email system. See Chapter 35 for a discussion of issues related to union communication and solicitation using the employer's email system. A precedent file following the format of the policy statement should be

developed to ensure the policy is being implemented in a consistent and fair manner.

(10) *Reemphasize Policy.* Periodically, employees should be reminded of the policy statement.

Despite having a carefully crafted policy statement, employers may inadvertently violate federal and/or state laws involving employee usage of workplace technology, such as computers, cell phones and pagers. For example, one city had a comprehensive policy statement, but was found by the 9th District Court of Appeals to have violated appellants' rights under the Fourth Amendment and the California Constitution.[7] In the same case, a text-messaging service provider was found by the Court to have violated the Stored Communications Act.[8]

Record Access and Security

Employers should designate at least three levels of security for access to employee information. A person receiving one or more of the three designations should be given the authorization in writing. The levels are:

- **Level One: Personnel Records.** Personnel records, whether in hard-copy form or in computer files, must remain secure at all times. There is no valid reason that any person should have access to an employee's personnel file unless that individual is required to work with information in the file for a legitimate purpose, such as accessing an employee's file for information on an accident for a workers' compensation claim. Even in these situations, employees should not be permitted to rummage through the employee's file, reviewing information which is not relevant to the workers' compensation case.

- Employees who are authorized to access personnel files should be required to sign confidentiality agreements requiring them to be responsible for maintaining the secrecy of any information they obtain from reading the files. Such agreement should require the employees to certify that they shall not release any information to any unauthorized individual. It should also should clearly indicate that the employees understand that any breach of confidentiality or other release of information in the personnel files shall be grounds for immediate dismissal and/or prosecution, if authorized by law.

- **Level Two: Employment Tests (Excluding Drug Tests).** The results of employment testing, whether for initial employment, promotions or reassignments, should be retained in a separate, secure location and maintained by an employee or employees who is/are specifically authorized to perform this function, whether on a full- or part-time basis.

- **Level Three: Medical Records and Drug Tests Results.** What is true for personnel files and employment tests is especially important for medical records and the results of drug testing. These records should be protected by extraordinary access limitations. In hard-copy form, medical records should be kept in separate, sealed folders with initials across the seal. No

---

[7] Ibid.   [8] Ibid.

one should be permitted to review medical records, even those who are regularly required to post information in personnel folders or files. The only individuals who should be permitted to see medical records are those specifically authorized in writing by the top HR manager. Medical records should be filed in a separate location, away from personnel records and employment testing records, under the custody of specifically designated individuals.

Computer Systems

Computer system access to personnel files should be coded and should have the same levels of access as discussed above.

Contract or Outsourced Work

The same standards for record access and control should apply to any work that is contracted to outside vendors. Such contractors should sign confidentiality agreements and have the same stringent system of record-keeping and controls that apply to in-house work.

Record Retention

One way to help prevent the unauthorized release of information is to strictly adhere to time limits for record retention. The two broad groups of regulations involving record retention are equal employment opportunity statutes and laws covering other subjects.

Equal Employment Opportunity Statutes

Generally, under U.S. Equal Employment Commission regulations personnel and employment records must be kept for one year, however, such records must be kept for one year following an employee's involuntary termination.[9] When a charge of discrimination is involved, records must be kept until the issue is resolved. In addition to this general regulation, these are record requirements under certain laws:

- *Age Discrimination in Employment Act.* Keep payroll records for three years. Keep employee benefit plans and written seniority or merit plans as long as they are in effect and one year following their termination.

- *Equal Pay Act.* Keep records for two years that apply to wage rates, job evaluation results, documentation of reasons for wage differences of female and male employees, seniority and merit procedures and provisions in collective bargaining agreements. (See the *Fair Labor Standards Act* for records that must be maintained for three years).

- *Americans with Disabilities Act.* Keep records for one year involving personnel actions such as new hires, promotions and disciplinary actions. Also keep for one year documentation on requests for reasonable accommodation. Keep for two years records pertaining to apprenticeship programs.

---

[9] U.S. EEOC, *A Charge Has Not Been Filed Against My Company. Do I Need To Keep Records or File Reports With the EEOC? n. d.* This is the source of record retention requirements under the Age Discrimination in Employment Act, the Americans with Disabilities Act, and the Equal Pay Act.

- *Rehabilitation Act of 1973.* Federal contractors must keep employment records for two years from the date of an employment decision or the making of a personnel record, whichever is later. Records include applications, job postings, job descriptions, employment offers, tests used, employment policies and procedures, interview notes and personnel records. Record retention is only one year for contractors who either have less than 150 employees or have contracts less than $150,000.[10]

- *Executive Order 11246.* Record and retention requirements are the same as those under the *Rehabilitation Act of 1973.*

- *Vietnam Era Veterans' Readjustment Assistance Act.* Record and retention requirements are the same as those under the *Rehabilitation Act of 1973.*

Other Statutes

- *Family and Medical Leave Act.* Keep records for three years for such documentation as any disputes about granting leave, dates and hours of leave taken, and written policies and procedures.

- *Occupational Safety and Health Act.* Keep records for five years after the calendar year ends to which the records apply. Records must be transferred to succeeding employer in the event the business is sold.

- *Labor-Management Reporting and Disclosure Act.* Keep records for five years from the date of the report.

- *H-1B & H-1B1 Visa Program.* Keep payroll records three years from the date they were created. Keep all other records required under the program for one year.

- *H-2A Visa Program.* Keep records for three years after the date the work contract is completed.

- *H-2B Certification for Temporary Nonagricultural Work.* Record retention requirements are the same as those under the *H-1B & H-1B1 Visa Program.*

- *McNamara-O-Hara Service Contract Act.* Keep records for three years after work on the contract is completed.

- *Davis-Bacon & Related Acts.* Keep records for three years after work on the contract is completed.

- *Copeland "Anti-Kickback" Act.* Keep records for three years after work on the contract is completed.

- *Employee Polygraph Protection Act of 1988.* Keep records for three years after the polygraph is conducted. Records include employer statements explaining the justification for examining an employee in conjunction with an investigation prompted by an economic loss.

- *Fair Labor Standards Act.* Keep records on non-exempt employees for three years that pertain to payrolls, collective bargaining agreements, sales and purchases. Keep for two years records used to compute non-exempt

[10] The source of retention requirements for all laws other than those noted in Footnote 15 was the U.S. Department of Labor.

employee wages, such as time cards, work schedules and the related. The law requires a significant amount of information that must be maintained.

Employee Records Disposal

Records should never be disposed of by means of ordinary trash removal. Once the time limitations noted above have been met, the records should be destroyed, either by shredding or incinerating the materials. Care should be taken to ensure that documentation of all record disposal is retained.

Drug Testing

Drug abuse is a serious concern for employers. Consequently, employers conduct drug testing under these six scenarios:

- As part of the employment process of job applicants.
- In the event of an accident involving an employee.
- In for-cause situations (other than accidents), such as when a workplace disturbance occurs involving the employee.
- In a regular testing regime, such as during routine annual physical examinations.
- Random testing, particularly for jobs involving security or safety.
- As a condition of an agreement between the employee and the employer, such as a return to work agreement, to ensure the employee is remaining drug-free in return for being allowed to work.[11]

Employers have valid reasons for implementing or considering the implementation of workplace drug testing. For example, according to the results of a study conducted by the Substance Abuse and Mental Health Services Administration, an estimated 10 million users of illicit drugs are employed.[12] The study's sample represented 81.8 million U.S. workers. In the same study, 74 percent of workers in large establishments said their employer had some kind (at hiring, randomly, upon suspicion or after an accident) of drug testing program. The percentages reported by workers in small and medium workplaces were 28 and 58, respectively. All the percentages were significant increases from 1994 when the study was last done.[13]

There is considerable sentiment in favor of workplace drug testing. Ninety-seven percent of employees in a Gallup poll agreed that under appropriate circumstances drug testing should be conducted at work.[14]

In addition to conducting pre-employment drug testing, some employers conduct background investigations of applicants' drug use. Sources for verifying applicants' contentions about their drug use include court records, drug tests, former employers, honesty tests, medical examinations, performance appraisal

---

[11] The National Clearinghouse for Alcohol and Drug Information, *Drug Testing in the Workplace,* 2001.

[12] Ibid.

[13] Substance Abuse and Mental Health Services Administration, *Worker Drug Use and Workplace Poli-*

cies and Programs: results from the 1994 and 1997 National Household Survey on Drug Abuse, 2001.

[14] The National Clearinghouse for Alcohol and Drug Information, *Drug Testing in the Workplace,* 2001.

results from former employers, personal references, police records, and polygraph testing (for those jobs where such tests can be conducted). Drug testing, which is the primary method of verifying drug use, is usually restricted to testing for cannabinoids, opiates, cocaine metabolites, amphetamines and phencyclidine. Employers in the private sector typically have the unrestricted right to conduct drug testing. Among the benefits of testing is to preclude hiring applicants whose use of drugs subjects the employer to the probability of increased utilization of employee benefits and unsatisfactory job performance. In fact, employers who employ individuals who are responsible for the safety of others would be expected to conduct such testing.

Legal Issues in Drug Testing

There are legal issues to consider in establishing drug testing programs. Two U.S. Supreme Court decisions indicate that drug testing among public sector employers is legal if the program is announced in advance and if there is reasonable cause for the testing. Possible reasons for drug testing include concern for public safety in case of accidents and law enforcement work involving drug enforcement.[15] The Department of Transportation requires drug testing for employees who are in one of these categories:

- Are members of a flight crew;
- Operate commercial motor vehicles in interstate commerce (subject to some limitations);
- Perform railroad services;
- Perform operating, maintenance, or emergency-response functions on a pipeline or liquid natural gas facility;
- Are crew members on a commercial vessel licensed, certified, or documented by the U.S. Coast Guard.

In the private sector, some states have enacted laws restricting drug testing or mandating use of specific testing procedures. The National Labor Relations Board has ruled that employers must bargain with a union before implementing a drug testing program for current employees in the bargaining unit.[16] While unionized employers are not required to bargain with unions on the subject of drug testing of job applicants, they are required to provide information to unions about such programs when requested.[17] Legal problems may also occur if no laws exist on the subject of testing. For example, an applicant could file a civil suit seeking recovery for damages due to an adverse employment decision resulting from a faulty drug testing method.

Testing Measures

At a minimum, employers with testing programs for job applicants, or those considering adopting them, are advised to ensure that the following types of precautions are taken:

---

[15] For more information on this issue see CCH HUMAN RESOURCES MANAGEMENT, *Personnel Practices/ Communications*, ¶ 326.

[16] CCH HUMAN RESOURCES MANAGEMENT, *Employment Relations*, ¶ 2078.

[17] Ibid.

- Checking for any legal requirements;

- Defining the conditions under which drug testing will be conducted;

- Ensuring that specimen collection, transportation and testing will be conducted with the utmost considerations for employee privacy, confidentiality, and scientific accuracy;

- Disseminating a copy of the drug policy statement to all employees;

- Obtaining consent forms, signed by applicants, giving permission for present and future drug testing;

- Utilizing testing laboratories certified by the Department of Health and Human Services; and

- Requiring that confirmatory tests be conducted if a positive finding occurs.

Security

As noted above, all drug testing results should be maintained with medical records or at the same level of security as medical records (Level Three).

Workplace Smoking

Historically, employers have been conscious of the safety risks posed by workplace smoking. Consequently, smoking was either banned or restricted where there was a danger of explosion or fire. More recently, in response to health hazards, cost considerations, local and state laws, and complaints from nonsmoking employees, employers have instituted policies to restrict workplace smoking or even to ban it altogether.

Smoking Laws

Most states have laws regulating workplace smoking. The provisions in these laws require employers to take one or more of the following actions:

- Accommodate the desires of nonsmokers;

- Post notices about workplace smoking, including smoke-free work areas;

- Prepare written policies about smoking; and

- Establish smoking and no smoking areas.

Some employers have attempted to bar employees from smoking while they are off-duty. A number of states have laws prohibiting employer actions against employees/job applicants for smoking off-the-job. About 30 states have such laws addressing hiring, discipline/discharge or discriminating against individuals for smoking away from work. An additional 11 states have similar laws restricting employer actions for smoking off-the-job unless there is a job-related reason of a bona fide occupational qualification. For some types of work, however, such as police officers and fire fighters, no-smoking requirements, both on and off the job, have been upheld by state courts.[18]

---

[18] "Smoking Ruled a Firing Offense," *Richmond Times-Dispatch* (October 21, 1997), p. 2.

Tort Claims

The legal theories most frequently used by employees claiming harm from workplace smoking are:

- *Battery.* In such a situation, the employee typically alleges that the actions of the smoker in the workplace were intended to harm the employee.

- *Contract.* Some employees have filed suit, alleging that a smoke-free workplace should be an inherent right of employment.

- *Discrimination.* In some states that require employers to either provide no-smoking work areas for employees requesting them or maintain smoke-free work environments, employers who permit employees to violate these laws may be charged with discrimination.

International Aspects of Workplace Smoking

In July 2007, England invoked a law prohibiting smoking in all enclosed and "substantially enclosed" workplaces. See Chapter 38 for a fuller discussion of this law.

See Chapter 21 for a discussion of wellness issues involving smoking.

Personal Life Intrusions

Generally speaking, there is no justifiable reason for employers to intrude in employees' personal lives, unless there is a valid job-related reason, such as conducting investigations of applicants for jobs in law enforcement. Specific areas of intrusion into an employee's personal life include the persons with whom the employee associates, his or her alcohol consumption, spending habits, financial obligations, and punctuality in paying bills.

Types of Personal Information

Various types of personal information obtained during the selection process need to be protected from disclosure.

Antisocial Behavior

Antisocial behavior includes a broad category of behavior ranging from chronic rudeness to felony assaults. If antisocial behavior is used to bar employment, it must be job related. Applicants for bank teller positions obviously should be trustworthy and must not have been discharged by a former employer for theft or have been convicted of theft. On the other hand, politeness may not be a job requirement for a warehouse worker who does not regularly come in contact with either customers or other workers.[19] Sources of information about an applicant's prior behavior include court records, credit reports, former employers, honesty tests, police records, and polygraph tests (where legal). The unauthorized release of this type of information could be the basis of a tort action.

[19] CCH HUMAN RESOURCES MANAGEMENT, *Equal Employment Opportunity,* ¶ 10,110.

Driver's License

For jobs that require a valid driver's license, the employer will need to confirm that the applicant is licensed and has no significant moving violations. Items of concern would include any convictions for reckless driving, driving under the influence of alcohol, or speeding. Because some of this information could be embarrassing to the applicant or employee if it were released, unauthorized disclosure should be prevented.

Financial Status

Depending upon job-related conditions, the types of financial information an employer might need to obtain include evidence of bankruptcy, garnishments, credit rating, financial obligations, rental or home ownership, car ownership, length of residence at present and past addresses, outstanding financial obligations, delinquencies in payment of taxes or other financial obligations, failure to pay alimony or child support, tax liens and judgments, and student loan obligations. This information is usually obtained through court records, credit reports, and personal references. Since some of this information could be embarrassing to an individual if it is disclosed, or it might be inaccurate, it should be not be released.

On-the-Job Injuries

Employers may have a legitimate right to know what accidents and injuries applicants have experienced in the past in order for an employer to determine whether applicants are able to perform the tasks in a job without risk to themselves or others. This information could be requested on the application and verified through credit reports, former employers, or the medical examination. Care should be taken not to inquire about workers' compensation claims until after a conditional offer of employment has been made. The same is true for the medical examination. Because the release of this information could affect an individual's subsequent employment prospects, unauthorized releases must be avoided.

Work Experience/Performance

Employment decisions frequently are dependent upon applicants' claims regarding their work experience and level of performance. Types of information generally collected include the dates of previous employment, job title(s) held, tasks performed, length of time these tasks were performed, and job-related training programs that were completed. Information is also collected about the level of applicants' past job performance, including the quantity and quality of work, attendance record, job safety, and conduct or behavior at work. Such information is obtained from various sources, including military records, results of performance appraisals completed by former employers, and personal references. A minority of former employers may also provide such information, only on the condition that the ex-employee authorizes the release of the information.

Court Records

A considerable amount of sensitive information can be obtained from court records, including local, county, state and federal courts. Various levels of courts have different jurisdictions over both the geographical area covered and the type of tort or criminal activity involved. Local courts may be restricted to traffic offenses and minor torts. County and state courts could involve non-federal offenses, ranging from torts to capital offenses. Federal courts involve bankruptcy cases, federal crimes and civil cases. Some court records, particularly those involving domestic cases and juvenile offenses, may be sealed and thus not available to the public. Most other court records are public; some courts even have on-line access.[20] In addition, employers may require an applicant to obtain information about any court records that they have. The sensitive nature of this information imposes an obligation upon the employer to ensure that it is not released.

Credit Report

There are two types of credit reports. A *consumer report* is a report on an individual's credit (including matters of worthiness, standing, or capacity), character, reputation, personal characteristics, or style of living that may affect an individual's employability. An *investigative consumer report* is a full or partial consumer report derived from interviews with people who know the individual, including friends, neighbors, and associates.

Employer Responsibilities

Employers have legal responsibilities under the Fair Credit Reporting Act. This law requires employers to give applicants a written notification that a credit report may be used on a form that is exclusively used for that purpose. The employer must also obtain a written approval from the applicants authorizing the employer to obtain the credit report (special procedures apply to employers in the trucking industry).[21] Before the credit reporting agency will send a credit report, the employer is required to certify that it has complied with the law and that the information will be used in accordance with applicable equal employment opportunity laws and regulations.

A negative employment decision, such as a denial of employment, reassignment or promotion, or a termination that results from information derived from credit report, is legally defined as an *adverse action*. Prior to taking an adverse action affected by a credit report, even if it is only in a minor way, the employer must send the individual a *pre-adverse action disclosure*. This disclosure must include a copy of the individual's consumer report and a copy of the document *A Summary of Your Rights Under the Fair Credit Reporting Act*. The credit reporting agency is responsible for providing the employer with a summary of consumer rights.

---

[20] CCH Human Resources Management, *Personnel Practices*, ¶ 335.

[21] For an explanation of the procedures see Federal Trade Commission, *FTC FACTS FOR BUSINESS Using Consumer Reports: What Employers Need to Know*, March 1999, p. 3.

After the employer has taken an adverse action, the person affected by the action must also be given an individual notice (orally, in writing, or electronically) that an *adverse action* has been taken. The notice must include:

- The name, address, and phone number of the credit reporting agency that supplied the report;

- A statement that the credit reporting agency did not make the decision to take the adverse action and cannot give specific reasons for it; and,

- A notice of the individual's right to dispute the accuracy or completeness of any information the agency furnished, and his or her right to an additional free consumer report from the agency upon request within 60 days.[22]

The law is enforced by the Federal Trade Commission, and there are significant legal consequences for employers who fail to comply with it.

Precautions

Because a considerable amount of the information obtained through a credit report could be potentially embarrassing to an individual, special precautions must be taken to ensure that such information is protected. This protection applies to information related to both job applicants and employees.

Disclosure of Personal Information

Special precautions must be taken by employers to protect any investigative information obtained for a job-related purpose. Policies should be established concerning the length of time such information is retained. Detailed procedures should explain what information is to be released and how it is to be released. This policy should also apply to those applicants for employment who are not hired due to information disclosed in any background investigation that was conducted.

Negligent Hiring or Negligent Retention

Negligent hiring and *negligent retention* can also subject an employer to a tort action. *Negligent hiring* is the potential liability of an employer for the actions of an employee who was selected for employment without adequately determining the person's qualifications for the job. *Negligent retention* is the prospective liability an employer faces by retaining employees who it knows (or should know) are not qualified to perform their job tasks or have mental or physical conditions or propensities that result in them being hazards to themselves or others.

There is evidence that some applicants do not provide correct information about themselves. For example, one study found that 80 percent of the resumes applicants submitted did not accurately report their job experience. In addition, the study found 30 percent of the resumes did not correctly show educational attainments.[23] There also is evidence that all employers do not fully verify the information furnished by applicants. A survey of 320 employers found that 18

---

[22] Federal Trade Commission, *Using Consumer Reports: What Employers Need to Know.* December 1997.

[23] CCH HUMAN RESOURCES MANAGEMENT, *Personnel Practices/Communications,* ¶ 332.

percent of them did not check the employment history of college graduates, and 21 percent did not verify the graduates' education.[24]

Serious, and even tragic, consequences may result from inadequately verifying whether applicants have the personal characteristics and other relevant qualifications for employment. In one case, the manager of an apartment complex selected an applicant to work in the maintenance department. An inadequate verification of the individual's background failed to disclose that he had a violent personality, including convictions for assault, and that he was wanted for probation violations. He raped and murdered a female tenant of the complex; the apartment owners were sued by the woman's parents for failing to adequately check the employee's past background. In another case, a woman raped by a cab driver obtained a judgment of $4,500,000 from the taxi company because it failed to discover that the driver had a criminal record and never should have been hired.[25]

Improving Accuracy of Applicant Information Provided

The accuracy of information furnished by applicants can be substantially improved by following two steps. First, advising applicants that accuracy is essential, since the information they furnish will have a direct bearing on their employability. In addition, instruct applicants that the information they furnish will be carefully verified. These two steps will decrease the inconsistency between information furnished by applicants and that which is obtained through verification.

For example, one organization required applicants for truck driver positions to list all traffic convictions that had occurred within the previous five years. Often, applicants would omit listing either some, or even all, of their traffic citations and convictions. The application form contained a statement in small print that read, *Information furnished by applicants is subject to verification.* The process of verifying traffic convictions took some time, particularly for those applicants who had lived in different cities and states. Consequently, to speed the employment process, applicants were given other selection procedures, such as road-driving and vision tests, while the information they provided on the applications was verified. On a number of occasions, applicants were hired when clean records were received from local police departments in those communities in which applicants *reported* they had lived. Later, however, state police verified that the "clean records" contained information that was either omitted or in error. Depending upon the seriousness of the conviction, this new information sometimes necessitated discharging the employee. The Personnel Director was concerned about the problem and he reworded the warning statement in larger print to read:

> All the information you furnish on this form will be checked, except that present employers will not be contacted if you specifically request it. Driving records will be thoroughly checked with local and state police departments. Other conviction information will also be verified and considered in evaluating your application, if it is

[24] Schellhardt, T.D., "What Personnel Offices Really Stress in Hiring," *The Wall Street Journal,* (March 8. 1991), p. B-1.

[25] Atwood, C.S. and Neel, J.M., "New Lawsuits Expand Employer Liability," *HR Magazine* (October, 1990), p. 74.

related to the job for which you are applying. Your failure to omit important information may bar you from employment.

In addition, employment interviewers were instructed to inform applicants of this statement:

We verify all information furnished on an application; this includes checking for driving and other conviction information from state and local police departments. We neither obtain nor consider such information unless it is specifically related to the job. Providing false information or omitting information may bar you from employment. With this in mind, would you like to review your application to be sure you did not omit any information.

These procedures significantly reduced errors, inaccuracies, and omissions.

The accuracy of information furnished by applicants can also be increased by requiring them to sign release forms holding previous employers harmless for any job-related information they furnish. Reviewing the release forms with applicants and explaining the types of necessary information, such as job title, length of employment, rehire eligibility, safety record, attendance record, quantity of work, conduct and quality of work, may also prompt the applicant to tell the interviewer about important information that was either omitted or incorrect. The interviewer should emphasize that any differences in the information provided by the applicant and former employers will delay, or even bar, their employment.

Adverse Impact in Verification

If an employment decision that was based on information used to verify applicants' qualifications results in adverse impact on a protected group, the employer will be required to show that the basis for the employment decision is job-related or is a bona fide occupational qualification. This issue is discussed in Chapter 14.

Failure to Disclose

Failure to disclose is a term used to explain the unwillingness of former employers to provide information about employees who left their employ to future employers. Failing to disclose pertinent information can be a double-edged sword. On the one hand, some employers refuse to release the information due to the fear of a defamation lawsuit. On the other hand, failing to disclose information, which later results in serious adverse employment consequences, may also result in tort actions.

Defamation

Defamation and *malice* are two of the major concerns former employers have for declining requests for information about previous employees. *Defamation* is damaging a person's reputation as the result of something said (slander) or something put in writing (libel) that is not true. *Malice* is wantonly or recklessly making statements about a person that are known to be false, causing damage to an individual's reputation.

Suits

The basis for a defamation suit may be groundless, but that does not spare the employer the expense and time required to prepare a legal defense. At the prospect of a possible lawsuit, some employers simply do not release any information about a former employee, except to confirm such information as the dates of employment and the job title. However, this practice can subject an employer to other tort actions, particularly if the employer had important information about the former employee that was not revealed, such as knowledge of violent acts the person committed in the workplace. If an unsuspecting employer hires the individual after contacting the previous employer, and that person commits a violent act, what liability might the former employer have? In one case, a court found that a former employer had no responsibility to honor a request for information about an ex-employee's violent propensities. In the absence of the information, the person was hired and subsequently murdered a co-worker.[26] However, there have been cases where employers were held to be liable for giving favorable references for former employers who were potentially violent.[27]

To help both the prospective and the former employer minimize their liabilities, the following courses of action may be helpful:

- The *prospective employer* should:
  - Put the request in writing.
  - Ask specific questions, such as, "Was the person ever disciplined for fighting?"
  - Seek only relevant information.
  - Include a signed release from the applicant.
  - If a former employer still refuses, consider these steps:
    - Call the employer and ask for the reason for the refusal.
    - Ask how the request should be made so it will be honored.
    - If the individual still refuses to release any information, state that a record of the call will be made and, if the information sought is so relevant that the applicant will not be hired unless it is obtained, the applicant will be told the reason that he or she was not hired was due to the failure of the former employer to cooperate.
- The *former employer* should:
  - Give only truthful information that can be documented.
  - Give only factual information, not opinions.
  - Ask separating employees to sign a release form holding the employer harmless for the release of job-related information. If an individual declines to sign the release, inform the individual that prospective employers will be told that no information can be released because the person did not sign the authorization form.

---

[26] CCH *Ideas and Trends in Personnel* (July 1, 1998), p. 112.

[27] CCH Human Resources Management, *Personnel Practices/Communications,* ¶ 1467.

Employment Discharges

Another significant area where tort actions may be brought are employment discharges. A *discharge* occurs when an employee is terminated due to performance deficiencies in such areas as productivity (amount of work produced), quality of work (including the number of errors made), safety (including the number of accidents and the amount of property damage), attendance pattern (including punctuality and regularity of attendance), and conduct (including an employee's personal behavior while at work or off-the-job, when the conduct affects the job). Discharges are reserved for only the most serious deficiencies and cases where employees do not improve, even after repeated efforts are made to correct their behavior through less serious forms of punishment, such as reprimands, suspensions, and demotions.

Discharges should be handled very carefully because they can have a profound impact upon an employee. For example, discharged employees who felt they were mistreated have sabotaged equipment, committed arson, and even murdered co-workers and their supervisors. One employee, who believed he had been fired after his supervisor told him to leave the business premises, murdered a co-worker. Often, deficient employees are troubled by such problems as substance abuse, marriage and family problems, and legal or financial difficulties. Due to their inability to cope with a discharge, such employees obtain vengeance against their employer or other person in the organization who they feel is responsible for the action.

Two types of discharges which may be illegal, depending upon state law, are:

- *Constructive discharge,* which occurs when an employer makes conditions so unbearable for an employee that he or she resigns. This is a type of involuntary separation.

- *Retaliatory discharge,* which occurs when an employee is discharged by an employer in retaliation for something, such as reporting a safety hazard.

Employment-at-Will

Most employees in the United States are employed under a historical common-law rule that they can be discharged "for any reason or for no reason at all." These employees thus depend upon the goodwill of their employers for continued employment. The doctrine in this situation is known as employment-at-will, meaning an employee is employed subject to the will of the employer. This subject is covered in detail in Chapter 37.

CHAPTER 9
JOB ANALYSIS

Chapter Highlights
- The job analysis process
- Job analysis purposes
- Job analysis methods
- Human resources management-job analysis relationships

Introduction

Virtually everything done within human resources management is related in some way to job analysis. For some activities, job analysis is essential, such as in the preparation of job descriptions, the development of selection methods, the validation of employment decisions and the evaluation of job worth. Job analysis is both a science and an art. The science is the relatively large body of knowledge about the various methods of job analysis, including how information can be effectively classified for decision-making purposes. The art of the process is knowing how to collect information from employees and applying the science to obtain valid and consistent results.

Job Analysis Process

Job analysis is the systematic process of obtaining, analyzing and interpreting valid job information.

"Systematic process" in the above definition means the analysis is planned to meet stated objectives using accepted methods. "Valid" means the job analysis provides accurate information about the job to meet the purpose for which the analysis was conducted. For example, if the purpose of the job analysis is to identify performance criteria to be used in a performance appraisal system, the criteria that are identified will be those that are representative of successful job performance.

Job analysis is performed by persons who are employed as job analysts or have other titles, such as compensation analysts.

Kinds of Information

All pertinent information about a job is obtained in a job analysis. These are illustrations of the major types of information which are obtained:

- *Task information,* which includes how often the tasks are performed or what percentage of an employee's time is spent performing them, how important each task is in relation to all other tasks performed, and which tasks are deemed "essential," as required in establishing selection procedures for persons with disabilities.

- *Products and services* provided in the job.
- *Physical demands* required in the job, including walking, lifting, stooping, crawling, and sitting.
- *Physical environment* in which the job is performed, including inside/ outside work, temperature and other climatic conditions.
- *Knowledge, skills, abilities, training, education,* and *experience* required to perform the job tasks.
- *Licenses.* including craft licensure and motor vehicle license needed in the job.
- *Machines, tools, equipment,* and *work aids* used in the job.
- *Relationships* encountered on the job, including peers, customers, governmental employees, and supervisors.

Role of Job Analysis

The role of job analysis in other HR activities is examined in the following sections.

Validity and Reliability

In adverse impact situations, the *Uniform Guidelines for Employee Selection Procedures* (*Guidelines*) require that the offending selection procedure be validated by job criteria obtained from a job analysis. A *partial* job analysis is required in criterion-related studies if production or error rates, or other measures, such as absenteeism or tardiness, are obtainable and important in the employment situation, or if an overall method of determining job performance can be shown to be related and important for job success. If this information is not obtainable, a *full* job analysis must be conducted. In addition, a *full* job analysis is required in all content or construct studies.

Job Structuring

Many aspects of job structuring, such as preparing job descriptions and job specifications and designing jobs to meet employee needs, depend upon information obtained through a job analysis. Job analysis studies are also important in organizational restructuring to prevent task redundancy and to ensure that tasks are not omitted.

Human Resource Planning

Human resource planning depends upon the outputs of job analysis, particularly the job descriptions which are prepared from the study, in the process of forecasting human resource needs and projecting human resource supply.

Recruitment

Recruitment is the first step in the selection process, often involving recruitment interviews and posting jobs within an organization so interested employees can apply for them. The information about the job that is supplied in both cases must be accurate. For example, recruitment interviewers study job descriptions and job specifications (prepared from a job analysis study) so they can determine the types of applicants they should recruit and answer questions prospective employees ask in recruitment interviews.

Selection

Selection methods are used that compare applicants' qualifications with the job specifications. If the job specifications derived from job analysis are inaccurate or omit important information, either the wrong person might be selected or the right person might be rejected. The types of selection decisions involved in these situations include hiring, promotions and other placement actions.

Performance Appraisal

All performance appraisal systems involve comparing employee performance with performance criteria. The information about tasks, which is in the job description, is obtained through job analysis. Other information collected in a job analysis includes important job behaviors and activities, the machinery and equipment used, and working conditions. From this information, performance criteria are established and used in a performance appraisal system.

Job Evaluation

Before a job can be evaluated, it must be analyzed to determine the relative amounts of compensable factors, such as the skill, effort, responsibility, and working conditions that are necessary to perform a job. The Equal Pay Act of 1963 requires employers to provide equal pay for women and men who perform the same work requiring the same skill, effort, and responsibility under similar working conditions.

Performance-Based Pay

Performance based pay methods, which include merit pay, bonus systems and contingency-based systems, such as pay for knowledge, are established from information collected through a job analysis study.

Safety and Health

One of the valuable outputs of a job analysis study is the identification of unsafe acts and unsafe conditions. This information is important in determining the causes of occupational accidents and illnesses. Preventing occupational accidents and occupational disease is a fundamental part of loss control in workers' compensation and in preventing human suffering.

Human Resources Development

Employee job training is based upon the duties that are a part of a job and the qualifications an incumbent must possess to perform them. Consequently, for the training to be job-related, the duties and qualifications must be obtained from a job analysis study. For example, an organization was experiencing both low productivity and excessive quality problems with newly trained machine operators. Neither the newly trained operators nor the operators' supervisors told the trainer what was causing the problems. The only feedback the trainer received was about the poor work performance of new trainees. The trainer decided to study the problem and he began by observing employees at work. He discovered that the routing diagram he was using in his training classes had been revised, but no one in production told him about the change.

Career Planning

Employees set their sights on career advancement by identifying the jobs that interest them. The next step is for the employees to obtain information about the necessary qualifications they need to obtain targeted jobs. All this information, including the tasks and the job specifications, are obtained from a job analysis study.

Research

Human resources research includes constructing, conducting and interpreting employee opinion surveys, which require information obtained from a job analysis study. For example, an important part of opinion surveys are questions related to job conditions. Research is also conducted in other HR activities, such as selection method validation, which also require job analysis studies.

Conducting a Job Analysis Study

Determine Purposes

The purpose of the job analysis should be determined so that information can be communicated to employees. Employees have a right to know why the study is to be conducted. Providing this information to them is important in both securing their cooperation and in preventing potential problems.

Secure Cooperation

Among the groups from which cooperation should be sought are employees, managers and, if employees are represented by a union, union representatives. Good faith efforts to inform employees about a prospective job analysis will greatly increase their diligence in providing accurate information.

Prevent Potential Problems

Some of the potential problems generated by a job analysis are employee hostility and fears, indifference, and overstating or understating job information. These problems can be prevented through a combination of measures. For example, informing employees about the purposes of the study should help prevent hostility. Indifference can also be alleviated by explaining to employees how important the results of the job analysis will be for such actions as job evaluation and merit pay.

Overstating tasks and job specifications is generally caused by the desire of either job incumbents or their supervisors to increase the pay level for the affected jobs. Auditing is the best method for controlling this problem. Employees and supervisors should be notified that direct observations will be conducted to verify the accuracy of information to be furnished.

Three-Step Process

As stated in the definition, job analysis is a three-step process that consists of collecting the information, analyzing the information and interpreting the information. The first step, *collecting information,* is accomplished by observing employees at work, interviewing employees about what they do or having them complete written instruments describing what they do. The second step, *analyzing the information,* is largely a mental process of understanding the information and obtaining any needed clarification or amplification. When the information is obtained from either an interview or from observation, usually the analysis is done at the same time. The analysis may also be completed when information is collected by the analyst using a checklist. For written instruments, such as position questionnaires or diaries, which are completed by the employees whose jobs are to be analyzed, the analyst may need further clarification of some of the information that was provided. The final step, *interpreting information* involves classifying the information into a logical framework.

Obtaining Information

These are three ways of obtaining job information:

- Through interviewing job incumbents and other employees;
- By observing employees as they perform their tasks; and,
- Through the submission of written information furnished by job incumbents and their supervisors.

In some situations, all three methods are used to obtain information.

Interviews

Usually, job analysis interviews are conducted away from the job site. The announcement notifying employees of the job analysis project should explain where interviews will be conducted. Exhibit 9-1 is an illustration of a notice announcing a job analysis project. A structured format should be used in conducting the interviews. The job analyst should review any available information about the job, such as existing job descriptions, before the interviewing begins. Sometimes, employees are apprehensive about job analysis interviews, so it is important for the analyst to exhibit positive nonverbal behavior. The interview should begin with an explanation of why the employee is to be interviewed and how the results of the interview will be used. The employee should be assured that the only object of the interview is to learn what the job entails. It is a good idea to explain to the employee that notes will be taken for later reference.

Sometimes employees have difficulty in explaining what their jobs entail. To help such employees, it is a good idea to simply have them explain the various tasks they perform. At various points in the interview, it is a good idea to use active listening techniques to summarize the explanations by rephrasing what the employee has said. After the employees are satisfied they have explained all their tasks, the analyst can go back over the list of tasks and categorize the information by chronology of performance. If the tasks are not performed in a chronological or other sequence, the tasks can be described in a functional manner, starting with the most important one, next most important one, and so on. Sometimes it is helpful to draw rough flowcharts during the interview to get a full understanding of the job and how it relates to other jobs. Before terminating an interview, the employee should be given the opportunity to explain or add anything or to ask questions.

Exhibit 9-1
Sample Announcement Notifying Employees of a Job Analysis
Project
ABC Company

To All Associates:

We are conducting a job analysis study to gather information to be used in revising job descriptions. Sheila Porter of Modern Management, Inc., is directing the project. Part of the project includes collecting information about the tasks performed in all jobs. Interviews, position questionnaires and on-the-job observations will be used in the study. Every employee will be interviewed by either Sheila or one of her associates. The purpose of the interviews will be to collect information directly from each employee.

Each associate has a key role in ensuring that Sheila has the information necessary to prepare accurate job descriptions that may affect such important subjects as the performance criteria for your job and the selection methods that will be used in the future in filling job vacancies. We are announcing this project in advance so you can be prepared for the interview. The specific date and time of your interview will be given to you later. Meanwhile, there are several things that you should do in preparation for the interview. First, you should carefully complete the ABC Position Questionnaire which will be given to you by your supervisor. The information you furnish on this questionnaire will be an important item for discussion during your interview, so you will need to have it fully completed prior to the interview. Discuss with your supervisor any problems that you may have in completing the questionnaire.

On-the-job observations will be conducted as necessary to obtain additional data or to verify information furnished on the questionnaire or provided during the interview. These observations are a fundamental part of the process in a project of this type. Many times essential information about job tasks can only be obtained through personal observation of the job. During these observations, only the tasks in the job will be reviewed. You are assured that your job performance will not be appraised. You will be notified in advance if your job is scheduled for observation and when it will be conducted.

Please cooperate with Sheila and others involved in this project to help ensure that maximum benefit will be received from it.

/s/ Larry Profitable

President

Inevitably, some issues are brought up during interviews which should be approached with caution. For example, if management problems are noted by employees, the analyst should not take sides. If the purpose of the analysis is to gather information for a job evaluation project, the analyst should avoid expressing an opinion about whether the job is adequately compensated or if any pay changes may be made. Another wise course of action is to avoid expressing opinions about the job, such as the relative importance of tasks in it or the adequacy of methods or equipment used in the job.

Individual and Group Interviews

Interviews can be conducted with an individual employee or in group settings. Group interviews usually consist of several employees who perform the same tasks or have the same job. Interviewing individual employees is more time-consuming, and there may be a tendency for some employees to overstate their tasks when they are interviewed alone. For these reasons, some analysts use group interviews to save time. Also, so the logic goes, having peers present in group interviews helps employees be completely honest about their tasks. Other reasons for group interviews include helping the analyst get a fuller picture of different tasks in a particular job. Group interviews also help the analyst see how various tasks relate to each other and, more importantly, identify any significant differences in tasks among employees who are thought to be performing the same ones.

Employee Sampling

Sometimes only a sampling of employees are interviewed to save time. Furthermore, interviewing can be disruptive to operations, and this is minimized when only a sample of employees are interviewed. Interviews of a sample of employees can be done on either an individual employee or group basis. Sampling may, however, cause employee concern. Employees, who are sampled, may wonder, "Why me?" Employees omitted from the sample may question, "Why not me?"

Observation

Observing employees as they perform their job tasks is probably the optimum method of collecting data, since the analyst obtains the information first-hand and there is no better way of understanding the tasks in a job than watching as the tasks are performed. Observation enhances employee acceptance of both an analyst's findings and other outputs derived from the job analysis, such as the results of a job evaluation project. This acceptance is partially due to the greater accuracy obtained from observation, but probably the biggest reason is the knowledge employees have that the analyst conducted the analysis at the work site instead of from an office.

Conducting Observations

Use the announcement publicizing the job analysis study to inform employees that observations will be used to collect information. Study any available information about the job, such as job descriptions, before observations are made. If possible, try to schedule observations for "typical" days, so the analyst can observe a representative sample of the tasks. Give employees ample notice before the observation is done. As with interviews, employees may be apprehensive about being observed, so it is important for the analyst to exhibit positive nonverbal behavior. Be as unobtrusive as possible. If feasible, observe the employee complete an entire work cycle before asking any questions. As needed, supplement the notes taken during the observation with flowcharts or other documentation to aid in your understanding of the job. Before leaving, give the employee the opportunity to explain or add anything.

Observation in Auditing

Sometimes the only feasible manner of collecting information is with a written instrument, such as position questionnaire or diary. To ensure the written information is accurate, audits are conducted. Of the two types of audits, *field* and *desk,* the former involves observing the employee while the job tasks are performed. The information obtained through observation is compared to the written data. Audits are discussed later in this chapter.

Disadvantages

One disadvantage of observations is the time required to observe every employee, although this is less of a problem than it seems for several reasons. First, analysts usually have some understanding of the jobs to be analyzed so the observation period need only be long enough to confirm this understanding or to obtain any supplemental information. Second, there are usually several and sometimes many employees who perform the same job, so even if the analyst is totally unfamiliar with a job, he or she will acquire a full comprehension of it after observing the first one or two employees. After these initial observations, each subsequent one will require less time. Third, if necessary, the analyst may only be able to observe a sample of employees, although the problems discussed above relative to sampling in interviewing would apply. Perhaps the biggest disadvantage of observations is that employees may be apprehensive about being watched while they are working.

Work Sampling

Work sampling is a method of selecting the tasks to be observed using random sampling. The workday is divided into equal time intervals; random samples of the intervals are taken, and the tasks performed at those intervals are recorded. Typically, the analyst is situated in an office close to where the jobs are to be analyzed. At the appropriate time, the analyst goes to the employee who is designated for observation during the time interval and records the task the employee is performing. Employees only know that recordings of different persons will be made throughout the day; they do not know which employees will be sampled. Since the intervals are sampled randomly, the analyst theoretically can get an accurate picture of a job's tasks without observing the job for an entire day, week or other period in which the sampling is done.

Work sampling is also used to determine the amount of time spent in performing the various tasks in a job. For example, a work sampling project was conducted in a hospital to determine the amount of time spent in performing tasks in different nursing jobs. One of the major objectives of the study was to determine the amount of time spent by registered nurses in performing tasks that could be performed by aides or licensed practical nurses.

Work sampling is used in time and motion studies as a prelude to setting pay, such as in a piece-rate system and is also employed in methods analysis to identify more efficient ways of accomplishing tasks. Work sampling is done in ergonomic studies as well, to determine how equipment and other technology can more effectively accommodate human needs and abilities.

There is a tendency for employees to resent work sampling because they may feel it treats them like subjects in a scientific experiment and ignores their human concerns. For example, employees may be apprehensive about going on a break or using the restroom for fear that the analyst will arrive at their work site to record what they are doing.

Written Instruments

Among the written instruments used to obtain task information are diaries, questionnaires and checklists.

Diary

The term "diary," as it is used in job analysis, is somewhat misleading. Typically, a "diary" consists of structured sheets on which employees record, in chronological sequence, their tasks as they are performed throughout the day(s) the job analysis is to be conducted. The typical information that is recorded includes a description of the task and the beginning and ending times spent on it. Diaries may be used alone or in conjunction with other methods of collecting job analysis information. There are many variations of diaries; one type is shown in Exhibit 9-2.

Exhibit 9-2
Example of Task Diary Sheet

Task diary sheets are used in job analysis to determine what tasks are performed in a job and how much time is spent doing them. The information you furnish on this form will be used for important purposes, such as preparing job descriptions and job specifications.

INSTRUCTIONS:

1. Show whole completed tasks rather than parts of them. The example below shows both the correct and incorrect ways of writing tasks.

2. Show any interruptions of tasks as they occur during the day if they involve more than a minute.

3. In the last column, show the priority of each task by using A for the most important, B for the next most important, and C for the least important.

4. On the back of the form you complete for the last day's entries, show any tasks that you typically perform that were not performed during the period in which you were completing the diary. For each task, show (1) the type of task, (2) the percent of time you spend doing it and (3) its priority, using the A, B and C coding.

5. Start a new sheet each day; use additional sheets as necessary.

6. Once the forms are completed, you may want to keep a copy for your personal analysis to see how you can improve the way you perform various tasks.

EXAMPLE:

"Task Diary"

EMPLOYEE NAME   DATE

JOB TITLE

	Time			Priority
TASK	*Start*	*Stop*	*Total*	*A, B, or C*
CORRECT ENTRY:				
Typed 3 driver accident forms from pencil copies	9:22	9:26	4 min.	A
INCORRECT ENTRY:				
Take accident forms from desk	9:22	9:23	1 min.	A
Typed one accident form from pencil copy	9:23	9:24	1 min.	A
Typed second accident form from pencil copy . .	9:24	9:25	1 min.	A
Typed third accident form from pencil copy	9:25	9:26	1 min.	A

The typical period of time in which diaries are used in a particular job analysis study is about one week, but this can vary considerably. Sometimes, the period consists of a random sample of days over a one-year period to get a more representative picture of job tasks.

Disadvantages. As in other forms of job analysis, diaries have some disadvantages. One of the biggest problems is *work storing*, which is the propensity of employees to accumulate work to do during the period when diaries will be maintained, because they fear they may have insufficient work to report on the form. This is a particular problem if employees are notified in advance (which they should be) of the contemplated date that diaries will be used. Storing work can be partially prevented by informing employees that it is known that there is a propensity to store work prior to completing diaries, but since it distorts the results, they are requested not to do it.

Recording their tasks as they are performed can be stressful for employees because of their apprehension about the use of the results, i.e., how it will affect their jobs and salary. Also, it is only natural for employees to be concerned about whether management will use the information for such purposes as determining how much work is produced and comparing the output of different employees. This perception, whether erroneous or not, can be a disadvantage to using diaries unless action is taken to prevent it, because it contributes to problems (see the discussion of work-storing above), and it can cause employees to misrepresent their tasks.

Another problem with diaries is that they are based upon the assumption that task information, collected during the week or so when the study is conducted, fairly represents all the tasks performed in a job. This period of time, even when it is randomly selected, does not necessarily represent every task performed, for example, during an entire year. This problem can be partially controlled by instructing employees to write in any tasks (and the percent of time spent doing them) that were not performed during the period the diaries were maintained.

Another shortcoming with diaries is that they typically do not require employee opinions about the job specifications necessary to perform the tasks. This is one reason that the use of diaries is generally supplemented with other job analysis methods that secure other information, such as job specification requirements.

Diaries are inappropriate for some jobs, such as assembly-line work or other jobs where entry recording would seriously disrupt the work routine. Finally, the preparation of diaries requires a fair amount of writing skills for employees to adequately describe what they do.

Advantages. In spite of their many problems, diaries have some real advantages. A diary is the only written method of collecting job analysis information where a record is maintained of job tasks as they are performed. Diaries can be used for multiple purposes, such as improving methods and procedures, preparing job descriptions and developing valid selecting procedures. Diaries are easy to prepare and economical to use. The diary entries provide a detailed picture of what employees do and how much time they spend doing it. From this type of information, the analyst can fairly accurately determine the percentage of time employees in different jobs spend on specific tasks. This information is especially important in job evaluation studies. The data furnished is usually more dependable than estimates of time that employees give on checklists, position questionnaires, and other methods used in collecting job information. Furthermore, the method is less obtrusive than observation. Diaries are more personal because employees are permitted to describe their tasks in their own words; this helps make the job analysis process, and outcomes from it, more meaningful to the employees who are involved. Finally, diary entries are more precise statements of accomplished work than are either generic checklists or broader task statements obtained though a position questionnaire.

Position Questionnaire

A *position questionnaire* is a generic instrument used to collect written information about a job encompassing a range of topics, such as a description of the work performed, equipment used in the job, contacts with other persons, instructions used in the performance of tasks, types of errors that occur and the responsibility for them, supervisory responsibilities, qualifications necessary to satisfactorily perform the job tasks and the tasks that are subject to review by others. There are numerous formats for position questionnaires. Some questionnaires are relatively concise while others are more detailed. An example of a questionnaire is illustrated in Exhibit 9-3.

Exhibit 9-3
Job Analysis Questionnaire

Instructions: This form is used to obtain information about your position. Please complete the form in your own words and be complete and accurate. Write N/A if an item on the form does not apply to your position. Do not use technical jargon, abbreviations or comments about work complexity or difficulty. Attach additional pages if you need more space. Give the form to your supervisor after you have completed it.

1.   Name: _____ 2. _____

       (Last)   (First)   (Job Title)

3.   Work Location: _____ 4. Work Telephone _____

5.   Work Schedule (Circle days normally
   worked)   Sun   Mon   Tues   Wed   Thur   Fri   Sat

          (Show the normal hours of work)   Start time _____ a.m./p.m. (circle one)

                                        End time _____ a.m./p.m. (circle one)

6.   Describe what you do, show the approximate percentage of time spent on each duty and the importance of the duty in relation to all others. This is an example:

     Answers inquiries and gives directions to customers: Greets customers at Information Desk and ascertains reason for visit to Credit Office. Sends customer to Credit Interviewer to open credit account, to Cashier to pay bills, to Adjustment Department to obtain correction of error in billing. Directs customer to other store departments on request, referring to store directory. (50%) (Importance = #2)

7.   List any machines, tools, equipment, work aids or vehicles which you need to operate in doing your job:

8.   List the job titles of those individuals in the company with whom you have contact and indicate if the contact is D=Daily, F=Frequently, O=Occasionally:

9.   Explain the physical demands in your job:

Lifting:

Bending, stooping, crawling and related:

Climbing:

Extreme temperatures:

Other:

10.   List any contacts you have with individuals outside the company and show the amount of contact D=Daily, F=Frequently, O=Occasionally:

Customers: _____

Contractors: _____

Government representatives: _____

Others: _____

11. List any licenses, registrations, certifications or related credentials you are required to have for your job:
_____

12. List the knowledge, skills, abilities, training, education and experience necessary to perform the tasks in your job. Do not indicate the amount you possess, but only the amount needed to do the job. Omit any requirements that can be acquired in a brief orientation period:

Knowledge:
_____
_____

Skills:
_____
_____

Abilities:
_____
_____

Training:
_____
_____

Education:
_____
_____

Experience:
_____
_____

13. Indicate how your work is accomplished by putting an (✓) where appropriate:
_____ My supervisor assigns me work and tells me how to do it.
_____ My supervisor assigns me work but I decide how to accomplish it.
_____ I know what my duties are and I am responsible for doing them.
_____ Other (please describe):
_____
_____

14. List the two most important mistakes that you could make in your job:
1. _____
2. _____

15. Explain the worst result for each of these two mistakes (show in the same order as above):
1. _____
2. _____

16. Indicate how many employees you directly supervise and their job titles:
_____

17. Explain anything else about your job that has not been covered above:
_____
_____
_____

18. Employee Certification:
I certify that all the information furnished on this Questionnaire is correct.
_____

        (Signature)   (Date)

19. Supervisor Concurrence:

I concur that the information furnished on this Questionnaire is correct with the exceptions noted below. Also, I have indicated on the listing of duties which ones are "essential."

_____   _____
(Signature)   (Date)

20.   Exceptions:

As necessary, a questionnaire can be constructed to meet the unique needs of an organization. Also, a questionnaire can be modified to meet the purpose of the job analysis, such as the development or validation of selection methods or the preparation of job descriptions. Customized versions can be modified to contain the terms and language of the organization, so it will appear less foreign to employees who are completing it. Previously, it was noted that employee acceptance is a problem in job analysis, particularly when task diaries or observation is used. Customized questionnaires do not guarantee employee cooperation and acceptance, but they do complement other efforts to achieve those objectives. Finally, generic questionnaires, whether customized or not, are economical to develop.

Questionnaires have some significant disadvantages, the foremost is that they require an extensive amount of time to complete. Employees should be given several weeks to complete them. Because questionnaires are also subject to manipulation by both employees and their supervisors, precautions, such as field audits, should be used to prevent this. Another problem with questionnaires is that they impose significant writing requirements upon employees.

Position Analysis Questionnaire

The *Position Analysis Questionnaire* (PAQ) (which is not to be confused with a Position Questionnaire), is a 195-item checklist that can be used for any job. The 195 items consist of 187 related to job tasks and eight that pertain to compensation questions, such as whether salary or tips are involved. The six major divisions of the PAQ are:

- *Information Input:* Where and how the worker gets the information that is used in performing the job.

- *Mental Processes:* What reasoning, decision-making, planning, and information processing activities are involved in performing the job.

- *Work Output:* What physical activities the worker performs and the tools and devices that are used.

- *Relationships with Other Persons:* The relationships with other people that are required in performing the job.

- *Job Context:* The physical and social contexts in which the job is performed.

- *Other Job Characteristics:* The activities, conditions, or characteristics other than those described above that are relevant to the job.

Typically, the analyst schedules an interview with those employees whose jobs are to be studied. In the interview, the analyst asks the employees the questions in the questionnaire. The analyst uses the information to make judgments in completing the checklist. Once completed, the PAQ code sheet can be computer scanned. Outputs include a brief job description and a point evaluation of job worth.

Professional and Managerial Position Questionnaire (PMPQ)

The PMPQ, which is a companion checklist to the PAQ, is intended for the analysis of managerial and professional jobs, such as engineers, instructors, scientists and staff professionals and technicians. The PMPQ is composed of 98 situations divided into these three categories:

- *Job Functions:* Planning/Scheduling, Processing of Information and Ideas, Exercising Judgment, Communicating, Interpersonal Activities and Relationships, and Technical Activities.

- *Personal Requirements:* Personal Development and Personal Qualities).

- *Other Information.*

The situations within the categories are evaluated using these four criteria:

- *Part-of-the-Job:* the extent to which the situation exists in the job.

- *Complexity:* how difficult or comprehensive the situation is in the job.

- *Impact:* the effect the situation has on the organization.

- *Responsibility:* the amount of responsibility in the job for the situation.

Department of Labor (DOL) Method

The DOL method of job analysis was developed by the U.S. Training and Employment Service. The method includes procedures, forms for recording information, and a system for classifying work in these terms:

- What the worker does in relation to data, people, and things (which is the Worker Function approach also used in the Functional Job Analysis described below).

- The methodologies and techniques employed.

- The machines, tools, equipment, and work aids used.

- The materials, products, subject matter, or services that result.

- The traits required of the worker.[1]

Occupational Information Network (O*NET)

O*NET, the Occupational Information Network, is the nation's new primary source of occupational information.[2] A sampling of the information offered by O*Net includes:

- types of skills that are in demand;

- assistance for workers with proven skills to transfer to new careers; and

- employment levels, occupational outlook, and wages.

O*NET is a comprehensive database system that collects, organizes, describes, and disseminates data on occupational characteristics and worker attributes. O*NET defines the key elements of an occupation, such as the description of the type of work and requirements of the work. Currently, there are over 1,100 occupations listed in O*NET, each with a unique title and code, and each is

---

[1] For more information on the DOL method, see U.S. Department of Labor, *The Revised Handbook for Analyzing Jobs,* 1991.

[2] Information on the O*NET Content Model was obtained from the U.S. Department of Labor, website.

electronically linked through O*NET to the eight major existing job classification systems. Designed, developed, and tested by scientific and technical experts under the leadership of the U.S. Department of Labor, O*NET is a collaborative effort to move beyond the 60-year-old structure of the Dictionary of Occupational Titles (DOT).

The database is based largely on data supplied by occupational analysts from sources such as the Dictionary of Occupational Titles (DOT). To develop information for this database, analysts evaluated and refined existing occupational data, then applied it to the O*NET Content Model.

O*NET products will help employers, workers, educators, and students use O*NET information to make informed decisions about education, training, careers, and work.

The O*NET Content Model. The six domains of the Content Model are:

- Worker Characteristics;
- Worker Requirements;
- Experience Requirements;
- Occupation Requirements;
- Occupation Specific Information; and
- Occupation Characteristics.

By using comprehensive terms to incorporate occupational definitions across all sectors of the economy, the O*NET structure standardizes the way that occupational information is defined and described. The data in O*NET forms a common ground of understanding on which public and private workforce initiatives can be brought together. O*NET is a communication link to help integrate learning, training, and work.

The O*NET system connects to these other occupational systems:

- Apprenticeship Information Management System (AIMS);
- 1990 Census Occupations (CEN);
- Classification of Instructional Programs (CIP);
- Dictionary of Occupational Titles (DOT);
- Guide for Occupational Exploration (GOE);
- Military Occupational Codes (MOC);
- Office of Personnel Management Occupations (OPM); and
- Standard Occupational Classification (SOC).

Functional Job Analysis

Functional job analysis (FJA) is an extension of the work of Sidney Fine, who was instrumental in the development of the Department of Labor method of job analysis. The FJA is not a complete method of job analysis, so it must be used with another approach. Two basic components of FJA are the categorization of work and a methodology of writing task statements.

Categorization of Work. In FJA, work is categorized into *Data, People,* and *Things.* These three components are called *Worker Functions,* hence the term Functional Job Analysis. According to Fine, all tasks, regardless of the type of organization or level within an organization, require workers to perform functions that relate to *Data, People* and *Things.* The hierarchy of these *Worker Functions* is shown in Exhibit 9-4.

Exhibit 9-4
Worker Functions in Functional Job Analysis

Data	People	Things
0 Synthesizing	0 Mentoring	0 Setting-Up
1 Coordinating	1 Negotiating	1 Precision Working
2 Analyzing	2 Instructing	2 Operating-Controlling
3 Compiling	3 Supervising	3 Driving-Operating
4 Computing	4 Diverting	4 Manipulating
5 Copying	5 Persuading	5 Tending
6 Comparing	6 Speaking-Signaling	6 Feeding-Offbearing
	7 Serving	7 Handling
	8 Taking Instructions	
	Helping	

Source: U.S. Department of Labor, *The Revised Handbook for Analyzing Jobs,* 1991.

The highest level of tasks in each function is designated by a O. Thus, Synthesizing is the highest possible level of tasks in conjunction with Data, Mentoring is the highest for People and Setting-Up is the highest level for the Things function.

Writing Task Statements. The FJA task statements in a job description are written in the format of a verb, immediate object of the verb, and an infinitive phrase. An example of three tasks for the job of Contract Assistant are shown in Exhibit 9-5.

Exhibit 9-5
Functional Job Analysis Task Statements

Verb (Worker Function)	Immediate Object (Data, People, or Things)	Infinitive Phrase	
		Infinitive	Object of Infinitive
Analyzes (Data)	agreement	to prepare	legal contract
Talks with (People)	legal representatives	to prepare	written contract
Handles (Things)	legal papers, writing materials	to write	contracts

Job Analysis Audits

Since the information provided through a job analysis is used for many important purposes, it is essential that controls be implemented to verify this information. The major way this is accomplished is through *office audits* and *field audits*.

Office Audit

An *office audit*, which is sometimes referred to as a *desk audit*, is performed by the analyst in his or her office, reviewing information obtained from the job analysis study. The major auditing dimensions of this review process consist of determining if requested information was provided and checking for discrepancies in written statements made by job incumbents, peers and supervisors.

Field Audit

A *field audit* is performed by observing an employee at work and comparing the information that is obtained with that furnished orally and/or in writing by the employee or the supervisor. For example, the employee may have completed a position questionnaire containing information which appears to conflict with information provided on questionnaires completed by other employees. The analyst may do a field audit to resolve the problem.

Sometimes employees request field audits when they believe their supervisors or other decision-makers do not fully understand what tasks they perform or the importance of the tasks. Inevitably this results in job evaluations which the employees feel is unfair. Analysts should honor these requests where possible to address employee perceptions of inequity. An audit can provide the information necessary to either help correct any inequities or to provide assurances that an inequity is not present. Furthermore, employees are more likely to accept the results of a job evaluation study, even if the audit fails to confirm their contentions, because they had the opportunity to demonstrate their job tasks to an analyst.

CHAPTER 10
JOB AND ORGANIZATION STRUCTURE

Chapter Highlights
- Job structuring and strategic management
- Job and organization structuring designs
- Employee scheduling methods
- Accommodating persons with disabilities
- Job descriptions and job specifications

Introduction

An *organization* is a group of people working together in a formal structure towards the accomplishment of goals. Several different methods of structuring organizations are used to more efficiently accomplish those goals. Ultimately, objectives are accomplished through the work of employees whose jobs may be structured in different ways, depending upon such factors as the assignment of tasks and the authority delegated for the accomplishment of them. Consequently, the efficiency of an organization is affected by the design of both the structure and the jobs within the structure. *Organizational charts* depict both the structure of the organization and the jobs within it.

Organization Structuring

Organization structuring is that part of the organizing function of management concerned with the arrangement of people and resources for the accomplishment of goals.

Structure Designs

There are several basic designs that U.S. firms use in structuring their organizations. Among the most frequently used design methods are *functional, divisional or product,* and *geographical.* In addition to these principal methods of organization designs, there are several micro-organizational designs. The main types of these micro designs are *matrix* and *team.* It is helpful to discuss these designs, but it should be noted that most firms use variations of them and even different combinations of several designs.

Functional Design

The *functional* structure is perhaps the oldest approach used in structuring organizations. An *organizational function* is a grouping of work in which the jobs are clearly distinguishable from others. For example, the work performed in manufacturing is clearly different from human resources work. Often, there is a particular body of knowledge which is unique to each function. Very large organizations may have the functional design at the executive level and other designs at lower levels. An example of a functional organization is illustrated in Chart 10-1.

Chart 10-1

Functional Organization Structure

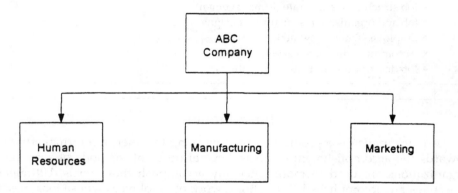

In the functional organization, all employees are assigned to a function, and they report to a manager who ultimately reports to the chief executive officer. Usually, the top manager in each function has the title of vice president. The basic appeal to the functional organization is a clear hierarchical ordering of jobs up to the chief executive. As organizations become much larger, however, problems emerge; for instance, communication becomes more difficult both within and among the various functions.

Divisional/Product Design

Some large organizations use *divisional* or *product* structures. For example, if a firm manufactures chemicals, plastics, and packaging materials, then each of the three product lines would constitute separate divisions. An example of a divisional structure is illustrated in Chart 10-2. If some products constitute a significant portion of a firm's business, each one could be organized in a separate structure. An automobile manufacturer might have separate divisional structures for different makes of automobiles, such as Cadillac and Chevrolet. The reasons for divisional structuring include more streamlined decision-making and the ability to develop marketing plans which appeal to the unique needs of customers.

Chart 10-2

Divisional/Product Organization Structure

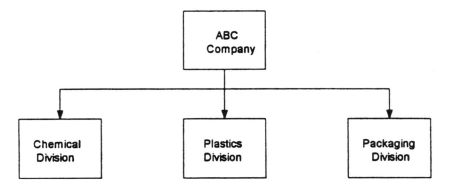

Considerable authority is delegated to the chief executive of each division. The executive team of the division makes fundamental decisions about human resources policy, marketing strategies, and manufacturing methods. For this reason, each division usually has separate departments for the various functions, such as human resources, marketing, and manufacturing.

Geographical Design

As firms grow and expand their market areas, consideration is given to adopting geographical structures, such as the example illustrated in Chart 10-3. The advantage to a geographical structure is closeness in physical proximity to the client base within each territory. The obvious disadvantage is the redundancy in management levels. In addition, sometimes arbitrary decisions are made in drawing the boundaries of each geographical area, thus causing many of the same transportation and other problems that existed in a centralized operation.

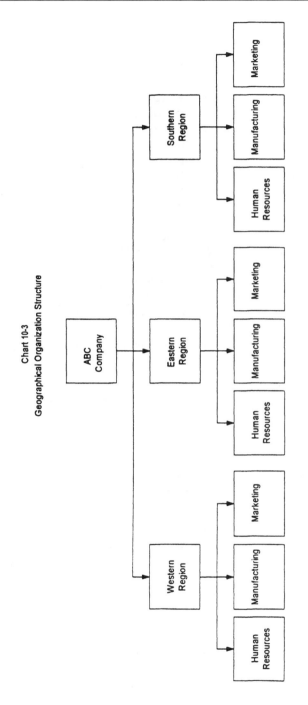

Chart 10-3
Geographical Organization Structure

Micro-Organizational Designs

Within the *functional, divisional,* and *geographical* structures, there are several types of organizational designs that are frequently used. The principal types of these microorganizational designs are the *matrix* and the *team* approaches.

Matrix. The *matrix* structure, which is sometimes also called a *project* structure, typically involves functional specialists who are assigned to either an *ad hoc* or a standing committee or project. Examples of two matrix structures are illustrated in Chart 10-4. Assume the Diversity Coordinating Committee was an *ad hoc* committee organized for the purpose of designing a diversity management program for ABC Company. The three members of the committee are Sue (from Human Resources), Tom (from Manufacturing) and Bill (from Marketing). During their tenure on the committee, all three individuals will report to the person who is directing the committee's work. In addition, they also report to their manager within their respective functions or departments. The other project shown in Chart 10-4 is the New Product Development committee that has a membership composed of Todd (from Human Resources), Gladys (from Manufacturing) and Linda (from Marketing). Sometimes disputes may erupt between the person directing the committee and the committee member's manager about who has priority over the functional specialist's time. In some organizations, highly talented functional specialists may be assigned to several projects at the same time. These situations exacerbate the reporting relationships and the potential for conflict.

Chart 10-4

Matrix Organization Structure

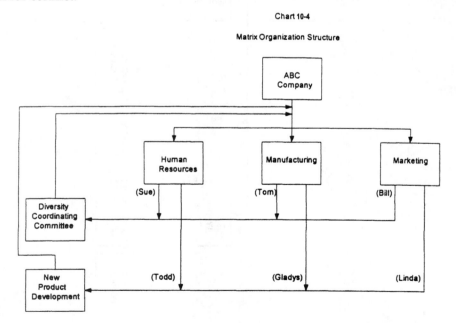

Team. An approach to organizational structuring used more frequently today is the *team* design. Typically, teams are used within a functional design, like the one illustrated in Chart 10-5. However, other designs are also used, such as teams consisting of members from each functional area. In the latter situation, the team resembles a matrix design. Teams may be assigned varying amounts of authority. For example, the team may actually select other team members when replacements are needed. The members may plan their work, assign individuals to various tasks, inspect their work, and even appraise each member's performance. Some teams are even given budgetary responsibilities. Some teams perform all these tasks and more. Other teams perform only those tasks related to work planning, assignment and control.

Chart 10-5

Team Organization Structure

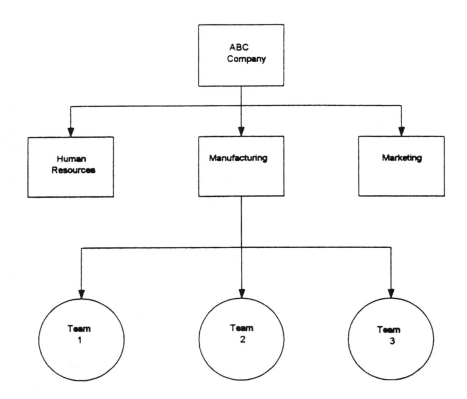

Restructuring Organizations

Mergers, acquisitions, and the need for efficiency improvements, such as reducing costs to remain competitive or better meet customer needs, may cause employers to restructure their firms. Some of the terms for this restructuring include *downsizing* and *rightsizing.* During the period January 1995 to December 1997, 3.6 million U.S. workers were displaced from jobs that they previously had held for a minimum of three years. This is an improvement from 1991-1994, when 4.2 million workers were displaced.[1] The reasons for the displacements included plant or company closings, insufficient work and job or shift abolishment. Typically, restructuring is traumatic to those affected by it. To reduce the resulting financial and psychological stress, many employers provide various incentives and assistance, such as outplacement counseling. There also are legal requirements for certain employers to forewarn or aid workers being terminated or laid-off.

Worker Adjustment and Retraining Notification Act of 1988 (WARNA)

WARNA applies to firms with 100 or more full time employees. Those employers must give employees (or their representative, if there is one) 60 days advance notice in the event of a *mass layoff* or a *plant closure.*

- A *mass layoff* is the loss of employment (which includes layoffs exceeding six months in duration and reductions in the hours of work of more than 50 percent during each month in a six-month period) within a 30-day period at a single site of either: (1) at least 33 percent of the full-time workforce and at least 50 full-time persons, or (2) 500 full-time employees.

- A *plant closure* is the permanent or temporary closure of one employment site or one or more facilities or operating units in a single site during a 30-day period in which 50 or more full-time employees lose their employment.

Employers must notify the state dislocated worker unit under Title III of the *Job Training Partnership Act* (superseded by the Workforce Investment Act of 1998) and the chief elected official of the local political unit in which the layoff or closing will occur. The 60-day notice period may be reduced for any of these conditions:

- The employer was attempting to secure financing, which would have prevented either the layoff or the closing, and the advance notice would have precluded the financing from being obtained.

- Business conditions prevented the employer from giving the advance notice.

- A natural disaster occurred that caused the layoff or closure.

Employers who fail to give the required notice are liable for back pay and benefits for each day of the required notice period and, in certain cases, civil penalties of $500 per day may be assessed.

Older Workers Benefit Protection Act of 1990

Older workers are targeted for job abolishment because they are usually among the most highly paid workers in an organization. Workers who are 40 and over are protected from employment discrimination resulting from such targeting by the Age Discrimination in Employment Act of 1967 (ADEA). Usually employers will provide incentives to such workers, so they will waive their rights to file discrimination charges under the ADEA. The Older Worker Benefit

---

[1] U.S. Department of Labor, *Worker Displacement, 1995-97 Survey* (1999).

Protection Act of 1990 prohibits employees who are 40 and over from waiving their rights under the ADEA, such as the right to file a charge of discrimination as part of an agreement between an employee and the employer, unless these conditions are met:

- The waiver offer is written so the average person to whom the waiver would apply can understand it.
- The waiver offer includes the specific rights employees have under the ADEA.
- The employee does not waive any rights that may exist after the date of the waiver.
- The waiver is in exchange for anything of value beyond which the employee is already entitled.
- The employee is advised in writing to consult with an attorney prior to executing the waiver.
- The employee is given 45 days to consider the waiver and the terms of the agreement if an incentive or other termination program is offered to a class of employees; otherwise, a 21-day consideration period is required.
- The employee is given seven days to revoke the waiver agreement after he or she has signed it.
- If an incentive or other termination program is offered, the employer must inform the employees at the beginning of the 45-day notice period of (a) the class of persons covered by the program, (b) the eligibility terms, (c) the time limits, and (d) the job titles and ages of those persons who are eligible or selected for the program and those who were not eligible or selected.

Consolidated Omnibus Budget Reconciliation Act of 1985 (COBRA)—Continuation of Health Benefits

Employers with 20 or more employees must offer continued health benefit coverage for 18 months for a reduction in hours or termination of employment. A person who becomes disabled within 60 days of being covered under COBRA can receive an additional 11 months (thus having 29 months of total coverage, the same as an employee who was disabled at the time of termination of employment) of COBRA coverage. The cost to the employee is 102 percent of the entire premium (150 percent for months 19 through 29, if disabled). COBRA benefits stop if:

- The employee becomes eligible for another health benefits plan and does not have pre-existing conditions that are excluded under the new plan.
- The employee becomes eligible for Medicare.
- The employer discontinues the health benefits plan.
- The employee does not pay scheduled premiums.

Job Structuring

Job structuring is that part of the organizing function of management concerned with the formal and informal processes of assigning tasks to jobs and delegating authority to accomplish them.

The formalization of task assignments is generally shown in the job description. Formalization means specific tasks are recognized as belonging to particular jobs. The purposes for this formal assignment are to ensure that tasks are properly assigned so goals are accomplished, to prevent duplication of effort, and to avoid confusion about task responsibility. Informal assignment of tasks may be made in a variety of ways. For example, an employee may be temporarily asked to assume the tasks of another job while the incumbent is away. Employees may also be given temporary tasks in *ad hoc* assignments, such as committee projects.

Job structuring can also be done to provide both intrinsic and extrinsic rewards. Employees may receive such rewards from work. Awards that are *extrinsic* include praise, letters of commendation, pay increases, bonuses, and promotions. *Intrinsic* rewards are those received from the job, such as challenge, satisfaction, autonomy, and the opportunity to use one's creative talents. All jobs have extrinsic rewards, but they all may not be intrinsically rewarding to different individuals.

Job Structuring and Organizational Behavior

Organizational behavior is employee responses to planned and unplanned stimuli within a formal structure.

Such responses may be desirable, such as meeting established performance standards, or undesirable, such as absenteeism. The manner in which jobs are structured has a profound impact upon employee motivation and behavior within an organization. For example, all employees do not necessarily want an intrinsically rewarding job. There is a problem, however, if an employee wants intrinsic rewards and does not receive them. Studies have demonstrated that monotonous and unchallenging work can result in employee expressions of job dissatisfaction, absenteeism, product defects, excessive errors, diminished production and high turnover.[2]

There also is evidence that job dissatisfaction can result in time theft and even sabotage. For example, an unhappy computer operator removed the tape labels on a number of computer tape reels, and many hours were required to sort out and identify the correct reels.[3] Employee crime is also linked to employee

---

[2] R.W. Walters, "Job Enrichment: Challenge of the Seventies," *Atlanta Economic Review* (July-August 1975): 32.

[3] E.J. Criscuoli, "What Personnel Administrators Should Know About Computer Crime," *Personel Administrator* 26 (September 1981): 54.

dissatisfaction; one third of the employees responding to a survey of 47 corporations said they stole company property. The study found that stealing was more likely among employees who were dissatisfied with their supervisors, and their organization's ". . . attitude toward the workforce."[4] Disgruntled employees have also committed serious acts of violence, including assault and murder.

There also is some evidence that working conditions can contribute to employee accidents. For example, one employee admitted that a boring and confining job with supervision that he termed "oppressive" caused him to continually be absent and argue with his peers and supervisors. His personnel record contained an abnormally high number of accident reports for non-disabling injuries involving minor scrapes and cuts. He also was a frequent visitor to the organization's health unit. Finally, he resigned and accepted a position as a salesperson in a department store, where he eventually was promoted to manage the housewares department. His work deficiencies and safety problems disappeared in his new sales job.

Job Structuring Strategies

Ergonomics

Ergonomics is the science of designing and arranging equipment and adapting environmental conditions to meet human needs. For example, minor adjustments in chairs and other equipment can reduce physical stress and discomfort. Dangerous work can be made safer through the introduction of equipment guards and negative reinforcers, such as lights and automatic cut-off switches. For example, tennis ball testers were experiencing tendon soreness. An analysis of the problem indicated the squeeze angle was the culprit; changing the work method eliminated the problem.[5] These improvements can result in increases in productivity and efficiency, but, more importantly, they demonstrate to employees that management is concerned about them. Ergonomic health hazard exposure is one of the types of health hazards that can cause occupational illnesses. Ergonomic illnesses, such as cumulative trauma syndrome, comprise a significantly increasing percentage of occupational illnesses. Among the job structuring strategies employers are implementing to prevent these types of illnesses are modifications in equipment, such as computer keyboards, and changes in the manner in which tasks are performed.

Job Rotation

Job rotation is the process of assigning employees to different job assignments to reduce boredom and eliminate fatigue caused by performing repetitive job tasks. Occasionally, employees are permitted to voluntarily exchange assignments or to rotate from one assignment to another. Critics argue the employees get little relief from boredom even when they rotate between a series of boring jobs. However, there are advantages to job rotation, particularly when employees are given the authority to control the rotation. There also is an advantage in

---

[4] N.A. "Survey Finds Pilferage by Workers Widespread," *Richmond Times-Dispatch* (June 11, 1983): A-11.

[5] S.L. Jacobs, "Industrial Hygienists Increase Firms' Output and Efficiency," *The Wall Street Journal* (March 5, 1984): 33.

changing assignments requiring different physical skills and abilities to help reduce fatigue. Sometimes, job rotation is used to prevent cumulative trauma syndrome. Also, delegating authority to employees to make job assignment changes gives them some personal autonomy over their work setting. Another advantage is that employees learn other jobs, which gives management some flexibility in making assignments during peak workloads or when employees are absent due to scheduled vacations or for unscheduled reasons, such as sickness.

Job Enlargement

Job enlargement is the process of broadening a job by including tasks from other jobs, usually at the same pay level. For example, a Personnel Department had four Personnel Assistants who performed specialized personnel tasks. One assistant was exclusively assigned to administer employee benefits, a second handled all employee interviewing, and the two remaining assistants handled the testing program. There was little cross-training of the four assistants so when one was absent, in particular the interviewer or the benefits assistant, their work went undone. To prevent this problem and to expand each employee's authority, all the work was incorporated into one job. The title and pay remained the same but each employee was trained to handle all the tasks.

Initially, the four employees were opposed to the broader job; however, after it was implemented, their skepticism disappeared because the work volume leveled out. Formerly, during certain periods, such as health benefits open season, when employees are permitted to make changes in their benefit plans, the employee benefits assistant worked weekends and nights to stay current. The assistants were similarly overloaded when hiring was initiated to staff a new shift or, conversely, when layoffs were ordered. With the new, generalized job description, the four assistants work together on all tasks; the result is a balanced workload for everyone, and work is completed in a timely fashion.

Job Enrichment

Job enrichment is the process of assigning employees more complex and varied tasks. Since these additional tasks are of a more responsible nature, some experts refer to job enrichment as *vertical loading*. This means the additional tasks (load) are of a higher level (vertical) of responsibility. *Job enlargement*, on the other hand, is called *horizontal loading* because the tasks are at the same level (horizontal) of responsibility as the existing ones. The five main parts of job enrichment are task variety, task identity, task significance, task autonomy and feedback.

- *Task variety* is the number of tasks in a job that involve different skills, abilities, and other qualifications.

- *Task identity* is the extent to which the tasks in a job relate to an entire end product.

- *Task significance* is the impact or significance that the tasks in a job have upon other people, such as peers, customers, and even the general public.

- *Task autonomy* is the freedom employees experience in being permitted to accomplish tasks that either customarily require supervisory approval or are actually performed by a supervisor.

- *Feedback* is input to the employee from a peer, supervisor, or customer concerning the quality or quantity of the employee's performance.

Employee Scheduling Methods

Employee scheduling is the arrangement of work hours and off-days in tours of duty. Employers have responded to employee needs for more creative scheduling by allowing freedom in workday scheduling and/or reducing either the work hours or workdays in a week. Some of the methods being used are flextime, the four-day and 40-hour work week, special weekend schedules, reduction of the 40-hour work week, job sharing, creation of part-time jobs and homework.

Flextime

Flextime is a work scheduling method that permits employees to begin and end their workday within a range of hours. Flextime provides a core period of 4 to 5 required hours each day when all employees must be present, combined with a $1^1/2$ to 2 hour flexible period before and after the core in which employees may vary their work schedule, as long as they work the required number of daily hours. *Core time* is the period of time in which all employees must be at work. *Bandwidth time* is the overall time in the schedule from the beginning to the end of the work day (including core time). The proportion of workers with flexible schedules in 2004 consisted of 27.5 percent of all full-time employees, which is less than the 28.6 percent figure in 2001 when the survey was last conducted. The usage in flexible work schedules was widespread across demographic groups, occupations, and industries.[6]

Flextime increases employee morale because it reduces inter-role conflict, such as those employees with parental responsibilities versus those without, and it increases the intrinsic satisfaction from work due to personal control over one's workday.[7] Other benefits from flextime are reduced tardiness and turnover. While employees have generally been more satisfied with flextime than traditional scheduling methods, some employers have not. The most prevalent employer complaint is the difficulty in coordinating meetings and employees' failure to work either the required number of core hours or the total number of hours per day. A few days' advance notice for meetings should eliminate the first problem, and management oversight should eliminate the latter.

Four-Day and 40-Hour Week

One way to reduce the number of workdays in a work week is to have employees work four 10-hour workdays. Another variation is the $4^1/2$ day work week. In this latter arrangement, employees work four 9-hour days with a half-day on Friday. Employees are generally receptive to this schedule because it

---

[6] Bureau of Labor Statistics. *Workers on flexible and shift schedules in 2004 summary* (July 1, 2005).

[7] G.W. Rainey, Jr. and L. Wolf, "Flextime: Short-Time Benefits; Long-Term . . . ?" *Public Administration Review 41* (January/February 1981), p. 52.

gives them an extra four-hour block of time on Friday, when they can avoid Friday afternoon traffic jams and tend to personal business.[8]

Reducing 40-Hour Work Week

Despite some efforts at reducing hours in the basic work week, the 40-hour work week applies to 83 percent of employees in medium and large firms. In such firms, four percent of employees are required to work 35 hours per week, one percent work between 35 to 37.5 hours, five percent work 37.5 hours, two percent work between 37.5 to 40 hours per week, and 3 percent work over 40 hours per week.[9] In the past several years, the required number of hours of work per week for most employees has increased slightly.

Job Sharing

The typical job-sharing arrangement involves two employees who share a 40-hour-per-week job, with one working the mornings and the other the afternoons. Four percent of the respondents in a sample survey of membership in the Society for Human Resource Management said their firms used job sharing.[10] Job-sharers benefit since it accommodates their parental or other roles. Retirees particularly like job-sharing because they can utilize their occupational skills without devoting their total energies to a full-time job.

Part-Time Employment

Job-sharing is a variation of part-time work, since employees work part-time in sharing a full-time job. Employees and employers both benefit from part-time schedules. Employers benefit, for example, because part-timers help prevent the excessive use of overtime for peak work periods. In addition, many kinds of jobs are not suitable for full-time staffing. For example, some parcel-delivery firms have a relatively brief period in the evening when parcels are centralized, unloaded, processed and loaded for either transportation to another distribution center or delivery in the local area. This work is ideally suited to part-time scheduling. Many jobs in service industries, such as fast-food businesses, are also suited for part-time employment.

Homework

Homework is a scheduling method in which employees with either part-time or full-time jobs perform some or all of their work at home. Approximately 21.4 million people, or 17.8 percent of the labor force, perform some work at home. Of this number, 17 percent are paid for their work, 51 percent are unpaid (these are individuals who took work home with them but were not paid for it), and 30.1 percent are self-employed.[11]

Among the advantages to employees are savings in commuting time, transportation expenses, and purchasing meals. Homeworkers also can forego the

---

[8] D. Stilley, "Half Fridays, Long Weekends Are Recruiting Plus For Catalytic," *Charlotte Observer* (Charlotte, N.C.: date unknown), 5B.

[9] *Employee Benefits in Medium and Large Firms, 1995* (Washington, D.C.: U.S. Government Printing Office, 1998), p. 14.

[10] CCH HUMAN RESOURCES MANAGEMENT, *1987 ASPA/CCH Survey*, June 26, 1987, p. 9.

[11] Bureau of Labor Statistics, *Job-related work at home on primary job: All workers by sex, occupation, industry, and pay status*, May 1997.

substantial investment in clothes for office work. Many people with childcare responsibilities who formerly did not work because of the expenses they incur simply to have a job, particularly for child care, can now work from home. Employers benefit from homework through a reduced need for parking facilities and office space requirements. Homeworkers also do not pose a problem in absenteeism, tardiness, and sick leave abuse. Most employees will readily admit their reluctance to either leave sick children unattended at home or drop them off at a childcare center. These are problems that employers of homeworkers do not have to face.

Homework does have its share of problems, due to union objections, confidentially concerns, distribution and collection of work, and communication difficulties. One firm was compelled to discontinue homework because clients disapproved of employees handling confidential records in their homes.[12] Unions oppose homework because they fear it will cause the reappearance of "sweatshop" conditions in which homeworkers are prodded to produce more work for reduced pay and/or to work longer hours. Unions also realize that homework would be detrimental to their long-term interests. For example, homeworkers would be more difficult and expensive to organize. In addition, even if homeworkers could be organized, unions would have a difficult time communicating with them. In sum, these problems would inevitably cause union membership to decline even further during a period in which union influence and membership rolls are waning.

Shift Scheduling

Among full-time wage and salary workers, 85 percent work regular day schedules. Fifteen percent usually work an alternative shift. By type of shift, 4.7 percent work evening shifts, 3.2 percent work night shifts, 3.1 percent work irregular shifts arranged by employers, and 2.5 percent work rotating shifts. Over half of the workers on these alternative shift arrangements do so because of the "nature of the job." As would be expected, the majority (over 50 percent) of workers on shift work are in service occupations, such as police, fire fighters, and security.[13]

People who work in the late night or early morning hours often feel sleepy and fatigued during their shift. This happens because their body rhythm (also called a *circadian rhythm*) tells them to be asleep at those times. Night workers also must sleep during the day when their circadian rhythm tells them to be awake. Because of this, day sleep is short and feels "light" or unsatisfying. Often, night workers do not sleep enough during the day to combat nighttime fatigue and sleepiness. Also, day workers sometimes must wake up very early to go to work. This might cause them to cut off their sleep, which makes them feel tired during the day.

Shift work takes a toll on most shift workers. For example, a study of employee sleep patterns found that permanent night workers slept an average of

[12] R. Johnson, "Rush to Cottage Computer Work Falters Despite Advent of Inexpensive Technology," *The Wall Street Journal*, (June 29, 1983): 37.

[13] Bureau of Labor Statistics. *Workers on flexible and shift schedules in 2004 summary,* (July 1, 2005).

5.8 hours, and rotating shift workers averaged 6.7 hours.[14] The sleep deprivation of shift workers causes " . . . weight gain, gastrointestinal disorders, higher incidence of injury, moodiness, and marital problems."[15] Work problems of shift workers include deficiencies in attendance, conduct, productivity, and work quality. Other problems are an excessive use of sick leave, mental disorders that include depression and manic depression, and alcohol and drug abuse.

Employers can help prevent the adverse effects of shift work by following the guidelines in Exhibit 10-1.

Exhibit 10-1
Shift Work Guidelines for Employee Orientation
& Management Procedures

Employee Orientation	Management Procedures
1. Use logs to determine sleep needs.	1. Discuss shift work needs with applicants to determine person-job compatibility.
2. Install room-darkening shades and ensure quietness by unplugging telephone.	2. Give employees advance notice in shift changes.
3. Get family commitment to respect sleep needs.	3. If possible, place employees on shift work who need less sleep than average.
4. Follow regular daily sleep-work-leisure cycle.	4. Change rotating schedules forward from morning to afternoon to night.
5. Avoid tobacco, coffee, and alcohol.	5. Provide counseling and/or placement assistance for employees who experience problems adjusting to shift work.

Many new employees have never performed shift work. To prepare for it, new employees should keep a daily log for one month indicating the amount of sleep they get each night *before* beginning shift work. The daily average number of hours for the month should be used as a target for sleep needs *after* employees begin shift work. Most standard window shades do not adequately darken a room for daytime sleeping; special room-darkening shades that are custom-cut to properly fit windows are worth the investment. Other precautions should be taken to prevent disturbances during sleeping hours, such as unplugging telephones and requiring other family members to respect sleeping areas as off-limits. Some shift workers find that window air-conditioners and ceiling fans block outside noise of passing cars and children playing. A top priority for the employee is to obtain a formal commitment from each family member to respect the shift worker's sleep periods. The shift worker should not allow any contingency to interfere with his or her regular sleep cycle. Family members have a tendency to infringe upon the worker's sleep periods; however, they should support and encourage regular sleep and pattern their activities around it. Finally, there is conclusive evidence that tobacco, coffee and alcohol interfere with sleep, so shift workers should avoid them.

---

[14] C. Timberlake, "Then There Is Shift Work . . . " *Richmond Times-Dispatch* (July 2, 1984), p. 1.

[15] N.A., "Researchers Say Perils Exist," *Richmond Times-Dispatch* (July 2, 1984), p. 1.

Initiatives to help shift workers include discussions with management concerning the advantages and problems of shift work. Based upon these discussions, the prospective shift worker and the supervisor should jointly determine if the person can adjust to shift work. Employees should receive as much advance notice as possible when their work schedules change to shift work or when shifts are being changed. Where possible, employees who require less sleep should be used on shift work. For example, one employee had over 20 years seniority, which was enough to secure a day job, but he preferred the night shift because he only required 5 $1/2$ hours sleep per day.

Management can also help the adjustment of employees on rotating shifts by rotating the schedules forward from morning to afternoon to night, so employees can rotate their sleeping periods forward. Finally, management can materially assist employees who have problems with shift work. This assistance includes identifying the problem source and recommending alternatives. Some symptoms of shift adjustment problems include excess tardiness and absence, irritability, and sleepiness. It may be necessary to reassign employees who are unable to adjust to shift work.

Job Structuring for the Disabled

The Americans with Disabilities Act (ADA) of 1990 states that 43 million Americans have one or more physical or mental disabilities. The ADA further states that discrimination in the employment area is a "serious and pervasive problem." A 1986 study found that two-thirds of persons with disabilities who were between the ages of 16 and 65 were unemployed.[16] Two of the major reasons for this high level of unemployment are discrimination and the failure of employers to structure jobs so people with disabilities can be accommodated. The Rehabilitation Act of 1973 and the ADA prohibit discrimination and require employers to make reasonable accommodation for the employment of otherwise qualified persons. See Chapter 12 for a discussion of reasonable accommodation.

Often, accommodating a person with a disability is relatively inexpensive. A survey of 2,000 contractors found that 81 percent of such changes did not cost over $500.[17] Among the kinds of changes that may be made are modifying bathroom facilities and lowering the height of tables by cutting the legs. To accommodate a person with multiple disabilities, a collection agency installed a turntable that rotates files and provided a non-slip desk surface and a telephone microphone that attaches to the employee's eyeglasses. The employee also designed some other simple devices to handle the work better. A side benefit from the job is that the employee has experienced an improvement in his arm mobility, which indicates that some movements required by a job may also be a form of physical therapy.

Jobs and Positions

A *job* is a collection of tasks grouped together in a formal assignment with a unique title and performed by one or more employees. *Positions* are the number

---

[16] Olivera, M., "Hire Smart, Hire the Disabled," *Working Woman* (February 1990).

[17] N.A., "Labor Letter," The Wall Street Journal (November 22, 1983), p. 1.

of personnel who can be hired for each job. For example, if there are 25 Automotive Technicians working in a car dealership there is one job, Automotive Technician, and 25 positions.

Job Descriptions

A *job description* has these basic parts:

- Job title;
- A short summary statement of the job;
- A detailed definition of tasks, typically shown in the chronological sequence of performance or by functional area;
- Identification as to whether the job is exempt or nonexempt from Fair Labor Standards Act requirements for overtime pay;
- Supervisory tasks or responsibilities (if any); and,
- Job specifications.

An illustration of a job description is shown in Exhibit 10-2.

Exhibit 10-2
Banks Department Store Job Description

Job Title: Information Clerk

Job Summary:

Answers inquires and gives directions to customers, authorizes cashing of customers' checks, records and returns lost charge cards, sorts and reviews new credit applications, and requisitions supplies. Work location is at the Information Desk in the Credit Office.

Description of Essential Tasks:

1. *Answers inquiries and gives directions to customers*: Greets customers at Information Desk and ascertains reason for visit to Credit Office. Sends customer to Credit Interviewer to open credit account, to Cashier to pay bills, to Adjustment Department to obtain correction of error in billing. Directs customer to other store departments on request, referring to store directory. (50%) (Importance=#2)

2. *Authorizes cashing of checks*: Authorizes cashing of personal or payroll checks (up to a specified amount) by customers. Requests identification, such as driver's license or charge card, from customers and examines check to verify date, amount, signature, and endorsement. Initials check and sends customer to Cashier. Refers customer presenting Stale Date (over 30 days old) check to bank. (5%) (Importance=#1)

3. *Performs routine clerical tasks in the processing of mailed change of address requests*: Fills out Change of Address form, based on customer's letter, and submits for processing. Files customer's letter. Contacts customer to obtain delivery address if omitted from letter. (10%) (Importance=#6)

4. *Answers telephone calls from customers reporting lost or stolen charge cards and arranges details of cancellation of former card and replacement*: Obtains all

possible details from customer regarding lost or stolen card and requests letter of confirmation. Notifies supervisor immediately to prevent fraudulent use of missing card. Orders replacement card for customer when confirming letter is received. (10%) (Importance=#3)

5. *Records charge cards which have inadvertently been left in sales departments and returns them to customer*: Stamps imprint of card on sheet of paper, using Imprinting Device. Dates sheet and retains for records. Fills out form, posting data such as customer's name and address and date card was returned, and submits to supervisor. Inserts card in envelope, and mails to customer. (5%) (Importance=#4)

6. *Sorts and records new credit applications daily*: Separates regular Charge Account applications from Budget Accounts. Breaks down Charge Account applications into local and out-of-town applications and arranges applications alphabetically within groups. Counts number of applications in each group and records in Daily Record Book. Binds each group of applications with rubber band and transmits to Accounting. (10%) (Importance=#5)

7. *Prepares requisitions and store supplies*: Copies amount of supplies requested by Credit Department personnel onto requisition forms. Submits forms to Purchasing Officer or Supply Room. Receives supplies and places them on shelves in department store storeroom. (10%) (Importance=#7)

Job Specifications:

Ability to follow instructions in dealing with standardized situations such as authorizing the cashing of customer checks.

Ability to perform simple addition in sorting and counting credit applications.

Ability to read and respond to requests for credit applications, and customer letters regarding address changes.

Ability to write requisitions and change of address forms.

Ability to speak with customers personally or via the telephone to answer questions, give information regarding credit cards, and refer customers to the proper office.

Ability to efficiently perform a variety of tasks, such as personally greeting customer, answering the telephone, approving checks, and preparing change of address forms.

Tasks

The *Uniform Guidelines for Employee Selection Procedures* (Guidelines) state that task descriptions should indicate all "important work behaviors" and should state both "their relative importance and their level of difficulty." The importance of each task that is part of the Information Clerk job illustrated in Exhibit 10-2 is shown in the parentheses. For example, authorizing check cashing is the most important task in the job. The Guidelines state that task descriptions should also include observable work behaviors and products and services produced and indicate the relative importance of the behaviors, products, and services so selection procedures can be accurately prepared.

The listing of tasks should indicate which of them are *essential* (these are referred to as *"essential functions"* in the *Regulations to Implement the Equal Employment Provisions of the Americans With Disabilities Act*). Employers are required to use only those tasks that are considered essential in making selection decisions. These are the criteria for employers to use in determining if a task is *essential*:

- The position exists to perform that function. For example, the job of Water Meter Reader exists to read meters so the task, "reads meters," is an essential function.

- If the number of employees who perform a task is limited compared to the volume of work to be done, then the task may be considered an essential function, since there is a limited opportunity to shift the task to other employees.

- Employees who perform the task have specialized qualifications and the task cannot be shifted to other employees who do not have the requisite qualifications, then the task could be considered an essential function.

- The time spent performing the task is a significant portion of the workday, then the task could be an essential function. For example, if persons employed as Water Meter Readers spend 60 percent of their total workday driving a vehicle, such as from one water meter to the next one, then the task, "driving a motor vehicle," would be an essential function.

- If the task is a part of a collective bargaining agreement, there is a greater likelihood that it is an essential function.

- If past and present employees in a particular job had work experience in performing certain tasks in the job, there is a greater likelihood that they are essential functions.

- If a task was not performed and the consequences of it not being performed have a serious impact on the job, it probably is an essential function.

Job Specifications

Job specifications are the qualifications a person must possess to satisfactorily perform the tasks in a job. Sometimes, the term *job specifications* is confused with *applicant qualifications*. The difference is that job specifications state what qualifications a person must possess to perform a job at a satisfactory level, while applicant qualifications are the experience, education and other credentials a person actually possesses.

There are various terms used in defining job specifications. The Guidelines use the terms *knowledge, skills, abilities,* and *training.* Most job specifications also designate *experience* and *education* requirements if specific levels are needed.

Ability

The Guidelines define *ability* as "a present competence to perform an observable behavior or a behavior which results in a observable product."[18] Thus, an ability is the capacity to perform either a required job behavior or a behavior which produces an observable product or service.

Skill

The Guidelines define *skill* as "a present, observable competence to perform a learned psychomotor act."[19] The definitions for ability and skill are very similar. *Ability* means the demonstrated capacity to do something; for example, the *ability* to make independent judgments in claim payments. *Skill,* however, is more than just ability since it involves the application of learning, generally compared to some standard. Some work behaviors may involve both an ability and a skill. For example, a clerk job may involve only incidental typing, so the job specification may state: "Ability to type." However, if specific levels of typing are important for success in the job, the typing requirements may be stated more explicitly as: "Skill in typing 40 correct words per minute."

Regardless of attempts to define *skill* and *ability* differently, it is often difficult to distinguish between them. For example, the Department of Labor method of job analysis defines the aptitude component of worker traits as "abilities required of an individual . . . "[20] However, many of the illustrative examples of various aptitudes demonstrate *skills* rather than *abilities.* For example, an illustration of verbal aptitude requires reading a written job order to accomplish this work element:

> Sets type by hand and machine, and assembles type and cuts gallery [galley], for printing articles, headings, and other printed matter; determining type size, style, and compositional pattern . . . [21]

This work element obviously requires a fair amount of skill. As a rule of thumb, the word *skill* should be used when some standard of performance exists or the work behavior or products of work behavior obviously require the application of learning beyond the routine.

Knowledge

The Guidelines define *knowledge* as "a body of information applied directly to the performance of a function."[22]

---

[18] 43 FR 38295,38314, Uniform Guidelines for Employee Selection Procedures, Section 16.

[19] Ibid.

[20] U.S. Department of Labor, *Handbook,* p. 8.

[21] Ibid.

[22] Ibid.

Education

    Education is conceptual learning, either formal or informal, that does not have a "specific occupational objective" but is needed to satisfactorily perform a job.[23]

Training

    Training is formal or informal instruction in the performance of specific tasks in a job.

Experience

    Experience is the work experience needed to adequately perform a job.

    Training, education, and experience requirements stated in job specifications must be job-related and validated if adverse impact exists. In addition, knowledge, skills and abilities (KSAs) that can be acquired in a brief orientation period shall not be used in the selection procedures for a job.

Competency-Based Job Dimensions[24]

    Competency-based job dimensions is a contemporary approach to job descriptions, including job specifications and assessment methods to measure the existence of those competencies in job applicants. A *competency* is "an observable, measurable pattern of skills, knowledge, abilities, behaviors or other characteristics that an individual needs to perform work roles or occupational functions successfully."[25] Two of the principal categories of competencies are *general competencies* and *technical competencies.*

General Competencies

    General competencies are those required, to some extent, in many types of jobs. The two domains of general competencies are *cognitive* and *noncognitive. Cognitive competencies* involve such areas as reading, writing, and mathematics. For the most part, these competencies comprise the knowledge areas in traditional job descriptions. An example of the types of cognitive competencies that might exist in a *Human Resources Consultant* position are shown in Exhibit 10-3.

    Noncognitive competencies are personal characteristics that are required for the job. Examples of these characteristics, which are required for all levels of Human Resources Consultant positions, as shown in Exhibit 10-3, are Oral Communication, Interpersonal Abilities, and Teamwork. For higher level Human Resources Consultant positions (Journey level and above), noncognitive competencies are required in Creative Thinking.

Technical Competencies

    Technical competencies are those required for a specific job. For example, as shown in Exhibit 10-3, General Human Resources Management competencies are required for all levels of Human Resources Consultant positions, in such activi-

---

[23] Ibid.

[24] For a fuller discussion of the concept and an example of the use of competency-based job dimensions, see United States Office of Personnel Management, *GS-0510, Accountant, Competency-Baes Job Profile,* April 2, 1999.

[25] Ibid.

ties as Staffing, Compensation, and Diversity. For positions that are Journey level and above, Specialized Human Resources Management technical competencies are required, as shown in Exhibit 10-3, in Organization Culture and Programmatic Management and Evaluation. For Senior Expert level positions, technical competency is required in Consulting.

Work Level Descriptors and Assessment Options

The Work Level Descriptors and Assessment Options section in Exhibit 10-3 defines the various levels of Human Resources Consultant jobs and the options that are available to assess applicant qualifications for various required competencies. The bottom section of the Exhibit explains the assessment options. For example, for an entry level Human Resources Management Consultant job, a behavioral interview would be used to assess applicants' cognitive and noncognitive competencies (General Competencies) and an Achievement or Knowledge Test (Option A) could be used to assess General Human Resources Management competencies in such areas as Staffing and Compensation.

Exhibit 10-3

Job Competency Profile

Occupation: *Human Resources Consultant* Positions

GENERAL COMPETENCIES:

Fundamental: (All levels) Reading, Writing, Mathematics, Learning, Memory

Communication/Coordination: (All levels) Oral Communication, Interpersonal Abilities, Teamwork

Business Acumen: (All levels) Decision Making, Reasoning, Problem Solving, Attention to Detail, Math Reasoning, Technology Application, Planning and Organizing, Evaluating, Multi-Task

Personal Awareness: (All levels) Self-Esteem, Integrity/Honesty, Ethics, Self-Management, Stress Tolerance, Flexibility

Innovation/Results: (Journey and above) Creative Thinking, Information Systems Management

Accountability: (All levels) Operational Budgeting; **(Intermediate and above)** Capital Budgeting; **(Journey and above)** Programmatic

TECHNICAL COMPETENCIES

General Human Resources Management: (All levels) Staffing, Compensation, Diversity, Performance Management, Legal Environment, Safety and Health, Human Resources Development, General Human Resource Management Principles and Practices; **(Intermediate and above)** Human Resources Planning Concepts and Principles, Career Planning, Labor and Employee Relations, Wellness ; **(Journey and above)** Strategic Management and Human Resources Planning; Organizational Structuring, Human Resources Cost/Benefit Analysis

Specialized Human Resources Management: (Intermediate and above) Support Organizational Mission, Functional Specialization and Competence; **(Journey and above)** Organizational Culture, Programmatic Management and Evaluation; **(Senior Expert)** Consulting

Competencies in Related Areas: Business Law; Information Technology Concepts, Tools and Systems; Management Principles, Tools and Techniques; Business Practices, Production, Finance and Marketing

WORK LEVEL DESCRIPTORS AND ASSESSMENT OPTIONS:

Entry: Tasks range from basic through somewhat difficult; tasks are performed under immediate to general supervision with some opportunity for the exercise of independent judgment. **Assessment Options:** A, B, C, D, G, H, I.

Intermediate: Tasks range from the moderately difficult to the considerably difficult performed under limited supervision which allows for considerable to wide latitude for the exercise of independent judgment. **Assessment Options:** A, C, D, E, G, H, I.

Journey: Tasks range from the highly difficult to the complex performed under little supervision which allows for the considerable exercise of independent judgment. **Assessment options:** A, C, D, E, G, H, I.

Senior Expert: Tasks are of the most demanding and difficult nature requiring complete independent judgment with little or no supervision. **Assessment options:** B, D, E, F, G, H, I.

COMPETENCY ASSESSMENT OPTIONS: An applicant must demonstrate proficiency in the required competencies. A combination of a structured behavioral interview (to assess General Competencies) and one or more of the following assessment options may be applied to measure Technical Competencies:

A. Assembled Assessment - Achievement or Knowledge Test	E. Professional Certification, e.g., PHR, CEBS, CCP	H. Unassembled Assessment (evaluate work history)
B. Assessment Center	F. Professional Activity, e.g., Publications	I. Solicited Recommendations from former Employers/others
C. Certification Program (In-House)	G. Work Sample Assessment	

D. Education/Experience - Completion of a four-year or Post-baccalaureate degree program in human resources management from an accredited institution, or a combination of education, training and experience that indicates proficiency in both the required general and technical competencies.

CHAPTER 11
HUMAN RESOURCES DIVERSITY

Chapter Highlights
- The changing, diverse nature of the U.S. labor force
- Several approaches to affirmative action
- How employers can achieve EEO goals

Introduction

The job of management involves interacting with diversity in many dimensions, such as meeting the needs of customers with different demands, meeting the needs of stockholders or owners who may have a variety of objectives for their investments, and complying with diverse laws emanating from all levels of government. Management also involves unifying employees, who have a multiplicity of backgrounds and needs, so that the organization can effectively meet its goals. This last dimension, managing human resources diversity, is the focus of this chapter.

For generations, people have come to the U.S. to experience economic and other freedoms. Immigrants came from countries with diverse languages and customs to enjoy the "land of opportunity." The influx into the U.S. continues to this day. Because of its diverse population, the U.S. has been called the "melting pot of the world."

For too many people, both immigrants and U.S. citizens, the reality of economic opportunity fell short of the dream. Too often in the past, the unfulfilled promise was due to both deliberate and unintended employment discrimination, as well as archaic attitudes, habits and practices. Clearly, public policy initiatives were needed, which resulted in fair employment legislation. Title VII of the Civil Rights Act has been providing the legal boundaries for a discrimination-free workplace for over 30 years. The objectives of this and other fair employment laws were the elimination of discrimination through equal employment opportunity and the development of strategies to increase and advance the employment of women and minorities through affirmative action initiatives. By no means have these laws eliminated discrimination, but they have provided—and they continue to provide—employment opportunities for millions of Americans.

Equal Employment Opportunity

Equal employment opportunity (EEO) is the identical treatment of people in all human resource management activities from recruitment to retirement without regard to race, color, age, gender, national origin, religion, veterans' status, or mental or physical disability.

Equal employment opportunity considerations should be an integral part of the fabric in all human resource (HR) systems; unfortunately, they are too often omitted, and discrimination results. Sometimes, the discrimination is simply the result of misguided intent, such as designing retirement plans that discriminate against women retirees who, due to their longer average lifespan, will receive less in monthly benefits than men who have the same length of service and income.[1] Ostensibly, the intent of such plans was to equalize retirement outcomes, since women would receive more total retirement pay than men, if the retirement annuities were the same, by virtue of women living longer. Federal courts have determined, however, that such discriminatory provisions are illegal.

In other cases, the discrimination may be intentional mistreatment, such as deliberately paying women employees less than men for performing the same tasks in a job. However, pay discrimination and benefit plans designed or administered to discriminate on the basis of national origin, race, color, religion, gender, age, disability, veteran's status or alien status are patently unfair and illegal.

Reasons for Equal Employment Opportunity

Effective Management Strategy

Competition is the strength of a free-market economy. Equal employment opportunity (EEO) laws ensure an ample supply of applicants for jobs, and this competition results in hiring employees who most capably perform job duties.

People have strong *conative* needs in a free-market society, where competition is heavily stressed. *Conation* is the need to try, and this basic human need is repressed when individuals are treated unfairly. Where EEO is not practiced, people tend to feel hopeless. This hopelessness leads to frustration, which can cause apathy or aggression, both of which are destructive to society and the organizations within it.

Legally Required

Fair employment practices are required by local, state, and federal laws, regulations and executive orders. There are severe penalties for violations of these legal requirements. Each year, enforcement agencies handle thousands of discrimination charges, in which the victims receive substantial awards totaling millions of dollars. In addition, other forms of relief, such as promotions and job assignments that were previously denied, may be available to those who have been treated unfairly.

Organizational Goals

Private sector organizations formulate long-term goals that affect stockholder interests, customer needs, employee opportunity and commitment to organizational success and social responsibility. As shown in Exhibit 11-1, practicing EEO supports organizational goals in all four areas.

---

[1] See *Arizona Governing Committee v. Norris,* 32 FEP Cases 233 (1983).

Exhibit 11-1
Effects of Practicing Equal Employment Opportunity on Organizational Goals

	Stockholders	Customers	Employees	Community Commitment
Organizational Goals	Insure short- and long-term shareholder wealth	Provide desired products and services at competitive prices	Fairly select, develop, and reward employees	Act socially responsible and be a good citizen
Effects on Organizational Goals of Implementing EEO Practices	Competitive present and future return on investment	Better products and services with desired features at lower prices	Competent, motivated and committed to organizational success	Self-governing, law-abiding and less government intervention

Shareholders

The purpose of a private-sector organization is to provide shareholders with short- and long-term wealth. Implementing equal employment opportunity in HR actions helps ensure that shareholders receive a return on their investment.

Customers

Organizations exist to satisfy the needs of customers. An expanding customer base is essential for the future viability of any profit-seeking venture. Incorporating equal employment opportunity into HR practices results in better products and services with desired features at lower prices. These characteristics are important to all customers.

Employees

Organizational goal statements articulate commitment to select, develop, and reward employees fairly. Using valid and reliable employee-selection methods results in a better qualified workforce. Practicing equal employment opportunity in HR policies and procedures helps achieve a workforce that is competent, motivated and committed to organizational success, resulting in better products and services at less cost.

Community Commitment

Employers recognize the importance of supporting the greater community in which they do business, since the maintenance of social orderliness, cohesion and stability are essential for business to be conducted efficiently. Conversely, lawlessness, chaos, and societal unpredictability inhibit business growth. Employers recognize the importance of acting in a socially responsible manner and being good corporate citizens. Along with such areas as environmental pollution, employers recognize the importance of voluntarily complying with nondiscrimination laws, including equal employment opportunity laws that prohibit discrimination on the basis of race, color, religion, gender, national origin, disability, age and veteran's status. The effect of commitment to voluntary compliance with equal employment opportunity laws is a business community that is self-governing and law-abiding. The end result of this self-direction is less government intervention.

Affirmative Action

Affirmative action refers to the planning and implementing of strategies to increase and advance the employment of women and minorities to overcome the effects of past or present practices, policies, or other barriers to equal employment opportunity.

Affirmative action (AA) means different things to different people. Some people equate the term with preferential or even mandatory hiring of people based upon classifications, such as their race, age, or gender. Some people also believe AA means hiring individuals in these classes, even if they are not qualified for the job. However, AA does not mean either preferential treatment or the hiring of unqualified persons. For example, the AA provisions of the Vietnam Era Veteran's Readjustment Assistance Act state that employers are not required to hire " . . . any particular job applicant or from any particular group of applicants . . . "

Affirmative Action Terms

Affirmative action efforts may include *quotas, goals,* and *good faith efforts.* Some people associate the term affirmative action solely with quotas. *Quotas* are numbers of employees or proportions of jobs that are arbitrarily assigned to groups of individuals, based on considerations such as their race or gender. In most cases, quotas are illegal, since they violate Title VII of the Civil Rights Act. In some situations, courts have found quotas to be legal. For example, a voluntary quota system established between a union and an employer was found to be legal.[2] Typically, where quotas existed, they were used to correct situations where gross employment discrimination existed.

Goals are desired results that an employer hopes to accomplish through planned actions. Federal regulations state that where protected groups, such as racial minorities, are underrepresented in specific job categories, employers must set goals and timetables to increase the employment of persons in protected groups. Furthermore, the regulations require employers to make a "good faith effort" to achieve the AA goals. Typically, good faith efforts to recruit more individuals from underrepresented groups result in a larger supply of qualified applicants who will compete with all other applicants. This larger supply of applicants will eventually increase the selection of persons from underrepresented groups.

There is ample evidence of the need for AA, such as the underrepresentation of women and minorities in the upper levels of management. The information in Exhibit 11-2 shows the relative absence of women and minorities in top manage-

---

[2] *United Steelworkers of America v. Weber* (U.S. Sup. Ct. 1979).

ment positions in the corporate headquarters of Fortune 1000 companies over a three-year period. Preventing this underutilization of women and minorities is the goal of the *Frances Perkins-Elizabeth Hanford Dole National Award for Diversity and Excellence in American Executive Management,* which is awarded annually to an organization that has demonstrated leadership in developing and promoting women and minorities.[3]

There is some evidence that the lack of minorities and woman on boards of directors is improving. A 1998 study of corporate boards found that 37 percent of the boards had directors that were African-American, an increase from the 31 percent of boards that had African-Americans members in 1991.[4]

Exhibit 11-2
Women and Minorities in Corporate Headquarters Positions in Fortune 1000 Companies

Type positions	No. of employees	% Female	% Minorities
All positions	147,179	37.2	15.5
All levels of management	31,184	16.9	6.0
Executive levels of management	4,491	6.6	2.6

Source: U.S. Department of Labor, *A Report on the Glass Ceiling Initative,* 1991.

Another indication of the need for AA is the disparity in pay of women who are employed in positions that are comparable to those of men. Exhibit 11-3 shows that, within five occupational groups, women's pay, as a percentage of men's, ranges from 70 percent to 79 percent.

Exhibit 11-3
Median Weekly Earnings of Full-Time Workers by Occupation and Gender, 2004

Occupation	Number employed (000s)		Median weekly earnings		Women's earnings as % of mens
	Men	Women	Men	Women	
Management & professional specialty	17,981	18,168	$1,098	$780	.71%
Sales & office	9,410	15,540	669	512	.77
Service	6,989	6,773	476	374	.79
Production, transportation & material moving	11,786	3,296	578	406	.70
Natural resources, construction & maintenance	10,835	445	626	453	.72

[3] This award was authorized by the Civil Rights Act of 1991.

[4] *The Wall Street Journal,* "Work Week: African-Americans expand presence on corporate boards" (April 14, 1998), p. 1.

Source: Bureau of Labor Statistics, 2006.

Clearly, there is much more that needs to be done to more effectively manage a diverse U.S. workforce, both in the increased utilization of women and minorities in higher-level positions and in pay equity between the sexes. Achieving objectives in both areas will require increased emphasis on EEO and AA.

Reverse Discrimination

In the main, placement actions, such as promotions, based on a person's race or gender violate Title VII.

One contradiction regarding this issue stems from court decisions that appeared to be in conflict but actually were based on different circumstances. In a 1989 decision, a Court of Appeals found that a procedure establishing a special register of eligibility for a group of 240 African-American employees who were specially targeted for promotion was legal, since it provided remedial relief. This procedure did not preclude the promotion of whites, who were on a separate register, because they were alternately promoted with the black employees.[5] In two other cases, employment decisions that were based on sex were found to be legal. In one of the cases, a minority candidate was selected for a job over a white applicant with more seniority, but the U.S. Supreme Court found it to be legal, since it was part of a union-management agreement.[6] In the other case, the U.S. Supreme Court found that promoting a woman on the basis of her gender was legal because it was part of a case-by-case approach, was not quota-based, did not bar consideration of male applicants, and was intended to rectify a situation in which 238 positions were held by men and none by women.[7]

In an apparently contradictory decision, the U.S. Supreme Court permitted a group of fire fighters to challenge a court-ordered quota plan because they were not a party to the original suit.[8] In another case, the U.S. Supreme Court held that the city of Richmond's practice of requiring prime contractors to award city construction subcontracts of at least 30 percent of the dollar amount of each contract to one or more "Minority Busines Enterprises" to be illegal. The Court stated that, since the plan was not justified by a compelling city interest and the city had no prior history of discrimination in awarding contracts, the 30-percent set-aside was not narrowly tailored to accomplish a remedial purpose.[9]

The salient facts that may have a bearing on whether a quota plan is considered nondiscriminatory are these:

- The plan is temporary;
- The rights of whites were not trammeled; and
- The plan is not implemented to establish and maintain a racial balance.

[5] *Howard v. McLucas* (CA-11 1989).
[6] *Kaiser Aluminum v. Weber* (1979).
[7] See *Johnson v. Transportation Agency, Santa Clara County* (1987) in Appendix 1.
[8] *Martin v. Wilks; Personnel Board of Jefferson County, Alabama v. Wilks;* and *Arrington v. Wilks* (U.S. Sup. Ct. 1989).
[9] See *City of Richmond v. J.A. Croson Co.* (1989) in Appendix 1.

The actual effects of reverse discrimination are minimal. The U.S. Department of Labor conducted a study of approximately 3,000 discrimination cases adjudicated in federal courts between 1990 and 1994. Reverse discrimination was involved in 100 of the cases, and only six involved situations in which minorities and females were unfairly favored over whites or males.[10]

Legal Requirements

Affirmative action is required by several federal laws and one executive order. Following is a discussion of the major provisions of these laws.

The National Apprenticeship Act of 1937. This law prohibits discrimination based on national origin, race, color, religion, and gender in recruiting, selecting, and training apprentices. Written AA plans, including goals and timetables, are required if the percentage of individuals in the labor market area is underrepresented in the firm's apprenticeship programs. Construction contractors are exempt from the written AA plan requirement. However, the OFCCP has established affirmative action plans for such contractors including a goal of 6.9 percent for the employment of females.

Covered under the law is any employer or organization employing or sponsoring an apprentice registered by the U.S. Department of Labor and evidenced by a Certificate of Registration as meeting the standards of the Department for apprenticeship. A sponsor is any person or organization operating an apprenticeship program, irrespective of whether such person or organization is an employer. The law does not include state apprenticeship programs.

Executive Order 11246 of 1965. Each non-construction contractor/subcontractor with contracts exceeding $10,000 may not discriminate in the employment of persons under the contract on the basis of national origin, race, color, religion or gender. These contractors/subcontractors must also develop a written Affirmative Action Program (AAP) for each of its establishments, within 120 days from the start of the Federal contract, if one of these conditions is met:

- Has a Federal contract or subcontract of $50,000 or more;
- Has government bills of lading which in any 12-month period totals $50,000 or more;
- Serves as a depository of Federal funds in any amount; or
- Is a financial institution that is an issuing and paying agent for U.S. savings bonds and savings notes.

An Employment Information Report (EEO-1), also known as Standard Form 100, that provides a demographic breakdown of the employer's work force by race and gender, must be filed annually with the EEO-1 Joint Reporting Committee by Federal contractors who meet these conditions:

- Have 50 or more employees, and
- Are prime contractors or first-tier subcontractors, and

---

[10] American Management Association, *HRfocus* (June 1995), p. 8.

- Have a contract, subcontract, or purchase order amounting to $50,000 or more; or serve as a depository of federal funds in any amount, or is a financial institution which is an issuing and paying agent for U.S. Savings Bonds and

Rehabilitation Act of 1973. A contractor who has a contract with the federal government for the purchase, sale or use of personal property or providing non-personal services (including a fund depository) of more than $10,000, cannot discriminate against persons with disabilities and must make reasonable accom-modation for their employment unless it would cause undue hardship. Such employers must also have a written AAP if one of these conditions is met:

- Has 50 or more employees and a federal contract of $50,000 or more;

- Serves as a depository for federal funds of $50,000 or more; or,

- Has an agreement valued at $50,000 or more to be an issuing and paying agent for savings bonds and notes.

Employers must also annually file EEO-1 if they meet the conditions out-lined under Executive Order 11246.

Vietnam Era Veteran's Readjustment Act of 1974. This law prohibits contractors or subcontractors, with contracts of $100,000 or more for the purchase, sale or use of personal property or non-personal services or serves as a fund depository or an issuing and paying agent for savings bonds and notes (for $100,000 or more), from discriminating in the employment of veterans who served on active duty in the U.S. military ground, naval, or air service in one of the following groups:

- *Special disabled veteran.* A "special disabled veteran" is a veteran (1) who was discharged or released from active duty because of a service-con-nected disability, or (2) is entitled to compensation (or who but for the receipt of military retired pay would be entitled to compensation) for certain disabilities under laws administered by the Department of Veter-ans Affairs (i.e., disabilities rated at 30 percent or more, or at 10 or 20 percent if the veteran has been determined to have a serious employment handicap).

- *Disabled veteran.* A "disabled veteran" is a veteran who (1) is entitled to disability compensation (or who but for the receipt of military retired pay would be entitled to disability compensation) under laws administered by the Secretary of Veterans Affairs, or (2) was discharged or released from active duty because of a service-connected disability.

- *Recently separated veteran.* A "recently separated veteran" is any veteran who served on active duty during the three-year period beginning on the date of such veteran's discharge or release from active duty.

- *Other protected veteran.* An "other protected veteran" is any other veteran who served during a war or in a campaign or expedition for which a campaign badge has been authorized, other than a special disabled vet-eran, veteran of the Vietnam era, or recently separated veteran.

- *Armed Forces service medal veteran.* An "Armed Forces service medal veteran" is a veteran who participated in a U.S. military operation for which an Armed Forces service medal was awarded pursuant to Executive Order 12985.

This law also requires covered contractors and subcontractors to take affirmative steps to employ qualified veterans in the above groups and to list their job openings with an appropriate employment service delivery system, including one-stop career centers.

Contractors must file Federal Contractor Veterans' Employment Report (VETS-100) that contains data on the number of veteran employees in the contractor's workforce by job category, hiring location, the number of new hires (veterans and non-veterans), and the maximum and minimum number of employees.

Contractors with 50 or more employees and a contract of $100,000 or more to serve as a depository of federal funds or as an issuing and paying agent for savings bonds and notes, must have a written AAP.

Americans with Disabilities Act of 1990. The Americans with Disabilities Act (ADA) applies to employers engaged in an industry affecting commerce who have 15 or more employees for each working day for at least 20 calendar weeks in the current or preceding calendar year. This law prohibits discrimination against a person with a disability and requires employers to exercise AA in making reasonable accommodation for the employment of an otherwise qualified person with a disability, unless it can be shown that it would pose an undue hardship. See Chapter 12 for a discussion of reasonable accommodation.

The OFCCP has coordinating authority under Title I of the ADA and the EEOC has primary authority for enforcing the ADA. Most Government contractors are covered by both the Rehabilitation Act and the ADA.

Reasons for Affirmative Action

Some of the major reasons for AA are:

- Enlightened employers recognize the detrimental effects of past discrimination and realize that responsible action is necessary. Many of the AA policies initiated by employers are due to their voluntary efforts. For example, if women have never been employed in particular jobs, an employer may realize that affirmative action is necessary to encourage women to apply for future vacancies.

- Court-mandated affirmative action may result from decrees, stemming from EEO discrimination cases. The action taken depends upon the circumstances in each particular case. In one case involving discrimination against women, the consent decree stipulated that the firm was required to take the following actions:

  - Establish five-year hiring and accession goals for women in clerical and professional jobs at various pay grades;

  - Develop a procedure for posting job vacancies in designated clerical and professional jobs;

- Implement an employee training program for advanced clerical jobs;

- Implement a training program for supervisors and managers, focusing on their responsibilities to both EEO principles and the actions they are required to fulfill under the consent decree; and,

- Establish a counseling program directed at motivating women employees to apply for professional job vacancies.[11]

- As noted previously, several laws and one executive order require employers to exercise AA in the employment of individuals from designated groups.

Equal Employment Opportunity and Affirmative Action

Achieving equal employment opportunity and affirmative action goals can be facilitated through decisive management.

Executive Commitment and Accountability

Executive commitment and accountability are the driving forces behind an organization's success in making EEO and AA a reality.

Environmental Scanning

The principal forces in the external environment that should be considered in dealing with EEO are applicable laws, regulations, and guidelines. Additional information about these requirements may be obtained from the Equal Employment Opportunity Commission (EEOC), state EEOC-affiliated agencies, consultants, and trade associations. An environmental scan should also include the demographics in the local labor force, including the racial composition and number of females seeking employment, the educational attainment of individuals in these groups, and any barriers to the recruitment and employment of individuals from the groups.

Strategic Action Plans

Strategic planning activities should incorporate equal employment opportunity in every dimension of the organization, including recruitment, training, performance appraisals, and compensation programs. EEO achievements should also be considered in evaluating the performance of managers. The following is an example of a plan that incorporates a goal, a policy, and an objective addressing EEO:

- *Goal*: ABC Company will provide employment opportunities fairly and without regard to national origin, race, color, religion, gender, disability, veteran's status, sexual orientation, and family status.

- *Policy*: ABC Company will identify those jobs in which minorities and women are underrepresented and establish action plans to increase their employment.

---

[11] *EEOC v. United States Fidelity & Guaranty Company. The State* (Columbia, SC: May 15, 1982).

- *Procedure*: Every college with large populations of minorities and women will be identified, and annual visits will be conducted in order to recruit qualified applicants for open positions with ABC Company.

Leadership

Employers should encourage the attainment of EEO by all managers, supervisors, and other employees. Business practices and reward systems should be structured to reinforce the organization's goals, policies, and practices. A key component is to link pay and performance in achieving equal employment. Employees who positively interact with and respect their peers should be rewarded. Conversely, those individuals whose behavior is discriminatory will be subject to disciplinary action or discharge.

Enter: Workplace Diversity

Over time, the U.S. labor force has become more diverse. This trend is projected to continue to the year 2014, as shown in Exhibit 11-4. The challenge to HRM is the effective utilization of this changing workforce. Men will outnumber women in the labor force by 2015 but the rate of increase, from 2005 to 2014, will be greater for women than men in all racial categories. Of all the groups, the largest rate of increase will be for Hispanic women.

Exhibit 11-4
Actual and Projected Labor Force, 2005-2014

Labor Force Group, 16 & over	2005 (000's)	2014 (000's)	% change
Total	149,132	162,100	8.7
Men	80,040	86,194	7.7
Women	69,092	75,906	9.9
White men	66,606	70,335	5.6
White women	55,654	59,601	7.1
Black men	8,052	9,075	12.7
Black women	8,801	10,359	17.7
Asian men	3,500	4,411	26.0
Asian women	2,975	3,893	30.8
Hispanic men	11,923	14,921	25.2
Hispanic women	7,992	10,839	35.6

Source: U.S. Department of Labor

The changing nature of the U.S. labor force will ultimately affect businesses. In addition, fair employment practices and the implementation of affirmative action planning will result in more diverse workplaces. As these changes occur, employers will need to focus on the effective utilization of the talents of such a workplace through *diversity management.*

Diversity management is the process of motivating employees who have diverse backgrounds to increase their interpersonal communication and cooperation to unify their efforts to optimize the organization's goals.

The objective of diversity management is the creation of a workplace in which people are unfettered by discrimination, lack of opportunity, and outmoded thinking.

Optimizing Diversity Management

Executive Commitment

As with equal employment opportunity and affirmative action, diversity management requires the support of top management leadership and direction.

Designate Responsible Person

Early on in the creation of any effort to unify a diverse workplace, the company must designate someone to be responsible for the program. In small organizations, these duties could be added to an existing job. In medium-sized firms with 100 or more employees, the logical person to whom to delegate this work is the HR Director. Very large organizations have special committees or a matrix-type of structure devoted to diversity. For example, Westvaco has a Workplace Diversity Forum, devoted to focusing diversity efforts on the firm's objectives. The firm's Manager of Organizational Effectiveness is the Chair of the Forum.[12] Some organizations have full-time positions to lead diversity management initiatives. For example, Smith Barney has a diversity program led by Johnnetta Cole, whose past employment history includes serving as the president of Atlanta's Spelman College.[13]

Adapt Organizational Culture

An organization's culture consists of the *values, beliefs, customs, rules* and *management philosophies* that exist in the organization. As needed, one or more of these components may have to be changed to make the organization's climate receptive to the goal of diversity management, that is, expediting communication and cooperation among employees so the organization can accomplish its goals.

For example, if the custom has been to consider older workers as "excess baggage" or "has-beens," it should not be surprising that the level of communication and cooperation among younger and older workers is minimal. Does the organization "value" the contributions of all employees, regardless of race, gender, or other characteristic? Do employees freely associate with other employees, including those who are different from them, such as those of a different national origin? Answers are needed to these and similar questions in order to measure the tenor of the culture and identify what changes are needed.

Use Focus Groups

Using employee focus groups of employees can help in defining the prevailing attitudes about the organization's culture. The groups can be used to address specific questions such as:

- What is the prevailing attitude toward the employment of women?

- What is the prevailing attitude toward employees with disabilities?

- What changes, if any, are needed to improve the attitudes of employees toward those and other groups that are different from each other?

- What is the level of communication among employees of different races, and what changes should be considered to improve such communication?

The focus group members can also be asked to respond to a questionnaire, designed to measure various components of the organization's culture. Additional focus group sessions can be scheduled to provide feedback on the results of the survey. Also, creativity techniques, such as brainstorming or the nominal group method, can be used to obtain ideas about resolutions to problems identified by the survey.

---

[12] *Richmond HRMA,* "Diversity and organizational effectiveness" (May 1998).

[13] *Richmond Times-Dispatch,* "Markets take holiday to honor King" (January 20, 1998), B-6.

Stress Economic Value

In today's business climate, employers are concerned about the cost/benefits of alternatives in which economic resources are being expended. Including diversity management in business operations is most desirable, since it improves organizational effectiveness. However, cost avoidances, such as expensive settlements of discrimination complaints, that can realistically be achieved through implementing diversity management, are powerful incentives motivating decision-makers to implement diversity programs. To support such diversity management proposals, research can be conducted into past discrimination charges filed against the organization. Also, the experiences of others in the industry or locality should be explored.

Develop and Conduct Training

The information acquired from the focus groups should be used to develop training programs to meet the unique needs of the organization. Training should begin with a short introduction by a member of top management, explaining the importance of diversity management to the attainment of the organization's goals. The results of the focus groups should be presented and discussed. Any misconceptions about the organization's culture should be examined and corrected. It is particularly important to stress that employees will be expected to conform to a culture that emphasizes communication, cooperation, and teamwork among all employees.

Training should also include a behavioral component to give employees experience in understanding people who may have different backgrounds and needs. Among the training methods that could be considered for this portion of the program are role playing and behavioral modeling. In the *role-playing sessions*, the participants can assume either assigned or unassigned roles. In *assigned* roles, the person is given a script and plays the role accordingly. In an *unassigned* role, the participant is allowed to assume whatever role he or she desires. Generally, unassigned roles better illustrate the way a person would handle an actual situation at work because he or she is not constrained by a script and, therefore, is not "acting" in a role. A role-playing situation involving workplace harassment could be set up in which one employee is assigned the role of the harasser and another plays the role of the employee being harassed.

In *behavioral modeling* training, trainees attempt to copy or reproduce the behavior of, or the procedures used by, an expert who "models" or demonstrates the proper way of performing some action. The demonstration may be in person, but usually it is conducted through an audiovisual medium, such as a film or videotape.

One variation of behavioral modeling involves the use of an expert who demonstrates how a particular workplace diversity issue might be handled. The trainees observe the demonstration, showing employees with different ethnic backgrounds establishing a communication dialogue. During the presentation, the trainees make a list of the behaviors exhibited by the expert that they believe were most conducive to the desired outcome. Next, the scene is replayed, and the instructor stops the session at points at which an important behavior is exhibited.

The trainees check and discuss their lists of behaviors and make any necessary changes to their lists. The trainees use their individual lists to prepare for role-playing sessions.

Both role playing and behavioral modeling give trainees active practice in applying what they have learned. Also, immediate reinforcement is available through self-assessment, peer assessment and instructor evaluation. These training methods give trainees practical ideas of ways to address diversity issues and experience in applying them.

Training programs can have a significant impact upon trainees' knowledge and understanding about diversity. The City of San Diego instituted a serious commitment to diversity that included a training component. After the training program was conducted, the participants " . . . gave high ratings to their knowledge of different cultures, understanding diversity issues and their ability to address such issues, based on their training."[14]

Ongoing Efforts

Since the concept and thrust of diversity management require significant change in employee behavior, it must become a daily issue in organizational life. This requires continuous efforts to encourage employee interpersonal communication. Committees are good vehicles for stimulating communication. Some examples are quality circles, employee suggestion committees, safety and health committees, good housekeeping committees, and employee transportation or parking committees. As necessary, short training sessions can be offered on running effective committee meetings, including eliciting employee communication. Membership on the committees should be periodically rotated to allow many employees the opportunity to participate. Other means of fostering interpersonal communication and cooperation are employee guest editorials in the firm's newsletter and company-sponsored sports or other leisure activities. In all of these ongoing efforts, the focus should be on encouraging employees to engage in dialogues with each other and to learn how to work together.

Initiatives should also be established that will encourage employees to reflect on diversity issues, such as recognizing special days, including Martin Luther King Jr. Day, or days set aside to recognize pioneers in women's issues. Other topics that may be emphasized through company newsletters, employee essay contests, posters, and free soft drinks, are the Special Olympics, or events featuring persons with disabilities or leading figures from minority groups.

Evaluate Efforts

Periodic evaluations should be conducted to gauge progress, including short questionnaires to assess employee opinions about the level of communication and cooperation. Trends determined from the responses may be used to determine the level of progress and any changes that may be needed. Quarterly reports may be prepared, showing the results achieved by various methods used

---

[14] American Association of Retired Persons, *How to Develop a Diversity Commitment* (Washington, DC, 1994).

to increase employee communication and cooperation. For example, attendance at various company-sponsored events may be tracked. Committee activities, such as safety and health committees, may also be tracked to determine how effective the committees are in accomplishing objectives, such as in accident reductions.

CHAPTER 12

PREVENTING EMPLOYMENT DISCRIMINATION

Chapter Highlights
- Learn what constitutes employment discrimination
- Introduce the major laws, executive orders and regulations affecting discrimination
- Understand the actions necessary to prevent discrimination

Introduction

Each year, the U.S. Equal Employment Opportunity Commission (EEOC), along with the state agencies responsible for ensuring that employers comply with state equal employment opportunity laws, receives thousands of charges from individuals, alleging discrimination in employment. The numbers of persons filing charges annually is increasing. In 1991, less than 64,000 persons filed charges. In 2007, the EEOC received 82,792 charges.

In fiscal year 2007, the EEOC obtained $290.6 million in monetary benefits for charging parties through settlement and conciliation. In the same year, the EEOC obtained $54.8 million in monetary benefits for discrimination victims through litigation. In addition to paying these monetary benefits, employers spend countless hours in responding to charges of discrimination and millions of dollars in legal fees and expenses in defending themselves in investigations and suits.

The EEOC's work in 2006 resulted in these awards and settlements:

- A court found that an employer who fabricates products used in the petrochemical and power industries failed to pay the minimum wages and overtime premiums required under the FLSA to a group of employees from India. The employees were also subjected to a hostile work environment and disparate terms and conditions of employment because of their race and national origin, that included numerous offensive comments about their ancestry, ethnic background, culture, and country. The court awarded a variety of damages under all claims, and the total recovery was approximately $650,000.

- Three stores in a restaurant chain engaged in sex and race discrimination retaliation that included subjecting female and black employees to a hostile work environment, and required black employees to wait on customers that white employees refused to serve and to work in the smoking section. Management failed to take effective corrective action to stop the harassment and other discrimination, and the company took no action in response to complaints reported to the company's complaint hotline. Under a 2-year consent decree, the defendants will pay $2 million into a settlement fund. They were also required to provide annual training to managers on discrimination, including harassment and retaliation issues, and to all employees on workplace harassment.

- A temporary employment agency and two of its clients engaged in various violations of Title VII, the Americans with Disabilities Act, and the Age Discrimination in Employment Act. These were among the alleged violations: (1) failing to refer applicants for temporary employment based on their race, gender, pregnancy, national origin, age, disability, and responses to pre-employment medical inquiries; (2) violating the EEOC's recordkeeping regulations by intentionally and systematically destroying documentary evidence during the EEOC's investigation; and, (3) requiring applicants for temporary employment to complete a pre-employment questionnaire that elicited information regarding potential disability. In addition, according to the suit, one client asked the temporary agency not to refer female applicants and another client asked the agency not to refer black or female applicants. Through separate consent decrees with the defendants, the case was settled for a total of $580,000 in monetary relief to be administrated through a claims fund. In addition, the employer agreed to comply with a number of remedial and affirmative actions.

- A union discouraged individuals age 40 and above from applying a apprenticeship program required for membership in the union. One of the eligibility criteria for admission was being "between the ages of 18 through 25." Application requests from a number of individuals in the protected age group were marked "too old." According to the suit, after the union dropped the age limit from the application form, it continued to exclude applicants in the protected age group. The lawsuit was resolved through a 5-year consent decree in which the union agreed to pay the aggrieved individuals $625,000 for lost wages. Remedial action in the decree included enjoining the union from imposing any upper age limit in recruiting applicants or admitting applicants to the apprenticeship program. The union was also enjoined from discriminating based on age (40 or older) against individuals who inquire about the program, apply for the program, or are enrolled in the program.

- A manufacturer of precision metal-formed products and assemblies refused to hire women and African Americans into laborer and machine operator positions at its plant because of their sex and race, and failed to retain employment applications. According to the suit, the manufacturer rejected qualified female applicants in favor of lesser qualified male applicants. Evidence showed that women were employed only as clericals and blacks were not employed at all. External measures of availability showed statistically significant disparities between defendant's employment of women and blacks in laborer and operative positions and their representation in the relevant labor market. In a consent decree, the employer agreed to pay $940,000 to compensate at least 19 individuals, and any additional potential claimants. The employer also agreed to make good faith efforts to increase recruitment of female and black applicants, and appoint an EEO Coordinator. The employer also agreed to retain extensive hard copy and computer records regarding its recruitment and hiring efforts and submit reports to the EEOC.

Legal Environment

Discrimination laws cover different protected groups and apply to employers with varying numbers of employees. Some laws apply to businesses that have contracts with the federal government that meet threshold dollar amounts. The following is a summary of the major federal laws prohibiting workplace discrimination.

Civil Rights Act of 1866

This law, which prohibits intentional race discrimination in the making and enforcing of contracts, has been used sparingly in the past but will be used more in the future in employment discrimination cases. It permits compensatory and punitive damages (if malice or reckless indifference is present) and must be used first for racial discrimination charges in which punitive and compensatory damages are being sought. There are no caps on the amount of damages that a plaintiff may be awarded, and the law applies to *all* employers, including those with only one employee.

Civil Rights Act of 1871

This law prohibits state laws from impacting upon individuals' rights, as guaranteed by federal law. The Act prohibits discrimination based on age, national origin, race, religion and gender.

The National Apprenticeship Act of 1937

This law prohibits discrimination based on national origin, race, color, religion, and gender in the recruiting, selecting, and training of apprentices. Written affirmative action plans, including goals and timetables, are required where the numbers of individuals in the market area are underrepresented in the firm's apprenticeship programs.

Equal Pay Act of 1963, as amended (EPA)

The Equal Pay Act is an amendment to the Fair Labor Standards Act of 1938. The law requires employers to pay male and female employees the same wages for jobs that are the same or substantially the same—that require equal skill, effort and responsibility and are performed under substantially the same working conditions. The law permits exceptions in the pay for male and female employees for pay based on (1) quality or quantity of work, (2) merit pay systems, (3) length of service, and (4) any basis other than gender.

Title VII must be used for allegations of discrimination in pay for dissimilar jobs performed by males and females; for example, men who are employed as janitors and females who are employed as maids. These situations involve the concept of *comparable worth*, which means that employers should provide equal pay to women and men for dissimilar jobs that have comparable value to the employer.

An aggrieved person is not required to file a charge with the EEOC to obtain relief under the EPA; such person may take the matter directly to court. Typically, when charges are filed with the EEOC, the person is advised that compensation charges should be filed under both the EPA and Title VII.

Title VI, Civil Rights Act of 1964

This law prohibits discrimination on the basis of race, color, religion, gender, and national origin in federally financed programs and activities. This Act formed the basis for the plaintiff's underlying lawsuit in the landmark case, *Bakke v. The Regents of the University of California*.[1]

Title VII, Civil Rights Act of 1964

This law, which is often referred to as simply "Title VII," prohibits employment discrimination on the basis of race, color, religion, gender, and national origin. The Act applies to employers engaged in an industry affecting commerce that have 15 or more employees for each working day for at least 20 calendar weeks in the current or preceding calendar year. See Chapter 7 for issues concerning the 15-employee requirement, including its use as a defense in federal court actions. The law also applies to apprenticeship programs, employment agencies, labor unions (including labor unions with 15 members) and state and local governments, including school districts. Title VII was amended by the Pregnancy Discrimination Act of 1978, which prohibits pregnancy discrimination, including the failure to hire or the discharge of pregnant women. It also bans compulsory leaves of absence for pregnancies.

There is an issue about the legality of employer-provided employee disability plans that do not extend coverage for pregnancy-related conditions. Title VII states pregnancy shall be treated the same for all employment-related purposes, including benefits under a fringe benefit program.[2] Furthermore, the EEOC *Guidelines on Discrimination Because of Sex* state "Disabilities caused or contributed to by pregnancy, childbirth, or related medical conditions, for all job-related purposes, shall be treated the same as disabilities caused or contributed to by other medical conditions, under any health or disability insurance or sick leave plan available in connection with employment . . . "[3] However, the U.S. Supreme Court ruled in a 1977 case that an employer's health insurance plan which provided benefits for any disability except pregnancy was not a violation of Title VII because the exclusion was not based upon gender.[4]

Charges alleging discrimination under Title VII must be filed with the EEOC within 180 days of the alleged unlawful practice. The unlawful practice is the discrete act of alleged discrimination – not the eventual adverse effects of the discrimination. The U.S. Supreme Court addressed this issue in Ledbetter v.

---

[1] 17 EPD ¶ 8402, 438 US 265 (1978).
[2] Civil Rights Act of 1964.

[3] U.S. Equal Employment Opportunity Commission, *Guidelines on Discrimination Because of Sex.*
[4] See *General Electric Co. v. Gilbert* (1977) in Appendix I.

Goodyear Tire & Rubber Co.[5] In this case, an employee (Ledbetter) alleged gender discrimination in that she was paid considerably less than men employed in the same job. She contended the differential in pay occurred from pay decisions based upon unfair performance appraisals in past years. Ledbetter did not charge discrimination within 180 days of any of the performance appraisals. Instead, after the time periods had expired, she alleged that several supervisors in the past had given her poor evaluations based on her sex, resulting in her being paid less than her male counterparts. The Court held that allegations of discrimination under Title VII must be filed within 180 days of the discrete act of discrimination. If this time limitation is not met, the Court held, a person cannot allege discrimination based on the effects of the alleged discriminatory acts.

If the charge is initiated with an authorized state or local agency, the charge may be filed with the EEOC 300 days from the practice or 30 days from receiving notice from the local or state agency that it is terminating its action, whichever is less. In *National Railroad Passenger Corporation v. Morgan* (2002) the U.S. Supreme Court held that charges alleging a hostile work environment are not time barred if they are part of an unlawful practice in which at least one act falls within the 300-day deadline.[6] Also, in *Edelman v. Lynchburg College* (2002) the U.S. Supreme Court held that a person alleging discrimination in a letter and not the required Form 5, may have met the 300-day deadline.[7]

Age Discrimination in Employment Act of 1967, as amended

The Age Discrimination in Employment Act (ADEA) prohibits discrimination against persons 40 years of age and older. The law prohibits mandatory retirement ages except in certain occupations, such as fire fighters and law enforcement personnel. Bona fide executives entitled to an immediate, non-forfeitable right to a retirement pension of $44,000 or more per year may be required to retire at age 65.

The ADEA applies to employers engaged in an industry affecting commerce that have 20 or more employees for each working day for at least 20 calendar weeks in the current or preceding calendar year. The law also applies to labor unions that have 25 or more members, employment agencies, and apprenticeship and training programs involved in interstate commerce.

The law also applies to state and local governments (including school districts). However, the U.S. Supreme Court decided that states are immune under this law for private suits brought by individuals (see *Kimel et al., v. Florida Board of Regents et al.*) in the Appendix.

Charges alleging discrimination on the basis of age must be filed with the EEOC within 180 days of the alleged unlawful practice. If the charge is initiated with a "deferral agency" (a state in which there is a law prohibiting age discrimination that has an agency empowered to obtain remedies), the charge may be filed with the EEOC no more than 300 days from the practice or 30 days

---

[5] See *Ledbetter v. Goodyear Tire & Rubber Co.* in Appendix 1.

[6] For further information see *National Railroad Passenger Corporation v. Morgan* (2002) in the Appendix.

[7] For further information see *Edelman v. Lynchburg College* (2002) in the Appendix.

from receiving notice from the local or state agency that it is terminating its action, whichever is less.

Title I, Civil Rights Act of 1968

This law prohibits interference with a person's application for employment or a person's actual employment.

Executive Order 11478

In 1969, President Richard M. Nixon signed Executive Order 11478, which prohibits federal agencies from engaging in discrimination in employment matters on the basis of national origin, race, color, religion, gender, age, and handicap. The Executive Order also requires agencies to establish and implement affirmative action programs for employees and applicants for employment in the federal service.

Civil Service Reform Act of 1978

This law contains a number of provisions, including one requiring federal agencies to establish affirmative action plans that include " . . . targeted recruitment activities wherever under representation is found in specific occupations or grade levels." For the first time, this law imposed the same requirements on federal agencies that had applied for over 13 years to certain private-sector firms contracting with those federal agencies.

Older Workers Benefit Protection Act of 1990

The Older Workers Benefit Protection Act amended the ADEA to permit employees to waive their rights under the ADEA, including the right to file a charge of discrimination, provided the employer has met certain conditions, such as giving employees the right to consult an attorney prior to executing the waiver.

Immigration Reform and Control Act of 1986

The Immigration Reform and Control Act was designed to stem the flow of illegal immigrants into the U.S., provide a means for certain aliens who were unauthorized to be in the U.S. to obtain legal status, and prevent discrimination against persons because of their national origin or citizenship status. This law:

- Prohibits the employment of persons who are in the U.S. without authorization;
- Requires new employees, within 72 hours of hire, to provide evidence of residence and employability and to complete Form I-9. Employers must retain Form I-9 for three years from date of employment or one year following termination of employment, whichever is later;
- Employers with 4 or more employees are prohibited from discriminating against any person (other than an unauthorized alien) in hiring, discharging, or recruiting or referring for a fee because of a person's national origin or citizenship status. Furthermore, employers with 15 or more employees may not - in addition to discrimination based on hiring, discharging or recruiting or referring for a fee - discriminate against any

person on the basis of national origin in assignment, compensation, or other terms and conditions of employment.

- An employer's obligation under IRCA begins when a person has been hired. The new employee is entitled to submit a document or combination of documents of his choice (from List A or a combination from List B and List C, shown on the reverse side of the I-9 form) to verify his identity and work eligibility. See Chapter 16 for a fuller discussion of these lists.

- The term *"hired"* means the commencement of employment. An employee is a person employed for wages or other remuneration (such as goods or services like food and lodging). The employee must complete Section 1 of the I-9 Form by the date of hire.

- Employers may not engage in *document abuse* which is

  -Demanding more or different documents than an employee chooses to present, provided that the documents presented are acceptable under the I-9 requirements.

  -Refuse to hire based upon documents having future expiration dates.

  -Reject reasonably genuine-looking documents.

- Charges alleging discrimination on the basis of national origin, citizenship, documentation abuse, or retaliation are handled by the EEOC except when all of the following conditions are met (in which case the charges are handled by The Office of Special Counsel for Immigration Related Unfair Employment Practices):

  (1) The charge alleges discrimination against the complainant with respect to his or her hiring, discharge, or recruitment or referral for a fee;

  (2) The charge is outside the jurisdiction of the EEOC in that the employer (a) does not have 15 or more employees for each working day in each of 20 or more calendar weeks in the current or preceding calendar year or (b) is an employer that is expressly excluded from coverage under Title VII; and,

  (3) The employer had at least 4 employees, including both full-time and part-time employees, on the date of the alleged discriminatory occurrence.

Genetic Information Nondiscrimination Act

Prohibitions: The Genetic Information Nondiscrimination Act (GINA), which is effective November 21, 2009, prohibits these actions:

- Employer use of genetic information in decisions affecting employee selection, termination, work assignment and promotions; and,

- Group health plans and insurers either refusing coverage or charging higher premiums to otherwise healthy individuals solely due to their genetic disposition to disease.

The law prohibits discrimination based upon knowledge of genetic information of an employee or an employee's family member. Discrimination is also prohibited based upon knowledge of an employee's or an employee's family member's disease or disorder.

Employer Coverage: These employers are covered by GINA:

- Government employees defined in the Government Employee Rights Act of 1991 (basically most federal legislative employees, presidential appointees, and employees of elected state officials)[8] ;

- Government employees covered by the Congressional Accountability Act of 1995 (employees of the U.S. Congress and related agencies);

- Employees in the federal executive branch (Title 3 of the U.S. Code);

- Private sector employers who have 15 or more employees as defined in Title VII of the Civil Rights Act; and,

- Employment agencies, labor organizations, and apprenticeship programs.[9]

Genetic Information: GINA prohibits discrimination based upon genetic information. *Genetic information* includes the following:

- Information from the genetic test results of either the employee or the employee's family member;

- Information of a disease or disorder afflicting an employee's family member;

- Information from a fetus' genetic test;

- Information obtained from an embryo by an individual using reproductive instruments that measures genetic information; and,

- Requests for genetic services or involvement in a clinical study.

Compliance Suggestions: Prior to the law's implementation compliance guidance will be forthcoming from the EEOC, the agency that will be enforcing the law. These are some suggestions to get ready for compliance:

- Include awareness of discrimination based on genetic information along with other forms of discrimination in training materials;

- Instruct applicable personnel of the necessity to avoid genetic discrimination, such as training employment personnel not to ask questions about genetic information, for example, "are there any diseases that run in your family?";

- Prepare scenarios of types of discrimination based on genetic information and how to avoid them; and,

- Safeguard all medical information.[10]

---

[8] EEOC, *Civil Rights Act of 1991*.

[9] "President signs law protecting employees' genetic information," *Human Resources: Management Ideas & Trends*, June 4, 2004, p. 84.

[10] CCH, *Human Resources Management: Ideas & Trends* (July 16, 2008), p. 111.

Disparate Treatment Violations: Violations of GINA are processed under the *disparate treatment* cause of action however, by November 21, 2015, a Commission will be formed to study the science of genetic testing and the related to determine if discrimination based upon genetic information could be subject to *disparate impact* analysis.

Processing Charges: Charges of discrimination will be handled by the same agencies shown in the above section titled Employer Coverage.

Remedies and Sanctions: Remedies and sanctions are the same under GINA as those provided by the laws noted in the above section, Employer Coverage. See the Remedies and Sanctions section of this chapter for a discussion of them. Like racial discrimination, however, for genetic discrimination there are no caps on compensatory and punitive awards for charges filed under Title VII.

Americans with Disabilities Act (ADA) of 1990

The preface to the ADA states there are 43 million Americans with disabilities. Of the several titles in the law, only one—Title I—concerns employment. Title I applies to employers engaged in an industry affecting commerce that have 15 or more employees for each working day for at least 20 calendar weeks in the current or preceding calendar year. The U.S. Supreme Court ruled in *Board of Trustees of the University of Alabama et al. v. Garrett et al.* that the ADA exceeds Congress' authority to abrogate the States' immunity under the Eleventh Amendment; therefore, state employees cannot use the ADA to collect money damages for allegations of discrimination.[11] This law prohibits discrimination against a person with a disability if the person is able to perform the *essential tasks* in the job. The three definitions of a person with a disability are discussed later in this chapter.

Other practices or conditions are prohibited by the ADA. Employers may not segregate persons with disabilities into certain work areas and other areas, such as lunchrooms. Employers cannot refuse to select persons with disabilities due to administrative considerations, such as a liability insurance policy that does not cover persons with disabilities. Furthermore, it is illegal for an employer to obtain insurance or secure other employee benefits from an organization that will not extend coverage to employees who have disabilities. The law prohibits discrimination against a person because of his or her association with an organization involving persons with disabilities or their relationship with a person with a disability.

In addition, employers are prohibited from conducting preemployment medical tests, preemployment inquiries, medical examinations of employees or inquiries about the disability of an employee *unless* such activities are job related and are necessary for business purposes. The U.S. Supreme Court held that a person who receives disability payments from Social Security is not prevented from seeking coverage as a person with a disability who is employable, with

---

[11] CCH HUMAN RESOURCES MANAGEMENT, *Ideas and Trends in Personnel* (March 7, 2001). Also see *Board of* *Trustees of the University of Alabama et al. v. Garrett et al.* in Appendix I.

reasonable accommodation, under the Americans with Disabilities Act.[12] Medical examinations of applicants, prior to their commencing work, is legal if all applicants are also examined, and the medical information remains confidential.

Americans with Disabilities Act of 2008

This amendment to the Americans with Disabilities Act of 1990, effective January 1, 2009, was enacted so courts would interpret the definition of a "person with a disability" in a manner consistent with how they had defined a "handicapped person" under the Rehabilitation Act of 1973. The amendment specifically made reference to two U.S. Supreme Court cases [*Sutton v. United Air Lines* (1999) and *Toyota Motor Manufacturing, Kentucky, Inc. v. Williams* (2002)] that narrowed the definition of a "person with a disability" beyond what Congress intended in the Americans with Disabilities Act of 1990. The amendment further states the EEOC's current regulations for the term "substantially" limits in the definition of a "person with a disability" are not consistent with Congress's intent since the standard is too high. These decisions of the court and the EEOC's definition are covered in the following sections of this chapter. The EEOC material will appear in a future edition of the *Guide* when the EEOC issues new regulations mandated by the ADA Amendments Act.

The ADA Amendments Act has these three definitions for a person with a disability:

1. Has a physical or mental impairment affecting one or more of life's major activities[13]

(a) Major life activities include, but are not restricted to caring for oneself, accomplishing manual tasks, seeing, hearing, eating, sleeping, walking, standing, lifting, bending, speaking, breathing, learning, reading, concentrating, thinking, communicating, and working.

(b) Major bodily functions including the immune system, normal cell growth, digestive, bowel, bladder, neurological, brain, respiratory, circulatory, endocrine, and reproductive functions.

(c) Disabilities that are episodic or in remission are covered if they would limit a major life activity when active.

(d) Determinations of whether impairments are covered shall be made without consideration of the ameliorative or mitigating effects of such measures as these:

(i) Medication, medical supplies, equipment, or appliances, low-vision devices (not including ordinary eyewear which are intended to fully correct visual acuity or eliminate refractive error), prosthetics, hearing aids, and cochlear implants or other implantable hearing devices, mobility devices, or oxygen therapy equipment and supplies.

---

[12] *Cleveland v. Management Systems Corp. et al.* 6 ADD ¶ 6-184, 120 F.3d 513 (SCt 1999). See also *Cleveland v. Management Systems Corp.* in Appendix 1.

[13] All of the following material is extensively quoted, including some direct quotes from the *ADA Amendments Act of 2008.*

      (ii) Assistive technology.

      (iii) Reasonable accommodations or auxiliary aids or services.

      (iv) Learned behavior or adaptive neurological modifications.

2. A record of an impairment shown in 1.a or l.b above.

3. Regarded as having an impairment.

    (a) An individual must show he/she has been subjected to a prohibited action because of an actual or perceived physical or mental condition whether or not it is perceived to limit a major life activity.

    (b) Such impairments must have an expected duration of more than six months.

Reasonable Accommodation

The ADA requires employers to make reasonable accommodation for the employment of an otherwise qualified person with a disability, unless it can be shown that this would pose an undue hardship.

Reasonable accommodation is a change in the employment application process, in the work environment or in the manner of providing the benefits of employment that would enable a qualified individual with a disability to enjoy equal employment opportunities.[14]

Discussing a Request for Reasonable Accommodation. An informal discussion between an employee and an employer, prompted by the employee's request for reasonable accommodation, will generally focus on these two issues:

- If the employee has a "disability" as defined by the ADA.
- Why the requested accommodation is needed.

Usually a simple conversation between the parties will resolve these issues. However, when the disability and/or the need for accommodation are not obvious, the employer may ask the employee for additional information, such as documentation from an appropriate health care or vocational rehabilitation professional to determine if the person has a disability that needs reasonable accommodation.

An employer that requests documentation should specify the types of information needed regarding the employee's disability, such as functional limitations, and/or the need for reasonable accommodation. In some instances, the employer may obtain needed information by asking the person to sign a limited release allowing the employer to submit a list of specific questions to the employee's health care or rehabilitation provider, or by having the employee submit the questions to the provider directly. Employers should ask questions relevant to a request for accommodation, such as these (assuming the employee is requesting accommodation because of asthma):

- What job tasks are limited by this employee's condition.

---

[14] Material on reasonable accommodation, including some full passages, obtained from *Enforcement Guidance: Reasonable Accommodation and Undue Hardship Under the Americans with Disabilities Act* (October 17, 2002).

- Does it affect her ability to breathe? To walk? Any other activities?
- Please indicate: 1) the degree of limitation, for example difficulty in breathing and 2) the frequency with which these limitations occur.

The employer should be clear about the purpose for asking such questions, i.e., they are designed to elicit information to enable the employer to determine if the person has an ADA "disability," why a reasonable accommodation is needed, and what possible accommodations might be made.

> **Example:** An employee who has low blood pressure begins to experience some problems with the condition. She requests that she be allowed to arrive at work at 10:00 a.m. and work later in the evening to accommodate her low blood pressure since it occurs more frequently prior to 10:00 a.m. She also requests a reclining chair in her office that would enable her to avoid sitting upright, thus preventing the onset of the low blood pressure and enabling her to continue working. The employer discusses the request with the employee and makes the following determinations: the employee's job involves numerous telephone conversations and significant amounts of reading, so she can use the reclining chair when her symptoms prevent sitting at her desk.

In situations like those in the example, the employer must decide if the accommodations can be reasonably made within the work environment. In some instances, it will immediately be clear whether a proposed accommodation will be effective. In other instances, an employer may have to consider more carefully whether an accommodation will work.

Types of Actions *Not* Required as Reasonable Accommodation. These are types of actions that are not required as reasonable accommodation:

- Removing an "essential function"—i.e., a fundamental job duty. Employers should be careful to distinguish essential functions from marginal functions—duties that are tangential or secondary to the primary job duties. While essential functions never have to be removed from a position, marginal functions may have to be removed as a reasonable accommodation if a person cannot perform them because of a disability.
- Lowering or eliminating production standards for essential functions.
- Replacing a supervisor.
- Withholding discipline, including discharges, warranted by poor performance or conduct.
- Providing "personal use" items needed to accomplish daily activities on the job, such as a wheelchair, hearing aid, or similar devices if they are also needed outside of the workplace.

Management May Choose Between Effective Accommodations. In many situations, more than one possible accommodation may meet the needs of an employee with a disability. The ADA requires that any accommodation chosen be reasonable and effective in eliminating the workplace barrier. While the employer should give fair consideration to a specific accommodation requested by an employee, the employer is not required to provide that accommodation.

The employer may select one accommodation among several reasonable accommodations as long as the chosen one is effective in eliminating the workplace barrier.

Example: An employee who is visually disabled requests to be moved to another office to avoid glare from a window. A spare office is available but the supervisor asks if window blinds will be equally effective. The employee agrees and the accommodation is made.

Limitation on Providing Reasonable Accommodation: Undue Hardship. An employer has no obligation to provide a specific form of reasonable accommodation if it will cause "undue hardship," i.e., significant difficulty or expense. Undue hardship must be determined on a case-by-case basis, taking into consideration the following factors:

- The nature and cost of the accommodation needed.

- The financial and other resources at the employer's facility where the request for reasonable accommodation is made. The number of persons employed at this site and the effect on expenses and resources.

- The overall financial resources, size, number of employees, and type and location of facilities at all sites of the employer.

Example: A firm based in New York has offices in four other cities, including Atlanta. The Atlanta office is considering hiring a blind attorney who has requested the following: a screen reader computer program that converts what is on the screen to speech; a computer program that scans written text and reads it aloud; a Braille printer; and a screen magnification program. In determining whether undue hardship exists, the Atlanta office must consider the resources of the entire firm, including those in the Atlanta.

If the employer determines that the cost of a reasonable accommodation constitutes an undue hardship, it should consider whether some or all of the cost can be offset. In some instances, state rehabilitation agencies or disability organizations may provide certain accommodations at little or no cost. An employer should also determine whether it is eligible for certain tax credits or deductions to offset the cost of the accommodation. But, an employer cannot claim undue hardship solely because it cannot obtain a reasonable accommodation at little or no cost, or because it is ineligible for a tax credit or deduction.

Undue hardship may exist if a particular form of reasonable accommodation actually disrupts the ability of other employees to do their jobs.

Example: A procurement officer seeks and is granted, a modified work schedule because of her disability. Her job requires that she work closely with other employees. As a result of her new schedule she often is not available when other employees need her assistance, thus resulting in missed deadlines and incomplete work. Also, other employees are handling more requests for assistance because of her new schedule. Her new schedule is causing an undue hardship on the employer because it adversely affects the ability of other employees to perform their essential functions in a timely manner.

These are the three categories of reasonable accommodation:

- Modifications to the job application process.

- Modifications to the work environment or manner of customarily performing the job.

- Modifications to the benefits of employment (such as training opportunities or social events) so they can be enjoyed by all employees including those with disabilities.

Generally applicants and employees with disabilities must request reasonable accommodation, rather than requiring employers to ask if accommodation is needed. To request a reasonable accommodation, the person must let the employer know that because of a medical condition a change is needed to the application process, to the job, or to a benefit of employment. The person only needs to make a "plain English" request for a change due to a medical condition. In some instances, a request for reasonable accommodation may come from a third party, for example a doctor's note outlining work restrictions.

Requests for reasonable accommodation may be made at any time during the application process or during employment. A person may choose to wait until a job offer is made before requesting a reasonable accommodation. Also, a person may raise the issue during the hiring process. Some employees may develop disabilities during their employment, thus prompting a request for reasonable accommodation.

Reasonable accommodation decisions should be made on a case-by-case basis to understand the nature of the accommodation(s) requested and the aspect of the application process, job, or benefit that poses a barrier.

Application Process Accommodations. Employers may note on applications that applicants may request reasonable accommodation during the application process and name the person responsible for receiving such requests. During an interview, employers may not generally ask applicants if they need reasonable accommodation to perform a job. However, if an employer knows a particular applicant has a disability, either because it is obvious or because the person has voluntarily revealed it, and the employer reasonably believes the disability might require accommodation to perform the job, the employer is entitled to ask the following two questions:

- Do you need reasonable accommodation to perform the job?

- If the answer is yes, what accommodation do you believe you need?

Some types of reasonable accommodation in the application process may include the following:

- Acquiring or modifying equipment (e.g., a TTY that would enable a deaf person to use a telephone relay service, or an assistive listening device that can help a person who is hard of hearing take a test).

- Providing tests or training materials in an alternative format, such as Braille or large print or on audiotape.

- Providing sign language interpreters for applicants who are deaf.

- Using restaurants that have facilities to accommodate applicants who use wheelchairs when a firm has the practice of taking applicants to lunch.

- Providing specialized computer software to accommodate applicants with vision impairments who use screen reading or magnification software.

Employers can assist applicants in assessing whether they will need an accommodation by making clear the job requirements, the duties to be performed, and the expected level of performance.

Work Environment Modifications/Accommodations. Employers can do a number of things to create a climate in which employees will request needed accommodation, such as the following:

- Adopting policies and procedures for handling accommodation and ensuring that the policies are well publicized and implemented.

- Making sure that both employees and managers know that company policy supports full compliance with the ADA and the provision of reasonable accommodation.

- Training supervisors, managers, and human resources professionals on handling requests for accommodation and other requirements of the ADA.

These are some examples of accommodations to the work environment:

- Physical changes, such as installing a ramp, widening a doorway, or reconfiguring a workspace.

- Job restructuring, such as removing a marginal function.

- Part-time or modified work schedules.

- Modifying workplace policies.

- Providing qualified readers or sign language interpreters.

- Changing the methods of supervision (e.g., a supervisor provides the employee with critiques of his work through e-mail rather than face-to-face meetings).

- Reassignment to a vacant position.

- Providing voice-recognition software to an employee with cerebral palsy which would make it easier for the person to use a computer and perform his/her work.

- Accommodating a temporary change in a person's disability by temporarily changing her work hours and removing several marginal functions.

Employees are *not* protected if they fail to either request a needed accommodation in a timely manner or to accept a proffered accommodation that could affect their job performance.

Example: An employee who has a disability does not want to disclose it but her job performance deteriorates. The firm follows its counseling and disciplining procedure for employees who are failing to meet minimum requirements, but these efforts are unsuccessful. During this period, the employee does not ask for reasonable accommodation. Finally, when the employer informs the employee that she will be fired, the employee informs the employer about her disability and requests accommodation. The employee's request is too late since reasonable accommodation is always prospective. An employer is not required to excuse performance problems that occurred prior to the accommodation request.

Denying Requests for Accommodation May Constitute Violations of the ADA.

Example: An employee with a learning disorder has been performing successfully for six months, but distractions which are caused by his disability are beginning to create some difficulties in his job. To help him control the distractions, he requests that a secretary be assigned to transcribe his work-related recordings. This accommodation helped him when he worked for a previous employer. Without discussing the request with the employee, the employer denies the request and the employee left the firm soon thereafter. If this accommodation would have permitted the individual to perform his job, without causing undue hardship to the firm, then the denial was a violation of the ADA.

Accommodation to Gain Equal Access to Benefits of Employment. Benefits and privileges of employment include, but are not limited to the following: (1) training that can lead to employee advancement (whether provided by the employer or an outside entity); (2) services (e.g., employee assistance programs, credit unions, cafeterias, lounges, gymnasiums, auditoriums, transportation); and (3) social and professional functions (e.g., parties to celebrate retirements and birthdays, company retreats, and outings to restaurants, sporting events, or other entertainment activities). Benefits and privileges of employment also include access to information communicated in the workplace, such as through e-mail, public address systems, or during meetings, whether or not that information relates directly to performance of an employee's essential job functions.

Example: A firm provides unassigned parking spaces for its employees. An employee has severe emphysema and asks for a parking space next to the door. His disability requires constant use of a portable oxygen tank which, in turn, restricts him from walking even relatively short distances. The employee is seeking an accommodation to use the employer-provided benefit. Therefore, the employer should reserve a parking space next to the door for use by the employee as a reasonable accommodation, if there is no undue hardship, in order to provide him equal access to the parking benefit.

Example: A firm provides paid parking for its employees. An employee with epilepsy does not drive because of her disability. She requests that the employer provide her with the cash equivalent of the parking subsidy as a reasonable accommodation so that she can use the money to pay for her transportation. The employer does not have to grant this request because the employee is asking the employer to provide her with a different benefit— subsidized use of public transportation. The employer has the right to choose to provide paid parking while not providing subsidies for use of public transportation. The fact that the employee's disability does not allow her to make use of the paid parking does not require the employer to provide her with a different benefit.

Some examples of accommodations regarding access to benefits of employment are these:

- Unpaid leave once an employee has exhausted all employer-provided leave (e.g., vacation leave, sick leave, personal days).
- Permitting telecommuting, even if the employer does not have an established telecommuting program or the employee with a disability has not met all the prerequisites to qualify for an existing telecommute program (e.g., length of service).
- Reassignment to a vacant position.

The U.S. Supreme Court has ruled in several cases on the issue of reasonable accommodation. In *US Airways v. Barnett*, the Court ruled that requests for accommodations which violated seniority systems, such as request to place a person with a disability in a job which is subject to bidding through a company seniority system, would typically be considered unreasonable and cause an undue hardship on the employer.[15] On a related matter, in *Chevron U. S. A. Inc. v. Echazabal* (2002), the Court decided employers could defend their actions not to employ a person with a disability if such employment would be in a job in which the person's disability would be a threat to the individual.[16]

Civil Rights Act of 1991

This law created the Frances Perkins-Elizabeth Hanford Dole National Award for Diversity and Excellence in American Executive Management, awarded annually to an organization that has demonstrated leadership in developing and promoting women and minorities. The law also contains provisions for handling allegations of discrimination by these groups previously exempt from federal laws:

- U.S. Senate employees (handled by Director, Office of Fair Employment Practices, who is a Senate employee);
- Previously exempt state employees (handled by the EEOC);
- Presidential appointees (handled by the EEOC or other entity designated by the President); and
- House of Representatives employees and agencies of the U.S. Congress (which includes both the House of Representatives and the Senate), who are subject to the Civil Rights Act of 1964 (subject to procedures and remedies as the House of Representatives and the agencies may design).

Federal Contractors

Some employers do not have sufficient numbers of employees to be covered by the federal equal employment opportunity laws, with the sole exception of the Civil Rights Act of 1866. For example, a painting contractor with 10 employees is not covered by any laws, except the Civil Rights Act of 1866. However, if

---

[15] *For more information see US Airways v. Barnett* in the Appendix.

[16] *For more information see Chevron U. S. A. Inc. v. Echazabal in the Appendix.*

that contractor obtains a contract with the federal government, such contractor may be required to adhere to equal employment opportunity practices in making employment decisions.

Rehabilitation Act of 1973

The Rehabilitation Act creates rights for persons who are physically and mentally handicapped. The law applies to federal agencies, recipients of federal grants or federally assisted programs, and employers that have contracts with the federal government of more than $10,000. The three definitions for a person who has a handicap are covered later in this chapter. As with the ADA, the Rehabilitation Act requires employers to make reasonable accommodations for people with disabilities, except when an undue hardship would result. See Chapter 11 for a fuller discussion of this law, including affirmative action requirements.

Vietnam Era Veteran's Readjustment Act of 1974

This law applies to employers that have contracts with the federal government of $100,000 or more. The law prohibits discrimination in the employment of certain veterans. The law also requires those employers to use affirmative action in the employment of such veterans. See Chapter 11 for a full discussion of this law, including affirmative action requirements and definitions of veterans covered under the law.

Executive Order 11246

This executive order prohibits discrimination on the basis of race, color, religion, gender, and national origin by contractors and subcontractors with federal contracts. See Chapter 11 for a full discussion of this executive order, including affirmative action requirements.

Equal Employment Opportunity Commissions' Guidelines

To interpret, establish procedures for, and aid in the implementation of equal employment opportunity and affirmative action, the EEOC issues regulations. These regulations assist employers in understanding the way that various provisions of equal employment opportunity laws should be interpreted and implemented. Four of the more significant regulations are discussed in the following sections.

Uniform Guidelines for Employee Selection Procedures

In 1978, the EEOC released this set of *Guidelines* on selection procedures to assist employers, labor organizations, employment agencies, and licensing and certification boards in complying with the requirements of federal anti-discrimination laws. These *Guidelines* cover a range of topics; including the forms of discrimination, methods for determining adverse impact, ways of justifying adverse impact, validation methods, technical standards for validity studies, and record-keeping and reporting requirements.

Guidelines on Discrimination Because of National Origin

These *Guidelines* prohibit job requirements that may discriminate against persons on the basis of national origin because of their physical characteristics or language ability, unless they are justified by bona fide occupational qualification, business necessity or a job validation study. Examples of suspect criteria are: height and weight requirements; the requirements for, or the denial of, employment because of foreign training or education; fluency in speaking the English language; and requirements for speaking only English. Employers are also held responsible for either verbal or physical forms of harassment, such as national origin slurs committed by employees and non-employees.

Guidelines on Discrimination Because of Religion

Employers must make reasonable efforts to accommodate both employees' and prospective employees' religious practices. *Reasonable* is interpreted to mean that the employer would not be expected to incur more than *de minimis* costs, such as the administrative costs in arranging shift swaps, infrequent overtime payments, or administrative costs in recording payroll record changes for employees whose assignments are changed. Employers must show that their failure to accommodate an employee's religious practices resulted from an undue hardship on the conduct of business.

Some methods employers can use to accommodate religious practices include: actively helping employees arrange assignment changes with other employees; giving employees time off without pay; placing employees in other jobs; and making schedule changes and providing scheduling arrangements, such as flextime work scheduling, flexible breaks, staggered shift hours, and alternative off-days and holidays. Examples of undue employer hardships are arrangements that either require frequent overtime payments or violate bona fide seniority systems, to the extent that other employee rights are adversely affected. Unions must also accommodate religious practices by permitting employees to donate to charity a sum equivalent to dues withholding if their religious practices prohibit them from joining a union. Although efforts to accommodate employees' and prospective employees' religious practices may seem to place an undue burden on an employer, the actual numbers of employees involved in such cases are usually quite small.

Guidelines on Discrimination Because of Sex

These *Guidelines* define the circumstances in which gender is a bona fide occupational qualification, such as employment conditions in which "authenticity or genuineness" is necessary, such as an actress for a female part in a play. Employers may not use state laws that conflict with Title VII as a defense in sex discrimination cases, such as state laws that limit female employment in occupations where certain lifting requirements are specified or constraints on hours of work are present. These *Guidelines* also prohibit such acts as:

- Separate seniority or progression lines for males and females;
- Discrimination against married women; and

- Designating "male" and "female" in job advertising, except where gender is a bona fide occupational qualification.

Employment agencies may not limit services to one gender, unless such service is based on business necessity. Agencies also violate the law if they fill vacancies on the basis of gender, and no bona fide qualification requirement is present.

Employers may not discriminate against women in employee benefits, including the benefits extended to employees' spouses and their families. Under this provision of Title VII, these employer practices have been declared unlawful:

- Offering spouses of female employees benefits that are not similarly offered to the wives of male employees;

- Requiring females to pay higher contributions for pensions;

- Requiring females to take reduced pension payments; and,

- Requiring pregnant employees either to commence annual leave or resign at a specified period of pregnancy, such as at the beginning of a certain month of pregnancy.

These *Guidelines* also address sexual harassment, which is defined as unwelcome sexual advances, requests for sexual favors, or other verbal or physical conduct of a sexual nature that is either an implied or an explicit condition of employment, is conveyed in a manner where acceptance or rejection of the gesture will affect the employee's status, causes an unfavorable job environment, or interferes with the employee's job performance. In sexual harassment investigations, all the conditions surrounding the complaint must be investigated. Employers are responsible for the actions of employees and may be held responsible for the actions of non-employees, such as subcontractors visiting an employer's premises to deliver goods or furnish services. An employee who is denied an employment opportunity may be eligible for relief if the opportunity was given to another employee solely because the person granted sexual favors to the decision maker.

Employment Discrimination

Employment discrimination occurs when an employer treats employees or job applicants who are members of a protected group less favorably than others.[17]

In general, it is illegal for employers to discriminate against protected group members in these areas:

- Hiring and firing;
- Compensation;
- Assignment or classification of employees;
- Transfer, promotion, layoff or recall;
- Job advertisements;
- Recruitment;
- Testing;
- Use of company facilities, such as lunchrooms and fitness facilities;
- Training and apprenticeship programs;
- Fringe benefits;
- Pay;
- Retirement plans and disability; and
- Other terms and conditions of employment.

Protected Groups

The following are the definitions of the various groups protected by federal equal employment opportunity laws and executive orders:

- **Age.** This group is defined as persons 40 years of age and older. Even if an employee who is 40 years of age or older is replaced by another employee who is also 40 or over, discrimination may be present. The U.S. Supreme Court held that a person who is in the protected age group of 40 or older does not have to have been replaced by someone under 40 for a *prima facie* case of discrimination to exist.[18]

- **Color.** Federal courts and the EEOC refer to a person's color as skin "pigmentation, complexion, or skin shade or tone."[19] Discrimination based on color occurs when an adverse employment decision is based upon these factors pertaining to a person's skin. Race and skin color may sometimes overlap but they are not the same. People of the same race or ethnicity may be subject to unlawful discrimination based on their skin color. Also, people of different races may experience discrimination on the basis of their color.

---

[17] CCH HUMAN RESOURCES MANAGEMENT, *Equal Employment Opportunity*, ¶ 101.

[18] See *O'Connor v. Consolidated Coin Caterers Corp.* (1996) in Appendix 1.

[19] Equal Employment Opportunity Commission, *Compliance Manual Section 15: Race and Color Discrimination* (April 19, 2006).

- **Handicapped/disabled.** A "person with a handicap" is the term used in the Vocational Rehabilitation Act; a "person with a disability" is used in the ADA. The terms "a person with a disability" or "a person with a handicap" are preferred in lieu of "disabled person" or "handicapped person," since they emphasize the person and not the disability or handicap. For both laws, the definitions are the same. A person with a handicap or disability is a person who meets one or more of these criteria:

  - *A person who has a physical or mental impairment that substantially limits one or more of a person's major life activities.* This first part of the definition applies to persons who have substantial (as distinct from minor) impairments that limit major life activities, such as seeing, hearing, speaking, walking, breathing, performing manual tasks, learning, caring for oneself, and working. An individual with epilepsy, paralysis, a substantial hearing or visual impairment, mental retardation, or a learning disability would be covered. Conversely, an individual with a minor, non-chronic condition of short duration, such as a sprain, infection, or broken limb, generally would not be covered.

  In several decisions, the U.S. Supreme Court systematically circumscribed physical conditions which substantially limit one or more of life's major activities:

  - *Bragdon v. Sidney Abbott* (1998). The Court ruled that a person infected with HIV is considered to be a person with a disability.[20]

  - *Sutton et al. v. United Air Lines* (1999). The Court ruled that twin sisters, who had severe myopia but, with corrective lenses, were employed as pilots by a regional airline were not disabled under the definition of the ADA after rejection for employment as pilots for a major commercial airline because they did not meet the airline's minimum uncorrected vision requirement. The Court ruled that the provisions of the ADA did not apply because the position for which they applied was a single job. There were other jobs for which they did meet the requirements; thus, their condition did not substantially limit their finding employment.[21]

  - *Albertsons, Inc. v. Kirkingburg* (1999). The Court ruled that Kirkingburg who had amblyopia, an uncorrectable condition which caused him to have 20/200 vision in one eye and effectively resulted in him having monocular vision, was not covered under the ADA because he had adapted to the condition and thus monocularity in his situation was not a disability under the ADA.[22]

  - *Murphy v. United Parcel Service* (1999). Murphy, who was a mechanic for the United Parcel Service (UPS), was required to drive commercial vehicles. His high blood pressure, though controllable through medication, exceeded the Department of Transportation (DOT) requirements, and caused UPS to discharge him. Murphy claimed he was protected by the ADA but the U.S. Supreme Court disagreed and ruled his

---

[20] See Court Cases in the Appendix.   [22] Ibid.
[21] Ibid.

condition, which prevented him from retaining a particular job because he did not meet DOT requirements, was not a disability since he could be employed as a mechanic in other jobs.[23]

- *Toyota Motor Manufacturing, Kentucky, Inc. v. Williams* (2002). The Court ruled that Williams, who as an employee of Toyota Motor Manufacturing, had carpal tunnel syndrome which prevented her from performing all the tasks required by her assembly line job, was not covered by the ADA because her condition did not substantially limit a "major life activity."[24]

- *An individual who has a record of such impairment.* This second part of the definition would include, for example, a person with a history of cancer that is currently in remission or a person with a history of mental illness.

- *Any person who is considered to have such an impairment.* This part of the definition protects individuals who are regarded and treated as though they have a substantially limiting disability, even though they may not have such an impairment. For example, this provision would protect a severely disfigured, qualified individual from being denied employment because an employer feared the "negative reactions" from others.[25]

- The ADA also prohibits discrimination against persons who have a known association or relationship with a person with a disability.

- **National origin.** This category includes a person's ancestors, place of origin, or physical, cultural or linguistic characteristics of a national origin group. The EEOC includes both religion and national origin under the term *ethnic*. The U.S. Supreme Court held that non-citizens of the United States are entitled to protection under Title VII and, furthermore, a requirement of U.S. citizenship may violate Title VII if it is intended to discriminate or results in discrimination based upon national origin.[26] National origin discrimination includes discrimination based on accent, manner of speaking, or language fluency. Also covered are rules requiring employees to speak only English in the workplace.

- **Race.** All people are protected from discrimination based on their race. Title VII does not include a categorization or definition of race. Federal agency forms used for collecting racial information have these five categories:
  - American Indian or Alaska Native
  - Asian
  - Black or African American
  - Native Hawaiian or Other Pacific Islander

---

[23] Ibid.
[24] Ibid.

[25] EEOC, *The ADA: Questions and Answers.* January 15, 1997.
[26] See *Espinoza v. Farah Mfg. Co.* (1972) in Appendix I.

- White

These federal forms have "Hispanic or Latino" as the only ethnicity category[27]

- **Religion.** This group includes religions, beliefs, observances, and practices (moral or ethical beliefs of right and wrong and sincerely held with the strength of traditional religious views). Employers are responsible for making reasonable efforts in accommodating employees' religious beliefs. The U.S. Supreme Court has ruled that an employer that provided a means of reasonably accommodating an employee's religious needs has met its requirements and does not have to meet the employee's preferred means of accommodation.[28]

- **Gender.** This group includes both male and female.

- **Veteran.** See Chapter 11 for a full discussion of "veterans" covered under federal law.

  Citizen or legal alien. This category includes persons who fall into one of the following categories:

  - Citizens or nationals of the U.S.;
  - Aliens who meet one of these conditions:
    - Those lawfully admitted for permanent residence;
    - Those who are granted the status of aliens lawfully admitted for temporary residence; or
    - Those who are admitted as refugees or granted asylum, and who evidence the intention to become citizens of the U.S. through completing declarations of intention to become citizens.

It is not illegal to hire, recruit, or refer an individual who is a citizen or national of the U.S. over another individual who is an alien, if the two individuals are equally qualified.

- **Genetic information**. This category includes knowledge of genetic information of an employee or an employee's family member. Also included is knowledge of an employee's or an employee's family member's disease or disorder.

Protection Under State or Local Laws

Some states and localities provide protection against discrimination on other bases, such as marital status, political affiliation, and sexual preference or orientation. The District of Columbia also prohibits discrimination on the basis of a person's status as a student.

Protection from Employment Discrimination in Federal Agencies

Job applicants and employees of federal agencies are protected from employment discrimination on the bases of race, color, religion, sex, national origin, disability and age. In addition, these individuals are protected from employment

---

[27] EEOC, *Questions and Answers About Race and Color Discrimination in Employment.*

[28] See *Ansonia Board of Education v. Philbrook* (1988) in Appendix 1.

discrimination on the bases of "sexual orientation, parental status, marital status, political affiliation, and conduct that does not adversely affect the performance of the employee."[29]

Exclusions

Volunteers, independent contractors, military personnel, partners, and shareholders are some of the major groups that are not protected under federal equal employment opportunity law. Under some circumstances, volunteers may be protected, if certain conditions are met. For example, if volunteer work typically leads to an offer of employment from the same employer, volunteers could conceivably be protected. Furthermore, monetary forms of compensation are not necessarily requisite for an employment relationship to exist in order for individuals to be protected under equal employment opportunity laws. For example, volunteers and others who receive lodging, food and other non-monetary forms of compensation may be considered to be protected under federal equal employment opportunity laws.

Independent Contractors

The regulations governing the determination of independent contractor status vary somewhat under the various federal laws. Independent contractor issues arise under federal tax law, the Fair Labor Standards Act, the Occupational Safety and Health Act, Title VII of the Civil Rights Act, and the National Labor Relations Act. Under equal employment opportunity laws, the determination of status as an employee (as opposed to an independent contractor) is generally somewhat less stringent, and strict adherence to the concept of power to control the work of the individual may not apply. If a person meets certain conditions, such as the work of the individual is assigned by the employer and the individual is paid by the employer, an employment relationship may exist.

Discrimination Theories

The two prominently applied theories of employment discrimination are *disparate treatment* and *disparate impact* (also referred to as *adverse impact* or *disparate effect*). The two theories, along with evidentiary models used to prove their occurrence, were developed in efforts to establish ways to identify discrimination.

Disparate Treatment

Disparate treatment occurs when one individual, or a group of individuals, experiences less favorable treatment as resulting from an employment decision than another individual or group of individuals on the basis of national origin, race, skin color, gender, religion, age, disability, veteran's status or alien status. A victim of disparate treatment must show that the employer had an unlawful motive or intent, and that the discriminatory motive or intent was the basis of the employment decision that adversely affected him or her. A discriminatory mo-

---

[29] U.S. EEOC, *Facts About Federal Sector Equal Employment Opportunity Complaint Processing Regulations (29 CFR Part 1614).*

tive is frequently reflected by the use of subjective criteria (standards residing only in the mind of the decisionmaker) in making employment decisions.

There are two primary evidentiary models in use for establishing disparate treatment. One is used generally for proving discrimination against individuals, while the other is used to show that a class or group of persons is the object of discrimination. It must be remembered that the burden of proving discrimination remains, at all times, with the person or persons claiming to be victims of the unlawful conduct.

Individual Case for Establishing Disparate Treatment

As to any individual case of employment discrimination, the U.S. Supreme Court in 1973 set up this three-stage procedure for handling the bias claim:[30]

First, the individual must present initial evidence supporting his or her claim. This can be done (for example, in a denial of hiring situation) by showing that:

1. The individual belongs to a protected group;

2. The individual was qualified to perform the job for which the employer sought applicants;

3. The individual was rejected, despite the qualifications; and

4. The position remained open and the employer continued to seek applications from persons having the same qualifications as the rejected individual.

Second, the accused employer must come forward with non-discriminatory explanations for the apparent discriminatory treatment of the complainant.

Third, after all the explanations have been presented, the individual complainant must be able to show that the reason(s) given by the employer for rejecting him or her are merely pretexts to cover a discriminatory motive. In such cases, it is not necessary for the individual to show that his/her qualifications were so superior ". . . as virtually to jump off the page and slap you in the face." Rather, a pretext of discrimination could be established by showing a reasonable person with impartial judgment would have selected the individual or a reasonable employer would have found the individual significantly better qualified for the position.[31]

Subordinate Bias Theory . In some situations, a protected group member's supervisor recommends an adverse employment action against a subordinate for no reason other than racial animus or other bias (hence the term subordinate bias theory). Before taking action on supervisor recommendations, employers are well advised to ensure they are based upon good cause. Chapter 37 contains a disciplinary procedure, if followed, will help prevent this type of discrimination. At a minimum, employees should be given the opportunity to explain their

---

[30] See *McDonnell Douglas Corp. v. Green* (1973) in Appendix 1. See also *Reeves v. Sanderson Plumbing Products, Inc* (2000).

[31] See *Anthony Ash et al. v. Tyson Foods, Inc.* (2006) in *Appendix 1.*

version of a situation before an adverse employment decision is made.[32] Such a procedure helps ensure fairness and prevents adverse employment actions based on capricious or discriminatory reasons.

Disparate Treatment Using Statistics

The secondary evidentiary model for establishing disparate treatment involves the use of statistical comparisons. This model is particularly suited to raise an inference that a large group of persons in a protected class, such as a group of females, has been treated disparately on account of their status (that is, as females).

To establish a violation under this model, the personnel action statistics, such as the number of selections for promotion, must show that the differences in the employment opportunities accorded members of the protected group (such as females), as compared to those accorded the non-protected group (in this case, males), are gross and long-standing. In other words, the disparity or differences reflected in the statistics must be statistically significant, and the offending employment practices must have been in use for some time.

Significant, in this context, refers to the rates of treatment; for example, the selection rates for the groups must differ at the .05 percent level of significance. This .05 difference would not be significant in more than five out of 100 instances. Employers may discredit these statistics or try to explain the differences. For the protected group to succeed, it must show that the statistics are correct and that any employer explanation for the differences lacks merit.

Disparate Impact

Disparate impact is a type of employment discrimination in which an employment practice, though fair in form and applied in a nondiscriminatory manner, operates to discriminate against members of a protected group. Thus, an employment selection criteria, such as a specified education level, may be neutral (nondiscriminatory) on its face but fall more harshly on members of a protected class, such as racial minorities or females. This theory, approved by the U.S. Supreme Court in 1971, is utilized by federal enforcement agencies to secure compliance with federal statutes, executive orders, and regulations. The U.S. Supreme Court held that Duke Power Company's requirement of a high school diploma and a written test were artificial, arbitrary, and unnecessary barriers to employment on the basis of race, in the absence of intent to discriminate, if they do not demonstrate a reasonable measure of relationship to job performance.[33]

In another case, the U.S. Supreme Court held that adverse impact analysis also applies to subjective systems of selection. In that case, Fort Worth Bank & Trust used subjective judgments of white supervisors in selecting white applicants for four promotions and rejecting Watson, who was black. The Court ruled that subjective or other discretionary systems of promotion may be subjected to disparate impact analysis. In so ruling, the Court rejected the contention that

---

[32] CCH, U.S. Supreme Court grants certiorari in subordinate bias theory case, *Topic Spotlight*, 2007.

[33] See *Griggs v. Duke Power Co.* (1971) in Appendix 1.

such systems can only be analyzed under the disparate treatment concept of discrimination.[34]

In another case, the Court gave guidance to those seeking recovery for disparate impact discrimination. The Court found the mere fact the number of individuals alleging discrimination (protected group) compared to other individuals (non-protected group) have a disproportionately smaller percentage of preferred jobs and a larger percentage of less preferred jobs does not constitute a *prima facie* case of disparate impact job discrimination. In such situations, the alleged victims of discrimination must show the disproportionate statistics are due to one or more selection practices and evidence must be shown of the significant disparate impact each practice has on the employment of the job applicants.[35]

In *Smith et al., v. City of Jackson, Mississippi, et al.,* the U.S. Supreme Court held that under the Age Discrimination in Employment Act, recovery was permitted under disparate impact cases comparable to that permitted under the Civil Rights Act of 1964 except that the apparent offending practice could be justified based on reasonable factors other than age. In this case, the City of Jackson gave pay raises which resulted in higher raises to younger police officers compared to most officers over 40 years of age. The City's rationale for this action was an attempt to bring the starting salaries of police officers and dispatchers up to the regional average. The Court determined that this purpose was a reasonable justification for the action which had a disproportionately adverse effect upon officers over 40 years of age.

In *Meacham et al., v. Knolls Atomic Power Laboratory, aka Kapl, Inc., et al.,* the U.S. Supreme Court found that an employer had the burden of production and persuasion for its "reasonable factors other than age" (RFOA) affirmative defense to a disparate impact suit. The employer instituted a lay-off plan in which employees would be appraised on their "performance," "flexibility," "critical skills," and points for years of service. Thirty of the 31 employees who were laid-off were at least 40 years old. Meacham and some others, who were at least 40 years old and laid-off, filed a disparate impact suit under the Age Discrimination in Employment Act. They used the results of an analysis conducted by a statistics expert to show that there was a statistically significant inverse relationship between the appraisals and age. The expert also found that the relationship was strongest with "flexibility" and "criticality" which were the two factors in which the evaluators had the most discretion. In essence, the Court's decision meant Knolls must show there is a reasonable relationship between the factors used in making the lay-offs and the lay-off decisions.[36]

Since it is the *effects* of the employment practice that constitute the harm felt by the protected group members, intent or motive on the part of the employer is irrelevant under disparate impact analysis. Good intent or the absence of dis-

---

[34] See *Watson v. Fort Worth Bank & Trust* (1988) in Appendix 1.

[35] For more information see *Ward's Cove Packing Co., Inc. v. Antonio* (1989) in Appendix 1..

[36] For more information see *Meacham et al., v. Knolls Atomic Power Laboratory, aka Kapl, Inc., et al.* (2008) in Appendix 1.

criminatory intent does not redeem employment procedures that operate as "built-in headwinds" for protected groups.

Educational requirements, hiring bans on persons with arrest records, or height and weight standards are some of the employment practices more frequently challenged under the disparate impact theory. An individual who is rejected for employment or denied a promotion for failure to satisfy either of such requirements may have a valid claim of unlawful discrimination if he or she can show that members of his or her race, gender, or other characteristic are disproportionately screened-out when compared with persons of other races, gender, or other characteristic.

Statistics may be used to show that a particular screening device or hiring requirement impacts disparately on protected individuals. Such a disparity will raise an inference that the device or requirement unlawfully discriminates against the affected individuals. As with instances of disparate treatment, the difference shown by the statistics (figures revealing that a greater percentage of persons in one of the protected groups are adversely affected than are persons belonging to the other groups) must be significant. The *Uniform Guidelines for Employee Selection Procedures* (*Uniform Guidelines*) contain a rule-of-thumb measure, or four-fifths rule (which is discussed below), for determining the existence of disparate impact.

The employer confronted with this challenge to a neutral employment practice may escape liability by showing that the hiring or promotion requirement is related to the successful performance of the job at hand. In other words, the challenged practice is necessary to the efficient conduct of the employer's business.

In some instances, employers have been held liable for using high school education requirements to screen employees for jobs requiring only basic skills, when the effect of the requirements was to screen out racial minorities at a higher rate than non-minorities. Likewise, the use of height and weight standards has been determined to discriminate unjustifiably against females and persons of certain national origins who statistically tend not to satisfy those requirements. Where liability was established in these cases, the employers were unable to show that the specified physical attributes were necessary to perform the jobs at hand.

Adverse Impact Analysis

Adverse impact occurs when a selection procedure[37] results in an employment decision which is substantially to the disadvantage of certain persons, based upon their national origin, race, color, religion, gender, age, or disability.

---

[37] The *Uniform Guidelines* defines a *selection procedure* as "any measure, combination of measures, or procedure used as a basis for any employment decision." Examples of selection procedures include all types of tests; physical, educational and work experience requirements; probationary periods; performance appraisal systems; and training programs required for job retention or advancement. For example, if performance appraisal system results are used for promoting or disciplining employees, then the employer would be required to determine whether adverse impact resulted from the system. If adverse impact was present, the employer would also be required to show that the appraisal system validly measured job performance to avoid the adverse impact form of discrimination.

The four-fifths rule is a method used to determine whether an adverse impact exists.

Four-Fifths Rule

The *four-fifths rule* is a rule-of-thumb measure for adverse impact. According to the rule, adverse impact is present when the selection rate for protected group applicants is less than $^4/_5$ (or 80%) of the selection rate for non-protected applicants.

EXAMPLE 1:

Group	# Job Applicants	# Applicants Hired	Selection Rate
Non-protected	300	30	10% or .10
Protected	200	10	5% or .05

The selection rate for the protected group should be 80% of 10% (.80× .10=.08 or 8%). Adverse impact exists, since 5% is less than 8%.

EXAMPLE 2: Adverse impact can also be calculated by dividing the selection rate for the protected group by the selection rates for the non-protected group. In the above example:

5% (or .05) ÷ 10% (or .10)=50% (or .50)

In this case, the selection rate for the protected group is 50%. The minimum selection rate for adverse impact not to exist is 80%.

Adverse impact can also occur in other personnel actions, including disciplinary actions, such as suspensions or discharges. In such cases, the discharge rate of the non-protected group cannot be less than 80% (or .80) of the discharge rate for the protected group.

EXAMPLE 3: Last year, at Apex Manufacturing, 10 of the 100 protected group members were suspended for performance problems. During the same period, four of the 200 non-protected group members employed by the firm were suspended for performance problems. Is there adverse impact in the administration of employee suspensions?

Suspension rate for the protected group=10%

Suspension rate for the non-protected group=2%

2% ÷ 10%=20%

Answer: Yes. Since 20% is less than 80%, there is adverse impact in the administration of suspensions. Therefore, the employer must show that the suspension policy is job-related.

Where Four-Fifths Rule Does Not Apply. The four-fifths rule is only a broad gauge to guide employers, particularly in cases where the numbers of selections are small. Where numbers of selections are large enough, the employer must use the appropriate statistical measures.

EXAMPLE 4: ABC Manufacturing Company requires newly hired employees to successfully complete a training program before they start work.

Over a two-year period, 520 of 1,020 males successfully completed the course. Of the females, 295 of 725 trainees were successful. The results are summarized in this table:

Group	Number Completed Training	Passed Course	Pass Rate
Males	1,020	520	.50
Females	725	295	.40

The pass rate for the protected group is 80 percent of the rate for the non-protected group. However, due to the large numbers of applicants, the two rates should be compared, using a normal distribution test, in which it is assumed that the two rates are equal. Readers are spared the mathematics, but for those who desire a further look, the solution is shown in the Chapter Appendix. The normal distribution statistical test indicates at the .05 level (the level required by the *Uniform Guidelines*) the pass rate for the protected group is significantly lower than the non-protected rate (even though it is 80 percent). Since this test shows adverse impact is present, the employer must justify the difference.

Bottom Line

In analyzing selection results, an employer may find that the overall results are racially balanced but one or more procedures in the process have an adverse impact. This issue was the basis of *Connecticut v. Teal*, in which the U.S. Supreme Court held that an employer is liable for racial discrimination when any part of its selection process, such as an unvalidated examination or test, has a disparate impact even if the final result of the hiring process is racially balanced. In effect, the Court rejects the "bottom line defense" and makes clear that fair employment laws protect the individual who is a victim of discrimination regardless of the total effect of a selection process.[38]

Business Necessity

Business necessity is often the reason advanced to support an employer's use of an offending or disparaging practice. It may sometimes take the form of a bona fide (good faith) occupational qualification (BFOQ); that is, a particular sex is a necessary qualification for the job, such as an actor or actress for a part in a play. Exhibit 12-1 contains a summary of the situations in which an adverse impact analysis must be conducted and whether business necessity can be used as a defense. A specific age level may also be a BFOQ for employment as an airline pilot, since the degenerative changes in the body associated with advancing age may adversely affect operative abilities and, thus, endanger the public. A business necessity is one where the practice or qualification standard is directly related to adequate job performance and is necessary to the efficient and safe operation of the business. BFOQ or business necessity can never be used as a

---

[38] See *Connecticut v. Teal* in Appendix I.

defense where adverse impact involves either race or color. BFOQ, however, *can* be asserted in cases of national origin, religion, or sex discrimination.[39]

Exhibit 12-1
Requirements for Adverse Impact Analysis
and BFOQ/Business Necessity Defense

Group	Adverse Impact Analysis	BFOQ/Business Necessity Defense
Age	Yes	Yes
Disability/handicap	Yes	Yes
Height/weight	Yes	Yes
National Origin	Yes	Yes, limited
Pregnancy	No	Yes
Race/color	Yes	No
Religion	Yes	Yes
Reproductive/fetal	No	Yes
Sex	Yes	Yes

Age as a BFOQ

Age requirements can be imposed as a BFOQ, if an employer is able to demonstrate a relationship between age and job performance. For example, airline pilots are not permitted to fly commercial airplanes after the age of 60.[40]

Disability/Handicap as BFOQ

The ADA and the Rehabilitation Act require covered employers to exercise affirmative action in the employment of persons with disabilities (ADA) or handicaps (the Rehabilitation Act). In limited situations, however, employers can use business necessity as a defense for failing to hire persons with disabilities, if their employment would cause significant personnel problems, impose significant costs or unnecessarily interfere with the operation of the business. For example, one appeals court ruled that an employer legally refused to hire a disabled applicant because many of the applicant's duties would have to be handled by a small number of other employees, thus imposing a hardship.[41] The number of workers available for work assignments and the size of the organization have a bearing on whether a particular accommodation would be deemed feasible. A court found it feasible for a state agency with a large budget to provide part-time readers to blind workers so that they could be employed.[42]

[39] Title VII, Section 704(b).

[40] CCH HUMAN RESOURCES MANAGEMENT, *Equal Employment Opportunity*, ¶2270.

[41] *Treadwell v. Alexander*, 32 EPD ¶33,690 (11th Cir 1983), 707 F2d 473; discussed at CCH HUMAN RESOURCES MANAGEMENT, *Equal Employment Opportunity*, ¶6218.

[42] *Nelson v. Thornburgh*, 32 EPD ¶33,857 (EDPa 1983); cert. denied, 35 EPD ¶34, 904, 105 SCt 955 (1985); discussed at CCH HUMAN RESOURCES MANAGEMENT, *Equal Employment Opportunity*, ¶6218.

Height/Weight Requirements as BFOQ

In the past some employers imposed height and weight requirements for certain types of jobs, such as firefighter, police officer, or correctional officer. The mistaken notion, in most of these situations, was that the jobs in question required incumbents to meet the minimum weight or height requirements so they could safely and effectively perform the job tasks. In 1997, the U.S. Supreme Court addressed this issue in a case involving a female applicant for the job of Correctional Counselor (prison guard) in an Alabama correctional institution. A female applicant (Rawlinson) was rejected for the job because she failed to meet the 120-pound minimum weight requirement. The State of Alabama contended the weight requirement, together with a minimum height requirement of 5 feet 2 inches, were necessary because they were associated with a candidate's strength, which in turn is an essential physical requirement for satisfactory job performance. The Court held that (1) the State of Alabama failed to show the requirements were job related, and (2) since the requirements would only exclude 1 percent of males but over 40 percent of the female population, they were unlawful.[43]

National Origin as BFOQ

Business necessity defenses involving national origin issues have been restricted to the implementation of English-only rules. A court found an English-only workplace rule for bilingual employees did not violate Title VII.[44]

Pregnancy as BFOQ

Employers who use pregnancy as the basis of an employment action, such as a termination of employment, must be able to justify the decision through business necessity; for example, if no alternative was available, this would have prevented the need to take the action.

Race/Color

Business necessity can never be used as a justification for an employment action, based upon either race or color.

Religion

Religion can be used as a basis for an employment action if justified due to business necessity. For example, a Catholic university was found to be acting lawfully in requiring teaching applicants to be Jesuits.[45]

Reproductive/Fetal Protection

Employment decisions that are based on the protection of the reproduction capabilities of women must be justified by business necessity. For example, one employer was not permitted to exclude fertile females from positions that

---

[43] CCH HUMAN RESOURCES MANAGEMENT, *Equal Employment Opportunity*, ¶8827.

[44] *Garcia v. Spun Steak Co.*, 62 EPD ¶42,456, 998 F2d 1480 (CA-9 1993); discussed at CCH HUMAN RESOURCES MANAGEMENT, *Equal Employment Opportunity*, ¶2684D.

[45] *Pime v. Loyola University of Chicago*, 35 EPD ¶34,667 (DC ND Ill. 1984), 585 FSupp 435, aff'd (CA-7 1986), 41 EPD ¶35, 567, 803 F2d 351; discussed at CCH HUMAN RESOURCES MANAGEMENT, *Equal Employment Opportunity*, ¶6216.

exposed them to hazardous chemicals because it proved a significant potential danger to unborn children.[46]

Sex

Sex can be used as a basis for employment decisions in circumstances in which employment of a specific gender is justified by business necessity. For example, the practice of the Alabama Correctional System of hiring only males to be correctional officers in all-male institutions was upheld by the court. The state's reason for this practice was that some inmates were sex offenders, so that hiring female correctional officers could precipitate inmate violence.[47]

Sometimes, employers' well-intentioned policies, such as using a defense of business necessity to justify a policy to the protect the health of women, are illegal. For example, the U.S. Supreme Court held that an employer's policy, which excluded women of child-bearing age from employment in jobs that exposed the worker to lead concentrations that exceeded the OSHA standard as critical for employees who planned to have children, was illegal.[48]

Remedies and Sanctions

Depending upon the circumstances, victims of employment discrimination may be entitled to remedies and/or sanctions.

Remedy

A *remedy* is non-punitive relief for either intentional acts or practices that have a discriminatory effect (that is either disparate treatment or disparate effect, respectively). These are the monetary forms of remedial relief which may be available to victims of employment discrimination based on national origin, race, color, religion, sex, disability and age:

- *Back pay*, which is giving a victim of discrimination any lost wages due for such reasons as being illegally deprived of a job;

- *Back pay with interest*, which awards interest on the amount of the back pay, intended to compensate the victim for the loss of the income for the period for which he or she was denied it; and

- *Front pay*, which is compensating the victim with monetary payments extended into the future. Front pay is awarded in several situations. One situation might involve an employee who was illegally denied a promotion. If the position was no longer vacant, the employee would receive the difference in pay in his/her present job and the higher level one. The front pay may be made until that position or a similar one becomes vacant, so that he or she can be assigned to it. Front pay is also used in situations

---

[46] *Automobile Workers (UAW) v. Johnson Controls, Inc.*, 51 EPD ¶39, 359 (7th Cir 1989); 111 SCt 1195, 55 EPD ¶40,605 (1991); discussed at CCH HUMAN RESOURCES MANAGEMENT, *Equal Employment Opportunity*, ¶2690.

[47] *Dothard v. Rawlinson*, 14 EPD ¶7632, 433 US 321 (SCt 1977); discussed at CCH HUMAN RESOURCES MANAGEMENT, *Equal Employment Opportunity*, ¶6216.

[48] See *International Union, United Automobile, Aerospace and Agricultural Implement Workers of America, UAW v. Johnson Controls, Inc.*, 51 EPD ¶39, 359 (7th Cir 1989); 111 SCt 1195, 55 EPD ¶40,605 (1991). Also see *International Union, United Automobile, Aerospace and Agricultural Implement Workers of America, UAW v. Johnson Controls, Inc.*, in Appendix 1.

where a person no longer desires to remain employed with the organization that discriminated against him or her, and an expert calculates how long it would take the victim to find a job making the same income as he or she would have made if the discrimination had not occurred. For example, if it was estimated that it would take the victim six months to find such employment, he or she would receive front pay equal to six months' pay.

Other remedies may include hiring, promoting, reinstating, making reasonable accommodation, or implementing other actions that will make an individual "whole" and thereby correct a condition caused by discrimination. Remedies also may include payment of: attorneys' fees, expert witness fees, and court costs. An employer may also be required to take other actions such as to post notices to all employees addressing any violations and advising them of their rights, such as to apply for relief or other awards without fear of retaliation. Other remedies include requiring the employer to take action to insure it will not recur and to conduct training of employees and managers to prevent future act of discrimination.

Sanction

A *sanction* is a penalty for failing to meet legal EEO/AA requirements. For cases involving intentional discrimination based upon race, color, religion, sex, national origin, genetic condition, or disability (but not age), the two types of monetary awards that are sanctioned against the employer are compensatory and punitive. There are two standards of liability, depending upon the sanction. For compensatory damages, a plaintiff must show that he or she was a victim of intentional discrimination on the part of the employer. A second and higher standard applies to punitive damages.[49]

- *Compensatory* monetary awards are given to recompense a victim of intentional discrimination. The two types of compensatory payments are pecuniary and nonpecuniary.

  - *Pecuniary* compensatory awards reimburse the victim for any expenses incurred as a result of the discrimination. For example, if the discrimination caused the victim to seek medical treatment, like counseling, a pecuniary compensable award might include reimbursing the victim for the cost of the counseling sessions.

  - *Nonpecuniary* compensatory awards make reparations to the victim of discrimination for any pain and suffering the person endured due to the discrimination.

- *Punitive* damages, where *malice* or reckless indifference is present, except in cases brought against federal, state, or local government employers, may also be awarded to victims of discrimination. The purpose of these damages are to penalize the perpetrator of the discrimination. "*Malice* is defined as a condition of mind which prompts a person to do a wrongful

---

[49] *Kolstad v. American Dental Association*, 75 EPD ¶ 45,887; SCt No. 98-208 (6/22/99). Also see *Kolstad v. American Dental Association* in Appendix 1.

act willfully, that is, on purpose, to the injury of another. Thus, discriminatory conduct is maliciously done if prompted or accompanied by ill will . . . either toward the injured person individually or toward all persons in one of more groups . . . of which the injured person is a member."[50]

- In cases concerning reasonable accommodation under the ADA, compensatory or punitive damages may not be awarded to the charging party if an employer can demonstrate that "good faith" efforts were made to provide reasonable accommodation.

Caps on Monetary Awards

There are no caps for remedial monetary payments. In addition, there are no caps on compensatory and punitive damages for racial discrimination, since the victims of this intentional discrimination typically file their complaints under the Civil Rights Act of 1866 and discrimination based on genetic information. For discrimination due to religion, gender, national origin, or disability, the caps on total monetary awards for both compensatory and punitive damages allowable under federal law are as follows:

- $50,000 for employers with 15-100 employees;

- $100,000 for 101-200 employees;

- $200,000 for 201-500 employees; and

- $300,000 for 500 or more employees.

The U.S. Equal Employment Opportunity Commission

The U.S. Equal Employment Opportunity Commission (EEOC) carries out its work at its headquarters and in fifty field offices located throughout the United States. The EEOC conducts investigations of employment discrimination, issues regulatory and other forms of guidance interpreting the laws it enforces, administers the federal sector employment discrimination program, provides funding and support to state and local fair employment practices agencies (FEPAs), and conducts broad-based outreach and technical assistance programs.

Charge Investigation Procedures

When a charge is filed, the employer is notified and these are among the ways the charge may be handled:

- Priority is given to charges that indicate a violation of law. When the evidence is less strong, a follow-up investigation may be conducted to determine if a violation has occurred.

- A charge can be settled at any stage if both parties have an interest in doing so. Investigations continue if a settlement attempt is not successful.

- Investigations may involve written requests for information, interviews, documents review, and, if necessary a personal visit to the facility where the alleged discrimination occurred.

---

[50] *Soderbeck v. Burnett County*, 752 F2d 285, 289 (7th Cir. 1985), *cert. denied*, 471 U.S. 1117 (1985);   discussed at CCH Human Resources Management, ¶ 10,086.

- When the investigations are completed a discussion of the evidence is conducted with both parties, as appropriate.

- Mediation may be an alternative, based upon the evidence and if both parties concur. Mediation is both confidential and voluntary, but if it is unsuccessful, the investigation resumes.

- Charges that do not establish a violation of law are dismissed with a notice giving the charging party 90 days in which to file a lawsuit on his/her behalf.

- If there is evidence of a violation of law both parties are informed in a letter and an attempt is made to conciliate the charge with the employer and develop a remedy for the discrimination.

- Cases that are successfully conciliated, mediated or settled may not be pursued in court by either the EEOC or the charging party unless the conciliation, mediation, or settlement agreement is not honored.

- If conciliation is unsuccessful, the EEOC may either bring suit in federal court or issue a notice closing the case and giving the charging party 90 days in which to file a lawsuit on his or her own behalf.

- A charging party may file a lawsuit under the following conditions:

  (1) Within 90 days after receiving a notice of a "right to sue" from EEOC, as stated above.

  (2) Under Title VII and the ADA, a request can be made for a notice of "right to sue" from the EEOC 180 days after the charge was first filed with the EEOC, and the suit can be brought within 90 days after receiving this notice.

  (3) Under the ADEA, a suit may be filed at any time 60 days after filing a charge with EEOC, but not later than 90 days after EEOC gives notice that it has completed action on the charge.

  (4) Under the EPA, a lawsuit must be filed within two years (three years for willful violation) of the discriminatory act, which in most cases is payment of a discriminatory lower wage.

EEOC's Alternative Dispute Resolution (Mediation)

As discussed above, mediation is an option to settle charges of discrimination, if both parties agree to its use. Since April 1999, when its mediation program was launched nationally, EEOC has mediated more than 50,000 cases with approximately 70% being successfully resolved in an average time of 85 days which is nearly half the time it takes to resolve a charge through the investigative process.

The EEOC also has Regional Universal Agreements to Mediate (RUAM) and National Universal Agreements to Mediate (NUAM). Over 100 NUAMs and RUAMs, have been consummated by the EEOC with various employers. In addition, EEOC district offices have over 800 mediation agreements with employers at local and regional levels. These mediation efforts have been successful since 13-20% of mediated cases are resolved on non-monetary issues. Also, some disputes are resolved in a single session.

State and Local Programs

Many states and localities have agencies responsible for enforcing state and local equal employment opportunity laws. Charges filed with these agencies, referred to by the EEOC as Fair Employment Practices Agencies (FEPA), are subject to a procedure to avoid duplication of effort in resolving discrimination complaints. The FEPA typically handles any charge filed with but it also files the charge with the EEOC if it is covered by federal law. Similarly, the EEOC typically handles any charge filed with it but it also files the charge with the appropriate FEPA if it is covered by state or local law.

U.S. Citizens Employed by Multinational Firms

Multinational Firms Operating in the U.S. U.S. equal employment opportunity laws apply to multinational firms in the United States, including American Samoa, Guam, the Commonwealth of the Northern Mariana Islands, Puerto Rico, and the U.S. Virgin Islands. An exception applies if the employer is covered by a treaty or international agreement, such as permitting the company to prefer its own nationals for certain positions.

U.S. Firms Operating Outside the U.S. Title VII, the ADEA and the ADA apply to U.S. citizens employed by U.S. firms operating outside the U.S. The laws do not apply to foreign nationals working for U.S. firms outside the U.S.

See Chapter 38 for a further discussion of the application of U.S. equal employment opportunity laws to U.S. employees employed in a different country.

Federal Sector Program

The EEOC is also responsible for enforcing the anti-discrimination laws in the federal sector. The EEOC conducts thousands of hearings every year for federal employees who have filed discrimination complaints. In addition, when a federal agency issues a final decision on a complaint of discrimination, the complainant can appeal such decision to the EEOC.

When the EEOC determines that a federal agency has engaged in illegal discrimination, the EEOC has the authority to require appropriate remedies, including hiring or reinstatement, with or without back pay. The EEOC also has the authority to require federal agencies to pay compensatory damages when they engage in employment discrimination.[51]

The Commission also ensures that federal departments and agencies maintain equal employment opportunity programs required under Title VII and the Rehabilitation Act. Moreover, under Executive Order 12067, the Commission provides leadership and coordination to all federal departments' and agencies' programs enforcing statutes, executive orders, regulations, and policies that

---

[51] *West v. Gibson*, 73 EPD ¶45,275, 137 F.3d 992 (1998); cert. granted Jan. 15, 1999.

require equal employment opportunity or that have equal employment opportunity implications.

Outreach Activities

The EEOC conducts extensive outreach activities to prevent employment discrimination. These activities include conducting meetings with employers and others, devoted to presentations by invited experts and stakeholders on specific bases of employment discrimination. EEOC Commissioners conduct numerous media interviews and address numerous stakeholder organizations across the country. The EEOC Commissioners also conduct special fact-finding missions on various topics, such as the "glass ceiling," and anti-immigrant, disability, race, and other types of workplace discrimination.

EEOC personnel conduct numerous technical assistance seminars to individuals in the private sector and state and local governments about EEOC-enforced laws. Agency staff also make numerous public presentations and respond to requests for technical assistance.

Chapter Appendix

The problem analysis of the two pass rates for the employee groups assumes they will be approximated by binomial probability distributions. The null hypothesis is that the pass rates are equal. The alternative hypothesis is that the pass rate for the protected group is significantly less than that of the non-protected group. A one-tailed test is appropriate. Since the EEOC requires testing at the .05 level, we will reject the null hypothesis (that they are equal) when $Z > 1.645$. The test statistic is:

$$Z = \frac{P_1 - P_2}{\sqrt{Rq \left(\dfrac{1}{n_1} + \dfrac{1}{n_2} \right)}}$$

$$Z = \frac{.509 - .407}{\sqrt{(.467)(.533) \left(\dfrac{1}{1020} + \dfrac{1}{725} \right)}}$$

$$= 4.25$$

Where: P_1 = the nonprotected group success rate
P_2 = the protected group success rate
R = $\dfrac{y_1 + y_1}{n_1 + n_2}$ = $\dfrac{520 + 295}{1020 + 725}$ = .467
y_1 = the number of nonprotected employees who successfully passed
y_2 = the number of protected employees who successfully passed
n_1 = the total number of nonprotected employees in training sampled
n_2 = the total number of protected empolyees in training sampled
q = $1 - R$

Solution:

Since the computed Z of 4.25 is greater than 1.645, the null hypothesis, that the two success rates are equal, is rejected, and it is concluded that the protected group pass rate is significantly lower.

CHAPTER 13
WORKPLACE HARASSMENT

Chapter Highlights
- Learn what constitutes harassment
- Understand the bases for harassment
- Explain how to prevent harassment

Introduction

Harassing people because of their age, disability, national origin, race, color, religion, gender, or veteran's status is wrong. More than anything else—even more than the economic costs of expensive court suits and settlements—harassment is humiliating and degrading to human beings. It is not only unfair, it is dehumanizing because it causes pain and suffering in innocent victims. Some victims carry the scars of harassment for their entire lives.

Workplace Harassment is Illegal

Harassment in the workplace is not only wrong; it is *illegal.* Each year, employers pay millions of dollars in legal expenses and remedial, compensatory and punitive awards to the victims of workplace harassment. The other economic costs of harassment are the untold hours lost in investigating and adjudicating harassment charges. There is no doubt about it; the costs of harassment are *significant.* These are dollars that deprive stockholders of dividends and prevent employees from receiving higher pay or better benefits. Furthermore, these costs inevitably cause consumers to pay more for goods and services.

Stopping Workplace Harassment

The fundamental steps in eliminating harassment are: (1) understanding what constitutes harassment; (2) requiring each employee to refrain from engaging in such behavior; and (3) taking prompt corrective action against any person who harasses others. Unfortunately, many people do not understand what harassment is and, consequently, they may be guilty of harassing others and not know it. For example, people who usually harass others because of their gender, race, religion, national origin, or for any other reason, may not believe their behavior is wrong, but it is.

Stopping workplace harassment must be everybody's concern—from top management to a entry-level employee. Management's role includes incorporating a harassment-free environment as part of the organization's strategic planning through long-term goal setting and policy formulation. Management should also assess and eliminate any dimensions of the organization's culture that may condone or unintentionally abet harassment. Operational implementation includes establishing short-term objectives to achieve a harassment-free workplace, conducting employee training, creating a procedure to investigate any complaints of harassment, and taking prompt action against any perpetrators. Employee responsibilities include acquiring an understanding of the behavior that constitutes harassment, assessing their own personal attitudes towards harassment, and ensuring that they do not engage in harassing conduct.

What is Harassment?

The two types of harassment are hostile environment harassment and *quid pro quo* harassment.

Hostile Work Environment Harassment

Hostile work environment harassment is intimidating, hostile, or offensive behavior towards employees, or the creation of such an environment for employees, because of their national origin, citizenship status, race, color, religion, sex, disability, veteran's status, age, or other protected status.

A hostile work environment is one in which the comments, conduct and other aspects of the work atmosphere are such that the victim perceives them to be hostile or abusive, and a "reasonable person" would also find them to be so. Some of the factors that could be considered in deciding whether an environment is "hostile" would be the severity, duration, and frequency of the abuse. In the case of *Harris v. Forklift Systems, Inc.*, the U.S. Supreme Court defined a hostile work environment as one in which a reasonable person would conclude that "the workplace is permeated with 'discriminatory intimidation, ridicule, and insult,' that is 'sufficiently severe or pervasive to alter the conditions of the victim's employment and create an abusive working environment.'"[1]

These are some examples of behavior that could be considered as intimidating, hostile, or offensive. *Intimidating* behavior toward a person because of his or her sex, for example, would be threatening to cause trouble if the person accepts employment in a job that in the past had only been filled by members of the opposite sex. An example of *hostile* behavior toward an older workers would be to give them assignments that were impossible for them to perform, in order to cause them to quit. Finally, an example of *offensive* behavior toward a person because of his or her religious beliefs would be ridiculing some practices of that person's religion.

A tangible adverse action, such as a demotion or discipline, is not a necessary condition for a harassed employee to obtain financial or other relief under equal employment laws. In *Faragher v. City of Boca Raton*, the U.S. Supreme Court held that an employer is liable for hostile-environment sexual harassment by a supervisor who has immediate authority over an employee, even though no tangible adverse employment action resulted from the harassment.[2] The affirmative defenses for this form of hostile-environment sexual harassment are discussed later in this chapter.

---

[1] 62 EPD ¶ 42,623, 114 SCt at 371 (1993).　　　[2] *Faragher v. City of Boca Raton*, 73 EPD ¶ 45,341, 118 SCt 2275 (1998).

Quid Pro Quo Sexual Harassment

Below is the Equal Employment Opportunity Commission's definition of *quid pro quo* sexual harassment.

Quid pro quo sexual harassment consists of unwelcome sexual advances, requests for sexual favors, and other verbal or physical conduct of a sexual nature, when submission to such conduct is made either explicitly or implicitly a term or condition of an individual's employment or submission to, or rejection of, such conduct by an individual is used as the basis for employment decisions affecting the person.

Quid pro quo means "something given in exchange for something else." *Quid pro quo* sexual harassment exists where sexual favors are requested or demanded in exchange for either an improvement in the terms and conditions of employment or the avoidance of an undesirable outcome involving such terms and conditions.

Victims of Quid Pro Quo Sexual Harassment

The victims of *quid pro quo* harassment are not confined to those individuals from whom sexual favors are demanded. The victims include individuals in these three groups:

- Employees who accede to demands and thereby receive benefits from their concession;
- Employees who refuse the demands and are deprived of the benefits because of their refusal; and
- Employees who were qualified for the benefits but were denied them because they were granted to others who yielded to the demands.

The typical improvements offered to individuals in exchange for a sexual favor involve employment advancement opportunities, better work scheduling arrangements, inflated performance appraisals, more employee benefits, higher pay, and human resource development opportunities.

Selections

Quid pro quo harassment victims who acquiesce to demands for sexual favors may be offered opportunities for promotions, temporary assignments, and reassignments. Individuals who rebuff the demands may be deliberately denied such opportunities. Granting opportunities in exchange for sexual favors prevents other employees from fairly competing for them.

Work Scheduling

Many organizations have opportunities for non-traditional work scheduling, such as flextime, job sharing, work-from-home, and part-time employment. *Quid pro quo* victims may be offered opportunities to arrange special work schedules which are not granted to other employees. Those employees who submit to the demands will receive the opportunities, while other employees will be denied them.

Performance Appraisal

Victims of *quid pro quo* harassment may be offered elevated performance appraisals. Victims may also be either implicitly or explicitly threatened that their performance will be appraised as unsatisfactory if they do not consent to the sexual demand.

Employee Benefits

Those employees who rebuff demands for sexual favors may be denied discretionary benefits, such as earned paid time-off. Victims may also be harassed when they request sick leave, requiring them to furnish medical evidence or a doctor's certificate when other employees are not subjected to the same requirements. One victim's supervisor routinely called the employee's doctor every time she used sick leave, demanding that the doctor send a statement justifying the reason for the absence. Employees who were absent more frequently were not subjected to the same abusive practice.

Pay

Harassment victims who decline *quid pro quo* advances may be paid less than their peers and/or their pay increases may be smaller. Alternatively, employees who grant sexual favors may receive higher paying jobs and/or larger pay increases than their job performance would warrant.

Opportunities for Development

Victims of *quid pro quo* sexual harassment may be denied opportunities for career development. One employee who resisted a supervisor's advances for sexual favors was told she could not go to a training class designed to prepare employees for promotion opportunities because "she was too good at her job and could not be spared."

Offers to Avoid Undesirable Outcomes

In exchange for a sexual favor, employees may be offered the opportunity to be spared from undesirable employment actions, such as pay cuts, disciplinary actions, or layoffs.

Harassment Perpetrators

Workplace harassment has been perpetrated by individuals in the following groups:

- Supervisors or other management personnel in the organizational hierarchy who have authority to affect the terms and conditions of employment of the person being harassed;
- Peers;
- Non-employees with whom the employee has work-related interactions, such as vendors who deliver supplies or service vending machines at the work site or contract personnel, including security officers and parking lot attendants; and

- Customers.

All four groups of individuals can engage in behavior that causes a work environment to be intimidating, hostile, or offensive. In addition, the individuals in the first group, such as supervisors or others higher in the organization who have the authority to influence victims' careers, may engage in *quid pro quo* harassment.

Types of Harassing Conduct

There are physical, verbal, visual, and written forms of harassment.

Physical Harassment

Physical harassment includes grabbing, handling, kissing, pushing, striking, and touching.

Verbal Harassment

The most common types of verbal harassment include whistling, making remarks about the victim's anatomy, telling obscene jokes, or making offensive comments that either are directed at the victim or are intended to emphasize some characteristic of the victim, such as the victim's stature or other physical characteristic. In one harassment case, the victim's supervisor made fun of her weight. Continually badgering a person, whether for sexual reasons, such as repeatedly asking a victim for a date or a sexual favor, or for other reasons, such as continually asking an older worker to retire, are types of verbal harassment. Verbal harassment may also include threats, unfounded criticisms, or disparaging remarks about a victim.

Visual Harassment

Visual harassment includes making facial expressions at someone, such as giving a female ogling looks. Hand, finger, or other bodily gestures that are obscene are also types of visual harassment. Whether obscene or not, however, such gestures can be harassment if they have sexual connotations or are meant to create a hostile or abusive work environment for the victim.

Written Harassment

Posting or disseminating cartoons that either refer to the victim or to some characteristic that the victim shares with others are examples of written harassment. Some cartoons or jokes are more blatant than others, such as obscene jokes directed at the victim or placed in a location where they will be seen by the victim. Other forms of written harassment include circulating notes about the victim, repeatedly giving notes to the victim, or placing notes in a location where they will be seen by the victim.

Harassment and Discrimination

The two types of unlawful employment discrimination are disparate treatment and disparate impact. *Disparate treatment* discrimination is intentionally treating a person less favorably in making an *employment decision* because of that individual's national origin, race, color, religion, gender, disability, age, citizenship or veteran's status. *Disparate impact* discrimination is using employment practices that, although fair in form and applied in a nondiscriminatory manner, nevertheless have an adverse impact upon individuals because of their national origin, race, color, religion, sex, disability, age, citizenship or veteran's status.

Since harassment is an intentional act, it is a type of disparate treatment discrimination. *Disparate treatment* typically involves an employment decision by an employee at a higher level than the ones experiencing the discrimination. Although harassment may involve these same circumstances, it may also involve non-employees or employees at any organizational level. Harassment may occur at the workplace or away from the immediate workplace, such as in the company parking lot or at an out-of-the-office, business-related event.

Statuses Protected From Harassment

Harassment based upon any of the following conditions is prohibited under federal law.

National Origin

Harassment founded on national origin includes intimidating, hostile, or abusive behavior toward a person because the individual's physical, cultural or linguistic characteristics are those of a certain national origin group or because of the individual's or the individual's ancestors' place of origin. Also included would be harassment that is grounded on any of the following:

- An individual's marriage or association with persons in a national origin group;

- An individual's membership in an organization supporting a certain national origin group; and

- Attendance or participation in schools and related activities attended by members of an origin group.

Examples of national origin harassment include ethnic slurs or other conduct, whether of a verbal or physical nature, which are intimidating, hostile, or offensive; which are intended to or have the effect of reasonably interfering with a person's job performance; or which negatively affect a person's job opportunities. Other examples include ridiculing an individual because of the person's accent, difficulty in speaking English, or foreign training or education.

Sex

Sex-based harassment can involve either sexual conduct or sexual harassment based upon a person's gender. The U.S. Supreme Court has ruled that same-sex sexual harassment is covered under Title VII.[3] *Sexual-conduct harassment* includes unwelcome sexual advances, requests for sexual favors, and other verbal or physical conduct of a prurient nature that meet one or more of these conditions:

---

[3] See *Oncale v. Sundowner Offshore Services Inc.* (1998) in Appendix 1.

- It is implicitly or explicitly stated that acceptance of the advances is a condition of employment (such as to retain employment in an organization);

- Acceptance or rejection of the advances is used in making employment decisions (such as to be promoted to another job the victim must grant a sexual favor); or

- The conduct creates a hostile, intimidating, or offensive environment or unreasonably interferes with an individual's job performance (such as making lewd jokes, obscene gestures, provocative remarks about a person's appearance, or sexual overtures).

Gender harassment occurs when the object of the harassment is the victim's gender, such as disparaging remarks about women in general (assuming the victim was a woman), for example, referring to women as "airheads."

Religion

Religious harassment includes creating a hostile, intimidating, or offensive environment towards an individual because of his or her religious beliefs or practices. Examples of religion-based harassment include making jokes about an individual's personal appearance or attire mandated by his or her religion, ridiculing a person's beliefs or religious diet, and using slurs in referring to an individual's religion.

Age

Age-based harassment that generates a hostile, intimidating, or offensive environment is legally prohibited when it is directed at persons 40 or more years of age. Regardless of the individual's age, such harassment is still wrong. Examples of age-based harassment include using slurs in describing older workers, such as "dead wood" or "old codgers." Ridiculing older workers and using erroneous stereotypes in referring to older workers by stating, "You can't teach old dogs new tricks," may also be illegal, if such comments create a hostile, intimidating, or offensive environment.

Persons with Disabilities

A person is protected from *disability harassment* if he or she has a physical or mental condition that substantially limits one or more of life's major activities, has a history or record of having such a condition, or is considered to have such a condition. Disability harassment would include using slurs in referring to particular disabilities, taunting individuals about their abilities, and criticizing persons who only perform the essential functions in a job.

Veterans

See Chapter 11 for a full discussion of the groups of veterans protected from harassment and other forms of discrimination.

Citizenship Status

Harassment of either a U.S. citizen or a legal alien on the basis of citizenship status is prohibited. A *citizen* of the United States is a person who is either native born or naturalized. A *legal alien* is a person who is lawfully admitted for permanent residence or granted the status of an alien lawfully admitted for temporary residence or admitted as a refugee, or granted asylum, and who evidences an intention to become a citizen of the United States through completion of a declaration of intention to become a citizen. Examples of citizenship-based harassment include making slurs about a person's country of origin and ridiculing a person's accent in speaking, or his or her difficulty or inability to speak, English.

Race

All people are protected from discrimination based on their race. Federal agency forms used for collecting racial information have these five categories:

- American Indian or Alaska Native
- Asian
- Black or African American
- Native Hawaiian or Other Pacific Islander
- White

These federal forms have "Hispanic or Latino" as the only ethnicity category.

There are several forms of racial harassment, including preferential treatment for a particular racial group or groups. Dealing more harshly with rules infractions committed by individuals in some racial groups is another form of race-based harassment. A particularly odious form of racial harassment is the use of racial slurs.

The U.S. Supreme Court held that the term "boy" may be evidence of racial animus depending upon the context, historical usage, custom and the speaker's inflection and tone of voice and does not need to modified by the words "black" or "white."

Other Prohibited Bases for Harassment

Some states have laws prohibiting harassment on other bases, such as marital status, personal appearance, matriculation, and sexual orientation.

Employer Responsibilities

Employers are liable for harassment against employees. An employer need not have *personally* known about the harassment to be liable. If the harassment is committed by agents or supervisors, employers are responsible, regardless of whether they knew or should have known of their occurrence. The employer will be responsible, even if the behavior was forbidden.

The employer is also responsible for acts of harassment committed by either fellow employees or non-employees, if the employer knew or should have known about the conduct, *unless* the employer took immediate and appropriate action. Mitigating circumstances with respect to non-employees includes the extent of the employer's control and any other legal responsibility which the employer may have had.

A *should have known* standard obviously sets a high level of responsibility for employers. Meeting this standard requires an extraordinary level of management planning, organization, direction, and control. The *planning* includes establishment of written policies that emphatically prohibit work-related harassment and effective procedures to stop any such behavior reported by employees. *Organization* activities include delegating authority to management personnel for both the prevention and correction of harassment, and disseminating the policy and procedures. Management activities involving *direction* include implementing the policy and procedures, conducting management and employee training, swiftly pursuing any complaints of harassment, and taking prompt, corrective action, which may include dismissing employees who engage in harassment. *Control* is the key to the elimination of harassment, since it involves checking that training is effective, that employees are working in a harassment-free environment, and that corrective actions are taken if necessary.

What Causes Some People to Harass Others?

From infancy, people are shaped by their environment. Family members, friends, teachers, and others have an impact upon the kind of person one becomes. Also, the material people read, the television programs they watch, the radio programs they listen to, the organizations they join, and numerous other experiences contribute to the complex process of making people who they are. The expression, "As the twig is bent, so inclines the tree," recognizes the importance of life experiences in shaping human behavior. However, it is important to note that people react to similar environments in unique ways. Thus, even members of the same family may have different opinions on the same subject.

All of a person's experiences on a particular subject form his or her *frame of reference* towards it. This frame of reference dictates a person's *attitude* about a subject; his or her *opinion* is an expression of that particular attitude. As noted above, people exposed to similar environments involving the same subject will not necessarily have the same frame of reference. This is due to both the unique makeup of each person and the way in which he or she learns from different experiences.

Role of Fact and Fiction

A frame of reference based upon facts is much easier to change than one based upon beliefs, perceptions, background and environment. For example, it would be difficult to change the frame of reference of a person who believes particular racial groups are superior to others, if that person was raised in an environment in which those opinions were strongly held. Since such prejudices are not based on facts, it is very difficult to change them, even upon the presentation of convincing evidence. On the other hand, a frame of reference based on facts may be changed, if the facts change.

Intra-Person Frames of Reference

The same person can have apparently contradictory frames of reference on similar subjects. For example, a person could have a frame of reference based on prejudice toward one racial group, such as Asians, but not another group, such as

Blacks. As noted previously, frames of reference based upon facts may be changed quite readily, if the facts change. The more important question is: "Can people's frames of reference change if they are based upon bias and prejudice?" The answer is YES, but they must want to change. In the workplace, management's role is to help that happen.

Organizational Culture and Harassment

An organization's culture can have a significant impact upon workplace harassment. Properly nurtured, such a culture may successfully contain harassment. To accomplish this, however, may require some fundamental changes in the various components that constitute an organization's culture. Organizations have unique cultures that evolve over time. This evolvement may occur by chance, as the result of deliberate management action or through a combination of the two. *Organizational culture* is the beliefs, customs, rules, values, and management philosophies that prevail in an organization.

Beliefs are the expectations and opinions that members of organizations acquire as they become acclimated. If, for example, through the process of organization enculteration, employees are made to believe that harassment is acceptable behavior through example and daily conduct, then, despite any administrative pronouncements to the contrary, they will be more likely to engage in this behavior. In addition, it is difficult to change employee beliefs once they become ingrained. For example, one organization that was experiencing serious problems with unscheduled absences issued a "get-tough" policy statement on the subject. This statement was accompanied by an elaborate procedure for the daily handling of employee absences. Management was surprised to learn that the unscheduled absence rate did not approve in the months following the memo. After making inquiries of several union representatives, management learned that employees generally did not believe that management really meant to implement the policy because unscheduled absences had been ignored for so long in the past.

Customs are the institutionalized expressions, habits, and ways of accomplishing things within an organization. Some organizational customs almost become ritualized, such as the type of clothing that is acceptable and the jargon that is used. Some organizations have literally their own vocabulary of expressions and terms for various dimensions of organizational life. As with other forms of behavior, harassment can inadvertently become customized within an organization. Thus, if employees become accustomed to engaging in a certain type of harassment, then they will continue doing it, despite efforts by management to stop it. The behavior will continue because it is part of the regular ritual of employee interactions. To change the custom requires planned strategies that are rigorously implemented.

Rules are written or unwritten standards to which employees are expected to conform. The types of rules that an organization develops, disseminates and enforces reflect what the organization considers to be important. If an organization's rules are silent on the subject of harassment, it should not be surprising that it occurs.

Values are the relative worth of intrinsic and extrinsic rewards within an organization. Management can significantly influence the value system by communicating the type of behavior that is desired and rewarding it.

Management philosophies are the prevalent attitudes toward different dimensions of the organization. Management commitment to implementing policies and procedures and vigorously ensuring that they are followed is one way of expressing management philosophy toward different subjects.

Management Strategic Planning

Preventing and correcting harassment begins with strategic planning, which includes the following:

- Assessing the organization's culture with regard to harassment and making any necessary changes;
- Establishing a harassment-free policy statement that is consistent with what the culture should be;
- Developing and disseminating a harassment complaint procedure; and
- Making the necessary organizational changes to implement and enforce the policy and the complaint procedure.

Changing the Organizational Culture

Sensitizing employees about the importance of maintaining a harassment-free work environment may require some alterations to an organization's culture. For example, conducting employee training on preventing and stopping harassment will be more effective if the training program is preceded by conscientious effort to ensure that the culture supports the training effort. When what employees are taught runs contrary to what exists in the organizational culture, the training becomes *encapsulated learning,* which means that it cannot be applied in the setting for which it was intended.

The first step in changing an organization's culture is to survey employees to measure the various cultural components that exist in the organization. What are the prevailing beliefs, customs, and values among employees regarding harassment subjects? Also, what are the perceptions of both employees and supervisors of the management philosophy toward harassment? Employee opinion surveys will help management become aware of employees' perceptions of the organization's culture towards harassment. In addition, management may learn about areas in which harassment may be occurring. Too often, top management is totally unaware of a harassment problem until a charge is filed with a regulatory agency. By that time, the problem may be too serious to prevent the filing of charges.

The second step is to communicate the survey results to employees, correct any misperceptions, and make any needed alterations to the organization's culture.

Step 1: Survey Employees

Survey questions should elicit employee opinions about the various components (beliefs, customs, rules, values, and management philosophies) of the organization's culture regarding harassment and whether they have witnessed harassment.

Here are two sample statements that could be included in a survey:

1. It is O.K. for employees to joke about women who are assigned to jobs that typically were done by men.

    — Agree

    — Slightly agree

    — Neither agree nor disagree

    — Slightly disagree

    — Disagree

2. I have seen employees who cannot speak English very well ridiculed for the way they speak.

    — Agree

    — Slightly agree

    — Neither agree nor disagree

    — Slightly disagree

    — Disagree

Step 2: Communicate Results and Change Culture

Employees should be informed of the results of the survey as soon as possible, and any erroneous perceptions about the organization's culture not consistent with management's intentions should be corrected. As necessary, those components of the culture should be changed. The following is a discussion of the components which explain why changes may be needed.

Change Management Philosophies. There are various reasons encapsulated learning occurs, as discussed earlier, such as when learning is contrary to the prevailing management philosophy. If any level of management, but specifically the level with which an employee daily interacts, condones any form of harassment, training employees to maintain a harassment-free workplace will be relatively ineffective. The employee is simply unable to apply what has been learned.

The force of a management philosophy on a particular subject depends upon how deeply feelings are held. In turn, the conviction with which the philosophy is dispatched throughout the organization also depends upon the intensity with which the philosophy is held. If management's commitment to a harassment-free workplace is tentative, superficial, or simply put in place to prevent legal problems, the resultant efforts will lack the fervor to make any substantive change a reality. For example, a policy statement on a harassment-free workplace will only be marginally effective without the wholehearted support of top management. Thus, the prevailing management philosophy is the most important dimension of an organizational's culture in creating a harassment-free environment.

Change Customs. Encapsulated learning will also occur if the organization has a custom of harassing employees, such as gender-based harassment of women who work in jobs that were traditionally filled only by men. In this case, it is the custom in the organizational culture that is causing the encapsulated learning. Sometimes, customs evolve from "making fun" of others, such as playing practical jokes on new employees. However, as the workplace becomes more diverse, the danger in practical joking is that it may create a harassing environment. For a harassment-free environment to exist in the workplace, management must be aware of the customs among employees, including those that involve the various levels of management, and take steps to change those that could constitute harassment.

Change Values. Values differ significantly among organizations. For example, some organizations value employee creativity, while other organizations emphasize the status quo. Obviously, few, if any, organizations have a culture that values employee harassment. So why is there a problem? This is the case because organizations do *not* have a value system in place indicating that harassment is *taboo*. Various management initiatives to prevent and correct harassment, such as issuing policy statements and training employees, will not be fully effective unless the value system is designed or modified to support a harassment-free work environment.

There are various actions that management can take to develop a value system for a harassment-free workplace. First, employees, and particularly supervisory personnel, should be rewarded through a formal performance appraisal system for behavior that supports the organizational policy on harassment-free conduct. Also, promotion procedures should include assessing employees' past behavior and attitudes towards non-harassment. Another way of rewarding harassment-free behavior is through recognition of employees who serve on committee assignments within the organization designed to promote non-discrimination and harassment-free behavior. Management can also ascribe value to a harassment-free work environment by establishing special events to recognize workplace diversity, such as an Equal Employment Opportunity Week or an Employee Diversity Week.

Change Beliefs. Although management may state the harassment is not wanted, employees may *believe* otherwise. These beliefs need to be identified in the survey, and corrective action must be taken. Employees must be convinced that management is serious about preventing harassment. This entails communicating the survey results to employees, correcting any misconceptions, establishing a policy on a harassment-free workplace, and taking prompt action against those who violate it. A practical way to change employees' beliefs is through *object lessons,* in which those who engage in harassment are punished, and those who support the policy are rewarded.

Change Rules. Controlling behavior, particularly the types of behavior that are not desirable, requires rule formulation and enforcement. This is particularly important for the prevention of harassment. Harassment is more likely to occur in the absence of such precepts. Consequently, a harassment-free strategy should include the formulation and enforcement of rules of conduct prohibiting harassment and stating that disciplinary and other types of actions that will be taken for violation of the directives. Rules for maintaining a harassment-free workplace can be included in the following documents:

- A policy statement containing the official position of the organization regarding the prohibition of harassment;

- An employee complaint procedure, in which employees report allegations of harassment;

- An employee code of conduct; and

- A statement of prohibited behaviors.

Harassment-Free Policy Statement

The policy statement and the organization culture should be consistent. Information obtained from the employee survey, discussed above, can be used in either formulating a new policy statement or in changing one that already exists. Appendix 2 contains a sample statement.

Harassment-Free Complaint Procedure

The best way to insure that employee complaints of harassment are internalized and promptly reported is to establish a complaint procedure and motivate employees to use it. Appendix 3 contains a sample procedure.

In addition to the fact that a harassment-free complaint procedure is good business practice, there are also solid legal reasons for establishing such a policy. In *Faragher v. City of Boca Raton*, the U.S. Supreme Court held that an employer is liable for hostile-environment sexual harassment by a supervisor who has immediate authority over an employee. If no tangible employment action results from the harassment, such as discharge or discipline of the employee, the employer can present an "affirmative defense" by showing that: (1) the employer exercised reasonable care to prevent and correct the harassment, and (2) the harassed employee unreasonably failed to take advantage of any opportunities provided by the employer to prevent or correct the harassment. An anti-harassment policy, including a complaint procedure, is not always required for this defense, but such a policy could be presented as evidence of an employer's good-faith effort to prevent and correct such harassment under the first defense, above. Normally, evidence that the harassed employee failed to use any complaint procedure provided by the employer would satisfy the employer's affirmative defense under (2), above. This affirmative defense cannot be used by employers if the supervisor's harassment results in a tangible employment action, such as discharge, demotion, or discipline.[4]

Policy and Complaint Procedure Implementation

The actions needed to implement the policy and complaint procedure include delegating authority to administer them and selecting and training investigators.

---

[4] *Faragher v. City of Boca Raton*, (97-282) 111 F.3d 1530. See also *Faragher v. City of Boca Raton* in Appendix 1.

Complaint Procedure Administrator

The person assigned to administer the complaint system should be effective and respected. Nothing is worse than a system that is clogged in paperwork, with a backlog of complaints awaiting investigation and/or adjudication of findings. An effective manager of such a system should be able to quickly determine the facts of an allegation and resolve it, either through a mediated settlement (for less serious cases) or a recommendation of appropriate action (for those allegations of a more serious nature). The person in charge of the system should also be respected for his or her impartiality.

Training of Investigators

Individuals who are selected as investigators in the complaint procedure should have interpersonal abilities in such areas as sensitivity, listening, stress tolerance, patience, flexibility, and tenacity. Sensitivity is very important, since investigators must be the type of people to whom others can relate their allegations of harassment. Often, harassment experiences have caused pain and suffering to the victims. The victims relive those experiences in relating the circumstances to others. Investigators must be sensitive to this possibility and present a demeanor of compassion and understanding.

Investigators must be trained in such areas as gathering facts, listening, and remaining impartial. There may be a tendency to take sides *before* the facts in a case are known; investigators must refrain from doing so. There typically are at least two points of view in harassment cases. An investigator should refrain from prejudging a case, or even giving such an impression, before the entire case has been investigated. The investigator is *not* an advocate for any party, including the victim or the alleged harasser. Investigators must be perceived as fair to all parties. Victims, alleged harassers, witnesses, and other principal players in harassment cases should believe that the investigator is a fair-minded person. As soon as investigators assume advocacy roles, their appearance of, if not their actual, impartiality is lost.

Investigators can be either in-house or contract personnel, depending upon the needs of an organization. A sufficient number should be selected and trained to ensure that an investigation is commenced within a minimal number of days after a complaint is received. If necessary, *ad hoc* investigators can be used to ensure complaints are handled in a timely manner.

Operational Commitment

Operational implementation includes the following steps:

- Sending a strong message that work-related harassment will not be tolerated;
- Conducting employee training;
- Taking steps to internalize harassment complaints through the organizational complaint procedure established for that purpose;
- Encouraging employees to submit complaints;
- investigating complaints promptly and vigorously; and

• Taking corrective action as soon as the investigations are completed.

Send a Strong Message

It is important that management send a strong message that work-related harassment will not be tolerated. The message, which should be directed to all employees, contract personnel, customers, and all other third parties with whom employees come into contact, should emphasize that harassment will not be tolerated and any reported acts of harassment will be vigorously investigated and prompt corrective action will be taken. Dissemination may occur through various channels, including memoranda, letters, permanent postings on all bulletin boards, and contract agreements.

Conduct Employee Training

Employee training includes explaining the company's sexual harassment policy statement and reviewing the complaint procedure for reporting harassment. Training seminars are also a good place to report the results of the employee survey concerning employees' perception of the organizational culture concerning harassment. Any changes that are proposed in the culture may be covered in training sessions. Key parts of the training should be devoted to starting the process of helping everyone change their attitudes. Harassment would not exist if everybody, including all employees, non-employees, customers and other third parties with whom employees come in contact during their work-related activities, acquired an *attitude* of good faith toward all people that, at a minimum, includes understanding and preventing harassment.

Make Prevention the Focal Point. It is easier to prevent harassment than it is to take corrective action once it occurs. Altering employee attitudes, while not a minor undertaking, is easier in the long run than investigating each reported instance of harassment and taking corrective action. In short, "An ounce of prevention is worth more than a pound of cure."

Help Employees Understand Themselves. How do employees feel about harassment? Do employees understand their own attitudes towards harassment? Are employees motivated to change their attitudes if they are harassment-prone? Answers to these and similar questions are needed for employees to learn about their personal feelings towards harassment and ways to change them. Typically, there is little incentive for people to change their attitudes, unless they are motivated to do so. Employers can motivate a change in *behavior* towards harassment since they have the authority to control employees' actions in the workplace. Whether the behavioral changes occur as a result of an *attitudinal* change may not be apparent. However, conducting sensitivity training and enforcing a policy of non-harassment are important steps in motivating attitudinal changes. Other areas the training should include are:

• *Understand individual differences.* All people are different, due to both nature and nurture; they differ because of their unique genetic composition and the environment to which they have been exposed. Employees should receive sensitivity training that stresses these facts so that they learn to understand workplace diversity.

- *Appreciate people for what they can do and not what they are.* Appearances are only skin-deep. The true value of people is their character. Employees need to understand this fundamental fact.

Internalize Harassment Complaints

Internalizing harassment complaints includes encouraging employees to file complaints when they experience such behavior, vigorously enforcing the no-harassment policy, and taking prompt action to stop it when identified. If an internal system of handling complaints does not exist, the only choices an employee will have are to remain in the organization and be victimized by the harasser; leave the organization; or take his or her complaint to an external source, such as the Equal Employment Opportunity Commission, or to an attorney. Since none of these alternatives benefits the organization, there are obvious advantages to internalizing complaints. Some of these advantages are greater employee satisfaction and prevention of financial losses due to legal expenses and court-mandated settlements.

Encourage Employees to Report Harassment

No harassment policy or procedure will be effective if employees do not report allegations of harassment. The word "allegations" is important because, while harassment may be blatant and obvious in some cases, it can be subtle and less overt in others. Also, harassment is, by definition, the creation of an environment that both the victim and "a reasonable person" consider hostile. Thus, a complaint does not represent a *prima facie* case of harassment. In no way, however, should the word "alleged" be construed as prejudging a complaint. Consequently, employees should be encouraged to report *any* instances they consider to be harassment and leave the actual determination to the person who is responsible for managing the complaint procedure.

Vigorously Investigate Complaints

Each complaint should be investigated in a timely manner. The victim should be contacted upon receipt of the complaint and told when the investigation is expected to commence.

Take Prompt Action

Regardless of the outcome of the case, prompt action should be taken. If the complaint is not substantiated, the employee should be told the reason for the decision immediately. When the facts in the case do support the allegation, quick, corrective action should be taken. This typically means, in less serious cases, that a negotiated settlement is reached that satisfies all the parties. Where more severe action is warranted, more drastic steps may need to be taken. Delays in handling and resolving complaints raise doubts about the fairness and effectiveness of the system.

CHAPTER 14
VALIDITY AND RELIABILITY METHODS

Chapter Highlights
- Introduce the concepts of validity and reliability
- Learn the methods of selection procedure validation
- Understand the methods of selection procedure reliability measurement

---

Introduction

Validity, as the term is used in selection procedures in an employment setting, means a selection procedure that is job related. All types of selection procedures, not just those used in selecting applicants for employment, can be validated.

A *selection procedure* is defined in the *Uniform Guidelines on Employee Selection Procedures* (*Guidelines*) as any measure, combination of measures, or procedure used as a basis for any employment decision. Selection procedures include the full range of assessment techniques from traditional paper and pencil tests, performance tests, and training programs or probationary periods and physical, educational, and work experience requirements on through informal or casual interviews and unscored application forms.[1]

Also considered as selection procedures in the *Guidelines* are initial screening measures, application blanks, medical examinations, background checks, interviews conducted by supervisors, work samples, and performance appraisals.[2]

In short, the *Guidelines* define a selection procedure as virtually any procedure used to make employment decisions about new hires, promotions, demotions, pay increases, disciplinary actions, layoffs, and selections for training programs or preferred assignments. The *Guidelines* stipulate that validation is required for any selection procedure that results in an adverse impact and cannot be justified by a bona fide occupational qualification. Generally, the *Guidelines* apply to employers with 15 or more employees.

A selection procedure used to hire new employees is valid if the results correlate[3] with job performance. For example, a selection interview is valid if the interviewer's predictions of applicants' job performance correlate with the actual

---

[1] CCH HUMAN RESOURCES MANAGEMENT, *Equal Employment Opportunity,* ¶8826 and ¶8827 (*Uniform Guidelines on Employee Selection Procedures*).

[2] CCH HUMAN RESOURCES MANAGEMENT, *Equal Employment Opportunity,* ¶8817 (*Uniform Guidelines on Employee Selection Procedures*).

[3] *Correlate,* as the term is used in this chapter, means a statistically significant relationship.

job performance of those applicants. A performance appraisal procedure used to make pay decisions or take disciplinary actions against employees is valid if the appraisal results correlate with job performance.

Reliability

The term *reliability*, when used in the context of selection procedure decision making in an employment setting, means the results obtained from the process are consistent. For example, a written test is reliable if there is a correlation in a person's scores when he or she takes the same test more than once. An interview is reliable when there is a correlation in the ratings given to the same interviewee in additional interviews by either the same or a different interviewer. A performance appraisal system is reliable if there are correlations among different appraisers using the system in their appraisals of the same employee's performance.

Why Use Valid and Reliable Selection Methods?

There are four main reasons for using valid and reliable selection methods.

Accomplishment of Organization Goals

Selecting the best qualified persons helps ensure that an organization will accomplish its goals. For example, the best qualified persons will produce more at less cost. In short, the best qualified employees will perform better and this will help the organization produce profits for stockholders or, in the case of public organizations, provide taxpayers with required services within budget constraints. The best qualified employees will also produce the quality of product or service the public demands. Employers that use valid and reliable selection methods are acting in a socially responsible manner because they are adhering to societal concerns about fairness codified in equal employment opportunity laws and regulations. Finally, using valid and reliable selection methods meets organizational goals by helping to ensure that employees are permitted to maximize their potentialities.

Maintenance of Goodwill

Maintaining public goodwill is another reason for using valid and reliable selection methods. The public looks more favorably upon organizations that treat people, such as job applicants, in a fair manner. Valid and reliable selection methods are fair and help build public goodwill.

Human Dignity

All persons are entitled to respectful and dignified treatment. This right particularly extends to employment selection decisions because of the intrinsic and extrinsic rewards people receive from their jobs. Human dignity requires employers to fairly consider all persons and to treat them as human beings with personal worth. Selection methods that are not valid or do not produce consistent results demean human dignity.

Legal Requirements

A final reason for using valid and reliable selection procedures is a legal one. In the event of an employment decision having an adverse impact, using valid and reliable selection procedures is the employer's best defense. If litigation over an employment selection decision occurs, and the selection procedure cannot be justified on the basis of a bona fide occupational requirement, the employer may be required to demonstrate that the selection procedure is validly related to the job in question. Adverse impact and bona fide occupational requirements are discussed in Chapter 12.

Selection Method Validation

The three types of selection method validation are criterion-related, construct, and content. Both *criterion-related* and *construct* validation require empirical evidence of a statistically significant correlation between the selection method and job performance. This evidence typically involves computing a coefficient of correlation. Coefficients of correlation measure both the strength and the direction of a relationship between two variables. *Strength* is determined by the size of the coefficient of correlation and a positive coefficient suggests a direct relationship between the variables.

EXAMPLE: Assume that a patterned selection interview correlates 0.4 with the dollar sales of Wholesale Grocery Sales Representatives. Dollar sales is considered the major measure of success in that job. In addition, a sales aptitude test correlates 0.5 with dollar sales. The aptitude test has a stronger relationship with dollar sales than does the interview.

The *statistical significance* of a coefficient of correlation, which is usually denoted by the letter r, is determined by the size of the sample and the selected significance level. The larger the sample, the greater the probability of a statistically significant relationship between the variables. The term *significant relationship* indicates the coefficient of correlation, such as 0.4, is statistically different from zero at some alpha level, such as .01. The .01 means a correlation of this magnitude (0.4) would not be significant in only one of 100 times. The *Guidelines* require that coefficients of correlation in selection method validation must be statistically significant from zero at a minimum of a .05 level.

The *coefficient of determination,* or r^2, is another statistical measure used in empirical validation. This coefficient indicates how much variation in one variable is attributable to another. For example, for $r = 0.4$ the coefficient of determination is $r^2 = 0.4^2 = 0.16$. This means that 16 percent of the variation in some performance variable, such as production differences in employees, is attributable to their scores on a test used to select them and 84 percent of the differences are attributable to other variables. This, of course, assumes a cause and effect relationship.

Criterion-Related Validation

Criterion-related validation is the process of demonstrating that a selection procedure is predictive of important elements of work behavior. Selection methods are the predictors or independent variables. Job performance criteria are the measures of job performance or the dependent variables.

EXAMPLE: ABC Company is a very large supplier of building materials. ABC's human resources manager uses sales experience as a predictor of salespersons' sales. These figures show the sales experience for each sales-person when he or she was first hired at ABC. Also shown are the average annual sales for the first three years after the person was hired.[4]

Exhibit 14-1
Experience and Sales Performance

Sales person	Years of Experience	Annual Sales (in thousands)
Jack	7	$ 90
Claire	5	100
Jean	1	20
Charles	3	20
Jody	4	30
Libby	5	60
Scott	4	40
Edythe	1	30
Phil	2	10
Hank	1	25
Mary	1	10
Peter	3	40
Rich	6	70
Walter	6	70
Marghy	4	80
Joel	1	15
Sallie	2	50
Ralph	2	40
Sharon	3	30
Total	60	$860

The mathematical relationship between selection method and job perform-ance typically is demonstrated through a correlation derived from a linear regression. For the above example, the coefficient of correlation is derived by the Pearson product-moment formula:

$$r = \frac{\Sigma d_x d_y}{n \sigma_x \sigma_y}$$

in which:

   d_x = difference in each value of x and the mean X (years of experience).
   d_y = difference in each value of y and the mean Y (annual sales).
   n = number of pairs
   σ_x = standard deviation of year of experience
   σ_y = standard deviation of annual sales

---

[4] Figures are from B.J. Mandel, *Statistics for Management* (Baltimore: Dangary Publishing Company, 1966), pp. 336-360.

Substituting the values in this formula results in a computed $r = .77$. (The arithmetic is omitted for space reasons.)

Often, a single independent variable, such as a test, or, in the case of ABC Company, the years of sales experience, is not sufficient alone in predicting success. There may be other important job specifications, such as education or certain skills, that should be considered in the selection process. For example, the coefficient of determination or r^2, described earlier, indicates how much variation in a dependent variable is attributable to variations in the independent variable. In the ABC Company example, $r^2 = 0.77^2 = 0.59$. This means that 59 percent of the variation in sales among ABCs' salespersons is attributable to differences in their sales experience. Conversely, 41 percent of the variability is unexplained. With a lower r, such as .4, only 16 percent of the variability is explained. One reason for this is that other variables, such as education or sales skills, may also be important in helping ABC salespeople make sales. For this reason, some employers use more than one method in making selection decisions.

> **EXAMPLE:** A state uses these job specifications and selection methods in selecting highway patrol officers:
>
> 1. High school graduate or GED equivalent;
>
> 2. 21-31 years of age;
>
> 3. Height up to 6'6" and weight proportional to height;
>
> 4. Eyesight 20/40, uncorrected in each eye and corrected to 20/20;
>
> 5. An agility test requiring removal of a 160-pound dummy from a car to a distance 50 feet away, to be accomplished within 35 seconds;
>
> 6. Successfully passing a medical examination;
>
> 7. Background investigation; and
>
> 8. Aptitude test that measures writing ability, judgment, and reading.

If the state validated these selection methods, several of them would have to be validated through criterion-related validation. For example, the state could validate the high school education requirement by conducting a means-difference test of the job performance of officers who were high school graduates or passed the GED test compared to those officers who neither graduated from high school nor passed the GED equivalency test.

> **EXAMPLE:** Assume one of the most important tasks of highway patrol officers is preparing accurate reports of vehicle accidents. Assume further that accident reports are reviewed by superiors, and records are maintained of the number of errors and omissions made by each officer. The high school education or GED equivalency requirement could be validated using a means-difference test.

Exhibit 14-2
Error Rates of Patrol Officers

High School Graduates or GED	Neither High School Graduate nor GED
32	35
31	37
29	35
25	28
34	41
40	44
27	35
32	31
31	34

The error rates could be compared using a means-difference test to determine if there is a significant difference in the errors of the two groups. The means and sums of squares of deviations are:

$\bar{x}_1 = 35.22$ (high school graduates)

$\bar{x}_2 = 31.56$ (*not* high school of GED)

$\sum(x_i - \bar{x}_1)^2 = 195.56$

$\sum(x_i - \bar{x}_2)^2 = 160.22$

Estimate formula for common variance, S^2 is:

$$S^2 = \frac{\sum(x_i - \bar{x}_1)^2 + \sum(x_i - \bar{x}_2)^2}{n_1 + n_2 - 2}$$

$= 22.24$

$S = 4.71$

The hypothesis is that the mean-error rate of high school graduates is no different than that of those without either a high school diploma or a GED equivalency. The alternative hypothesis is that the mean error rate of high school graduates is less than that of those persons without either a high school diploma or a GED equivalency. Thus, we would use a one-tailed test of the t distribution or:

$$t = \frac{\bar{x}_1 - \bar{x}_2}{S\sqrt{\dfrac{1}{n_1} + \dfrac{1}{n_2}}}$$

$$t = 1.65$$

The computed t of 1.65 is less than the table value of 1.746, so we conclude high school graduates do not have lower error rates than those employees who have neither a high school diploma nor a GED high school equivalency.[5]

The other job specifications for patrol officers must either be validated or evidence produced of a bona fide occupation qualification (BFOQ). For example, the requirements concerning age, height, eyesight, medical examination, and background investigation would require the state to show BFOQ. The agility test will be discussed later in this chapter.

Criterion-related validation could be used with the aptitude test by correlating test scores with some summary measure of job performance, such as the supervisor's report of the patrol officers' performance in days absent, sick days used, accidents, number of citations issued, and the average number of miles driven each shift.

Exhibit 14-3
Test Scores and Job Performance Summary

Employee	Test Score	Job Performance Summary
Tom	39	65
Sue	43	78
Frank	21	52
Joan	64	82
Bob	57	92
Greg	47	89
Franklin	28	73
Scott	75	98
Don	34	56
Jack	52	75

The coefficient of correlation, r, is .84, using the formula described above. This r value is at a confidence level above the required 0.05 alpha level, so that the aptitude test for highway patrol officers is significantly related to the supervisors' Job Performance Summary.

---

[5] The values in this example are from W. Mendenhall, *Introduction to Probability and Statistics* (Belmont, California: Wadsworth Publishing Company, Inc., 1967), p. 199.

Concurrent and Predictive Criterion-Related Validation

Criterion-related validation may be performed by either concurrent or predictive studies. *Concurrent* validation uses existing employees as study subjects. The most expedient way to approach *criterion* validation might be to first conduct studies with existing employees. Current employees should be tested and the results correlated with their performance. If correlation is not present; that is, if test scores do not correlate with job performance at the 0.05 level, it is probably unwise to proceed further with using this test.

Concurrent Criterion Validation. The process of using existing employees to validate a selection method for a job they *currently* have, is called *concurrent criterion validation.* The obvious problem with concurrent validation is that the study subjects are existing employees and not applicants. Thus, unsuccessful applicants have already been screened out. Some of these applicants may have been successful in the job, but that cannot be determined. In addition, some applicants who were selected may have left the job for various reasons, including poor job performance—again, this information is not available. These conditions obviously limit the feasibility of generalizing any correlation or other validation study using a concurrent approach. For this reason, the *Uniform Guidelines on Employee Selection Procedures* state that concurrent validation:

> . . . assumes that the findings from a criterion-related validity study of current employees can be applied to applicants for the same job. Therefore, if concurrent validity is to be used, differences between the applicant and employee groups that might affect validity should be taken into account. The user should be particularly concerned with those differences between the applicant group and current employees in the research sample that are caused by work experience or other work related events or by prior selection of employees and selection of the sample.[6]

Predictive Criterion Validation. *Predictive criterion validation* uses applicants, in lieu of employees, as the study subjects. An example of predictive validation would be testing highway patrol officer applicants and hiring them, regardless of their test score. In fact, the test scores are safeguarded, so that only the persons conducting the validation study would have access to them. Later, at various time intervals, such as three, six, nine, and twelve months, the test results for each applicant are correlated with his or her accident report error rate or other performance criteria.

The obvious problem with predictive criterion validation in outside hiring situations is the necessity of hiring the applicants in the study sample. This requirement results in hiring a number of applicants who will not perform satisfactorily. For some jobs, such as the highway patrol officer, hiring unqualified applicants could have serious adverse results. In addition to making excessive error rates on accident reports, they may also perform deficiently in other areas. This may also mean discharging deficient performers.

---

[6] CCH HUMAN RESOURCES MANAGEMENT, *Equal Employment Opportunity,* ¶ 8829 (*Uniform Guidelines on Employee Selection Procedures*).

These are some of the adverse effects of predictive validation. If the negative consequences are too great, and if concurrent validation is not feasible, management may choose one or more of these alternatives: discontinue the test; use the test and risk adverse impact with possible discrimination charges filed by applicants who are not hired; or find another selection method, perhaps even a different test, that can be validated through content validity, which is discussed later in this chapter.

Predictive validation studies for in-house placement of personnel do not pose problems of the same magnitude as hiring personnel from outside the organization. For example, assume that the state highway patrol was validating a test for selecting supervisors, such as sergeants or lieutenants. The applicants would be existing highway patrol officers; selecting all applicants, regardless of test score, would not have the serious consequences as before because officers could be temporarily promoted and later demoted if they failed to adequately perform as supervisors. However, the process of discharging employees who were initially hired because of the validation study is more difficult.

Disadvantages of Criterion-Related Validation

There are three main disadvantages of criterion-related validation. First, predictive studies may be required, and this means employers must tolerate hiring some applicants who will fail.

Second, the number of study subjects must be "substantial," which could be as large as 100 or more for the statistical evidence to be conclusive.[7] This requirement eliminates the possibility of conducting criterion-related studies in small firms. This disadvantage may be offset by using standardized tests that have been previously validated for the same job by other employers, who could use the study results to show criterion validation, provided the jobs are essentially the same and job behaviors used in the validation were the same.

Sometimes, test suppliers have conducted validation studies that might be useful for employers that purchase the test. There is a risk in using the results of validation studies conducted by others. The studies may be faulty or the jobs may not be similar enough. The employer that uses a criterion-related selection method is ultimately responsible for ensuring that it is job related. For example, the *Guidelines* stipulate the test user, not the test supplier, must produce the validation evidence.[8]

A third disadvantage is that cross-validation studies may be necessary. *Cross-validation* is the process of conducting additional studies to show whether similar results occur.

Construct Validation

Constructs are human characteristics, such as leadership, intelligence, and creativity, that may be necessary for satisfactory job performance. *Construct validation* is the process of demonstrating a significant relationship between one or more constructs and job performance.

---

[7] *Ibid.*, ¶ 8829. [8] *Ibid.*, ¶ 8828.

EXAMPLE: Management in an advertising agency believes *creativity* is an important construct for successful performance in one of their jobs titled Advertising Account Representative (AAR). Employees who are AARs work with clients in developing newspaper, magazine, and television advertisements. Agency management considers these two criteria the most important for successful performance as an AAR: (1) agency revenue generated by the AAR; and (2) clients' opinions of AAR effectiveness in meeting their advertising needs. Through experience, agency management has determined that both of these criteria depend upon the AAR's creative ability or skill to develop advertising campaigns that successfully communicate a client's product or service. Also, creativity is needed to effectively interpret a client's ideas and philosophies through advertising. One of the methods the agency uses in selecting AARs is a commercial test of creativity. To be considered for employment, applicants are required to achieve a minimum score of 90 on the test.

The *Guidelines* require employers to produce evidence of a significant relationship between a construct test and job performance, if adverse impact exists, and if the test does not result in measuring the skill or ability through an observable product or service similar to those actually produced on the job. The commercially prepared creativity test used by the agency does not result in an actual or a simulated work sample or a simulation of a work behavior. The agency must show a significant relationship between test scores (specifically achieving a minimum score of 90) and the two criteria of job success. The study would entail a means-difference test in which subjects are categorized into two groups—those who score below 90 and those who score 90 or above. The dollar revenue of sales would be compared for the AARs in the two groups. A similar comparison would be made for the client's opinion of AAR effectiveness.

The legality of construct validation was demonstrated in a case reviewed by the U.S. Supreme Court involving a test of verbal skill that the District of Columbia used in the selection of police officers. The test had an adverse impact on African-American applicants. The U.S. Supreme Court found the test was legal, since there was a relationship between scores on the test and performance in a training program required of new police officers.[9]

Construct validation can be performed either concurrently (with existing AARs) or predictively (using job applicants). The concurrent and predictive criterion validity problems discussed earlier, also apply to construct validation.

Content Validation

A selection method is *content valid* if it requires applicants to produce products, provide services, or display behaviors essential for satisfactory job performance. These products, services, and behaviors may either be simulations or samples of job task performance.

---

[9] *Washington v. Davis,* 11 EPD ¶10,958, 426 U.S. 229 (1976).

A *job simulation* selection method simulates the work environment, such as the previously noted agility test for highway patrol officers that requires the removal of a 160 lb. dummy from a car to a distance of 50 feet within 35 seconds. Obviously, the tasks of highway patrol officers may involve removing people from cars, but it is doubtful that they would ever remove dummies. However, the test simulates a task considered essential in the job.

A job *sample* requires applicants to perform some task or behavior actually required on the job. An example of a job sample test would be requiring applicants for the job of Automobile Transmission Mechanic to diagnose the problems in an inoperable transmission.

These examples illustrate how content validity is a relative quality on a continuum with simulations on one end and work samples on the other.

Typically, content validity is highest with task samples; thus, employers should use them when a option exists. For example, either a sample or a simulation test could be given to applicants for an accounting clerk position that requires verifying the accuracy of figures on purchase orders, such as checking the billing and payment dates to ensure that the proper discount was taken, verifying prices of items by comparing them with price lists, checking the multiplication of extensions, and verifying totals. A sample test would require applicants to perform these tasks, using copies of actual vouchers. A simulation test would require applicants to perform the same tasks, but the test materials would be forms that simulate purchase orders. Both tests involve checking figures, addition, and multiplication. However, the sample test involves performing those tasks with the actual materials used on the job. Another example of the differences in simulation and samples is professional football teams using scrimmages and preseason games to select football players. Scrimmages are simulations of actual games. During preseason games, coaches try out players to select those who will make the final squad. This selection process involves task samples because it is performed under actual game conditions.

There are three important advantages to content validation. First, content-valid selection procedures are job-related, so that applicants can demonstrate whether they can produce a required product or service or display a behavior necessary for satisfactory job performance. Another reason is that such methods have high *face validity.*

Face validity means a selection method *appears* to measure what should be measured in a selection process.

In other words, a selection method has face validity to applicants to the extent that they can see it is related to the job they are seeking. Job sample and simulation selection methods have this authenticity. As a result, applicants are more motivated to perform well or, conversely, withdraw their application if they cannot perform the task. Face validity is not a substitute for criterion, construct, or content validity. However, proper attention to face validity will help guide decisionmakers in their choices of which selection methods to use and how to structure them.

If possible, employers should substitute content validation for either criterion or construct validation because it does not require statistical analysis. This advantage eliminates sampling problems, the use of controls, and other costly concerns like selecting applicants in predictive criterion studies.

Finally, content validation does not require cross-validation studies.

In short, content validation is easier, has less adverse impact, has higher face validity, is less disruptive to the organization, and is less costly than criterion or construct validation.

Differential Validity

There may be occasions when members of one sex or racial group may attain lower scores on average than members of the other sex or racial group(s). A problem arises when these differences are not reflected in commensurately lower differences in job performance. In such cases, the selection procedure would be deemed to be *unfair*. On the other hand, if the differences in scores in a selection procedure are related to job performance, then the procedure has *differential validity*. Employers have the responsibility of ensuring that selection procedures are fair to members of all groups.

Unfairness Defined

According to the *Uniform Guidelines On Employee Selection Procedures*, a selection procedure is *unfair*, "When members of one race, sex, or ethnic group characteristically obtain lower scores on a selection procedure than members of another group, and the differences in scores are not reflected in differences in a measure of job performance . . . "[10] Generally, employers who have a large number of employees or applicants for a job will be under a greater obligation to conduct analyses of test fairness because it will be more technically feasible for them to do so. "The greater the severity of the adverse impact on a group, the greater the need to investigate the possible existence of unfairness. Where the weight of evidence from other studies shows that the selection procedure predicts fairly for the group in question . . . for the same or similar jobs, such evidence may be relied on in connection with the selection procedure at issue."[11]

Cutoff Scores

When technically feasible and a group represents a significant portion of the labor market, "data must be generated and results separately reported for minority and nonminority groups . . . "[12] A selection procedure that has differential validity may be used where it is valid and not used for groups where it is not valid. Furthermore, if the procedure is valid for all groups but one or more groups typically scores higher without a corresponding difference in job performance, then cutoff scores must reflect the same probability of job success for all groups.

---

[10] *Uniform Guidelines In Employee Selection Procedures*, 1978, Section 14B(7).

[11] Ibid.

[12] Ibid.

Validation and Job Analysis

According to the *Guidelines,* a job analysis is required prior to conducting a validation study. A *full* job analysis is required in all content or construct studies and in some criterion-related studies. A *partial* job analysis is required for criterion-related studies if production or error rates or other measures, like absenteeism or tardiness, are obtainable and important in the employment situation or if an overall method of determining job performance can be shown to be related and important for job success.

Selection Method Reliability

The three main types of reliability measures are split-half, test-retest, and equivalent forms.

Split-Half Reliability

Split-half reliability is accomplished by dividing a test in half and correlating the responses for the even-numbered questions with the odd-numbered ones. This correlation is a measure of a selection method's internal consistency. One method of testing for this type of reliability is the Spearman-Brown formula.

EXAMPLE: 500 applicants for a job as software trainee took a 100-question test measuring aptitude to learn software-training materials. The employer conducted a split-half reliability measure of the test. Correlating the answers of the 500 applicants to the even-numbered questions with their answers to the odd-numbered questions is how the split-half measure was conducted.

Test-Retest

Test-retest is administering the same selection method to the same individuals and correlating the two scores. Reliable methods should yield about the same results.

EXAMPLE: All applicants for a technician trainee position are given an aptitude test to determine how well they can be expected to perform in a technician training class. Two weeks later, the test is given to the same group of applicants. The results of the two tests are correlated to see how consistent the scores are.

The statistical test used in this case is the *Pearson* r. Another name for this test is the *coefficient of stability* because it measures the coefficient of correlation over time. One problem with this reliability measure is people change over time, so the interval between testings should not be too long. On the other hand, if the interval is too short, the applicants may remember how they responded to various items and/or selection personnel may recall how the applicant was evaluated on particular items. This recall obviously contaminates the results. Another problem is that people may have different emotional moods or be in different conditions of health that cause their performance to vary from one day to another.

Equivalent Forms

The *equivalent forms* method of reliability correlates applicants' scores on two different but equivalent versions of the same selection method.

> **EXAMPLE:** A written job knowledge test is given to all applicants for the position of accountant. A test bank of 400 items is constructed and numbered. From this bank, two tests, called A and B, are prepared with 150 items in each. The items are randomly selected from the bank and alternatively assigned to the two tests. Both tests are given on successive days to all applicants, and the scores are correlated.

The coefficient of correlation for this type of reliability study is sometimes called the *coefficient of equivalence.* This is the most demanding of all reliability correlation methods because of the difficulty in constructing two forms of a selection method that are fully equivalent.

CHAPTER 15
RECRUITMENT

Chapter Highlights
- Learn why success in recruitment depends upon an organization's reputation
- Understand the steps in designing a recruitment program
- Learn the internal and external sources of recruitment
- Learn the methods of recruitment interviewing

Introduction

Recruitment is the human resource management activity that develops sources of qualified applicants. Some recruitment tasks interface with the selection process. For example, newspaper recruiting advertisements typically include some job specifications that motivate potential applicants to evaluate their personal qualifications. Presumably, many underqualified applicants decide not to apply after this self-analysis. A more significant interaction of selection and recruitment occurs when interviews are conducted. For example, many organizations send recruiters to colleges and technical schools to conduct interviews. These initial screening interviews are the first step in the selection process.

Importance of the Organization's Reputation

Recruitment success is influenced by an organization's reputation, which is determined by these four groups: (1) the employees; (2) the public; (3) the customers; and (4) the competition.

Employees

Employees are the best sales and public relations people an organization can have, since satisfied employees positively influence an organization's reputation. Employers that are concerned about their reputations build employee loyalty and commitment and capitalize on them through employee testimonials in recruitment literature and advertising campaigns. Some organizations even temporarily assign employees to recruitment campaigns. For example, one school district used classroom teachers to recruit new teachers. These recruiters received some basic skills training, but the biggest advantage was their enthusiasm about their profession and their school district.

Public

Corporate citizenship has many long-term effects, such as its impact upon an organization's image as an employer. Applicants are attracted to organizations that are socially responsible and fulfill their obligations to the community. Both large acts (obeying laws and supporting community projects) and small ones (buying advertising space in a local high school newsletter) contribute to the organization's image and reputation. A roofing company in one city supported youth athletic teams in basketball and baseball. Many young people started their sports careers through these company-sponsored programs.

Customers

Customers want good products and services at fair prices; when they do not receive them, the result is unhappiness and occasionally some grief for the organization. An accumulation of negative events will ultimately affect the organization's reputation and image. One outcome of this situation is a decline in the number of well-qualified job applicants. In addition, employees do not appreciate working for an organization that has an unfavorable reputation with its customers.

Competition

It is not unreasonable for an organization to be concerned about its reputation with competing firms when recruitment strategies are contemplated. For example, the best employees within a discipline or industry want to work for organizations that are the leaders in the field. This explains why the exceptional organizations are exceptional; they are able to recruit and retain exceptional talent. This situation does not occur by chance; industry leadership is earned by effective long-term strategic management that includes treating employees as responsible partners.

Employees know the top organizations within a field, and they do not hesitate to apply for employment with them and to refer others. One talented computer scientist knew the well-earned reputation of a competitor and took the opportunity, while on vacation in the area, to visit one of the competitor's plants. Company representatives were quite hospitable and gave the scientist a brief orientation. The tour corroborated the scientist's prior opinions. He was so impressed he applied for a job and was hired the same day. Eventually, several of his former colleagues also resigned and joined the scientist at the same company. Sometimes, critics label these interfirm personnel moves as "raiding" or "proselytizing," but the biggest motivation for these changes is the gaining organization's reputation as a leader in the field. Top-level talent is not attracted to organizations that disregard the human element. Furthermore, top people will not refer their friends and associates to firms with this reputation.

Designing a Recruitment Program

A recruitment program should include:

1. Recruitment planning;

2. Assignment of recruitment responsibilities, either full-time or part-time, to one or more jobs;

3. Development of recruitment sources;

4. Consideration of special recruitment concerns; and

5. Analysis of various recruitment questions, such as the organization's major recruiting advantages.

Recruitment Planning

Recruitment planning includes defining recruiting goals, policies and procedures.

Defining Goals, Policies, and Procedures

Recruitment goals are part of the long-term strategic planning of the organization. These goals address key matters such as career opportunities for employees, equal employment opportunity, and the competitiveness of the organization's pay and benefits.

The following is an example of a recruitment goal:

> *ABC Manufacturing will ensure equal employment opportunity in the recruitment and employment of protected group members.*

Recruitment policies are broadly written guidelines that address various recruitment subjects, such as career advancement, that are included in goal statements. This is an example of a recruitment policy that addresses equal employment opportunity:

> *College recruitment will include annual interviewing at colleges with large populations of students in protected groups.*

Recruitment procedures are detailed instructions specifying how recruitment activities will be conducted. This is an example of a recruitment procedure addressing equal employment opportunity:

> *College recruiters will identify every college with a large population of protected-group students in the geographical recruiting area, meet the director of student placement at those schools, explain our commitment to equal employment opportunity, and schedule annual recruitment visits.*

Delegating Recruitment Tasks

Large organizations have full-time recruiters. Most other organizations delegate parttime recruiting tasks to an employee in the human resources department. In the smallest companies, recruiting activities are performed by the owner-manager. Often, organizations contract with public or private employment agencies that perform various recruitment and/or selection functions.

The person to whom recruitment responsibilities are delegated should be the focal point for recruitment within the organization. Some organizations select a person from a functional area other than human resources/personnel management to perform recruiting activities. Regardless of the function from which they are selected, candidates for recruiter assignments should be able to communicate with prospective employees. In addition, recruiters should possess any special qualifications necessary to recruit from specific recruitment sources. For example, college students appear to be favorably disposed toward recruiters who are friendly, knowledgeable about the jobs for which they are recruiting applicants, demonstrably interested in the applicants, and truthful.

Training Recruiters. Recruiters need training in several areas before they commence work. For example, recruiters should understand these three purposes of a recruitment interview: (1) obtain information from the applicant, such as her/his qualifications and career interests; (2) give information about the job and the company, such as tasks, reporting relationships, and products/services produced; and (3) make a friend. The last purpose is important because applicants should leave the interview with a positive opinion of the interviewer and the organization. Applicants may be disappointed if they are not selected for a job, but they do not easily forgive an organization whose interviewers mistreat them.

Rapid-fire questions and a stress-induced interviewing environment have no place in the average recruitment interview. Introducing some stress may be necessary in preparing interview questions for jobs that require the ability to tolerate stress, such as meeting time deadlines, handling customer dissatisfactions, and resolving crisis situations. However, even interviews that cover these subjects can be tactfully handled.

One interviewee related how an interviewer commenced an interview by asking, "Why should we hire you?" There weren't any of the customary preliminary questions, just this one direct question. The interviewee explained how he was initially dumbfounded by the abrupt question but somehow managed to explain qualifications he had that he felt the organization would need. After he finished, the interviewer responded by asking further, "Why do you think that should make us interested in hiring you?" Needless to say, the organization did not make a friend. Problems such as these are largely attributable to a lack of training.

Recruitment Sources

Applicants may be obtained through both external and internal sources. According to the results of the 1999 SHRM/CCH Recruiting Practices Survey, advertisements in the daily and Sunday newspapers are the top recruitment methods used for most jobs. Table 15-1 shows the top five methods used for various types of occupations.

Table 15-1
Top Five Recruitment Methods

Occupation	Recruitment Method				
Officers & Managers	Promotions	Sunday paper ads	Search agency	Personal contract	Contingency agency
Professionals	Sunday paper ads	Daily paper ads	Employee referral	Contingency agency	Search agency
Technicians	Sunday paper ads	Daily paper ads	Internet job posting	Employee referral	Diversity referral
Technology	Sunday paper ads	Internet job posting	Employee referral	Daily paper ads	Search agency
Sales	Sunday paper ads	Daily paper ads	Personal contact	Search agency	Employee referral
Office & clerical	Sunday paper ads	Daily paper ads	Temp to hire	Employee referral	Job hotline

Occupation	Recruitment Method				
Skilled	Sunday paper ads	Daily paper ads	Promotions	Employee referral	Personal contact
Semi-Skilled	Sunday paper ads	Daily paper ads	Job hotline	College visits	Promotions
Laborers	Sunday paper ads	Daily paper ads	Employee referral	Temp to hire	College visits
Service	Sunday paper ads	Daily paper ads	College visits	Employee referral	Public employment agency

Source: CCH Incorporated, *Ideas and Trends in Personnel*, June 16, 1999, p. 91.

Internet Applicants

The U.S. Department of Labor for the purposes of the Office of Federal Contract Compliance Programs, which includes the Vietnam Era Veteran's Readjustment Assistance Act, Executive Order 11357, and Rehabilitation Act, defines an "Internet Applicant" as an individual to whom these four criteria are satisfied:

- The individual submits an expression of interest in employment through the Internet or a related technology, such as an email, commercial and internal resume databanks and employer Web sites;

- The contractor who receives the expression of interest, considers the individual for employment in specific position;

- The individual's expression indicates he/she is qualified for the position; and,

- The individual does not remove himself/herself from the selection process.

Contractors must maintain the following information:

- Retain all expressions of interest for employment received through Internet and related technology; and,

- If the person is an" internet applicant", as defined above, the employer must "attempt to collect race, gender, and ethnicity information and run an adverse impact analysis" for any job for which they are considered[1]. Examples of adverse impact analyses are demonstrated in Chapter 12.

Sources of Internet Applicants. Internet or related electronic data technologies include these sources of applicants:

- Electronic mail/email

- Resume databases

- Job banks

- Electronic scanning technology

- Applicant tracking systems

---

[1] CCH, On-line recruiting carries particular recordkeeping requirements HR should be aware of, *Human Resources Management: Ideas & Trends* (January 24, 2007), p. 13.

- Applicant service providers
- Applicant screeners[2].

These procedures apply to federal contractors and subcontractors under the laws and Executive Order shown above.

Data Recording Requirements. There are significant data recording requirements under the "Internet Applicant" procedures. Except for resumes, see Chapter 5 for the types of information to be collected and time periods for which it is to be retained.

Record Requirements for Resumes. Data must be obtained for resumes regardless of whether the individuals who submitted the resumes met the definition of an "Internet Applicant." These individual' names must be recorded on each occasion they are contacted to determine their interest in a particular job. There are other record requirements depending upon whether the resumes are in internal or external databases.

- **Record requirements for Internal resumes.**
  (1) A copy of each resume added to the database
  (2) Date each resume was added
  (3) The position for which each resume database search was conducted
  (4) The date each database search was conducted
  (5) The criteria used in conducted each search
- **Record requirements for External resumes.**
  (1) Record of the position subject to a database search
  (2) The search criteria used
  (3) The date of the search
  (4) Resumes (or copies) of any persons who were considered and met the job's basic qualifications

Strategies to Reduce Record Requirements. Employers can reduce the instances in which resumes are obtained from Internet Applicants and thus reduce the data recording requirements, by following these actions:

- Don't accept or review applications and resumes received through the internet and related technologies unless they are submitted under an employer-defined protocol, such as to a specific website where job vacancies are posted (thus eliminating unsolicited applications and resumes submitted via email). Instead, return the applications and resumes and refer the senders to the website that contains information on any job vacancies.
- On the defined website, persons should be informed applications are only being accepted for whatever jobs are available. Job postings should be carefully crafted to show the essential functions and basic qualification

---

[2] U.S. Department of Labor, *Internet Applicant Recordkeeping Rule.*

requirements persons must meet to be considered. The posting should clearly state only persons who meet the qualification requirements and agree to perform the essential functions will be considered. Persons should be required to indicate they meet these two conditions. This will reduce the number of persons who submit applications without regard to either their personal qualifications for a specific position or interest in performing the job's essential functions. Persons who meet the two conditions should be requested to complete a voluntary self-identification tear-off section on the application on which they can identify their race, gender and ethnicity.

- If the number of applications submitted by persons who meet the two conditions for a particular job is too large then reduce the number by an objective means such as taking a random sample that will yield a more manageable applicant pool.

Problems with Resumes. As discussed above and in Chapter 5, the "Internet Applicant" rule has significant record requirements for employers who maintain resume databases. The strategies outlined above will help limit record retention and the required activities related to it.

In the larger picture, this rule warrants a more rigorous examination of the role and utility of resumes. In the past, the resume occupied a unique place in traditional recruitment and selection. Many books, pamphlets, training seminars, Internet websites and the related have been devoted to preparing effective resumes. College entrants into the market labor diligently attempt to perfect a resume that would place them ahead of others in obtaining a job interview. In the past, applicants sent their resumes to a limited number of employers, usually those with the greatest prospect of providing employment offers. This changed when universal access to the Internet opened the gate for applicants to flood employers with unprecedented numbers of resumes. To efficiently handle this surge, many employers purchase resume processing software to perform various functions ranging from acknowledging receipt of resumes to integrating them into an accessible database.

Typically, a resume is a generic document and as such is not submitted for a specific job. Oftentimes persons submitting resumes have not constructed the resumes to provide basic information about their qualifications for a particular job. Also, persons submitting resumes do not know the essential tasks in various jobs, the hours of work and the work location.

Due to the Internet applicant recordkeeping rules that apply to resume databases, and the limited utility of the resume in a selection process, employers may want to reexamine their policies regarding maintaining such databases.

Internal Sources

There are advantages and disadvantages to the use of internal sources for job applicants. Among the advantages are providing career advancement opportunities for existing employees and utilizing the qualifications of employees, without incurring the expenses of recruiting someone from outside the organization.

There are also several distinct disadvantages to exclusively relying upon internal recruitment. First, filling all higher-level positions from within the organization prevents an infusion of new ideas, which is needed to counter stagnation. Examples of this condition are found in some public and quasi-public agencies. While most of the top executive-level federal jobs change with new presidential administrations, these executives must depend upon long-term bureaucratic careerists for the implementation of policy changes. Accomplishing these changes requires considerable patience and leadership in working through sticky rules and procedures. Some external recruitment at initial, middle, and upper levels helps prevent this stagnation.

Another problem with exclusively relying upon internal recruitment is that it may prevent or retard the achievement of equal employment opportunity goals. If an organization already has adverse impact in its selection process, exclusive reliance upon internal recruitment may exacerbate the condition.

Present Employees

Existing employees are an immediate source of applicants to fill vacancies through promotions or reassignments. Some organizations have a policy of initially attempting to fill all vacancies from their employee populations. The advantages of filling vacancies from within include increased employee morale, reduced expenses for recruitment and orientation training, and better employee utilization. Employee utilization is a factor because organizations have fluctuating needs for human resources. For example, one firm produces products for consumer, manufacturing, and construction markets. When the home building market was depressed, the firm had surplus employees available for reassignment to other divisions. This is an example of human resource planning that reduces the need for layoffs and, consequently, eliminates excessive expenditures for unemployment compensation and other benefits such as supplemental unemployment insurance.

Present employees are also a resource for recruiting their friends and relatives. Usually, since friends and relatives of employees possess similar qualifications and interests as the employees, employers actively encourage this source of recruits. Some firms in industries with a scarcity of qualified applicants have special programs to induce employees to find and refer recruits. As shown in Table 15-1, employee referrals are among the five methods that firms use to recruit applicants for the following types of positions: professional; technical; technology; sales; office and clerical; skilled and unskilled labor; and service.

Some firms use financial incentives to induce employees to make referrals. One firm pays the referring employee $150 when the referred employee commences work. Three months later, the referring employee is paid an additional $150 if the referred employee is still employed. Another firm pays a referral bonus of $250 upon employment of the referred employee. This bonus is followed with another $250 after six months, contingent upon the referred employee being employed at that time.[3]

---

[3] CCH Incorporated, *Ideas and Trends in Personnel,* June 16, 1999, p. 91.

Job Posting. Normally, internal recruitment is accomplished through the posting of job vacancies. Some firms use a computer system to list any job vacancies, allowing employees access to the system through their personal computers at work or through their home computers.[4] Job posting consists of publicizing vacancies through notices that contain information such as the job description, salary, job specifications, and the work schedule. Job vacancies are typically posted for periods ranging from 10 to 30 days. Many firms are using information technology in job posting. According to the 1999 SHRM/CCH Recruiting Practices Survey, 52 percent of the respondent firms use intranet or e-mail internal job postings.[5]

Application Process. One problem with job posting is the length of the period required to fill the initial vacancy and any subsequent vacancies that result from filling the initial one. Job posting is also time consuming because each applicant's qualifications must be studied to select the best qualified person. This process is considerably shortened when jobs are filled on the basis of seniority; however, this practice normally is used only in companies with union contracts. Also, even if seniority is used to fill vacancies, there is some delay, since the jobs are usually awarded on the basis of the senior *qualified* bidder.

One way of substantially shortening the time delay is to use an application process in which employees apply beforehand for any jobs in which they have an interest. Applicants' qualifications can be evaluated before a vacancy occurs, and unqualified employees can learn where their qualifications are deficient. This process permits each vacancy to be filled almost immediately, since no posting is required, and all the applicants' qualifications have already been evaluated. Employees are responsible for keeping management informed of any changes in their qualifications that are pertinent to those jobs in which they have an interest.

Career Planning. Through career planning, applicants are advised of various job opportunities. Interested employees complete interest questionnaires and self-analysis profiles and compare the results with the specifications of the jobs in which they are interested. Employees are also given career counseling and informed about the ways that they can obtain any additional skills they may need.

External Sources

External sources of job applicants include newspaper advertisements, employment agencies, college placement offices, the CareerOneStop, direct mail, shopping center kiosks, computer databases, retirees, walk-ins, military veteran organizations, and trade associations.

Newspaper Advertisements

As shown in Table 15-1, Sunday newspaper advertisements are among the most frequently used methods to recruit applicants for all types of work. Furthermore, daily newspaper advertisements are among the most frequently used methods for all types of positions, except for officers and managers. Some firms

---

[4] Moravec, M., "Effective Job Posting Fills Dual Needs," *HR Magazine* (September 1990), p. 77.

[5] CCH Incorporated, *Ideas and Trends in Personnel*, June 6, 1999, p. 99.

use the ads to publicize their products or services or to point out some distinctive features. This type of ad performs two functions. First, it attempts to motivate applicant interest by educating readers about some unique characteristics of the organization, such as its management philosophy, product technology, or career opportunities. In addition, the ads are intended to build goodwill and/or consumer demand by stressing distinctive features of various products or services.

Preparing an effective and legal employment ad is more involved than it appears. Several preliminary guidelines may ensure an ad's success. First, check the job description and job specifications to be sure that they are correct; conduct a job analysis if there is any doubt about their accuracy. Incorrect specifications may inadvertently result in adverse impact by improperly eliminating applicants who do not meet the advertised specifications but, nevertheless, could perform the job tasks. Second, the ad should be written so that it can be read, omitting technical jargon. Third, recruitment ads are sales devices and should be written accordingly—to sell the job to prospective applicants. This means the ad must be appealing in both structure and content. Structural items, such as the ad's printing style, borders, and layout are important for aesthetic appeal. Content items concern the way the ad is written, such as factual statements that highlight the job's major features. There is a tendency to fill ads with too much information about the company, location, and related items.

This information is important, but applicants are mainly interested in the type of job, what the job entails, the challenges, and any promotional or career opportunities. The ad's opening sentence or paragraph should be written to gain reader attention. Subsequent information should explain major job tasks.

Some ad experts contend that more specific information, such as staff and budget responsibilities, should also be included.[6] Unfortunately some ads do not contain even basic job information. One job searcher reported his frustrations with ads such as this one:

> *Director opportunity with prestigious Fortune 100 organization committed to providing rapid advancement opportunities to fast-track achievers who can continue to enhance a state-of-the-art human resource function. This high profile individual, who possesses excellent managerial and intervention skills, technical achievements and dynamic personal characteristics, will interface with executives recognized for their growth-oriented business results. Initiative, potential and progression through meaningful exposure is more important than years of experience. Respond in strict confidence to. . . .[7]*

The same job searcher read job advertisements in newspapers from the largest cities in the U.S., and only one of the "thousands" of ads he read clearly stated what the job actually required, the pay, and how to apply.[8]

Employee benefits can be a selling feature but they must be presented properly. For example, the statement "a very competitive benefits package" is

---

[6] CCH Incorporated, *Ideas and Trends in Personnel* (July 13, 1984) p. 77.

[7] L.O. Baier, "Job Searching and the Advertising Dilemma," *Personnel Administrator* 29 (April 1984), p. 22-23.

[8] *Ibid.*, p. 23.

not as clear as "full benefits are offered including company-paid pension, tuition-reimbursement, and medical and dental plan."

Similarly, salary levels should be stated; statements such as "competitive salary" or "attractive salary" are of little value. The most direct way of communicating salaries is to show the salary range or indicate the approximate pay such as "salary in low $50's." Sometimes, ads indicate salary is "negotiable" or "salary commensurate with qualifications."

Geographical designations are appropriate provided they are specific. For example, "south" can range from New Mexico to Florida. The job searcher mentioned above concluded that "SB" means the Sunbelt and it can range " . . . from California (on good days) in a straight line east to Georgia and includes all areas south to the Gulf of Mexico."[9]

Finally, every ad should adhere to equal employment opportunity requirements. Ad statements, such as "high school student wanted for grocery bagging," "mature female college student wanted for office work" and "man with experience" are discriminatory. Ads may not stipulate requirements regarding national origin, race, color, religion, sex, disability and age; to do so risks charges of discrimination. In addition, certain federal contractors may not make reference to veteran's status. Some local jurisdictions, such as Washington, D.C., also prohibit references to marital status, sexual preference, and political affiliation. The wise course, and the one observed by socially responsible employers, is to omit reference to any of these characteristics.

Employment Agencies

Employment agency is a generic term that includes firms that recruit, screen, and refer applicants to employers. There are several types of agencies. Some deal solely with placing temporary help and others are very specialized, dealing with placing managerial talent within a specific industry. Employment agencies perform some selection functions in addition to recruiting applicants. For example, they interview applicants and determine their employment interests and qualifications. In addition, they may administer job skills and knowledge tests and verify applicant qualifications.

Fees charged by employment agencies vary considerably from industry to industry. Sometimes, fees are charged on a flat rate basis, but, more typically, they are based upon 10 to 30 percent of the job's annual salary. Although fees are occasionally paid by the applicant, most agencies work only with employer-paid fees. In these situations, the agency normally guarantees the employer that the applicant will perform satisfactorily for a minimum period, or the fee is refunded.

As in other human resource areas, the employment agency field is undergoing some changes. Employment agencies also are facing, more frequently, the dual-career family. This topic is discussed later in the chapter. Employment agencies are subject to various employment laws, including those that apply to equal employment opportunity, so that they must ensure their selection proce-

---

[9] *Ibid.*, p. 22.

dures are valid and reliable. The National Association of Personnel Services (NAPS) established the Certified Personnel Consultant (CPC) and the Certified Temporary-Staffing Specialist (CTS) designations to address these challenges and increase the professionalism in the field.

Employment agencies, as with any other recruitment source, are not appropriate for every situation. For example, agencies have little to offer the recent college graduate with little or no salable job experience, unless the person has majored in a field with immediate job application, such as accounting or engineering. Recent graduates who know that they want to work in the sales field find jobs through employment agencies; however, the business major who wants a management trainee position will not likely have much luck through an agency. After a graduate secures a job and is moving along in a career, an employment agency may be a viable source for further advancement opportunities. This also applies to individuals who are seeking career changes, but employment agencies have little to offer these persons unless a client firm intends to make a training commitment to a new hire. However, employers go to a college placement office when they want to recruit and train a person for a specific job, not to an employment agency. On the other hand, when employers want to recruit an experienced applicant, they typically use the services of employment agencies.

Staffing Firms

Staffing firms recruit and employ individuals who are assigned to client firms that wholly or partially control the employees' working conditions. According to the National Association of Temporary and Staffing Services, in 1997 approximately 2.3 million individuals were employed by staffing firms;[10] a 100 percent increase since 1991. *Staffing firms* include temporary employment agencies, contract employment firms, facilities staffing firms, and leasing or payrolling firms.

Temporary Employment Agencies. Unlike a standard agency, a *temporary employment agency* employs the individuals it places in temporary jobs at its clients' worksites. The agency recruits, screens, hires, and sometimes trains its workers. The agency sets and pays the wages when the worker is placed in a job assignment, withholds taxes and social security, and provides workers' compensation coverage. The agency also bills the client for the services performed. While the worker is on a temporary job assignment, the client typically controls the individual's working conditions, supervises the individual, and determines the length of the assignment.

Contract Firms. Under a variety of arrangements, contract employment firms perform services for clients on a long-term basis and place its employees, including supervisors, at the client's worksite to perform the work. Examples of contract firm services include security, landscaping, janitorial, data processing, and cafeteria services. As with a temporary employment agency, a contract firm typically recruits, screens, hires, and trains its workers. It sets and pays the wages

---

[10] Equal Employment Opportunity Commission, *EEOC Notice Number 915.002*, December 12, 1997.

when the worker is placed in a job assignment, withholds taxes and social security, and provides workers' compensation. The primary difference between a temporary agency and a contract firm is that a contract firm takes on full operational responsibility for performing an ongoing service and supervises its workers at the client's worksite.

Facilities Staffing Firms. This type of firm provides one or more workers to staff a particular client's operation on an ongoing basis, but does not manage the operation as under the contract firm arrangement.[11]

Payrolling or Leasing Firms. This is an employment arrangement in which the employees of a firm are hired by a leasing company and leased back to the former employer. The concept was first seen in 1972.[12] The leasing company performs all administrative activities for payroll and benefits. Leasing companies charge from 126 to 136 percent of payroll costs; this includes an administrative fee (which can be from five to 10 percent of payroll or a monthly fee per employee) and the cost of employee benefits.[13]

Direct Mail

Direct mail is an efficient method for recruiting applicants in specialized types of jobs. Initially, the applicant population and potential sources of applicant's names and addresses are identified. The sources may be membership lists rented from a peer or other type of organization. If an organization will release its mailing list, usually it will also prepare mailing labels at a reasonable cost.

An attractive mailing piece should be prepared; this can be accomplished through a desktop publishing program or an advertising agency.

One organization that used a direct mail recruitment campaign received 80 responses in a mailing to 5,000 persons. The end result was the selection of an "exceptionally gifted" employee.[14]

Executive Search

An *executive search recruiter* typically specializes in the recruitment of applicants for executive-level jobs. Executive recruiters may perform services on either a contingent or retainer basis. In the contingent arrangement, the recruiter is paid when a placement is made. Recruiters who are on retainers are paid regardless of whether a placement is made. In both arrangements, the typical fee, which is always paid by the employer, is about 35 percent of the total compensation for the job.[15]

Shopping Centers

Job information kiosks may be set up by employers in shopping center malls to generally inform persons about employment opportunities and to recruit for

---

[11] The definitions for these staffing firm arrangements were obtained from *EEOC Notice Number 915.002*, published by the EEOC (December 3, 1997).

[12] *Press Release,* "Marvin R. Selter, Chairman of the Board, National Staff Network" (Van Nuys, CA: National Staff Network, n.d.).

[13] Keaton, P.N., and Anderson, J., "Leasing Offers Benefits to Both Sides," *HR Magazine,* (July 1990), p. 58.

[14] Bargerstock, A.S., "Recruitment Options that Work," *Personnel Administrator* (March 1989), p. 53.

[15] VanMaldegiam, N.E., "Executive Pursuit," *Personnel Administrator* (September 1988), p. 96.

specific positions. The booths can also serve the purpose of educating the public about the firm and its products or services.

Job Fairs

As the name implies, a *job fair* is a group of employers assembled in one location, such as at a college or a convention center, in order to attract applicants for many different types of jobs. Usually, advertising costs for the fair are shared among the participating firms. Any rental expenses for recruitment booths are based upon the amount of space used. Sometimes, job fairs have a particular theme that is emphasized, such as recruiting for jobs within a specific industry or field. In such cases, the participating firms would be employers who recruit for vacancies in the selected fields. Applicants may be attracted to job fairs because they have the opportunity of talking to many recruiters from different firms— and all in the same location.

Computer Databases

On-line employment services are revolutionizing the recruiting activity of human resources management. On-line recruiting is a quick and efficient method of both publicizing vacancies and accessing qualified applicants. Databases come in all forms, ranging from trade association systems that specialize in particular functional areas to government databases composed of jobs and applicants in virtually every field of employment. In addition, some employers have in-house databases of job vacancies for employees to access.[16] A well-known job search computer resource is *Monster.com*. A government-sponsored system is the *Career-OneStop*. Both databases have ancillary systems to help employers list job openings and to guide applicants in preparing their resumes. The *CareerOneStop* is discussed below in the section on the U.S. Employment Service.

Retirees

Retirees are an excellent source of recruits for all types of jobs. As the U.S. population continues to age, and as the youth labor market continues to decline, employers will increasingly be seeking applicants from among the retired sector of the population. One supermarket makes extensive use of retirees for various jobs, including bagging groceries. Among the advantages to hiring retirees are their strong work ethic, regularity in attendance, and job skills.

Walk-Ins

Walk-ins are a nearly universal form of recruitment for some jobs. The obvious advantage to walk-ins is that the employer is spared the expenses inherent in most other sources of recruitment.

Military Veterans

Military veterans, particularly those who were only recently discharged or are approaching the date of their discharge, may be a source of applicants for all types of jobs, particularly those related to their military specializations. The

---

[16] Herren, L.M., "The Right Recruitment Technology for the 1990s," *Personnel Administrator* (April 1989), p. 48.

obvious advantages to veterans are the training and discipline they received during their military service.

College Recruitment

College recruitment is big business in the United States. For example, 1,700 college career services offices in college, technical, and graduate schools in the U.S. are members of the National Association of Colleges and Employers (NACE), which is a national organization serving as " . . . the leading source of information for career services practitioners on college campuses who advise students and alumni in career development and the employment process and for human resources professionals who recruit and hire college graduates."[17] An additional 1,700 individuals are also members, representing business, industry, nonprofit organizations and government.

Principles for Professional Conduct. The NACE has some principles of professional conduct that apply to career services professionals, employment professionals and third-party recruiters. These are some of the principles that apply to the various groups:[18]

Career Services Professionals:

- Career services professionals, without imposing personal values or biases, will assist individuals in developing a career plan or making a career decision.
- Career services professionals will know the career services field and the educational institution and students they represent and will have appropriate counseling skills.
- Career services professionals will provide students with information, a range of career opportunities and types of employing organizations. They will inform students of the means and resources to gain access to information that may influence their decisions about an employing organization. Career services professionals will also provide employing organizations with accurate information about the educational institution and its students and about the recruitment policies of the career services office.

Employment Professionals:

- Employment professionals will refrain from any practice that improperly influences and affects job acceptances. Such practices may include undue time pressure for acceptance of employment offers and encouragement or revocation of another employment offer. Employment professionals will strive to communicate decisions to candidates within the agreed-upon time frame.
- Employment professionals will know the recruitment and career development field, as well as the industry and the employing organization that they represent, and will work within a framework of professionally accepted recruiting, interviewing, and selection techniques.

[17] National Association of Colleges and Employers, May 28, 2000.

[18] For all the principles applying to the various groups see the NACE webpage (http://www.naceweb.org/about/principl.html).

- Employment professionals will not serve alcohol as part of the recruitment process.

Third-Party Recruiters:[19]

- Third-party recruiters will be versed in the recruitment field and will work within a framework of professionally accepted recruiting, interviewing, and selection techniques.

- Third-party recruiters that directly charge students for services are not following accepted professional practices and will not be given on-campus recruiting privileges.

- Third-party recruiters will disclose the following information to students and career services practitioners:

- The name of the client, or clients, that the third-party recruiter is representing and to whom the student's credentials will be disclosed. Career services will be permitted to verify this information by contacting the named client or clients. In the case of a resumé referral entity, a list of clients that use the services of the entity must be made available.

- The types of positions for which the third-party recruiter is recruiting. Resumé referral firms do not have to disclose this information.

U.S. Employment Service

The U.S. Employment Service (USES) is part of the Employment and Training Administration of the U.S. Department of Labor. USES has a national office, but most of its work is accomplished through affiliated state employment agencies located in each state. The affiliated state agencies operate about 2,000 local Employment Service offices. Each year, the state offices assist millions of job seekers and employers. In addition, some area offices also provide job training and other services. All employment assistance provided to both job seekers and employers is free. Most of the cost of operating the services of the agencies comes from trust funds collected under the Federal Unemployment Tax Act.

The USES sponsors **CareerOneStop** which is a Web site that offers career resources and workforce information to job seekers, students, businesses, and workforce professionals to foster talent development. The site helps individuals explore career opportunities to make informed employment and education choices. The site features user-friendly occupation and industry information, salary data, career videos, education resources, self-assessment tools, career exploration assistance, and other resources that support talent development[20]

Professional Associations

Many professional organizations offer placement services for their members. The services provided differ among organizations. For example, the Society for Human Resource Management has an on-line directory of available job vacancies for its members. The directory also has a free notification process that advises members when additional job openings are posted.

---

[19] See the above webpage for a full definition of third-party recruiter, as defined by NACE.

[20] Quoted from *CareerOneStop* web site.

Special Recruitment Concerns

Dual-Career Couples

A *dual-career couple* is one in which both spouses are employed. There are estimates that 80 percent of all households are dual-career.[21] The dual-career couple represents a special recruitment problem for employers because often a well-qualified applicant will accept a job offer only on the condition that suitable employment is found for the applicant's spouse. Employers may more readily recruit employees who are dual-career couples by meeting their special needs, such as providing some form of childcare assistance. Another way employers can aid the recruitment of dual-career family members is by assisting in the spouse's career search. The employer may choose to pay the spouse's expenses incurred in visiting prospective employers. Other aids include helping the spouse find potential employers and arranging interviews.

Noncompete Agreements

A *noncompete agreement* is a contract between a firm and a current or prospective employee that restricts the employee, should he or she leave the firm, from competing with it. For example, a marketing executive left one firm and went to work for another in the same industry. He immediately began making sales calls on some of the same clients he worked with at the former firm. When he was threatened with a lawsuit for breaching a noncompete agreement, he discontinued contact with the former clients.

In the example above, the executive did comply with the noncompete agreement. That does not always happen, requiring the former employer to take legal action. Courts may be unwilling to require compliance if the agreement is not reasonable. Agreements that unnecessarily restrict either competition in an industry or the ability of a former employee to make a living may be considered a restraint of trade or otherwise unreasonable. In addition, an agreement that does not limit the geographical area in which a former employee may not compete may be viewed with disfavor by the courts.

Some considerations that may affect the legality of a noncompete agreement are:

1. How long it is to be in effect;

2. Which industry (or industries) it affects;

3. What the former employee received in exchange for the agreement;

4. How much training the employee received at the expense of the former employer;

5. What resources of the former employer the employee used in the present employment; and

6. What resources, such as those in (5), that were legally obtained.[22]

---

[21] CCH HUMAN RESOURCES MANAGEMENT, *Ideas and Trends in Personnel* (March 22, 2000).

[22] Bequai, A., "Ties to Employers Can Be Broken," *HR Magazine* (June 1990), p. 160.

Sign-On Bonuses

A *sign-on bonus* is a lump-sum cash payment used as an inducement in recruiting employees with specialized qualifications. These bonuses help prevent internal pay inequity since the starting salary is typically consistent with the salary of current employees who have the same experience and other qualifications as the newly recruited person. The amount of the bonus is usually a percentage of base pay and may range from $1,000 to 25,000.[23]

Consider Recruitment Questions

Who are Our Recruits and Who Should They Be?

Among the difficult recruitment issues for an organization to consider is determining whether the recruits are the types of employees the organization wants. An organization's effectiveness is largely determined by the quality of recruits who seek employment.

Employee quality is difficult to measure, but some indicators are productivity, work quality, safety records, employee conduct, and attendance patterns. Indices for these variables, such as production levels, error rates, accidents, grievances, and absenteeism may be computed for the organization and compared with those of other organizations in the industry. Another way of measuring applicant quality is to compute selection ratios, which give the number of qualified applicants for each vacancy. For example, if there are two vacant positions for the same job that are filled within a year and there are 10 qualified applicants for the two positions, the selection ratio is:

$$\frac{\text{number of hires for each job}}{\text{number of qualified applicants for each job in the year}} = \frac{2}{10} = .20$$

Selection ratios are indicators of a recruitment program's effectiveness. The ratio also indicates whether the employer is attracting a sufficient number of quality recruits, since quality is a function of the number of qualified applicants.

Another way of determining if qualified applicants are recruited is to check training records and performance appraisal results. Quality recruits require less initial and remedial training, which saves money. Also, quality recruits perform better, which should be evident in the results of formal performance appraisal systems. Quality recruits require less discipline for deficiencies in attendance, conduct, productivity, safely, and work quality. Finally, quality recruits are more stable and not prone to job-hopping, so that their rate of turnover is lower.

There are various ways to compute turnover. A relatively straightforward method is:

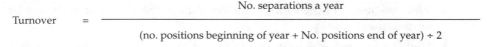

$$\text{Turnover} = \frac{\text{No. separations a year}}{(\text{no. positions beginning of year} + \text{No. positions end of year}) \div 2}$$

[23] Dossin, M.N., and Merritt, N.L., "Sign-On Bonuses Score for Recruiters," *HR Magazine* (March 1990), p. 42.

EXAMPLE: If there are 20 separations in one year and the number of authorized positions was 309 at the beginning of the year and 315 at the end, the turnover rate for the year would be:

$$\frac{20}{(309 + 315) \div 2} = .064\% = 6.4\%$$

Turnover and selectivity ratios may be used to measure recruit quality and to determine if recruitment strategy changes are needed. For example, the turnover rate was about 25 percent in a police department with 114 police officers. The chief of police wanted to reduce the rate, which he felt was too high. A consultant's study found that low pay and dissatisfaction with departmental policies were the principal reasons for the turnover. In the past, the City Council had refused to raise the pay because of budgetary problems. The consultant found that state law required each new officer to complete six weeks of training at a state training institution. Furthermore, the law required that the training had to be completed within the first year of an officer's employment. Since 28 (25 percent turnover×114 officers) new officers were hired during the study year, and each had to train six weeks at the state academy, a total of 168 weeks of training time was spent during the year. This meant that the equivalent of 3.5 full-time police officers were involved in state training each year. The figure of 3.5 was derived by dividing the 168 weeks by 48, which is the number of weeks in one police officer's work year (52 weeks minus the sum of two weeks vacation and nine paid holidays). The 3.5 officers represent 3 percent (3.5 ÷ 114) of the total police department.

The consultant recommended an immediate pay increase of 3 percent and demonstrated that the cost of the increase would be more than offset by a reduction in both the turnover, which would reduce the training time at the state academy, and overtime pay for officers who had to cover for new recruits who were to be trained. The excessive overtime also caused morale problems among the police force.

How Is Our Organization Viewed and How Should It Be?

One government agency paid a consultant to compare its compensation (salaries and benefits) plan to plans offered by its competitors. Agency management found it was paying almost 20 percent above the market rate, but was astounded because it felt the quality of new employees was low based on error rates, training expenditures, and other indices. However, the problem with recruit quality was the low regard the public had for the agency. Surveys indicated consumer dissatisfaction with the agency. Specific areas of dissatisfaction included perceptions of employee slothfulness, carelessness, indifference, and incompetence. Agency management wanted to be seen as efficient, productive, competitive, and socially responsible. The agency tried a major and expensive campaign through the news media, but a snafu caused it to be a financial flop. In addition, reporters were surprised to learn that their salaries were less than the starting pay for unskilled, newly hired employees in the agency.

There are no easy methods for developing a public image as a good employer. Every employee must be conscious of his or her impact upon the public. Public relations efforts should include training employees in the impact their performance has upon public opinion.

Where Are We Heading and Where Do We Want to Be?

Quality recruits seek employment in organizations that are leaders in their fields. Employers must realize that quality applicants do not want jobs in stagnating industries or in companies that are not progressive. These demands help explain why recruitment depends upon strategic management decisions that determine the direction of an organization.

What Major Advantages Do We Enjoy?

Recruitment advantages include an organization's present market demand, its share of the industry, its technological position relative to the competition, and the prospects for long-term market growth. Other advantages include geographical location, employee compensation and benefits, career growth potential, and working conditions. All employers have one or more of these or related advantages that must be identified, so that recruiting brochures can describe them. One organization had a difficult time attracting recruits because of its isolated location. However, the organization's recruitment efforts were more successful when it began to emphasize its recreational advantages, such as the availability of hunting, fishing, and boating and its convenient location to an ocean resort area.

Interviewing

Recruitment screening interviews are part of every recruiting effort. This indispensable recruitment tool is made more effective by following some basic guidelines and understanding the principal methods of recruitment interviewing.

Screening Interview Guidelines

Some of the guidelines for conducting initial recruitment screening interviews are as follows:

1. Demonstrate positive nonverbal communication by smiling, offering a warm handshake, and extending normal courtesies.

2. Stay on schedule, allowing sufficient time for each interview, but making sure that other applicants are not made to wait for extended periods.

3. Record impressions immediately after each interview.

4. Initially explain the purposes of the interview with a statement, such as "The purpose of this interview is for us to learn something about you and for you to learn about our company so that we can see if there is a match between our needs and your interests."

5. Before closing the interview, ask the applicant: "This about covers the subjects I wanted to discuss, but before we close the interview do you

have any questions or anything further you would like to say that we may have not covered?"

6. Finally, respond promptly with a decision as to whether the applicant is still under consideration for the job.

Types of Recruitment Interviews

Patterned Interview

A *patterned interview* consists of a set of specific questions, the answers to which are presumed to be relevant to job performance. The questions are prepared from information obtained from a job analysis and from employees and supervisors who have comprehensive knowledge about that job. Each question is designed to help the interviewer make a sound decision. The questions are precisely written to avoid ambiguity. After each question are examples of more and less qualified responses, as shown in Exhibit 15-1.

Nondirective Interview

The *nondirective interviewing* technique is based upon the concept of nondirective counseling developed by Carl Rogers.[24] Nondirective interviewing typically follows these steps:

1. The interviewer structures questions in response to the unique needs and qualifications of the applicant;

2. The applicant is permitted to talk freely; and

3. The interview topics are determined by the interviewer, but the interviewee is allowed sufficient time to develop his or her individual responses.

---

[24] C.R. Rogers, *Counseling and Psychotherapy* (New York: Houghton Mifflin Company, 1942).

Exhibit 15-1
Sample Questions in a Patterned Interview for Route Sales Representatives

1. *MOTIVATION*

(Note to interviewer: This job requires high motivation because successful Route Sales Representatives set ambitious goals for sales calls, sales volumes, and generating new customers).

Relate some examples in your work experience or background that demonstrate your motivation.

Response:

More qualified: Leadership positions, academic achievements, extracurricular activities, community/religious activities involvement, promotions, pay increases, commendations, and related accomplishments. Work experience in sales that shows progression in results or places applicant among the top producers is especially good.

Less qualified: Unable to relate any specific incidents of motivation above what might be expected.

2. *SAFE DRIVER*

(Note to interviewer: Employee spends 40 percent of time driving a station wagon that is assigned for both personal and business use).

Tell me about your experiences and training in driving vehicles.

Response:

More qualified: No preventable accidents, safe driving awards, preferred risk for automobile insurance, courses in defensive driving, no violations, pride in personal vehicle appearance, and regular maintenance.

Less qualified: Chargeable accidents, violations for speeding and related offenses, high risk insurance group.

Nondirective interviewing is based on humanistic psychology, which assumes that people are responsible for and capable of controlling their lives and can accomplish their potentialities, provided the environment is structured to permit it. Applying these and other humanistic concepts to nondirective interviewing results in letting applicants know what a job entails and the requisite qualifications. Applicants respond and describe their qualifications for the position. Humanistic psychology suggests that people will correctly compare their qualifications and interests to the job tasks and specifications because they want to accept responsibility in determining whether they are qualified for a job and whether the job is compatible with their needs. Undoubtedly, all interviewing embraces these concepts to some degree; however, in nondirective interviewing, they are fundamental.

Group Interview

In a *group interview,* two or more people simultaneously interview an applicant. Group interviews are also called *panel interviews.* Typically, each panel member asks the applicant at least one question.

There are three main reasons for group or panel interviews. First, some technical jobs may require the input of experts in several fields. For example, a municipality used group interviews to evaluate applicants for the position of captain in the fire department. There were three panel members. One panel member was from the state Fire Marshal's office; his role was to evaluate the applicants' technical knowledge of state fire regulations. Another member was a management consultant whose responsibility was to evaluate applicants' knowledge of management and leadership concepts (the Fire Captain position had significant management responsibilities). The final panel member was the Assistant Fire Chief, whose role it was to evaluate applicants' knowledge about the local fire department, such as operating fire equipment.

Another reason for group interviews is to include at least one panel member who is a member of a protected group. For example, the U.S. Postal Service frequently uses panels to interview applicants for promotion. Invariably, one of the panel members represents a protected group. This is done to ensure that the interests of protected group members are met and to demonstrate to applicants that interview panels are representative of the employee population.

A final reason for using group interviews is they may be less biased than those conducted by one interviewer.

There are also disadvantages to using panel interviews. First, applicants are more intimidated by a group interview than one conducted by a single individual. There are valid reasons for these feelings. For example, it is more difficult for an applicant to maintain eye contact with several panel members than just one person. Also, a panel interview environment tends to be more formalized and impersonal than an interview with one person. Usually, there is more physical distance between a panel and the applicant than there is when only one interviewer is present. Applicants also tend to feel overwhelmed when they must answer questions from a group of interviewers instead of just one. For example, it is not uncommon for one panel member to ask a question and appear to be satisfied with the applicant's response, while another panel member may either disagree with the response or request clarification.

Another problem with panel interviews is staying within set time constraints. Invariably one panel member in a group interview will dominate the interview, using a disproportionate amount of time. As a result, either other panel members must omit some of their questions or the interview schedule will be delayed. On one occasion, the time schedules for each interview were exceeded and the accumulated delays resulted in applicants waiting for several hours. The last applicant was finally interviewed at 8:30 p.m., when the interview had originally been scheduled for 3:30 p.m. The tension and suspense from prolonged delays such as this add to the intimidation of group interviews.

Stress Interview

A *stress interview* is an interview in which questions are purposely posed to induce stress. Some interviewers create stress in an interview for obscure reasons, such as to gauge an interviewee's ability to function under stress. In actuality, however, the position for which the applicant is interviewed may have minor or no stress in it. Other interviewers create stress by confrontational or antagonistic behavior. Sometimes, interviewers do not realize the stress their questioning may cause. For example, a female was interviewed by a panel for a customer service position. One panel member felt that personal appearance was an important requirement for the job, and he startled the applicant (and the other panel members) by asking her, "Why do you always wear such loud clothes and all that gaudy jewelry?" The applicant was flabbergasted by the question, and the stress it caused prevented her from demonstrating her qualifications in response to additional questions during the rest of the interview. She filed a discrimination charge several weeks after she was notified that another applicant had been selected for the position.

Some jobs require the ability to tolerate considerable amounts of stress. In these situations, it is appropriate to ask stress-inducing questions, preferably ones that simulate the actual work environment. Using this technique helps the applicant decide whether he or she would be comfortable with the job. Also, the interviewer can determine if the applicant can reasonably be expected to meet the job demands. Since all interviews produce varying amounts of stress, care should be exercised to see the amount of stress deliberately caused is not so excessive the interviewee is unable to demonstrate his or her qualifications.

Depth Interview

A *depth interview* is a structured interview in which questions thoroughly measure an interviewee's qualifications for a specific task. For example, a city manager wanted to hire police officers who were sensitive to human conflicts, such as domestic squabbles, and were able to resolve them through negotiation and without resorting to excessive force. Recruitment interviews were structured to measure this sensitivity in police officer applicants. Actual situations from police reports were described to applicants, and their responses were evaluated to determine whether they were consistent with the correct ones of the officers who actually handled the incidents. Interviewers also had examples of inappropriate responses.

In depth interviews, the interviewer asks follow-up questions that thoroughly explore important job dimensions. For example, if the police officer applicants, in the interview situation described above, did not completely describe how they would handle hypothetical domestic conflicts, the interviewer would continue probing the subject through additional questions until the interviewee's proposed solution was clearly understood. Another depth interviewing technique is to ask additional questions or propose other actual or hypothetical situations to the interviewee and check for response consistency.

The redundancy and thoroughness of depth interviewing in exploring carefully selected topics help ensure interviewees are qualified in the most important job functions. This means the important job tasks are well-defined, so both the interviewer and the applicant can decide if the applicant is properly suited for the job. The disadvantages of the depth interview approach include limiting the number of subjects that can be discussed. Depth interviews give a detailed picture of an applicant in selected areas; however, other less important areas are neglected. Consequently, precautions must be taken to ensure the interview subjects are, in fact, the most important ones.

Computer Interview

In a *computer interview,* the interviewee uses a keyboard or touch screen to respond to a set of questions in a computer file. At the conclusion of the interview, the interviewee's score is determined and communicated via the screen. Typically, these interviews are initial screening interviews that save time for both the applicant and the employer. Those applicants who "pass" this initial effort are scheduled for live interviews or informed about the next step in the selection process.

Video Interview

A *video interview* is conducted live through video teleconferencing, usually involving a panel of interviewers. The time and place of the such a teleconference is agreed upon several weeks in advance. Video interviewing is typically used when there are significant distances or costs involved for candidates' or interviewers' travel to a location where a personal interview could be arranged.

Behavioral Interview

A *behavioral interview* is a type of employment interview in which questions about job requirements are posed to applicants, and they are asked to give examples of situations in their past where they have had experience dealing with them. Usually, this involves explaining to applicants various job requirements, such as different situations in which a particular skill would be required, and having them explain similar situations they faced in the past and how they exhibited the skill. Also, applicants might be told about a particular behavior that is required on the job; then the applicants are asked to give examples of situations in their past in which the same behavior was required and how they exhibited this behavior. This is an example of a question that might be used in a behavioral interview:

Competency: Leadership

Read to applicant: This job requires the ability to motivate team members to identify courses of action and pursue them to successful conclusion. Give me an example of a situation in your past where you exercised such an ability.

Record applicant's response:

Situational Interview

A *situational interview* is a type of interview in which questions about job situations are posed to applicants and they are asked to explain how they would respond. For example, a potential job situation could be described, in which a particular skill or behavior might be required, and they are asked how they would respond. This is an example of a question that might be used in a situational interview:

Competency: Stress Tolerance

Read to applicant: This job has a considerable amount of stress. Explain how you would handle the stress you would experience in this job.

Record applicant's response:

Obviously, there is some similarity in the *behavioral* and the *situational* interviews. The major difference is the former requires the applicants to give specific examples from their past where they had experience meeting the job requirement. The *situational* interview, on the other hand requires applicants to explain how they might be expected to react to job conditions. The main difference in the two approaches can be summarized in "how did I do it" versus "how would I do it."

Multiple-Approach Interviews

Depending upon the situation, recruitment interviewers use all the methods described above. Each method is appropriate for certain situations. As with most human resource management decisions, the important consideration is when to use each one.

Interviewer Perceptual Errors

Improperly trained interviewers may commit a number of perceptual errors that may influence their decisions. These same errors also may occur when supervisors are completing performance appraisal reviews or evaluating employee qualifications for a promotion. Educating interviewers and supervisors to avoid these potential errors may help prevent them.

Central Tendency

Central tendency is the propensity of untrained interviewers to use "the comfortable middle" in rating interviewees, avoiding either very low or very high ratings. Some supervisors commit the same error in completing formal written performance appraisals.

"Just Like Me" or "Similar to Me"

"Just like me" or "similar to me" is the tendency of interviewers to give higher ratings to persons they perceive as having qualities or qualifications similar to their own.

Halo Effect

Halo effect is the tendency of raters to rate a person high in all categories, based upon one positive characteristic. *Horn effect* is the reverse, that is, the tendency to rate a person low in all categories because of one negative characteristic.

> **Example of Halo Effect:** The interviewer concludes the interviewee is an excellent candidate because he is appropriately dressed for the interview.

> **Example of Horn Effect:** The interviewer determines the interviewee is unsuited for the position because she has a "cold fish" handshake.

Implicit Personality Theory

Implicit personality theory is the tendency of raters to imply certain things about a person, based upon one or more characteristics; for example, implying that a person is highly stress tolerant because he or she worked while attending college.

Leniency or Strictness Effect

Lenient raters look at people through rose-colored glasses and this causes their evaluations of people to be in error. Strict raters, who are at the opposite end of the spectrum, make statements, such as "I've never interviewed (or appraised) an outstanding applicant." Both lenient and strict interviewers have unrealistic views of people.

First Impression

First impression is the tendency of raters to base their subsequent opinions about people upon their first impression of them.

> **EXAMPLE:** An interviewee is well-dressed and confidently enters the interviewing room. She makes an excellent response to the interviewer's first question: "Why do you want to work for ABC Company?" The interviewer is so favorably impressed that he scarcely noted the interviewee's responses to the remaining questions.

First impression can also work in reverse if the initial impression is unfavorable.

> **EXAMPLE:** The interviewee is a few minutes late for the interview because the receptionist gave the wrong information. The interviewer is unaware of the receptionist's error and concludes the interviewee is at fault.

The initial unfavorable impression causes the interviewer to negatively perceive the interviewee's qualifications.

Contrast

Contrast is the tendency of raters to grossly misjudge people because those persons' characteristics differ somewhat from others. For example, a rater interviews two candidates who are significantly underqualified for a job and later interviews a person who is marginally qualified. By misjudging the contrast in the candidates, the marginally qualified person may be given a much higher rating.

Stereotyping

Stereotyping is the tendency of raters to make favorable or unfavorable conclusions about applicants because of some particular characteristic that the applicants share with others or with groups to which they belong.

Recency Effect

Recency effect is the tendency of raters to make judgments based upon the most recent event. For example, if an employee had performed satisfactorily during an entire performance period but recently made a mistake, recency effect would come into play if the rater used only the recent error in giving the employee a poor rating.

Inconsistency Error

Inconsistency is the tendency of raters not to ask the same questions or use the same variables or standards in evaluating people.

Cultural Noise

Interviewees also can cause interviewers to come to erroneous conclusions through *cultural noise,* which is the tendency of applicants to give answers or behave as they believe the interviewer or appraiser expects them to respond.

Nonverbal Bias

Nonverbal bias is the tendency of raters' judgments to be influenced by an applicant's mode of dress or personal appearance.

Interview Reliability and Validity

Interview *validity* occurs when an interviewer makes accurate judgments about an interviewee. In an employment setting, this means that an interviewer makes accurate predictions about how well (or poorly) an applicant ultimately will perform on a job. There are two types of interviewer reliability. *Intra-interviewer* reliability is the degree of consistency in an interviewer's decision-making. In short, a reliable interviewer consistently reaches the same or similar conclusions in successive interviews of applicants who have the same qualifications.*Inter-interviewer* reliability is the degree to which two or more interviewers rate interviewees equally.

A *patterned interview,* with content-valid questions, helps ensure interview validity and reliability. Training interviewers to avoid perceptual errors also helps increase validity and reliability. This training may include conducting mock interviews that are videotaped, so that the results can be reviewed and critiqued.

CHAPTER 16
SELECTION

Chapter Highlights
- Introduce the major types of selections
- Explain the procedures used to select employees
- Review the risk aspects of selection

Introduction

Selection is the HRM activity concerned with choosing people for jobs or assignments. The six types of employment selections are accessions, promotions, temporary assignments, demotions, training assignments, and reassignments.

Accessions

Accessions are new hires of applicants from outside the organization.

Promotions

Promotions are vertical placements from one job to another of greater rank and responsibility. Sometimes, the terms pay increase, job reevaluation, and reclassification are confused with the term promotion.

EXAMPLE 1: Tracy is a secretary, which is a pay grade 12, with a salary range $18,500—$23,000 per year. Based upon her job performance, her pay is increased from $19,200 to $21,000; this action is a *pay increase.*

EXAMPLE 2: Tracy's job is analyzed, and the pay grade is increased from a grade 12 to a grade 13, with a salary range $20,2000—26,200. This action is a *job reevaluation.*

EXAMPLE 3: Tracy's boss changes her job by adding more important tasks to it that require Tracy to assume more responsibilities. Her job title and pay grade are changed to Administrative Assistant, at a pay grade 15, with a salary range $26,200—$33,800; this action is a *reclassification.*

EXAMPLE 4: Tracy applies for a job of Assistant Manager, pay grade 17, salary range $32,200—$41,800. There are 10 other applicants for the job, but she is selected as the best qualified. This action is a *promotion.*

Temporary Assignments

Temporary assignments are selection actions that: (1) place an employee in a light duty assignment or a job other than his or her own while recuperating from an illness or injury; (2) temporarily assign an employee in a higher-level job for reasons such as the absence of the incumbent or until a replacement is selected; and (3) place an employee in a special project or assignment.

Demotions

Demotions are vertical placements to jobs at a lower level of rank and responsibility. There are various reasons for demotions; for example, an employee may request a demotion because the job is too stressful. Management may demote employees who are unable to perform the tasks in a job at a higher pay grade. Sometimes, reorganizations result in a job abolishment, and the employee affected by the action either requests a reassignment to a job at an equivalent pay grade or a demotion to remain employed with the organization.

Training Program Selections

There are three types of *training program selections*. First, applicants may be selected for a job that requires the successful completion of a training program as a condition of continued employment. Examples include air traffic controllers and police officers. This type of selection is typically made from external recruitment sources. A second type of training selection is for skilled trades apprenticeship courses that require both on-the-job and classroom instruction, such as a machinist apprenticeship course. The third type of training selection is for management development programs.

Reassignments

Reassignments are lateral placements from one position to another at the same job evaluation level.

EXAMPLE: Beth is an accountant, in a pay grade 16, with a salary range of $29,900—$37,900, and she applies for the position of auditor, with the same pay grade and salary range. Beth is selected for the auditor job; this action is a reassignment.

Selection Authority

The process of making selection decisions is typically shared by the HRM department and other departments affected by the decisions. In some organizations, the HRM department selects several top candidates for a job, but the final selection is made by the manager of the newly hired individual. Some organizations include several individuals in the decisionmaking process. For example, in the Lincoln Electric company, a nationally known manufacturer of welders and electric motors, the personnel department does the initial selection, but the final decision is made by four vice-presidents who must unanimously agree, after each one has interviewed the applicant.[1] In other organizations, the HRM department makes the final selection for some or all jobs, depending upon the type of job, its pay grade, and the person to whom the employee would report.

Selection Procedure

As discussed in Chapter 14, a *selection procedure,* as defined in the *Uniform Guidelines on Employee Selection Procedures* (*Guidelines*) is " . . . any measure, combination of measures, or procedures used as a basis for any employment

---

[1] Perry, T.A., "Staying With the Basics," *HR Magazine* (November 1990), p. 73.

decision (including) the full range of assessment techniques, . . . traditional paper and pencil tests, performance tests, training programs, or probationary periods, . . . physical, educational, and work experience requirements, . . . informal or casual interviews, . . . unscored application forms, . . . initial screening measures, application blanks, medical examinations, background checks, interviews conducted by supervisors, work samples and performance appraisals."[2] In short, a selection procedure is virtually anything done that affects an employment decision.

The Selection Process

A selection procedure is one step of the selection process, such as an employment interview, used to guide management in making selection decisions. A *selection process* is the systematic arrangement of selection procedures used in choosing people for positions or assignments. The selection process may differ for different types of jobs and for different types of selections. The selection process used to fill a Senior Vice President for Human Resources position will obviously be different from one used to a select a Human Resources Assistant. Similarly, the process used for internal selections will typically differ from one used for external selections.

Legal Environment

Selection Procedure Decisionmaking

The federal laws that apply to employment selection decisionmaking are covered in Chapter 7. Basically, employers engaged in commerce that have 15 or more employees for each working day in 20 or more weeks in the current or preceding year may not make employment decisions on the basis of national origin, race, color, religion, sex, and disability. Employers that are engaged in commerce and that have 20 or more employees for each working day in 20 or more weeks in the current or preceding year may not discriminate against individuals age 40 and over in making employee selection decisions. Other federal legal requirements apply to contractors. See Chapters 7 and 11 for a full discussion of the federal contractor responsibilities in selecting employees.

Fair Credit Reporting Act of 1997

This law requires employers to inform applicants if a credit report will be obtained and receive their consent before requesting it. See Chapter 7 for a full discussion of the law's provisions.

Immigration Reform and Control Act

The Immigration Reform and Control Act of 1986 was one of a number of amendments made to the Immigration and Nationality Act (INA). Some of the provisions in the following material, such as the unfair immigration-related practices in employment are covered under the INA[3].

---

[2] CCH Human Resources Management, *Equal Employment Opportunity*, ¶ 8817.

[3] U.S. Citizenship and Immigration Services, *Public Laws Amending the INA*, http://www.uscis.gov/portal/site/uscis/template.print/menuitem.eb1d4c2a3e5b9ac89243c6a7543.. 9/22/08.

Purposes of the Law. These are the purposes of the law:

- Ensure that employees hired after November 6, 1986 are legally employable in the U.S. and have an I-9 completed by the date of their employment.
- Prohibit employers with 4 or more employees from discriminating against workers based upon their national origin or citizenship status.

Completion of I-9. Employees and employers have responsibilities in the completion of the I-9.

- Employee responsibilities:
  - (1) Section 1
    - ☐ Must complete Section 1. If the employee is unable to complete Section 1, the **Preparer/Translator Certification** must be completed by the person who completes it. The employee must sign Section 1, regardless of who completes it.
    - ☐ Section 1 must be completed when the person is hired, which is the beginning of employment.
  - (2) Section 2
    - ☐ Present one original document from List A or one original document from both List B and List C within three business days of starting work.
    - ☐ Present a receipt for the application of the documents if they cannot be furnished within three business days and then provide the actual documents within 90 days.
  - (3) Section 3
    - ☐ Complete Block A if the employee's name has changed.
    - ☐ Provide documents showing employment eligibility if rehired within three years of the date the Form I-9 was originally completed and work authorization has either expired or about to expire (reverification).
- Employer responsibilities
  - (1) Section 1
    - ☐ Although the employee (or a "preparer/translator") is responsible for completing Section 1, the employer is responsible to see that it is timely and properly done.
    - ☐ In completing the I-9, the term "employer" includes recruiters and others who refer employees for a fee, including agricultural associations, farmers, and labor contractors.
  - (2) Section 2
    - ☐ Complete Section 2 by examining evidence of employability and identity within three business days of starting work.

☐ If employees cannot produce the required documents, the employer is responsible to see they present a receipt for the application of the documents within three days of employment and present the actual documents within 90 days.

☐ Complete Section 2 when employment begins if the period of employment is less than three days in duration.

☐ This is the evidence employers must record in Section 2:

— Document title;

— Issuing authority;

— Document number;

— Any expiration date; and,

— Date employment begins.

(3) Record Retention/Production

☐ Retain the Form I-9 for three years after the date of an employee's employment or one year after the employment ending date, whichever is later.

☐ The Form I-9 must be produced for inspection by applicable U.S. government officials during the retention period.

☐ At their discretion, employers may make copies of the documents from Lists A, B and C furnished by the employee for retention with the completed Form I-9.

(4) Section 3

☐ Update/re-verify information as required, such as for rehire or expiration of document establishing work authorization.

☐ Complete Block A for employee name change.

☐ Complete Block B and the signature block if the employee is eligible for reemployment on the same basis when the Form I-9 was originally completed and is rehired within three years.

☐ Complete Blocks B and C if the employee is rehired within three years of the date of the original Form I-9 and the employee's work authorization has expired or is about to expire (re-verification). Also complete the signature block.

There are documents that provide evidence of identity, right to work, and identity and employability. These are the documents:

List A Documents —That establish both identity and employment eligibility:

- U.S. Passport (unexpired or expired)

- Permanent Resident Card or Alien Registration Receipt Card (Form I-551)

- An unexpired foreign passport with a temporary I-551 stamp

- An unexpired Employment Authorization Document that contains a photograph (Form I-766, I-688, I-688A, I-688B)

- An unexpired foreign passport with an unexpired Arrival-Departure Record, Form I-94, bearing the same name as the passport and containing an endorsement of the alien's nonimmigrant status, if that status authorizes the alien to work for the employer.

List B Documents —Documents that establish identity:

- Driver's license or ID Card issued by a state or outlying possession of the United States provided it contains a photograph or information such as name, date of birth, sex, height, eye color, and address
- ID card issued by federal, state, or local government agencies or entities provided it contains a photograph or information such as name, date of birth, sex, height, eye color, and address
- School ID card with a photograph
- Voter's registration card
- U.S. military card or draft record
- Military dependent's ID card
- U.S. Coast Card Merchant Mariner Card
- Native American tribal document
- Driver's license issued by a Canadian government authority

For persons under age 18 who are unable to present a document in List B above:

- School record or report card
- Clinic, doctor or hospital record
- Day care or nursery school record

List C Documents —that establish employment eligibility:

- U.S. Social Security Card issued by the Social Security Administration (other than one stating it is not valid for employment)
- Certificate of Birth Abroad issued by the Department of State (Form FS-545 or Form DS-1350)
- Original or certified copy of a birth certificate issued by a state, county, municipal agency, or outlying possession of the U.S. bearing an official seal
- Native American tribal document
- U.S. Citizen ID Card (INS Form I-197)
- ID Card for Use of Resident Citizen in the U.S. (INS Form I-179)
- Unexpired employment authorization document issued by the DHS (other then those listed under List A)

Document Review

The employer must review and accept documents that reasonably appear to be genuine and relate to the person presenting them (e.g., the name on the Social Security card should be compared to the name on the state driver's permit and the photo on the driver's permit compared to the appearance of the person who presented the documents).

Employers may reject documents it they do not reasonably appear to be genuine and ask employees who present questionable documentation for other documentation that satisfy the I-9 requirements. Employees who are unable to present acceptable documents should be terminated. Employers who choose to retain such employees may be subject to penalties for improper completion of the form or for "knowingly continuing to employ" unauthorized workers if such workers are in fact unauthorized. Such employers may be ordered by the Department of Homeland Security (DHS) to "cease and desist" from such activities and pay the following penalties for each unauthorized alien:

- First Offense – from $375 up to and including $3,200;
- If the employer has been previously in violation – from $3,200 up to and including $6,500; and,
- If the employer was subject to more than one cease and desist order – from $4,300 up to and including not more than $16,000.[4]

Pattern of Knowingly Employed Undocumented Workers. Employers who engage in a practice of knowingly employing or continuing to employ unauthorized aliens may face fines up to $3,000 per employee and/or six months imprisonment.

Record Retention

The civil penalties for violations of I-9 requirements, such as improper completion or not making them available for inspection are from $110 up to and including not more than $1,100 for each person for which there is a violation.[5]

Document Fraud

Employers who knowingly use false documents, including documents under another person's name are subject to fines and/or five years of imprisonment. These are the fines for each document and instance of document use:

- Fraudulent use, acceptance or creation: $375 - $3,200.
- Where a cease and desist order was previously issued: $3,200 - $6,500[6].

I-9 Not Required

Form I-9 is not required for the following:

— Employees hired before November 6, 1986, and continuously employed by the same employer;

— Individuals performing casual employment who provide domestic service in a private home that is sporadic, irregular or intermittent;

— Independent contractors; and,

[4] CCH, *Human Resources Management: Management Ideas & Trends* (March 19, 2008), p. 42.
[5] Ibid.
[6] Ibid.

— Workers provided to employers by individuals or entities providing contract services, such as temporary agencies (in such cases, the contracting party is the employer for I-9 purposes)

Missing I-9 Forms

An employer who discovers that an I-9 form is not on file for a given employee should request the employee to complete section 1 of an I-9 form immediately and submit documentation as required in Section 2. The new form should be dated when completed. When an employee does not provide acceptable documentation, the employer must terminate employment to avoid penalties for "knowingly" continuing to employ an unauthorized worker if the individual is not in fact authorized to work.

Discovering an Unauthorized Employee

An employer who discovers that an employee has been working without authorization should reverify work authorization by allowing such an employee another opportunity to present acceptable documentation and complete a new I-9. However, employers should be aware that if it knows or should have known that an employee is unauthorized to work in the U.S., they may be subject to serious penalties for "knowingly continuing to employ" an unauthorized worker.

Successive Employers and Reorganizations

Employers that acquire a business as a result of a corporate reorganization, merger, or sale of stock or assets, and retain the predecessor's employees are not required to complete new I-9's for those employees, however, the successor employer will be held responsible if the predecessor's I-9s are deficient or defective.

IMAGE

Image, which is an acronym for *ICE Mutual Agreement between Government and Employers*, is a U.S. Department of Homeland Security program designed to increase cooperation between employers and the government to improve hiring methods and reduce the employment of illegal aliens. The advantage to employers is the that the U.S. Citizenship and Immigration Service, which is the lead agency in implementing the program, will give training in such areas as hiring methods, detecting document fraud related to the I-9, use of the E-Verify program and preventing employment discrimination.

To become "IMAGE Certified," employers must do the following:

- Complete a self-assessment questionnaire;
- Enroll in E-Verify;
- Enroll in the Social Security Number Verification Service;
- Follow the IMAGE Best Employment Practices;
- Have an I-9 audit by Immigration and Customs Enforcement (ICE); and,
- Sign an IMAGE agreement with ICE.

An Associate Membership is available to employers who are interested in becoming IMAGE Certified, but want two-years to complete the requirements.

Best Employment Practices. Employers must follow these best employment practices to be IMAGE Certified:

- Use E-Verify for all hiring;
- Establish an internal training program on completing the Form I-9, detecting fraudulent documents and using E-Verify;
- Restrict the I-9 and E-Verify processes to trained employees;
- Have annual I-9 audits by outside firms or qualified in-house personnel who are not involved in the I-9 process;
- Conduct self-audits and have a system to report any violations to the ICE;
- Develop a system for handling no-match letters from the Social Security Administration (SSA);
- Establish a hot-line for employees to report I-9 violations and a procedure to handle them;
- Establish a system to prevent discrimination;
- Establish a system for contractors/subcontracts to follow the "best employment practices;" and,
- Annually report to the ICE the results of IMAGE program participation.[7]

E-Verify Program. This is a web-based system to electronically verify if new employees are eligible for employment. The DHS and the SSA are partners in the program which is overseen by the U.S. Citizenship and Immigration Services. With the system, employers can electronically compare I-9 information furnished by new employees against information for over 425 million records in the SSA' database and 60 million records in the DHS' database. Each comparison is completed within seconds. Naturalization data is also available so citizenship status information can be instantly obtained; this helps prevent the major source of SSA mismatches. E-Verify's Photo Screening Tool is the first step in a comprehensive biometric identification procedure for identity fraud.[8]

Discrimination Prohibition

Employers with 4 or more employees are prohibited from discriminating against any person (other than an unauthorized alien) in hiring, discharging, or recruiting or referring for a fee because of a person's national origin or citizenship status. Furthermore, employers with 15 or more employees may not - in addition to discrimination based on hiring, discharging or recruiting or referring for a fee - discriminate against any person on the basis of national origin in assignment, compensation, or other terms and conditions of employment.

---

[7] U.S. Immigration and Customs Enforcement, *IMAGE: ICE Mutual Agreement Between Government and Employers,* (September 8, 2008), http://www.ice.gov/partners/opaimage/index.htm.

[8] U.S. Immigration and Customs Enforcement, *E-Verify Program Highlights*, (July 16, 2008), http://www.uscis.gov/portal/site/uscis/template.PRINT/menuitem.eb1d4c2a3e5b9ac89243c6a7543.

Charges alleging discrimination on the basis of national origin, citizenship, documentation abuse, or retaliation are handled by the EEOC except when all of the following conditions are met (in which case the charges are handled by The Office of Special Counsel for Immigration Related Unfair Employment Practices):

(1) The charge alleges discrimination against the complainant with respect to his or her hiring, discharge, or recruitment or referral for a fee;

(2) The charge is outside the jurisdiction of the EEOC in that the employer (a) does not have 15 or more employees for each working day in each of 20 or more calendar weeks in the current or preceding calendar year or (b) is an employer that is expressly excluded from coverage under Title VII; and,

(3) The employer had at least 4 employees, including both full-time and part-time employees, on the date of the alleged discriminatory occurrence.

Penalties and corrective actions differ for violations handled by the EEOC and those handled by the Office of the Special Counsel. See Chapter 12 for the charges handled by the EEOC.

These are corrective actions and penalties for employment discrimination violations handled by the Office of the Special Counsel:

- Corrective actions including stopping the discriminatory practice and one or more of the following:
  - ☐ As appropriate, hire or reinstate (with or without back pay) the victims of discrimination;
  - ☐ Post notices of employer obligations and employee rights; and,
  - ☐ Train personnel who make selection decisions about compliance with the law.
- Penalties for each victim of discrimination are these:
  - ☐ First Offense: At least $375, but not more than $3,200;
  - ☐ Second Offense: At least $3,200, but not more than $6,500; and,
  - ☐ Third Offense: At least $4,300, but not more than $16,000.

The penalty for failing to complete, keep and/or show I-9 documents to inspectors ranges from $110 to not more than $1,100 for each employee's document.[9]

Negligent Hiring

Negligent hiring is the potential liability of an employer for the actions of an employee who was selected for employment without adequately determining the person's qualifications and background characteristics for the job. The two essential elements of negligent hiring are: (1) administering the proper selection methods to determine whether a person is adequately qualified to satisfactorily perform the tasks in a job; and (2) verifying essential information supplied by the person, relative to his or her qualifications. An employer may be found negligent

---

[9] CCH, *Human Resources Management: Management Ideas & Trends* (March 19, 2008), p. 42.

in hiring a person who seriously injures either himself or herself or others because the employer failed to use the proper selection methods to determine if the person was qualified to safely perform the tasks in the job. The judicious use of the selection methods discussed in this chapter and the verification of applicants' backgrounds and qualifications, which are discussed in Chapter 17, will help prevent the liability posed by negligent hiring.

Selection Methods

Recruitment Methods

Some recruitment methods, such as newspaper advertisements and job postings, are selection methods because they screen potential applicants by describing job specifications and job tasks. Applicants who review the job specifications and job tasks perform a self-assessment to determine whether they are interested in the job and are qualified for it. This self-assessment is a preliminary and inexpensive selection method that saves employers the expense of reviewing applications of obviously unqualified or disinterested applicants. In addition, applicants are spared investing their time and money in applying for a position for which they are neither qualified nor interested. For this reason, employers should carefully prepare recruitment notices and include essential information about the job specifications, tasks, pay, and benefits.

Pre-Application Screening

Applicants who have not read recruitment notices announcing a vacancy are typically neither fully aware of the tasks and specifications of the job, nor have they critically compared their qualifications and interests to those tasks and specifications. For example, an applicant may want to apply for a sales position, until he or she realizes the job involves overnight travel in an assigned territory. At the pre-application screening stage, applicants are greeted and given complete descriptions of job tasks. Specifications, such as licensing or certification requirements, should be highlighted. Applicants are instructed to review this information and, if they feel that they are qualified and are interested in the job, the next step is to complete an application.

Application Forms

There are two basic types of application forms. The common version is an *application form* on which applicants are requested to furnish basic information, such as name, address, job title, experience, and education.

ABC Company
Employment Application

ABC Company is an equal employment opportunity employer to qualified applicants without regard to national origin, race, color, religion, sex, disability, veteran's status, age, genetic composition, sexual orientation or any other non-employment related condition.

INSTRUCTIONS: Please print your answers to all parts of the application.

Last name	First name	Middle name	Other last &/or first names used

Current address: Number   Street   City   State   Zip   How long?

Previous address: Number   Street   City   State   Zip   How long?

Social Security Number: Telephone number: Area Code and number
_ _ _ _ _ _ _ _ _   (   )

EMPLOYMENT DESIRED

Position sought: _____

Applying for:	Salary desired:	Date available	Accept temporary job?
□ Full time	$ _____	to start work	□ Yes
□ Part time		_____	□ No

EMPLOYMENT AVAILABILITY

Work nights?	Weekends?	Relocate?	Shift work?	Overnight travel?	Overtime work?
□ Yes	□ Yes	□ Yes	□ Yes	□ Yes	□ Yes
□ No	□ No	□ No	□ No	□ No	□ No

WORK EXPERIENCE

Please provide your work experience for the past 10 years. List in chronological order beginning with your present (or most recent employer, if currently unemployed). Show periods of unemployment and state the reason. Attach additional sheets as necessary, providing the same information.

Name of Employer	Dates of employment From: Mo. Yr. To: Mo. Yr.	Name of Supervisor
No. and Street: City, State, Zip Code: Phone number: ( )		Your Job Title
Salary/Pay : Start: End:	Reason for leaving	

List jobs held, tasks performed, competencies required, promotions and recognition received.		
Name of Employer	Dates of employment From: Mo. Yr. To: Mo. Yr.	Name of Supervisor
No. and Street: City, State, Zip Code: Phone number: ( )		Your Job Title
Salary/Pay : Start: End:	Reason for leaving	

List jobs held, tasks performed, competencies required, promotions and recognition received.		
Name of Employer	Dates of employment From: Mo. Yr. To: Mo. Yr.	Name of Supervisor
No. and Street: City, State, Zip Code: Phone number: ( )		Your Job Title
Salary/Pay : Start: End:	Reason for leaving	

List jobs held, tasks performed, competencies required, promotions and recognition received.

MILITARY SERVICE

If a member of a reserve unit or the national guard show:

Branch: _____ Specialty:_____ Rank: _____

If active duty service show:

Branch: _____ Specialty:_____ Rank: _____

Date of discharge _____ Type of discharge _____

EDUCATION

	Name, City and State of School	Dates Attended				Diploma/Degree & Major
		From		To		
		Mo	Yr	Mo	Yr	
High School						
College/University						
College/University						
Other						
Other						

Honors/Awards/Leadership/Grade Point Average

OTHER CREDENTIALS

Professional Designations/Registrations:

Computer Skills:
Other Competencies:

PERMISSION TO CONTACT PRESENT EMPLOYER

May we contact your present employer?   □ YES   □ NO
If yes, whom should we contact?
Name: Position: Telephone number: (   )

REFERENCES

Please list three individuals who we can contact who have person knowledge about your qualifications.		
Name	Address	Telephone No.
Name	Address	Telephone No.
Name	Address	Telephone No.

PERSONAL HISTORY

What do you consider your most important personal achievement?
Have you ever had your driver's license revoked?   □ Yes   □ No
If yes, please explain the details.
Have you ever been convicted of a crime? □ Yes   □ No
If yes, please explain the details.

Have you ever been suspended, disciplined, asked to resign or discharged from employment?
□ Yes □ No
If yes, please explain the details.

ACKNOWLEDGMENT & AUTHORIZATION

I acknowledge that all information furnished on this application is true and that any error or omission will be grounds for immediate dismissal. I understand that the information I have provided here will be verified and I authorize *ABC Company* to use the means necessary to obtain such verification.

According to the Immigration Reform and Control Act of 1986, all persons, including citizens and nationals of the U.S., who are hired by *ABC Company* within three business days of employment, must present either documents of their employment eligibility and identity or a receipt for a replacement of such documents (in the case of lost, stolen or destroyed documents) *and* sign a completed Employment Eligibility Verification form (Form I-9). If a receipt for replacement of documents is furnished, the actual documents must be produced to *ABC Company* within 90 days of the date employment begins. Documents must be genuine and photocopies will not be accepted-the only exception is for certified copies of birth certificates. Persons who do not follow these procedures will be terminated.

I authorize all educational institutions, other organizations, and previous employers to give information to *ABC Company* concerning my educational background (dates of attendance, degrees earned, disciplinary records, and school activities), work history and other qualifications. This includes contacting my present employers if I have so indicated in this application. I release all institutions, organizations, and previous employers, and my present employer if I have indicated contact could be made, from any liability as a result of such contact.

I agree to exclusively settle through final and binding arbitration by an impartial arbitrator all claims, disputes or dissatisfactions resulting from my application for employment and any and all conditions resulting from my employment or separation from employment with *ABC Company*. This includes all claims under federal, state, local and any other laws or statues, including, but not restricted, to claims under the Civil Rights Act of 1964, as amended, the Age Discrimination in Employment Act, and the Americans with Disabilities Act.

Applicant's Signature _____   Date _____

IMPORTANT NOTICE: CREDIT CHECK AUTHORIZATION REQUIRED

As part of the employment application process, I understand that a consumer credit report relating to me will be obtained from a consumer credit reporting organization. I understand that any information in the credit report will not be used in violation of any federal, state or local law. I also understand before any adverse action is taken on my application that in any way is based upon information obtained in the credit report that I will be provided, without charge, a copy of the report and a written summary of my rights under the Consumer Credit Reform Act. My signature below authorizes *ABC Company* to obtain a copy of my credit report.

Applicant's Signature _____   Date _____

Several studies have found employers asking potentially improper questions on applications, such as an applicant's age or date of birth. Asking these questions is not illegal, unless employers use the information to discriminate against job applicants. This type of discrimination is called *disparate treatment.* Sometimes, *intent* is not present even though a disparate effect, as measured by computations of adverse impact, has occurred. In such cases, employers may be asked to justify their reasons for including improper questions on the application, explaining why the item is on the application and what use is made of the information.

There are some other questions frequently found on employment application forms that may be difficult to justify and could encourage discrimination complaints:

- Arrests;
- Availability for Saturday and/or Sunday work;
- Number of children or children under 18;
- Citizenship of a country other than the U.S.;
- Credit record or personal financial information;
- Color of eyes or hair;
- Whether a fidelity bond has ever been refused;
- Garnishment record;
- Height and weight;
- Marital status;
- Gender; and
- Spouses's name and whether he or she is employed

Some of this information is required for EEO/AA reporting. When that is the purpose of collecting the information, it is advisable to use a tear-off sheet attached to the application.

The standard application form may yield information needed to adequately compare an applicant's qualifications to the job specifications. However, an improperly structured form is practically useless and may cause an employer trouble. In view of the potential problems, employers are encouraged in determining whether a question should be included by asking: "How does this question help make a selection?" Questions should be discarded if they are not demonstrably related to selection decisions.

Red Flag Items

Red flag items on an employment application include gaps in years of employment experience and qualifications that indicate a person is clearly overqualified for the job for which they are applying.

Weighted Application Blanks

Another type of application form is the *weighted application blank (WAB),* which is used to evaluate the relative value of biographical information. Other terms for a WAB are *biographical inventories* or *biographical information blanks,* also known as *BIBs*. There are several ways of constructing a WAB. One way is to conduct an *item analysis* of each application question to determine the relative worth of different responses to each question. If the responses are *nominally scaled*, such as yes or no, the analysis includes searches for the responses of successful job performers.[10]

> **EXAMPLE:** Assume one question on a WAB is, "Did you work at any time while attending college?" A study of 100 applicants was conducted. Fifty of them answered yes, of which 35 were successful on the job and 15 were not successful. In such a case, a "yes" answer has a weight of 35/50, or .70. Fifty applicants answered no to the question; 10 were successful and 40 were not. Thus, a "no" answer has a weight of 10/50 or .20.

Ratio-scaled information, such as the number of years of education or the years of employment, may also be weighted by correlating the resulting values with different levels of job performance. This process results in assigning weights based upon the applicant's response. For example, the weight may increase proportionately to the number of years of employment experience.

WABs have been used in varied occupations, such as the amount of sales for life insurance sales representatives, job turnover among bank clerks, naval personnel performance in a divers' training course, and research scientists's productivity.[11] WABs have proved effective in predicting job performance in many jobs, including unskilled employees, " . . . office clerks, . . . service station dealers, . . . chemists, engineers, and high level executives."[12]

WABs, as with other selection methods, also have disadvantages. They require a lengthy and somewhat involved construction process. A large number of study subjects are necessary for validation; usually, a minimum of 150 is required.[13] In addition, different jobs typically require the development of unique WABs.[14] Consequently, development costs prohibit using a WAB for jobs that are seldom vacant. Another disadvantage to WABs is that they require criterion-related validation and the problems inherent in that method of validation, such as large samples, predictive studies, and cross-validations, would apply.

Interviews

Paradoxically, the interview is the most frequently used but least valid selection method. In Chapter 15, the purposes of interviewing and the types of interviews are discussed. Despite validity and reliability problems with interviews, they can be made more valid and reliable by using patterned interview formats and properly training interviewers.

Tests

A *test* is a generic term encompassing various methods of measuring applicant qualifications. Types of tests administered to applicants include written

---

[10] See Chapter 6 for an explanation of scaling methods.

[11] A. Anatasi, *Psychological Testing* (New York: Macmillian Publishing Co., 1976), p. 615.

[12] *Ibid.*

[13] C.H. Lawshe and M.J. Balma, *Principles of Personnel Testing* (New York: McGraw-Hill Book Co., 1966), p. 161.

[14] *Ibid.*, p. 159.

instruments, oral questions, performance of exercises, and manipulation of objects. Tests may either be commercially prepared or custom-constructed by an employer or a consultant. Tests can be validated through content, construct or criterion studies.

Care should be taken to ensure a test, regardless of its name, accurately measures a job's essential functions. One firm used a test called a *Work Tolerance Screen* to test the strength of applicants. A Circuit court found the test to be discriminatory because it had a disparate impact on women and was not based on business necessity. An expert witness concluded the test was more difficult than the job[15]. The types of validation are discussed in Chapter 14. Also discussed in Chapter 14 is the requirement that a full job analysis be performed before conducting a validation study.

Commercially Prepared Tests

There are commercially prepared tests for virtually every employment selection decisionmaking situation. Many different organizations publish tests. Usually, test publishers provide norm data. *Norms* are the test results from a group of individuals who took the test. Depending upon the test, the group may be representative of a typical pool of applicants for which a test is designed. Included in norm data is the range of scores and the percentages of subjects achieving them. norms are helpful but they are not a substitute for validation and reliability data. Some publishers provide validity and reliability data on one or more of their tests. Whether the data is furnished, the *Guidelines* stipulate that if adverse impact results from a test, the test user is responsible for ensuring that the test is valid and reliable for the purpose for which it is used. Consequently, test users should thoroughly research a test before it is used.

There are several authoritative sources of information on commercially prepared tests. *The Mental Measurement Yearbook* (*MMY*) contains information on over 1,000 employment tests.[16] Included for each test is a comprehensive review by one or more independent reviewers. The reviews include information on validation and reliability studies and other information, such as how the test is constructed and administered. Some reviewers also critique the test by noting any significant advantages and disadvantages. A second reference source, *Tests In Print (TIP)*, is a companion book to the MMY.[17] The TIP contains information on many commercial tests in the U.S. Each entry contains the title, author, explanation of groups for which the test is applicable, publication date, publisher, cross references, and miscellaneous information, such as foreign adaptations.

---

[15] CCH, Did pre-employment strength test unlawfully impact female employees? *Human Resources Management: Ideas and Trends* (April 11, 2007), Issue 652, p. 55.

[16] O.K. Buros, ed., *The Eighth Mental Measurements Yearbook* (Highland Park, New Jersey: The Gryphon Press, 1978).

[17] J.V. Mitchell, ed., *Tests in Print III* (Lincoln, Nebraska: The University of Nebraska Press, 1983).

Commercial Occupational Tests

Occupational tests can be grouped into these categories: achievement; aptitude; behavioral/personality; interest inventory; manual dexterity/motor; mental ability; performance; and sensory.

Achievement Tests. *Achievement tests* measure the extent of a person's knowledge or competence within a field. An example of an achievement test is the American Institute of Certified Public Accountants *Achievement Test II*, which is used to select applicants for accounting positions or to assess the training needs of accountants.

Aptitude Tests. *Aptitude* tests measure innate or acquired capacities to learn an occupation. Sometimes, mental ability tests are included in the definition of aptitude tests. In this book, both mental ability and manual dexterity tests are classified separately from aptitude tests. Two of the major aptitudes measured with tests are *clerical* and *mechanical* aptitudes. The *SRA Clerical Aptitudes* and the *MacQuarrie Test for Mechanical Ability* are, respectively, examples of a clerical aptitude test and a mechanical aptitude test.

Behavioral/Personality Tests. *Behavioral* or *personality* tests purport to measure emotional characteristics, mental stability, and personality traits. For example, the *Comprehensive Personality Profile* is intended to measure emotional intensity in candidates for sales jobs. The *Minnesota Multiphasic Personality Inventory* (*MMPI*) is used to identify mental problems. The *16PF Personality Profile* is used to measure personality traits, such as shrewdness and dominance.

The three main concerns in using behavioral or personality tests are validity, adverse impact potential, and invasion of privacy. These tests would seem to have more validity for certain types of jobs. For example, it might be important to know about the mental health of applicants for high stress jobs, such as those in law enforcement work. One might question the validity, however, of measuring personality traits, such as shrewdness or dominance, if applicants are seeking employment as house painters. In any event, since the tests are typically used to measure constructs, they should be validated through empirical studies, particularly, if adverse impact occurs.

Another problem with personality tests is questions that may invade an applicant's privacy. Several court cases on this privacy issue are currently pending, and more may be expected in the future. According to a survey conducted by the National Consumer League, 80 percent of 1,007 persons surveyed said that they were asked questions that they felt invaded their privacy when they were seeking employment.[18] Some questions on personality tests may also constitute grounds for charges of discrimination. For example, the Rhode Island Commission for Human Rights directed that three questions involving sin and the afterlife be removed from the MMPI when the test is given to applicants for law enforcement jobs in that state.[19]

---

[18] Marlowe, G., "How Personal Can An Application Be?" *Richmond Times-Dispatch* (January 21, 1990), p. 1.

[19] "Labor Letter," *The Wall Street Journal* (February 19, 1991), p. 1.

In a federal court of appeals decision, a panel of judges found the MMPI to be a "medical examination under the ADA" and not job related for the purpose it was being used by the employer.[20]

Interest Inventory. An *interest inventory*, while nominally a test, is more a self-assessment of occupational interests. The interests could be those of individuals who are successfully employed in various occupations or those individuals who are seeking employment in a particular field. The *Strong-Campbell Interest Inventory* is an example of an interest inventory test.

Manual Dexterity/Motor Tests. *Manual dexterity* or *motor tests* measure a number of motor functions including reaction time, quickness of arm movements, multi-limb coordination and finger dexterity. Some tests in this category, such as the *Hand-Tool Dexterity Test*, require the use of small tools to disassemble and reassemble bolts and other hardware. Other manual dexterity tests, such as the *Purdue Pegboard,* do not involve the use of tools.

Mental Ability. *Mental ability* tests measure a person's ability to reason, perceive relationships, understand numerical properties, and solve quantitative problems. Two well-known mental ability tests are the *Wonderlic Personnel Test* and the *Wesman Personnel Classification Test.*

While there is a place in selection for general ability tests, the HRM professional must understand how they should be used. Improper use results from the assumption that jobs can be classified by the amount of intelligence required. Mental ability tests should be used where intelligence is an important determinant of some measure of job success. However, where other qualifications, such as mechanical aptitude, are the important ones for job success, a mental ability test is not appropriate. In the words of one expert:

> For many occupations . . . tests of special aptitudes will serve as better predictors of achievement than will the general intelligence tests. This point is not always adequately stressed in the test manuals. In fact, some test manuals tend to create the erroneous impression that the . . . (mental ability) test can be used to predict success in almost every type of industrial work.[21]

Performance Tests. *Performance* tests measure demonstrated competence, learned through training or experience, usually on a piece of equipment. Examples of performance tests are typing, shorthand, and computer hardware tests. Sometimes, manual dexterity or motor tests are also called performance tests but, in this book, they are separately categorized. The *SRA Typing Skills* test is an example of a performance test.

Sensory Tests. *Sensory* tests measure hearing and vision, including color vision. Some marine, aviation and railroad jobs require the ability to interpret colored signals. Hearing is also important in jobs involving radio and telephone communications. An example of a sight test is the *AO Sight Screener.* The *Dvorine Color Vision Test* is an example of a test that measures color vision.

---

[20] *Steven L. Karraker, et al. v. Rent-A-Center, Inc., J. Ernest Tally, and Associated Personnel Technicians* 4-2881 (7th Cir 2005).

[21] Anastasi, *Psychological Testing,* p. 440.

Situational Exercises

A *situational exercise* is a generic term for exercises that measure an applicant's responses to work-life situations. Situational exercises are typically constructed to measure abilities that are important for job success. Among the more common situational exercises are leaderless group situations, in-basket exercises, computer games, and role-playing sessions.

Leaderless Group Situations

Leaderless group situations typically involve a group of applicants in a group project in which their behavior is observed and recorded by trained observers. Sometimes, the situation involves building something; other situations involve reaching a consensus on planning or organizing a project. Sometimes, the group simply discusses a topic. In some situations, each applicant is assigned a role in the discussion. Other times, roles are unassigned.

In one federal agency, leaderless group discussions were used as one part of a selection process to fill management trainee positions. For the exercise, six applicants were seated around a table discussing topics presented by an observer. The topics involved both hypothetical and real management situations in the agency. The behavior of the applicants was unobtrusively observed and assessed. Among the skills that were evaluated were oral communication, sensitivity, leadership, flexibility, initiative, problem analysis, judgment, and decisiveness.

In-Basket Exercise

An *in-basket* exercise tests the ability of applicants to handle an average amount of work representative of that which would be encountered in the job they are seeking. Applicants are given an hour or more to handle the basket of work. Later, in an individual interview with an observer, the applicants explain their rationale for the order in which they handled the work and how they accomplished it. Sometimes, these interview sessions are modified and observers use previously structured questions, such as introducing "what if" situations to see how the applicant would respond. Other variations include questioning applicants why they handled a situation a certain way.

Computer Games

Computer games measure the ability of applicants to evaluate information, usually quantitative data, plan responses, and make decisions. Normally, several iterations of a problem are made, since the computer quickly interacts with the applicant's decision and presents a different set of events resulting from the previous decision. Computer games are work-life situational to the extent the database and programming are representative of the actual job environment.

Role Playing

Role playing (RP) typically involves two persons playing assigned roles. Most often, RP is used to measure applicant knowledge, training, skills, and abilities to handle employee performance appraisal interviews, evaluate employee ideas, assist employees in receiving help for personal problems, and resolve disciplinary problems. These tasks, involving one-on-one confrontations with employees, are among the most important ones that managers must face. RP exercises are effective in both measuring applicants' abilities in performing these tasks and training them to perform them.

Assessment Centers

An *assessment center* (*AC*) is a selection method in which participants engage in multiple exercises, some of which are simulations, and their performance is appraised by pooled-assessments of trained assessors. The typical AC lasts one day, during which participants engage in both group and individual exercises. According to the *Standards for Ethical Considerations for Assessment Center Operations,* the following conditions must be met for a selection method to qualify as an assessment center: (1) multiple assessment techniques are used, at least one of which is a simulation; (2) multiple assessors are used who are specially trained; (3) assessors' judgments of participants' employability, promotability, and developmental needs must be accepted; (4) final assessments of participants must be made at a time other than when their behavior is observed; and (5) a job analysis must be used to determine that the job specifications are assessed.[22]

The exercises used in an AC may either be custom developed or consist of off-the-shelf exercises that are commercially prepared. In some organizations, candidates either nominate themselves or are nominated by their supervisor to attend the AC. Typically, participants are assessed and categorized according to their readiness for promotion. Names of those who are considered to be immediately ready are placed on an eligibility list for promotion as vacancies occur. Those participants who are non-promotable are advised of the areas in which they are deficient, and they are given suggestions for self-development. For example, a participant who demonstrates weak oral communication skills may be advised to enroll in a speech class or a *Toastmaster's Club*. All participants receive feedback in a private, post-assessment center interview.

The typical procedure for an AC begins with a job analysis to determine the job specifications that will be used to develop AC exercises. Experts within the occupational field of the job may be consulted in preparing the exercises. Next, assessors are selected and trained in certain areas, such as how the exercises are used, what specifications various exercises measure, how to observe and record behavior, how rating forms are completed, and that ethical standards are employed. Assessors are also observed in their training to ensure that they are capable of fulfilling their duties.

Participants receive advance notification of the objectives of the AC, the participant selection process, background information about the assessors, general information about the conduct of the center, the exercises to be used, and reassessments (if any). A reassessment opportunity relieves the stress of the pass/fail situation, in which participants are restricted to one assessment. Reas-

---

[22] Task Force on Development of Assessment Center Standards, "Standards for Ethical Consideration For Assessment Center Operation," in *Applying* *The Assessment Center Method*, edited by J.L. Moses and W.C. Byham (New York: Pergamon Press, 1977), pp. 304-305.

sessment, however, is not feasible for vacant jobs that are filled from external sources of applicants.

Participants and assessors arrive about 30 minutes early on the assessment day. This period is used for socializing, where participants and assessors get acquainted and have soft drinks or coffee. The AC usually starts with one of the less-threatening exercises, such as a leaderless group discussion. In this exercise, one assessor usually observes the behavior of two participants. The day's events are carefully scheduled and timed. Assessors are rotated among participants, so that an assessor does not develop an "advocacy" relationship with any one participant. The day after the AC is conducted, all the assessors assemble to complete the evaluation reports. Finally, participants are privately given the results in post-assessment interviews. Exhibit 16-1 shows the schedule for an AC used to fill the job of Director of Public Affairs. The participants were asked to evaluate the AC.

ACs are a proven selection method, provided that they are properly prepared and conducted. Over 3,000 public and private organizations use ACs, or some variation of them, for selection purposes.[23] No court cases have challenged the content validity of ACs.[24]

Exhibit 16-1
Assessment Center Schedule

9:30	Social
10:00	Introduction
10:15	Leaderless Group Discussion
11:00	Field House Session
11:15	Break
11:30	Field House write-up
12:15	Lunch
1:15	Personal Interview
1:45	In-Basket Exercise
3:15	In-Basket Interview
3:45	Break
4:00	Alumni News Layout
5:00	Field House Evaluation
6:00	Assessment Center Evaluation
6:15	Dismiss

Realistic Job Preview

A *realistic job preview* is a video description of a job that is given to job applicants. The purpose of the realistic job preview is to inform the applicants about the important dimensions of a job, including the tasks that are performed and the environment in which work is performed. Sometimes, descriptions of the

[23] W.E. Souder and A.M. Leksich, "Assessment Centers Are Evolving Toward A Bright Future," *Personnel Administrator* (November 1983), p. 80.

[24] S.D. Norton, "The Assessment Center Process and Content Validity: A Reply to Dreker and Sackett," *Academy of Management Review* (November 4, 1981), p. 563.

work or interviews with employees are videotaped, so that applicants can get an even more realistic idea of the job. Realistic job previews help reduce unpleasant surprises new employees often experience. This may result in helping to prevent job dissatisfaction among new employees and the resulting turnover.

Performance Appraisal Results

Performance appraisal results are used in two major ways in employment selection decisionmaking. First, the results of prior performance appraisals are sometimes used in selecting existing employees for promotion, reassignment, or for a training program. These uses often exceed the capability of performance appraisal systems, since they are typically intended to measure *existing* job performance and do not *assess* a person's capability to perform another job. Predictions of success should be based upon comparisons of applicant qualifications with job specifications. These comparisons are not typically incorporated in performance appraisals. Nevertheless, there are occasions when performance appraisal results may be effectively used in a selection process, particularly when the jobs are similar to or are in the same occupation field.

The second way in which performance appraisal results are used may be to verify the qualifications of job applicants. This use of performance appraisals is discussed in Chapter 17.

Graphology

Graphology, also known as *handwriting analysis,* is the process of analyzing handwriting traits, such as writing pressure and slant, to determine human characteristics. It is estimated that over 1,000 firms in the U.S., and 85 percent of European firms, use graphology.[25] The International Graphoanalysis Society trains analysts through course work and other teaching methods; approximately 10,000 persons have been certified by the Society since its founding in 1929.[26]

Graphoanalysts typically require handwriting samples to be original work, to be written with a ballpoint pen (so that writing characteristics are more discernible), and to be at least one page in length. In addition, if the analysis is used in selecting applicants for employment, the analyst usually requests a job description and a personal interview with the applicants.[27]

There is considerable anecdotal evidence about the effectiveness of graphology, such as employers that state the method has proven successful to them. However, there is virtually no conclusive empirical evidence that graphology is a *valid* predictor of job success. On the contrary, several well-designed studies have found that graphology was not valid in predicting job performance.[28]

---

[25] Rafaeli, Anat, and Klimoski, R.J., "Predicting Sales Success Through Handwriting Analysis: An Evaluation of the Effects of Training and Handwriting Sample Content," *Journal of Applied Psychology* (68, No. 2), p. 212.

[26] Taylor, M.S., and Sackheim, K.K., "Graphology," *Personnel Administrator* (May 1988), p. 71.

[27] *Ibid.*

[28] See Rafaeli and Klimoski, "Predicting Sales Success," and Ben-Shakhar, Gershon, Maya Bar-Hillel, Yoram Bilu, Edor Ben-Abba, and Anat Flug, "Can Graphology Predict Occupational Success? Two Empirical Studies and Some Methodological Ruminations," *Journal of Applied Psychology,* 71 (1986), pp. 645-653.

Drug Testing

According to the results of a study conducted by the Substance Abuse and Mental Health Services Administration, which was a sample representing 81.8 million U.S. workers, 74 percent of the workers in large establishments said their employer had some kind (at hiring, randomly, upon suspicion or after an accident) of drug testing program. The percentages reported by workers in small and medium workplaces were, respectively, 28 and 58. All the percentages were significant increases from 1994 when the study was last done.[29] In another study, 97 percent of employees contacted in a Gallup poll agreed under appropriate circumstances drug testing should be conducted at work.[30]

For a fuller discussion of drug testing, see Chapter 8.

HIV Testing

Human immunodeficiency virus (HIV) is the virus that causes acquired immunodeficiency syndrome (AIDS). It is presumed that anyone who is infected with HIV, whether or not he or she has AIDS, can infect others with HIV. HIV is transmitted through intravenous drug use, sexual contact, perinatal transmission, and blood products contaminated with the virus.

AIDS and HIV infection are recognized as disabilities under the American with Disabilities Act (ADA) and the Rehabilitation Act (RA), so that employers who are covered by the ADA (those with 15 or more employees), as well as those covered by the RA (employers with federal contracts of $25,000 or more), may not discriminate in the employment of persons who are infected with HIV or who have AIDS. Employers covered by either law are also required to make reasonable employment accommodation for persons who are infected with HIV or who have AIDS.

In addition to these federal laws, a number of states and cities have banned discrimination against persons who are infected with HIV.[31] Because of these laws, employers should carefully contemplate the potential negative consequences of including a HIV testing protocol as part of a selection process. In addition, using an AIDS test as a strategy to prevent infection is not scientifically justified, since the disease is not spread through casual contact in the workplace. Finally, although workers in the health care field would presumably be at greatest risk for such infection, unless an exposure occurs the Centers for Disease Control does not recommend that they be tested.[32]

Genetic Testing

Genetic testing is an emerging medical practice that tests for genes that cause diseases and addictive behaviors. The results of genetic tests may indicate the

---

[29] Substance Abuse and Mental Health Services Administration, *Worker Drug Use and Workplace Policies and Programs: results from the 1994 and 1997 National Household Survey on Drug Abuse*, 2001.

[30] *The National Clearinghouse for Alcohol and Drug Information, Drug Testing in the Workplace*, 2001.

[31] For a discussion of these legal provisions as well as thorough discussion of the employment issues involving AIDS and HIV, see CCH HUMAN RESOURCES MANAGEMENT, *Personnel Practices/Communications*, ¶ 4200.

[32] However, several cases involving the transmission of HIV infection occurred during an invasive dental procedure in Florida.

predisposition of persons to certain diseases. Genetic testing involves ethical issues, such as whether to hire persons for certain types of jobs if they have a genetic predisposition to a disease such as cancer, and there is a chemical health hazard present in the work environment.

A new medical field called *genetic counseling* has been created to assist people in understanding the significance of genetic tests. Obviously, a part of genetic counseling involves workplace issues, such as job placement and protection from human hazard exposures.[33] A number of states have laws prohibiting employers from using the results of tests in making employment decisions.[34]

The Genetic Information Nondiscrimination Act (GINA) prohibits the use of genetic information in decisions affecting employee selection, termination, work assignment and promotions. See Chapter 12 for a discussion of these provisions.

In addition to GINA, there is a compliance manual and two other laws related to genetic discrimination. In its compliance manual, the EEOC extended the provisions of the Americans with Disabilities Act to cover genetic information. The rationale for this extension was the third definition of a person with a disability; that is, that the person is perceived to have or is regarded as having a disability. Thus, the use of genetic testing for employment reasons is suspect and, unless there are valid job-related reasons for it, the practice would be illegal. Generally, however, many discrimination cases, which are based on the argument that an employer has discriminated against workers by regarding them as disabled, have not been well received by the courts. Nevertheless, in 2002, the Equal Employment Opportunity Commission reached a $2.2 million settlement with Burlington Northern and Santa Fe Railway Co. involving genetic testing. This was the first case involving the application of the Americans with Disabilities Act to genetic testing. The Company had initiated a program to conduct genetic tests as part of its effort to study workers' claims of carpal tunnel syndrome. Employees had contended the Company was conducting the tests without their knowledge. The Company stopped the testing immediately when the EEOC filed suit requesting the practice be stopped.[35]

The two other laws that apply to genetic testing are the Civil Rights Act of 1964 and the Health Insurance Portability and Accountability Act of 1996 (HIPAA). The Civil Rights Act of 1964 prohibits discrimination based upon race. Thus, the use of any genetic tests to deny employment to an individual for a genetic disorder that is racially based would be illegal.[36]

Executive Order 13145 prohibits genetic testing among federal employees. The order prohibits discrimination based upon genetic information regarding employees' compensation, hiring and firing decisions, promotions, and other

---

[33] "Genetic Counseling Track Now Offered," *VCU Voice* (November 16, 1990), p. 1.

[34] CCH Human Resources Management, *Ideas and Trends in Personnel* (June 13, 2001), p. 90.

[35] Society for Human Resource Management, *HR News* (June 2002), p. 18.

[36] Department of Labor, Department of Health and Human Services, Equal Employment Opportunity Commission, and the Department of Justice, *Genetic Information and the Workplace*, January 20, 1998.

employment conditions. Federal agencies are also required to maintain the confidentiality of federal employees' genetic information.[37]

Thirty-five states have laws regulating the use of genetic testing in the workplace. Generally, these laws restrict the employers' use of genetic information in employment testing and in decision-making affecting the terms and conditions of employment.[38]

Medical Examinations

Due to the cost involved, medical examinations that are part of a selection process are administered as the last step in the process. Employers typically use one of two strategies to ensure that they receive adequate medical information concerning an applicant's employability. First, large organizations employ a physician on either a full- or part-time basis. Smaller organizations may either employ a physician on a retainer basis or utilize a selected group of physicians and pay them a set fee for each examination. Normally, physicians employed under one of these arrangements are also used for other medical services, such as job-related accidents, fitness for duty examinations, and disability retirement examinations. Establishing relationships with one or more physicians is cost-effective because the physician better understands the physical requirements of various jobs, is able to render a quicker opinion about an applicant's employability, and can more easily complete the required paperwork.

In addition, utilizing the services of a selected number of physicians provides a greater opportunity for dialogues among employment personnel and physicians on a range of medically related topics. Consequently, there is a likelihood that a physician will represent the employer's interests, or at least ensure that such interests are properly considered in medical matters pertaining to an applicant's employability. Applicants' personal physicians often either fail to adequately understand the medical requirements of a job or advocate for applicants in their efforts to secure employment.

Pre-employment Medical Examinations

Pre-employment medical examinations are expressly prohibited under the Americans with Disabilities Act. Furthermore, an employer may not require an applicant to answer medical inquiries or questions about workers' compensation claims filed prior to a job offer. If a medical examination is required, it must be given after an offer of employment has been made (but prior to commencement of work), provided that it is required of all person employed in the same job. If a person with a disability is denied employment because the post-offer medical examination indicates that he or she is not qualified for employment, the employer must show that the reason for denial is job-related and that reasonable accommodation was not possible.

---

[37] CCH HUMAN RESOURCES MANAGEMENT, *Newsletter, Benefit-News*, #221-10 (February 22, 2000).

[38] American College of Physicians. *Establishing Federal Protections Against Genetic Discrimination.* Philadelphia: American College of Physicians; 2008: Position Paper.

Probationary Periods

People might assume that the selection process ends when an applicant is hired. However, successful completion of a *probationary period* is typically the last step. Estimating applicants' potential to satisfactorily perform in a job is not a precise process. In spite of the best efforts to predict success, some applicants will not make satisfactory employees. The purpose of the probationary period is to allow management to determine if a newly selected employee should be retained in the job he or she was hired to do. This trial period also helps employees decide if a job suits them. Management must validate any measurement instruments, such as a performance appraisal system, used to decide whether an employee should be retained beyond the probationary period. In addition, the EEOC considers probationary periods as selection procedures, so that they also must be validated.[39]

Special Selection Considerations

Special selection considerations involve matters such as residency or licensing requirements, certification or accreditation, and successful completion of a training course required for job retention or advancement. Often, public employment jobs, such as the federal civil service, require an applicant to be a U.S. citizen. Some cities require that employees live within the city limits. Sometimes, an applicant is employed on the condition that he or she will pass an examination for a certain type of license, such as life insurance or real estate, within a certain period.

Training courses are special selection methods if employees are required to pass them as a condition of remaining employed. The EEOC interprets training courses as " . . . a selection procedure if passing it is a prerequisite to retention or advancement."[40] All these special selection considerations must be validated if they have an adverse impact upon protected persons. Normally, this is accomplished through content validation.

---

[39] *Ibid.*, ¶8817.

[40] CCH Human Resources Management, *Equal Employment Opportunity*, ¶8831.

CHAPTER 17
VERIFYING APPLICANTS' QUALIFICATIONS

Chapter Highlights
- Understand the processes in verifying applicants' qualifications
- Review the risk dimensions of verifying applicants' qualifications
- Learn how to address former employers' failure to release information about applicants
- Understand the methods of verifying applicants' qualifications for employment

Introduction

Verifying applicants' qualifications is the process of corroborating the information that applicants furnish, determining if any important facts were omitted, and obtaining other relevant information about the applicants' employability. *Reference checking* is a term used for some of the activities involved in verifying applicants' qualifications. A term used for checks on an applicant's employment experience is *employment verification*. While both of these activities are important, verifying the qualifications of applicants extends beyond checking references and verifying previous employment experience.

Risk Issues in Employment Verification

As noted in Chapter 16, *negligent hiring* is the potential liability of an employer for the actions of employees who were selected for employment without adequately determining their qualifications and verifying the accuracy of the information they provided. Some applicants do not provide correct information about themselves. For example, one study found that 80 percent of the resumes applicants submitted did not accurately report their job experience. In addition, the study found 30 percent of the resumes did not accurately show the applicant's educational attainments.[1] There also is evidence that all employers do not fully verify the information furnished by applicants. A survey of 320 employers found that 18 percent of them did not check the employment history of college graduates and 21 percent did not verify the graduates' education.[2]

Serious, even tragic, consequences may result from inadequate verification of applicants' personal characteristics and other relevant qualifications. A manager of an apartment complex selected an applicant to work in the maintenance department. The check of the individual's background failed to disclose that he had a violent personality, including convictions for assault; he was also wanted for probation violations. He raped and murdered a female tenant of the complex

---

[1] CCH HUMAN RESOURCES MANAGEMENT, *Personnel Practices/Communications*, ¶ 332.

[2] Schellhardt, T.D., "What Personnel Offices Really Stress in Hiring," *The Wall Street Journal* (March 8. 1991), p. B-1.

where he worked. The apartment owners were sued by the woman's parents for failing to adequately check the employee's past background. In another case, a woman who was raped by a cab driver obtained a judgment of $4,500,000 from the taxi company because it failed to learn that the driver had a criminal record.[3] The verification procedures discussed in this chapter will help to prevent negligent hiring and ensure that those applicants who are hired are qualified to perform their work efficiently and safely.

Adverse Impact in Verification

If an employment decision, based on information used to verify applicants' qualifications, results in adverse impact on a protected group, the employer is required to show that the decision was job-related or was a bona fide occupational qualification.

Improving Accuracy of Applicant Provided Information

The accuracy of information furnished by applicants can be substantially improved by following two steps. First, inform applicants of the importance of accuracy, explaining that the information they furnish will have a direct bearing upon their employability. In addition, applicants should understand that the information they furnish will be carefully verified. These two steps will help decrease the inconsistency between information furnished by applicants and that obtained through verification. For example, one organization required applicants for truck driver positions to list all traffic convictions that occurred within the previous five years. Often, applicants would omit listing either part or all of their traffic citations and convictions. The application form contained a statement in small print that read, *Information furnished by applicants is subject to verification.* The process of verifying traffic convictions took some time, particularly for those applicants who had lived in different cities and states. Consequently, to speed up the employment process, applicants took part in other selection procedures, such as road-driving and vision tests, while the information they provided on the applications was verified. On a number of occasions, applicants were hired when clear records were received from local police departments in those communities in which they *reported* they had lived. Later, however, state police verifications revealed conviction information that was either omitted or in error. Depending upon the seriousness of the conviction, this sometimes necessitated discharging the employee. The personnel director was concerned about the problem and he reworded the warning statement in larger print to read:

> *All the information that you furnish on this form will be checked, except that present employers will not be contacted if you specifically request it. Driving records will be thoroughly checked with local and state police departments. Other conviction information will also be verified and considered in evaluating your application, if it is related to the job for which you are applying. Your failure to include important information may bar you from employment.*

---

[3] Atwood, C.S. and Neel, J.M., "New Lawsuits Expand Employer Liability," *HR Magazine* (October, 1990), p. 74.

In addition, employment interviewers were instructed to inform applicants as follows:

> *We verify all information furnished on an application; this includes checking for driving and other conviction information from state and local police departments. We neither obtain nor consider such information unless it is specifically related to the job. Providing false information or omitting information may bar you from employment. With this in mind, would you like to review your application to be sure that you did not omit any information?*

These procedures significantly reduced errors, inaccuracies, and omissions.

The accuracy of information furnished by applicants may also be increased by having them sign release forms holding previous employers harmless for any job-related information they furnish. Reviewing the release forms with applicants and explaining the types of information desired, such as job title, length of employment, rehire eligibility, safety record, attendance record, conduct and quality of work, may prompt the applicant to tell the interviewer about important information that was either omitted or incorrect. The interviewer should emphasize that any differences in the information provided by the applicant and former employers will delay, and may even bar, employment.

What Information Should be Verified?

Virtually all the qualifications of applicants may be either directly or indirectly verified, but, as a practical matter, only essential information that is job-related is checked. *Directly verified* means the information is first-hand. For example, an applicant may state in an interview or write on an application that he or she has a baccalaureate degree. A college transcript that is prepared and notarized by the college's registrar and mailed to the employer is a direct verification of the applicant's education at that college. On the other hand, an honesty test administered to an applicant may not be able to directly verify a statement made in an employment interview, such as that the applicant never stole anything from a prior employer. A direct verification in this case might be a statement signed by former supervisors indicating, to the best of their knowledge, that the applicant did not steal from the employer. Where possible, direct sources of proof should be sought. Care should be taken to separate *facts* from *opinions* when employment information is verified.

Some of the major types of information that employers should check and the sources used for verification are shown in Exhibit 17-1.

Antisocial Behavior

Antisocial behavior includes a broad category of behavior, ranging from chronic rudeness to felony assaults. Antisocial behavior used to bar employment must be job-related. Applicants for bank teller jobs should be trustworthy and not have been discharged by a former employer for theft or have been convicted of theft. On the other hand, chronic rudeness may not be job-related for a warehouse worker who does not regularly come in contact with either customers or other workers.[4] As shown in Exhibit 17-1, sources of information about an applicant's prior behavior include court records, credit reports, former employers, honesty tests, police records, and polygraph tests (only legal in limited circumstances). These verification sources are discussed later in this chapter.

Exhibit 17-1
Types of Applicant Information Verified
and Source of Verification

Information to be Verified	Verification Source												
	Court records	Credit report	Dept. motor vehicle	Drug test	Former employers	Honesty test	Medical exam	Military records	Performance appraisals	Personal references	Police records	Polygraph	Schools/universities
Antisocial behavior	✓	✓			✓	✓		✓	✓	✓	✓	✓	
Driver's license			✓										
Driving record	✓	✓	✓		✓						✓		
Drug use	✓			✓	✓	✓	✓			✓	✓	✓	
Education													✓
Financial status	✓	✓								✓			
On-the-job injuries	✓				✓		✓		✓				
Work experience/ performance					✓			✓	✓	✓			

Driver's License

For jobs that require a valid driver's license, an important item on the verification list is to check whether the applicant is licensed and whether there are any significant moving violations. *Red-flag* items are any convictions for reckless driving, driving under the influence of alcohol, or speeding. Some states have special licenses for chauffeuring duties and driving trucks over a certain tonnage. The department of motor vehicle licensing in the state would be source for checking an applicant's driving license.

Driving Record

Important information about an applicant's driving record would include, in addition to the information discussed above, any preventable on-the-job vehicle accidents, evidence of safe driving awards, number of years of driving experi-

---

[4] CCH HUMAN RESOURCES MANAGEMENT, *Equal Employment Opportunity*, ¶ 10,110.

ence, the types of vehicles driven, and the completion of driver training courses. Sources of information to prove an applicant's driving record include court records, credit reports, state department of motor vehicle records, former employers, and police department records.

Drug Use

Drug abuse is a serious concern for employers. Sources for checking applicants' contentions about their drug use include court records, drug tests, former employers, honesty tests, medical examinations, performance appraisal results from former employers, personal references, police records, and polygraph testing. Drug testing is the primary method of verifying drug use. Drug testing usually involves cocaine, amphetamines, methamphetamines (ecstasy), opiates (heroin, morphine), pcp (angels dust, hog) and tetrahydrocannabinol (marijuana, hashish).

Education

The types of educational information that can be authenticated include a high school diploma or GED equivalency. Usually, authentic copies of those two documents are sufficient proof. College educational requirements require more documentation. Depending upon the job, the verification of college credentials includes evidence of matriculation at the institution, name and date of degree obtained, major course of study, and dates of enrollment. If specific course work and/or grades are required for the job, a transcript may be needed to prove that the requirements are met. The source for verifying this information is school or university records.

Financial Status

The types of financial information, depending upon job-related conditions, that an employer might need to verify include evidence of bankruptcy, garnishments, credit rating, financial obligations, rental or home ownership, car ownership, length of residence at present and past addresses, outstanding financial obligations, delinquencies in payment of taxes or other financial obligations, failure to pay alimony or child support, tax liens and judgments, and student loan obligations. Financial information furnished by the applicant may be checked through court records, credit reports, and personal references. The Bankruptcy Act prohibits employers from rejecting job applicants just because they have declared bankruptcy.[5] In addition, as discussed below, there are procedures required by the Fair Credit Reporting Act that employers must observe in using credit reports for employment decisionmaking purposes.

On-the-Job Injuries

Employers have a legitimate right to know what accidents and injuries applicants have experienced in the past. This information is important in order for an employer to determine whether applicants are able to perform the tasks in a job without risk to themselves or others. This information may be requested on

---

[5] CCH HUMAN RESOURCES MANAGEMENT, *Personnel Practices*, ¶ 335.

the application and verified through credit reports, former employers, or a medical examination. Care should be taken not to inquire about workers' compensation claims until after a conditional offer of employment has been made. The same is true for requesting a medical examination.

Work Experience/Performance

Employment decisions are frequently dependent upon applicants' claims regarding their work experience and level of performance. The types of information that may be checked include the dates that the person was employed, the job title held, the tasks performed and the length of time they were performed, and job-related training programs that were completed. Of equal importance is the level of applicants' job performance in their job history. Questions to be answered include the quantity of work, work quality, attendance record, job safety, and conduct or behavior at work. The best source of this information is former employers, military records, the results of performance appraisals completed by former employers, and personal references.

Other Types of Information

Other types of information that should be verified include professional licenses or certifications and any other special requirements necessary for the job. The sources for confirmation would depend upon the special requirement, such as the organizations that granted the licensure or certification.

Verification Sources

Court Records

Court records include local, county, state, and federal courts. The various levels of courts have different jurisdictions over both the geographical area covered and the type of tort or criminal activity involved. Local courts may be restricted to traffic offenses and minor torts. County and state courts may only oversee non-federal offenses, ranging from torts to capital offenses. Federal courts handle bankruptcy cases, federal crimes, and civil cases. Some court records, particularly those involving domestic cases and juvenile offenses, may be sealed and, therefore, may not be available to the public. Most of the other records of courts are public, and some courts even have on-line access.[6]

Credit Report

There are two types of credit reports. A *consumer report* is a inquiry into an individual's credit (worthiness, standing, or capacity), character, reputation, personal characteristics, or style of living that may affect an individual's employability. An *investigative consumer report* is a full or partial consumer report derived from interviews with people who know the individual, including friends, neighbors, and associates.

---

[6] CCH HUMAN RESOURCES MANAGEMENT, *Personnel Practices*, ¶ 335.

Employer Responsibilities

Employers have legal responsibilities under the Fair Credit Reporting Act. This law requires employers to give applicants written notification on a form exclusively used for that purpose, stating that a credit report may be used. The employer must also obtain written approval from the applicants, authorizing the employer to obtain the credit report. Before the credit reporting agency will send a report, the employer is required to certify that the law has been complied with and the information will be used in accordance with applicable equal employment opportunity laws and regulations.

A negative employment decision, such as a denial of employment, reassignment, promotion, or termination resulting from information derived from a credit report, is defined in the law as an *adverse action*. Prior to taking an adverse action, which, even in a minor way, was affected by a credit report, the employer must send the individual a *pre-adverse action disclosure*. This disclosure must include a copy of the individual's consumer report and a copy of the document, *A Summary of Your Rights Under the Fair Credit Reporting Act*. The credit reporting agency is responsible for providing the employer with a summary of consumer rights.

After the employer has taken an adverse action, the person affected by such action must be given an individual notice, orally, in writing, or electronically, that an adverse action has been taken. The notice must include:

- The name, address, and phone number of the credit reporting agency that supplied the report;

- A statement that the credit reporting agency did not make the decision to take the adverse action and cannot give specific reasons for it; and

- A notice of the individual's right to dispute the accuracy or completeness of any information furnished by the agency, and his or her right to an additional free consumer report from the agency upon request within 60 days.[7]

The law is enforced by the Federal Trade Commission, and there are significant legal consequences for employers that fail to comply with it.

Department of Motor Vehicles Records

The state department of motor vehicles is a valuable resource for the verification of information, such as traffic violations, driving offenses, and type of license.

The Driver's Privacy Protection Act of 1994 contains provisions regulating the release and use of certain personal information from state motor vehicle records. Among the permissible uses includes release of such information to businesses that are verifying the accuracy of personal information submitted by the individual. In certain situations defined in the law, written consent is required of the individual to whom the information applies.[8]

---

[7] Federal Trade Commission, *Using Consumer Reports: What Employers Need to Know* (December 1997).

[8] Federal Driver's Privacy Protection Act (18 U.S.C. Section 2721 et. Seq).

Drug Test

As noted in Chapter 8, drug use among employees and potential employees is a concern for employers. For example, 73 percent of all current drug users age 18 and older (8.3 million adults) were employed in 1997. Furthermore, an unknown, but presumably large, percentage of drug and alcohol abusers are under the influence of drugs or alcohol at work. According to a national survey conducted by the Hazelden Foundation, more than 60 percent of adults know workers who have gone to work under the influence of drugs or alcohol. For these and other concerns, a 1996 survey conducted by the American Management Association found that 81 percent of the businesses that were surveyed conduct some form of applicant or employee drug test.[9]

Legal Issues in Drug Testing

There are legal issues to consider in establishing drug testing programs. Two U.S. Supreme Court decisions indicate that drug testing among public sector employers is legal, if the program was announced in advance and there is reasonable cause for it, such as accidents involving the public safety or for law enforcement work involving drug enforcement.[10] The Department of Transportation requires drug testing for employees who:

- Are flight crew members;
- Operate commercial motor vehicles in interstate commerce (subject to some limitations);
- Perform railroad services;
- Perform operating, maintenance, or emergency-response functions on a pipeline or liquid natural gas facility; or
- Are crew members on a commercial vessel licensed, certified, or documented by the U.S. Coast Guard.

In the private sector, 41 states have laws regulating the use of drug tests. Some of these laws prohibit drug testing, while other laws establish guidelines for such testing. These guidelines specify the conditions under which applicants or employees can be tested. In some states, the laws apply to both applicants and employees. Some states have guidelines that are voluntary. Among the issues addressed by state laws are posting and general notice requirements, the consequences for refusal to take a test, the timing of testing, testing procedures, results and confidentiality, and limitations of testing to specific jobs or employment situations.[11]

The National Labor Relations Board has ruled that employers must bargain with a union before implementing a drug testing program of current employees in the bargaining unit.[12] While unionized employers are not required to bargain

---

[9] U.S. Department of Labor. "Facts and Figures about Drugs and Alcohol in the Workplace," November 6, 1998, pp. 1 and 2.

[10] For more information on this issue see CCH HUMAN RESOURCES MANAGEMENT, *Personnel Practices/ Communications*, ¶ 326.

[11] CCH HUMAN RESOURCES MANAGEMENT, *Personnel Practices*, ¶ 327A.

[12] CCH HUMAN RESOURCES MANAGEMENT, *Employment Relations*, ¶ 2078.

with unions on the subject of drug testing of job applicants, they are required to provide information to unions about such programs, when requested.[13] Legal problems may also occur even if no laws govern the subject of drug testing. For example, an applicant may file a civil suit seeking recovery for damages due to an adverse employment decision resulting from a faulty drug testing method.

Testing Measures

At a minimum, employers with testing programs for job applicants, or those considering them, are advised to ensure that the following precautions are taken:

- Check for any legal requirements;
- Define the conditions under which drug testing will be conducted;
- Ensure that specimen collection, transportation, and testing is conducted with the utmost consideration for employee privacy, confidentiality, and scientific accuracy;
- Disseminate a copy of the drug policy statement to all employees;
- Obtain consent forms, signed by applicants, giving permission for present and future drug testing;
- Utilize testing laboratories certified by the Department of Health and Human Services; and
- Require confirmatory tests be conducted for all positive test results.

Former Employers

Previous employers are important sources of information about job applicants. Unfortunately, many employers are reluctant to reveal anything but basic facts about a former employee. *Failure to disclose* is a term used to explain the unwillingness of former employers to reveal information to future employers about those who have left their employ. The major reason for this reluctance is fear of defamation suits. In the opinion of experts, the best defense for defamation suits is to tell the truth.[14] Failing to disclose relevant information to a prospective employer may subject a former employer to a lawsuit, although, in one case, a court found that a former employer had no responsibility to honor a request for information about an ex-employee's violent propensities. In the absence of the derogatory information, the person was hired and subsequently murdered a co-worker.[15] Risk aspects of employee selection and retention include *defamation,* which is damaging a person's reputation as the result of something said (slander) or something put in writing (libel) that is not true, and *malice,* which is wantonly or recklessly making statements about a person that are known to be false.

The following steps will help elicit former employers' cooperation in supplying information:

- Put the request in writing;

---

[13] *Ibid.*

[14] For a complete discussion of defamation suits, see CCH HUMAN RESOURCES MANAGEMENT, *Personnel Practices/Communication,* ¶ 1467.

[15] *Ibid.*

- Ask specific questions, such as, "Was the person ever disciplined or discharged for fighting?" and, "Was the person ever disciplined or discharged for drug or alcohol use?";

- Limit requests for information to those subjects relevant to the employment decision; and

- Include a release form signed and dated by the applicant specifically stating: (1) the applicant has read all the information requested by the prospective employer; (2) the applicant agrees to the release of all the information that was requested; (3) the applicant requests that the previous employer comply with the request for information; and (4) the applicant holds the previous employer harmless for any information that is furnished, regardless of the decision the prospective employer makes based upon it.

Of course, applicants are the best source of valid information about themselves. Often, merely having applicants read and sign the release form will prompt them to reveal information they did not include on the application form. Consequently, prior to having them sign the release form, it is a good idea to ask them to review their application and make sure that all the information is correct.

Even after following these steps, some former employers may still refuse to cooperate. If this happens:

- First, the principal person responsible for the previous employer's human resources function should be telephoned to determine why the request for information was not honored;

- Second, the person should be asked how a request should be made, so that it will be honored; and

- Third, if the person still refuses to cooperate, he or she should be informed that the failure to disclose information will be documented, with the date and time of the call and the name of the person who would not comply with the request for information. The person also should be told that, in the event the missing information was so relevant that the applicant would not be hired without it, the applicant will be informed that the previous employer's failure to cooperate was the reason that he or she was not hired.

Honesty Test

The demand for instruments that measure the propensity of individuals to engage in antisocial behavior at work, such as stealing from the employer, abusing drugs while working, or committing workplace violence, rose appreciably with the significant decline in the use of "lie detectors," as a result of the Employee Polygraph Protection Act. Instruments in this category include *honesty tests* used to measure characteristics such as an applicant's inclination to steal from an employer or to cause trouble at work.[16]

---

[16] CCH HUMAN RESOURCES MANAGEMENT, *Ideas and Trends,* (December 26, 1990), p. 6.

The Office of Technology Assessment (OTA) conducted a study on honesty tests and concluded there is not sufficient evidence of their validity. Furthermore, the OTA was concerned about potential abuses that could result from using honesty tests, such as reaching inaccurate conclusions from test results and invading applicants' privacy. Another study found evidence of the predictive validity of honesty tests.[17]

Other tests are used to predict applicant's propensity to commit acts of violence at work. Employers that use these tests should review the results of validity studies conducted by the test manufacturer or others who use the tests. The test user is responsible for ensuring that a selection procedure is valid if adverse impact results.

At least two states have laws regarding the use of honesty tests. Massachusetts defines a *lie detector test* as "any test using a polygraph or any other device, mechanism, instrument or written examination, that is used or interpreted by an examiner to detect deception, verify truthfulness, or to render a diagnostic opinion regarding the honesty of an individual."[18] The law further states that it is unlawful for any employer to subject or request applicants for employment or employees to take "a lie detector test, or to discharge, not hire, demote or otherwise discriminate against" such persons for asserting their rights under the law. The provision also applies to persons who are applying for employment as police officers. The law also requires that all employment applications must contain this statement:

> It is unlawful in Massachusetts to require or administer a lie detector test as a condition of employment or continued employment. An employer who violates this law will be subject to criminal penalties and civil liability.

Rhode Island also has a law restricting the use of honesty tests. This law defines a *lie detector test* as "any test utilizing a polygraph or any other device, mechanism, instrument or written examination that is operated, or the results of which are used or interpreted by an examiner to detect deception, verify truthfulness, or render a diagnostic opinion regarding the honesty of an individual."[19] The actual effects of the law on honesty tests are somewhat softened, since written examinations measuring deception, truthfulness and related concepts may be used if the results are not used as the primary reason for an employment decision.

Medical Examination

In accordance with the Americans with Disabilities Act (ADA), an applicant may not be given a medical examination until after a conditional job offer has been extended. The information from the examination may be used to help verify an applicant's drug use and any previous on-the-job injuries.

---

[17] Sackett, P.R., Burris, L.R., & Callahan, C., "Integrity Testing for Personnel Selection: An Update," *Personnel Psychology*, 42, 491-529 (1989).

[18] CCH HUMAN RESOURCES MANAGEMENT, *State-Laws*, ¶ 22-8800.

[19] CCH HUMAN RESOURCES MANAGEMENT, *State-Laws*, ¶ 41-8800.

Military Records

The DD 214 is a brief record of an individual's military service, particularly the period of service and the type of discharge. This document may be used to verify any behavioral problems applicants may have had while in the military. For example, any discharge, other than an honorable one, should be explained by the applicant. The DD 214 also shows the military occupational code, which may be used to determine the type of work the applicant did while in the military.

Performance Appraisals

If employers fail to cooperate in providing information about the job performance of applicants, the next best alternative is to review the performance appraisal forms that the former employers completed on the applicants. These forms may provide information about any antisocial behavior that the applicant may have exhibited. In addition, performance appraisals may verify information about on-the-job injuries, work experience, and work performance.

Personal References

In the narrowest sense, *references* are reports by those individuals listed by an applicant who can furnish pertinent information about the applicant's qualifications. Normally, references are requested on *application forms.* References are erroneously viewed as valueless because applicants only use persons who they feel will give favorable information to a selection official.

Another perceived problem with references is that information furnished by them is usually subjective and/or not related to job specifications. These and other problems with using personal references can be neutralized by placing several constraints on applicants. First, applicants should be instructed to list only those references who have known the applicant for at least a set period, such as one or two years, and have direct knowledge of the applicant's qualifications as they relate to the job specifications. This requirement may be reinforced by requesting the applicant to briefly justify why the reference is qualified to provide this information. Second, applicants should be requested to sign releases waiving their rights to review information furnished by a personal reference. References should be sent a copy of the document, indicating whether the review rights were waived. Third, references should be sent a copy of the job specifications and requested to use their knowledge to compare the applicant's qualifications with the job specifications. Finally, when useful, references should be contacted by telephone to discuss an applicant's qualifications or to verify information.

Police Records

Some employers check for evidence of an applicant's criminal record for selected jobs, such as security guards. Typically, the information is requested on the employment application. This information is verified from police department records where the applicant has lived. In some states, the information may be obtained through the state criminal records repository. This approach would preclude contacting the police department in each locality where the applicant has lived. Most local law enforcement agencies will check an applicant's police record and give the information to the applicant who, in turn, may present it to the prospective employer. Depending upon the state's regulations, the information may be sent either to an employer after a form requesting it is signed by the applicant, or to the applicant who may present it to the prospective employer.

Inaccurate Records

Criminal record information, even that supplied by law enforcement agencies, may not always be accurate. The information may be incorrect due to mistaken identity or failure to post changes or reflect the outcome of the case. For example, criminal records may show arrests without indicating the final disposition of the case (whether the person was convicted).

Arrest Information

Some states do not have laws regulating employers' use of applicants' criminal record information. However, many states prohibit employers from requesting any information that did not result in a conviction. In addition, the EEOC contends that excluding applicants solely on the basis of arrests, without a job-related correlation, may be discriminatory.[20] In addition, in *Gregory v. Litton Industries* (1972) a federal circuit court held that using arrest information in cases where no conviction resulted is a violation of Title VII if adverse impact results.[21]

Fingerprinting/Criminal Records

While some states are silent on the subject of fingerprinting applicants or employees, others, such as New York, prohibit employers, except for those in specified occupations, from requiring the fingerprinting of applicants or employees as a condition of employment. A number of states require fingerprinting of employees in certain fields of work, such as law enforcement, child care, private security or detective agencies, and state gambling agencies.[22]

Polygraphs

A *polygraph* is an instrument that monitors respiration (rate of breathing), blood pressure, and electrical conductivity of skin surfaces (also known as galvanic responses or perspiration). The use of polygraph tests among private sector employers is controlled by both federal and state law. The federal law on the subject, the Employee Polygraph Protection Act of 1988 (EPPA), prohibits the use of all lie detectors, except for the polygraph. This law only permits certain employers to *request* applicants to take a polygraph test. Employers are also permitted, under restricted conditions, to request that employees take a test in the event of an economic loss. The law also stipulates requirements and qualifications for polygraph examiners. Violations of the EPPA are subject to money damages, such as lost wages and benefits, court orders to stop violations, and civil fines up to $10,000.

[20] CCH Human Resources Management, *Personnel Practices/Communications*, ¶ 338.
[21] CCH Human Resources Management, *Equal Employment Opportunity*, ¶ 8827.
[22] For an analysis of state laws, see CCH Human Resources Management, *Personnel Practices/Communications*, ¶ 325.

In addition to the EPPA, 20 states and the District of Columbia have laws restricting the use of polygraph tests in an employment setting. The EPPA does not preempt state laws that are more restrictive.

According to a national survey conducted by the U.S. Department of Labor, less than two percent of employers use polygraphs in selecting employees.[23]

Polygraphs for Job Applicants

The EPPA prohibits private sector employers from administering, to applicants or employees, a deceptograph, voice stress analyzer, psychological stress evaluator, or any similar test.[24] The act also prohibits private sector employers from administering a polygraph test to job applicants. The sole exception is that applicants may be requested to take a polygraph test if they are applying for work with *either:* (1) security firms (armored car, alarm, and guard) if they will be engaged in security work, *or* (2) manufacturers, distributors, or dispensers of controlled substances, if the applicant will have direct access to the manufacture, storage, distribution, or sale of such substances. Neither applicant refusal to take a polygraph test nor the analysis of the results of a polygraph test may be the sole basis for denying employment. Applicants who consent to polygraph testing may terminate the test at any time and may not be asked questions in specific areas, such as sexual behavior. Employers are required to give applicants written notice, informing them that they may not be required to take the test as a condition of employment.

Polygraphs for Economic Losses

Private sector employers may request that employees take a polygraph test in conjunction with an ongoing investigation involving economic loss or injury to the employer's business, such as theft, embezzlement, misappropriation, or an act of unlawful industrial espionage or sabotage. The only employees that may be requested to take a polygraph test are those that had access to the property that is the subject of the investigation, or if the employer has reasonable suspicion that the employee was involved in the incident or activity under investigation. The employer is also required to give a signed statement to the employee, who is requested to take the polygraph, specifically explaining the incident or activity to be investigated and the basis for testing that particular employee.

No employee may be disciplined, discharged, denied employment or promotion, or otherwise discriminated against on the basis of an analysis of a polygraph test or the refusal to take the test, without additional supporting evidence. An employee who consents to polygraph testing may terminate the test at any time and may not be asked questions in specific areas, such as sexual behavior. Employers must give employees written notice, informing them that they may not be required to take the test as a condition of employment.

---

[23] *Human Resource Policies and Practices in American Firms* (Washington, DC: U.S. Government Printing Office, 1989), p. 13.

[24] CCH HUMAN RESOURCES MANAGEMENT, *Employment Relations,* ¶ 5686.

Schools/Universities

To secure information from a school or university, the employer must either obtain a signed consent statement from the applicant or have the applicant request that the institution furnish the information directly to the employer. The latter is the most economical method.

Pre-employment Verification Companies

Some companies provide verification services that include checking job experience, work performance, attendance, training and education, criminal convictions, motor vehicle driving records, and Social Security reports. In addition to verifying information, these companies also conduct pre-employment searches of applicants' backgrounds and provide comprehensive reports. These searches may include workers' compensation claims, credit bureau records, bankruptcy filings, and interviews with co-workers and neighbors to determine an applicant's reputation in areas such as honesty and alcohol or drug abuse. Such services are subject to the Fair Credit Reporting Act discussed previously. The fees for these services depend upon how much investigation is done. For a modest fee, some companies will conduct comprehensive verifications covering all of the areas noted above. Most of the firms cover the previous five years of an applicant's history.

CHAPTER 18
COMPENSATION PLANNING

Chapter Highlights
- Compensation planning process
- Compensation plan design
- Human resource/compensation management relationships
- Changing patterns in compensation

Introduction

Compensation has always been a top priority for both employers and employees, but that importance has dramatically increased in recent years and will undoubtedly continue to increase. The major concerns for employers are domestic and international competition compelling them to reduce compensation costs, new laws placing additional obligations on employers in such areas as health care and employee leave, and the need to find new methods of compensating employees. Top concerns among employees are the slow growth in pay increases, reductions in employer-provided benefit programs, and ominous rumblings about the future of Social Security retirement and Medicare. The convergence of these forces (that is, what employees want and what employers provide) within a dynamic political, social, and economic environment has enormous import for compensation management.

Compensation is the process of directly and indirectly rewarding employees, on a current or deferred basis, for their performance of assigned tasks.

Pay

Pay, the *direct* or monetary rewards for job performance, represents about 70 percent of total compensation costs.[1] Employers that have large numbers of employees generally have more generous benefit programs; for them, pay represents a smaller percentage of total compensation than for the average-sized employer. Pay includes all forms of monetary compensation, such as wages, salaries, bonuses, overtime pay, commissions, and profit-sharing cash disbursements

Monetary payments are made for either the amount of time worked, such as the number of hours worked in a pay period, or some other measure, such as the number of units produced in a piece-rate production system.

[1] This figure is the average of all private sector firms with one or more employees. U.S. Department of Labor, Bureau of Labor Statistics, June 2008.

Pay includes both current and deferred monetary payments. The semi-monthly paycheck is an example of a *current* monetary payment. What are *deferred* monetary payments? Profit-sharing earnings paid when employees end their working careers and retire is an example of a *deferred* monetary payment.

Pay is the direct or monetary forms of current or deferred compensation.

Benefits

Employees today are keenly aware that *benefits* are the other component of compensation. There are valid reasons for this awareness; cost considerations are motivating employers to reduce the benefits in their employee benefit programs, shift the costs of one or more benefits to their employees, and even eliminate programs.

The awareness of the importance of employee benefits, particularly health benefits, is having a significant impact upon employees. There is considerable evidence that the fear of losing health insurance coverage is a major factor in some employee decisions not to change employers. A law, the Health Insurance Portability and Accountability Act of 1996 (HIPAA), is intended to help address this concern.

Employee benefits, also called *indirect compensation*, consist of current and deferred non-pay entitlements that employees receive as a condition of their employment.

Job-site child care provided by the employer is an example of a current benefit. An employer-funded retirement plan is an example of a deferred benefit. Employee benefits may or may not necessitate monetary payments by employers. Health benefits, educational reimbursements, and employer-funded child care subsidies do require monetary payments. Merchandise discounts to employees are an example of a benefit that does not involve expenditures.

Benefits Include Services

Some benefit programs consist of *services* that are provided to employees. An *employee assistance program* (EAP) is a service that employers provide to assist employees who are suffering from personal problems, including alcoholism and alcohol abuse, other forms of drug addiction, gambling, legal problems, marriage and family problems, financial problems, and mental or emotional problems. Other types of services offered to employees are wellness and recreation programs.

Compensation Management

As we have seen, compensation consists of both paying employees for the work they do and providing benefits to them that help make their lives more secure and enjoyable. The four major processes involved in compensating employees are:

- *Planning* the systems to pay employees and provide them with various benefits. This process includes determining the types of pay and benefits that will best meet the organization's objectives.

- *Establishing* the pay systems and benefit programs, which includes preparing the pay structures and negotiating with providers of health benefit plans.

- *Administering* the systems and programs, such as placing employees within a pay grade, adjusting employees' pay, and enrolling employees in the employer's retirement plan.

- *Evaluating* the systems and programs to ensure that they meet the planned objectives. Evaluation is an increasingly important process, as objectives are refocused and costs mandate changes.

Compensation management is the function of planning, establishing, administering, and evaluating pay and benefit programs.

Total Compensation Planning

Total compensation is the value of pay, benefits, and services employees receive for their work performance. Historically, various dimensions of compensation were emphasized during different eras. Early in the 20th century, the emphasis was on the use of incentives, such as Frederick W. Taylor's task and bonus system. Later, the concept of job classification came into vogue. In the 1930s, the importance of retirement income prompted the enactment of the Social Security Act. In the 1950s, voluntary benefits, such as employer-provided health benefits and life insurance, were emphasized. Gradually, this myopic perspective on the individual components of compensation broadened to include both pay and benefits. These are some of the major conditions that changed the focus from this narrow perspective to total compensation:

- Spiraling compensation costs;

- The realization that employer-provided benefits, such as medical expense and retirement plans, are not entitlements but must be earned;

- Increased employee mobility; and

- The development of flatter organizations that are more responsive to all organizational dimensions.[2]

Total compensation planning is the process of establishing a system of pay and benefits that best meet an organization's compensation objectives.

---

[2] Scott, Miriam Basch, "Future of employee benefits features changed employer-employee relationship," *Employee Benefit Plan Review,* Vol. 49, No. 9 (March 1995), pp. 46-47.

Compensation and Culture

In the past, compensation plans were established to be consistent with the organization's culture. Some organizations adopted every new compensation program created, regardless of the cost. Employees expected that the practice would continue, but, beginning in the late 1980s, compensation practices began to change. General pay increases were abandoned for more performance-related pay systems. Benefit plans were assessed as well to find ways of reducing costs without significantly cutting benefits.

Today, compensation plans are not created to be consistent with an outmoded corporate culture; instead, the culture is changed to accommodate desired behavior, and compensation plans are developed to support the culture.[3] Changing corporate culture is not easy, and there is considerable resistance to it, but unprecedented demands facing both public and private organizations demand that it be done.[4]

Employee Benefit Planning

Employee benefits have become a significant part of the work rewards provided to employees. Thus, for maximum effectiveness in meeting an employee's needs and an employer's objectives, it is essential that employee benefits be analyzed as a whole. A piecemeal approach leads to gaps or overlaps in coverage. Proper planning and organizing ensures that employee benefits are appropriately integrated and consistent with the employer's total compensation philosophy.

Steps in Employee Benefit Planning

The steps in employee benefit planning are:

- Defining the employer objectives;
- Designing a program of benefits consistent with those objectives;
- Implementing the program (which includes communicating the program to employees); and
- Monitoring the plan to make changes when necessary.

Defining Objectives

The first step in the planning process is to determine what are the employer's objectives influencing the design of employee benefit plans. Objectives vary among individual firms, as a result of differences in size, location, type of industry, collective bargaining agreements, and the employer's basic philosophy on issues, such as cost and the company's obligation to employees. If a consultant is used in benefit planning, clearly defined objectives are needed in order for the consultant to make appropriate recommendations. Clearly defined objectives also provide guidance to the firm's in-house benefit specialists in making decisions about various components of the plan. Sometimes, consultants, who also represent product offerings, suggest their products to meet various objectives.

---

[3] n.a., "Today's structure: yesterday's pay," *Risk Management*, Vol. 42, No. 5 (May 1995), p. 8.

[4] Foote, David, "The New Breed," *CIO*, Vol. 10, No. 3 (November 1996), pp. 38-42.

The objectives, however, should be independent of a consultant's product offerings. The following discussion represents some of the objectives that a firm may have in designing a benefit plan:

Fulfill Social Obligation to Employees. When an employee, or his or her survivor(s), suffers a financial hardship as a result of death, injury or sickness, the employer and fellow employees have a genuine desire to assist. If an employer provides coverage for these basic risks, the employer's obligation is discharged in a consistent manner, and fellow employees are relieved of the financial burden of "passing the hat," which was the prevalent method years ago.

Attract and Retain Good Employees. The employer must determine which benefits are best suited to the types of employees it desires to hire and retain. Industry norms are often more appropriate for skilled and professional positions, where employees change jobs often within the same industry. The norms in the local geographical area are typically used for semiskilled and unskilled jobs.

Economic conditions within an industry or geographical area may necessitate offering a benefit package that is better than the ones offered by competitors. An employer might also include benefits that are not yet prevalent among its competitors to give it a competitive edge in the labor market. Of course, factors other than benefits are important in attracting and retaining employees. The pay system, working conditions, work location, commuting distance, and opportunities for development and advancement are also important in competing for qualified personnel.

Increase Employee Morale and Productivity. To the extent that employee benefits reduce financial worry for the employee, their presence improves morale and efficiency. This effect may vary, depending upon the type of benefit. Group health coverage, for example, is more important as a worry eliminator than group life coverage. Retirement security will generally be more appreciated by older employees than by younger ones.[5] To achieve its desired objectives, an employer must consider the employees' perceived needs and wants.

There is less of a belief today, however, that the goal of increased employee morale and efficiency can be obtained from an employee benefit plan. Most benefits are more accurately viewed as maintenance-type benefits; that is, their presence does not have a strong positive impact on productivity, but their absence is likely to have a negative effect. Examples of maintenance-type benefits are disability, death, and medical expense coverage.

Benefits that are linked to the performance of the company, such as stock purchase and profit-sharing plans, will provide a stronger stimulus for increased productivity than the maintenance-type benefits. Other types of benefits may actually produce the opposite results. Liberal disability benefits, for example, can provide the employee with an incentive to stay home.

[5] The publicity surrounding the Social Security program's problems in the past and fears regarding its future have made younger persons more aware and concerned about their retirement security than their counterparts of previous generations.

Some benefits can assist in increasing morale and productivity by solving the problems that cause absenteeism and tardiness. Certain types of day care benefits are a good example; if they give the employees a dependable place for their children or elderly parents to stay while they work and/or provide quality care that gives them peace of mind.

Obtain Insurance at Low Rates. Employee benefits are often established because employers of owner-controlled firms view them as a way of acquiring insurance and qualified retirement plans at low group rates. The tax deductibility of premiums reduces the cost further.

For larger firms that are essentially manager-controlled, the decision making executives purchase the employee benefits with corporate dollars. Generally, the cost of group benefits are less than an individual would have to pay for separate coverage.

Take Advantage of Favorable Tax Treatment. Employers generally try to design their plans to maximize the tax benefits. Many employee benefits can qualify for favorable tax treatment because they are deductible business expenses for the employer. In some instances, the employer's cost is either not taxable or is tax-deferred income for the employee.[6] In addition, investment earnings on retirement and savings plans are not subject to taxation until benefits are distributed. Lump-sum distributions may qualify for favorable income tax treatment.

From a tax standpoint, employer-provided benefits are particularly attractive to employees when compared to salary increases. The after-tax value of benefits is greater than the same dollar amount in a salary increase, assuming that the employee desires to purchase the benefit individually.

If paid out in wages, the employee first pays taxes on the entire amount and buys the benefit with the remaining dollars. Receiving employee benefits in lieu of direct wages has several monetary advantages. First, the employer is purchasing the benefit with before-tax dollars. In addition, the group cost of benefits is often less than the cost for an individual purchase. Finally, for many benefits, employer-provided benefits as compensation are not taxable as wages would be.

Provided that total compensation is "reasonable and necessary," the employer can deduct employee compensation as a business expense, whether it is in the form of direct wages or employee benefits. In that case, what would be the tax advantage to the employer? The answer is that employee benefits that are paid in *lieu of* direct wages have the effect of reducing the employer's payroll-based taxes on these legally required benefits: Social Security, unemployment compensation, and worker's compensation.

Finally, it should be recognized that the employee tax advantage of benefits is greatest for higher-paid (thus, higher-taxed) executive personnel who are quite often the persons who are making the employee benefit decisions.

---

[6] There continue to be proposals to substantially restrict or eliminate the income exemptions of many employee benefits. Some legislators argue that income exemptions give a greater subsidy to higher-income employees because they receive more benefits and they are in a higher income tax bracket. There is considerable opposition to these proposals, however, from employers, labor unions, and the insurance industry.

Replace Income. The objective of income replacement is to substitute pay that is foregone due to an employee's retirement or disability. In determining the level of disability income or retirement income benefits, many employers establish a goal as to the percentage of pre-disability or pre-retirement income that the benefit should replace. Typically, this goal is less than 100 percent replacement, particularly for disability benefits, in order to discourage misuse of the benefit. For disability plans, replacement ranges are commonly from 50 to 70 percent. Short-term disability plans are more common than long-term versions. In addition, the replacement goal for short-term plans is higher. For example, a *salary continuation plan* or *sick leave plan* usually continues the employee's full salary for up to one year. Some governmental plans permit employees to accrue up to several years of sick leave benefits at full pay.

To minimize costs, employers will frequently coordinate income replacement plans, both disability and retirement plans, with Social Security benefits. This coordination is known as *integration*.

Simplify Administration. Another employer objective is administrative simplicity. Employers are especially concerned with administrative involvement as a result of increased government regulations and requirements associated with the Employee Retirement Income Security Act, the Health Insurance Portability and Accountability Act, the Mental Health Parity Act, and others. Administrative difficulties, for example, are frequently cited by employers as their major reason for not establishing a flexible benefit plan. However, administrative costs generally are not a significant proportion of total benefit costs. Good plan design that fulfills the employer's other objectives should not be sacrificed for the sole objective of administrative simplicity and low administrative cost.

Benefit Plan Design

In designing an employee benefit plan, there are tradeoffs. Some objectives may conflict with others. For example, an employer may have the objective of providing a benefit plan that is competitive with the plans offered by other firms in the area. Another objective the employer wants to achieve is a plan that is simple to administer. A conflict in these objectives may result if most of the other firms in the market area offer comprehensive flexible benefit plans that give employees a number of options in designing benefits plans that best fit their individual needs.

To design a competitive plan, an employer may need to consider establishing a flexible plan. However, the employer may conclude, from a preliminary study of flexible plans, that they are difficult to communicate to employees and even more difficult and expensive to administer. In this eventuality, the employer has two objectives that conflict. An alternative is to have a flexible plan that limits the number of options employees will have in designing their plans.

Legal Requirements

In designing employee benefit plans, there are several important laws to consider. Among the most important of these laws are Title VII of the Civil Rights Act, the Age Discrimination in Employment Act, the Americans with Disabilities Act, the Employee Retirement Income Security Act, the Health Insurance Portability and Accountability Act, the Mental Health Parity Act, and the Newborns' and Mothers' Health Protection Act.

Age Discrimination in Employment Act. The Age Discrimination in Employment Act (ADEA) prohibits discrimination against persons age 40 and over in the administration of retirement plans. The Act prohibits maximum retirement ages, except for bona fide executive personnel, fire fighters, law enforcement personnel, and employees in other types of jobs in which bona fide occupational age qualifications can be demonstrated. Many plans provide for a reduction in some benefits, such as life insurance, when employees reach a specified age, commonly 65 years old. If a firm employs 20 or more persons, any reduction of benefits for active employees 40 years of age and older is prohibited by the ADEA.

Further, under the "equal cost—equal benefits" provisions, either the benefits older workers receive or the expenditures made by employers to provide benefits must be equal to those provided younger workers.

Title VII. Title VII prohibits discrimination based upon race, color, religion, sex or national origin in any aspects of retirement plans or other benefits. It is illegal to require women to make higher contributions than men in order to receive the same annuity payment upon retirement. It is also illegal for an employer to offer a choice of gender-based annuities at retirement.

Employee Retirement Income Security Act (ERISA). ERISA establishes basic safeguards for covered employees, requires employers to disclose essential information, ensures that plans are for the benefit of employees and their dependents and prohibits discrimination in favor of highly compensated employees. Other provisions in the law that apply to benefit planning are:

- Age of participation for retirement plans;
- Any exclusions of classes of employees;
- Vesting schedules that will be used;
- Length of service requirement for participation;
- Reporting requirements;
- Plan termination requirements; and
- Coverage tests.

A full discussion of these provisions is found in Chapter 22.

Continuation of Health Benefits (COBRA). Benefit planning should include the initial notification and the eligibility requirements of COBRA. These provisions are covered in Chapter 19.

Health Insurance Portability and Accountability Act of 1996 (HIPAA). The benefit planning implications of this law involve:

- *Medical Savings Accounts* were established.
- Penalty-free withdrawals for medical expenses from Individual Retirement Accounts were allowed.

- Portability requirements were instituted that apply to medical care coverage (which does not include limited scope dental or vision, long-term care, nursing or home health care, care for a specific disease, or hospital indemnity or supplemental coverage offered independently of the medical care plan) for newly hired employees (and their families) in non-governmental group health plans with two or more participants on the first day of the plan year.

- Limitations on preexisting conditions were introduced. A medical care plan may not exclude coverage for a preexisting condition (where medical advice, diagnosis, care or treatment was received within a six-month period ending on the enrollment date in the new employer's medical care plan) for more than 12 months (18 months for late enrollees, those who do not enroll at the first opportunity).

- Individuals subject to the 12-month exclusionary clause for preexisting conditions may have this period reduced for each month of health care coverage (called "creditable coverage" in the Act) under a prior health care plan, provided that there is no more than a 63-day break in coverage from the former to the new plan.

- Employers must track coverage for certification.

This law is covered more extensively in Chapter 19.

Mental Health Parity Act of 1996. The Mental Health Parity Act, which was effective for group health plans beginning January 1, 1998, applies to employers with more than 50 employees, but employers are exempt if the effect of the law increases the employers' health plan costs by more than one percent. The law does not require employers to provide mental health coverage, but, where coverage is provided, the plan must either include services for mental illness coverage in the lifetime or annual limits that the plan will spend for medical or surgical benefits or have a separate limit for mental illness services that is not less than that provided for medical or surgical services.

Newborns' and Mothers' Health Protection Act of 1996. This law went into effect on January 1, 1998. Under the Act, group health plans are not permitted to restrict postpartum hospital stays to less than 48 hours for a normal delivery and 96 hours for a caesarean section. It applies to both self-insured and insured plans, but only applies to health care plans that provide hospital-stay maternity benefits for mother and child.

The Women's Health and Cancer Rights Act of 1998. This law was effective for health benefit plans for years beginning on or after October 21, 1998. The law applies to all plans that provide medical and surgical benefits with respect to a mastectomy. The Act requires that mastectomy benefits include breast reconstruction (if desired by the participant or beneficiary). Benefit coverage, in connection with the mastectomy, is extended for the following procedures:

- reconstruction of the breast on which the mastectomy has been performed;

- surgery and reconstruction of the other breast to produce a symmetrical appearance; and

- prostheses and coverage for physical complications of all stages of the mastectomy, including lymph edemas, in a manner reached through consultation with the attending physician and the patient.

Deductibles and coinsurance provisons may apply but must be consistent with other benefits provided by the plan. Plan administrators are required to notify participants of the benefit.

Minimize Adverse Selection

An important consideration in planning employee benefits, particularly group life and health insurance, is to minimize *adverse selection* (the tendency of those with a greater chance of a claim to seek insurance) and, thereby, minimize the cost of insurance. To accomplish this objective, these underwriting principles may be applied to both life and health group insurance:

- *The existence of the group is for other than insurance coverage.* This usually is not a problem for the employer-employee type of group, but it may be for association type of groups. If the purpose of forming the group is primarily for obtaining insurance, the potential for adverse selection is too great.

- *There is a steady flow of persons through the group.* This means that young employees will enter while older employees leave. If this does not occur, the group becomes progressively older, and the cost of insurance becomes prohibitively high.

- *The group has a large number of employees.* A large number in the group reduces the chances of a disproportionate number of impaired lives and spreads fixed costs over a larger base. Insurers will vary with regard to the minimum number of employees that are needed to make up a group. Rates will also vary according to the number of employees in the group.

- *There is a predetermined schedule of benefits.* Individual employees should not have the freedom to select the amount of life insurance they desire. If they did, those insureds with health problems would select the greatest amount of insurance. Instead, a schedule is established that determines the level of benefits for each employee.

- *There are specified enrollment periods.* Employees who do not sign up for insurance during a specified time after employment, or during specified enrollment periods, should be required to show proof of insurability if they are permitted to join at other times.

- *There are participation requirements.* Participation requirements encourage a large enough number of members and minimize adverse selection. If the plan is *noncontributory* (the employer pays the full cost), 100 percent of the employees are usually required to participate. If the plan is *contributory* (the employee pays part of the premium), generally 75 percent participation is required.

- *The employer shares in the cost.* It is highly desirable that the employer pay part of the premium. This helps ensure that the cost will be attractive to all employees, especially the younger ones. If the premium is not low enough, the young and healthy employees will not join, and the group will consist of members with a high probability of loss.

Plan Implementation

Implementing either a new plan or changes to an existing one requires a carefully planned communication effort. Many employees are misinformed about their employee benefit entitlements. In fact, most employees do not realize how expensive benefits are until, for example, they receive a COBRA notification, explaining how much they will have to pay for continuing health benefits coverage. Since benefits represent 30 cents for every dollar of employee compensation in an average firm, a comprehensive communication program should be planned for a year or more in advance, explaining various components of the benefits plan. Among the communication methods that are successfully used for this purpose are employee newsletters, paycheck inserts, benefits fairs, hotline telephone numbers, and interactive voice response systems.

Another important component of plan implementation is benefit delivery. Decisions must be made considering which providers will be selected to deliver the various benefits and how they will be selected.

Benefit Plan Monitoring and Evaluation

Plan monitoring and evaluation compare how well the implemented plan is meeting the employer's objectives using operational data and/or assessments.

- *Operational data* consists of quantitative information, such as the amount of production, the number of errors or rejects, the dollar value of scrap, and the number or dollar value of accidents. Other operational data includes turnover rates and selection ratios that show whether the plan is effective in recruiting and retaining employees.

- *Assessments* are the opinions of people, including employees and customers.

The actual design of the evaluation plan using these two variables would depend upon the type of benefit that is offered and the objectives that the plan was intended to accomplish. This concept is illustrated in Exhibit 18-1.

Exhibit 18-1
Illustration of Benefit Plan Objectives, Design, and Evaluation

Objectives	Type of Benefit	Plan Evaluation
Attract good applicants Increase morale	Medical expense	Operational data: Selection ratios*
		Assessments: Employee satisfaction with plan
Income replacement	Disability income	Operational data: Replacement rates of
		employees receiving disability income during the past year

* See Chapter 15 for a method of computing selection ratios.

Exit interviews of employees may include questions about the level of satisfaction with various components of the benefits plan. Employee opinion surveys may serve a dual purpose, both informing employees about their benefit plans and also measuring their experience and satisfaction with them. Chapter 6 gives some ideas about how employee surveys can be conducted and sample items for inclusion in a survey.

Pay Planning

The pay planning process is the same as the one used in benefit program planning; that is, defining the objectives, designing a pay plan that is consistent with the objectives, implementing the program, and monitoring and evaluating the plan.

Defining Objectives

Objectives for pay systems vary among individual firms as a result of differences in size, location, type of industry, and management philosophy. These are the objectives employers set for their pay systems:

- *Reward employees equitably.* Employees receive intrinsic and extrinsic rewards in return for their task performance. *Equity* is an employee's perception of the fairness of this exchange. These perceptions differ among people. For example, employees typically make self-assessments of how fair their job intrinsic and extrinsic rewards are in relation to their job performance.

  In addition, employees also compare their reward-job performance outcomes with those of other employees. For example, employees may believe their reward-job performance exchanges are equitable; however, this opinion may change when they compare their exchange with those of their peers. On the other hand, employees may feel their personal exchanges are inequitable, until they compare them with the exchanges of others. And, lastly, employees compare their reward-performance outcomes with those occurring in jobs outside their organization.

- Equity comparisons cause employees to react in a number of ways. Perceptions of reward fairness promote employee loyalty to the firm, job satisfaction, low absenteeism, and low turnover. Perceptions of reward inequities cause the opposite reactions. In addition, reward inequities may also cause employee frustration and aggressive behavior that may lead to criminal acts, such as stealing company property or destroying records. In view of the enormous importance of reward-performance equity, employers attempt to achieve it through *internal equity* and *external equity.*

- *Internal equity* is the goal of reward systems designed to ensure employees are equitably rewarded for their performance within the organization. Job evaluation methods, which are discussed in Chapter 26, are examples of reward systems designed to achieve internal equity.

- *External equity* is designed to ensure employees are equitably rewarded for their performance in relation to reward-performance exchanges existing in other organizations. One way employers attempt to achieve external equity is through market pay surveys, which are discussed in Chapter 25.

- *Pay equity.* Pay equity involves the equitable treatment of members of both sexes in pay administration. Pay equity includes both equal pay for equal worth and equal pay for work that is comparable within the firm. Pay equity is discussed in Chapter 26.

- *Attract and retain good employees.* Pay systems that are both internally and externally equitable are essential in recruiting and retaining good employees. The type of job is important in determining the extent of the market area in setting competitive pay levels. Larger geographical areas are used for managerial, skilled, and professional positions where employees change jobs frequently within the same industry. The norms in the local geographical area are typically used for semiskilled and unskilled jobs. Other factors that are important in attracting and retaining employees include working conditions, work location, commuting distance, and opportunities for development and advancement.

- *Increase employee morale and productivity.* Equitable pay systems are important in maintaining employee morale. Some pay systems, such as gain-sharing plans, are directly linked to productivity improvement.

- *Simplify administration.* Pay systems should not be so complicated that employees do not understand them. If more sophisticated systems are used, extra efforts should be made to explain them in readily understandable language. For example, the formulas used in some profit-sharing plans are so complicated that employees do not understand at what threshold of profits the sharing begins. Pay plans that are not understood are less effective in achieving the objectives for which they are intended.

Consider Legal Requirements

Among the laws to consider in planning a pay system are the Fair Labor Standards Act (including the Equal Pay Act), the Age Discrimination in Employment Act, Title VII of the Civil Rights Act, and the various laws and Executive Orders that apply to federal contractors.

Fair Labor Standards Act (FLSA). The FLSA provisions that apply to pay systems are the minimum wage rate, overtime pay, and equal pay for equal work regardless of sex (the Equal Pay Act). An important decision in designing pay systems is the classification of workers as *exempt* or *nonexempt* from the FLSA's overtime provisions.

Age Discrimination in Employment Act. This law prohibits discrimination against persons age 40 and over in pay decisionmaking.

Title VII of the Civil Rights Act. Title VII prohibits discrimination in pay matters on the basis of race, color, religion, sex, and national origin. Equal pay for members of both sexes for dissimilar work that has comparable worth to the employer is also covered under Title VII, but no comparable worth cases have resulted in the plaintiff prevailing.

Establishing the System

In establishing a pay system, employers will need to conduct pay surveys if external equity is an important objective. Similarly, if internal equity is a key objective, in-house studies need to be conducted on the perceived equity of pay within the firm. Job evaluation is one way of achieving internal equity, but other systems, including those involving pay for performance, can also be used.

Other objectives, such as increasing productivity, involve the consideration of pay for performance systems. Gainsharing, such as Improshare or Rucker plans, are examples of bottom-line, pay-for-performance plans that focus on productivity.

Implementing the System

The type of pay system, and the corresponding objectives that the pay system is intended to achieve, will largely determine how the system is to be implemented. Pay systems that motivate and reward productivity will require significant employee cooperation and commitment. Training sessions, focus groups, and feedback meetings will be needed to get everyone involved. Special implementation protocols should be followed prior to implementing productivity-sharing plans, such as Scanlon, Rucker, and Improshare. As an example, these are the steps involved in the installation of a Scanlon plan:

- *Step 1:* The plan should be limited to organizations, such as plants or firms that have less than 3,000 employees. The reason for the employee limitation of the plan is because the plan relies heavily upon employee participation through councils and committees. Also, communication and cooperation are essential, and these are difficult to achieve in larger units.

- *Step 2:* Research should be conducted on organizations that are using Scanlon plans.

- *Step 3:* A consultant should be selected who has installed Scanlon or similar types of gainsharing plans, and the consultant should recommend one or two firms with Scanlon plans that would be willing to indoctrinate a top management team from the company.

- *Step 4:* The company's top management team should visit the indoctrinating company. The indoctrination typically requires one day. The first half-day is devoted to a general orientation covering the mechanics and potential benefits. For the remainder of the day, the visitors are educated about their individual roles by their indoctrinating company counterparts. This indoctrination is very important because it answers questions and helps dispel opposition.

- *Step 5:* The visiting team returns home and prepares its Scanlon plan for presentation to the Board of Directors.

- *Step 6:* After the Board's approval, a committee should be selected, consisting of about 15 employees representing different functions and organizational levels of the firm, for example, from Sales Manager to production employee. This group is sent to the indoctrinating company for the same exposure as the top management group. Again, the employee committee will spend half of the day on orientation and the other half with their counterparts at the indoctrinating company.

- *Step 7:* The plan developed in step five is implemented. Promotional campaigns and extensive employee communication sessions are held, with various members of the 15-member employee team speaking about their experiences and their commitment to the plan. Production, cost, sales, and other performance data are posted to keep employees informed of the progress that is made. The committee identifies areas that need attention. Gradually, the plan begins to have an effect, as employee work teams cooperate to increase efficiency.

If a pay system is to be developed based on input from the external market, a market pay survey should be conducted. The steps involved in conducting such a survey are discussed in Chapter 25.

Evaluation and Monitoring

As with the process involved in the evaluation of employee benefit plans, evaluating pay plans also involves the use of operational data and/or assessments. As discussed above, operational data consists of quantitative information, such as turnover rates, selectivity ratios, the number of units produced, the number of errors or rejects, the dollar value of scrap, and the number or dollar value of accidents. Assessments are opinions of people, including employees and customers. The actual design of the evaluation plan, using these two variables, would depend upon the type of pay plan and the objectives that the plan was intended to meet. An example is illustrated in Exhibit 18-2.

Exhibit 18-2
Illustration of Pay Objectives, Plan Design, and Plan Evaluation

Pay Plan Objectives	Type Pay Plan	Plan Evaluation
Increase productivity Increase morale	Rucker	Operational data: Monthly sales value of production Assessments: Employee satisfaction with plan
Internal equity Decrease turnover	Factor job evaluation	Operational data: Turnover rates Assessment: Employee perceptions of equity

Compensation Planning/Human Resource Relationships

Compensation strategic planning is linked to virtually all other HR activities. The major linkages in these relationships are depicted in Exhibit 18-3.

Equal Employment Opportunity. *Equal employment opportunity* considerations should be an integral part of the fabric of all compensation systems but, unfortunately, they are too often omitted, and discrimination results. Sometimes, the discrimination is simply the result of misguided intent, such as designing retirement plans, so that women retirees, due to their longer average longevity, will receive less in monthly benefits than men who have the same length of service and income. Ostensibly, the intent of such a plan is to equalize the retirement outcomes, since women would receive more total retirement pay than men, if the retirement annuities were the same, by virtue of the fact that women live longer. Federal courts have determined, however, that such provisions are illegal.[7]

In other situations, the discrimination may be due to intentional mistreatment, such as paying women employees less than men for performing the same tasks in a job. Obviously, discriminating in pay matters and designing or administering benefit plans on the basis of national origin, race, color, religion, sex, age, and disability are patently unfair and illegal. Consequently, as shown in Exhibit 18-3, pay and benefit plans must be designed to conform to equal employment opportunity laws.

Human Resource Planning. *Human resource planning* is the process of determining human resource needs, comparing those needs to the human resources available, and establishing plans to fill the shortages or make the needed reductions. This process is preceded by an environmental scan that includes defining the political, social, and economic environment in which the organization exists. Human resource planning is also involved in decisionmaking that affects the structure of the organization, such as the types of jobs needed to most effectively perform available work and the resulting reporting relationships.

As shown in Exhibit 18-3, compensation strategic planning and human resource planning are interactive. The outputs from human resources planning, such as identifying human resource needs, are included in the compensation strategic planning process for defining the benefit and pay systems required—for example, finding a way to recruit and retain qualified personnel and to be competitive in the market. Strategic compensation outcomes are considered in future human resource planning efforts. Strategic compensation management also affects job structuring, pay systems, and employee benefit programs.

---

[7] See *Arizona Governing Committee for Tax Deferred Annuity and Deferred Compensation Plans v. Norris,* 32 EPD ¶ 33,696, 463 U.S. 1073 (SCt 1983).

Exhibit 18-3
Human Resource Management/Compensation Management Relationships

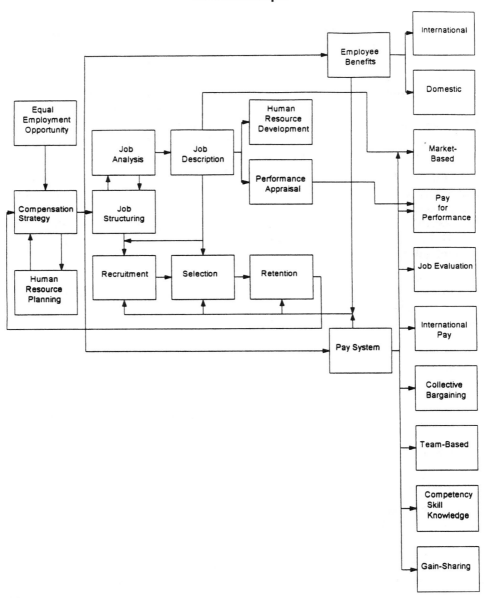

Job Structuring. *Job structuring* is the process of assigning tasks to jobs. The compensation of jobs is determined through compensation strategic planning. This compensation information and task data derived from job analysis is used in recruiting, selecting, and retaining employees.

Efforts to increase the intrinsic worth of work, improve the opportunity for rewarding effort and facilitate organizational efficiency have fundamentally increased the importance of job structuring. Expanding the number and complexity of tasks in jobs are two ways of increasing the intrinsic worth of work. Skill-based pay, pay for knowledge, and competency-based pay systems provide greater opportunities for employees to utilize their personal initiative, to increase their qualifications, and receive rewards for their accomplishments. Downsizing, job reengineering, and other means of restructuring work share the common goal of increasing organizational efficiency.

Job Analysis. *Job analysis* is the systematic process of obtaining, analyzing, and interpreting job information. Job analysis is a fundamental antecedent of compensation systems. Other HR activities also require inputs from job analysis; for example, job descriptions are derived from job analysis. Job worth is determined through job evaluation, using information on job descriptions or obtained through job analysis.

As shown in Exhibit 18-3, the process of job structuring is interactive with the process of job analysis. The information used to assign tasks to jobs is derived from job analysis. After the desired structure is formulated, job descriptions are prepared that contain this information:

- Job title;

- Job summary;

- Description of tasks; and

- Job specifications (knowledge, skills, abilities, training, education, experience, and special qualifications).

Job description information is used in informing job applicants about tasks and requirements, determining training needs, and in establishing performance appraisal criteria.

Human Resource Development. Information in the job description, such as job tasks and training needs, is used in training employees to provide satisfactory job performance.

Performance Appraisal. The performance appraisal process should include establishing performance criteria (preferably in writing), communicating the criteria to employees, and informing employees how their performance meets the criteria.

Performance criteria is obtained from the job description. As shown in Exhibit 18-3, pay-for-performance systems use the results from performance appraisals in pay decisionmaking. In addition, employee job safety and health practices and outcomes are frequently important determinants in pay decisions.

Recruitment. As noted above, recruiters use task information to inform applicants about job duties and to make preliminary selection assessments. Pay and benefits are primary considerations in attracting qualified applicants.

Selection. Selection methods are used to measure applicants' abilities and skills to satisfactorily perform the job tasks. Job offers are extended to the best qualified applicants. Job acceptances are predicated upon applicants' satisfaction with various considerations, including the organizational culture, working conditions, and job opportunities. In addition to those three factors, pay and benefits are among the major, if not the ultimate, considerations in most acceptance decisions.

External compensation equity, which asks whether pay and benefits are competitive in the external market, are important in recruiting and selecting new employees. Retaining employees necessitates pay and benefit programs that are both externally and internally equitable. Information and feedback about recruitment, selection, and retention outcomes, as a result of perceptions of internal and external equity, are included in future compensation strategic decisionmaking.

Compensation Planning Issues

No other activity of human resource management is undergoing the rate of dynamic change experienced in compensation management. Changes are necessitated by new laws, pressures of marketplace competition, benefit cost increases in both voluntary and compulsory programs, and changing perceptions of employee and employer workplace responsibilities.

Changing Patterns in Benefits and Services. William Walters worked for the same employer for 25 years and, suddenly, his job was abolished. He was 67 years old, with no income except Social Security, because the employer did not have a retirement plan.[8] For many workers of Mr. Walters' generation, the only source of retirement income is Social Security, so he certainly is not an exception. The American dream of retirement is financial independence and the good life of relaxation and perpetual vacationing. As so often is the case, the dream and the reality bear no resemblance to one another. Part of the problem is many employees do not have the opportunity to participate in benefits and services at work. As shown in Exhibit 18-4, in 2008 only 61 percent of employees in private sector firms had access to an employer-sponsored retirement plan. Health benefit plans were available to 71 percent of employees and 59 percent of employees had access to employer-sponsored life insurance. The percentages of employees with access to other benefits and services are also shown.

---

[8] Moss, Michael, "Golden Years? For One 73-year-old, Punching Time Clock Isn't a Labor of Love," *The Wall Street Journal* (March 31, 1997).

Exhibit 18-4
Percentage of Employees in Private Industry With Access to Selected Employee Benefits and Services,
2005 and 2008

Benefit	Percentage of employees with access		
	2005	2008	% change
Retirement plans	60	61	1.6
Health benefit plans	70	71	1.4
Life insurance	47	59	25.5
Paid holidays	77	77	n/c
Short-term disability	40	39	-2.5
Long-term disability	30	31	3.3
Paid vacations	77	78	1.3
Paid personal leave	36	37	2.7
Educational assistance, work-related	49	50	2
Wellness programs	23	25	8.6
Employee assistance programs	40	42	5.0

Source: U.S. Department of Labor, *Employee Benefits in Private Industry, 2005 and 2008,* Washington, D.C., U.S. Government Printing Office.

Having access to benefit programs is one thing—more important, is the extent to which employees take the opportunity to participate in them. As shown in Exhibit 18-5, in 2008, 61 percent of employees had access to retirement plans but only 51 percent were participating. Twenty percent of employees were participating in defined benefit plans (21 percent had access to them)[9] but only 43 percent of employees were participating in defined contribution plans (56 percent had access to them). One reason for the difference in the rate of participation for the two types of plans is that defined contribution plans, such as 401(k) plans, often require employees to make a monetary contribution as a condition of participation. For example, for employees in private sector firms in 2008, 66 and 3 percent, respectively, were required to make contributions to the defined contribution and defined benefit plans in which they were participating.

These data show that a significant percentage of employees in private firms are not electing the opportunity at work to assume a personal role in providing for their financial future in retirement. This is occurring while many Americans are questioning the long-term viability of the Social Security retirement program.

---

[9] U.S. Department of Labor, *National Compensation Survey: Employee Benefits in Private Industry in the United States,* March 2006, p.6. Note: The total is less than the sum of the two types of plans since some employees have access to both..

Exhibit 18-5
Percentage of Employees in Private Industry With Access and Participating in Selected Employee
Benefits and Services, 2008

Benefit	Percentage of employees		
	with access	participating	% difference
Retirement plans	61	51	6.1
Defined benefit	21	20	5
Defined contribution	56	43	23.2
Health benefit plans	71	53	25.3
Life insurance	59	56	5
Short-term disability	39	38	2.5
Long-term disability	32	30	6.2

Source: U.S. Department of Labor, *Employee Benefits in Private Industry, 2008,* Washington, D.C., U.S. Government
Printing Office.

Health benefits insurance is also problematic since 46.6 million Americans
do not have coverage. Many of these individuals have access to coverage at work
but have elected not to participate. As shown in Exhibit 18-5, 71 percent of
employees in private sector firms have access to health benefits coverage but
only 53 percent participate. Cost of coverage is one factor in employee decisions
about participating. The percentages of participating employees who must share
in the cost of their single and family coverage are 77 percent and 87 percent,
respectively. The average flat monthly contribution required of participating
employees is $87.69 for single coverage and $330.99 for family coverage.

Exhibit 18-4 shows the percent of employees who have access to other types
of employee benefits and services. Some benefits and services, such as paid
vacations, wellness programs and employee assistance programs are without
cost to employees so they would be expected to participate should they be so
inclined. Other benefits, such as life insurance and disability may require an
employee contribution. These benefits are shown in Exhibit 18-5.

Financial Accounting Standards Board (FASB)

FASB is the private sector organization governing the standards for financial
accounting and reporting in the preparation of financial reports. The standards
issued by the FASB are recognized as authoritative by the Securities and Exchange Commission and the American Institute of Certified Public Accountants.
These are some of the major standards that apply to employee benefits:

- *Standard No. 112.* This standard requires employers in financial statements to account for liabilities associated with post-employment benefits.
  If the amount cannot be reasonably estimated, the financial statement
  must so indicate.

- *Standard No. 106.* For other than retirement benefits (which are covered
  under *Standard Nos. 87* and *88*) employers are required in financial statements to account for liabilities associated with post-retirement benefits.

- *Standard No. 123.* This standard requires employers in financial statements to account for stock-based compensation plans for employees, such
  as stock purchase plans, stock options, restricted stock, and stock appreciation rights.

- *Standard No. 132.* This standard covered "disclosure requirements for pensions and other postretirement benefits" and required more information about changes in financial obligations of benefit plans and "fair values of plan assets."[10]

---

[10] Financial Accounting Standards Board, *Statement No. 132 Employers' Disclosures about Pensions and Other Postretirement Benefits, an amendment of FASB Statements No. 87, 88, and 106,* February 1998.

CHAPTER 19

HEALTH BENEFITS, INSURANCE, AND PERQUISITES

Chapter Highlights
- Types of group life insurance
- Types and providers of medical expense benefits
- Features of disability and sick leave benefits
- Legal requirements affecting benefits
- Provisions in benefit plans

Introduction

Employee benefits have evolved from earlier years, when employees viewed them as a gratuitous gesture on the part of their employers, to a form of compensation that they now have come to expect. In recent years, a new emphasis has been placed on this expectation of employee benefits, as we witness more and more support for proposals in Congress that mandate employers to provide minimum levels of health care coverage for their employees and dependents.

Group benefits provided through employment often represent a substantial part of an employee's insurance portfolio. For many individuals, group benefits are their only protection against the risks of death, illness, injury, and unemployment. The increasing cost of employee benefits has been an important concern for most employers. It has led to the active involvement of employers in the design and maintenance of their benefit plans and in formulation of strategies to contain costs.

Employee benefits are the current and deferred forms of compensation, other than monetary payments, that employees receive as a condition of their employment.

Trend in Employee Contributions

A *contributory plan* is one in which the employee is required to share in the cost of the benefit, such as in the premium for the medical expense benefits plan. In contrast, a *noncontributory plan* is a plan in which the premium is fully paid by the employer. The current trend in employee benefits is toward contributory plans, thus requiring employees to shoulder all or part of the costs of their benefit plans.

Group Life Insurance

Life insurance is provided in many employee benefit plans. For many employees, group life insurance is the only life insurance they possess. To meet this need, employers use several different types of plans.

One-Year, Renewable Term Insurance

The most common form of life insurance used in group plans is one-year, renewable term insurance. This coverage provides protection for one-year periods. In group plans, one premium is developed, based on the age distribution of the group. The annual premium increases each year as a function of the employees' ages. Term insurance does not build up cash values and remains in effect only as long as premiums are paid.

Paid-Up Insurance

Paid-up insurance is a permanent life insurance policy with cash value that is paid-up at a certain time, usually at the holder's normal retirement age. The insurance accumulates cash value, which sometimes is used to help fund retirement benefits.

Ordinary Life

Ordinary life, which is another type of permanent insurance coverage, is paid over the employee's working life, so that it is never completely paid-up. Ordinary life also accumulates cash value that can be used to help fund retirement benefits. Both paid-up insurance and ordinary life insurance were introduced as affordable means of providing death protection that can continue after the employee retires.

Universal Life

A more recent offering that also provides employees with a permanent form of coverage is group universal life insurance. This is a type of life insurance contract with an investment portion and a life insurance portion, in which the interest rate, mortality rate, and expense loading factors are permitted to vary to reflect current market conditions. As a result, it provides more flexibility than either paid-up or ordinary life policies. Group universal is generally offered as supplemental insurance paid for by the employees through payroll deductions.

Split Dollar Plans

Split dollar plans are life insurance plans, typically used with executives, in which the premium is shared by the employer and the employee. Upon the death of the employee, the death benefits are "split" (hence the name "split dollar plans") between the beneficiary and the employer.

Other Life Insurance Coverage

Other forms of group life insurance offered by employers are:

- *Survivor income benefit insurance,* which is offered by a small number of employers, provides a death benefit in the form of a monthly income. The income is payable only to qualified survivors. Typically, qualifying survivors are an unmarried spouse and unmarried children up to a specified age. Spousal benefits cease upon remarriage or the attainment of a certain age, usually 65. Some plans provide for one or two additional years of benefit upon remarriage, as an incentive to report the marriage.

- *Dependent life insurance* permits employees to purchase limited amounts of term life insurance on their spouses and dependent children. Generally, the full cost is borne by the employee. Maximum coverage is usually $1,000 to $5,000 on spouses, with a lower limit on each child. The employee is automatically the beneficiary on dependent coverage.

- *Supplemental life insurance,* which is offered in many group life plans, permits the employee to purchase additional coverage. The amount of additional coverage permitted is predetermined just as the basic life is. For example, the plan may allow the employee to purchase one-half, one, or one and one-half times the employee's salary up to a specified maximum amount.

- *Accidental death and dismemberment coverage* is frequently included in group life plans. The amount of coverage is a multiple of the basic group term. Loss of one limb or eye may result in a reduced lump-sum payment. The coverage may be for both occupational and nonoccupational injuries or death. Often, employers provide a higher pay out if the employee is traveling on company business.

Eligibility

Group underwriting focuses on the characteristics of the group. Ratings will vary by type of business and some businesses may not be acceptable risks. In contrast to personal insurance, in group plans individual employees generally do not have to show evidence of insurability.[1] To be eligible for coverage, an existing or new employee must be in the class of employees covered by the plan. In addition, the employee generally must be actively at work on the date the coverage is effective.

Amount of Insurance

The group insurance plan may specify the same amount of life insurance for all employees or it may provide different amounts of insurance for different classes of employees. To minimize the effect of adverse selection, it is important that the level of insurance is not solely determined by the individual employee. Benefit schedules may be based on the employee's earnings, position, length of service, or be a flat amount for all employees. Employers may also determine benefits by a combination of the above elements.

The most common type of benefit schedule is one in which the life insurance is based on earnings, particularly for white-collar workers. The amount of life insurance will increase automatically with raises in salary. Most employees have life insurance equal to one to two times their annual earnings.

---

[1] Plans for small employers may require simplified underwriting on individual employees. The plan is not a "true" group plan, but, rather, a multiple-employer trust (MET) or franchise insurance.

Beneficiary Designation

The employee may name and change the beneficiary as desired unless the beneficiary was named irrevocably (in which case the beneficiary must consent to a change) or an assignment of this ownership right was made. An insurance assignment is the transfer of all or part of the ownership rights of a policy from one party to another. A change of beneficiary is made by filing a written notice with the insurer. The insurer is not responsible if proceeds are paid out before a notice of change is received. In many states, group life statutes prohibit naming the employer as the beneficiary.

Assignment

In most states, the employee is permitted to transfer any and all rights of ownership under the group life insurance contract to another party. Assignments are usually made to remove the policy proceeds from the insured's estate for federal estate tax purposes.

Conversion Privilege

If an employee terminates employment, he or she generally has the right to convert, within 31 days, to individual life insurance without showing evidence of insurability. The employee is issued an individual contract and premiums are set at the insurance company's standard rates for the employee's attained age. The amount of insurance may not exceed the amount of group coverage that the employee had. If the employee dies within the 31-day conversion period, and before application for conversion has been made, the group death benefit is payable (even if the employee had not intended to convert). It is the employer's responsibility to notify the terminating employee of his or her right to convert.

Disability Benefits

Group life contracts generally contain a provision for continuation of life insurance if the employee becomes disabled. The most common method is the *waiver of premium* provision. Under this provision, the life insurance is continued in force without premium payments for as long as the employee is disabled, up to a specified age.

Settlement Options

Typically, group death benefits are paid out in a lump sum. However, the beneficiary (or employee before death) may select an alternative form of payment such as installments or a life annuity.

Continuation of Coverage

Most contracts now permit terminated employees to continue their group coverage for an extended period of time. The employee may be required to pay the complete cost of coverage. Continuation provisions are useful to fill gaps between changes in employment or for temporary interruptions of employment with the same employer.

Life Insurance for Workers Over Age 65

Many plans provide for a reduction in life benefits when employees reach a specified age—commonly 65 years old. If a firm employs 20 or more persons, any reduction of benefits for active employees 40 years of age and older is subject to the Age Discrimination in Employment Act (ADEA), as amended in 1978. Employers are permitted to reduce benefits if the reduction is not greater than the increased cost of providing benefits for the older worker.

Life Insurance During Retirement

Employees may have a need to continue life insurance at retirement if they have dependents or need life insurance for estate liquidity. The employee is entitled to convert the group term to an individual form of permanent life insurance. The cost of purchasing permanent life insurance at retirement age, however, may be prohibitive. In some situations, employers may voluntarily provide employees with life insurance during retirement using several different approaches, such as reducing the amount of the insurance. The permanent forms of life insurance mentioned previously, if purchased during the employee's working years, can also provide continuing coverage during retirement.

Taxation

An employer's contribution for an employee's group term life insurance is tax deductible as an "ordinary and necessary" business expense. Benefits paid out to beneficiaries, in the event of the employee's death, in most cases are exempt from federal income tax. Employees are not subject to federal income tax on amounts of group term life insurance up to $50,000. The employee includes the cost of life insurance in excess of $50,000 in his or her taxable income. The cost is based on a rate schedule provided by the Internal Revenue Service. Any employee contributions are subtracted from this cost. The employer includes the net reportable amount on the employee's W-2 form.

Medical Expense Benefits

Introduction

As with life insurance benefits, medical expense benefits are available to many employees. Due cost considerations, however, a significant percentage of employees elect not to participate.

Legal Requirements

Family and Medical Leave Act (FMLA)[2]

Employees may take job-protected, unpaid leave or substitute appropriate paid leave if the employee has earned or accrued it as follows:

(1) For up to a total of 12 workweeks in any 12 months for these reasons:

- The birth of a child.

---

[2] Most of the material on this law is verbatim from the *Final Rule on Family and Medical Leave Act* which is effective January 16, 2009.

(a) Both the mother and father are entitled to FMLA leave for the birth of their child.

(b) A husband and wife who are eligible for FMLA leave and are employed by the same covered employer may be limited to a combined total of 12 weeks of leave for the birth of a child or to care for the child after birth.[3]

(c) If one spouse is ineligible for FMLA leave, the other spouse would be entitled to a full 12 weeks leave.

(d) The mother is entitled to FMLA leave for incapacity due to pregnancy, for prenatal care, or for her own serious health condition following the birth of the child. Circumstances may require that FMLA leave begin before the actual date of birth of a child.

- For a qualifying exigency arising out of the fact that the employee's spouse, son, daughter, or parent is a covered military member on active duty (or has been notified of an impending call or order to active duty) in support of a contingency operation. See section below titled **Military Duty**.

- To care for a family member (child, spouse, or parent) with a serious health condition or incapacity.

(a) "Serious health condition" means an illness, injury, impairment or physical or mental condition that involves inpatient care or continuing treatment by a health care provider. "Incapacity" means inability to work, attend school or perform other regular daily activities due to the serious health condition.

(b) "Treatment" includes (but is not limited to) examinations to determine if a serious health condition exists and evaluations of the condition. Treatment does not include routine examinations.

(c) A regimen of continuing treatment includes, for example, a course of prescription medication (e.g., an antibiotic) or therapy requiring special equipment to resolve or alleviate the health condition (e.g., oxygen).[4]

(d) The medical certification provision that an employee is "needed to care for" a family member or covered servicemember (see 2. below) encompasses both physical and psychological care. It includes situations where, for example, because of a serious health condition, the family member is unable to care for his or her own basic medical, hygienic, or nutritional needs or safety, or is unable to transport himself or herself to a doctor.

- For the placement of a child with the employee for adoption or foster care.

---

[3] See Department of Labor, *Final Rule on Family and Medical Leave Act* for a fuller discussion.   [4] Ibid.

(a) A father, as well as a mother, can take family leave for the placement for adoption, or foster care of a child for a combined total of 12 weeks.

(b) An eligible employee may use intermittent or reduced schedule leave (for definitions see **Employee Notice Requirements for Foreseeable FMLA Leave** below) after the placement of a healthy child for adoption or foster care only if the employer agrees. Thus, for example, the employer and employee may agree to a part-time work schedule after the placement for bonding purposes.

(c) If the employer agrees to permit intermittent or reduced schedule leave for the placement for adoption or foster care, the employer may require the employee to transfer temporarily during the period to an alternative position for which the employee is qualified and which better accommodates recurring periods of leave than does the employee's regular position. When the employee no longer needs to continue on leave and is able to return to full-time work, the employee must be placed in the same or equivalent job as the job he or she left when the leave commenced.

(2) For up to a total of 26 workweeks in a single 12-month period to care for a covered servicemember with a serious injury or illness if the employee is the spouse, son, daughter, parent, or next of kin of the servicemember. "Covered servicemember" means a current member of the Armed Forces, including a member of the National Guard or Reserves, who is undergoing medical treatment, recuperation, or therapy, is otherwise in outpatient status, or on the temporary disability retired list, for a serious injury or illness incurred in the line of duty on active duty. "Serious injury or illness" means an injury or illness incurred by a covered servicemember in the line of duty on active duty that may render the servicemember medically unfit to perform the duties of the member's office, grade, rank, or rating.

Determining 12-month Period

Absent a State requirement, an employer is permitted to choose any one of the following methods for determining the "12-month period" in which the 12 weeks of leave entitlement occurs:

(1) The calendar year;

(2) Any fixed 12-month "leave year," such as a fiscal year, a year required by State law, or a year starting on an employee's "anniversary" date;

(3) The 12-month period measured forward from the date any employee's first FMLA leave begins; or,

(4) A "rolling" 12-month period measured backward from the date an employee uses any FMLA leave.

The alternative chosen must be applied consistently to all employees. If an employer fails to select an option then the one providing the most beneficial outcome for the employee will be used. An employer who changes to another alternative is required to give at least 60 days notice to all employees, and the transition must occur so employees retain the full benefit of 12 weeks of leave under the method giving the greatest benefit to the employee.

Covered Employers

An employer covered by FMLA is any person who employs 50 or more employees for each working day during each of 20 or more calendar workweeks in the current or preceding calendar year.

Any employee whose name appears on the employer's payroll will be considered employed each working day of the calendar week, and must be counted whether or not any compensation is received for the week. The FMLA applies only to employees who are employed in the United States, including the District of Columbia or any Territory or possession of the United States. Employees on paid or unpaid leave, including FMLA leave, leaves of absence, and disciplinary suspension are counted as long as the employer has a reasonable expectation that the employee will later return to active employment. Employees on temporary or permanent lay-off are not counted. Part-time employees are considered to be employed each working day of the calendar week, as long as they are maintained on the payroll.

Once a private employer meets the 50 employees/20 workweeks threshold, the employer remains covered until it reaches a future point where it no longer has employed 50 employees for 20 (nonconsecutive) workweeks in the current and preceding calendar year. For example, if an employer who met the 50 employees/20 workweeks test in the calendar year as of September 1, 2008, subsequently dropped below 50 employees before the end of 2008 and continued to employ fewer than 50 employees in all workweeks throughout calendar year 2009, the employer would continue to be covered throughout calendar year 2009 because it met the coverage criteria for 20 workweeks of the preceding (i.e., 2008) calendar year.[5]

The legal entity which employs the employee is the employer under FMLA. Thus, a corporation is a single employer rather than its separate establishments or divisions.

An "employer" includes any person who acts directly or indirectly in the interest of an employer to any of the employer's employees. Individuals such as corporate officers "acting in the interest of an employer" are individually liable for any violations of the FMLA.

All public agencies are covered by the FMLA regardless of the number of employees; they are not subject to the coverage threshold of 50 employees carried on the payroll each day for 20 or more weeks in a year. However, employees of public agencies must meet all of the requirements of eligibility, including the

---

[5] See Ibid. for information on Joint Employer coverage.

requirement that the employer (e.g., State) employ 50 employees at the worksite or within 75 miles.[6] Public as well as private elementary and secondary schools are also covered employers without regard to the number of employees employed.

A "Professional Employer Organization" (PEO) is an organization that contracts with client employers to perform administrative functions such as payroll, benefits, regulatory paperwork, and updating employment policies. The determination of whether a PEO is a joint employer is based upon the facts, such as the right to hire, fire, assign, or direct and control the client's employees, or benefits from the work that the employees perform.[7]

In joint-employment relationships, only the primary employer is responsible for giving required notices to its employees, providing FMLA leave, and maintenance of health benefits. For employees of temporary placement agencies, for example, the placement agency usually would be the primary employer. In cases in which a PEO is the joint employer of a client's employees, the client employer would only be required to count employees of the PEO (or employees of other clients of the PEO) if the client employer jointly employed those employees.

Job restoration is the primary responsibility of the primary employer, but a secondary employer is also responsible for compliance with the prohibited acts provisions with respect to its jointly employed employees, whether or not the secondary employer is covered by FMLA.

Determining Whether 50 Employees Are Employed Within 75 miles

Generally, a worksite is either a single location or a group of contiguous locations. Structures which form a campus or industrial park, or separate facilities in proximity with one another, may be considered a single site of employment. Separate buildings or areas which are not directly connected or in immediate proximity are a single worksite if they are in reasonable geographic proximity, are used for the same purpose, and share the staff and equipment. For example, if an employer manages a number of warehouses in an area, but regularly shifts the same employees among them, the multiple warehouses would be a single worksite.

For employees with no fixed worksite such as construction workers, transportation workers (like truck drivers, seamen, pilots), and salespersons, the "worksite" is the site to which they are assigned as their home base, from which their work is assigned, or to which they report. An employee's personal residence is not a worksite, such as salespersons, who travel a sales territory and who generally leave to work and return from work to their personal residence, or employees who work at home, as under the concept of flexiplace or telecommuting. Rather, their worksite is the office to which they report and from which assignments are made.

The 75-mile distance is measured by surface miles, using surface transportation over public streets, roads, highways and waterways, by the shortest route

---

[6] See Ibid. for additional information on public, including federal employer coverage.　　[7] Ibid.

from the facility where the employee needing leave is employed. Absent available surface transportation the distance is measured by using the most frequently utilized mode of transportation such as airline miles.

Employees of educational institutions who are employed permanently or who are under contract are "maintained on the payroll" during any portion of the year when school is not in session.

Eligible Employee

An "eligible employee" is an employee of a covered employer who:

(1) Has been employed for at least 12 months, and

(2) Has been employed for at least 1,250 hours of service during the 12-month period immediately preceding the commencement of the leave, and

(3) Is employed at a worksite where 50 or more employees are employed by the employer within 75 miles of that worksite.

The 12 months need not be consecutive months, except employment periods prior to a break in service of seven years or more need not be counted. However, if an employer chooses to recognize such prior employment, the employer must do so uniformly, with respect to all employees with similar breaks in service. Employment periods preceding a break in service of more than seven years must be counted where the employee's break in service is occasioned by:

- The fulfillment of his or her National Guard or Reserve military service obligation. The time in the military service must be counted in determining if the employee has been employed for at least 12 months by the employer. However, this section does not provide any greater entitlement to the employee than would be available under the Uniformed Services Employment and Reemployment Rights Act (See Chapter 7).

- A written agreement, including a collective bargaining agreement, exists concerning the employer's intention to rehire the employee after the break in service, like an employee furthering his or her education or for childrearing purposes.

If an employee is maintained on the payroll for any part of a week, including periods of paid or unpaid leave (sick, vacation) during which other benefits are provided by the employer, such as workers' compensation and group health plan benefits, the week counts as a week of employment. For purposes of determining whether intermittent/occasional/casual employment qualifies as "at least 12 months," 52 weeks is deemed to be equal to 12 months.

Whether an employee has worked the minimum 1,250 hours of service is determined according to the principles established under the Fair Labor Standards Act (FLSA) for determining compensable hours of work. See Chapter 21 for the provisions of the FLSA

An employee returning from a National Guard or Reserve military obligation shall be credited with the hours of service that would have been performed but for the period of military service. Accordingly, a person reemployed following military service has the hours that would have been worked for the employer added to any hours actually worked during the previous 12-month period to meet the 1,250 hour requirement. To determine the hours that would have been worked during the period of military service, the employee's pre-service work schedule can generally be used for calculations.

In the event an employer does not maintain an accurate record of hours worked by an employee, the employer has the burden of showing that the employee has not worked the requisite hours. An employer must be able to clearly demonstrate, for example, that full-time teachers of an elementary or secondary school system, or institution of higher education, or other educational establishment or institution (who often work outside the classroom or at their homes) did not work 1,250 hours during the previous 12 months in order to claim that the teachers are not eligible for FMLA leave. See Chapter 5 for record-keeping requirements.

The determination of whether an employee has worked for the employer for at least 1,250 hours in the past 12 months and has been employed for at least 12 months must be made as of the date the FMLA leave is to start. An employee may be on "non-FMLA leave" at the time he or she meets the eligibility requirements, and in that event, any portion of the leave taken for an FMLA-qualifying reason after the employee meets the eligibility requirement would be "FMLA leave."

Whether 50 employees are employed within 75 miles to ascertain an employee's eligibility for FMLA benefits is determined when the employee gives notice of the need for leave. Once an employee is determined eligible in response to that notice, the employee's eligibility is not affected by any subsequent change in the number of employees employed at or within 75 miles of the employee's worksite, for that specific notice. Similarly, an employer may not terminate employee leave that has already started if the employee-count drops below 50. For example, if an employer employs 60 employees in August, but expects that the number of employees will drop to 40 in December, the employer must grant FMLA benefits to an eligible employee who gives notice in August for leave to begin in December.

Employees cannot waive, nor may employers induce employees to waive, their prospective rights under FMLA. For example, employees (or their collective bargaining representatives) cannot "trade off" the right to take FMLA leave against some other benefit offered by the employer.

Designation of FMLA Leave.

Employer responsibilities. The employer's decision to designate leave as FMLA-qualifying must be based only on information received from the employee or the employee's spokesperson (e.g., if the employee is incapacitated, the employee's spouse, adult child, parent, or doctor may provide notice to the employer of the need to take FMLA leave). If the employer does not have sufficient information about the reason for an employee's use of leave, the employer should inquire further. Once the employer has acquired knowledge that the leave is being taken for a FMLA-qualifying reason, the employer must notify the employee. Form WH-381 (see copy of form in Appendix 4) can be used for this purpose.

The employer must notify the employee of the amount of leave that will be counted against the employee's FMLA leave entitlement, such as the number of hours, days, or weeks. Form WH-382 (see copy of form in Appendix 4) can be used for this purpose. If it is not possible to provide this information in advance, then the employer must provide notice of the amount of leave counted against the employee's entitlement upon request by the employee, but no more often than once in a 30-day period if leave was taken in that period. This notice may be oral or in writing. If such notice is oral, it shall be confirmed in writing, no later than the following payday (unless the payday is less than one week after the oral notice, in which case the notice must be no later than the subsequent payday). Such written notice may be in any form, including a notation on the employee's pay stub.

Employee responsibilities. An employee giving notice of the need for FMLA leave needs to state a qualifying reason and satisfy notice requirements.

An employee using accrued paid leave must explain the reason for the leave so the employer is aware and may appropriately count the paid leave against (substituted for) the employee's FMLA leave entitlement. Similarly, an employee using accrued paid vacation leave who seeks an extension of unpaid leave for a FMLA-qualifying reason will need to state the reason. If this is due to an event which occurred during the period of paid leave, the employer may count the leave used after the FMLA-qualifying reason against the employee's FMLA leave entitlement.

Disputes. Employer and an employee disputes as to whether leave qualifies as FMLA leave should be resolved through discussions between them. Such discussions and the decision must be documented.

Retroactive designation. If an employer does not designate leave as required, the employer may retroactively designate leave as FMLA leave with appropriate notice to the employee, provided that the employer's failure to timely designate leave does not cause harm or injury to the employee. In all cases where leave would qualify for FMLA protections, an employer and an employee can mutually agree that leave be retroactively designated as FMLA leave.

Remedies. If an employer's failure to timely designate leave causes the employee to suffer harm, it may constitute an interference with, restraint of, or denial of the exercise of an employee's FMLA rights. An employer may be liable for compensation and benefits lost by reason of the violation, for other actual monetary losses, and for appropriate equitable or other relief, including employment, reinstatement, promotion, or any other relief tailored to the harm suffered.

Substitution of Paid Leave. Generally, FMLA leave is unpaid leave. However, FMLA permits an eligible employee to choose to substitute accrued paid leave for FMLA leave. If an employee does not choose to substitute paid leave for FMLA leave, the employer may require it. The term "substitute" means that the paid leave provided by the employer, and accrued pursuant to established policies of the employer, will run concurrently with the unpaid FMLA leave.

Accordingly, the employee receives pay pursuant to the employer's applicable paid leave policy during the period of otherwise unpaid FMLA leave. An employee's ability to substitute accrued paid leave is determined by the terms of the employer's normal leave policy. When an employee chooses, or an employer requires, substitution of accrued paid leave, the employer must inform the employee that he/she must satisfy any procedural requirements of the paid leave policy. If an employee does not comply with the additional requirements in an employer's paid leave policy, the employee is not entitled to substitute accrued paid leave, but remains entitled to take unpaid FMLA leave. Employers may not discriminate against employees on FMLA leave in the administration of their paid leave policies.

If neither the employee nor the employer elects to substitute paid leave for unpaid FMLA leave under the above conditions, the employee will remain entitled to all the paid leave which is earned or accrued under the terms of the employer's plan.

If an employee uses paid leave under circumstances which do not qualify as FMLA leave, the leave will not count against the employee's FMLA leave entitlement. For example, paid sick leave used for a medical condition which is not a serious health condition or serious injury or illness does not count against the employee's FMLA leave entitlement.

Leave taken pursuant to a disability leave plan would be considered FMLA leave for a serious health condition and counted in the leave entitlement permitted under FMLA. In such cases, the employer may designate the leave as FMLA leave and count the leave against the employee's FMLA leave entitlement. Because leave pursuant to a disability benefit plan is paid, the provision for substitution of the employee's accrued paid leave is inapplicable, and neither the employee nor the employer may require the substitution of paid leave. However, employers and employees may agree, where state law permits, to have paid leave supplement the disability plan benefits, such as in the case where a plan only provides replacement income for two-thirds of an employee's salary.

FMLA provides that a serious health condition may result from injury to the employee "on or off" the job. If the employer designates the leave as FMLA leave the leave counts against the employee's FMLA leave entitlement. However, employers and employees may agree, where state law permits, to have paid leave supplement workers' compensation benefits, such as in the case where workers' compensation only provides replacement income for two-thirds of an employee's salary. If the health care provider treating the employee for the workers' compensation injury certifies the employee is able to return to a "light duty job" but is unable to return to the same or equivalent job, the employee may decline the employer's offer of a "light duty job." As a result the employee may lose workers' compensation payments, but is entitled to remain on unpaid FMLA leave until the employee's FMLA leave entitlement is exhausted. As of the date workers' compensation benefits cease, the substitution provision becomes applicable and either the employee may elect or the employer may require the use of accrued paid leave.

As is the case with leave taken for other qualifying reasons, employers may retroactively designate leave as leave to care for a covered servicemember.

The FLSA permits public employers under prescribed circumstances to substitute compensatory time off accrued at one and one-half hours for each overtime hour worked in lieu of paying cash. The FLSA limits the number of hours of compensatory time accumulations depending upon whether the employee works in fire protection or law enforcement (480 hours) or elsewhere for a public agency (240 hours). In addition, under the FLSA, an employer always has the right to cash out an employee's compensatory time or to require the employee to use the time. Therefore, if an employee requests and is permitted to use accrued compensatory time to receive pay for time taken off for an FMLA reason, or if the employer requires such use pursuant to the FLSA, the time taken may be counted against the employee's FMLA leave entitlement.

Military Duty

Eligible employees may take FMLA leave for a "qualified exigency" while a "covered military member" is on "active duty or called to active duty status" for a "contingency operation."

Covered Military Member. A "covered military member" means the employee's spouse, son, daughter, or parent on active duty or call to active duty status. A "son or daughter on active duty or call to active duty status" means the employee's biological, adopted, or foster child, stepchild, legal ward, or a child for whom the employee stood in loco parentis[8] and is of any age.

Contingency Operation. A "contingency operation" is a military operation that:

- Is designated by the Secretary of Defense as an operation in which members of the armed forces are or may become involved in military actions, operations, or hostilities against an enemy of the United States or against an opposing military force; or

- Results in the call or order to, or retention on, active duty of members of the uniformed services under the United States Code, or any other provision of law during a war or national emergency declared by the President or Congress.

The active duty orders of a covered military member will generally specify if the duty is in support of a contingency operation.

Active Duty or Call to Active Duty. "Active duty or call to active duty status" means a call or order to active duty (or notification of an impending call or order to active duty) in support of a contingency operation pursuant to the United States Code that authorizes ordering:

- To active duty retired members of the Regular Armed Forces and members of the retired Reserve who retired after completing at least 20 years of active service;

---

[8] Persons who are "in loco parentis" include those with day-to-day responsibilities to care for and fi-nancially support a child. A biological or legal relationship is not necessary.

- All reserve component members to active duty in the case of war or national emergency;

- Any unit or unassigned member of the Ready Reserve, Selected Reserve and certain members of the Individual Ready Reserve to active duty;

- The suspension of promotion, retirement or separation rules for certain Reserve components;

- The National Guard into federal service in certain circumstances;

- The National Guard and state military into federal service in the case of insurrections and national emergencies; and,

- Any other provision of law during a war or national emergency declared by the President or Congress so long as it is in support of a contingency operation.

Employees are eligible to take FMLA leave because of a qualifying exigency when the covered military member is on active duty or call to active duty status in support of a contingency operation as either a member of the reserve components (Army National Guard of the United States, Army Reserve, Navy Reserve, Marine Corps Reserve, Air National Guard of the United States, Air Force Reserve and Coast Guard Reserve), or a retired member of the Regular Armed Forces or Reserve.

An employee whose family member is on active duty or call to active duty status in support of a contingency operation as a member of the Regular Armed Forces is not eligible to take leave because of a qualifying exigency.

A call to active duty for purposes of leave taken because of a qualifying exigency refers to a Federal call to active duty. State calls to active duty are not covered unless under order of the President of the United States pursuant to one of the provisions of law identified above in support of a contingency operation.

Qualifying Exigencies. Following are the FLMA-qualifying military exigencies.

(1) Short-notice deployment.

    (i) To address any issue that arises from the fact that a covered military member is notified of an impending call or order to active duty in support of a contingency operation for seven or less calendar days prior to the date of deployment; and,

    (ii) Leave taken for this purpose can be used for a period of seven calendar days beginning on the date a covered military member is notified of an impending call or order to active duty in support of a contingency operation.

(2) Military events and related activities due to active duty or call to active duty status of a covered military member:

    (i) To attend any official ceremony, program, or event sponsored by the military; and,

    (ii) To attend family support or assistance programs and informational briefings by the military, military service organizations, or the American Red Cross.

(3) Childcare and school activities for a covered military member's biological, adopted, or foster child, a stepchild, or a legal ward, or a child for whom a covered military member stands in loco parentis, who is either under age 18, or age 18 or older and incapable of self-care because of a mental or physical disability at the time that FMLA leave is to commence, necessitated by the active duty or call to active duty status of a covered military member:

    (i) To arrange for alternative childcare;

    (ii) To provide childcare on an urgent, immediate need basis (but not on a routine, regular, or everyday basis);

    (iii) To enroll in or transfer to a new school or day care facility when enrollment or transfer is necessitated; and,

    (iv) To attend meetings with staff at a school or a daycare facility, such as meetings with school officials regarding disciplinary measures, parent-teacher conferences, or meetings with school counselors, when such meetings are necessary.

(4) Financial and legal arrangements.

    (i) To make or update financial or legal arrangements to address the covered military member's absence while on active duty or call to active duty status, such as preparing and executing financial and healthcare powers of attorney, transferring bank account signature authority, enrolling in the Defense Enrollment Eligibility Reporting System (DEERS), obtaining military identification cards, or preparing or updating a will or living trust; and,

    (ii) To act as the covered military member's representative before a federal, state, or local agency for purposes of obtaining, arranging, or appealing military service benefits while the covered military member is on active duty or call to active duty status, and for a period of 90 days following the termination of the covered military member's active duty status.

(5) Counseling. To attend counseling provided by someone other than a health care provider for oneself, for the covered military member, or for the biological, adopted, or foster child, a stepchild, or a legal ward of the covered military member, or a child for whom the covered military member stands in loco parentis, who is either under age 18 or age 18 or older and incapable of self-care because of a mental or physical disability at the time that FMLA leave is to commence, provided that the need for counseling arises from the active duty or call to active duty status of a covered military member.

(6) Rest and recuperation. Eligible employees may take up to five days of leave for each instance of rest and recuperation to spend time with a

covered military member who is on short-term, temporary, rest and recuperation leave during the period of deployment.

(7) Post-deployment activities.

(i) To attend arrival ceremonies, reintegration briefings and events, and any other official ceremony or program sponsored by the military for a period of 90 days following the termination of the covered military member's active duty status; and,

(ii) To address issues that arise from the death of a covered military member while on active duty status, such as meeting and recovering the body of the covered military member and making funeral arrangements.

(8) Additional activities. To address other events which arise out of the covered military member's active duty or call to active duty status provided that the employer and employee agree that such leave shall qualify as an exigency, and agree to both the timing and duration of such leave.

FMLA Notice Requirements – Employer Obligation

Employers must inform employees of FMLA notice requirements by the proper posting of the required notice WHD Publication 1420 (see copy of form in Appendix 4) at the employee's worksite and placing the requirements in either an employee handbook or other written material for employee distribution.

Advance Notice for Foreseeable and Unforeseeable FMLA Leave

Before taking leave an employer generally has a right to advance notice from the employee, but may waive the FMLA notice and/or the employer's own notice requirements. If an employer does not waive employee's obligations under its leave rules, the employer may take appropriate action for violations, if it does so consistently and does not discriminate against employees taking FMLA leave. The employer may require an employee to submit certification to substantiate that the leave is due to the serious health condition of the employee or the employee's covered family member, due to the serious injury or illness of a covered servicemember [Form WH-385 (see copy of form in Appendix 4) may be used for this purpose], or because of a qualifying exigency [Form WH-384 (see copy in Appendix 4) may be used for this purpose]. Failure to comply with these requirements may result in a delay in the start of FMLA leave. The requirements depend upon whether the need for leave is foreseeable or unforeseeable. When an employee seeks leave for the first time for a FMLA-qualifying reason, the employee need not expressly assert rights under the FMLA or even mention the FMLA. When an employee seeks leave due to a qualifying reason, for which the employer has previously provided the employee FMLA-protected leave, the employee must specifically reference either the qualifying reason for leave or the need for FMLA leave.

Employee Notice Requirements for Foreseeable FMLA Leave.

Foreseeable Leave--30 days. When the need for FMLA leave is clearly foreseeable at least 30 days in advance and an employee fails to give timely advance notice with no reasonable excuse, the employer may delay FMLA coverage until 30 days after the date the employee provides notice. Some qualified events are clearly not foreseeable, for example, knowledge that an employee would receive a telephone call about the availability of a child for adoption at some unknown point in the future would be sufficient to establish the leave was clearly unforeseeable 30 days in advance.

Foreseeable Leave--Less Than 30 days. When the need for FMLA leave is foreseeable fewer than 30 days in advance and an employee fails to give notice as soon as practicable, the extent to which an employer may delay FMLA coverage for leave depends on the facts of the case. For example, if an employee reasonably should have given the employer two weeks' notice but instead only provided one week notice, then the employer may delay FMLA-protected leave for one week.

Amount of Advance Notice. An employee must provide the employer at least 30 days advance notice before FMLA leave is to begin if the need for the leave is foreseeable based on an expected birth, placement for adoption or foster care, planned medical treatment for a serious health condition of the employee or of a family member, or the planned medical treatment for a serious injury or illness of a covered servicemember.

If 30 days notice is not practicable, such as because of a lack of knowledge of approximately when leave will be required to begin, a change in circumstances, or a medical emergency, notice must be given as soon as practicable. For example, an employee's health condition may require leave to commence earlier than anticipated before the birth of a child. Similarly, little opportunity for notice may be given before placement for adoption. For foreseeable leave due to a qualifying exigency, notice must be provided as soon as practicable, regardless of how far in advance such leave is foreseeable. Notice need only be given one time.

Content of Notice. An employee shall provide at least verbal notice sufficient to make the employer aware that the employee needs FMLA-qualifying leave, and the anticipated timing and duration of the leave. The employer should inquire further of the employee if necessary to have more information about whether FMLA leave is being sought and obtain details of the leave to be taken. Failure to respond to reasonable employer inquiries regarding the leave request may result in denial of FMLA leave if the employer is unable to determine if it is FMLA-qualifying.

Complying with Employer Policy. An employer may require an employee to comply with procedural requirements for requesting leave, absent unusual circumstances. For example, an employer may require that written notice set forth the reasons for the requested leave and the anticipated start and duration of the leave. An employee also may be required to contact a specific individual. Unusual circumstances would include situations including when an employee is unable to comply with the employer's policy such as there is no one to answer a call-in number. Where an employee does not comply with notice and procedural requirements without justification, FMLA-protected leave may be delayed or denied.

Scheduling Planned Medical Treatment. When planning medical treatment, the employee must consult with the employer to make a reasonable effort to schedule the treatment so it will not unduly disrupt operations. Requests for "intermittent leave" or leave on a "reduced leave schedule" must be medically necessary due to a serious health condition or a serious injury or illness. "Intermittent leave" is leave taken in separate blocks of time due to a single qualifying reason. A "reduced leave schedule" is a leave schedule that reduces an employee's usual number of working hours per workweek, or per workday, normally adjusting the employee from full-time to part-time. An employee shall advise the employer, upon request, of the reasons the intermittent/reduced leave schedule is necessary and of the schedule for treatment. The employee and employer shall attempt to work out a leave schedule that meets the employee's needs without unduly disrupting the employer's operations, subject to the approval of the health care provider.

Employee Notice Requirements for Unforeseeable FMLA Leave

Failure to Provide Notice. When the need for FMLA leave is unforeseeable and an employee fails to give notice the extent to which an employer may delay FMLA coverage for leave depends on the facts of the case. For example, if it would have been practicable for an employee to have given the employer notice of the need for leave very soon after the need arises, but instead the employee provided notice two days after the leave began, then the employer may delay FMLA coverage of the leave by two days.

Timing of Notice. When the approximate timing of leave is not foreseeable, an employee must provide notice to the employer as soon as practicable which usually is within the time prescribed by the employer's customary notice requirements. Notice may be given by the employee's spokesperson (e.g., spouse, adult family member, or other responsible party) if the employee is unable to do so personally. For example, if an employee's child has a severe asthma attack and the employee takes the child to an emergency room, the employee would not be required to leave his or her child to report the absence while emergency treatment is being administered. However, if the child's asthma attack required only the use of an inhaler at home, the employee would be expected to call the employer promptly after ensuring the child has used the inhaler.

Content of Notice. An employee shall provide sufficient information for an employer to reasonably determine whether the FMLA may apply to the leave request. Such information may include that a condition renders the employee unable to perform the functions of the job; that the employee is pregnant or has been hospitalized overnight; or a family member is a covered servicemember with a serious injury or illness. Calling in *sick* without providing more information is insufficient notice. The employer will be expected to obtain any additional required information through informal means. An employee has an obligation to respond to questions to determine whether an absence is potentially FMLA-qualifying. Failure to respond to reasonable employer inquiries may result in denial of the leave.

Complying with Employer Policy. When the need for leave is unforeseeable, an employee must comply with the employer's notice and procedural requirements for requesting leave, absent unusual circumstances. For example, an employer may require employees to call a designated number or a specific individual to request leave. However, if an employee requires emergency medical treatment, he or she would not be required to follow the call-in procedure until his or her condition is stabilized and can make the phone call. Similarly, in the case of an emergency requiring leave because of a FMLA-qualifying reason, written advance notice may not be required. If an employee does justify not complying with the employer's usual notice and procedural requirements, FMLA-protected leave may be delayed or denied.

Certification: General Rule

Generally, an employer may require certification by a health care provider that an employee's leave is necessary to either care for the employee's covered family member with a serious health condition, or due to the employee's own serious health condition. An employer may also require that an employee's leave because of a qualifying exigency or to care for a covered servicemember with a serious injury or illness be supported by a certification [Forms WH-384 and WH-385, respectively (see copies in Appendix 4), are available for these certifications]. Another document containing the same basic information may be used by the employer; however, no information may be required beyond that specified on the two forms. An employer must give written notice of a requirement for certification.

Timing. In most cases, the employer should request that an employee furnish certification at the time the employee gives notice of the need for leave or within five business days thereafter, or, in the case of unforeseen leave, within five business days after the leave commences. The employer may request certification at some later date if there is reason to question the appropriateness of the leave or its duration. The employee must provide the requested certification to the employer within 15 calendar days after the employer's request, if practicable, unless the employer provides a longer period.

Contents. If the certification provided by the employee is insufficient the employer shall state in writing what additional information is necessary. An insufficient certification includes information that is vague, ambiguous, or non-responsive. The employer must give the employee seven calendar days, if practicable, to cure any deficiency or the FMLA leave may be denied. This provision applies to an initial certification, a recertification, a second or third opinion, or a fitness for duty certificate.

Annual medical certification. Where the employee's need for leave due to the employee's own serious health condition, or the serious health condition of the employee's covered family member, lasts beyond a single leave year the employer may require the employee to provide a new medical certification in each subsequent leave year.

An employer may require medical certification from a health care provider that contains the following information:

(1) The name, address, telephone number, and fax number of the health care provider and type of medical practice/specialization;

(2) The approximate date when the serious health condition began, and its probable duration;

(3) A statement of medical facts to support the need for FMLA leave;

(4) Information sufficient to establish that the employee cannot perform the essential functions of her/his job, the nature of any other work restrictions, and the likely duration of such inability;

(5) If the patient is a covered family member, information sufficient to establish that care is needed and an estimate of the frequency and duration of the leave required;

(6) Information sufficient to establish the medical necessity for intermittent or reduced schedule leave, if requested by the employee and an estimate of the treatment dates and duration;

(7) If an employee requests leave on an intermittent or reduced schedule basis for the employee's serious health condition, including pregnancy, that may result in unforeseeable episodes of incapacity, information sufficient to establish the medical necessity for such leave and an estimate of the frequency and duration of the episodes of incapacity; and

(8) If an employee requests leave on an intermittent or reduced schedule basis to care for a covered family member with a serious health condition, a statement that such leave is medically necessary to care for the family member and an estimate of the duration of the required leave.

The DOL has two optional forms (Form WH-380E and Form WH-380F) for use in obtaining medical certification, including second and third opinions, from health care providers that meet FMLA's certification requirements. Form WH-380E (see Appendix 4 for a copy of the form) is for use for the employee's serious health condition and Form WH-380F (see Appendix 4) is for leave to care for family member's serious health condition. These forms or another form containing the same basic information may be used by the employer; however, no information may be required beyond that specified.

If an employee is on FMLA leave running concurrently with a workers' compensation absence, and the provisions of the workers' compensation statute permit the employer or the employer's representative to request additional information from the employee's workers' compensation health care provider, the FMLA does not prevent the employer from following the workers' compensation provisions and information received under those provisions may be considered in determining the employee's entitlement to FMLA-protected leave.

An employer may request additional information in accordance with a paid leave policy or disability plan if the employer informs the employee that the additional information only needs to be provided in connection with receipt of such payments or benefits. Any information received pursuant to such policy or plan may be considered in determining the employee's entitlement to FMLA-protected leave.

If an employee's serious health condition may also be a disability within the meaning of the Americans with Disabilities Act (ADA), as amended, the FMLA does not prevent the employer from following the procedures for requesting medical information under the ADA. Any information received pursuant to these procedures may be considered in determining the employee's entitlement to FMLA-protected leave.

While an employee may choose to comply with the certification requirement by providing the employer with an authorization, release, or waiver allowing the employer to communicate directly with the health care provider of the employee or his or her covered family member, the employee may not be required to provide such an authorization, release, or waiver.

Second and Third Opinions. If an employee submits a complete and sufficient certification signed by the health care provider, the employer may not request additional information from the health care provider. If deficiencies exist, the employer may contact the health care provider to cure any deficiencies. Such contact must be made by a health care provider, a human resources professional, a leave administrator, or a management official other than the employee's direct supervisor. "Authentication" means providing the health care provider with a copy of the certification and requesting verification that the information was provided and/or authorized by the health care provider who signed the document; no additional medical information may be requested. The requirements of the Health Insurance Portability and Accountability Act ("HIPAA") Privacy Rule, which governs the privacy of individually-identifiable health information created or held by HIPAA-covered entities, must be satisfied when individually-identifiable health information of an employee is shared with an employer by a HIPAA-covered health care provider. If an employee chooses not to provide the employer with authorization allowing the employer to clarify the certification with the health care provider, and does not otherwise clarify the certification, the employer may deny the taking of FMLA leave.

Second Opinion. An employer who has reason to doubt the validity of a medical certification may require the employee to obtain a second opinion at the employer's expense. Pending receipt of the second (or third) medical opinion, the employee is provisionally entitled to unpaid leave benefits, including maintenance of group health benefits. If the certifications do not ultimately establish the employee's entitlement to FMLA leave, the leave shall not be designated as FMLA leave and may be treated as paid or unpaid leave under the employer's established leave policies. The same consequences will apply if the employee or the employee's family member fails to authorize his or her health care provider to release all relevant medical information.

The employer is permitted to designate the health care provider to furnish the second opinion, but the selected health care provider may not be employed on a regular basis by the employer.

Third Opinion. If the opinions of the employee's and the employer's designated health care providers differ, the employer may require the employee to obtain certification from a third health care provider, again at the employer's expense. This third opinion shall be final and binding. The third health care provider must be designated or approved jointly by the employer and the employee. The employer and the employee must each act in good faith to attempt to reach agreement on the selection. If the employer does not attempt in good faith to reach agreement, the employer will be bound by the first certification. If the employee does not attempt in good faith to reach agreement, the employee will be bound by the second certification. For example, an employee who refuses to agree to see a doctor in the specialty in question may be failing to act in good faith. An employer that refuses to agree to any doctor on a list of specialists in the appropriate field provided by the employee and whom the employee has not previously consulted may be failing to act in good faith.

Copies of Opinions. The employer is required to provide the employee with a copy of any second and third medical opinions, upon request by the employee. Requested copies are to be provided within five business days unless extenuating circumstances prevent such action.

Travel Expenses. If the employer requires the employee to obtain either a second or third medical opinion the employer must reimburse an employee or family member for any reasonable "out of pocket" travel expenses incurred to obtain the opinions. The employer may not require the employee or family member to travel outside normal commuting distance for purposes of obtaining the second or third medical opinions except in very unusual circumstances.

Recertifications. Recertifications for leave taken because of an employee's own serious health condition or the serious health condition of a family member.

- 30-day rule. An employer may request recertification no more often than every 30 days.

- More than 30 days. If the medical certification indicates that the minimum duration of the condition is more than 30 days, an employer must wait until that minimum duration expires before requesting a recertification.

- Less than 30 days. An employer may request recertification in less than 30 days if:

    (1) The employee requests an extension of leave;

    (2) Circumstances described by the previous certification have changed significantly.

Timing. The employee must provide the requested recertification to the employer within 15 calendar days after the employer's request, where practicable.

Maintain Health Benefits

An employee on FMLA leave is entitled to have health benefits maintained while on leave as if the employee had continued working. An employee would continue paying his or her share of premiums during the leave period. The employer may recover its share only if the employee does not return to work for a reason other than the serious health condition of the employee or the employee's covered family member, the serious injury or illness of a covered servicemember, or another reason beyond the employee's control.

Employee Failure to Pay Health Plan Premium Payments. In the absence of an established employer policy providing a longer grace period, an employer's obligations to maintain health insurance coverage cease under FMLA if an employee's premium payment is more than 30 days late. In this case to drop coverage for an employee the employer must provide written notice to the employee that the payment has not been received. Such notice must be mailed to the employee at least 15 days before coverage is to cease, advising that coverage will be dropped on a specified date at least 15 days after the date of the letter unless the payment has been received by that date.

Return to Work

An employer may require an employee on FMLA leave to report periodically on the employee's status and intent to return to work. If an employee gives unequivocal notice of intent not to return to work, the employer's obligations under FMLA to maintain health benefits (subject to COBRA requirements covered later in this chapter) and to restore the employee cease. However, these obligations continue if an employee indicates he or she may be unable to return to work but expresses a continuing desire to do so. The taking of FMLA leave cannot result in the loss of any benefit that accrued prior to the start of the leave.

Certificate of Fitness to Return to Work. Under a uniformly applied policy, the employer may also require that an employee present a certification of fitness to return to work when the absence was caused by the employee's serious health condition. The employer may delay restoring the employee to employment without such certificate.

Employee Right to Reinstatement. On return from FMLA leave, an employee is entitled to be returned to the same position the employee held when leave commenced, or to an equivalent position with equivalent benefits, pay, and other terms and conditions of employment. An employee is entitled to such reinstatement even if the employee has been replaced or his or her position has been restructured to accommodate the employee's absence.

Equivalent Position. An equivalent position is one that is virtually identical to the employee's former position in terms of pay, benefits and working conditions, including privileges, perquisites and status. It must involve the same or substantially similar duties and responsibilities, and entail substantially equivalent skill, effort, responsibility, and authority. If an employee is no longer qualified for the position because of the employee's inability to attend a necessary course, renew a license, fly a minimum number of hours, etc., as a result of the leave, the employee shall be given a reasonable opportunity to meet requirements upon return to work.

Equivalent Pay. An employee is entitled to any unconditional pay increases which may have occurred during the FMLA leave period, such as cost of living increases. Pay increases conditioned upon seniority, length of service, or work performed must be granted in accordance with the employer's policy on equivalent leave status for other than FMLA leave. An employee is entitled to be restored to a position with the same or equivalent pay premiums, such as a shift differential and opportunity to earn overtime pay.

Equivalent pay includes any bonus or payment, whether discretionary or non-discretionary. However, if a bonus or other payment is based on the achievement of a specified goal such as hours worked, products sold or perfect attendance, and the employee has not met the goal due to FMLA leave, then the payment may be denied, unless otherwise paid to employees on an equivalent leave status for a reason that does not qualify as FMLA leave.

Equivalent Benefits. "Benefits" include all benefits available to employees including group life insurance, health insurance, disability insurance, sick leave, annual leave, educational benefits, and pensions. At the end of an employee's FMLA leave, benefits must be resumed in the same manner and levels as provided when the leave began, subject to any changes occurring during the period of FMLA leave affecting the entire workforce. Upon return from FMLA leave, an employee cannot be required to requalify for any benefits enjoyed before FMLA leave began. Accordingly, some employers may find it necessary to modify life insurance and other benefits programs in order to restore employees to equivalent benefits upon return from FMLA leave, make arrangements for continued payment of costs to maintain such benefits during unpaid FMLA leave, or pay these costs subject to recovery from the employee on return from leave.

An employee may, but is not entitled to, accrue any additional benefits or seniority during unpaid FMLA leave. Benefits accrued at the time leave began, however, (e.g., paid vacation, sick or personal leave to the extent not substituted for FMLA leave) must be available to an employee upon return from leave. If, while on unpaid FMLA leave, an employee desires to continue life insurance, disability insurance, or other types of benefits for which he or she typically pays, the employer is required to follow established policies or practices for continuing such benefits like other instances of leave without pay. If no established policy, the employee and the employer are encouraged to agree upon arrangements before FMLA leave begins.

With respect to pension and other retirement plans, any period of unpaid FMLA leave shall not counted toward a break in service for purposes of vesting and eligibility to participate. Also, if the plan requires an employee to be employed on a specific date in order to be credited with a year of service for vesting, contributions or participation purposes, an employee on unpaid FMLA leave on that date shall be deemed to have been employed on that date. However, unpaid FMLA leave periods need not be treated as credited service for purposes of benefit accrual, vesting and eligibility to participate.

Employees on unpaid FMLA leave are to be treated as if they continued to work for purposes of changes to benefit plans is if no leave had been taken except those which may be dependent upon seniority or accrual during the leave period.

An employee who returns to work for at least 30 calendar days is considered to have "returned" to work. An employee who transfers directly from taking FMLA leave to retirement, or who retires during the first 30 days after the employee returns to work, is deemed to have returned to work. When an employee elects or an employer requires paid leave to be substituted for FMLA leave, the employer may not recover its (share of) health insurance or other non-health benefit premiums for any period of FMLA leave covered by paid leave.

Key Employee

A "key employee" is an FMLA-eligible employee who is among the highest paid 10 percent of employees within 75 miles of the employee's worksite. In determining which employees are among the highest paid 10 percent, year-to-date earnings are divided by weeks worked (including weeks in which paid leave was taken). Earnings include wages, premium pay, incentive pay, and non-discretionary and discretionary bonuses. Earnings do not include incentives whose value is determined at some future date, such as stock options, or benefits or perquisites. The determination of whether a salaried employee is among the highest paid 10 percent shall be made at the time the employee gives notice of the need for leave.

Leave Denial. Key employees may be denied FMLA leave if the restoration of the employee to employment will cause "substantial and grievous economic injury" to the operations of the employer, not whether the absence of the employee will cause such injury. In determining such injury an employer may take into account its ability to replace on a temporary basis or temporarily do without his/her services. If permanent replacement is unavoidable, the cost of reinstating the employee can be considered in evaluating whether substantial and grievous economic injury will occur from restoration; in other words, the effect on the operations of the company of reinstating the employee in an equivalent position.

A precise test cannot be set for the level of hardship or injury to the employer which must be sustained. If the reinstatement of a "key employee" threatens the economic viability of the firm, that would constitute "substantial and grievous economic injury." A lesser injury which causes substantial, long-term economic injury would also be sufficient. Minor inconveniences and costs that the employer would experience in the normal course of doing business would not constitute" substantial and grievous economic injury." FMLA's "substantial and grievous economic injury" standard is different from and more stringent than the "undue hardship" test under the ADA.

Rights of a Key Employee. An employer who believes that reinstatement may be denied to a key employee, must give written notice to the employee at the time the employee gives notice of the need for FMLA leave (or when FMLA leave commences, if earlier) that he or she qualifies as a key employee. At the same time, the employer must also fully inform the employee of the potential consequences with respect to reinstatement and maintenance of health benefits if the employer should determine that substantial and grievous economic injury to the employer's operations will result if the employee is reinstated from FMLA leave. If such notice cannot be given immediately because of the need to determine whether the employee is a key employee, it shall be given as soon as practicable after being notified of a need for leave (or the commencement of leave, if earlier). In most circumstances there will be no desire that an employee be denied restoration after FMLA leave and, therefore, thus no need to provide such notice. However, an employer who fails to provide timely notice will lose its right to deny restoration even if substantial and grievous economic injury will result from reinstatement.

When an employer makes a good faith determination that substantial and grievous economic injury to its operations will result if a key employee is reinstated, the employer shall notify the employee in writing of its determination, that it cannot deny FMLA leave, but that it intends to deny restoration to employment on completion of the leave. It is anticipated that an employer will ordinarily be able to give such notice prior to the employee starting leave. Notification will either be in person or by certified mail and must explain the basis for the finding that substantial and grievous economic injury will result. If leave has commenced the employee must have a reasonable time to return to work, taking into account the circumstances, such as the length of the leave and the urgency of the need for the employee to return.

If an employee on leave does not return to work in response to the employer's notification of intent to deny restoration, the employee continues to be entitled to maintenance of health benefits and the employer may not recover its cost of health benefit premiums. A key employee's rights under FMLA continue (including the right to health benefits) until the employee either gives notice that he or she no longer wishes to return to work, or the employer actually denies reinstatement at the conclusion of the leave period.

After notice to an employee has been given that substantial and grievous economic injury will result if the employee is reinstated to employment, an employee is still entitled to request reinstatement at the end of the leave period even if the employee did not return to work in response to the employer's notice. The employer must then again determine whether there will be substantial and grievous economic injury from reinstatement, based on the facts at that time. If it is determined that substantial and grievous economic injury will result, the employer shall notify the employee in writing (in person or by certified mail) of the denial of restoration.

Special Rules for School Employees

Special rules apply to employees of "local educational agencies," including public school boards and elementary and secondary schools under their jurisdiction, and private elementary and secondary schools. The rules do not apply to other kinds of educational institutions, such as colleges and universities, trade schools, and preschools.

The usual requirements for employees to be "eligible" apply, including employment at a worksite where at least 50 employees are employed within 75 miles. For example, employees of a rural school would not be eligible for FMLA leave if the school has fewer than 50 employees and there are no other schools under the jurisdiction of the same employer (usually, a school board) within 75 miles.

Groups of School Employees. These are the two groups of school employees:

(1) *Instructional employees* who are those whose principal function is to teach and instruct students in a class, a small group, or an individual setting; this includes teachers, athletic coaches, driving instructors, and special education assistants such as signers for the hearing impaired. It does not include teacher assistants or aides who do not have as their principal job actual teaching or instructing.

(2) *Non-instructional employees* who are auxiliary personnel such as counselors, psychologists, curriculum specialists, cafeteria workers, maintenance workers, and bus drivers.

These are the FMLA areas with special rules for school employees:

(1) Intermittent or leave on a reduced schedule;

(2) Limitations on leave taken near the end of an academic term;

(3) The duration of the FMLA leave; and,

(4) Restoration to an equivalent position.

Intermittent or Leave on a Reduced Schedule. If an instructional employee needs intermittent or leave on a reduced schedule to care for a family member with a serious health condition, to care for a covered servicemember, or for the employee's own serious health condition, which is foreseeable based on planned medical treatment, and the employee would be on leave for more than 20 percent of the total number of working days over the period the leave would extend, the employer may require the employee to choose either to:

(i) Take leave for a period or periods of a particular duration, not greater than the duration of the planned treatment; or

(ii) Transfer temporarily to an available alternative position for which the employee is qualified, which has equivalent pay and benefits and which better accommodates recurring periods of leave than does the employee's regular position.

These rules apply only to a leave involving more than 20 percent of the working days during the period over which the leave extends. For example, if an instructional employee who normally works five days each week needs to take two days (or 40 percent) of FMLA leave per week over a period of several weeks, the special rules would apply. Employees taking leave which constitutes 20 percent or less (one day or less) of the working days during the leave period would not be subject to transfer to an alternative position.

"Periods of a particular duration" means a block, or blocks, of time beginning no earlier than the first day for which leave is needed and ending no later than the last day on which leave is needed, and may include one uninterrupted period of leave.

In addition, if an instructional employee does not give required notice of foreseeable FMLA leave to be taken intermittently or on a reduced leave schedule, the employer may require the employee to take leave of a particular duration, or to transfer temporarily to an alternative position. Alternatively, the employer may require the employee to delay the taking of leave until the notice provision is met.

Intermittent leave taken by instructional and non-instruction employees for a period that ends with the school year and begins the next semester is leave taken consecutively rather than intermittently. The period during the summer vacation when the employee would not have been required to report for duty is not counted against the employee's FMLA leave entitlement.

Limitations on Leave Near the End of an Academic Term. Regular FMLA rules apply to instructional employees except in these circumstances:

(1) The employee begins leave more than five weeks before the end of a term. The employer may require the employee to continue taking leave until the end of the term if--

 (i) The leave will last at least three weeks, and

 (ii) The employee would return to work during the three-week period before the end of the term.

(2) The employee begins leave during the five-week period before the end of a term because of the birth of a son or daughter; the placement of a son or daughter for adoption or foster care; to care for a spouse, son, daughter, or parent with a serious health condition; or to care for a covered servicemember. The employer may require the employee to continue taking leave until the end of the term if--

 (i) The leave will last more than two weeks, and

 (ii) The employee would return to work during the two-week period before the end of the term.

(3) The employee begins leave during the three-week period before the end of a term because of the birth of a son or daughter; the placement of a son or daughter for adoption or foster care; to care for a spouse, son, daughter, or parent with a serious health condition; or to care for a covered servicemember. The employer may require the employee to continue taking leave until the end of the term if the leave will last more than five working days.

"Academic term" means the school semester, which typically ends near the end of the calendar year and the end of spring each school year. In no case may a school have more than two academic terms or semesters each year for purposes of FMLA. An example of leave falling within these provisions would be where an employee plans two weeks of leave to care for a family member which will begin three weeks before the end of the term. In that situation, the employer could require the employee to stay out on leave until the end of the term.

Duration of FMLA Leave. If an instructional or non-instructional employee chooses to take leave for periods of a particular "duration" in the case of intermittent or reduced schedule leave, the entire period of leave taken will count as FMLA leave. In the case of an employee who is required to take leave until the end of an academic term, only the period of leave until the employee is ready and able to return to work shall be charged against the employee's FMLA leave entitlement. The employer has the option not to require the employee to stay on leave until the end of the school term. Therefore, any additional leave required by the employer to the end of the school term is not counted as FMLA leave; however, the employer shall be required to maintain the employee's group health insurance and restore the employee to the same or equivalent job including other benefits at the conclusion of the leave.

An instructional employee who is on FMLA leave at the end of the school year must be provided with any benefits over the summer vacation that employees would normally receive if they had been working at the end of the school year.

Restoration to "An Equivalent Position." The determination of how an instructional and non-instructional employee is to be restored to "an equivalent position" upon return from FMLA leave will be made on the basis of "established school board policies and practices, private school policies and practices, and collective bargaining agreements." The "established policies" and collective bargaining agreements used as a basis for restoration must be in writing, must be made known to the employee prior to the taking of FMLA leave, and must clearly explain the employee's restoration rights upon return from leave. Any established policy which is used as the basis for restoration of an employee to "an equivalent position" must provide substantially the same protections as provided in the Act for reinstated employees. In other words, the policy or collective bargaining agreement must provide for restoration to an "equivalent position" with equivalent employment benefits, pay, and other terms and conditions of employment. For example, an employee may not be restored to a position requiring additional licensure or certification.

Enforcement

An employee has the choice of filing a complaint with the Secretary of Labor, or filing a private lawsuit within two years after the last violation or three years if the violation was willful. If an employer has violated one or more provisions an employee may receive one or more of the following: Wages, employment benefits, or other compensation denied or lost due to the violation; or, where no tangible loss has occurred, such as when FMLA leave was unlawfully denied, any actual monetary loss sustained by the employee as a direct result of the violation, such as the cost of providing care, up to a sum equal to 26 weeks of wages for the employee in a case involving leave to care for a covered servicemember or 12 weeks of wages for the employee in a case involving leave for any other FMLA qualifying reason. In addition, the employee may be entitled to interest on such sum, calculated at the prevailing rate. An amount equaling the preceding sums may also be awarded as liquidated damages unless such amount is reduced by the court because the violation was in good faith and the employer had reasonable grounds for believing the employer had not violated the Act.

When appropriate, the employee may also obtain appropriate equitable relief, such as employment, reinstatement and promotion. When the employer is found in violation, the employee may recover a reasonable attorney's fee, reasonable expert witness fees, and other costs of the action from the employer in addition to any judgment awarded by the court.

Definitions

- Spouse means a husband or wife as defined or recognized under State law for purposes of marriage in the State where the employee resides, including common law marriage in States where it is recognized.

- Parent means a biological, adoptive, step or foster father or mother, or any other individual who stood in loco parentis to the employee when the employee was a son or daughter as defined in this section. Does not include parents "in law."

- Son or daughter means a biological, adopted, or foster child, a stepchild, a legal ward, or a child of a person standing in loco parentis, who is either under age 18, or age 18 or older and "incapable of self-care because of a mental or physical disability" at the time that FMLA leave is to commence.

- "Next of kin of a covered servicemember" means the nearest blood relative other than the covered servicemember's spouse, parent, son, or daughter, in the following order of priority: blood relatives who have been granted legal custody of the covered servicemember by court decree or statutory provisions, brothers and sisters, grandparents, aunts and uncles, and first cousins, unless the covered servicemember has specifically designated in writing another blood relative as his or her nearest blood relative for purposes of military caregiver leave under the FMLA.

- "Adoption" means legally and permanently assuming the responsibility of raising a child as one's own.

- Foster care is 24-hour care for children in substitution for, and away from, their parents or guardian. Such placement is made by or with the agreement of the State.

- "Son or daughter on active duty or call to active duty status" means the employee's biological, adopted, or foster child, stepchild, legal ward, or a child for whom the employee stood in loco parentis, who is on active duty or call to active duty status, and who is of any age.

- "Son or daughter of a covered servicemember" means biological, adopted, or foster child, stepchild, legal ward, or a child for whom the servicemember stood in loco parentis, and who is of any age.

- "Parent of a covered servicemember" means biological, adoptive, step or foster father or mother, or any other individual who stood in loco parentis to the covered servicemember. Does not include parents "in law."

- "Health care provider" is:

   (i) A doctor of medicine or osteopathy who is authorized to practice medicine or surgery (as appropriate) by the State in which the doctor practices; or

  (ii) Any other person determined by the Department of Labor to be capable of providing health care services.

- Others "capable of providing health care services" include only:

   (i) Podiatrists, dentists, clinical psychologists, optometrists, and chiropractors (limited to treatment consisting of manual manipulation of the spine to correct a subluxation as demonstrated by X-ray to exist) authorized to practice in the State and performing within the scope of their practice as defined under State law;

  (ii) Nurse practitioners, nurse-midwives, clinical social workers and physician assistants who are authorized to practice under State law and who are performing within the scope of their practice as defined under State law;

 (iii) Christian Science Practitioners listed with the First Church of Christ, Scientist in Boston, Massachusetts. Where an employee or family member is receiving treatment from a Christian Science practitioner, an employee may not object to any requirement from an employer that the employee or family member submit to examination (though not treatment) to obtain a second or third certification from a health care provider other than a Christian Science practitioner except as otherwise provided under applicable State or local law or collective bargaining agreement.

  (iv) Any health care provider from whom an employer or the employer's group health plan's benefits manager will accept certification of the existence of a serious health condition to substantiate a claim for benefits; and

   (v) A health care provider listed above who practices in a country other than the United States, who is authorized to practice in accordance with the law of that country, and who is performing within the scope of his or her practice as defined under such law.

- "Authorized to practice in the State" as used in this section means that the provider must be authorized to diagnose and treat physical or mental health conditions.

- Continuing treatment by a health care provider means any one of the following:

   (1) Incapacity and treatment is a period of more than three consecutive, full calendar days, and any subsequent treatment or period of incapacity relating to the same condition that also involves:

      (i) Treatment two or more times, within 30 days of the first day of incapacity, unless extenuating circumstances exist, by a health care provider, by a nurse under direct supervision of a health care provider, or by a provider of health care services (e.g., physical therapist) under orders of, or on referral by, a health care provider; or

(ii) Treatment by a health care provider on at least one occasion, which results in a regimen of continuing treatment under the supervision of the health care provider.

(iii) The requirement in paragraphs (1)(i) and (ii) of this definition for treatment by a health care provider means an in-person visit to a health care provider. The first in-person treatment visit must take place within seven days of the first day of incapacity.

(iv) Whether additional treatment visits or a regimen of continuing treatment is necessary within the 30-day period shall be determined by the health care provider.

(v) The term "extenuating circumstances" means circumstances beyond the employee's control that prevent the follow-up visit from occurring as planned by the health care provider. Whether a given set of circumstances are extenuating depends on the facts.

(2) Pregnancy or prenatal care is incapacity due to pregnancy, or for prenatal care.

(3) "Chronic condition" is any period of incapacity or treatment for such incapacity due to a chronic serious health condition. A "chronic serious health condition" is one which:

(i) Requires periodic visits (defined as at least twice a year) for treatment by a health care provider, or by a nurse under direct supervision of a health care provider;

(ii) Continues over an extended period of time (including recurring episodes of a single underlying condition); and,

(iii) May cause episodic rather than a continuing period of incapacity (e.g., asthma, diabetes, epilepsy, etc.).

(4) "Permanent or long-term conditions" is a period of incapacity due to a condition for which treatment may not be effective. The employee or family member must be under the continuing supervision of, but need not be receiving active treatment by, a health care provider. Examples include Alzheimer's, a severe stroke, or the terminal stages of a disease.

(5) "Conditions requiring multiple treatments" is a period of absence for a condition (including any period of recovery) by a health care provider or by a provider of health care services under orders of, or on referral by, a health care provider, for:

(i) Restorative surgery after an accident or other injury; or

(ii) A condition that would likely result in a period of incapacity of more than three consecutive full calendar days in the absence of medical intervention or treatment, such as cancer (chemotherapy, radiation, etc.), severe arthritis (physical therapy), kidney disease (dialysis).

(6) Absences attributable to incapacity under paragraphs (2) or (3) of this definition qualify for FMLA leave even though the employee or the covered family member does not receive treatment from a health care provider during the absence, and even if the absence does not last more than three consecutive full calendar days. For example, an employee with asthma may be unable to report for work due to the onset of an asthma attack or because the employee's health care provider has advised the employee to stay home when the pollen count exceeds a certain level. An employee who is pregnant may be unable to report to work because of severe morning sickness.

Record-Keeping

See Chapter 5 for the recording-keeping requirements of the FMLA.

Health Insurance Portability and Accountability Act of 1996 (HIPAA)

HIPAA was enacted to:

- Prevent discrimination against persons in obtaining group health care coverage;
- Establish portability provisions to facilitate employees changing jobs without the fear of losing health insurance for themselves and their families;
- Restrict exclusions for preexisting conditions when obtaining group health insurance coverage;
- Allow newly hired employees the opportunity to apply credits accumulated from prior health insurance coverage to reduce the period of exclusions for preexisting conditions required for coverage under a new plan;
- Modify existing COBRA requirements for disability and dependent coverage; and
- Prevent persons from illegally obtaining, using, and/or disclosing health information about an individual.

Medical Savings Accounts. HIPAA authorizes the establishment of medical savings accounts. These accounts, now called Archer Medical Savings Accounts, and other types of tax-favored health plans are covered later in this chapter.

IRA Withdrawals. The law authorizes penalty-free withdrawals for medical expenses under certain conditions from Individual Retirement Accounts (IRAs).

Self-Employment. HIPAA permits increased deductions for the health expenses of self-employed persons and requires that individual health insurance coverage be guaranteed to be renewable.

Prevention of Discrimination. A group health plan may not discriminate in coverage or premiums charged to persons and/or their dependents, based solely on health status, physical or mental medical condition, claims' experience or receipt of health care, medical history, genetic information, or evidence of insurability.

Wellness Program Requirements. Three federal agencies issued Health Insurance Portability and Accountability Act (HIPAA) nondiscrimination provisions governing the use of incentives for health care coverage of participants in wellness programs.[9] A number of employers provide such participants with incentives, such as premium reductions and lower deductibles contingent upon goal attainment. According to these agencies about 30,000 plans with 1.1 million participants vary premiums among similarly situated participants based upon the attainment of goals related to a health factor.[10] The agencies estimate that about 13,000 plans with 460,000 participants vary benefits and/or lower deductibles, among similarly situated employees based upon goal attainment. On their face, incentives appear to be health factor neutral, but conditions like heredity, may stymie the most diligent efforts, for example, to reduce low density lipoprotein cholesterol levels.

To level the playing field, the HIPAA nondiscrimination provisions which were generally effective January 1, 2008 do the following:

"prohibit a group health plan . . . from denying an individual eligibility for benefits based on a health factor (such as requiring a higher deductible) or from charging an individual a higher premium than a similarly situated individual based on a health factor. Health factors include: health status, medical condition (including physical and mental illnesses), claims experience, receipt of health care, medical history, genetic information, evidence of insurability . . . and disability."[11]

Under HIPAA, a *Wellness Program* is one that promotes health or prevents disease, regardless of the name. Wellness programs may have various titles, such as, Smoking Cessation Program, Fitness Program, Health Program or Employee Assistance Program. The HIPAA nondiscrimination procedures do not apply to a wellness program that neither provides an incentive nor bases an incentive on an individual meeting a standard. Accordingly, the nondiscrimination provisions would not apply in these situations:

- The program reimburses individuals for health/fitness club membership;
- Individuals are given a reward for undergoing medical diagnostic testing, but the reward is not contingent on test results;

  Example: Alabama state employees pay $25 monthly for self-only health benefits coverage. In 2009, employees will be offered free health screenings. The premium will increase to $50 in 2010 for those employees who either decline the screening or do not seek medical treatment should a health issue be found during the screening. The premium will remain at $25 for employees who either accept the screening and no health issues are found or accept the screening and seek free medical treatment if a health issue is found.[12]

---

[9] Departments of the Treasury, Labor and Health and Human Services, *Nondiscrimination and Wellness Programs in Health Coverage in the Group Market: Final Rule*, December 13, 2006.

[10] Ibid.

[11] Ibid.

[12] CNN.com, *Alabama to Link Premium Costs to Workers' Health*, http://www.cnn.com/2008/HEALTH/diet.fitness/09/19/alabama.obesity.insurance/index.html.

- Individuals are encouraged to engage in preventive care by waiving the deductible for medical treatment, such as prenatal care;
- The program pays for the cost of smoking cessation programs; and,
- Individuals are rewarded for attendance at health information seminars.

Depending upon answers to the following questions the HIPAA nondiscrimination provisions may apply to a wellness program:[13]

(1) The wellness program is part of a health benefit plan?

(2) Rewards are offered in the health benefit plan, such as a lower premium or deductible to participants who meet a health factor (as defined above) goal in the wellness program?

(3) The health benefit plan rewards are based upon discriminatory health factors?

(4) The amount of the health benefit plan award is limited to 20 percent of the employee-only applicable cost of coverage?

(5) Health promotion or disease prevention is reasonably related to participation in the wellness program?

(6) Eligible participants in the wellness program are afforded the opportunity at least annually to qualify for the rewards?

(7) All similarly situated persons are eligible to participate in the rewards?

(8) Reasonable alternatives for participation in the rewards are disclosed in the program?

Portability Requirements. The portability requirements apply to medical care coverage for newly hired employees (and their families) in non-governmental group health plans with two or more participants on the first day of the plan year. This coverage does not include limited-scope dental or vision care, long-term care, nursing or home health care, care for a specific disease, or hospital indemnity or supplemental coverage that are offered independently of the medical care plan.

Preexisting Conditions. A medical care plan cannot exclude coverage for a preexisting condition (where medical advice, diagnosis, care, or treatment was received within a six-month period ending on the enrollment date in the new employer's medical care plan) for more than 12 months (18 months for late enrollees, such as those who do not enroll at the first opportunity).

A newborn child, adopted child, or a child placed for adoption under age 18 is exempt from preexisting requirements if he or she becomes covered under creditable coverage within 30 days of the birth, adoption, or adoption placement. Also exempt from preexisting requirements are pregnant employees or pregnant dependents of employees, even if there is a break in any coverage.

Creditable Service. Individuals subject to the 12-month exclusionary clause for preexisting conditions may have this period reduced for each month of health

---

[13] Ibid., for a discussion of the questions, including scenarios.

care coverage (called "creditable coverage" in the Act) under a prior health care plan, provided that there is no more than a 63-day break in coverage from the former to the new plan. The following conditions apply:

- If a break of 63 days has occurred, only the coverage after the break is creditable.

- Waiting periods and/or affiliation periods required for new coverage are not considered breaks in coverage.

- Creditable coverage may be earned under a variety of health plans, such as group health plans, individual policies, HMOs, Medicare, and government health plans (such as Medicaid, military health care plans, Indian Health Service plans, and a state health benefits risk pool).

- Employers must track coverage for certification.

- Health plans and health insurance group offerers must certify the period of creditable coverage under their plans, coverage under a COBRA health benefits continuation provision, and any waiting or affiliation period required by their plans.

The penalty for failing to follow the portability provisions is $100 per day for each person for each noncompliance.

Privacy Rules of the Health Insurance Portability and Accountability Act of 1996

An important component of the Health Insurance Portability and Accountability Act are safeguards against the improper disclosure of an individual's health information. The Department of Health and Human Services (DHHS) is responsible for providing procedures to protect against any improper disclosures. As part of this responsibility, DHHS issued *Privacy Rules* (Rules). Firms and others covered (called "covered entities") by the Rules may use or disclose individuals' *Protected Health Information* (PHI) only with their written consent.

Covered Entities. Under the *Administrative Simplification* regulations of the Rules a covered entity generally includes any of the following:

- a health care provider that conducts certain transactions in electronic form (called a "covered health care provider");

- a health care clearinghouse; and,

- a health plan.

All entities in these categories are not necessarily covered. For example, a health plan that has fewer than 50 participants and is self-administered is not covered. In addition, a health care clearinghouse is covered only if it provides this function for another legal entity. To facilitate the process of determining which entities are covered, a series of decision tools or flowcharts are available to assist in the process.[14]

Covered Information. The Rules cover individually identifiable PHI in any format including electronic, paper, or oral including demographic data, relating to:

---

[14] DHHS, *Covered Entity Charts*, July 7, 2003.

- past, present or future physical or mental health;
- health care provided; or,
- payment for provided health care.

Also included is any information that can be reasonably expected to identify an individual, such as name, address, birth date, and Social Security Number.[15] PHI excludes health information in employment records maintained by an employer and education and certain other records defined in the Family Educational Rights and Privacy Act.[16]

Authorized Disclosures. A covered entity may use and disclose PHI, without an individual's authorization if the disclosure is to the individual or for the person's own treatment, payment, and health care operations or "...for the treatment activities of any health care provider, the payment activities of another covered entity and of any health care prover, or the health care operations of another covered entity involving either quality or competency assurance activities or fraud and abuse detection and compliance activities, if both covered entities have or had a relationship with the individual and the protected health information pertains to the relationship."[17] These entities may obtain written consent from the individual for these purposes even though such consent is not required.

Required Employer Administrative Actions. Employers are required to take the following actions in complying with the Rules:

- develop and implement written privacy policies and procedures consistent with the Rules.
- prepare and disseminate a notice of policies and practices regarding PHI.
- designate a privacy official responsible for developing and implementing policies and procedures, and a contact person responsible for receiving complaints and providing individuals with information on privacy practices.
- train employees on privacy policies and procedures.
- institute a procedure of sanctions for policy violations and take appropriate sanctions against employees who violate the policies.
- take action to reduce any harmful effect caused by improper disclosures of PHI or violations of policies.
- maintain reasonable safeguards to prevent unauthorized use or disclosure of PHI and to limit incidental use and disclosure by appropriate safeguards such as shredding documents containing PHI before discarding them and securing medical records with locks.
- have complaint procedures available for use regarding issues about compliance with privacy policies. These procedures must be in an entity's privacy practices notice.

---

[15] 45 C.F.R. § 160.103
[16] 20 U.S.C. § 1232g.

[17] DHHS, OCR *"Treatment, Payment, Health Care Operations" Guidance.*

- identify the individuals who will administer the complaint procedures and explain that complaints also can be submitted to the Secretary of HHS.

- prevent any retaliation against a person for exercising rights provided by the Rules, for assisting in an investigation by HHS or another appropriate authority, or for opposing an act or practice that the person believes in good faith violates the Rules.[18]

No individual may be required to waive any right under the Rules as a condition for obtaining treatment, payment, and enrollment or benefits eligibility.

Documentation and Record Retention. Records must be maintained until six years after the later of the date of their creation or last effective date. Records include privacy policies, notices, disposition of complaints, and other activities that require documentation.

Fully-Insured Group Health Plan Exception. The only administrative obligations for a fully-insured group health plan that has no more than enrollment data and summary health information is to prohibit retaliatory acts and a waiver of individual rights and to document any disclosure of protected health information to the plan sponsor by a health insurance issuer or HMO that services the group health plan.

Civil Money Penalties. Penalties may be imposed of $100 per failure to comply with a Rules requirement. That penalty may not exceed $25,000 per year for multiple violations of the same Rule in a calendar year. Penalties may not be imposed in specific cases, such as when a violation is due to reasonable cause and did not involve willful neglect and was corrected within 30 days of when it became known.

Criminal Penalties. A person who knowingly obtains or discloses PHI can be fined $50,000 and imprisoned up to one year. Criminal "...penalties increase to $100,000 and up to five years imprisonment if the wrongful conduct involves false pretenses, and to $250,000 and up to ten years imprisonment if the wrongful conduct involves the intent to sell, transfer, or use individually identifiable health information for commercial advantage, personal gain, or malicious harm. Criminal sanctions will be enforced by the Department of Justice."[19]

Mental Health Parity Act of 1996

This act applies to employers with more than 50 employees but such employers are exempt if the effect of the law increases the employer's health plan costs by more than one percent. The law does not require employers to provide mental health coverage, but where such coverage is provided, the plan must either:

- Include services for mental illness coverage in the lifetime of the employee, or place annual limits on what the plans will spend for medical or surgical benefits, or

---

[18] For additional information regarding these administrative actions, see 45 C.F.R. § 164.

[19] See 45 C.F.R. § 164.

- Have a separate limit for mental illness services that is not less than that provided for medical or surgical services.

The law neither requires employers to provide mental health coverage nor does it apply to the type, amount and duration of such benefits. Employers are permitted to limit the number of days of coverage and the number of office visits. Employers may also limit the scope of mental health benefits, including cost sharing and requirements regarding medical necessity. The law does not extend benefits for substance abuse or dependency.

Newborns' and Mothers' Health Protection Act of 1996

The law became effective on January 1, 1998. Group health plans are not permitted to restrict postpartum hospital stays to less than 48 hours for a normal delivery and 96 hours for a caesarean section. The Act applies to both self-insured and insured plans, but only to those plans that provide hospital stay maternity benefits for mother and child.

The Women's Health and Cancer Rights Act of 1998

This law was effective for health benefit plans for years beginning on or after October 21, 1998. The law applies to all plans that provide medical and surgical benefits with respect to a mastectomy. The Act requires that mastectomy benefits include breast reconstruction (if desired by the participant or beneficiary). Benefit coverage, in connection with the mastectomy, is extended for the following procedures:

- reconstruction of the breast on which the mastectomy has been performed;

- surgery and reconstruction of the other breast to produce a symmetrical appearance; and

- prostheses and coverage for physical complications of all stages of the mastectomy, including lymph edemas, in a manner reached through consultation with the attending physician and the patient.

Any deductibles and coinsurance provisions must be consistent with other benefits provided by the plan. Plan administrators are required to notify participants of the benefit.

Uniformed Services Employment and Reemployment Rights Act of 1994

A person who was called into service and allows his employer's health plan to lapse, while he was away since he enrolled in military health coverage, may qualify for coverage under the employer's plan upon return from the period of service. Under USERR, both the returning service member and his family should be able to resume coverage under the employer's plan. Furthermore, the plan cannot impose a waiting period or other exclusion period if health coverage had been provided except for the military service. However, the plan can exclude from coverage any illness or injury that was caused or aggravated by the period of military service since it is covered by a military health plan.

Genetic Information Nondiscrimination Act of 2008

The health care provisions of the Genetic Information Nondiscrimination Act (GINA) are effective for plan years beginning after May 21, 2009. GINA amends ERISA to prohibit genetic discrimination in all group health care plans. These are some prohibitions:

- Premium adjustments cannot be based upon genetic information;
- Health plans cannot ask covered individuals to have a genetic test except;

    □ Health professionals may ask such individuals to have such a test;

    □ A health plan can use such a test to determine payment; and,

    □ A health plan may ask individuals to have a genetic test for research purposes provided:

    — Participation is voluntary and refusal will not affect enrollment status;

    — Genetic information is not used in underwriting; and,

    — The plan informs the Secretary of Health and Human Services of the nature of the research.

- Health plans cannot use genetic information for underwriting or regarding an individual's enrollment.

There are extensive penalties for violations of GINA's provisions.

Basic Group Medical Expense Coverage

Basic medical expense benefits consist of three separate types of coverage:

- Hospital expense benefits;
- Surgical expense benefits; and
- Physician's visits expense benefits.

Today, most medical expense plans have extended coverage to include a much broader array of services. In addition, gaps caused by limitations or exclusions under these basic types of coverage are frequently filled by major medical coverage.

Hospital Expense Benefits

Hospital expense coverage pays for room and board charges and other in-hospital services specified in the contract. These services, when ordered by a physician, may include operating room charges, anesthesia, drugs and other supplies, x-rays, and laboratory fees. Hospital room and board charges may be covered on the basis of:

- A specified dollar amount per day; or
- Room classification, usually semi-private accommodations.

The latter approach is the most common and the one used by Blue Cross plans.

Maximum Number of Days. Blue Cross and some private carriers specify a maximum number of days of hospital coverage. Charges for other in-hospital services my be covered in full, with or without a dollar maximum. The plan may pay 100 percent of charges, up to a specified amount, and a reduced percentage for charges in excess of that amount.

First-Dollar Coverage and Deductible. Frequently, basic hospital benefits are covered on a *first-dollar* basis; that is, the employee does not have to satisfy a deductible before benefits are paid. A *deductible* is the amount of covered medical expenses that must be paid by the covered person before he or she will receive benefits under the plan.

Outpatient Services. In the past, outpatient hospital services typically were not covered by hospital expense plans. In recent years, however, the emphasis on health care cost containment has led many insurers to provide reimbursement for services performed on an outpatient basis. Normally, services performed on an outpatient basis are less costly than the same services performed on an inpatient basis.

Disincentives and Coinsurance. It is not uncommon for insurers to include disincentives for hospitalization by applying a deductible and coinsurance for certain in-hospital services that could have been performed as effectively on an outpatient basis. *Coinsurance* is the sharing of expenses between the insurer and the employee. A typical coinsurance clause is 80/20, where the insurer pays 80 percent of the expense and the employee pays 20 percent.

Surgical Expense Benefits

Surgical expense benefits cover charges for surgical procedures performed as a result of accident or sickness, either in or out of the hospital. As with hospital expense benefits, recent trends in group coverage provide greater benefits for surgery performed on an outpatient basis. The benefits may be paid according to a predetermined schedule of fees, based on the surgical procedure performed, or the actual charges may be paid in full. Typically, the latter method pays up to "usual, customary, and reasonable" (UCR) charges. To determine UCR charges, the insurers survey the charges of physicians in a geographical area. Some insurers define the geographic area by zip codes. The more narrowly defined the area and more frequent the updating of the charges, the more representative the UCR charges are of the actual prevailing rates.

Second Opinions. The plan may provide for a second opinion before certain elective and non-emergency surgery is performed. It may be a voluntary or mandatory provision. Under the voluntary provision, the plan will pay the cost of the second, and even a third, opinion if there is a disagreement between the first two. There is no financial impact, however, if the employee does not obtain a second opinion. Under plans with the mandatory provision, a reduction in benefits occurs if a second opinion is not obtained for the specified types of surgery. In either case, the final choice regarding surgery is left up to the employee. Also, many larger groups are now requiring a preadmission review for non-emergency hospitalizations. Failure to obtain a preauthorization can result in a substantial reduction in benefits.

Exclusions. Virtually all plans contain exclusions for some types of surgery. Normally, surgery for occupational disease or injury, cosmetic surgery, and certain dental surgery are not covered.

Physician's Visits Expense Benefits

Physician's visits, both in the hospital and in the physician's office, if covered, usually have a maximum dollar limit per visit. Covered office visits are those resulting from an accident or sickness. Generally, regular checkups or physical examinations are not covered. Some plans do provide coverage for well-baby checkups.

Major Medical Coverage

The purpose of major medical coverage is to pay for a broad range of services and a substantial portion of expenses associated with catastrophic illness. Services both in and out of the hospital are covered. Frequently, the employee shares in the cost of services through a deductible and coinsurance provision. There are two methods of providing major medical coverage.

- *Supplemental* major medical plans are coordinated with basic coverage. They cover expenses that are not included in, or in excess of, the basic coverage. Frequently, there is a deductible paid after the maximum limit on the basic coverage is exhausted before the expenses are paid under the major medical coverage. There are several variations in this type of coverage. For example, certain "other medical expenses" may be covered as major medical expenses and not as a basic expense. In this case, expenses over an initial deductible are covered.

- *Comprehensive* plans are those in which a single contract covers all medical expenses. These plans offer greater simplicity, both in administration and in the ability to communicate their provisions to employees. These plans cover all expenses, in excess of any deductible, subject to the coinsurance provision, if any.

Stop Limit

Many plans have a *stop limit*; that is, after the employee incurs a specified dollar amount in out-of-pocket expenses, the plan pays 100 percent of all covered expenses.

Cost Containment

Consideration is often given to cost containment in designing major medical plans. The employer can include incentives, in the form of higher reimbursement levels for less costly types of medical care. For example, full reimbursement may be given to outpatient surgery, while inpatient surgery is subject to the deductible and coinsurance provisions.

Federal Taxation

Employer contributions to a medical expense plan are tax deductible for the employer. Generally, an employer's contributions are not taxable income to the employee. If, however, the benefits are self-funded by the employer, the plan must meet certain nondiscrimination rules for highly compensated employees, so that employer contributions may be excluded from the highly compensated employees' taxable income.

Dental Expenses

Dental plans have long been designed to cover preventive care as a means of reducing more costly dental expenses later. Thus, most plans cover preventive procedures, such as checkups, cleaning, and x-rays. Typically, there is a small deductible and a yearly maximum dollar limit on dental services covered. The type of services that may be covered include:

- Examination and x-rays;

- Cleaning and fluoride treatment;

- Restorative procedures: fillings, periodontal care, inlays, root canal work;

- Orthodontic expenses;

- Oral surgery; and

- Denture and bridgework.

Most dental plans pay a percentage (frequently, 80 percent) of "usual, customary, and reasonable" (UCR) charges, subject to an initial deductible and exclusions. The percentage of expenses paid by the insurer may depend upon the category of the expense. Preventive care will have the highest level of reimbursement. More extensive services, such as crowns, dentures, and inlays, are typically paid at 50 percent. Many plans do not cover orthodontic services.

Some dental plans pay according to a schedule, with maximum dollar amounts for each type of dental service. Services are usually paid on a first-dollar basis and not subject to coinsurance. These plans, however, typically have smaller maximums than would be payable under the UCR method. A small percentage of employers offer an incentive form of benefit payment, allowing that if an employee is examined regularly by a dentist, the percentage of expenses paid by the carrier increases each year.

Predetermination of Benefits

A common feature in most insured dental plans is the *predetermination of benefits* provision. With this provision, the insurance company reviews the procedures and costs for expenses that will be over a specified amount. The dentist completes a claim form, and the insurance company advises the dentist and employee of the amount that it will pay of the proposed cost. The company may consider some of the procedures unnecessary or suggest alternative procedures.

Other Medical Expense Benefits

Other types of benefits offered in medical expense plans include prescription drugs, vision and hearing care, mental and nervous disorders, inpatient alcohol and drug rehabilitation, nursing home and hospice care, and home health care visits. The last three services mentioned are alternatives to hospital care, and their popularity is expected to increase as employers seek to control health care costs.

Contract Provisions

Most of the group insurance provisions discussed under life insurance benefits are also applicable to medical expense contracts. In addition, there are other provisions unique to health coverage, discussed below.

Coordination of Benefits

Many group plans have a provision for the manner in which benefits will be paid in the event that participation is covered by more than one plan. This is known as a *coordination of benefits* (COB) provision. Duplicate coverage can occur when both spouses in a family are employed, and each has coverage with their respective employers. One or both plans may provide dependent coverage as well and, thus, cover family members. If dependent coverage is contributory and the husband and wife have children, they will usually select dependent coverage under one of the plans. Duplicate coverage may also occur when an employee has two jobs or when benefits are provided from some other source, such as automobile insurance, that provides medical benefits in cases of a vehicle accident.

If neither plan contains a COB provision, benefits are paid out under each plan as if no other insurance is involved. When a plan does contain a COB provision, its coverage is secondary to any other plan *without* the COB provision. Thus, the plan without the provision is said to be "primary" and pays a claim first, according to its coverage. The plan with the COB provisions pays the claim, according to its coverage *up to* the amount of the claim.

Most plans, however, do have a COB provision. Each plan's provision will specify the priority of payment in the event that the employee or dependent is covered by more than one plan. Each spouse's medical expenses will be primary under their own employer's plan. Most plans provide for the children's medical expenses to be primary under the plan of the spouse whose birthday falls earliest in the year, although some still provide for the father's plan to be primary for the children's expenses. The COB provision also specifies which plan is primary in the event the spouses are divorced.

Medicare Coordination. Medical expense benefits are also coordinated with Medicare, in the event that the employee or the dependent has Medicare coverage. Any covered individual who is 65 years old is eligible for Medicare, whether or not they are actually retired. Employers must offer the same plan to active employees over age 65 that is offered to younger employees. Unless the employee elects otherwise, the employer's plan is primary and Medicare is secondary. (Generally, the employer plan has better coverage, and the employee will not elect Medicare as primary coverage.) Employer-provided health care coverage for retirees can be secondary to Medicare.

Preexisting Conditions

A *preexisting condition* is defined as an illness or injury for which the participant received medical treatment during a specified period of time (typically, from three to 12 months) immediately preceding eligibility to join the plan. The purpose of refusal to cover preexisting conditions is to minimize adverse selection against the plan by those persons with a need to utilize it. After a period of time, if the participant has not received medical care, the condition will no longer be considered a preexisting condition.

It is common for a preexisting condition clause to be waived for all eligible employees on the effective date of a new plan. All future employees who become participants of the plan, however, are subject to such provision. Preexisting conditions clauses are subject to HIPAA provisions. See the discussion of the Health Insurance Portability and Accountability Act of 1996 (HIPAA) above.

Dependent Eligibility

In contrast to group life insurance, it is very common for group medical expense plans to provide coverage for certain members of the employee's family. Also, unlike group life plans, benefits under medical expense plans are generally the same for both employees and their dependents. Most plans do not require employees to share in the cost of their own coverage. Part or all of the cost of coverage for dependents, however, is often paid by the employee.

Maternity Benefits

The Civil Rights Act was amended in 1978 to require employers to treat pregnancy and childbirth-related expenses the same as any other type of illness. In addition to the requirement of equal treatment for maternity care expenses, the following rules have been developed:

- If the plan provides dependent coverage, such coverage must be the same for dependents of male employees and dependents of female employees. Thus, a plan may provide a lower level of benefits for pregnancy-related conditions for male employees' wives than for female employees, if all benefits for spouses of both male and female employees are lower than for employees. The plan may also exclude maternity benefits for female dependent children, provided that the exclusion applies to the children of both male and female employees.

- Abortions need not be covered, unless they are performed because the mother's life is endangered. Complications from any abortion must be covered.

- Extension of medical expense benefits beyond the employee's termination must apply equally to all conditions. Thus, if benefits continue for a pregnancy that commenced before the employee's termination, extensions must apply to other medical conditions that commence before the employee's termination.

The one area in which the 1978 amendment had a negative impact for women is with regard to the last item listed above. Traditionally, pregnancy has been covered by the plan in existence when the pregnancy commenced, even if the participant is no longer covered by the plan at the time of pregnancy termination. However, in order to continue providing extension of pregnancy-related benefits, the plan would also have to cover all medical conditions that commenced during employment; the cost impact of such a provision could be devastating, especially for illnesses that continue indefinitely. The uncertainty of the amount of loss and the increased exposure to loss has led most employers to discontinue providing extended benefits for pregnancy-related conditions.

Conversion Right. Conversion to individual coverage without evidence of insurability is required by most states. Employees normally have 31 days in which to purchase individual insurance at individual rates. Individual coverage benefits may not be as broad as those under the group coverage.

Benefits Upon Termination of Plan Eligibility (COBRA)

Typically, medical expense plans provide coverage until the last day of the month in which employment terminates. An extension of benefits is often provided for employees who are totally disabled at the time of termination. There are also a number of circumstances in which the employee's dependents are no longer eligible for coverage under the plan; for example, when children marry or reach a specified age. Death and divorce can result in termination of coverage. As a result of the Consolidated Omnibus Budget Reconciliation Act of 1985 (COBRA) and its subsequent amendments, group medical, dental, and vision plans must now permit employees and covered dependents to elect continuation of coverage at group rates following an event that would otherwise terminate their coverage.

Covered Employers. Employers with 20 or more employees on more than 50 percent of the typical business days in the previous calendar year must offer continued health benefit coverage for employees and qualified beneficiaries who are presently covered but who lose their coverage due to qualifying events. The employee must have been covered by the employer's health plan on the day before the qualifying event. "Qualified beneficiaries" include the employee's spouse and dependent children, if they were covered by the employer's health plan on the day before the qualifying event.[20]

Periods of Coverage. COBRA specifies that continued coverage must extend to the earliest of:

- 18 months for employees and their qualified beneficiaries for a reduction in hours or termination of employment, except when the termination is for gross misconduct. An employee who becomes disabled within 60 days of coverage under COBRA, as determined by Title II or XVI of the Social Security Act, can receive an additional 11 months of coverage. Thus, the employee will have 29 months of total coverage, which is the same number of months as an employee who was disabled as determined by Title II or XVI of the Social Security Act at the time of termination of employment. The employee's qualified beneficiaries are also entitled to the additional 11 months of coverage.

- 29 months for an employee (and his or her qualified beneficiaries) if the employee is determined to be disabled under Title II or XVI of the Social Security Act.

---

[20] U.S. Department of Labor, *Health Benefits Under the Consolidated Omnibus Budget Reconciliation Act (COBRA)*, July 1999.

- 36 months for qualified beneficiaries of an employee who dies, becomes divorced or legally separated, or becomes enrolled in Medicare. This includes children who are newborn or adopted during the period of COBRA coverage.

- 36 months for a qualified beneficiary who loses "dependent child" status under the rules of the plan.

Cost of Coverage. The cost for the coverage can be up to 102 percent of the entire group premium (150 percent for months 19 through 29 for persons who are eligible due to a disability).

Benefit Cessation. COBRA benefits stop if:

- The employee or dependent becomes eligible for another health benefits plan, and the employee or dependent do not have pre-existing conditions that are excluded under the new plan. However, if other group health coverage is obtained prior to the COBRA election, COBRA coverage may not be discontinued, even if the other coverage continues after the COBRA election.

- The employee or spouse becomes eligible for Medicare after the COBRA election. However, if Medicare is obtained prior to the COBRA election, COBRA coverage may not be discontinued, even if the other coverage continues after COBRA election.

- The employer discontinues the health benefits plan.

- The employee does not pay scheduled premiums.

However, if the former employee is already covered under his or her spouse's benefit plan as a dependent, the former employee would still be qualified for COBRA benefits from the previous employer.[21]

Notice Requirements. COBRA rights must be described in the summary plan description (SPD) that all participants receive. The SPD must be furnished within 90 days after a person becomes a participant or a beneficiary begins receiving benefits. An initial notice describing COBRA rights must be furnished to covered employees and their spouses at the time that coverage under the plan commences. Other notification requirements are:

- Employers must notify plan administrators of a qualifying event within 30 days after an employee's death, termination, reduced hours of employment or entitlement to Medicare.

- A qualified beneficiary must notify the plan administrator of a qualifying event within 60 days after divorce or legal separation, resulting in a child ceasing to be covered as a dependent under plan rules.

---

[21] See *Geissal v. Moore Medical Corp.* (SCt 1998, Docket No. 97-689), in which the U.S. Supreme Court held that Geissal, who was terminated from employment by Moore Medical Corp., was eligible for COBRA benefits from Moore Medical Corp., even though he was covered as a dependent under his wife's medical expense benefits plan at her place of employment prior to the termination of employment at Moore Medical Corp.

- Plan administrators, upon receiving notice of a qualifying event, must provide an election notice to the qualified beneficiaries within 14 days after receiving notice that such qualifying event has occurred.

- Qualified beneficiaries seeking the additional 11 months of coverage must notify the plan administrator of the disabled beneficiary's Social Security determinations. The notice must be made within 60 days of a disability determination and prior to expiration of the 18-month period of COBRA.

Other COBRA Provisions. Employees and qualified beneficiaries must be given at least 60 days for the election of COBRA benefits. The 60 days is the later of the coverage loss date or the date that the COBRA election notice is provided. COBRA coverage is retroactive if it is elected and paid for by the employee or qualified beneficiary.

Conversion Rights. If an employee chooses to continue group coverage, as provided under COBRA regulation, he or she still has the right to convert to an individual plan when the continuation coverage terminates.

Medical Expense Benefits Providers

Medical expense benefits are provided through Blue Cross-Blue Shield, commercial insurance companies, managed care programs,[22] or an employer's self-funded plan. *Managed health care* is an organized program that coordinates the financing, as well as the delivery of, health care to its employees through specified providers. The concept of managed care is becoming more popular among large employers that are attempting to control their high cost of health care. Managed care programs include health maintenance organizations (HMOs), preferred provider organizations (PPOs), and point-of-service (POS) plans, which are discussed below.

Blue Cross-Blue Shield and Commercial Insurers

Characteristics of the two major providers of benefits, insurance companies and Blue Cross-Blue Shield (the Blues), are different, but have become somewhat similar over the years, as a result of intense competition. The Blues are comprised of a network of more than 60 independent companies, referred to as *plans*. The Blues use community-based pricing, establishing arrangements with local hospitals and physicians. The Blues offer health care benefits to 25 percent of Americans.

Originally, the Blues were nonprofit organizations but, in recent years, some of the plans in various states have been reorganized into either for-profit organizations or charitable trusts. An example of the former is Blue Cross/Blue Shield of Virginia, which converted to the for-profit organization known as Trigon Blue Cross/Blue Shield of Virginia which was later sold. In Colorado, California, and New York, the plans were converted to charitable trusts.

Taxation. In most states, the Blues are treated as nonprofit organizations and, thus, are frequently exempt from state income and/or premium taxes. The

---

[22] Many of these plans are owned by commercial insurers or Blue Cross and Blue Shield.

degree of tax exemption varies by state. In addition, the Blues receive favorable federal income tax treatment, giving the Blues a distinct cost advantage over insurance companies.

Expense Reimbursement. Another major distinction between the two providers of coverage is the manner in which reimbursement of expenses is made. Insurance companies have traditionally reimbursed participants directly for expenses they must pay to the providers of service. In the case of hospital care services, the hospital usually requires the patient to assign the benefits to it, so that the insurer will reimburse the hospital directly.

The Blues generally make payment directly to the hospital or physician rather than to the patient. Participating providers agree to accept a predetermined charge from the Blues as payment in full for the service. If the patient goes to a nonparticipating provider, he or she is responsible for amounts in excess of the Blues' scheduled fees. This negotiation with providers generally results in lower charges than those charged to patients with commercial insurance coverage.

Rating System. Traditionally, the Blues have used a *community-rating* system that charges the same premium rates to all policyholders in a given area. In contrast, insurance companies use an *experience-rating* approach that considers past claim experience in determining premium rates for large groups. For better than average experience, employers can obtain lower rates from an insurance company than they can from the Blues. The Blues, to be competitive, were forced to adopt an experience-rating system. However, the community-rating approach is still used by the Blues for small groups and individual health products.

Operating Characteristic. Each Blue Cross and Blue Shield plan operates as an independent, autonomous unit over a specified geographic area. Most of the large insurance companies operate on a national basis.

Health Maintenance Organizations (HMOs)

A *health maintenance organization* is an organized system of health care financing and delivery of health care services. For a preset fee, an HMO promises to provide comprehensive health care services.

HMOs became popular in the early 1970s due to the influence of the HMO Act of 1973.[23] The percentage of employees covered by HMOs increased rather significantly from 1993 to 1995, but declined in 2003, as shown in the following table.

Exhibit 19-1
Employee Coverage by Employer Medical Expense Plans in Private Industry Firms with 100 or More Employees, 1993-2003

Type of plan	% of employees covered

---

[23] The origins of the HMO concept (traditionally referred to as *group prepaid practice plans*) go back to two early plans that have had continued strong success: the Ross-Loos Medical Group in Los Angeles and the Kaiser Foundation Health Plan, which operates in California and several other states.

	1993	1995	2003
Traditional fee-for-service	50	37	7
Preferred provider organization	26	34	67
Prepaid health maintenance organization	23	34	24

Source: BLS, U.S. Department of Labor

Characteristics of HMOs. An HMO is an organized system of health care. HMOs finance health care but, unlike the Blues and insurance companies, they deliver health care services as well.

Comprehensive Benefits. HMOs provide extensive medical care as part of a standard benefit package.

Prepaid Fixed Fee. In contrast to the traditional "fee-for-service" approach to paying for health care, the HMO charges one fixed fee, regardless of the type or amount of services received. In some cases, there may be an additional nominal charge. For example, the patient may be required to pay an additional $1 to $5 for each physician's visit, or there may be a $2 charge for each prescription. These charges are in addition to the fixed, prepaid monthly premium. The additional fee is the same regardless of the services provided.

Network of Providers. Typically, to receive care under an HMO, the member must go to a participating provider.

Specified Geographical Area. An HMO operates over a defined geographic area. Thus, if an employee is not within a reasonable distance of the HMO, it is not favorable for him or her to enroll. Most HMOs have a provision for employees who are treated by a non-HMO provider of service outside of the HMO's geographical area. Typically, the service must be for an emergency or a life-threatening situation. Some HMOs that have several locations are beginning to offer reciprocal services at any of the locations.

Types of HMOs. The basic types of HMOs are:

- *Group model* approach, which contracts with physicians to provide services for members. Care is provided in a central location by physicians practicing in a group practice.

- *Network model* approach, in which care is provided by a network of two or more independent group practices.

- *Individual practice* approach, which contracts with independent physicians to provide some services to HMO members. Care is provided by these physicians practicing in their own offices; the physicians usually contract with the HMO through an individual practice association.

- *Staff model HMOs,* which is an approach where care is provided in a central location by physicians and other health care professionals who are salaried employees of the HMO.

HMOs may do business under more than one of these models.

State and federal law. Most states have enacted specific laws pursuant to which HMOs are organized or licensed. While there is also a federal HMO Act of 1973, the standards under that Act are voluntary, and many HMOs have chosen not to seek federal qualification. HMOs are required, in many state, to undertake substantial utilization review and quality assurance activities.

On occasions, employees have been unhappy with decisions made by particular HMO's concerning whether claims, such as surgical procedures will be covered. When these disputes wind up in court, the HMOs' typical defense has been that they are covered by ERISA and thus exempt from state law. In *Rush Prudential HMO, Inc. v. Moran et al.* (2002), the U.S. Supreme Court ruled that ERISA did not preempt Illinois state law (the Illinois HMO Act).[24]

Gatekeeper provision. HMOs and the more recent *point-of-service* (POS) plans have a "gatekeeper" provision that requires members to select a primary care physician who gives authorization to a member who needs to see a specialist. With the traditional HMO, the member will not be reimbursed for medical care obtained outside of the provider network without the primary care physician's authorization. There are criticisms that these arrangements may result in a rationing of health care and even result in delays in providing referrals to medical specialists in order to keep costs low.

Medical Specialties. Often, an HMO plan may not be large enough to have a full-time physician in certain specialties. The HMO contracts with a specialist in the area to provide services as needed. In this case, the specialist is normally paid on a per-service basis.

Physician Compensation. Compensation approaches vary, but they usually provide incentives for cost effectiveness by service providers. Salaried physicians, for example, may receive bonuses if the experience of the plan is better than expected.

Advantages of HMOs. HMOs have several advantages to individuals and to society. The HMO offers potential cost control advantages, such as physical checkups, well-baby care, and other well-patient services that frequently are not provided in traditional insurance plans. Also, the HMO treats patients in the early stages of illness in an attempt to avoid more costly service later.

The HMOs flat-fee payment structure for service providers is also a financial disincentive for medical personnel to perform unnecessary services. These and other measures have produced results that indicate that the HMO approach has reduced the cost of health care. Savings in health care costs may be passed on to the employer and employees through lower premiums and more comprehensive services.

For the individual, the HMO offers "one-stop" health care services and the elimination of claim filling and delays or hassles over payment of services. Often, the services provided are more extensive than in a traditional plan.

---

[24] See *Ragsdale et al. v. Wolverine World Wide, Inc.* (2002) in the Appendix.

Disadvantages of HMOs. One of the main oppositions to the HMO is for the employee who already has an established relationship with a physician who is not participating in the HMO.[25] Often, such an employee is unwilling to switch to a new physician. Critics of the HMO concept contend that the patient-doctor relationship is lost entirely, and that it is similar to going to a clinic. Most HMOs, however, have a number of general practitioners. Patients or family members are assigned to one general practitioner as their primary care physician. These individuals have the option of assignment to a different physician, if they so desire.

Another potential problem arises if a patient needs care outside of the HMO area. Although most HMOs have provisions for such contingencies in emergency situations, there can be a disagreement over what constitutes an emergency. Furthermore, there are usually other requirements when emergency care is needed, such as time limits in reporting or getting preauthorization for the care.

One of the primary advantages of an HMO, its cost efficiency, can result in a disadvantage to the patient if a physician delays or does not perform necessary tests or treatment in an effort to contain costs. As explained previously, the method of compensation to physicians discourages service providers from performing additional treatment.

Preferred Provider Organizations (PPOs)

PPOs are "networks of individual physicians and hospitals that discount fees in exchange for an increased volume of business. In effect, PPOs work as brokers to arrange contracts between employer-purchasers and health care providers."[26] The owners of a PPO may be an insurance company, a Blue Cross and Blue Shield organization, a private entrepreneur or even a group of health care providers who organize their own PPO and contract directly with employers. PPOs offer employees greater flexibility and freedom to choose doctors and other health care providers than do HMOs. Unlike HMOs, which are maintained on a prepaid basis, PPOs are fee-for-service arrangements. Also unlike an HMO, PPOs do not have gatekeepers, so a member can directly receive services from a specialist and have the services paid at the regular fee arrangement. However, if the specialist is not within the network, the reimbursement rate is lower, unless prior permission was obtained.

Point-of-Service (POS) Plans

Point of service (POS) plans have a "gatekeeper" feature that requires employees to select a primary care physician. The primary care physician gives authorization to employees who need to see a specialist. This is similar to the HMO, except that with a traditional HMO, the employee will not be reimbursed for medical care obtained outside of the provider network without the primary care physician's authorization. The POS permits the employee to obtain medical attention outside the provider network at a lower reimbursement rate (unless prior authorization is received from the primary care physician).

---

[25] Recently, some "open-ended" HMOs have been established, which enable a patient to go to a nonparticipating provider.

[26] CCH HUMAN RESOURCES MANAGEMENT, *Compensation*, ¶ 3134.

Health Insurance Purchasing Cooperatives

Health insurance purchasing cooperatives buy medical expense benefits from providers for a group of employers. These arrangements help employers, particularly smaller employers, to obtain medical services at lower prices.

Self-Funding

Self-funding is an alternative to insurance as a means of financing employee benefits. Benefit claims are paid directly from the employer's own assets. Payment may come from the current cash flow, or funds may be set aside in advance for potential future claims. The decision to self-fund is a financial one. Generally, competition and consumer sophistication (relative to the individual market) keep insurers' profit margins low. Commission rates are also negotiable in the group market. However, if the employer can provide the promised benefits less expensively than an insurance provider, it should consider self-funding.

The larger a group is, the more predictable is its loss experience and, thus, it is more likely to self-fund. Predictability is a major factor that makes some types of benefits better candidates for self-funding than others. In a comparison of financing alternatives, consideration is given to savings realized by having the use of the funds that would otherwise go to the insurance company. Other savings include the state's premium tax. Earnings could also be made on the remaining portion of the premium, until it is needed to pay claims and expenses. Self-funding also gives the employer control of the reserves that would be established by insurers and of the float on deposits and withdrawals. Other health care plan cost savings are realized because self-insurers are not subject to the various state-mandated provisions that insured plans are required to provide for covered employees.

In addition to the costs associated with changing from an insured to a self-funded plan, the employer should consider the additional ongoing costs. Executives and other personnel will need to acquire competence in a field that is not related to the employer's business. A qualified staff is necessary. There are additional fees for actuarial guidance, medical reviews, audit reviews, legal work, internal reporting and disclosures, and paperwork necessary for regulatory compliance.

The conversion feature, which entitles an employee to convert to individual coverage, is required by many states. Few employers have the financial ability to offer permanent individual coverage on their own. Thus, it is necessary to have an agreement with an insurer for the conversion provision.

Self-funding of health benefits requires direct involvement of the employer with medical providers and cost containment efforts. The employer must develop UCR guidelines, aggressive claims administration, detection of fraud, and other methods to keep costs down.

The increase in employer self-funding during the late 1970s and 1980s has resulted in the development of many employer coalitions. These *coalitions* are groups of employers who are pooling their knowledge and developing methods of health care cost containment.

Although self-funding *may* increase cash flow, there is also greater uncertainty in predicting those cash flows. Reserves set aside by an employer to meet unforeseen contingencies are not tax deductible, unless the employer divests control of the funds by establishing a trust that is annually audited by a certified public accountant.

Another disadvantage of self-funding may be possible problems related to claims administration. If a claim is denied, the employee sees the employer, rather than the insurer, as the "bad guy." Often, borderline claims are decided in favor of the employee—particularly in strong union situations—to avoid employee dissatisfaction. Furthermore, claims administration is usually a function far removed from the employer's main line of business. Inexperience leaves the employer ill-prepared to handle a job formerly handled by an insurance company whose primary business is claims administration. For these reasons, most employers who self-fund will continue to have claims administered by an insurance company (or the Blues). This type of contract is referred to as an *Administration Services Only* or ASO. The employer still bears all the risk of claims with an ASO contract except at contract termination. The insurer typically assumes the responsibility for claims filed after the contract has terminated. The premium tax is imposed on the fees paid to the insurer for the ASO contract.

A fully insured and a self-funded plan represent the two opposite extreme approaches to financing employee benefits. Insurers have designed numerous financing alternatives that may be more suitable than either of the two extremes. These other alternatives attempt to lower the amount of money that the employer must pay to the insurer up front via lower premiums, delay of the premium due date, and reserve reduction arrangements.

Medical expense plans and pension plans are the two major employee benefits that are most often self-funded. Death benefits are least likely to be self-funded, because the probability of death is more difficult for most employers to estimate. A firm may go many years without a death. When more than one death occurs in a particular year, the large amount of the benefit may place a strain on the employer's cash flows.

In summary, an employer's funding choice should consider these issues:

- The employer's willingness to assume risks;
- Cash flow improvements resulting from additional investment income and cost savings versus increased administrative costs;
- Tax and legal implications; and
- The effect on employees.

Health Savings Accounts and Other Tax-Favored Health Plans

These are the types of tax-favored health plans:

- Health Savings Account.
- Archer Medical Savings Account.
- Flexible Spending Arrangement.
- Health Reimbursement Arrangement.

Health Savings Account. A *Health Savings Account* (HSA) is a tax-exempt account that a person can establish with a trustee (such as a bank, insurance company, credit union or anyone approved by the IRS to be a trustee for an IRA or Archer MSA) to pay for certain medical expenses.

These are the advantages to a HSA:

- Contributions are tax deductible even if deductions are not itemized.
- Contributions made by an employer are excluded from income and employment taxes.
- Contributions remain in the account until used.
- Interest or earnings on amounts in the account are tax-free.
- Distributions from the account are tax-free for qualified medical expenses.
- It is portable from one employer to another.

These are the requirements to establish a HSA:

- An individual must have a high deductible health plan (HDHP). A HDHP is one in which the minimum annual deductible for 2008 is at least $1,150 (deductibles and co-pays cannot exceed $5,500) for the individual or $2,300 for the individual and his/her family (deductibles and co-pays cannot exceed $11,600). An HDHP can provide preventive care, with or without a deductive, such as periodic health evaluations, immunizations, and screening services such as for heart or musculoskeletal disorders.
- An individual cannot have any other health coverage (excluding coverage for dental care, vision care, accidents, disability and long-term care).
- An individual cannot be enrolled in Medicare.
- An individual cannot be a dependent on someone else' tax return.
- There cannot be joint HSAs. Each spouse who is eligible to establish her/his own HSA must do so.

These are the maximum contributions:

- For an individual's HSA (including all amounts contributed, by the individual and any other person like his/her employer) the maximum is $2,850 not to exceed the amount of the annual HDHP deductible.
- For a family's HSA the maximum is $5,950 not to exceed the amount of the annual plan deductible.

	In addition to these contributions, individuals who are age 55 and older can make these "catch-up" contributions annually:

- 2008 - $900
- 2009 and later - $1,000

These are some other major provisions of HSAs:[27]

- Amounts from Archer MSAs can be rolled over into a HSA and are not subject to the contribution limits.

---

[27] For a complete discussion of HSAs, see IRS Publication 969.

- Records must be kept of distributions from an HSA and reported on annual tax returns.

Expenses that qualify for disbursement include most medical care and services, dental and vision care, prescribed medications, including most over-the counter drugs such as aspirin. Medical insurance premiums are not covered, except these:

- Any health plan coverage while receiving federal or state unemployment benefits.

- COBRA continuation coverage after leaving employment with a company that offers health insurance coverage.

- Qualified long-term care insurance.

- Medicare premiums and out-of-pocket expenses, including deductibles, co-pays, and coinsurance for Part A (hospital and inpatient services), Part B (physician and outpatient services), Part C (Medicare HMO and PPO plans), and Part D (prescription drugs).

- Medical expenses for a spouse or dependent children (even if they are not covered by the person's HDHP).

Any amounts used for purposes other than to pay for "qualified medical expenses" are taxable as income and subject to an additional 10% tax penalty. Examples of non-qualified expenses are cosmetic surgery and health insurance other than that described above. After age 65, the 10% additional tax penalty no longer applies. Also, upon becoming disabled and/or enrolling in Medicare, the account can be used for other purposes without paying the additional 10% penalty[28].

Archer Medical Savings Account. An *Archer Medical Savings Account* (MSA) is a tax-exempt account established with a trustee (such as a bank, insurance company, credit union or anyone approved by the IRS to be a trustee for an IRA or MSA) used exclusively to pay for future medical expenses.[29]

These are the benefits of an MSA:

- Contributions are tax deductible even if deductions are not itemized.

- Contributions made by an employer are excluded from income.

- Contributions remain in the account until used.

- Interest or earnings on amounts in the account are tax-free.

- Distributions from the account are tax-free for qualified medical expenses.

- It is portable from one employer to another or if a person leaves the workforce.

These are the requirements to establish a MSA:

- A person must be either of the following:

---

[28] Source with some direct quotes, U.S. Department of the Treasury, *Health Savings Accounts* (November 2006).

[29] For a complete discussion of MSAs, see IRS Publication 969.

—1. Employed by a firm, with an average of 50 or fewer employees during either of the prior two years, that maintains an individual or family High Deductible Health Plan (see the following table for limits in 2007).

Type of Coverage	Minimum annual deductible	Maximum annual deductible	Maximum annual out-of-pocket expenses
Self-only	$1,900	$2,850	$3,750
Family	$3,750	$5,650	$6,900

— 2. Is self-employed and has an individual or family HDHP.

- An individual does not have any health coverage that is not HDHP except for a specific disease, coverage for a fixed daily (or period) of hospitalization, and coverage for accidents, disability, dental care, vision care, or long-term care.

These are other requirements for a MSA:

- An employer and an employee can make contributions to an employee's MSA but an employee and an employer cannot make contributions in the same year.

- Contributions do not need to be made each year.

- The annual contribution limit (the individual or the employer) for family coverage is 75 percent (65 percent for only individual coverage) of the HDHP's deductible.

    Example: The deductible for Joe's family HDHP is $4,000. The maximum annual contribution allowed is .75 × $4,000 = $3,000.

- An employee cannot contribute more than he/she earned during the year from the employer.

- Individuals enrolled in Medicare cannot contribute to a MSA (but they can contribute to a Medical Advantage MSA—See IRS Publication 969 for the requirements).

- Contributions to a MSA must be reported on the employee's federal income tax form.

- Upon request, plan trustees will make disbursements from the MSA for qualified medical expenses until the HDHP's deductible is reached (at that point, medical expenses are paid by the HDHP).

- Examples of medical expenses that qualify for MSA disbursement are doctor's fees, prescription and non-prescription medicine and hospital services not paid for by insurance incurred by the individual, the individual's spouse, all dependents claimed on the individual's tax return and others that could have been claimed as dependents.

Flexible Spending Arrangement. A *flexible spending arrangement* (FSA) is an employer established fund comprised of pretax contributions by employees (and sometimes employers) to reimburse employees for medical expenses.

These are the advantages to a FSA:

- Employer contributions are excluded from employees' income.

- No federal income or employment taxes are deducted from contributions.

- Withdrawals are tax-free for qualified medical expenses, such as doctors' fees, prescription and non-prescription medicines and hospital services.[30] No withdrawals are permitted for amounts paid by health insurance or for health plan or long-term care coverage or expenses.

- Withdrawals may be made from an FSA even if the funds have not yet been placed in the account.

These are the requirements pertaining to FSA contributions:

- There are no limits on the amounts that employees can contribute to an FSA but the plan must designate either the maximum dollar amount or percentage of salary that can be contributed.

- At the beginning of the plan year employees designate how much they want to contribute (usually this entails estimating how much will be spent from the FSA since unspent amounts are typically forfeited).

- Unless there is a change in employment or family status, employees cannot change the amount they want to contribute during the year to the FSA.

- Employers withhold contributions from employees' pre-tax pay.

These are the requirements pertaining to distributions:

- The maximum amount that can be distributed for qualified medical expenses is the amount designated for contribution to the FSA at the beginning of the plan year.

- A statement from a third-party must be sent to the FSA indicating the expense amount and that it has not been paid by any other health coverage.

- FSAs are "use it or lose it" plans so any balance remaining at the end of the plan year is forfeited except the plan can provide for a 2 $1/2$ month grace period at the end of the plan year during which employees can spend any balances in their funds for qualified expenses.

Health Reimbursement Arrangement. A *health reimbursement arrangement* (HRA) is a plan funded solely by employers to provide tax-free reimbursements to employees for qualified medical expenses.

These are the advantages to an HRA:

- Contributions made by employers are excluded from employee' gross income.

- Reimbursements for qualified medical expenses are tax free to employees.

- Unused amounts in an HRA can be carried over to the next plan year.

These are other features of an HRA:

- There is no limit on the amount of contributions an employer can make for an employee.

---

[30] See IRS Publication 502.

- Reimbursements can be made for the following:

  —Current and former employees.

  —Spouses and dependents of employees.

  —Any person claimed on the employees' return who earned less than $3,300.

  —Any person who could have been claimed as a dependent but was claimed by someone else.

  —Spouses and dependents of deceased employees.

- Examples of qualified medical expenses include doctors' fees, prescription and non-prescription medicines, and hospital services not covered by insurance. In addition, qualified medical expenses include health insurance premiums, amounts paid for long-term health coverage and amounts not covered under another health plan.

Disability Income and Sick Leave Benefits

Disability income coverage provides periodic income in the event that the employee is unable to work due to injury or sickness. Disability is one of the greatest risks facing an individual. The probability of disability for an employee is greater than the probability of dying during his or her entire working life. Furthermore, disability is often more financially devastating than death. While both events result in the loss of income, disability involves the wage earner's continued support and the potential for health-related expenditures.

In spite of these facts, employers are less likely to provide nonoccupational disability income coverage than they are to provide benefits for medical expenses and death. Employees may be covered for disability under Social Security; however, Social Security has a very strict definition of disability. Also, an employee must have the required number of covered quarters and wait five months before eligibility for benefits. Benefit payments start at the beginning of the *next* month. The amount of benefits may also be insufficient to provide for the employee's pre-disability standards of living.

Benefit Period

The benefit period is the maximum length of time for which benefit payments will continue.

Short-Term Disability Benefits

Short-term disability benefits were the earliest type provided by employers and are still the most prevalent type. Short-term coverage may be an uninsured salary continuation plan or a formal short-term disability plan that replaces a portion of the employee's salary. A *salary continuation plan* or sick-leave plan continues the employee's full salary for short periods of time, ranging up to one year. The maximum period is frequently a function of the employee's length of service. These plans are more common for nonunion employees, since union employees are usually covered under an insured plan. The short-term plan most commonly provides benefits for 26 weeks or less.

Long-Term Disability Benefits

Long-term disability plans continue benefit payments for extended periods of time. Often, the plan continues payments until retirement age. Many employers that do not have a separate long-term disability plan have a disability benefit in their pension plan. If an employee becomes permanently disabled, he or she may retire on a disability benefit. A major drawback to this approach, when used exclusively, is the long period of employment (i.e., five years) that is required before the employee becomes eligible for any benefits.

Waiting Period

The *waiting period* is the length of time after the onset of a disability before benefit payments will begin. A short-term plan may have a shorter waiting period for a disability resulting from an accident than it does for a disability resulting from sickness. It is not uncommon to have first-day benefits for accidents. Waiting periods may be longer for disabilities due to sickness. Since it is easier to feign a sickness than an accident, the longer waiting period discourages unwarranted absences. It also lowers costs by eliminating claims for less serious ("sniffle") illnesses.

If an employer has both a short-term and a long-term plan, it is generally wise to have the waiting period of the long-term plan be equal to the benefit period of the short-term plan. By doing so, payments under the long-term plan begin when short-term benefits are exhausted, and there is no duplication or gap in benefits.

Definition of Disability

Contracts specifically define disability for the purpose of qualification for benefit payments. An attending physician's statement is required for proof of disability, as well as a statement by the employer indicating the date that active employment terminated. The insurance company may require a periodic physician's statement to verify the employee's continued disability. The insurer may also retain the right to have the employee examined by a physician of its choosing at its expense. Disability may be defined for short- and long-term plans as follows:

- *Short-Term Plans.* The definition of disability for short-term plans is fairly uniform. Plans typically specify *disability* as the employee's inability to perform the substantial duties of his or her regular occupation at the time of the disability. Most plans limit benefits to nonoccupational disabilities, as the employee is usually eligible for worker's compensation for disabilities that arise out of the employee's work.

- *Long-Term Plans.* A few long-term plans define disability as described above. Most plans, however, have more restrictive definitions. Typically, disability under these plans is defined in either of two ways:

  - The employee's inability to perform the substantial duties of an occupation for which he or she is reasonably trained, educated, or experienced; or

  - The inability to perform any gainful occupation.

The majority of long-term plans combine these definitions and pay benefits for a stated period (often, two years) if the employee is unable to perform his or her regular occupation. Thereafter, disability is defined as the inability to perform any gainful occupation. Most long-term plans provide benefits for both occupational and nonoccupational disabilities.

Amount of Benefits

The amount of benefit payments is frequently based on a percentage of earnings. The level of disability benefits is an important decision that the employer must make. If payments are too high, relative to the employee's predisability earnings, they provide a disincentive for the employee to return to work. Typically, the level of disability benefits ranges from 50 to 70 percent of gross earnings.

Coordination of Benefits

To further minimize the potential of over-insurance, most group disability plans are coordinated (or integrated) with other disability benefits to which the employee may be entitled. Benefits provided under the group contract are often reduced by all or a portion of benefits received under Social Security or worker's compensation and other employer-provided disability benefits. Group benefits are *not* reduced by any amounts payable under an employee's own individual coverage.

Exclusions

There are always some exclusions for which benefits will not be paid, even if the employee satisfies the definition of disability. It is normally required that the employee be under the care of a physician, unless the employee's condition is not expected to improve by such care. In the latter case, a periodic physician's statement would still be required. Other common exclusions are disabilities resulting from war, intentionally self-inflicted injuries, and preexisting conditions.

As noted previously, employers subject to the Civil Rights Act cannot exclude disabilities resulting from pregnancy. Benefits must be the same as for disabilities from any other cause. Keep in mind, however, that pregnancy in and of itself does not ensure a benefit. The employee must still satisfy the plan's definition of disability.

Rehabilitation

Many plans provide reimbursement for rehabilitation services, such as educational tuition and books or physical training to learn new skills. Benefit payments continue during retraining. A trial work period, with no cessation of payments, may be provided to encourage the employee to return to work.

Administrators

Some employers use third parties to administer various benefits, such as disability benefits. In one situation an insurance company was both the administrator and insurer for a firm's long-term disability insurance plan. In fulfilling the dual roles of administrator and insurer, respectively, the insurance company both determined the validity of employee' claims and then paid benefits to employees with valid claims. An employee initially received disability benefits after she was diagnosed with a heart disorder. Later the insurer determined she could perform sedentary work and denied her claim for further disability benefits. The U.S. Supreme Court concluded that a potential conflict of interest exists when a benefits administrator both determines the validity of a claim and pays benefits on it. Whether the conflict is fairly resolved depends upon the administrator's actions, which in this case the Court determined were unreasonable.[31]

For ethical reasons and to prevent legal problems arising from conflicts of interest like the one described above, these factors should guide administrator decisions:

- Process claims "solely in the interests of the (plan's) participants and beneficiaries."[32]
- Resolve issues fairly and impartially.
- Be open in decision-making.
- Provide opportunities for appeals of decisions.

Federal Taxation

Employer contributions to a disability plan are a tax-deductible business expense for the employer. These employer contributions are not taxable income to the employee.

Other Group Benefits

Group Legal Services Plans

A *group legal service plan* is an arrangement whereby a group of individuals contract with one or more attorneys to provide legal services for members of the group. A trust or insurance may also be established to fund for the services in advance of the need. Legal service plans are an attractive employee benefit for several reasons. Employer contributions are tax deductible as a business expense, and a portion of the employer contributions may be excluded from an employee's taxable income.

Many of the legal services provided in a legal service plan are expenses that an individual would have to pay for on an after-tax basis. The employer can provide these services at a fairly low cost, and it is generally a very appreciated benefit, particularly for those employees who have an occasion to use it. The benefit also provides legal services for many individuals who would not otherwise seek legal assistance or may not be able to afford it.

Types of Plans

In addition to being either insured or non-insured, a legal services plan may provide for *automatic* or *voluntary enrollment*. Generally, there is a higher utilization rate among participants in a voluntary plan. A plan may have either a closed or open panel of attorneys. In a *closed panel plan*, employees must use one of the

---

[31] For more information see *Metropolitan Life Insurance Co. et al. v. Glenn* (2008) in Appendix 1.

[32] Ibid.

plan's selection of staffed attorneys (fully closed) or outside attorneys (partially closed). In a *fully open plan,* employees are free to choose their own attorney. A modification to the open panel occurs when the employee's choice of attorney agrees in advance to an established maximum fee.

Services

Typical legal services provided for are wills, real estate transactions, adoptions, small claims proceedings, felony or misdemeanors, divorce, and bankruptcies.

Exclusions

Common exclusions are for services for any action against the employer, class action or similar suits, business activities, and tax-related matters. Any fines or penalties are also exclusions.

Financial Planning Services

Financial planning services have been provided as a benefit to a limited class of employees for some time. This benefit has traditionally been referred to as *financial counseling services.* The term "financial planning services" is used here to avoid confusion with counseling for employees in financial difficulty. Furthermore, "financial planning" is more descriptive of the services provided. Financial planning is for those employees with a high enough income to benefit from the service. For that reason, the plans are more prevalent among white-collar workers than blue-collar workers.

A *financial planner* evaluates an individual's financial situation and gives advice on appropriate fund allocation among financial services alternatives, such as insurance, mutual funds, and other investments. Estate planning and preparation of tax returns may also be a part of plan benefits. The financial services may be provided by a firm's own employees, outside specialists, such as attorneys, accountants, or insurance agents, or by outside providers whose advice are professional and unbiased. Using the firm's own employees has several pitfalls. The employer may be held liable for poor or bad advice. Further, employees may be hesitant to avail themselves of the services because of the confidential nature of the subject. The safest policy is for the employer to disassociate the firm from the financial planning services and simply provide reimbursement for services rendered.

Perquisites and Other Benefits

In addition to the major types of employee benefit plans already discussed, there are numerous other benefits that are often provided to employees. Taken together, these "minor" benefits may indeed be substantial. They include: automobiles; country club and professional organization dues; educational assistance; stock purchase options; purchase discounts for goods and services; credit unions; holidays; vacation days; military, jury, and other time excused; rest periods; lunch periods; subsidized lunches; child day care; and fitness health programs.

Paid Lunch and Rest Periods

Most employers do not pay their employees for their lunch break, but they do pay for rest periods. Typically, these are two 10- or 15-minute breaks each day.

Paid Holidays

Most full-time employees are provided with an average of nine paid holidays. Many plans provide "floating" days that allow employees to choose which paid holidays they want.

Paid Vacations

Most employers provide paid days of vacation after the worker has been employed a specified length of time. Typically, the average number of days are nine days for one year of service, 16 days for 10 years of service, 20 days for 20 years of service, and 22 days for 30 years of service. White-collar employees average a higher number of days than do blue-collar employees.

Dependent Day Care

As the number of dual-job parents and single-parent families continues to grow, child care becomes an increasing concern. Working parents experience stress when they worry about the care their children receive during working hours. In addition, many employees have the responsibility of caring for an elderly parent. As the number of the population over 65 years old grows, elder care will become a bigger issue.

Inadequate dependent care is an issue that affects employers. Studies show that problems associated with dependent care result in absenteeism, tardiness, and low productivity for both men and women. Also, projected labor shortages will increasingly force employers to address dependent care concerns as a means of increasing their available labor pool.

Employer day care assistance may be provided in the following ways:

- On-site or near-site facilities;
- Financial subsidies to employees who purchase day care or arrange for group discounts from day care providers;
- Information and referral services to help employees locate providers;
- Emergency child care services;
- Parental leaves; and
- Flexible work schedules that can accommodate employees in their efforts to meet day care responsibilities.

On-site or near-site facilities may be operated by the employer (or a subsidiary formed for that purpose) or by an independent agency. There are also some facilities that have been established by a consortium of employers. However, building or renovating facilities can be expensive, and this alternative can pose liability issues for the employer.

Alternatively, subsidies may be provided in the form of reimbursements for day care expenses at a facility of the employee's choosing. An employer may also establish flexible spending accounts that permit employees to set aside a portion of their incomes on a before-tax basis. The employee is reimbursed from the fund for actual day care expenses.

Several firms provide temporary child care services in emergency situations when an employee's regular child care arrangement is unavailable, such as when the child is ill. Generally, it is these short-term, unexpected situations that are the cause of most parents' absenteeism and tardiness. The Women's Bureau of the U.S. Department of Labor in Washington, D.C., provides considerable information and technical assistance for employers that are interested in establishing family-related employment programs. This assistance can aid in the design of a program and give examples of actual employers' programs in operation.

Flexible Spending Accounts

The Internal Revenue Code (IRC) permits the establishment of *flexible spending accounts*, also known as *flexible spending arrangements* or *flexible reimbursement accounts*, that permit employees to pay for certain types of benefit expenses with pretax dollars. Separate accounts may be established each year for these types of IRS-qualified plans:

- Medical plans (IRC Section 105);

- Accident and health plans (IRC Section 106);

- Group legal plans (IRC Section 120);

- Dependent care (IRC Section 129), subject to a $5,000 maximum for married persons filing a joint return and $2,500 for those filing a single return;

- Group life insurance plans, up to $50,000 in insurance (IRC Section 79);

- Deferred compensation plans (IRC Section 401(k)).

- Transportation expenses (IRC Section 132(f)).

The transportation provision permits employers to offer employees the opportunity to set aside a portion of their salary to pay for mass transportation and parking expenses. The limit for mass transportation expenses, such as fares for buses, subway and trains, is $110 per month. Parking expenses are limited to $215 per month. Separate accounts must be maintained for both types of expenses; that is, they cannot be co-mingled.

For most flexible spending accounts, employees must determine the funding amount prior to the beginning of a plan year. All elections by employees are irrevocable during the year. Unused funds are forfeited and cannot be transferred from one account to another or received in cash. There is an exception to this "use or lose it" rule for transportation expenses. Amounts that are left over in the reimbursement accounts for transportation expenses are refunded to the employee in the following year.

Long-Term Care

The cost of long-term care is becoming an increasing concern to Americans. People are living longer, and the number of individuals over 65 is expected to increase as the "baby boom" generation ages. Nursing home care is expensive, and coverage is generally excluded under health care plans. Social Security does not cover extended stays in nursing homes. Still, few employers provide long-term care insurance. Most employers offer it only on an employee-pays-all basis. Care for or worry about the health of an aged parent may have a negative impact on an employee's productivity. As the number of elderly individuals in our society increases, this employment issue will become a greater concern to employers.

Educational Assistance

Educational assistance programs are a popular benefit for employees. Some employers require that reimbursement be for a job-related course. Many employers, however, reimburse employees for any course used to fulfill the requirement of a related course of study, such as a business degree. Reimbursement may include tuition only or tuition plus books. Subject to a maximum limit of $5,250, employer-supplied educational assistance for both graduate and undergraduate courses is excludible from employee income for federal taxes.[33] Some employers provide loans, educational leaves of absence, and scholarships for dependents.

---

[33] CCH Human Resources Management, *Ideas and Trends in Personnel* (June 13, 2001), p. 92.

CHAPTER 20
COUNSELING

Chapter Highlights
- Personal problems of employees
- Costs of troubled employees
- Preventing and assisting employee problems
- Types of counseling programs

Introduction

There is a long history of employers providing counseling assistance to employees to help them reach their employment goals and deal with their personal problems. In fact, personnel administration, which was the original term for HRM, was an outgrowth of industrial social work. Ordway Tead, who was originally an industrial social worker, was a pioneer in the field of personnel administration. Over time, counseling programs have become more formalized.

Types of Counseling

The three types of counseling are:

- *Giving basic information,* such as informing a supervisor of the best way to complete a performance appraisal form;

- *Providing technical advice and assistance,* such as counseling an employee about career planning; and

- *Administering professional therapy,* such as drug rehabilitation counseling.

Effective HRM incorporates all three types of counseling. Counseling programs may be staffed with either in-house personnel or external providers. Some programs have a combination of in-house staffing and external operation. In-house programs may be operated either full- or part-time, depending upon such variables as the commitment of top management, the size of the organization, the professional expertise available in-house, and the perceived need. In most cases, professional therapy, such as alcoholism or mental illness counseling, is administered by external service providers.

Counseling is basic, technical, and, in some cases, professional assistance given by qualified individuals.

Counseling subjects can be categorized into personal problems and career-related problems. Exhibit 20-1 shows the subjects in the two groups.

Exhibit 20-1
Counseling Programs

Personal Problem Counseling	Career-Related Counseling
Alcohol	Career planning
Compulsive gambling	Dual careers
Drugs	Expatriation/repatriation
Emotional and mental	Leisure
Family and marital	Mid-life
Financial	Outplacement
Legal	Performance appraisal
	Relocation
	Retirement
	Wellness

Employee Personal Problem Counseling

Twenty percent of the U.S. workforce is troubled by one or more personal problems to the extent their work is adversely affected. This group of employees, although only 20 percent of a typical employer's workforce, cause 80 percent of all employee deficiencies in attendance, conduct, productivity, safety, and work quality. Exhibit 20-2 illustrates the potential problems and losses caused by troubled employees.

A few examples will demonstrate the costs caused by employee personal problems. One study found that alcoholic employees seek assistance from health benefit plans three times more frequently than nonalcoholic employees.[1] Another study found that 65 percent of terminations involved employees with emotional problems.[2] Other studies found the rate of employee absences for alcoholics was double that for nonalcoholics, and problem employees had accident rates that were 3.6 times higher than a control group of non-problem employees.

Exhibit 20-2
Problems and Losses of Troubled Employees

Accidents	Attendance	Conduct	Crime
Damage	Emergency absences	Apathetic	Assault
Disability payments	Failure to report	Cursing	Embezzlement
Insurance claims	Leaving assignment	Failure to follow	Murder
Insurance premiums	Personal needs abuse	instructions	Sabotage
Lawsuits	Tardy	Moody	Security breaches
Medical expenses		Unkempt appearance	Theft

---

[1] Marchesini, E.P., "The Advantages of Employee Assistance Programs," *Labor-Management Alcoholism Journal* 10 (May/June 1981), p. 237.

[2] Liebowitz, B., "Employee Assistance Programs as an Employee Benefit and as Risk Management," *Employee Benefits Journal* (March 1982), p. 15.

Discipline	Health	Productivity	Work Quality
Discharge	Disability payments	Below standard	Complaints
Grievance	Insurance claims	Decline	Defects
Suspensions	Insurance premiums	Erratic	Errors
Warning letters	Sick leave	Wastes time	Lawsuits
			Rejects
			Waste

There is also abundant evidence that troubled employees lead unhappy, if not tragic, lives. Experts believe most of the suicides occurring in the U.S. each year are caused by depression. In one case, a father wrote a note, stating that he could not cope with "severe money problems." He killed his wife and three children before committing suicide.[3]

History of Helping Troubled Employees

There is a rich history of employer initiatives to assist employees in the workplace. From 1875 to 1930, many firms employed psychologists, counselors, psychiatrists, and "welfare secretaries" to establish industrial human service programs. Some employers used industrial social workers to counter union organizing. The major reason that human service practitioners left industrial positions was that they felt that employer demands upon them, such as opposing employee unionization, compelled them to compromise their professional training and standards.

Employers also used human service professionals to assist in the selection and placement of personnel. Still others, such as the R.H. Macy Company, used various professionals, including psychiatrists, social workers, psychiatric case workers, and psychologists, to assist troubled employees. Macy's approach used job deficiencies to identify troubled employees. Treatment for troubled employees included counseling and job reassignment, if it appeared that job conditions were either causing or contributing to an employee's problem.

Among the other early efforts to assist workers was the famous personnel counseling study in the Hawthorne Works of the Western Electric Company. The study started in 1927 when one personnel counselor position was established for each 300 employees. The role of the counselors was to assist employees with personal problems, work pressures, formal organizational changes, changes in technology, and job change problems.

Another early form of employee assistance was *pastoral counseling*, also known as *industrial chaplaincy*. These programs were started during World War II because of the personal and family problems caused by relocations, the stress of working long hours in factories, and the separation from family members in the military. Today, there are approximately 48 full-time industrial chaplains employed in different organizations.

The roots of modern-day employee assistance counseling can be traced to industrial alcoholism programing that began at E.I. du Pont Nemours in 1942. A

---

[3] "Police Say Money Woes May Cause Deaths," *Richmond Times-Dispatch* (April 6, 1983), p. B-4.

program was established by Dr. George Gehrmann, who was the company's Medical Director. Supervisors confronted deficient employees and, if they were thought to have problems with alcohol, the individuals were referred to Dr. Gehrmann. Dr. Gehrmann would make an assessment of the individuals and refer those with alcohol problems to Alcoholics Anonymous. This approach is no longer used. Today, supervisors focus on performance deficiencies, referring deficient performers to the firm's counselor, who assesses whether a personal problem is contributing to the deficiency.

One of the biggest boosts to employee assistance programming was a 1971 federal grant for each state to hire two occupational program consultants. The principal tasks of the consultants were to assist employers in establishing programs to prevent, treat, and rehabilitate employees who were alcoholics or alcohol abusers. These consultants were extremely successful in educating employers about the existence of alcoholism and alcohol abuse among employees. The consultants also were effective in demonstrating how occupational assistance programs could use the performance appraisal system as an instrument for confronting deficient performers and referring them to a counselor trained to handle the denial syndrome of alcoholics and to refer them for treatment. This performance-confrontation model is still an essential part of the operating philosophy of contemporary employee assistance counseling. Gradually, the focus on alcoholism and alcohol abuse widened to include other personal problems, including compulsive gambling, indebtedness, and mental illness.

Employee Assistance Programs

A Strategy to Help Troubled Employees

Employers implement employee assistance programs (EAPs) to prevent and treat the problems of troubled employees and, thereby, reduce the costs and job deficiencies they cause, and to prevent and reduce the suffering that they experience. As noted in Chapter 18, 40 percent of employees in private industry have access to an employee assistance program.[4]

Employee assistance programs are employer-provided programs operated either in-house or by external sources to prevent employee problems and treat and rehabilitate troubled employees.

There are several different forms of EAPs. Some programs handle only one or two problems, usually alcohol and drug abuse. Other programs handle all types of personal problems. Some programs operate exclusively through a hotline telephone service. Other programs have on-site EAP counselors, supported by in-house and external medical professionals and specialists. The typical "staff" of an EAP consists of a counselor, who is either an employee of the organization or employed by an external provider, who provides counseling

---

[4] Bureau of Labor Statistics, *National Compensation Survey: Employee Benefits in Private Industry in the United States, March 2006*, (March 2006), p. 30.

services. Most often, supervisors refer all deficient performers to the counselor, who assesses any problems the employee may have and refers the person to a qualified service provider. Some counselors are also qualified to render treatment, such as certified alcohol counselors or marriage counselors.

EAPs can be operated exclusively by the employer, by employer-union cooperative arrangements, or exclusively by unions. Some union or peer programs also have a confrontation component, in which specially trained union members are alert for behavioral symptoms and job deficiencies that indicate that a member needs help. One program of this type is operated by the Association of Airline Flight Attendants.

EAPs receive referrals from various sources. In addition to supervisory referrals and referrals by peers or union members, cooperation is solicited from family members. Most programs also try to motivate self-referrals of troubled employees. Many programs, especially those where employee acceptance is high, have a large proportion of self-referrrals in their client caseload.

Confidentiality

Confidentiality of client/counselor discussions is an important component in employee assistance counseling. Employees must have confidence that information disclosed in counseling sessions remains confidential. Federal courts have ruled matters discussed between employees and counselors in EAP sessions are privileged.[5] In addition, some states have laws protected the confidentiality of EAP counseling sessions.[6]

An important component of the Health Insurance Portability and Accountability Act was safeguards against the improper disclosure of an individual's health information. The Department of Health and Human Services (DHHS) is responsible for providing procedures to protect against any improper disclosures. As part of this responsibility, DHHS issued *Privacy Rules* (Rules). Firms and others covered (called "covered entities") by the Rules may use or disclose individuals' *Protected Health Information* (PHI) only with their written consent. There are both civil and criminal penalties for violating these provisions. See Chapter 19 for a full discussion of the requirements.

Drugs in the Workplace

A survey conducted by the Substance Abuse and Mental Health Services Administration found that 15 percent of employees who were illicit drug users and 6 percent of employees who were heavy alcohol users said they went to work high or a little drunk during the past year.[7] Studies have shown substance-abusing employees are:

- Six times more likely to be absent from work.
- Nine times more likely to use sick leave.
- Five times more likely to file workers' compensation claims.[8]

---

[5] *Oksana Oleszko v. State Compensation Insurance* (2001), 9th U.S. Court of Appeals, 99-15207.

[6] Ibid.

[7] Substance Abuse and Mental Health Services, *Fact Sheet: Workplace Substance Abuse*, November 1998.

[8] Ibid.

Drug-Free Workplace Act of 1988

The Drug-Free Workplace Act applies to employers with federal contracts of $100,000 or more. The act requires employers to:

- Publish a policy statement that the unlawful manufacture, distribution, dispensation, possession, or use of a controlled substance is prohibited in the workplace and setting out the actions that will be taken for policy violations;

- Establish a drug-free awareness program to inform employees about the dangers of drug abuse, the employer's policy about a drug-free workplace, the existence of an EAP to help employees with drug-related problems, and the penalties for drug abuse violations;

- Provide each employee with a copy of the policy statement;

- Affirm that employees must abide by this policy and notify the employer of any violations within five days of convictions for drug violations that occurred in the workplace;

- Notify the agency that awarded the contract of any reported violation;

- Impose sanctions or require drug treatment by any employee who violates the policy; and

- Make a good-faith effort to maintain a drug-free workplace.

Return to Work Agreements

Sometimes, when employees have been disciplined or placed on leave without pay while receiving treatment for drug use, an employer will negotiate a *return to work* agreement with the employee. These arrangements are agreements between an employer and employee in which the employee agrees to certain stipulations, such as regular attendance at counseling sessions and submission to drug testing, in return for continued employment. Such agreements also specify that any violation will result in the employee's discharge.

Career-Related Counseling

Career-related counseling subjects are shown above in Exhibit 20-1. Several of these subjects are covered elsewhere in this book. *Career planning* is discussed in Chapter 34, *expatriation/repatriation* counseling is covered in Chapter 38, *performance appraisal* counseling is explained in Chapter 29, and *wellness* counseling is examined in Chapter 21.

Dual-Career Counseling

Dual career marriages are those in which both spouses are employed. Approximately 80 percent of all households are dual-career households.[9] One reason for the increase in dual-career marriages is the increased participation of women in the labor force. By 2014, women in the labor force are projected to number approximately 79 million for a 9.9 percent increase from 2005. The number of

---

[9] CCH INCORPORATED, *Ideas and Trends in Personnel,* March 22, 2000.

men is projected to total 86 million, which is a 7.7 increase during the same period.[10]

Husbands in dual-career marriages must adjust to new household roles, such as cooking, baby-sitting, and house cleaning. They also must adjust to their wives' work roles, which will likely involve some or all of the following: overnight travel, office problems, long work hours, and work that is brought home at night and on weekends.

In addition to marital problems caused by adjustments to a dual-career marriage, some job deficiencies may appear. Most notably, attendance problems may occur as both spouses must share child care responsibilities, such as staying home to care for an ill child. Sudden out-of-town trips or extraordinary work commitments of one spouse may shift all the household responsibilities to the other spouse. These additional family burdens may be evident on the job through substandard productivity and work quality. Dual-career marriages may also constrain an employee's mobility.

Employers can assist dual-career couples by providing child care assistance, by using special work scheduling methods, by providing flexible benefit plans that help dual-career couples choose benefits to fit their unique situations, and by counseling spouses on such subjects as household and child care responsibilities, lifestyles and career goals, and stress-related problems.

Leisure Counseling

Leisure counseling is the process of helping people meet their leisure needs, such as autonomy and creativity, in both their private and work lives. Employers have traditionally provided leisure assistance to employees, such as company-sponsored athletic teams, which provide constructive outlets for employees' physical needs. They also help build employee morale and company loyalty and increase efficiency. Some employers believe that leisure programs help prevent potential problems, such as grievances and union organizing. Employers also develop leisure programs to fulfill their social responsibilities to help employees develop their potentialities. Finally, these programs can help create public good-will and/or publicize the company's products.

The eight typical properties of leisure are: (1) autonomy, (2) intrinsic rewards, (3) personal commitment, (4) time unconsciousness, (5) physical or mental escape, (6) use of personal creativity, (7) freedom from structure, and (8) anticipated or actual excitement. The priorities of these eight properties vary among people and vary at different times for the same person. Some or all of these eight properties can be present in either work or nonwork experiences. For some people, their work is their leisure. Robert Frost, the poet, once remarked that his vocation was his avocation.

Job enrichment characteristics, such as autonomy and task significance, are similar in some ways to leisure properties. Through techniques such as job enrichment, management can structure jobs so that they are more enjoyable to

---

[10] U.S. Bureau of Labor Statistics, *Total Labor Force: 2005 - 2014.*

perform. Through informal counseling programs and discussions with individual employees, employers can determine whether employees are properly placed or whether reassignments or other changes can be made to ensure a better job-person fit.

Midlife Career Counseling

Midlife career counseling is the process of assisting employees with the physical, social, and psychological adjustments of midlife, affecting both work and nonwork life. Midlife occurs between 35 and 45 years of age and is a major transitional period in the personal and career lives of most individuals. In one study, 80 percent of 1,000 male managers and professionals admitted experiencing midlife transition problems; 16 percent of them also reported that they never fully adapted to the change.[11]

Midlife Counseling Purposes

There are two basic purposes motivating employers to assist employees with midlife career counseling. First, the self-doubt and personal unhappiness that often appear in midlife are frequently reflected in diminished job performance. Second, employers also have humanitarian motives for helping employees through this major transition in life. These two purposes are not antithetical, since helping employees for humanitarian reasons will generally have a favorable impact upon organizational efficiency.

Internal Causes of Midlife Crisis

People with midlife problems exhibit a number of symptoms, First, midlifers begin to question their values and their ideas of the meaning of success. These feelings occur even among highly successful managers and professionals. In fact, these groups also tend to feel uncomfortable about their career success.[12] This disquietude causes two self-assessments. First, particularly in their late 30s, midlifers experience the feeling that they have one last opportunity to be really successful in their careers. A second self-assessment comes a few years later, when they realize that one's work life is half over, and there is insufficient time left to accomplish either those long-sought goals or those newly developed from a reappraisal of the meaning of success.

Midlifers also are frustrated by their personal convictions of job fulfillment, yet they find themselves growing stale or performing routine and monotonous work. These feelings cause considerable internal conflict. Midlifers want to seek new careers, but they feel compelled to remain in their current jobs because of fear of the unknown and fear of financial loss. Midlifers know their jobs, even though they are bored with them, and they fear starting a new career. Most importantly, they fear failure. Often, they have accumulated substantial pension rights, and they dread the prospects of losing them. Another financial obstacle is

---

[11] Sheehy, G., *Passages, Predictable Crises of Adult Life* (New York: Bantam Books, 1976), p. 350.

[12] Korman, A.K., Wittig-Berman, V., and Lan, D., "Career Success and Personal Failure: Alienaton in Professionals and Managers," *Academy of Management Journal* 24 (June 1981): 342.

their current income; midlifers usually have moderate or better incomes, and they fear risking them for the unknown.

Midlife is also a period in which minor physical problems surface, which are unpleasant reminders of the aging process. Bifocals may become necessary, stamina is probably reduced, new wrinkles appear and old ones deepen, hairlines may recede, and chronic aches and pains start to appear. These physical symptoms, when combined with society's emphasis upon youth, contribute to feelings of inadequacy and unattractiveness.

Finally, midlife is the period when the inevitability of death becomes apparent. A friend or associate may suffer a terminal illness or other affliction, such as a heart attack. Midlifers, for perhaps the first time in their lives, realize their mortality. Experts believe that, prior to age 30, individuals give little or no thought to death; however, this changes in midlife.

External Causes of Midlife Crisis

The three major external causes of midlife crisis are societal emphasis upon youth, myths about aging, and employment discrimination against midlifers. The U.S. is a youth-orientation culture; this leads to the view that older people are more of a burden than an asset. This emphasis upon youth tends to perpetuate the myths that people over the age of 40 are inflexible, lack creativity, and lack commitment. None of these myths are supported by documented studies, but they still persist. When such myths spill over into the work environment, they may result in considerable discrimination.

Assisting Midlife Employees

Employers can assist midlifers through both career and personal counseling. Some counseling subjects are shown in Exhibit 20-3. In the area of career planning, employers should assist midlifers to reassess their interests. Job opportunities should be made available to midlifers on the same basis as they are to other employees. Training and development courses should also be offered to midlifers, just as they are to other employees. Midlifers should be encouraged to apply for career opportunities without fear of job discrimination.

Exhibit 20-3
Counseling Midlife Employees

Career	Personal
Assess interests	Midlife stages
Job opportunities	Cathartic relief
Training & development	Recognize accomplishments
Encouragement	Future goals
Nondiscrimination	Professional referral

Counseling for midlifers should include educating them about the various fears people experience in midlife. The counselors should encourage a free exchange of information and, thereby, provide some cathartic relief. As with all other individuals, midlifers need to be recognized for their accomplishments and should also be encouraged to formulate or refocus their goals for the future. Where necessary, counselors should obtain professional assistance for midlifers who are profoundly depressed or who exhibit other symptoms requiring treatment.

Outplacement Counseling

Outplacement counseling is the process of ending a person's employment in one organization and assisting him or her in securing a position in another one. The purposes of outplacement programs are to:

- Help exiting employees secure employment;
- Reduce the stress on exiting employees;
- Promote goodwill;
- Prevent legal problems; and
- Aid managers.

Secure Employment

A primary purpose of outplacement counseling is to help exiting employees find other jobs. Many separations, particularly layoffs, can be planned to allow a sufficient lead period for employees to remain employed until other jobs are found. Often, employees are unaware of labor markets and do not know the best way to begin a job search. Outplacement counselors can facilitate the process by helping employees develop leads and arrange employment interviews.

Reduce Stress

Separations are stressful, regardless of the reason. For example, layoffs can be as stressful as discharges, since both situations cause loss of income and economic uncertainty. Involuntary separations, such as layoffs and discharges, are ranked eighth out of 43 different stressful social situations. This stress can produce various reactions, ranging from mild ones, such as anxiety and feelings of inadequacy, to the more serious, including substance abuse to severe depression. Involuntary separations may cause employees to question their abilities and their self esteem. Paradoxically, this is an inopportune time for these feelings to occur, since job searches and interviews require mental discipline and self-confidence. Outplacement counseling does not eliminate the stress, but it helps by providing the employee with emotional and financial support and professional training in locating a suitable job.

Promote Goodwill

Outplacement assistance can promote goodwill among remaining employees, as well as those who will be outplaced. Layoffs and discharges, particularly when they appear to be done in a capricious and arbitrary manner, cause disquietude among employees, who may wonder, "Will I be next?" Also, employees who feel that they have been treated unfairly may harbor grudges. Officials of internal security firms caution employers about the dangers of causing employees to feel embittered towards them. Vandalism, theft of company property, deliberate errors, stolen records, and other types of negative behavior have resulted from employee hostility caused by discharges.

Prevent Legal Problems

Outplacement counseling may also help prevent legal problems. For example, outplacing employees may dissuade them from filing lawsuits, alleging violations of implicit or explicit employment contracts. Outplacement may also prevent equal employment opportunity complaints, if employees who are separated from service are members of protected groups. Where unions are involved, employees may access grievance procedures to delay the implementation of layoffs and discharges. Some state laws and state courts have imposed limitations on the employer's right to discharge employees. These constraints typically regulate wrongful discharges for such reasons as allegations of minimum wage violations or discriminatory acts. Furthermore, case law is broadening to include some instances of employer bad faith in discharging employees. Outplacement can help prevent these negative outcomes.

Any actions to lay off, reduce hours, or terminate employees must be taken in compliance with the Older Workers' Benefit Protection Act and the Worker Adjustment and Retraining Notification Act. COBRA rights may also be involved in these actions.

Older Workers Benefit Protection Act

Often, older workers are targeted for job abolishment because they are usually among the most highly paid workers in an organization. Workers who are age 40 and over are protected from employment discrimination resulting from such targeting by the Age Discrimination in Employment Act (ADEA). Usually, employers will provide incentives to older workers to encourage them to waive their rights to file discrimination charges under the ADEA. However, the Older Worker Benefit Protection Act prohibits employees who are age 40 and over from waiving their rights under the ADEA, such as the right to file a charge of discrimination, as part of an agreement between an employee and the employer unless these conditions are met:

- The waiver offer is written so that the average person to whom the waiver would apply can understand it.

- The waiver offer includes the specific rights employees have under the ADEA.

- The employee does not waive any rights that may exist after the date of the waiver.

- The waiver is in exchange for something of value beyond which the employee is already entitled.

- The employee is advised in writing to consult with an attorney prior to executing the waiver.

- The employee is given 45 days to consider the waiver and the terms of the agreement, if an incentive is offered or other termination program is offered to a class of employees; otherwise, a 21-day consideration period is required.

- The employee is given seven days to revoke the waiver agreement after he or she has signed it.

- If an incentive or other termination program is offered, the employer must inform the employees at the beginning of the 45-day notice period of the class of persons covered by the program, the eligibility terms, the time limits, and the job titles and ages of those persons who are eligible or selected for the program and those who were not eligible or selected.

Worker Adjustment and Retraining Notification Act (WARNA)

WARNA applies to firms with 100 or more full-time employees. Employers must give employees (or their representative, if there is one) 60 days' advance notice in the event of a mass layoff or a plant closure.

- A *mass layoff* is the loss of employment (which includes layoffs exceeding six months in duration and reductions in the hours of work of more than 50 percent of employees during each month in a six-month period) within a 30-day period at a single site of either: (1) at least 33 percent of the full-time workforce and at least 50 full-time persons, or (2) 500 full-time employees.

- A *plant closure* is the permanent or temporary shutdown of one employment site or one or more facilities or operating units in a single site during a 30-day period in which 50 or more full-time employees lose their employment.

Employers must notify the state dislocated worker unit and the chief elected official of the local political unit in which the layoff or closing will occur. The 60-day notice period may be reduced for any of these conditions:

- If the employer was attempting to secure financing that would have prevented either the layoff or the closing, and the advance notice would have precluded them from obtaining financing;

- If business conditions prevent the employer from giving the advance notice; or

- If a natural disaster occurred that caused the layoff or closure.

Employers that fail to give the required notice are liable for back pay and benefits for each day of the required notice period and, in certain cases, civil penalties of $500 per day.

Consolidated Budget Reconciliation Act (COBRA): Continuation of Health Benefits

Employers with 20 or more employees must offer continued health benefit coverage for 18 months after a reduction in hours or termination of employment. A person who becomes disabled within 60 days of coverage under COBRA can receive an additional 11 months (thus having 29 months of total coverage, the same as an employee who was disabled at the time of termination of employment) of COBRA coverage. The cost to the employee is 102 percent of the entire premium (150 percent for months 19 through 29, if disabled). COBRA benefits stop if:

- The employee becomes eligible for another health benefits plan and does not have pre-existing conditions that are excluded under the new plan;

- The employee becomes eligible for Medicare;
- The employer discontinues the health benefits plan; or
- The employee does not pay scheduled premiums.

For a full discussion of COBRA, see Chapter 19.

Aid Managers

Outplacement can reduce the pressure managers experience when they discharge employees. Undoubtedly, some managers avoid discharging employees because they cannot handle the stress and/or the employee's reactions to the discharge. These managers tolerate unacceptable performance because they are psychologically unable or unwilling to communicate a discharge decision. Outplacement does not eliminate the stress, because the manager still must tell an employee he or she will be discharged. However, the manager is able to counter some employees' reactions, such as tears or anger, by offering outplacement assistance.

Reasons for Outplacement

The need for outplacement is motivated by the causes for employee separations, as shown in Exhibit 20-4, below.

Employee Reasons

Employees have various reasons for leaving a job. Initially, one might question the wisdom of giving outplacement assistance to an employee who voluntarily is seeking another job. Some employers even have a policy of immediately discharging an employee who is suspected of looking for another job. Such a policy is a bad practice, since it causes employees to use secrecy in their job search and generates retribution motives in discharged employees.

Exhibit 20-4
Reasons for Employee Separations

| Employee | Organizational | | |
	Employment Needs	Deficient Performance	Other
Career	Product demand	Incompatibility	New team
Family	Business cycle	Personal problems	No confidence
Financial	Plant relocation	Job growth	New blood
Health	Technology		
Climate			
Physical			
Transitional			

There are valid reasons both for employees to seek a change of employment and for employers to provide those employees with outplacement assistance in their job searches. First, employees may have career reasons for getting in the job market. The employee may be seeking a job opportunity that does not exist with the present employer. For example, an employee may have recently earned a college degree and wants a job that will permit him to use this education. Employers would be foolish to impede such an employee's job search, if they are unable to offer a suitable job opportunity. An employee may also simply want to change careers or enter a new field of work. The employee may feel burnt-out or need rejuvenation in a different employment setting. Other career reasons are dissatisfaction with a current field of work or failure to adapt to new developments. Regardless of the reason, employers are advised to offer some basic form of outplacement assistance.

Family considerations may also motivate an employee to seek a job with another employer; for example, in order to live near an elderly parent or to move after a traumatic family event, such as a divorce. Financial reasons, such as assuming a financial burden due to medical expenses or even receiving an inheritance, may motivate a desire for a job change. Sometimes, financial counseling can help in such cases, but, in the final analysis, the employee must make the decision whether to change jobs.

As the population gets older and as more elderly employees remain in the workforce, employers can expect an increase in job changes due to health and other reasons. Often, the reason for the job change may be to relocate to a warmer climate.

Employees may have transitional reasons for seeking jobs with other employers. For example, an employee approaching retirement may want to reduce her employment obligations through either a reduction in work hours or a reversion to a less-demanding job.

Organizational Reasons

Employers may be compelled to outplace employees due to a change in employment requirements caused by declines in product/service demand, a downswing in the business cycle, or a plant relocation. In some industries, changing technology is a major reason for a decline in employment levels. Robotics and new production methods have also increased the need for outplacement, as employment opportunities decline. Some experts believe that the rate of technological displacement will substantially increase in the future.

Human resource planning will reduce, but not eliminate, the problem of excess staffing. For example, market surveys and other demand projections can help anticipate reductions in employment levels. When these trends are observed, various strategies, such as using temporary or part-time help and allowing normal attrition to reduce the excess in the workforce, can preclude some outplacement.

Typically, job deficiencies are considered the major cause of outplacement. If possible, job reassignment, additional training, or even a job restructuring should be considered before a decision is made to outplace a deficient employee. This recognizes that performance deficiencies may result from employee-job incompatibility. A reassignment may eliminate the problem by moving the employee to a job he or she can perform. In addition, the environment or demands of the job, such as regular overnight travel, may cause family problems that spill over into the employee's work performance.

In some cases, the deficiencies may be due to unrealistic job expectations or inadequate training. For example, a college accounting student on a work internship was assigned a complex role on an audit team for a major accounting firm. The team leader was an exceptional person who assumed everyone knew as much as he did. This assumption was reflected in the inadequate orientation the student received from the team leader. The student was embarrassed to ask for additional explanations, and he did not demonstrate his true capabilities in either the quality or quantity of work he produced.

Finally, job deficiencies can result when job demands change, but the employee is not capable of adapting to them. This problem occurs with greater frequency in high technology fields, where conditions are continually changing and employees continually face challenges that increase in intensity. An employee may have been well-qualified for the job when initially hired but, due to rapid changes, the job gradually outdistances him or her. A similar situation occurs when employees are promoted, based upon their present job performance, rather than an assessment of their potential for a new job. The humane way to handle these mismatches is through reassignment or job restructuring; outplacement should be the last alternative.

When top management is replaced, the newcomers often start to work on recruiting a "new team." Inevitably, this means outplacement for some managers. Often, poor performance or a major problem within a plant or division means that, "Some heads will roll," and outplacement counselors begin work. Sometimes, a "lack of confidence" in a manager or simply a perceived need for "new blood" results in outplacement for someone. Many of these reasons lack validity, but they do occur.

Employment During Outplacement

While an employee is involved in outplacement, the employment arrangements with the existing employer differ among firms. Non-managerial employees who receive advance notices of pending layoffs remain employed until they either find another job or the layoff date is reached. Typically, managerial employees continue receiving their existing salary until they are outplaced. However, they do not normally remain in their old jobs because the outplacement activities require their full energies.

Performing Outplacement

Outplacement may be performed internally or externally, by outplacement and consulting firms. Some outplacement assistance may also be offered either solely by unions or jointly by unions and management. The two types of internal outplacement are individual outplacement and group outplacement.

Individual Outplacement

Individualized outplacement varies considerably, depending upon the size of the organization. Some of the very largest organizations have in-house specialists who work full-time outplacing employees. Smaller organizations either use functional specialists to assist in certain outplacement activities or assign all outplacement tasks to one person. Using functional specialists has some advantages because they have expertise within specific areas. For example, placement and recruiting personnel usually know which organizations have vacancies.

These specialists also know their counterparts in other organizations and/or they belong to groups, such as the Employment Management Association, that focus on employment-related activities. These contacts can be beneficial in helping an outplaced employee develop employment leads. Employment specialists also can give advice on various steps in the application process, such as preparing resumes, applying for jobs, preparing for job interviews, and dressing in appropriate attire for employment interviews.

Many of these skills, while rudimentary, are forgotten when a person has been employed for awhile and is not searching for a job. Other applicant skills may also be deficient, such as how to respond to interviewer questions, what questions to ask the interviewer, and what conditions, if any, the applicant should seek if a job is offered. In-house human resource development specialists can help in these areas by conducting mock interviews and role-playing sessions.

Other internal specialists can provide advice and assistance; for example, compensation and benefit specialists can explain what benefits, such as group life insurance, that the outplaced employee may have. Conversion provisions that give outplaced employees the right to change from group to individual benefit plans can be explained. Compensation personnel can also brief the outplaced employee on current pay and benefit trends within the employee's occupation. This information can help the employee formulate realistic compensation expectations and can help him or her determine any changes that may be needed in the family budget.

Finally, EAP counselors can help the employee with any personal problems precipitated by the outplacement. Employees can divulge their feelings to the counselor and receive assistance in such areas as financial counseling and stress reduction. Professional assistance, such as mental health therapy, can be provided or appropriate referrals may be made. Moderate or severe reactions, including substance abuse and emotional problems, often accompany job loss. Personal problem counseling can treat this suffering and prevent the tragic consequences that may result.

General Outplacement Services

Generalized outplacement services are not necessarily less effective simply because they are not specifically or individually designed for each outplaced employee. For example, a consumer products manufacturer abolished a manufacturing facility. Employees were given almost a full year's notice of the planned action. During the interim, the company placed announcements in the help-wanted section of the local newspaper. The ads explained the reason for the job abolishments and the types of employees involved, and encouraged prospective employers to contact the company.

Some companies also provide on-site interviewing space for prospective employers' convenience. General assistance typically includes group meetings, where outplaced employees are advised of their rights to benefits, and workshops, where basic job-seeking skills, such as interviewing and preparing applications, are taught. Sometimes, general assistance also includes job clearinghouse functions, such as posting notices of job vacancies in the community.

Outplacement Firms

Several points should be considered in selecting an outplacement firm. First, there may be advantages to selecting a local firm over a national one, provided that the local job market contains sufficient employment opportunities for the employees targeted for outplacement. If the local job market is too small or if the jobs involved require searching in a broader geographical areas, a regional or national firm may be best.

Second, some experts feel a firm that only deals in outplacement is preferable to one that offers a variety of management consulting services. The rationale is that consulting firms may have a conflict of interest if they are providing both outplacement and employee search services. A few associations of recruiting firms have ethical codes prohibiting members from providing outplacement services.

It is also advisable to check the track record of an outplacement firm before contracting with it. Reference information might include the percentage of individuals who received job offers, the number of placements, the starting salary of those who were placed, and an opinion survey from former employees who received the firm's services.

These are the typical services provided by outplacement firms (it should be noted that not every firm provides all these services):

- Meet the client and provide an orientation of outplacement, including the procedures and role responsibilities of both the client and the outplacement firm;
- Administer diagnostic instruments, including vocational interest questionnaires and self-assessment profiles;
- Discuss the diagnostic test results with the client and select the jobs that best match the client's income needs, interests, and qualifications;
- Help the client prepare resumes;
- Give the client advice on proper attire and use interview role-playing to prepare the client for employment interviews;
- Help the client develop employment leads through former business associates, professional associations, and known job vacancies;
- Educate the client in on-line recruiting networks, including *CareerOneStop,* and *America's Talent Bank*;
- Review the client's progress in mailing resumes, making follow-up telephone calls, and developing a network of employment leads;
- Conduct additional role-playing specifically designed for particular job interviews or negotiating employment conditions;
- Review the clients' efforts in securing leads and arranging interviews and positively reinforce progress; and
- Terminate relationship when the client obtains a job.

Outplacement firms also offer a range of other services for both employers and clients. Some of the employer services include reviewing the adequacy of severance arrangements and advising management on the optimum methods for conducting termination interviews. Care should be taken to avoid any conflict of interest between services provided to employees and commitments made to employers. For example, one outplacement firm was accused of acquiescing to an employer's demand to steer ex-employees away from employment opportunities with competitors.[13] Employee services include financial counseling, administrative and clerical assistance for resume preparation, answering services for telephone messages, and office space and telephone service. Some outplacement firms also maintain job banks to aid clients' job search activities.

Relocation Counseling

For most employees in fast-track positions, destined for higher level ones, relocation is a frequent requirement. Also, some employees are relocated due to the discontinuance of their jobs. *Relocation counseling* assists employees in the economic, social, and psychological adjustments required by job relocations. An employee may be relocated for any of the following reasons:

- The employee is considered the best qualified for the vacancy that occurred;

- The relocation will provide the employee with work experience in a specific area or function or in a particular job; or

- The employee requests the relocation.

Effects on Employees

Relocation affects virtually every dimension of an employee's life. Some effects are positive, while others are negative. The major effects are on the employee's career, financial condition, family relations, and lifestyle. Career changes usually involve greater job challenge, more responsibility, and other increased intrinsic rewards. Extrinsic rewards also usually result from a relocation because of increased pay and more perquisites. Relocations usually have a profound impact upon an employee's economic position, in addition to changes in pay. Some of these changes are due to changes in state and local taxes, real estate values and interest rates, moving expenses, and commuting and other transportation expenses.

The employee's family is also profoundly affected by relocations. Seventy-five percent of firms that report employee unwillingness to relocate cite family resistance as the reason.[14] Dual-career families are especially affected, particularly when the partners are on career-tracks in their respective organizations. Paradoxically, a relocation for either a promotion or a career-development purpose may substantially advance the career of the relocated spouse, while it forces the other spouse to abandon a promising career and start another one in the new location. Some spouses in dual-career marriages only accept relocation assignments on the condition that their partners find acceptable positions in the new location.

---

[13] Lublin, J. S., "Memo Reveals Dual Allegiances of Outplacement Firm," *The Wall Street Journal* (January 27, 1995), p. B-1.

[14] Employee Relocation Council, *Transfer Volume and Cost Survey*, April 1999.

Relocations compel employees' children to leave their friends and schools and start new lives in different communities. This uprooting can be psychologically disturbing. Spouses of relocated employees also have their routines and lifestyles turned topsy-turvy. Employees and their spouses must cultivate new friendships as they sever old ones. Unquestionably, relocation is unsettling to family life.

Lifestyle changes are necessitated by relocation. Recreational pursuits may be changed, as well as leisure activities. The economic changes resulting from the relocation may result in either an improvement or deterioration in the family's lifestyle.

The end result for both spouses is an increased amount of stress resulting from a relocation. Exhibit 20-5 contains the results of one survey about the levels of stress from relocations experienced by both employees and their spouses.

Exhibit 20-5
Stress from Relocations

Amount of Stress	Employee	Spouse
Not too/not at all stressful	35%	14%
Somewhat stressful	50	52
Very stressful	15	34

Relocation Assistance

Some very large firms have full-time relocation administrators who handle the firm's relocations, including the formulation and administration of policies. Other firms contract with an external service provider to assist employees in the relocation process. Typical relocation assistance includes moving expenses, hotel or other types of temporary lodging reimbursement, travel expenses, cost of meals, assistance with mortgages or closing expenses, general relocation expense reimbursement, assistance with rentals, and reimbursements for realty expenses. The average cost of relocating a homeowner/employee exceeds $53,000;[15] the relocation cost for an employee/renter is substantially less.

Relocation assistance is an important benefit in recruiting new personnel for some types of work. According to a results of the 1999 SHRM/CCH Recruiting Practices Survey, relocation assistance is considered as one of the top five incentives in recruiting executives, managers, and professionals.[16]

Research studies indicate that the benefits of relocation counseling and assistance are substantial. A group of employees who attended a relocation workshop were absent an average of 3.8 days in the four months after relocation; the rate was 8.7 days for transferred employees who did not attend the workshop. The company health unit also found that individuals in the workshop group exhibited less stress-related symptoms.[17]

[15] *Ibid.*

[16] CCH INCORPORATED, *Ideas and Trends in Personnel,* June 16, 1999.

[17] Johnson, A. A., "Relocation: Getting More for the Dollars You Spend," *Personnel Administrator* (April 1984), p. 30.

Retirement Counseling

The transition from work to retirement is difficult because it causes financial, psychological, and social problems. *Retirement counseling* is the process of preparing employees for this transition. *Pre-retirement counseling* is another term for the same process, although sometimes it is used for long-term programs, starting 10 years or more before retirement. The logic behind this is that *pre*-retirement programs help employees prepare long-term retirement plans. The purposes of retirement counseling are:

- To systematically inform prospective retirees about their rights to retirement benefits offered by the employer;

- To offer a relatively inexpensive employee benefit;

- To prepare older employees for retirement; and

- To enable management to obtain some indication of employees' retirement plans.

Retirement counseling can be provided for any age group. Some retirement counselors think that 10 to 15 years prior to retirement is an optimum time for employees to start planning. While long-term planning is a worthwhile objective, most retirement programs are short-term oriented. Usually, there are three criteria for retirement counseling eligibility:

- When employees reach a set age, such as 55 or 60;

- When employees are within one or two years of optional retirement; or

- When employees are within one or two years of mandatory retirement, such as commercial airline pilots and fire fighters.

Sixty-two percent of the respondents in a national survey of HR departments indicated their firms offered retirement/pre-retirement counseling. In 83 percent of the firms the HR department was responsible for the counseling.[18]

Outside Speakers

Most retirement counseling programs include some use of outside experts. Counselors from the local chapter of the Consumer Credit Counseling Service are available to discuss budgeting and credit. Recreation specialists from a school or local government may cover a range of subjects, including leisure options, exercise programs, and volunteer groups. Clinicians from publicly funded agencies in mental health are qualified to discuss the mental and emotional problems often associated with retirement. Pastoral counselors are usually available to speak about marriage and family problems that may be precipitated by retirement. Local Social Security Administration representatives can give informed presentations on the latest developments in Social Security. Life insurance representatives, stock brokers, real estate professionals, and similar experts in related fields usually honor requests to discuss their specialties as they apply to retirees. Some programs have a session on menu planning and food preparation, conducted by a home economist employed at a local school or government. Legal

---

[18] The Bureau of National Affairs, *Human Resource Activities, Budgets, & Staffs* (June 28, 2001), p. S-7.

matters are usually discussed by a representative from Legal Aid or a retired attorney. Other outside organizations that usually are interested in making presentations are the American Association of Retired People (AARP), Golden Age clubs, Service Corps of Retired Executives, and various volunteer organizations. Representatives from the state employment service can present a session on part-time employment opportunities.

Retirement Program Subjects

Money and health are probably the two principal concerns for retirees. These two concerns, along with the following concerns, are commonly included in retirement planning programs:

- Social Security, including retirement, survivor benefits, Medicare, and Medicaid;

- Health benefits, including premiums, COBRA benefits, conversion rights to individual plans, and benefit provisions for the retiree and his or her family;

- Life insurance, including any reductions in coverage, premiums, conversion rights, and medical examination requirements;

- Pension plan, including survivor options, and benefit provisions at different retirement ages;

- Legal planning, including wills, trusts, and estate planning;

- Taxes, including income, pensions, Social Security benefits, inheritance, tax deferred income, and tax shelters;

- Financial planning, including insurance, stocks, and bonds;

- Credit counseling, including credit cards, counseling services, bankruptcy statutes, and budgeting;

- Diet, including nutrition, aging and dietary needs, menu planning, and food preservation;

- Exercise, including health clubs, weight control, and exercise methods;

- Leisure, including self-assessment techniques and leisure options;

- Employment, including second jobs, part-time work, homework, and training opportunities;

- Relocation, including moving arrangements, retirement communities, personal relationships, and climate and health;

- Real estate, including selling/buying, "total-care" facilities, rent versus buy, home maintenance, and home inspection before purchase;

- Substance abuse, including alcohol, legal and illegal drug abuse, Alcohol Anonymous, and Al-Anon;

- Family and marriage, including divorce, family deaths and illnesses, and living with grown children;

- Stress, including retirement-induced stress, coping mechanisms, and preventive aspects;

- Aging myths, including intelligence, flexibility, creativity, and physical condition;

- Special interest groups, including American Association of Retired People; and

- Volunteer associations, including United Way, Red Cross, and Service Corps of Retired Executives.

Counseling Format

Retirement counseling is offered in several formats.

Individual Counseling

Individual counseling is one-on-one counseling between an employee and a specialist who gives advice and information on a particular topic. This type of counseling is normally used for employer-provided benefits. Usually, the counselor has an itemized list of subjects that are explained to the prospective retiree. The retiree completes various retirement forms after they are explained, such as options for survivor's benefits and health benefit coverage.

Group Counseling

Group counseling is used in more formalized programs that are conducted after working hours. Sessions are usually offered regularly, with a different subject presented every month or so. Any employee is permitted to attend. Depending upon the number of subjects covered, it may take up to two years to complete an entire cycle. Usually, popular subjects, such as employer-provided retirement and health benefit plans, Social Security, financial planning, diet, and exercise, are offered more frequently. Various inducements are used to encourage participation, such as free soft drinks and framed certificates for those who complete the program.

Well-organized group sessions, presented on a well-timed schedule, will help develop camraderie among the participants, including spouses. Spousal participation is encouraged for several reasons. Retirement may have a profound impact upon the family because of changes in routine and income. It is important for the spouse to know about these changes. The employee may have difficulty in adjusting to retirement, so that it is helpful if the spouse is informed and knows how to help the employee get assistance. During these sessions, the spouse may also learn about his or her rights to survivor benefits.

Commercial Retirement Materials

Some employers obtain subscriptions to commercial retirement materials. Every month, employees who are approaching the eligibility age for retirement are sent a brochure on a different retirement subject.

Limited and Comprehensive Programs

Exhibit 20-6 illustrates the differences in limited and comprehensive retirement planning programs. Limited programs are confined to only basic economic subjects, such as pension matters and Social Security benefits. Usually, limited programs are individually conducted and are initiated when an employee announces an intention to retire. There is little or no advance preparation or planning.

In contrast, more comprehensive programs significantly help prepare employees for one of life's major transitions—retirement. These programs cover many subjects, dealing with the economic, social, and personal dimensions of retirement. Usually, the employee's spouse is invited to attend all sessions. Sometimes, commercial materials are purchased to supplement the program.

Exhibit 20-6
Differences in Limited and Comprehensive Retirement Planning Programs

Characteristics	Type of Program	
	Limited	Comprehensive
Subjects	Several	Many
Participants	Employee	Employee and spouse
Lead time	Little/none	Several years
Topic	Economic	Economic, social, and personal
Setting	Individual	Group and individual
Procedure	Upon need	Scheduled speakers
Commercial services	No	Sometimes
Counseling subjects	Few	Many

Retirement Counseling Effectiveness

Retirement counseling effectiveness can be measured by determining how well it meets the purposes defined earlier in this chapter. A study analyzed the effects of a retirement counseling program upon a group of participants, as compared to a nonparticipant group. The two groups did not differ in either their work attitudes or job involvement, but the group that participated in retirement counseling did have a significantly more favorable attitude toward retirement.[19]

[19] Morrow, P. C., "Retirement Planning Programs: Assessing Their Attendance and Efficiency," *Aging and Work* 4 (Fall 1981), pp. 244-48.

CHAPTER 21
WELLNESS

Chapter Highlights
- Explain the concept of wellness
- Describe the purposes of wellness programs
- Discuss the benefits of wellness programs
- Diagram the various roles in achieving wellness

Introduction

Traditionally, employee health was considered to be a personal matter. Today, however, employers realize that a person's job has a profound influence upon his or her health. For example, working conditions and job structuring may either positively or adversely affect employee health. Unsafe or unhealthy working conditions cause unnecessary occupational disease and injuries that may result in disability and death. Furthermore, unhealthy employees cause employers to incur unnecessary expenditures for health benefits. Unhealthy employees also have a proportionately larger percentage of deficiencies in productivity, work quality, attendance, and work conduct.

Employees have major responsibilities for their personal health. Personal health needs differ among people; each person has unique needs that may change over time or in response to daily living. For example, a person with diabetes may have distinctly different dietary needs than a person who does not have the disease. People also differ in the amounts and kinds of exercise they need. These and other lifestyle choices, such as leisure pursuits, diet, tobacco and alcohol use, and other risky behavior, are individually determined by personal preference and other considerations that make people unique.

Lifestyle encompasses all aspects of a person's non-work and work life; it can be described as behavior toward or away from wellness. A lifestyle is healthy if it provides personal well-being and is not detrimental to the lifestyle of others.

In sum, wellness requires the combined efforts of both the employer and the employee.

Wellness is employee mental and physical well-being as a result of employer and employee commitment to complete human health in both non-work and work life.

Purposes of Wellness

Wellness supports the missions and goals of organizations toward stockholders, customers, human resources, and the public. Healthy employees are

more efficient, which reduces costs and increases productivity, thereby ultimately increasing stockholders' profits. Healthy employees produce quality
products at competitive prices, so that customers are better able to maximize
their incomes. A goal of most organizations is to help employees develop their
potential, and wellness is vitally important in achieving that objective. Healthy
employees' desire to help build a healthy society can contribute to an organization's social responsibility.

Wellness programs also serve other purposes; for example, they improve
employee morale and contribute towards the recruitment of new employees.

Incidence of Wellness Programs

As discussed in Chapter 18, 25 percent of employees in private sector firms
have access to wellness programs. Thirteen percent of employees in these firms
also have access to fitness centers.[1]

Wellness Roles

While the employer and the employee have roles in achieving wellness,
society and the family also have important responsibilities. Exhibit 21-1 illustrates the various components of those roles.

Exhibit 21-1
Roles in Wellness

Society	Employer	Family	Employee
Freedom	Health strategy	Wellness support	No smoking
Laws	Fair treatment	Love/caring	Alcohol discipline
Nondiscrimination	Job design	Refuge	Sexual behavior
Parks	Safety and health		Personal problems
Cultural facilities	Smoking policies		Nutrition
Education institutions	Job stress		Exercise
Healthy People 2010	Cumulative trauma		Professional care
	Employee assistance		Stress management
	Education		Stress control
	Exercise		

Societal Role

Society must be structured so that citizens can express freedom in their work
and non-work choices. Also, laws must exist to protect these individual rights.
For example, religion is an essential part of many individuals' non-work lives.
However, there are times when religious beliefs may also affect a person's work
life, such as taking time off from work in order to celebrate religious holidays.
Title VII protects these rights and prevents employers from discriminating
against a person unless there is a bona fide occupational reason. Title VII and
other laws provide other protection for people in both their non-work lives and
work lives. For example, no-smoking laws affecting public places prevent exposure to secondhand smoke. Also, more restrictive laws involving alcohol con-

---

[1] Bureau of Labor Statistics, *National Compensation
Survey: Employee Benefits in Private Industry in the
United States, March 2007*, p. 14.

sumption and driving protect individuals from intoxicated drivers. Society also aids wellness lifestyle development by providing recreational parks, cultural facilities, and educational and training institutions.

Healthy People 2010

Healthy People 2010, built from the comments of more than 11,000 individuals and organizations, is the prevention agenda for the U.S. that identifies the most significant preventable threats to health and focuses public and private efforts to address them. Ongoing involvement is ensured through the *Healthy People Consortium,* an alliance of 350 national membership organizations and 250 state health, mental health, substance abuse, and environmental agencies. Its goals are to increase years of healthy life and reduce disparities in health among different population groups. To achieve these goals, the agenda has multiple objectives, organized into 28 focus areas, which are: Access to Quality Health Services, Cancer, Chronic Kidney Disease, Educational and Community-Based Programs, Environmental Health, Family Planning, Food Safety, Heart Disease, Injury and Violence Prevention, Medical Product Safety, Physical Activity and Fitness, Tobacco Use, Vision and Hearing, and Immunization and Infectious Diseases.[2] Success is measured by positive changes in health status or reductions in risk factors, as well as in improved provisions for certain services.

Employer Role

Employers have a profound influence upon employee wellness. Developing corporate strategies is an integral part of an employer's wellness program. Below is a list of 12 corporate health strategies that employers can adopt to address employee wellness:

- Implement employee lifestyle change programs, such as smoking cessation, physical fitness activities, improved nutrition, lower back care, stress reduction;

- Institute a corporate health risk appraisal and counseling program;

- Develop a corporate health promotion mission statement, in order to demonstrate management support of health promotion;

- Develop an organization culture that is flexible, socially supportive, and responsive to employee needs, including training in team-building, conflict resolution, and violence prevention skills;

- Establish a corporate policy to maintain a smoke-free and drug-free work site;

- Form an employee health and safety committee;

- Regularly monitor health promotion programs' effectiveness, costs, benefits, and participation rates;

- Promote corporate compliance with federal, state, and local laws and regulations;

---

[2] *Healthy People 2010* (webpage: http://www.health.gov/healthy people/PrevAgenda/whatishp.htm)

- Offer a program of flexible employee medical and disease prevention benefits that includes clinical preventive services, such as immunizations for employees and their dependents;

- Offer occupational safety and health training programs that are targeted to the requirements of particular jobs and industries;

- Create and maintain health promotive facilities by conducting workplace environmental quality audits at regular intervals and taking steps to address identified problem areas by ensuring closer adherence to ergonomic, safety, signage, and clean air standards in the workplace; and

- Communicate regularly with employees regarding health promotion through meetings, newsletters, posters, e-mail, payroll inserts.[3]

Wellness Practices

Employers can encourage employee wellness by offering employee benefits, including recreational programs, lifestyle change programs, and safety training programs. Other ways employers can contribute to employee wellness are through the fair treatment of employees and job design.

Fair Treatment

Theory X and similar types of management styles are antithetical to wellness because they cause excessive stress, emotional problems, and a reduction in feelings of self-worth. Autocratic managers reproduce their management style in their supervisors and employees. This type of management causes dissatisfaction and deviant behavior in the workplace. Bosses who use unfair supervisory methods cause employees to be sick. Autocratic and unfair supervisors should be identified and trained to modify their behavior and observed to be sure that they do so.

Job Design

Management can also promote wellness through proper job design. For example, redesigning a job to make it less stressful or more safe is preferable to teaching employees how to cope with a stressful or unsafe job. The two ways to achieve person-job congruence are by changing either the person or the job. When an employee is unhappy in a job that cannot be redesigned, the next option is to reassign the employee. Sometimes, it is easier to reassign an employee than it is to change the job.

Frederick W. Taylor, the father of scientific management, conducted many studies with different types of jobs. From these experiences, he concluded that all employees are exceptional performers at some type of work. Management has a responsibility to help employees find the job where they can be first-class performers. The economic gains are significant for both the employer and the employee, since top performers produce from two to three times more and are paid proportionately more.

---

[3] This listing was adapted from *The UCI Health Promotion Center's Top-12 List of Corporate Health Strategies,* Social Ecology Research Group Listing, Department of urban and Regional Planning, School of Social Ecology, University of California, Irvine, 1997.

Safe and Healthful Work Environment

Another management role in achieving employee wellness is providing a safe and healthful work environment. This responsibility includes facilities design, such as a work layout, which prevents employee exposure to hazardous conditions. Work methods include equipment and procedures that prevent physical stress on employees, such as unnecessary heavy lifting. Safety and health also includes employee training in correct methods of performing job tasks. Some companies emphasize safety and health concerns by including employee accident rates in supervisors' performance appraisals.

Smoking Policies

Studies have shown that smokers incur more medical expenses than do nonsmokers. A study of a South Dakota firm found that the health benefit claims of smokers were 24 percent greater than nonsmokers.[4] In response to the health hazards and economic costs caused by employee smoking, employers have implemented various initiatives.

Historically, employers have been conscious of the safety risks posed by workplace smoking. Consequently, smoking was either banned or restricted where there was a danger of explosion or fire. More recently, in response to health hazards, cost considerations, local and state laws, and complaints from nonsmoking employees, employers have instituted policies to either restrict or ban workplace smoking. In addition, some employers charge smokers more for their health benefits.

See Chapter 8 for a discussion of the legal issues involving smoking, both on- and off-the-job.

Smoking Cessation. Employer efforts to help employees stop smoking include initiatives, such as smoking cessation programs. These programs may cost up to $200 per person. Commercially available programs have various formats, usually meeting from one to two hours per week for eight weeks. A national survey of adult smokers who attempted to quit smoking in the previous 10 years found that 47.5 percent of those who quit "cold turkey" (without any type of assistance) were successful. For organized smoking cessation programs, the success rate was 23.6 percent. For purposes of the study, "quitting" was defined as abstinence from smoking for at least one year.

Pharmacotherapy is also used to help smokers quit. The relative effectiveness of these therapies varies widely. A study, which was conducted by the U.S. Department of Defense, found that effectiveness (defined as quitting smoking for at least one year) varied from a low of 10 percent for inhalers to 33 percent for a combination of a patch and Bupropion.[5]

Job Stress

Stress is a nonspecific bodily reaction to a stimulus. All stress is not necessarily harmful; it can create the impetus to accomplish tasks that might take

---

[4] Winslow, R., "Some Firms Put a Price On Smoking," *The Wall Street Journal* (March 6, 1990), p. B-1.

[5] "Relative Cost-Effectiveness of Smoking Cessation Pharmacotherapies," *PEC Update* (October 1999), p. 1.

a longer amount of time absent such stress. Excessive stress, however, can cause harm, because it overtaxes the body and impairs the ability to repair itself. Under extreme and prolonged conditions, the result can be illnesses and job problems. A five-year study of nearly 3,000 workers found a direct link between work-related demands that create problems for workers at home, resulting in lower productivity at work.[6]

Control Over Job Performance. One medical study found that men in stressful jobs, with minimal control over their task performance, had heart conditions which were precursors to disease and elevated blood pressure.[7] Apparently, two main conditions influencing disease and stress are: (1) the amount of job stress, and (2) the degree of control the job incumbent has over how the job is performed. Employers can help address this area of employee stress by giving employees more control over their work environment.

Control Over Physical Environment. Depending upon the employee, the manner in which the job is structured, such as too much repetition of tasks or too much autonomy, may cause stress for employees. Job conditions that can cause stress include extremes in temperature, noise, exposure to toxic substances, exposure to weather conditions, vibration from equipment, and unsafe conditions. Providing protective clothing and protective equipment will help prevent some of the physical conditions contributing to employee stress.

Cumulative Trauma Disorders

Carpal tunnel syndrome was the major cause of disabling illnesses resulting in the most median days away from work. Repetitive motion, such as scanning groceries, was the most frequent cause of events or exposures resulting in the longest absences from work occurring in 2005.[8]

Employers can help prevent these causes of illnesses by incorporating ergonomics in designing and arranging equipment and adapting environmental conditions to meet human needs. Some areas that benefit from ergonomics include keyboard design, desk height, and the type of chair used. Some employers also rotate employees among different assignments, if different physical movements are required in other jobs.

Employee Assistance Programs

Employers can provide employee assistance programs (EAPs) to help prevent and treat employees' personal problems. The recovery rates for various personal problems are higher when treatment is administered in the early stages of the disease; for example, alcoholism can be successfully treated in 85 percent of the cases when treated in the beginning stages. Family members, supervisors, peers, and union representatives must be informed about various personal problems, so that they can recognize the symptoms and refer troubled employees

---

[6] "Job-Related Stress Comes Home," *Richmond Times-Dispatch* (April 15, 1998), p. B-1.

[7] "Powerless Jobs Fuel Worst Stress," *Richmond Times-Dispatch* (April 11, 1990), p. 1.

[8] Bureau of Labor Statistics, *Nonfatal Occupational Injuries and Illnesses Requiring Days Away From Work, 2005*, November 17, 2006.

to a counselor. Supervisors also should use the performance appraisal system to confront deficient employees and refer them to a qualified professional.

Employers can encourage treatment and rehabilitation by either paying for it or by providing insurance coverage. One of the best excuses an employee has for not seeking treatment is that he or she cannot afford to pay for it. Employers do benefit by paying for treatment, since some studies show that such assistance returns from $2 to $4 in increased productivity for each dollar spent.[9]

Educational Programs

Educational programs on wellness issues may include classes on various subjects, articles in employee newsletters, posters and announcements posted on employee bulletin boards, paycheck inserts, and periodic mailings to employees' homes. Extensive formal educational programs involve a personal interview with a health professional and usually include needs assessment, health appraisal, and courses for changing behavior.

Some organizations have more elaborate testing, such as electrocardiograms, heart stress tests, and physical examinations and medical tests that measure weight, height, blood pressure, cholesterol, body fat percentage, lung function, blood count, blood chemistry (triglycerides, high density lipoprotein cholesterol, and blood sugar), and liver and kidney functioning. The information gathered from the assessment process is analyzed, and an individualized wellness program is prepared for each employee, including an interview that involves frank discussions on such topics as an employee's alcohol consumption, smoking, diet, obesity, and general physical condition.

Wellness health prescriptions are specific action plans tailored to the needs of each employee; for example, smoking clinics to help employee/smokers quit. Employers should also educate and train employees in the working conditions that may cause occupational illnesses or injuries, utilizing OSHA training standards, for example.

Exercise

Despite the small percentage of firms offering fitness centers to employees, as discussed at the beginning of this chapter, a sizable portion of employers do offer fitness-types of benefits. For example, 83 percent of the respondents in a survey of HR professionals, indicated their organizations offered recreation/ social programs to employees.[10] Many of these programs incorporate one or more of these eight types of exercise:

- Team sports, such as baseball or volleyball;
- Cycling;
- Horseback riding;
- Skiing;
- Gymnasium exercising, such as aerobic dancing;

---

[9] Myers, D. W., "Measuring EAP Cost Effectiveness: Results and Recommendations," *EAP Digest* (March/April 1984), p. 23.

[10] The Bureau of National Affairs, *Human Resource Activities, Budgets, & Staffs* (June 28, 2001), p. S-7.

- Ballroom dancing, including folk dancing;

- Swimming; and

- Track exercising, such as walking and running.

Some employers provide on-site exercise facilities, while others either rent facilities or pay all or part of membership fees to health clubs. Still others conduct wellness orientation programs and encourage employees to exercise on their own. Some owners of office parks or corporate centers install jogging or walking paths, fitness centers, gyms, tennis courts and other types of sports facilities. There are several advantages to such facilities. First, they are features that attract corporate tenants. Also, some facilities, such as racquetball and tennis courts, can be an additional source of income, if fees are charged.

While some employers offer organized sports, including basketball, some experts believe competitive sports should be avoided because they are more likely to cause injuries; also, such competition can increase stress for participants. Employees who participate in company-related sports programs should consider the President's Council on Physical Fitness and Sports, 200 Independence Ave. SW, Humphrey Building, Room 738H, Washington, D.C. 20201. The President's Council has information to help a person decide if they are physically fit to engage in sports activities. Included in this information are self-administered questionnaires about personal fitness and advice about contacting one's personal physician.[11]

Health Insurance Portability and Accountability Act (HIPAA) Nondiscrimination Provisions Applying to Wellness Programs

Traditionally, some employers have used some components of wellness programs to motivate employees to reduce health care costs. For example, some employers have offered financial incentives to employees that meet certain fitness goals. See Chapter 19 for a discussion of the nondiscrimination requirements of HIPAA applicable to wellness programs offered by group health plans.

Role of the Family

Family Accommodations

Support of wellness may require some changes in family member roles and expectations. For example, a spouse may not support an employee's decision to attend classes at night in order to make a career change. Also, some spouses may resist changing menus to accommodate an employee's desire or need for a salt-free or reduced-cholesterol diet. Exercise programs inevitably interfere with other family routines, such as the regular evening meal. Even the employee who goes to bed early to exercise before work must try to sleep while family members stay up to read or watch television. The next morning, the same employee must exercise while trying to avoid waking the family.

---

[11] Website address is http://www.fitness.gov/contact/contact.html

Love and Support

Family members must give love and support to other members who are embarking upon a wellness lifestyle. A healthy lifestyle requires self-discipline, sacrifice, and work. Family opposition, or simply a lack of support for the employee, may be sufficiently discouraging for the employee to abandon it.

The family also aids employee wellness by offering a refuge from the stresses and strains of daily living. Home is a place for relaxation and revitalization for the next day. People need loved ones who care about them, someone they can talk to, and, most of all, friends who will listen without criticizing or directing. Such interactions provide catharsis, which is important in order to maintain equilibrium. Often, the employee in search of wellness simply needs a sounding board, someone to listen to his or her feelings and aspirations.

Employee's Role

Individual employees are ultimately responsible for their personal wellness. Society can provide the opportunities for personal health, organizations can provide programs and employment potential, and the family can offer love, encouragement, and support, but the final decisions about the type of lifestyle selected rests with the employee. Employees must develop the self-discipline to eat properly, get adequate sleep, exercise, educate themselves, and maintain the motivation to continue a wellness lifestyle.

Lifestyle and Death

As illustrated in Exhibit 21-2, most of the 10 major causes of death in the U.S. are related to lifestyle. For example, a number of factors (exercise, cholesterol, diet, alcohol use, tobacco use, and stress) associated with heart disease are lifestyle-related. Among the things that employees can do to help prevent heart disease are exercise regularly, control diet and cholesterol levels, limit tobacco use, and control stress.

Exhibit 21-2
Ten Major Causes of Death in the U.S.
and Lifestyle Factors, 2006

Cause of Death		Deaths in 2006	Lifestyle Factors
1.	Heart disease	629,191	Cholesterol Diet Exercise Tobacco use Stress
2.	Malignant cancers	560,102	Diet Tobacco use
3.	Cerebrovascular disease	137,265	Cholesterol Diet Exercise Tobacco use Stress
4.	Chronic obstructive pulmonary diseases and allied lung conditions	124,614	Exercise Smoking
5.	Accidental injury	117,748	Alcohol use Safety procedures
6.	Alzheimer's disease	72,914	None
7.	Diabetes mellitus	72,507	Diet Exercise
8.	Pneumonia and influenza	56,247	Smoking
9.	Nephritis, nephrotic syndrome, and nephrosis	44,791	None
10.	Septicemia	34,031	None

Source: Centers for Disease Control and Prevention, *National Vital Statistics Report* (June 11, 2008).

Smoking

About 46 million adult Americans smoke, but this minority suffers a dispro-portionate share of agonizing disease and death.[12] According to the Surgeon General, cigarette smoking is a major cause of disease and death in the U.S. Differences in the magnitude of risk for various diseases are directly related to smoking patterns.

Smoking cessation. Approximately 70 percent of smokers want to stop smoking, but only 2.5 percent actually succeed. Smokers use various methods to try to quit smoking; some employers give assistance to those smokers who want to quit. Methods employees use include hypnotism, acupuncture, and group therapy. Probably the most common method is to simply stop smoking, also called going "cold turkey."

---

[12] Centers for Disease Control and Prevention, *Adult Cigarette Smoking in the U.S.: Current Estimates* (May 2004).

Employees also seek medical advice in their efforts to stop smoking. In response to their patients' needs, some physicians may prescribe medications to help combat withdrawal symptoms. There is reason to be optimistic about the prospects of quitting, since more than 45 million ex-smokers ultimately do succeed in stopping.

Alcohol Abuse

In 2002, approximately 54.9 percent of the adult population reported drinking at least one drink in the past month. About 45 million engaged in binge drinking and 12.4 million were heavy drinkers.[13] Alcohol abuse is a disease and a serious health problem. It can cause suicides and homicides and is a major cause of cirrhosis. In addition, impaired-alcohol use is involved in 31.7 percent of all motor vehicle car crashes resulting in a fatality, as shown in Exhibit 21-3. Because of both the human tragedy and the economic costs of alcohol abuse, employers establish employee assistance programs to assist the recovery of alcoholics; these programs are covered in Chapter 20. However, employees have the ultimate responsibility for their personal consumption of alcohol.

Exhibit 21-3
Total Fatalities and the Number and Percent of Alcohol-Impaired Driving Fatalities in the United States, 1996-2007

Crash Type	1996	2007	Change	% Change
Alcohol-Impaired Driving Fatalities[1]	13,431	12,998	433	-3.2%
Total Traffic Fatalities	41,709	41,059	650	-1.6%
Percent of Total	32.2%	31.7%	—	—

[1] Blood Alcohol Concentration (BAC) = 0.08 or higher
Source: NHTSA Fatality Analysis Reporting System, 2008

Sexual Behavior

Risky sexual behavior can lead to disease and premature death, primarily due to the human immunodeficiency virus (HIV). Approximately 1,056,400 to 1,156,000 people currently living in the United States are infected with HIV and about 40,000 new infections occur each year.[14]

As shown in Table 21-4, HIV is spread by sexual contact with an infected person, and by sharing needles and/or syringes (primarily for drug injection) with someone who is infected. Less commonly (and now very rarely in countries where blood is screened for HIV antibodies), HIV is spread through transfusions of infected blood or blood clotting factors. Babies born to HIV-infected women may become infected before or during birth or through breast-feeding after birth[15].

---

[13] Centers for Disease Control and Prevention, *General Alcohol Information* (n.d.).

[14] CDC, *HIV Prevalence Estimates –United States, 2006* pp. 1-6.

[15] Quoted from *HIV and Its Transmission*, CDC, July 1999.

Health care workers have been infected with HIV after being stuck with needles containing HIV-infected blood or, less frequently, after infected blood gets into a worker's open cut or a mucous membrane (for example, the eyes or inside of the nose). There has been only one instance of patients being infected with HIV by a health care worker in the U.S.; this involved transmission from one infected dentist to six patients. Investigations involving more than 22,000 patients of 63 HIV-infected physicians, surgeons, and dentists have found no other transmission of this type in the United States[16].

HIV causes acquired immunodeficiency syndrome (AIDS), which destroys the immune system, thus making a person susceptible to one or more opportunistic diseases and conditions that may be fatal. Approximately 952,629 cases of AIDS have been reported to the Centers for Disease Control and Prevention since reporting started in 1981; 421,873 of these persons are still living.[17]

Table 21-4
Transmission Categories of Adults and Adolescents with HIV/AIDS Diagnosed in 2005

Categories	Male	Female
Male to male sexual contact	67%	n/a
Heterosexual contact	15%	80%
Injection drug use	13%	19%
Male to male sexual contact and injection drug use	5%	n/a
Other	<1%	1%
Total	100%	100%

Source: *A Glance at the HIV/AIDS Epidemic*, CDC, June 2007

Virtually 100 percent of the adult/adolescent cases of AIDS are lifestyle-related and can be prevented through abstinence from sex, safe sexual behavior, and refraining from intravenous drug use.

Personal Problems

Personal problems include alcoholism and alcohol abuse, drug use, compulsive gambling, marital and family problems, financial problems, and mental and emotional problems. Preventing these problems is the highest priority. Employee responsibilities include learning about such problems, recognizing any symptoms and seeking professional help as early as possible. Employee assistance programs and counseling alternatives are discussed in Chapter 20.

Nutrition

Most people realize the wisdom of the adage, "You are what you eat." The evidence is convincing that diet is a lifestyle factor in four of the 10 major causes of death, as shown in Exhibits 21-2. Heart disease and cancer, the two primary causes of death, are linked to diet. Studies have shown that the reduction in the

---

[16] *Ibid.*

[17] Centers for Disease Control and Prevention, *A Glance at the HIV/AIDS Epidemic*.

death rate due to heart attacks is attributable to lower blood cholesterol levels. Poor nutrition causes obesity, a condition that affects 20 percent of all children and 16 percent of the adult population.

Dietary programs are a wellness responsibility that employers and employees can share. As many as 200 companies offer diet programs, either in addition to or as part of a wellness program. Diet and nutrition programs include offering weight reduction classes, serving reduced calorie or reduced fat foods in company cafeterias, employing nutritionists to advise employees, and offering employees diet analyses. Weight reduction classes often use behavior modification techniques to reinforce proper eating, menu planning, and caloric requirements. Employees' cafeterias and food vending machines offer other ways to help employees eat the right foods by including a salt-free daily food special low in both calories and cholesterol and displaying caloric information on all menu items. Most companies with nutrition components also have some type of nutritional questionnaire to help employees monitor their dietary preferences.

Exercise

Employees need the self-discipline to establish a regular exercise routine and stick with it. Sophisticated exercise equipment is not necessary for good health. A daily walk is one of the best exercise routines. Employers can promote employee exercise through a variety of programs, from motivational information campaigns, to establishing a walking path on company property, to providing on-site exercise classes and weight rooms.

Professional Care

Professional care includes a range of medical services, such as physical examinations, physiological testing, eye examinations, and hearing tests. Medical care is another wellness responsibility that employees and employers share. For example, preventive medical services that an employer may provide include periodic hearing tests, immunizations, health education, and health counseling, either in the company health unit or in connection with a wellness component, such as an exercise program. Occupational medical services include periodic health screening in occupations with hazardous conditions; an example is blood-lead-level testing in jobs where employees are exposed to lead, such as battery repairers or smelter workers. Occupational medical personnel also screen jobs for potentially harmful agents and unsafe conditions.

Stress Management

The amount of stress an individual experiences is a function of factors such as role conflict, neglect of one's health, and personal problems.

Role Conflict

Role is defined as the behavior expected from someone because of his or her social position. The *role set* are the people with whom a person regularly interacts and who dictate how that person will assume a particular role. People assume different roles; some of them may conflict. These role conflicts include:

- *Intra-person role conflict*, which occurs when a person's expected role is incompatible with his or her values or beliefs. For example, a recruiter may be required to use a particular type of test in the employment process, but she may personally believe the test is unfair or invalid.

- *Intra-role conflict*, which occurs when members of a role set differ on how a person's role should be performed. For example, the human resources director in one organization has the final authority in adjudicating employee grievances. Employee-grievants expect the director to be impartial, but supervisors involved in the grievance expect the director to support them because the director's job is part of management.

- *Inter-role conflict*, which is caused by people fulfilling multiple roles that conflict. For example, a single working parent of young children is expected to care for them *and* to be reliable in attendance at work.

Personal Health

Neglecting personal health care can also impede the body's defenses against stress. These areas of health care include alcohol use, caffeine, diet, drugs, exercise, rest, and smoking.

Personal Problems

Personal problems, such as mental or emotional problems, also contribute to both physiological and psychological stress.

Stress Control

The two basic strategies for stress control are: (1) to prevent and reduce it, and (2) to learn how to cope with it. The preferred strategy is to identify the sources of stress and either eliminate or reduce them. If stress cannot be prevented or reduced, these are some techniques to learn how to cope with it:

- *Biofeedback training* uses electronic equipment to monitor a person's reactions to stressors. Biofeedback helps individuals learn how they are reacting to stress and teaches them how to control those reactions.

- *Behavior modification* involves classroom training, in which operant conditioning measures, such as positive reinforcement and punishment, help a person learn new coping skills.

- *Psychotherapy* includes professional counseling by a trained therapist to help a person learn how to handle various stressors.

- *Meditation* teaches a person relaxation techniques; it can be used for short periods periodically during the day.

- *Time management skills* include learning to set priorities, identify wasted time, and how to work efficiently.

Effectiveness of Employer Wellness Programs

Wellness lifestyles can produce positive results for both the employee and the employer. Tenneco established a fitness center in 1982 and found that employees who use the center at least twice a week file only 50 percent as many health benefit claims as those employees who do not use it. Compared to nonusers, the users also received higher performance appraisals and were absent 30 percent less. A division of DANA Corporation established a wellness program, and, after two years of operation, the program produced the following results:

- 76 percent of the firm's employees are active participants in various parts of the program;

- The cost of medical claims dropped an average of $451 per employee;

- Tobacco use declined 54 percent;

- The number of employees with elevated cholesterol declined 12.5 percent;

- 76 percent of the employees changed to more healthy eating habits;

- 47 percent of the employees who were diagnosed with high blood pressure made changes in their lifestyles to reduce it;

- The use of seat belts increased 77 percent; and

- Employee work attendance averaged 99 percent.[18]

---

[18] Petersen, C., "Wellness Pays At This Firm," *Managed Healthcare* (March 1996), p. 36.

CHAPTER 22
RETIREMENT PLANS

Chapter Highlights
- Major types of retirement plans
- Legal and regulatory requirements
- Eligibility, funding and administration provisions

Introduction

Retirement plan is a generic term for an employee benefit that provides income for employees upon reaching an age at which they neither desire to continue working nor are able to continue working. Often, the term *pension* is used either interchangeably with, or in lieu of, the term *retirement*. As discussed in Chapter 18, 61 percent of employees have access to retirement plans but only 51 percent are participating.[1]

Retirement Plans

The two types of retirement plans are defined contribution plans and defined benefit plans.

Defined contribution retirement plans specify the amount (either the dollar amount or the percentage of the employee's salary or company profits) that the employer will contribute to the plan on behalf of each participant.

A defined contribution plan does not specify the benefit the employee will receive upon retirement, since it would be contingent upon the amount of funds that have accumulated on behalf of the employee upon reaching retirement age. Separate accounts are maintained for the contributions made for each employee, although funds may be commingled for investment purposes.

Defined benefit retirement plans obligate an employer to provide retirement benefits that are calculated by a formula that specifies the amount of benefit the employee will receive upon retirement.

Benefits generally are based on salary, years of service, or a combination of the two. An employer usually has considerable latitude in financing the benefits.

---

[1] Bureau of Labor Statistics, *National Compensation Survey: Employee Benefits in Private Industry in the United States, March 2008,* (March 2008).

Defined Contribution Plan Advantages

Defined contribution plans are easier to administer and are subject to fewer regulations than defined benefit plans. Because of these advantages, defined contribution plans have become more prevalent.

Defined Benefit Plan Advantages

Defined benefit plans are better than defined contribution plans for meeting desired income replacement objectives.

Contributory/Noncontributory

A plan that does not require employees to make contributions is known as a *noncontributory plan*. A plan that does require employee contributions is a *contributory* plan.

Portability

Employee mobility, that is, movement from one employer to another, is occurring more frequently today than it did 20 years ago. There are some estimates that the average employee will change jobs as many as eight times in his or her working career. The concern among employees about losing their pension rights is a key factor in preventing mobility. To some extent, this concern is addressed through *vesting*, which is a pension participant's right to benefits that, upon termination of employment or upon reaching the normal retirement age, becomes nonforfeitable. In some situations, a better alternative to vesting is portability of retirement benefit rights. *Portability* is the ability to move one's vested rights in a retirement or savings plan from one employer to another. Unfortunately, few retirement plans afford this option to employees.

Laws That Affect Retirement Plans

Age Discrimination in Employment Act

The Age Discrimination in Employment Act (ADEA) prohibits discrimination against persons age 40 and over in the administration of retirement plans. The ADEA prohibits maximum retirement ages except for executive personnel, fire fighters, law enforcement personnel, and employees in other types of jobs in which bona fide occupational qualifications can be demonstrated.

Title VII

This law prohibits discrimination based upon race, color, religion, sex or national origin in any aspect of retirement plans. In *City of Los Angeles, Department of Water and Power v. Manhart*, the U.S. Supreme Court held that the contributory plan involved in the case could not require women to make higher contributions than men in order to receive the same annuity payment upon retirement. In *Arizona Governing Committee v. Norris*, the U.S. Supreme Court held that the plan could not offer a choice of gender-based annuities at retirement.

Uniformed Services Employment and Reemployment Rights Act of 1994

Under USERRA, a period of active duty is neither considered a break in employment for retirement calculation purposes nor affects participation eligibility, vesting or benefit accruals. However, accrued benefits resulting from employee contributions are restricted to those the employee actually makes to the plan. Employers are not required to make contributions to an elective deferral plan, such as a 401(k) plan, while the employee is on duty, however, upon return to employment, the employer must make the contributions that would have been made had the employee remained employed. If employee contributions are either required or permitted under the plan, the returning service member has a period equal to the lesser of three times the period of military service or five years to make the contributions. Also, the employer must contribute any matching payments according to the plan's provisions.

Employee Retirement Income Security Act (ERISA)

The most significant law affecting retirement plans is ERISA. Prior to ERISA's passage, employees had little protection to ensure that they would receive the pensions that employers had promised. The purposes of ERISA are:

- To establish basic safeguards for covered employees;
- To provide for the disclosure of essential information; and
- To ensure that plans are maintained for the benefit of employees and their dependents.

Administration of ERISA

ERISA is a complex law that provides considerable tax incentives for both employers and employees. In addition, this law establishes a system of insurance that protects the retirement benefits of employees and mandates recordkeeping and administrative requirements. To accomplish the purposes and procedures required by ERISA, three federal agencies administer various provisions of it:

- *The Internal Revenue Service* determines whether plans meet specific requirements necessary to receive tax advantages. Two major requirements ensure that plans do not discriminate in favor of the highly compensated employees in a firm and guaranty that minimum funding requirements are met.

- *The U.S. Department of Labor* administers the non-tax aspects of the act, such as deciding whether plans are covered by ERISA, granting exemptions to ERISA provisions and conducting investigations of ERISA violations.

- *The Pension Benefit Guaranty Corporation (PBGC)* ensures that participants in defined benefit plans are protected in the event that a plan is terminated. Employers pay premiums to the PBGC, which are used to provide benefits in the event of a loss caused by a partial or full termination of a retirement plan. Single-employer plans pay a flat rate premium of $33 per year per plan participant, plus $9 for each $1,000 of unfunded vested benefits per participant per year. Participants and beneficiaries of terminated plans who have reached the retirement age required by the plan are entitled to PBGC benefits, subject to a maximum amount.

Automatic Enrollment

For private sector employers can automatically enroll employees in 401(k) plans provided they are given a notice explaining their rights. Employers can make decisions about the default contribution amount but employees must be given time to either opt-out or select an alternative amount.[2]

Favored Tax Treatment: "Qualified Plans"

In order to receive favorable tax treatment, *qualified* retirement plans must meet the requirements established by the Internal Revenue Code and ERISA. Most employers structure their retirement plans for qualification because of the tax benefits afforded to both employers and employees. Employers enjoy a current tax deduction for their contributions to fund future retirement income, and employees are not taxed on the employer's contributions until benefits are actually received. Retirement benefits for employees receive favorable tax treatment under certain circumstances, typically when they are actually paid. Investment income earned on funds set aside are not currently taxed.

General Requirements

In addition to specific requirements regarding employee eligibility, coverage and termination rights, a qualified plan must:

- Be operated for the exclusive benefit of a broad classification of employees;
- Be in writing and communicated to employees; and
- Be established with the intent to be permanent.

Participation Requirements

Employees must be permitted to participate in the plan if they have attained age 21 and have one year of service. The service requirement may be as long as three years, if the employee is immediately vested in all of the employer's contributions. A year of service in a retirement plan is any 12-month period in which an employee works 1,000 or more hours.

Exclusions

The plan may be designed to permanently exclude certain classes of employees, such as seasonal or part-time workers.

Vesting Requirements

Vesting is a participant's nonforfeitable right to benefits upon termination of employment. Employees are always fully vested in their own contributions to a plan; ERISA vesting requirements pertain only to the employer's contributions. Employers must design the vesting requirements of their retirement plans, so that they are at least as liberal as one of the two following vesting schedules:

---

[2] CCH, *CCH Tax Briefing: Pension Protection Act of 2006*, (August 17, 2006), p. 3.

- *Three-Year Vesting (Cliff Vesting).* The employee is fully vested at the end of three years. Under this schedule, there is no vesting before this time period has elapsed.

EXAMPLE: ABC Company has a defined benefit, noncontributory retirement plan with a cliff vesting schedule. The company has a defined benefit plan that pays two percent per year of employment, multiplied by the average of the highest three years of income.

Situation 1: Charles was employed by the company for two years. What is Charles' vested right to a pension? The answer is that Charles does not have a vested right to a pension because he did not complete at least three years of service.

Situation 2: Hank was employed by the company for six years, and the average of his highest three years of income is $40,000. He resigns to work for another company. What is Hank's vested amount to a pension at ABC? The answer is that when Hank reaches the retirement age designated by plan, he has a vested right to a pension computed as follows: 2% × 6 years × $40,000 = $4,800 per year.

- *Two-to-Six-Year Vesting (Graduated Vesting).* Under this schedule, an employee does not have any vested rights prior to the completion of two years of employment. The employee is vested in 20 percent of his or her pension rights at the end of the second year of employment; he or she has an additional 20 percent vested rights at the end of each of the next four years (20 percent at the end of the third, fourth, fifth and sixth years). Thus, the employee would be fully or 100 percent vested at the end of six years.

EXAMPLE: ABC Company has a two-to-six-year vesting schedule for its retirement plan. The plan pays a retirement benefit of two percent for each year of employment, multiplied by an average of the employee's highest three years of income with the company.

Situation 1: Cody left the company after one year of employment. What vested right to a pension does Cody have? The answer is that she does not have any vested rights to a pension, since she did not complete at least two years of employment.

Situation 2: Philomena left the company after five years of service. The average for her highest three years of income was $60,000. What is her vested benefit with the company? When Philomena reaches the retirement age designated by the plan, she has a vested right to a pension computed as follows: 2% × 5 years × $60,000 × 80% = $4,800.

Funding Requirements

Employers are required to fund their retirement plans to guarantee that promised benefits will be paid when employees reach the retirement age designated by the plan. Unfortunately many plans are under-funded which in the past resulted in employees losing all or a significant portion of their benefits. To help correct this situation, the Pension Protection Act of 2006 requires employers with underfunded plans to gradually fully fund them within a seven-year period starting in 2008. There are two exceptions to the gradual funding requirement. For example, plans that more significantly under-funded must fully fund more quickly. Another exception is for plans in the airline industry: two airlines (Delta and Northwest) have 17 years to achieve full funding; and other airlines have 10 years.[3]

Maximums

Defined Benefit Plans. The maximum annual retirement benefit an individual can receive from a defined benefit plan in 2008 is the *lesser* of $185,000 or an amount equal to the average compensation of the individual's three highest years while a participant in the plan.

Defined Contribution Plans. The maximum amount that can be contributed in 2008 to a participant's defined contribution plan is the *lesser* of $46,000 or 100 percent of the employee's annual compensation. This amount is adjusted for inflation in increments of $1,000. This maximum includes all contributions (those made by the employer and the employee) made in behalf of an employee. Some employers have more than one defined contribution plan, such as a noncontributory pension plan and a 401(k) plan to which both the employee and the employer contribute. The sum of all these contributions cannot exceed the above limit.

Plan Terminations

Employers have the right to terminate pension plans. Previous tax deductions are not disqualified, provided that the IRS deems that the employer's original intent was to establish a permanent plan. Plans in force for several years usually are not questioned by the IRS. The only plan assets that can revert to the employer are those funds in excess of those needed to provide employee benefits.

Plan Administration

Plan administration is an important aspect of ERISA. It includes filing governmental forms, appropriate recordkeeping of employees' benefits, disclosure requirements to employees and other benefit recipients and claim and investment administration. The reporting requirements include:

- *Annual Report Form 5500*, below, which must be filed each year with the IRS. Exhibit 22-1 is a copy of Form 5500.

---

[3] Ibid., p.2.

Exhibit 22-1

Form **5500** Department of the Treasury Internal Revenue Service Department of Labor Pension and Welfare Benefits Administration Pension Benefit Guaranty Corporation	**Annual Return/Report of Employee Benefit Plan** This form is required to be filed under sections 104 and 4065 of the Employee Retirement Income Security Act of 1974 (ERISA) and sections 6039D, 6047(e), 6057(b), and 6058(a) of the Internal Revenue Code (the Code). ▶ Complete all entries in accordance with the Instructions to the Form 5500.	Official Use Only OMB Nos. 1210 – 0110 1210 – 0089 **1999** This Form is Open to Public Inspection

Part I	**Annual Report Identification Information**

For the calendar plan year 1999 or fiscal plan year beginning   ,   and ending   ,

A This return/report is for: (1) ☐ a multiemployer plan;   (3) ☐ a multiple-employer plan;
    (2) ☐ a single-employer plan (other than a   (4) ☐ a DFE (specify) _____
        multiple-employer plan);

B This return/report is: (1) ☐ the first return/report filed for the plan;   (3) ☐ the final return/report filed for the plan;
    (2) ☐ an amended return/report;   (4) ☐ a short plan year return/report (less than 12 months).

C If the plan is a collectively-bargained plan, check here . . . . ▶ ☐

D If you filed for an extension of time to file, check the box and attach a copy of the extension application . . . . ▶ ☐

Part II	**Basic Plan Information** — enter all requested information.

1a Name of plan

1b Three-digit plan number (PN) ▶

1c Effective date of plan (mo., day, yr.)

2a Plan sponsor's name and address (employer, if for a single-employer plan)
(Address should include room or suite no.)

2b Employer Identification Number (EIN)

2c Sponsor's telephone number

2d Business code (see instructions)

Caution: A penalty for the late or incomplete filing of this return/report will be assessed unless reasonable cause is established.

Under penalties of perjury and other penalties set forth in the instructions, I declare that I have examined this return/report, including accompanying schedules, statements and attachments, and to the best of my knowledge and belief, it is true, correct, and complete.

_____   _____   _____
Signature of plan administrator   Date   Typed or printed name of individual signing as plan administrator

_____   _____   _____
Signature of employer/plan sponsor/DFE   Date   Typed or printed name of individual signing as employer, plan sponsor or DFE as applicable

For Paperwork Reduction Act Notice and OMB Control Numbers, see the Instructions for Form 5500.   v2.3   Form **5500** (1999)

Form 5500 (1999)   Page **2**

3a Plan administrator's name and address (If same as plan sponsor, enter "Same")

3b Administrator's EIN

3c Administrator's telephone number

4 If the name and/or EIN of the plan sponsor has changed since the last return/report filed for this plan, enter the name, EIN and the plan number from the last return/report below:

a Sponsor's name

b EIN

c PN

5 Preparer information (optional)   **a** Name (including firm name, if applicable) and address

b EIN

c Telephone no.

6 Total number of participants at the beginning of the plan year **6**

7 Number of participants as of the end of the plan year (welfare plans complete only lines **7a, 7b, 7c,** and **7d**)

a Active participants. **7a**

b Retired or separated participants receiving benefits **7b**

c Other retired or separated participants entitled to future benefits **7c**

d Subtotal. Add lines **7a, 7b,** and **7c** **7d**

e Deceased participants whose beneficiaries are receiving or are entitled to receive benefits **7e**

f Total. Add lines **7d** and **7e** **7f**

g Number of participants with account balances as of the end of the plan year (only defined contribution plans complete this item) **7g**

h Number of participants that terminated employment during the plan year with accrued benefits that were less than 100% vested **7h**

i If any participant(s) separated from service with a deferred vested benefit, enter the number of separated participants required to be reported on a Schedule SSA (Form 5500) **7i**

8 Benefits provided under the plan (complete **8a** through **8c,** as applicable)

a ☐ Pension benefits (check this box if the plan provides pension benefits and enter the applicable pension feature codes from the List of Plan Characteristics Codes (printed in the instructions)):

b ☐ Welfare benefits (check this box if the plan provides welfare benefits and enter the applicable welfare feature codes from the List of Plan Characteristics Codes (printed in the instructions)):

c ☐ Fringe benefits (check this box if the plan provides fringe benefits)

9a Plan funding arrangement (check all that apply)
- **(1)** ☐ Insurance
- **(2)** ☐ Section 412(i) insurance contracts
- **(3)** ☐ Trust
- **(4)** ☐ General assets of the sponsor

9b Plan benefit arrangement (check all that apply)
- **(1)** ☐ Insurance
- **(2)** ☐ Section 412(i) insurance contracts
- **(3)** ☐ Trust
- **(4)** ☐ General assets of the sponsor

Form 5500 (1999)   Page **3**

10 Schedules attached (Check all applicable boxes and, where indicated, enter the number attached. See instructions.)

a Pension Benefit Schedules
- **(1)** ☐ **R** (Retirement Plan Information)
- **(2)** ☐ ___ **T** (Qualified Pension Plan Coverage Information)
  If a Schedule T is not attached because the plan is relying on coverage testing information for a prior year, enter the year . . . . ▶ ___
- **(3)** ☐ **B** (Actuarial Information)
- **(4)** ☐ **E** (ESOP Annual Information)
- **(5)** ☐ **SSA** (Separated Vested Participant Information)

b Financial Schedules
- **(1)** ☐ **H** (Financial Information)
- **(2)** ☐ **I** (Financial Information -- Small Plan)
- **(3)** ☐ **A** (Insurance Information)
- **(4)** ☐ **C** (Service Provider Information)
- **(5)** ☐ **D** (DFE/Participating Plan Information)
- **(6)** ☐ **G** (Financial Transaction Schedules)
- **(7)** ☐ **P** (Trust Fiduciary Information)

c Fringe Benefit Schedule
- ☐ **F** (Fringe Benefit Plan Annual Information)

- *Summary Plan Description,* which must be furnished to participants 120 days after a plan is established or 90 days after an employee becomes eligible for the plan.

- *Summary Annual Report,* containing the financial data of the plan, which must be furnished to participants and pension plan beneficiaries receiving benefits within 120 days after the start of the plan year. If the plan has serious financial funding problems, the notification must state the nature of such problems and the procedure to obtain a copy of the plan to correct them.[4]

- *Summary of Material Modifications,* containing any changes to the plan, which must be furnished to participants within 210 days of the date that the plan is changed.

- *Individual Benefits Statements,* containing information on total accrued benefits and nonforfeitable pension benefits (if any) must be furnished to participants and beneficiaries every three years for defined benefit plans and annually for defined contribution plans.[5]

Nondiscrimination Requirements

Qualified plans may not discriminate in favor of highly compensated employees. A person who meets any one of the following definitions is considered to be a *highly compensated employee*:

- Who was a five-percent owner at any time during the year or the preceding year or

- Who had compensation from the employer in excess of $100,000 and was in the top-paid group of employees for the preceding year. The $100,000 threshold is indexed for inflation. An employee is in the top-paid group if he or she is among the 20 percent of employees ranked highest, based on the amount of compensation paid during the year.

Coverage Tests

For a retirement plan to be qualified it must meet one or more of the following tests:

- *Percentage test.* To meet this test, 70 percent or more of non-highly compensated employees must be covered by the plan.

- *Ratio test.* The percentage of non-highly compensated employees covered by the plan must be at least 70 percent of the percentage of highly compensated employees who are covered in order to qualify under this test.

- *Average benefits test.* To meet this test, the plan must cover a "fair cross section" of employees and not discriminate in favor of highly compensated employees, and the average benefit percentage for non-highly com-

---

[4] U.S. Senate Republican Policy Committee, *Legislative Notice: H.R. 4—Pension Protection Act of 2006,* p. 11.

[5] Ibid.

pensated employees must be at least 70 percent of that for highly compensated employees.

Defined Benefit Plans

Due to their complexity and regulatory requirements, the number of defined benefit plans are declining somewhat in favor of defined contribution plans. In 2008, 20 percent of employees in private industry were participating in defined benefit plans and 43 percent were participating in defined contribution plans.[6] Defined benefit plans are also referred to as *unit benefit trusteed or insured plans.* These plans provide retirement benefits, based upon the accumulation of units of retirement credits earned from years of service or the amount of earnings, or a combination of the two. Several formulas are used to calculate benefits. These formulas, with examples of benefit calculations, are discussed below.

Defined benefit plans are quite complex to establish and administer. Some considerations involved in the establishment of defined benefit plans are:

- Benefit formulas;
- Coordination with Social Security;
- Maximum and minimum benefit;
- Methods of payment;
- Survivor rates;
- Replacement rates;
- Disability provisions;
- Vesting;
- Participation requirements;
- Portability; and
- Postretirement pension increases.

Employee Contributions

Few employers that offer defined benefit retirement plans require contributions by employees. Only three percent of employees in private sector firms who are participating in defined benefit plans are required to contribute.[7]

Participation Requirements

Most private sector retirement plans that have a participation requirement stipulate employees must have one year of service and be 21 years of age. These are the most restrictive requirement permitted by ERISA.

Other Provisions

Two other important provisions for employees enrolled in retirement plans concern early retirement and disability retirement. Virtually all employees participating in defined benefit plans may retire before the normal retirement age and

---

[6] Bureau of Labor Statistics, *National Compensation Survey: Employee Benefits in Private Industry in the United States, March 2008.*

[7] Bureau of Labor Statistics, *National Compensation Survey: Employee Benefits in Private Industry in the United States, March 2008.*

receive an immediate, but reduced, annuity. Disability retirement benefits typically differ for blue-collar and white-collar workers. Blue-collar employees generally are in plans that provide immediate disability benefits. In contrast, white-collar workers usually have long-term disability benefits paying up to 60 percent of replacement income; such benefits are usually provided until retirement or for a specified number of years.

Defined Benefit Plan Formulas

The four types formulas for computing retirement benefits in a defined benefit plan are:

- Earnings-based;
- Flat-dollar amount;
- Percent-of-contribution; and
- Cash account.

Usually, different formulas are used for different classes of employees. For example, earnings-based formulas are used for white-collar employees, and flat-dollar formulas are used for blue-collar.

Earnings-Based Formulas

The most common formulas for defined benefit plans are *earnings-based,* paying a flat percent of the employee's annual earnings for each year of employment. The two principal types of these formulas are these:

- Final pay, also known as terminal earnings formula; and
- Career average formula.

Final Pay Formula. For most plan participants with earnings-based formulas, pensions are based upon earnings in the final years of employment. Known as *final pay* or *terminal earnings formulas,* the retirement benefit is based upon the average income of the last number of years of service, typically the last five years, multiplied by a percentage amount for each year of service. Often, these formulas specify the use of the five consecutive years, with the highest earnings out of the last 10 years of employment.

> **EXAMPLE:** ABC Company provides a retirement benefit of two percent for each year of service multiplied by an average of the employee's highest five years' pay. William is 65 years old, and he is retiring. He has 25 years with the company; the average of his highest five years of pay is $40,000. William's retirement pay from the plan will be $20,000 (25 years × .02/year × $40,000).

Some plans with terminal-earnings formulas have benefit formulas that vary according to service, earnings, or a combination of the two factors. As an example, the formula might credit an employee with one percent of earnings up to the first $12,000 in each year of employment, plus 1.5 percent of earnings exceeding that amount, multiplied by the number of years of employment.

> **EXAMPLE:** William had 30 years of employment with ABC Company. The company retirement plan credits employees with one percent of earn-

ings up to the first $10,000 in the last year of employment plus 1.5 percent of earnings above that amount in the last year, multiplied by the number of years of employment. William had 30 years of employment, and his pay for the final year was $50,000. William's retirement pay from the plan will be: {[(1.0%× $10,000) + (1.5% × $40,000)]× (30) = $21,000.

Career Average Formula. There two basic *career average formulas*. They are:

- Percentage of pay for each year of service covered by the plan:

   EXAMPLE: John's company has a retirement benefit of two-percent of pay for each year of employment. In the first year of employment, John earned $20,000; thus, he earned $400 that year toward his retirement ($20,000 × .02 = $400). The following year, his pay was $22,500, which earned him another $450 toward his retirement. The same procedure would be followed for subsequent years of employment.

- Average pay over the employee's working career, multiplied by a percentage amount for each year of service:

   EXAMPLE: Joan's company provides a retirement benefit of two percent for each year of service, multiplied by an employee's average career earnings with the company. Joan is 65, and she is retiring after 30 years with the company. Her average earnings for the 30 years are $35,000. Her retirement from the company will be $21,000 (30 years × .02/year × $35,000).

Flat-Dollar Formula

The flat dollar formula provides a benefit that is a specified dollar amount for each year of service.

   EXAMPLE: Beth's company provides a retirement benefit of $40 per month of retirement income for each year of service. Beth is 59 years old and is retiring after 28 years of employment with the company. Beth's monthly retirement income from the company's plan is $1,120 (28 years × $40).

Percentage-of-Contribution Formula

This formula specifies a periodic contribution to be made by the employer. Some plans also require the employee to make a contribution. Benefits are a percent of total accumulation.

   EXAMPLE: Scott's company has a percentage-of-contribution defined benefit plan that pays a monthly retirement benefit of two percent of the total contributions that accumulate in an account for Scott. The employer contributes one percent of Scott's pay into the account. Scott is not required to contribute to the account. Scott is retiring, and the account totals $90,000. Scott's monthly retirement will be $1,800 ($90,000 × .02).

This formula resembles the formulas in defined contribution plans, but the IRS classifies it as a defined benefit plan because the employer guarantees a certain level of benefits.

Cash Account Pension Formula

This formula specifies a certain periodic contribution that will be made by the employer, plus a rate of interest on the contribution. Benefits are computed as a percent of each employee's account balance upon retirement.

> **EXAMPLE:** Madge's company has a cash account pension defined benefit plan that pays a monthly retirement benefit of three percent of the total contributions that accumulate in an account for her. The employer contributes one percent of Madge's pay into the account, which earns an annual interest rate of five percent. Madge is retiring, and the account totals $100,000. Madge's monthly retirement benefit will be $3,000 ($100,000 × .03).

Like the percent-of-contribution formula, the cash account pension formula resembles the formulas in defined contribution plans but, once again, because the employer guarantees a certain level of benefits, the IRS classifies it as a defined benefit plan.

Hybrids

Both the *percentage-of-contribution* and the *cash account pension plans* are often referred to as *hybrids* because they have some similarities to both defined benefit and defined contribution plans. They resemble defined contribution plans because the employer agrees to contribute a certain percentage of the employee's pay to fund a retirement plan, and they resemble defined benefit plans because the employer agrees to provide a certain level of benefits. Another term for these hybrids is *cash balance plans*.

Social Security Coordination

Virtually all employers are required to make contributions to Social Security on behalf of their employees; in addition, some employers make contributions to a retirement plan on behalf of employees. For this reason, many employers feel that pension benefits should not duplicate what is provided under Social Security. To preclude this, some employers integrate their pension plans with Social Security. This integration is accomplished through either an offset plan or a step-rate excess plan.

Offset Plan

In an *offset plan,* part of the Social Security benefit is subtracted (or offset) from the pension benefit.

> **EXAMPLE:** ABC Company's retirement plan is integrated with Social Security benefits, through a reduction in the retirement benefit of 50 percent of the Social Security benefit. Joel, who is retiring, is entitled to a $1,600 per month pension from the company's retirement plan. In addition, he is entitled to a monthly Social Security retirement benefit of $1,000. ABC Company's pension plan reduces Joel's benefit by 1/2 of the Social Security benefit (or $500). Thus, Joel's monthly retirement income, from both the pension plan and Social Security, is $2,100 ($1,600 − $500 + $1,000).

Step-Rate Excess Plan

Another way of integrating a pension with Social Security is through a *step-rate excess plan,* which calculates the pension benefit at a lower rate for earnings below the Social Security taxable wage base and at a higher rate for earnings above the base.

> **EXAMPLE:** William has been employed by ABC Company for 30 years. The company retirement plan, which is integrated with Social Security, credits employees with one percent of earnings up to the first $106,800 (which is the taxable wage base for 2008) in the last year of employment, plus 1.5 percent of earnings above that amount in the last year, multiplied by the number of years of employment. William retired in 2009; his pay for the final year was $150,000. William's retirement pay from the plan will be $51,480 [(1.0%× $106,800) + (1.5% × $43,200)] × (30).

Methods of Payment

All the benefit formulas discussed above are used to calculate a *straight-life annuity,* which is a regular annuity for the life of the retiree, with no adjustments for survivors. If a retiree is married, the law requires that a *joint-and-survivor annuity* be used, which provides an annuity for the surviving spouse should the retiree die. Both the retiree and the spouse have the option of selecting a straight-life annuity in lieu of a joint-and-survivor annuity, but only upon written approval of both the retiree and the spouse.

The retiree may also opt for a lump-sum settlement, in which case no monthly annuity would be received. Another option is for a partial lump-sum settlement, plus a reduced monthly annuity. In both of the above options, the amounts the employee receives are the actuarial equivalent of a regular monthly annuity for the retiree's life.

Survivor Benefits

ERISA requires that a surviving spouse receives at least 50 percent of the retiree's annuity after his or her death; the result is that the retiree receives a lower retirement annuity. Most plans also offer the survivor preretirement benefits in the event that an employee dies before retiring.

Replacement Rates

Replacement rate is the amount of the retiree's final year's pay that is interchanged with the retirement annuity. Generally, the lower the level of income of the retiree prior to retirement, the higher the replacement rate. For example, an employee who was employed for 30 years, earning $25,000 a year and retiring at 65, would receive, from his or her pension and Social Security combined, approximately 72 percent of his or her preretirement earnings. A person who had the same amount of service and had attained the same retirement age (65), but who was earning $65,000 at retirement, would only receive a retirement income from both sources of approximately 50 percent of his or her preretirement income.

Vesting

Over 89 percent of defined benefit plans use *cliff vesting.*[8]

Postretirement Pension Increases

Retirement plans with flat-dollar benefits have been seriously affected by inflation. Some plans address the issue of preretirement inflation by periodically adjusting benefits upward. Increases in wages during the working years also help keep up with inflation.

Few private plans, however, adjust postretirement benefits on a predetermined basis because of the uncertain cost commitment. Instead, some plans make *ad hoc* increases in benefits. A few plans link benefits to the asset values of the retirement investment fund.

Automatic *cost-of-living adjustments,* known as COLAs, which are provided in a few private plans, link increases in benefits to changes in the Consumer Price Index. COLAs are more often found in public plans, such as the Social Security program, as well as the Civil Service Retirement and military retirement systems.

Defined Contribution Plans

Defined contribution plans are easier to administer and have fewer regulatory requirements than defined benefit plans; therefore, it should not be surprising that more employers are shifting to defined contribution plans. The level of employer contributions is specified but not the manner in which benefits will be determined. Individual accounts are established for each participant, and contributions, either a percentage of salary or some other method, are used to credit the accounts. In addition, the funds in the account earn interest, which, in turn, is credited to each participant.

Employee Contributions

Most defined contribution plans require employees to make contributions; in contrast, few defined benefit plans require employee contributions. Some organizations have both defined benefit and defined contribution plans; in such cases, employees may be required to contribute to one plan but not to the other.

Types of Plans

The types of defined contribution plans are:

- Savings and thrift plans;
- Deferred arrangement plan;
- Deferred profit-sharing plans;
- Money purchase pension plans; and
- Employee stock ownership plans.

---

[8] Bureau of Labor Statistics, *National Compensation Survey: Employee Benefits in Private Industry in the United States, 2005,* May 2007, p. 77.

Savings or Thrift Plans

Savings or thrift plans are defined contribution plans that require employee contributions, which the employer matches, up to a specified percentage. Thus, the plans provide an incentive for employees to save. The contributions are usually in pretax dollars and are invested in financial instruments, such as stocks, bonds, and money market funds, as directed by the employer or the employee and provided by the plan. Withdrawals are permitted for specific reasons, such as medical or educational expenses. In addition, employees are permitted to borrow from their individual plans. Some plans also permit newly hired employees to "roll over" balances that accrued in savings and thrift plans from previous employers, without having to incur a tax liability.

Employees are permitted to vary the rates of contributions on a pretax basis, unless the plan is a 401(a) plan, discussed below. In addition, employees are sometimes offered the option of participating in more than one plan. At retirement, payouts are usually in a lump sum or an annuity, paid over the retiree's lifetime.

Vesting. Savings and thrift plans are subject to the same vesting requirements under ERISA as other qualified retirement plans.

401(a) Plan

The 401(a) plan is a savings plan in which the employee's contributions are in after-tax dollars, instead of pretax dollars, as with the 401(k). The principal reason for employees electing a 401(a), rather than the 401(k), is that the 401(a) plan permits the withdrawal of funds without having to justify a hardship condition. However, since the earnings on the savings are not currently taxable, both the federal income tax and a 10-percent federal excise tax is due for any premature withdrawals attributable to earnings on the savings. Some employers offer both the 401(a) and the 401(k) plans; employees are permitted to enroll in either or both.

Cash or Deferred Arrangement Plan

A *cash or deferred arrangement plan*, sometimes referred to as a *CODA*, permits employees to choose between receiving taxable income from their pay or deferring taxation on a portion of their pay and using it to fund a retirement plan. Two types of cash or deferred arrangements are the 401(k) plan and the 403(b) plan.

Salary Reduction or 401(k) Plans

Salary reduction plans, usually called *401(k) plans,* permit employees to direct a portion of pretax salary to savings plans. Starting in the mid-1980s, employers increasingly added 401(k) plans to their defined contribution plans or established new plans with 401(k) provisions. Employer contributions to such plans are important in motivating employees to participate. For example, in 2008, 43 percent of employees in the private sector were participating in plans that had employer contributions.[9]

There are significant tax advantages to 401(k) plans, since federal withholding taxes are based on the employee's gross salary after 401(k) contributions. Social security taxes and unemployment taxes are based on the employee's gross salary before the reduction for the 401(k) is made. A person who contributes to a savings plan is much better off with a deferred savings plan than they are trying to save a similar amount after taxes.

EXAMPLE: Assume an individual's gross income is $40,000, and the federal tax rate is 25 percent. The employee wants to save $1,000 a year and has to decide whether to contribute to a 401(k) plan or to a private savings account in a credit union. Assume the savings for both alternatives earn an annual compound interest rate of 10 percent.

Alternative 1—401(k) plan: The employee saves the $1,000 through contributions to a 401(k) plan at work; thus, the employee receives a gross salary of $39,000. The 401(k) earnings are tax deferred so they accrue in the account.

Alternative 2—Private plan: The employee receives the salary of $40,000; however, only $750 remains of the $1,000 the employee wants to save, because the other $250 was paid in federal taxes. The private investment is not tax-deferred; therefore, the after-tax rate of return is only 7.5 percent.

Results: The effect of the two types of savings methods are shown in Exhibit 22-2, below. The amount accumulated through the 401(k) is more than twice that which could be accumulated through the after-tax private investment.

Exhibit 22-2
Accumulations in 401(k) v. Private Investment Plans

	Amount accumulated	
Number of years accumulated	*401(k)*	*Private investment*
10	$15,937	$10,610
20	57,275	32,479
30	164,494	77,550

Safe Harbor 401(k) Plan

A safe harbor 401(k) plan is like the regular 401(k) plan but there are several differences which may make it more appealing to smaller firms because it does not require annual discrimination testing to determine if the plan favors highly compensated employees. However, to avoid this and other complex tax rules, the plan must meet these conditions:

- Employer contributions must be fully vested when made to employee accounts.

- Employer contributions must be made under one of these two methods:

[9] Bureau of Labor Statistics, *National Compensation Survey: Employee Benefits in Private Industry in the United States, 2008* (March 2008).

- The first method is to match each employee's contribution on a dollar for dollar basis up to 3 percent of the employee's pay and 50 cents for each dollar of each employee's contributions that exceeds 3 percent but not more than 5 percent of pay.

- The other method is to make a nonelective contribution of 3 percent of pay to each eligible employee's account.

Another requirement is for the employer to annually make either the matching or nonelective contributions to employee accounts.[10]

Safe Harbor for Plans with Automatic Enrollment.

There is another safe harbor provision for plans following the automatic enrollment of employees if they meet minimum and maximum rates of contribution up to 10 percent. The minimum rates are graduated one percent increases beginning with 3 percent in the first year up to 6 percent in the four and subsequent years. Full vesting must be after two years in the plan.

The 403(b) Plan or Tax-Sheltered Annuity

Tax-exempt organizations do not have the same tax incentive to provide a pension plan for employees as do taxpaying businesses. As a result, it was believed that employees of tax-exempt organizations would not have adequate retirement coverage. This concern gave Congress the impetus to enact Section 403(b) of the Internal Revenue Code, which permits employees of public schools and certain other nonprofit organizations, as described under Section 501(c)(3) of the Code, to set aside funds on a tax-deferred basis. These plans are also referred to as *tax-sheltered annuities*.

Eligibility. The types of organizations that may offer a 403(b) plan are:

- Nonprofit organizations, such as charitable, religious, educational and scientific private organizations; and

- Public schools and colleges.

Organizations that are not eligible to offer 403(b) plans are government agencies, recreational clubs, and credit unions.

Types. There are 2 types of 403(b) plans: those provided by employer-paid contributions to covered employees and those provided by employees' contributions through a salary reduction arrangement. The first type of plan is not commonly used. Under the salary reduction plan, the employee has the option to divert some of his or her salary to the 403(b) plan. A written salary reduction agreement is executed in which the employee directs the employer to reduce his or her salary by a specified amount or percentage and to remit the funds to a financial institution which the employee has designated to receive the funds. At retirement, the employee may select a lump-sum distribution or periodic payments. Income is taxed at ordinary income tax rates in the year it is received.

---

[10] U.S. Department of Labor, *401(k) Plans for Small Businesses* (no date), p. 2 & 3.

Section 457 Plans . Section 457 plans are defined contribution plans that only apply to employees of state and local governments and tax-exempt organizations.

Individual Retirement Account (IRA). These are the major types of IRAs:

- *Traditional IRA*. A *traditional IRA*, sometimes called an "ordinary IRA" or a "regular IRA," can be established if an individual has taxable income and was not age 70 by the end of the year. Contributions are deductible and earnings are not taxed until distributed. The individual's spouse also qualifies for a *traditional IRA* subject to income and age provisions. The deduction for the individual and/or the spouse may be reduced or phased out if either is covered by a retirement plan at work and their modified adjusted gross annual income exceeds certain limits.

- *Roth IRA*. A *Roth IRA* can be established at any time, even after reaching 70 and the amounts in the plan can be left as long as the individual lives. Unlike a *traditional IRA* contributions to a *Roth IRA* are not tax deductible. Subject to specific age and length of time rules since the plan was established, earnings and distributions are not taxable. Contributions to a *Roth IRA* are subject to modified adjusted gross annual income limitations.

- *Simple IRA*. A *Simple IRA* is a tax-favored retirement plan that certain small employers (including those who are self-employed) can establish for their employees. Employees must be allowed to participate if they received at least $5,000 in compensation during any two years prior to the current year and are reasonably expected to receive $5,000 in compensation during the calendar year in which contributions will be made.

- *Simplified Employee Pension (SEP)*. A SEP is a plan that permits employers to make contributions towards their own retirement (if they are self-employed) and their employees. These contributions are made to a *traditional IRA* (see above) that is set up for each employee (these are called *SEP-IRAs*). Each employee controls his/her own SEP-IRA. Employees are qualified for a SEP if they are 21, have worked for the employer for three of the past five years and received a minimum amount of compensation (in 2009 the amount was $550).

Maximum Contributions. For Traditional IRA plans, the maximum pretax contributions in 2008 are $5,000 ($6,000 for persons age 50 and above). Beyond 2007, the maximum is indexed for inflation.

For Simplified Employee Pension (SEP) plans, the maximum pretax contributions in 2008 cannot exceed the lesser of 25 percent of compensation or $46,000. Special rules apply to contributions by self-employed individuals. Beyond 2008, this maximum is indexed for inflation.

The maximum amount of pretax contributions that can be made by participants in 401(k), 403(b) and 457 plans are:

For taxable year:	Amount
2003	$12,000
2004	$13,000
2005	$14,000
2006	$15,000
2007 and 2008	$15,500

Beyond 2008 the maximum will be indexed for inflation.

For SIMPLE IRAs and SIMPLE 401(k) plans, the maximum pretax contributions are:

For taxable year	Amount
2003	$8,000
2004	$9,000
2005	$10,000
2006	$10,000
2007 and 2008	$10,500

Beyond 2008 the maximum will be indexed for inflation.

For Roth IRAs the maximum contributions (after-tax) are:

For taxable year	Amount
2003	$3,000
2004	$3,000
2005	$4,000
2006	$4,000
2007	$4,000
2008	$5,000

Beyond 2008 the maximum will be indexed for inflation

Catch-Up Contributions

Additional pre-tax contributions, above the maximum contributions shown above, can be made by plan participants who are age 50 before the end of the taxable year.

SIMPLE IRAs and SIMPLE 401(k) Plans

The dollar limit on these additional contributions for SIMPLE IRAs and SIMPLE 401(k) plans are:

For taxable year:	Catch-up
2003	$1,000
2004	$1,500
2005	$2,000
2006-2010	$2,500

Plans other than SIMPLE IRAs and SIMPLE 401(k) Plans

For other than SIMPLE IRAs and SIMPLE 401(k) plans (such as 403(b) and 457 plans) the limits are:

For taxable year:	Catch-up
2003	$2,000
2004	$3,000

For taxable year:	Catch-up
2005	$4,000
2006-2010	$5,000

Traditional and Roth IRAs

Additional contributions to a traditional and Roth IRA are also permitted for persons who are age 50 before the end of the taxable year:

For taxable year:	Catch-up
2003-2005	$500
2006-2010	$1,000

Deferred Profit-Sharing Plans

A *profit-sharing plan* is funded by contributions from employers that agree to share profits with employees. A profit-sharing plan may be either a *cash plan,* in which the proceeds are currently taxable income to employees, or a *qualified deferred plan,* in which plan contributions accumulate for later retirement years, and the tax consequences are deferred until retirement. Deferred profit-sharing plans have the same basic objectives as other types of retirement plans, but they are particularly suited for the purpose of motivating employees to increase efficiency and productivity, by demonstrating a link between their increased efforts and the contributions made on their behalf. Some profit-sharing plans are a combination of both a cash and deferred retirement plan.

Requirements

As with other types of retirement plans, ERISA requires that profit-sharing plans be in writing, be communicated to employees, be for the exclusive benefit of employees, and be nondiscriminatory and permanent in nature. Minimum eligibility and vesting requirements are also the same. In practice, however, eligibility and vesting requirements are usually more liberal, because of the employer's objective of using the plan as an incentive for increased employee productivity and morale.

Employer Contributions

Although a profit-sharing plan must be established with the intent to be permanent, a contribution need not be made for a year in which profits do not justify one. The regulations state that contributions must be "substantial and recurring" in order to fulfill the permanency requirement. Implicit in this definition is an understanding that a contribution may not be made in a given year, unless there are sufficient profits to share. Often, employer contributions are determined by a formula, such as three percent of profits, if the sales for the firm are over $10 million but less than $15 million. The percentage of profits shared may increase to six percent, if the sales are over $15 million. In other plans, the amount to be shared depends upon the employer's discretion, without any predetermined formula.

Allocating Shares

Often, profits are shared with each employee in the same proportion as the employee's pay is to total pay for all employees. Thus, each employee's share=[Employee's pay ÷ Total pay]×Profit-sharing pool.

> **EXAMPLE:** ABC Company has a deferred profit-sharing plan in which each employee's share of the profits is equivalent to the percentage of his or her pay to total pay of all employees. Amounts are credited annually to each employee's retirement fund. Last year, the combined pay for all employees was $6,000,000; the profit-sharing pool was $500,000. Marge Brown's pay was $30,000. What amount is credited to Marge Brown's retirement account? The answer is

Profit-sharing pool=$500,000

Combined pay for all employees=$6,000,000

Employee Marge Brown's pay=$30,000

Marge's share=[$30,000 ÷ $6,000,000]×$500,000=$2,500

Money Purchase Pension Plans

Money purchase pension plans are funded through a fixed contribution from the employer. Each employee has a separate account, and a fixed percentage of each employee's pay (for instance four percent annually) is credited to the account. These contributions, plus earnings, are distributed at the employee's retirement.

Typically, employee contributions are not permitted, nor do employees participate in investment decisions. Withdrawals for any reason are usually not permitted prior to retirement. Instead, the accumulated funds are used to purchase an annuity, often from an insurance company, that guarantees a retirement income for life, or the accumulated amount in the employee's account may be paid out in a lump sum or periodically for a fixed period of time.

A variation of the money purchase plan is a group-deferred annuity. A *group-deferred annuity* is a defined contribution retirement plan in which the employer purchases incremental paid-up retirement annuities from an insurance company for employees after specified periods of time, such as on a annual basis.

Stock Plans

Two types of stock plans, which are considered defined contribution plans, are employee stock ownership plans and stock bonus plans.

Employee Stock Ownership Plans

An *employee stock ownership plan (ESOP)* is an arrangement whereby the employees in a company are given various amounts (up to 100 percent) of ownership in a company through the issuance of stock. The plans are usually wholly employer financed and are invested in the company's stock. Often, ESOPs are used to arrange financing to purchase the company, with the stock as collateral. As the loan is repaid, the stock is released back to the company and distributed to employees.

Advantages. Chief among the advantages of ESOPs is that employees become owners of the firm. In addition, employees receive profits from the firm, which are distributed as dividends, based upon the relative amount of their stock holdings. As a retirement arrangement, the dividends and the stock distributions are credited to each employee's retirement account and used to finance a retirement income.

Disadvantages. Unfortunately, not all the results of an ESOP are good ones. There are several reasons that the arrangement may go sour. First, some ESOPs are designed to prevent a company from failing. When the ESOP is used for this purpose, employees are usually required to make financial sacrifices, such as wage and benefit rollbacks and concessions in work rules and employment conditions. Employees grudgingly agree to these arrangements, either to protect their jobs or for the promise of future stock ownership, dividend accumulations, and appreciation of their stock holdings. Sometimes, these promises are not fulfilled, or at least not to the employees' expectations. For example, in one company, the Board of Directors postponed sharing profits with employees because they were needed for capital expenditures. While employees who were on the Board resisted the proposed action, they were outvoted. The result was a work slowdown and a new union contract that dramatically raised costs and threatened the company's future.[11] In another case, employees agreed to wage freezes and the discontinuance of their pension plan, but the company continued to lose money, despite a 20-percent improvement in productivity. In this same company, three employees served on the Board of Directors, and employees elected a majority of the Board members. Paradoxically, union leaders at this company accused management of inefficiencies and other failures.[12]

Some important lessons may be learned from these experiences. First, an ESOP is not a panacea for labor-management strife and poor communication. If anything, an ESOP requires the utmost in trust and shared information. Companies would be well-advised to carefully plan employee communications before they initiated action for an ESOP. Second, employees cannot be expected to indefinitely forego some profit distributions; they must be able to benefit from their labor and any financial sacrifices they made. In short, there is little incentive to own stock in a company if there are no profits to share or realized profits are not shared.

Stock Bonus Plans

A *stock bonus plan* is funded through distributions in either company stock or cash. Plan contributions are made either solely by the employer or by the employee and the employer. These contributions are made to a separate trust fund for each employee who invests in various securities.

Insider Trading

Unfortunately, in the past some unscrupulous executives and directors have used their inside knowledge of business operations to engage in stock trading

---

[11] Myers, D.W., *Compensation Management* (Chicago: CCH, 1989), p. 523.

[12] *Ibid.*, p. 524.

during blackout periods in which other employees were prohibited from making trades. In response to this abuse, the SEC issued rules prohibiting, during a blackout period, any actions by a director or executive officer to directly or indirectly, "purchase, sell, or otherwise acquire or transfer any equity security...(of the firm that was)...acquired...in connection with his or her employment as a director or executive officer."[13] The SEC rule explains the reason for the prohibition is to prevent the unfairness of restricting employees from engaging in any trades of their holdings acquired as a reason of their employment with the firm, while directors and executive officers have engaged in such trading.

Non-qualified Retirement Plans

A *non-qualified retirement plan* does not qualify for favorable tax treatment under the Internal Revenue Code. These plans may discriminate in favor of highly compensated employees.

Safeguarding Pensions

A major concern to employees is the safety of their retirement contributions. Among the concerns are fraud, failure of the fiduciary to safeguard funds and employer bankruptcy. The Pension and Welfare Benefits Administration (PWBA), U.S. Department of Labor is responsible for administering ERISA. One of ERISA's purposes, noted at the beginning of this chapter, is to establish safeguards for employee retirement plans. In addition, employees in both defined benefit and defined contribution plans have responsibilities to help protect their retirement plans.

Wise Investments

Employees must recognize their obligation to make wise investment decisions if a plan gives them the option. Selecting an investment strategy depends upon several important considerations. For example, some mutual funds are riskier than others so while the potential for rewards may be higher - the reverse is also true. Also, some people have a greater tolerance for risk than others. In addition, a probable retirement date is an important consideration in choosing among investment alternatives.

Educating Participants

The Pension Protection Act of 2006, contained an important provision requiring employers to educate employees about their pensions and to help prevent employees from making uninformed investment decisions where they have right to make such judgments in 401(k) plans, IRAs and others. Under this law, employers are required to educate employees about their pensions including making investments, their rights and responsibilities, payout alternatives and tax consequences.[14] Furthermore professional investment advice can be provided to employees but the fees for such advice must either be independent of the type of investment selected or based upon a computer model.

---

[13] Securities and Exchange Commission, *Insider Trades During Pension Fund Blackout Periods* (January 26, 2003), p. 1. See this rule for the definition of the terms director and executive officer.

[14] CCH, *CCH Tax Briefing: Pension Protection Act of 2006*, (August 17, 2006), p. 3.

Monitor Contributions

In qualified retirement plans, employers make contributions on behalf of employees and/or withhold funds from employee pay for retirement purposes. Unfortunately, there have been situations where employers did not make contributions to retirement plans, as required. Employees have responsibilities in these and similar situations. First, they should confirm all deductions for retirement purposes have in fact been sent to the plan's trust. They should review their individual benefit statements and verify amounts withheld from their pay equal contributions to their retirement plans. Also, they should ensure funds are being wisely invested. Employees who have questions about these matters should contact the nearest office of the PWBA.

Bankruptcy

Typically, employee retirement contributions are safe in the event of employer bankruptcy since employers are required to keep pension funds apart from a firm's other assets and be held in trust or invested in an ensured contract such as an insurance annuity. Defined benefit retirement plans have an additional layer of protection since the promised benefits are ensured either partially or fully by the Pension Benefit Guaranty Corporation, which is a corporation of the Federal Government.

Plan Administrators

Under ERISA plan administrators have fiduciary responsibilities to plan participants. These responsibilities differ somewhat for defined benefit and defined contribution plans. Typically an administrator's misconduct in a defined benefit plan will not adversely affect a participant's benefit unless it increases the likelihood of the entire plan's failure. Conversely, an administrator's misconduct in an individual's defined contribution plan could have serious ramifications for the individual. In a 2008 decision, the U. S. Supreme Court succinctly addressed the distinction in misconduct involving the two types of plans:

"Misconduct by . . . a plan's administrators will not affect an individual's entitlement to a defined benefit unless it creates or enhances the risk of default by the entire plan. For defined contribution plans, however, fiduciary misconduct need not threaten the entire plan's solvency to reduce benefits below the amount that participants would otherwise receive."[15]

The Court's decision went on to state that certain provisions of ERISA do "authorize recovery for fiduciary breaches that impair the value of plan assets in a participant's individual account."[16] As defined benefit plans are increasingly being replaced by defined contribution plans, plan participants are well-advised to monitor the actions of their plan administrators. This decision by the U. S. Supreme Court shows federal courts will support such vigilance if losses in individual' assets in defined contribution plans are due to administrator misconduct.

---

[15] For more information see *LaRue v. DeWolff, Boberg & Associates, Inc.* (2008) in Appendix 1.   [16] Ibid.

Financial Accounting Standards Board

The Financial Accounting Standards Board (FASB) is covered in Chapter 18. FASB issues standards pertaining to the accounting practices of publically held firms. *Standard Nos. 87 and 88* require employers to accurately reflect in financial statements liabilities associated with retirement benefits. This helps ensure that employers are accruing or setting aside reserves for employee pension obligations.

Qualified Domestic Relations Order

A *Qualified Domestic Relations Order* (QDRO) is an order "that creates or recognizes the existence of an 'alternate payee's' right to receive, or assigns to an alternate payee the right to receive, all or a portion of the benefits payable with respect to a participant under a pension plan."[17] According to Federal law, a QDRO may "assign some or all of a participant's pension benefits to a spouse, former spouse, child, or other dependent to satisfy family support or marital proper obligations if . . . the order is a 'qualified domestic relations order.'"

These are the provisions a QDRO *must not* contain:

- "Require the plan to provide an alternate payee or participant with any benefit not provided by the plan."

- "Require a plan to provide increased benefits based on an actuarial value."

- "Require a plan to pay benefits to an alternate payee that are required to be paid to another alternate payee under a previous QDRO."

- "Require a plan to pay benefits to an alternate payee in the form of a qualified joint and survivor annuity for the lives of the alternate payee and his/her subsequent spouse."[18]

A QDRO may be "issued by a state agency or instrumentality with the authority to issue judgments, decrees, or orders, or to approve property settlement agreements, pursuant to state domestic relations law." A QDRO does not have to be issued by a state court.[19]

A QDRO *must* contain the following:

- "The name and last known mailing address of the participant and each alternate payee."

- "The name of each plan to which the order applies."

- "The dollar amount or percentage of the benefit to be paid to the alternate payee."

- "The number of payments or time period to which the order applies."[20]

---

[17] Pension Benefit Welfare Association, U.S. Department of Labor.
[18] Ibid.
[19] Ibid.
[20] Ibid.

CHAPTER 23
MANDATED BENEFIT PLANS

Chapter Highlights
- Social Security
- Workers' compensation
- Unemployment compensation
- State compulsory disability

Introduction

Many factors are responsible for making employees unable to work and earn salaries. The major contingency, one that ultimately affects all workers, is death. Some workers experience periodic intervals of unemployment due to economic conditions or become disabled through a work-related condition or from an incident occurring away from work. Mandated benefit programs are intended to protect workers and their dependents from the economic consequences of these events. The federally mandated benefit programs are Social Security, workers' compensation, and unemployment insurance. In several states, employers are required to provide disability insurance to protect employees and their dependents in the event of nonoccupational disability.

Social Security

Social Security is a significant benefit, since it replaces a portion of earnings lost as a result of death, disability, or retirement. Benefits are also payable to qualified survivors. Medical care insurance is difficult for many persons to obtain, but individuals who meet certain requirements are entitled to receive Medicare benefits, the medical expense benefit portion of Social Security.

Old Age Survivors and Disability Insurance is the portion of Social Security that provides retirement benefits, protection for the survivors of persons covered by Social Security and disability insurance in the event of total and permanent disability. The *Medicare* portion of Social Security provides hospital insurance, prescription drug coverage and supplementary medical insurance.

While the benefits and coverage under Social Security are significant, so are the costs of financing them. The cost of Social Security is paid primarily through payroll taxes. An equal amount is contributed by the employer and the employee. In 2009, the Social Security tax rate was 6.2 percent on the first $106,800 of income, plus 1.45 percent tax on all income for Medicare.

For years prior to 1991, the Medicare rate was applied in the same way as the OASDI rate; that is, it was subject to a *wage base cap,* beyond which earnings were not taxed. In 1991, due to funding deficiencies for Medicare, the wage base cap was increased above that which applied to OASDI. Several years later, the cap was removed and the Medicare rate was applied to all income. Exhibit 23-1, later in this chapter, illustrates a brief history of Social Security tax rates, wage bases, and maximum employee taxes.

Both the employer and employee pay 6.2 percent of income for OASDI (12.4%) and 1.45 percent for Medicare (2.9%). Thus, in 2009, assuming an employee made $120,000, the employer's and the employee's taxes paid in behalf of the employee would be [(12.4% × $106,800) + (2.9% × $120,000)] = $13,243.20 + $3,480 = $16,723.

Coverage

Most workers are covered by Social Security. Some employees who are not covered include most federal employees who were hired before 1984 (however, since January 1983, all federal employees have paid the Medicare hospital insurance part of the Social Security tax), railroad employees with more than 10 years of service, employees of some state and local governments that chose not to participate in Social Security and children under age 21 who work for a parent (except children age 18 and over who work in their parent's business).

Eligibility: Earning Credits

To be eligible for Social Security benefits, a covered individual must earn a sufficient number of credits, depending upon the benefit. Credits are earned when a covered person works in a job in which Social Security taxes are paid.

Each year, the amount of earnings needed for one credit increases. For example, in 2009, one credit was received for each $1,090 of earnings. The maximum number of credits that can be earned in a year is four. Consequently, in 2009, a person who earned at least $4,360 received four credits. Self-employed individuals receive credits in the same way. Special rules apply to the self-employed who have earnings less than $400 and individuals employed in domestic work, farm work or a church or church-controlled organization that has been exempted from payment of Social Security taxes.

Credits Needed and Benefits Provided

The number of credits needed for benefits depends upon a covered person's age and the type of benefit.

Retirement benefits. Everyone who was born in 1929 or later needs 40 credits to be eligible for retirement benefits. In addition, the covered worker must meet certain age requirements (see the section below on Age and Retirement Benefits). If the covered individual is eligible to receive benefits, the following types of dependents are also eligible for retirement benefits:

- *Husband or wife.* The husband or wife of the covered individual is entitled to benefits if the husband or wife (including a divorced husband or wife who was married to the covered worker for at least 10 years and has not remarried) is age 62 or older (unless the husband or wife collects a higher Social Security benefit on his or her own record). The amount of benefits a divorced spouse receives has no effect on the amount of benefits that a current spouse can receive.

- *Husband or wife with certain childcare responsibilities.* The husband or wife of the covered individual is entitled to benefits, regardless of the husband's or wife's age, if he or she is caring for the covered individual's child who is either under 16 or is disabled and receiving Social Security benefits.

- *Dependent children.* Dependent, unmarried children of the covered worker can receive benefits if they are:

  - children who are under age 18 (or age 19 if they are attending an elementary or secondary school full time); or

  - children who are 18 or older and who were severely disabled before age 22;

Disability benefits. A covered worker who becomes disabled and is unable to engage in any substantial gainful work (either full- or part-time) and has not been able to do so for the past five months is eligible for disability benefits if the disability is expected to last at least 12 months or is expected to result in death within 12 months. The disabled worker must wait five *full* consecutive months before becoming eligible for the first month's benefit. The disabled worker will receive that month's benefit on the third of the following month. Thus, a disabled worker might have to wait up to seven months before actually receiving the first benefit check.

> **EXAMPLE:** If an application for disability is approved, Social Security benefits will be paid for the **sixth full month** after the date the disability began. For example, if a disability began on January 15, the first disability benefit will be paid for the month of July. Because Social Security benefits are paid in the month following the month for which they're due, the July benefit would be received in August.

In addition to meeting the disability requirements, the number of credits a covered worker needs to collect disability benefits depends upon the person's age when he or she became disabled, as follows:

- *Disabled before age 24.* Generally, six credits are needed during the three-year period ending when the disability begins.

- *Disabled between age 24 and 30.* Generally, credits are needed corresponding to one-half of the time period between age 21 and the time that the person becomes disabled.

- *Disabled at age 31 or older.* The individual must have earned at least 20 of the credits in the 10-year period immediately before becoming disabled *and* must have credits as set out below:

Disabled At Age	Credits Needed
31 through 42	20
44	22
46	24
48	26

Disabled At Age	Credits Needed
50	28
52	30
54	32
56	34
58	36
60	38
62 or older	40

- *Spouses.* If the covered person is receiving disability benefits, spouses are also eligible for disability benefits:

  - if the husband or wife is age 62 or older (unless he or she collects a higher Social Security benefit on his or her own record); or

  - if the husband or wife, regardless of age, is caring for the covered individual's child who is either under 16 or is disabled and receiving Social Security benefits.

- *Dependent children.* If the covered person is receiving disability benefits, dependent unmarried children can receive benefits:

  - until they reach age 18 (or age 19 if they are attending an elementary or secondary school full time); or

  - if they are 18 or older and became severely disabled before age 22.

Monthly survivor benefits. Spouses, parents and dependent children of a covered worker who is deceased may be eligible for monthly survivor benefits under certain conditions:

- *Spouses.* If the deceased worker was born in 1929 or before, the worker must have had one credit for each year after 1950, up to the year of death. If the deceased worker was born in 1930 or later, one credit is needed for each year after the year in which the worker reached 21, up to the year of death. If the deceased worker met the credit requirements, the individual's widow or widower can receive survivor benefits if he or she is:

  - 60 or older;

  - 50 or older and disabled; or

  - caring for a child under age 16 or a disabled child who is receiving Social Security benefits, regardless of the spouse's age.

- *Parents.* If the deceased worker met the same credit requirements as outlined above for spouses, the deceased worker's parents can also receive survivor benefits if they were dependent upon the deceased worker for at least half of their support.

- *Dependent children.* Dependent, unmarried children can receive benefits if the deceased worker had six credits in the three years before his or her death and the children are:

  - under age 18 (or age 19 if they are attending an elementary or secondary school full time); or

  - age 18 or older and severely disabled before age 22.

Limitations on Monthly Benefits

The monthly benefits for survivors and dependents equal up to 50 percent of the covered person's retirement or disability rate. However, there is a limit to the total amount of money that can be paid to a family on the covered person's Social Security record. The limit varies, but it is generally equal to about 150 to 180 percent of the covered person's retirement benefit (it may be less for disability benefits). If the sum of the benefits payable on the covered person's account is greater than the family limit, the benefits to the family members will be reduced proportionately. The covered person's benefit is not affected.

Age and Retirement Benefits

Workers who were born in 1937 or before receive full retirement benefits at age 65. Workers who were born in 1960 or later receive full benefits at age 67. For workers who were born between 1937 and 1960, the years (and months) of age for full benefits are graduated. Workers may retire as early as 62 and receive a permanently reduced benefit that is 80 percent of the full benefit. Benefits are permanently larger if the worker does not begin receiving them until after the age at which full benefits can be received. Delaying the receipt of benefits beyond age 70, however, does not result in any further increase in benefits.

Maximum and Average Benefits in 2009

The maximum retirement benefit for a worker retiring at age 65 and 10 months (full retirement age in 2009) in 2009 was $2,323. The average monthly benefit for a retired worker in 2009 was $1,153; for a retired couple, $1,876; and for a disabled worker, $1,064.

Exhibit 23-1
History of Social Security Tax Rates and Wage Base

Calendar Year	OASDI[1] Rate	Medicare Rate[2]	Combined Rate	Self-Employed Tax Rate[3]	Wage Base
1937-49	1.00 %				$ 3,000
1950	1.50				3,000
1951-53	1.50			2.25 %	3,600
1954	2.00			3.00	3,600
1955-56	2.00			3.00	4,200
1957-58	2.25			3.375	4,200
1959	2.50			3.75	4,800
1960-61	3.00			4.50	4,800
1962	3.125			4.70	4,800
1963-65	3.625			5.40	4,800
1966	3.85	0.35 %	4.20 %	6.15	6,600
1967	3.90	0.50	4.40	6.40	6,600
1968	3.80	0.60	4.40	6.40	7,800
1969-70	4.20	0.60	4.80	6.90	7,800
1971	4.60	0.60	5.20	7.50	7,800
1972	4.60	0.60	5.20	7.50	9,000
1973	4.85	1.0	5.85	8.00	10,800
1974	4.95	0.90	5.85	7.90	13,200
1975	4.95	0.90	5.85	7.90	14,100

Calendar Year	OASDI[1] Rate	Medicare Rate[2]	Combined Rate	Self-Employed Tax Rate[3]	Wage Base
1976	4.95	0.90	5.85	7.90	15,300
1977	4.95	0.90	5.85	7.90	16,500
1978	5.05	1.00	6.05	8.10	17,700
1979	5.08	1.05	6.13	8.10	22,900
1980	5.08	1.05	6.13	8.10	25,900
1981	5.35	1.30	6.65	9.30	29,700
1982	5.40	1.30	6.70	9.35	32,400
1983	5.40	1.30	6.70	9.35	35,700
1984[4]	5.40	1.30	6.70	11.30	37,800
1985	5.70	1.35	7.05	11.80	39,600
1986-87	5.70	1.45	7.15	12.30	43,800
1988-89	6.06	1.45	7.51	13.02	45,000
1990	6.20	1.45	7.65	15.30	51,300
1991 and after	6.20	1.45	7.65	15.30	106,800[5]

[1] Old-Age, Survivors, and Disability Insurance tax rate for employer and employee.
[2] Hospital Insurance began in 1966.
[3] Self-employed persons not covered until 1951.
[4] Employers paid 7.00% in 1984 (5.70%; OASDI[1] and 1.30%, Hospital Insurance).
[5] Social Security maximum for 2009; No maximum on Medicare rate.

Medicare Eligibility

These groups qualify for Medicare:

- The first group consists of these individuals who are *automatically* eligible. These are workers who are eligible for Social Security retirement benefits (and anyone eligible for Railroad Retirement Benefits). These individuals are automatically eligible for Medicare at age 65 (the worker need not be receiving retirement benefits). Other persons who are automatically eligible are those who have been receiving disability benefits for two years or individuals who are receiving dialysis treatment or have had a kidney transplant.

- The second group of individuals are those who are *not automatically* eligible but elect to receive Medicare coverage during the period three months before and after they reach age 65.

Exhibit 23-2, on the following page, summarizes qualifications for benefits that apply to the employee and the employee's spouse, dependent children, and dependent parents.

Disability Benefits and the Americans with Disabilities Act

The Social Security Administration considers a person eligible for disability benefits if the claimant is unable to engage in any substantial gainful activity by reason of any medically determinable physical or mental impairment that can be expected to result in death or which has lasted or can be expected to last for a continuous period of not less than 12 months. Under these provisions, a person is entitled to disability benefits if his or her impairment is so severe that he or she is not only unable to do his or her previous work but cannot, considering his or her age, education, and work experience, engage in any other kind of substantial gainful work which exists in the national economy.

The Social Security Administration (SSA) acknowledges that its standards for the determination of disability may differ from those of other regulatory authorities. SSA regulations state that a decision by any other entity about whether an individual is disabled is based on the other entity's rules and may not be the same as the SSA's determination, which is based on Social Security law.

The SSA's definition of disability is inherently different from the definition used in the Americans with Disability Act (ADA), as discussed in the next sections of this chapter.

Exhibit 23-2
Qualifications for Benefits

Type of Benefit	Employee		Employee's Spouse[1]		Employee's Dependent Children	Employee's Dependent Parent(s)
Retirement	Age 62 and older	(1)	Age 62 and over; or[2]	Unmarried and:		No Benefit Available
		(2)	Any age, if caring for	(1)	under age 18;	
			worker's dependent	(2)	under age 19 if a full-time	
			child under age 16 or		student; or	
			child disabled before	(3)	over age 18 if child	
			age 22		became disabled before	
					age 22	
Disability	Any age	(1)	Age 62 and over;	Unmarried and:		No Benefit Available
		(2)	Any age, if caring for	(1)	under age 18;	
			worker's dependent	(2)	under age 19 if a full-time	
			child under age 16 or		student; or	
			child disabled before	(3)	over 18 if child became	
			age 22		disabled before age 22	
Survivor	N/A	(1)	Any age, if caring for	Unmarried and:		Age 62 and older if
			dependent child under	(1)	under age 18;	receiving at least half of

Type of Benefit	Employee	Employee's Spouse[1]	Employee's Dependent Children	Employee's Dependent Parent(s)
		age 16 or child disabled before age 22; or	(2) under age 19 if full-time student; or	support from worker and worker was fully
		(2) Age 60 and over, if worker was also fully insured; or	(3) over age 18 if disabled before age 22	insured
		(3) Age 50 and over if spouse is disabled and worker was also fully insured		
Medicare Part A: Hospital Insurance	(1) Age 65 whether or not on retirement benefits yet; (2) A disability benefit recipient for 2 years; or (3) On dialysis or received a kidney transplant	Age 65	No Benefit Available	No Benefit Available
Part B: Supplementary Medical Insurance	Optional upon becoming eligible for Part A. requires monthly premium	Age 65—optional upon becoming eligible for Part A	No Benefit Available	No Benefit Available

[1] Includes divorced spouse, if married to the employee for at least 10 years and has not remarried.
[2] Divorced spouse must have been divorced for at least two years; eligible if former spouse is eligible regardless of whether he/she is receiving benefits.

Individualized inquiry. The ADA requires an individualized inquiry into the ability of a particular person to meet the requirements of a particular position. The SSA considers some conditions to be presumptively disabling. The individual person's condition is not considered in making a decision on the issue.

Customary job requirements. The SSA looks at the customary requirements of jobs as usually performed in the national economy without focusing on the essential functions of a particular position. Thus, a person who is able to perform the essential functions of a particular position, but not the marginal functions, may be found to be unable to work and eligible for SSA benefits. Under the ADA definition, however, the person may be employable, since he or she can perform the essential functions in the job.

Reasonable accommodation. Unlike the requirements of the ADA, the SSA definition does not consider whether the individual could work with reasonable accommodation. Interpretive regulations issued by the SSA, regarding the effect of the ADA on the SSA's disability determination process, state that whether an individual may be able to perform work if an employer makes accommodations is not relevant in determining if the individual meets the SSA definition of disabled. Thus, the SSA may find that a person is unable to do any work that exists in the national economy even though he or she could work with a reasonable accommodation. In short, the SSA may find a claimant to be disabled, but the person may also be entitled to protection under the ADA.[1] The U.S. Supreme Court held that a person who receives disability payments from Social Security is not prevented from seeking coverage as a person with a disability who is employable, with reasonable accommodation, under the ADA.[2]

Replacement Amount

Social Security disability benefits are reduced for any worker whose combined disability benefits from workers' compensation and any federal, state, or local government disability plan exceed 80 percent of the worker's pre-disability earnings. Also subtracted are any payments from these same sources that are received by the family due to the worker's disability. Payments received from private insurance disability plans are not deducted.

Social Security Disability and Supplemental Security Income Disability. Social Security disability is financed by taxes paid by employers, employees, and the self-employed. Benefits are determined by workers' earnings. Supplemental Security Income (SSI) disability is financed by general tax revenues, not by Social Security trust funds. SSI benefits are paid to individuals who are disabled and do not have much income or property.[3]

Working and Receiving Retirement Benefits

Covered workers who begin receiving retirement benefits at age 65 may continue working without either a loss or a reduction in their Social Security benefits.

Taxation of Benefits

Some recipients of Social Security pay taxes on their benefits if their income exceeds specified amounts.

EXAMPLE: An individual filer who has an income (which is the sum of his or her adjusted gross income plus nontaxable interest plus one-half of his

---

[1] Comparison information on the ADA and Social Security Administration's determinations of "disability" was obtained from *EEOC Enforcement Guidance on the Effect of Representations Made in Applications for Benefits on the Determination of Whether a Person Is a "Qualified Individual with a Disability" Under the Americans with Disabilities Act of 1990*, EEOC Notice 915.002 (February 12, 1997).

[2] *Cleveland v. Policy Management Systems Corp. et al.*, 6 ADD ¶ 6-184, 120 F.3d 513 (Sct 1999, Docket No 97-1008). See also *Cleveland v. Policy Management Systems Corp. et al.* in Appendix 1.

[3] Social Security Administration, 2003.

or her Social Security benefits) between $25,000 and $34,000 may have to pay taxes on 50 percent of his or her Social Security benefits. If the income is above $34,000, up to 85 percent of the Social Security benefits is subject to income tax.

> **EXAMPLE:** Joint filers who have a combined income (as constituted above) that is between $32,000 and $44,000 may have to pay taxes on 50 percent of their Social Security benefits. If the combined income is more than $44,000, up to 85 percent of the benefits are subject to taxation.

Working and Receiving Disability Benefits

The Social Security Administration evaluates the work activity of persons either filing claims for or receiving disability benefits. In 2009, a person who is eligible for benefits can earn $980 a month from employment and remain eligible. A person who is blind and eligible for benefits can earn $1,640 a month and remain eligible. These earnings limits are automatically adjusted to national wage index increases.[4]

Cost-of-Living Adjustments

Each January, benefits increase automatically if the cost of living increases.

Death Benefits

If a covered worker dies, a $255 one-time lump-sum benefit is paid to one of the following, in this order of priority:

- The widow(er) who was living with the worker at the time of death;
- The widow(er) who was not living with the worker at the time of death, but is eligible on the worker's earnings record; and
- A surviving child who is eligible for benefits.

International Social Security Agreements

Work overseas may be used to qualify for U.S. benefits if it was covered under a foreign Social Security system. The United States has Social Security agreements with a number of other countries. One of the main purposes of these agreements is to help people who have worked in both the United States and the other country, but who have not worked long enough in one country or the other to qualify for Social Security benefits.

Under the agreement, work credits in the other country can be counted to qualify for U.S. benefits. However, the credits will not be counted if a person already has enough credits under U.S. Social Security to qualify for a benefit. If foreign work credits are counted, a person may receive a partial U.S. benefit that is related to the length of time worked under U.S. Social Security.

Although work credits in the other country are counted, they are not actually transferred from that country to the United States. They remain on the person's record in the other country. It is therefore possible for the person to qualify for a separate benefit payment from both countries.[5]

---

[4] Social Security Administration, 2008.   [5] Social Security Administration, 2004.

Medicare Benefits

If the employee is covered under Medicare (as discussed previously), the employee's spouse is also covered at age 65.

Part A Benefits

Part A benefits are available without charge to those who are *automatically eligible*. The group that is not automatically eligible for Part A benefits must pay a monthly premium of $443.

Hospital treatment. Hospital treatment includes tuberculosis hospitals, psychiatric hospitals, and Christian Science sanatoriums, but psychiatric hospital benefits have a lifetime limit of 190 days. Subject to a deductible, hospital services including almost all hospital costs (two- to four-bed rooms, unless private rooms are medically required, nursing services except private-duty nursing, the usual drugs and supplies, and diagnostic and therapeutic services) up to a maximum of 90 days in a "benefit period." For the 61st through the 90th day, the patient must pay a coinsurance charge, in addition to the deductible. Beyond 90 days in a hospital, the patient pays an additional co-pay per day for up to 60 more days.

Benefit period. A *benefit period* is each period of illness that begins with the first day of hospital treatment and ends 60 days after the last day of treatment in a hospital or skilled nursing facility. In sum, a person must not receive any treatment in a hospital or skilled nursing facility for 60 days to start a new benefit period.

Lifetime reserve. A *lifetime reserve* of an additional 60 days of hospital treatment may be used if the 90-day period is exhausted. There is a coinsurance payment for each of the 60 days.

Skilled nursing facility treatment. Treatment in a skilled nursing facility is provided for up to 100 days in a benefit period when preceded by at least three consecutive days in a hospital for the same condition and the person was admitted within 30 days after discharge from the hospital. There is neither a deductible nor a coinsurance payment for the first 20 days. Each day after the 20th day requires a coinsurance payment.

Home health care. An unlimited number of home health care services under a doctor's treatment plan are covered for therapy (physical, occupational, or speech), part-time assistance of nursing aides, medical supplies (excluding drugs), and durable medical equipment.

Hospice care. *Hospice care* is a program of care for terminally ill patients who have a life expectancy of six months or less. The person must elect to receive hospice care instead of most other Medicare benefits. The benefits included are the typical ones received in a hospital setting, including drugs and supplies.

Part B Benefits

Services covered under Part B include physicians' fees, diagnostic tests, physical therapy, drugs that are not self-administered, necessary ambulance service, radiation therapy, and medical equipment rental or purchase. The patient must pay an annual deductible of $135 of medical expenses. Above that amount, Medicare pays 80 percent of covered expenses.

Part B Premium. The premium for Part B is based upon income as shown in Exhibit 23-3.

Exhibit 23-3
Monthly Premiums for Medicare Part B

Premium	Yearly Income	
	Single	Married Couple
$96.40	$85,000 or less	$170,000 or less
$134.90	$85,001-$107,000	$170,001-$214,000
$192.70	$107,001-$160,000	$214,001-$320,000
$250.50	$160,001-$213,000	$320,001-$426,000
$308.30	Above $213,000	Above $426,000

Source: Social Security Administration, *Medicare Part B monthly premiums in 2009.*

Part C Benefits

In lieu of Part A and B benefits, covered individuals may select a Part C Medicare Advantage Plan (MAP). Part C benefits include those covered by both Part A and Part B. The providers of MAPs include Preferred Provider Organizations, Health Maintenance Organizations, Private Fee-for-Service Plans, Medical Savings Account Plans, and Special Needs Plans. Typically these plans have copayments, coinsurance and deductibles like Part A and Part B plans. The plans may offer services not provided by Part A and Part B plans, such as vision, hearing, and dental benefits. Referrals are often needed to see specialists and some MAPs require participants to stay within provider networks to receive services or to avoid paying part of the cost. Typically, Part D benefits (prescription drug coverage) are covered by MAPs. To enroll in a MAP a participant must be within the plan's service area. Special rules apply to individuals with end-stage renal disease and a kidney transplant.[6]

Part D Benefits

Part D benefits are prescription drug coverage for both brand-name and generic prescription drugs at participating pharmacies. Everyone with Medicare is eligible for Part D Benefits.

Medicare established a "standard of coverage" for prescription drugs. Within each state, various organizations compete for eligible persons to enroll in their prescription drug plans by offering drug benefits that are at least as good as the "standard of coverage." These plans are funded by both Medicare and enrollees. The monthly premium enrollees pay depends upon the benefits in the plan they select. Medicare's payment is based on the "standard of coverage" so all plans receive the same funding from Medicare.

[6] Department of Health and Human Services, *Medicare and You* 2009, p. 50..

Workers' Compensation

Workers' compensation provides medical expenses, monthly income replacement, and rehabilitation benefits for job-related injuries and sickness. Survivor benefits are available in the event a worker's death is job-related.

Workers' compensation benefits are designed to provide broad coverage in the event of occupational injuries and illnesses and to encourage safety in the workplace. Workers' compensation laws exist in all 50 states. Similar legislation covers federal civilian employees, residents of the District of Columbia, and harbor and longshore workers. Most employees are covered; however, there are exclusions in virtually all states for some types of workers such as farm, domestic, and casual workers. In several states, employers are excluded if they employ fewer than a minimum number of employees, typically three or fewer.

History

Prior to the enactment of state workers' compensation laws, it was very difficult for employees or their survivors to receive compensation for job-related injuries and disease. Only the worker was permitted to sue an employer. Survivors could not sue even in the event of a wrongful death. Another problem was that employees had to prove that the employer was at fault. In addition, if an employee received benefits, the right to them ceased upon the employee's death. Furthermore, employers were permitted to use these three common law defenses against any suits that were filed against them:

- The fellow-servant rule;

- The doctrine of contributory negligence; and

- The doctrine of assumption of risk.

Fellow-Servant Rule

Under the *fellow-servant* rule, an employee was unable to recover damages resulting from a job-related injury or illness if the injury or illness was caused by the actions of a fellow employee.

Doctrine of Contributory Negligence

Under the *doctrine of contributory negligence,* if the employee's own negligence even partly contributed to the injury, no matter how slightly, the employee could not recover any damages from the employer.

Assumption of Risk Doctrine

The *assumption of risk doctrine* contended that an employee assumes the normal risks of a job by accepting employment. This doctrine assumes that dangerous jobs carry a higher wage that compensates the employee for the added risk. Further, if it can be shown that an employee was aware of unsafe working conditions, he or she assumed the risk by continuing to work on the job.

Result of Common Law Provisions

The result of the above conditions was considerable hardship to employees who suffered the misfortune of becoming ill or injured due to work-related conditions. Similar hardships were experienced by the dependents and survivors of these employees. Litigation, even in those cases that were successful, resulted in long delays and little compensation after attorneys were paid.

As the economy became more industrialized, the number of workplace accidents increased. Unfortunately, too many employers were relatively unconcerned with the occupational safety and health of their workers. Eventually, workers' compensation laws were developed, based on the premise that an entire society benefits from industrialization and should bear the costs of industrial accidents. Today, liability is imposed upon the employer without regard to fault and the cost of compensating workers who become ill or injured due to work-related conditions is passed on to consumers as a cost of production. In return for the absolute liability imposed upon the employer, the employee, with few exceptions, must accept compensation per the applicable state's statue.

Variation in State Laws

In recent years, a greater uniformity among state workers' compensation laws has emerged. However, there remain variations among states in the amount of benefits, the manner in which initial and continuing eligibility for benefits is determined, and, to a lesser extent, the categories of employees excluded under the law. The states also differ in the manner in which benefits may be financed.

Benefit Eligibility

Workers' compensation benefits are provided to covered employees for injuries and disease that arise out of and in the course of employment. Generally, coverage does not extend to the period that the employee is going to and from work. Injuries are excluded that result from such causes as the employee's horseplay, intoxication, or intentional self-injury. An employee who is not wearing or using required safety apparel or equipment may also be denied benefits.

Occupational Disease Coverage

All states now include coverage for some occupational diseases, but the extensiveness of this coverage varies widely among states. In some states, there is a specific listing of diseases covered. The diseases that are covered usually include those arising out of exposure to a harmful substance or a condition that is associated with the particular employment as compared to employment in general. It is much more difficult, however, to prove a causal relationship between the employee's disease and occupation than it is to establish a relationship between an injury and an occupation.

Some states use the same prescribed limitation period for filing claims of either injuries or illnesses. Many states use a *discovery rule*, which means that the limitation period for filing a claim depends upon when the employee acquired knowledge ("discovered") that his or her symptoms or illness were related to employment. Claims for disease represent a small but growing percentage of total workers' compensation claims.

Administration of Laws

Benefits are paid out to employees by their employer or the applicable funding source. When disagreement arises over eligibility for benefits, the case is heard before a board or commission. In a few states, the law is administered by courts. States vary widely in how they administer the law.

Types of Benefits

The four major types of benefits provided by workers' compensation laws are:

- Medical care;
- Income replacement for disability;
- Survivors' benefits; and
- Rehabilitation services.

Medical Care

Necessary medical treatment is provided in all states. Medical benefits are unlimited. In some states, services must be provided by a doctor selected from a panel. About one-third of workers' compensation claim payments are for medical expenses.

Income Replacement for Disability

The employee is provided with a weekly income for disabilities that are a result of a covered injury or sickness. Under certain circumstances, the benefit may be in the form of a lump-sum payment. The amount and duration of benefit payments will depend on the nature of the employee's disability. In some states, benefit payments are based on actual wage loss suffered by the injured employee. This method is becoming the trend in benefit payments.

These are the four categories of disability:

- *Temporary total disability.* The employee is unable to perform the duties of his or her occupation, but the employee is expected to return to work. This is the most frequent form of disability claim filed.

- *Temporary partial disability.* The employee can perform some, but not all, of the essential duties of his or her occupation. It is expected that the employee will be able to resume full responsibilities.

- *Permanent total disability.* An employee is unable to perform the duties of his or her occupation and is expected to remain totally disabled.

- *Permanent partial disability.* An employee has a permanent injury, but still can perform some of the duties of his or her occupation or be retrained in another occupation. Loss of a body part is an example of a permanent partial disability.

Survivors' Benefits

In addition to a lump-sum burial allowance that typically ranges up to several thousand dollars, a weekly income is provided to the surviving spouse and dependent children of a worker whose death is job-related. Some states have a maximum number of weeks for which benefits will be paid. A spouse's benefits cease upon remarriage. A few states offer a cash payment as an incentive to report remarriages. Benefits to dependent children cease upon marriage or attainment of a specific age. Where there is a maximum on the number of weeks for which the benefit will be paid, benefits may cease before the dependency period ends.

Rehabilitation Services

All states have provisions for rehabilitation services that assist the worker in returning to employment in the same or a different occupation. These services may include medical care, physical therapy, vocational training to learn new skills, and psychological counseling. Income replacement payments generally continue during rehabilitation efforts. In most states that require rehabilitation services, unjustified refusal to accept the services may result in the suspension of the employee's benefit payments.

Weekly Benefits

Income benefits for disability (or death payments to survivors) are calculated as a percentage of the employee's *average weekly wage* (AWW). Weekly wages are averaged over a specified time period, such as over the preceding 13 weeks. Typically, the AWW averages around 70 percent of the employee's wages, with some states paying a larger percentage and others paying a smaller percentage. Payment amounts are less than 100 percent of AWW to prevent malingering and to provide an incentive for workers to return to work if they are able.

Waiting Period

Disability income payments begin after the employee has satisfied a *waiting period*, which is typically three to seven days in duration. The purpose of the waiting period is to reduce compensation costs for less serious problems and minimize the potential for dishonest claims. If time lost due to an injury or illness exceeds a specified time, such as two weeks, benefits will be paid retroactively to cover the waiting period.

Duration of Benefits

In many states, income benefits continue for the duration of the disability. Some states, however, place a time limit on income payments for either permanent or temporary disabilities or on both. The maximum time limits range from about 300 weeks for temporary total disability to approximately 600 weeks for temporary or permanent disability.

Dollar Limits

Every state has a maximum dollar limit on weekly income benefits. Permanent partial benefits are usually paid out in a lump sum. The cash benefit is equivalent to the total income benefit for a specified number of weeks. For example, the loss of a thumb may entitle the worker to 60 weeks of disability benefits. The weekly disability benefit is computed as usual, such as two-thirds of the worker's AWW. This amount is multiplied by 60 to determine the amount of the lump-sum payment.

Cost-of-Living Increases

A number of states have a provision for automatic cost-of-living increases in income benefits. The increase is usually based on the Consumer Price Index. The adjustments increase the weekly maximum benefit provided by the state and also increase the amount of benefits received by current recipients.

Offsets by Other Benefits

In a number of states, workers' compensation benefits may be reduced for any disability benefits the worker is receiving from Social Security. Thus, Social Security is the primary source of disability income for workers in these states. It is in the best interest of the employer to assist an employee in qualifying for Social Security if the potential savings in workers' compensation costs will exceed the cost of providing the assistance. Workers' compensation benefits are not reduced by payments from an employer's disability plan or retirement plan. The employer's plan, however, may have a provision for offsetting benefits by amounts received under workers' compensation laws.

Second-Injury Funds

In most states, the loss of two eyes or two limbs is deemed a total disability. Situations arise, however, when a partial injury leaves the worker totally disabled because of a prior partial occupational injury. For example, assume a worker lost one arm in an accident. Assume further that after recuperation, the worker is not able to return to work for his former employer because that employer was unable to find a suitable job, even after making efforts at reasonable accommodation. However, the worker finds employment with another employer and then, tragically, loses the other arm in another accident. Even though the second accident resulted in the loss of one arm, the worker is left totally disabled as a combined result of both accidents. Benefits for a permanent and total disability will greatly exceed those for a permanent and partial disability. This would mean that the second employer would be obligated to provide total disability benefits to the worker, even though the loss of an arm is a total partial disability.

To remedy this inequity and to encourage employers to hire individuals with disabilities, most states have established *second-injury funds*, which provide reimbursement to employers for the difference between the total compensation benefits and the partial compensation benefits that would have been paid had it not been for the previous injury. These second-injury funds are financed through assessments paid by employers and insurance companies.

Taxation

The cost of workers' compensation is a deductible business expense for the employer. Premiums paid to insurance companies or state funds are deductible in the year in which they paid. Self-insurers may also take deductions in the year that benefits are paid. In some cases, self-insurers may deduct contributions to reserve accounts. Workers' compensation benefits are not taxable income to the recipients.

Financing Benefits

The direct cost of workers' compensation is paid by the employer. Employees do not make any contributions.

Methods of Funding

Depending upon the state's requirements, the cost of benefits may be funded in the following ways:

- Private insurance;
- Self-insured by the employer;
- State workers' compensation fund; or
- A combination of any of the above.

Several states have exclusive state funds and employers are not permitted to purchase private insurance. This type of funding is known as *monopolistic state funds*. A few states have this type of funding, but permit employers to self-insure if they have the financial ability to do so. Some states have *competitive state funds.* In these states, employers may self-insure, if they qualify, purchase private insurance, or insure with the state fund. The remaining states typically require employers to either purchase insurance or self-insure.

Most workers' compensation benefits, however, are paid by private insurers. State funds are the next most frequent payer of benefits.

Factors Affecting Cost

The primary factors determining the cost of benefits are the nature and administration of the state's law, the number of employees, and the frequency and severity of occupational injuries and disease. The more liberal a state is in requiring the payment of benefits and in administering the law, the higher the cost is to employers. The frequency and severity of claims are a function of the degree of occupational hazard and the employer's loss prevention and control efforts. Sound safety and health management practices have a significant effect upon workers' compensation costs.

Workers' Compensation and the Americans with Disabilities Act

Under workers' compensation, a worker is generally considered to be "totally disabled" when the injury or illness is found to render the worker temporarily or permanently unable to do any kind of work for which there is a reasonably stable employment market. In such a situation, the person may still qualify for protection under the Americans with Disabilities Act (ADA). The following are some other differences in workers' compensation provisions and the ADA.

Individualized Inquiry

Unlike the ADA, which requires an individualized inquiry into the ability of a particular person to meet the requirements of a particular job, some workers' compensation statutes presume that some conditions are so severe as to prevent the claimant from doing any kind of work. For example, under some statutes a person who has lost vision in both eyes or lost both arms or legs may have a "permanent total disability" and be deemed unable to work. That person, however, can perform the essential functions of some jobs with or without accommodation.

Consideration of Essential Functions

The ADA requires that employers consider only the essential functions in a job in determining whether an individual is employable. Workers' compensation definitions of "disability" do not distinguish between marginal and essential functions and do not consider whether an individual can work with reasonable accommodation. In some workers' compensation cases, a person has a "total disability" when he or she is unable to do certain tasks, even if those tasks are marginal functions or if he or she could perform them with reasonable accommodation. Thus, a person may be "totally disabled" for workers' compensation purposes and still be able to perform a position's essential functions, with or without reasonable accommodation.

Availability of Work

Some statutes permit a finding of "total disability" if a person can work but the work that he or she can do is of such limited availability that a reasonably stable and continuous market for that work does not exist. This determination, however, does not mean there is no work available that the person can perform with or without reasonable accommodation. Consequently, a person receiving workers' compensation may also be entitled to protection under the ADA.[7]

Unemployment Insurance

Unemployment insurance provides benefits to qualified workers during periods of involuntary unemployment.

Unemployment insurance laws are created, financed, and administered by the individual states but influenced by federal guidelines and standards. This is part of the Social Security Act of 1935. Employers are covered by the Federal Unemployment Tax Act (FUTA) if they employ one person for 20 calendar weeks in a year or pay wages of at least $1,500 in any calendar quarter in the current or preceding year. If an employer meets the FUTA requirement any time during the year, it is required to pay the tax on all wages from January 1 of the year. Once qualified, an employer remains qualified for two calendar years.

FUTA funds are deposited into the Unemployment Insurance Trust Fund. Monies in the Fund are invested and maintained by the U.S. Treasury. Separate accounts are kept for each state agency, and money may be withdrawn by the states only for the payment of unemployment benefits.

---

[7] Comparison information on the ADA and workers' compensation was obtained from *EEOC Enforcement Guidance on the Effect of Representations Made in Applications for Benefits on the Determination of* *Whether a Person Is a "Qualified Individual with a Disability" Under the Americans with Disabilities Act of 1990*, EEOC Notice 915.002 (February 12, 1997).

Benefits Eligibility

To qualify for benefits, the employee must be partially or totally unemployed for at least one week, and:

- Be able and available for work. To collect benefits, the unemployed worker must be physically and mentally able to work. The worker is required to file a claim for unemployment compensation and register for work in person at the respective state unemployment office. Unjustified refusal to work may disqualify the worker for benefits.

- Be actively seeking work. Registration for a job at the state employment office is the first requirement demonstrating that the worker is actively seeking work. In addition, most states require periodic reporting of the worker's efforts to locate employment.

- Have been employed for a minimum required period and have sufficient earnings during the period. All states require previous earnings and covered employment in a *base period* to qualify for benefits. In most states, the base period is the first four of the last five completed calendar quarters immediately preceding the individual's benefit year. The qualifying amount of wages and number of weeks worked varies by state.

- Be registered with the required employment service (except if the unemployment period is expected to be a short period or if work opportunities are received through a union), and not otherwise be disqualified for benefits.

Financing Benefits

In most states, unemployment compensation benefits are financed by taxes imposed upon employers. There are a few states in which employees must also contribute. The plan is funded through contributions by employers, who pay 6.2 percent of the first $7,000 of each employee's income, plus the state unemployment tax.

Cost Containment

All state tax rates are *experience rated;* that is, the tax rate is, to some extent, a function of the individual employer's own unemployment experience. An employer with a lower incidence of unemployment claims will pay a lower tax rate than an employer with a higher level of claims. This creates an incentive for employers to contain costs since, if their unemployment insurance account is current, they receive a 5.4 percent credit (they don't have to pay it on the first $7,000 of each employee's income); the other .8 percent goes to the federal government for administration of the plan. Typically, an employer's experience rating is determined by comparing the amount of benefit expenditure to total payroll.

Notification of Eligibility

States have different provisions concerning employer obligations to notify the state's unemployment compensation agency when employees become unemployed. Some states require the employer to notify the employees involved, to notify the state agency, or to respond to the agency, presumably after unemployed employees contact the agency.

Filing for Benefits

Unemployed employees file a claim for benefits with the appropriate state agency. The agency determines if the individual is entitled to benefits. Benefits are based upon past earnings and employment. Benefits are paid for 26 weeks, which is the regular state program. An additional 13 weeks of *extended benefits*, which is a federal-state program, may be provided during periods of high unemployment.

Benefit Amounts

The weekly benefit amount is computed according to individual state formulas. Several different formulas base the payment on a percentage of the worker's earnings during some part of the base period. All states have minimum and maximum dollar limits on benefits.

Waiting Period

Most states have a waiting period, typically one week, before benefits begin. There is no provision for the retroactive payment of benefits. By eliminating very short periods of unemployment, waiting periods help reduce the cost of unemployment insurance and permit the allocation of funds to longer terms of unemployment, which is when workers' needs are the greatest.

Employees on Strike

States may provide unemployment benefits to employees on strike. In most states, unemployment benefits are only permitted if the business continues functioning with striker replacement workers and/or supervisory personnel because the strike would not have resulted in a "curtailment of work" or a "stoppage of work," which are the conditions that typically must prevail for benefits to be denied to strikers. If the business is essentially stopped due to the strike, strikers are not entitled to benefits.

Denial of Benefits

Benefits can be temporarily or permanently denied, or totally or partially reduced for the following reasons:

- The employee quits a job without good reason;
- The employee was fired for misconduct;
- The employee was receiving workers' compensation or Social Security benefits;
- The employee was receiving compensation from a former employer;
- The employee had a license or bond that was required for employment revoked or suspended;
- The employee is part of a labor dispute, if the business does not continue functioning with replacement workers and/or supervisory personnel;

- The employee has invalid reasons for not accepting work for which the person is suited; or

- There is fraudulent misrepresentation connected with an unemployment insurance claim.

Employer Rights

Employers may appeal decisions by the state unemployment agency granting unemployment compensation to former employees and other decisions of the agency, such as the calculation of an employer's experience rating.

Taxation

Employers may take a deduction for unemployment taxes paid. Employees who are required to contribute to the financing of benefits may claim an itemized deduction on their federal income tax return. Unemployment benefits that employees receive may be subject to federal taxation. The amount that is taxable depends upon the amount of the benefit and the amount of other income that the employee receives.

State Compulsory Disability Laws

A contingency that is not covered by either Social Security or workers' compensation is temporary nonoccupational injuries or sickness. Currently, six jurisdictions have laws requiring employers to provide insurance to protect employees in the event of such contingencies. The six are California, Hawaii, New Jersey, New York, Rhode Island, and Puerto Rico. In addition, employers in the railroad industry are required to provide such benefits.

CHAPTER 24

BENEFITS COST CONTAINMENT

Chapter Highlights
- Examining the costs of employee compensation
- Establishing baseline data
- Reviewing the phases of cost containment
- Designing benefit plans to prevent and contain costs

Introduction

Costs for Employee Compensation

In 2008, total employer costs for employee compensation for both private industry and government workers (excluding federal workers) averaged $28.48 per hour worked. Wages and salaries constituted $19.85 or 69.7 percent of the cost, and benefits represented $8.64, accounting for the remainder. Exhibit 24-1 shows the total costs of these expenditures by type of benefit.

Exhibit 24-1—Employer costs per hour worked for employee compensation and costs as a percent of total compensation: Civilian workers, by major occupational and industry group, June 2008

Compensation component	All workers[1]		Management, professional, and related		Sales and office		Service	
	Cost	Percent	Cost	Percent	Cost	Percent	Cost	Percent
Total compensation	$28.48	100.0	$47.57	100.0	$21.70	100.0	$15.57	100.0
Wages and salaries	19.85	69.7	33.32	70.0	15.41	71.0	11.05	71.0
Total benefits	8.64	30.3	14.25	30.0	6.29	29.0	4.52	29.0
Paid leave	1.99	7.0	3.90	8.2	1.43	6.6	0.87	5.6
Vacation	0.94	3.3	1.78	3.7	0.69	3.2	0.42	2.7
Holiday	0.65	2.3	1.26	2.7	0.48	2.2	0.28	1.8
Sick	0.31	1.1	0.66	1.4	0.21	1.0	0.14	0.9
Personal	0.08	0.3	0.19	0.4	0.05	0.2	0.03	0.2
Supplemental pay	0.76	2.7	1.23	2.6	0.52	2.4	0.28	1.8
Overtime and premium[4]	0.26	0.9	0.17	0.4	0.14	0.7	0.17	1.1
Shift differentials	0.07	0.2	0.11	0.2	0.02	0.1	0.05	0.3
Nonproduction bonuses	0.43	1.5	0.96	2.0	0.35	1.6	0.07	0.4
Insurance	2.39	8.4	3.57	7.5	1.94	9.0	1.33	8.6
Life	0.05	0.2	0.10	0.2	0.03	0.2	0.02	0.1
Health	2.25	7.9	3.32	7.0	1.85	8.5	1.28	8.3
Short-term disability ..	0.05	0.2	0.08	0.2	0.04	0.2	0.02	0.1
Long-term disability ..	0.04	0.1	0.08	0.2	0.03	0.1	(5)	(6)
Retirement and savings ..	1.25	4.4	2.41	5.1	0.71	3.3	0.58	3.8
Defined benefit	0.75	2.6	1.44	3.0	0.32	1.5	0.44	2.8
Defined contribution .	0.50	1.8	0.97	2.0	0.39	1.8	0.14	0.9
Legally required benefits .	2.25	7.9	3.14	6.6	1.70	7.8	1.45	9.3
Social Security and Medicare	1.62	5.7	2.60	5.5	1.28	5.9	0.94	6.0
Social Security[7] ...	1.29	4.5	2.05	4.3	1.03	4.8	0.75	4.8
Medicare	0.33	1.1	0.55	1.2	0.25	1.2	0.19	1.2
Federal unemployment insurance	0.03	0.1	0.02	(6)	0.03	0.1	0.03	0.2
State unemployment insurance	0.14	0.5	0.13	0.3	0.13	0.6	0.11	0.7
Workers' compensation	0.47	1.6	0.38	0.8	0.25	1.2	0.36	2.3

Compensation component	Occupational group							
	All workers[1]		Management, professional, and related		Sales and office		Service	
	Cost	Percent	Cost	Percent	Cost	Percent	Cost	Percent

See footnotes at end of table.

Compensation component	Occupational group				Industry group			
	Natural resources, construction, and maintenance		Production, transportation, and material moving		Goods-producing[2]		Service-providing[3]	
	Cost	Percent	Cost	Percent	Cost	Percent	Cost	Percent
Total compensation	$30.41	100.0	$23.30	100.0	$31.59	100.0	$27.84	100.0
Wages and salaries	20.67	68.0	15.50	66.5	21.09	66.8	19.59	70.4
Total benefits	9.75	32.0	7.80	33.5	10.50	33.2	8.25	29.6
Paid leave	1.59	5.2	1.39	6.0	1.99	6.3	1.99	7.1
Vacation	0.84	2.8	0.71	3.0	1.06	3.4	0.92	3.3
Holiday	0.52	1.7	0.49	2.1	0.71	2.3	0.64	2.3
Sick	0.16	0.5	0.16	0.7	0.17	0.5	0.33	1.2
Personal	0.06	0.2	0.04	0.2	0.04	0.1	0.09	0.3
Supplemental pay	0.99	3.2	0.85	3.6	1.30	4.1	0.65	2.3
Overtime and premium[4]	0.68	2.2	0.51	2.2	0.58	1.8	0.20	0.7
Shift differentials	0.05	0.2	0.10	0.4	0.10	0.3	0.06	0.2
Nonproduction bonuses	0.28	0.9	0.23	1.0	0.62	2.0	0.39	1.4
Insurance	2.60	8.5	2.41	10.4	2.89	9.2	2.29	8.2
Life	0.05	0.2	0.04	0.2	0.06	0.2	0.05	0.2
Health	2.44	8.0	2.28	9.8	2.69	8.5	2.16	7.8
Short-term disability . .	0.08	0.3	0.06	0.3	0.10	0.3	0.04	0.2
Long-term disability . .	0.03	0.1	0.03	0.1	0.04	0.1	0.04	0.1
Retirement and savings . .	1.49	4.9	0.91	3.9	1.45	4.6	1.21	4.3
Defined benefit	1.01	3.3	0.55	2.3	0.83	2.6	0.74	2.6
Defined contribution .	0.48	1.6	0.37	1.6	0.63	2.0	0.47	1.7
Legally required benefits .	3.08	10.1	2.23	9.6	2.87	9.1	2.12	7.6
Social Security and Medicare	1.74	5.7	1.32	5.7	1.80	5.7	1.58	5.7
Social Security[7] . . .	1.40	4.6	1.07	4.6	1.45	4.6	1.26	4.5

Compensation component	Occupational group				Industry group			
	Natural resources, construction, and maintenance		Production, transportation, and material moving		Goods-producing[2]		Service-providing[3]	
	Cost	Percent	Cost	Percent	Cost	Percent	Cost	Percent
Medicare	0.33	1.1	0.25	1.1	0.35	1.1	0.32	1.2
Federal unemployment insurance	0.03	0.1	0.03	0.1	0.03	0.1	0.03	0.1
State unemployment insurance	0.18	0.6	0.16	0.7	0.20	0.6	0.13	0.4
Workers' compensation	1.14	3.7	0.71	3.1	0.84	2.7	0.39	1.4

Includes workers in the private nonfarm economy excluding households and the public sector excluding the Federal government.

Includes mining, construction, and manufacturing. The agriculture, forestry, farming, and hunting sector is excluded.

Includes utilities; wholesale trade; retail trade; transportation and warehousing; information; finance and insurance; real estate and rental and leasing; professional and technical services; management of companies and enterprises; administrative and waste services; educational services; health care and social assistance; arts, entertainment and recreation; accommodation and food services; other services, except public administration; and public administration.

Includes premium pay for work in addition to the regular work schedule (such as overtime, weekends, and holidays).

Cost per hour worked is $0.01 or less.

Less than .05 percent.

Comprises the Old-Age, Survivors, and Disability Insurance (OASDI) program.

Note: The sum of individual items may not equal totals due to rounding.

Hidden Costs

In addition to dollar expenditures, there often are hidden costs involved in employee benefits. For example, having an employee on disability compensation may require an employer to pay both the benefit and the hidden costs of the services of a replacement employee. The emphasis on cost containment efforts has been directed at rapidly increasing health care costs. However, cost control need not be limited to health benefits, since the costs of other benefit programs, including both voluntary ones, such as retirement plans, and mandatory programs, such as workers' compensation, can be contained as well.

Benefit Cost Containment Management

Employee benefit cost containment is that part of compensation planning involving the implementation of strategies to prevent and control unnecessary costs in the benefits portion of employee compensation.

Benefit Need

Concerns about the costs of employee benefit programs are motivating many employers to consider some very fundamental questions about the programs. The most basic of these questions concerns the objectives that employers have for providing employee benefits. As discussed in Chapter 18, these objectives are to fulfill social obligations to employees, attract and retain good employees, increase employee morale and productivity, obtain insurance at low rates, take advantage of favorable tax treatment, income replacement, and administrative simplicity. Each of these objectives should be considered in developing a comprehensive cost containment program. The following are some questions that should be asked about each objective.

- *Fulfill social obligations to employees.* Employers increasingly expect employees to assume more responsibility for their own obligations. For example, the evidence is clear that employee health is lifestyle related. The most extensive medical expense benefit program available will not keep employees healthy if they do not do their part. Undoubtedly, some employer dissatisfaction with wellness programs is due to the failure of employees to take an active role in their own wellness. This is one reason some employers are discontinuing their wellness programs. Exhibit 24-2 contains data on the percentage changes in employee coverage for wellness programs and other major employee benefit programs in firms with 100 or more employees from 1995 to 2007.

- *Attract and retain good employees.* The recruitment and retention of employees is, to a considerable extent, dependent upon the compensation practices of other employers in the market area. The need to compete for employees prevents employers from discontinuing employee benefit programs unless the competition takes the same action. In effect, as the trend for employers to discontinue various components of their benefit plans occurs, other employers that have not been so inclined in the past will consider similar actions.

Exhibit 24-2
Percentage of Employees in Firms with 100 or More Employees
with Access to Selected Employee Benefits and Services, 2008 and 1995

Benefit	Percentage of Employees Covered		
	2008	*1995*	*% Change*
Retirement plans	79	80	−1.2
Defined benefit	35	52	−32
Defined contribution	71	55	29
Medical care benefits	84	77	9
Dental benefits	64	57	12
Paid time off			
Holidays	86	89	−3.3
Vacations	86	96	−10.4

Personal leave	50	22	127.2
Funeral leave	82	80	2.5
Jury leave	84	85	−1.1
Long-term disability insurance	45	42	7.1
Life insurance	77	87	−11.4
Employer assistance for child care	26	8	225
Adoption assistance	19	11	72.7
Wellness programs	42	34	23.5
Employee assistance programs	66	58	13.7
Educational assistance			
Job-related	67	65	3.0
Non-job-related	23	18	27
Flexible benefits plans	26	12	116
Healthcare Reimbursement plans	52	38	36.8

Sources: Bureau of Labor Statistics, *National Compensation Survey: Employee Benefits in Private Industry in the United States, March 2008*. Bureau of Labor Statistics, *BLS Reports on Employee Benefits in Medium and Large Firms, 1995* (July 27, 1997).

- *Increase employee morale and productivity.* Presumably, employee benefits are important in maintaining employee morale, but there are no comprehensive studies indicating the extent of the relationship. The fact is, many employers have reduced benefits, and even discontinued entire benefit programs, with no apparent negative effect on employee morale. The relationship between employee benefits and productivity is even more suspect. Most likely, employee benefits are something that employees learn to expect, rather than earn, since they are not related to employee behavior.

- *Obtain insurance at low rates.* Obtaining insurance at low rates is becoming an increasingly difficult task for employers, which is the reason that efforts to contain costs have increased.

- *Take advantage of favorable tax treatment.* Even by shifting part of the burden of financing benefits to employees, employers can establish programs, such as 401(k) savings plans and reimbursement plans, that will permit employees to obtain the value of favorable tax treatment. Fortunately, as shown in Exhibit 24-2, the percentage of employees in firms with 100 or more employees who are covered by healthcare reimbursement plans increased 36.8 percent from 1995 to 2008.

- *Replace income.* Employees are expected to shoulder an increasing share of the burden in providing replacement income for themselves for such contingencies as short- and long-term disability. In addition, employers are opting for defined contribution plans and are expecting employees to provide for their eventual retirement through participation in 401(k) and thrift plans.

- *Simplify administration.* This objective is a major reason for shifting from defined benefit retirement plans to defined contribution plans. In addition, flexible benefit plans have proven to be more complex to administer than was previously thought. This is a major reason that the percentage of employees covered by such plans has remained flat during the past 10 years.

Baseline Comparative Data

The preliminary step before designing cost containment programs is to develop baseline cost information for each benefit program. Employers can use survey data from consulting firms to assist in comparing themselves with others. The Employment Cost Index is a national measure of employment cost increases that employers can use to gauge how their costs are increasing in relation to other employers. If an employer's costs are higher than others in the industry, research may be needed to determine if the compensation program, including both pay and benefits, is higher than the industry average. If the total compensation package is competitive with the industry, cost containment measures need to be considered. The same approach should be used in comparing a firm's claim experiences with others in its industry. The claim information should include rates of hospital admissions, the duration of stay, and charges for different procedures.

Cost Containment Phases

The management of employee benefits cost containment involves the following phases:

- *Plan design.* It is important to clearly define the various provisions in each benefit program to avoid litigation and unnecessary expenditures in resolving disputes over what various plan provisions mean. It is also a good idea to check for ambiguities in plan provisions. Prior to plan design or redesign, wording should be tested with employees to ensure clear intent. Future contingencies, such as mergers or divestitures, should be taken into account, so that any results will not adversely affect plan costs.

  Carefully define the term "employee" in plan documents. Approximately 3.5 million individuals are employed by staffing firms.[1] These firms include temporary employment agencies, contract employment firms, facilities staffing firms, and leasing or payrolling firms. In addition, the use of staffing firms is projected to increase significantly in the next five years. Employers are also outsourcing work to independent contractors. The benefit plan language should be unequivocal in excluding those individuals from coverage, if that is the intent of the employer. Failure to make this distinction can result in expenses to resolve disputes about coverage. Definitions of dependents should also be clear; if the term "spouse" is used, the definition should be clear.

---

[1] Bureau of Labor Statistics, *Employment Services,* March 2004.

- *Benefits duplication.* One of the early steps in cost containment is to view the employee benefit program as a whole. Before examining the specifics of each plan, the employer can determine if costly duplications in benefits exist. Exhibit 24-3 illustrates the events or contingencies that employees may face and the types of benefits that are intended to assist them. The exhibit highlights the redundancies in benefits that can occur if the overall employee benefit program is not properly coordinated, increasing employers' costs. Furthermore, duplication of benefits can lead to unnecessary utilization or even fraudulent claims. For example, excessive benefits provided for disability can motivate individuals to resist efforts to get them to return to work or even cause them to feign disability.

Exhibit 24-3
Benefits Provided for Employee Contingencies

Contingency	Medical Expense Plan	Disability Income Plan	Life Insurance	Pension	Social Security	Workers' Compensation	Compulsory Disability	Unemployment Compensation
Death								
Occupational			x	x	x	x		
Nonoccupational			x	x	x			
Disability								
Occupational		x	x	x	x	x		
Nonoccupational		x	x	x	x		x	
Medical care								
Occupational	x				x	x		
Nonoccupational	x				x			
Retirement	x		x	x	x			
Unemployment								x

- *Claim administration.* All claims should be administered equally, that is, no class of employees should receive more favorable treatment than any other class, unless the plan specifically provides for such treatment. This can occur if the plans are administered in-house instead of by an outside source. For example, a highly paid executive may ask for special treatment under a dental plan, when claims filed by other employees for the same treatment were denied in the past. This treatment not only increases the cost of the benefit, but it may evoke employee disputes that can be costly and time-consuming to resolve. The best policy is to treat everyone equally in administering claims.

  Plan provisions should explicitly state the time limitation for filing claims. This precludes the possibility of claims filed long after an event has occurred and for which documentation is not available.

- *Active employee involvement.* To minimize plan administration costs, such as the cost involved in answering employee questions about various provisions and even the cost involved in handling plan investments, give employees choices about various benefits, particularly if they are incurring part of the cost. For example, allow employees to designate how their funds are to be invested in savings plans. In addition, permit employees to change their investments, including changes within funds and among different funds.

- *Employee communication.* Keep employees informed about the costs of various benefits. This communication should be intelligently formulated to arouse employee interest in reading the material, so that they will understand what costs the employer is incurring in providing various benefits. Also, employees should be kept informed about any matters relevant to the areas in which they are participating in the decision-making about their benefits.

  Employees should be informed about the measures they can take to help contain the costs of their benefits. Most people object to sections of benefit plans dealing with exclusions and limitations of benefits, but this information is very important in ensuring that the plans are meeting their objectives without obligating the employer to unintended consequences.

  Communication methods include seminars, audiovisual presentations, posters, newsletters, paycheck stuffers, employee benefit fairs, and hotlines. Employee communication should be a continual strategy.

Retirement Plans

The strategies for containing retirement plan costs include converting to defined contribution plans, using formulas such as the cash account formulas for defined benefit plans, selecting lower replacement rates for retirement plan payouts, and implementing retirement plans that are linked to employee performance

Defined Contribution Plans

Defined contribution plans are easier to administer, are less costly, and have less regulatory requirements than defined benefit plans, so that it should not be surprising that more employers are shifting to them as a cost containment strategy. In addition, most defined contribution plans require employees to make contributions. In contrast, few defined benefit plans require employee contributions.

Lower Replacement Rate

Replacement rate is the amount of a retiree's final year's pay that is replaced by the retirement annuity. Generally, the lower the level of income of the retiree prior to retirement, the higher the replacement rate. For example, an employee who had 30 years of service, was earning $25,000 a year at retirement, and retires at 65 would receive from her pension and Social Security combined approximately 72 percent of her preretirement earnings. A person with the same amount of service and with the same retirement age who was earning $65,000 at retirement would only receive a retirement income from both sources of about 50 percent of his preretirement income.

The higher the replacement rate of preretirement income is in the retirement income objective, the greater the funding needed to provide the benefit. Setting lower replacement rates from the employer-funded plan, and communicating with employees about the importance of preparing for their own retirement through tax-deferred savings plans, is an important strategy in controlling retirement plan costs.

Performance Links

Implement retirement plans that have a gainsharing element to them, such as profit-sharing plans, so that employees have the incentive to apply themselves more diligently because of their motivation to contribute to their own retirement program.

Profit-sharing plans permit employers to create account balances for employees. They can be used in any business. There is no model form for the establishment of a profit-sharing plan; advice from a financial institution or employee benefit advisor would be necessary to formulate one. Annual filing of IRS Form 5500 is required (see Exhibit 22-1 in Chapter 22 for a copy of the form). The employer contribution level can be determined on a yearly basis. The plan must be offered to all employees who are at least 21 years old and who worked at least 1,000 hours in the previous year. Employer contributions are based upon the terms of the plan.

Cash Account Pension Formula

For employers that want to retain their defined benefit plans instead of converting to a defined contribution plan, consideration should be given to using a *cash account pension formula.* This formula specifies a certain periodic contribution that will be made by the employer, plus a rate of interest on the contribution. Benefits are computed as a percentage of each employee's account balance upon retirement. This formula resembles the formulas in defined contribution plans, but because the employer guarantees a certain level of benefits, the Internal Revenue Service classifies it as a defined benefit plan. This formula is discussed more fully in Chapter 22.

Social Security Coordination

Virtually all employers are required to make contributions to Social Security on behalf of their employees. These contributions are significant expenditures for employers. The contributions represent 6.2 percent of pay up to a maximum that increases annually (see Chapter 23 for the current maximum). Some employers also make contributions to a retirement plan on behalf of their employees. For these reasons, many employers feel that pension benefits should not duplicate what is provided under Social Security. To preclude this from happening, about one-half of all employees in firms with 100 or more employees integrate their defined benefit plans with Social Security. The two ways this integration is accomplished are through an *offset plan* or a *step-rate excess plan*. These plans are discussed more fully in Chapter 22.

Postretirement Pension Increases

Retirement plans with fixed dollar benefits have been seriously affected in the past by inflation. Some plans address the issue of preretirement inflation by periodically adjusting benefits upward. Increases in wages during the working years also help keep up with inflation. Few private plans, however, adjust postretirement benefits on a predetermined basis because of the uncertain cost commitment. Instead, some plans make *ad hoc* increases in benefits.

Medical Expense Benefits

Medical expense plans are a major focus of benefits cost containment. Among the reasons for the high cost of medical expense plans are:

- Efforts to motivate employees to use outpatient in lieu of inpatient treatment has not been effective enough. In addition, while some employees are choosing this form of treatment, the costs of outpatient services have significantly increased.

- The widespread increase in medical clinics operated by health care corporations has made health care more accessible to individuals.

- More sophisticated treatment programs, due to advances in medical technology, are more expensive than the traditional forms of care.

- Health maintenance organizations, preferred provider organizations, and similar types of medical service delivery have not produced the promised reductions in health care costs.

- As human services programs, such as Temporary Assistance to Needy Families, relief for indigent persons, and similar programs are phased-out, relatives of the individuals adversely affected by these phase-outs are required to provide assistance. In some cases, this has resulted in accepting individuals as dependents of employees and receiving medical expense benefit coverage from their employers.

- As the age of the population grows older, the demand for medical services is increasing.

Discontinuing Health Benefit Plans

The ultimate approach to medical expense cost containment is to discontinue offering medical expense plans to employees. As shown in Exhibit 24-2, the number of employees in firms with 100 or more employees who are covered by medical care plans decreased nine percent during the interval 1995 to 2007.

Healthy Employees

A major way to reduce the costs of medical expense plans is through cost prevention by keeping employees healthy. As discussed in Chapter 21, employers have numerous opportunities to help employees remain healthy. These opportunities include developing a health strategy, treating employees fairly and thereby fostering good mental health, designing jobs to challenge employees, developing sound safety and health programs to prevent occupational injuries and illnesses, encouraging employees to stop smoking, assisting employees in addressing job stress, establishing work methods to prevent cumulative trauma illnesses, organizing employee assistance programs to prevent and treat employee personal problems, and educating employees about the importance of eating wisely and exercising. There are significant cost advantages to helping employees stay healthy. One employer developed a wellness program and the cost of its medical claims dropped an average of $451 per employee.[2]

Healthy People 2010. Employers can get ideas about ways of keeping employees healthy by participating in the *Healthy People 2010* initiative, discussed in Chapter 21.

Coordination of Benefits

Many group plans have a provision for the manner in which benefits will be paid in the event participants are covered by more than one plan. This is known as a *coordination of benefits* (COB) provision. Duplicate coverage can occur when both spouses in a family are employed and each has coverage with their respective employers. One or both plans may provide dependent coverage as well and, thereby, cover family members. If dependent coverage is contributory, and the husband and wife have children, they will usually select dependent coverage under one of the plans. Duplicate coverage may also occur when an employee has two jobs or when benefits are provided from some other source, such as automobile insurance, that has medical benefits provided in cases of a vehicle accident.

If neither plan contains a COB provision, benefits are paid out under each as if no other insurance is involved. When a plan does contain a COB provision, its coverage is secondary to any other plan *without* the COB provision. Thus, the plan without the provision is said to be "primary" and pays a claim first,

---

[2] Petersen, C., "Wellness Pays At This Firm," *Managed Healthcare* (March 1996), p. 36.

according to its coverage. The plan with the COB provisions pays, according to its coverage *up to* the amount of the claim.

Most plans, however, do have a COB provision. Each plan's provision will specify the priority of payment in the event that the employee or dependent is covered by more than one plan. Each spouse's medical expenses will be primary under his or her own employer's plan. Most plans provide for the children's medical expenses to be primary under the plan of the spouse whose birthday falls earliest in the year. Some plans provide for the father's plan to be primary for the children's expenses. COB provisions also specify which plan is primary in the event the spouses divorce.

Medicare Coordination

Medical expense benefits are also coordinated with Medicare in the event the employee or dependent has Medicare coverage. Any covered individual age 65 or older is eligible for Medicare whether or not they are actually retired. Employers must offer the same plan to active employees over age 65 that is offered to younger employees. Unless the employee elects otherwise, the employer's plan is primary and Medicare is secondary. Generally, the employer plan has better coverage, and the employee will not elect Medicare as primary coverage. Employer health care coverage for retirees can be secondary to Medicare.

Cost Control Coalitions

The extent of employer efforts to organize cost control campaigns is not precisely known. Some employers have formed local health care cost control coalitions to share ideas. Other employers have implemented individual cost control strategies. For the most part, however, some research indicates that these efforts have been of minimal value in controlling medical expense cost increases.

Employee Cost Sharing

Medical expense costs are contained through more employee cost sharing, by increasing the amount of deductibles and copayments. Exhibit 24-4 shows the percentages of employees in firms with 100 or more employees in which the contributory provisions were increased for coverage for employees alone. From 1988 to 2008, the percentage of health benefits that were wholly financed by the employer declined from 57 percent of all employees in firms with 100 or more employees to 17 percent in such firms. The percentage of family coverage wholly financed by employers declined from 31 percent to 10 percent. Similar trends are apparent in the increased amount of deductibles and higher percentages of copayments which employees must incur.

Exhibit 24-4
Wholly Employer Benefit Plan Financing
Firms With 100 or More Employees, 1988 & 2008

Benefit	Wholly Employer Financed (%)		
	1988	2008	% Change
Medical care for employees	57%	17%	−70.1%
Medical care for family	31	10	−67.7
Life insurance	87	95	9.1
Short-term disability	80	82	2
Defined benefit pension	94	96	2.1

Sources: Bureau of Labor Statistics, *National Compensation Survey: Employee Benefits in Private Industry in the United States, March 2008,*; Bureau of Labor Statistics, *Employee Benefits in Medium and Large Firms,* 1988.

Note: Data for Short-term disability in the 2007 column is from 1997.

Retiree Coverage

As a major cost containment strategy, employers are less likely to offer health benefits to retirees. Furthermore, those employers that do offer such coverage are expecting retirees to pay for it. For example, in 1993, 52 percent of employees in firms with 100 or more employees had health benefit plans with coverage for retirees. By 2003, this figure declined to 19 percent for retirees under the age of 65 and 15 percent for retirees age 65 and over[3].

Cost Shifting v. Cost Reduction

Cost sharing strategies reduce employer costs for the delivery of medical care services, but they do not necessarily decrease overall health costs in the economy. Assuming the same medical costs would be incurred, regardless of who paid them, cost sharing simply shifts more of the medical expense to the employee. The theory is that cost sharing motivates employees to be more astute users of medical services, in that they will substitute less expensive forms of medical care in place of more expensive ones. Furthermore, if increased cost sharing would cause the employee to ration medical services, employer costs would be similarly reduced. A disadvantage is that increased cost sharing may result in an employee postponing or neglecting needed medical services, which could have a serious impact upon an employee's health and/or increase medical expenses in the longer term when the employee's condition worsens.

Alternatives to Retrospective Reimbursement

Retrospective reimbursement for medical payments is the traditional method of claim paying. It is the payment of medical expenses after the charges have been incurred. *Prearrangement of payments,* which is an alternative to retrospective reimbursement, is an arrangement in which a provider agrees to provide a

[3] Bureau of Labor Statistics, *National Compensation Survey*, March 2003.

service for a flat amount regardless, for example, of how complicated the employee's condition or how long a stay is required in a medical facility.

The Medicare program involves a prospective pricing system. Standard rates have been developed for various types of diagnoses. When a covered patient is hospitalized, Medicare pays the hospital the fixed amount for the patient's diagnosis, without regard to the actual services provided or the length of the patient's stay. If the hospital exceeds the Medicare payment, it is responsible for the remaining cost. If the hospital's cost is less, they still get the established fixed payment. This practice encourages the hospital to be cost-efficient. The two set rates of prearranged payments are a *rural set* and a *urban set*. Some hospitals have exemptions from the procedures due to the mission they fulfill.

Health maintenance organizations (HMOs) also use a system of prearrangement of payments. HMOs establish a prepaid, fixed fee for all services provided. Since the provider is not paid for providing additional care, there is an incentive to keep the employee well and to provide less costly treatment when needed.

Exclusive Provider

For employers that self-insure, an exclusive contract with a single provider may help lower medical expense costs. This type of arrangement involves contracting with a single provider for a set fee and, in turn, requires the provider to negotiate a fee arrangement with a network of treatment providers that will ensure stable costs for a stipulated period of time.

Incentives for Less Costly Care

Traditionally, medical care plans have contained disincentives for lower-cost services. For example, the plan may have paid for surgery performed in a hospital but will not pay for the same surgery if it is provided in the lower-cost setting of a physician's office. To reduce these disincentives, plans have increasingly been restructured to include incentives for less costly forms of care, such as reimbursement for outpatient services and surgery in a physician's office. A more effective incentive is to provide a higher reimbursement for outpatient care than for inpatient care. Other less costly substitutes for in-hospital care are birthing centers, skilled nursing facilities, and hospice and home health care.

Gate-Keeping

Many medical expense benefit plans have provisions requiring various gate-keeping functions, such as obtaining second opinions before receiving surgery. The frequency of use of these cost containment measures is shown in Exhibit 24-5.

Exhibit 24-5
Cost Containment Measures
for full-time employees, non-HMO plans, private industry, 2000

Cost containment feature	% Employees in firms with feature
Preadmission certification requirement	63
Penalty for not obtaining preadmission certification	94
Second surgical opinion provisions	44
Penalty for not obtaining second surgical opinion	10
Utilization concurrent review	39
Preadmission testing	26
Nonemergency weekend admission restriction	9
Hospital audit program	5

Source: Bureau of Labor Statistics, *National Compensation Survey: Employee Benefits in Private Industry in U.S., 2000.*

Preadmission Certifications

Preadmission certification is the process of having an insured person and/or his or her personal physician obtain authorization (or certification) prior to hospitalization for nonemergency and nonmaternity medical treatment. The request for hospitalization is typically reviewed by a medical peer who renders a decision after considering the employee's medical condition and the proposed length of hospitalization. Employees are exempted from such requirements for emergency treatment, but evidence may be required that a real emergency condition existed. The insured's physician is often also required to get permission to extend the period of hospitalization beyond the period that was approved.

Most plans impose penalties for failing to obtain the preauthorization. Typically, the penalties consist of reducing the coinsurance and imposing deductibles, usually around $300. A minority of plans, about five percent, will not provide any benefits if a certification is not obtained.

Second Opinions

There is often a disparity in opinions among physicians as to the necessity of surgery. For example, a team of medical researchers who analyzed 400 bypass operations in three hospitals found that 56 percent of them were proper, given the medical condition of the patient, 30 percent were "equivocal," and the other 14 percent were considered to be inappropriate.[4] The significance of this study is more apparent when one considers that about 300,000 of these procedures are performed each year at a cost of more than $25,000 each. Similar results were obtained when the researchers analyzed the medical histories of patients who received other types of surgery. The percentage of cases in which the surgery was determined to be inappropriate ranged from six percent to 23 percent, depending upon the type of surgery performed.

[4] Ruffenach, G., "Study Contends Bypass Surgeries Often Unneeded," *The Wall Street Journal* (July 22, 1988), p. 21.

One way of controlling unnecessary surgery is by requiring second opinions. Plans with second-opinion provisions usually pay for the cost of the second opinion, plus a third opinion if the first two conflict. In those plans that have a second opinion requirement, a failure to obtain one usually results in reducing the coinsurance portion. Much less frequently used is the imposition of a deductible. A small percentage of plans do not provide any benefits if the required second opinion is not obtained.

Concurrent Reviews

Concurrent reviews monitor care while the patient is hospitalized. Thirty-nine percent of full-time employees in private industry are enrolled in health benefit plans that have the requirement for monitoring care to ensure that only proper services are provided.

Preadmission Testing

Preadmission testing is administering required medical tests for the purpose of diagnosing a person's physical problems before admission to a hospital. This process saves the costs of hospital room charges during the period in which the tests are conducted, particularly if different tests are conducted over a period of several days. About 26 percent of full-time employees in private industry have provisions requiring such testing. Failure to obtain preadmission testing usually results in reducing the coinsurance, incurring a somewhat higher deductible, and, in a small percentage of cases, withholding benefits.

Claims Administration

Claim administration should include monitoring fees, utilization patterns, and length of stay in hospitals. Monitoring helps to pinpoint problem areas and to determine where plan changes will be the most effective. Monitoring is also important in helping detect benefit fraud.

Self-Admissions

On occasion, persons may become ill over a weekend and be unable to contact their regular physician. Sometimes this results in people admitting themselves to hospitals. Some plans specifically contain a provision restricting this practice. Increasingly, medical plans have provisions requiring the imposition of second deductibles, usually between $200 and more than $500 for each admission, to discourage unnecessary hospitalizations.

Audits

Audits are an essential component of health care cost containment. Audits should be performed by both claims administrators and patients.

Employee Audits

Employees who are patients are better able to catch those errors pertaining to the delivery of services, since they are usually more knowledgeable about whether they received a service for which the plan is charged. In addition, an employee who is knowledgeable about the costs of various services, particularly when he or she receives multiple amounts of service, can determine whether the amount that is charged is correct. Consequently, some employers have instituted *employee self-audit programs* in which the employee verifies whether he or she actually received the services billed by providers. Sometimes employees are given a specified percentage of any billing errors they find in excess of some small amount, such as $10. Employers that have initiated self-audit programs have been pleased with the results. Some employers contend they save between $2 and $3 for each $1 of audit cost.

Trained Auditors

Some employers either employ or contract with specialists to audit large bills. These specialists, as well as claims adjusters and other claim personnel, can detect obvious billing errors, such as claims that are significantly outside the typical range of charges for the service that was performed. Claims personnel should conduct periodic reviews on randomly selected claims of different types to test the effectiveness of claims administration. These audits should check for errors in:

- The claimant's eligibility for benefits;

- The appropriateness and necessity of services relative to the diagnosis;

- Paid and unpaid expenses relative to the plan provisions;

- Excessive charges, which can be detected by comparing them with the "usual, customary, and reasonable" charges for such services in the locale. This area of claims review can be facilitated through computer programs;

- The benefit calculation;

- The application of deductibles, coinsurance, and plan maximums;

- The applicability and proper computation of the coordination of benefits provisions; and

- Payment to the wrong party.

Fraud Detection

Health insurance fraud is a major reason for increases in health benefit costs. Health care expenditures in the U.S. are more than $2 trillion per year, which is about 15 percent of the gross domestic product. There are estimates that as much as three percent of the expenditures or $60 billion dollars can be attributed to fraud and abuse[5]. Fraud is committed by both patients and service providers. Of the two groups, it is probably more difficult to detect provider fraud. To cope with this problem, insurance companies employ special fraud units and train claims personnel in how to detect fraud, such as observing patterns in the filing of certain types of claims and any noticeable tampering with information provided on claim forms.

---

[5] National Health Care Anti-Fraud Association, *Consumer Info & Action: What is Health Care Fraud,* 2007.

Repercussions of Cost Containment

Health care costs are a significant component in total compensation, so that employer efforts to contain these costs are necessary. Employers must, however, be mindful of the long-term effects of cost containment. Overzealous strategies to reduce health care costs can be expected to result in public policy action. Some federal legislation that has been implemented in response to employer actions includes the Health Insurance Portability and Accountability Act of 1996 (HIPAA) and the Newborns' and Mothers' Health Protection Act of 1996 (NMHPA). Both laws, which were effective in 1998, were at least partially in response to employer initiatives to contain health benefit costs. For example, HIPPA was due in part to employer efforts to expand exclusionary provisions that applied to new employees who had preexisting health conditions and to obtain and use health information about employees. The NMHPA became law due to public disclosures about the danger of health care plan requirements that mandated restrictions on postpartum hospital stays for normal and caesarean section deliveries.

Workers' Compensation

Workers' compensation costs can be contained both through prevention and properly responding to employee claims for benefits.

Prevention

Among the principal preventive methods for containing workers' compensation costs is an effective safety and health program designed to prevent occupational injuries and illnesses. There are no great mysteries to having a safe and healthful work environment. Successful programs are not appendages but rather are an essential part of the management philosophy and operating characteristics of an organization. Studies have found that the companies with the lowest accident and illness rates have the following characteristics:

- Top management direction in the safety and health program;
- Safety personnel who had formal training in safety and health subjects;
- Employees' family involvement in safety consciousness;
- Extensive safety communication for employees;
- The use of safety incentives;
- The use of less severe forms of discipline for safety violations. In this conjunction, the philosophy is not to punish employees for violating safety rules; rather, the emphasis is on explaining why the rules exist and the importance of complying with them;
- A work force that is a little older than the industry average. The work force in the U.S. is getting somewhat older as the population ages but, obviously, an employer cannot wait for employees to mature. The key here is to establish networks where older workers who have the best safety records can mentor younger workers;
- Formalized safety and health training programs;
- Safety officials who report to top management;

- Investigations of all accidents to determine the causes(s), the failure sources, and the actions necessary to prevent such accidents in the future;

- Frequent safety inspections; and

- Safety and health reviews conducted on facility construction and modifications projects. The key here is to "build-in" safety, that is, design the facilities to help prevent accidents.

Reacting to Claims

A fundamental step in containing the cost of claims filed under workers' compensation is obtaining accurate and timely information. The importance of prompt reporting of all occupational injuries and illnesses where workers' compensation is requested cannot be over-emphasized. Timely reporting permits prompt accident investigations, so that relevant facts can be obtained. This process includes interviewing witnesses and gathering evidence.

Fraud Detection

Fraudulent claims for workers' compensation is a significant factor in workers' compensation cost increases. Among the actions employers can take to control this needless expense is the prompt reporting of claims, so that an early investigation can be conducted. In addition, trained investigators should be assigned to investigate suspected cases involving fraud.

Return to Work

Once an employee begins receiving benefits, management should make special efforts to get the person to return to work as soon as possible. Some of these efforts include designing light-duty assignments that can accommodate the employee's condition, providing rehabilitation to speed the employee's return to gainful employment, and redesigning jobs, so that ill or injured employees are able to perform the required tasks.

Sick Leave/Short-Term Disability

Sick leave and short-term disability plans are provided to continue an employee's pay for short periods, typically up to one year, when an employee is disabled due to illness or injury. As with workers' compensation, there are preventive and reactive methods for controlling the costs of these plans.

Preventing Sick Leave/Short-Term Disability Costs

Effective strategies to prevent the costs of sick leave or short-term disability are educating employees about the value of conserving their sick leave, giving employees retirement credit for the unused portion of their earned sick leave credits, and implementing employee wellness programs that include such subjects as smoking cessation, fitness training, and diet and nutrition programs. Another important strategy is to broaden the definition of disability for purposes of determining when an employee can receive benefits. One encompassing definition of disability is "the inability to perform any job for which you can be reasonably trained and which can be made to accommodate your condition."

Coordination of Benefits

To minimize the potential for overinsurance, disability plans should be coordinated (or integrated) with other disability benefits to which the employee may be entitled. The plan should be established, so that benefits provided under the group contract are reduced by any benefits received under any other employer-provided plan, Social Security, or workers' compensation. These decisions should be guided by the employers' objectives regarding the income replacement rate.

Preventing Abuse

A problem with short-term disability and sick leave plans is the propensity of some employees to abuse the *benefit.* The word benefit is italicized because that is what the plans are—benefits—for use when employees are really too incapacitated to work. Unfortunately, some employees believe that they have a right to benefit from the provisions of such plans, whether they are sick or not. For some employees, this belief can be modified through educational programs and following the other preventive methods discussed above. For other employees, more drastic actions are necessary, such as restricting the use of sick leave privileges by requiring medical documentation (a doctor's certificate) when sick leave is taken. In more severe cases of abuse, employee sick leave privileges can be withdrawn or the employee can be disciplined, including discharge, for the abuse.

Unemployment Insurance

All state tax rates for unemployment insurance are *experience rated,* and the tax rate is, to some extent, a function of the individual employer's own unemployment experience. An employer with a lower incidence of unemployment claims will pay a lower tax rate than an employer with a higher level of claims. This provides incentives for employers to contain costs since, if their unemployment insurance account is current, they receive a 5.4 percent credit (they don't have to pay it on the first $7,000 of each employee's income); the other .8 percent goes to the federal government for administration of the plan. Typically, an employer's experience rating is determined by comparing the amount of benefit expenditure to total payroll.

Like cost containment for other types of benefits, unemployment insurance costs can be contained through both prevention and control strategies.

Preventing Claims

The principal ways of preventing unemployment insurance claims are:

- *Plan for human resources needs.* Long-term planning of the need for human resources will help prevent unnecessary layoffs. Through such planning any excess personnel that may result from future actions, such as the introduction of labor-saving equipment or other technology, can be handled through normal attrition.

- *Avoid overstaffing.* Overstaffing may result in layoffs during slack economic periods. A better alternative is use part-time staffing agencies to fill in during peak periods.

- *Use overtime.* Using overtime in lieu of hiring additional workers will also help prevent the need for laying off workers.

Document Separations/Discipline

Former employees who were discharged for good cause should be denied unemployment insurance benefits. The reasons for a denial of benefits usually must involve "willful misconduct." If the employer is able to show that this standard was met, and that the employee in effect caused his or her own separation, a denial of benefits decision is more likely. To aid in this process, the reasons for employee separations should be thoroughly documented. For example, if an employee was separated for cause, such as for fighting or for a poor attendance record, that information should be documented in the employee's record. This information can be provided to the state unemployment commission to support a request for denial of benefits.

CHAPTER 25

COMPENSATION SURVEYS AND EXTERNAL EQUITY

Chapter Highlights
- Review the purposes for conducting compensation surveys
- Examine sources of survey information
- Introduce the procedures involved in conducting a compensation survey

Introduction

Achieving *external equity* is one of the two (the other being *internal equity*) main goals employers consider in establishing compensation systems. *External equity* is the degree to which an organization's compensation program rewards employees relative to their contributions compared to the rewards received for similar contributions by employees of other employers in the labor market.

Virtually all employers consider the external labor market when establishing and revising their compensation plans. This consideration should be expected, since the compensation practices of other firms in an industry and/or labor market have a profound impact upon the quality and quantity of labor that a particular firm will be able to recruit and retain.

A *compensation survey* is a method used in compensation planning in which the employers in a labor market are surveyed to determine the monetary payments and benefit programs they are providing to their employees.

Types of Surveys

The two types of compensation surveys are indirect compensation or benefits surveys and direct compensation or pay surveys. Occasionally both types of surveys are combined in one study of the market, but more typically, the practice is to conduct them independently. The major reason for separate surveys is that they are less complex, which means that the survey instrument is simpler, shorter, and requires less time for respondents to complete. These advantages result in greater respondent cooperation and hence better response rates and more accurate data.

Purposes for Conducting Compensation Surveys

Employers have various purposes for conducting surveys, such as to establish compensation practices, obtain pay information on benchmark jobs, assist in the evaluation of jobs, and plan for future collective bargaining sessions.

Establishing Compensation Practices

Some employers use compensation surveys as the sole means of determining their compensation practices. These employers are concerned with ensuring that they are compensating their employees at a level commensurate with other firms that are competing for the same type of employees. Determining what to pay in relation to the market depends on the company's compensation philosophy. For example, an employer may have a goal of providing compensation that is competitive with those firms in the top quintile in the market. Other firms may be content with providing compensation consistent with the average of the market.

Benchmark or Key Job Pay

Pay surveys are sometimes used when establishing job evaluation systems to determine if the pay of benchmark or key jobs is competitive with the external market. A *benchmark* or *key* job is a job commonly found across organizations. It is used to guide the process of establishing a fair system of the relative worth of all the jobs in an organization. Chapter 28 discusses how the information furnished from a pay survey is used to establish a pay system which is externally equitable and also meets stated objectives.

Unique Jobs

Sometimes, unique jobs which are performed by only one or two employees are difficult to evaluate internally because of their distinct characteristics. Because these one-of-a-kind jobs may also exist in other firms in the labor market, a market survey can provide valuable information about their relative worth.

Collective Bargaining

Compensation surveys are an important part of preparing for upcoming collective bargaining sessions. For example, to anticipate what demands a particular union might make during forthcoming negotiations, an employer might consider surveying those employers who negotiated agreements with the union within the past year to gain information prior to the commencement of negotiations. An employer might want to know the union's initial proposals, management's counterproposals, and the terms of the final agreement. This information could be used in conjunction with relevant cost, revenue, or production data to indicate limits on concessions during the forthcoming round of negotiations.

Sources of Survey Information

Survey information can be obtained from trade associations, the federal government, consulting firms, or by conducting an independent survey.

Trade Associations

Various associations routinely conduct compensation surveys. Sometimes, the survey results are provided free, but typically the members are charged a fee for the results—albeit at a reduced rate compared to those charged to a nonmember. The principal advantage of such surveys is the better-than-average response rate obtained from the association's membership. Another advantage is the cost-sharing involved in underwriting the survey, which reduces the price of the results to the members. One disadvantage is validity problems if the survey is confined to association members, who might not fairly represent the employers in some labor markets for one or more jobs.

Federal Government

The federal government is the biggest single source of compensation survey information. The advantages of federal surveys are the validity of the information, the comprehensive coverage of occupations which are surveyed, the representativeness of geographical areas, and the nominal charge for copies of the results.

Consultants

Consultants interact with compensation surveys in several ways. One way is for the consultant to assist an organization in conducting a study. This assistance might include helping to design the survey, giving advice on the types of information to collect, ensuring that the objectives of the study are well-defined, and/or analyzing the data. This type of arrangement is used when the employer prefers to conduct the study with in-house personnel but wants consultant assistance to be certain that the output will be valid and reliable. Sometimes, consultants are contracted to completely plan and conduct the study and make recommendations for any necessary changes. In both of these situations, the consultant is performing services for a particular employer.

Consulting firms, as opposed to individual consultants, provide extensive services to employers. In addition, they independently conduct compensation studies in various industries and market the results to employers. In other situations, a consulting firm with a large client base may conduct a survey specially designed for a specific group.

An advantage of using consultants is their expertise, which helps ensure the validity and reliability of the survey results. Also, the use of consultants may be less expensive than attempting to conduct a survey through the exclusive use of in-house personnel.

When purchasing compensation survey information from some consulting firms, ensure that the results are representative of the relevant labor markets, and not simply the results of a survey of the firm's client population.

Employer-Conducted Surveys

Surveys conducted by individual employers have distinct advantages and equally distinct disadvantages. First, the particular jobs and market areas can be precisely defined, so that the specific objectives of the survey can be focused upon. Also, the survey can be tailored to meet any unique needs that the organization may have. One of the major disadvantages is the significant cost of planning and conducting a survey. Depending upon the size of the project, the cost can be prohibitive. A valid survey requires expertise not available in every organization.

Published Surveys

Most nationally conducted surveys are confined to either benefits or pay. Some surveys include both dimensions.

Benefits Surveys

The best-known national surveys of employee benefits are the annual benefit survey conducted by the U.S. Chamber of Commerce and the annual benefits surveys conducted by the U.S. Department of Labor.

U.S. Chamber of Commerce Survey

The Chamber of Commerce survey has been conducted for over 50 years. Since 1981, the survey has been published annually.

U.S. Department of Labor Survey

The Department of Labor conducts these employee benefits surveys:

- *Employee Benefits in Private Industry*;
- *Employee Benefits in State and Local Governments.* Included in this survey population are all state and local governments.

Both surveys include both full-time and part-time employees. The sample sizes for the surveys are quite large and representative of the populations sampled. Part-time and full-time employees are covered in all 50 states and the District of Columbia.

Within each surveyed establishment, data is collected for a sample of all occupations in the establishment. The occupations are selected randomly. The probability of any occupation's selection is related to its employment size relative to total employment in the surveyed establishment. Exhibit 25-1 is a summary report for employee participation in selected benefits other than retirement plans. Exhibit 25-2 is the summary report for employee participation in defined contribution retirement plans from the same survey.

Exhibit 25-1 Percent of workers with access to quality of life benefits, by selected characteristics, private industry, National Compensation Survey, March 2005

Characteristics	Total[1]	Employer assistance for childcare			Adoption assistance	Long-term care insurance	Flexible work-place	Employer-provided home PC	Subsidized commuting
		Employer-provided funds	On-site and off-site child-care	Child-care resource and referral services					
All workers	14	3	5	10	9	11	4	3	5
Worker characteristics									
White-collar occupations	19	5	7	14	14	17	7	4	7
Blue-collar occupations	8	2	2	6	7	6	2	1	3
Service occupations	9	2	4	5	2	4	1	1	2
Full time	16	4	6	11	11	13	5	3	6
Part time	8	1	3	5	4	6	2	1	2
Union	18	3	7	16	13	15	2	2	6
Nonunion	14	3	5	9	9	11	4	3	5
Average wage less than $15 per hour	9	2	3	5	5	7	2	1	2
Average wage $15 per hour or higher	21	5	8	16	15	18	7	5	8
Establishment characteristics									
Goods producing	13	3	4	11	10	10	3	4	4
Service producing	14	3	6	10	9	12	4	2	5
1 to 99 workers . .	5	1	2	3	3	4	3	1	2
100 workers or more	26	5	9	19	17	21	5	4	8
Geographic areas									
Metropolitan areas	15	3	5	11	10	12	5	3	6
Nonmetropolitan areas	7	2	3	3	3	5	1	1	1
New England . . .	16	2	7	13	12	12	3	2	8
Middle Atlantic . .	16	4	6	11	13	13	6	5	7
East North Central	16	4	7	11	10	11	3	2	3
West North Central	15	2	7	8	10	9	2	2	4
South Atlantic . .	11	3	4	8	9	12	3	2	2
East South Central	11	4	5	7	5	7	4	2	3
West South Central	15	3	5	10	9	13	5	3	4
Mountain	15	4	3	12	7	10	6	2	7
Pacific	12	2	3	9	7	13	4	2	8

[1]The total is less than the sum of individual childcare provisions because many employees have access to more than one of the benefits.

Exhibit 25-2. Percent of workers participating in defined contribution plans with selected attributes, by selected characteristics, private industry, National Compensation Survey, March 2005

Characteristics	Employee contribution requirement			Employee contribution pretax option		
	Required	Not required	Not determinable	Pretax	Not pretax	Not determinable
All workers	61	31	8	72	18	10
Worker characteristics						
White-collar occupations	60	31	9	72	18	11
Blue-collar occupations	63	31	6	73	17	10
Service occupations	60	34	6	72	19	9
Full time	61	31	8	72	18	10
Part time	61	32	8	72	19	8
Union	51	36	13	67	17	16
Nonunion	62	31	7	73	18	10
Average wage less than $15 per hour . .	59	36	5	71	21	8
Average wage $15 per hour or higher	62	28	9	72	15	12
Establishment characteristics						
Goods producing . .	64	29	8	76	13	11
Service producing .	60	32	8	71	19	10
1 to 99 workers . . .	59	32	9	71	17	12
100 workers or more	63	31	7	73	18	9
Geographic areas						
Metropolitan areas .	61	31	8	72	18	10
Nonmetropolitan areas	62	31	7	74	17	9
New England	64	31	6	70	18	12
Middle Atlantic . . .	56	35	9	73	13	13
East North Central .	56	38	6	72	21	7
West North Central	59	34	7	77	15	8
South Atlantic	65	25	10	70	18	12
East South Central .	71	24	5	79	13	8
West South Central .	60	34	6	71	19	10
Mountain	63	30	7	73	19	8
Pacific	64	26	10	69	19	12

NOTE: Because of rounding, sums of individual items may not equal totals. Where applicable, dash indicates no employees in this category or data do not meet publication criteria.

Pay Surveys

The two most comprehensive pay surveys are conducted by the Bureau of Labor Statistics, U. S. Department of Labor. These surveys are the National Compensation Survey and the Occupational Employment Statistics survey. Both of these surveys contain occupational wage and salary information but each has particular strengths which are discussed in the following sections.

National Compensation Survey

The National Compensation Survey (NCS) includes pay information for about 480 occupations in 85 metropolitan and non-metropolitan areas. In addition to other formats, pay information is shown by industry, union/nonunion status, private industry, state and local government and size of organization. NCS pay information is more detailed than that provided by the Occupational Employment Statistics program since it includes pay for different levels of work for the same occupation. For example, the tasks of Architect may vary considerably from one firm to another and even from one job to another. Consequently, each job should be evaluated to determine its pay. This is shown in Exhibit 25-3.

In addition to providing pay information, the other major parts of the NCS are these:

- The Employment Benefits Survey, which is discussed above;
- The Employment Cost Index, which measures price changes in employee compensation and is discussed later; and,
- The Employer Costs for Employee Compensation, which is discussed in Chapter 24, is a measure of the average costs of employee compensation.

Occupational Employment Statistics

The Occupational Employment Statistics (OES) program is broader than the NCS since it includes pay information for over 800 occupations from 1.2 million establishments. Approximately 200,000 establishments are surveyed each six months so it requires about 3 years to collect data from all 1.2 million. The survey includes all workers in nonfarm industries in the U.S. Pay and employment information is available for the nation, the individual States and for 409 metropolitan areas. This is an advantage to OES pay data. The disadvantage is the pay information is not leveled reflecting different levels of pay for differing responsibilities in the same occupation.

Summary

These are the major similarities/differences and advantages/disadvantages in the OES and NCS surveys:

- Both surveys include market pay information for full-time and part-time workers in various occupations.
- The OES survey includes the entire U.S. and estimates the number of workers employed within each occupation. The NCS does not contain occupational employment estimates and the scope of the survey is more limited.

- OES data is available for 800 occupations at the national level, by state and for 409 areas of the U. S. (all occupations are not available for all 409 areas). NCS data is available for 480 occupations at the national level, for nine broad geographic areas and for 85 areas (all 480 occupations are not available for all 85 areas).

- OES data is obtained from a mail survey; NCS data is obtained by Bureau of Labor Statistics' (BLS) Field Economists who visit each employer in the survey and evaluate each occupation.

- For OES data, the surveys returned by the employers are analyzed and wages and salaries for each occupation are summed and an average is calculated. For example, the pay for a Human Resources Manager is included with the pay for the same occupation (including both the largest and smallest firm) from all other firms; then averages are calculated. One problem with OES data is that invalid comparisons may occur, for example, when an employer compares the pay for a Human Resource Manager in his/her firm with the average pay in the OES data.

- In the NCS survey, BLS' Field Economists visit each employer in the study and evaluate each occupation using the BLS' *Point Factor Leveling* method of job evaluation. The *Point Factor Leveling* method is briefly discussed in Chapter 26. As discussed above the pay levels for several occupations are shown in Exhibit 25-3.

- OES data should be used if pay is needed for a large number of occupations in different occupational areas and average pay is sufficiently accurate. NCS data is preferable if a more precise measure of pay is needed and expertise in the *Point Factor Leveling* method is available to evaluate in-house occupations.

Exhibit 25-3 **Occupations and levels, West South Central: Mean hourly earnings and weekly hours, private industry and State and local government, National Compensation Survey,[4] June 2005**

Occupations and levels	Total			Private industry			State and local government		
	Hourly earnings		Mean weekly hours	Hourly earnings		Mean weekly hours	Hourly earnings		Mean weekly hours
	Mean	Relative error[5] (percent)		Mean	Relative error[5] (percent)		Mean	Relative error[5] (percent)	
White collar -Continued									
Administrative support, including clerical- Continued									
Supervisors, general office -Continued									
8	$25.95	6.3	40.2	$27.15	4.0	40.1	-	-	-
Supervisors, financial records processing . . .	23.13	10.2	40.0	23.23	10.1	40.0	-	-	-
Supervisors, distribution, scheduling, and adjusting clerks	24.46	16.0	40.0	24.58	15.8	40.0	-	-	-
Computer operators . .	15.87	3.7	39.9	-	-	-	-	-	-
Secretaries	14.93	3.1	38.8	15.74	4.5	38.6	$12.87	3.4	39.3
3	10.23	2.7	39.2	10.04	2.4	39.2	10.76	4.6	39.0
4	14.67	2.8	38.2	15.64	3.9	37.6	12.92	3.4	39.3
5	16.62	3.3	38.6	17.44	3.6	38.5	13.74	5.3	39.0
6	18.47	5.0	39.4	19.93	3.8	39.2	14.02	5.2	39.8
7	20.24	2.5	39.9	20.86	2.2	40.0	17.05	3.8	39.3
Not able to be leveled									
. . . .	15.58	4.0	39.9	15.62	4.3	39.9	-	-	-
Stenographers	16.18	19.7	40.0	-	-	-	-	-	-
Typists	13.14	7.9	39.2	14.23	7.9	39.1	-	-	-
4	13.46	8.9	39.0	-	-	-	-	-	-
Interviewers	10.74	5.2	38.7	10.33	5.1	38.2	11.63	11.7	40.0
3	10.61	4.0	36.1	10.36	2.6	34.3	-	-	-
4	12.29	10.0	40.0	-	-	-	-	-	-
Hotel clerks	8.68	9.8	36.9	8.65	10.1	36.8	-	-	-
2	8.53	10.2	36.5	8.53	10.2	36.5	-	-	-
Transportation ticket and reservation agents	14.46	7.6	34.0	14.46	7.6	34.0	-	-	-
2	11.04	12.1	34.2	11.04	12.1	34.2	-	-	-
3	15.70	10.8	40.0	15.70	10.8	40.0	-	-	-
Receptionists	10.10	3.5	37.0	10.04	3.5	36.9	11.45	11.5	39.0
1	7.12	8.5	27.9	7.12	8.5	27.9	-	-	-
2	9.58	3.5	37.3	9.50	3.9	37.3	-	-	-
3	10.54	4.4	38.5	10.50	4.5	38.5	11.04	14.6	39.7
Information clerks, n.e.c.									
. . . .	12.33	5.8	39.6	12.34	6.2	39.6	12.07	6.4	38.9
3	10.26	3.1	39.4	10.03	2.9	39.4	-	-	-
4	13.00	4.9	40.0	13.02	4.9	40.0	-	-	-

Occupations and levels	Total			Private industry			State and local government		
	Hourly earnings		Mean weekly hours	Hourly earnings		Mean weekly hours	Hourly earnings		Mean weekly hours
	Mean	Relative error[5] (percent)		Mean	Relative error[5] (percent)		Mean	Relative error[5] (percent)	
Order clerks	13.76	12.0	38.4	13.76	12.0	38.4	-	-	-
2	8.62	7.4	36.1	8.62	7.4	36.1	-	-	-
3	10.13	5.8	38.4	10.13	5.8	38.4	-	-	-
4	13.39	12.8	39.4	13.39	12.8	39.4	-	-	-
5	17.05	8.1	39.8	17.05	8.1	39.8	-	-	-
Personnel clerks, except payroll and timekeeping	14.86	7.9	39.8	14.49	7.0	39.8	-	-	-
4	12.77	6.4	39.4	-	-	-	-	-	-
Library clerks	10.99	5.2	34.4	12.05	16.6	37.6	10.62	3.6	33.5
3	10.60	5.1	37.5	-	-	-	11.25	1.1	37.5
File clerks	11.74	4.1	39.3	12.09	2.6	39.8	9.71	4.9	36.7
2	12.29	7.4	39.6	-	-	-	-	-	-
3	10.99	7.4	40.0	-	-	-	-	-	-
Records clerks, n.e.c. . . .	12.04	4.5	39.0	12.07	5.7	38.7	11.97	3.1	39.7
2	10.46	2.8	39.6	-	-	-	10.86	4.4	40.0
3	9.96	3.3	39.1	9.99	4.1	38.9	9.89	7.0	39.8
4	11.88	6.5	39.5	11.17	4.0	39.8	13.66	11.0	38.9
5	15.88	3.5	40.1	15.89	4.7	40.3	15.85	3.8	39.6
6	14.09	6.6	38.7	-	-	-	-	-	-
Bookkeepers, accounting and auditing clerks . . .	13.67	2.6	38.4	13.80	2.9	38.1	13.10	9.2	39.7
2	9.29	4.9	31.5	9.29	4.9	31.5	-	-	-
3	10.93	5.7	36.5	10.86	6.2	36.3	11.96	2.5	40.0
4	12.80	1.8	39.5	13.25	2.9	39.4	12.04	7.9	39.6
5	14.00	4.0	39.4	14.01	4.5	39.3	-	-	-
6	18.19	3.6	38.7	18.48	3.9	38.3	-	-	-
Billing clerks	12.33	3.8	39.4	12.31	3.7	39.3	-	-	-
3	10.46	3.8	38.6	10.50	4.0	38.6	-	-	-
4	13.48	3.0	39.8	13.45	3.1	39.8	-	-	-

Surveys for Tracking Inflation

A major concern among employers is how their compensation plans are affected by price increases. The major measures of inflation are the Employment Cost Index, Employer Costs for Employee Compensation, and the Consumer Price Index.

Employment Cost Index

The Employment Cost Index (ECI) is a quarterly index that measures the change in the cost of labor, free from the influence of employment shifts between occupations and industries. It measures the change for total compensation (wages, salaries, and employer costs for employee benefits). Wages and salaries are defined as the hourly straight-time wage rate, or straight-time earnings divided by the corresponding hours. Straight-time wage and salary rates are total earnings before payroll deductions, excluding premium pay for overtime and for work on weekends and holidays, shift differentials, and nonproduction bonuses such as lump-sum payments.[3]

Benefits covered by the ECI include paid leave, supplemental pay, insurance benefits, retirement and savings benefits, and legally required benefits.

The ECI covers the civilian economy, which includes the private and public sectors, excluding farms, private households, the self-employed, and the federal government. Data are provided separately for the public and private sectors.

Data is collected each quarter from a probability sample. The sample establishments are classified by industry, using specific job categories which are selected to represent broad occupational definitions. Exhibit 25-4 is the quarterly report for the period 2001-2002, showing percentage changes in total compensation, wages and salaries, and benefits, by industry.

[3] Information on the ECI was obtained from U.S. Department of Labor, *Compensation and Working Conditions* (Summer 1997).

Exhibit 25-4
Table 1. Employment Cost Index for total compensation[1], wages and salaries, and benefit costs by industry and occupational group
(Seasonally adjusted data)

Industry and occupational group	Indexes (June 1989=100)		Percent changes for 3-months ended·							
	Dec. 2001	Mar. 2002	Jun. 2000	Sep. 2000	Dec. 2000	Mar. 2001	Jun. 2001	Sep. 2001	Dec. 2001	Mar. 2002
TOTAL COMPENSATION										
Civilian workers	156.9	158.2	1.0	0.9	0.9	1.1	1.0	1.0	1.0	0.8
State and local government . . .	154.9	156.0	.7	.5	1.0	1.0	1.1	1.4	.6	.7
Private industry	157.3	158.7	1.2	1.0	.9	1.1	1.0	.9	1.0	.9
Industry										
Goods producing[2]	154.8	156.2	1.2	1.0	.6	1.1	.9	.8	.9	.9
Construction	153.3	154.3	1.3	1.4	1.4	1.0	1.1	1.0	1.2	.7
Manufacturing	154.8	156.4	1.1	1.0	.5	1.1	.9	.6	1.0	1.0
Durables	155.6	156.8	1.2	.9	.6	.9	.8	.7	1.0	.8
Nondurables	153.6	155.6	.9	1.2	.3	1.4	1.0	.5	.9	1.3
Service producing[3]	158.6	159.9	1.1	1.0	1.0	1.1	1.0	1.0	1.1	.8
Transportation and public utilities	155.8	157.3	1.2	1.2	.8	1.3	1.2	.7	1.6	1.0
Wholesale trade	159.4	162.2	.8	.5	1.4	.7	1.4	.8	.4	1.8
Retail trade	153.8	153.4	1.0	1.0	.8	1.0	.6	.8	2.1	−.3
Finance, insurance, and real estate[4]	161.3	165.2	.7	1.4	.3	1.4	1.0	.9	.2	2.4
Services	161.2	162.6	1.2	1.0	1.0	1.4	.8	1.3	.9	.9
Nonmanufacturing	157.9	159.2	1.2	1.1	1.0	1.1	1.0	1.0	1.1	.8
Occupational group										
White collar	160.5	161.8	1.2	1.0	.9	1.1	1.0	.9	1.2	.8
Blue collar	152.2	153.6	1.0	1.0	.9	1.0	.7	1.1	.9	.9
Service	154.4	156.2	1.1	.8	1.1	1.2	.8	1.0	1.4	1.2
WAGES AND SALARIES										
Civilian workers	153.4	154.7	1.0	.9	.8	1.0	1.0	.8	.9	.8
State and local government . . .	153.4	154.5	.8	.8	.9	.9	1.0	1.0	.7	.7
Private industry	153.4	154.8	1.0	.9	.8	1.0	1.0	.7	.9	.9
Industry										
Goods producing[2,4]	150.5	151.7	1.2	.9	.6	1.2	1.1	.6	.7	.8
Construction	146.6	147.1	1.2	1.2	1.2	.9	1.0	1.0	1.1	.3
Manufacturing[4]	151.7	153.1	1.0	.9	.5	1.4	1.0	.5	.7	.9
Durables[4]	152.6	153.9	1.2	1.0	.8	1.2	1.0	.7	.7	.9
Nondurables	150.5	151.7	.9	.9	.3	1.2	1.1	.3	.7	.8
Service producing[3]	154.7	156.1	1.0	1.0	.9	.9	.9	.9	1.0	.9
Transportation and public utilities	149.2	150.7	.9	.9	.8	1.1	1.2	.7	1.8	1.0
Wholesale trade	154.6	157.7	.9	.3	1.2	.5	1.3	.1	.3	2.0
Retail trade	151.2	150.8	.9	.9	.8	.8	.5	.7	1.7	−.3
Finance, insurance, and real estate[4]	156.0	160.3	.5	1.5	.0	1.5	.5	.8	.1	2.8
Services	158.3	159.4	1.3	.9	.9	1.2	.9	1.2	.8	.7

Industry and occupational group	Indexes (June 1989=100)		Percent changes for 3-months ended·							
	Dec. 2001	Mar. 2002	Jun. 2000	Sep. 2000	Dec. 2000	Mar. 2001	Jun. 2001	Sep. 2001	Dec. 2001	Mar. 2002
Nonmanufacturing	153.7	155.0	1.0	1.0	.9	.9	.9	.9	1.1	.8
Occupational group										
White collar	156.3	157.7	1.1	0.9	0.8	1.0	0.9	0.7	1.0	0.9
Blue collar[4]	148.3	149.6	1.0	1.0	.6	1.3	.9	1.1	.5	.9
Service[4]	150.6	152.0	1.1	.7	1.0	1.0	.8	.8	1.3	.9
BENEFIT COSTS										
Civilian workers	165.3	166.9	1.2	1.0	1.1	1.2	1.1	1.5	1.2	1.0
State and local government . . .	158.5	159.6	.5	.1	.9	1.1	1.2	2.2	.8	.7
Private industry	166.8	168.6	1.3	1.2	1.1	1.3	1.1	1.4	1.3	1.1
Industry										
Goods producing[2]	163.1	165.4	1.3	1.2	.6	.9	.8	1.0	1.4	1.4
Manufacturing	161.0	163.2	1.1	1.0	.2	.8	.6	.7	1.4	1.4
Service producing[3]	169.0	170.4	1.3	1.3	1.4	1.4	1.3	1.6	1.2	.8
Nonmanufacturing	169.4	170.8	1.4	1.3	1.4	1.5	1.3	1.5	1.3	.8
Occupational group										
White collar	172.0	173.1	1.4	1.4	1.1	1.6	1.4	1.4	1.5	.6
Blue collar	159.4	162.3	.9	1.0	.8	.9	.3	1.3	.8	1.8
Service	166.1	168.8	1.3	1.2	1.3	1.9	1.0	1.4	1.7	1.6

....

[1] Includes wages, salaries, and employer costs for employee benefits.

[2] Includes mining, construction, and manufacturing.

[3] Includes transportation, communication, and public utilities; wholesale and retail trade; finance, insurance, and real estate; and service industries.

[4] No identifiable seasonality was found for this series.

Employer Costs for Employee Compensation

Data from the ECI survey is used to calculate the Employer Costs for Employee Compensation (ECEC), which is a measure of the average cost of employee compensation. The Bureau of Labor Statistics has been publishing data on the ECEC annually since 1987. These data, with a reference period of March each year, show the cost per hour worked to employers for wages, salaries, and employee benefits. Exhibit 24-1 is the quarterly report for June 2008.

Consumer Price Index

No review of pay survey data would be complete without a discussion of the Consumer Price Index (CPI). Many union agreements have cost-of-living-adjustment (COLA) clauses that provide for pay increases that are dependent upon changes in the CPI. In addition, Social Security benefits and many public and private pension plans have COLA clauses that increase benefits, based upon changes in the CPI.

There are two CPIs. One is the CPI-U, which is the Consumer Price Index for All Urban Consumers. This index measures the purchases of 87 percent of U.S. consumers. Included in this index are changes in prices affecting the self-employed, professional workers, white-collar and salaried workers, retired persons, the unemployed, and individuals who are not in the labor force.

The other measure is the CPI-W, which is the Consumer Price Index for Urban Wage Earners and Clerical Workers. This index represents a subset of the CPI-U population, that is, the expenditures by urban households that derive more than one-half of their income from clerical or hourly wage occupations. These households comprise about 32 percent of the total U.S. population.

Both CPIs measure the average change in prices for a "market basket of goods and services." The term "market basket" is misleading, since the groups of goods and services in the indexes include many items that obviously would not fit in a market basket. The groups are food and beverage (the only true market basket category), housing, apparel, transportation, medical care, recreation, education and communication, and other goods and services. These major groups are further subdivided into smaller groups. Periodically, the lists of items are reviewed and changes are made. Some items on the lists are dropped if they are no longer appropriate. Other items are added to the list when they begin appearing on the market. The indexes are computed for national changes in prices, as well as changes in prices in various cities and regional areas in the U.S.

The CPIs are tools that simplify the measurement of changes in prices over time. By selecting an appropriate reference base and setting the average index level for that time period equal to 100, it is possible to compare this month's (or last year's) price index level with the reference base period or to any other period. The current standard reference base period is 1982-1984 = 100; that is, all price changes are measured from a base (100) that represents the average index level of the 36-month period encompassing 1982, 1983, and 1984. Exhibit 25-5 shows some of the changes in prices for the past several years.

Exhibit 25-5
Consumer Price Index—All Urban Consumers

Year	Jan	Feb	Mar	Apr	May	June	July	Aug	Sep	Oct	Nov	Dec	Year
1998	161.6	161.9	162.2	162.5	162.8	163.0	163.2	163.4	163.6	164.0	164.0	163.9	163.0
1999	164.3	164.5	165.0	166.2	166.2	166.2	166.7	167.1	167.9	168.2	168.3	168.3	166.6
2000	168.8	169.8	171.2	171.3	171.5	172.4	172.8	172.8	173.7	174.0	174.1	174.0	172.2
2001	175.1	175.8	176.2	176.9	177.7	178.0	177.5	177.5	178.3	177.7	177.4	176.7	177.1
2002	177.1	177.8	178.8	179.8	179.8	179.9	180.1	180.7	181.0	181.3	181.3	180.9	179.9
2003	181.7	183.1	184.2	183.8	183.5	183.7	183.9	184.6	185.2	185.0	184.5	184.3	184.0
2004	185.2	186.2	187.4	188.0	189.1	189.7	189.4	189.5	189.9	190.9	191.0	190.3	188.9
2005	190.7	191.8	193.3	194.6	194.4	194.5	195.4	196.4	198.8	199.2	197.6	196.8	195.3
2006	198.3	198.7	199.8	201.5	202.5	202.9	203.5	203.9	202.9	201.8	201.5	201.8	201.6
2007	202.4	203.4	205.3	206.6	207.9	208.3	208.2	207.9	208.4	208.9	210.1	210.0	207.3
2008	211.0	211.6	213.5	214.8	216.6	218.8	219.9	219.0	218.7				

Source: Bureau of Labor Statistics, 1982-84 = 100

Conducting a Compensation Survey

These are the steps in conducting a compensation survey:

- Defining objectives;

- Selecting the topics of the survey;

- Defining the labor market;
- Selecting employers in the respective labor markets;
- Designing the survey questionnaire;
- Pretesting the survey questionnaire;
- Securing potential respondent cooperation;
- Mailing the questionnaire and follow-up; and
- Analyzing responses and present findings.

Define Objectives

As basic as it seems, the formulation of objectives is often overlooked in conducting compensation surveys. One organization contracted with a consultant to conduct a compensation survey. The consultant was told the purpose of the study was to compare the organization's pay and benefit plans with other employers in the labor market. Later, when the results of the study were presented, the consultant was asked for recommendations concerning changes in both the pay and benefit plans. The breakdown in communications occurred because the chair of the compensation subcommittee failed to communicate the objectives to the consultant's company contact.

Questions to Consider

In defining the objectives of the survey, these questions should be considered:

Why is the survey being conducted?

What information is to be obtained?

What compensation issues should the survey address?

How can a survey help resolve compensation problems we are experiencing or may be expecting in the future?

What is our organization's policy regarding compensation concerning such issues as providing benefits or pay compared to our competitors or to others competing from the same labor market?

How does our organization view itself regarding the labor market for potential employees?

Select Survey Topics

Some items to consider in selecting survey topics are which topics are the most important. Also consider whether respondents should be asked what changes they are proposing to make to their compensation plans.

Survey Topics

What specific topics will be included in the study? These are among the many topics which should be considered:

- The monetary values in pay structures for both exempt and nonexempt personnel;
- The number of job incumbents in each job in the survey;

- The frequency of payments for wages, salaries, and gainsharing plans;
- The types of performance-based pay methods used;
- Minimum, midpoint, and maximum pay for pay grades for each job in the study; and
- The actual lowest, average, and highest pay for incumbents in each job.

Getting Information on Planned Changes

Sometimes, surveys request information on any planned implementation of new or changing approaches to compensation. Examples of such approaches that have appeared in the past include flexible spending accounts, performance-based pay plans, two-tier pay arrangements, and reductions in pay and benefit plans.

Deciding Upon Survey Topics

In deciding upon the number of topics to include in any survey, consider that the response rate from potential respondents is somewhat inversely related to the complexity and size of the survey instrument they are asked to complete. To obtain an acceptable rate of response, the survey instrument should be concise. To accomplish this, tight constraints on the number of topics should be imposed.

Define the Labor Market

A major step in conducting compensation surveys is determining the appropriate labor market areas to be considered in the survey, such as the geographical area and the types of organizations within the area. Decisions on these subjects largely depend upon the policies of the organization. For example, if the policy is to select employees from among the best qualified applicants within a specific area, such as a state, the market area is that particular state. The geographical area of the labor market largely depends upon the type of job involved. For example, the labor market is smaller for bank tellers than it is for computer engineers. In the former case, a city may be a sufficient area, while the entire U.S. or a multistate region may be the market area for computer engineers.

The organization's policy also determines which employers the organization competes with for labor. An organization may have the policy of competing only with the recognized leading or largest employers within an industry. Using the organization's policies to define the labor market saves time, prevents misunderstandings, and increases the validity of the survey findings.

Select Employers to Survey

A major problem in conducting compensation surveys is determining which employers should be included in the study. The following sections discuss some points to consider in addressing that issue.

Same or Different Industries

Should the survey include employers in selected industries or all industries in the labor market? The answer to this question depends upon the purpose of the study and the sponsoring organization's compensation policies. If the study is conducted to prepare for collective bargaining negotiations, the employers' population would include those organizations with employees represented by the respective union. In a similar fashion, if the organization's policy is to provide compensation that is competitive within a particular industry or a group of industries or even all industries, the designated survey population must be consistent with that policy.

Sampling

Employers should be randomly selected for the survey unless all of them will be included. If different jobs have different labor market areas, separate samples of employers may be needed. If the labor market is stratified, such as by dollar amount of annual sales, annual production output, number of employees, or other characteristics, a stratified random sample should be used. Appropriate methods of sampling must be used to insure the validity of the survey results.

Watch for Bias

Bias, whether intentional or not, can distort the information in a survey. For example, in one compensation study, a consultant who was conducting the project asked several members of the organization's compensation committee to suggest organizations that should be included in the survey. These members had a vested interest in the outcome of the survey, since it would affect their compensation, so that they suggested only organizations that were known to have liberal pay and employee benefit policies.

One way that unintentional bias can occur is by assuming that the information furnished by respondent organizations represents the labor market. For example, if all of the organizations do not respond to the request for information, the possibility exists that the respondent data may not be representative of the market. Respondent cooperation is typically a problem in compensation surveys, and precautions must be taken to avoid making misleading conclusions when summarizing data from too few respondents.

Design the Survey Questionnaire

The design of the survey instrument may vary somewhat, depending upon the circumstances of the project (i.e., the employers involved, the purposes of the study, and the type of information to be collected). The following are some of the major issues that should be considered in the design of a survey questionnaire.

Purpose of the Survey

The purpose explains who is conducting the survey, in what areas is it conducted, which jobs are included, and a deadline for returning the requested information. Sometimes, this section also explains what organization or consultant has been retained to direct the study. This is an example of a statement:

> *Purposes of the Survey.* This compensation survey is conducted for ABC Company to determine market pay information on 16 jobs. The study is also conducted to secure information on health benefits provisions. Your assistance and cooperation are needed to make the survey results more valid.

Contact Person

This section includes the name, address, and telephone number of the person to whom the completed questionnaire is to be returned and to whom any questions about the survey should be addressed.

Definition of Terms

The varying use of terms in compensation management can corrupt an otherwise well-designed survey. Sensitivity to the possibility of different interpretations of terminology is the first step in recognizing the importance of specificity in defining terms. Respondents want to give the right information and are impeded in doing so, if they do not understand which information is requested. This is a suggested format:

> *Definition of Terms.* Please use these definitions of various terms in preparing your responses:
>
> - *Cost of living* is a pay increase granted to employees in response to changes in the Consumer Price Index for All Urban Consumers.

Relying Upon Job Titles

A frequent problem with compensation surveys, particularly the pay component of them, is that they rely too heavily upon job titles. People experienced in conducting compensation surveys know the folly of using only job titles to elicit pay and other types of information about compensation. For example, Job A in one organization may have the same title as Job A in another organization but there may be distinctive differences in the tasks in the two jobs. These are some measures to help prevent receiving pay information on a job that is significantly different:

- Send the respondent a copy of the job description for the jobs surveyed and request that the respondent compare them with the jobs in their organizations for which pay information is sought.

- Ask the respondent to include copies of the company's job descriptions with the return of the questionnaire.

- Prepare a concise five- or six-sentence summary of each job in the survey, and ask the respondent to delete tasks not included in their jobs and to add tasks that are not shown.

All three of these measures have some shortcomings. Some employers do not have job descriptions or, if they do have them, they are not current or are superficial. Also, asking respondents to furnish copies of their job descriptions may be unreasonable if a number of jobs are included in the study. This request virtually dooms any chances of securing respondents' cooperation. To some extent, the same fate awaits surveys requesting respondents to wade through a pile of job descriptions they are asked to use in supplying pay information.

Furnishing brief summaries is the best alternative, but the problem is the difficulty of realistically reducing a job description to several statements. Exhibit 25-6 is an example of job summary statements used by the Department of Labor in conducting pay surveys. Note that the job summary information includes a general statement about the nature of Computer Systems Analyst work. In addition, three different levels of such work are defined to help the respondents determine which level of work corresponds with their jobs and the appropriate levels of pay for them.

Exhibit 25-6
Examples of Job Description Summaries
Professional and Technical

COMPUTER SYSTEMS ANALYST, BUSINESS

Analyzes business problems to formulate procedures for solving them by use of electronic data processing equipment. Develops a complete description of all specifications needed to enable programmers to prepare required digital computer programs. Work involves *most of the following:* Analyzes subject-matter operations to be automated and identifies conditions and criteria required to achieve satisfactory results; specifies number and types of records, files, and documents to be used; outlines actions to be performed by personnel and computers in sufficient detail for presentation to management and for programming (typically this involves preparation of work and data flow charts); coordinates the development of test problems and participates in trial runs of new and revised systems; and recommends equipment changes to obtain more effective overall operations. (NOTE: Workers performing both systems analysis and programming should be classified as systems analysts if this is the skill used to determine their pay.)

Does not include employees primarily responsible for the management or supervision of other electronic data processing employees, or systems analysts primarily concerned with scientific or engineering problems.

For wage study purposes, systems analysts are classified as follows:

Computer Systems Analyst I

Works under immediate supervision, carrying out analyses as assigned, usually of a single activity. Assignments are designed to develop and expand practical experience in the application of procedures and skills required for systems analysis work. For example, may assist a higher level systems analyst by preparing the detailed specifications required by programmers from information developed by the higher level analyst.

Computer Systems Analyst II

Works independently or under only general direction on problems that are relatively uncomplicated to analyze, plan, program, and operate. Problems are of limited complexity because sources of input data are homogeneous and the output data are closely related. (For example, develops systems for maintaining depositor accounts in a bank, maintaining accounts receivable in a retail establishment, or maintaining inventory accounts in a manufacturing or wholesale establishment.) Confers with persons concerned to determine the data processing problems and advises subject-matter personnel on the implications of the data processing systems to be applied. *OR*

Works on a segment of a complex data processing scheme or system, as described for level III. Works independently on routine assignments and receives instruction and guidance on complex assignments. Work is reviewed for accuracy of judgment, compliance with instructions, and to insure proper alignment with the overall system.

Computer Systems Analyst III

Works independently or under only general direction on complex problems involving all phases of systems analysis. Problems are complex because of diverse sources of input data and multiple-use requirements of output data. (For example, develops an integrated production scheduling, inventory control, cost analysis, and sales analysis record in which every item of each type is automatically processed through the full system of records and appropriate follow-up actions are initiated by the computer.)

Source: U.S. Department of Labor

Formatting Data Collection Forms

Care in formatting the questionnaire will help increase the probability of respondent cooperation. In addition, data collection forms should be formatted to facilitate data input. Exhibit 25-7 is an example of a data collection form. Where necessary, explanations should be given. The forms should be designed to be as self-explanatory as possible.

A word of caution is necessary regarding coding data fields. Although this practice does facilitate data input, it may cause confusion for potential respondents. In addition, printing data fields on survey instruments generally make them appear more complicated than they really are, which also can reduce the response rate. For these reasons, the data fields should be written on the survey instruments when they are received from respondents. The modest increase in input time resulting from this extra step is generally well worth the effort.

Exhibit 25-7
Example of Pay Survey Collection Form

Job Title	# in Job	Hours in Workweek	Hour	Week	Month	Annual	Minimum	Midpoint	Maximum	COLA	Merit	General Increase
				Pay Status				Pay Range			Planned Increase (%)	
Finance Director I												
Finance Director II												
Finance Director III												
Buyer I												
Buyer II												
Buyer III												
Clerk I												
Clerk II												
Clerk III												
Programmer I												
Programmer II												
Programmer III												
Programmer IV												

Pretesting the Questionnaire

Pretesting, also known as *field testing,* a questionnaire is the process of submitting the instrument to several respondents to obtain their reaction before it is finalized and sent to all respondents in the survey sample. There are both advantages and disadvantages to pretesting. The big advantage is that any problems with it can be detected and resolved before it is sent to all potential respondents. Pretesting also can save embarrassment by identifying errors and other deficiencies, such as conflicting or misleading instructions.

The main disadvantage with pretesting is the time it takes. Often, time is a major constraint in conducting compensation surveys and a pretesting phase simply cannot be squeezed in.

Securing Respondent Cooperation

Respondent cooperation is required, since the validity of survey data depends upon the response rate and the accuracy of the information provided. There are some steps that can help secure this cooperation.

Telephone Potential Respondents

Sometimes, respondent cooperation is sought before a survey instrument is sent. The logic behind this step is that it will result in an increased response rate, more diligence on the part of the respondents in completing the questionnaire, and, thus, more and better data.

The typical approach used in securing respondent information is to telephone the person in each organization who will be responsible for furnishing the information. The caller explains the purpose of the survey, how extensive it is, the deadline for responding, and the importance of the respondent's cooperation. Sometimes, an additional inducement to secure cooperation is to offer a summary of the survey results to all respondents who participate in it.

Follow-up Telephone Calls

Another way of securing cooperation after the survey instrument is mailed is to make follow-up telephone calls to answer any questions and check on the respondent's progress in completing the questionnaire.

Use Go-Betweens

Consultants may have more difficulty in securing cooperation from respondents if they are not well-known within the industry or localities in which the survey is conducted. The typical way of securing cooperation in these situations is to have a representative of the firm contact his or her counterparts in other firms and explain the need for their help. Another way is to secure the endorsement of a well-known person in the industry and have him or her communicate with potential respondents and request their cooperation.

Mail Questionnaire and Follow-up

After the questionnaire is mailed, it is a good idea to follow up with the intended respondent to see if it was received. This contact is necessary to ensure that the right person received the questionnaire and that it did not get sidetracked within the respondent's organization. Also, this communication refreshes the respondent's memory about the survey and gives him or her an opportunity to ask any questions about it.

Analyze Responses and Present Findings

Survey data can be analyzed in various ways. One way is to simply show the data from each organization, as shown in Exhibit 25-8. Due to possible antitrust implications, codes should be used in lieu of the actual names of the organizations participating in the study. These antitrust concerns are discussed below. Summarizing data by each organization is more suitable if the number of respondents and/or the topics in the survey are limited. Either respondents or topics should be less than 10 and the other should not be over 30 or so, if reports are formatted by organization. If the number of organizations is quite large (several hundred or more), a more suitable format would be to categorize the data by quartiles or quintiles, as shown in Exhibit 25-9.

Exhibit 25-8
Reporting Market Pay Survey Data by Respondent

	Respondent											
Job	A		B		C		D		E		Our Firm	
	Min.	Max.	Min.	Max.	Min.	Max.	Min.	Max.	Min.	Max.	Min.	Max.

Job	A		B		C		D		E		Our Firm
Accounting Clerk	xxx	xxx	xxx	xxx	xxx	xxx	xxx	xxx	xxx	xxx	

Exhibit 25-9
Reporting Market Pay Survey Data in Quintiles

| Job | Quintiles | | | | | | | | | | Our Firm | |
| | Lowest | | 2nd | | Middle | | 4th | | Highest | | | |
	Min.	Max.	Min.	Max.	Min.	Max.	Min.	Max.	Min.	Max.	Min.	Max.
Accounting Clerk	xxx	xxx	xxx	xxx	xxx	xxx	xxx	xxx	xxx	xxx		

Using Narratives for Job Differences

The question of comparable jobs was discussed earlier in this chapter. As noted, comparability is only a problem if a job surveyed differs enough among employers to affect its compensability. Of course, the only way to determine that is to check the tasks of the jobs. Usually, it is difficult to determine if the jobs in a particular survey are the same or similar to those in an organization to be studied. This is a major weakness with virtually all compensation surveys, even those conducted by in-house personnel. Part of the answer is to obtain information such as job descriptions or, at a minimum, short summary descriptions of the jobs in the survey.

More realistically, a better approach, as mentioned earlier, would be to include a short six- to eight-sentence summary of each job for which pay information is requested and ask the respondent to line-out any tasks not performed in the job in the respondent's organization. In addition, several blank lines can be included in the summary, and the respondent can be asked to include any important tasks in the job in his or her organization which are not on the summary. The person compiling the data from the survey can prepare short descriptions summarizing the results of the information furnished by the respondents.

> **EXAMPLE:** A pay survey among public utilities include the job of Gas Repairer. The tasks for this job varied somewhat among the different organizations included in the survey. In one organization, the job was confined to responding to customer complaints about gas leaks and to lighting pilot lights. The job in other organizations was restricted to installing, repairing, and replacing gas meters. In another organization, the job tasks were limited to reading gas meters. In the latter situation, the job title should have been Meter Reader or something akin to it—but the title was Gas Repairer. The consultant who was conducting the study used the approach suggested above. This is an illustration of a summary statement the consultant compiled from the information furnished by the respondents:

> *Gas Repairer.* In Company A, the tasks are restricted to meter reading. In Company B, the tasks are primarily confined to investigating complaints on the customer's side of the meter, which is checking for leaks and lighting pilot lights but not repairing customer-owned furnaces. In Companies D, E, and F, the tasks are restricted to installing repairing and replacing gas meters. In the remainder of the firms, they confined the tasks to repairing inoperable meters brought into the shop.

Summarizing Benefit Data

Summarizing employee benefit data is more involved and requires a number of different report formats to present the data, so that it is understandable. The most obvious reason for this situation is the wide variation in most employee benefit plans. An example of this variation requires report formats, such as the one shown in Exhibit 25-10, below.

Compensation Surveys and Antitrust Law

U.S. antitrust laws prohibit employer practices that are intended to monopolize an industry or are in restraint of trade. While these laws typically apply to suppliers of goods and services, they have also been used to attack employers' compensation surveys. The most obvious antitrust violations are such practices as employer collusion to fix employee wages and benefits. Some practitioners suggest the following procedures for employers to use in avoiding the possibility of antitrust action:

- Define a policy statement concerning the purposes and intended uses of survey data, particularly how such data relates to the employer's overall compensation policies;

- Do not discuss with other employers the salaries of individual employees;

- Avoid publishing survey results by employer name;

- Do not ask for information about prospective pay rates; and

- Do not enter into agreements with other employers about compensation rates for various jobs.

Exhibit 25-10
Paid vacations: Number of days by service requirement,[1] private industry workers National Compensation Survey, March 2007
(All workers with paid vacations = 100 percent)

Vacation policy	Total	Less than 5 days	5 days	Over 5 but under 10 days	10 days	Over 10 but under 15 days	15 days	Over 15 but under 20 days	20 days	Greater than 20 days
					Percent with paid vacation days by length of service[2]					
All workers										
After 1 year	100	7	36	5	33	5	5	4	2	4
After 3 years	100	3	11	5	54	7	8	5	3	5
After 5 years	100	2	7	4	33	6	30	5	5	9
After 10 years	100	2	6	2	13	3	37	5	17	14
After 15 years	100	1	6	2	11	3	20	4	35	18
After 20 years	100	1	6	2	11	2	15	3	33	26
After 25 years	100	1	6	2	11	2	14	3	26	34
Management, professional, and related										
After 1 year	100	5	11	2	43	7	12	7	5	9
After 3 years	100	2	3	2	42	9	17	9	6	10
After 5 years	100	1	1	2	18	6	35	7	12	18
After 10 years	100	1	1	1	7	3	28	6	26	27
After 15 years	100	1	1	1	6	2	14	5	39	31
After 20 years	100	1	1	1	6	2	11	3	35	40
After 25 years	100	1	1	1	6	2	10	3	27	49
Service										
After 1 year	100	12	44	7	21	5	2	5	1	4
After 3 years	100	6	18	8	43	7	4	7	2	5
After 5 years	100	4	12	7	27	5	22	8	3	12
After 10 years	100	3	12	6	14	4	26	4	12	19
After 15 years	100	3	12	5	13	3	17	4	21	22
After 20 years	100	3	12	5	13	2	15	4	20	25
After 25 years	100	3	12	5	13	2	15	3	18	29
Sales and office										
After 1 year	100	6	36	4	37	4	4	4	2	3
After 3 years	100	3	8	5	61	6	7	5	2	4
After 5 years	100	2	4	4	35	6	33	4	4	8
After 10 years	100	2	4	2	13	3	42	5	17	12
After 15 years	100	1	4	1	11	2	19	4	41	15

Vacation policy	Percent with paid vacation days by length of service[2]									
	Total	Less than 5 days	5 days	Over 5 but under 10 days	10 days	Over 10 but under 15 days	15 days	Over 15 but under 20 days	20 days	Greater than 20 days
After 20 years	100	1	4	1	11	2	15	3	40	22
After 25 years	100	1	4	1	11	2	15	3	31	32
Natural resources, construction, and maintenance										
After 1 year	100	7	54	5	27	4	1	1	([3])	1
After 3 years	100	2	25	6	54	5	3	2	1	1
After 5 years	100	1	17	4	44	6	20	2	2	4
After 10 years	100	1	15	2	21	3	40	4	9	5
After 15 years	100	1	15	2	19	3	24	4	26	7
After 20 years	100	1	15	1	19	3	20	2	25	14
After 25 years	100	1	15	1	19	3	20	2	15	24
Production, transportation, and material moving										
After 1 year	100	7	53	6	29	3	2	1	([3])	1
After 3 years	100	3	12	7	66	5	4	1	([3])	1
After 5 years	100	2	7	5	46	7	28	2	2	2
After 10 years	100	2	5	2	15	5	48	4	15	4
After 15 years	100	2	5	2	12	3	27	6	37	6
After 20 years	100	2	5	2	12	3	18	3	35	21
After 25 years	100	2	5	1	12	3	17	3	28	29

[1] Employees either are granted a specific number of days after completion of the indicated length of service or accrue days during the next 12-month period. The total number of days is assumed to be available for use immediately upon completion of the service interval. Periods of service are chosen arbitrarily and do not necessarily reflect individual provisions for progression. For example, changes after 20 years reflect changes in provisions between 15 and 20 years.

[2] Employees eligible for paid vacations but who have not fulfilled the minimum service requirement are included as receiving less than 5 days.

[3] Less than 0.5 percent.

NOTE: Because of rounding, sums of individual items may not equal totals. Where applicable, dash indicates no employees in this category or data do not meet publication criteria.

CHAPTER 26
JOB WORTH AND INTERNAL EQUITY

Chapter Highlights
- Discuss how pay affects behavior
- Explain the legal requirements regarding pay
- Review the components of pay
- Examine the methods of job evaluation

Introduction

Employees cannot live on bread alone, but they certainly cannot live without it. Pay systems provide the means for employees to meet their requirements for living and other things besides. Employers use pay to increase employee loyalty and to recognize superior job performance. Sometimes, pay for superior performance systems involve one-time payments, such as the Superior Accomplishment Awards used in the federal service. Other systems, such as the Lincoln Electric Company's annual profit-sharing distribution, are based upon employees' total performance. Finally, pay systems may also be used to stimulate increased productivity. Salespersons' commissions, piece-rate production pay systems, and profit-sharing plans are examples of pay methods used to motivate employee productivity.

Internal Equity

Employees bring to the job their motivation, personal qualifications, and accomplishments in their task performance; in return, employees receive various rewards. Employees assess the fairness of the exchange of what they put into a job and what they receive from it. In addition, they compare their exchanges with those of their co-workers. Their assessments of the fairness of these exchanges is their perception of *internal equity*.

Internal equity is the degree to which an organization's compensation program rewards employees relative to their contributions within the organization.

The focus of this chapter is on the various methods employers use to achieve internal equity.

Federal Laws Regarding Pay

Fair Labor Standards Act of 1938

The Fair Labor Standards Act (FLSA) provisions cover:

- Minimum wages;
- Overtime pay;
- Child labor restrictions; and
- Equal pay for equal work regardless of sex.

State and Territorial Coverage

The FLSA applies to all 50 states, plus Washington, D.C., Puerto Rico, the Virgin Islands, Outer Continental Shelf lands, American Samoa, Wake Island, Eniwetok Atoll, and Johnston Island.

Coverage

Employees are covered by FLSA under either *enterprise coverage* or *individual coverage*.[1]

Enterprise Coverage

All employees of the following enterprises/organizations are covered by FLSA:

- A company/organization with annual dollar volume of sales or receipts in the amount of $500,000 or more.

- A federal, state, or local government agency. While employees of state and local governments are covered by FLSA, there is a question about the enforcement of the provisions of the law. This is due to a 1999 case in which the U.S. Supreme Court held that states are immune from private lawsuits to enforce the rights of employees of state governments to the minimum wage and overtime pay provisions of FLSA.[2] The case involved parole officers employed by the state of Maine, which had refused to pay overtime to the officers, prompting the private suit by them. The Court's decision left open the question of whether a federal agency could use legal action to enforce the provisions of FLSA. In a subsequent case decided in 2000, the Supreme Court held that states and their political subdivisions can compel employees to use compensatory time in lieu of overtime payments under the Fair Labor Standards Act. Since this latter case was after the 1999 decision, presumably, FLSA applies to state and local governments, but they are immune from private lawsuits affecting the application of the law.[3]

- A hospital or an institution primarily engaged in the care of the sick, the aged, or the mentally ill or developmentally disabled who live on the premises; it does not matter if the hospital or institution is public or private or is operated for-profit or not-for-profit.

- A pre-school, elementary or secondary school or institution of higher learning (e.g., college), or a school for mentally or physically handicapped or gifted children; it does not matter if the school or institution is public or private or operated for-profit or not for profit.

---

[1] The information in the following sections on FLSA was obtained from *FLSA Advisor*, Wage and Hour Division, U.S. Department of Labor, 1999.

[2] *Alden v. Maine*, 138 LC ¶ 33,890 (SCt 1999).

[3] *Christensen et al. v. Harris County et al.*, 140 LC ¶ 34,043 (SCt 2000).

An enterprise may be covered on an *enterprise coverage* basis if the coverage provisions of FLSA's 1989 amendments apply. When the law was changed in 1990, the definition of a covered enterprise changed. Enterprises that were covered by FLSA's 1989 Amendments on March 31, 1990, continue to be subject to the record-keeping, overtime pay and child labor requirements, and the $3.35 per hour minimum wage requirement (the minimum wage in effect on March 31, 1990). This is called *grandfather coverage*. Included in grandfather coverage are construction/reconstruction enterprises and laundry/dry cleaning enterprises, as well as certain other enterprises with less than $500,000 in annual sales or receipts.

Individual Coverage

Individual employees are covered under FLSA if they fall into any of the categories discussed below.

Engagement in Interstate Commerce. An employee is covered on an individual basis in every workweek in which he or she performs any work constituting *engagement in interstate commerce*. *Interstate commerce* means any work involving or related to the movement of persons or things (including intangibles, such as information) across state lines or from foreign countries. An employee may be individually covered in one workweek and not covered in the following workweek. Also, some employees of an employer may be covered, and others not.

Examples of covered employees who are engaged in interstate commerce include:

- An employee, such as an office or clerical worker, who uses a telephone, facsimile machine, the U.S. mail, or a computer e-mail system to communicate with persons in another state;

- An employee who drives or flies to another state while performing his or her job duties;

- An employee who unloads goods that came from an out-of-state supplier; and

- An employee, such as a cashier or waitress, who uses an electronic device to authorize a credit card purchase.

Employees of businesses that are engaged in interstate commerce or instrumentalities of interstate commerce are also generally covered. An instrumentality of interstate commerce includes railroads, highways and city streets, pipelines, telephone and/or electrical transmission lines, airports, bus/truck/steamship terminals, radio or TV stations and rivers/streams/waterways over which interstate or foreign commerce regularly moves.

Employees who perform support functions for these instrumentalities of interstate commerce are so closely related to interstate commerce that they are also considered to be engaged in interstate commerce. It does not matter who employs these workers; it is the work that is important. Examples of covered employees who are also considered to be engaged in interstate commerce include:

- A security worker at an airport;

- A custodian who works for a janitorial contractor that cleans a bus terminal; and

- A laborer or mechanic who performs maintenance or repair work or improvements to a city street.

Engagement in the Production of Goods for Interstate Commerce. Employees are covered on an individual basis when they are engaged in the production of goods for interstate or foreign commerce. The word *production* means producing, manufacturing, mining, handling, transporting or in any other way working on goods. The word "goods" means all products, commodities, merchandise, wares, articles or any ingredient thereof. *Interstate commerce,* as used in this context (as opposed to *engagement in interstate commerce,* as discussed above), means that goods are produced for trade, sales, transportation, transmission or communication across state lines.

Examples of covered employees under this definition are:

- An employee of a small garment company who sews buttons onto shirts that are eventually sold to a retailer in another state;

- An employee who works in his or her own home making the wings to a decorative art object that, when complete, is sold to an out-of-state wholesaler;

- A production employee who works for a small firm that makes electrical on/off switches and sells them to a local lighting factory, which ships its lamps to customers in many states; and

- A migrant farm worker who picks cucumbers, which are then graded and sold to a processor who, in turn, makes them into pickles and markets the product in other states.

Employees who do not directly engage in producing goods for interstate or foreign commerce are also covered on an individual basis, if they provide services that are closely related and directly essential to the production of goods for interstate commerce. Examples of covered employees included in this category are:

- A bookkeeper who does the payroll for a small garment manufacturing company that makes shirts that are sold to a retailer in another state;

- A guard-service employee who guards a lamp factory that ships its products across state lines; and

- A maintenance employee who repairs a pressing machine at a nearby garment factory that sells its products in other states.

Construction Employees. Construction employees may be individually covered by FLSA when they engage in interstate commerce or in the production of goods for interstate commerce or work in a job that is closely related and directly essential to such production. To determine whether an employee is covered, the character of the work must be analyzed. FLSA covers the following:

- Construction work in or on a channel or facility of interstate commerce (i.e., highway, telephone lines, and related work);

- Construction work that is closely tied with the process of producing goods for interstate commerce; for example, construction that improves, replaces, or expands a covered production facility that ships its products across state lines;

- Repair, maintenance, and construction of instrumentalities of interstate commerce, such as railroads, highways and city streets, pipelines, telephone and/or electrical transmission lines, airports, bus/truck/steamship terminals, radio or TV stations and rivers/streams/waterways over which interstate or foreign commerce regularly moves; and

- Repair, maintenance, reconstruction, redesign, improvement, extension or enlargement of an existing facility engaged in the production of goods for interstate commerce; the construction of a new production facility would not be a covered project.

Domestic Service Employment. FLSA covers domestic service employment, which refers to services (temporary or permanent) of a household nature performed by an employee in or about a private home of the person by whom he or she is employed. Included are cooks, waiters, butlers, valets, maids, housekeepers, governesses, nurses, janitors, laundresses, caretakers, handymen, gardeners, footmen, animal groomers and chauffeurs of automobiles for family use. Also included is babysitting that is not on a casual basis (e.g., babysitting that is not irregular or intermittent).

Child Labor

Child labor restrictions on youth 14 – 16 years of age.

Youth 18 years of age or older. No restrictions on hours or type of work, even if hazardous.

Youth 16 and 17 years of age. May be employed for unlimited hours in any occupation except for those in hazardous occupations, such as baking and operating food slicers.[4]

Youth 14 and 15 years of age. May only work outside of school hours, no more than three hours on a school day and 18 hours in school weeks (this may be extended to 23 hours for an approved Work Experience and Career Exploration Program). May work eight hours on a non-school day and 40 hours in a week when school is not in session. Work must be performed between 7 a.m. and 7 p.m. except during the period from June 1 to Labor Day when the evening hour can be extended to 9 p.m. These youth may not be employed in hazardous occupations.

Youth Employment in Agriculture. Special rules apply to the employment of youth in agricultural jobs.[5]

---

[4] See U.S. Department of Labor for a complete list of the hazardous occupations.   [5] Ibid.

Violations of Youth Hours and/or Hazardous Jobs/Tasks Provisions. These are the penalties for these violations:

- Each violation is subject to a penalty of no more $11,000 for each employee involved; or,

- If the violation resulted in the death or serious injury of the person, the penalty shall not exceed $50,000.

"Serious injury" is defined as this:

☐ Permanent loss or substantial impairment of (1) one of the senses (sight, hearing, taste, smell or tactile sensation); or (2) the functions of a bodily member, organ, or mental faculty, including the loss of all or part of an arm, leg, foot, hand or other body part.

☐ Permanent paralysis or substantial impairment that causes loss of movement or mobility of an arm, leg, foot, hand or other body part.[6]

Penalties can be doubled for repeated or willful violations.

Employer Precautions. Following are two actions employers can take to minimize their risk of incurring penalties for violations of youth employment noted above.

- **Certificates of Age.** To help prevent violations of youth hours and hazardous jobs/tasks provisions, employers should maintain unexpired certificates attesting to an employee's age. The FLSA provides that any employer who has such a certificate showing the employee can be legally employed without violation thus has sufficient proof of compliance. Regardless of what an employee states as his age, particularly for employees who state they are two years older than the minimum age that applies for the job in question, a bona fide Certificate of Age should be obtained prior to employment.

  EXAMPLE: An employee who is working in a hazardous job is found to be 16 years old, but the employer produces a valid Federal certificate of age authorized by the Wage and Hour Administrator that shows the employee is 18. The certificate attests that a violation of the law did not exist.

  Among the information contained in a Certificate of Age includes, name and address of the individual, place and date of birth, sex, name and address of person's parents, name and address of the employer if the person is under 18, signature of issuing person and issuing date.[7]

- **Safe Work Acts/Conditions/Job Training.** Obviously, to prevent serious occupational injuries and deaths, the first line of defense is requiring safe work acts performed in safe working conditions. In addition, employees need to be trained in the safe acts and conditions.

[6] GovTrack.us.H.R. 493-110th Congress (2007): *Genetic Information Nondiscrimination Act of 2008*. Some information in these sections is direct quotes from the law.

[7] See U.S. Department of Labor for more specific information on Certificates of Age, including the states authorized to issue them.

Violations of Minimum Wage and Overtime Pay Provisions. Each violation of the minimum wage and overtime pay provisions shall be subject to a penalty of no more than $1,100.

Calculating Penalties for Youth (Hours and Job/Tasks) and Minimum Wage and Overtime Pay Violations. The amount of the penalty shall include consideration of the size of the business and the seriousness of the violation.

Minimum Wage

The minimum wage was 25 cents per hour when FLSA was passed in 1938. It increases to $7.25 effective July 24, 2009. Many states have higher minimums that employers in those states must meet.

Rates below the minimum wage can be paid to:

- Learners, apprentices, messengers, handicapped workers, and student workers in retail or service establishments, on farms, or in institutions of higher learning, if approved by the Wage-Hour Administrator, as required to prevent curtailment of employment opportunities.

- Newly hired workers under the age of 20 may be paid an "opportunity wage" ($4.25/hour) for the first 90 days of employment.

Tipped Employees. Tipped employees are those who customarily and regularly receive more than $30 a month in tips. The following must be kept in mind:

- For employers of tipped employees, the maximum credit against the minimum wage is $3.72 but employers must pay such employees a direct hourly wage of at least $2.13 if a tip credit is claimed.

- The employer that elects to use the tip credit provision must inform the employee in advance and must be able to show that the employee receives at least the minimum wage, when direct wages and the tip credit allowance are combined. If an employee's tips, combined with the employer's direct wages of at least $2.13 an hour, do not equal the minimum hourly wage, the employer must make up the difference.

- Employees must retain all of their tips, except to the extent that they participate in a valid tip pooling or sharing arrangement.

Overtime Pay

FLSA generally requires covered employers to pay time and one-half for all hours worked in excess of 40 per week. The overtime pay is based upon their regular rate of pay. *Regular rate of pay* includes base pay, shift premium, non-discretionary bonuses (discretionary bonuses are not included), pay for unworked hours, commissions, and non-cash gifts that are typically valued at less than $25. However, the reasonable cost of non-cash payments in goods and facilities must be included in the regular rate. Income from employer-provided stock options, stock appreciation rights or stock purchase plans is excluded from the regular rate of pay for overtime purposes, provided that certain conditions are met.[8] Rest periods of five to 20 minutes are counted as work-time, but meal periods of 30 minutes or more are not counted. *Not* included as work-time is time for sick leave, vacation, or jury leave. Overtime is not required to be paid to employees who are asked to stay by the telephone at home or to be available by beeper. Overtime is not required for insignificant amounts of time before or after work (such as time to wash hands before going home). Travel to work-related events is counted as work-time.

In no case may an agreement between an employee and employer waive the employer's responsibility to pay overtime. For example, an agreement that only eight hours of work per day will be counted as work is not permissible under the FLSA. Similarly, an announcement by management that no overtime will be permitted or no overtime will be paid unless approved in advance is not permissible.

Donning and Doffing Safety Gear. In IBP, Inc. v. Alvarez, individually and on behalf of all others similarly situated, et al, the U.S. Supreme Court held that employees must be compensated under the FLSA for the time to doff specialized protective gear, walk to their work locations and commence working. At the end of the day, the employees must also be compensated for the time required to walk to the location where the gear is doffed, as well as the time required to actually doff it.

Training. Time spent in training is work-related *unless* these four conditions are met:

- The training is voluntary;

- The training is outside work hours;

- The training is not job-related; or

- No productive work is performed.

Compensatory Time. Compensatory time, in lieu of overtime, may be used (but it is earned at the rate of one and one-half hour for each hour worked on overtime) in these situations:

- In the public sector, employees can accrue 240 hours (480 hours for police officers and fire fighters), and then overtime must be paid.

- In the private sector, compensatory time can be used if it is part of an established plan and is taken in the pay period it is earned.

Calculating Overtime. For some employees, the regular rate may vary from week to week. However, it can never be less than the minimum wage rate. Regardless of the system under which the employee is paid, the regular rate is an hourly rate, figured by dividing the total remuneration for employment in a workweek by the total hours actually worked in such workweek. Bonuses, paid idle time, and premiums paid under custom or contract work also enter into overtime pay calculations.

---

[8] See CCH HUMAN RESOURCES MANAGEMENT, *Compensation*, at ¶1118 for discussion of the provisions of the Worker Economic Opportunity Act of 2000 (P.L. 106-202).

EXAMPLE: Sally works 40 hours a week and is paid $320 per week. Her hourly rate is $8 an hour. She works 42 hours one week and is paid $344 for the week [(40 × $8) + (2 × $12) = $344].

EXAMPLE: Fred is a dispatcher for a truck company and is paid $320 a week, regardless of the number of hours he works. One week, he works 42 hours, and the next week he works 46. His regular rate of hourly pay for 42 hours a week is $7.62 ($320 ÷ 42), so that his pay is $327.62 [($320 + (2 × $3.81)]. For the 46-hour week, his regular rate of pay is $6.96 per hour ($320 ÷ 46) so that his pay is $340.88 [$320 + (6 × $3.48)].

Fixed Sum for Varying Amounts of Overtime: A lump sum paid for work performed during overtime hours without regard to the number of overtime hours worked does not qualify as an overtime premium even though the amount of money paid is equal to or greater than the sum owed on a per-hour basis.

EXAMPLE: No part of a flat sum of $90 to employees who work overtime on Sunday will qualify as an overtime premium, even though the employees' straight-time rate is $6.00 an hour and the employees always work less than 10 hours on Sunday.

EXAMPLE: Where an agreement provides for 6 hours pay at $9.00 an hour regardless of the time actually spent for work on a job performed during overtime hours, the entire $54.00 must be included in determining the employees' regular rate.[9]

Exemptions

Some groups of employees are *exempt* from FLSA; the provisions of FLSA do not apply. The exemptions for different FLSA provisions depend upon the occupation. Some examples include:

1. Employee unions (except when acting as employers), which are exempt from all provisions;

2. Offshore fishing industry employees, who are exempt from the minimum wage, equal pay, and overtime provisions;

3. Executives, administrators, and professionals, including academic administrators and elementary and secondary school teachers, who are exempt from minimum wage and overtime pay provisions; and

4. Employees delivering newspapers to customers, who are exempt from all four FLSA provisions, namely, minimum wage, equal pay, overtime pay, and child labor provisions.

There are also a number of full and partial overtime pay exemptions for specified groups of employees.

Independent Contractor Exemptions

The U.S. Supreme Court has reviewed cases involving independent contractors and has ruled that no single definition or factor covers the employer-employee relationship under the FLSA. Rather it should be based upon whether

---

[9] U.S. Department of Labor.

the individual is independent and engaged in his own business. These are the factors the Court considers significant, although no single one is regarded as controlling:

1. "The extent to which the worker's services are an integral part of the employer's business (examples: Does the worker play an integral role in the business by performing the primary type of work that the employer performs for his customers or clients? Does the worker perform a discrete job that is one part of the business' overall process of production? Does the worker supervise any of the company's employees?);"

2. "The permanency of the relationship (example: How long has the worker worked for the same company?);"

3. "The amount of the worker's investment in facilities and equipment (examples: Is the worker reimbursed for any purchases or materials, supplies, etc.? Does the worker use his or her own tools or equipment?);"

4. "The nature and degree of control by the principal (examples: Who decides on what hours to be worked? Who is responsible for quality control? Does the worker work for any other company(s)? Who sets the pay rate?);"

5. "The worker's opportunities for profit and loss (examples: Did the worker make any investments such as insurance or bonding? Can the worker earn a profit by performing the job more efficiently or exercising managerial skill or suffer a loss of capital investment?); and"

6. "The level of skill required in performing the job and the amount of initiative, judgment, or foresight in open market competition with others required for the success of the claimed independent enterprise (examples: Does the worker perform routine tasks requiring little training? Does the worker advertise independently via yellow pages, business cards, etc.? Does the worker have a separate business site?)."[10]

Are Trainees Employees?

Individuals are trainees and thus not employees subject to the FLSA if <u>all</u> of the following criteria:

1. "The training, even though it includes actual operation of the facilities of the employer, is similar to that which would be given in a vocational school;"

2. "The training is for the benefit of the trainees;"

3. "The trainees do not displace regular employees, but work under close supervision;"

4. "The employer that provides the training receives no immediate advantage from the activities of the trainees and, on occasion, his operations may even be impeded;"

---

[10] U.S. Department of Labor.

5. "The trainees are not necessarily entitled to a job at the conclusion of the training period; and"

6. "The employer and the trainees understand that the trainees are not entitled to wages for the time spent in training."[11]

Are Volunteers Employees?

Under the FLSA employees cannot volunteer their services to "for profit" firms but they can volunteer for "not for profit" organizations, such as public service or religious organizations and thus are not considered as employees of such groups that receive their services.

Exemptions from Overtime Compensation[12]

Employees in some occupations are exempt from overtime compensation. The title of an occupation is usually not a sufficient basis to form a judgment regarding exemption. Rather specific tests must be met to determine if an occupation is exempt.

Executive, Business Owners, Administrator, Professional (Learned or Creative), and Highly Compensated. Employee Exemption. To qualify for the executive employee exemption, all of the following tests must be met:

- The employee must be compensated on a *salary basis* (as defined below) at a rate not less than $455 per week;

- The employee's primary duty must be managing the enterprise (such as selecting, training, and appraising employees), or managing a customarily recognized department or subdivision of the enterprise;

- The employee must customarily and regularly direct the work of at least two or more other full-time employees or their equivalent (one full-time employee and two part-time employees is the equivalent of two full-time employees); and

- The employee must have the authority to hire or fire other employees, or the employee's suggestions and recommendations as to the hiring, firing, advancement, promotion or any other change of status of other employees must be given particular weight.

Salary basis means an employee regularly receives a predetermined amount of compensation (but not less than $455 per week) each pay period on a weekly, or less frequent, basis. The predetermined amount cannot be reduced because of variations in the quality or quantity of the employee's work. Subject to exceptions listed below, an exempt employee must receive the full salary for any week in which the employee performs any work, regardless of the number of days or hours worked. Exempt employees do not need to be paid for any work week in which they perform no work. If the employer makes deductions from an employee's predetermined salary, i.e., because of the operating requirements of the business, that employee is not paid on a "salary basis." If the employee is ready,

---

[11] Ibid.

[12] Due to the technical nature of these definitions, most of the material is verbatim from various U.S. Department of Labor sources.

willing and able to work, deductions may not be made for time when work is not available.

Business Owners. A person who owns at least 20 percent of a business and is actively engaged in its management, is considered a bona fide exempt executive.

Administrative Exemption. To qualify for the administrative employee exemption, all of the following tests must be met:

- The employee must be compensated on a *salary* or *fee* basis at a rate not less than $455 per week. *Fee Basis* means an employee is paid an agreed sum for a single job, regardless of the time required for its completion. Administrative, professional and computer employees may be paid on a "fee basis" rather than on a salary basis. Executive employees must be paid on a *salary basis* as defined above. A fee payment is generally paid for a unique job, rather than for a series of jobs repeated a number of times and for which identical payments repeatedly are made. To determine whether the fee payment meets the minimum salary level requirement, the test is to consider the time worked on the job and determine whether the payment is at a rate that would amount to at least $455 per week if the employee worked 40 hours. For example, an artist paid $250 for a picture that took 20 hours to complete meets the minimum salary requirement since the rate would yield $500 if 40 hours were worked.

- The employee's primary duty must be the performance of office or non-manual work directly related to the management or general business operations (meaning assisting with the running or servicing of the business, such as work in functional areas like finance; accounting; tax; budgeting; auditing; insurance; quality control; purchasing; procurement; advertising; marketing; research; safety and health; personnel management; human resources; employee benefits; labor relations; public relations; governmental relations; computer network, Internet and database administration; legal and regulatory compliance; and similar activities) of the employer or the employer's customers; and

- The employee's primary duty includes the exercise of discretion and independent judgment with respect to matters of significance.

Educational establishment employees meet the duties requirement if they are performing administrative functions directly related to academic instruction or training.

Financial services industry employees generally meet the duties requirements for the administrative exemption and are not entitled to overtime pay if their duties include work such as:

- Collecting and analyzing information regarding the customer's income, assets, investment or debts;

- Determining which financial products best meet the customer's needs and financial circumstances;

- Advising the customer regarding the advantages and disadvantages of different financial products; and,

- Marketing, servicing or promoting the employer's financial products.

An employee whose primary duty is selling financial products does not qualify for the administrative exemption. In applying the exemption, it does not matter whether the employee's activities are aimed at an end user or an intermediary. The status of financial services employees is based on the duties they perform, not on the identity of the customer they serve.

For *insurance claims adjusters* to qualify for the administrative employee exemption, the three conditions required of administrators must be met.

Learned Professional Exemption. To qualify for the learned professional employee exemption, <u>all</u> of the following tests must be met:

- The employee must be compensated on a *salary* or *fee* basis at a rate not less than $455 per week;

- The employee's primary duty must be the performance of work requiring advanced knowledge, defined as work which is predominantly intellectual in character and which includes work requiring the consistent exercise of discretion and judgment;

- The advanced knowledge must be in a field of science or learning; and

- The advanced knowledge must be customarily acquired by a prolonged course of specialized intellectual instruction.

Professional work is different from work involving routine mental, manual, mechanical or physical work. Advanced knowledge cannot be attained at the high school level. Fields of science or learning include law, medicine, theology, accounting, actuarial computation, engineering, architecture, teaching, various types of physical, chemical and biological sciences, pharmacy and other occupations that have a recognized professional status and are distinguishable from the mechanical arts or skilled trades where the knowledge could be of a fairly advanced type, but is not in a field of science or learning.

The learned professional exemption is restricted to professions where specialized academic training is a standard prerequisite for entrance into the profession. The best evidence of meeting this requirement is having the appropriate academic degree. However, the word "customarily" means the exemption may be available to employees in such professions who have substantially the same knowledge level and perform substantially the same work as the degreed employees, but who attained the advanced knowledge through a combination of work experience and intellectual instruction. This exemption does not apply to occupations in which most employees acquire their skill by experience rather than by advanced specialized intellectual instruction.

Attorneys or physicians who have a valid license or certificate permitting the practice of law or medicine, respectively, are exempt if they are actually engaged in such a practice. An employee who holds the requisite academic degree for the general practice of medicine is also exempt if he or she is engaged in an internship or resident program for the profession. The salary and salary basis requirements do not apply to bona fide practitioners of law or medicine.

Registered nurses who are paid on an hourly basis should receive overtime pay. However, registered nurses who are registered by the appropriate State examining board generally meet the duties requirements for the learned professional exemption, and if paid on a salary basis of at least $455 per week, may be classified as exempt.

Licensed practical nurses and other similar health care employees, however, generally do not qualify as exempt learned professionals, regardless of work experience and training, because possession of a specialized advanced academic degree is not a standard prerequisite for entry into such occupations, and thus are entitled to overtime pay.

Technologists and technicians, such as engineering technicians, ultrasound technologists, licensed veterinary technicians, avionics technicians and other similar employees are not exempt from the minimum wage and overtime requirements because they generally do not meet the requirements for the learned professional exemption.

Creative Professional Exemption. To qualify for the creative professional employee exemption, all of the following tests must be met:

- The employee must be compensated on a *salary* or *fee* basis at a rate not less than $455 per week;
- The employee's primary duty must be the performance of work requiring invention, imagination, originality or talent in a recognized field of artistic or creative endeavor.

Exemption as a creative professional depends on the extent of the invention, imagination, originality or talent exercised by the employee. The requirements are generally met by actors, musicians, composers, soloists, certain painters, writers, cartoonists, essayists, novelists, and others as set forth in the regulations.

Journalists/reporters may satisfy the duties requirements for the creative professional exemption if their primary duty is work requiring invention, imagination, originality or talent. Journalists are not exempt creative professionals if they only collect, organize and record information that is routine or already public, or if they do not contribute a unique interpretation or analysis to a news product. However, employees may be exempt creative professionals if their primary duty is to perform on the air in radio, television or other electronic media; to conduct investigative interviews; to analyze or interpret public events; to write editorial or opinion columns or other commentary; or to act as a narrator or commentator. Thus, journalists' duties vary along a spectrum from the nonexempt to the exempt. The less creativity and originality involved in their efforts, and the more control exercised by the employer, the less likely journalists are to be considered exempt.

Teachers are exempt if their primary duty is teaching, tutoring, instructing or lecturing in the activity of imparting knowledge, and if they are employed and engaged in this activity as a teacher in an educational establishment. Exempt teachers include, but are not limited to, regular academic teachers; kindergarten or nursery school teachers; teachers of gifted or disabled children; teachers of skilled and semi-skilled trades and occupations; teachers engaged in automobile driving instruction; aircraft flight instructors; home economic teachers; and vocal or instrument music teachers. The salary and salary basis requirements do not apply to bona fide teachers.

Highly-Compensated Workers. Highly-compensated workers who are paid total annual compensation of $100,000 or more are exempt from overtime if:

- The employee earns total annual compensation of $100,000 or more, which includes at least $455 per week paid on a *salary* basis;

- The employee's primary duty includes performing office or non-manual work; and,

- The employee customarily and regularly performs at least one of the exempt duties or responsibilities of an exempt executive, administrative or professional employee.

Thus, for example, an employee may qualify as an exempt highly-compensated executive if the employee customarily and regularly directs the work of two or more other employees, even though the employee does not meet all of the other requirements in the standard test for exemption as an executive.

The required total annual compensation of $100,000 or more may consist of commissions, nondiscretionary bonuses and other nondiscretionary compensation earned during a 52-week period, but does not include credit for board or lodging, payments for medical or life insurance, or contributions to retirement plans or other fringe benefits.

Computer Employee Exemption. To qualify for the computer employee exemption, the following tests must be met:

- The employee must be compensated either on a salary or fee basis at a rate not less than $455 per week or, if compensated on an hourly basis, at a rate not less than $27.63 an hour;

- The employee must be employed as a computer systems analyst, computer programmer, software engineer or other similarly skilled worker in the computer field performing these primary duties:

- The application of systems analysis techniques and procedures, including consulting with users to determine hardware, software or system functional specifications;

- The design, development, documentation, analysis, creation, testing or modification of computer systems or programs, including prototypes, based on and related to user or system design specifications;

- The design, documentation, testing, creation or modification of computer programs related to machine operating systems; or

- A combination of the aforementioned duties, the performance of which requires the same level of skills.

The computer employee exemption does *not* include employees engaged in the manufacture or repair of computer hardware and related equipment. Employees whose work is highly dependent upon, or facilitated by, the use of computers and computer software programs (e.g., engineers, drafters and others skilled in computer-aided design software), but who are not primarily engaged in computer systems analysis and programming or other similarly skilled computer-related occupations identified in the primary duties test described above, are also not exempt under the computer employee exemption.

Outside Sales Exemption. To qualify for the outside sales employee exemption, *all* of the following tests must be met:

- The employee's primary duty must be making sales, or obtaining orders or contracts for services or for the use of facilities for which a consideration will be paid by the client or customer; and

- The employee must be customarily and regularly engaged away from the employer's place or places of business.

The salary requirements of the regulation do not apply to the outside sales exemption. An employee who does not satisfy the requirements of the outside sales exemption may still qualify as an exempt employee under one of the other exemptions under executive, administrative, or professional.

"Sales" includes any sale, exchange, contract to sell, consignment for sales, shipment for sale, or other disposition. It includes the transfer of title to tangible property, and in certain cases, of tangible and valuable evidences of intangible property.

Obtaining orders for "the use of facilities" includes the selling of time on radio or television, the solicitation of advertising for newspapers and other periodicals, and the solicitation of freight for railroads and other transportation agencies. The word "services" extends the exemption to employees who sell or take orders for a service, which may be performed for the customer by someone other than the person taking the order.

An outside sales employee makes sales at the customer's place of business, or, if selling door-to-door, at the customer's home. Outside sales does not include sales made by mail, telephone or the Internet unless such contact is used merely as an adjunct to personal calls. Any fixed site, whether home or office, used by a salesperson as a headquarters or for telephonic solicitation of sales is considered one of the employer's places of business, even though the employer is not in any formal sense the owner or tenant of the property.

Promotion work may or may not be exempt outside sales work, depending upon the circumstances under which it is performed. Promotional work that is actually performed incidental to and in conjunction with an employee's own outside sales or solicitations is exempt work. However, promotion work that is incidental to sales made, or to be made, by someone else is not exempt outside sales work.

Drivers who deliver products and also sell such products may qualify as exempt outside sales employees only if the employee has a primary duty of making sales. Several factors should be considered in determining whether a driver has a primary duty of making sales, including a comparison of the driver's duties with those of other employees engaged as drivers and as salespersons, the presence of absence of customary or contractual arrangements concerning amounts of products to be delivered, whether or not the driver has a selling or solicitor's license when required by law, the description of the employee's occupation in collective bargaining agreements, and other factors set forth in the regulation.

Construction Workers. Manual laborers or other "blue collar" workers, including non-management construction workers, who perform work involving repetitive operations with their hands, physical skill and energy are nonexempt. Such nonexempt "blue collar" employees gain the skills and knowledge required for performance of their routine manual and physical work through apprenticeships and on-the-job training, no through the prolonged course of specialized intellectual instruction required for exempt learned professional employees.

Blue-Collar Workers. The minimum pay and overtime exemptions do not apply to manual laborers or other "blue-collar" workers who perform work involving repetitive operations with their hands, physical skill and energy. Such nonexempt "blue-collar" employees gain the skills and knowledge required for performance of their routine manual and physical work through apprenticeships and on-the-job training.

Non-management employees in production, maintenance, construction and similar occupations such as carpenters, electricians, mechanics, plumbers, iron workers, craftsmen, operating engineers, longshoremen, construction workers and laborers are entitled to minimum wage and overtime premium pay and are not exempt no matter how highly paid they might be.

Police Officers, Fire Fighters and Other First Responders. Police officers, detectives, deputy sheriffs, state troopers, highway patrol officers, investigators, inspectors, correctional officers, parole or probation officers, park rangers, fire fighters, paramedics, emergency medical technicians, ambulance personnel, rescue workers, hazardous materials workers and similar employees ("first responders") who perform work such as preventing, controlling or extinguishing fires of any type; rescuing fire, crime or accident victims; preventing or detecting crimes; conducting investigations or inspections for violations of law; performing surveillance; pursuing, restraining and apprehending suspects; detaining or supervising suspected and convicted criminals, including those on probation or parole; interviewing witnesses; interrogating and fingerprinting suspects; preparing investigative reports; and other similar work are not exempt under Section 13(a)(1) or the regulations and thus are protected by the minimum wage and overtime provisions of the FLSA.

First responders generally do not qualify as exempt executives because their primary duty is not management. They are not exempt administrative employees because their primary duty is not the performance of office or non-manual work directly related to the management or general business operations of the employer or the employer's customers. Similarly, they are not exempt learned professionals because their primary duty is not the performance of work requiring knowledge of an advanced type in a field or learning customarily acquired by a prolonged course of specialized intellectual instruction. Although some first responders have college degrees, a specialized academic degree is not a standard prerequisite for employment.

Veterans. Veterans are not exempt administrative, executive or professional employees based upon their status as veterans. Military training, for example, generally is not sufficient to meet the requirements for the professional exemption. No amount of military training will satisfy the requirements of the learned professional exemption because the exemption applies only to employees who are in *occupations* that have attained recognized professional status, which requires than an advanced specialized academic degree is a standard prerequisite for entrance into the profession.

Docking Pay

Exempt employees' pay may be "docked" or their pay may be offset for these reasons:

- Full day for personal absences;
- Full day absence for illness, provided that the employer has a plan, policy, or practice of providing compensation for loss of salary due to sickness or disability, but the employer need not pay the employee for days of absence before the employee has qualified for compensation under the plan, such as a waiting period, or after the employee has exhausted benefits under the plan;[13]
- Covered absence due to illness (the employee is compensated for the absence by state or private disability plan that covers the employer);
- Covered absence due to an occupational accident (if the employee is compensated for the absence by a state or private plan which covers the employer);
- Week-long absence for jury duty, witness attendance, or military duty, though no deductions may be made for absences of less than one week, but the employer may offset the employee's salary for any jury duty, witness fees or military pay received for that week;[14]
- For penalties imposed in good faith for infractions of safety rules of major significance;
- For unpaid disciplinary suspensions of one or more full days imposed in good faith for workplace conduct rule infractions; and,
- Vacation or sick leave credits (salary deductions can be made for any credits given for vacation or sick leave with pay, provided the overall pay for the week is not reduced).

[13] CCH HUMAN RESOURCES MANAGEMENT, *Compensation*, "Quick Answers: Docking Pay and Leave from Exempt Employees."

[14] CCH HUMAN RESOURCES MANAGEMENT, *Compensation*, ¶430.

The full salary of exempt employees need not be paid in the initial of terminal week of employment, or for weeks of unpaid leave under the Family and Medical Leave Act.

Effect of Improper Deductions from Salary

The employer will lose the exemption if it has an "actual practice" of making improper deductions from salary. Factors to consider when determining whether an employer has an actual practice of making improper deductions include, but are not limited to:

- The number of improper deductions, particularly as compared to the number of employee infractions warranting deductions;
- The time period during which the employer made improper deductions;
- The number and geographic location of both the employees whose salary was improperly reduced and the managers responsible; and,
- Whether the employer has a clearly communicated policy permitting or prohibiting improper deductions.

If an "actual practice" is found, the exemption is lost during the time period of the deductions for employees in the same job classification working for the same managers responsible for the improper deductions. Isolated or inadvertent improper deductions will not result in loss of the exemption if the employer reimburses the employee for the improper deductions.

Safe Harbor

An employer will not lose the exemption for any employee if the following conditions have been met:

- A clearly communicated policy is in place prohibiting improper deductions and including a complaint mechanism;
- Employees are reimbursed for any improper deductions;
- A good faith commitment is made to comply in the future; and
- The employer does not willfully violate the policy by continuing the improper deductions after receiving employee complaints.

Maintaining Records

Employers must keep FLSA records for three years. In addition, they must keep supplementary records, including time cards, work schedules, and pay tables for two years. Violations include up to two years of overtime pay (three years for willful violations) and may include doubling of overtime pay. The statue of limitations is two years (three years for willful violations).

Violations

FLSA, with the exception of the EPA, is enforced by the Wage and Hour Division of the U.S. Department of Labor (DOL). In spite of the fact that this law has been in existence for nearly 50 years, violations occur more frequently than one might expect. To enforce the law, the DOL uses court injunctions, criminal penalties, and monetary relief, in the form of unpaid wages and an equal amount in liquidated damages. It is also against the law to retaliate against an employee for filing a complaint under the Act. The Equal Employment Opportunity Commission (EEOC) enforces the provisions of the EPA.

Equal Pay Act of 1963

The Equal Pay Act (EPA) requires equal pay for both sexes for performing job tasks that are substantially the same within the same establishment. The tasks need not be identical, but they must be substantially the same and require substantially the same skill, effort, responsibility, and working conditions. Generally, the EPA applies to the same employees covered under FLSA; however, executives, administrators, professionals, and outside salesmen are covered by the EPA but not by FLSA.

The EPA provides several situations for men and women performing similar tasks to be paid differently. Differentials are permissible where pay is based upon:

- A seniority system or length of employment;

- A merit system;

- The quality or quantity of production; and

- Any factor other than sex, such as pay given to employees for ideas submitted through a suggestion program that are adopted.

Seniority applies in situations where pay increases, sometimes called step increases, are conditional upon satisfactory completion of a period of employment, such as six months or a year. Merit pay systems are typically associated with performance appraisal systems, in which an employee's overall job performance is judged, using such factors as attendance, conduct, safety, and productivity. Pay increases are granted, based upon the overall merit appraisal.

Other Equal Employment Opportunity Legislation

Title VII

Title VII of the Civil Rights Act prohibits employers from discriminating in pay matters on the basis of race, color, national origin, religion, and sex. Title VII prohibits claims of sex-based pay discrimination which are permitted by the Equal Pay Act. This provision in Title VII, sometimes referred to as the *Bennett Amendment*, does not allow claims of sex-based pay discrimination which are permitted under the Equal Pay Act, namely pay differentials which are based upon merit pay, quality or quantity of work, seniority, and any factor other than sex.

Age Discrimination in Employment Act

The Age Discrimination in Employment Act prohibits discrimination in compensation (including both pay and benefits) for persons age 40 and over.

Americans with Disabilities Act

The Americans with Disabilities Act prohibits discrimination in pay on the basis of a person's disability.

Uniformed Services Employment and Reemployment Act of 1994

A service member who is returning to work after being called to active duty is entitled to general wage increases he/she would have received if not called to active duty. Such persons are also entitled to any pay increases due to seniority and to the current rate of pay if such pay is an attribute of the job. Returning service members are not entitled to any pay increases attributable to merit.

Wage Laws for Federal Contractors

Certain federal contractors for the supply of materials and equipment (Walsh-Healey Act), the supply of services (McNamara-O'Hara Service Contract Act), and public works construction (Davis-Bacon Act) must meet certain compensation requirements. In addition, Executive Order 11246 prohibits certain federal contractors from discriminating in matters of compensation on the basis of national origin, race, color, religion, and sex. These requirements are enforced by the DOL.

Walsh-Healey Act of 1936

The Walsh-Healey Act (W-HA) applies to all contractors that deal with the federal government for supplies, materials, articles, and equipment in which the contract exceeds $10,000. Generally, such contractors are required to pay the FLSA-mandated minimum wage and overtime for work over 40 hours per week. No person under 16 years of age may be employed by the contractor. The law prohibits the contractor from permitting employees to work in conditions deemed by the Occupational Safety and Health Administration (OSHA) to be unsanitary, dangerous, or hazardous to employee health and safety. The W-HA covers all employees of the contractor who are engaged in federal government work, except those employed in these occupations: executive, administrative, professional, office, custodial, and maintenance. However, if FLSA applies to the employer, office, custodial, and maintenance workers must be paid in accordance with those provisions.

Davis-Bacon Act of 1931

The Davis-Bacon Act applies to all federal or federally financed contracts of more than $2,000 for construction, alteration, or repair, including painting and decoration of public buildings or public works. This law applies only to laborers and mechanics employed on the job site. Laborers and mechanics are generally interpreted as employees who work with their hands; therefore, accounting clerks, timekeepers, guards, and similar occupations are not covered. The two main provisions require employers to pay wages and fringe benefits that *are prevailing* in the locality. These prevailing wages and benefits are determined by the DOL and in no case are the wages to be below the FLSA minimum.

Copeland Act of 1934

The Copeland or "Kickback" Act prohibits the use of force, intimidation, threat of dismissal from employment, or any other means to induce an individual employed in the construction, completion, or repair of any public building, public work, or building or work financed in whole or in part by loans or grants from the U.S., from giving back any part of the compensation to which the individuals are entitled under the contract.

Service Contract Act of 1965

The Service Contract Act applies to all contractors with the federal government for services in which the contract exceeds $2,500. This law requires the payment of wages and fringe benefits that are prevailing in the locality for all employees performing work under the contract. Employees under 16 years of age may be employed under restrictions similar to FLSA. The prevailing wages and fringe benefits to be paid are determined by the DOL. All contractors, even those with contracts less than $2,500, must at least pay the FLSA minimum.

Executive Order 11246

Executive Order 11246 applies to all employers with contracts with the federal government of $10,000 or more. The Executive Order prohibits contractors from discriminating in pay matters on the basis of race, color, national origin, religion, and sex.

Pay Components

Exhibit 26-3 shows the four components of pay, which are:

- The base rate of pay for a job, such as the pay grade for the job or the salary commission structure for sales jobs;

- Within-grade pay increases, excluding promotions and demotions but including periodic pay grade merit increases or cost-of-living pay increases;

- Special pay conditions, such as overtime pay and shift differential payments; and

- *Ad hoc* payments, such as suggestion system awards or superior accomplishment awards.

Exhibit 26-3
Components of Pay

Base Rate	*Within Grade Increases*	*Special Pay*	*Ad Hoc Pay*
Job evaluation	Merit increases	Overtime	Suggestion awards
Performance based	Cost of living	Shift differential	Superior achievement
		Hazardous work	
Market surveys		Holidays	
Collective bargaining agreements			

Method of Base Pay Determination

Exhibit 26-3 indicates base pay rates are determined by one or a combination of these four methods:

- Job evaluation;
- Market surveys;

- Performance; or
- Collective bargaining.

Job evaluation is discussed later in this chapter. Performance-based pay methods are covered in Chapter 29. Collective bargaining is covered in Chapter 36.

Within-Grade Increases

The two major types of within grade pay increases are merit pay increases and cost-of-living (COLA) increases. Merit pay increases are covered in Chapter 29. Within-grade increases determined by market surveys are covered in Chapter 25. Collective bargaining agreements typically include provisions for pay increases, including COLA clauses.

Special Pay Conditions

Special pay provisions are used to compensate employees for performing job tasks under atypical conditions. Four of the more common types are shown in Exhibit 26-3.

Overtime pay is usually based on the Fair Labor Standards Act requirement of 150 percent of base pay on all work in excess of 40 hours per week. Some employers also pay the 150-percent rate for all work over eight hours per day; this may be a state's legal requirement or it may be adopted as a pay policy either voluntarily or because of a collective bargaining agreement.

Shift differentials typically are provided for work performed before 6 a.m. and after 6 p.m., or for any shift other than the customary day shift of 8 a.m. to 4:30 p.m.

Hazardous work pay is additional pay for tasks performed in extreme weather conditions or when the job involves hazardous materials or conditions. Hazardous work pay may involve a pay premium, such as a stipend paid each month, or it may be included in setting the base pay for the job. Collective bargaining agreements usually specify special pay conditions.

Ad Hoc Pay

Single-occasion payments, such as cash awards for employee suggestions and special achievement or accomplishment awards, are examples of *ad hoc* payments, which are covered in Chapter 30.

Collective Bargaining

The pay of workers represented by unions (excluding federal employees not in the U.S. Postal Service) is primarily determined through collective bargaining.

Job Evaluation

Job evaluation is the process of applying predefined compensable factors to jobs to determine their relative worth, with the goal of achieving internal pay equity among them.

Job evaluation is both a science and an art. There are proven methods of evaluating jobs, but using these methods requires considerable subjective judgment. Job evaluation does not consider the job performance, seniority, and related personal qualifications or characteristics of employees performing a job. For example, in determining the relative worth of the education required to perform a job, the evaluator does not consider the amount of education of employees who perform the job; rather, such worth is determined by how much education is actually needed. In addition, the level of the employee's performance is not considered in evaluating the worth of a job. Such competence is recognized through the organization's performance appraisal plan and rewarded with merit or other types of pay increases.

Methods of Job Evaluation

The four methods of job evaluation are:

- Classification;
- Ranking;
- Factor; and
- Point.

Compensable Factors

All methods of job evaluation involve compensable factors. A *compensable factor* is a characteristic used to compare the worth of jobs in job evaluation. The EPA requires employers to consider these compensable factors in setting pay for similar work performed by both females and males:

1. skill,
2. effort,
3. responsibility, and
4. working conditions.

Virtually all job evaluation methods incorporate these same compensable factors, although different terms may be used. Below are sample definitions of these terms:

- *Skill* includes subfactors such as ability, education, experience, and training;
- *Effort* is the mental and physical exertion required to perform the job tasks;
- *Responsibility* is the accountability required by a job, such as supervising work performed by others and managing assets or funds;
- *Working conditions* consists of two subfactors: surroundings and hazards. *Surroundings* include the environment in which work is performed. *Hazards* refer to the physical dangers or risks involved.

Classification Method

The *classification method* of job evaluation involves grouping similar or like positions into classes, based upon such considerations as the same pay grade, the same or similar job task description, and similar job specifications. Some organizations use the terms *job classification* or *position classification* for the classification method they use. To some extent, classification is used in all job evaluation methods; that is, similar jobs are grouped together, with one job title and job description.

Classification is used most frequently in government, from the federal government down to state and local governments. There has been some decline, however, in the number of organizations using the classification method in favor of point or point/factor methods.

A *class* is a group of positions which are similar or the same in these areas:

- The kind or subject area of work;
- The difficulty and responsibility in job tasks; and
- The job specifications (the knowledge, skills, and abilities required to perform the jobs).

A *pay grade* identifies a specific pay range, usually with minimum and maximum dollar figures.

Steps in Preparing a Classification System

These are the steps in constructing a classification system:

1. Evaluators start a classification project with the confidence that millions of positions have been classified in different organizations, covering virtually every conceivable kind of job. Also, since most of this body of knowledge is in the public sector, an evaluator can easily access it. Public managers willingly respond to requests for such information as job descriptions, job class series descriptions, and copies of classification procedures.

2. The assignment of jobs to pay grades or salary ranges should be determined. For example, one county government uses the classification method to evaluate jobs, conducts wage and salary surveys and uses the results to set pay grade ranges for various jobs.

3. Once the method of pricing the jobs is known, a job analysis is conducted. If internal compensable factors are used in setting pay levels, the analysis must provide information regarding them.

4. The job analysis information is used to classify jobs by type of subject matter, level of difficulty, responsibility in job tasks, and kinds and levels of job specifications. Evaluators are careful not to rely upon job titles in performing classification because they are often misleading.

5. Once jobs are classed by similar duties, difficulties, responsibilities, and specifications, job descriptions and job specifications are prepared. Also, if compensable factors are used to determine pay grade levels, concise descriptions for each compensable factor are put together.

6. Pay grades are assigned to each job class. If compensable factors are used, the grading process consists of comparing the evaluation task factors for the job with compensable factor descriptions. Once appropri-

ate matches are found, the pay grade is assigned. Sometimes, grade descriptions are compared to the job descriptions in order to find the correct grades.

Ranking Method

The ranking method of job evaluation puts the jobs in order, from the least to the most valued. The whole job must be considered in developing the rankings. In making ranking decisions, the evaluator can consider a global statement, such as:

Of the jobs under consideration, select the one that is worth the most overall, based upon skill, effort, responsibility, and working conditions.

For example, an employer could use a ranking method in evaluating these jobs: laborer, janitor, truck driver, forklift operator, computer assistant, secretary, supply assistant, printer, accountant, electrician, and human resource director. Using a global statement, such as the one above, the rankings would look like this (in descending order, with 1 as most valued):

1. Human Resource Director;
2. Electrician;
3. Accountant;
4. Printer;
5. Supply Assistant;
6. Secretary;
7. Computer Assistant;
8. Forklift Operator;
9. Truck Driver;
10. Janitor; and
11. Laborer

Evaluators may have a difficult time using the ranking method with a global statement, since only rarely does one job require most of the compensable factors. For example, of the jobs shown above, most people would agree that the laborer job should be ranked higher on working conditions than a human resource director, because laborer tasks require working in intemperate conditions. One way of addressing this problem is to use a worksheet to perform the ranking, showing each job and each compensable factor. The results of this process are shown in Exhibit 26-4.

Exhibit 26-4
Ranking Method of Job Evaluation: Four Compensable Factors

Benchmark Job	Compensable Factor			
	Skill	*Effort*	*Responsbility*	*Job Conditions*
Laborer	1	2	1	8
Janitor	2	3	2	3
Truck Driver	3	1	3	4

Benchmark Job	Compensable Factor			
	Skill	Effort	Responsbility	Job Conditions
Forklift Operator	4	4	5	2
Computer Assistant	5	5	4	9
Secretary	6	8	6	6
Supply Assistant	7	7	9	1
Printer	8	6	10	10
Accountant	9	10	8	7
Electrician	10	9	7	11
Human Res. Dir.	11	11	11	5

Ranking methods can be systematized by carefully defining each compensable factor, so that the evaluator has a standard for making judgments. Also, the job descriptions may include a section with headings for each compensable factor and a description of the compensable factors for the job tasks.

The factors shown in Exhibit 26-4 appear to have the same weight. If this condition does not represent the wishes of management, weights can be assigned to each factor, depending upon how management views their relative importance. After all the jobs are ranked, the next step is to assign pay ranges to them. Each job usually does not have a separate pay range. For example, an organization with 35 different jobs would not have 35 different pay ranges. Typically, the 35 jobs would be collapsed into 12-15 pay ranges. This procedure substantially reduces the difficulty of explaining fine distinctions that separate jobs that are closely ranked. For example, it is difficult to explain why one job is ranked 32 and another one 33. That explanation is unnecessary when both of them are placed in the same pay grade, which occurs when fewer pay grades are used. This does not mean that rankings cannot or should not be documented; they can and they should, but the discussions are academic when groups of closely ranked jobs are assigned the same pay level.

The process of establishing pay structures with pay grades is covered in Chapter 28.

Factor Method of Job Evaluation

The factor method evaluates jobs by adding up the individual dollar values of each compensable factor. These dollar values are determined by using the factors of benchmark jobs for comparison purposes. *Benchmark* or *key* jobs are those jobs used in making job evaluation decisions. These are the steps in conducting a factor job evaluation:

1. The compensable factors used in the job evaluation project should be determined.

2. A job analysis should be conducted and job descriptions prepared that include the type and amount of each compensable factor present in each job.

3. Key or benchmark jobs should be selected; guidelines for making these selections are as follows:

a. The jobs should represent the full range of pay levels, from the lowest to the highest. It is usually not feasible to represent every pay level, but it is important that the entire range be represented.

b. All organization functions should be represented.

c. Benchmark jobs should have low turnover rates. This requirement ensures that pay rates are adequate to retain personnel. High turnover rates may indicate that the pay is too low to keep fully qualified employees from leaving.

d. The selection ratio should be at least .3 or .4, which means there are at least three or four fully qualified applicants for each vacancy. An adequate number of qualified applicants is an indication the job pay is competitive in the labor market.

e. Where possible, benchmark jobs should represent all job families.

Sometimes, an evaluator can choose among several jobs that meet all the other conditions described above. In such cases, different kinds of jobs, representing various classes of work, should be selected.

Finally, where a choice exists, jobs should be selected that represent the preponderance of positions in the organization. For example, in most organizations, five to ten jobs represent 75 percent of the work performed. Where possible, some of these jobs should be chosen, if they meet other requirements for benchmark jobs.

Exhibit 26-5
Hourly Monetary Values Used in Factor Job Evaluation

Benchmark Job	$ Monetary Value for Compensable Factor				
	Skill	Effort	Responsbility	Working Conditions	$ Hourly Rate
Laborer	.50	2.00	1.00	8.00	11.50
Janitor	1.50	3.00	2.00	5.00	11.50
Truck Driver	2.50	1.00	3.50	5.50	12.50
Forklift Operator	3.00	4.00	5.00	4.00	16.00
Computer Assistant	4.00	4.50	4.00	8.50	21.00
Secretary	5.00	6.50	6.00	6.50	24.00
Supply Assistant	6.00	5.50	8.00	2.00	21.50
Printer	7.00	5.00	10.00	9.00	31.00
Accountant	7.50	8.50	7.00	7.00	30.00
Electrician	8.00	7.50	6.50	10.00	32.00
Human Resource Director	9.50	10.50	11.00	6.00	37.00

4. A worksheet form is used for listing the dollar values for each compensable factor in each benchmark job; an example is found in Exhibit 26-5. The steps are as follows:

   a. The current wage for each benchmark job should be listed, as seen in the last column. Since benchmark jobs have low turnover rates and reasonably high selection ratios, it is assumed the current wages paid by the organization approximate the market rate and, therefore, are appropriate; this is a critically important assumption, since the pay of all other jobs in the organization is related to the pay of benchmark jobs.

   b. All benchmark jobs are compared on all the compensable factors, and each job is ranked on each factor. This is done by comparing the factor descriptions for each job. Due to length considerations, neither the factor descriptions for each job nor the factor level descriptions are discussed herein.

   c. Monetary values are assigned to each factor for each job by estimating the dollar portion of the total wage attributable to each factor and recording those amounts on the worksheet. Columns 2 through 5 on Exhibit 26-5 are the factor attributions for the jobs.

5. A *factor value scale,* also called a factor wage comparison scale is prepared, using the dollar figures on the worksheet. Exhibit 26-6 illustrates the scale and factor values for the jobs shown in Exhibit 26-5. The values are rounded to the nearest increment of 50 cents. Other scaling differentials may be used, depending upon the circumstances. Ideally, a sufficient number of benchmark jobs are used containing enough differences in factor values that the value scale will have numerous examples for all of the factors.

6. The final step is to evaluate all the other jobs (nonbenchmark) in the organization. Each factor in every job is individually evaluated. The evaluator narrows the comparison to several benchmark jobs, refers to the factor value scale and decides which monetary value best equates to the factor.

EXAMPLE: The job of Accounting Clerk is to be evaluated. The evaluator reads the factor description for the factor *Skill* in the job description. She compares the description with the various level descriptions for *Skill.* and determines that the *Skill* factor in Accounting Clerk is the lowest level. She refers to the factor value scale in Exhibit 26-6 and compares the Accounting Clerk *Skill* description to those of Forklift Operator and Computer Assistant. She determines the *Skill* requirements are above Forklift Operator but below Computer Assistant, and selects $3.50 cents as the appropriate wage value. She follows the same procedure for the other three factors, totals the values, and computes the wage for the job.

Exhibit 26-6
Factor Value Scale Used in Factor Job Evaluation

		Compensable Factor		
Value	Skill	Effort	Responsibility	Working Conditions
.50	Laborer			
1.00		Truck Driver	Laborer	
1.50	Janitor			
2.00		Laborer	Janitor	Supply Assistant
2.50	Truck Driver			
3.00	Forklift Operator	Janitor		
3.50			Truck Driver	
4.00	Computer Assistant	Forklift Operator	Computer Assistant	Forklift Operator
4.50		Computer Assistant		
5.00	Secretary	Printer	Forklift Operator	Janitor
5.50		Supply Assistant		Truck Driver
6.00	Supply Assistant		Secretary	Human Res. Dir.
6.50		Secretary	Electrician	Secretary
7.00	Printer		Accountant	Accountant
7.50	Accountant	Electrician		
8.00	Electrician		Supply Assistant	Laborer
8.50		Accountant		Computer Assistant
9.00				Printer
9.50	Human Res. Dir.			
10.00			Printer	Electrician
10.50		Human Res. Dir.		
11.00			Human Res. Dir.	
11.50				

Point Method

Point or point/factor systems are the most widely used method of job evaluation. The steps in preparing a point system are these:

1. The compensable factors used in the evaluation project should be determined. Most point systems also have subfactors; for example, the factor *Knowledge* might be composed of such subfactors as *Education* and *Experience*. Point systems also have various degrees of each subfactor.

   Example:

KNOWLEDGE	1st Degree	2nd Degree	3rd Degree	4th Degree	5th Degree
1. Education	12	24	36	48	60
2. Experience	20	40	60	80	100

   Each degree is described for every subfactor, so that the evaluator can compare the job analysis information and the degree descriptions and select the appropriate number of points for the job. This example describes each of the five degrees for the subfactor, *Education:*

   1st Degree: Simple arithmetic, basic English, reading and writing, and following step-by-step instructions.

   2nd Degree: Use of fractions, letter and memorandum composition, and operation of a 10-key keyboard with the touch system.

   3rd Degree: Technical knowledge of a specialized field, measuring instruments, preparation and interpretation of technical reports.

   4th Degree: Knowledge typically acquired through a pertinent baccalaureate program involving concepts, principles and skills of a professional or administrative occupation.

   5th Degree: Relevant graduate study and mastery of a professional field, developing new hypotheses or methods and conducting independent research.

2. The compensable factors are weighted, depending upon their importance in job performance. In the Example above, the subfactor *Experience* is weighted higher than *Education.*

3. Benchmark jobs are chosen, analyzed, evaluated, and the points totaled for all the factors. The process of selecting benchmark jobs is discussed in the previous section on the *Factor* method.

4. A wage schedule is constructed. As with the *Factor* method, the current wage rates of benchmark jobs are considered as representative of market rates. The point totals for each benchmark job are equated to the wage. As an intermediate step, various point totals for the benchmark jobs are used to establish pay grades.

Point Range	Grade	Hourly Wage
up to 117	1	$6.80
118-140	2	7.50
141-163	3	8.50
164-186	4	9.70
187-209	5	11.30

Point Range	Grade	Hourly Wage
210-232	6	13.25
233-255	7	15.80
etc.		

The pay grades, in turn, correspond to the wage rates of the benchmark jobs. Pay ranges with minimum, midpoint, and maximum wages are established.

5. The nonbenchmark jobs are analyzed and job descriptions are prepared, including factor descriptions.

6. Nonbenchmark jobs are evaluated, using their factor descriptions, the factor descriptions of benchmark jobs, and the degree descriptions of the subfactors. The points are totaled for the subfactors, and they are equated to a pay grade and wage.

Three Specific Job Evaluation Methods

Three well-known methods of job evaluation are the Point Factor Leveling method used by the U.S. Bureau of Labor Statistics, they Hay Guide Chart-Profile method and the American Association of Industrial Management method.

Point Factor Leveling Method of Job Evaluation

The *Point Factor Leveling* (PFI) method of job evaluation is used by the U.S. Bureau of Labor Statistics (BLS) to determine pay grade levels for occupations in a number of cities, regions and the Nation. Employers can use the PFI method to calculate the pay grades for jobs in their organizations and compare the results with BLS survey data. In addition, employers can use the PFI method to establish a pay structure within their organizations. The four compensable factors in the PFI method are Knowledge, Job Controls and Complexity, Contacts and Physical Environment.[15]

Hay Guide Chart-Profile Method of Job Evaluation

The Hay Guide Chart-Profile Method of Job Evaluation (Hay method) was developed from the early job evaluation work of Edward N. Hay, a pioneer in job evaluation. The method was conceived in the early 1950s. The three factors in the system are know-how, problem solving, and accountability. As the need exists, another factor, additional compensable elements (ACES), can be considered if special conditions in a job, such as potential health exposures and physical hazards, need to be incorporated into the compensation for the job. ACES are not a part of the core job evaluation but consist of additional compensation to reflect job conditions.[16]

---

[15] To learn how to use the PFL method consult the publication *National Compensation Survey: Guide for Evaluating Your Firm's Jobs and Pay*, Bureau of Labor Statistics, October 2003.

[16] For exhibits of the Hay Guide-Chart Profile method, see Myers, Donald W. and Patten, Thomas, H., Jr., *Exercises for Developing Human Resources Management Skills* (Chicago: CCH Inc., 1996).

Know-How

Know-how is defined as the sum total of every kind of capability or skill, however acquired, necessary for acceptable job performance. The three aspects of know-how are:

1. *Knowledge,* ranging from practical procedures to scientific disciplines. The seven levels of this knowledge are (in ascending order):

   a. Primary;

   b. Elementary vocational;

   c. Vocational;

   d. Advanced vocational;

   e. Basic technical-specialized;

   f. Seasoned technical-specialized;

   g. Technical-specialized mastery; and

   h. Professional mastery.

   Depending upon the organization, there could be as few as four levels, particularly when only nonexempt jobs are involved, or as many levels as necessary. For example, very specialized, unique scientific jobs may require more than the seven levels of technical know-how listed above.

2. *Managerial know-how,* consisting of either consulting on or performing the managerial functions of organizing, planning, executing, controlling, and evaluating. There are four levels of this know-how, but the actual number of levels could vary, from two up to as many as necessary, depending upon organizational management layers and the content of the jobs to be evaluated. The four levels of managerial know-how are:

   a. Minimal;

   b. Related

   c. Diverse; and

   d. Broad.

   Human relations skills, which involve active personal relationships. The three levels, in ascending order, are:

   a. Basic;

   b. Important; and

   c. Critical.

Problem Solving

Problem solving is viewed as partially a function of know-how because identifying, defining, and resolving problems begins with knowledge. Consequently, problem solving is evaluated as a percentage of know-how. There are two levels of problem solving:

1. *The environment in which problems are solved.* The ascending order of this environment is:

   a. Strict routine;

   b. Routine;

   c. Semi-routine;

   d. Standardized;

   e. Clearly defined;

   f. Broadly defined;

   g. Generally defined; and

   h. Abstractly defined.

2. *How the problem challenges thinking.* The five levels of this challenge are:

   a. Repetitive;

   b. Patterned;

   c. Interpolative;

   d. Adaptive; and

   e. Uncharted.

Accountability

Accountability is the third compensable factor and is the responsibility for the consequences of actions. Accountability is composed of these three levels:

1. degree of personal freedom to take action or commit resources;

2. effect of the job on results; and

3. the dollar magnitude of accountability.

Additional Compensable Elements

The *additional compensable elements* (ACES) factor is used to reflect any special conditions in a job, such as physical conditions or working on an evening shift. Originally, this fourth compensable factor was called *working conditions,* but this term was inappropriate in some situations, such as an employee switching from the night shift to the day shift. With the ACES factor, the employee is compensated for certain factors, such as working a night shift, without including them in the core job. ACES is not part of the job evaluation process, but instead is determined through specific means, such as prevailing practice and market pay surveys.

Applying the Hay Guide Chart-Profile Method

The terms in the Hay system appear to be technical but, with training, people can readily learn to use them. The system is very adaptable to all types of jobs and organizations; this universal application explains why over 7,000 public and private organizations use the Hay method, making it the most widely used job evaluation system in the world.

The AAIM Point Factor Method

Virtually all point methods are a combination of points and factors; in reality, they are point/factor methods. Probably the oldest surviving point/factor method is the one offered by the American Association of Industrial Management (AAIM), which was developed in the 1930s by a group of the

Associations' engineers. Originally, the plan was called the National Metal Trades Association method, which was AAIM's former name.

The AAIM point/factor system has two manuals. The first covers production, maintenance, and service occupations; the second manual covers clerical, technical, engineering, administrative, sales, and supervisory occupations. The compensable factors differ in the two manuals. The factors used in the manual covering production, maintenance, and service occupations are *Skill, Effort, Responsibility*, and *Job Conditions*, the same compensable factors specified in the EPA.

Pay Issues

Pay Equity

Pay equity is the concept involving the equitable treatment of members of both sexes in pay administration. Originally, *pay equity* was restricted to mean comparable worth. However, the definition has been expanded to include all aspects of sex-based pay differences. *Comparable worth* is paying members of both sexes equally for dissimilar jobs that have the same relative worth to an employer. Pay equity concerns both similar and dissimilar jobs and the causes of pay differentials between the sexes.

Decreases in Compensation

Increasing competition is compelling employers to reduce costs, including employee compensation. Handling these decreases in an equitable manner to reduce employee dissatisfaction requires foresight and creativity. Some employers make such decreases on a *quid pro quo* basis, so that employees receive a benefit, such as a profit-sharing plan, in return for reduced pay.

Two-Tier Compensation

Two-tier compensation plans provide one level of compensation, usually the existing one, for current employees and a new, lower one for employees who are hired after the arrangement is established. This arrangement is shown in Exhibit 26-12.

Exhibit 26-7
Monthly Pay
Step

	1	2	3	4	5
Pay Grade 6 (Tier 1) (old)	$2,000	$2,100	$2,205	$2,315	$2,431
Pay Grade 6 (Tier 2) (new)	$1,800	$1,890	$1,984	$2,083	$2,187

The major advantage of two-tier pay grades is that the organization may reduce costs without decreasing pay to existing employees. The disadvantage is the perception of internal inequity generated in new employees, who are performing the same tasks as other employees paid at the higher tier. One way of correcting this problem is by gradually reducing the difference in the pay grades, as employees gain more experience with the firm, until the two tiers are the same. This arrangement is shown in Exhibit 26-13.

Exhibit 26-8
Monthly Pay
Step

	1	2	3	4	5
Pay Grade 6 (Tier 1) (old)	$2,000	$2,100	$2,205	$2,315	$2,431
Pay Grade 6 (Tier 2) (new)	$1,800	$1,900	$2,100	$2,225	$2,431

Pay Compression

Pay compression is the narrowing of pay differences for reasons other than sound pay administration.

These are common types:

- *Pay grade compression* the condition of having too small a differential in the pay of higher grades compared to lower ones.

    EXAMPLE: A firm's pay range for the job, Truck Driver, is Pay Grade 6, starting pay is $35,500 and the maximum pay in the range is $49,700. The pay for the job, Supervisor, Truck Drivers, is Pay Grade 7, starting pay is $36,000 and the maximum is $50,400. The pay grade for the job of Supervisor is compressed since there is too small a differential in the pay of the job compared to a job which it supervises.

- *Pay range compression* which is the condition of having too small a differential in the pay ranges of higher pay grades compared to those in the lower grades.

    EXAMPLE: For ABC Company, the range of pay from the minimum to the maximum in each grade for Grades 1 through 10 is a gradual increase of 40 percent. However, for each grade in the top Grades 11 through 14, the range from minimum to maximum is only 25 percent. The within grade pay ranges in grades 11 through 14 are compressed compared to grades 1 through 10.

- *Employee pay compression* (also called *"labor scarcity compression"*) which is the condition of having too small a spread in the pay of an employee who is better qualified or has more experience compared to another employee who is less well qualified or has less experience. This type of compression is often caused by labor market conditions, namely a scarcity of qualified applicants.

    EXAMPLE: A school system cannot recruit enough new teachers because the pay in Step 1 (the starting pay for new employees) of the pay scale is too low. To correct the problem, the School Superintendent raises the starting pay for new teachers to Step 3. Normally, it requires two years of service before a teacher is in Step 3. With the change, the pay of teachers with two years of service in the system is compressed since they are in the same step (Step 3) as new teachers with no experience in the system.

- *Pay grade "creep" compression* which is a condition resulting from increasing the pay range in a grade without increasing the range in the immediately higher pay grade.

    EXAMPLE: DEF Company conducts a job evaluation of all the jobs in Pay Grade 8 and decides to increase the pay range for the grade (that is the minimum to maximum pay). The firm does not conduct a similar job evaluation on the jobs in Pay Grade 9 and makes no change in the pay range. Consequently, Pay Grade 9 is compressed after the change is implemented.

Pay Secrecy

    Some employers have personnel rules or provisions in employee handbooks prohibiting employees from discussing wages or pay matters among themselves. The usual reasons for such rules are to prevent employee perceptions of inequities if they learn a peer is earning more and to avoid employee complaints. Regardless of the rationale, these policies are illegal because they "tend to interfere with, restrain, or coerce employees in the exercise of (their) rights" to engage in protected concerted activity which is provided by the National Labor Relations Act.[17]

Pay Terminology

Compa-Ratio

    The *compa-ratio* is the ratio of an individual's pay to the midpoint of the person's pay grade. The ratio is computed by dividing the employee's pay by the midpoint of the pay range. A compa-ratio of 1.00 means that an employee's pay is at the midpoint of the salary range. A ratio which is less than one, such as 0.95 means the employee is .05 percentage points below the midpoint; conversely, 1.10 means the employee's pay is .10 percentage points above the midpoint. The significance of the midpoint is that employees whose pay is above the midpoint (greater than 1.00) are expected to perform at higher levels of performance to warrant a pay increase. Compa-ratios can also be computed, for example, for an entire of group of employees in the same job or for all the employees in the same job in a specific department or other organizational unit. Compensation software can readily calculate compa-ratios for desired situations.

Pay for Professionals

    Many employers use special pay methods to compensate professionals, technical and scientific personnel. Two of the most common methods involve *dual career ladders* and *maturity curves.*

    Dual career track. As discussed in Chapter 34, Career Planning, a *dual career ladder*, which is sometimes called a *dual career track*, is a career progression in which professionals can elect to remain within their discipline, as a chemical engineer for example, or to move into a management position. Several levels of progression are possible and, at each level, the professional can choose either to

---

[17] CCH HUMAN RESOURCES MANAGEMENT, *Employment Relations*, ¶ 194. See also U.S. Department of Labor, *Rule Prohibiting Employees from Discussing Wages Violated the National Labor Relations Act, Court Holds* (June 2, 2001).

move into a comparable management position or to stay in the profession. The pay is also comparable, so that the income of the professional would not suffer if he or she moved into a management job instead of remaining in the profession. The reverse would also be true. This system continues to reward the individual for remaining within the profession, while leaving open the option to him or her to enter into a management position without loss of income.[18]

Maturity curves. Another approach to paying professionals is to compensate them either for the number of years of experience within their respective professions or for the number of years that have elapsed since they received their last professional degree. These are essential points of *maturity curves:*

- The years of experience or years since receiving the last degree are shown on the x-axis, and salary is shown on the y-axis.

- Salary rises rather rapidly at first and then gradually decreases as the number of years approaches 15.

- Around 20 years of experience or of the amount of time since the last degree, the curve begins to flatten as the salary remains the same.

- The curve reflects the phenomenon that professionals, as a group, have less to contribute as the time elapses from their last professional degree, unless they add to their competence by obtaining additional education.

- The curve represents the profession and not necessarily the salary history for any particular individual.[19]

Pay "Circling"

Inevitably, due to restructuring and changing pay plans, some employees' pay will not be consistent with their existing pay ranges. The following are some terms used to describe these and related conditions:

- *Red circle* is freezing an employee's pay at the maximum of the pay range;

- *Green circle* is paying an employee at a lower rate of pay than the minimum of the pay range (the opposite of red circle);

- *Silver circle* is paying an employee above the maximum of the pay range as a reward for super-seniority or long tenure; and

- *Gold circle* is a condition of giving an employee a merit pay increase above the maximum of the range to reward performance.

[18] Milkovich, G. T. and Newman, J. M. *Compensation* (Chicago: Irwin, 1996), pp. 594-596.

[19] Henderson, R. I. *Compensation Management: Rewarding Performance* (Englewood Cliffs, N.J.: Prentice Hall, 1994), pp. 219-220. See also Milkovich, G. T. and Newman, J. M. *Compensation* (Chicago: Irwin, 1996), pp. 596-597.

CHAPTER 27
EXECUTIVE COMPENSATION

Chapter Highlights
- Objectives of executive compensation plans
- Roles of executive compensation committees
- Legal issues in executive compensation
- Types of executive compensation plans

Introduction

Executive compensation includes base pay, incentives, long-term compensation, and perquisites. The incentives or performance-based component is a known as *contingent compensation,* since payouts are contingent upon the executive meeting specific performance objectives, such as a certain level of profitability or budget performance. Another major part of executive compensation is long-term compensation, typically various forms of stock options. The final component is *perquisites,* which are special employee benefits given to executive-level management, such as paid country club dues. As with other forms of compensation, executive compensation methods are changing; this chapter examines both the major components of this type of compensation and the changes that are occurring.

Executive Compensation Objectives

The major objectives of executives' compensation plans are:

- To provide protection in the event of job loss, whether through takeovers or reorganization;

- To reward performance;

- To achieve external equity;

- To minimize the impact of income taxes; and

- To protect proprietary information.

Executive personnel include all those who are employed in the top jobs in each functional area of the organization, up to and including the chief executive officer. Some examples of executive-level jobs are the top jobs in human resources management, marketing, finance, engineering, operations/production, research, advertising, and administration. Other jobs at the executive level are controller, treasurer, executive vice president, chief operating officer, and corporate secretary.

Provide Protection Contingent Upon Job Loss

In recent years, the prospect of job loss due to business takeovers, financial insolvency, and other reasons is a continuing reality for many executives. To lessen the effects of this contingency, various types of severance arrangements, including monetary payments, are among the fastest growing types of executive compensation. These forms of compensation, often referred to as *golden parachutes,* are intended to provide some financial compensation in the event of a premature loss of employment.

Reward Performance

Ostensibly, rewarding performance is one of the major, if not the major, objective of executive compensation plans. However, there are critics who argue that executive pay, more pointedly the pay of chief executive officers, is only indirectly linked to performance. For example, one compensation consultant, who used a number of operational and performance variables in studying the compensation of chief executive officers of the largest companies in the U.S., concluded that many companies really do not reward performance.[1] This researcher found that when a firm does well, the chief executive is extremely well rewarded, but when the fortunes of the business sag, the executive is still rewarded, though not as well.[2]

In spite of these criticisms, rewarding performance is a major objective motivating boards of directors in their choice of the compensation systems they implement to reward executives. Some of the specific results that these boards seek from their executives involve the short term, such as annual profitability, as well as long-term accomplishments, including market share and stock prices.

Achieve External Equity

To some extent, other compensation objectives, such as rewarding performance, providing contingent compensation in the event of job loss, and minimizing the impact of income taxes, impact upon the objective of achieving external equity. If other firms in the same labor market are providing compensation to meet these objectives, it behooves the individual firms to offer them, in order to be competitive in recruiting executive talent.

The competition for executive talent is keen, particularly for those who get high marks for savvy and motivation. To attract and retain these executives requires a combination of job conditions, including job challenge and autonomy, as well as a competitive compensation package.

Some critics argue that the unrealistic expectations of compensation committees in the U.S. have boosted chief executive officer compensation beyond what is necessary. One critic contends that fully one-third of compensation committees set the objective of paying their chief executive officers at the 75th percentile of the market, with the other two-thirds of the committees paying their executives at the median level or just above it. This practice, according to various research-

---

[1] Crystal, G.S., "The Wacky, Wacky World of CEO Pay," *Fortune* (June 6, 1988), p. 76.   [2] *Ibid.*

ers, is one of the main reasons for the disproportionate increases in the pay of chief executives compared to the rest of the employee population.[3]

Minimize Income Tax Impact

A major objective of executive compensation plans is reducing or otherwise minimizing the tax burden for the executive. To help executives get the full tax benefit from various compensation strategies, compensation committees typically seek the advice of tax accountants and tax attorneys.

Protect Proprietary Information/Prevent Competition

During their tenures of employment, executives acquire substantial information about their employing firms. This information includes client data, technological advances, research findings, and new product development. Executives leaving firms pose two significant threats to their previous employers. First, they will reveal this sensitive information to their new employer, a competitor. Second, they will establish their own businesses and use such information to compete against their former employers. To protect against these two possibilities, employers adopt various strategies, such as requiring executives to sign non-disclosure or secrecy agreements, entering into contracts with the executives noncompetition clauses, and preparing compensation systems that reward the executives for their ideas; in return, the executive relinquishes all future rights to them.

Compensation Committees

Most organizations, both private and public, designate compensation committees to research the compensation of executives and to make recommendations. Included in the work of these committees is engaging the services of compensation consultants and overseeing their work. Other tasks of compensation committees include recommending performance criteria for appraising the work of executives and developing various instruments to track performance.

Sometimes, the top executives meet with various members of the compensation committee to exchange ideas about such subjects as:

- Definitions of proposed objectives and goals;
- Formulation of strategies to achieve those plans;
- Establishment of criteria to measure performance toward the accomplishment of the plans; and
- Compensation systems to be used to reward performance.

In addition, the compensation committee chairperson, and, on occasion, members of the compensation committee, meets with the executives to evaluate their progress toward goal accomplishments.

There are times when the entire board of directors (in private sector organizations) and the council (or other governing body in public sector organizations)

---

[3] *Ibid.* See also, Reibstein, L., "Consultants' Influence on Compensation Is Pervasive—and Controversial," *Wall Street Journal* (May 28, 1986), p. 27.

will formulate general guidelines for the operation of the compensation committee. In addition, these bodies may also give the compensation committee some objectives to be used in compensating executives.

A key role of the compensation committee is the formulation of compensation contracts for executives.

Director Ethics

Revelations about corruption and malfeasance of corporate officers have increased the responsibilities of directors to exercise more oversight in the management of public corporations. In addition, the Sarbanes-Oxley Act of 2002 prohibits, in the words of the Securities and Exchange Commission (SEC) rules implementing the Act " . . . officers and directors of an issuer, and persons acting under the direction of an officer or director, from taking any action to coerce, manipulate, mislead, or fraudulently influence the auditor of the issuer's financial statements if that person knew or should have known that such action, if successful, could result in rendering the financial statements materially misleading."[4]

Among the types of direct or indirect conduct that the SEC considers improper to influence auditors are these:

- Offering bribes, future employment and contracts for non-audit services.
- Giving incorrect or misleading information to an auditor.
- Issuing threats to cancel auditing and non-auditing contracts if an auditor raises questions about the firm's accounting.
- Trying to remove an auditing firm's partner from an audit if the partner object's to the firm's accounting.
- Blackmailing.
- Making physical threats.

Compensation Contracts

A *compensation contract* is an agreement between an executive and the Board of Directors, in which the executive agrees to provide certain services for a stipulated period of time in return for various compensation provisions. The typical clauses contained in a salary contract are:

- The first clause usually states the employer's intention to hire the executive for a designated period of time.
- The second clause expresses the executive's determination to render his or her best efforts in meeting the organization's mission and purposes.
- The third clause defines the compensation arrangements, including base salary, contingent compensation that is related to job performance, and other financial provisions.

---

[4] Securities and Exchange Commission, *Final Rule: Improper Influence on Conduct of Audits.* Effective June 27, 2003.

- The fourth clause explains the requirements for business expenses, such as the type of accommodations for airplane travel, hotel, and lodging.

- The fifth clause describes the financial arrangements in the event of job abolishment or job restructuring due to a merger or other type of consolidation.

- The sixth clause contains provisions concerning the executive's agreement not to compete with the firm during the life of the contract and for a designated period after the contract is terminated.

- Other clauses may contain provisions regarding such matters as the way that cost of living adjustments are made and the manner in which death benefits are paid to the executive's dependents.

Types of Executive Compensation

The seven types of executive compensation are:

- Base pay or salary;
- Short-term compensation, other than base pay;
- Deferred compensation;
- Long-term pay incentives, which are primarily stock options and variations;
- Employee benefits and perquisites;
- Health and welfare plans; and
- Retirement plans.

Base Pay or Salary

Base pay or salary represents the major portion of executive compensation. For all levels of executives, ranging from the top jobs in each functional area up to the chief executive officer, salary is approximately 60 percent of the total direct compensation. Salary represents the following percentage for these jobs:

- Chief executive officer and chief operating officer—45 percent;
- Executive vice president—60 percent; and
- Vice presidents of functions—60 to 70 percent.[5]

The proportion of total direct current compensation that is base salary also varies inversely with the size of the organization. For example, base salary averages about 40 percent of compensation among chief executive officers (CEOs) in organizations with revenues from $1 billion to $5 billion; the average increases to 50 percent for organizations with $10 million to $25 million in revenue.

Differences also exist in base pay as a percentage of total compensation in high- versus low-performing firms. In firms judged as high performing, based on earnings and stock price, base salary is 20 percent of CEO pay. The base pay of CEOs in low-performing firms represents about 50 percent of pay.[6]

[5] Based upon a random review of 1998 proxy statement for firms in various industries.

[6] Saccomano, A., "Incentives emphasized," *Richmond Times-Dispatch* (September 14, 1997).

There is a significant trend in executives opting more for incentive compensation in lieu of base salary. Two executives, the CEO and the President and Chief Operating Officer for Capital One, cut their salaries to just one dollar for the years 1998-2000, in return for stock options valued at $14.5 million and $9.7 million, respectively.[7]

Legal Issues

Both Internal Revenue Service (IRS) regulations and Securities and Exchange Commission (SEC) disclosure requirements have had an impact on the use of base salaries to compensate executives.

IRS Regulations. IRS regulations restrict executive compensation to $1 million, unless it is related to performance. This regulation is one reason for the decreases in base pay as a percentage of total direct compensation. Some experts, however, feel that this regulation has not had any affect on CEO total compensation. These critics argue that Boards of Directors have simply established bonus plans that are contingent upon the easily attainable performance objectives; thus, executives suffer no reduction in total compensation.

SEC Disclosure Rules. Disclosure rules issued by the SEC require publicly traded firms to disclose all compensation, including base salary, contingent-based pay, stock options, and awards for the CEO and the other four highest-paid executives in the firm. The information must be disclosed in the annual proxy statements. Such information must also be disclosed about any individuals who served as CEO during the previous year and at least two other departing officials who, had they remained with the firm, would have been among the four highest-paid persons. The information is to be disclosed in a tabular format, with two tables for stock options and stock appreciation rights. One table must show the number of options granted and the terms of the grant. The other table must show a summary of the employees' stock options, including the number exercised and unexercised.

The rules also require a graph in the proxy statement to show the total cumulative return to shareholders during at least the previous five years. Comparative information must also be included on the same graph, composed of returns to shareholders for stocks in the S&P 500 or, if the firm is not on the index, a broad index that includes the firm's stock and any nationally recognized industry index or group of peer firms.

Also mandated by the rules is a report by the Board of Directors or the Compensation Committee of the Board, if there is one, outlining factors of the firm's performance used in developing the firm's executive compensation plan. Some of the factors to be included in the report are market share, sales growth, profitability, and return on equity.

Sarbanes-Oxley Act of 2002. In response to various types of corporate management and auditor malfeasance, such as insider trading and fraud resulting in the loss of employee investments, the Sarbanes-Oxley Act (SOX) was

---

[7] Beausoleil, M., "Pay cuts now, profits later?" *Richmond Times-Dispatch* (February 11, 1998).

enacted into law in 2002. Among the provisions covered by the law include rules in such areas as:

- Attorney's conduct;
- Record retention;
- Disclosure of off-balance sheet arrangements;
- Auditor independence;
- Ownership reports and trading by officers, directors and the related;
- Corporate audit committee responsibilities; and,
- Insider trading during pension fund blackout periods.[8]

With specific reference to the last bulleted item, the SEC issued rules prohibiting, during a blackout period, any actions by a director or executive officer to directly or indirectly, "purchase, sell, or otherwise acquire or transfer any equity security...(of the firm that was)...acquired...in connection with his or her employment as a director or executive officer."[9] The SEC rule explains the reason for the prohibition is to prevent the unfairness of restricting employees from engaging in any trades of their holdings acquired as a reason of their employment with the firm, while directors and executive officers do engage in such trading.

A "blackout period" is three consecutive (business) days when no more than 50 percent of participants in the firm's plan are able to institute equity transactions, such as buying or selling securities or otherwise make changes in their 401(k) plans. Participants must be given a 30-day advance notice of the blackout period. The advance notice must contain the following:

- The reasons for the blackout;
- A description of participants' rights that will be suspended during the blackout;
- The beginning and ending dates of the blackout; and,
- A statement advising participants to assess their investments with the view that they will not be able to make any changes during the blackout period.[10]

As noted previously, identifying malfeasance by a firm's management and auditors is a top priority in SOX. Naturally, managers and auditors may be reluctant to report their own malfeasance. Similarly, employees who possess knowledge of nefarious schemes may be reluctant to report them for fear of retaliation. To address these issues, audit committees have the responsibility under the law to establish procedures for employees to make "confidential, anonymous submission . . . of concerns regarding questionable accounting or auditing matters."[11]

---

[8] Securities and Exchange Committee, *Spotlight on Sarbanes-Oxley Rulemaking and Reports* (no date), pp. 1-4.

[9] Securities and Exchange Commission, *Insider Trades During Pension Fund Blackout Periods* (January 26, 2003), p. 1. See this rule for the definition of the terms director and executive officer.

[10] U.S. Department of Labor, *Labor Department Issues Final Rules on Disclosure of Pension Plan "Blackout Periods,"* (January 23, 2003), p. 1.

[11] Securities & Exchange Commission, *Final Rule: Standards Relating to Listed Company Audit Committees.*

Increases in Base Pay

Increases in base pay are granted to executives through either a lump-sum payment or, more typically, a percentage increase in the base salary. Salary increases are awarded in order to implement the results of a compensation survey, to reward executives for their overall successful performance, and to adjust the real income of executives by offsetting any price inflation, as measured by a particular price index.

Merit Pay Increases

Merit pay is a generic term for an incentive rewarding job performance, typically through some overall measure. Merit pay increases are one way of increasing the base salary of executives. In recent years, the use of merit pay increases is declining, due to the growing importance of bonuses and other methods of rewarding performance, such as stock options.

Trends in Base Pay Increases

Corporate boards have generally increased the base pay of executives significantly more than the percentage increases to other employees, including managerial and non-managerial employees. Generally, in the past several years, these pay changes have been related to changes in the fortunes of the firm.

Effects Upon Compensation Objectives

To some extent, base salary affects several of the compensation objectives discussed above. Contingent pay for the discontinuance of employment is affected because severance arrangements are based upon the executive's salary. Base salary increases do help achieve external equity, if they are implemented as a result of a market compensation survey.

On the other hand, base salary has little or no effect upon rewarding performance or protecting proprietary information, except in cases where the executive's salary contract contains noncompetition clauses, as discussed above.

Base salary has a neutral or somewhat negative effect upon income taxes, depending upon how salary increases are handled in relation to the use of other forms of compensation, such as stock options, that defer taxes.

Bonuses

Bonus is a generic word used in pay incentives to describe cash payments for the attainment of objectives in a range of performance variables. Next to base salary, bonuses represent a major portion of executive compensation.

Methods of Using Bonuses

The two major ways bonuses are used to reward executives are overall organizational performance, such as the earnings per share of stock, and individual performance of departments or functions. Of the two, rewarding overall organizational performance is the one that is most popular. Some examples of the types of performance variables that are used to determine the overall performance of the organization are:

- Amount of pretax profits above a certain percentage of pretax return on stockholder's equity;

- After-tax profits above a certain percentage;

- Productivity above a designated level in the executive's performance plan;

- Increase in market share above a targeted amount;

- Achievement of forecasted budget; and

- Accomplishment of other specific objectives, as defined by the compensation committee.

Performance variables used in awarding bonuses also include both the individual executive's performance and the overall performance of the firm. Variables that focus on an individual's performance include meeting a budget, attaining the projected figures for a profit-center, achieving a specified level of productivity in the executive's functional area, keeping below a certain level of complaints or errors, and meeting established levels of customer service.

Sometimes, the two ways of using bonuses, that is, the overall organizational performance and individual performance within a functional area, may be combined. In one firm, three variables are used to determine each executive's bonus. Two of them are related to the overall performance of the organization, and the other one is tied directly to the individual's performance. One-third of each executive's bonus amount depends upon the executive's attainment of the objectives in each of the three performance categories. If the objectives in two of the three categories are achieved, the executive receives two-thirds of the bonus.

Performance Incentive Pay

Performance incentive pay is a method of awarding bonus payments to executives who achieve specific performance objectives. The performance variables in these incentive pay plans may include sales, production, work quality, and service standards. The amount of the bonus depends upon the executive's accomplishments in relation to those objectives.

Sign-On Bonus

As an incentive to recruiting executives in tight labor markets, more firms are using sign-on bonuses. The amount of the bonus depends upon the job and the executive's qualifications. One firm used a $1.5 million bonus to hire a CEO.[12]

Deferred Compensation

A *deferred pay plan* is one in which compensation is postponed to a later date, such as retirement, when the executive should be in a lower tax bracket and, thus, be able to retain more of it. Some examples of such plans are pensions, profit-sharing plans, and annuities. If the deferred compensation plan is limited to executives and/or discriminates in the favor of higher-paid employees, the tax

---

[12] Schellhardt, T. D., "Relocating Mom: a Primer of New Perks," *The Wall Street Journal* (June 23, 1998), B1.

benefits to employers under qualified plans would not be allowed. Some forms of stock options are also deferred compensation plans, if the executive waits until retirement to sell them.

Contractual Arrangements

Unqualified deferred compensation plans require that the taxes be paid by the employer, either when the funds are set aside for the executive or when the executive receives the compensation at a future date. While a deferred plan may not qualify for tax benefits, it still may be necessary for the employer to meet certain conditions under Title I of the Employee Retirement and Income Security Act of 1974 (ERISA). These conditions involve the adequacy of funding and participation and vesting requirements.

Types of Deferred Pay Plans

Among the various types of deferred pay plans are the excess benefit plan and the deferred bonus plan.

Excess Benefit Plan

An *excess benefit plan* provides benefits in excess of the maximum allowable under qualified plans by the IRS. Another term for these plans is *supplemental executive retirement plans.*

Deferred Bonus Plan

Another type of deferred pay plan is the *deferred bonus.* Under this arrangement, bonuses earned in current years, such as through a pay-for-performance plan, are paid in later years. Sometimes, the bonus is paid in smaller increments, made over a span of several years. Another way of handling the bonus is to simply defer the entire amount until the executive retires. In either case, the terms of the arrangement can be specified in a contract. The basic type of deferred bonus contract is one in which the firm agrees to provide a certain amount of compensation for a designated period of time after the executive retires.

Effects upon Compensation Objectives

Deferred compensation does provide contingent compensation in the event that the executive's employment with the firm is severed. The extra retirement income possible through these plans provides more than a modest amount of income security and peace of mind. Deferred pay plans do reward performance, particularly if they are funded through bonuses that are performance-related, such as profitability targets or return on stockholder's equity. Deferred compensation is effective in helping the organization achieve external equity, with adjustments to remain competitive with the market. In addition, unless there are vesting requirements in the plan, a deferred compensation plan, particularly one with substantial amounts of deferred pay, can serve as a disincentive for the executive to look for employment elsewhere.

Deferred pay plans are perhaps one of the most effective means of helping the executive minimize the impact of income taxation. There are substantial benefits accruing to the executive who is able to defer income to his or her retirement years, when the marginal taxes are lower.

Finally, deferred pay plans are effective in protecting proprietary information and preventing competition if the executive is, for example, granted deferred royalties to patents and inventions resulting from his or her work with the firm. Also, compensation contract provisions can include nondisclosure and noncompete clauses, which make deferred compensation payments contingent upon the executive meeting stipulated requirements.

Long-Term Compensation

Long-term compensation is typically based upon the performance of a firm in one or more areas, such as earnings per share of stock, over a period of four or more years. Virtually all firms use long-term compensation plans in executive contracts. Furthermore, the trend towards the use of such plans appears to be increasing, as employers continue to emphasize long-term goals.

Types of Plans

The most common type of long-term compensation plan is the stock option. Other types of plans that have some properties of stock options are phantom stock plans and restricted stock plans.

Stock Options

A *stock option* is an agreement by the firm to sell the executive a certain number of shares of stock at a designated price within a specified period of time.

> **EXAMPLE:** Scott Lewis, CEO of Alert Alarm Company, is given the option of buying 5,000 shares of Alert Alarm stock at $7.50 per share, provided that he makes the purchase within three years of the date the option is presented to him. Twenty-seven months later, Alert Alarm stock is selling for $10.50 a share; Scott exercises the option for the 5,000 shares and makes $15,000 on the deal.

The obvious incentive for the executive with a stock option is to make decisions that positively influence the business, so that the price of the stock increases.

Among the types of stock options are nonqualified or nonstatutory stock options, restricted stock options, restricted stock plans, incentive stock options, stock appreciation rights, performance shares, phantom stock, and employee stock purchase plans. As discussed above, restricted stock plans and phantom stock plans have some properties of stock option plans. To some extent, performance shares and employee stock purchase plans are related to stock options.

Nonqualified or "Nonstatutory" Stock Option

A *nonqualified* or *"nonstatutory" stock option* is one that does not qualify for preferential tax treatment. Stock options that meet specific IRS requirements permit eligible employees to pay capital gains instead of ordinary income tax rates on income received from the sale of stock and/or defer the taxes until later when the stock is sold. Stock options meeting these requirements are called *qualified stock options*.

Restricted Stock Option

A *restricted stock option* is no longer is used, but it is mentioned here because it is sometimes confused with *restricted stock plans*.

Restricted Stock Plans

A *restricted stock plan* is a type of deferred compensation plan in which an employer gives stock to an executive that is subject or "restricted" to the executive meeting certain conditions. One of the conditions or restrictions typically requires him or her to complete a certain period of employment with the firm. Other restrictions may prohibit the executive from selling the stock for a certain period of time or until he or she retires. The deferred income provision of restricted stock plans states that the executive can defer selling the stock until a later date, such as retirement, when his or her income will presumably be lower and, thus, less taxes will accrue on the sale of the stock.

Incentive Stock Options

An *incentive stock option (ISO)* is a stock option that an employer grants to an executive for the purpose of either motivating the person to accomplish certain objectives or meet certain requirements, such as fulfillment of an employment contract.

Stock Appreciation Rights

Stock appreciation rights (SARs) are options in which the executive is given the "right" to any appreciation in the value of a stipulated number of shares of stock at the end of a certain period of time. The executive is never required to exercise the option (that is, to actually buy the stock), but instead receives any increase in the value of the stock from the period in which the rights were given to the end of that designated period. The executive also receives any dividends paid on the stock during the intervening period.

In effect, SARs are win-win propositions. The executives win because they are not required to make the substantial outlay of capital required to exercise options under other forms of stock option plans. The employer wins because SARs provide an incentive for the executives to make business decisions necessary to improve the public's perception of the stock as a good buy, elevate the demand for it, and, as a result, increase its price. Stockholders gain because improving the value of their shareholdings increases their wealth.

Performance Shares

Performance shares are incentives made to executives in the form of bonuses, stock options, or a combination of the two, for the accomplishment of specific long-term goals. The term performance shares comes from the fact that executives "share," through stock options or other incentive, in any improvement in the "performance" of those variables upon which goals are established. Since either bonuses or stock options, or both, are used to reward executives, performance shares have considerable flexibility.

The advantages of performance shares to executives is that, as with SARs, they are not required to make large capital outlays when stock options are exercised. Another advantage unique to performance shares is that they can be tied to performance variables, such as profitability or return on investment, instead of related to stock price alone. Where feasible, goals can be set for a combination of several variables, including stock prices.

Phantom Stock

A *phantom stock option* is a pay incentive, with the appearance of a stock option, in which a stipulated number of fictitious shares of stock, based upon the value of actual stock, are given to an executive. The word "phantom" is derived from the fact that the shares of stock assigned to the executive do not actually exist. The fact that the stock is fictional is of no consequence, however, since the executive receives dividends on it, as though it were real. In addition, the executive receives any increase in the value of the stock. Various arrangements can be made for distribution of the dividend earnings and the appreciated value of the stock. Typically, the benefits are accumulated and paid out in a series of payments upon the retirement of the executive.

In return for the phantom shares, executives sign agreements providing for their continued employment for a certain number of years. The agreements also may contain clauses in which the executive agrees not to engage in competition with the firm after leaving it.

Effects upon Compensation Objectives

As with other forms of compensation, there are advantages and disadvantages to the use of stock options in helping an organization achieve its objectives. First, stock options, particularly those with provisions deferring payment until the executive retires, can provide income, contingent upon the executive's premature severance of employment. To some extent, stock options do reward performance; however, most of them, with the exception of performance shares and stock appreciation rights, exclusively focus on stock values. Thus, other performance measures, such as profitability and productivity, are ignored.

A major problem with stock options as a reward mechanism is the relative volatility of stock prices. This argument has particular relevance due to the stock market crash in October of 1987, in which some executives saw the value of their options drop by 50 percent or more. This situation was particularly traumatic for those executives planning to retire within several months of the market's crash.

Stock options can help achieve external equity for executives, depending upon the compensation plans of competitors in the labor market. To some extent this "keeping up with the Joneses," is necessary for a firm's compensation package to remain competitive.

One area in which stock options make an important contribution toward the accomplishment of compensation objectives is in minimizing the impact of income taxes. Executives may defer negotiating their options until retirement, thus avoiding the payment of taxes on the appreciated value in the stocks. In addition, the potential tax liability is reduced at retirement, since the executive's marginal tax rate is lower.

Stock options are also effective in protecting proprietary information and preventing competition from former executives. The major hedge against these two contingencies are stock appreciation rights and phantom shares, since they typically are accompanied by contractual arrangements in which the executive agrees not to compete with the firm for at least a minimal period of time after leaving it.

Trends in Stock Options

Stock options are a major component of most executive compensation plans, and certainly one of the most popular. As long as stock prices increase, the stock option will have appeal, both as a method of medium-term income and as a solid retirement instrument. The problem with deferrals, however, is the potential volatility in stock prices. The executive with a vault full of stock options for impending retirement is naturally apprehensive about his or her economic future during periods in which downturns are projected. At the same time, an employer must consider the effectiveness of an executive whose livelihood is largely dependent upon stock prices that fluctuate with economic news of every variety, ranging from the national debt to international trade balances.

Employers also have some problems with stock options. In small firms, stock options can dilute the voting strength of owners. In addition, sales of options, particularly those involving large numbers of shares, may, under certain conditions, adversely affect the market price.

Employee Benefits and Perquisites

As discussed earlier in this chapter, only those employee benefits and perquisites unique to executives are discussed here; compensation in categories that apply to all employees is covered in Chapters 20-23.

Types of Benefits/Perquisites

Some of the main types of benefits specially offered to executives include "golden parachutes," company cars, financial counseling, country club membership, health club membership, special officers' liability insurance, first-class air travel, spouse' traveling expenses when accompanying the executive on the firm's business, and housing and renovation allowances. Several of the more notable of these benefits are discussed below.

Golden Parachutes

A *golden parachute* is special compensation provided to executives in the event of a hostile takeover by another firm. Two reasons for using golden parachutes are:

- They help the firm retain valued executives who, fearing the possibility of discharge, might prematurely leave the firm whenever the prospect of a hostile takeover appears on the horizon.

- The total financial cost of golden parachutes might be significant enough to prevent a hostile takeover from occurring.

For these and other reasons, including an increase in hostile takeovers, such arrangements are a popular perquisite.

Excessive Payments

Accompanying the growth in these financial arrangements was a significant increase in the size of golden parachute payments to executives. The adverse publicity resulting from some of the more exorbitant of such payments prompted the U.S. Congress to provide tax rules governing them in the Tax Reform Act of 1984. Prior to this law, employers could deduct all parachute payments as customary and necessary business expenses. Without getting into the particulars of the law, it basically disallows a tax deduction to the firm and imposes an excise tax of 20 percent on the executive for parachute payments that equal or exceed 300 percent of the executive's annual gross income in any of the five preceding taxable years. Parachute payments include stock options and other forms of property transfers.

Effects Upon Compensation Objectives

Golden parachutes are effective at providing compensation in the event of a hostile takeover, since that is precisely what they are designed to do. Parachutes do little to meet other objectives, however. They do not reward performance, they offer no income tax relief, they do not protect the organization from an executive entering into competition with the firm after leaving it, and they do little to help the firm achieve external equity, since many, if not most, firms do not have such provisions in their executives' compensation programs.

Flexible Plans

More firms are opting for flexible perquisites that permit executives to choose according to their individual needs. Among such perquisites are family clothing allowances, private school tuition for children, chauffeur-driven automobiles, temporary housing expenses, and stipends for allowances. According to one study, eight percent of firms use flexible perquisites.[13]

Other Executive Benefits/Perquisites

Some perquisites, notably financial counseling, physical examinations, club memberships, and company-provided personal computers for home use, are increasingly provided by employers. Physical examinations are also popular perquisites.

Because of the increasing emphasis upon wellness, firms are becoming more concerned about the health of their executives. One indicator of that concern is the "thousands of executives and professionals" in the U.S. who are receiving thorough, one-day physical examinations, euphemistically referred to as "executive health assessments."[14] For a fee of up to $1,000, executives receive a range of diagnostic services, including body-fat analysis, resistance to fatigue, a blood-chemical analysis, proctoscopy, and cardiovascular analysis. While some may

---

[13] Ibid.

[14] Russell, M. "More Executives Take Special Physicals, But Some Question Their Value and Cost," *Wall Street Journal* (October 6, 1986), p. 33.

question the cost of the benefit, an increasing number of executives are getting these "health assessments," which is evidence enough of their personal concern about health matters.

Retirement Plans

Mandatory Retirement Age

Due to amendments to the Age Discrimination in Employment Act, employers with 20 or more employees cannot establish a mandatory retirement age, except for certain types of occupations or unless there is a bona fide qualification for doing so. One of the exceptions to this law is that it permits organizations to retire executives who have attained the age of 65 and who, for the two-year period immediately prior to such retirement, have been employed in bona fide executive or high policymaking positions. Such executives must also be entitled to an immediate nonforfeitable annual retirement benefit from a pension, profit-sharing, savings, or deferred compensation plan (or any combination of such plans) of at least $44,000.

Nondiscrimination Requirements

A *tax-qualified* retirement plan must be operated for the exclusive benefit of a broad classification of employees and not discriminate in favor of selected groups, such as the firm's executives. Employers cannot implement special plans for executives without considering the retirement needs of other employees, if they want the plans to qualify for income tax deductibility.

Employee Welfare Plans

An *employee welfare plan* is any plan or benefit provided by employers to employees and/or their dependents. Examples of welfare programs include virtually all the types of benefits provided to employees, such as medical benefits, disability benefits, vacation pay, and unemployment insurance. For these plans to be tax-qualified, they cannot discriminate in favor of highly compensated employees.

"Golden Handcuffs"

There are two different definitions for the term *golden handcuffs.* One definition is that a golden handcuff is any compensation plan, such as a bonus for exceptional performance or a perquisite (including the exclusive use of a company-owned airplane) used as an incentive to keep an executive with the firm.

The second, and perhaps more commonly accepted definition, is that a golden handcuff is an employer-imposed condition requiring an executive to defer some direct compensation to a later date, with the further requirement that the amount will be forfeited should the executive leave the organization before that date. Usually, such provisions, if agreed to by the parties, are contained in the employment contract. These provisions can be applied to any form of compensation, not just bonuses.

The rationale for golden handcuffs is that they help maintain stability in executive jobs, and they provide an incentive for executives to remain with the firm. This explanation seems appropriate for the first definition and, few would argue with it. Critics of the second definition contend that the term "handcuffs" aptly describe what they do to an executive. The opposition further believes that, rather than an incentive to stay with a firm, golden handcuffs, are a disincentive to leaving, resulting in an unhappy executive, shackled to a job that he or she does not want.

CHAPTER 28
PAY STRUCTURE MANAGEMENT

Chapter Highlights
- Discussing the process of developing a pay structure
- Studying how to develop a pay line
- Incorporating external pay data in an internal pay structure

Introduction

How important is the pay structure in an organization? Perhaps no other component of the employment relationship is more important than an equitable pay structure to build employee loyalty and trust.[1]

A *pay structure* is a method an organization uses to determine the monetary value of work performed by employees.

Different structures may be used to compensate different types of work. Commission structures, for example, are often used to compensate salespeople, and bonus and incentive stock arrangements are used with executives. Executive pay methods are covered in Chapter 27. Union members are typically compensated with pay structures achieved through collective bargaining. Union-management negotiated pay structures are included in Chapter 36. Some pay methods, such as gainsharing plans and overseas service premiums, are used in addition to basic pay structures. International pay is included in Chapter 38, and gainsharing plans are covered in Chapter 30.

Developing a Pay Structure

The process of developing a pay structure includes a consideration of these variables:

- Internal and external equity;
- Type of structure;
- Relation of pay grades to the job evaluation system and/or to a market-integrated or market-based system;
- Width of the pay range for the minimum and maximum rates of pay in each pay grade;
- Number of structures;
- Contingencies for knowledge, skills, or competencies; or
- Rewards for team effort.

---

[1] Mullen, James X., "What's fair?" *Adweek* Vol. 36, No. 20 (May 15, 1995); p. 49.

The Goal of Equity

Equity is the perceived fairness of the intrinsic and extrinsic rewards that employees receive in exchange for the work they do. *Internal equity* is the goal of reward systems, designed to ensure that employees are equitably rewarded for their work within the organization. The objective of *job evaluation* and *contingency-based* pay structures is to achieve internal equity in the evaluation of job worth. The goal of *external equity* is to ensure that the organization's compensation programs are competitive with the compensation of other employers in the labor market. Employers use market compensation surveys to help them achieve external equity. Internal methods of establishing pay structures, combined with market surveys, are used by employers to achieve both internal and external forms of equity.

Type of Structure

The pay structures covered in this chapter are:

1. Job evaluation-based;
2. Market-based;
3. Job evaluation and market-based; and
4. Contingency-based.

Job Evaluation-Based Structure

The methods of job evaluation are described in Chapter 26. In this chapter, pay structures derived from the factor, point, and classification methods of job evaluation are described.

Factor Pay Structure

In the factor evaluation method, a *factor value scale* is developed, which contains the monetary values of the compensable factors for key jobs. In organizations with the factor method of job evaluation, the factor value scale is the pay structure for determining the pay for all jobs. Exhibit 28-1 is an example of a factor value scale, with the monetary values for each factor for 11 key jobs.[2] Exhibit 28-2 shows the total hourly pay and the monetary value of each compensable factor for the 11 jobs.

---

[2] The process involved in creating a *factor value scale* is covered in Chapter 26.

Exhibit 28-1
Factor Value Scale
Factor Job Evaluation

	Compensable Factor			
Value	*Skill*	*Effort*	*Responsibility*	*Working Conditions*
.50	Laborer			
1.00		Truck Driver	Laborer	
1.50	Janitor			
2.00		Laborer	Janitor	Supply Assistant
2.50	Truck Driver			
3.00	Forklift Operator	Janitor		
3.50			Truck Driver	
4.00	Computer Assistant	Forklift Operator	Computer Assistant	Forklift Operator
4.50		Computer Assistant		
5.00	Secretary	Printer	Forklift Operator	Janitor
5.50		Supply Assistant		Truck Driver
6.00	Supply Assistant		Secretary	Human Res. Dir.
6.50		Secretary	Electrician	Secretary
7.00	Printer		Accountant	Accountant
7.50	Accountant	Electrician		
8.00	Electrician		Supply Assistant	Laborer
8.50		Accountant		Computer Assistant
9.00				Printer
9.50	Human Res. Dir.			
10.00			Printer	Electrician
10.50		Human Res. Dir.		
11.00			Human Res. Dir.	
11.50				

**Exhibit 28-2
Hourly Monetary Values
Factor Job Evaluation**

Benchmark Job	$ Monetary Value for Compensable Factor				$ Hourly Rate
	Skill	Effort	Responsibility	Working Conditions	
Laborer	.50	2.00	1.00	8.00	11.50
Janitor	1.50	3.00	2.00	5.00	11.50
Truck Driver	2.50	1.00	3.50	5.50	12.50
Forklift Operator	3.00	4.00	5.00	4.00	16.00
Computer Assistant	4.00	4.50	4.00	8.50	21.00
Secretary	5.00	6.50	6.00	6.50	24.00
Supply Assistant	6.00	5.50	8.00	2.00	21.50
Printer	7.00	5.00	10.00	9.00	31.00
Accountant	7.50	8.50	7.00	7.00	30.00
Electrician	8.00	7.50	6.50	10.00	32.00
Human Resource Director	9.50	10.50	11.00	6.00	37.00

To determine the pay for a non-key job, the job in question is analyzed to determine the extent to which the compensable factors are present. The factor value scale is used to compare the monetary value of each factor, one at a time, in the non-key job with those in the key jobs. The comparison narrows to several key jobs; the tasks of these jobs are compared to those of the non-key job. The objective is to select the key job with tasks having the same compensable worth as the non-key job. Once that objective is accomplished, the "$ monetary value" for the factor is selected from the Factor Value Scale in Exhibit 28-1, above. The same process is repeated for each compensable factor. The dollar value of the non-key job is determined by totalling these monetary values.

EXAMPLE: The information in Exhibit 28-1 was developed for ABC Company. The new job of Warehouse Supervisor has been established, and a rate of pay for the job needs to be determined. The job is analyzed, and general information is obtained, pertaining to the four compensable factors. This compensable factor information for the Warehouse Supervisor job is subjectively compared with relative amounts of the compensable factors in key jobs in the Factor Value Scale at Exhibit 28-1, above. Assume that the skill required for the Warehouse Supervisor job is concluded to be comparable to the skill required for the job of Accountant, so that $7.50 is selected for the Skill factor. The Effort factor in the Warehouse Supervisor job does not completely fit any of the key jobs, since it appears to be somewhat less than that in the job of Electrician, but more than a Secretary, $7.00 is selected. Responsibility of the job is on the same level with the job of Supply Assistant, so that $8.00 is selected. Finally, working conditions in the Warehouse Supervisor job are believed to be more than that of an Accountant but less than a Computer Assistant, so that $7.50 is selected.

Adding the four values ($7.50 + $7.00 + $8.00 + $7.50) equals $30.00, which is the hourly pay for the Warehouse Supervisor job.

Point Pay Structure

Pay structures that are established with both the point and the classification methods of job evaluation entail the use of pay grades.

A *pay grade* is a single plateau in a pay structure with a pay range. A *pay range* is the minimum and maximum dollar amounts in a pay grade. A *pay grade number* is a unique number assigned to each pay grade.

Sometimes, in addition to minimum and maximum levels of pay, a midpoint value of pay is also shown for each pay grade. Graded pay structures are either *stepped,* like the sample structure shown in Exhibit 28-3, or *unstepped,* with only minimum and maximum amounts of pay in the structure, as in the example in Exhibit 28-4.

Exhibit 28-3
Sample Graded Pay Grade Structure (Stepped)

Pay Grade	1	2	3	4	5	6	7	8	9	10	11
1	$12,038	$12,439	$12,480	$13,241	$13,642	$14,043	$14,444	$14,845	$15,246	$15,647	$16,048
2	13,513	13,963	14,413	14,863	15,313	15,763	16,213	16,663	17,113	17,563	18,013
3	15,118	15,622	16,126	16,630	17,134	17,638	18,142	18,646	19,150	19,654	20,158
4	16,851	17,413	17,975	18,537	19,099	19,661	20,233	20,785	21,347	21,909	22,471
5	18,726	19,350	19,974	20,598	21,222	21,846	22,470	23,094	23,718	24,342	24,966
6	20,739	21,430	22,121	22,812	23,503	24,194	24,885	25,576	26,267	26,958	27,649
7	22,907	23,671	24,423	25,199	25,963	26,727	27,491	28,255	29,019	29,783	30,547
8	25,226	26,067	26,908	27,749	28,590	29,431	30,272	31,113	31,954	32,795	33,636
9	27,716	28,640	29,564	30,488	31,412	32,336	33,260	34,184	35,108	36,032	39,956
10	33,218	34,325	35,432	36,539	37,646	37,753	39,860	40,967	42,074	43,181	44,288
11	39,501	40,818	42,135	43,452	44,769	46,086	47,403	48,720	50,037	51,354	52,671
12	46,679	48,235	49,791	51,347	52,930	54,459	56,015	57,471	59,127	60,683	62,239
13	54,907	56,737	58,567	60,397	62,227	64,057	65,887	67,717	69,547	71,377	73,207
14	64,397	66,544	68,691	70,838	72,500	73,660	75,765	77,870	79,975	82,080	84,185
15	73,958	76,423	78,888	81,353	83,818	86,283	88,748	91,213	93,678	96,143	98,608

Exhibit 28-4
Sample Graded Pay Structure
(Unstepped)

Pay Grade	Pay Range	
	Minimum	Maximum
1	$12,038	$15,647
2	13,513	17,565
3	15,118	19,654
4	16,851	21,909
5	18,726	24,342
6	20,739	26,958
7	22,907	29,783
8	25,226	32,795
9	27,716	36,032
10	33,218	43,181
11	39,501	51,354
12	46,679	60,683
13	54,907	71,377
14	64,397	82,440

A pay structure for the *point* method of job evaluation consists of a table of points in increasing intervals corresponding to commensurate increases in pay grades, as shown in Exhibit 28-5.

To determine the pay grade, the following steps would be taken:

1. The job would be analyzed;
2. The tasks in the job would be compared with each of the levels and/or degrees of the compensable factors in the point system used,
3. The appropriate number of points would be selected,
4. The points selected for each compensable factor would be totalled, and
5. The points would be converted to a pay grade, using a conversion chart similar to the one in Exhibit 28-5.[3]

---

[3] An explanation of the processes involved in the point system of job evaluation is covered in Chapter 26.

Exhibit 28-5
Point/Grade Conversion
Table

Pay Grade	Job Evaluation Points	
	Minimum	*Maximum*
1	190	250
2	255	450
3	455	650
4	655	850
5	855	1,100
6	1,105	1,350
7	1,355	1,600
8	1,605	1,850
9	1,855	2,100
10	2,105	2,350
11	2,355	2,750
12	2,755	3,150
13	3,155	3,600
14	3,605	4,050
15	4,055	up

Classification Pay Structure

Organizations using the *classification* method of job evaluation have graded pay structures. Some of these organizations use points for determining pay grades; other organizations determine the pay grade for jobs by using compensable factor descriptions for each grade. Exhibit 28-6 is an example of a grade description for a hypothetical Pay Grade 5 in a classification pay structure with these five compensable factors: *Knowledge Required, Supervision Required, Work Complexity, Personal Contacts,* and *Work Environment.*

Exhibit 28-6
Example of a Pay Grade Description

Pay Grade: 5

Knowledge Required

Knowledge of basic principles, concepts and methodology of an administrative occupation, and skill in applying this knowledge in completing elementary assignments.

Supervision Required

Administrative direction in broadly defined missions or functions.

Work Complexity

Varied duties, requiring many different and unrelated processes and methods applied to a broad range of tasks.

Personal Contacts

Personal contacts with employees in the immediate job vicinity. Contacts with the public or other parties in highly structured situations.

Work Environment

Simple risks of a daily nature requiring normal precautions. Environment adequately lighted with sufficient ventilation and heat and cooling.

If the pay structure has 15 pay grades, there would be separate pay grade descriptions for each of the 15 grades. The pay for a job is determined by analyzing the job, preparing short summaries of the amount of each compensable factor required in the job, and comparing these summaries to the pay grade descriptions. The appropriate pay grade for a job is the highest one in which the grade descriptions for all the compensable factors are met.

Market-Based Pay Structure

A *market-based pay structure* contains job titles and "level of pay" in the market that the employer decides to pay his or her employees. Pay for the same type of jobs differs among employers in a labor market; furthermore, the pay ranges for these jobs also typically differ among firms. One firm in a market area may have the lowest minimum level of pay for a job but may have a higher-than-average midpoint or maximum pay level because it has a higher-than-average factor used in calculating minimum to maximum pay. An employer considers these factors in deciding upon the level of pay in the market used to establish a pay structure.

As discussed in Chapter 25, the manner in which a firm responds to labor market influences in setting pay is decided in strategic compensation planning. Among the important factors included in this decisionmaking process are:

- *The organization's ability to pay.* Obviously, some firms are more profitable than others, so that they are among the top-paying employers in the market.

- *Competition in the market for qualified applicants.* The supply and demand for applicants by firms in a labor market area vary over time. For example, in a certain year, the supply of teachers may far exceed the demand in a metropolitan area; thus, the existing starting pay was sufficient to recruit teachers for the school system. However, five years later, the supply of teachers seeking employment may be insufficient to meet the demand, primarily if a smaller number of new teachers graduated from the state's colleges. This would prompt that school system to significantly increase starting pay in order to recruit the minimum number of new teachers needed.

- *The importance of a job to the employer.* There are situations in which a particular job may have extreme importance to an organization. For example, if an organization is entering a new market, it may be necessary to have a starting rate of pay that is the same or even above the top-paying firms, in order to recruit "essential" personnel to lead the effort to gain entrance into the new market.

- *The image that the employer wants to communicate.* A firm may define a long-term image for pay and benefits that it wants to communicate to the market, such as having the best employee benefits program or paying top-dollar salaries in the community. There may be many reasons for cultivating such an image, including the perception of the company as an asset to the community, the recruitment of new employees, and morale-building for employees, who see themselves working for an organization that is highly regarded in the community.

Some of the tasks involved in conducting and analyzing pay survey data include obtaining and arranging survey information in a format suitable for decisionmaking purposes.[4] For example, assume that Firm ABC conducts a pay survey to determine what other employers in the market area are paying their Human Resource Directors. A hypothetical report of pay information obtained from the 15 employers who responded to the survey is shown in Exhibit 28-7. For comparison purposes, Firm ABC's pay is shown in the bottom row.

The data in Exhibit 28-7, while important, can be analyzed and/or arranged in different formats to make it more valuable for decisionmaking purposes in preparing a pay structure.

---

[4] The process of planning and conducting pay surveys is covered in Chapter 25.

Exhibit 28-7
Hypothetical Results of Market Pay Survey

Results of Pay Survey for Human Resource Director
Array of Respondent Firms

Respondent (Coded)	Yearly Pay		
	Minimum	Midpoint	Maximum
1	$33,218	$42,352	$51,487
2	35,432	51,198	59,731
3	36,539	45,260	53,981
4	37,646	45,551	53,457
5	38,232	47,790	57,348
6	39,860	48,828	57,797
7	39,900	51,870	63,840
8	40,137	47,160	54,184
9	40,834	52,063	63,292
10	41,525	53,982	66,440
11	42,665	51,198	59,731
12	44,769	55,961	67,153
13	50,377	61,711	73,046
14	63,587	81,073	98,559
15	67,117	78,862	90,607
Mean (En÷N)	43,455	54,323	64,710
Median	40,137	51,870	63,292
Firm ABC's Pay Range	37,200	46,035	54,870

One method of analysis is to compare the organization's existing minimum, midpoint, and maximum pay for the surveyed job with the *arithmetic means* or the *medians* for the same three figures in the data set.[5] As shown in the second and the third rows from the bottom in Exhibit 28-7, the means for the minimum, midpoint, and maximum values in the pay ranges shown are, respectively:

 $43,455 $54,323 $64,710

The three median values, as shown in the Exhibit, are:

 $40,137 $51,870 $63,292

Presently, ABC Firm's pay range for Human Resource Director is $37,200—$54,870, with a midpoint of $46,035. Assume the employer decides to use the market midpoint pay figure for comparison purposes. The question is, which market midpoint figure should be selected? The median figure ($51,870) indicates that seven firms paid more than this and seven other firms paid less. Selecting this figure as a benchmark would require the employer to increase the existing pay for the job by $5,825 dollars. If the arithmetic mean was selected, the pay would have to be increased $8,288, or an additional $2,463 dollars above the median value.

Instead of using averages, the employer may want to see a more detailed analysis of how the pay for Firm ABC's Human Resource Director compares to other firms. One way to do this would be to arrange the data by quartiles or quintiles. This might also be done, for example, if the employer wanted to compensate the Human Resource Director within a certain percentile of the market, such as among the top 40 percent of firms. Exhibit 28-8 contains quintile data for the 15 firms.

Would an employer want to use the same market reckoning point in setting pay for all jobs? The answer is, "Not necessarily," due to the four factors in strategic compensation planning mentioned above. In other words, a firm may be required to offer pay at the top end of the market scale, if necessary, in order to attract and retain talent for the firm to succeed. Due to economic reasons, however, the employer may not be able to adopt the same pay posture for all jobs. The result would be that the pay for some jobs might lead the market, while pay in other jobs might lag, and the pay in the remaining jobs might be relatively even with the average of the market.

---

[5] The formula for the mean is the familiar mean = $\Sigma n \div N$. The median is the middle in an array of numbers arranged from the lowest to the highest value. It is a good idea to compute both values to see if there is a significant difference between them. For further discussion on this subject, see Kerlinger, Fred N. *Foundations of Behavioral Research* (New York: Holt, Rinehart and Winston, Inc., 1973).

Exhibit 28-8
Quintiles of Pay Survey Means
Hypothetical Example

Results of Pay Survey Averaged[1] and Arrayed by Quintiles

Job	Lowest			Second			Middle			Fourth			Highest			Firm ABC's Pay Range		
	Min.	*Midpt.*	*Max.*	*Min.*	*Midpt.*	*Max.*	*Min.*	*Midpt.*	*Max.*	*Min.*	*Midpt.*	*Max.*	*Min.*	*Midpt.*	*Max.*	*Min.*	*Midpt.*	*Max.*
HRDir	35063	46270	55066	38069	47389	56200	40290	50364	60438	42986	53713	64441	60360	73882	87404	37200	46035	54870

[1] Pay for the 15 firms was arranged in an array, then grouped into quintiles. The values (minimum, midpoint, and maximum) in each quintile were averaged. The results in the Exhibit are the averages.

The judgments involved in establishing pay structures, from obtaining market data to the problems in designing and conducting market surveys, such as getting accurate responses from other firms (as discussed in Chapter 25), are two of the main reasons that market pay structures are so challenging to develop and use.

Job Evaluation and Market-Based Pay Structure

The principal reason that employers adjust their job evaluation systems to reflect pay in the market is to ensure that they are externally equitable. Pay structures for different job evaluation systems that are market-based share a common feature and differ somewhat in other aspects. This common feature is the inclusion of *key* or *benchmark* jobs for obtaining market pay data.[6] The differences are due to the unique features of different job evaluation methods. One such difference is the manner in which the key job survey results are used in the factor, point, and classification methods of job analysis.

Factor Job Evaluation Method

Key jobs are used to prepare the factor value scale. If internal equity is the only consideration, the existing pay for the key jobs is used to prepare the scale. If the structure is to be market-based, however, the market pay for the jobs is obtained through a survey and the results, such as the midpoint pay levels, may be used to prepare the scale. The pay for the non-key jobs is calculated, using the scale values as reckoning points. The objective of this approach is a system that is externally based and internally equitable.

Point and Classification Job Evaluation Methods

The objective of incorporating market pay data with the point and classification methods of job evaluation is to recalibrate the pay ranges in the pay grades, so that the pay structure is externally equitable. This is accomplished by using key jobs, as described previously. Typically, a key job from each pay grade is included in the survey.

Establishing pay structures that incorporate market pay data with the point and classification methods of job evaluation is somewhat more involved than for the factor method. The two main reasons for this situation are: (1) several outcomes from survey data may complicate the way in which the information is used; and (2) market pay information must be integrated with the internal pay grade structure.

Market Outcomes

It would be quite helpful if the outcomes from a market survey could be neatly incorporated in the organization's existing pay structure; unfortunately, that is not likely to occur for two reasons. First, some jobs that are evaluated higher than others in the firm may be ranked lower than those same jobs in the market. This situation concerns the positioning of the *relative monetary worth* of

---

[6] The use of key jobs in job evaluation is discussed in Chapter 26.

the jobs within the firm, as compared to the positioning of them in the market. This outcome is depicted in the hypothetical information shown in Exhibit 28-9.

EXAMPLE: Assume that Firm ABC used the pay grade midpoints in its existing pay structure to convert the market survey pay information (the market pay figures in Exhibit 28-9 are the arithmetic means of the midpoints of the responding firms) to the firm's pay structure. This is accomplished by converting the survey midpoint pay for each job to the pay grade with the closest midpoint in the firm's pay structure. This is done to discern any differences in how the jobs in the survey would be graded in the market compared to the firm. Exhibit 28-9 shows the pay grade rankings for 15 key jobs for both Firm ABC and the market. Several differences are apparent. Janitor is ranked in the lowest pay grade for Firm ABC, but it is next to the lowest in the respondent firms. Conversely, Shipper is in a higher pay grade in Firm ABC than in the rest of the market.

When these types of differences occur, some decisions must be made. Should the job's existing pay grade be maintained, or should it be modified to be more consistent with the market? In making these decisions, consideration should be given to the source of the differences. For example, the differences may be due to incorrect job evaluations. On the other hand, compensation surveys are difficult to conduct. Problems, such as determining whether the tasks in the jobs of the respondent firms are comparable with those in the firm and/or whether the firms providing pay information are representative of the market, may affect the validity of survey outcomes. Obviously, the greater the inconsistencies between a firm's evaluation of job worth and the market pay for the same jobs, the greater the need to investigate the cause.

Another common outcome is when the firm's pay for one or more jobs is significantly different from the pay for equivalent jobs in the market. Once again, when differences occur, some decisions must be made, including investigating the cause and determining whether to conduct additional job evaluations or further analyze the survey results.

Exhibit 28-9
Comparison of Market and Firm ABC's Pay and Pay Grades for Key Jobs
Hypothetical Example

Job Title	Pay Grade		$ Annual Pay	
	Firm ABC	Market	Firm ABC	Market
Laborer	2	1	14663	14043
Janitor	1	2	12935	15763
Mail Clk	4	3	18844	17638
Elec. Helper	3	4	16623	19661
Picker	5	5	21361	21846
Packer	6	6	24216	24194
Shipper	8	7	31119	26727
Driver	7	8	27451	29431
Forklift Operator	9	9	35227	32336
Analyst	10	10	39991	37753
Senior Analyst	11	11	45334	46086
Buyer	12	12	51391	54459
Engineering Dir.	14	13	66042	64057
Accounting Dir.	13	14	58258	73660
Human Res. Dir.	15	15	74866	86283

Integrating Market Pay Data

Integrating market pay data into the pay grades for the firm's existing pay structure begins by preparing tabular and graphical comparisons of the pay structure and the survey data. Exhibit 28-10 is a comparison of the midpoint values for both the firm and the data from the survey. As shown in the "Difference" column, the firm pays less than the market rate from pay grades 1 to 5; however, beginning with pay grade 6, the firm's pay is progressively greater, until pay grade 10, when the trend is reversed and the market pay becomes progressively greater. Thus, the firm pays significantly more than the market for pay grades 8 through 10 but pays significantly less in grades 1 through 3 and 12 through 15. The firm's pay is considerably below the market for the latter four grades, particularly grade 15.

Exhibit 28-10
Comparison of Firm and Market Pay
Hypothetical Example

Pay Grade	Annual Pay		Difference
	Firm	Market	
1	12935	14043	−1108
2	14663	15763	−1099
3	16623	17638	−1015
4	18844	19661	−817
5	21361	21846	−484
6	24216	24194	22
7	27451	26727	725
8	31119	29431	1689
9	35227	32336	2942
10	39991	37753	2238
11	45334	46086	−751
12	51391	54459	−3067
13	58258	64057	−5798
14	66042	73660	−7617
15	74866	86283	−11416

As noted above, the existing pay structure and survey pay data is also graphed, so that the pay lines can be viewed and compared, and decisions may be made about which analytical models (curvilinear or linear) to use in testing for the best fit and symmetry. Often, scatter diagrams, such as the one shown in Exhibit 28-11, are used to graphically depict the general relationship of pay grades and monetary values. The scatter diagram in Exhibit 28-11 is a plot of pay grades and corresponding midpoint pay from the market data shown in Exhibit 28-10.

Exhibit 28-11

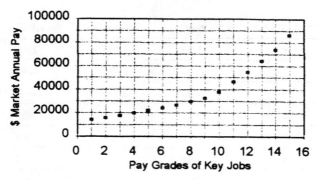

Scatter Diagram of Market Pay Survey
15 Key Jobs

Exhibit 28-12, which is simply a line connecting the data points in the scatter diagram, graphically depicts monetary worth gradually increasing as the pay grade increases to about pay grade 9. Above pay grade 9, however, the monetary worth increases more sharply as the pay grade increases. Typically, pay lines do curve upward, since pay amounts increase at a greater rate at higher pay grades. A straight line would mean the percentage change in pay is the same for all pay grades.

Exhibit 28-12

Market Pay Survey Results
15 Key Jobs

A *pay line* is a graphical depiction of the relationship between monetary pay and pay grades.

The next step in integrating market pay data in a firm's pay structure is to compare the firm's existing pay line with a pay line using the survey results.

Exhibit 28-13, which is a plot of the firm's pay grades and corresponding midpoint pay shown in Exhibit 28-10, is the pay line for the existing pay structure.

Exhibit 28-13

Firm ABC Pay Grade Payline

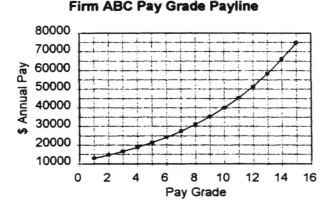

Exhibit 28-14 is a comparison of the pay line for the existing structure and the pay line from the survey. This graph depicts the differences shown in Exhibit 28-10.

Exhibit 28-14

Comparison of Firm and Market Paylines

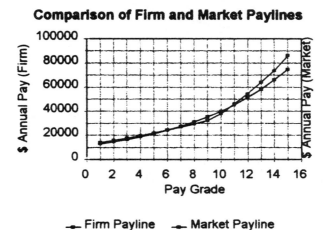

Finally, a pay structure is prepared after the market data is obtained, converted to pay grades for the key jobs, and any significant problems are corrected. The objective is to develop a structure that is consistent with the employer's pay objectives, such as internal and external equity and symmetry. To accomplish competing considerations mandates some compromises, since a pay structure cannot be symmetrical if a decision is made to increase the pay in all the middle pay grades (such as pay grades 6 through 10) 15 percent above the market midpoint, but to keep the top one-third of the pay grades at the market midpoint.

How is a final pay structure developed? The first step would be to prepare a pay line that best fits the employer's objectives. For ease of illustration, assume that the employer of Firm ABC decides to make an initial effort to develop a pay structure, using the midpoint pay data obtained from the survey. However, the employer wants the pay line changed so that the largest differences in the firm's and the survey's pay grades can be reduced.[7]

This decision can be accomplished by smoothing the survey data, using an exponential model. Exhibit 28-15 shows the effects of the exponential smoothing of the survey data. How well does the exponential pay line compare to the existing pay structure? Actually, as shown in Exhibit 28-15, the two curves are quite similar, and the exponential pay line does correct for most of the major differences in the firm's and survey's pay grades.

Exhibit 28-15

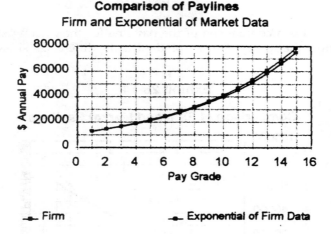

Comparison of Paylines
Firm and Exponential of Market Data

Assuming that the employer of Firm ABC accepts the exponential smoothing, the next step in developing the pay structure is to convert the midpoints of the exponential pay line to pay grades.[8] The completed pay structure for Firm ABC is shown in Exhibits 28-16 and 28-17.

---

[7] The data shown in Exhibit 28-9 is realistic of what could result from a pay survey. That is, an employer may compensate some jobs higher and others lower than other firms in the market. Typically, an employer may have valid reasons for bringing the pay of some jobs closer in line with the market while permitting the pay of others to vary from it. As noted previously, this may be due to a variety of reasons, such as internal equity or a unique condition within the firm. The assumption that an employer would use the entire results of a survey to develop a pay structure is, therefore, un-

realistic, but it is done here to simplify how a pay structure is developed using an employer's objectives and market data.

[8] Other changes could be made to make the pay line more consistent with the employer's objectives. This would simply entail changing the pay in one or more pay grades and using the exponential model to smooth the pay line. All the modeling and calculations in these examples were done with relative ease using *Quatro-Pro* software. Other spreadsheet programs can also accomplish the same work.

Pay Range: Minimum-Maximum

An issue in developing pay structures is how wide the range should be from the minimum to the maximum pay in each grade. The pay range percentages for the various levels in Exhibit 28-16 are realistic of what could be expected with a curvilinear pay line. The lowest one-third of the pay levels would typically have a 25- to 35-percent difference from the minimum to the maximum in the pay range. These percentages would increase to about 40 to 50 percent for the middle pay grades, moving up to 55 to 70 percent in the top pay grades.

Exhibit 28-16
Firm ABC's New Pay Structure
Hypothetical Example

Pay Grade	Annual Pay			% Max/Min
	Minimum	Midpoint	Maximum	
1	11578	13120	14692	1.27
2	13014	14910	16823	1.29
3	14628	16944	19263	1.32
4	16442	19255	22058	1.34
5	18482	21881	25258	1.37
6	20774	24866	28922	1.39
7	23350	28257	33117	1.42
8	26247	32112	37921	1.44
9	29502	36492	43442	1.47
10	33161	41470	49721	1.50
11	37274	47126	56934	1.53
12	41897	53554	65193	1.56
13	47094	60859	74651	1.59
14	52935	69161	85480	1.61
15	59501	78595	97880	1.65

Exhibit 28-17

Firm ABC Pay Line (Market Adjusted)
Hypothetical Model

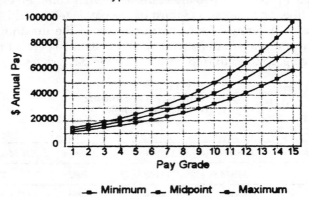

How Many Pay Structures?

   How many pay structures should an organization have? Separate structures can be prepared for different types of work, such as clerical/administrative, sales, scientific and professional, maintenance and skilled, managerial, and executive. In organizations with unionized employees, there might be separate structures for different bargaining groups.

   The obvious problem with multiple pay structures is the difficulty in maintaining internal equity among the jobs in different structures. Another problem is the expense of maintaining multiple structures; that is, changing all of the structures when one or more other structures change. In spite of these problems, there may be valid reasons for multiple structures in some organizations. For example, a municipality might want separate structures for fire fighter personnel, law enforcement personnel, and school teachers. These structures might be separate from and in addition to a fourth structure, which would be set up to cover all other jobs in the municipality.

   Some factors to consider in deciding the number of pay structures that are necessary include:

   • *The differential from highest- to lowest-paid employee.* This ratio would be computed for those jobs that historically have been compensated with the same pay structure. If the ratio is greater than 15, consideration should be given to a second pay structure. Jobs at the executive level of management would be excluded, since they invariably are paid under very different arrangements from non-executives.[9]

---

[9] These methods include special bonuses, stock options, and long-term forms of pay that are often restricted to the executive fulfilling specific require- ments. Executive compensation is covered in Chap- ter 27.

- *The number of pay grades to be included in one pay structure.* The larger the number, such as more than 30, the greater the likelihood that more than one pay structure is needed.

- *Whether special arrangements, in addition to the basic pay structure, may be used to reward employees.* For example, a basic pay structure that includes sales personnel could apply to all employees, if any extraordinary forms of sales compensation were calculated through an "add-on" algorithm.

- *The implementation of broadbanding or contingency-based pay structures.* Career broadbanding, which is discussed below, typically necessitates multiple pay structures. Also, contingency-based pay, such as competency-, knowledge-, or skill-based pay plans, involves multiple structures.

In the United States, the emphasis is on reducing the number of traditional hierarchical pay structures, and replacing them with contingency-based structures, such as skill-based plans. The U.S. is also experiencing a trend toward reducing the number of pay grades as broadbanding gains more acceptance. In other parts of the world, the trend is toward more pay structures. For example, researchers found that 70 percent of the 57 private sector firms that were studied in the United Kingdom had more than one pay structure, with the majority of them having two or three.[10]

Broadbanding

What is broadbanding, why is it used, and when is it appropriate to use a broadbanded structure?

Broadbanding is a pay structure with either: (1) a smaller number of pay grades with large pay ranges, called a pay grade broadband, or (2) a separate pay band for several occupational groups or families in which all jobs are categorized, called a career broadband.

Pay Grade Broadband. A *pay grade broadband* is a pay structure with a small number of pay grades (typically, about five) and a maximum amount of pay in each grade that is from one to two times the pay of the minimum. A broadband structure might be thought of as collapsing a multi-graded structure, with 15 or more grades, into five grades. For example, a broadband pay structure for the structure in Exhibit 28-3 might look like this:

Pay Grade	Minimum Pay	Maximum Pay
1	12,038	27,649
2	16,485	36,956
3	22,907	54,671
4	33,218	79,207
5	46,679	96,143

---

[10] n.a. Collective bargaining and pay determination levels: a survey. *IRS Employment Review.* No. 601 (February 1996): pp. 4-9.

In the traditional pay structure, salary increases within a pay grade are typically based upon length of service or, in some cases, upon job performance, such as in a merit pay system. Movement within a broadbanded pay grade, on the other hand, is typically based upon the acquisition of additional skills, knowledge, or competencies.[11] Thus, broadbanding results from rethinking the reward system and not just from the mechanical process of compressing multiple pay grades into a few grades.

This revision of the method of rewards is perhaps the most significant advantage of broadbanding. It motivates employees to refocus their attention from job tenure or the often nebulous concept of "merit" to more tangible outcomes, such as increasing their job knowledge, and, thus, increasing the value of their contributions to the organization. Among the other advantages of a pay grade broadband is the ease of pay structure maintenance; that is, only five grades need to be changed when the structure is redesigned, rather than 15. Also, requests from employees to have their jobs re-evaluated are infrequent, since each pay grade consists of at least three times the number of pay grades that exist in the typical pay structure. Finally, there is less need for re-evaluation requests, since employees can progress within their respective grades by achieving the requisite milestones.

Career Broadband. In the traditional pay structure, each job (though not each position) is assigned to a pay grade, based upon either the internal worth of the job tasks determined by the organization's job evaluation system or the external worth of the job, based upon what other employers in the labor market are paying for the same work. Through a third approach, which is the typical model, the internal job evaluation scheme is adjusted for external market conditions. Job tasks, not the person(s) who perform the tasks, are the focus of all three of these approaches. Multiple pay grades provide decisionmakers with several alternatives in order to compensate the tasks in the job. Determining the internal and/or external equity of the pay for each job is the objective.

In the *career broadband* pay structure, each broad occupational group or category of jobs is placed in a separate pay grade. For example, a pay structure was changed in a credit union, and the number of pay grades were reduced from 22 to four. The four grades were career-banded into these four occupational groups:

- Member service representatives;
- Lending service representatives;
- Service support staff; and
- Managers.[12]

---

[11] n.a. NIKE pushes the limits with LifeTrek. *Compensation & Benefits Review*, Vol. 27, No. 1 (January/February 1995); pp. 74-76.

[12] Vogt, Peter. Broad bands of pay. *Credit Union Management*, Vol. 19, No. 5 (May 1996); pp. 34-37.

Hypothetically, the pay ranges for these bands might look like this:

Occupational Band	Pay Range (Minimum to Maximum)
Member service representative	$15,000—45,500
Lending service representatives	18,000—52,250
Service support staff	21,500—63,000
Managers	38,000—82,500

Typically, the jobs clustered within a career band range from the basic to the most advanced. The objective of career broadbanded pay structures is to reward employees for what they do or know how to do. This procedure motivates employees who are so inclined to learn how to do more tasks and, thus, be eligible to be paid more. Broadbanding tends to strengthen both intrinsic and extrinsic rewards, since employees are challenged to learn more and be rewarded for it. The emphasis in the broadbanded structure is on *the individual*.

In the typical pay structure, on the other hand, employees are paid for the tasks required in their jobs. To earn more pay for performing tasks at a higher pay grade, employees must be promoted to the higher pay grade. The emphasis in the traditional pay structure is *the job*.

Broadbanding is also used in other countries. Researchers in one study found that seven firms in the United Kingdom successfully used broadbanding to accomplish several goals, including reassigning pay decisionmaking from the human resources management department to line management.[13]

---

[13] Brown, Duncan. Broadbanding: a study of company practices in the United Kingdom. *Compensation and Benefits Review*, Vol. 28, No. 6 (November/December 1996); pp. 41-49.

CHAPTER 29

JOB PERFORMANCE MANAGEMENT

Chapter Highlights
- Understand the dimensions of performance appraisal
- Learn the multiple purposes of performance appraisal
- Review the methods of performance appraisal
- Learn how to design and implement a performance appraisal system

Introduction

Performance appraisal is the process of establishing written standards of performance criteria, telling employees about those standards and frequently informing them how they are performing in relation to them.

Sometimes, the term *performance evaluation* is used either in lieu of or interchangeably with the term performance appraisal. There is growing evidence that performance appraisal of all employees is becoming a top priority today. A national survey of 400 human resource practitioners concluded that performance appraisal was done in 95 percent of the respondents' firms for both managerial and nonmanagerial employees.[1]

Dimensions of Performance Appraisal

These are the five dimensions of performance appraisal:
- The purposes of the system;
- The variables used in the system;
- The appraisal method;
- The design of the system; and
- The procedures used to implement and maintain the system.

Purposes of Performance Appraisal

The purposes of performance appraisal are shown in Exhibit 29-1. Organizations differ in what they attempt to accomplish through performance appraisal.

[1] Bureau of National Affairs, Inc. "SHRM-BNA Survey No. 62: Human Resource Activities, Budgets, and Staffs," 1996-97, *Bulletin to Management* (June 26, 1997).

Exhibit 29-1
Major Purposes of Performance Appraisal

Management Decisions	Employee Information	Customer Service	Stockholder Interests
Pay matters	Performance criteria	Product quality	Return on investment
Personnel actions	Performance feedback	Service	Investment security
Job evaluation	Recognition	Prices	
Training needs	Discipline	Product	
Career planning	Personality development	development	
Employee relations			
Validation			

Management Decisions

Managers use appraisal results to aid their decisionmaking in a number of areas, including making pay increases, implementing personnel actions, conducting job evaluations, determining training needs, conducting career planning for employees, handling employee relations issues, and validating selection methods.

Pay Increases

Planning and implementing pay increases is a major purpose of performance appraisal.

Personnel Actions

Performance appraisal is frequently used to guide management decisionmaking regarding personnel actions, such as transfers and assignments. For example, a reassignment to another job may be necessary if information received through the appraisal system indicates that an employee is performing poorly in his or her present job.

Performance appraisal results are often used in making promotion decisions. However, relying too heavily upon appraisal information in making promotions can result in incorrect decisions. For example, a truck driver whose performance appraisal file indicates that he or she is an outstanding employee may not be able to perform at that same level as a supervisor of truck drivers, since the two jobs require different skills. Using appraisal information in promotion deliberations is proper, provided that it is not given undue consideration. A reasonable approach is to consider performance appraisal results, along with other information developed while evaluating the qualifications of the various candidates for the promotion.

Job Evaluation

A properly evaluated job helps to ensure that there is a reasonable supply of qualified applicants for vacancies, and that such employees will perform well and have relatively stable tenures of employment. The performance appraisal system is also one of the major indicators of whether the pay level for a job is reasonably in accord with the market. The pay for a job may be too low if the appraisal system indicates that too many employees are substandard performers.

Other indicators that the job pay rate is too low are a high turnover rate among employees in that position and few qualified applicants for any vacant positions.

Training Needs

Performance appraisal is used to determine if job training is adequate, to determine training needs, and to plan training activities. Often, employees may perform some of their duties inadequately because they are not properly trained. Performance appraisal information is instrumental in determining whether job skills training and other employer-provided training are effective or whether modifications are needed. A major difficulty with many training programs is determining their effectiveness. Employee performance, as measured through the appraisal system, is one way to evaluate training effectiveness.

Some appraisal methods, such as management by objectives, provide for employee input in planning the training needed to achieve specific objectives during the appraisal period. Usually, this personal appraisal planning also includes defining the developmental activities planned for the year, such as attendance at seminars, college courses, or technical training.

Career Planning

Performance appraisal results are important in career planning because they may be used to help determine an employee's strengths and developmental needs. This information is used in counseling employees and helping them make career decisions. One organization required all employees in the career planning program to maintain discipline-free employment records and receive above-average performance appraisal reports. Employees who were enrolled in the career planning program reported to the career counselor on a regularly scheduled basis to review their accomplishments. This career planning system was an incentive for employees to remain proficient in their jobs.

Employee Relations

There are multiple links between the activities of employee relations and performance appraisal, since grievances, discipline, discharges, and employee attitudes are related to employee performance. Employee job performance is a valid indicator of employee attitudes. For example, studies have demonstrated a relationship between employee attitudes and employee attendance, conduct, safety, and work quality.

Validation

Validation studies are required if adverse impact exists from employment decisions, such as promotions or the selection of applicants for vacant positions. In such situations, tests, interviews, probationary periods, training programs, and other selection procedures must be validated against job performance criteria, including attendance, conduct, productivity, safety, and work quality. The source of this information is the formal performance appraisal system.

Employee Information

Performance appraisal is used to provide information to employees in such areas as the criteria used to measure performance, feedback about the level of performance, recognition for work accomplishment, discipline for failing to meet job requirements, and reinforcement to aid personality development.

Performance Criteria

Giving employees information about criteria that will be used to measure their performance helps to ensure the accomplishment of desired outcomes. This also helps prevent misunderstandings about what is expected. Often, disagreements between supervisors and employees result from such misunderstandings, including the relative priority of work to be accomplished.

Performance Feedback

Appraisal systems provide a convenient basis for informal and formal communication with employees about their performance. Informal communication is composed of the daily discussions with employees on various performance-related topics, such as work quality or attendance. Formal communication consists of scheduled performance appraisal reviews between the supervisor and the employee.

Both informal and formal communication is needed for employees to compare their perceptions of performance requirements with supervisory expectations. Consistent informal feedback prevents "surprises" when formal performance reviews are conducted. Employee unhappiness may cause conflicts and complaints of unfairness to arise when employees are surprised by their supervisors' appraisals. This unhappiness is not restricted to bad appraisals. For example, an employee may be unhappy with a "good" appraisal, when he or she felt the appraisal should have been "excellent." Supervisors unwittingly contribute to such misunderstandings by failing to consistently inform employees about their performance, regardless of the level.

Recognition/Discipline

Performance appraisal systems provide a convenient method of recognizing employee performance, both desired and undesired. Employees receive both intrinsic and extrinsic rewards from work. Intrinsic rewards are those associated with the job tasks, such as task autonomy and task significance. Extrinsic rewards are those received from others, particularly from supervisors, in recognition of the way a task was performed.

A performance appraisal system is requisite for an effective disciplinary system. Through performance appraisal, supervisors set performance standards that are used as the bases of comparison for actual performance. Deficient performance is self-evident, so that employees will exercise self-discipline in adjusting their behavior. The importance of self-assessment is often overlooked or misunderstood in disciplinary systems because of the assumption that discipline is the most effective and economical way of correcting behavior. A performance appraisal system encourages employees to keep their own account of their strengths and deficiencies, so that they can adjust their behavior to conform with expectations. This does not mean that supervisors can ignore the responsibility for employee discipline. However, a self-disciplined workforce reduces the need for supervisory discipline. Furthermore, a performance appraisal system facilitates discipline administered by supervisors because confrontation interviews are more objective and, thus, are less likely to cause arguments.

Personality Development

A content-valid performance appraisal system helps foster personality development and growth. For example, informing employees of performance standards displays human concern. Some appraisal systems, such as management by objectives, allow employees to participate in setting performance standards. This approach treats employees as responsible and self-motivated adults who will exercise responsibility in determining their own goals and objectives. Most employees who are treated as responsible human beings will tend to be responsible in their behavior. Reward systems that are based upon a performance appraisal system that treats employees as responsible human beings build self-confidence and shape future behavior.

Customer Service

Performance appraisal helps to build customer service through a combination of product quality, efficient service delivery, competitive prices, and desired product features. These purposes are typically included in an organization's long-term goals, and a performance appraisal system is one way of accomplishing them. Product quality, for example, depends upon such variables as employees' attention to detail and the motivation to do a thorough job. These and related measures of quality, such as the amount of wasted materials and errors, are tracked, using the performance appraisal system.

Stockholder Interests

Stockholders are concerned about the return on their investment, as reflected in the value of their stock holdings and the security of their investment. These interests are directly dependent upon the productivity of employees and the quality of the product or service they provide, both of which are measured through performance appraisal.

Performance Variables

The second dimension of appraisal systems is comprised of the variables used to set standards and track performance; typical variables include attendance, safety and health, conduct, productivity, and work quality.

Attendance

Attendance is a generic term that includes punctuality, consistency in reporting for work, sick leave usage, and unscheduled absences. Attendance also refers to the presence of the employee at his or her job, instead of prolonged or frequent absences from the job or leaving an assignment without a supervisor's permission.

Safety and Health

Safety and health performance variables focus on how safely an employee performs his or her tasks. Safety involves a concern for personal and coworker safety. Accidents and health hazard exposures are prevented by adhering to work rules, properly using equipment, and following safety procedures.

Conduct

Conduct is a performance variable that covers a range of employee behaviors, including cooperativeness, honesty, appearance, and motivation. If conduct is used in an appraisal system, caution must be exercised to limit an appraiser's subjectivity in judging it. One way to accomplish this is to require supervisors to document critical incidents that are both good and bad examples of an employee's conduct during the appraisal period.

Productivity

Productivity is a measure of an employee's output. Two criteria must exist to adequately measure productivity. First, some standards of output must be adopted. For delivery drivers, this may be the number of parcels delivered. For animal control officers, it could be the number of citizen complaints handled. Regardless of the job, some objective unit of output must be defined before it is possible to measure productivity. Second, output levels must be designated that represent the various categories of performance, ranging from unacceptable to superior. One organization adopted output levels that were so lenient that employees could easily meet daily requirements. Make-shift or soft standards are useless. Sometimes, easy standards are set under the mistaken notion that any standard, even an easy one, is better than none. The reverse, however, is probably better; no standard is better than an easy one. The reason is simple: employees interpret easy standards as management's lack of commitment to productivity. Once standards are established, supervisors can track employees' productivity relative to the standards.

Work Quality

Work quality is a major focus of contemporary management. Excessive rejects, waste, product recalls, and customer complaints are some of the reasons for this concern. Perhaps the two biggest reasons, however, are lawsuits resulting from products that are improperly designed and/or constructed and the increasing foreign competition that has made significant inroads in U.S. basic industries.

Some indicators of work quality are scrap material, reject rates, customer satisfaction, and errors. These measures of quality are largely related to the actual production of the product or service. Other measures of employee efforts towards quality improvement are participation in quality circles and employee ideas for improving product or service quality. There are various ways of appraising work quality, such as defining unit measures of quality, establishing performance levels ranging from unacceptable to exceptional performance, and, finally, keeping score.

Methods of Performance Appraisal

The third dimension of performance appraisal is the appraisal method(s) used in the system. An outline of the most commonly used methods of performance appraisal follows:

- Rating Scales
  - Graphic Rating Scales
  - Weighted Graphic Rating Scales
  - Behaviorally Anchored Rating Scales
  - Behavior Observation Scales
- Ranking
  - Straight Ranking
  - Alternation Ranking
- Checklists
  - Basic Checklist
  - Weighted Checklist
  - Forced-Choice Checklist
- Forced Distribution
- Pair Comparison
- Essay
- Critical Incidents
- Management by Objectives
- Field Review
- Competency-Based
- 360°

Graphic Rating Scales

Of the four types of rating scales, the simplest is the *graphic rating scale (GRS)*. With this method, the appraiser typically notes an employee's performance by circling a number or marking a box. Generally, several performance variables are used, such as productivity, work quality, attendance, job knowledge, cooperation, initiative, and safety. Exhibit 29-2 is an example of a graphic rating scale used for two of these variables.

Exhibit 29-2
Example of a Graphic Rating Scale

ABC Company
Performance Appraisal Form

(Employee)	(Date)	(Supervisor)

Instructions: Use this scale to indicate the level of the employee's performance in each category by circling the appropriate letters.

SE =   ·   Substantially exceeds expectations
EE =   Exceeds expectations
ME =   Meets expectations
BE =   Below expectations
SB =   Substantially below expectations

Productivity
Appraise the output of this employee.	SE	EE	ME	BE	SB

Work Quality
Indicate the quality of work produced.	SE	EE	ME	BE	SB

Safety
Evaluate this employee's safety record.	SE	EE	ME	BE	SB

Conduct
Appraise the employee's conduct.	SE	EE	ME	BE	SB

Attendance
Evaluate the employee's attendance record.	SE	EE	ME	BE	SB

The GRS is the most commonly used method of performance appraisal in the United States, primarily because it is the simplest of all the methods. The main advantages to the GRS are that they are easy to learn, require minimal training, easy to implement, and easy to use. The principal disadvantages of GRS are susceptibility to subjective ratings and rater errors, such as central tendency and the halo/horn effect.

Weighted Graphic Rating Scales

Each performance appraisal variable, such as productivity or quality of work, has equal weight with simple graphic rating scales. Often, this is unrealistic, since some criteria are more important than others. In these cases, it is difficult to obtain employee and supervisory acceptance for GRS because they do not understand why a more important performance variable is given the same weight as other, less significant, ones. *Weighted graphic rating scales (WGRS)*, as shown in Exhibit 29-3, address this problem by assigning a value, or weight, to each variable depending upon its perceived importance.

Exhibit 29-3
Example of a Weighted Graphic Rating Scale

ABC Company
Performance Appraisal Form

(Employee)	(Date)	(Supervisor)

Instructions: Weight the importance of each category as a percentage of 100 percent. Place the percentages in the weight boxes. The combined weights must total 100 percent. Use this scale to indicate the level of the employee's performance in each category by circling the appropriate letters.

SE =	Substantially exceeds expectations
EE =	Exceeds expectations
ME =	Meets expectations
BE =	Below expectations
SB =	Substantially below expectations

Weight						
☐ %	**Productivity** Appraise the output of this employee.	SE	EE	ME	BE	SB
☐ %	**Work Quality** Indicate the quality of work produced.	SE	EE	ME	BE	SB
☐ %	**Safety** Evaluate this employee's safety record.	SE	EE	ME	BE	SB
☐ %	**Conduct** Appraise the employee's conduct.	SE	EE	ME	BE	SB
☐ %	**Attendance** Evaluate the employee's attendance record.	SE	EE	ME	BE	SB
100%						

The advantages of the WGRS are that more important performance criteria can be emphasized and that communication between managers and employees concerning the relative priority of different performance variables is improved. Just as with GRS, WGRS's disadvantages are susceptibility to rater subjectivity and rater errors.

Behaviorally Anchored Rating Scales

Behaviorally anchored rating scales (BARS) are sophisticated modifications of graphic rating scales, in which different scale values in performance areas are "anchored" in explanations or illustrations of "behavior." Exhibit 29-4 is a BARS example for one dimension for the job of employee benefits assistant.

Exhibit 29-4
Example of Performance Dimension in a BARS Appraisal Form
for the Job of Employee Benefits Assistant

ABC Company
Performance Appraisal Form

_____ _____ _____
(Employee) (Date) (Supervisor)

Instructions: Circle the number corresponding to the typical performance of this employee in each job dimension.

Job Dimension: Benefit Planning

7	Independently conducts benefit surveys using the latest survey methods.
6	Keeps current of benefit trends by consulting literature and participating in surveys conducted by others.
5	Attends benefit planning seminars to keep knowledgeable.
4	Forecasts benefit plan needs by projecting trends of historical in-house experiences.
3	Conducts benefit planning in some areas but neglects others, particularly newer programs.
2	Fails to document planning recommendations.
1	Frequently misses important deadlines in submitting benefit plan proposals.

BARS are not necessarily superior to other appraisal methods; however, "anchors" do provide some measure of various levels of performance. The guides would appear to ensure inter-rater reliability, but no research is available to support this opinion.

There are disadvantages to BARS. BARS are complex to construct. Because BARS are job-specific, separate ones must be constructed for each job. A project to develop BARS for every job would be a major undertaking. Prudence would lead one to question the advisability of such a project, since BARS have not proven to be more valid than simpler methods.

Behavioral Observation Scale

A _behavioral observation scale_ (BOS) is similar to BARS in that a behavior is anchored to scale values, except that the frequency of the employee's perform-ance is used by the appraiser to determine which value to select. This gives the appraiser flexibility in selecting the behavior that most appropriately typifies the employee's performance. Like BARS, there are multiple statements within each performance dimension. This is an advantage over the typical graphical rating scales, where the appraiser simply makes a global assessment of an employee's performance in each dimension. Exhibit 29-5 is an example of a BOS for the job dimension of attendance.

Exhibit 29-5
Example of Performance Dimension in a BOS Appraisal
Form

ABC Company
Performance Appraisal Form

(Employee)	(Date)	(Supervisor)

Instructions: Circle the number corresponding to the typical performance of this employee in each job dimension.

Job Dimension: Attendance	Frequency				
	Never				*Always*
Contacts office if late	1	2	3	4	5
Schedules leave in advance	1	2	3	4	5
Returns from lunch and breaks on time	1	2	3	4	5
Reports for work at the scheduled time	1	2	3	4	5

A BOS also requires more time to construct than the simpler graphic rating scales. Also, like BARS, BOSs are job-specific, so that a separate one would have to be prepared for a job dimension dealing with productivity and another dealing with the type of performance and the relative quality of it. Like BARS, a project to develop a BOS for every job would require a significant investment of time. Some performance dimensions, such as attendance or safety, may be the same, or nearly the same, for different jobs, which would make it unnecessary to prepare scales for every dimension.

Ranking Methods

The two ranking methods of performance appraisal are straight ranking and alternation ranking.

Straight Ranking

Straight ranking is an appraisal method characterized by the systematic ordering of employees from best to worst, based upon some single global statement, such as "Rank all employees based upon their overall job performance." The appraiser places each employee's name on a continuum from highest to lowest. Appraisers separately list the names of those employees that they are unable to rank for various reasons, such as those who are newly hired or have recently been assigned to the appraiser. Exhibit 29-6 is an example of a hypothetical straight ranking form.

Exhibit 29-6
Example of a Straight Ranking Appraisal Form

ABC Company
Performance Appraisal Form

_____   _____

     (Date)   (Supervisor)

Instructions: Rank all the employees that you supervise from the highest to the lowest performers, using your opinion of their overall job performance. Use #1 for the best performer, #2 for the next best, and so on. On the reverse of this form, list the name(s) of those employees you are not qualified to rank and explain why.

Rank	Employee Name
#1	
#2	
#3	
.	
.	
.	
.	
.	
.	

Alternation Ranking

Alternation ranking uses the same basic approach as straight ranking, except that the appraiser alternates the ranking, starting with the best employee and then the lowest performing employee, continuing with the second best and the next-to-the-lowest performer. Exhibit 29-7 is an example of a typical alternation ranking form.

Exhibit 29-7
Example of an Alteration Ranking Appraisal Form

ABC Company
Performance Appraisal Form

(Date)	(Supervisor)

Instructions: Alternatively rank all the employees you supervise from the highest to the lowest performers, using your opinion of their *overall job performance*. First, rank the best performer, using #1 at the top of the form. Next, rank your lowest performer, using #1 at the bottom of the form. Continue the process of ranking the next highest and then the next-to-the-lowest performer, until you have ranked all employees. On the reverse of this form, list the name(s) of those employees you are not qualified to rank and explain why.

Rank	Employee Name
Highest #1	
Highest #2	
Highest #3	
.	
.	
.	
#3	
#2	
Lowest #1	

The advantages of ranking methods are:

1. They are simple and easy to use;

2. Appraisers are required to distinguish the best and the worst performers;

3. They help appraisers make clear choices among all of their employees; and

4. They help prevent certain appraiser errors, including central tendency.

Among the principal disadvantages of ranking methods are:

1. They rely upon single measures (global or one variable) of employee performance;

2. They are ineffective for employee development purposes; and

3. They cannot be used to aid employees in performance planning.

Basic Checklist

A checklist is a generic term for three appraisal methods that contain lists of statements indicating various levels of favorable and unfavorable performance.

In the *basic checklist* method, the appraiser reviews the lists of statements and checks those descriptive of the employee. Exhibit 29-8 is an example.

Checklists help correct for rater errors. Other advantages are that the appraiser must read each statement, and they are easy to use and score. As with other appraiser methods, basic checklists have some disadvantages; a good deal of time is required to prepare them, the method does not help employees plan their performance, and it does not provide a basis for regular feedback to employees about their performance.

Exhibit 29-8
Example of a Basic Checklist Appraisal Form for Parcel Delivery Driver

ABC Company
Performance Appraisal Form

(Employee)	(Date)	(Supervisor)

Instructions: Circle all the numbers corresponding to the items that fully describe the employee's job performance.

Number	Item
#1	Obtains customer signatures on delivery receipts.
#2	Operates truck in an unsafe manner.
#3	Does not exceed time limits for breaks and meals.
#4	Requires assistance to complete route deliveries.
#5	Is punctual in attendance.
#6	Submits ideas for improvement of operations.
.	
.	
.	
#10	Makes frequent errors in deliveries

Weighted Checklist

A *weighted checklist* is an appraisal method that entails the use of lists of statements with different assigned weights, representing various levels of favorable and unfavorable performance. One procedure for weighting statements is to prepare a list of various performance levels for each variable, using a panel of experts to assign values to them. This procedure results in a weight for each statement in a performance category. For example, the top attendance category may be assigned a value of 5, while the lowest might be worth a value of 1. Weights can also be prepared for performance categories. Attendance, for example, may be weighted 25 percent and work quality may be assigned a weight of 40 percent. The motive for using weights is so that each variable is assigned a value that corresponds to its contribution towards organizational objectives.

Weighting also shows management concern for different performance variables. A manufacturer of toxic chemicals, for example, expresses concern for safety by weighting it five times higher than job knowledge and three times higher than all other variables, including productivity.

The advantages of weighted checklists are that they show the relative priority of performance variables and they help prevent appraiser errors, such as central tendency and halo effect. Weighted checklists have the same disadvantages as basic checklists, except, as noted above, that they do give more credit for those contributions deemed to be of greater important.

Forced-Choice Checklist

A *forced-choice checklist* consists of several groups, from four to six statements each, representing different levels of performance. The statements in each group are not confined to one performance variable to help prevent rater errors, including central tendency. Appraisers review each group of statements and select the one statement that best typifies the employee's performance. Some forced-choice systems require appraisers to check two statements; one for the statement that best characterizes the employee's performance and another for the statement that least typifies an employee's performance. The appraiser follows the same procedure for all groups of statements. If five performance levels of eight variables are used, the checklist will consist of 10 clusters of four items. Exhibit 29-9 is an example of two clusters.

There are several advantages to this method. The items in each cluster are all positive, all negative, or a combination of positive and negative items, so that appraisers must carefully read them to discern which one(s) apply. This process corrects for rater errors, including central tendency. Appraiser reliability can be determined by correlating appraiser responses to cluster items, which can determine appraiser inconsistencies. Also, performance items have different values; thus, the system recognizes distinctions in contributions towards organizational objectives.

Forced-choice checklists also have some disadvantages, such as the amount of time required to prepare them. In addition, supervisors are not told the values of various statements so that they cannot use the information to slant appraisals. This mistrust causes supervisors to "play games" with the method. For example, appraisers can usually "beat the system" by imagining a profile of an ideal employee. The appraiser compares these ideal characteristics with the forced-choice items and selects those items, depending upon the way that the supervisor intends to appraise the employee. Another disadvantage is that the method is inappropriate for performance feedback until the formal appraisal is completed.

Exhibit 29-9
Example of Two Clusters in a Forced-Choice Checklist Appraisal Form
for Parcel Delivery Driver

ABC Company
Performance Appraisal Form

_____   _____   _____
(Employee)   (Date)   (Supervisor)

Instructions: Read each of the four statements in each cluster and use a check mark (✓) to denote the one item **most** descriptive of the employee. Next, check the statement in each cluster which is **least** descriptive of the employee.

Most	Least	Cluster
☐	☐	Notifies the office when unable to report for work.
☐	☐	Uses safety equipment when instructed.
☐	☐	Follows directions in completing work.
☐	☐	Researches work methods and accurately describes improvements.
☐	☐	Conducts vehicle safety inspections.
☐	☐	Completes route assignments before scheduled time.
☐	☐	Accepts work methods and procedures without complaining.
☐	☐	Promptly corrects errors when notified.

Forced Distribution

Forced distribution is a ranking method in which appraisers are required to place employees in proportion to a normal population distribution. As a result, from two to five percent of the employees receive the highest appraisal and an equal percentage receive the lowest appraisal. An additional 60 percent are appraised in the middle or average, and the remaining 30 to 35 percent are equally divided into two groups; 15-17 percent are above average and the same percentages are below average. The rationale behind the forced distribution is that most human characteristics, when sampled in sufficient quantities, will display a bell-shaped curve. Consequently, appraisers are required to conform to a normal distribution in preparing formal appraisals of their employees. Exhibit 29-10 is an example of a forced-distribution appraisal form.

Exhibit 29-10
Example of the Forced Distribution Method of Performance Appraisal

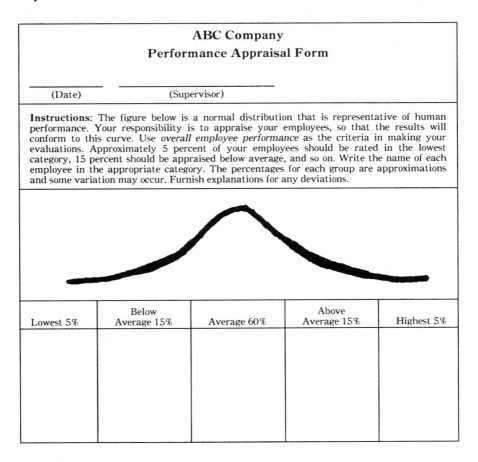

Lowest 5%	Below Average 15%	Average 60%	Above Average 15%	Highest 5%

Within the form:

ABC Company
Performance Appraisal Form

_____   _____
(Date)   (Supervisor)

Instructions: The figure below is a normal distribution that is representative of human performance. Your responsibility is to appraise your employees, so that the results will conform to this curve. Use *overall employee performance* as the criteria in making your evaluations. Approximately 5 percent of your employees should be rated in the lowest category, 15 percent should be appraised below average, and so on. Write the name of each employee in the appropriate category. The percentages for each group are approximations and some variation may occur. Furnish explanations for any deviations.

Deviations Permitted

Normally, forced-distribution appraisals are not as unequivocal as they seem, since appraisers are permitted to deviate from the percentage groupings if they have sufficient justification for it. There are various reasons for installing forced-distribution appraisal systems. They may be used to correct past practices of inflated appraisals. Sometimes, management does not trust appraisers to fairly perform appraisals. Another reason is that the forced-distribution system provides a method of categorizing employees, so that management may use appraisals to award salary increases. For example, one organization established a merit pay budget for each manager to use in granting merit pay increases. The managers distributed individual pay increases, based upon set percentages, depending upon where an employee was slotted in the distribution. Pay increases were given only to employees who were appraised as at least average.

Advantages

The forced-distribution method has several advantages, such as the ease with which it can be used. The method also corrects for rating errors, including central tendency. The theory of forced-distribution appraisals is sound in that human characteristics do conform to a normal curve. If supervisors can be educated to understand the concept and apply it, more valid and reliable appraisals will result.

Disadvantages

Forced distribution appraisal also has several disadvantages, such as a lack of validity. The logic behind forced distribution is sound, but, as with other statistical concepts, it is only valid when several criteria are present. First, the sample size must be large enough. Second, the subjects must be representative of a population group. In most situations where forced-distribution appraisals are used, neither of these criteria apply. For example, a work group of 20 employees supervised by one manager may not be a representative sample because it is too small. Consequently, the system may be patently unfair in a specific situation. In other words, while a forced distribution may be appropriate in depicting the performance of all the employees in an organization, it may not be equally appropriate when applied in one work section. Thus, pay increases and other administrative decisions within those work sections may be inequitable if they are based upon a forced-distribution appraisal.

Another problem with forced distribution is that, when the method is used alone, it does not provide a logical explanation for an employee to be slotted in a particular distribution category. The method also cannot be used for performance planning or regular performance feedback. Supervisors resent being compelled to follow arbitrary performance systems unless they provide some means of documentation or other support that will help them in tough situations, such as explaining why an appraisal decision was made. Forced-distribution appraisals do not provide that support. Finally, the word "forced" connotes distrust, since, in effect, it says, "I don't trust you to fairly distribute your appraisals, so I am forcing you to do so with this system." The result is the system tends to generate ill-will and opposition from supervisors.

Pair Comparison

Pair comparison is an appraisal method in which all employees are paired with each other and compared by the appraiser, using some performance measure, usually a global one, such as, "Which of these two employees performs the job best?" The number of pairs is determined by the formula $N(N-1)$ divided by 2, where N is equal to the number of employees appraised. The number of appraisals increases geometrically as the number of appraised employees increases arithmetically. For example, 36 comparisons are required when a work group has nine employees. The number of comparisons increases to 45 with the addition of one more employee.

The pair comparison method of performance appraisal has a number of advantages. It is statistically valid. Also, appraiser reliability is an advantage because the method reduces rater errors, including central tendency, and requires appraisers to randomly consider all employees with each other. Another advantage is that the ratings are convertible to an overall performance index, permitting comparisons of employees' index ratings, even if they work for different supervisors.

Among the disadvantages of the method is the tedium involved in the process of comparing each employee with every other one. In addition, preparing, handling, and storing the comparison bundles is a nuisance. However, this could be somewhat reduced through the use of computers. The main criticisms of the method are the same ones that apply to all ranking methods: the difficulty in explaining ratings to employees, the lack of documentation to justify the ratings, and insufficient employee feedback.

Essay

The *essay* method involves the writing of narrative descriptions of employee performance. The *pure* form of an essay performance appraisal is several paragraphs of information describing an employee's performance. The *open-ended form* of the essay method is written comments in response to statements of employee performance in selected areas.

Most appraisal methods make some use of essay responses. Sometimes, the method requires the appraiser to comment on the employee's performance or to explain why a particular rating was assigned. For example, most graphic rating scale appraisal methods require appraisers to use written comments to explain or justify their ratings. Sometimes these essay requirements are quite modest, particularly when appraisers are not required to use specific examples in substantiating opinions.

The use of essays, alone or in combination with other methods of performance appraisal, may be effective if appraisers:

- Use specific examples of employee performance;
- Write objective facts in preference to subjective opinions; and
- Use quantitative data where possible.

Advantages

To be fully effective, the essay method requires appraisers to document performance, particularly the significantly good and bad performance events occurring during the appraisal period. Another advantage is that narrative descriptions of performance may be used to explain to employees why their performance warrants a particular appraisal. This documentation can also be used to justify or document significantly high or low appraisals. Furthermore, appraisers will be more careful in preparing appraisals, particularly those using graphic rating scales or a checklist, if the rating in each category requires some objective substantiation.

Disadvantages

A major disadvantage of the essay method is the possibility that appraisers will substitute verbosity for substance in writing performance narratives. In such situations, the appraisals become time-consuming and meaningless. Another problem results from the lack of feedback inherent in the method. A final problem is certainly a human one; appraisers generally do not like writing narrative appraisals. It is much easier to check blocks, such as those used in graphic rating scales.

Critical Incidents

The *critical incidents* method is a narrative style of appraisal, using incidents occurring during the appraisal period that are examples of significantly good or bad task performance. In addition to being a significant event, critical incidents must be:

- Observable; and

- Verifiable.

Appraisers are required to determine when a significant behavior (critical incident) occurs and immediately document it. Copies of the documentation are placed in employees' critical incident files (also called performance review files or incident files) and given to the employee. Some organizations permit employees to submit an explanation, if the critical incident is negative. Occasionally, an incident may be so significant as to warrant additional action, such as a letter of commendation for a positive event or a counseling or a warning letter for a negative one. Appraisers are encouraged to keep their files current, since the formal appraisal will be based on a summary of the year's events.

Used in Other Methods

The critical incidents method can be used with any other appraisal method. For example, critical incidents are often used to substantiate or document appraiser's opinions in rating scales appraisal methods or in the essay method. However, there is a fundamental distinction, because an essay can consist of various examples of performance, some of which may not be the most significant or critical incidents. In addition, a critical incident formal appraisal is simply prepared by summarizing the year's incidents. An essay formal appraisal, however, contains a summary of the person's performance, using factual data to support the appraisers' conclusions.

Advantages

A major advantage to the critical incidents method is its timeliness and job-relatedness. These features help ensure the content validity of the method. Subjectivity is a major problem with performance appraisal, and the critical incidents method can effectively control it. Consistent feedback is a second advantage. An intermittent flow of critical incident reports gives employees a good idea of how their supervisors view their performance. Employees can keep their copies of the incidents and prepare their own summary of how the final year-end formal appraisal should look. This prevents surprises in the formal appraisal review. Regular feedback also indicates to employees what areas of their performance need corrective action before the final appraisal is prepared.

Disadvantages

One disadvantage with critical incidents is that the method does not focus on any specific performance variable, only those in which significant events occur. Consequently, the method offers no format for performance planning. Employees do not know which specific variables are to be measured, unless the critical incident method is supplemented by some other system of performance appraisal in which performance categories are shown. In short, the critical incident method is unexcelled in chronologically recording significant performance events, but it is deficient in informing employees of what performance events are desired, unless they do not occur at all or they occur in a significant number.

Management by Objectives

Management by objectives (MBO) is a performance appraisal method with subordinate-supervisor interaction and various degrees of mutual decisionmaking in establishing task priority, preparing performance criteria and objectives, defining operational strategies, monitoring progress, and evaluating results on a scheduled review date.

Implementing MBO

There are different approaches to MBO. For example, assume that the budget objective for the year at ABC Company is a five-percent cut in total operating expenses. Here are three different MBO approaches to address this objective:

- In the first approach, all supervisors are required to cut their expenses by five percent, and their MBO appraisal planning would involve listing the specific cost-saving plans they intend to implement, so that the reduction would be achieved.

- A second MBO approach permits more supervisory latitude. The same five-percent budget reduction objective is defined by the organization; however, supervisors are permitted to negotiate with their superiors concerning what percent reduction they plan to achieve. This approach assumes that all supervisors have different opportunities for budget-cutting and, in fact, some may actually need budget increases.

- A third MBO approach permits supervisors to prepare objectives independent of those established for the organization. In this approach, supervisors normally respond to at least some organizational objectives, even though they are not required to do so. A modification of this approach requires responses to some, but not all, organizational objectives. For example, top management may set organization objectives for cost reductions, service improvements, error reduction, safety improvements, sales increases, and capital investment changes. Field supervisors may be required to respond to those objectives involving costs, service standards, errors, and safety.

Confusion About MBO

The many approaches to MBO are one reason for the confusion about it. Two different organizations may use MBO but chances are that an independent observer would have a difficult time discerning any similarities in the methods used. Another reason for apparent inconsistencies in MBO use among organizations is a misunderstanding concerning what it entails. For example, 40 percent of the respondents in a survey of 217 companies stated MBO was the method used in appraising lower-level management. This was the most commonly mentioned method, followed by the essay method with 37 percent and graphic rating scales with 17 percent. The authors of the study were puzzled when they attempted to compare the questionnaire responses with copies of appraisal forms that the respondents submitted with the questionnaire. The survey authors found "... fully a third do not seem to correspond ... to the approach reported on the accompanying questionnaire ... thus ... it is possible that the conventional rating scale is the most commonly used approach to managerial performance appraisal."[2]

Exhibit 29-11 is an example of an MBO form that was prepared for a school district.

Advantages

MBO has a number of advantages. First, the method provides a clear understanding between the supervisor and the employee concerning performance criteria, the priority of various job tasks, planned objectives, and strategies for achieving the objectives. Another advantage is that employees tend to be more committed to accomplish objectives that they help to set. A third advantage is the extensive planning that typically accompanies the process, which causes proactive, rather than reactive, employee performance. Thus, accomplishments occur according to plan, instead of as a reaction to unplanned events. A fourth advantage is the feedback employees receive as they monitor their own progress towards accomplishing objectives. A fifth advantage is that employees allocate their time and resources as they see fit in performing tasks. This self-discipline precludes the need for extensive supervisory observation and direction. In short, employees know what tasks are to be done, the order of priority of them, and when they must be done. Finally, MBO treats employees as mature adults who are responsible for their behavior.

Disadvantages

Among the disadvantages of MBO is the considerable stress that may result if employees commit to unattainable objectives. Setting objectives is one thing; accomplishing them is quite another. A second problem is overzealous supervisors who use MBO improperly, such as imposing objectives upon employees without negotiation. Ultimatums leave subordinates with little or no personal choice. When input is constrained, the objective-setting process becomes a farce. Employees who survive one or two rounds of objectives being imposed by their managers usually resort to arguing over objectives or building elaborate excuses, complete with documentation, about why objectives are not feasible. A third problem is employee skepticism. Employees may view MBO as a manipulative

---

[2] R.I. Lazer and W.S. Wikstrom, *Appraising Managerial Performance* (New York: The Conference Board, 1977), p. 7.

system instituted in order to get more work out of them, an attitude common in organizations with a history of treating employees unfairly.

Exhibit 29-11
Example of MBO Appraisal Form

ABC School District

Performance Planning and Appraisal Form for _____

_____
(Employee)

Instructions: Write your objectives for the year and the strategies you intend to use to accomplish them. Be specific with planned actions, dates, and accomplishments. Negotiate the final terms of your plan with your supervisor. Both you and the supervisor should sign the form on the reverse and send a copy to Human Resources. Use this form to guide your performance during the year.

		Performance	
Duties (Show the priority, using #1 for most important)	**Self-Development** (Show any development you plan to pursue)	**Your Objectives**	**Your Strategies to Achieve the Objectives**	**Accomplishments**

(Additional space on the reverse)

Some organizations implement MBO programs and fail to follow through on them. In the latter case, managements' intentions may be honorable, but they fail to establish controls to monitor the program or they underfund it. In these situations, employees may protect themselves by agreeing only to easy objectives or by offering excuses why an objective was not met. These disadvantages demonstrate that MBO can be manipulated by both supervisors and subordinates.

Competency-Based Appraisal

A *competency* is a skill, ability, or behavior that is considered relevant to effective job performance. Examples of competencies are communication skills, critical thinking skills, teamwork skills, facilitation skills, abilities to participate in group decisionmaking, and the ability to simultaneously deal with several projects or problems. Most appraisal methods include competencies in some manner, typically in the area of conduct or personal or interpersonal skills. Some competencies are obviously important in many jobs. For example, leadership is important in supervision, oral communication is important in customer representatives, and motivation is important for account sales executives. The difficulty with competencies is the ability to measure them in an objective and standardized manner.

A competency-based system is not a different method of performance appraisal, such as graphic rating scales or ranking. Rather, the approach involves the incorporation of competencies in one of the methods, which previously have been discussed. A performance appraisal system that is competency-based would typically involve the use of graphic rating scales or a variation of them, such as behaviorally anchored rating scales or behavior observation scales. For example, types of competencies that could appear on a graphic rating scales might include *leadership performance* or *multi-task performance*. The appraiser would evaluate the employee by checking a box indicating the extent to which the employee exhibits leadership on the job. If a behaviorally anchored scales method was used, there would be examples of leadership behavior to guide the appraiser in rating the employee. For behavior observation scales, the frequency of the behavior would be used to guide the appraiser in rating the employee.

360°Appraisal

During the past 15 years, management has become more aware of the impact of various constituencies on the success of both public and private organizations. For example, for the private business, customers, peers, and supervisors have contact with employees and could provide important information about their performance. In an effort to obtain that information, some organizations have established formal methods of performance appraisal consisting of separate components for appraisal input from the important groups that interact with the employee. Several methods of performance appraisal, such as rating scales or essay, may be used to obtain the input.

While the objectives of global appraisals are worthy, the mechanics of implementation are unwieldy for most organizations. Criticisms of the concept include the difficulties in coordinating the inputs, in obtaining cooperation from the various constituencies, and in communicating the information to employees so that they can use it.

Designing a Performance Appraisal System

The fourth dimension of performance appraisal is designing the system. The important steps in designing an appraisal system are:

1. Define the system's purposes;

2. Conduct a job analysis to ensure that the system is job-related and valid;

3. Provide a mechanism for employee input and feedback;

4. Use objective measures that limit subjectivity;

5. Standardize the process; and

6. Provide for the documentation of performance.

Define Purposes

Performance appraisal is intended to accomplish one or more of the purposes described at the outset of this chapter. These purposes should be clearly defined, stated in writing, and published with the procedures and other materials that are used to educate all employees about the system.

Conduct Job Analysis

Job analysis is conducted to collect the information related to the purposes of the system. If the purpose is to measure the quality of employee performance, the job analysis must obtain information about work quality, such as errors, scrap, waste, and complaints. Once the quality variables are identified, measurement units and performance standards are developed. These steps result in an appraisal system that is job-related, so that the purposes can be accomplished.

Validation is the process of ensuring that the performance appraisal system is job-related. Serious consequences can result if protected group members are adversely impacted by an invalid performance appraisal system. In *Albermarle Paper Company v. Moody,*[3] the U.S. Supreme Court stated that it was illegal to validate a selection method, using performance appraisal results, if a job analysis had not been conducted. If an appraisal system is used for administrative purposes, such as promotions, discipline, and pay increases, a job analysis should be conducted to ensure the performance criteria are job-related.

Employee Input and Feedback

Performance appraisal is foremost a method of communicating with employees about performance standards. At a minimum, input means that the employee has the opportunity to discuss performance criteria before the appraisal period begins. Periodic feedback means the employee is informed at various intervals concerning how he or she is performing in relation to the appraiser's expectations.

---

[3] *Albemarle Paper Co. v. Moody,* 422 U.S. 405 (1975).

System Objectivity

Performance appraisal, as with many other management decisionmaking processes, requires subjective judgment. No appraisal system is entirely free of some appraiser subjectivity. However, where possible, this should be constrained by using measurable job-related criteria.

Standardized Appraisal System

Standardized means that, among the personnel in the organization, there is commonality in appraisal system definitions, units of measurement, performance criteria, and interpretations of performance. In *Brito v. Zia,*[4] the employer's appraisal system was ruled unfair because standardized scoring was not used. Without some standardization, appraisers independently select the variables to use in appraising employees. Experience also shows that without standards, supervisors use individualized systems of weights for different variables. Standards will help control these and other problems, including the application of differing definitions to different performance variables.

Documentation

Documentation is the process of recording significant information pertaining to an employee's performance. Documentation can aid management decision-making in such areas as personnel actions, promotions, and pay increases. An area of increasing importance is the role of documentation in justifying those decisions which may precipitate EEO complaints. One author suggested these guidelines for following in documenting employee performance:

- Be accurate;
- Document facts and not opinions;
- Base documentation on direct observation and not on hearsay;
- Be timely in preparing the documentation;
- Be specific in describing behavior; and
- Be consistent in documenting facts.[5]

Field of Play as Performance Management Tool: Confidence Builders International

While managers and senior human resource executives expect employees to perform at high levels, they are sometimes disappointed with actual results. One of the ongoing dilemmas managers face is how to effectively define and measure productivity and performance.

Some managers micromanage; however, that usually yields undesired results. Employees decry micromanaging as a poor management technique since it implies a lack of trust. Some managers ignore a situation until a crisis occurs and then step in as the hero who solves the problem. Some simply leave results to chance.

---

[4] 5 EPD (CCH) ¶ 8626.

[5] M. Smith, "Documenting Employee Performance," *Supervisory Management* 24 (September 1976), p. 31.

We recommend a different approach, called the Field of Play, see Exhibit 29-12. Field of Play is based on the theory that employees work best when they have a crystal clear vision and precise understanding of what is expected of them. Then they are encouraged to work out details of how the job will be performed. The manager monitors the work at selected intervals, but does not interfere with methods used unless the employee goes completely off track.

How does Field of Play work? For purposes of clarity, we use an image of a football field. Around the perimeter of the field we describe every aspect of a particular job, ranging from goals, reporting relationships, budgets, legal and ethical issues, accountabilities, authorities, responsibilities, etc. The manager and employee openly discuss each of the restrictions or boundaries and how each will be measured. Nothing is left to chance. At the end of the conversation, both parties agree that the employee will be evaluated based on the agreements reached. All critical elements are clearly identified.

It should be noted that the size of the Field of Play changes from employee to employee. For example, with new hires, the field will be very small and monitored closely; for more senior executives, it will be large and may contain fewer restrictions.

During the course of the conversation, opportunities arise to discuss expectations based on a common vocabulary and a deep understanding of the areas that will be evaluated. For Field of Play to work properly, the manager must possess two attributes: complete understanding of job requirements and willingness to fully turn the job over to the employee to perform in his or her own way.

It is imperative that the manager and employee meet periodically to measure ongoing results. If handled correctly, this would not be considered micromanaging. If course corrections are necessary, it is relatively simple, based on the information provided in the Field of Play discussion, to quickly identify an area that requires attention. If other areas are moving along as planned, there is no need to spend time to discuss those.

The Field of Play model can yield powerful results. When employees see and understand the parameters of the job and are told to go ahead and do it their way, a light goes on and productivity increases. To be effective, Field of Play must be based on mutual trust. It becomes one of the most powerful management tools a manager can use.

Dorothy Lynn is co-founder with her daughter, Jessica Selasky, of Confidence Builders International, with offices in Ohio and Florida. Confidence Builders concentrates on the people side of the enterprise. www.confidencebuilders

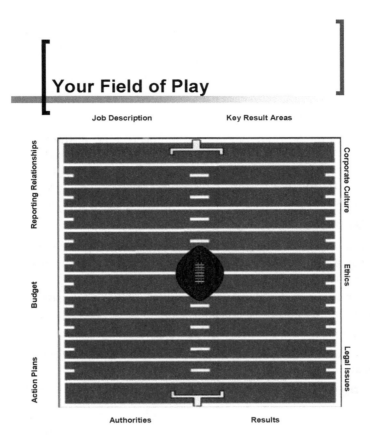

Implementing the Appraisal System

The final dimension of performance appraisal is the implementation of the system. The steps involved in performance appraisal implementation are:

1. Train appraisers;
2. Train employees;
3. Set standards;
4. Check performance;
5. Communicate results frequently;
6. Take required actions; and
7. Evaluate the system.

Training Appraisers

Training supervisors in performance appraisal is important for the system to be successful. Through training, supervisors learn the procedures required in the system. Also, the training should include the legal issues in performance appraisal. Training sessions are the opportune place to standardize the system; that is, to ensure that there is a uniformity among the supervisors concerning various levels of performance, interpretation of performance, and evaluation of performance. Where possible, quantified standards should be used and communicated during the training programs. Training also prevents some of the apprehensions that supervisors may have about conducting performance appraisal reviews.

Training Employees

While it is often ignored, employees should receive, at the minimum, orientation training explaining the purposes of the appraisal system, the mechanics of the system, the disposition of the information gathered (including how long it will be retained), and the way in which the system will affect such matters as employee pay, developmental and promotional opportunities, and job tenure.

Setting Standards

Standards are important in obtaining employee acceptance of a performance appraisal system. In order for a system to be accepted, employees should answer "Yes" to these three questions:

1. Do you know the standards by which your supervisor evaluates your performance and the expected results?
2. Do you feel your contribution and performance are measured fairly?
3. Has your supervisor assisted you in evaluating your strengths and weaknesses for future performance improvements?[6]

Checking Performance

The process of checking performance entails the almost daily task of observing employees at work. Where possible, computerized monitoring systems should be used, such as attendance programs that tally and record information on variables, such as punctuality, unscheduled absences, and sick leave use. Such systems can be programmed to submit reports when the rates in any of these attendance variables indicate that action is needed.

Computerized records can also be used to monitor other performance variables, including productivity, accidents, and work quality. In addition to easing supervisors' burdens, computers have other advantages over manual records. Computer databases are more accurate, they save space, and they can be regularly updated. These databases also significantly aid management decisionmaking, either through programmed exception reporting or by providing the information necessary to make decisions.

Communicating Results

Where possible, systems should be used that continually keep employees informed regarding their performance. Through an MBO system, for example, employees are generally well-informed about their status because they know

---

[6] R.R. Ball, "What's the Answer to Performance Appraisal?" *Personnel Administrator* 23 (July 1978), p. 44.

what their objectives are and how they are doing in relation to them. Self-monitoring systems are the best form of feedback communication because an employee knows what the target is and is able to personally judge his or her progress. Self-monitoring supplements other communications systems, such as supervisory feedback.

Appraisal Interviews

Appraisal interviews include: goal-setting or other type of appraisal orientation interview; counseling interviews, in which the employee's deficient performance is reviewed with the individual; and the formal appraisal interview, conducted at the end of the appraisal period.

Goal-Setting Interview

The *goal-setting interview* is normally associated with the MBO appraisal method. The purpose is to finalize the employee's performance plans for the year. For other types of appraisal systems, the initial interview is conducted to orient the employee in the appraisal system and to explain the performance variables and expected levels of performance. Informal goal-setting occurs in this process when the employee is asked to commit to meeting the requisite performance levels.

Counseling Interview

Counseling interviews are conducted for the purpose of reviewing an employee's unsatisfactory performance with him or her and explaining what improvement is expected. Also, during the counseling interview, the employee is expected to explain any problems that he or she is experiencing that are preventing the employee from achieving the desired level of performance.

Because counseling appraisal interviews cause supervisors stress, they tend to avoid them. This avoidance simply increases the stress, since deficient employees will continue their unsatisfactory performance patterns. Avoidance also causes other problems, such as lowering the morale of employees who are not deficient. Eventually, the situation prompts the frustrated supervisor to overreact and impose severe disciplinary measures. The employee resists the severe measures and may charge the supervisor with unfairness. In sum, the employee's performance has not improved, organizational effectiveness is reduced, and a grievance may need to be resolved if the employee alleges unfair tactics by the supervisor.

Formal Appraisal Interview

The *formal appraisal interview* is typically conducted at the end of the appraisal period, usually at the year's end. If procedures have been observed during the year, such as informing employees of critical incidents and conducting counseling interviews as needed, the formal appraisal interview should simply formalize what the employee and the supervisor already know. The result is that there are no surprises and no stress when the supervisor reviews the form with the employee before both of them sign it.

Taking Required Actions

Performance appraisal systems are established to accomplish purposes. The entire process is consummated through the actions required to make those purposes a reality.

Evaluating the Appraisal System

The process of evaluating an appraisal system consists of comparing the results of the system with the system's purposes. If a purpose of the appraisal system is to determine whether training is adequate for new employees, there should be some documentation of dialogue among supervisors and training personnel. Some tangible evidence linking extrinsic rewards to appraisal results should be available for review, if the appraisal system is intended to recognize and reward employees who meet or exceed performance expectations.

CHAPTER 30
PERFORMANCE-BASED PAY

Chapter Highlights
- Review contemporary concepts in pay and performance
- Explain the different types of performance-based pay plans
- Learn how to plan and implement a gainsharing plan
- Review sales compensation plans
- Examine competency-based pay methods

Introduction

The traditional graded pay structure, adjusted for external equity, is the predominant system to standardize employee pay both in the U.S. and abroad.[1] The simplicity of the system, ease of implementation and administration, and employee acceptance, are major reasons for the extensive use of graded pay structures. The problem is that graded pay structures reward the importance of job tasks performed in an organization but do nothing to reward how well those tasks are performed. Gradually, these structures will be transformed from pay for positions to pay for outcomes. The outcomes may be productivity, profits, sales, knowledge, competencies, and skills. Learning how to effectively implement and administer these new systems to obtain optimal results is a challenging area of compensation.

Performance-based pay is a form of direct compensation, using an immediate and/or deferred monetary payment based upon a desired outcome.

Purposes of Performance-Based Pay

The purposes of performance-based pay are to increase the organization's efficiency, improve service, enhance employee job satisfaction, and meet social responsibilities.

Increase Efficiency

Performance-based pay is intended to increase organizational efficiency. For private sector businesses, this purpose includes increasing shareholder wealth by increasing productivity and decreasing the costs per unit of output. In public organizations, performance-based pay is intended to increase the return on services, products, or constituent payments, whether they are donations to human services organizations or taxes and fees paid to governments.

---

[1] Welch, Jilly, "Pay plans worry civil servants," *People Management*, Vol. 2, No. 17 (August 29, 1996), pp. 6-7.

Improve Service

A second purpose of performance-based pay is to improve the quality of services and goods provided to customers and constituencies. Service purposes also include reducing the costs of services and goods, increasing the variety offered, expanding the utility of those goods and services, and developing new ones to better meet future needs.

Enhance Employee Job Satisfaction

A major purpose of performance-based pay is to increase employee job satisfaction. Some benefits of improved employee job satisfaction are reduced turnover, absenteeism, and accidents and better job performance. Performance-based pay also facilitates the recruitment of better qualified applicants. Performance-based pay accomplishes this purpose by providing employees with pay that is competitive in the market. Performance-based pay also equitably rewards performance within the organization.

Meet Social Responsibility

A review of the discussions on performance-based pay provides a convincing case of its role in fostering and perpetuating free enterprise capitalism.[2] These arguments include strengthening the domestic economy through producing goods and services that are competitive in world markets. Pay incentive advocates also believe some pay incentive systems, such as profit-sharing plans and dividend distributions through employee stock ownership plans, strengthen the capitalistic system by permitting employees to share in economic gains. Another practical way incentive pay meets this purpose is by relating rewards to contributions. Competition is the bulwark of a free enterprise system, and performance-based pay fosters healthy and fair competition by rewarding employees according to their contributions.

Making Performance-Based Pay Work

For performance-based pay methods to accomplish their purposes, consideration should be given to such factors as job structuring and employee training.

Job Structuring

For performance-based pay to achieve the desired effect, each job must be properly designed and described and the work methods should be efficient. Therefore, prior to implementing an incentive pay plan, management should conduct a complete work methods analysis and staffing study to develop the optimum work methods and the most efficient staffing levels.

Train Employees

As simplistic as it sounds, employees must be trained in the optimum work methods. In addition, if the pay incentive concerns performance variables like

---

[2] See Lincoln, J.F., *Incentive Management* (Cleveland, Ohio: The Lincoln Electric Company, 1951). Also see Kelso, L.O. and Hetter, P., *How to Turn* *Eighty Million Workers Into Capitalists on Borrowed Money* (New York, Random House, 1967).

attendance or safety, employees should be oriented in the procedures that will be followed in tracking their performance in those areas.

Product Design

Performance-based pay is not a panacea for the ills of a firm that is producing a product or providing a service that customers do not want. In order for performance-based pay to work, the product or service must have the features to make it competitive in the market. At the risk of oversimplification, it should be noted that there are two sides for a firm to make a profit. Costs, which are one side, are affected by employee productivity which in turn is positively influenced by performance-based pay. The other side of profitability is total revenue, which is dependent upon customer demand. While it is true that demand for a product is related to price, which in turn incorporates costs, customers will not purchase a product, regardless of price, if it does not contain the features they want.

Performance-based pay is not a substitute for management strategies to improve a product's market position through greater expertise, superior design features, effective advertising, and specialization. Incentive pay is most effective in companies that can capitalize on a propitious niche in a market.

Provide an Incentive

Performance-based pay will not work if it does not provide an incentive for employees to do those things that the system is designed to influence. For example, implementing a profit-sharing plan to motivate employees to produce more and better products will not work for a firm that is not making any profits. In this situation, a bonus plan based upon productivity improvement or a Scanlon plan, which is designed to reduce labor costs as a percentage of the value of output, would provide an incentive to employees.

System Equity

Incentive systems do not work in an environment in which the procedures are subject to the capricious whims of management or where the opportunities to realize rewards are constrained by barriers beyond the employee's control. For example, piecework pay rates should not be unilaterally raised by management unless there is adequate justification, such as a significant change in work methods or technology. Changing piece rates is a disincentive when employees are consistently earning bonuses for surpassing quotas.

Performance-Based Pay Philosophy

A pay-for-performance plan is simply a procedure. Making it work requires managers who have the requisite philosophy. This philosophy should include such considerations as the potential of human performance.

Human Potential

A pay incentive philosophy recognizes the virtually limitless potential of employee performance. This belief applies to every aspect of employee performance, such as productivity, work quality, and creativity. For example, employee ideas for improvement represent a vast untapped resource in most organizations. These ideas range from quality improvements to cost reductions. Employee creativity nurtures additional ideas as employees become skilled at identifying subjects that need improvement.

Productivity improvements are also limitless. F.W. Taylor, the father of scientific management and a leader in pay incentive management, found through numerous studies in different industries that incentive pay systems can motivate employees, after they are properly placed and trained, to produce two to three times more than they formerly did.[3] He used the term *first-class workers* to describe these high performers. The possibility of increasing productivity is always present due to changes in technology, methods, and in the products and services demanded.

Every Employee a High Performer

F.W. Taylor found in his employment experiences that every employee is a first-class worker at some job. Effective selection and placement insures employees are placed in jobs for which they are suited. However, selection and placement cannot be accurate in every such action because of the inadequacies in selection methods. Follow-ups after selection, probationary periods, and performance appraisals are designed to spot incorrect placements. Also, human resources management professionals must be alert for other evidence of employee-job congruence problems. Through personnel placement actions like reassignments and other human resources management activities, such as training, employees become qualified as top performers.

High Pay with Incentives

Incentive pay may result in high wages and salaries. First-class workers should be paid from 30 to 100 percent more than average employees. For example, the average production employee at the Lincoln Electric Company receives about $50,000 in base salary plus an additional $19,000 in incentive pay. The highest paid production worker earns about $130,000 per year.[4] Higher pay under incentive schemes does not equate to high labor costs, if the system is properly planned and administered. This is a tenet of incentive pay plans that is difficult for many people to understand. Higher pay is a bargain when compared to the 200 to 300 percent increase in productivity that is attainable under incentive pay systems.

Employee-Management Cooperation

Adversarial relationships have no place in pay-for-performance systems. For example, if piece rates are used, employees must trust management to set fair base rates. Without such trust, employees will quibble over rates, under the assumption that management is manipulating them. Profit-sharing plans also require trust, so that employees will believe management is not cheating on how profits are shared. This spirit of cooperation is evident in the term "classless society" used by Gordon E. Forward, President of Chaparral Steel Company, to describe the employee-management relations existing in that company. As an

---

[3] Taylor, F.W., *Scientific Management* (New York: Harper and Brothers, 1947).

[4] Ahladas, D., Personal interview with Mr. Richard Sabo, Director of Communications at the Lincoln Electric Company (November 5, 1997).

example of that philosophy, all of Chaparral employees are included in a profit-sharing pay plan.[5]

Other examples of teamwork in pay incentive systems are the willingness of employees to contribute their ideas to improve operations, products, and services. Management provides the climate for these contributions by expressing confidence in employees' creative talents and asking for help.

Cooperation is also developed through information-sharing. There are many types of information shared with employees, such as productivity figures, changes in profitability, accident rates, suggestions submitted, and the dollar benefit value of adopted ideas, product quality rates, customer complaints, sales figures, and how the company compares with the competition.

Employee Acceptance Takes Time

Employees have generally been exposed to management styles such as "a day's work for a day's pay," and "employees perform according to what you inspect, not what you expect." In addition, they may have experienced various management manipulation schemes to boost productivity, such as unfair incentive rate increases prompted by employees collecting bonuses. Also, there may be a history of adversarialism in a particular work environment. For these and other reasons, management cannot expect employees to quickly embrace an incentive pay system and put 100 percent effort into their performance. Many employees will take a "wait and see" attitude when an incentive pay plan is initially installed.

Many incentive pay plans fail because management did not explain the system to employees and gradually convert them to it. F. W. Taylor called this conversion the "mental revolution" and he said it was accomplished through "object lessons." An *object lesson* was what each worker experienced when he discovered the rewards were indeed greater under the new system. A *mental revolution* is a summation of the object lessons of many employees. Taylor cautioned that incentive pay systems may take as long as several years to fully convert employee thinking. If the other concepts of the philosophy discussed in these chapter sections are followed, managers can expect to see some immediate improvement. However, the largest gains will take time.

Pay-for-Performance Benefits All

There are no losers with performance-based pay. The organization gains through cost reductions, increased productivity, and improved employee attitudes. The long-term benefits are increased profitability and organizational survival. Eventually, depending upon the performance variables used in the incentive pay system, other results occur such as an increase in sales due to employees' ideas to improve the utility of a product or service.

Customers also benefit from incentive pay systems through lower prices, better quality products and services, and improved product features. The lower prices result from productivity and efficiency improvements. For example, as

[5] *Ibid.*

noted above, employees under pay incentive systems produce two to three times more and are paid from 30 to 100 percent more. Part of the productivity improvement is shared with customers through lower prices.

Stockholders also gain through pay for performance by sharing in some of the productivity and efficiency increases. Stockholders benefit through increased dividends and an appreciation in the price of their stock due to the company's improved performance. Citizens or taxpayers gain in public organizations through an improvement in service and lower taxes and fees.

Gainsharing

Among the bold methods of performance-based compensation is *gainsharing*, in which employers are translating their beliefs about employee partnerships into action.

Gainsharing plans are performance-based pay plans that "share gains" among employees for improvements in productivity, profitability, or efficiency.

The term *gainsharing plan* is usually reserved for bottom-line pay incentive systems that are based upon some overall measure of organizational performance like profitability or productivity, as noted above. In a more realistic sense, most performance-based pay methods involve some measure of gainsharing. For example, cash awards given to employees for ideas submitted through a suggestion system involve gainsharing, since the employer shares with the employee-suggester the gains realized from his or her idea. In a similar manner, piecework plans involve gainsharing, since employers share with employees the gains resulting from any increased output. In fact, one of the earliest uses of the word "gainsharing" was in conjunction with the Halsey Premium incentive pay plan which was introduced in 1891 and was the first such plan in North America. The Halsey plan guarantees employees an hourly wage and gives them the option of earning a premium based upon standard task times set from records of employees' past performance.[6]

Types of Gainsharing Plans

These are some of the major types of gainsharing plans and a brief explanation of how they are unique.

- *Employee stock ownership plans.* In these plans, employees share in the gains of their efforts in the form of dividends and the increased value of their stock.

- *Improshare plans.* In these plans, employees share in the gains in productivity resulting from their performance.

- *Profit-sharing plans.* In these plans, employees share in a portion of the profits that they help generate.

---

[6] Roe, J.W. and Lytle, C.W., "Operation Study and Rate-Setting," *Management's Handbook,* edited by L.P. Alford, (New York: The Ronald Press Company, 1924), p. 929.

- *Rucker plans.* These plans give employees the opportunity of sharing in the value added by production operations.

- *Scanlon plans.* With these plans, employees share in any savings in labor costs that result from their performance.

- *Employee stock purchase plans.* These plans permit employees to share in the gains of stock they purchase at prices below the existing market price.

Employee Stock Ownership Plan

An *employee stock ownership plan* (ESOP) is an arrangement in which employees are given various amounts, up to 100 percent, of company ownership through the issuance of stock. As defined by the Internal Revenue Service, an ESOP is a qualified stock bonus plan or a qualified stock bonus and money purchase plan. There are two types of gainsharing involved in an ESOP. The first type of sharing is in the form of profits that employees receive, not as employees in the company (such as through a profit-sharing plan), but as owners of the business who receive dividends on their investment in a business. The second form of gainsharing that employees receive through an ESOP is in the appreciation of a stock's value. ESOPs are discussed in more detail in Chapter 22.

Employee Stock Purchase Plans

An *employee stock purchase plan (ESPP)* is a stock option that permits employees to purchase stock at a reduced price and to sell it and receive preferential tax treatment, provided that certain conditions are met. This type of stock option is not limited to executives; in fact, one of the conditions which the plan must meet to qualify for tax benefits is that the option must be made available to virtually all of a firm's employees.

An ESPP should not be confused with two other types of stock plans for employees. An *employee stock plan (ESP)* is offered by employers in which employees agree that periodic deductions may be made from their paychecks in order to purchase stock in the firm. When a sufficient amount of deductions have accrued, a share of stock is purchased in the name of the employee and issued to him or her. Salary will be withheld for additional purchases until the employee halts it. An *employee stock ownership plan (ESOP)* is an arrangement whereby the employees in a company are given various amounts of ownership in a company (up to 100 percent) through the issuance of stock.

Advantages to ESPPs. There are two advantages to an ESPP. The first advantage is the prospect of favorable tax treatment. Under certain conditions, some of the gain received on the sale of the stock is taxable as a long-term capital gain instead of as ordinary income. The other advantage to an ESPP is that employees receive any gain in the selling price of the stock when they exercise the stock option.

Requirements for ESPPs. There are nine requirements that an ESPP must meet in order for any gains on the sale of the stock to receive favorable tax treatment. Without describing the fine points of each requirement, they essentially provide the following:

1. The plan must be provided to virtually all full-time employees;

2. Only employees of the firm may be granted the options;

3. Generally, the option price for the stock must be less than 85 percent of the market value;

4. Typically, the period of the option cannot exceed five years;

5. The plan must be approved by the firm's stockholders;

6. The plan cannot discriminate in favor of any group of employees;

7. Owners of more than five percent of the firm's stock cannot be granted an ESPP option;

8. Generally, no employee can purchase more than $25,000 of stock; and

9. The option is not transferable.

Improshare

The term *Improshare* is an acronym for *IM* proved *PRO* ductivity through *SHAR* ing. Mitchell Fein, created Improshare in 1974 as a means of sharing with employees the increased productivity resulting from their labor. The basic concept of Improshare is that every product can be evaluated in terms of the hours of labor or work hours that are required to produce it. The two essential factors in the system are work hour standards, which are than converted into standard value hours and the base productivity factor.

Work Hour Standard and Standard Value Hours

The *work hour standard* is the average number of hours or fraction of an hour which is necessary to produce one unit of output over a base period. For example, if 20,000 work hours of labor (20 employees working 40 hours per week for 25 weeks) were necessary to produce 40,000 units of Product A, the work hour standard for that product is: 20,000 divided by 40,000 = 0.5 work hours per unit.

The *standard value hours* are simply the number of hours allotted to produce a set amount of output and are determined by multiplying the number of units of output of a product by the work hour standard for it.

Standard value hours = # units of output × work hour standard

The standard value hours for the above example can be determined by substituting the values in the equation.

20,000 = 40,000 × 0.5

If several products are involved, a separate work hour standard is prepared for each of them and the standard value hours are computed by combining the results of the equations.[7]

EXAMPLE: Forty production employees work for Apex Manufacturing, a company that produces two products, Product A and Product B. Over a 25-week period, 20 of these employees work only on Product A, and the

---

[7] The following examples were adapted from information obtained from *Productivity Sharing Programs: Can They Contribute To Productivity* *Improvement?* (Gaithersburg, Maryland: U.S. Government Accounting Office, 1981), p. 11.

other 20 work only on Product B. Here are the calculations of the work hour standards for the two products:

Product A = 20,000 ÷ 40,000 units = 0.5 hours per piece

Product B = 20,000 ÷ 80,000 units = 0.25 hours per piece

Here are the calculations of the combined standard value hours for the two products:

Product A	=	.5 × 40,000	=	20,000		
Product B	=	.25 × 80,000	=	20,000		
				40,000	=	Total standard value hours

As noted above, after the work hour standards are determined, the total standard value hours are computed. *Total standard value hours* are the number of production hours in a base period that are required for a specified amount of output.

It is important to note that in computing the work hour standard and the standard value hours, only the work hours of those employees who are actually engaged in the production of the product are included.

Base Productivity Factor

Before defining the base productivity factor, the components of it will be examined. As noted above, in computing the work hour standards and the standard value hours, the units of output and only the work hours of employees actually engaged in the production of the product are included in the calculations. In determining the *base productivity factor* (BPF) the work hours of all employees are included, both non-production and production workers. This is the formula for the BPF:

BPF = Total production and non-production hours ÷ Total standard value hours

EXAMPLE: Using the same data in the previous example, assume five non-production employees were included in this plant that produced the Products A and B. Applying the BPF formula for the 40 production workers (20 workers producing only Product A and 20 workers producing only Product B) and the five non-production workers would be:

BPF

=45 workers × 40 hours/week × 25 weeks ÷ 40,000

=45,000 ÷ 40,000

=1.125

Defining the Base Productivity Factor. After describing the components of the BPF, and working with an example of it, it should be apparent that the BPF is, for the established base period, the ratio of all the plant's work hours (both production and non-production) to the number of production hours.

Improshare Hours. The Improshare hours are computed with this formula:

Total standard value hours × BPF = Improshare hours

EXAMPLE: Using the above example where 40,000 = Total standard value hours;

40,000 × 1.125 = 45,000 = Improshare hours

Computing the Improshare Bonus

Bonuses are earned under an Improshare plan when the Improshare hours are less than the actual production and non-production work hours. Savings are shared on some ratio, such as 50/50, between the company and the employees. Each employee's share is derived by his or her hours as a percent of the total work hours for the month, times his or her hourly rate.

EXAMPLE: During Y month, the employees in Apex Manufacturing produced 2,000 units of Product A and 3,000 units of Product B. Assume the sharing is 50/50 between the company and the employees. Also assume during the month the actual work hours were 1,700. For this production here is the bonus calculation for Apex Manufacturing for the month:

Product A =	0.5 hours × 2,000 units × 1.125	=	1,125	
Product B =	0.25 hours × 3,000 units × 1.125	=	843	
			1,968	= Improshare hours
Less: actual hours worked during Y month =			1,700	
Gained hours =			268	
Employees = share: (50% of hours gained) =			134	

Each employee's share of the 134 hours would be determined by his or her hours for the month as a percent of the total work hours for the month, times his or her hourly rate. For example, assume Bert worked five percent of the total hours worked in month Y, and his regular rate of pay is $32.50 per hour. This would be his bonus for the month:

.05 × 134 × $32.50 = $217.75

Advantages to Improshare Plans

Improshare plans have some notable advantages over other gainsharing methods.

Improshare Emphasizes Productivity. More so than other gainsharing methods, Improshare emphasizes the one hard and unchanging statistic of employee efficiency—productivity. One advantage to this approach is that items like the costs of raw materials, changes in prices, and the use of other factors like utilities are not involved. For example, as we shall see later in this chapter, profit-sharing plans, as well as Rucker and Scanlon plans, do involve changes in product prices. If other things remain equal and only the price of the product changes, employees will receive a bonus even though they have done nothing to warrant receiving one.

Constant Factor. Another advantage to Improshare is that work hours are constant—no dollar figures are involved. Consequently, productivity measures from one month or year to the next can be compared.

Profitability Is Not a Factor. Another advantage to Improshare is that it can be used to motivate improvements in employee productivity when other methods such as a profit-sharing plan would not work. For example, if a plant is not making any profits (the total costs of producing and marketing the plant's production are greater than the revenue it generates), there are no profits to share with employees regardless of how productive they are. For profit-sharing plans, this situation is a "Catch 22" in that employees are not motivated to be more efficient because there are no profits to share. To complete the cycle, no profits occur because employees do not work harder and smarter to produce them.

Profit-Sharing Plans

Profit-sharing is the oldest known method of gainsharing. The first documented use of profit-sharing was in February 12, 1843, when Edme-Jean Leclaire, owner of a French painting and decorating business and the father of modern gainsharing, held a meeting with his employees and plunked down on a table a bag with 12,266 gold francs, which was their share of profits that the business gained through their efforts.[8] In 1840, Leclaire introduced the concept to his 300 employees after first determining how much they could save him through a combination of better use of their time, not wasting materials, and using tools more carefully so that they would not break or lose them. He discussed these potential savings with his employees and explained his plan to share a percentage of the savings with them through the increased profits that would result. The plan was successful and still functioning almost 70 years later although the firm had changed names.[9]

Types of Profit-Sharing Plans

The two principal types of profit-sharing plans are *immediate* and *deferred*. Some plans use a combination of these two. An immediate plan makes cash disbursements from a company's profits, usually on a semiannual or annual basis. A deferred plan is on the order of a pension plan. The motivation associated with profit-sharing is stronger with the immediate plan, since employees can associate the rewards with performance.

Deferred plans have some advantages too. For example, under certain conditions they receive special tax concessions. In addition, the amount of funds in any employee's deferred profit-sharing account can be used for other purposes, such as to purchase annuities or life insurance. In addition, deferred profit-sharing plans have some advantages over qualified pension plans, since they can be used to provide an employee with funds in the event of a layoff. Also, under certain conditions, employees may withdraw funds if the plan permits it.

---

[8] Metzger, B.L., *Profit Sharing as a Motivator* (Chicago: Profit Sharing Research Foundation, 1984), p. 9.

[9] Roe, J.W. and Lytle, C.W., "Wage Payment and Timekeeping," *Management's Handbook*, edited by L.P. Alford (New York: The Ronald Press Company, 1924), p. 967.

Arguments Against Profit-Sharing

Some critics argue against the use of profit-sharing as a pay incentive because of the difficulty in associating rewards to performance when they are made on an annual or semiannual basis. This is why advocates of Scanlon, Rucker, Improshare, and other types of gainsharing plans believe management should make monthly calculations of savings and immediately distribute them to employees. Nevertheless, some companies, such as the Lincoln Electric Company, believe annual profit-sharing is an inducement to employee performance.

Employee Participation

In 2003, 21 percent of employees in private sector firms were participating in deferred profit sharing plans.[10]

Scanlon Plan

The Scanlon plan was developed by Joseph N. Scanlon, a local union president in an Ohio steel company. Allegedly, he developed the plan to protect the company from failing. A Scanlon plan is a gainsharing plan that shares with employees any gains resulting to the organization from a reduction in payroll costs as a percentage of the value of production.

Scanlon Plan Principles

The three principles forming the basics of a Scanlon plan are employee participation, bonus payments, and employee identification with the business or plant.[11]

Employee Participation. Employee participation in the plan is realized through involvement with the company-sponsored suggestion system and two committees with some shared responsibilities. Through the suggestion system, employees are expected to investigate various productivity-related problems and suggest solutions. Sometimes this aspect of the plan is emphasized through suggestion system campaigns in which different shifts or work locations in a plant are pitted against each other. Another way of stimulating participation is through brainstorming sessions with supervisors. Employees define the various types of problems affecting their productivity and groups are formed to find solutions to the different problems.

The two committees have various names depending upon the organization, such as Production or Executive Committee. Employees are elected by their peers to serve on the committees. Typically, the committees meet monthly to address various matters pertaining to the Scanlon plan. For example, the Production Committee, which has a more operational role, meets with supervisors from various departments to review data on such subjects as production rates by various shifts or departments, error rates, and other quality control information and employee suggestion participation. Another role this committee fulfills is evaluating employee suggestions, recommending approvals or disapprovals, and giving explanations for their decisions. In some situations, these committees may

---

[10] Bureau of Labor Statistics, *National Compensation Survey: Employee Benefits in Private Industry in the United States*, March 2004, p. 74.

[11] *Productivity Sharing Plans*, p. 8.

be delegated authority to approve suggestions within certain cost limitations. Obviously, the structure, membership tenure, mode of operation, and many other characteristics of this type of committee can vary considerably among different organizations. The important consideration is organizing and operating the committee in a manner that will optimize employee input and involvement.

The second committee, which can be called the Executive Committee, fulfills a higher role than the Production Committee. This committee, which also usually meets monthly, has the task of reviewing data on bonuses, employee productivity, and product quality. This committee may also have more authority to approve employee suggestions with a greater cost impact.

Principle of Bonus Payments. The second of the three principles that form the foundation of the Scanlon plan is the payment of bonuses to employees who have increased productivity, reduced costs, or accomplished a combination of the two, so that a gain has been realized. The essence of this principle is the Scanlon ratio:

Scanlon ratio = Labor costs ÷ Sales value of production

The ratio is derived from a careful analysis of labor cost and production data over a base period ranging up to seven years.

Principle of Employee Identification with the Firm. Gainsharing plans rely upon effective formal and informal communication systems in which management and employees are able to share ideas and cooperate with each other. Many years ago, Mary Parker Follett said that, for labor and management to coordinate their efforts and work as a team, they must first be able to cooperate, and that, in turn, requires that they must be able to communicate.[12]

The true success of any type of employee involvement, whether gainsharing is involved or not, is employee-management harmony and understanding. Regardless of how simple a plan is, how well-designed it is, and how well trained all the players are, it will not work if an atmosphere of trust and mutual respect is not the underlying theme behind it. To achieve this goal often requires much diligence, creativity, and hard work.

Installing a Scanlon Plan

The installation of a Scanlon plan entails several steps.

Size of Organization. First, the size of the organization or organizational unit should be manageable. Some experts suggest any size under 3,000 employees is sufficient. The purpose for limiting the size is because the plan relies heavily upon employee participation through councils and committees. Also, as discussed previously, employee communication and cooperation are essential. This cooperation, communication, and participation are too difficult to achieve in very large organizations. This is one reason most organizations define smaller units, such as plants, in which Scanlon plans are implemented.

---

[12] *Dynamic Administration: The Collected Papers of Mary Parker Follett,* edited by H.C. Metcalf and L. Urwick (New York: Harper & Brothers, 1940).

Research. The second step is to conduct research on operating Scanlon plans, including visiting several organizations that are using them.

Retain Consultant. The third step is ask a consultant who has installed Scanlon plans to recommend one or two companies with such a plan that would be willing to indoctrinate a top management team from the company installing a new plan. The company may also want to retain the consultant to plan and implement the plan.

Visit Indoctrinating Company. In the fourth step, the company's top management team visits the indoctrinating company. The indoctrination typically requires one day. The first half-day is a general orientation covering the mechanics and potential benefits, and in the second half-day, the visiting group members are oriented about their roles by their indoctrinating company's counterparts. This indoctrination is very important because it helps dispel both covert and obvious opposition, such as helping to convince skeptics about the effectiveness of the plans.

Prepare Plan. The fifth step consists of the top management team returning home and preparing a Scanlon plan which is presented to the company's board of directors.

Select Committee. After the board's approval, the sixth step is selecting a committee of 15 or so employees who represent different functions and organizational levels, from finance director to production employee. This group is sent to the indoctrinating company for the same exposure the top management group received (one-half day on orientation and the other half with their counterparts).

Implement Plan. The seventh step is the implementation of the plan, including the development of promotional campaigns and extensive employee communication in which the 15-member committee plays the lead role. Production, costs, sales, and other performance data are posted to keep employees informed of the progress that is made. The committee identifies areas that need attention. Gradually, the plan begins to have an effect as employee work teams cooperate to increase efficiency.[13]

Developing the Scanlon Ratio

> **EXAMPLE:** Assume over a five-year base period that labor costs have averaged $600,000 and the sales value of production averaged $1,000,000. The Scanlon ratio would be:
>
> $600,000 ÷ $1,000,000 = .60

Applying the Ratio

Assume the Scanlon ratio for a firm is .60, as computed above. This means labor is entitled to 60 cents for each $1 dollar of the sales value of production. Now assume in a given month the sales value of production was $100,000 and labor costs were $50,000, so that labor costs were only 50 percent or .50 of the sales value of production. This is an improvement in the Scanlon Ratio (because .50 is lower than the Scanlon Ratio of .60). Labor was entitled to $60,000 (.60 ×

---

[13] *Productivity Sharing Plans*, p. 33.

$100,000), but the actual labor costs were lower ($50,000), so that savings resulted. Usually 75 percent of the savings is distributed to employees. The remainder is placed in a pool (sometimes called a "balancing account") to be used in months when deficits occur. If there are any funds left in the pool at the end of the plan year, they are distributed and the plan starts again for the next year. Each employee's percentage of the gain is the same as the employee's pay as a percent of total pay for the period. Bonuses are paid monthly. Employees are kept regularly informed of production, work quality, sales value of production, and other performance variables to induce them to improve production and save labor costs.

> **EXAMPLE:** ABC Company has a Scanlon plan with a Scanlon ratio of labor cost to sales value of production of .70, meaning that labor is entitled to 70 cents for every $1 of sales value of production that is produced by the employees. At the end of the month of November, assume the sales value of production was $500,000 and labor costs were $300,000. Labor was entitled to $350,000 ($500,000 × .70 = $350,000). Therefore, the savings were $50,000 ($350,000 − $300,000). The company shares .75 (75 percent) of the savings with employees. The amount to be shared was $37,500 (.75 × $50,000). Assume Linda' s pay for the month was one percent of the total payroll for the month. Linda's share of the $37,500 is $375 (.01 × $37,500).

Rucker Plan

The Rucker plan was developed in 1933 by Allen Rucker, a cost accountant, who found through a historical analysis of aggregate manufacturing firm data for the period 1899 through 1932 that there was an almost constant ratio of labor costs to the value added by manufacture. He conducted other studies involving individual firms and single plants of larger firms and found the same result. From this research, he concluded that this ratio could be used as a convenient yardstick for employers to share any gains with employees. Before the calculations of the method are discussed, it would be useful to examine the concept of "value added by manufacture," since it is important to an understanding of the Rucker plan.

Value Added by Manufacture

"Value added by manufacture" is a term used in economics for the value that is added to a product through manufacture. Another way of expressing this is the value added to materials, services, and supplies by a production operation. In the case of a plant that makes steel automobile frames, the values produced are the frames the plant makes and sells after paying for the steel that is bought from a steel mill.

A typical example used to explain a sequence of "values added by manufacture" is the progression of events in growing wheat, milling it, adding it to other ingredients to make bread, and marketing the bread to the ultimate consumer. First, a farmer grows the wheat and sells it to a miller. The *added value* is the difference in the income the farmer receives for his wheat and the costs he incurred for seed, fertilizer, fuel, and other supplies. The miller, in turn, buys the wheat from the farmer, mills it, and sells it to a bakery. The difference in the cost of buying the wheat and the price it is sold for to the bakery is the amount of "value" the miller "adds" in the milling process. The same process is repeated by the baker, as the flour which was milled by the miller is mixed with other ingredients and is sold as bread to either the consumer or to a retailer who in turn sells it to the consumer. The baker "adds value" by blending in the other ingredients to the flour and baking the bread. If the bread is sold to the consumer through a retailer, the retailer also "adds value" by buying the bread from the bakery, transporting it to a store convenient for the consumer, displaying the bread and selling it. The total of all the *added values* from each step along the way equals the total contribution to the overall economy from the whole chain of events.

Consistent Ratios of Labor Costs and Value Added

As noted above, Allen Rucker found that manufacturing businesses tend to have very consistent ratios between the labor costs incurred at a given site and the amounts of "value added" produced at the same site.

> **EXAMPLE:** In a recent year, the ABC Company had net sales of $5,000,000. The company paid $2,000,000 for materials, $300,000 for various supplies, and another $200,000 for such services as utilities and subcontractors. The "value added" was $2,500,000, which is the difference between the $5,000,000 it took in and the $2,500,000 it paid out to its various suppliers.

Rucker Formula

This is the formula for the Rucker ratio:

Rucker ratio = TEC ÷ (SVP–COMSS)

Where:

TEC = total employment costs of the employee population in the plan, including wages, salaries, payroll taxes, and all benefits;

SVP = net sales value of current production; and

COMSS = costs for materials, supplies, and services consumed.

The numerator is the employment cost associated with the same output. The denominator is the value added by the given production operation.

> **EXAMPLE:** Carrying on with the earlier example of the ABC Company numbers, assume that a long-term pattern showed $2,500,000 of value added, accompanied by spending $1,500,000 on total employment costs. The Rucker formula or ratio is $1,500,000 divided by $2,500,000, or .60.

Bonus and "Balancing Account"

In recognition of the fact that not all months will produce bonuses and to guard against possible audit adjustments or inventory shrinkages, the Rucker plan uses a "Balancing Account" or reserve from the bonuses in months in which they are earned to offset any "bad" months in which bonuses are not earned. Typically, one-third of all bonuses in the months in which they are earned are placed in the Balancing Account. The remaining two-thirds of the bonuses are paid as soon as practical in the following month.

Generally, a company should expect one to three bad months in even a well-performing bonus-making operation. Sometimes the total of bad months may be as high as four or five during the first year of a plan start-up, particularly if the company is in a deficit condition, which is not uncommon in gainsharing plans. The typical bad months are during vacation seasons, in hot months, during the holiday seasons, and during periods of epidemic illness.

The funds left in the Balancing Account at the end of the year, after any deductions or additions for the contingencies described above, are distributed to the employees in a separate check. If the employees have received a bonus check each month, receiving this 13th one is a very pleasant event.

Calculating a Bonus

Like the Scanlon plan, the Rucker Ratio is derived from a base period. Any improvements (meaning reductions or savings) in the ratio are shared with employees, both managerial and non-managerial. Each employee's percentage of the gain is the same as the employee's pay as a percent of total pay for the period. Bonuses are paid monthly. Employees are kept regularly informed of production, work quality, sales, waste, and other performance variables. Calculations are similar to the Scanlon plan.

EXAMPLE: ABC Company has a Rucker plan with a ratio of labor costs to the value added through manufacture (sales value of production minus the costs of outside goods and services) of .80. Thus, labor is entitled to 80 cents for every $1 of sales value of production added through manufacture. In December, the labor costs were $460,000, the sales value of production was $800,000, and the costs of outside goods and services was $200,000. Labor was entitled to $480,000 [($800,000 − $200,000) × .8], so that the savings were $20,000 ($480,000 − $460,000). The company shares .75 of any gain with employees. The amount to share among employees is $15,000 ($20,000 × 75). Assuming Frank's pay for the month was eight percent of the total payroll for the month, he is entitled to $1,200 ($15,000 × .8).

Conditions Influencing Rucker Formula Variables

The four variables in the Rucker formula are employment costs, sales value of production, purchases of outside services, and purchases of supplies and materials. Following are some examples of conditions that could affect those variables. These examples are for illustration purposes only, since some of them could affect more than one variable.

- *Labor Costs.* Labor costs are affected by hiring additional personnel, by reducing personnel through attrition due to productivity improvements, by either increases or decreases in either pay or benefits, and by changes in overtime usage. These are some other examples of conditions that could increase or decrease labor costs, depending upon the outcome:
  - Stand-by time;
  - Employee training;
  - Reworking to correct errors or bring products up to standard;
  - Changes in work methods; and

- Capital investment projects that change the demand for employee's time.

- *Sales Value of Production.* The sales value of production is affected by output and/or price increases or decreases. Price changes are often influenced by such variables as employment costs and the costs of purchased services, materials, and supplies. Some conditions that influence output are:

  - Capital investment projects, such as changes in plant and equipment;

  - Changes in work methods;

  - Product changes, such as the design or features that affect consumer demand; and

  - Changes in sales procedures, such as credit requirements or warranty provisions that affect consumer demand.

- *Purchases of Outside Services.* Purchases of outside services are affected by changes in subcontracting, utility rates, regulatory matters, and other conditions, such as capital investment in plant and equipment that changes the demand for outside services.

- *Purchases of Supplies and Materials.* Purchases of supplies and materials are affected by changes in prices charged by vendors, waste, defects, errors, and changes in procedures or work methods. These are some other conditions that affect supplies and materials:

  - Purchasing economics;

  - Employee theft;

  - Inventory accuracy and procedures; and

  - Changes in product design.

Sales Pay Plans

Among the objectives that are accomplished with sales pay plans are market share and profitability, customer service, and employee acceptance.

Market Share and Profitability

The factors impacting market share and profitability include sales volumes, new business, retaining business, product mix, and selling expenses.

Sales Volume

Sales volume objectives simply stipulate the amount of sales targeted for specific time periods. Sales are the lifeblood of most organizations, so that the importance of such an objective is obvious. In recognition of this importance, in most sales jobs sales volume is the sole means of compensating personnel through performance-based pay.

The advantages of using sales volume as the sole means of paying sales personnel is that it is relatively easy to plan, easy for employees to understand, easy to track and administer, and it focuses on the revenue portion of an organization's profitability. On the other hand, the disadvantages of using sales volume alone in the application of performance-based pay is that it ignores customer service, does not consider costs, fails to include profitability, and ignores the long-term viability of the firm.

New Business

New business objectives involve setting targets for sales from customers who have not made purchases from the firm before. This objective reinforces the need to bring new business into the firm. This focus may cause sales personnel to change their sales methods by directing part of their efforts from old to new business.

The advantages of using this objective is that it motivates sales personnel to overcome any anxieties they may have in attempting to penetrate new markets for potential customers. Also, it focuses attention on the need for the firm to open up new markets and secure new customers. The extra efforts required to develop new business can be compensated through the pay plan.

New business objectives can also have their limitations, such as the additional cost that may be involved in developing new sources of customers. Also, if the performance-based pay plan disproportionately rewards new business compared to old business, existing customers may be neglected.

Retaining Sales

A retaining sales objective rewards personnel with performance-based pay for sales that are repeat business from existing customers. This objective is particularly important in industries that are experiencing a major transition in technology or in other areas, such as an unexpected increase in the number of new competitors.

The advantages of a retained sales objective is that it emphasizes to sales personnel the importance of treating customers in such a manner that will ensure repeat business. Another advantage is that sales personnel will give more service and try a little harder to retain business, instead of following the tactic of "taking the customer's money and run." This objective also recognizes the importance of customer goodwill.

Like other sales objectives, used alone, the retaining sales objective has disadvantages. First, it tends to make sales personnel apathetic about developing new sources of customers. Prospecting and calling on new customers is hard work and emphasizing repeat business provides little incentive for a salesperson to perform those chores.

Product Mix

Product mix objectives are intended to motivate sales personnel to consider all product lines and not just those that they are the most comfortable selling or those that they have the most success in selling. Employers are concerned about sales personnel knowing all the products in a line, so that the business can be more profitable. Diversification is often the key to business survival. While one or two products may be the major source of income for a firm, the continuing success of it depends upon introducing new products and making the necessary changes in others, so that they will remain competitive in the market. In order for a business to achieve those conditions, it is not enough to simply produce the products. Sales personnel must be knowledgeable about the new products and be creative in selling them.

Learning the characteristics of products, including their different properties and operating features, takes time and perseverance. Some sales personnel have to be motivated to make the effort to gain this knowledge. A pay plan that rewards efforts made in this manner is more likely to gain some results.

The advantages to a product mix objective are: it helps ensure the profitability and continued existence of the business; it motivates sales personnel to expend the effort necessary to learn the firm's products; and, in the long term, it improves the income of sales personnel. This objective provides a motivation for sales personnel to become knowledgeable in a firm's products. A firm can build a better mousetrap but if sales personnel will not learn about it, so that they can sell it, the costs involved in the development of the product are not recouped. A product mix objective helps prevent that contingency.

The disadvantages of a product mix objective include the possibility of increased training costs. In addition, in the short term, there could be some reduction in sales for those sales personnel who are devoting extra time to orienting themselves about the characteristics of various products.

Win-Back Sales

The win-back sales objective focuses the attention of sales personnel on the importance of obtaining business from former customers who are presently buying from a competitor. One organization that has an assertive "competitive win-back" sales objective component in the sales personnel performance-based pay program doubles the value of sales for each dollar of "qualified" win-back sales.

A win-back sales objective is often used when the competition is especially keen in an industry. Other situations in which a win-back objective is particularly appropriate is trying to regain sales lost because of an advantage a competitor once had, but which has been neutralized due to a new product or strategy recently introduced by the business.

The advantages of a win-back objective include focusing sales employees' attention on the competition within an industry. Sometimes sales personnel can become indifferent to the competition. This is particularly true when the firm has traditionally held a significant competitive advantage over competing firms. Another advantage is that it helps motivate sales personnel to emphasize to customers how the firm has regained an advantage or become competitive. In some cases this means the salesperson must update their knowledge or training in the firm's procedures, products, or other dimensions that resulted in the firm regaining a competitive posture. A sales objective providing pay incentives for win-backs is often enough motivation for sales personnel to gain that knowledge or training.

Selling Expenses

Selling expenses include all the fixed and operating expenses attributable to the sales function. To the extent that is feasible and accurate, these expenses are sometimes tracked by each salesperson. The typical types of such expenses are lodging, travel, meals, entertainment, postage, printing, office supplies, and samples. Other types of expenses that are sometimes related to selling include technical support, and administrative and typing assistance.

Care must be exercised when including selling expenses in a pay plan because of the differences in sales territories, assigned customer/client bases, and product assignments. For example, one sales representative for a major corporation had a territory located a considerable distance from her residence. In addition, the larger cities, which represented the major portion of her potential customers, were 75 miles from each other. Understandably, her selling expenses were considerably larger than those of other representatives.

Controlling Sales Expenses

Some organizations compute a sales/expense ratio to compare the relative sales efficiency of different sales personnel. Caution should be exercised in using such ratios, however, because they can be very misleading. For example, assume Joe has a ratio of .10 and Julia's is .11; using the ratio alone, one might conclude that Joe is the more efficient salesperson. However, that opinion would no doubt change with the extra knowledge that Julia sold 15 times more merchandise than Joe did.

There are several ways of using a pay system to control selling expenses. One way is to establish expense budgets based upon sales objectives. The employee would be compensated for a portion of the budgetary savings, assuming the sales targets were reached. Another way is to use expenses to sales ratios and share any savings with the employee.

The obvious advantage of including selling expenses in a pay plan for sales personnel is the positive effect it will have on controlling those expenses. Instead of staying at a premium hotel, a sales representative will more likely stay at a lower-price accommodation, if there is an incentive to do so. Other expenses can be similarly affected through pay incentives.

The disadvantages of a pay system designed to control selling expenses is the problem of unfairness discussed above. Determining comparability, be it expenses or even sales prospects, is difficult to achieve when sales territories are constructed. While equity considerations would demand comparability, achieving that goal is often elusive. Another disadvantage is the possibility that sales representatives will cease entertaining clients, stay in substandard accommodations that will adversely reflect upon the image of the firm, and engage in similar tactics in other areas to save expenses.

Sales Returns

Sales returns, credits for damaged or unwanted merchandise, and similar types of transactions are deductions from sales. In addition to a reduction in sales, some transactions, if they involve returning merchandise that is shopworn or used, represent a cost, since the items cannot simply be returned to inventory and resold. In addition, there are expenses involved in handling returned goods. These types of expenses can occur in many industries. For example, in life insurance sales, a policy that lapses before the end of the first year of coverage not only reduces premium income but it causes the company to incur a disproportionate amount of expenses due to the underwriting expenses, including any medical examinations that were incurred in issuing the policy.

The advantages of including sales returns or actions of a similar nature that represent a reduction in sales and/or increased costs in a pay plan are that they decrease the likelihood that sales personnel will simply sell something to a customer and forget the important roles of meeting the customer's need and providing service. The salesperson will be more attuned to what the customer really needs and less concerned about simply making a sale. The other obvious advantages is that giving an incentive for reducing returns and related actions will reduce costs.

Like other types of pay system variables, there is a flip side to including returned merchandise in a performance-based compensation plan. The principal disadvantage, which is especially applicable if the penalty is excessively high, is the propensity of salespeople to not make a sale if there is a risk of a return.

Customer Relations

An essential dimension of any sales pay plan is customer relations. Firms want to keep their customers happy. This philosophy is behind the age-old motto, "The customer is always right." Some of the variables involved in measuring customer service include customer commendations or expressions of satisfaction with a salesperson, survey instruments that measure customer satisfaction, and the percentage of time spent in assisting customers.

Customer Calls

A proxy for customer service is the number of sales calls made to customers. This could be the average number of calls made or some similar measure. The logic behind such a variable is that the probability of helping customers is in some degree related to the number of calls made to them. As some customers lament to their sales representatives, "The only time I see you is when you want to make a sale."

The advantage to including the number of calls in a sales incentive program is that it emphasizes to sales personnel that customer service is important to the firm. Another advantage is that customer service is increased when sales representatives make calls. A byproduct benefit from making calls, whether they are simply goodwill calls or calls to render service, is the probability of additional sales.

A disadvantage to using customer calls in a pay system is that some sales personnel will interpret the variable to mean that sales calls, and not customer service, is what is important in the business. Another disadvantage is that sales calls, as such, really accomplish little. The important aspect of a sales call is the quality of what transpires during the call, be it the service that is rendered, the goodwill that is obtained, or the additional sales that are received.

Employer Objectives

Employers have various objectives affecting employees' acceptance of pay plans. Some of these objectives are to motivate sales personnel, to have a plan that is easy to communicate to employees and is equally easy for them to understand, and to construct a plan that can be easily administered.

Plan Comprehension

Plan comprehension is a function of the number of variables in the plan, the complexity of the plan, and the instrument used to communicate the plan. The top official in one organization told a consultant that he wanted a pay plan that was so simple that employees could mentally calculate how well they were doing in it while they were driving to work. After several attempts, the consultant did develop such a plan that included four objectives, some of which were similar to those discussed above.

Plan Communication

Plan communication may include both a written instrument that explains the various features of the plan and a briefing session in which the plan is formally introduced and endorsed by the top management of the firm. The plan may also be communicated in an orientation session that is conducted by someone from the human resources management department.

Plan Administration

About 50 percent of firms delegate the responsibility for performance-based pay plans to the HR department. In the other 50 percent, the responsibility is jointly shared by the HR department and others.[14] These administrative functions include conducting the above-mentioned orientation sessions, interpreting various provisions, and recommending any needed changes. In some organizations, it is necessary to differentiate the administration of the plan, as discussed above, from the other essential activities of tracking performance in the different variables included in the plan and making payments for that performance.

Usually the activities performed under the second category above are delegated to the accounting function. For example, each salesperson generally completes weekly activity reports. This information, together with other quantitative data, like sales invoices, credit slips, etc., are routed to the accounting department, where the data is entered into various accounts. Depending upon the information system used, the data is coded by a salesperson, so that periodically (not less than monthly) each salesperson receives a report of the status of all the variables in his or her account. Any data directly affecting periodic paychecks is summarized on a statement accompanying the check.

Employee Motivation

Finally, a major objective of a sales personnel compensation plan is to motivate sales employees to meet those other objectives for which the plan has also been designed. Consequently, the manner in which the other objectives are

---

[14] The Bureau of National Affairs, Inc., "SHRM-BNA Survey No. 62: Human Resource Activities, Budgets, and Staffs: 1996-97," *Bulletin to Management* (June 26, 1997).

designed in the plan has a profound effect upon the motivation of sales personnel to do those things necessary to accomplish them.

Sales Compensation Methods

The major methods of compensating sales personnel are salary and performance-based pay. Most sales personnel are on a combination of salary plus some
form of incentive. Some types of sales jobs are paid exclusively through incentives; for example, most life insurance sales jobs are paid totally through commissions on premiums for insurance sales. In addition, commercial real estate sales
jobs are paid exclusively from commissions earned on leases consummated or
real estate sales.

Some organizations use salary as the sole method of paying sales personnel.
For example, for a number of years all sales personnel at Digital Equipment were
paid only salaries; pay incentives were not used.[15]

Rationale for Salary Only

Organizations have various reasons for placing sales personnel on salaries
without incentives.

Unnecessary Sales. First and perhaps foremost, a firm with this policy may
be concerned about sales personnel selling products or services to clients/
customers who do not need them. There is validity to this concern when pay
incentives constitute a significant portion of a salesperson's pay, and there are
inadequate controls to prevent unnecessary or improper selling from occurring.
The problem of control is more significant in these types of selling situations:

- *Situation 1:* The product requires considerable technical training and
  experience to understand, so that the customer relies upon the judgment
  of the salesperson in making the purchasing decision.

- *Situation 2:* The sales personnel have a number of options to meet the
  needs of a customer, and some have disproportionately large pay
  incentives.

- *Situation 3:* The firm is a monopoly with few, if any, substitutable
  products.

- *Situation 4:* The product is new to the market and technologically
  advanced.

In Situation 1, the customer essentially depends upon the goodwill of the
salesperson. For example, a customer shopping for a piece of equipment to help
his niece write term papers at college may be totally ignorant of the various
options available to him. In this situation, one alternative is to buy a word
processor; another is a personal computer. Still a third option is to buy an electric
typewriter; a fourth is to buy an electronic typewriter. Since the generous uncle
does not even know how to type, let alone have knowledge of word processing
software capabilities and the degrees of "user-friendliness" provided by the
various types of equipment, he expects the salesperson to act as both a sales

---

[15] n.a., "Digital Equipment to Pay Bonuses to Top
Salesmen," *Wall Street Journal* (June 17, 1986), p. 6.

consultant/counselor and a seller of equipment. Too often, the two roles cause confusion and dissatisfaction. The buyer expects the salesperson to be impartial, but too often those expectations are unrealistic. To prevent this contingency, some employers simply pay sales personnel salaries.

In Situation 2, a problem may occur if the sales incentive on the various types of equipment differs. For example, if the sales commission on the electronic typewriter was twice that of the personal computer, the salesperson would be motivated to push the typewriter, even though it may not be the best alternative for the customer. Some employers avoid this conflict of interest by using straight salary with no pay incentives to compensate sales personnel.

Situation 3 occurs when there are no competitive products on the market and a salesperson can take advantage of the customer because there is no alternative source to meet the customer's need.

The problem in Situation 4 is the increased possibility that customers will be uninformed about the product and must rely exclusively upon the salesperson for this information. In this situation, the motto, *caveat emptor*, is relatively meaningless. To prevent the sales personnel from taking advantage of customers, some employers compensate sales employees by paying them a salary alone.

Organizational Image. Another reason some firms use salary only for sales personnel is to impress upon the customer that the salesperson is solely motivated by meeting the customer's need. Pay incentives may pose an ethical dilemma for sales personnel. Money, particularly when there is considerable amount of it involved in a transaction, can interfere with a salesperson's judgment. In addition, some customers do not like the idea of buying from personnel who are paid an incentive for selling it. In these cases, the customer fears the employee is unduly influenced by the incentive. This feeling is reinforced if the salesperson is too assertive in making the sale and not mindful enough of the customer's pocketbook and needs.[16]

Establishing Base Salary

Base salary in sales jobs is determined through job evaluation, assigned territory and/or product, client or customer base, and service responsibilities.

Job Evaluation. *Job evaluation* is the process of applying compensable factors to job tasks to determine the relative worth of jobs within an organization with the goal of achieving internal pay equity among them. Determining the pay grade for a sales job using job evaluation entails studying the job using one or more job analysis methods, and applying the job evaluation method to the information obtained. Job evaluation is discussed in Chapter 26.

Assigned Territory/Product. Establishing a base salary by territory gives recognition to the differences that may exist in different territories or locations. It is difficult to set geographical boundaries so the various sales territories will be equal. Some of the differences that occur most frequently in territories are the

---

[16] Allen, M., "Sales Commissions Attract Fans, Opponents," *Richmond Times-Dispatch* (September 13, 1987), p. F-1.

type of customer, the customer income/sales potential, the distance between customer locations, the travel time necessary to serve customers, and the cost of living. Since many of these differences are related to the sales potential of a territory, the base salary is adjusted accordingly.

The type of product assigned to a salesperson may also affect the salary. For example, some products are more difficult to sell, have no potential for repeat business, require extraordinary amounts of sales personnel training and preparation, and require more customer service. To compensate for these differences, some organizations make the necessary adjustments in the base salary.

Some organizations fill vacant sales jobs in territories by offering them to sales personnel usually based on seniority. This selection process is particularly appealing to sales personnel in firms that do not use base salary differentials for the various territories or use differentials that do not accurately reflect significant differences in the characteristics of the territories.

Some of the advantages of using assigned territories include the decreased selling expenses by having only one salesperson call on a customer, the opportunity for sales personnel to develop closer professional relationships with their customers, and the prevention of customers becoming annoyed by having more than one salesperson calling on them. The principal disadvantage is the tendency for sales personnel to become complacent in serving the needs of their customers. Another disadvantage is the possibility that a customer may dislike a particular salesperson and refuse to do business with the firm.

Client/Customer Base. Sometimes base salary is determined by the client or customer base. The customer base could be established in a number of ways, such as by industry or client name. In the industry example, all the firms within an industry are assigned to a specific salesperson who is responsible for all sales activity in those firms. The base salary may depend upon past revenue generated in the industry.

In other situations, specific clients are assigned to different sales personnel. The reasons for this practice are the same as for territorial divisions, namely, to prevent more than one salesperson from contacting the customer and to provide an opportunity for each salesperson to develop a relationship with his or her assigned customers.

Service Responsibilities. Some sales jobs require sales personnel to perform a certain amount of service work with customers. The services may be answering questions or training the customer's employees. The salary for a job in these situations depends upon the amount of service that is required.

Commission

A *commission* is a pay incentive that is based upon a percentage of the selling price of a product or service. Usually, sales jobs are paid either partially or totally by commission.

Salary Plus Commission. As noted above, some sales jobs involve various tasks in addition to selling. For example, clothing salespeople place price tags on items, straighten stock, take inventory, and perform other administrative tasks.

Typically, selling jobs that involve non-selling tasks have a salary schedule, in addition to sales commissions. The salary compensates employees for these non-selling tasks. The percentage of salary and commission in the total pay for a job depends upon the relative importance of each in compensating job tasks.

Among the various types of commissions are *straight commission, graduated commission,* and *multiple-tiered commission.*

Straight Commission. A *straight commission* is a pay incentive with a fixed percentage of the sales price of the product/service. For example, a hardware store clerk is paid a straight commission of 10 percent for all sales. A straight commission is used in many types of sales jobs, such as real estate, department store sales personnel, and retail shoe sales.

Graduated Commission. A *graduated commission* is a pay incentive with increased percentage rates for successively higher sales volumes. Usually, the commission percentages increase at regular intervals, such as these:

Sales	Commission
up to $100,000	6 %
100,000 up to 200,000	7
200,000 up to 300,000	8
300,000 up to 400,000	9
400,000 up to 500,000	10
500,000 up to 600,000	11
600,000 and over	12

Graduated commission structures are an additional incentive for sales personnel to increase their sales. This incentive rewards those sales personnel who marginally add to a firm's profitability.

Multiple-Tiered Commission. A *multiple-tiered commission* is similar to graduated ones except the employee is paid at the higher rate for all sales. For example, some brokerage firms pay their stockbrokers a 25 percent commission on total annualized stock sales of a certain dollar amount. However, once the stockbroker's sales exceed that level, the commission jumps to 35 percent and the stockbroker receives the higher percentage on all sales.[17]

Like the graduated commission, multiple-tiered commissions provide a strong incentive for sales personnel to sell more. Also, like the graduated commission, the multiple-tiered commission rewards sales personnel who marginally add to the profitability of the firm. In addition to the two features that multiple-tiered commissions share with the graduated commission, they have two others that are different. First, the multiple-tiered commission exerts a very strong incentive for sales personnel to exceed the base, since all sales, including those in the base, qualify for the higher commission rate. Second, multiple-tiered commissions are intended to penalize lower producers by causing them to bear their share of the administrative costs caused by their lower sales volumes.

---

[17] McMurray, S., "Brokerage Firms Push Salespeople To Produce More or Face Penalties," *Wall Street Journal* (June 19, 1984), p. 31.

Commission Terminology

In the following sections, some of the terms related to commissions are discussed.

Commission-with-Draw. A *draw* is an advance payment made to a salesperson that is deducted from his or her future commissions. An *earned draw* is an advance payment against commissions that have been earned but not paid. An *unearned draw,* by contrast, is an advance payment against commissions that have not been earned. Sometimes, the term *advance* is used in lieu of draw. In other situations, the term *advance* is used to denote a payment to salaried employees who need money either for an emergency situation that cannot wait until the regular payroll date or because their paycheck was not issued due to some administrative error. Some firms do not give unearned draws as a matter of policy. Other firms do not use draws at all because of the administrative work that is entailed in them, such as writing extra checks and making accounting entries in payroll records.

Commission-Splitting. *Commission-splitting* is the process of dividing an earned commission among more than one sales personnel for their efforts in either assisting in the sale or for fulfilling the role of broker in the sale.

Charge-Backs. A *charge-back* is a deduction from a person's pay for a previously paid commission which was voided by a sale not consummated or withdrawn.

Partial Commission Payment. Some organizations have a policy of not crediting an entire sale to a salesperson until a certain period has elapsed. This is used as a precaution in the event the sale is not consummated, such as when the customer returns the item for a credit or in some way fails to meet the conditions of the sale. A *partial commission payment* is that part of the commission that the salesperson does receive.

Bonus

A *bonus* is a generic term used to describe cash payments in pay-for-performance plans. Bonuses are given to employees in all types of jobs, including those in sales. Bonuses are paid on various schedules ranging from daily to annual payments. In some cases, the word *bonus* is used to describe annual payments made under profit-sharing plans or monthly payments made under Scanlon or Rucker plans. A *bonus* for sales personnel is typically a lump sum payment for meeting a quota or a specific performance objective. Some of the various types of bonuses used in sales jobs are discussed in the following sections.

Quotas

A *quota* is a quantified objective in such areas as sales or production that is to be accomplished by one or more persons within a certain time period. In sales jobs, quotas can be set on any of the variables discussed above, such as total sales, repeat sales, win-back sales, or new business. Quotas can also be established for sales of different product lines.

Setting Quotas. Several different methods can be used to set quotas. One way is for the manager to independently set the quota for each salesperson. The problem with this approach is the lack of sales personnel input, which causes resentment. Another way is for the sales employee and the manager to jointly develop a sales quota for the individual. The obvious advantage of the latter approach is the greater tendency of a person to accept a quota if they have a role in setting it. Sometimes organization-wide goals are established and these are used as guides for quota-setting.

Quotas can be based upon such data as sales trends in a salesperson's performance, growth in sales in a particular market or product, or market forecasts. Some of the sources of information considered in establishing quotas include market surveys, demographic data of customers, and various economic statistics, like regional and national projections of the gross domestic product or an industry section thereof.

Establishing the Bonus Pool. A *bonus pool* is the amount of funds available for distribution to employees through a pay-for-performance plan. Some organizations establish a specific amount of funds that will be available for incentive pay purposes. For example, one national organization provides a $3,000 bonus to each salesperson who achieves his or her annual objectives which includes sales quotas in various categories and planned accomplishments in such areas as personal development. The bonus pool is simply the number of sales personnel multiplied by $3,000. In some organizations, the size of the bonus pool depends upon the combined efforts of all employees eligible for a bonus, including sales personnel.

Types of Bonus Arrangements

There are various types of bonus arrangements that include sales volume, profit performance, and overall job performance.

Sales Volume. As the term implies, a sales volume bonus is a lump sum payment made to a salesperson who achieves a designated minimum in sales volume during a stipulated time period. The purpose of this type of bonus is to motivate sales personnel to reach a sales target. As noted previously in this chapter, some types of sales commission plans, such as the graduated or multiple-tiered commission structure, are intended to accomplish this same purpose. To some extent, however, the bonus is particularly effective in this regard because the lump sum payment represents a significant reward for meeting the target.

Profit Performance. A bonus for profit performance is especially effective in group bonuses, in which a bonus pool is used to reward a group of employees for achieving a specified level of profitability. One organization has several different profit-making product lines. Because of the manner in which the organization is structured, achieving profitability in those lines requires the combined efforts of several key employees, including the principal salesperson. To encourage teamwork among those key players, the organization has a bonus plan in which part of each of the player's bonus depends upon the total financial plan.

Setting a bonus on profit performance may require some special reporting arrangements if individual instead of group bonuses are to be used. This means "profit centers" must be established for each salesperson. Under this arrangement, the costs, revenues, and resulting profit for each salesperson are planned and the bonus is based on the resultant figures.

Accomplishing Performance Objectives. *Performance objectives bonuses* are annual cash payments for performance that exceeds set performance objectives, such as the number of sales calls, dollar amount of win-back sales, or self-development accomplishments.

Overall Job Performance. Some organizations employ a bonus plan that incorporates multiple features to reward overall job performance.

Special Purpose Bonus Plans

Sometimes organizations use bonuses for special purposes. For example, one organization that already had an annual overall job performance bonus established a special bonus plan in a particular sales category to stimulate sales in a product line. The bonus amounts were relatively modest ($300 was awarded to the top salesperson, $200 to the next best, and $100 to the third best). The bonus eligibility period consisted of three specific months. Awards were made at a special breakfast at the conclusion of the contest.

Special purpose bonuses are very effective in piquing the interest of sales personnel in selected areas of sales performance. The different ways in which these bonuses can be used are only constrained by the creativity of management.

Types of Bonus Payments

The three main types of bonus payments are percentage of salary, fixed amount, and graduated or scaled amounts.

Percentage of Salary. Under the percentage of salary arrangement, management announces to employees the terms of the bonus, including the maximum percentage of salary that an employee can earn as a bonus. This method can be inequitable if the same or similar performance objectives are set for all sales personnel, such as all employees having the same dollar objective for sales volume. This arrangement would obviously be inequitable if some employees have a larger base salary than others. The method is most equitable when the salary of each salesperson equitably rewards his or her base level of performance and the performance objectives for a bonus are relative to the performance justifying the base salary.

Fixed Amount of Bonus. A fixed amount of bonus is fair in situations where sales personnel have approximately the same objectives and about an equal chance of accomplishing them. For example, if all the sales territories were the same or similar in sales potential and other variables included in the bonus plan, it would be fair to use a fixed bonus amount of $3,000 for each employee who achieved a five percent improvement in their base for the same variables.

Fixed bonuses are also fair if sales personnel have equal access to all customers in a market. For example, paying a $1,000 bonus to the home insulation salesperson who sells the most in an eight-week sales contest is fair if all the home insulation sales personnel in the firm are permitted to call on any customer.

Graduated and Multiple-Tiered Bonus Plans. The terms *graduated* and *multiple-tiered* have already been defined above. Both percentage of salary and fixed amount bonus plans can be graduated or multiple-tiered. The following is an example of a graduated percentage of salary bonus plan based upon a sales volume objective:

% of Sales Volume Objective	% of Salary Bonus
below 90	0
90	5
91	6
92	7
93	8
94	9
95	10
96	11
97	12
98	13
99	14
100	15
over 100	20

A multiple-tiered bonus can also be used in pay plans. In the above example, there are the following three tiers. Tier 1 entails sales performance that is below 90 percent of the sales volume objective in which no bonus is paid. The second tier involves a graduated one percentage point increase in the bonus for the same one percentage point increase at 90 percent or better of the sales volume objective. In the third tier, the bonus jumps from 15 percent of salary for achieving 100 percent of the sales volume objective to 20 percent for exceeding 100 percent.

Contingency-Based Pay Structure

Among the new performance-based pay systems that have been adopted by companies are competency-based pay, pay-for-knowledge, and skill-based pay. These new systems are used in a variety of settings.

Competency-Based Pay

A *competency* is a skill possessed by a person that is required for successful performance on the job.

A *competency-based* pay structure equates pay or pay grades to specific, defined competencies that must be demonstrated to earn the pay or pay grade.

How does a competency-based pay plan differ from the traditional plans? The principal difference in a competency-based pay structure and a traditional job evaluation or market pay structure is the focus of the pay. In a competency-based system, the focus is on what the employee does and is thus rewarded for it.

In the traditional job evaluation pay structure, the focus is on the job tasks; employees are rewarded for the tasks they are required to perform but not on what they actually do or how well they do it.

Thus, a competency-based pay structure is both a job worth and performance appraisal pay-for-performance plan. A job evaluation or market pay structure has only the job worth component.

A fundamental step in designing a competency-based pay structure is a comprehensive job analysis of the jobs that will be included in the plan. This analysis involves identifying all levels of critical competencies.[18] For example, for an in-house computer programmer who designs programs to meet the information systems requests of personnel within the organization, a competency might be this:

> *Design computer programs that meet the computer information needs of in-house personnel.*

Programmers would be rewarded based upon the degree of this competency they possessed and demonstrated on the job. Exhibit 30-1 is a hypothetical example of a pay structure designed to reward programmers for this competency.

Exhibit 30~1
Competency-Based Pay Structure for Programmers
Hypothetical Example

Pay Grade	Competency: Design computer programs.
8	Level 1: Basic programming applications, such as a job applicant tracking system.
12	Level 2: Intermediate programming applications, such as accounting for employee contributions to the 401(k) plan.
14	Level 3: Advanced programming applications, such as a human resource planning system.

Employers are using competency-based pay systems in a variety of settings. A large university is using competency-based pay for computer programmers. Healthcare organizations are using competency-based pay to broaden job tasks, motivate employees to assume more skills, and encourage initiative.[19] Sometimes, a competency-based pay structure is used for some groups of employees and a traditional job evaluation pay structure is used for other jobs.

Knowledge-Based Pay

In the context of a work environment, *knowledge* is a body of information applied directly to the performance of a task or function. Thus, knowledge is the

---

[18] Nemerov, Donald W., "How to design a competency-based pay program," *Journal of Compensation & Benefits*, (March/April 1994), Vol. 9, No. 5: pp. 46-53.

[19] Sachs, Robert H. and Spreier, Scott W., "Reward ceremonies: compensating people to perform new roles finally takes center stage," *Hospitals and Health Networks*, Vol. 70, No. 17 (September 5, 1996): pp. 26-38.

possession of facts or data which are necessary for the satisfactory performance of job tasks.

A *knowledge-based* pay structure equates pay or pay grades to the number of different jobs or the number of different tasks in one job that an employee is capable of performing.

The distinction in jobs and tasks is important. Some organizations, such as the Westinghouse Nuclear Fuel plant, have one job with different levels (six at this Westinghouse plant) of tasks that cover all production employees.[20] Six different levels of pay are equated with the six levels of tasks. Employees who have the knowledge to perform the tasks at level six receive the highest level of pay. Other organizations reward employees for knowing how to perform the tasks in additional jobs. In some situations, employees are required to demonstrate that they possess the knowledge they claim to have. Once this assertion is validated, the employees are paid for this knowledge regardless of what job they are assigned to perform.

Skill-Based Pay

A *skill* is a present, observable competence to perform a learned psychomotor act.[21] Typically, skill-based pay is used for skilled jobs like electrician and electronics technician. The more skills employees possess, the more value they provide to the organization. A skill-based pay system rewards employees for acquiring more skills.

A *skill-based* pay structure equates pay or pay grades to the number of skills an employee possesses.

A hypothetical example of a skill-based pay structure is demonstrated in Exhibit 30-2.

---

[20] n.a., "HRM update: team skills," *Personnel Administrator*, Vol. 32, No. 1 (January 1987), p. 22.

[21] U.S. Equal Employment Opportunity Commission, *Uniform Guidelines for Employee Selection Procedures.*

Exhibit 30~2
Skill-Based Pay Structure
Hypothetical Example

Pay Grade	Skill
6	Electrician I
7	Electrician II
9	Electronics Technician

Some employers reward employees for the highest skills they demonstrate, regardless of the type of skill they typically apply. For example, employees who possess the skills of an Electronics Technician are paid at Pay Grade 9 regardless of the type of work they do. Other employers compensate the employee only for the skill required in the job that is performed. For example, an employee who has the skills to perform the Electronics Technician job, but is currently working as an Electrician I, would be paid at Pay Grade 6. Both settings motivate employees to acquire more skills to earn more money. The motivation is much greater in the first example.

Organizations use skill-based pay models to motivate employees to acquire additional skills that increase their investment in the job, give them the opportunity to earn more pay, and provide the organization with greater flexibility in employee assignments. These pay systems also help lower absenteeism and turnover, and are associated with improved work output and quality.[22]

Team-Based Pay

The "Lone Ranger" is an anachronism in today's work environment where interaction and collaborative effort are essential. Some employers reward coordination and collaboration or "teamwork" through the performance appraisal system. Where work performance requires a higher level of interaction, employers establish work teams. The distinction between "teamwork" and a "work team" is more than a play on words. Work teams demand a higher level of commitment and even personality adjustment by individual team members. "I'ism" gives way to "we'ism" and independency is transformed to interdependency. In this environment, communication in both giving and receiving information is of paramount importance. Mary Parker Follett[23] was among the earliest management philosophers to define this link between performance and communication:

communication → cooperation → coordination

Reduced to the bare essentials, Mary Parker Follett found in any effort involving more than one person that people must be able to communicate with

---

[22] Shenberger, Ron, "Still paying for hours on the job? Think again," *Journal for Quality and Participation.* Vol. 18, No. 1 (January/February 1995), pp. 88-91.

[23] Metcalf, Henry C. and Urwick, L., *Dynamic Administration: The Collected Papers of Mary Parker Follett* (New York: Harper & Brothers, 1940).

each other before they could learn to cooperate. Furthermore, active cooperation was requisite for people to be able to coordinate their efforts. She rightly recognized that during the period in which she was doing her research (the 1920s) that individual effort was the touchstone of final performance. Coordination was important to the accomplishment of work but was secondary to individual effort. Thus, worker coordination supplemented individual performance:

			Individual Effort	—↓
			+	Output
Communication →	Cooperation→	Coordination→	Group Effort	—↑

Work teams have somewhat transformed this progression, since final work accomplishment depends upon coordination:

communication → cooperation → coordination → work culmination

In short, the culmination of work performance among work teams depends upon team member communication, cooperation, and coordination. Team members know what they have to do, assign tasks among themselves, communicate with each other as the work is performed, cooperate to resolve any problems that may occur, and coordinate their roles as necessary. The final product is the culmination of their team efforts.

The changing nature of work outcomes from the individual to the work team necessitates changing the focus of rewards from the individual to the work team. Pay structures that slot workers into specific pay grades and reward performance through a performance appraisal system are not appropriate for work team members.[24] New systems are needed that reward team outcomes and thereby motivate employee communication, cooperation, and coordination of effort. Work team rewards or team-based pay is based upon the attainment of specific group goals in such areas as production, quality, or financial outcomes. Successful team-based pay systems use criteria which can be directly influenced by team performance.[25]

---

[24] Johnson, Sam T., "High performance work teams: one firm's approach to team incentive pay," *Compensation and Benefits Review.* Vol. 28, No. 5 (September/October 1996), pp. 47-50.

[25] Lindsay, Fred, "All for one," *Credit Union Management,* Vol. 18, No. 2 (February 1995), pp. 25-27.

CHAPTER 31
SAFETY AND HEALTH

Chapter Highlights
- Learn the causes of accidents and occupational exposures
- Study how to compute accident and illness rates
- Examine the purposes of OSHA
- Review the major components in an effective safety and health program

Introduction

Safety and health are major concerns of employers, since unsafe and unhealthy acts and conditions cause human suffering due to injury, illness, disability, and death, and also cause economic costs that must be borne by employees and their families, employers, and the general public. In 2007, a total of 4 million occupational injuries and illnesses were reported in private industry. In 2007, there were approximately 2 million occupational injuries and illnesses in the private sector workforce that were serious enough to either cause the worker to miss work or have his or her work tasks reduced. Because of the long-term effect of occupational illnesses, they can have serious repercussions for both employers and employees. In 2007, there were about 206,300 newly reported cases of occupational illnesses in private industry.

Death is the unfortunate ultimate price some employees pay while at work. In 2007, there were 5,488 fatal work injuries[1]. The human tragedy caused by job-related injuries and illnesses is enormous. Pain, suffering, temporary and permanent incapacitation, and the premature loss of life are the human costs.

Safety and Health Definitions

Safety is the process of providing working conditions and requiring work acts that prevent occupational injuries.

An accident is an unexpected and undesirable occurrence that may result in property damage and/or an occupational injury, disability, or death.

Virtually all accidents are preventable. A very small number of accidents, perhaps one or two percent, are considered nonpreventable because of unpredictable acts of nature. For example, a business insurer conducted an analysis of

---

[1] U.S. Department of Labor, *National Census of Fatal Occupational Injuries in 2008.*

claims filed during a three-year period. The 1,169 losses for the period totaled $172 million. Researchers found 97.9 percent of the losses were "related in some manner to human failure."[2]

Health is the absence of illness or disease.

A healthy work environment is one that helps produce employee physical and mental well-being. Occupational illnesses result from conditions or acts that are unhealthy. Like accidents, virtually all occupational illnesses are preventable.

Occupational Injury and Occupational Illness

Occupational injury. An *occupational injury* is any injury, such as a cut, fracture, sprain, amputation, or other related injury, resulting from a work accident or from a single instantaneous exposure in the work environment. Conditions resulting from animal bites, such as insect or snake bites, and from one-time exposure to chemicals are also considered to be injuries.

Occupational illness. An *occupational illness* is any abnormal condition or disorder (other than one caused by an occupational injury), caused by exposure to environmental factors associated with employment. It includes acute and chronic illnesses or diseases that may be caused by inhalation, absorption, ingestion, or direct contact. The following are the categories of recordable occupational illnesses:

- *Skin diseases or disorders* caused by exposure to chemicals, plants or other substances, such as contact dermatitis, eczema or rash.

- *Respiratory disorders* caused by breathing hazardous biological agents, chemicals, dust, gases, vapors, or fumes, such as silicosis, asbestosis, pneumonitis, and tuberculosis.

- *Poisoning* caused by breathing or absorbing toxic substances into the body to the extent abnormal concentrations are present in tissue, bodily fluids and the related, due to such materials as lead, mercury, gases, organic solvents, insecticide sprays or other chemicals.

- *Hearing loss*

- *All other illnesses*, such as heatstroke, frostbite, decompression sickness, nonionizing radiation, cumulative trauma and bloodborne diseases.[3]

These definitions of injury and illness are those used by the Occupational Safety and Health Administration (OSHA). In some cases, the classification system, based upon whether a condition was caused by a single incident or a prolonged exposure may appear arbitrary. For example, the disease rabies, which results from an animal bite, is considered an injury because it is caused by a single incident.

---

[2] *Overview: Management Programs for Loss Prevention and Control* (Toronto, Ontario: Industrial Risk Insurers, n. d.), p. 1.

[3] For a complete listing, see Occupational Safety and Health Administration, *Protecting the Safety and Health of America's Workers: Major Changes to OSHA's Recordkeeping Rule*, 2002.

The effects of unsafe and unhealthy acts and/or conditions are depicted in Exhibit 31-1.

Exhibit 31-1
Consequences of Unsafe and Healthy Acts and Condition

Act and/or Condition	Result of Act and/or Condition	Consequence
Unsafe	Accident	Injury, disability, death or property damage
Unhealthy	Exposure	Illness, disability or death

Variables Related to Occupational Injuries and Illnesses

Research has identified the following variables that are related to injuries and illnesses:

- The age of the employee (new employees have higher incident rates);
- The length of time on the job (employees who are new on a job have higher rates);
- The size of the firm (in general, medium-sized firms have higher rates than either smaller or larger firms);
- The type of work performed (incidence and severity rates vary significantly by SIC code); and
- The use of hazardous substances in the workplace.
- Research also indicates employees who have personality problems or difficulties in accepting supervisory authority may cause accidents either deliberately or as a means of retaliation.[4]
- Troubled employees also have higher accident rates, since their problems, such as alcoholism, drug abuse, financial difficulties, legal problems, marriage and family problems, and mental or emotional disturbances, may prevent them from following proper safety procedures. For example, studies have found that compared to nonalcoholic employees, alcoholic employees have more accidents and are absent longer after an accident. In addition, another study found that troubled employees had both off-and on-the-job accident rates 3.6 times higher than a nontroubled control group. The same study found the troubled employee group had loss-time accidents six times the rate of the nontroubled control group.[5]

Analyzing Occupational Accident Causes[6]

OSHA defines an *accident cause* as any behavior, condition, or act, whether due to negligence or otherwise, without which an accident would not have occurred. This definition recognizes that some accidents may involve an interac-

---

[4] Miner, J.B. and Brewster, J.F., "The Management of Ineffective Performance," *Handbook of Industrial and Organizational Psychology* (Chicago: Rand-Mc-Nally College Publishing Co., 1976), p. 1005.

[5] Myers, D.W., *Establishing and Building Employee Assistance Programs* (Westport, CT: Greenwood Press, 1984), pp. 48 and 276.

[6] See *Investigating Accidents in the Workplace* (Washington, D.C.: U.S. Department of Labor, 1977).

tion with events or conditions that otherwise would be safe were it not for the accident. Exhibit 31-2 shows the three types of accident causes and six sources of failure that may contribute to the causes.

Exhibit 31-2
Causes and Failure Sources of Occupational
Accidents

Cause	Failure Source
Basic	Human
Direct	Technical data
Indirect	Organizational
	Material
	Design
	Natural

Basic causes

The *basic causes* of accidents are:

- *Poor management practices,* such as encouraging employees to work without using safety equipment, such as safety glasses; as a result, a splinter from a wood planing machine causes an eye injury.

- *Personal factors,* such as a young and inexperienced employee who operates a machine without adequate training.

- *Environmental factors,* including snow, fog or wet roads.

Each of these basic causes may also lead to indirect causes, as discussed below.

Direct causes

The *direct causes* of accidents are the unplanned release of energy and/or hazardous material. A metal ladder touching a high voltage electrical line results in the person holding the ladder receiving an electrical charge. The direct cause of this accident is the electrical charge that the person receives. In this situation, the basic cause of the accident may be management's failure to train the employee about using metal ladders around electrical lines.

Indirect causes

The *indirect causes* of accidents are the unsafe acts and unsafe conditions that existed at the worksite.

Unsafe acts include those that should have been performed but were not, as required by law or procedure. Unsafe acts also include those that are improper, hazardous, and illegal. These are some examples of unsafe acts:

- Operation of equipment too fast or too slow;
- Interference with operations;
- Hazardous motion or position, such as bending at the waist to lift a heavy object;
- Overloading of a person or a machine;

- Lack of attention, including failure to be alert for possible evasive reaction; and

- Incorrect action to prevent or reduce the consequences of an impending accident after it was noticed.

Unsafe conditions are conditions at the worksite that contributed to the accident. These are some examples of unsafe conditions:

- Poor housekeeping in the work area, such as empty boxes littering the floor of a shipping department, which might cause a tripping hazard; and

- Defective conditions in buildings, equipment, or vehicles, such as defective brakes, which may cause a vehicle to skid when they are applied.[7]

Sources of Failure

The six failure sources are shown in Exhibit 31-2, above.

Human failure includes physical, mental, and physiological deficiencies. Examples are failure to follow instructions, sickness, or excessive stress. Two problems confound determining if human failure is present. First, employees may protect themselves and their peers by covering up for specific acts. Second, once a human failure is determined, it may not be possible to find out why it occurred.

Technical data failure results from errors and omissions in instructions and operating data.

Organizational failure could be more appropriately called management failure, since it is a deficiency of management in providing instructions, planning, and training.

Material failure is the physical or chemical breakdown of any material or component.

Design failure is a deficiency in the design of a structure or component.

Natural failure is an act of nature.

Maintaining Injury and Illness Incident Rates

Safety and health management requires the maintenance of incident rates. These rates are important for several reasons such as determining whether a disproportionate number of injuries and illnesses are occurring by comparing the rates of various organizational units, such as shifts, plants, and departments. In addition, the rates of one firm can be compared with those of the industry as a whole, and incident rates can be tracked over time to determine trends. Also, incident rates can be used to determine where interventions, such as training programs, are necessary. Finally, incident rates are evidence of the effectiveness of various management strategies, such as incentive pay systems linked to employee safety and health.

---

[7] The source of material on accident causes was obtained from the U.S. Department of Labor, *Accident Investigation*, no date supplied.

Occupational Safety and Health Administration (OSHA)

OSHA uses three incident rate formulas. All three formulas calculate incident rates per 200,000 employee hours. The 200,000 employee-hour multiplier is based upon 100 full-time employees working 50 weeks a year and 40 hours per week. The purpose of using the 200,000 hour multiplier is so that incidence rates are expressed as the number per 100 employees. The multiplier permits comparisons of rates among industries, firms, and even work units within firms.

The formulas are:

Where:

EWH = The total workhours of all employees during the year.

1. *Total injuries & illnesses rate* = [# injuries & illnesses × 200,000] ÷ EWH

2. *Lost workday injury & illness rate* = [# injuries & illnesses with lost workdays × 200,000] ÷ EWH

3. *No lost workday injury & illness rate* = [# injuries & illnesses without lost workdays × 200,000] ÷ EWH

Cases Involving Days Away From Work or Restricted Work

Under OSHA procedures, separate counts are maintained on:

- Cases where the accident/illness caused the employee to be away from work for at least one day.

- Cases where the accident/illness caused the employee to have restricted work activity. This includes shortened work hours, a temporary change in the job to accommodate the employee's inability to do his/her normal job or the temporary elimination of some job duties, such as bending or lifting.[8]

Days do not need to be counted beyond 180 days under either of the two definitions above.

Recording Cases

The second item of concern in OSHA incidence rate computation is recordability. Only recordable cases are included in OSHA rates. Basically, all work-related cases are recorded if they result in a death, illness, or injury involving medical treatment other than first-aid, loss of consciousness, restriction of work or motion, and/or transfer to another job.

The following work-related conditions must also be recorded:

- Any significant injury or illness diagnosed by a health care professional.
- Cancer.
- Chronic irreversible disease.
- Fracture or cracked bone.
- Punctured eardrum.

[8] Bureau of Labor Statistics, *Workplace Injuries and Illnesses in 2000*, (December 18, 2001), p. 3.

- Needlestick injury or cut that is contaminated with another person's blood or potentially infectious material.

- A condition requiring an employee to be medically removed due to an OSHA health standard.

- Tuberculosis infection identified by results from a skin test or physician's diagnosis.

Work-Related Injury or Illness Defined

An injury or illness is work-related if the work environment caused or contributed to it or aggravated it. An injury or illness is presumed to be work-related if occurring from events or exposures in the workplace. A "work environment includes the establishment and other locations where one or more employees are working or are present as a condition of their employment."[9]

Medical Treatment Defined

Medical treatment includes the process of "managing and caring for a patient for the purpose of combating disease or disorder."[10]

These are not medical treatment and thus not recordable:

- Visits to a health professional for observation or counseling.

- Diagnostic procedures or administering medications for such purposes.

- First aid, which includes the following:

  — Using non-prescription medications

  — Tetanus immunizations

  — Cleaning wounds on the surface of the skin

  — Using bandages

  — Administering hot/cold therapy

  — Drilling a fingernail to relieve pressure

  — Administering fluids to relieve heat stress[11]

Vehicle Reporting Not Separated

The third item of concern about OSHA incidence rates is that they do not have special provisions to isolate vehicle accident rates. Consequently, firms with vehicle fleets, such as trucking or delivery companies, and others where vehicle use is a major portion of employee tasks would want to develop separate reporting procedures.

The Occupational Safety and Health Act of 1970

This act created two federal agencies: the National Institute of Safety and Health (NIOSH) and the Occupational Safety and Health Administration (OSHA). NIOSH, an agency of the Department of Health and Human Services,

---

[9] Occupational Safety and Health Administration, *Protecting the Safety and Health of America's Workers: Major Changes to OSHA's Recordkeeping Rule*, 2002.
[10] Ibid.

[11] For a complete listing, see Occupational Safety and Health Administration, *Protecting the Safety and Health of America's Workers: Major Changes to OSHA's Recordkeeping Rule*, 2002.

conducts safety and health research and assists OSHA in technical areas, such as investigating toxic substances in the workplace and providing relevant criteria to evaluate the substances and recommending standards.

The act applies to all employers with one or more employees. The following are excluded:

- Self-employed persons;
- Farmers whose only employees are members of the immediate family;
- State and local governments; and
- Employers whose employees are covered by other federal statutes, such as the Mine Safety and Health Act of 1977.

OSHA Purposes

The five purposes of OSHA are:

- Motivate employers and employees to reduce hazards and develop safety and health programs;
- Develop employer and employee responsibilities and rights for improved safety and health conditions;
- Implement and monitor a workplace injury and illness reporting system;
- Prepare and enforce safety and health standards; and
- Help states develop approved occupational safety and health programs.

To accomplish these purposes, OSHA develops various programs and procedures. The remainder of this section focuses on each purpose and examines some of these programs and procedures.

Purpose 1—Motivating Employers and Employees to Reduce Hazards and Develop Safety and Health Programs

Two programs OSHA implemented encouraging voluntary safety and health efforts by both management and labor are the *OSHA Strategic Partnership Program* (OSPP) and the *Voluntary Protection Programs* (VPP).

Strategic Partnership Program

The *OSHA Strategic Partnership Program*(OSPP) is an expansion of OSHA's efforts to develop formal voluntary programs with employers and applicable stakeholders. OSHA enters into partnerships to "encourage, assist, and recognize" employers' "efforts to eliminate serious hazards and achieve a high level of worker safety and health."[12] These partnership arrangements do not reduce OSHA's enforcement responsibilities.

Most partnerships consist of small firms with an average of 22 employees. Employers in various industries together with a number of different unions have also developed partnerships. The OSHA approval process for a partnership depends upon the geographical reach of the partnership. These are the two types of partnerships:

---

[12] OSHA, *What Is An OSHA Partnership*, p. 1.

- *Comprehensive partnership.* The distinctive features of these partnerships are "management leadership and employee involvement, hazard analysis, hazard prevention and control, safety and health training, evaluation and compliance with applicable OSH Act requirements."[13] Comprehensive partnerships must contain all these elements:

  — Situation Analysis

  — Identification of Partners

  — Partnership Goal

  — Leveraging

  — Safety and Health Programs

  — Employee Involvement/Rights

  — Stakeholder Involvement

  — Measurement System

  — OSHA Incentives

  — Verification

  — OSHA Inspections

  — Evaluation

  — Termination[14]

- *Limited partnership.* As the term implies, limited partnerships typically focus on one goal or the elimination of a particular hazard. They must contain as many of the elements above to ensure the partnership is effective. Furthermore, they must contain specific elements, such as OSHA Inspections and they must submit to a rigorous application process similar to the one for comprehensive programs

Voluntary Protection Program

In a *Voluntary Protection Program*(VPP), a relationship is established among management, employees and OSHA in an environment with an effective safety and health program.[15] Three voluntary programs are *Star, Merit,* and *Demonstration.*

Star Program. The *Star Program* focuses on employers who have effective safety and health programs in place in their firms. Companies may participate if their three-year average incidence and lost-workday case rates are at or below the national average for their industries. They must also meet requirements for extensive management systems. Construction firms must maintain strong employment participation programs. Star participants are evaluated every three years, but their incident rates are reviewed annually.

Merit Program. This program is for employers who are seeking entrance in the Star Program. Such employers may have general management systems but they must set goals for meeting Star requirements. While there are less stringent

---

[13] Ibid., p. 2.

[14] Ibid., p. 3.

[15] OSHA, *An Overview of VPP.*

rate requirements for the Merit Program, applicants must agree to meet specific goals for reducing rates to below the average for their industry. Merit participants are evaluated onsite annually.

Demonstration Program. The *Demonstration Program* is for employers who are open to new or creative approaches towards employee safety and health programming. Approaches that are successful are considered for inclusion in the Star Program.

Reasons for Participation

Employers have several reasons for seeking membership in these programs. First, membership indicates a firm is a leader in occupational safety and health. Second, the programs are a constructive channel for achieving employer-employee cooperation. Third, improving employee safety and health shows a humanitarian concern for employee suffering. Fourth, reducing accidents and illnesses saves the firm's economic resources. Finally, program participation demonstrates to all employees and managers that safety and health is a top priority.

Purpose 2—Employer and Employee Responsibilities and Rights

Examples of the responsibilities and rights of employers are:

Employer Responsibilities

1. Meet the "general duty" responsibility to provide a workplace free from recognized hazards that are causing or are likely to cause death or serious physical harm to employees and to comply with standards, rules, and regulations issued under the act.

2. Be familiar with mandatory OSHA standards and make copies available to employees for review upon request.

3. Inform all employees about OSHA.

4. Examine workplace conditions to make sure they conform to applicable standards.

5. Minimize or reduce hazards.

6. Make sure employees have and use safe tools and equipment (including personal protective equipment) and that such equipment is properly maintained.

7. Use codes, posters, labels, or signs to warn employees of potential hazards.

8. Establish or update operating procedures and communicate them, so that employees follow safety and health requirements.

9. Provide medical examinations when required by OSHA standards.

10. Report to the nearest OSHA office any fatal accident or one resulting in the hospitalization of five or more employees.

Employer Rights

1. Seek advice and off-site consultation as needed by writing, calling, or visiting the nearest OSHA office.

2. Be active in industry association's involvement in job safety and health.

3. Request and receive proper identification of the OSHA inspector prior to inspection.

4. Be advised by the inspector of the reason for an inspection.

5. Have an opening and closing conference with the inspector.

6. File a Notice of Contest with the OSHA area director within 15 working days of receipt of a notice of citation and proposed penalty.

7. Apply to OSHA for a temporary variance from a standard if unable to comply because of the unavailability of materials, equipment, or personnel needed to make necessary changes within the required time.

Employee Responsibilities

1. Read the OSHA poster at the job site.

2. Comply with all applicable OSHA standards.

3. Follow all employer safety and health rules and regulations, and wear or use prescribed protective equipment while engaged in work.

4. Report hazardous conditions to the supervisor.

Employee Rights

1. Protect against punishment or discrimination for complaining about job safety and health, for filing safety and health grievances, for participating in job safety and health committees, for involvement in union activities regarding job safety and health, and for participating in OSHA inspections or other OSHA activities.

2. Review copies of appropriate OSHA standards, rules, regulations, and requirements that the employer should have available at the workplace.

3. Request information from your employer on safety and health hazards in the area, on precautions that may be taken, and on procedures to be followed if an employee is involved in an accident or is exposed to toxic substances.

4. Request the OSHA area director to conduct an inspection if you believe hazardous conditions or violations of standards exist in your workplace.

5. Have your name withheld from your employer, upon request to OSHA, if you file a written and signed complaint.

6. Be advised of OSHA actions regarding your complaint and have an informal review, if requested, of any decision not to inspect or to issue a citation.

7. Have your authorized employee representative accompany the OSHA inspector during the inspection tour.

8. Respond to questions from the OSHA inspector, particularly if there is no authorized employee representative accompanying the inspector.

9. Be paid for any time you spend on OSHA inspection activity.

10. Observe any monitoring or measuring of hazardous materials and have the right to see these records, as specified under the act.

11. Have your authorized representative, or yourself, review the Log and Summary of Occupational Injuries (OSHA No. 200) at a reasonable time and in a reasonable manner.

12. Request a closing discussion with the inspector following an inspection.

13. Submit a written request to the NIOSH for information on whether any substance in your workplace has potential toxic effects in the concentrations that are used, and have your name withheld from your employer if you so request.

14. Object to the abatement period set in the citation issued to your employer by writing to the OSHA area director within 15 working days of the issuance of the citation.

15. Be notified by your employer if it applies for a variance from an OSHA standard, testifies at a variance hearing, and appeals the final decision.

16. Submit information or comment to OSHA on the issuance, modification, or revocation of OSHA standards and request a public hearing.

Purpose 3—Injury and Illness Reporting System

All employers with more than 10 employees must record occupational injuries and illnesses. Earlier in this chapter case recordability and occupational injuries and illnesses are defined. Employers must keep records on a calendar year basis and must retain them for five years. Each recordable injury or illness must be recorded on OSHA Form 301 (Exhibit 31-3) within seven calendar days from the time the employer has knowledge of it. OSHA Form 300 (Exhibit 31-4) must also be completed. A summary, OSHA Form 300A (Exhibit 31-5), must be completed and posted by February 1 of the year after the year covered by the OSHA Forms 300. The Form 300A must remain posted until April 30.

Exhibit 31-3

OSHA's Form 301

Injury and Illness Incident Report

Form approved OMB no. 1218-0176

U.S. Department of Labor
Occupational Safety and Health Administration

Attention: This form contains information relating to employee health and must be used in a manner that protects the confidentiality of employees to the extent possible while the information is being used for occupational safety and health purposes.

This *Injury and Illness Incident Report* is one of the first forms you must fill out when a recordable work-related injury or illness has occurred. Together with the *Log of Work-Related Injuries and Illnesses* and the accompanying *Summary*, these forms help the employer and OSHA develop a picture of the extent and severity of work-related incidents.

Within 7 calendar days after you receive information that a recordable work-related injury or illness has occurred, you must fill out this form or an equivalent. Some state workers' compensation, insurance, or other reports may be acceptable substitutes. To be considered an equivalent form, any substitute must contain all the information asked for on this form.

According to Public Law 91-596 and 29 CFR 1904, OSHA's recordkeeping rule, you must keep this form on file for 5 years following the year to which it pertains.

If you need additional copies of this form, you may photocopy and use as many as you need.

Completed by _____

Title _____

Phone (____) ____ – ____ Date ____/____/____

Information about the employee

1) Full name _____

2) Street _____
City _____ State ____ ZIP ____

3) Date of birth ____/____/____

4) Date hired ____/____/____

5) ☐ Male
☐ Female

Information about the physician or other health care professional

6) Name of physician or other health care professional _____

7) If treatment was given away from the worksite, where was it given?
Facility _____
Street _____
City _____ State ____ ZIP ____

8) Was employee treated in an emergency room?
☐ Yes
☐ No

9) Was employee hospitalized overnight as an in-patient?
☐ Yes
☐ No

Information about the case

10) Case number from the Log _____ (*Transfer the case number from the Log after you record the case.*)

11) Date of injury or illness ____/____/____

12) Time employee began work ____ AM / PM

13) Time of event ____ AM / PM ☐ Check if time cannot be determined

14) **What was the employee doing just before the incident occurred?** Describe the activity, as well as the tools, equipment, or material the employee was using. Be specific. *Examples:* "climbing a ladder while carrying roofing materials"; "spraying chlorine from hand sprayer"; "daily computer key-entry."

15) **What happened?** Tell us how the injury occurred. *Examples:* "When ladder slipped on wet floor, worker fell 20 feet"; "Worker was sprayed with chlorine when gasket broke during replacement"; "Worker developed soreness in wrist over time."

16) **What was the injury or illness?** Tell us the part of the body that was affected and how it was affected; be more specific than "hurt," "pain," or sore." *Examples:* "strained back"; "chemical burn, hand"; "carpal tunnel syndrome."

17) **What object or substance directly harmed the employee?** *Examples:* "concrete floor"; "chlorine"; "radial arm saw." *If this question does not apply to the incident, leave it blank.*

18) **If the employee died, when did death occur?** Date of death ____/____/____

Public reporting burden for this collection of information is estimated to average 22 minutes per response, including time for reviewing instructions, searching existing data sources, gathering and maintaining the data needed, and completing and reviewing the collection of information. Persons are not required to respond to the collection of information unless it displays a current valid OMB control number. If you have any comments about this estimate or any other aspects of this data collection, including suggestions for reducing this burden, contact: US Department of Labor, OSHA Office of Statistics, Room N-3644, 200 Constitution Avenue, NW, Washington, DC 20210. Do not send the completed forms to this office.

Exhibit 31-4

OSHA's Form 300

Log of Work-Related Injuries and Illnesses

You must record information about every work-related death and about every work-related injury or illness that involves loss of consciousness, restricted work activity or job transfer, days away from work, or medical treatment beyond first aid. You must also record significant work-related injuries and illnesses that are diagnosed by a physician or licensed health care professional. You must also record work-related injuries and illnesses that meet any of the specific recording criteria listed in 29 CFR Part 1904.8 through 1904.12. Feel free to use two lines for a single case if you need to. You must complete an Injury and Illness Incident Report (OSHA Form 301) or equivalent form for each injury or illness recorded on this form. If you're not sure whether a case is recordable, call your local OSHA office for help.

Attention: This form contains information relating to employee health and must be used in a manner that protects the confidentiality of employees to the extent possible while the information is being used for occupational safety and health purposes.

Year 20___

U.S. Department of Labor
Occupational Safety and Health Administration

Form approved OMB no. 1218-0176

Establishment name _____
City _____ State _____

Identify the person | **Describe the case** | **Classify the case**

(A) Case no.
(B) Employee's name
(C) Job title (e.g., Welder)
(D) Date of injury or onset of illness
(E) Where the event occurred (e.g., Loading dock north end)
(F) Describe injury or illness, parts of body affected, and object/substance that directly injured or made person ill (e.g., Second degree burns on right forearm from acetylene torch)

Using these four categories, check ONLY the most serious result for each case:
(G) Death
(H) Days away from work

Remained at work
(I) Job transfer or restriction
(J) Other recordable cases

Enter the number of days the injured or ill worker was:
(K) On job transfer or restriction ___ days
(L) Away from work ___ days

Check the "Injury" column or choose one type of illness:
(M)
(1) Injury
(2) Skin disorder
(3) Respiratory condition
(4) Poisoning
(5) All other illnesses

Page totals ▶

Be sure to transfer these totals to the Summary page (Form 300A) before you post it.

Page ___ of ___

Public reporting burden for this collection of information is estimated to average 14 minutes per response, including time to review the instructions, search and gather the data needed, and complete and review the collection of information. Persons are not required to respond to the collection of information unless it displays a currently valid OMB control number. If you have any comments about these estimates or any other aspects of this data collection, contact: US Department of Labor, OSHA Office of Statistics, Room N-3644, 200 Constitution Avenue, NW, Washington, DC 20210. Do not send the completed forms to this office.

Exhibit 31-5

OSHA's Form 300A

Summary of Work-Related Injuries and Illnesses

Year 20 ___ ___

U.S. Department of Labor
Occupational Safety and Health Administration

Form approved OMB no. 1218-0176

All establishments covered by Part 1904 must complete this Summary page, even if no work-related injuries or illnesses occurred during the year. Remember to review the Log to verify that the entries are complete and accurate before completing this summary.

Using the Log, count the individual entries you made for each category. Then write the totals below, making sure you've added the entries from every page of the Log. If you had no cases, write "0."

Employees, former employees, and their representatives have the right to review the OSHA Form 300 in its entirety. They also have limited access to the OSHA Form 301 or its equivalent. See 29 CFR Part 1904.35, in OSHA's recordkeeping rule, for further details on the access provisions for these forms.

Number of Cases

Total number of deaths

(G)

Total number of cases with days away from work

(H)

Total number of cases with job transfer or restriction

(I)

Total number of other recordable cases

(J)

Number of Days

Total number of days of job transfer or restriction

(K)

Total number of days away from work

(L)

Injury and Illness Types

Total number of . . . (M)

1) Injuries

2) Skin disorders

3) Respiratory conditions

4) Poisonings

5) All other illnesses

Establishment information

Your establishment name _____

Street _____

City _____ State ___ ZIP ___

Industry description (e.g., Manufacture of motor truck trailers) _____

Standard Industrial Classification (SIC), if known (e.g., SIC 3715) _____

Employment Information (If you don't have these figures, see the Worksheet on the back of this page to estimate.)

Annual average number of employees _____

Total hours worked by all employees last year _____

Sign here

Knowingly falsifying this document may result in a fine.

I certify that I have examined this document and that to the best of my knowledge the entries are true, accurate, and complete.

_____ Company executive ___ Title

_____ Phone ___ Date

Post this Summary page from February 1 to April 30 of the year following the year covered by the form.

Public reporting burden for this collection of information is estimated to average 50 minutes per response, including time to review the instructions, search and gather the data needed, and complete and review the collection of information. Persons are not required to respond to the collection of information unless it displays a currently valid OMB control number. If you have any comments about these estimates or any other aspects of this data collection, contact: US Department of Labor, OSHA Office of Statistics, Room N-3644, 200 Constitution Avenue, NW, Washington, DC 20210. Do not send the completed forms to this office.

Purpose 4—Prepare and Enforce Safety and Health Standards

The two major OSHA functions for accomplishing this purpose are developing standards and workplace inspections.

Developing Standards

OSHA standards are divided into four groups; General Industry, Maritime, Construction, and Agriculture. OSHA develops standards on its own and in conjunction with other federal agencies, such as the National Institute of Safety and Health. Once a determination is made that a standard is required, OSHA uses either standing or ad hoc committees, whose membership is composed of representatives from management, labor, state agencies, and the Department of Health and Human Services. Representatives may also be obtained from occupational safety and health professions and the public. Once a standard is developed, it is published in the Federal Register for public response and hearings are held, if they are requested. At the conclusion of the response period and after hearings are held, OSHA publishes a final decision, with an explanation, in the Federal Register. There are provisions for implementing temporary standards, for appealing standards and requesting variances of standards. The various provisions involved in setting standards are to ensure employees' safety and health are protected without infringing on the rights of others or imposing standards that are arbitrary and capricious.

Workplace Inspections

OSHA inspections are conducted without advance notice, except in special cases, such as when inspections are conducted outside the normal business hours of the firm. If an employer refuses to consent to the inspection, it cannot be conducted without an inspection warrant. These are the priorities that are observed in making inspections:

- *Imminent Danger.* These situations have the top priority. This is any condition in which there is reasonable certainty a death or serious harm could immediately result. The conditions could be either a safety or health problem.

- *Fatality and Catastrophe Incidents.* These are situations resulting in a fatality or the hospitalization of three or more employees. Employers must report these situations to OSHA within eight hours of occurrence.

- *Complaints.* Complaints involve allegations of unhealthy conditions or violations of OSHA safety regulations. Employees may request anonymity when making such complaints.

- *Referrals.* Referrals of allegations of unsafe and unhealthy conditions may be made by several sources including government agencies, individuals, organizations and even media representatives.

- *Follow-ups.* Follow-up inspections are conducted to ensure past violations have been corrected or employer plans to make such corrections have been accomplished.

- *Planned and Programmed Inspections.* These are primarily inspections of high hazard industries based on the highest injury and illness rates, previous citations, and employee exposures to unsafe and unhealthy conditions.[16]

Inspection Process

Following are the typical steps in the inspection process:

- Normally, inspections are conducted without giving the employer advance notice.

- The inspector presents his or her credentials to the employer's representative.

- If the employer refuses to admit the inspector, the next step is to obtain an inspection warrant.

- Once admitted, the inspector meets with employees or employees' representatives and the employer or the employer's representative to state the purpose of the inspection. The inspector explains the methods to be used in the inspection and the areas of the workplace and records to be inspected. The employer may designate the areas in which trade secrets are located. Inspectors are bound by OSHA regulations to protect any trade secret information they acquire during an inspection. The employer may designate that only employees who are permitted access to trade secret areas be allowed to accompany the inspector in those areas.

- If the inspection was initiated by an employee's complaint, a copy of the complaint is given to the employer with the employee's name deleted, if anonymity was requested by the employee.

- The employer and employees are permitted to accompany the inspector during the "walkaround" inspection.

- During the walkaround, the inspector may offer suggestions for the abatement of violations that are found but the employer is not bound to accept the suggestions.

- After the walkaround, the inspector holds a closing conference with the employer and the employees' representatives.

- The inspector advises the employer of any apparent violations for which a citation may be issued and suggests methods for the abatement of them.

- The employer has the opportunity to give any explanation or share relevant information with the inspector.

- The inspector explains the citation procedures and how to contest citations.

Violations and Penalties

Types of violations and the penalties. These must be posted by the employer for three days or until the violation is corrected (abated).[17]

---

[16] Occupational Safety and Health Administration, *OSHA Fact Sheet,* n. d.

[17] Information for the next several sections was obtained from OSHA, OSHA Inspections (2002) and OSHA, *CPL 2.45B CH 4- Changes to the Field Operations Manual* (no date).

- *Other-Than-Serious Violation.* This violation has adverse safety and health consequences that do not constitute a negligible risk but is less than serious harm. Penalty can be up to $1,000 and can be adjusted by as much as 95 percent based on Penalty Factors described below.

- *Serious Violation.* This violation is issued for conditions in which there is a high probability that death or serious harm could occur. Penalty can be from $1,500 to $7,000.

- *Willful Violation.* This is a violation that is knowingly committed by the employer. Penalties up to $70,000 can be imposed; a minimum penalty is $5,000 for each willful violation. Conviction in a criminal proceeding resulting in an employee's death, may result in fines up to $250,000 (or $500,000 if a corporation).

- *Repeated Violation.* This is a repeated violation of the same standard. Penalties up to $70,000 can be imposed.

- *Failure to Abate.* This is a separate type of violation issued for a failure to bring equipment or a condition into compliance. Penalties up to $7,000 for each day the condition is not corrected beyond the date that abatement was required.

- *Posting Violation.* This is the failure to post the various requirements of the Occupational Safety and Health Act. Penalty can be $7,000.

Penalty Factors

Penalties are assessed based on these factors:

- The "gravity" of the violation which is the primary basis for calculating the size of the penalty.

- The size of the business.

- The good faith of the employer (demonstrated efforts to comply with the Act).

- The employer's history of violations.

Penalty Calculation

The amount of the initial penalty for a violation is determined by OSHA using a *gravity-based penalty* (GBP) procedure, which is based upon these two factors:

- The "gravity" of the violation, based upon a *severity assessment* (high severity, medium severity, low severity, and minimal severity).

- The *probability assessment* that an illness or injury could result (assessments are classified as either "greater" or "lesser" depending upon such factors as the number of workers in the situation and proximity of employees to the hazard).

The GBP can be reduced by as much as 95 percent for such factors as the size of the business, good faith of the employer, and the employer's history of violations. Reductions are not made for citations involving willful violations.

describe how a respirator works and when it should be used," instead of *"The employee will understand how to use a respirator."*

- Design learning activities. The learning situation should simulate the actual work environment to facilitate learning reinforcement and application. Arrange the training in the sequence of the actual performance of tasks on the job.

- Conduct training. Motivate the employee to learn by:

  - Explaining the goals and objectives of the instruction;

  - Relating the training to the interests, skills, and experiences of the employees;

  - Outlining the main points to be presented during the training sessions; and

  - Pointing out the benefits of training (e.g., the employee will be better informed, more skilled, and thus more valuable both on the job and in the labor market) and/or the employee will be at less risk in performing the tasks on the job.

- Determine the effectiveness of the training by evaluating it. Methods to use in the evaluation may include employee/trainees' opinions, supervisors' observations of employee performance, both before and after the training, and workplace improvements through reductions in occupational injury and illness rates.

- Revise/improve the training. Make any necessary revisions, based on feedback from employees, supervisors, and others, and include other results from the evaluation phase.

- Establish a priority for employees who will receive training. If training cannot be given to all employees due to budget or other constraints, establish a priority for such training, which includes these considerations:

  - Train employees who have the greatest need to be trained; and

  - Train employees in the most hazardous occupations.

Developing an Effective Safety and Health Program

There is no great mystery to having a safe and healthful organization. Successful programs are not appendages but are rather an essential part of the organization. Following are organizational components that exist to some degree in all effective programs.

Top Management Commitment

An organization's occupational injury and accident rate is a reflection of the chief executive officer's concern for employee safety and health. All of the other safety program features are only marginally effective without this top leadership commitment. The first step is getting the top executive's attention. This is accomplished by illustrating the benefits of an effective safety program, such as reduced costs and improved cooperation among all employees and managers. The next step is for the top manager to incorporate safety and health throughout the organization. In larger organizations this may mean establishing a full-time position for safety and health tasks. This employee coordinates safety and health tasks, makes recommendations, and develops plans and systems as directed by management.

Organizations with ineffective safety and health programs typically view them as staff functions. In these situations, supervisors often consider safety personnel as nuisances who impede them in accomplishing their work. The top executive can change this attitude by incorporating safety and health functions into line management through such methods as including safety and health as variables in appraising supervisory performance. Another way is for the top executive to be visibly involved in safety and health matters. For example, one facility did not have a lost time injury in over three million work hours. This outstanding accomplishment was in the chemical industry, which has a high potential for illnesses and injuries. The reason for this outstanding six-year record was attributable to the company's president who established a firm policy, assigned responsibility, and used various measures to maintain control.[18]

Functional Responsibility for Safety and Health

Many HR departments have significant safety and health responsibilities. Ninety-one percent of the firms in a national study of HR activities have safety training programs and 90 percent have safety inspection/OSHA compliance programs. In these firms, the HR department is either solely responsible (29 percent of the firms) or responsible in conjunction with other departments (40 percent of firms) for the safety training. HR has similar rates of responsibilities for safety inspections/OSHA compliance (solely responsible in 26 percent of the firms and responsible in conjunction with other departments in 37 percent of the firms).[19]

Safety and Health Reporting Systems

Effective safety and health management depends upon an accurate reporting system. Among the variables included in such a system are injury and illness incidence rates, safety and health inspections, and accident reporting. Furthermore, accident, injury, and illness data should be maintained in a database, so that reports can be generated for these categories:

- Employee name;
- Supervisor name;
- Shift;
- Work area;
- Substance/material involved;
- Operation/machine;
- Basic, direct, and indirect cause(s) of the accident;

---

[18] Diekemper, R.F., "Faculty Corporate Philosophy Can Be Responsible For Accidents," *Business Insurance* (July 1983), p. 39.

[19] SHRM-BNA Survey No. 65: Human Resource Activities, Budgets and Staffs, 1999-2000. *Bulletin to Management*, The Bureau of National Affairs (June 29, 2000), p. S-7.

- Failure source (human, technical data, organizational, material, design, and natural);
- Job title; and
- Costs, including health benefits, worker's compensation, paid sick leave, and lost production.

Safety and Health Committee

The principal functions of a safety and health committee are to:

- Provide an opportunity for employees to assist management in maintaining a safe and healthy work environment.
- Increase the involvement of employees in job safety and health.

These committees are more prevalent in unionized settings, and often the structure of the committee, membership selection, and committee responsibilities become the subject of collective bargaining finalized in the union-management contract. Provisions for these committees existed in 29 percent of the 744 agreements that have expired or will expire between 1997 and 2007. Such agreements represent 1,000 or more workers.[20] Among the functions of the committees were to study chemical and air conditions, industrial hygiene, noise abatement and hazard communications. The union is usually permitted to name the employee representatives who will serve on the committee. In some cases, different occupations are represented by different unions, so that each union selects one committee member. Members usually serve one or two years. In large establishments, the committee may meet as often as monthly. Meetings are less frequent, perhaps only quarterly, in smaller facilities.

Management representatives usually chair the committee and serve as recorder or secretary. The recorder function is important in committees that maintain minutes. Each item in the minutes is usually numbered if it involves an "action" item, such as a report of an unsafe condition. Directions are given to the recorder concerning to whom the action items should be referred. Exhibit 31-7 is an example of a minute item.

Committee meetings are almost always held on company time. The meeting dates and times are set by the committee members.

Safety and health committees can be effective channels of communication between employees and management. To help ensure this, committee members should be publicized in newsletters. Employees should be encouraged to discuss their safety and health concerns with committee members. Some unions have their committee representative write columns in the local union newsletter and make presentations at union meetings. These actions help communicate safety and health concerns.

Sometimes, committee representatives serve staggered terms to prevent a complete turnover of all members when their terms expire. Usually new members are oriented in their duties and receive a short but intensive instruction in

---

[20] Gray, G., Myers, D. W., and Myers, P. S., "Collective Bargaining Agreements: Safety and Health Provisions," *Monthly Labor Review* (May 1998), pp. 13-35.

safety and health principles. Members are kept informed of safety and health matters through a briefing from the management representatives on the committee. In addition, their names are occasionally placed on a mailing list to receive safety and health materials.

Safety and health committees are an important component in an overall safety program. When properly organized and administered, they are invaluable in obtaining employee cooperation.

Exhibit 31-6
Example of a Safety and Health Committee Minute Item
Seneca Hospital Safety and Health Committee Minutes
January 15

Attendance: Sue Gardner, Paperworkers Union; Jacob Ginns, IBEW; Murial Roswell, Paperworkers Union; Roy Senn, Safety Officer, Jennings Sisky, American Nurses Association; and Josephine Waters, Human Resources Director.

Action Items (old business):

#22—Mopping the floor during shift changes on Saturdays causes a slipping hazard. Item referred to Joe Landrigan in Plant Maintenance. *Action:* Mr. Landrigan sent memo to the committee stating the mopping will be done on the second shift when the staffing levels are lowest and when most patients are sleeping.

Union Involvement

Unions are keenly interested in employee safety and health. If anything, this interest has significantly increased with the greater public awareness of employee exposure to occupational toxins. For example, unions in the healthcare industry are using audio-visual materials, pamphlets and other publications, and safety and health training courses to teach employees about the safety and health hazards in healthcare facilities. Unions are also encouraging legislators to introduce legislation aimed at tougher safety and health laws. Union officials also are pressuring decisionmakers at the Department of Labor to reduce the exposure limits on hazardous substances and materials. Union leaders are especially watchful of any lessening in the enforcement of safety and health laws, regulations, and standards.

The vigorous activities of unions in safety and health matters might lead to the erroneous conclusion that union-management cooperation is not feasible, but nothing could be further from the truth. First, union participation is essential in safety and health committees. Union cooperation can also be sought in special campaigns, such as identifying unsafe and hazardous conditions. Union representatives also generally serve on committees conducting feasibility studies about establishing employee assistance programs (EAPs). EAPs treat troubled employees, who incur occupational injuries and illnesses at a much greater rate than the rest of the employee population. Union cooperation is vitally important in making EAPs successful.

Occupational Disease Prevention Program

Occupational disease is a major health concern. One medical study listed 50 disease conditions linked to the working environment.[21] These diseases range from hepatitis to mesothelioma, a type of cancer caused by exposure to asbestos. The human suffering and economic costs of occupational illnesses are enormous. For example, one study of 645 workers exposed to asbestos determined the costs due to death and disability averaged $254,000 per employee.[22]

Unfortunately, occupational disease is neglected by both employers and the medical profession. For example, many employers are generally ignorant of the health effects of various workplace disease hazards. In addition, physicians do not receive adequate medical training in occupational diseases.

Employers can establish occupational disease prevention programs through several measures.

Identifying Health Hazards

The first place to start in occupational disease prevention is to identify health hazards. To assist in this effort, an employer can acquire the services of an occupational epidemiologist, a specialist who studies the causes of occupational disease. Some large companies have full-time epidemiologists on their staffs to research potential health problems. The types of occupational illnesses resulting from health hazard exposures are discussed earlier in this chapter.

After the hazards, agents, and conditions are identified, the employer should take corrective measures to either eliminate the hazard or implement procedures to prevent the agent from causing an occupational disease. A major part of this effort is informing employees about occupational hazards. Many states have right-to-know laws that require employers to inform employees, and in some cases the community in which a product is produced, of any health hazards.

Hazard Communication Standard

In 1983, OSHA issued the Federal Hazard Communication Standard, which requires manufacturers and importers of chemicals to analyze the hazards of any chemicals they produce, label containers of hazardous chemicals, and provide employers with completed Material Safety Data Sheets on any hazardous chemical. Exhibit 31-8 is an example of a Material Safety Data Sheet.

Under the standard, all employers are required to prepare a written hazard communication program that lists the hazardous chemicals used. The program must also include the following:

- Explain that hazardous chemicals will be labeled.
- State that Material Safety Data Sheets will be prepared.
- State employees will be trained.

---

[21] Rutsetein, D.D., Mullan, R.J., Frazier, Halperin, W.E., Melius, J.M., and Sestito, J.P., "Sentinel Health Events (Occupational): A Basis for Physician Recognition and Public Health Surveillance," *American* *Journal of Public Health* 73 (September 1983), pp. 1054-1062.

[22] Lambrinos, J. and Johnson, W.G., "Robots to Reduce the High Cost of Illness and Injury," *Harvard Business Review* 30 (May-June 1984), p. 28.

- Indicate that employees will be informed of hazards and chemicals.
- Explain that other employees at multi-employer worksites will be informed of hazards.

Employers are also required to take those actions described in the written program, such as label chemicals, prepare Material Safety Data Sheets, and train employees.

Exhibit 31-7

Material Safety Data Sheet	**U.S. Department of Labor**	
May be used to comply with OSHA's Hazard Communication Standard, 29 CFR 1910.1200. Standard must be consulted for specific requirements.	Occupational Safety and Health Administration (Non-Mandatory Form) Form Approved OMB No. 1218-0072	

IDENTITY *(As Used on Label and List)*	Note: Blank spaces are not permitted. If any item is not applicable, or no information is available, the space must be marked to indicate that.

Section I

Manufacturer's Name	Emergency Telephone Number
Address *(Number, Street, City, State, and ZIP Code)*	Telephone Number for Information
	Date Prepared
	Signature of Preparer *(optional)*

Section II - Hazard Ingredients/Identity Information

Hazardous Components (Specific Chemical Identity; Common Name(s))	OSHA PEL	ACGIH TLV	Other Limits Recommended	%(optional)

Section III - Physical/Chemical Characteristics

Boiling Point		Specific Gravity (H_2O = 1)	
Vapor Pressure (mm Hg.)		Melting Point	
Vapor Density (AIR = 1)		Evaporation Rate (Butyl Acetate = 1)	
Solubility in Water			
Appearance and Odor			

Section IV - Fire and Explosion Hazard Data

Flash Point (Method Used) ·	Flammable Limits	LEL	UEL
Extinguishing Media			
Special Fire Fighting Procedures			
Unusual Fire and Explosion Hazards			

(Reproduce locally)   OSHA 174, Sept. 1985

Section V - Reactivity Data

Stability	Unstable	Conditions to Avoid	
	Stable		
Incompatibility *(Materials to Avoid)*			
Hazardous Decomposition or Byproducts			
Hazardous Polymerization	May Occur	Conditions to Avoid	
	Will Not Occur		

Section VI - Health Hazard Data

Route(s) of Entry:	Inhalation?	Skin?	Ingestion?
Health Hazards *(Acute and Chronic)*			
Carcinogenicity:	NTP?	IARC Monographs?	OSHA Regulated?
Signs and Symptoms of Exposure			
Medical Conditions Generally Aggravated by Exposure			
Emergency and First Aid Procedures			

Section VII - Precautions for Safe Handling and Use

Steps to Be Taken in Case Material is Released or Spilled
Waste Disposal Method
Precautions to Be taken in Handling and Storing
Other Precautions

Section VIII - Control Measures

Respiratory Proctection *(Specify Type)*			
Ventilation	Local Exhaust		Special
	Mechanical *(General)*		Other
Protective Gloves		Eye Protection	
Other Protective Clothing or Equipment			
Work/Hygienic Practices			

Occupational Disease Prevention

Another way of preventing occupational disease is through well-defined job specifications, including training requirements for jobs involving toxic and hazardous substances. For example, three occupational diseases existing in work involving the manufacture and repair of automotive batteries are toxic encephalitis, inflammatory and toxic neuropathy, and acute or chronic renal failure. All three of these diseases, which are caused by improper exposure to lead, may be prevented through employee training and the use of protective clothing.

Employee training

OSHA regulations require employers to assume responsibilities for employee safety and health information, and OSHA believes that providing employees with information and training can help them take steps to protect themselves. Safety and health training is conditioned upon employees' motivation to learn and their ability to understand what is taught. For example, a person employed as a battery repairer may improperly use a respirator because of lack of knowledge that exposure to airborne lead is dangerous and lack of understanding of how a respirator is used.

There are several ways to determine whether employees' failure to adhere to safe and healthful work practices is due to poor motivation. First, poor motivation is usually the culprit if employees are able to properly perform their tasks but do not do so. This means they know the proper methods but lack the motivation to use them. Low motivation may also exist if employees seem unconcerned about safety and health matters. A third way of determining whether motivation is a problem is to see whether employees can properly do a task if asked.

Several steps can help motivate employees to learn and use safe working practices. First, specify safety and health objectives and communicate them to employees. Where possible, these objectives should be part of the reward systems in pay administration and pay incentives. These payments can be a part of a pay system, based upon performance appraisal which, in turn, considers safety performance as one variable. Another method is to provide annual payments, stipends, or bonuses for not having accidents. Another way of motivating employees to use safe and healthful practices is to determine what conditions may exist in the work environment that are reinforcing unsafe practices. Learning theory assumes behavior is reinforced, so there is a possibility that employees are conditioned to perform their tasks unsafely. Unsafe behavior may be reinforced by a supervisor who is encouraging employees to ignore safety and health.

Another way of motivating employees to follow safety and health procedures and regulations is through discipline. Discipline can be meted by either withholding a desired outcome, such as a pay increase, or by administering an unpleasant stimulus, such as a warning letter or a suspension. Discipline can be effective if safety and health rules are stated in writing, employees are trained in the rules, discipline is administered promptly when deficiencies occur, and the discipline is appropriate for the deficiency. Discipline is not a substitute for rewards. Also, rewards should occur much more frequently than disciplinary actions.

Skills in safety and health training. Skills training can be administered both on- and off-the-job. The assumption in skills training is that employees are motivated to learn. The best on-the-job training methods are coaching and modeling. In *coaching*, the trainer, be it a supervisor or a peer-trainer, assumes the role of a helpful person. Employees should be coached in both how *and why* a safe and healthful procedure or regulation should be followed.

Modeling is training in which the employee learns safety and health methods by observing the behavior of others. Modeling can have a strong influence on employee performance. For example, peer behavior, such as following safety and health procedures, influences both the motivation and the behavior of individual employees. Supervisors also are role models.

Safety and health incentives

Incentives for employee safety and health performance can range from pay bonuses to prizes. The Lincoln Electric Company considers an employee's safety performance as one of several variables in determining the amount of an employee's annual bonus. Other companies use prizes, such as key chains, pens, and clothing items like jackets and hats. Another incentive used effectively by some companies are chances to play games, like Bingo, and compete for prizes. The rules for these games vary: one company permits all employees to play during any week in which no accidents occur.[23] A bus company furnishes free coffee and donuts when no accidents occur in a month. One company uses monthly drawings for a $50 U.S. Savings Bond. There are two different drawings. One drawing is open to all employees who report at least one unsafe act or condition, submit a safety suggestion, or furnish some safety advice applicable to either the job or at home. To be eligible for the other drawing, an employee must have neither a lost-time injury during the month nor been disciplined for a safety violation during the period.[24]

Organizations can get maximum effect from incentives by publicizing them extensively, making frequent awards, making award presentations before the winners' peers, and by including top management in award presentations. Some companies use annual awards and present them at dinners celebrating significant safety and health milestones. For example, the president of the company discussed earlier in this chapter commemorated the attainment of three million workhours without an accident by presenting $15,000 in awards at a special reception.[25]

Safety and Health Audits and Inspections

A safety audit is a comprehensive evaluation of an organization's entire safety and health program. A *safety inspection* is a periodic evaluation of various

---

[23] Crapnell, S.G., "For Prize-Winning Programs, Try Awards and Incentives," *Occupational Hazards* (August 1982), pp. 35-40.

[24] *Ibid.*

[25] Diekemper, "Faulty Corporate Philosophy," p. 29.

departments or operational units to determine if any unsafe conditions exist and whether safety and health procedures are followed.

Audits

Safety audits typically scrutinize many areas of the safety and health program, ranging from an examination of program goals to a review of evaluation procedures. Among the topics included in an audit are:

- Determining the extent of safety and health involvement in both top management and operational planning;
- Analyzing the qualifications of safety and health personnel and preparing recommendations for personal and professional development;
- Evaluating the effectiveness of safety and health programs in such areas as work practices, housekeeping, maintenance, storage practices, condition of facilities and operating equipment, and employee selection and training;
- Reviewing the adequacy of safety and health reporting systems; and
- Evaluating the organization's effectiveness in complying with OSHA procedures and standards.

Safety audits can be performed either internally or externally. For example, some consulting firms perform safety audits. There are advantages to using external sources in safety audits. First, external personnel give an unbiased viewpoint. Using internal personnel to conduct an audit can be self-serving. A second advantage is that outside personnel have experience in many different organizations, so that they may have a range of ideas of how safety and health programs can be improved.

Sometimes audits are restricted to specific topics, such as safety incentives or an organization's occupational medical program. An OSHA compliance audit is another area in which employers use external consultants to determine if any potential problems exist. Sometimes safety and health audits are conducted by the organization's workers' compensation insurer. These audits are intended to help prevent unnecessary workers' compensation claims by identifying and eliminating potential safety and health problems.

Inspections

Safety and health inspections are the foundation of a comprehensive safety and health program. Inspections are virtually always conducted in-house. The frequency of these inspections vary; some organizations conduct them annually or semiannually. Other employers conduct inspections as often as monthly.

Generally, the inspections are conducted by the supervisor in his or her area of responsibility. Usually, a checklist is used to guide the supervisor. Sometimes organizations assign in-house safety personnel to either conduct unannounced inspections or assist supervisors in their inspections. These steps are taken to ensure integrity in the inspection process.

Generally, all completed inspection forms are sent to the safety and health department, if there is one. The forms are reviewed and any deficiencies are noted, together with the corrective action. In smaller organizations, this review function is performed by the personnel manager or other designated person. The inspection process can easily become a paper mill in which functions are marginally performed. To prevent this eventuality requires top manager attention, such as visible evidence that supervisors are expected to diligently conduct their inspections.

Accident Investigations

Prompt accident investigations are designed to quickly assess the causes and the failure sources of accidents. One reason for promptly conducting accident investigations is to immediately get a written record of what happened, how the accident was caused, and why it happened. Another important reason is to determine whether similar causes and sources exist elsewhere in the organization, so that other potential accidents can be prevented. Other reasons include determining whether safety regulation violations were involved and, if so, whether disciplinary action is warranted. Finally, written investigations that are well-documented may be needed in the event of legal action.

Two of the most common problem-solving techniques in accident investigations are *change analysis* and *job safety analysis*.

Change analysis. This is a technique in which the investigator looks for deviations from the norm. These are the steps in the technique:

- Define the problem (what happened);

- Establish what the norm is (what should have happened);

- Identify, locate, and describe the change from what happened to what should have happened (what, where, when, to what extent did it happen);

- Specify what was and what was not affected;

- Identify the distinctive features of the change;

- List possible causes (*basic*, *direct*, and *indirect*); and

- Select the most likely causes.

Job safety analysis. This is a technique in which the job is broken down into basic steps, and the hazards associated with each step are identified. Controls are established for each identified hazard. A chart is prepared, listing the basic steps and the controls. The chart is used to determine the events and the conditions that led to the accident, such as the failure to follow a step or the failure to control for a hazard.

Accident Report

After an accident is investigated, a report should be prepared containing the following information:

- *Background information,* including where and when the accident occurred, who and what was involved, and the operating personnel and other witnesses;

- *Account of the accident,* including what happened, such as the sequence of events, the extent of damage, the type of accident, and the source of energy or hazardous material;

- *Discussion (analysis) of the accident,* including the *direct causes* (energy sources and hazardous materials), *indirect causes* (unsafe acts and conditions), and *basic causes* (management policies or personal or environmental factors); and

- *Recommendations,* including what should be done immediately to prevent a recurrence and any long-range action to remedy the *basic*, *indirect*, and *direct causes.*

CHAPTER 32

SECURITY AND WORKPLACE VIOLENCE

Chapter Highlights
- Review the types of acts and perpetrators of workplace crime and violence
- Understand a strategic and operational approach to preventing workplace crime

Introduction

The top security concern for business is workplace violence. This conclusion was the result from the 2003 annual survey of security professionals employed in Fortune, 1000 firms.[1] Business Interruption/Disaster Recovery was ranked number two Computer Crime: Internet/Intranet Security was ranked number three and the Threat of Terrorism (global and domestic) was ranked number four in the security professionals' opinions.[2]

The role of security management is to identify security concerns and take action to prevent or control them.

Security is the protection of an organization's assets, its employees, and the property of employees while on the employer's premises.

Workplace Crime and Violence

Violence occurs all too frequently in the workplace. In 2006, 13.6 percent of crimes of violence occurred when the victim was working or on duty. An additional 4.6 percent of such crimes occurred while the victim was on the way to or from work.[3] Crimes of violence include rape/sexual assault, robbery, aggravated assault and simple assault. Crimes of violence also include workplace homicide which increased by 13 percent to 607 in 2007, but in spite of the increase, the number was 44 percent less than the high of 1,080 in 1994.[4] Crimes of violence also include injuries that are self-inflicted in the workplace.

Most violent acts, excluding homicide and suicide, do not result in injury. Approximately 88 percent of the victims are not injured. Of the 12 percent of

---

[1] Pinkerton, *Top Security Threats and Management Issues Facing Corporate America: 2003 Survey of Fortune 1000 Companies, p. 2, 2003.*

[2] Ibid.

[3] U.S. Department of Justice, *Criminal Victimization in the United States, 2006* (August 2008), Table 64.

[4] Bureau of Labor Statistics, *National Census of Fatal Occupational Injuries in 2007* (August 20, 2008), p. 2.

victims who do experience injuries, 1.2 percent are serious and 25 percent of these receive medical treatment.[5]

Nonviolent criminal acts also occur in the workplace. Such acts include embezzlement and fraud and theft.

Assaults

There are two types of assault:

- *Aggravated assault,* which is an attack or an attempted attack with a weapon, regardless of whether an injury occurred; this also includes an attack without a weapon when serious injury occurs; and

- *Simple assault,* which is an attack without a weapon, resulting in no injury, in a minor injury or in an undetermined injury requiring less than two days' hospitalization; this also includes attempted assault without a weapon.

Each year, during the seven year interval (1993-99) mentioned previously, an average of 325,000 aggravated assaults and 1,311,700 simple assaults occurred in the workplace.

Exhibit 32-1
Violent Acts Against Employees
Resulting in Days Away from Work, 2000

Violent Act	Total Cases	Women as % of Total
Hitting/kicking/beating	8,132	59 %
Squeezing/pinching/& related	1,649	71
Biting	316	80
Stabbing	156	52
Shooting	289	41
Threats and verbal assaults	123	76
Other	12,841	51
Total	23,506	59

Source: U.S. Department of Labor

Women often are the victims in workplace assault. A summary of the types of acts, showing women victims as a percent of the total are shown in Exhibit 32-1, above. The violent acts shown in this Exhibit include rape, which is part of the "Other" category.

Homicide

In 2007, homicide was the fourth major cause of workplace fatalities following transportation incidents, being struck by objects or equipment and falls.[6][7]

Homicide is the willful and unlawful killing of a person by another.[8]

---

[5] Duhart, D., *National Crime Victimization Survey: Violence in the Workplace, 1993-1999*, U.S. Department of Justice (December 2001), p.6

[6] U.S. Department of Labor, Bureau of Labor Statistics, *Census of Fatal Occupational Injuries, 2008.*

[7] Ibid, p. 6.

[8] Duhart, D., *National Crime Vicitimization Survey: Violence in the Workplace, 1993-1999*, U.S. Department of Justice (December 2001), p. 12.

The circumstances in which the homicides occurred are shown in Exhibit 32-2.

Exhibit 32-2
Circumstances/Alleged Perpetrator
Workplace Homicides, 2000

Circumstances/alleged perpetrator	Number	Percent
Robberies and other crimes	281	41
Work associates	73	11
Relatives	32	5
Other	291	43
TOTAL	677	100

Source: U.S. Department of Labor

Occupations of Perpetrators and Victims

In studying both assaults and homicides, researchers have found that victims are typically found in particular types of work. The occupations with the highest violent victimizations (rate per 1,000 workers), excluding homicide, are:

- police personnel (260.8)
- corrections (155.7)
- taxicab drivers (128.3)
- private security (86.6)
- bartender (81.6)
- mental health custodians (69.0)
- special education teacher (68.4)
- gas station sales personnel (68.3)
- mental health professionals (68.2)
- junior high teacher (54.2)
- convenience store sales personnel (53.9)[9]

For all occupations, the rate of violent victimizations per 1,000 workers is 12.6.

The relative frequencies of homicides among occupations differ somewhat from nonfatal but violent victimizations. These are the occupations with the highest frequencies of homicide (homicide as a percent of total fatalities occurring in the occupation):

- cashiers (82%)
- managers, food serving and lodging establishments (67%)
- taxicab drivers and chauffeurs (60%)
- supervisors and proprietors, sales occupations (59%)

---

[9] Ibid., p. 4.

- guards, including supervisors (46%)
- police and detectives, including supervisors (35%)
- executive, administrative, and managerial occupations (29%)
- administrative support occupations, including clerical (29%)
- cleaning and building services (15%)[10]

For all occupations, homicides represent 11% of all fatalities.

Based upon a comparison of rates for nonfatal violent victimizations and homicides among occupations, police personnel, corrections personnel, taxicab drivers, cashiers and gas station sales personnel are among the most violent.

Arson

Arson is willfully burning, or attempting to burn, a house, building, or other property, regardless of whether there is an attempt to defraud. No data is available about the number of job-related instances of arson.

Embezzlement and Fraud

Both employees and individuals with company business relationships, such as vendors and suppliers, may commit embezzlement and fraud. Effective risk management measures, such as verifying the credentials and experiences of outside contractors, can help spot potential problems. In addition, unannounced audits can help identify fraud and/or embezzlement.

Internal fraud and embezzlement are frequently linked to troubled employees. For example, employees experiencing financial problems may resort to embezzlement. A stockbroker embezzled $16 million from his clients and a bank where his father was president. In court, he confessed that he was a pathological gambler. In one study, 80 percent of the pathological gamblers admitted that they committed various crimes to secure gambling funds.[11]

Suicide

Suicide " . . . is a conscious act of self-induced annihilation . . . "[12] In 2007, 189 employees died at work due to self-inflicted injury.[13] While little is known about the circumstances surrounding workplace suicide, there is some evidence that co-worker perpetrators of workplace homicide are likely to commit suicide. This is more common when the co-worker has committed multiple homicides. Suicide is an extremely complex issue, typically involving inescapable psychological pain, feelings of abject hopelessness, and a chronic history of frustrated ambitions.[14] The manner in which employers respond to workplace suicide is

---

[10] Bureau of Labor Statistics, *National Census of Fatal Occupational Injuries in 2000*, (August 14, 2001), p. 8.

[11] Myers, D.W., *Establishing and Building Employee Assistance Programs* (Westport, CT: Quorum Books, 1984), p. 63.

[12] Leenaars, A.A. and Wenckstern, S., "Suicide in the School-Age Child and Adolescent," *Life Span*

Perspectives of Suicide, edited by Leenaars, A.A. (New York: Plenum Press, 1991), p.96.

[13] Ibid, p. 7

[14] For a thorough analysis of suicide, see Leenaars, A.A., *Life Span Perspectives of Suicide* (New York: Plenum Press, 1991).

important to prevent "copycat" suicides and to help co-workers recover from the trauma they may experience following a suicide.

Rape and Sexual Assault

Rape is forced sexual intercourse, including psychological coercion, as well as physical force. This definition includes attempted rapes, with male as well as female victims, and both heterosexual and homosexual rape.[15]

Sexual assault includes a wide range of victimizations, separate from rape or attempted rape. These crimes include attacks or attempted attacks, generally involving unwanted sexual contact between victim and offender. Sexual assaults also include verbal threats.

Rape and sexual assaults are no strangers to the workplace. Each week during the period of 1993-99, 702 workers suffered rape or sexual assaults. Eighty percent of the victims were women.

Robbery

Robbery is an act, whether attempted or completed, which involves theft, directly from a person, of property or cash by force or threat. Robbery may occur with or without a weapon whether or not an injury occurs. During the period of 1993-99, an annual average of 70,000 robberies occurred in the workplace in which the victim was robbed of personal property.[16] In 2000, 291 workers were the victims of homicide committed during a robbery.[17]

Methods of Robbers

These are the methods often used by robbers:

- The robber will select an establishment that is an easy target and where the robber does not know the victim;

- Usually, perpetrators will make a minor purchase while assessing whether to rob the victim;

- Often, the perpetrators have accomplices;[18] and

- In about one-third of all robberies; the victim is injured.

Motives of Robbers

Perpetrators have various motives for committing robbery; money is most the obvious reason. Research on the subject has also found support for the hypothesis that robbers are motivated by the need to exercise authority over someone; that is, to make someone do something they do not want to do. Common wisdom states that the victim should concede to the demands of the robber, which may help to fulfill the robber's need to exercise authority.

---

[15] Warchol, G., *National Crime Victimization Survey: Workplace Violence, 1992-96*, U.S. Department of Justice (July 28, 1998), p. 8.

[16] These figures differ from the FBI's Uniform Crime Reports (UCR), since the UCR includes robberies in which establishments or individuals were robbed of property.

[17] U.S. Department of Labor, *National Census of Fatal Occupational Injuries, 2000.*

[18] n.a., "How to protect yourself, your employees and your business from robbery," *Profit-Building Strategies for Business Owners* (23:3), pp. 5-7.

Terrorism

The material on terrorism in this chapter focuses on domestic acts. See Chapter 37 for a full discussion of international acts of terrorism, including how terrorism is defined.

Usually, domestic acts of terrorism are aimed against organizations involved in international business, or those involved in some economic, political, or social issue. For example, abortion clinics have been the object of threats and bombings by anti-abortion extremist groups.

The 2001 terrorist attacks on the World Trade Center, the Pentagon and the airliner that crashed in Pennsylvania, apparently due to passengers' interventions, dramatically affected the tranquility of U. S. workplaces both domestically and abroad. These monstrous crimes inflicted enormous suffering on the victims, their family members, and public safety personnel who either died or were hurt in the course of duty. This event will long-live in the American psyche paralleled by few other historical events. The long-run effects of the crimes while unknown are obviously enormous and will dramatically effect the workplace.

Typically, outsiders perpetrate terrorism. However, HR personnel should be alert for terrorists who attempt to infiltrate their organizations and create problems from within. To help address this problem, applicants' qualifications and references should be verified. Naturally, for jobs posing more significant security risks, such verifications should be as thorough as possible.

There are some acts that do not meet the typical definition of terrorism, but may disrupt an organization's operations, including bomb threats, harassing telephone calls, and making false alarms, such as calling the fire department about a bogus fire. These problems are more widespread than they might seem.

All companies should have contingency plans to deal with emergencies, such as bomb threats. This type of threat should also be part of a security audit to identify potential problems.

Theft

Some researchers estimate that 30 percent of all business failures are due to employee theft. One security expert contends that the major reasons for employee theft are, in order of importance: (1) gambling, (2) drug and alcohol use, (3) extramarital affairs, (4) economic need, (4) "trying to keep up with the Joneses," and (5) following an example set by the boss.[19]

Internal theft can be prevented through a combination of HR strategies. Employment verifications can help identify those applicants who have stolen from other employers and/or have been convicted of theft. This does not necessarily bar such individuals from employment in any job. In such cases, the employment decision should be based upon the date of the conviction, the type of job, and the experiences of the applicant since the conviction. Finally, employers should be sensitive to employees who are troubled by such problems as gambling, substance abuse, financial problems, and marital difficulties. This

---

[19] *Ibid.*

group, which constitutes 20 percent of the employee population, represents the biggest internal theft risk for employers.

Sabotage/Vandalism

Sabotage is the deliberate destruction of organizational assets. *Vandalism* includes a number of willful acts by employees, such as the destruction or defacement of real or personal property. Present or former employees commit virtually all sabotage, with computer operations particularly vulnerable. For example, one disgruntled computer operator programmed a computer to erase all accounts receivable six months after he quit the firm.[20] Some experts contend employee vandalism is one of the biggest threats to computer security.[21] Security experts warn employers not to cause employees to become disgruntled because of unfair treatment or other grievances. Such dissatisfaction may provoke employee sabotage. Sometimes, indifferent or inconsiderate treatment by management causes frustration and aggressive behavior by employees, resulting in sabotage.

Under-Reporting

As bad as these statistics are, some experts believe most workplace violence is *never reported* to the police. According to a U.S. Department of Justice study, 56 percent of all violent victimizations occurring at work were not reported to the police. When asked why the incidents were not reported, 20 percent of the victims felt the incident was a personal or private matter and 29 percent of the victims reported the incident to an organization representative, such as a security guard.

International Problem

Neither the problem of workplace crime and violence nor the under-reporting of it is confined to the United States. Researchers in Australia, for example, found that workplace violence affects about 40 percent of employees, although only about 20 percent of incidents are reported.[22]

Employer Response

Some contend workplace crime and violence are inevitable extensions of crime and violence in society. These and similar types of arguments are undoubtedly the reason that more employers do not have programs or policies in place to address workplace crime. For example, 71 percent of the respondents in a survey of human resources management professionals, conducted by the Society for Human Resource Management, indicated that their organization had neither a policy nor a program to deal with the possibility or the aftermath of workplace violence.[23]

---

[20] *Ibid.*

[21] Rushinek, A. and Rushinek, S., "Selecting Password/File Access Software," *Corporate Controller* (Jul./Aug. 1992), pp. 37-39.

[22] Wakefield, H., "Get ready for some workplace violence," *Australian Business Monthly* (14:2), pp. 130-131.

[23] Society for Human Resource Management, *Workplace Violence: Business As Usual? Survey Reveals Escalating Violence.* (Alexandria, VA: November 1993).

Effects of Workplace Crime and Violence

Psychological Effects on Employees

The three main psychological effects of workplace violence on employees are:

- The worry and stress caused by the anxiety of the prospect of crime, particularly violence;
- The pain and suffering experienced as a result of crime and violence; and
- Depression and other symptoms that are experienced during recovery from a criminal act.

Economic Effects

According to the U.S. Department of Justice, employees who are victims of workplace violence lose about 1.7 million workdays per year, for an average of 3.5 days per crime. These lost workdays result in more than $55 million in lost pay each year, not including compensation for sick and annual leave. Other economic effects are due to insurance claims, medical expense plan charges, and workers' compensation benefits. The economic costs of work-related homicide include survivors' benefits and liability suits. Insurance expenses include claims for disability benefits for persons recuperating from an act of workplace violence. Survivors' benefits must be paid if homicide is involved. Workers' compensation claims may include medical expenses and replacement income for workers who are unable to work due to the act of workplace violence. If the injury is severe, expenses may be incurred for rehabilitation, such as vocational physical therapy, so that employees can either return to their old jobs or find employment in other occupations.

Medical expense plan charges may include costs for medical treatment that is not covered by workers' compensation. Survivor's expenses may include workers' compensation and life insurance benefits, as previously noted.

Employers must also be cognizant of the economic costs of liability suits filed by either the victims of workplace violence or their survivors, alleging negligence for hiring or retaining a worker who committed an act of violence or for failing to provide safeguards to protect persons from acts of violence. Some researchers contend that a single suit for a work-related homicide can cost an employer $250,000. Some experts believe the total costs of workplace violence are in excess of $4 billion per year.[24]

---

[24] Smith, S.L., "Violence in the workplace: a cry for help," *Occupational Hazards* (October 1993).

Perpetrators of Workplace Crime and Violence

The types of perpetrators of workplace crime and violence are shown Exhibit 32-3.

Exhibit 32-3
Perpetrators of Workplace Crime and Violence

Employment Related	Contractors	Crime Related	Social/Family Related	Product/Service Related
Employee	Contractor	Arsonist	Boy/girlfriend	Perceived victim
Former employee	Service provider	Assailant	Ex-boy/girlfriend	
		Murderer		Client
Job applicant	Vendor	Rapist	Family member	Customer
		Robber		Protagonist
		Terrorist	Spouse	
		Vandal	Other friend	

Employees

Employees who may become perpetrators include personnel employed at all levels of an organization, regardless of their job title. An employee may be a peer, a subordinate, or a supervisor. This classification also includes leased or temporary workers, as well as individuals who work part-time. Employees who have problems with drug abuse, family and marriage difficulties, gambling, legal entanglements, financial difficulties, and mental or emotional conditions are particularly susceptible to resorting to crime and violence. Employee assistance programs are intended to prevent and treat the problems of troubled employees

Applicants for employment. Included in this group are individuals who applied for a job but were denied employment and are dissatisfied with the decision.

Former employees. Former employees who commit workplace violence include those who are disgruntled concerning some condition surrounding their former employment. A discharged employee who is still disgruntled over the situation is a prime example of an employment-related perpetrator. Every year, approximately three percent of all assaults in the workplace are committed by former employees. Also, about 2 percent of all employee harassments every year are caused by former employees. Former employees perpetrated 56 workplace homicides in 1997.[25] These homicides involve business disputes with a co-worker or former co-worker, usually resulting from an employment discharge.

Contractors/Vendors/Service Providers

Contractors, vendors, service providers, and other nonemployees are potential perpetrators of crime. These individuals are employed by others but come into contact with employees and customers in the workplace. Vendors delivering supplies or personnel providing services in the workplace, including parking lot

---

[25] U.S. Department of Labor, Bureau of Labor Statistics, *National Census of Fatal Occupational Injuries,* 1992-1997, p.3.

attendants, are examples of this category of potential perpetrators. These nonem-ployees could work full-time at the employer's place of business, such as a security guard, or work part-time, such as contract cleaning personnel.

Crime-Related Perpetrators

Crime-related perpetrators are those individuals outside the organization who have a criminal motive for committing such an act. The principal types of crimes involved are arson, assault, homicide, rape, robbery, terrorism, and van-dalism. This group includes perpetrators who commit a violent act toward either an employee or property while they are engaged in another workplace crime. For example, a robber who murders a convenience store employee during the rob-bery is a crime-related perpetrator.

Social/Family-Related Perpetrators

This group includes those who are connected with an employee either socially, such as a current or former boyfriend or girlfriend or through marriage, such as a current or former spouse.

Present/Past Friends and Spouses of Employees . Persons in this group include individuals who commit a violent act primarily because of their dissatis-faction, jealousy, or related feelings toward an employee. In 1998, there were 26 homicides of employees in the workplace that were committed by a husband/former husband, boyfriend/former boyfriend or other personal acquaintance.[26]

According to another study, there are in excess of 13,000 acts of violence annually against employees that are caused by domestic problems or romances that have gone sour. In virtually all of these cases, the victim was a female employee.[27] Frequently, attacks related to jealousy and other feelings occur at work because it is the one place where the victim can be found by the attacker. A threatened individual may make arrangements to stay at friends or relatives to avoid the attacker during off-hours but generally must return to the workplace to maintain employment.

Thirty-six percent of all workplace victimizations were committed by per-sons known by the victim. The figures for known attackers differ considerably between the sexes. Male victims knew 30 percent of their attackers, but female victims were acquainted (either intimately or casually) with 49 percent of their attackers.[28]

In an effort to prevent or treat the problem of domestic violence, several firms, including Liz Claiborne, Reebok, and Ben & Jerry's Ice Cream, have consolidated their efforts to raise $100,000 to fund the Domestic Violence Action Committee. The mission of this committee is to conduct research on the causes of domestic violence.[29]

---

[26] U.S. Department of Labor, Bureau of Labor Statistics, *Census of Fatal Occupational Injuries,* 1998.

[27] Silverstein, S., "Stalked by violence on the job," *Los Angeles Times* (August 8, 1994).

[28] Warchol, G., *National Crime Victimization Survey: Workplace Violence, 1992-96,* U.S. Department of Justice (July 28, 1998), p. 4.

[29] Marmon, L., "Domestic violence: the cost to business," *Working Woman* (April 1994), p. 17-18.

Product/Service-Related Perpetrators

The three groups of persons in this category are: (1) disgruntled clients, customers, and patients; (2) alleged victims of the product or service produced by the organization; and (3) extremists or militant activists who are compelled for various reasons, such as their beliefs or principles, to commit violent acts against the organization and/or its employees.

Disgruntled Customers, Clients, and Patients. This category includes persons who commit a violent act against employees because of their dissatisfaction with a product or service. A customer who assaults an employee because the employee refused to give the customer credit for merchandise that the customer wanted to return is an example of a disgruntled customer perpetrator. A patient who assaults a physician because he or she is unhappy with the outcome of a surgical procedure performed by the physician is a disgruntled patient perpetrator.

In 1998, there were approximately 35 work-related homicides perpetrated by customers or clients, usually involving a dispute in which the person was asked to leave the employers' premises.[30]

Perceived Victims. Included among this category are individuals who feel they have been adversely affected by an act of an owner or employee of an organization and commit a violent act against that owner or employee. A defendant in a lawsuit, angered by the outcome of a trial, who murders the plaintiff's attorney is an example of this type of perpetrator.

Extremists or Militant Activists. This category includes those who commit violent acts because of their dissatisfaction or disagreement with the mission of an organization, such as anti-abortion advocates who cause damage to abortion clinics and injure clinic personnel. Also in this group are conservationists and wildlife preservationists who perform various acts of violence, including nailing spikes in trees that are scheduled to be logged by timber companies.

Profile of Violence-Prone Person

Is there a profile of a person who is prone to commit a criminal act? A national survey of human resource management practitioners found that only 37 percent of the respondents who reported that their workplace had experienced a violent act stated that they could have identified the perpetrator as having the potential for violence; 63 percent said they could not have identified the potential of the person to commit a violent act.[31] One reason that such perpetrators could not be identified prior to the act is that few, if any employees, have been trained to spot such violence-prone individuals. Thus, the issue of whether a co-worker who committed violence could have been identified before the incident depends upon whether HR personnel were trained in recognizing the personal factors associated with violence.

Some researchers contend there are several profiles of potential violence-prone individuals, depending upon the type of crime or violence.

---

[30] U.S. Department of Labor, Bureau of Labor Statistics, *Census of Fatal Occupational Injuries,* 1998.

[31] "SHRM survey reveals extent of workplace violence," *EAP Digest* (14:3), p. 25.

Legal Requirements to Prevent Workplace Crime and Violence

Federal Laws

The General Duty responsibility of the Occupational Safety and Health Act of 1970 requires employers to provide a workplace free from recognized hazards that cause, or are likely to cause, death or serious physical harm to employees. The only other federal law that specifically applies to workplace violence is the Bank Protection Law of 1968, mandating security requirements in the banking industry. The Occupational Safety and Health Administration has issued guidelines to employers to protect health care and social workers from workplace violence.

State Laws

Several states, including Florida and Washington, have enacted legislation mandating security provisions to protect employees. These states' laws focus on convenience stores. California enacted a law in 1995 requiring hospitals to implement plans to prevent workplace violence, which was prompted by a study that found almost 60 percent of the hospitals in the five largest cities in California had experienced workplace attacks on hospital personnel, patients or visitors.[32]

Property Laws

A number of states have laws prohibiting computer-related crimes, such as sabotaging computer records, data, or software and hardware systems. While most of these state provisions are intended to punish outsiders, they could presumably be used against employees who commit violent acts against computers and related property.

Judicial Awards

"Negligent security" is a doctrine used in some courts for employer liability to provide for the safety of employees. According to one consultant, the average jury award for failing to adequately provide for security to employees is $1.2 million. The awards for non-jury cases average $600,000.

Preventing Workplace Crime and Violence

Prevention should be the focus of management's attention in addressing workplace crime. Prevention begins with strategic and operational planning that incorporates such functions as human resources management, risk management, and security management. This holistic approach is the optimal one because it incorporates contributions from different disciplines to address the common problem of workplace crime. Among the contributions from security management are security protocols and security devices. Risk management contributions include methods in avoiding, preventing and controlling, and transferring the risk of workplace crime. Human resources management contributions to workplace crime include the traditional ones involving the careful selection of employees and employee assistance programming. Other less-well known human

---

[32] Dunkel, T., "Newest danger zone: your office,"
Working Woman (August 1994).

resources methods to control workplace violence include establishing networks and changing organization culture.

Strategic Planning and Workplace Crime and Violence

Strategic and operational planning are needed to address workplace crime and violence. The factors to consider in this planning are shown in Exhibit 32-4 on the following page.

Changing the Culture to Prevent Workplace Violence

Maintaining a violence-free work environment may require some changes in an organization's culture. For example, conducting employee training on preventing and stopping crime and violence will not be effective unless the training program is preceded by a conscientious effort to ensure the culture supports the training effort. If what the employees are taught runs contrary to the organizational culture, the training becomes *encapsulated learning*, which means that such learning cannot be fully implemented to accomplish the purposes for which it was intended.

Exhibit 32-4
Strategic and Operational Planning
to Prevent Workplace Crime and Violence

Strategic Planning	*Operational Planning*
Mission statement	Define procedures
Goal establishment	Dispute Resolution
Organization culture	Grievance procedure
Policy formulation	Handling complaints
Authority delegation	Hot-line
Employee Assistance Program	Crime incident response
Job structuring	Objectives setting
Crime Prevention Team	Performance appraisal
Violence Response Team	

How to Change Organization Culture

To change the organization culture, management should survey employees and conduct a self-assessment of its philosophies and the rules used to guide and judge behavior.

Survey Employees

The first step in changing an organization's culture is to survey employees, in order to measure various components regarding workplace violence that currently exist in the organization. For example, what are the prevailing beliefs, customs, and values among employees regarding violence? Also, what are the perceptions of both employees and supervisors of the management philosophy toward stopping violence? Finally, what management philosophies exist that may impede goals to prevent workplace violence?

The second step is to use the results of the survey to make changes in the organization's culture that management feels are necessary in order to stop workplace violence.

Employee opinion surveys will accomplish two purposes:

1. Management will become aware of employees' perceptions of the organization's culture towards workplace violence; and,

2. Management will also learn about potential areas in which workplace violence may occur.

Too often, top management is caught totally unaware of workplace crime or violence, or the potential for such acts, until they occur. A survey of employee opinions can help prevent this.

Communicate and Take Action on Survey Results. Employees should be informed of the results of the survey as soon as possible and told about any components of the culture that are not consistent with management's intentions, such as certain beliefs employees may have. Also, employees should also be informed of plans to correct such misunderstandings.

Conduct a Self-Assessment of Management Philosophies

Management will need to assess whether the prevailing management philosophies, such as leadership styles and human resources management practices, are conducive to accomplishing the goals related to the prevention of workplace crime and violence.

Authority Delegation

Authority delegations commence with deciding which person(s) should be responsible for accomplishing the organizational goals regarding the prevention of workplace crime and violence, along with any other work assignments relevant to the achievement of the organizational goal. These types of decisions would be followed by decisions regarding the amount and type of authority to delegate to the various jobs.

Employee Selection

Preventing co-worker violence may be partially achieved through careful selection of employees. The selection methods that are typically used include application forms, interviews, tests, exercises, assessment centers, reference checking, polygraph testing, honesty/integrity tests, fingerprinting, arrest records, drug testing, verification of applicant's information, medical examinations, and probationary periods. Each of these methods may be designed to include information about any criminal acts or violence that the applicant may have committed or might have a propensity to commit.

Application Form

The application form should contain a statement for the applicant to read and acknowledge with a signature and date, stating as follows:

> The information that you furnish on this application will be *verified*, which will include checking with your references and former employers and having you provide copies of any court records in which you were a defendant. Also,

you will be asked to sign a release form authorizing us to obtain the above information.

The above statement ensures the applicant is forthcoming in revealing personal information necessary to make a valid hiring decision.

Ask Specific Questions

The application form should contain explicit questions asking the applicant about her/his past behavior. These are some examples:

Have you ever been convicted of any offense in a court or other legal proceeding? If the answer is yes, provide the details in the space below.

Have you ever been disciplined by an employer or discharged from employment for your conduct or behavior? If so, provide the details in the space below.

What types of controlled substances, whether legal or illegal (including alcohol), do you currently use? You will be given a drug test prior to employment.

Require Residence Information

The application form should require a list of all addresses for the past 10 years. Furthermore, the application should require the applicant to furnish evidence of the residency at those locations. Such information may be used to check the applicant's conviction record in the localities named on the application.

Interviews

Employment interviews should include questions about the applicant's qualifications for the job. A sample question might be:

Relate some examples in your work experience that demonstrate your ability to handle stressful situations.

More qualified: The applicant is able to relate experiences in which self-control was shown, or where he or she was not easily upset or displayed a high frustration tolerance.

Less qualified: The applicant is unable to relate any specific incidents or related incidents in which self-control was exhibited, situations in which he or she did not become easily upset or had a low level of frustration tolerance.

Results of Past Performance Reviews

As part of the application process, applicants should be required to furnish copies of their past performance appraisals, which may be reviewed to determine if they contain any information about criminal or violent propensities. If the applicant contends that performance appraisals were not used by prior employers, such information can be verified.

Tests

There are commercially prepared tests that can measure personal characteristics and predict how applicants will respond to job conditions. If desired, employers can consult the *Mental Measurement Yearbook* before using such a test. This reference contains information on over 1,000 tests, including reviews of the validity and reliability of the tests.

Reference Checking

References are individuals listed by an applicant who can furnish pertinent information about the applicant's qualifications. Normally, the names of references are requested on application forms. Applicants should be instructed to list only those references who have known the applicant for at least one or two years and who have direct knowledge of the applicant's qualifications in relation to the job. Applicants should sign releases that authorize references to furnish requested information and waive the applicant's rights to review information furnished by a reference. References should be sent a copy of the release form. References should be asked specific information about the applicant, including past conduct and behavior, and specific examples to support the reference's opinion should be requested.

Polygraph Testing

The Employee Polygraph Protection Act of 1988 (EPPA) restricts the use of polygraphs in the selection process to jobs with: (1) security firms (armored car, alarm, and guard); and (2) manufacturers, distributors, or dispensers of controlled substances, if the applicant will have direct access to the manufacture, storage, distribution, or sale of such substances. Neither refusal by the applicant to take a polygraph test nor the analysis of the results of a polygraph test shall be the sole basis for denying employment. The EPPA also stipulates requirements and qualifications for polygraph examiners.

Honesty/Integrity Tests

Honesty or integrity tests are pencil-and-paper instruments that measure applicant's inclination to steal from an employer or to cause trouble at work. The demand for such tests increased when polygraph testing was curtailed for selection purposes due to the EPPA.

Fingerprinting

A number of states require fingerprinting of employees in certain fields of work, such as law enforcement, child care, private security or detective agencies, and state gambling agencies. Some states prohibit employers from requiring the fingerprinting of applicants, except for certain occupations, such as those noted above.

Police Records

Most local law enforcement agencies will check an applicant's police record and give the information to the applicant who, in turn, may present it to the prospective employer. The same type of check can also be done for a person's vehicle driving record. Depending upon the state's regulations, the information may be sent directly to an employer upon receipt of a request signed by the applicant, or it may be sent to the applicant who may present it to the prospective employer.

Care should be taken to distinguish between arrests and convictions. Obviously, conviction information should only be used for employment purposes where it is relevant to the job.

Drug Testing

Although there are some indications of improvement, drug use continues to be a serious problem in the U.S., based on the results of national surveys conducted by the U.S. Department of Health and Human Services. The 1999 survey found that:

- The total number of current (at least once in the past month) illicit drug users in the United States age 12 and older remained level since 1992.[33]

- For the past three years, adolescents' use of illicit drugs has moderated after dramatic increases in the early 1990s.

- The use of illicit drugs and marijuana among teenagers remained stable or declined for the fourth year in a row.

- Drug-related emergency room visits have declined over the past five years for the general population. There has been an 11 percent decline in such visits among 12- to 17-year-olds.

In response to public disapproval over drug use, not to mention the increased risks posed by drug users, 96 percent of employers with 50 or more employees had worksite drug policies in 1995. Ninety-two percent of such employers also had alcohol policies.[34] Furthermore, according to a survey conducted by the American Management Association, more than 76 percent of businesses were conducting employee drug testing in 1996.[35]

There are a number of safeguards that employers should follow in a implementing a drug testing program, such as ensuring that specimen collection, transportation and testing will be conducted with the utmost of considerations for employee privacy, confidentiality, and scientific accuracy. Employers in six transportation industries are required to comply with drug testing provisions issued by the U.S. Department of Transportation.

Verifying Information

Verification is the process of checking the accuracy of information furnished by applicants. Verification is the *key* to having a solid violence prevention program. Virtually every qualification an applicant offers for employment consideration may be verified. Verification sources include previous employers, schools, colleges, military records, certifying or licensing bodies, and public records (records from courts, law enforcement departments, licensing departments, tax assessors, and financial departments). Release forms and waivers signed by the applicant are typically used to secure the cooperation from various sources of information.

Medical Examinations

Medical examinations are typically the last step in the selection process. Under the ADA, a medical exam that elicits information about a person's mental

---

[33] U.S. Department of Health and Human Services, *Substance Abuse—A National Challenge: Prevention, Treatment and Research at HHS* (December 14, 2000), p. 2.

[34] U.S. Department of Health and Human Services, *Healthy People 2000 Review*, 1998-1999, p. 62.

[35] 1996 AMA Survey, *Workplace Drug Testing and Drug Abuse Policies, Summary of Key Findings.*

or physical condition may only be conducted after a conditional offer of employment has been made. Where feasible, it is better to have a physician, or a select group of physicians, conduct the medical examination. In this manner, the physician may become knowledgeable about the types of jobs and their physical and mental requirements and, thus, be better qualified to render an informed opinion about the employability of applicants. In addition, utilizing the services of one physician, or a select number of physicians, provides a greater opportunity for dialogue among employment personnel and physicians on a range of medically related topics.

Probationary Periods

Successful completion of a probationary period should be a requisite to permanent employment. Estimating applicants' potential to satisfactorily perform in a job is not a precise process. In spite of the best efforts to predict success, some applicants are not satisfactory employees. This trial period gives the employer the opportunity to determine if the newly selected employee should be retained. During the trial period, the employee's behavior, particularly any indications of or propensity to commit crime or violence, should be observed.

Controlling Personal Causes of Workplace Violence

Employers may not be able to *control* all the factors in workplace crime and violence, but they can take actions to help *prevent* the acts. As an example, an employer may not be able to influence either the state of an employee's mental health or the internal needs motivating the employee's behavior; however, co-workers and others may be taught to observe employee behavior. Thus, if an employee is obviously agitated, acting differently, or not performing up to past levels, it may be necessary to recommend that the employee seek help.

Job Structure

The manner in which a job is structured may cause employee dissatisfaction, if the employee's needs are not met. Repetitive tasks in a job may cause dissatisfaction for employees who need variety or challenge. Research has shown that employees who become bored with task repetition may express their dissatisfaction through hidden means, such as absenteeism, or through more overt means, such as sabotage.

Some employees cannot handle challenging jobs. For individuals who prefer repetition or less demanding work, a challenging job may lead to excessive stress.

Other aspects of job structuring, such as a lack of opportunities for promotion, may also cause employee dissatisfaction. Lack of control over the means of accomplishing work is directly correlated to job stress. Studies have shown that such stress is highest among such jobs as stenographer, in which job incumbents have little or no control over their activities.

Working Conditions

Among the working conditions contributing to workplace violence are:

- Excessive temperatures, including either too hot or too cold or sudden and severe changes in temperatures;

- Excessive noise;

- Exposure to toxic substances;

- Exposure to weather conditions such as rain, snow and the sun;

- Vibration from equipment; and

- Unsafe equipment processes or procedures.

Some job conditions may have a more pronounced effect upon behavior than others. Chemical substances, for example, can cause changes in personality that an employee may not be able to control.[36]

Management Methods

Management methods that contribute to workplace violence include the procedures to:

- Select employees;

- Restructure the organization;

- Administer discipline;

- Resolve employee dissatisfactions;

- Prevent employee problems;

- Assist troubled employees;

- Address risk issues; and

- Implement security protocols and security devices.

External Causes

External causes of violence primarily refer to criminal acts, such as robberies, where the perpetrator typically makes some assessment of the situation before committing the act. Two of the major situation-related determinants that perpetrators consider are:

1. the *opportunity to successfully accomplish the act*, such as the ease with which the act could be accomplished; and

2. the *riskiness or probability that they will be caught*.

These determinants are the reasons that robberies usually occur during off-peak times when other conditions are present, such as the availability of cash and the lack of significant barriers to a fast getaway.

---

[36] Prince, J.J., "Fuming over workplace violence,"
Security Management (37:3), pp. 64-65.

Opportunity-Related Situation

Studies have been conducted of inmates who were serving sentences for robberies. The most appealing, opportunity-related characteristics of most robberies were:

1. lots of cash;
2. only one clerk on duty, who preferably was female;
3. a remote area;
4. no safe; and
5. no customers.[37]

Risk Assessment-Related Situation

The same studies also reflected a common theme in robber determinations of circumstances that decreased the risk of being caught. The low-risk situations included:

1. ease of entrance and exit;
2. unobstructed windows;
3. no alarm;
4. poor lighting; and
5. no video or other types of security cameras.

Employee Assistance Programs

Employee assistance programs (EAPs), sponsored by an employer and/or a union, are operated either in-house or by external consortia or contractors in an effort to prevent employee problems and treat or rehabilitate troubled employees. The purposes of EAPs are to help prevent and reduce the human suffering of troubled employees and to prevent job deficiencies and other problems, including workplace violence.

Among the strategic decisions that must be made regarding EAPs is whether to establish one and, if so, whether it should be operated in-house or by an external provider. Other decisions concern the linkages to be established between and among other organizational programs, such as performance appraisals and disciplinary procedures.[38]

Crime Prevention Team

A *crime prevention team* (CPT) consists of a group of employees selected by management and given functional and staff authority to accomplish a variety of purposes, including development and implementation of plans to achieve the goal of a nonviolent workplace. Usually, team members are selected from different areas of the organization, such as human resources, security, risk management, and production. For example, Abbott Laboratories has a Workplace

---

[37] *Violent Crimes in Convenience Stores: Analysis of Crimes, Criminals and Costs,* Virginia Crime Prevention Center, Department of Criminal Justice Services, Commonwealth of Virginia, 1993.

[38] For information on the strategic implications of establishing and maintaining employee assistance programs, see Myers, D.W. *Establishing and Building Employee Assistance Programs* (Westport, CT: Greenwood Press, 1984).

Violence Prevention team, consisting of representatives from employee assistance, employee health, human resources, legal, public affairs, and security.[39] Sometimes, violence prevention teams consist of representatives of management and unions, such as the National Committee on Violence and Behavior in the Workplace, formed by the U.S. Postal Service.[40]

The purposes of CPTs vary significantly. A CPT may be a sounding board to alert management of any areas in which violence may occur. A CPT may also serve an even more basic function, as an information conduit through which employees can express their concerns to management about workplace violence. Some CPTs, such as the one operating at Abbott Laboratories, serve mainly to identify and intervene in situations in which violence may erupt, such as when an employee reports a potentially violent situation.[41]

More fundamental purposes of CPTs are, as stated in the definition at the outset of this section, to develop and implement plans to prevent workplace nonviolence. Following these purposes, a CPT would have a more proactive role and would require training in problem identification, using creative methods, such as brainstorming, and solution analysis, including flowcharting.

Violence Response Team

A *violence response team (VRT)* is a group of employees selected by management from different functional areas of the organization to prevent or respond to acts of violence. According to this definition, a VRT fulfills a very different role from that of a CPT. Members of a VRT would need training in incident investigation, so that they would know what to look for and how to get information. The members would also need training in interpersonal relations in order to defuse a potentially violent situation. Some basic training in counseling might also help team members to render initial counseling assistance in potentially violent situations, such as calming down a potentially violent person or aiding a victim.

Send a Strong Message

The organizational commitment includes sending a strong message that workplace violence will not be tolerated. This message can be disseminated through various channels, including announcements, training programs, memoranda, letters to employees' homes, permanent postings on all bulletin boards, and, where appropriate, in contract agreements with customers, suppliers and contract personnel. This message, which should be directed to all relevant personnel with whom employees come into contact, should state unequivocally that workplace violence will not be tolerated, that any reported acts of violence will be vigorously investigated, and that prompt corrective action will be taken.

---

[39] Dainas, C., Beien, L., and Powell, J., "The team approach to preventing violence," *Human Resources Professional* (Jul./Aug. 1994).

[40] n.a., "Postal Service promises new management style," *Occupational Hazards* (Oct. 1993).

[41] Dainas, C., et al., "The team approach to preventing violence."

Establishing a Nonviolent Workplace Policy

The nonviolent workplace policy statement must be consistent with the organization's culture. Exhibit 32-5, below, is an example of a nonviolent workplace policy statement.

Institute Dispute Resolute Procedures

A *dispute resolution procedure (DRP)* is an internally or externally provided method for employees to resolve job dissatisfactions beyond their control, but which management has the means and the authority to correct. Approximately 70 percent of employees in the U.S. do not have access to a DRP. The 30 percent of the labor force that is covered by a DRP includes most local, state, and federal employees, virtually all employees in unions with grievance procedures, and a relatively small number of private sector employers.[42]

Establish a Crime and Violence-Prevention Hotline

A *violence prevention hotline* is an toll-free telephone number for employees to report criminal or violent behavior anonymously. Some employees know about such violent acts but do not want to reveal their names. The hotline number can be posted on employee bulletin boards and/or communicated in other ways, such as employee newsletters. The reports could be answered by a contractor, such as a contract security firm, or by other means, such as a telephone answering service or an employee assistance contractor. In-house personnel, including those employed in the human resources department or an in-house employee assistance program, may also be used to answer the hotline calls.

Conduct Employee Training

Employee training is needed to identify the potential perpetrators, the acts, and the causes of workplace violence, as well as the security devices, the security protocols, and the employer policies and procedures necessary to maintain a nonviolent workplace. It is also important to train employees to understand their personal feelings and the reasons for them.

Preventing Violence Caused by Layoffs

The term *layoff* traditionally meant a temporary suspension or dismissal of am employee for lack of work. A person who was laid off typically would be "called back" to work when business "picked up." Today, the term more accurately depicts a situation of prolonged unemployment and, in many cases, permanent job loss. For most contemporary workers, a layoff is a major disruption in their lives; some, however, view a layoff as a *catastrophe,* which can result in violence.

---

[42] Myers, D.W. *Human Resources Management: Principles and Practice* (Chicago: CCH INCORPORATED, 1992).

Exhibit 32-5
Sample-Nonviolent Workplace Policy Statement

I. Purpose

The purpose of this policy statement is to formally acknowledge that workplace violence *will not be tolerated*. Any employee who commits an act of violence at work against a person or property will be immediately dismissed and, where appropriate, the matter will be referred to legal authorities for prosecution. In addition, any employee who fails to comply with designated security protocols or fails to use security devices will be subject to disciplinary action, including immediate discharge.

Workplace violence is conduct in the workplace against employers and employees committed by persons who either have an employment-related connection with the establishment or are outsiders, involving:

1. Physical acts against persons or employer property;
2. Verbal threats or profanity, or vicious statements meant to cause harm or create a hostile environment;
3. Written threats, profanity, vicious cartoons or notes, and other extremely negative written materials meant to threaten harm or create a hostile environment; or
4. Visual acts that are threatening or convey injury or hostility.

Workplace violence can and must be prevented! To achieve this goal requires the combined efforts of all employees. Total commitment on the part of all employees is vital in order to eliminate workplace violence. The company is committed to see that workplace violence is prevented if at all possible. The five keys to prevention for employees are:

1. Understand what violence is;
2. Understand themselves, including their attitudes, motivations, and decision-making styles, so that they will not resort to violence;
3. Follow prescribed security protocols;
4. Use designated security devices; and,
5. Report any persons who may commit or have committed a violent act.

II. Employee Coverage

All employees are entitled to perform their work free from the threat of violence, regardless of location, whether on the employer's premises or elsewhere.

III. Non-Violent Workplace Assurance Procedure

A detailed procedure, called the *Non-Violent Workplace Assurance Procedure*, has been implemented that includes background information on workplace violence, such as the kinds of perpetrators, types of violent acts, profiles of victims, procedures to use in reporting potential or actual acts of violence, and procedures to follow should a violent act occur. *All* employees are expected to know these procedures. In addition, *all* employees are expected to report any suspicions they have about any potential acts of violence. All such reports shall be fully investigated. No reprisals will be taken against any employee who makes such a report. Any employee who retaliates against a person who reports any act of violence or a suspicion of violence, regardless of the magnitude of such retaliation, shall be subject to immediate discipline, including discharge.

IV. Performance Appraisal

The annual performance appraisal system includes an evaluation of each employee's conduct in complying with this policy. Failure to follow the provisions of this policy will be considered in such decisions as pay increases, promotions and career development.

V. Non-Violent Workplace Awareness Training

All employees will receive training concerning their roles and responsibilities in maintaining a nonviolent workplace.

VI. Audit Procedure

Audits will conducted periodically to ensure adherence to this policy.

VII. Violations

Prompt action will taken against any person who violates this policy.

VIII. Policy Implementation Responsibilities

All employees are expected to comply with this policy. However, management personnel must assume extraordinary responsibility to ensure that both the spirit and intent of the policy are met. In addition, managers are responsible for both (1) preventing, and (2) stopping violent harassment. Due to the pernicious nature of harassment, managers will be held to a higher standard of responsibility in both preventing and stopping it.

The Vice President of Human Resources Management is functionally responsible for the implementation and the overall enforcement of the policy.[43]

Downsizing/Right-sizing

Layoffs for lack of work or job abolishment were a hallmark of the 1980-99 era. Millions of jobs were lost due to a combination of factors, including mergers, consolidations, efficiency strategies, job redesign initiatives, organizational restructuring, and foreign competition. Terms created for reducing the number of jobs during this era, such as *downsizing* and *right-sizing,* have become part of the permanent lexicon of management.

Most industries have been affected in this drive to "compete in the global marketplace." Even employees in corporate giants with long-standing "no layoff" policies were not spared the grief of job loss.

---

[43] Myers, D.W. *Stop Workplace Violence* (Chicago: CCH INCORPORATED, 1995).

Preventing Violence Caused by Employment Discharges

For many people, a *discharge*, or *being fired from a job*, is the employment equivalent of a death penalty. Other terms that are occasionally used for the same action are *termination* or *separation*. All four terms mean losing a job, whether or not for just cause. For many people, such a scenario is difficult to contemplate, particularly during the turbulent economic times experienced in the U.S. during the past decade.

Violence can erupt even when the discharge is handled with compassion and understanding. Too often, however, the discharge is somehow mismanaged, with tragic results. In many instances, the fired employee behaves in a violent manner, simply selecting the victims at random. On other occasions, the victims are carefully selected.

Preventing Violence Caused by Disciplining Employees

The word *discipline* connotes employee learning that promotes self-control, dedication and orderly conduct. Usually, the term discipline is used synonymously with the word punishment, but the two words have different meanings. *Punishment* is:

1. Administering an unpleasant stimulus, such as suspending an employee for excessive tardiness; or

2. Withholding a reward, such as an employee's scheduled pay increase, for making too many errors.

The term *progressive discipline* means the application of more stringent types of punishment to employees for their repeated instances of job performance deficiencies or singular acts of a more serious nature.

Punishment for Performance Deficiencies

Performance deficiencies are instances in which performance requirements are not met, whether intentional or otherwise. Usually deficiencies involve:

1. *Conduct,* such as failing to follow instructions or disobeying a supervisor's instruction;

2. *Attendance,* including tardiness and unscheduled absences;

3. *Productivity,* such as failure to meet production standards;

4. *Safety,* including the failure to wear safety equipment; and

5. *Work quality,* such as excessive errors.

Punishing employees for performance deficiencies typically results in employee unhappiness; if handled incorrectly or without adequate consideration of other factors affecting an employee's behavior, it may result in violence of the most tragic proportions. For example, an employee, furious over a suspension he received for talking with his wife (also employed by the same firm), took a gun and knocked a guard unconscious. He entered the plant, shot five supervisors, killing four of them, including the one who suspended him, and then killed himself.[44]

Preventive Actions by Supervisors

The following actions may be used by supervisors to prevent violence:

1. Know the rules and performance criteria expected of employees.

2. Inform employees of performance expectations and rule conformance. Employees have the right to know what is expected of them. A major reason for employees' unhappiness when they are punished is that they were not adequately apprised of expectations.

3. Check periodically to see how well employees are performing in relation to the performance criteria. Give positive feedback to employees who are meeting requirements.

4. Enforce performance requirements in a uniform manner. Do not overlook a deficiency and expect it to go away; although that may happen, the greater likelihood is that it will recur.

5. Be sure the all information is factual and complete before taking action for any performance deviations. Talk to the employee to get his or her explanation. An employee who is punished for a deficiency may disagree with the type of punishment, but the facts used to make that decision should not be in dispute.

6. Make sure that the employee is compatible with job tasks before instituting punishment.

   Be sure that the employee has an aptitude for the job. Enough emphasis is not given to the fact that the final step in the selection process is the probationary period. Every new employee is entitled to assistance to adjust to a new job; however, if these efforts are not successful, action must be taken.

7. Take prompt and consistent action. Punishment is most effective when it is promptly administered. Prolonged waiting causes employee apprehension. Delay also is associated with indecisiveness, causing employees to question whether the supervisor is serious about performance standards.

8. Be positive in administering discipline. Being *positive* means treating employees as adults, instead of children, when they do not measure up to job requirements, offering constructive criticism instead of finding fault when employees have performance problems, and holding your temper with deficient employees.

9. Exhibit warm and humane nonverbal behavior. Show compassion, understanding, and friendliness. It may seem inconsistent to be friendly when administering discipline, but there is no reason to be angry with

---

[44] n.a., "Suspended worker fires, killing 4, self in factory," *The Richmond Times-Dispatch* (March 17, 1985), p. A-18.

an employee just because discipline is necessary. In fact, that is the best time to show compassion and friendliness.

Sometimes, supervisors show extreme reluctance to discipline employees; when they do, they tend to exhibit displeasure that the disciplined employees interpret as directed toward them. This may provokes response from the employees, who are unhappy at such disciplinary action in the first place. The final outcome of such confrontation could be violent.

10. In administering discipline, supervisors should be conscious of an employee's nonverbal behavior. Employees who are obviously agitated should be "handled with kid gloves," not with a "mailed fist."

Preventing Violence Caused by Disagreements

Disagreements among co-workers, customers, clients, and other related parties may erupt into workplace violence *if* certain long-term (predisposing) conditions and/or other short-term (precipitating) conditions are present.

Disagreements may result in simple verbal exchanges or, under extreme conditions, more severe violence. According to one study, about 75 percent of workplace violence was in the form of fist fights, most of which were caused by disagreements.

In 1998, 63 deaths occurred on the job as a result of business disputes among co-workers or former co-workers. In addition, 35 homicides occurred due to disputes between customers/clients and employees. How many of these deaths could have been prevented? No one knows for sure, but the evidence suggests there are steps that can be taken to minimize the risk of co-worker homicide and other forms of violence when disputes occur.

Security Management

Two major areas of *security management* are security protocols and security devices. Exhibit 32-6 illustrates examples of both areas.

Exhibit 32-6
Workplace Security Management

Security Protocols	Security Devices
Remain in secure building	Employee identification method
Precautions in travel status	Biometrics
Sign-in system for visitors	X-ray scanners
Centralized visitor clearance	Metal detectors
Centralized employee entrance	Coded door locks/keyless entry
Violence drills	Closed circuit/security video
High crime time intervals	Bullet-resistant enclosures
Employing minors	Drop safes
Restrict get-away opportunity	Security lighting
Open work areas	Security fencing
Business-like work areas	Hot-line security telephone
Well-lighted work areas	Silent alarm

Security Protocols	*Security Devices*
Unobscured view or work area	
Limited cash on-hand	
Signage	
Limited cash on-hand	
Drop safe use	
Security escort personnel	
Van service	

Security Protocols

Restriction to Secure Building in the Evening

Employees should be instructed not to leave a secure building for nonessential purposes, such as to empty trash cans, except during daylight hours. If it is necessary to leave the building at dark, security personnel should accompany the employee. Obviously, this protocol may assume greater importance depending upon several considerations, such as the area in which the building is located and whether the employee's job involves handling cash or other valuables that would make the employee a convenient target for a robber.

Precautions During Travel Status

Employees traveling for their employers should be instructed to refrain from risky behavior, such as jogging in the early morning hours, at dusk and in the evening. An employee on company business in another city was jogging near her motel when she was abducted and repeatedly raped. The rapist was caught and punished, but the victim was required to relive the entire nightmare during her testimony at his trial. Employees also should be instructed to be careful about where they travel in unfamiliar cities. Other normal precautions they should observe include parking in well-lighted areas at motels and observing their surroundings upon entering and leaving their automobiles.

Sign-in System for Visitors

All visitors should be required to sign-in at a centralized checkpoint, staffed by a receptionist or someone who could perform other activities as well, such as handling incoming telephone calls or performing clerical tasks. The employee should be alert for any visitors who are obviously distressed or troubled and notify a designated person, such as a security guard, if the need arose. This protocol is less expensive than a centralized clearance system for visitors, staffed by security personnel.

Centralized Clearance for Visitors

Depending upon the business of the organization, it may be advisable to require all visitors to be cleared before they are permitted to leave the lobby. Typically, this would require a centralized security desk at a single entrance. Visitors would be required to state whom they wished to see and, in turn, permission would have to given by that person before the visitor would be allowed to leave the security area.

This protocol is particularly important for organizations engaged in activities with a greater probability of provoking violence, such as law firms handling domestic matters (including divorce), child support enforcement agencies, and firms engaged in controversial issues. Once visitors sign in and are cleared to enter the building, they are usually assigned a badge that must be worn while they are on the premises. Such badges must be surrendered to the centralized security desk before the visitor leaves the building.

Centralized Entrance/Exit for Employees

Centralized employee entrances and exits are typically used in conjunction with an employee identification system. Both measures are basic protocols to help prevent violence. A centralized entrance and exit helps prevent unauthorized personnel from gaining access to employees and employer assets. Such an entrance also allows surveillance of off-duty personnel, including employees who might try to gain entrance to work areas to cause violence after disagreements with co-workers. Additionally, controlled employee entrances and exits help prevent former employees, particularly those who were discharged from employment, from gaining access to personnel with whom they might have a personal grudge.

Violence Drills

Violence drills train employees how to effectively respond to an act of violence. Among the topics covered in such drills are:

1. Telephone numbers of organizations to call in the event of violence;

2. Location of telephones;

3. Location of emergency exits, depending upon where the violence occurs;

4. Work areas in which violence is most likely to occur;

5. Safe areas in the event an employee is trapped in a building and cannot get out; and

6. Secure routes to those safe areas.

Violence drills may also cover interpersonal communication, including effective ways to deal with personnel, customers, or others who are obviously agitated.

High Crime Time Intervals

For businesses that remain open during high-crime intervals, typically 11:00 P.M. to 6:00 A.M., special precautions may need to be taken. A few proven simple precautions include restricting customer access where possible, using uniformed security personnel and adding extra personnel. For example, many gasoline stations use a special outside window for customers to pay for their purchases. Employing uniformed security personnel has been shown to reduce crime in many nighttime businesses. Convenience stores often have extra employees who stock shelves and perform other housekeeping duties at night.

At least one study of robbers found that convenience stores with one female clerk on duty were more appealing to robbers than stores with one male clerk.[45] Some employers might respond to such information by assigning additional personnel to stores where women were employed, and others might try to restrict employment to men if only one person was needed.

Obviously, a decision to restrict employment of women to certain hours or place other such restrictions different from the employment of men might conceivably be in violation of the Civil Rights Act. Rather than hire only men, consideration should be given to using other security protocols and/or devices that would provide adequate protection for female employees who are alone.

Employment of Minors During Daylight Hours

According to the Fair Labor Standards Act, children under 14 years of age may not be hired for employment, under most circumstance. Children 14 and 15 years of age may be employed in nonhazardous occupations, provided that the work:

1. Is performed outside of school hours;
2. Does not exceed a maximum of three hours on a school day or eight hours on a non-school day;
3. Does not exceed 18 hours in a payroll week while school is in session and 40 hours when it is not; and
4. Is performed between 7 A.M. and 7 P.M., except for the period between June 1 and Labor Day, when the evening hour is extended to 9 P.M.

There are no work-hour restrictions for children who are 16 or 17 years old.

Generally, children under 18 years of age, and more particularly if they are female, are perceived as more vulnerable than adults. Consequently, prudence suggests that only adults should be assigned to work at night. Furthermore, as noted previously, females who are employed alone at night should be provided with sufficient security to protect them from violence.

Restriction of Get-Away Opportunities

Several of the protocols discussed above, such as centralized employee entrances and exits and centralized clearance procedures for visitors, reduce the potential for workplace violence. Perpetrators will have less opportunity to avoid apprehension, and, presumably, will be less likely to carry out the violent act. Other measures that restrict getaway opportunities, such as circuitous exit routes or physical barriers to quick exits, may also be effective in preventing violence.

Open Work Areas

Open work areas are more likely to prevent violence, since there is a greater probability the perpetrator will be seen committing the violent act. Physical barriers, such as walls that fulfill no functional purpose, should be removed.

---

[45] *Violent Crimes in Convenience Stores: Analysis of Crimes, Criminals and Costs,* Virginia Crime Prevention Center, Commonwealth of Virginia, 1993.

Neat and Business-Like Work Areas

Work areas which are cluttered and dirty tend to invite violence, since they give the impression of ineptitude. Businesslike work areas, on the other hand, tend to be more imposing to a would-be perpetrator, since they connote efficiency.

Well-Lighted Work Areas

Darkness and dimly-lighted areas tend to invite violence if, for no other reason, that the perpetrator is less at risk of being seen by the victim and by bystanders. Thus, some states, such as Washington State, require certain types of establishments operating between 11:00 P.M. and 6:00 A.M. to have outside lighting that is at least one-foot candle.[46]

Unobscured Views

Owners of retail establishments, particularly convenience stores, liquor stores, and related businesses, should keep shrubbery and trees trimmed so there is a clear view of the business. Other organizations that may be a target for violence, such as clinics in which abortions are performed or other organizations which have taken controversial positions on volatile topics, should also have an unobstructed view of their buildings.

Limited Cash

Maintaining even modest amounts of cash on hand is a risky business practice. A potential robber may make a small purchase to determine whether the amount of cash available is worth taking. Enforcing a policy to require that excess cash be placed in a drop-safe may prevent a robbery. Florida's Convenience Store Security Act requires the establishment of a cash management policy to limit cash between the hours of 9:00 P.M. and 6:00 A.M. in convenience stores.

"Limited Cash on Premises" and "Drop Safe" Signage

Signage about limited cash holdings and the use of drop safes is legally required for certain types of establishments in both Florida and the State of Washington. Employers in other states should consider adopting similar signage procedures to curtail the risk of robbery.

Security Escort Personnel

Some office buildings provide escort service to parking areas for tenant personnel. In addition, employers typically have escort service for employees walking to parking areas. Some employers also have restricted access to parking areas and closed-circuit television cameras in parking areas.

Van Service

Employer-provided van service and car-pooling were initiated during the era of gasoline shortages in the late 1970s. Since some employers found the

---

[46] *Violent Crimes in Convenient Stores: Analysis of Crimes, Criminals and Costs,* Virginia Crime Prevention Center, Commonwealth of Virginia, 1993.

benefit especially attractive to employees for security as well as other reasons, they continued the practice after the gasoline shortage ended. Environmental concerns and legislation have also made this practice more attractive. In a typical van-pooling arrangement, the van is provided by the employer, and the designated employee-driver is permitted to take the van home after all passengers are dispatched. Another way that employers provide transportation assistance to employees is by establishing an internal clearinghouse for employees to develop car-pools. Both van service and car-pooling provide security for employees during an often-ignored interval for violence—between the place of business and the parking lot.

Security Devices

Security devices are special equipment or systems that prevent violent acts. These are some examples of such devices and systems include:

1. Employee identification badges and security cards;

2. Biometrics;

3. X-ray scanners and metal detectors;

4. Coded door locks and keyless entry systems;

5. Closed circuit and security camera systems;

6. Bullet-resistant barriers and enclosures;

7. Drop safes;

8. Security lighting;

9. Security fencing;

10. Security hotlines; and

11. Silent alarms.

Employee Identification Badges/Security Cards

Employee personal identification security systems, such as identification or security cards, are an essential component in an organizational security program. These identification systems help prevent unauthorized personnel from gaining access to an employer's premises. Usually, such identification systems are used in conjunction with centralized employee entrances and exits.

Biometrics

The general definition of biometrics is the use of statistics to analyze biological information. In security management, *biometrics* is the utilization of technology for the identification of people. Personal characteristics subject to biometrics technology include face prints, fingerprints, hand prints, retinas, signatures, and voice prints.[47]

These systems use scanners, which feed information to computers that access its database to determine if there is a match. These high-tech systems are

---

[47] For a discussion of the various biometrics methods, see Sherman, R.L., "The right look can open doors," *Security Management* (October 1992), p. 83.

used in very sensitive situations, such as highly secret research and development facilities.

X-Ray Scanners/Metal Detectors

Scanners and/or metal detectors for checking briefcases, pocketbooks, and similar items are common in airport terminals, some courthouses, and some government buildings. These devices have been extremely effective, for example, in preventing people from carrying contraband into airport terminals, but there are obvious disadvantages, such as the inconvenience they cause and the number of personnel needed to operate them.

A variation of the use of scanners or metal detectors is to require visitors to indicate whether they have any contraband and to conduct searches of briefcases and related items. Again, the disadvantages to such systems include the inconvenience they cause people, the cost to maintain them, and the degree to which they interfere with the transaction of business. For these and other reasons, most organizations use centralized visitor systems rather than scanners or searches of personal property.

Coded Door Locks/Keyless Entry Systems

A relatively common security innovation that is appearing increasingly more often at workplaces is the coded door lock or keyless entry system. No keys are necessary, and the system offers great flexibility, since combinations can be changed easily whenever the code has been compromised. Some organizations periodically change codes to avoid security breaches by former employees and others.

Keyless entry systems can be activated through a code on a keypad or through coded security cards. Both systems have advantages and disadvantages.

Closed Circuit or Security Video Cameras

Closed circuit cameras are typically monitored in a centralized location, such as a security office. Security video cameras constantly film an area or areas of a particular location. The Convenience Store Security Act in Florida requires certain local governments to adopt ordinances requiring convenience stores that are open between 10:00 P.M. and 5:00 A.M. to install a security camera video system.

Security cameras can be a deterrence to violent behavior; they can also be instrumental in identifying the perpetrators of violence. A computer-based information system installed by Southland Corporation, owner of 7-Eleven convenience stores, resulted in a 50-percent reduction in robberies since 1976.[48] Southland Corporation's newest security innovation is a computer-integrated closed circuit camera and alarm system.

---

[48] Menagh, M., "Under the gun," *Computerworld* (June 20, 1994), p. 104.

Bullet-Resistant Barriers/Enclosures

In 1993, 95 taxicab drivers and chauffeurs were murdered at work,[49] 43 in New York City alone. To counter the threat to drivers in these occupations, the New York City Taxi and Limousine Commission voted to require installation of bullet-resistant partitions in taxicabs to separate the driver from passengers. The effectiveness of the partitions is significant: no driver whose taxi is equipped with such a partition has been a homicide victim.[50]

Bullet-resistant barriers would appear to provide an extra margin of safety for personnel employed in convenience and liquor stores, particularly those open during peak crime periods.

Drop Safes

Drop safes are fixed security containers, mounted into the building or vehicle, with a slot into which excess cash is periodically deposited. They are typically used in certain retail establishments, such as convenience stores and liquor stores, to avoid potential loss in the event of a robbery. They are also used in taxicabs and in locations in which there is a greater potential for robbery. Designated management personnel open the safe during the day when extra personnel are on duty. No other employees have either a key or the combination to the safe. Drop safes are a deterrent to robbery when signs stating that no more than $50 in cash is maintained, and drop safes are used that cannot be accessed by employees.

The Late Night Retail and Workers Crime Protection regulations in the State of Washington mandate the use of drop safes and signage in certain retail establishments that are open between 11:00 P.M. and 6:00 A.M. Florida's Convenience Store Security Act also mandates use of drop safes or other types of cash management devices.

Security Lighting

Security lighting may be used to illuminate such places as employee parking lots and perimeter areas around an employer's building or place of business. The use of lighting to dramatize landscaped areas is generally not suitable for security purposes. The laws in Florida and the State of Washington require the use of security lighting in designated areas by certain retail establishments.

Security Fencing

Security fencing is primarily used for employee parking lots to restrict and/or control entrance and egress.

Security Hotline

A hotline security telephone or telephone number gives employees the opportunity to quickly report any criminal acts. The telephone is typically connected directly to an in-house security unit or to an external security contrac-

---

[49] *Violence in the Workplace Comes Under Closer Scrutiny*, U.S. Department of Labor, August 1994.

[50] Purdy, M. "Workplace Murders Provoke Lawsuits and Better Security," *The New York Times* (February 14, 1994).

tor. An employee merely needs to lift the receiver and the telephone will ring at the other end of the line. A security hotline telephone number requires employees to dial the designated number; the advantage is that the security designee may be called from any telephone.

Silent Alarm

Silent alarms are connected to police departments, in-house security units or security firms with centralized response offices that are open 24 hours per day, seven days per week. Florida law requires certain retail establishments that are open between the hours of 10:00 P.M. and 5:00 A.M. to have silent alarms that are connected to local police department.

Instituting Procedures to Aid Victims

About one-third of the respondents in a survey of human resources professionals said that violent acts in the workplace had not affected their organizations. The remaining two-thirds believed workplace violence had these effects:

- 41 percent felt that it caused more stress at work;
- 20 percent stated that it caused more paranoia;
- 18 percent said that it reduced trust among co-workers;
- 14 percent felt that it increased the anger in employees; and,
- 12 percent said that it lowered productivity.[51]

There also is evidence that workplace violence can triple employee turnover.[52] Depending upon the type of act, employees, their families and close friends may experience several types of loss: self-esteem, safety and security, personal identity, and interpersonal relationships.

The Canadian Imperial Bank of Commerce, which experiences about 250 robberies each year, has conducted extensive research on the effect that robberies have on bank employees. Those employees who experience robberies have flashbacks, persistent fears, and physical problems, including headaches, stomach aches, and fatigue. Job deficiencies among this group of employees include absenteeism, decreased productivity, more errors, and difficulty in responding to customer demands. Some employees request reassignment to positions removed from the threat of robbery; other employees resign.[53]

A job-related death of a co-worker may profoundly affect peers in a myriad of ways, including " . . . shock, anger, sadness, guilt, apathy, increased cravings for drugs and alcohol, cynicism, and a jungle of other emotions."[54] Both the severity and duration of the response depends upon how the death occurred, whether violence was involved, the extent to which others were or are threatened by the same cause, and the outlets available for employee expressions of grief.

[51] Society for Human Resource Management, *Workplace Violence: Business as Usual? Survey Reveals Escalating Violence* (Alexandria, VA: November 30, 1993).

[52] Frolkey, C., "Critical incidents and traumatic events: the differences," *EAP Digest* (May/June 1992).

[53] Curnock, C.A., "Trauma response: beyond broadbrush," *EAP Digest* (March/April 1991).

[54] McManus, M.L., "When a co-worker dies on duty," *EAP Digest* (May/June 1992).

Stages of Recovery

A victim's progression through the various stages of recovery also determines how long recovery will take and the likelihood of success. For example, victims who do not progress beyond the "realization" stage of recovery, may become "stuck" with constantly reliving the impact of the act; if this continues too long, a condition known as *post-traumatic stress disorder* becomes an increasing possibility.[55]

There are various theories concerning the number of stages in recovery, involving from three to as many as seven stages.[56] There are a number of symptoms in each stage, but victims do not necessarily experience each one. Also, the magnitude of various symptoms, such as grief during the shock stage, depends upon many variables, including the type of violent act, its duration, and any injury suffered.

Shock/Denial Stage

This is the initial stage after the violent act has occurred. Victims are in a state of shock and disbelief in which they cannot totally comprehend what has occurred. This stage is where grieving begins and loss is experienced.

Realization Stage

In this stage, the person feels a range of emotions, depending upon the circumstances. If it is a robbery, the victim may have feelings of helplessness or vulnerability. In assault cases, the victim may feel anger toward the perpetrator or others they perceive to be responsible. Some scapegoating may occur, especially if the victim believes the employer should have provided more protection. Victims may become depressed as they contemplate the magnitude of the violent act and may experience feelings of helplessness to prevent future acts.

Acceptance Stage

Victims who successfully negotiate their way through the earlier stages and overcome feelings of shock and anger will begin to accept the consequences of the event and, thus, will start to heal, both mentally and physically. At this point, victims are ready to put the traumatic event behind them and get on with their lives.

---

[55] Wolf, K.L., Leonhardi, M., Polancih, D., and Knight, M., "Helping employees recover from the trauma of workplace violence," *EAP Digest* (March/April 1994).

[56] Griggs, W.S., Jr., "Employee grief and loss counseling," in Myers, D.W., *Employee Problem Prevention and Counseling.* (Westport, CT: Greenwood Press, 1985).

CHAPTER 33
HUMAN RESOURCES DEVELOPMENT

Chapter Highlights
- Learn the continuing need for human resources development
- Understand the stages in human resources development
- Learn the major on-the-job and off-the-job methods of human resources development
- Review the methods of evaluating human resource development programs
- Examine the principal theories of learning

Introduction

Training employees to perform their jobs is essential for several reasons. First, inadequate training can cause tragic results. For example, ten hotel guests were killed by dense smoke when a fire erupted in a room on the fourth floor. Some guests reported to fire investigators that they never heard a fire alarm. Other guests said they heard the alarm but only for brief intermittent periods. Several guests said they pulled the alarm but nothing happened. A deputy fire chief found that the alarm activated a buzzer at the front desk. A clerk heard the buzzer, called the fire department, and switched off the buzzer. The clerk had not been *trained* on the alarm system, so that he did not know that cutting off the desk buzzer deactivated the entire alarm system in the hotel.[1]

Work Quality Affected

Inadequate training can also affect work quality. For example, management in a freight company became concerned with an increasing rate of damaged freight and customer complaints about delays. An analysis of these problems revealed that dock handlers were never *trained* in the correct way of loading trailers and drivers were never *instructed* to read the delivery times for shipments entered under a guaranteed delivery program initiated by the company.

Widespread Deficiencies

Training employees is even more important today because of widespread deficiencies in their abilities. For example, a survey conducted in 1997 by the National Association of Manufacturers found that more than two-thirds of manufacturers were experiencing problems in improving employee productivity and implementing technology because of workers' deficient job skills.[2]

---

[1] n.a., "10 Die in Hotel Fire," The State (March 7, 1982), p. 1.

[2] CCH INCORPORATED, "Shortage of skilled workers called emerging crisis." *Ideas and Trends in Personnel* (February 11, 1998), p. 23.

Fundamentally, the latest National Adult Literacy Survey, conducted in 1992 by the Educational Testing Service for the U.S. Department of Education, found that from 21 to 23 percent of American adults, age 16 or older, were at the lowest level of literacy (Level 1 on a scale of Level 1 to Level 5).[3] Adults at Level 1 can usually perform many simple tasks, such as signing their name or totaling a bank deposit entry, but they have difficulty in reading, writing and computational skills that are requisite for fully functioning in life. For example at Level 1, individuals cannot usually perform the following:

- Locate an intersection on a street map;

- Locate two pieces of information from a sports article;

- Identify and enter background information on a social security card application; and

- Calculate total costs of purchases from an order form.

Literacy is a fundamental ability for performing tasks in a technological economy. In addition, an illiterate employee is a potential risk problem. For example, an illiterate supervisor failed to properly assemble the safety components on a new piece of equipment. He was trying to complete the assembly by looking at an illustration of the equipment. The result: a worker's hand was severed.

These examples help explain why U.S. firms spend $100 billion each year in human resource development.[4] This development ranges from basic literacy abilities to advanced study in management, science, and engineering. Undoubtedly, human resources development is one of the most challenging areas in management.

Human resource development (HRD) is the process of preparing employees to maximize both their utility to the organization and their job satisfaction.

Education, Training, and Learning

HRD involves education, training, and learning.

- *Education* is formal or informal conceptual learning that does not have a specific occupational objective, but is needed to satisfactorily perform a job.

- *Training* is formal or informal instruction to qualify a person to perform a job at a satisfactory level.

- *Learning* is the act of acquiring knowledge, skills, and abilities through education, training, and experience. Thus, learning is the outcome of HRD efforts.

---

[3] National Institute for Literacy, *The State of Literacy in America*, no date, p. 3.

[4] "Firms Spend Billions on Teaching Workers," *Richmond Times-Dispatch* (January 28, 1985).

Skills, Abilities, Knowledge, and Experience

HRD involves preparing employees in the *skills, abilities,* and *knowledge* needed in a job. HRD also includes assisting employees in acquiring the *experience* needed to perform a job.

Roles of HRD

HRD has a fundamental role in many of the activities in HR. HRD has a particularly important role in improving employee job performance, qualifying employees for advancement, meeting the staffing needs of the organization, assisting in the career planning process, and aiding in diversity management goals.

Job Performance

HRD is used to improve employee performance in such areas as attendance, conduct, productivity, work quality, and safety. The improved performance increases employees' utility to the organization through increased productivity, reduced waste, and improvement in product quality. In addition, this improved performance results in increased employee satisfaction. For example, an increase in productivity resulting from an HRD program may mean an increase in pay if pay incentives or a merit pay system is used. Increased job performance also helps employees realize their potential, assume greater responsibilities, and accept increasing job challenges. These results help develop employee satisfaction as employees realize more intrinsic rewards from their work.

Career Advancement

HRD helps qualify employees for advancement into more responsible jobs. This increases their utility to the organization, since they are able to make contributions at a higher level. Of course, not all employees want to advance to a higher level, but for those that do, HRD helps make their plans a reality. Promotions increase employee satisfaction through intrinsic and extrinsic rewards. Intrinsic rewards include the opportunity to accept greater responsibility, have more autonomy, and use more of one's creativity. Extrinsic rewards include recognition and higher pay.

Staffing Needs

HRD increases employees' utility to the organization by insuring that qualified employees are available to meet future staffing needs. These needs may exist at all organizational levels. Recognizing this need is one reason organizations have implemented management succession plans to provide for the orderly replacement of top-level managers. Staffing needs are determined through the human resource planning process.

Career Planning

HRD is an essential part of career planning. Once employees make known their career aspirations, HRD is necessary to assist them in obtaining the training, education, and experience required to qualify them for job advancement.

Diversity Management

HRD helps an organization achieve equal employment opportunity and affirmative action objectives. For example, through HRD an employer is able to demonstrate equal opportunity by giving all interested employees the opportunity to develop themselves. Typically, the process is initiated by employees participating in career planning, in which their interests are identified and their qualifications are compared to the job specifications of those jobs in which they are interested. Next, their developmental needs are determined and HRD commences.

Employers can demonstrate affirmative action by encouraging protected group members to seek HRD opportunities through both in-house and externally-provided training and educational courses and programs. Affirmative action is also demonstrated by giving protected group members opportunities to gain employment experience in jobs through temporary assignments.

HRD Program Characteristics

HRD programs are either continual or ad hoc. For example, a truck driver training program for new drivers is typically an ongoing program; the same is true for orientation programs. Often, newly appointed supervisors receive a basic one- or two-week ongoing training course before they assume their supervisory tasks.

- *Continual* HRD programs are learning programs designed to meet a continual need and offered on a regular schedule. The format and subject matter of continual programs are relatively constant and only justifiable changes are made. Usually, these changes occur when the programs are reevaluated each year or so.

- *Ad hoc* HRD programs are those programs designed to meet a specific need. For example, a catalog discount store noticed a sizable increase in returned merchandise caused by shipping errors. The problem was caused by a failure to adequately train warehouse stockers in a new catalog numbering system. The stockers were using the old numbers, especially for less-frequently ordered items. A short training course was designed that included a test each warehouse stocker was required to pass on the new catalog numbering sequence.

Three Major Areas of HRD

The three major learning areas of HRD are cognitive, noncognitive, and psychomotor.

Cognitive

Cognitive learning deals with facts, data, and methods. For example, job specifications state the knowledge an applicant must possess to successfully perform a job. This knowledge is acquired through cognitive learning. Management is both a science and an art. The *science* of management consists of the knowledge of management principles, functions, and techniques. For example, to be able to apply management by objectives (MBO), a manager must first learn the principles of this performance appraisal method and how they can be applied. The actual application of MBO involves noncognitive learning.

Noncognitive

Noncognitive learning deals with behavioral abilities, such as leadership, sensitivity, and creativity. The art of management is demonstrated through the abilities a person possesses in applying the science or knowledge of the subject. For example, to use MBO effectively requires a manager to be *sensitive* to subordinates' needs in setting objectives. A manager must also exercise creativity in understanding a subordinate's ideas for plans or tactics to accomplish various objectives. HRD uses various methods, such as roleplaying exercises, to help a person develop noncognitive abilities and learn how to apply them.

Psychomotor

Psychomotor learning is involved in acquiring a competence to operate equipment or to perform tasks in which objects are manipulated. For example, psychomotor learning is involved in learning how to type or repair an automobile transmission. Some job tasks require cognitive, noncognitive, and psychomotor training. For example, a person who wants to be a dental hygienist must learn cognitive information, such as the names and functions of various dental instruments used in cleaning teeth. The person must also learn certain noncognitive skills, such as sensitivity to the fears of children, particularly in their initial appointments. Hygienists must also be proficient in the psychomotor skills of using dental instruments.

The HRD Process

The process involved in HRD consists of the following steps:

- Determine needs;
- Set objectives;
- Define criteria;
- Select methods;
- Implement the program; and
- Evaluate the program.

Determine HRD Needs

The author was asked by the training director of a financial institution to present a proposal for team-building workshops for first-level supervisors. The training director was asked how he determined team-building was needed and more specifically, what aspects of team-building he had determined were most needed. He responded that while he had not received any specific requests for team-building, he *felt* the training was needed to help supervisors learn how to build teams among their employees.

Often, HRD activities are commenced with only an intuitive need motivating the action. Many times this results in HRD that is not needed. HRD initiated without conducting an objective needs analysis is often needless and a waste of organizational resources.

Methods of Determining Needs

Some of the most frequently used methods of determining needs are assessment centers, career planning programs, critical incidents, employee performance appraisal results, human resource planning, needs surveys, and operational data. HRD needs determinations involve short-term, intermediate, and long-term periods.

- *Short-term* is HRD that can be met within a year;

- *Intermediate* HRD involves times periods ranging from one to three years; and

- *Long-term* HRD typically involves periods in excess of three years.

Assessment Centers. In an assessment center, participants are assessed for their abilities and job skills. Approximately one or two weeks after the assessments are conducted, each participant receives feedback on his or her performance in a private interview. Participants are told both the strengths and weaknesses they demonstrated in the various exercises. Where weaknesses or HRD needs are evident, the participant is given suggestions for self-improvement. For example, the participant might be advised to take some college writing courses if adequate writing skills were not demonstrated.

Career Planning. *Career planning* is the process of identifying employee career interests within an organization and designing an HRD program to help them achieve those careers. Once an employee identifies his or her career interests, the next step is to compare the employee's qualifications with the job specifications. This results in determining an individual's intermediate and long-run HRD needs.

Critical Incidents. *Critical incidents,* which are examples of significantly good or bad job performance, can be used to determine HRD needs. For example, if an employer uses the critical incident method of performance appraisal, managers can be requested to document the specific HRD needs that either caused or contributed to an undesired critical incident. Chapter 29 explains the critical incident method of performance appraisal.

A hospital uses a modified version of critical incidents to determine training needs.[5] This procedure consists of selecting various HRD topics, such as communications, and having each prospective trainee in the target audience use a 3×5 card to write specific (critical) incidents in which they were not an effective communicator. Usually, this is done in a group setting, and the employees are given 10 minutes for the assignment. Next, the employees are asked to explain what specific deficiencies they had that caused the ineffective communication. This information is recorded on a separate card. This same procedure is repeated 8-10 more times for other HRD subjects, such as planning or decision-making. All the cards are collected and the employees are divided into two groups of four persons. Each group is given two packets of cards. One packet is for the

---

[5] Stein, D.S., "Designing Performance-Oriented Training Programs," *Training and Development Journal* (January 1981), pp. 12-16.

undesirable incident and the other for the deficiencies that contributed to the incident. Each group's task is to identify the five most frequently noted deficiencies contributing to the incident. These lists of deficiencies are the HRD needs for each incident, and appropriate HRD methods are prepared to meet them.

Employee Performance Appraisal. The results of performance appraisals can be used to determine employee HRD needs. For example, formal performance appraisal systems are used to detect if an employee is deficient in one or more of the performance variables involving attendance, conduct, productivity, safety, and work quality. Some appraisal systems have a section for the employee and/or the appraiser to note any HRD needs that may be causing a deficiency or may need attention for the employee to perform adequately. An example of this appraisal feature is shown in the MBO system discussed in Chapter 29. In that chapter, the instructions in the exhibit describing the MBO system provide for the employee and the supervisor to concur on: (1) the skills needed to perform various job tasks, and (2) any plans the employee has for improving his or her skills.

Some performance appraisal systems also have a separate section in which the supervisor evaluates employees' potential for advancement. This second part typically includes space for the appraiser to assess any HRD needs that need attention for the employee to be promotable. Sometimes, the assessment of advancement potential is formally acknowledged on the appraisal form; the supervisor discusses the assessment with the employee and makes HRD recommendations.

Managers can also determine HRD needs through the daily observation of employee performance. In fact, the most common HRD method, on-the-job instruction, results from the daily supervisory observation of employees.

Human Resource Planning. Human resource planning involves determining human resource needs and checking the available supply of personnel to ensure the needs are met. HRD may be necessary to develop the talent to meet the need. More specifically, an important aspect of HRD is to insure qualified employees are available to meet the employer's future needs for human resources. Short-run needs may involve specific skill training in one job. Succession planning is an example of long-run developmental needs.

HRD Needs Surveys. Some organizations conduct annual HRD needs surveys. The survey input is provided by supervisors. The surveys can be either structured or unstructured. Exhibit 33-1 is a survey form for identifying management training needs. Similar forms can be used to survey training needs in other occupations, such as clerical, technical, and craft jobs. The advantages of these forms include directing the surveyed individual's attention to specific topics. Also, the form results can be tallied more readily to determine the frequency of responses to various subjects. An unstructured needs survey may simply consist of a memorandum to all managers asking them to submit any items in which they feel an HRD need exists.

Exhibit 33-1
Survey of Management Training Needs

| (Name) | (Department) | (Date) |

I. Check the appropriate column indicating the need you think exists for training in the subject.

Subjects	Definite Need	Some Need	No Need
1. Performance appraisal			
2. Safety			
3. Decision-making			
4. Planning			
.			
.			
.			
.			
.			
.			
.			
20. Disciplinary procedures			

II. Indicate below any subjects you feel are needed,
but not shown above.

1.
2.
3.
4.
5.
6.
7.
.
.
.
.
.
20.

Operational Data. Operational data include such information as accident incident rates, productivity rates, the amount of scrap or wasted material, customer complaints, and the rate of unscheduled absences. Unsatisfactory trends in these and similar indices may signal HRD needs. For example, an increase in accident rates over several consecutive months may or may not mean safety training is needed. A more thorough analysis of accident causes would reveal whether HRD was needed, and if so, what type. For example, an analysis may show the overall increase in the accident incident rate is due to the improper operation of a new machine. In this case, the HRD could simply consist of a brief on-the-job training session for the machine operators. On the other hand, an analysis of the accidents may fail to detect one or more particular direct, indirect, or basic causes. This might mean HRD is not needed because a specific training need cannot be identified.

Set Objectives

Objectives are the purposes of an HRD program. Conducting HRD programs without setting objectives or purposes is risky because the entire effort may be purposeless. Each objective should be written and specify what is to be done, and when, how, and where it is to be done. Exhibit 33-2 shows several examples of objectives for an Account Executive training course for a communications firm.

Exhibit 33-2
**Examples of Selected Subjects, Objectives, and Criteria
for Account Executive Training Course**

Training subject	Learning Objective(s)	Criteria
1. Personal computer operation	1. Learn computer sales procedure after 4 hours of instruction.	1.1 Score 100% on personal computer knowledge test after 4 hours of instruction.
		1.2 After 4 hours instruction use applicable software to make presentation.
2. Selling skills	2.1 Learn sales procedure for fiber coaxial cable and network after 6 hours of instruction.	2.1 Score 100 percent on sales skills test after 6 hours of instruction.
	2.2 Learn how to handle most frequently asked questions from customers after 2 hours of instruction.	2.2 Pass a role-play session handling questions from judges after 2 hours of instruction.
	2.3 Learn cable hourly charges for all network connections after 4 hours of instruction	2.3 Pass a videotaped sales presentation on cable charges after 4 hours of instruction with 2 instructors as judges.

Define Criteria

Criteria are the accomplishments that determine whether an objective has been met. Some examples of criteria are shown in Exhibit 33-2. Careful planning of criteria helps ensure HRD success because they become the targets for accomplishing objectives. Furthermore, HRD procedures, such as training outlines, are structured toward meeting the criteria.

HRD Methods

To some extent, all learning methods, whether college classroom courses or apprenticeship programs, involve some cognitive, noncognitive, and psychomotor learning. For example, a computer manufacturer's classroom course for its sales personnel includes teaching the various characteristics of the company's line of computers, such as their data storage capacities. This is cognitive learning. In addition, the course includes teaching the sales personnel how to operate the computers (psychomotor learning). Finally, the course also uses role-playing exercises to teach sales personnel how to be creative in making sales presentations to motivate customers to buy computers (noncognitive learning).

The most frequently used methods of on-the-job HRD are:

- Apprenticeship;
- Coaching;
- Internship/Trainee;
- Job instruction method;
- Job rotation; and
- Mentoring.

The most frequently used methods of off-the-job HRD are:

- Audiovisual;
- Behavioral modeling;
- Case method;
- College courses;
- Conference;
- Correspondence;
- Lecture;
- Professional education;
- Programmed instruction;
- Role playing;
- Simulation; and
- Vestibule training.

Apprenticeship

Registered apprenticeship is a proven training strategy that combines on-the-job training with related classroom instruction to prepare highly skilled workers for business and industry. In the apprenticeship agreement, the apprentice agrees to participate in the on-the-job training and related instruction components of the program. The on-the-job component is structured, supervised hands-on training consisting of at least 2,000 hours, depending on the occupation. Apprenticeship programs are registered with the Bureau of Apprenticeship and Training, U.S. Department of Labor. In the U.S., some 34,500 program sponsors offer registered apprenticeship training to approximately 367,700 apprentices. Currently, two-thirds of all apprenticeship training positions are in the construction and manufacturing industries. Experts agree, however, that apprenticeship has the potential to benefit numerous other industries, as well, including those in service, retail, and public sectors.[6]

These are some of the basic standards under the Code of Federal Regulations that apply to apprenticeship programs:

- All individuals have a full and fair opportunity to apply for apprenticeship;

- The program includes a schedule of work processes in which an apprentice is to receive training and experience on the job;

- The program includes organized instruction designed to provide apprentices with knowledge in technical subjects related to their trade, with a minimum of 144 hours per year normally considered necessary;

- The program includes a progressively increasing schedule of wages;

- Proper supervision of on-the-job training is provided, with adequate facilities to train apprentices;

- Apprentices' progress, both in job performance and related instruction, are evaluated periodically, and appropriate records are maintained; and

- No discrimination in any phase of selection, employment, or training is allowed.

Coaching

Coaching is the process by which a knowledgeable person assists employees in either adjusting to a job environment or learning how to perform job tasks. Coaching is performed by both peers and supervisors. Peer coaching is particularly effective in aiding the job adjustment of new employees. Sometimes, this is informally done, such as when a supervisor assigns a new employee to work with a senior employee. In other instances, the coaching arrangements are a formal HRD method used by the organization. For example, one government agency specially selected and trained a group of employees to serve as coaches of new employees. These coaches participated in the orientation of the employees to whom they were assigned and generally helped them in adjusting to their jobs.

To be a coach requires special qualifications, depending upon the assignment. For example, if the coach is to aid the employee's adjustment, the person should be sensitive to the needs of others and be a good listener. Coaches who perform job instruction, on the other hand, should be experts in their work.

To some extent, all supervisors perform some coaching, since a major supervisory task is guiding subordinates in the efficient accomplishment of objectives. Some supervisors are more adept at coaching; they relate better to their employees and build strong coach-player relationships. These are the supervisors who knit strong team relationships with high efficiency and morale.

---

[6] Information about apprenticeship programs was obtained from the Bureau of Apprenticeship and Training, U.S. Department of Labor.

Intern/Trainee

Intern or trainee programs are formalized HRD programs in which employees are rotated through a series of planned job assignments to prepare them for higher level responsibilities. Usually, intern or trainee job specifications require a Bachelor's degree. In some cases, particularly those in which the eventual target jobs are at middle management or higher, applicants are required to have a Master of Arts or a Master of Business Administration degree.

Educational Background. The relative value for managerial jobs of liberal arts, engineering, and business degrees is the subject of much speculation but little hard research. However, AT&T conducted several major studies with employees in which their management abilities and potential were assessed and their progress tracked over 25 years.[7] The assessments produced evidence that liberal arts majors were superior in interpersonal abilities, such as leadership and oral communications. In addition, these majors were equal to business majors, and ahead of engineering majors, in management functions, such as planning and organizing. The one area in which liberal arts majors were weakest was in quantitative abilities. The AT&T researchers found that after 25 years the liberal arts majors had progressed more quickly, and 46 percent were considered promotable for middle management jobs. The percentages for business and engineering degree graduates were 31 and 25 percent, respectively.

Development Period. Management trainee or intern jobs usually entail a one- or two-year developmental period. Normally, the program begins with an overall orientation lasting from several weeks to a month, depending upon the size of the organization. After the orientation, the trainee is assigned to a series of work projects in various organization functions. However, this is not always the case for trainees who are in development for specific organization functions, such as finance trainees or human resource management trainees. For these specialist trainees, their work assignments after the orientation are usually restricted to the respective function.

Coordinator Role. Normally, trainees are assigned to a coordinator who handles salary and administrative matters and communicates with each trainee about future assignments. The coordinator also maintains records on each trainee's progress. Usually, trainees are required to submit monthly reports to the coordinator explaining the status of a project and what has transpired since the previous report. Trainees are encouraged to keep daily logs or diaries to help them keep records of their activities. The coordinator uses the reports to gauge a trainee's progress on various projects and to ensure that the functional manager to whom the trainee is assigned is not subverting the trainee's development by assigning him or her to menial or make-work projects.

Advantages and Disadvantages. There are both advantages and disadvantages to management trainee programs. A major disadvantage some critics charge is that they create prima donnas who expect preferential treatment and

---

[7] "AT&T Studies Show Liberal Arts Majors Excel in Many Managerial Skills," *Management Review* (January 1982), p. 31.

automatic promotions. This criticism is especially prevalent among managers who progressed through the ranks, often starting at the lowest level job. To satisfy this group of managers and to give each trainee a degree of humility, many trainee programs require a tenure of one or two months in the "trenches" in which the trainee works on assembly lines and in the warehouse, and performs other unskilled and semiskilled tasks in a regular 40-hour-per-week job. Another disadvantage is that trainee jobs limit the promotion opportunities for in-house personnel. To counter this, most organizations encourage qualified employees to apply for trainee jobs.

The advantages of management trainee programs include the orderly development of a cadre of individuals who have an overall understanding of the organization and have been carefully developed to assume more responsible jobs. Another advantage is that the organization reaps the benefits from having bright and energetic men and women who have fresh ideas, and the motivation and the initiative to meet the challenges of the rapid changes facing today's organizations.

Job Instruction Method

Job instruction method (JIM) is an on-the-job training method in which written instructions for operating a machine or following a procedure are listed in a series of successive steps. Usually, the instructions are on a card or in a manual. Sometimes, the instructions include a flowchart portraying alternative steps for different conditions. The JIM is used for all types of jobs ranging from unskilled to professional work, but is most frequently used in skilled maintenance jobs where the instructions are prepared by manufacturers. Usually, the instructions are supplemented by the experiences of employees who discover more efficient ways of accomplishing tasks. Exhibit 33-3 is a hypothetical example of a JIM.

Exhibit 33-3
Selected Example of the Job Instruction Method
of Training for a Fictitious Transmission Adjustment

NEUTRAL START SWITCH ADJUSTMENT
1. Raise the transmission with a # 4 jack.
2. Place the transmission machine gear to interface with ventilating fan.
3. Remove the transmission lever retaining nut.
4. Loosen the inhibitor switch attachment.
5. Remove the screw from the alignment pin drop at the end of the switch.
6. Slowly rotate the switch and insert an alignment pin in the alignment pin hole.
7. Hold the switch assembly while inserting the screw in alignment pin drop.
8. Tighten the inhibitor switch attachment.
9. Replace the transmission lever retaining nut.
10. Lower the transmission.

The JIM is effective in quickly qualifying replacements to assume important job tasks. The method can also illustrate how various aspects of a task should be performed. For example, a purchasing officer used the method to prepare instructions for buyers concerning the different procedures to follow for various types of purchases, such as requests for proposals, sole source purchases, and blanket purchase agreements. The method is also effective in simplifying and streamlining tasks, since repetitious steps can be identified and eliminated.

Job Rotation

Job rotation is a HRD method in which employees are purposively rotated among various jobs to gain experience in performing tasks in them. A variation of job rotation is temporarily assigning employees to higher level jobs to help qualify them for promotion when vacancies occur. Usually, these temporary assignments, also known as *details,* are made when the incumbents are absent due to illness or when they are on vacation. Sometimes, details are made in conjunction with a career planning program, so that employees who are either qualified for the job except for the experience or are pursuing developmental activities, such as taking college courses are able to obtain the experience they lack.

The typical procedure used in job rotation is rotating employees among different jobs at the same pay level. While HRD purposes are often one reason for making the rotations, an equally important one is to ensure there are sufficient qualified personnel to perform each job should an employee become ill or a job otherwise becomes vacant. Some employees enjoy job rotation because they enjoy performing a variety of tasks. Other employees are not so keen on the idea because they have set routines that they do not enjoy having changed.

Mentoring

Mentoring is similar to coaching except that the mentor-protege relationship is more personal and involved. *Mentoring* is the process "... in which less-experienced technicians, managers, and professionals are formally or informally assigned to mature and highly qualified individuals in similar occupations ..." for the purposes of obtaining knowledge (cognitive learning) and/or to develop noncognitive abilities, such as leadership and decisionmaking.[8] Mentoring is a proven method for developing people. With few exceptions, all successful people in fields ranging from science to the military acknowledge the role of one or more mentors in their lives.

Types of Assistance. Mentors may assist their mentees in several ways. First, mentors chiefly assist their mentees in occupational matters, such as obtaining job assignments that will facilitate their development. Mentors also give their mentees advice on a myriad of subjects, such as how to handle tough problems and what to consider in making important decisions. Mentors seldom make decisions for their mentees, but they do give them guidance and advice. More importantly, the best mentors have an almost mystical ability to shape the critical noncognitive abilities of their mentees and thereby move them ahead. Mentors also teach their mentees the realities of internal politics. In some cases they help their mentees maneuver through the political maze of organizations; more importantly, they help them develop the "right" political affiliations.

---

[8] Myers, D.W. and Humphreys, N.J., "The Caveats in Mentorship," *Business Horizons* (July/August 1985).

Love Relationship. Sometimes, the mentor-mentee bond becomes so strong a love develops, similar to that which exists among immediate family members. These strong relationships result in mentors becoming involved to some degree in mentees' personal lives. These involvements may consist of personal advice about family problems and confidential discussions about intimate matters.

Effectiveness. Studies have been conducted indicating the effectiveness of mentoring in developing employees. For example, researchers found in a study of 300 Honeywell managers that 80 percent of their learning was obtained on-the-job or from personal contacts which primarily involved their mentors.[9]

Problems. Employers do experience some problems with mentoring. These problems entail the mentee selection method, the process used to develop mentees, and the eventual outcomes of the mentoring process. Selection problems arise when mentees are selected because of favoritism or nepotism. The mentoring process also can result in problems when mentors are tyrants or poor role models. The mentoring outcome may be less than successful when mentors' careers suffer setbacks. This result may occur because mentees often share the fates of their mentors, whether good or bad. For example, an employee's career can become permanently delayed because his or her mentor was fired or lost an internal political campaign.

Audiovisual Methods

Audiovisual methods range from materials, such as cassette tapes designed to constitute a complete learning package, to transparencies and special purpose films that supplement other learning methods, including lectures or role-playing. Videotaping gives trainees the type of immediate feedback and reinforcement that can dramatically influence behavioral change.

Closed-Circuit Television

Closed-circuit television (CCTV), particularly involving interactive video technology, is a learning method with wide application and practicality. Courses are offered via CCTV through vocational schools and colleges on a broad range of subjects, including graduate courses. CCTV is also used in the district and branch offices of national organizations to conduct training and to disseminate information.

Behavioral Modeling

Behavioral modeling is a learning method in which participants attempt to replicate either the behavior or the procedure of an expert who "models" or demonstrates the proper way a task should be accomplished. The demonstration or model performance may be in person but is usually conducted though an audiovisual medium, such as a film or videotape. Behavioral modeling is especially effective in developing interpersonal abilities. Behavioral modeling sometimes involves the use of symbolic coding or rule coding.

Symbolic Coding. In *symbolic coding*, trainees observe the model demonstration (such as how to conduct a performance appraisal interview) and they make

---

[9] Ibid.

a list of the behaviors exhibited by the expert that they believe were most effective in achieving the desired outcome. Next, the scene is replayed and the instructor stops the recording at those points where an important behavior is exhibited. The trainees check their lists of behaviors and add the item if they missed it. The trainees use their lists of behaviors to prepare for a role-playing session, which is usually videotaped. Frequently, this preparation includes a rehearsal, so that the trainee has practiced the behaviors on the list. Next, the role-playing sessions are videotaped and replayed for the trainee to critique his or her performance using the previously prepared checklist of behaviors. The instructor also participates in the critique offering suggestions and reinforcement for appropriate behavior.

Rule Coding. *Rule coding* follows the same procedure as is used in symbolic coding except the trainees are instructed to watch the model demonstration and prepare sequenced lists of rules that should be followed in handling the situation. For example, if the demonstration was a performance appraisal interview, the first rule might be to get prepared, the second rule could be to inform the employee in advance of the interview, and the third rule might be to warmly greet the employee when he or she arrives for the interview. As noted above, the trainees use their lists of rules to prepare for a videotaped role-playing session. The rest of the procedure is the same as the one used in symbolic coding.

Case Method

The *case method* involves using actual or fictional workplace situations, so that trainees can apply their knowledge. Cases are either vignettes or comprehensive descriptions of situations. Cases also may either focus on a specific area or be comprehensive and cover a range of topics. Specific cases and vignettes are usually used in learning situations where a specific topic is reinforced. General and comprehensive cases typically are used in management classes where trainees are required to analyze the situation and define a number of variables.

Immediate Application. The case method helps trainees immediately apply learning, which gives them actual practice. Cases also help reinforce learning if presentations are critiqued and trainees understand how they were right and wrong. Often, cases require both written and oral presentations that help build abilities in these areas, provided they are critiqued. Uncritiqued analyses, particularly those involving general cases, have marginal value even in group discussions, since trainees merely pool their opinions. All cases have optimum outcomes, pertinent facts bearing on those outcomes, and involve specific knowledge. Trainees should be advised of these conditions once they have presented their analyses and decisions. This feedback provides the reinforcement necessary for trainees to benefit from the experience. Unfortunately, cases are often used that are only tangentially related to a topic; this makes it difficult for trainees to relate them to their prior learning. Also, critiques are sometimes omitted with the explanation, "There is no optimum solution to this case." If this is true, one can logically question why the case was used, since its only value is for discussion purposes. To help control these problems, the HRD *objectives* and *criteria* should be specified before a case is selected.

College Courses

College courses, as used here, include technical and vocational courses offered above the high school level. College courses are an essential part of most HRD activities ranging from skilled work preparation to postgraduate courses in business, engineering, science, and other fields. Colleges have generally demonstrated significant flexibility in developing courses designed to meet specific needs. Some colleges even develop special purpose courses for an employer, provided there is sufficient demand for them.

Colleges have been particularly responsive to the needs for managerial and executive level development. In metropolitan areas, there are full offerings of evening courses in virtually every business subject. These evening courses are intended to make education more readily available to those students who are employed and on career tracks within their chosen fields. In addition, Master of Business Administration courses are offered in a variety of nontraditional ways to meet the needs of managers and executives. These schedules include weekends and full-time one- and two-week courses.

Colleges also offer non-degree courses in continued education. These may either be repeated offerings in selected subjects, such as business communications, or specific courses that are offered upon demand. Some colleges will assist employers in conducting a HRD needs analysis and designing special courses to meet those needs.

Conference

Conference instruction is a generic term encompassing learning situations ranging from an organization's staff conferences, in which management trainees are invited to attend and observe, to professional conferences, such as the annual national conference of the Society for Human Resource Management. Conferences typically involve other learning methods, such as lectures, films, and videotaped presentations. The unique feature of conferences are that they usually are dedicated to a specific activity or function. Another unique feature is the broad range of learning purposes that conferences can fulfill.

Generally, conference instruction is restricted to cognitive learning, although workshop sessions in skill development are sometimes conducted in conjunction with a professional conference. Also, most professional conferences have several rooms reserved for vendors of state-of-the-art technology, procedures, and techniques. These displays help practitioners learn the latest developments in the field.

Correspondence Courses

Correspondence courses are available for many learning situations, ranging from taking a required college course to learning how to repair electronic equipment. Some organizations have in-house correspondence courses. For example, many insurance companies provide correspondence courses to help agents learn both the concepts of different types of insurance and the various products the organization offers. Some organizations require employees to successfully pass correspondence courses before they will be permitted to enroll in organization-sponsored classroom courses.

Correspondence courses are an excellent way to obtain cognitive learning. Trainees can learn at their own pace and in the comfort of their residences. This is convenient, and it helps keep down the cost to the trainee, since transportation expenses and the time spent in commuting to classes are avoided. The principal problem with correspondence courses is reinforcement, since considerable time can elapse between submitting lessons to be graded and receiving them back after they are graded. Also, correspondence courses tend to be impersonal. Some organizations successfully address this problem by telling the trainee who the grader is and encouraging the trainee and the grader to communicate with each other. Correspondence courses are not effective in either noncognitive or psychomotor learning.

Lecture

Lecture is a teaching method in which trainees receive information through the oral presentations of the instructor. This method is unexcelled in the economy and speed of presenting material to trainees. The effectiveness of the method depends upon such factors as the trainees' motivation to listen and learn, the oral communication skills of the teacher, and the complexity of the subject matter. The method is unsuitable for both noncognitive and psychomotor learning. In addition, in straight lecture sessions, trainees do not have the opportunity to practice what they are learning, and there is no reinforcement.

The many disadvantages with lecturing explain why it is generally always supplemented by other learning methods, such as using a blackboard or flipchart to write items offered by trainees. The method is also usually supplemented by discussions and audiovisual materials, such as showing transparencies on overhead projectors.

Professional/Continuing Education Courses

Professional and continuing education courses are offered by numerous suppliers, such as colleges and professional organizations. Professional and continuing education courses are quite expensive. Fees run from $300 or so for a one-day workshop up to $1,500 or more for programs lasting a week or more. Additional costs include transportation, lodging, and meals if the course is offered at a location outside a participant's commuting area. The value of these courses ranges from minimal to extensive, depending upon such things as applicability and the degree to which they meet a need. Employers generally do not give adequate attention to determining course content and objectives and relating them to HRD needs. Without this type of analysis, the experience may be a waste of time and money. Large organizations can ensure getting their money's worth by doing a need analysis and asking various suppliers to submit proposals on how they intend to meet that need, the training methods that will be used, and the price.

Continuing Education Unit. To help establish standards in this area, the International Association for Continuing Education and Training publishes criteria for organizations that conduct continuing education programs. Those organizations that meet the criteria can award Continuing Education Units (CEU). One CEU is defined as "... ten contact hours of participation in an organized continuing education experience under responsible sponsorship, capable direction, and qualified instruction."[10] The contact hour is a full 60 minutes of instruction, exclusive of breaks, meals, or business meetings. The purpose of the CEU is to provide a permanent record of a person's continuing education participation. The criteria for an organization to follow in awarding the CEU relate to program sponsorship and program content.

Programmed Instruction

Programmed instruction (PI) is a learning method in which both the speed and repetition of learning are determined by the trainee. Subject matter is usually spaced into small integrated segments, starting with more elementary or basic material. Gradually these segments increase in difficulty, but ideally the transition is so gradual the learning is unimpeded. At the conclusion of each small segment, the trainee is asked questions to test comprehension of the material just covered. The trainee answers the questions and must turn the page (in the case of PI books or other printed materials) or hit a key (when either computers or training consoles are used) to see the correct answers. If the answers are wrong, the trainee is referred back to a previous section (for printed material) or is immediately shown material (computers and training consoles) explaining the correct answer. If the trainee's responses are correct, the text may congratulate the person and invite him or her to proceed with the next segment. This immediate reinforcement is a major plus for PI because it builds trainee confidence, encourages learning, and corrects any misunderstandings, so that time spent on subsequent material is not wasted if the trainee misunderstood some basic principles or concepts.

Limitations. With PI, trainees learn more quickly and learn better than they do with other methods. However, PI also has some limitations. First, while it is extremely effective for cognitive learning, it cannot be used for either noncognitive or psychomotor learning. Another limitation is the cost of preparing courses and buying training consoles and computer terminals. Material specifically prepared for computer-assisted PI is very expensive because of the costs of computer programming.

Role Playing

Role playing is a learning method in which trainees assume roles in simulated exercises to obtain practice in applying skills necessary for daily job situations. For example, sales trainees role play making sales representations and supervisors role play conducting performance appraisal interviews.

Defined/Undefined Roles. Role playing can be conducted with either defined or undefined roles. In *defined roles,* the trainee is given a script and plays the role according to it. An *undefined role* allows the trainee freedom to assume the role as he or she desires. Generally, undefined roles better illustrate how a person

---

[10] International Association for Continuing Education and Training, *What Is IACET?*

would handle an actual situation at work because the trainee is not constrained by a script and/or is not "acting" in a role.

Skill-building. Role playing is particularly good at building trainee skills. For example, one study found that supervisors who were given a role-playing training experience in goal-setting interviews were perceived by trained evaluators as more effective in videotaped, goal-setting interviews than a comparison group of supervisors who did not receive the role-playing training.[11] In addition, there was a significant difference in the attitudes and job performance of employees of the two groups of supervisors. For example, employees of trained supervisors experienced more intrinsic job satisfaction, performed better in one of two quantifiable performance variables, and perceived their supervisors as more supportive and better at clarifying goals in goal-setting sessions.

Learning Application. Role playing gives trainees active practice in applying learning and provides an environment in which immediate reinforcement is available through a combination of self-assessment, peer assessment, and instructor evaluation. Role playing helps trainees gain confidence in various interpersonal situations, such as resolving performance problems with employees.

Simulation Methods

Simulation is a generic form of HRD encompassing a number of work-life situations. Among the techniques used in simulations are these:

- Leaderless group situations;
- Competitive group exercises, in which teams of trainees compete against other teams;
- In-basket exercises; and
- Computer games.

Role playing is also a simulation. Different techniques are used, depending upon the developmental need. For example, *leaderless group situations* are often used to teach cooperation and communication. A typical project might entail developing a formal marketing strategy for a fictional company. The trainees are only given minimal instructions about how the task is to be accomplished; they must organize themselves, communicate, assign authority and responsibilities, and cooperate in completing the task.

In-Basket Simulations. *In-basket* training uses a work basket of tasks, such as memoranda, letters, reports, and telephone messages. Normally, an hour or two is allotted for the trainee to handle the basket of work. In a group setting, each trainee relates the priority with which the work was accomplished and how it was accomplished. Fellow trainees and the instructor critique each presentation. In-basket training is especially effective in teaching noncognitive abilities, such as planning, organizing, oral communication, and decisionmaking. Trainees are motivated to learn, particularly if the exercises parallel events that actually occur in the workplace. In-basket gives immediate reinforcement and gives

[11] Ivancevich, J.M. and Smith, S.V., "Goal Setting Interview Skills Training: Simulated and On-the-Job Analysis," *Journal of Applied Psychology 66* (December 1981), pp. 697-705.

trainees actual practice, experience, and training in handling work situations. Sometimes, in-basket exercises are used in time management courses to help teach trainees how to establish work priorities and allocate their time.

Computer Gaming

Computer gaming gives trainees experience and training in evaluating quantitative information, planning alternative strategies, and making decisions. Occasionally in training programs lasting several days the computer game is interspersed with other HRD activities. Trainees receive information, evaluate it, and make a decision. This information is fed into the computer, and while outputs are generated, the trainees are engaged in some other scheduled activity, such as role playing or a case study. Later in the day, printouts are distributed to the trainees and they see the effects of their previous decisions and make other decisions. Computer gaming can be realistic to the extent the database and programming represent work-life events, data, and situations.

Vestibule Training

A *vestibule* is an outer room or a passage from the outside into a main room. This definition is also appropriate in describing vestibule training because it takes place in an outer room, or at least in a space away from the work floor. This training also involves equipment, such as training consoles and machines, that are either replicas, simulators, or actual models of what are used on the work floor. The object of vestibule training is to provide the trainee with the equipment, if not the environment, in which the actual work is done, but without the stress and pressure from attempting to learn to operate a machine or perform other tasks while actually producing a product or service.

Vestibule training is usually used in situations where the training period is relatively long for employees to reach a satisfactory level of output. Also, the training is relatively complex and requires the trainee to concentrate and be away from distractions. Sometimes, the equipment and/or the materials used are expensive; in such cases, it is more efficient to use simulated machines that have operational features close to the actual machinery. Also, in a simulated environment, the employee can make mistakes without the fear of damaging equipment or ruining expensive raw materials. Flight simulators for commercial airline pilot training teach pilots to fly airplanes without endangering passenger lives or tying up expensive aircraft on extended training flights.

Evaluation

Evaluation is included in the initial stages of HRD planning because this helps ensure that purposes are met. For example, if a purpose of a training program for a group of shipping clerks is to decrease the error rates in invoices, a measurement must be taken of the error rates prior to the training, so that a basis for comparison can be established. These are among the major determining factors of evaluations:

- *Were the needs met?*

- *Was the training process conducive to learning?* The process includes the facilities in which a training program was conducted, the materials used in the training, and the teaching methods of the instructor.

- *Did the evaluation aid the instructor?* Evaluation aids the instructor, the facilitator, or other people responsible for the HRD. A training assistant who prepares material for correspondence courses can improve those courses by considering the ideas of students and implementing the workable ones.

Two Types of Evaluation

Two types of HRD evaluation are process evaluations and effect evaluations.

Process Evaluations. *Process evaluations* concern participant opinions of the manner in which the HRD was accomplished. For example, trainees could evaluate the process used in a computer simulation by asking whether the simulation was realistic and the instructions were adequate. An example of a process evaluation is shown in Exhibit 33-4. Ideally, process evaluations should be conducted at the end of each training activity to evaluate its effectiveness. Also, administering process evaluations immediately after the training helps ensure the accuracy of them, since the trainees are better able to remember and give valid opinions.

Exhibit 33-4
Example of an HRD Process Evaluation

INSTRUCTIONS: Check the space that best describes your opinions of the process used in the training program.

	Strongly Agree	Agree	Neutral	Disagree	Strongly Disagree	Not Applicable
1. Instructions were adequate	_____	_____	_____	_____	_____	_____
2. The facilities were right for learning	_____	_____	_____	_____	_____	_____
3. The instructor was prepared for class	_____	_____	_____	_____	_____	_____
4. Effective teaching materials were used	_____	_____	_____	_____	_____	_____
5. Tests were fairly graded						

Effect Evaluations. *Effect evaluations* measure employees' learning in cognitive, noncognitive, and psychomotor areas. In short, an effect evaluation indicates the effect the learning had on a trainee's knowledge (cognitive), abilities (noncognitive), and skill in operating something (psychomotor). Effect evaluations can be conducted through either *formative* or *summative* assessments.

- *Formative assessments* are periodic, usually informal, measures of learning during a course or training program to guage participants'/trainees' progress. Examples of formative assessment methods are pop quizzes, short exercises, class discussions of topics, or student presentations of subject matter. Trainers/facilitators use student/participant performance on these formative measures of learning to evaluate progress being made toward learning objectives.[12] From this evaluation any adjustments can be made, for example, in the manner in which training materials are being presented.

- *Summative assessments* are typically conducted at the conclusion of a course, training program, or independent module of a program or course, and provide a summary account of a student's/participant's learning. Examples of summative assessment methods include final examinations, students'/participants' assessments of learning accomplishments, or operation/maintenance of equipment which was the subject of the training

Evaluation Data

Three types of data used to evaluate HRD programs are assessments, tests, and performance data.

Assessments. Assessments are subjective opinions by a trainee concerning the manner (*process evaluation*) in which the learning method was accomplished or how much was learned (*effect evaluation*). Exhibit 33-4 is an example of a process assessment instrument. Effect assessments can be used to measure the perceived amount of cognitive, noncognitive, or psychomotor learning that resulted from the training. These assessments can be made by the trainee, the trainee's supervisor, or by the instructor. Exhibit 33-5 is an example of a trainee self-assessment evaluation instrument concerning the effects of a training program on the trainee's cognitive learning.

Exhibit 33-5
Example of Self-Assessment Evaluation of the Effects
of an HRD Program Upon Trainee Cognitive Learning

INSTRUCTIONS: Check the space that best describes your opinion of the process used in the training program.

	Strongly Agree	Agree	Neutral	Disagree	Strongly Disagree	Not Applicable
1. I learned how to assign rates	————	————	————	————	————	————
2. I learned what caused freight damage	————	————	————	————	————	————
3. I learned how to pack crates for shipping	————	————	————	————	————	————

Exhibit 33-6 is an example of a trainee self-assessment evaluation instrument of the effects of a training program on the trainee's noncognitive learning. There is research evidence demonstrating that self-assessments of noncognitive abilities are valid. One study, for example, found a significant correlation in self-assessments of noncognitive abilities and assessments of the same subjects conducted by specially trained psychologists.[13]

---

[12] Schweizer, Heidi, *Designing and Teaching an On-Line Course* (Boston: Allyn and Bacon, 1999), pp. 29-34.

[13] Mosea, J.L. and Byham, W.C., *Applying the Assessment Center Method* (New York: Pergamon Press, 1977).

Exhibit 33-6
Example of a Self-Assessment Evaluation of the Effects
of an HRD Program Upon Noncognitive Learning

INSTRUCTIONS: Check the space that best describes your opinion of what you learned in this training program.

	Strongly Agree	Agree	Neutral	Disagree	Strongly Disagree	Not Applicable
1. I learned how to plan loads	———	———	———	———	———	———
2. I learned to use initiative in loading trailers	———	———	———	———	———	———
3. I learned to be sensitive to customer complaints	———	———	———	———	———	———
4. I learned how to be an effective team player	———	———	———	———	———	———

Tests. Written tests are an efficient way to evaluate cognitive learning, particularly when the learning situation involves extensive amounts of information, such as a college course or a preparatory class for professional certification, accreditation, or licensing. *Skills* tests, such as those involving driver training or machine or instrument use, are used to evaluate psychomotor learning. As discussed in Chapter 14, learning tests must be validated if they are used as a selection procedure in making employment decisions.

Performance Data. *Performance data,* which includes accidents, productivity errors, and other quantitative data, are used to evaluate the effects of a training program on those variables. Performance data are considered essential in HRD evaluation because experimental studies involving the use of control and treatment groups depend largely upon numerical data. In addition, performance problems, such as error rates, are determined from performance data. Where possible, the evaluation should include performance data because of its relevance to work situations.

Levels of Learning

The level of learning a person possesses on different subjects varies. Few people have a mastery of all subjects. Typically, on some subjects a person may have very high levels of learning, while on other subjects the person's learning may be elementary. Obviously, there is a direct relationship between the amount of learning one possesses on a subject and the capability to responsibly handle more challenging tasks dealing with that subject. For example, a person who only has knowledge about some basic features of a computer software product could not be reasonably expected to render a comprehensive evaluation of it. Benjamin Bloom, a noted educator, developed a scale with six levels depicting outcomes associated with successive higher levels of learning.[14] This is the scale:

[14] Bloom, Benjamin and Broder, Lois, *Problem Solving Processes of College Students* (Chicago: University of Chicago Press, 1950).

- Level 1 is *knowing* facts or information about a subject. Typically, this requires memorization and recall. For example, to be able to use a spreadsheet software program, it is necessary to know particular keystrokes necessary to enter and manipulate data. Sometimes acquiring basic knowledge is a challenge for both learners and facilitators/instructors unless certain conditions exist, such as the learner is motivated to learn or is able to see or understand how the learning is related to an outcome.

- Level 2 is *comprehending* information by being able to interpret or explain what has been learned. For example, a person demonstrates comprehension of a spreadsheet software program by being able to translate or explain in everyday language to an uninformed person how to use the software.

- Level 3 in the learning hierarchy is *applying* the learning to the extent that problems can be solved, such as being able to resolve "glitches" that occur from time to time in using, for example, spreadsheet software.

- Level 4 is *analyzing* the information that has been learned in situations that are different from those in which the learning was originally attained. An example of the analytical level of learning as applied to the spreadsheet discussions above might involve using the software in a situation that is substantially different from the one in which the learning originally occurred. For example, a person might have learned how to use a spreadsheet software product in an accounting setting. An analytical level of learning might be using the same spreadsheet software to develop a database of information acquired in a field study of the causes of industrial accidents in a large firm.

- Level 5, *synthesizing*, is creating new adaptations or uses of previously learned information. This level of learning requires competencies in both creative processes and comprehensive cognitive knowledge in a subject. For example, some spreadsheet software does not readily permit a user to integrate columnar data into word processing software, except within rather rigid contraints. A sythesizing level of learning might be developing a protocol in which the user can use the spreadsheet data in multiple formats. Like all the other levels of learning, synthesizing can occur in any type of work, from the simplest to the most sophisticated.

- Finally, Level 6, *evaluating*, is the highest level of learning since it requires a person to develop criteria or other means of measuring what has been learned. In addition, to be able to judge learning in such areas as cognitive information, noncognitive competencies, and psychomotor skills, an evaluator must be able to develop valid evaluation systems.

Learning Settings

Researchers have found that trainees learn several times more in classroom settings compared to on-the-job learning, but they typically enjoy the classroom less. For groups of different sizes, different settings should be used. Use circle or rectangle seating for small groups involved with interactive learning. For large groups, use classroom/theater/banquet seating arrangements.

Learning Principles

Learning principles are used in HRD to help ensure the stated objectives will be accomplished. Among the important learning principles are reinforcement, feedback, practice, and application.

Reinforcement

Reinforcement is the process of recognizing and responding to behavior, so that desired acts will be learned and repeated and undesired ones will not. Reinforcement is based upon the *law of effect*, which states that people learn and repeat acts that are rewarded and will avoid acts that are punished. The reinforcement responses that influence learning are:

- Positive reinforcement;
- Punishment;
- Negative reinforcement; and
- Extinction.

Positive Reinforcement

Positive reinforcement is rewarding a desired response. The reward could be praise, a letter of commendation, and/or a pay increase. Positive reinforcement helps ensure desired responses are learned. For example, employees in a federal agency were trained as machine operators. The training program had ten different modules that employees had to learn before they were qualified as machine operators. At the end of each module, the employees were tested and, if they failed to achieve a score of 98 percent, they had to repeat the module. Progress was tracked on a large board showing each employee's name. Gold stars were used to indicate which modules an employee had completed. Prizes were given when an employee successfully passed a test. In addition, all the employees were competing for a large cash prize to be awarded to the first five employees who successfully passed the test for all ten modules. The stars, prizes, and cash awards were positive reinforcers.

Punishment

Punishment is the process of either administering an unpleasant stimulus, such as a warning letter, or withholding a reward, such as not granting a prize to a machine operator trainee for failing a test on one of the ten modules. In the machine operator example above, employees were given three attempts to pass the test for each module. The first failure resulted in an oral counseling. A warning letter was given on the second failure informing the employee that he or she would be removed from the training program upon a third failure. The oral counseling, warning letter, and the withholding of prizes are examples of punishment.

Negative Reinforcement

Negative reinforcement is an unpleasant stimulus intended to induce a person to perform a desired act and avoid or not do an undesired one. Punishment also involves an unpleasant stimulus; the difference is that punishment is administered *after* an undesired behavior occurs and a negative reinforcer is administered *before* it occurs. There are many learning situations in which a negative reinforcer would be appropriate. For example, automobile seat belt lights and buzzers are negative reinforcers intended to prevent a vehicle operator from driving without fastening the seat belt.

Extinction

Extinction is taking no action in response to a behavior. There are both correct and incorrect ways of using extinction in learning situations. For example, if a mentee typically completes all assignments in a timely manner, a mentor might be advised to ignore (extinction) one occasion in which a project is not done on schedule. This is a positive use of extinction. A negative use is if a mentor failed to properly recognize a mentee for doing a job in an exceptional manner.

Feedback

Feedback is the learning principle in which the consequences of a behavior which is in reaction to a learning situation are made known. Immediate feedback, for example, which is frequently used in computerized programmed instruction, is best because the person can quickly correct an error or, if a response was correct, proceed with his or her learning. Short pop quizzes in a classroom also have immediate feedback if the correct answer is discussed immediately following administration of the quiz. People do not like to be kept in the dark waiting for confirmation about their learning; the quicker the response, the better the effect.

Practice

Practice is a self-explanatory principle of learning. "Practice makes perfect" is an old but accurate adage. In the Pacific theater of operations during World War II, the first amphibious landings of U.S. troops on Japanese-held islands were near-disasters. Amphibious invasions that were conducted later, after many practice sessions, were much more successful with markedly reduced causalities.

Whole v. Part

Trainees can become so absorbed in the individual parts of learning that they fail to see the whole picture. Gestalt psychology states that learning is best when a person understands the integrated whole of a physical, biological, or psychological event. The analogy for this is seeing the forest for the trees. Looking down from an airliner at 30,000 feet, we get the big picture and can see the outline of an entire forest and how it is situated in relation to the surrounding country. That picture is difficult to imagine when we are in a valley of a forest and have trudged for 15 miles along a rough trail. People in a learning environment should periodically be given the big picture at critical junctures in their learning.

Chaining. Sometimes, when there are a number of parts involved in a very complex subject, the learning can be expedited through *chaining*, which is learning to do something by linking the learning of various operations.

Mass v. Distributed

Some professional or continuing education courses force large amounts of material into a 16- or even 40-hour course condensed into a period of from two to five days. There is an old training adage that states, "The mind can learn no more than the seat can endure." An author cannot write a book at one sitting, but he or she can accomplish the task by writing two pages or so each day. HRD should be segmented into logical and consumable pieces. Periodically, the learning should digress with an explanation of how the various pieces relate to the whole.

Immediate v. Delayed

Many times, teachers have heard, "I understood it when you were explaining it last week but last night, when I tried to do the assignment, I couldn't remember what you wanted." Virtually everyone has had the same experience. Our minds are not playing tricks on us; they simply have other things we ask them to do. They stored that prior knowledge, so that the immediate recall could be used for current matters. Ideally, practice should immediately follow the presentation of concepts or techniques. The longer the delay after initial exposure, the greater the likelihood of recall problems.

Learning Application

Applicability is using what one has learned. Applicability is enhanced if the learning methods used include practice sessions in which the trainee gets experience applying the concepts. This is particularly important in learning methods so novel or different that trainees may be afraid to attempt them because of the risk of appearing foolish. These practice sessions should include considerable reinforcement, so that the trainee can gain confidence in applying the concepts.

Application of learning will also occur if trainees see they will benefit by using it. To accomplish this requires comparing learning objectives with learning needs and using precise language, quantifiable if possible, to explain the specific benefit that will accrue to the trainee by applying the learning. Finally, trainees can only apply the learning they are permitted to apply. *Encapsulated learning* is a term describing situations in which a trainee is prevented from applying what has been learned. There are various conditions that either inhibit or prevent the application of learning, such as standard methods that do not permit deviation and supervisors who capriciously reject new methods or ideas that have been learned by trainees.

Transference of Learning

Transfer of learning also involves the application of learning, but more directly, it is applying the learning to a situation more or less different than the one for which the learning was originally intended. For example, assume a supervisor attends a course on accident investigation. Part of the course includes listening techniques used in interviewing employees involved in accidents. Applicability is demonstrated by the supervisor actually using the listening techniques in interviewing employees when accidents occur. Transfer of learning is the supervisor using the same listening techniques in conducting employee performance appraisal interviews.

Multiple Discrimination. *Multiple discrimination,* as applied to learning, is learning how to differentiate among similar but different categories of things.

Learning Retention

The more meaning the training has for participants, the better it is learned and retained. Also, the better the training content is learned during the initial training, the better it is retained.[15] Following are the percentages of information typically retained from different training methods:

- *Lecture.* About 10 percent of the material is retained by the listeners.

- *Reading.* Approximately 20 percent is retained.

- *Demonstration.* Watching a demonstration of a subject results in about a 30-percent retention.

- *Discussion.* Discussing a subject results in a 45-percent retention.

- *Practice.* As might be expected, practice yields a high retention rate of 75 percent in trainees.

- *Immediate application.* Applying what is learned has the highest retention rate at 90 percent.

Adult Learning

Andragogy is the science of how adults learn. *Pedagogy* is the science of how children learn. Persons engaged in learning for adults should consider that adults:

- Possess a large body of knowledge and experience that can be shared with other adults, and they can also learn from other adults;

- Appreciate the opportunity of assuming responsibility for their own learning; and

- Learn best when the learning focuses on immediate utility in addressing problems they are experiencing.[16]

In recent years, the claim that learning should differ for children and adults has been challenged.[17] More realistically, trainers should consider that different learning techniques are needed for different situations, whether the trainees are children or adults.

Conducting HRD Experiments

HRD is expensive; many times there are not sufficient funds to implement all the programs that are desired. In addition, on most occasions several alternatives seem appropriate for a particular need, so that the tough decision is choosing the most effective one. The word *effective,* depending upon the circumstances, could mean the lowest cost, the quickest method, or the method that best meets the criteria. Sometimes, it is feasible to experiment or conduct pilot studies

---

[15] Wexley, K.N., & Latham, G.P., *Developing and training human resources in organizations* (Glenview, IL: Scott, Foresman, 1981).

[16] Knowles, M. *The Adult Learner: A Neglected Species* (Houston: Gulf Publishing, 1978).

[17] Zemke, R. and Zemke, S. "Adult learning: what do we know for sure?", *Training* (June 1995), pp. 31-40.

with a particular method to determine how effective it is before implementing it throughout the organization.

Treatment and Control Groups

Pilot studies or experiments involve treatment and control groups. A *treatment* group is the one receiving the HRD. A *control* group consists of individuals who have the same or similar characteristics as the treatment group but do not receive the HRD. The control group is used to compare any effects the HRD had on the treatment group, including its effectiveness in meeting the criteria. Other terms used in pilot studies are subjects and random selection. *Subjects* are the employees involved in the study. *Random selection* is the process of using a table of random numbers or some other recognized method of randomly placing subjects in treatment and control groups. Randomness is important in pilot studies because the subjects must fairly represent the groups from which they are selected if the experimental results are to be valid.

Internal and External Validity

If a pilot study is conducted, precautions should be taken to ensure it is valid. The two types of validity are internal validity and external validity.[18]

Internal Validity

Internal validity concerns the question of whether the HRD program produced a desired change in the treatment group. These are eight errors that can affect internal validity:

- *Historical error* is any incident(s) occurring during the period that the HRD program is conducted that might influence the trainees' performance.

- *Maturation error* is any change(s) in the subject(s) during the time period that the HRD program is conducted.

- *Testing error* is any effect(s) of a pretest, such as a knowledge test, given to all the subjects in an HRD course that affects their performance upon a second test.

- *Measuring instruments error* includes any change(s) in the method of measuring the subjects. For example, if the subjects are tested before and after the HRD, the measurement methods must be the same.

- *Statistical regression error* occurs when subjects are not randomly selected from a group and instead are selected from the extremes. For example, selecting either the best or worst truck drivers for a driver training course may bias the results, since the best drivers may show no significant improvement after the training, while the poorest drivers may show sizable improvement.

- *Subject selection error* results if characteristics of the subjects differ in the control and "treatment" groups. This also occurs when the study subjects in the control or the "treatment" groups, or both, are not representative of

[18] Campbell, D.T. and Stanley, J.C., *Experimental and Quasi-Experimental Designs For Research* (Boston: Houghton Mifflin Co., 1963).

the employee population. For example, using volunteers to measure the effectiveness of a training program may produce invalid conclusions because volunteers have motives, such as a special interest in the program, that prompt them to learn and that may not exist in the average employee.

- *Subject loss error*, also called *experimental mortality*, is the loss of subjects, such as resignations or dropouts due to illness or personal reasons, while the study is conducted or before it is completed.

- *Errors interaction* includes any of the seven errors above interacting with the treatment group. For example, volunteers are used for the treatment group but subjects are randomly selected for the control group.

External Validity

External validity is the extent to which a study's findings can be generalized. For example, management would want to include the findings of an HRD pilot study in deciding whether the program should be implemented throughout the company. In other words, can the results obtained from the pilot study be generalized to the whole organization? The four errors that inhibit a pilot study's generalizability are:

- *Pretesting sensitivity error*, also called the *interaction effect of testing*, is the effect of pretesting upon pilot subjects' performance compared to that of other employee groups of the same population who are not pretested. As noted above, testing can be an internal validity error if pretesting sensitizes the subjects in the pilot study to what is expected or desired in an HRD program. Thus, the subjects may not have performed as they did if the pretest had not been administered. If pretesting is used in a pilot study, and if it had an effect upon subjects' performance, the results of the pilot study may not be generalized to future groups of employees who receive the same HRD, unless they also are pretested.

- *Selection error* is a possible error if the pilot study subjects are not representative of the entire employee population.

- *Hawthorne error*, also called *Hawthorne effect*, is when the subjects in a pilot study, especially those in the treatment groups, attempt to produce the desired results. In this case, the pilot study results will not be externally valid unless the same motivation is present in other groups in the employee population that receive the HRD.

- *Multiple-treatment error* is subjecting a treatment group to multiple treatments, which prevents discerning the effects of a particular treatment. For example, in response to an increase in errors, an employer conducted a pilot training course on error reduction, using both a treatment and a control group. In addition, the employer initiated a program of self-inspection for errors and installed error detection testing equipment. Due to the multiple actions taken to correct the error problem, the employer would be unable to generalize the results of the pilot training course.

Experimental Designs

An observation (O) is obtaining data about the subjects in a pilot study. Observations can be conducted before (pretest) and after (post test) a treatment is given. Where possible, subjects should be randomly (R) assigned to treatment and control groups.

> **EXAMPLE:** For several consecutive months, an airline experienced a progressive increase in accidents among the 5,000 baggage handlers throughout the system. Management decided to conduct a safety training class for all handlers. However, before the class is implemented over the entire system, the company decided to conduct a pilot study with a treatment and a control group. This is the experimental design:
>
> $R\ O_1 \times O_2$ (Treatment Group)
> $R\ O_1\ O_2$ (Control Group)

Where:

R	=	random selection of subjects
O_1	=	pretest
×	=	the training class
O_2	=	post test

In this example, a pretest does not involve an internal validity problem with testing error, as discussed above, because the pretests were *unobtrusive;* that is, they were based upon each subjects' accidents filed in the employees personnel files. However, suppose the pretest was a written test on safety topics. In this situation, there is a possibility the pretest could sensitize the subjects and influence their scores on a post test given after the training was conducted. To prevent this potential testing error, this design could be used:

$R \times O_2$ (Treatment Group)
$R\ O_2$ (Control Group)

A more rigorous design that is used to determine and control the effects of internal and external validity is this 4-square design that entails the random selection of four groups instead of just two:

Group 1 $R\ O_1 \times O_2$
Group 2 $R\ O_1\ O_2$
Group 3 $R \times O_2$
Group 4 $R\ O_2$

CHAPTER 34
CAREER PLANNING

Introduction

Most employed adults never made a deliberate choice and followed a career plan that resulted in the job they currently hold.[1] Due to changes in technology, an employee's knowledge and skill base becomes obsolescent within two years without serious investments in career development. In addition, jobs are changing, mandating career changes by employees to protect their future employability. Few adults realize the abundant resources available to help them make the difficult decisions about their vocational future. Among the on-line resources available are CareerOneStop, Monster.com, and O*Net. CareerOneStop and Monster.com are discussed in Chapter 15. These resources are available to help employers learn about career planning and develop a career planning process.

Career planning assists employees in defining their career interests and preparing for career changes through human resource development.

Career Changes

Career changes may entail a move to a different occupation, a promotion within an existing occupation, or changing the tasks in an existing occupation. Career planning may be either *voluntary* or *required*. Voluntary career planning is prompted by employees who are seeking a promotion or career change to a different job at the same pay grade. Required career planning is initiated by an employee to avert temporary lay-off or permanent displacement, due to such reasons as job abolishment caused by a change in technology or a decline in consumer demand.

The term *career development* is sometimes used to describe the phase of career planning in which employees are engaged in various human resource development (HRD) methods, such as taking college courses, to qualify them for a career advancement, or other career changes. The major methods of HRD are discussed in Chapter 33.

---

[1] Goodman, Jane, "Career Development for Adults in Organizations and in the Community," *The National Career Development Guidelines* (National Occupational Information Coordinating Committee, June 1991).

Career Planning Purposes

The two principal purposes of career planning (CP) are to influence employee intrinsic and extrinsic job satisfaction in a positive manner and to help the organization prepare for and meet its future human resource needs.

Employee Job Satisfaction

Career planning is important in maintaining employee job satisfaction. Some employees view career planning as an opportunity to progress in an occupation. Others see it as a way of obtaining more autonomy and challenge in a job. Still other employees may be concerned about their future employment prospects and see career planning as a way of ensuring that they will stay qualified for other work, should their current job be abolished. As these examples illustrate, employee motives for career planning are diverse.

Meet Organizational Needs for Human Resources

Employers provide career planning to meet both short- and long-term human resources needs. Changes in methods, the addition of new products/services, job vacancies, and changes in demand for a product/service may influence these needs.

Method Changes

A government agency changed its mainframe computer system for a modern one. The old system had been in place for ten years, so that computer center employees anticipated a change would be made. Nevertheless, phasing out the old system and implementing the new one required several career planning strategies. First, the new system required operator retraining. Some of the more senior personnel openly expressed doubts about their abilities to learn the new methods. In addition, the agency decided it was more cost-effective to do all programming in-house, so that a top priority was given to training and filling the programmer jobs that were created.

New Products/Services

Management of a package delivery firm decided to offer a new overnight delivery service to augment its regular service plans. Two key strategies, among several others, were necessary to make the new system work. First, package acceptance facilities were leased in central locations in metropolitan areas and personnel hired to staff them. In addition, small courier vans were purchased specifically for delivering overnight packages. Second, sales personnel were hired to call on potential large volume customers and sell the service. Prior to implementing the service, the company made a special effort to internally fill the new jobs created by the service. This included posting notices about the vacancies and discussing career opportunities with interested applicants.

Job Vacancies

To remain competitive, management in a large chemical manufacturing company determined that several thousand positions would have to be eliminated during a period of several years. The company decided the best way to reduce staff was by encouraging the early retirement of senior employees. To achieve this objective, the company substantially increased the retirement benefits of employees who elected to retire early. The number who actually accepted the retirement offer was far in excess of the planned reduction. The company immediately stepped up the career development plans of selected employees, so that they would be qualified to fill some of the vacancies, particularly those in which the need was most critical.

Some employee turnover events, such as premature deaths and resignations, are not predictable, but others, including persons who express an intention to retire, can be anticipated. In both conditions, career planning helps ensure qualified replacements are available.

Changes in Consumer Demand

Increases or decreases in consumer demand can occur unexpectedly or in a gradual and predictable fashion. For example, a cigarette manufacturer gradually reduced employment levels, due to a decrease in the demand for cigarettes. The reduction in the number of employees was carefully planned and handled through attrition. Also, career planning was used to retrain production employees interested in remaining with the company in other jobs.

Increases in product demand may prompt sudden increases in the demand for employees. Companies accustomed to these surges typically use career planning to have qualified employees available to meet the need.

Career Planning Focuses

Not all employees seek career changes or even changes in their job tasks. This explains why many employees are content to perform the same job throughout their working lives. For example, certain jobs, such as firefighters, police officers, teachers, clerks, truck drivers, and the bulk of the other jobs in the U.S., remain relatively unchanged. Most persons employed in them perform the same basic tasks until they eventually retire. In some industries, however, jobs do change. These changes may simply be adding or deleting tasks. In other situations, particularly where technology changes are frequent or competitive conditions fluctuate, such as the computer industry, many jobs change. Employees either must change with them by learning new skills or face the prospects of layoffs or job abolishment.

Employers use career planning to help employees adapt to these changes by providing them with opportunities in other jobs if they successfully meet the job qualifications. For career planning purposes, this group of employees could be called *steady state* employees, since they do not actively seek career changes.[2]

On the other hand, some employees want career changes. There are three subgroups in this group of employees, each of which has a different idea of what career advancement means. Some individuals see career advancement as a progression of successively higher level jobs within the same field. This group could be called *linear career* employees. Other people have career interests in moving to jobs in different occupations. This group could be called *spiral career*

[2] I. M.A. Von Glinow, M.J. Driver, K. Brousseau, and J. B. Prince, "The Design of a Career Oriented Human Resource System," *Academy of Management Review* 8 (January 1983), pp. 23-32.

employees. Finally, some individuals envision their careers as a series of moves among different organizations in which the occupations may be similar or different. The term *transitory career* employees could be used to describe the last subgroup.

Exhibit 34-1 contains information about the characteristics and career planning focuses for these four groups.

Exhibit 34-1
Characteristics and Career Planning Focuses
of Major Career Groups

Career Group	Major Characteristic	Career Planning Focus
Steady state	Status quo	Retraining
Linear	Progression	Career paths
Spiral	Multiple occupations	Succession planning and cross-training
Transition	Multiple employers/occupations	Outplacement and networking

Steady State Career

Steady state employees have career interests that emphasize increased competency in the existing job, recognition of the value of the tasks they perform, and continued employment. Career planning for this group should also focus on these three dimensions.

Job Competency

Job competency is acquired through HRD, such as on-the-job experience. For most steady state careerists, experience is the principal route to achieving job competency. However, there are other ways to accomplish this, such as job knowledge and psychomotor skills courses. Also, competency can be acquired through skills courses and through refresher training courses or journeyman level courses leading to a license, such as a master electrician's license.

Steady state careerists exist at all organizational levels ranging from laborers to managers. Steady state managers may originally have been in one of the other career groups but eventually were promoted to a level where they wanted to remain. Some critics argue that steady state managers should be targeted for demotions or outplacement because they are content to remain in their existing jobs. This reasoning falsely assumes that a person who does not want a promotion lacks career ambition or has insufficient on-the-job initiative or motivation. In sum, the thinking goes, a person who does not want to be promoted also lacks the qualifications to perform well in his or her existing job. This thinking is unfortunate because it assumes that all employees want to be promoted and fails to understand that employees have a range of career ambitions. For some, these ambitions simply consist of performing well in their existing jobs.

Recognition of Role Value

The steady state careerist values the idea of long and faithful tenure, typically in the same job. Some employers recognize this role value through non-pay awards, such as service pins and commendations. Pay incentives are also used, including bonuses and piece rate systems that reward top performers.

Maintain Employment

The steady state careerist is more job security-oriented than employees in other groups. This need is met through assisting them in remaining employed. Employers accomplish this through human resource planning in which future employment needs are determined. Where anticipated changes are imminent, action is taken.

Typically, the career planning will not involve any extraordinary programming unless conditions arise in which the prospects of job abolishment exist. When this occurs, the career planning consists of identifying the employee's career interests through such methods as assessment instruments and interviews. Usually, the employee's career interests are modest and can be met through retraining for a job similar to the one the person presently has. In these situations, career counseling is conducted in a private interview with each employee. Among the subjects discussed in these interviews include when the layoff or job abolishment is contemplated, what employment opportunities are available, and what retraining is needed. The interviewer also compares the employee's qualifications to the job specifications of the jobs in which the employee is interested. From this comparison, a HRD plan is prepared which explains what development is necessary, if any, to qualify the employee to perform the job. Usually this HRD planning includes a second interview after the employee contemplates his or her options.

During the initial interview, other options are also presented to the employee, such as early retirement and outplacement. Sometimes these are the only alternatives, particularly in situations in which no suitable vacancies exist or when an entire operation is closed. Both of these counseling subjects are covered in Chapter 20.

Linear Career

The linear careerist has career ambitions focusing on an orderly progression of promotions within an occupation. Exhibit 34-2 is an example of such a progression which is similar to one used for equipment maintenance jobs within a government agency.

Selection for Jobs

Exhibit 34-2
Career Progression of Equipment Maintenance Jobs

Electronic Technician II
Pay grade 11

↑

Electronic Technician I
Pay grade 9

↑

Maintenance Mechanic II
Pay grade 7

↑

Maintenance Mechanic I
Pay grade 5

↑

Junior Mechanic
Pay grade 4

↑

Mechanic Helper
Pay grade 3

↑
Start

Selections for jobs in a career progression are made in the same manner as any other selections; an applicant's qualifications are compared to the job specifications. Conceivably, this means a qualified applicant could enter the progression at any point. In reality, this is true for the lower-level jobs but may not apply to higher-level ones, particularly where organization-unique qualifications apply. For example, the Electronic Technician I and II jobs, shown in Exhibit 34-2 above, require the successful completion of special training courses offered by the agency. This training, conducted at the agency's technical training center, consists of several months of learning specifically directed to installing and maintaining electronic equipment used in the agency. To receive the training, an employee must first successfully complete some preliminary courses in several subjects, such as electricity and mathematics. In addition, applicants must have work experience in a job similar to either the Maintenance Mechanic I or II jobs.

Because of these and other job specifications, all applicants initially enter the career progression as either a junior mechanic or a mechanic helper. Career progressions exist for many occupations, such as finance, marketing, and human resources management.

Common Entry Point

Some progressions have common basic or entry-level jobs and branch to more specialized ones. An example of this progression is shown in Exhibit 34-3.

Exhibit 34-3 does not indicate any movements among the three specialized areas above the assistant level. In practice, some inter-specialist moves do occur, but the number is limited, since above the assistant level the technical knowledge requirements become quite specific. For example, incumbents in benefits jobs above the assistant level probably have commenced specialized or certification training in benefits. The same training activities may also be undertaken by incumbents employed above the assistant level in the HRD and employment areas.

Exhibit 34-3
Example of Career Progression in HRM With Common Entry-Level Jobs

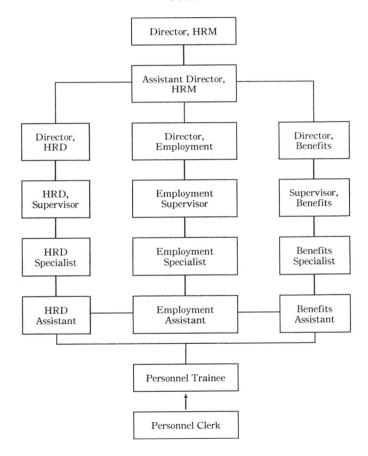

Knowledge/Skill Levels

Other versions of linear career progressions include the use of different knowledge or skill levels in the same generalist job. For example, a chemical manufacturer has one job, Production Operator, with five different pay levels. Employees employed in this job, and who know only the basic tasks, receive the first and lowest level of pay. Employees are moved into higher pay grades as they acquire the specified qualifications. Employees at the top pay level are qualified to perform all Production Operator tasks in the plant, and are paid the top pay rate regardless of which tasks they are scheduled to perform.

Some critics may question whether enlarged jobs, such as those described in the previous paragraph, offer employees a career progression. The response is a resounding, "Yes." For example, in one plant the job of machine repairman has been transformed, and the incumbents also perform tasks in pipe fitting, sheet metal work, and tool repair. In return for these additional tasks, employees receive higher pay. This *pay-for-knowledge* procedure gives employees a career progression in which they get paid for knowing how to perform more tasks. The concept has very broad applications. For example, one assembly line job classification in this plant combines the tasks performed by as many as 75 job classes found in other auto parts manufacturing facilities. Management benefits, since there is more flexibility in work scheduling. Workers also benefit because their pay is predicated upon the number of tasks they can perform. Pay for knowledge is also covered in Chapter 30.

Spiral Career

The employee who envisions his or her career as a movement among different occupations faces some tough obstacles, particularly in moving to production management positions from functional areas, including human resources management and marketing. These obstacles include:

- A bias that some production management personnel have toward functional specialists. Also, functional specialists tend to quickly become labeled as a finance person or a marketing person, and it is difficult to rid oneself of this label.

- Difficulty in learning the subject matter in diverse fields. For example, an HRD Director would require an extensive learning period to become technically knowledgeable as a Marketing Director. Furthermore, this knowledge gap has become more universal because the functional areas have become more complex.

In spite of these obstacles, career changes among different functional areas can be accomplished, particularly at the less-specialized lower pay levels and at the managerial levels where job tasks are more managerial and less technical. In addition, changes are much more feasible within a function, such as moving from a director of employee benefits to a director of compensation. These changes are more feasible because there is a much greater degree of knowledge transfer among jobs.

Career Strategies

Since most spiral career moves exist among managerial levels, employers can provide career opportunities through several strategies.

Succession planning. One of these strategies is developing a succession plan for replacing personnel at the highest management levels. In succession planning, selected candidates are rotated through a series of management assignments in different organizational functions. These assignments are specially selected to meet each manager's developmental needs.

Management trainee/executive intern jobs. To a limited extent, management trainee programs prepare persons for a variety of future jobs. This preparation also entails rotational assignments in various organizational functions. The level of the assignments differ from those in succession planning, since management trainees perform at a lower organizational level. However, so-called "fast track" executive intern programs involve progressively more responsible jobs.

Usually applicants for these programs are recruited from among MBA graduates. The distinguishing features of the programs are a relatively long development period, rapid progression, and a variety of assignments. The programs typically last three or four years. The programs have high rewards because employees generally are promoted rapidly; some programs even guarantee a job at a fairly high level to those who successfully finish. On the other hand, the demands are great, due to assignments in progressively more demanding jobs. This feature is one in which executive intern programs, sometimes called management associate programs, differ from management trainee jobs. Executive interns are assigned to vacant jobs and are appraised in their performance of the job tasks. Management trainees, however, usually are assigned project work, although sometimes they are placed in vacant jobs. These placements are typically at lower and less demanding jobs. The executive intern is under considerable pressure to learn quickly and perform exceptionally well in a variety of assignments.

Transition Career

Some employees see their careers as movements among different organizations in either the same or different occupations. This occurs frequently within functional areas, such as HRM and among top-level managers. It is not uncommon, for example, to find HRM specialists who have worked in HRM jobs in several different organizations. Typically, these moves are motivated by promotions and pay increases.

There are various resources to help employees who seek interorganizational job changes, such as professional organizations and employment agencies. Most professional organizations maintain some form of membership employment services. The Society for Human Resource Management, for example, provides job information for its members.

Employer assistance. Employers do not have an obligation to assist the transition careerist who is seeking external employment opportunities. Some employers view such job hunting as a form of disloyalty; a few employers take reprisals against any employee who is found either seeking outside employment or helping others find such employment. These attitudes are regrettable because they cause hard feelings, result in employees secretly arranging outside interviews, and can cause unfair actions against employees merely because of suspicions. Furthermore, it is doubtful that this philosophy ever deterred an employee from seeking a job with another employer if he or she was really earnest about it.

The more enlightened view today is to help transition careerists find jobs with other employers if they seek such help. The spirit motivating this assistance is based on the belief that employees can find jobs that better match their needs and qualifications. Employers with this view take an active role in helping employees find the jobs they desire, even if it means looking outside the firm. The method used most frequently in such cases is outplacement assistance. For example, one bank uses both internal placements and external outplacement as an essential part of its career planning process. Outplacement counseling is covered in Chapter 20.

Employer Career Planning Responsibilities

Exhibit 34-4 reflects the major responsibilities employers have for assisting employees in career planning.

Exhibit 34-4
Employer and Employee Responsibilities for Career Planning

Employer	Employee
Assess interests	Assess interests
Define opportunities	Select target jobs
Evaluate qualifications	Become qualified
Prepare development plan	Perform well
Aid development	Periodic feedback
Review progress	Compete for vacancies
Provide career opportunities	

Assess Interests

Employers should help employees assess their career interests. This step is unnecessary when employees are aware of what their interests are. In other cases, a formal assessment of interests is beneficial. Among the methods used in helping employees conduct self-assessments are workshops, career planning classes, workbooks, and scored instruments.

Workshops

One- or two-day workshops are among the most effective ways to involve employees in career planning. Workshops typically include activities that permit employees to see various dimensions of themselves through self-assessment instruments, feedback from workshop leaders, and discussions with the leaders and fellow participants. Among the subjects covered in career planning workshops are:

- Defining work and non-work values;

- Organizational culture, including values and norms;

- Exploring the organizational and employee commitments to career planning;

- Relating the ramifications of life stages to career decisions, particularly for the midlife careerist;

- Defining the personal skills needed for successful career self-management; and
- Career goal-setting and strategy formulation.

Planning Classes

Career planning classes are more intensive than workshops because they usually last several weeks and cover a broader variety of topics. For example, some courses are eight weeks in length and cover such subjects as work and non-work values, interests, attitudes, and personality characteristics. The methods used to obtain this information include self-assessment instruments, such as the *Strong-Campbell Interest Inventory* and the *Myers-Briggs Type Indicator,* homework assignments, creative exercises using fantasy situations, group experiential exercises, and class discussions. The final four weeks are devoted to formulating career strategies directed toward goal accomplishment, improving administrative abilities, such as decision-making, and learning techniques to secure employment.

Workbooks

There are both organization-specific and general workbooks. The organization-specific ones are specially developed to assist employees in formulating their career plans within a company. General workbooks help employees identify a career either within or outside their present employer.

Scored Instruments

As noted above, scored instruments are used in conjunction with career planning workshops and career planning classes. In addition, many career planning counselors use these instruments for various purposes, such as to help employees identify their career interests and understand their personal values.

Define Opportunities

Management should designate someone to be responsible for career planning. Generally, even large organizations do not have sufficient career planning activities to warrant a full-time person. For example, in one organization with 5,000 employees, career planning tasks were easily accomplished as an additional responsibility by a Personnel Assistant. Career planning tasks could be assigned to someone in either the HRD or in the employment function, although the latter is probably preferable because employment HR personnel deal on a daily basis with job descriptions and employment matters, such as recruitment and selection. Also, these specialists have experience in comparing applicant qualifications to job specifications. Employment specialists also are in frequent touch with their counterparts in other organizations, so they have general knowledge about current information in external job markets. Finally, employment personnel have the expertise, skills, and experience in interviewing and communicating with people about employment matters.

Make Announcement

Generally, when an employer starts a career planning program, an announcement is circulated. This notice instructs employees how to enroll in the program and the name of the counselor. Interested employees are invited to contact the counselor and arrange an interview.

Career Planning Interview

Early in the career planning interview, the counselor should stress any developmental activities that the employee pursues are voluntary and that *potential* career opportunities are not employment promises or commitments. The counselor can relate past case examples of employees who obtained their employment objectives through the career planning program, however, promising or making employment commitments may cause disappointments. There are several reasons commitments cannot be made, such as anticipated vacancies may not result according to plan. Also, employees generally compete for vacant jobs and there may be occasions when several employees, all of whom are enrolled in the organization's career planning program, will be competing for a position that was either newly created or recently vacated. Also, position planning is usually not precise enough to make commitments. Finally, the employee should be told that the bulk of the career planning efforts are on the employee and unless the employee obtains the training, education, experience, and other qualifications, he or she cannot attain vocational targets.

Career Assessment

Next, the career assessment begins. The counselor may schedule the employee to attend a career planning workshop or simply have him or her complete a career planning workbook or a career measurement instrument, such as the *Strong-Campbell Interest Inventory*. This step may be skipped if an employee is firmly convinced of his or her career path.

Job Opportunities

Once the assessment phase is completed, the employee's career interests are compared to job opportunities within the firm. Job opportunity projections are based upon human resource planning forecasts, which include estimates of product/service demands, anticipated human resources needs, and supplies. Chapter 3 discusses several methods used to make projections of anticipated human resources needs. Sometimes there may be anticipated opportunities in several fields in which an employee is interested. This should not be surprising, since people tend to have aptitudes in several areas. Employees can compare their preferences to the relative probabilities for employment in different areas.

Evaluate Qualifications

After an employee has determined his or her career interests and compared them to employment opportunities that may exist in the organization, the next step is to select some employment objectives. At this stage, the counselor obtains a complete summary of the employee's qualifications, so that they can be compared with the job specifications. This analysis is easily done for certain types of qualifications, such as education, training, and experience, but it is more difficult for knowledge, skills, and abilities.

Of these three, knowledge can be measured most readily, provided a knowledge test or some other quantifiable measure of knowledge is used. In the absence of such a measure, an employee's knowledge must be determined by following a miniature version of a selection method, such as an interview or a job simulation test. Skills and abilities may also be difficult to measure unless they involve a psychomotor skill or an ability, such as typing or written communication skills. Some organizations use assessment centers to determine employee's skills and abilities and to identify their developmental needs. Assessment centers are discussed in Chapter 16.

Prepare a Development Plan

A development plan is designed individually for each employee, since it is derived from a comparison of qualifications with career objectives. Exhibit 34-5 is an example of a worksheet that can be used for this purpose. The worksheet includes the employee's plans to acquire any qualifications he or she lacks. The employee is advised where or how these qualifications can be obtained and is assisted in formulating realistic plans.

Exhibit 34-5
Sample Career Development Worksheet

Career Development Worksheet for	_____	_____
	(Employee name)	(Position sought)

INSTRUCTIONS: Complete the worksheet by listing the job specifications for the position sought. Place the employee's qualifications and the qualifications that must be acquired. Suggest alternatives where the needed qualifications can be obtained and list the employee's plans to acquire them.

Job Specifications	Employee Qualifications	Qualifications Needed	Plan(s) to Acquire

Performance Counseling

Counseling at this stage includes reviewing the results of the employee's formal performance appraisals. Any performance deficiencies are noted and the employee is advised of the importance of correcting them and meeting job performance requirements. The employee is told that other employees are also pursuing career development plans and that he or she can expect considerable competition for any vacancies that occur. Consequently, an employee's record of job performance generally must be very good in such performance variables as productivity and work quality. In addition, the employee must have an exemplary record in variables, including attendance, conduct, and safety. Employees readily answer "yes" to this question, "If you were the boss, wouldn't you promote the employee with the best work record, particularly with regard to attendance and conduct, if the other qualifications of applicants were about equivalent?" This question sets the stage to ask the employee about personal job performance and discuss what actions he or she intends to take to correct any deficiencies.

Excellent results can be attained with this approach in helping employees achieve their career objectives. Employees should be frankly advised that there is no chance of advancement until their job performance is exemplary. Career counseling should also include giving employees suggestions about how to improve their performance, encompassing frank discussions with their supervisor, admitting past shortcomings, explaining their interest in career planning, and stating the actions they intended to take to improve their performance.

This career counseling approach has excellent by-product benefits for both the employee and the organization. The employee begins to see his or her job as a potential means to a desired career goal. Also, employees experience a self-renewal as they apply themselves more diligently in their existing jobs. Employees also see changes in their supervisors' attitudes towards them. The organization benefits from the employees' improved job performance.

Aid Career Development

The organization aids career development in many ways, including providing training opportunities. Some employers either partially or fully reimburse employees for educational and training expenses. Employers also may need to accommodate employee requests for shift changes, so that the employee can attend classes. Employers can help employees obtain the experience they lack by providing them with opportunities for special assignments. For example, one employer lists the names of those employees seeking career changes and uses them to make assignments when a job is temporarily vacant when the incumbent is out sick or on vacation.

Review Progress

When a development plan is prepared, progress review dates are set by the employee. At the progress review interviews employees inform the counselor about their progress. The counselor compares the progress with planned accomplishments and uses praise to reinforce the employee's efforts. Notations are made as milestones are achieved, such as completing a required course. Any adjustments in planned accomplishments are also made in these review sessions.

The employee's job performance is also discussed, including significant achievements and any problems. Any observable trends are discussed, such as gradual productivity improvements. If the employee had any recorded instances of unsatisfactory past performance, the employee explains what corrective actions have been taken. Employees are commended for improvements and encouraged to continue their efforts. These performance review and feedback sessions are often very fulfilling experiences for both employees and the counselor. For this reason, career planning, when conducted along the lines of the procedures discussed here, can be one of the most rewarding activities in HRM.

The review sessions also include discussions about anticipated vacancies in jobs the employee has targeted for career advancement.

Provide Career Opportunities

Career planning is a futile exercise if it does not produce some tangible results for employees. Employees undertake career planning with the knowledge that career opportunities are not promised and must be earned. They also are candidly informed about the realistic prospects of advancement. However, employees must see some results, either in their own promotions and assignments or those of other employees. In sum, there must be some success stories.

Employers can help provide career opportunities through using internal recruitment methods to fill jobs. Some employers give first preference to qualified in-house personnel before commencing external recruitment. Posting and application procedures are the most effective ways of filling vacancies internally. These procedures are explained in Chapter 15. Employers also help employees find career opportunities by providing outplacement assistance. This assistance is either provided by internal personnel or it is performed by outplacement consultants retained by the firm.

One HRM director was criticized by his boss for expending corporate resources in outplacing employees. The director's response to the criticism was, "Look, we have more employees enrolled in our career planning program than we can provide jobs for. Helping employees get ahead is good for employee morale and it actually increases the number of employees who want to enter our program because they know we won't stand in their way of getting ahead. Furthermore, they know we will help them when we can." Outplacement purposes and methods are discussed in Chapter 20.

Dual Career Ladders

The potential loss of talented employees is a challenge facing many organizations in which technology is ever-changing. This potential problem is especially prevalent among employees in technical, professional and scientific fields who possess considerable knowledge and experience but are stymied by a lack of career opportunities within an organization. These employees may be motivated to seek employment in the market, to pursue management opportunities or to gain more knowledge within their respective fields. A *dual-career ladder,* sometimes also called a *dual-career track,* is an arrangement in which employees, who typically are employed in professional, technical or scientific fields, are given the opportunity of pursuing their careers either within their field (profession, technology or science) or through management jobs. The purpose of the arrangement is to motivate highly qualified employees to remain with the firm, in lieu of seeking career opportunities elsewhere. Employees who elect not to pursue management tracks are given the opportunity of acquiring more specialized knowledge within their fields. Conversely, management opportunities are made available to those employees choosing to pursue careers as managers. The opportunities in both career ladders are accompanied by commensurate increases in monetary rewards and job challenge and satisfaction.

Generally, dual-career ladders are successful. One survey found that approximately 90 percent of respondent firms used dual-career ladders. The respondents indicated that the major reason for establishing such arrangements was to retain the best employees. Most employers were satisfied with dual-career ladders, but about 13 percent of the respondents indicated the arrangements did not meet desired objectives, typically because responsibilities on the non-managerial tracks were not clearly defined. The respondents also indicated the dual-career ladders had either three or four levels, and the costs of the dual-career ladder were about the same as a single ladder.[3]

Employee Career Planning Responsibilities

Exhibit 34-4 shows the six major responsibilities employees have for their career development. As stated above, employees are primarily responsible for their own development. The employer can provide career planning counseling and career opportunities, but in the final analysis, employees must accept personal responsibility for planning their own careers and engaging in the necessary development activities.

Assess Interests

Self-assessments may require employees to enroll in workshops and/or complete assessment instruments to identify their interests, values, and needs. This means employees must expend the time and have the initiative to engage in these activities.

Select Target Jobs

Employees must be realistic in selecting target jobs. For example, an employee may want to be Vice President, Planning, but he or she must realize to achieve that goal requires obtaining a college degree and acquiring the requisite experience. A more realistic approach would be first to aim for more immediate occupational objectives, with the ultimate goal of becoming a Vice President. Some employees are unable to select specific targets; consequently, they make half-hearted attempts at many career development activities and never finish any of them. The career planning counselor can help provide guidance, but the ultimate decision is the employee's.

Become Qualified

The tough part of career planning is implementing the plan, since it requires considerable personal sacrifices by the employee. The best advice early in career planning is to inform employees that "To get something, you must give up something." Often, employees decide the *potential* rewards are not worth the investment. Among the sacrifices employees may have to make are paying tuition fees and buying books for required college classes and technical school courses. Also, time is required to attend class and study homework assignments. Employees may also have to make changes in their work routines, shifts, and days off to meet class schedules. Many of these changes will affect their personal lives. For example, family members must be understanding when an employee has to study or fulfill other career development commitments, such as attending class.

Sometimes career development plans may require the employee to accept different work assignments or to accept additional responsibilities to acquire needed experience. Most employees do not realize that a promotion is accompa-

---

[3] CCH Human Resources Management, *Personnel Practices*, ¶1173.

nied not only by compensation increases, but also by added task responsibilities. For example, a promotion may result in a 10 percent increase in pay but, also, a 100 percent increase in job responsibilities.

In spite of the many obstacles, sacrifices, and personal commitments, career development can be a very rewarding experience for those employees who will persevere long enough to reap the satisfaction of scoring well on a test or completing a new job task. Some employees become discouraged when they fail to see immediate improvements or quick promotions. These employees should be persuaded to give their developmental activities sufficient time and effort to show results.

Perform Well

Employees also have the responsibility to perform well on their current jobs. For the marginal or poor performer, this means turning over a new leaf. Some employees want a promotion or other career opportunity without having to work for it. As noted above, these individuals must be frankly told such aspirations are unrealistic. In these cases, career planning can be the instrument that motivates employees to begin paying attention to their jobs and making improvements in their job performance.

Periodic Feedback

Here, feedback means interviews in which employees report their progress to the career planning counselor. Feedback sessions give employees an opportunity to show what they have accomplished towards their career objectives. These sessions also can be used to reassess employees' targets. Progress reports give the career counselor an opportunity to reinforce employees' progress and to determine whether their vocational goals are realistic. These feedback sessions give employees the chance to demonstrate their motivation and initiative to independently pursue career objectives.

The information given to the counselor includes grades achieved in college or vocational courses, completion of programmed instruction materials or correspondence courses, and work accomplishments in details or special assignments.

Compete for Vacancies

As noted previously, employees are not promised promotions when they enroll in a career planning program. Consequently, they must compete with other employees for vacancies. Sometimes this causes disappointments for employees who, despite their diligent pursuit of career development objectives, are not selected for vacant jobs. This is unfortunate and may make the career counselor unhappy. However, the counselor must reassure the disappointed employee to continue trying. The counselor should offer encouragement and inspiration and remind the employee that it is seldom easy to achieve worthwhile goals.

Career Planning Software Applications

There are a number of software programs to help the HRM professional in career planning. Some of these programs are closely related to human resource planning because of the strong relationship between the two activities.

Transition Probability Matrix

The Transition Probability Matrices, shown in Chapter 3, track career movements among related jobs. This information is used for several career planning purposes, such as analyzing retention and exit rates and EEO/AA planning.

Retention/Exit Rate Analysis

Transition probabilities, based upon recent human resource movements, are used to determine in which jobs vacancies are anticipated. This report also shows which jobs have low exit rates. This information is used in advising employees about the expected future opportunities in different jobs. When the opportunity is limited in a particular job, an employee may want to pursue another occupational goal. Exhibit 34-6 is a human resource planning report projecting for three years the expected hiring for selected jobs.

Exhibit 34-6
Example of Human Resources Planning Projections
and Career Planning Readiness for Selected Jobs

Job	Expected Hiring				Readiness of Employees in Career Planning Program			
	1 year	2 year	3 year	Now	1 year	2 year	3 year	Now
Accounting Assistant	11	17	30	15	19	24	38	11
Buyer	12	27	36	8	11	31	42	7
Financial Analyst	8	14	27	4	10	13	13	5
HR Coordinator	10	16	29	7	9	9	9	4
Maintenance Technician	18	31	54	11	27	41	44	10
Marketing Manager	8	19	31	2	5	11	14	6
Sales Trainee	43	91	142	33	38	71	67	28
Technical Representative	2	3	5	0	1	3	4	2

The expected hiring information is obtained from projections of past hiring, the anticipated demand for various jobs, and projections of separations. Estimations of the readiness of employees enrolled in career planning programs are based upon the information counselors receive in follow-up career planning interviews in which employees relate their accomplishments toward career objectives, such as the courses they have completed and the experience they obtained. The counselor updates the career planning database using information furnished in these follow-up interviews.

The career counselor uses the information in Exhibit 34-4 to guide employees in their career planning decisions. Based upon this information, employees may change their career plans. For example, a clerical employee who is interested in becoming an accounting assistant may decide to select another target job when he or she realizes there are more employees pursuing that job than there are anticipated vacancies during each of the next three years. Conversely, the employee may decide to continue with his or her career plan, and take a chance he or she will be selected over other applicants. The decision is up to the employee, and furnishing dependable information, obtained through dynamic human resource information systems, helps the employee make the best decision based upon current job information.

Diversity Planning

Transition planning includes an analysis of the effects of career moves upon organizational diversity planning. For example, the computer-generated transition matrix information shown in Chapter 3 can be reported by employees' race, age, and sex to show any changes and/or trends in the composition of employees grouped by one or more of these variables. In addition, this information can be combined with the records of employees in various stages of career development and projections can be made of anticipated staffing levels by group. These projections can be compared with past records to determine trends. Exhibit 34-7 is an example of a computer-generated staffing report incorporating this information.

Exhibit 34-7
Actual and Projected Staffing, by Sex

Job	Actual					Expected Separations								Career Planning Readiness								Projected Staffing					
	Last year		Present year		This year		Year 1		Year 2		Year 3		This year		Year 1		Year 2		Year 3		Year 1		Year 2		Year 3	
	M	F	M	F	M	F	M	F	M	F	M	F	M	F	M	F	M	F	M	F	M	F	M	F	M	F

Employee Career Development Progress

Human resource information systems are used in career planning to record employee development needs and to track employee accomplishments toward meeting those needs. An example of a report format with this information is shown in Exhibit 34-8. This information could be recorded on manual records but it is much more readily done on a computer, and the information can be used to compile other reports, such as projected employment levels.

Exhibit 34-8
Career Development Report

Career Development Plan	*Mary Doe*	*Maintenance Specialist*
	(Employee Name)	(Target Job)
Development Needed	**Development Source/Method**	**Action/Progress**
Aptitude Test	not applicable	Passed 4/25
Basic Mechanics Course	Correspondence Course No. 21A	Completed 8/21
Basic Electricity Course	Correspondence Course No. 21D	Completed 10/22
Basic Carpentry Course	Correspondence Course No. 21G	Completed 11/15
Power Tool Safety Course	Power Tool Course Midland Vocational Tech	Enrolled and attending class
Heating, Ventilating and Air Conditioning Systems (HVAC)	Maintaining HVAC Systems Midland Vocational Tech	Scheduled for Spring Semester
Six months experience as Maintenance Assistant	On-the-job training	In progress

CHAPTER 35
LABOR RELATIONS

Chapter Highlights
- Review a history of the labor movement
- Discuss the major laws affecting labor relations
- Examine the process of union recognition and decertification
- Review trends in union membersihp in the public and private sectors

Introduction

A *union* is an organization of employees who have some common interests, such as collectively bargaining with their employer over the terms and conditions of employment in such matters as pay, benefits, job security, safety, and health. While the term union is used in this book, most laws affecting unions call them labor organizations and do not use the word "union." This is the reason the term *labor relations* is generally used to refer to the HRM activity involving unions. In this book, union is used interchangeably with labor organization.

Labor relations is the human resources management activity concerned with union recognition and collective bargaining with labor organizations.

History of the AFL and the CIO

The American Federation of Labor

The American Federation of Labor (AFL) was organized in 1886 as a loose association of autonomous national labor unions. Samuel Gompers was the first president and served until his death in 1924. Gompers defined the following basic tenets of the AFL:

1. The organization of union workers along craft lines;
2. The confinement of union activities to economic issues instead of political ones; and
3. National union autonomy.

These tenets were formed because of the unsatisfactory experiences of other national level unionization efforts, most notably the Knights of Labor (Knights). The Knights was a labor organization composed of both skilled and unskilled members with the purpose of converting the U.S. economic system into cooperatives owned by employees. Gompers realized that the Knights failed because they organized all types of workers, skilled and unskilled, and this caused continual internal dissention as the various factions competed for power. Gompers correctly saw that members could be unified more readily when membership was restricted to distinct crafts.

In addition, Gompers saw that the political ambitions of unionists, particularly among groups dominated by the communists, provided a convenient target for employer groups opposed to unionism. These employer groups used the unionists' political and social reform ambitions to turn public opinion against unionism. In short, unionists were seen as radicals who wanted to overthrow the political and social systems of the U.S. Gompers saw that these strategies were self-defeating, so he wanted no part of political unionism. Instead, he argued the job of unions was economic only, that is wages and working conditions. These "bread and butter" issues were the early hallmarks of the AFL. Finally, Gompers could secure cooperation from the powerful national unions by assuring them autonomy in running their internal affairs.

While Gompers' philosophies, and those of his followers, were appropriate until the early 20th century, they became less relevant as the U.S. increasingly industrialized and vast numbers of semiskilled workers remained unorganized.

The Congress of Industrial Organizations

The three basic tenets of unionism, as defined by Gompers, guided organizing efforts until 1938 when the Congress of Industrial Organizations (CIO) was formed by 30 unions that were expelled from the AFL. The major cause of the split was a disagreement over craft versus industrial unionism. Advocates of industrial unionism, such as John L. Lewis of the United Mine Workers, wanted single unions composed of all workers within an industry, regardless of the craft. Craft union advocates, on the other hand, wanted the workers in each industry divided among the crafts depending upon the work they did. Thus, carpenters in an industry would belong to the carpenters' union, machinists to the machinists' union, and so on. Industrial union leaders were naturally opposed to splitting their unions into various crafts. Both sides were adamant and when efforts to reach a compromise failed, the AFL expelled the industrial unionists.

The CIO organizing campaigns were extremely successful and the membership rolls dramatically increased. From 1938 to 1955, the AFL and the CIO went their independent ways. Gradually, however, as new leaders, such as George Meany in the AFL and Walter Reuther in the CIO, assumed dominant roles within their organizations, talks began in 1953 to unite the two groups. The merger was consummated in December 1955 with an understanding that organizations of both craft and industrial workers were appropriate.

Structure of the AFL-CIO

The American Federation of Labor and Congress of Industrial Organizations, commonly known as the AFL-CIO, is an organization composed of 68 unions, representing more than 13 million of the 16 million union members in the U.S.

Union Structure

Unions are often structured by the type of work the members do. Two of the principal organizational structures of unions are the national union and the local.

Type of Work

The three general types of work in which unions exist are crafts, industrial work, and white collar work.

Craft unions are composed of members within a skill or trade, such as electricians or carpenters.

Industrial unions generally represent all the employees within a specific industry, such as the United Auto Workers (UAW) union that represents auto workers.

So-called *white-collar* unions are those concerned with such groups as teachers and clerical and administrative employees. The American Federation of Teachers (AFT) is an example of a white collar union. White collar unions have less of a common interest than either craft or industrial unions. The reason for their diversity is because of the range of interests the unions serve.

National Unions

National unions form the real nucleus of unionism in the United States. National unions that are members of the AFL-CIO are, nevertheless, independent from it. These unions are autonomous in all their internal affairs, such as conducting their conventions, electing officers, setting dues, making assessments upon locals and members, and setting salaries for their officers.

All national unions are not members of the AFL-CIO. For example, the United Mine Workers and the International Brotherhood of Longshoremen are not affiliated with the AFL-CIO. The membership in these unions ranges from less than 1,000 members, for the American Radio Association, to more than one million members for the Teamsters.

National unions provide various services for their locals, such as helping them in conducting local collective bargaining and helping them administer their finances. In return for these services, national unions exercise considerable authority over local unions in various matters. Examples of this control are national office approval before a strike occurs or national office agreement to the terms of a collective bargaining agreement before it can be accepted by the local representatives.

Local Unions

Locals are typically operated on the basis of a single unit or a craft. For example, all the assembly auto workers at the General Motors plant in Doraville, Georgia, belong to the same local of the United Auto Workers. Craft locals, such as the carpenters, cover a geographical area so they include carpenters who are employed by a number of employers. Some employers have employees who are represented by several different unions. For example, the Atlanta, Georgia, post office has one union representing the letter carriers, another one that represents clerks, and a third one representing rural letter carriers.

Management Structure

Locals have their own management structure. Typical jobs may include business agent, president, vice-president, treasurer, chief steward, and steward.

A *business agent* is a full-time paid employee who manages the affairs of the local office. This job exists more frequently among craft unions. Most white-collar unions use the title of *president* instead of business agent. The president may be either a part- or full-time position, depending upon the size of the local. In smaller locals, the president is unpaid and is reimbursed for any expenses incurred such as using a personal auto on union business. Vice-president positions are usually used to groom a candidate for presidency. *Stewards* handle any grievances that arise. The *chief steward* is generally a senior steward who has shown competence in resolving grievances in the union's favor.

There are some promotional opportunities for union officials. For example, a local officer might aspire to be a full-time employee of the national union. Some unions, such as the National Rural Letter Carriers Association, have a sequence of positions through which union representatives typically progress to reach national jobs. This progression helps ensure a union representative is properly prepared for national leadership.

Most local union representatives, excluding the business agent, are typically unpaid and spend a considerable amount of their personal time on union business. The motivations for this service vary; some individuals do it for the pleasure of helping their co-workers, others for the power it gives them, and still others have ambitions of becoming a national figure.

Initiation Fees and Dues

Union members pay initiation fees and dues to belong to a union. An *initiation fee* is a one-time expense for becoming a union member. The fee is intended to cover the administrative costs of memberships. *Dues* are periodic payments, usually monthly, that each member pays to support the union. Besides paying for the expenses of the local, part of the dues is sent to the national office. The national office in turn sends some monies to the AFL-CIO in the form of a per capita tax on each member of an affiliated union.

Labor Relations Law

Labor relations laws are complex because of distinctions in the application of the laws, exceptions to them, and judicial interpretations of various provisions. Adding to the problem is the relationship between federal and state laws. Generally, federal laws have precedence over parallel state laws, but there are situations where state laws either compliment or supplant federal law. For example, Section 14(b) of the National Labor Relations Act gives states the power to pass and implement so-called "right-to-work" laws that diminish union security by giving employees the right to choose whether they will join a union representing their employer's workforce. "Right-to-work" laws are covered later in this chapter. Also, states have extended labor relations laws to groups of employees not covered by federal law. For example, California has a law giving agricultural employees labor relations rights, and about 35 states have passed laws governing labor relations matters for public employees.

Generally, differing federal labor laws apply to these broad categories of employees:

- Most private sector employees, except those employed by rail and air carriers;
- Air and rail carrier employees;
- Most categories of federal government employees, except those in U.S. Postal Service; and
- Employees of the U.S. Postal Service.

Employees in the first category are covered by the National Labor Relations Act, the Labor-Management Relations Act, and the Labor-Management Reporting and Disclosure Act. Air and rail carrier employees are covered under the Railway Labor Act and the Labor-Management Reporting and Disclosure Act. Federal government employees, exclusive of those in the U.S. Postal Service, have union recognition and collective bargaining rights under Title VII of the Civil Service Reform Act. Finally, U.S. Postal Service employees have their labor relations rights defined in the National Labor Relations Act and the Postal Reorganization Act of 1970, and the Labor-Management Reporting and Disclosure Act applies to them, as well.

State and local public employees are not covered by federal labor relations laws. As mentioned above, however, most states have laws providing such rights to state and local public employees.

National Labor Relations Act of 1935

The National Labor Relations Act (NLRA) of 1935 was amended by the Labor-Management Relations (Taft-Hartley) Act of 1947 (LMRA) and the Labor-Management Reporting and Disclosure (Landrum-Griffin) Act of 1959 (LMRDA). It is important to remember that both the LMRA and LMRDA contain provisions *in addition* to those amending the NLRA.

Employers Covered by the NLRA

These are the revenue requirements for some groups of employers covered by the NLRA:

- Retail businesses with $500,000 gross volume of business;
- Non-retail businesses in general with $50,000 in goods or services either sent outside the state or received from outside the state, either (a) directly to or from someone outside the state, or (b) indirectly through someone inside the employer's state;
- Office buildings with $100,000 gross revenue, of which $25,000 comes from organizations on this list (the National Labor Relations Board [NLRB] does not count a non-retail business unless its inflow or outflow is $50,000 directly to or from an out-of-state source);
- Colleges and universities with $1,000,000 gross revenue for operating expenses of private, nonprofit colleges and universities;
- Employers who deal with other employers above and have $50,000 in goods or services provided to employers on this list (the NLRB does not count goods and services supplied to a non-retail business unless its inflow or outflow is $50,000 directly to or from an out-of-state source);

- Hotels and motels with $500,000 gross revenue (does not include motels and hotels that get 75 percent or more of their income from guests staying longer than one month, or whose rooms are 75 percent or more occupied by guests staying more than one month);
- Hospitals with $250,000 gross annual revenue; $100,000 gross annual revenue for nursing homes and visiting nurses associations; $250,000 revenue for child care centers; and other health care institutions;
- Law firms with $250,000 gross volume;
- Newspapers and communications systems with $100,000 gross volume for television and radio stations, telegraph, and telephone companies; $200,000 gross volume for newspapers (newspaper must also carry news purchased from an interstate service, nationally syndicated features, or advertising of nationally sold products);
- Public utilities with $250,000 gross volume, or non-retail standard (above);
- Residential, cooperative, or condominium apartments with $500,000 gross volume;
- Transit systems with $250,000 gross volume (except taxicabs, which come under the $500,000 retail test); and
- Associations; national defense involvement; and businesses in Washington, D.C. For purposes of deciding whether to assert jurisdiction, the NLRB will treat an association as an individual employer, and apply an appropriate test from this list. The Board will assert jurisdiction over any national defense contractor or subcontractor that has a "substantial impact" on national defense. The Board will assert jurisdiction over any private sector employer in Washington, D.C., regardless of size.[1]

Employers Not Covered by the NLRA

There are also some categories of employers and employees that are not covered by the NLRA:

1. The U.S. Government, including employees of private contractors employed under a federal contract and for labor relations purposes are under the federal government;

2. Federal Reserve Banks;

3. State and local governments, including employees of private contractors employed under a contract to these governments, if the governments are in charge of labor relations;

4. Businesses, such as airlines and railroads, covered by the Railway Labor Act; and

5. Labor unions, except in their capacities as employers.

---

[1] For a full listing and discussion of employers covered by the National Labor Relations Act, see National Labor Relations Board, *An Outline of Law and Procedure in Representation Cases.*

Employees Not Covered by the NLRA

These groups of employees are specifically excluded from the Act:

1. Agricultural laborers;

2. Domestic workers employed in private homes;

3. Any individual employed by a parent or spouse;

4. Independent contractors;

5. Supervisors; and,

6. Any person employed by an employer subject to the Railway Labor Act.

National Labor Relations Board

The NLRA provides for a National Labor Relations Board (NLRB) to oversee implementation of the Act. The NLRB is composed of five members selected by the President and who are responsible for implementing the Act. These are the principal functions of the NLRB:

1. The prevention of statutorily defined unfair labor practices by employers and labor organizations or their agents;

2. The conduct of secret ballot elections among employees in *appropriate* collective bargaining units to determine whether or not they want to be represented by a labor organization. The subject of appropriate bargaining units is covered in Chapter 36;

3. The conduct of secret ballot elections among employees represented by a union, when those employees show they want union representation to be revoked;

4. The resolution of jurisdictional disputes among various groups of employees concerning which group shall be assigned the work in dispute; and

5. The conduct of secret ballot elections among employees in situations involving a national emergency.

Rights of Employees

These are some principal rights the NLRA gives to employees:

1. Right to self-organize;

2. Right to form, join, or assist unions;

3. Right to bargain collectively through representatives of their own choosing;

4. Right to engage in other concerted activities for the purpose of collective bargaining or other mutual aid or protection. Rights to engage in concerted activity also extends to nonunion employees. To be covered, however, two or more employees need to act in concert. For example, assume two employees are unhappy about their employer's changing their work schedules and present the dissatisfaction to the employer. If the employer refuses to meet and then discharges them, the employer's actions are in violation of Section 7 of the NLRA. The Act grants all

employees (both union and nonunion) the right to act in concert and forbids employers from retaliating against employees who exercise those rights[2] ; and

5. Right to refrain from any or all such activities, except to the extent that such right may be affected by an agreement requiring membership in a labor organization as a condition of employment.

The right, shown in #5, above, is amended by Section 14(b) of the NLRA, which states employees will not be required to join a union as a condition of employment in any state or territory in which such a requirement is prohibited by law. Section 14(b) applies to so-called right-to-work laws. These are the 23 states with such laws:

Alabama, Arizona, Arkansas, Florida, Georgia, Idaho, Iowa, Kansas, Louisiana, Mississippi, Nebraska, Nevada, New York, North Carolina, North Dakota, Oklahoma, South Carolina, South Dakota, Tennessee, Texas, Utah, Virginia, Wyoming

The law in New York applies only to employees of para-mutual harness race tracks.

The NLRA gives employees the right to either self-organize or refrain from such activity. California Govt. Code Ann. §§ 16645.2(a), 16645.7(a) prohibited "employers that receive state grants or more than $10,000 in state program funds per year from using the funds 'to assist, promote, or deter union organizing.'" Some organizations, including the Chamber of Commerce of the United States of America, sued to prevent the enforcement of these provisions contending they are pre-empted by the NLRA in that they inhibit free debate in union organizing. The U.S. Supreme Court ruled the provisions are pre-empted by the NLRA.[3]

Employer Unfair Labor Practices

The NLRA bars employers from engaging in the following procedures:

1. Interfering with, restraining, or coercing employees in the exercise of their rights;

2. Dominating or interfering in the formation or administration of a labor organization or providing financial or other support to it;

3. Discriminating in hiring or the tenure of employment or any term or condition of employment to encourage or discourage membership in any labor organization;

4. Discharging or otherwise discriminating against an employee because he has filed charges or given testimony under the Act; or

5. Refusing to bargain collectively with employee representatives as provided by the Act.

Union Unfair Labor Practices

The NLRA prohibits unions from engaging in the following practices:

---

[2] CCH Inc., HR pros shouldn't assume NLRA is just about unions, Human Resources Management, *Ideas and Trends*, (November 7, 2001) p. 168.

[3] See *Chamber of Commerce of the United States of America et al.* v. Brown, Attorney General of California, et al. (2008) in Appendix 1.

1. Restraining or coercing employees in the exercise of their rights;

2. Restraining or coercing an employer in the selection of his representatives for the purposes of collective bargaining or the adjustment of grievances;

3. Causing an employer to discriminate against an employee;

4. Refusing to bargain collectively with an employer, provided the union is the representative of the employer's employees;

5. Engaging in or inducing employees to engage in a strike or a refusal in employment, to use, manufacture, process, transport, or otherwise handle or work on any goods, articles, materials, commodities, or to do any services where the object is one of these purposes: to force an employer or self-employed person to join an organization; to induce a person to refrain from doing business with another person; to force an employer to bargain with an organization; or to force an employer to assign work to employees in a particular labor organization or particular trade, class, or craft rather than to employees in another labor organization, trade, class, or craft;

6. Charging membership fees that are excessive;

7. Causing employers to pay for services that are not performed; or

8. Picketing or threatening to picket an employer unless the organization is the certified representative of the employees, and when certain conditions are present, such as the employer has legally recognized another organization.

9. Threats of economic reprisals.

10. Featherbedding (requiring an employer to hire unnecessary workers).

11. Fail to provide fair representation.

    a. The union must represent <u>all</u> employees in the bargaining unit for which it (the union) has exclusive bargaining authority.

    b. The union cannot settle grievances involving employees without informing them.

    c. The union must keep employees informed of the outcome of arbitration proceedings.

    d. Members can sue their unions for failing to provide representation when unions have exclusive recognition.

12. Threats to employees that they will lose their jobs unless they support the union's activities.

13. Refusing to process a grievance because an employee has criticized union officers.

14. Fining employees who have validly resigned from the union for engaging in protected activity following their resignation.

15. Seeking the discharge of an employee for not complying with a union shop agreement, when the employee has paid or offered to pay a lawful initiation fee and periodic dues.

16. Refusing to make a referral or giving preference in a hiring hall on the basis of race or union activities.

17. Threatening employees that they will lose their jobs unless they support the union's activities.

18. Refusing to process a grievance because an employee has criticized union officers.

19. Fining employees who have validly resigned from the union for engaging in protected activity following their resignation.

20. Seeking the discharge of an employee for not complying with a union shop agreement, when the employee has paid or offered to pay a lawful initiation fee and periodic dues.

21. Refusing referral or giving preference in a hiring hall on the basis of race or union activities.

Procedure for Filing Unfair Labor Practice . The following information must be provided when an allegation of an unfair labor practice is filed:

- Must include the name and address of the employer or union against whom the charge is being filed.

- State the nature of the complaint.

- State the name and address of the person making the charge; that person must also sign the charge.

Once the charge is received and documented the NLRB will take the following actions:

- A copy of the charge will be served upon the named employer or union.

- Evidence will be received in support of the charge.

- If sufficient evidence is revealed to warrant continuation of the investigation, the Board agent assigned to the case will contact other witnesses who possess relevant information and the charged union or employer.

- Following the investigation, a review of the evidence will be made. If it appears that no violation of the NLRA has taken place, the Board agent will ask the complainant to withdraw the charge. If the complainant declines to withdraw the charge, the Regional Office will dismiss the charge and the decision may be appealed the Office of Appeals in Washington, D.C.

- If, after reviewing the evidence it appears that a violation has occurred, the charged employer or union will be asked to remedy the violation. If the charged party refuses to voluntarily remedy the matter, a formal complaint will be issued against the charged party and the case will be set for a hearing before an Administrative Law Judge. During the hearing, evidence will be presented concerning the allegations of the complaint. The result of the hearing before the Administrative Law Judge and its possible review by the Board or U.S. Courts will determine what, if any, remedy the charging party may receive.

Secondary Picketing

Secondary picketing is picketing an employer's (Company A or secondary employer) premises because the employer does business with another employer (Company B or primary employer) with which the union in question has a labor problem. Unlawful secondary picketing can be examined from two perspectives: unlawful activities, such as a work stoppage that includes threats and coercion, and the objective of the picketing, such as inducing a company or person to cease doing business with another one or to get the primary employer to recognize a union.

Legalized Secondary Picketing. Secondary picketing is legal in restricted situations; for example, when the employers occupy the same premises, such as on a construction site. The term for this situation is *common situs* picketing, and under stipulated conditions, such as limiting the picketing to the times when the primary employers' employees are on the premises, it is legal. Secondary picketing is also legal in these situations:

- The secondary employer is an ally of the struck employer (*ally doctrine*).

- The secondary employer is the same employer as the one that is struck (*single employer doctrine*), is a joint employer with the one that is struck (*joint employer doctrine*), or is the alter ego of the struck employer (*alter ego doctrine*).

- The secondary employer is a *double-breasted* employer (the employer has one operation that is unionized and one that is not, but both have common management).

- The same employer controls both sites and one is a phase of the other (*straight-line operations*).

- The secondary employer's products are consumer products and the picketing informs consumers about the strike.

Secondary Boycotts

A *secondary boycott* is a more generic term than secondary picketing, since it includes the latter. In addition, it includes activities other than picketing, which are directed at a secondary employer to induce the employer to take action that pressures the primary employer to concede to a union demand. A secondary boycott can include threats and refusals to work. In other words, secondary boycotts include a union representative threatening a secondary employer or instructing employees not to report for work for a secondary employer to obtain concessions from another employer. These activities are illegal unless the secondary employer is an "ally" of the primary employer and helping it in the labor dispute.

Other Prohibitions

The NLRA also generally prohibits hot cargo contracts and the closed shop.

Hot Cargo Contracts. A *hot cargo contract* is an agreement between a company and union stating the company will not handle a product or do business with another company in an effort to achieve a union objective. While these contracts are generally illegal, they are legal, under certain conditions, in the construction and the clothing and apparel industries. For example, the NLRA provides for such contracts or agreements between a labor organization and an employer in the construction industry relating to the contracting or subcontracting of work to be done at the construction site or for the alteration, painting, or repair of a building, structure, or other work.

The exemptions from the hot cargo prohibitions are much broader for the apparel and clothing industry because employers in this industry have traditionally contracted work to piecework contractors, who operate what unions call "sweatshops." Congress felt employees needed protection from this type of arrangement, so the law permits "hot cargo" agreements if the employer that is undergoing pressure from the union works on goods owned by the jobber or manufacturer, performs this work on the jobber's or manufacturer's premises, and the work that is performed is part of an integrated manufacturing process.

Closed Shop. A *closed shop* is an arrangement where applicants for employment must be members of the union representing the employees of such employer; it is an illegal arrangement.

Types of Union Security Clauses

Employers and unions are permitted to make agreements, called *union security agreements*, that require employees to make certain payments to the union to retain their jobs. The agreement cannot require applicants for employment to be members of the union, which is a *closed shop*, as discussed above.

Under a union security agreement, individuals choosing to be dues-paying members may be required, as may employees who actually join the union, to pay full initiation fees and dues within a period of time (a grace period) after the collective bargaining contract takes effect or after a new employee is hired. This grace period cannot be less than 30 days, except it may be seven days for employees in the building and construction industry and 60 days for employees subject to the Railway Labor Act.

The most that can be required of nonmembers who inform the union that they object to the use of their payments for non-representational purposes is that they pay their share of the union's costs relating to representational activities, such as collective bargaining, contract administration, and grievance adjustment.

These are the types of union security clauses:

- *Prehire agreements.* Such agreements permit an employer to sign a union security agreement without the union's having been designated as the representative of its employees. The agreement may be made before the employer has hired any employees for a project and will apply to them when they are hired. These agreements are unlawful, except in the construction industry. However, such agreements in the building and construction industries may also include:

- A requirement that the employer notify the union concerning job openings;

- A requirement that gives the union an opportunity to refer qualified applicants for such jobs;

- Job qualification standards, based on training or experience; and

- A requirement for priority in hiring, based on length of service with the employer, in the industry, or in the particular geographic area.

- *Union shop.* A *union shop* is a union security arrangement in which continued employment is conditional upon the employee becoming a member of the union representing the employer's workforce. Generally, new employees have 30 days in which they must become a union member. However, in *NLRB v. General Motors Corporation* (1963), the U.S. Supreme Court held that, in a union shop arrangement, employees who want to neither join the union nor become involved in the union in the respective bargaining unit can satisfy the union shop requirement simply by paying union initiation fees and dues, without actually becoming union members.[4] Furthermore, unions are constrained somewhat concerning how monies received from dues and fees are spent. In *Communications Workers v. Beck*, (1988), the U.S. Supreme Court held that unions can only assess members for dues and fees necessary to perform their duties as exclusive bargaining representatives in dealing with employers on labor-management issues.[5]

- *Maintenance of membership.* In this arrangement, employees who either are union members when a union-management contract is accepted by both parties, or join the union after the contract is accepted, must remain union members during the life of the contract. The union shop and maintenance of membership arrangements are legal under the NLRA except in the 22 states noted above where so-called "right to work" laws are enacted as provided for by Section 14(b) of the NLRA.

- *Agency shop.* This is an arrangement permitted by the NLRA under which employees are not required to join a union, but they must pay an initiation fee and dues to a union to remain employed. States may regulate agency shop agreements as they do union shop and maintenance of membership agreements.

Religious Beliefs

Employees may have religious objections to joining or providing financial support to a union. The NLRA has a provision that permits such employees not to join a union and to refrain from paying dues and initiation fees provided they pay equal sums to charitable organizations under conditions defined by the Act. Unions representing such employees may also charge them the reasonable cost of any grievances processed at the employees' request.

---

[4] *NLRB v. General Motors Corporation*, 47 LC ¶18,285, 373 US 734 (SCt 1963). See also *NLRB v. General Motors Corporation* in Appendix 1.

[5] *Communication Workers v. Beck*, LC ¶10,548 (SCt 1963). See also *Communication Workers v. Beck* in Appendix 1.

Open Shop and Merit Shop

Open shop and *merit shop* are two other terms used to describe conditions involving union membership.

- *Open shop.* As the term implies, a place of work that has an "open shop" does not require union membership as a condition of employment.

- *Merit shop.* The definition for merit shop changed from the original one which essentially meant "open shop." Some individuals have retained that restricted definition. Others, such as the Associated Builders and Contractors (ABC), expanded the definition to include both union and open shop firms. The ABC's philosophy of the merit shop is summed up in these terms: as a "force for economy and efficiency in construction, regardless of labor affiliation. The merit shop is union and open shop firms working side by side, free of interference, providing on-time, on-budget construction with safety, quality and cost effectiveness as our goal."[6]

Labor Management Relations Act of 1947

The Labor Management Relations Act of 1947 (LMRA), also known as the Taft-Hartley Law, amended the NLRA. The LMRA contains the following provisions:

1. Establishes the Federal Mediation and Conciliation Service;

2. Provides for the establishment of fact-finding boards, called *boards of inquiry*;

3. Directs the Department of Labor to maintain copies of collective bargaining agreements and have them available for the research and guidance of interested parties;

4. Provides for the conciliation of disputes in the healthcare industry;

5. Authorizes suits by and against labor organizations;

6. Permits suits against labor organizations for violations of contracts between an employer and labor organization representing employees;

7. Places restrictions on payments and loans to employee representatives or unions by employers or any persons acting for employers; and

8. Permits suits by persons who are injured by a violation of the union unfair labor practices section of the NLRA.

Federal Mediation and Conciliation Service

The Federal Mediation and Conciliation Service (FMCS) is an independent federal agency with these principal functions:

1. To facilitate the resolution of disputes between the parties in collective bargaining by encouraging them to use their own resources;

---

[6] Associated Builders and Contractors, *Who Looks Out for Your Business Other Than You?* n.d.

2. To encourage states to establish facilities to help labor and management in settling their disputes;

3. To offer its services in settling disputes between labor and management (except in situations covered by the Railway Labor Act) when a significant interruption of commerce is threatened;

4. To offer its services in situations involving either government procurement contracting affecting the national defense or disputes in the healthcare industry that threaten national health and safety; and

5. To maintain a roster of labor arbitrators who meet the FMCS' established criteria and to furnish the names of arbitrators upon request from the parties in a dispute.

Assisting in the Settlement of Disputes

The FMCS principally assists in the settlement of disputes through conciliation, mediation, and the establishment of Boards of Inquiry.

- *Conciliation* is the process of encouraging the disputing parties to continue bargaining.

- *Mediation* is a more active process in which compromises and solutions are offered to the parties. Conciliation is intended to keep the negotiators bargaining, while mediation involves taking an active role in the bargaining such as serving as an intermediary in offering proposals to the two sides and offering suggestions to aid in reaching a settlement.

- *Boards of Inquiry.* When a dispute occurs in the healthcare industry, Section 213 of the LMRA authorizes the FMCS Director to establish a Board of Inquiry to investigate the areas in dispute between management and labor and make recommendations to settle them. The Board is given 15 days to make a report. For 30 days the parties in the dispute must maintain conditions existing prior to the dispute. This period includes 15 days for the Board to prepare its report plus 15 days after the report is issued.

Timeline for Assistance

FMCS' assistance in settling a dispute is typically provided when one of the parties to an agreement propose to end or modify it. The party wanting to end or modify an existing agreement must follow these provisions:

1. Serve upon the other party to the contract a written notice of the proposed end or modification 60 days before the expiration of the contract;

2. Offer to meet and confer with the other party to negotiate a new contract or a contract containing the proposed modifications;

3. Notify the FMCS by filing Form F-7 within 30 days after such notice of the existence of a dispute, and also notify any state or territorial agency established to mediate and conciliate disputes within the state or territory where the dispute occurred, provided no agreement has been reached by that time; and

4. Continue in full force and effect, without resorting to either a strike or a lockout, all the terms of the existing contract for a period of 60 days after such notice is given or until the expiration date of the contract, whichever occurs later.

After the FMCS receives the notice described above, the LMRA requires it to promptly communicate with the parties and use its best efforts, through mediation and conciliation, to bring them to an agreement. The LMRA requires the parties to participate fully and promptly in such meetings as set by the FMCS to settle the dispute.

Exceptions for Healthcare Institutions. If the contract involves employees of a healthcare institution, the notice periods for #1 and #3, above, are 90 days and 60 days, respectively. In addition, the contract period in #4, above, is extended to 90 days.

Exceptions for Initial Agreement. If the bargaining is for an initial agreement following certification or recognition by the NLRB, at least 30 days notice of the existence of a dispute will be given by the union to the FMCS and the state or territorial agencies noted in #3, above.

Court Injunctions

The FMCS also is involved in cases where a federal district court issues a court injunction enjoining the parties in a labor dispute from either a strike or a lockout because those actions may imperil or threaten to imperil the national health or safety. Neither party is required to accept any proposal made by the FMCS, but both parties are required to try to adjust and settle their differences.

National Defense

The FMCS is required to provide services in any labor-management disputes directly involving government procurement contracts necessary to the national defense.

Healthcare Industry

Two provisions specifically apply to the healthcare industry. First, Section 8(d) of the NLRA requires the FMCS to use its best efforts to help the employer and the union reach an agreement. Second, as noted above, Section 213 of the LMRA authorizes the FMCS Director to establish a Board of Inquiry to investigate the areas in dispute between management and labor and make recommendations to settle them.

Rosters of Arbitrators

The LMRA requires the FMCS to establish a roster of arbitrators for referral upon request of union and management representatives. *Arbitration* is the process of using a third party to settle disputes between labor and management. There are two basic types of arbitration. Both situations are covered under FMCS procedures.

- Arbitration of disputes under an existing contract; and
- *Interest arbitration*, which involves collective bargaining disputes in modifying a contract.

Standards for Arbitrators

Arbitrators must meet several standards to be listed on the FMCS roster.

- First, the arbitrator must comply with FMCS rules and regulations regarding arbitration.

- Second, arbitrators must adhere to the ethical standards in the Code of Professional Responsibility for Arbitrators of Labor Management Disputes, which is approved by the Joint Steering Committee of the National Academy of Arbitrators.

- Third, arbitrators must meet these general criteria:

    1. Possess demonstrated experience and competence in making decisions, which are acceptable to the parties, involving the resolution of labor relations disputes;

    2. Possess experience in collective bargaining; and

    3. Possess the ability to conduct hearings in an orderly manner, analyze evidence, and prepare logical and precise findings within a reasonable period.

The arbitrators on the FMCS rosters are not employees of the federal government. Rather, they serve the parties in disputes and are paid by them. Arbitrators who are placed on the roster may be removed from it if they fail to meet the requirements of the FMCS.

Railway Labor Act of 1926

The Railway Labor Act (RLA) originally covered only interstate railroads, but it was amended in 1936 to include air carriers. The entire provisions of the RLA apply to both railroads and air carriers, except that each has a separate board to handle disputes between unions and carriers. The railroad board is the National Railroad Adjustment Board, and the air carrier board is the National Air Transport Adjustment Board.

The RLA is basically "the NLRA of interstate railroads and air carriers." The Act provides the rights of employees to organize and bargain collectively, permits agreements between carriers and unions to establish a union shop and dues check-off, establishes a National Mediation Board, and provides a procedure for arbitrating disputes if the carrier and union involved agree to such arbitration.

While the RLA has some provisions similar to those found in the NLRA, there also are some significant differences.

Adjustment Boards

The two adjustment boards (National Railroad Adjustment Board and National Air Transport Adjustment Board) are composed of an equal number of members representing the carriers and the unions (17 of each for the railroads and two each for air carriers). A major purpose of these boards is to provide an opportunity for each industry (individually) to settle their disputes before resorting to outside parties. No such provision is provided by the NLRA.

Dual Roles for National Mediation Board

The National Mediation Board is authorized by the RLA to perform the same tasks as the NLRB under the NLRA concerning the designation of unions to represent employees through elections. However, this Mediation Board also provides some services similar to those provided by the FMCS under the LMRA; it is empowered to mediate disputes between the unions and the carriers and if those efforts fail, to try to induce the parties to resolve the disputes through arbitration. If the parties agree upon arbitration and the Mediation Board's services are chosen (the parties, however, can either decline the offer of arbitration or select their own means of arbitration), there are specific steps in selecting a board of arbitrators to hear the dispute.

State "Right-to-Work" Laws

State "right-to-work" laws enacted under Section 14(b) of the NLRA do not apply to parties covered by the RLA.

Labor-Management Reporting and Disclosure Act of 1959 (Landrum-Griffin Act)

During the period 1956-1958, several labor union leaders were found guilty of various illegal acts, including the illegal use of union pension funds. These and other illegal or improper practices motivated Congress to pass the Labor-Management Reporting and Disclosure Act (LMRDA). The Act requires the reporting and disclosure of union financial records and administrative acts to both prevent union officials from failing to fulfill their proper roles and to provide for the orderly conduct of union elections. Contrary to both the NLRA and the LMRA, this Act also applies to unions covered by the Railway Labor Act.

Bill of Rights

The LMRDA Bill of Rights specifies that every union member will have an equal right to nominate candidates, vote, and attend meetings. In addition, unions cannot increase the dues and/or initiation fees without a majority vote of the membership voting in a secret election. This section also makes it illegal for a union to limit some members' right to institute action either in court or in an administrative agency. Finally, unions cannot take action against a member, such as fining or expulsion (except for nonpayment of dues), without giving the member written charges and a reasonable period to answer them in a hearing.

Reporting Requirements of Unions

The Act imposes upon unions extensive requirements for reporting information to the Secretary of Labor. Included in this reporting are the dues, fees, and other payments required of members, membership qualifications, assessments, insurance and benefit plan participation, authorizations for disbursing union funds, financial audits, authorization of both bargaining demands and/or strikes, and terms for the ratification of contracts. Also, annual reports must be filed showing assets and liabilities, the source and amount of receipts, and salaries and other disbursements to officers and employees who earned more than $10,000 annually from the union. Unions must also report any loans of $250 or more to an officer, employee, or member.

Reporting Requirements of Union Officers and Employees

Union officers and employees are required to report to the Secretary of Labor any stock, bond, security, or other interest and any income or other benefit with monetary value that the individual receives from either an employer (or the employer's consultant) of employees represented by the union or from a business that does business with such an employer. The reporting requirement also includes any such transactions involving the spouses and minor children of union officers and employees. In addition, the income of union employees and union officers or their spouses and minor children must be reported if it was derived from a business dealing with their union.

Reporting Requirements of Employers

Employers are also required to file annual reports with the Secretary of Labor for any payments of money or other things of value that they make to union officers, representatives, and union employees. Employers must also report such payments made to employees to persuade them in voting for union representation or to obtain information about union activities involving a dispute with the employer. Finally, employers are required to report any arrangement and payments made to consultants who are employed to persuade employees in organizing campaigns or to obtain information for the employer about union activities involving a labor dispute with the employer.

Reporting Requirements of Consultants

The LMRDA imposes reporting rights on the consultants mentioned in the previous paragraph. That is, these individuals must file within 30 days of entering into an agreement with an employer, information such as the terms of the agreement. These same individuals must annually report the payments received for such services, their sources, and any disbursements made in rendering the services.

Labor Relations Law in the Public Sector

Public sector labor relations law can be examined by dividing public employees into three groups:

- All federal employees except those in the U.S. Postal Service;
- U.S. Postal Service employees; and
- State and local public employees.

Title VII of the Civil Service Reform Act

Federal employees, other than postal employees, are covered by Title VII of the Civil Service Reform Act of 1978. This Act does not apply to agencies involved primarily in intelligence, investigative, or security work such as the Federal Bureau of Investigation. The Act also does not apply to the U.S. Postal Service. The Act also excludes several other agencies such as the Tennessee Valley Authority and the Foreign Service of the United States.

The major provisions of the Act cover the recognition of unions, determining appropriate bargaining units, national consultation rights of labor organizations, unfair labor practices, the resolution of impasses, the creation of a Federal Labor Relations Authority, and grievance procedures.

Federal Labor Relations Authority (FLRA)

The FLRA is an independent federal agency responsible for administering the labor-management relations program for 1.9 million federal employees worldwide. The mission of the FLRA is to promote stable and constructive labor-management relations that contribute to an efficient government. These are the three agencies that comprise the FLRA:

- *The Authority*, which is a quasi-judicial body, with three full-time members appointed by the President for five-year terms. Responsibilities of the Authority include adjudicating disputes that arise under the statute, deciding whether proposals for collective bargaining are appropriate for negotiations, handling appeals regarding unfair labor practices, and administering exceptions to grievance arbitration awards. The Authority also provides guidance concerning rights and responsibilities under the statute and conducts secret ballot elections for unions that are requesting exclusive recognition or national consultation rights, as follows:

  - *Exclusive recognition* is accorded those unions that receive a majority vote of the employees in an appropriate bargaining unit. Unlike the NLRA, a majority vote is required for all employees in the unit, not just for those who are voting. Unions with exclusive recognition have the same rights as those with national consultation; in addition, they have the right to negotiate bargaining agreements with the federal agency. The subjects for negotiation are restricted to personnel policies, procedures, and working conditions, subject to federal law and regulations. Some of the substantive issues of collective bargaining in the private sector, such as pay and benefits, may not be negotiated.

  - *National consultation* is afforded to unions with memberships that constitute a substantial number of employees of the agency. National consultation is not accorded to a union if another union has exclusive recognition for the same group of employees. National consultation entitles a union to be notified of proposals involving substantial changes in personnel matters affecting its members. The union is also given the opportunity to comment on the proposals. Such recognition also gives the union the right to suggest changes in personnel policies.

- *The Office of the General Counsel*, who is appointed by the President for a five-year term and is responsible for the management of the FLRA's seven regional offices. Responsibilities of the position include investigating and settling or prosecuting all unfair labor practice complaints and managing the work of the seven Regional Directors in processing representation petitions and supervising representation elections.

- *The Federal Service Impasses Panel (the Panel)*, which has seven members, who are appointed by the President and serve part-time in resolving impasses between federal agencies and unions arising from collective bargaining negotiations under the statute, the Federal Employees Flexible and Compressed Work Schedules Act, and the Panama Canal Act of 1979. If mediation provided by the Federal Mediation and Conciliation Service proves unsuccessful, the Panel has the authority to recommend procedures and take action to resolve the impasse.

Resolving Impasses. The U.S. Supreme Court held that the FLRA has the responsibility to resolve issues involving the negotiation of subjects presented during collective bargaining, such as whether midterm collective bargaining may be required.[7]

There is a special procedure for settling impasses that arise during the course of negotiations. The Federal Mediation and Conciliation Service (FMCS) or other third party mediation may be used. If this effort is unsuccessful, either party may request assistance of the Federal Service Impasses Panel. This panel has several alternatives: it may order a settlement of the impasse; it may recommend a settlement; or it may direct the parties to use arbitration. The parties may not voluntarily use arbitration without the Panel's approval.

Postal Reorganization Act of 1970

Employees of the U.S. Postal Service may organize and bargain collectively under the Postal Reorganization Act of 1970 (PRA). The Act places postal employees and their unions under the NLRA and LMRDA. Consequently, postal unions can bargain on similar subjects that are bargainable in the private sector, such as wages, hours, and working conditions.

The NLRB handles recognition elections, and the FMCS is involved in labor disputes. However, should the customary FMCS efforts fail, the PRA provides settlement procedures that include compulsory and binding arbitration. The first step in the procedure is for the Director of the FMCS to name three persons to a fact-finding panel. This panel has about 45 days to investigate the dispute and make a report. The panel may at its discretion include recommendations for settling the impasse. If this effort fails, the matter is submitted to arbitration.

State and Local Public Employees

There are no federal laws requiring public sector employers either to recognize labor organizations or to conduct bargaining with them. However, there are many state laws on these subjects. For example, in Virginia it is legal for state employees to join a union, but it is illegal for the state to engage in collective bargaining with unions. To determine specifically what rights public employees have in various states, it is necessary to check the respective state laws and regulations.

Union Recognition and Decertification

There are three ways under the NLRA that unions become recognized or designated as a bargaining agent for a group of employees.

---

[7] *Federal Employees v. Department of the Interior,* 132 F.3d 157 (SCt Docket No. 97-1184). Also see *Federal Employees v. Department of the Interior* in Appendix 1.

- *Employer consent.* The first and less common way is through employer consent; the employer simply agrees to let a union represent his or her employees.

- *Win a certification election.* The second way is when a union wins an election conducted by the National Labor Relations Board (NLRB).

- *Court-ordered recognition.* The third way, which rarely occurs, is if the NLRB issues an order for recognition upon demand from a union because of an employer's unfair practices during the period in which the organizing campaign and representation election was conducted.

Neutrality Agreements

A *neutrality agreement,* also sometimes referred to as a "private recognition agreement," is an arrangement between a union and an employer in which an employer agrees to remain neutral in the event the union seeks to represent his/ her employees. These are some of the typical stipulations in an agreement:

- A set of procedures which both parties will abide by, such as an agreement not to say anything negative about each other.

- Employers agree to inform their employees of their neutrality on the issue of representation by the union.

- Employers agree to give union representatives access to their employees to inform them about the organizing campaign.

- Employers agree to the voluntary recognition of the union should a majority of their employees sign authorization cards.[8]

Employers and unions have various reasons for consummating neutrality agreements. Unions are spared the expense of conducting organizing campaigns. Employers do not experience the acrimony and disruption that frequently accompanies unionizing elections. Both sides want the firm to remain viable to protect jobs and be profitable. For example, one agreement contained this provision:

> The Union, the Company and its employees will work together in a spirit of teamwork, cooperation and mutual understanding to improve product quality, productivity, improve working conditions, enhance the opportunities of the work force, and grow the business to increase job security and shareholder value. Both the Company and the Union are committed to increase investment opportunities, increase return on investment and grow the facilities that are competitive and profitable. The Company and the Union believe in the interdependent relationship of quality, operating efficiency and empowerment of people to job security.[9]

---

[8] Davies, George N., *Neutrality Agreements: Basic Principles of Enforcement and Available Remedies*, paper presented to the American Bar Association.

[9] National Labor Relations Board, Division of Judges (JD-24-05), *Dana Corporation and International Union, United Automobile, Aerospace, and Agricultural Implement Workers of America (UAW), AFL-CIO v. Gary L. Smeltzer, Jr. et al.*

Stages in a Representation Election

These are the stages involved in an NLRB representation election:

- Union initiative or employee request for union interest;

- Handbilling;

- Authorization cards solicitation;

- NLRB election; and

- Certification/decertification.

Union Initiative or Employee Request for Union Interest

An employer becomes a target of a union organizing effort through various methods. A union may take the initiative to send out some "feelers" to see if the climate within the company is conducive to organizing. This includes learning the names of some employees and carefully probing to see if there is interest in a union. Sometimes a union will conduct an organizing "blitz" and attempt to organize all of the employees within an area.

A common method of generating union interest is for one or more employees to contact a union and request information or help in getting a union recognized to represent them and their coworkers. This latter method gives union representatives a head start because these employees can become key people in the organizing campaign. For example, they can help the union representatives determine the main reasons for employee dissatisfactions such as low pay, unfair treatment, or poor working conditions. This information is extremely important in helping the union formulate a winning campaign by stressing those dissatisfactions and explaining how the union will correct them. The contact employees can also help the union identify other employees who sympathize with the union and will help in the organizing effort. These employees can be helpful in many other ways, such as helping the union get the names, addresses, and telephone numbers of all employees. This information is particularly valuable so support can be solicited through telephoning and mailings during the campaign. More important, the employee contacts can help the union identify employees who might keep management informed of various union developments and/or tell management which employees support the organizing effort.

Salt/Salting Agent

Sometimes the unions will pay persons to get a job with a firm for the sole objective of helping the union organize the firm's employees. These persons are sometimes referred to as *salts* or *salting agents*. The U.S. Supreme Court ruled that it is illegal for an employer to refuse to hire job applicants who are union members, even if the union pays the workers to help it organize the firm's employees.[10]

---

[10] *NLRB v. Town & Country Electric, Inc.* (1995), CCH Human Resources Management, *Employment Relations*, ¶ 868.

Handbilling

Handbilling is the distribution of union materials to employees. The distribution may be at a company gate, through the mail, or at union organizing meetings. This distribution occurs early in the organizing. Later activities consist of organizers contacting employees at their homes. The purpose of handbilling is to educate employees in what the union is attempting to do, such as meeting identified employees' needs.

Card Solicitation

As a campaign gathers momentum, organizers begin to solicit authorization cards. There are two types of such cards: one is a single purpose card, and the other is a dual purpose card. A *single purpose authorization card* clearly states the signor selects the union as his or her representative. *Dual purpose authorization cards* designate the union as the employees' bargaining agent and contain a statement requesting the NLRB to hold an election.

Employees are generally permitted to conduct union solicitations in nonwork areas during nonwork time. Examples of nonwork time are mealtimes, break periods, and before and after scheduled work periods. Examples of nonwork areas generally consist of lunchrooms and cafeterias, lobbies, lounges, and parking lots. Union solicitation may be conducted at these times and places even though the employer has a general rule prohibiting solicitation on company premises. Nonemployee union solicitors may be prohibited from the workplace if the employer has a rule prohibiting nonemployees from entering the premises and if the union representatives have other means of effectively reaching employees.

Union Communications. Unions use various means of communicating with members, such as bulletin boards, mailings, and telephone messaging. Email is a more technologically advanced method of communication and unions are increasingly resorting to its use, but legal issues arise when the email system used belongs to the employer. In one ruling, a majority of the National Labor Relations Board ruled that employers may prohibit employees from using the employer's email system to engage in union-related activities.[11] In the case, the employer had permitted employees to use its email system for personal communications, but not with outside organizations. The Board ruled the union was an outside organization so the employer was consistent in denying it access to its email system.

Subsequent to the Board's decision the NLRB's Office of the General Counsel issued five decisions in other cases to ensure consistency.[12]

- Case 1: The employer permitted the union to use its email system for union business but lawfully restricted the use to company managers within the local facility.

---

[11] National Labor Relations Board, *The Guard Publishing Company d/b/a The Register-Guard and Eugene Newspaper Guild, CWA Local 37194*, December 16, 2007.

[12] NLRB, Office of the General Counsel, *Report of the General Counsel (involving the decision in The Guard Publishing Company, d/b/a The Register Guard 351 NLRB No. 70 (2007).*

- Case 2: The employer unlawfully prohibited the use of the company-owned email system for union-related solicitation since it allowed non-union individual and institutional commercial solicitations.

- Case 3: The employer disciplined an employee for using its email system for union solicitation in violation of a handbook provision restricting the system's use to "reasonable and responsible business purposes and is not intended for personal use, and that employees may not solicit during working time for any purpose." The employer's action(s) were unlawful since employees (including managers and supervisors) frequently used the system for a variety of non-business related purposes, including jokes and non-business related solicitations.

- Case 4: In this case a group of employees were dissatisfied with a number of working conditions and one of the individuals communicated the dissatisfactions via several emails (both anonymously and otherwise) to the firm's Board of Directors. The Executive Director upon learning the identity of the individual fired him. The Executive Director also fired a supervisor who knew about the emails but did not report them. The Executive Director's actions were determined to be unlawful since the employee was engaged in "protected concerted activity" and the firm's email policy "allowed reasonable personal use of the employer's computer . . . internet, e-mail and other company equipment for . . . personal purposes."

- Case 5: Rather than email usage, this case involved bulletin board postings about union issues on company boards. The employer did not have a policy restricting use of the boards, but it was changed after the postings were made. The employer's actions were illegal since they were motivated by anti-union sentiment.

Filing a Petition

Filing a petition with the NLRB is the first step in obtaining an election. The petition can be filed by one or more employees, a union, or an employer. Within 48 hours, the union, employee, or group of employees that filed the petition must produce evidence of employee interest, usually authorization cards signed by at least 30 percent of the employees in the unit where representation is sought. Other types of evidence are records of union membership such as membership lists and union dues receipts. Employers who file petitions must furnish evidence within 48 hours of filing the petition that a union has made a demand for recognition.

Designating Appropriate Bargaining Unit

Upon receipt of a petition and either evidence of interest or proof of a union demand for recognition, the NLRB decides the *appropriateness* of a bargaining unit. The National Labor Relations Act authorizes the NLRB to determine appropriate bargaining units. The NLRB is only required to designate an *appropriate* unit, it does not have to be the optimum one. A unit must have at least two employees, otherwise size is not usually a factor. These are some factors the NLRB considers in designating a bargaining unit:

- The type of work performed;
- The skills required to perform the work;
- The bargaining history of the employer;
- The geography of the employer;
- Whether employees have a community of interest, that is have the same or substantially similar interests concerning wages, hours, and working conditions;
- How employees are presently organized; and,
- Employee requests for unit recognition.

The NLRB only includes professional employees with nonprofessional employees when a majority of the professionals desire it. Plant guards may not be included in the same bargaining unit with other employees. Also prohibited is a plant guard bargaining unit if the labor organization has members who are non-guard employees or if it is "affiliated directly or indirectly" with an organization that has members who are non-guard employees.[13]

In certain circumstances, the NLRB also considers the number of bargaining units. For example, in the health care industry the NLRB is guided by Congress' concern about preventing disruptions in the delivery of health care services, and its directive to minimize the number of appropriate bargaining units.

Elections

There are two types of recognition elections:

- **Consent election.** In a *consent election*, both sides agree to an election and, thus, waive the right to a pre-election hearing.
- **Directed election.** In a *directed election*, the NLRB conducts a pre-election hearing and decides whether an election should be held; if so, the NRLB orders that an election be held.

An NLRB election is by a secret ballot vote in which employees decide whether they want to be represented by a union. During the campaign and before the election, the union and management vigorously attempt to persuade the employees to vote to accept or reject the union, respectively. This campaign in many ways is similar to a political contest. Below are some things that employers can and cannot do during the campaign.

Employers *can:*

1. Explain that joining a union may result in income loss due to strikes, initiation fees, and dues;
2. Explain what happened in other companies when employees selected a union to represent them, such as a strike or a plant closing;
3. Tell employees how their wages, benefits, and working conditions compare with those offered at other companies;

---

[13] National Labor Relations Board.

4. Tell employees about any untrue statements the union made in various campaign materials;

5. Inform employees that management would prefer to communicate directly with them instead of through a union; and

6. Explain that a union cannot require an employer to do anything it chooses not to do.

Employers *cannot:*

1. Ask employees how they intend to vote regarding a union;

2. Provide any benefits to or withhold any benefits from employees for either encouraging or discouraging employees to vote for a union;

3. Threaten to close the business or take other reprisals if the union is selected to represent the employees;

4. Take reprisals, such as discipline, against employees who support the union; or

5. Use spies, informers, or supervisors to monitor union activities.

Providing Names of Potential Voters. Within seven days after the NLRB's approval of a consent-election or directing an election, the employer is required to send the Regional Director of the NLRB a list of the names and addresses of the firm's employees who are eligible to vote in the forthcoming election. This list, known as the *Excelsior list,* is named after the firm (Excelsior Underwear, Inc.) that originally contested the NLRB rule requiring employers to furnish a list of employee names and addresses to the NLRB. The U.S. Supreme Court held that the NLRB decision was valid and the employer was required to comply with it and if the list was not furnished, the NLRB could subpoena it.

Employee Eligibility to Vote. Employees who are eligible to vote are those who are on the employer's payroll in the pay period just before the date of the directed election (as explained above) and are also on the payroll before the date of the election. The NLRB rules take into consideration the fact that employment is typically irregular in certain industries, such as construction, so there are formulas designed to permit those employees having a substantial continuing interest in their employment conditions to vote. Eligible employees include those who are on temporary lay-off, sick leave, vacation, or military leave who appear in person at the polls. Ineligible employees are those who are on permanent lay-off or leave of absence and those who have been discharged. Economic strikers who have been replaced by bona fide permanent employees are eligible to vote if the election is held within 12 months after the strike begins. The bona fide replacement workers are also eligible to vote provided they meet the other requirements defined above.[14]

---

[14] National Labor Relations Board, *A Guide to Basic Law and Procedures Under the National Labor Relations Act,* 1997, p. 26.

Definition of Supervisor

The National Labor Relations Act (NLRA) does not cover employees who are supervisors. Over the years the issue of whether a specific job was supervisory has been contentious. According to the NLRA, a supervisor is a person who has authority in the interest of the employer to perform at least one these 12 supervisory functions: ".. . hire, transfer, suspend, lay off, recall, promote, discharge, assign, reward, or discipline other employees, or responsibly to direct them, or to adjust their grievances, or effectively to recommend such action". These functions must not be performed in a merely routine or clerical manner and must require the use of independent judgment[15].

Any employees classified as supervisors reduce the size of the bargaining unit. Employers who believe employees are supervisors are wont to contest National Labor Relations Board' (NLRB) decisions placing them in bargaining units because they fail to meet the conditions of the above definition.

In a recognition case involving a residential care facility, the NLRB determined that registered nurses in the facility were not supervisors because rather than using independent judgment as required by the above definition, they exercised, ". . . ordinary professional or technical judgment in directing less-skilled employees . . ." The employer disagreed with the NLRB's decision and the case ultimately was appealed to the U.S. Supreme Court. The Court held that the NLRA does not differentiate in different kinds of independent judgment so the NLRB erred in determining that the registered nurses' use of "professional" judgment was not independent judgment[16]. Due to the Court's decision, in 2006, the NLRB issued three decisions (referred to as the "Kentucky River" decisions due to the U.S. Supreme Court's decision in that case).

Certification

Certification is the process of the NLRB certifying that a union has been chosen to represent an employer's employees. The union is certified as the employees' representative if a majority of those voting vote for the union. The law does not specify a majority of the employer's employees, but rather, a majority of *those voting* in the election. If a union is declared as the exclusive bargaining representative by a majority of the voting employees, the *Certification of Representatives* is issued. If the union is not selected as the representative, a *Certification of Election Results* is issued.

Union Decertification

Decertification is the process of a union representing a group of employees that is to be removed as the employees' representative. Petition for decertification must be filed between 60 and 90 days before contract expiration. The decertification process is the same as the one followed when a group of employees is seeking union representation. Employees must obtain authorization cards from 30 percent of the workforce. These cards requesting that the union not be the employees' representative are submitted with a petition for an election to the

---

[15] National Labor Relations Act, *Section 2 (11).*   [16] *National Labor Relations Board v. Kentucky River Community Care, Inc., et al (2001).*

NLRB. The NLRB schedules an election. The union is decertified if a majority of the voting employees vote not to retain the union as their representative. Employers may not be involved in any efforts to obtain the authorization cards from employees indicating they request an election for decertification.

Decertification v. Deauthorization. *Deauthorization* is when employees request that a compulsory union security clause, such as a union shop, be rescinded. The procedure for deauthorization is the same as the one for decertification except a petition cannot be filed by a union or an employer. In addition, the majority vote must be comprised of union members, not just employees, as permitted by a decertification vote.

Bars to Election

A contract for a period of less than three years will bar an election for the period of the contract. If the contract period is for more than three years, an election may not be held either within the three years of for three years beyond the contract period.

A representative certified by the NLRB is binding for at least one year and no other elections may be held during that period. Furthermore, if an election is held and no representative is certified, no further elections may be held for one year.

Setting Aside an Election

An election will be set aside if it was accompanied by conduct that the NLRB considers to have created an atmosphere of confusion or fear of reprisals, and thus interfered or tended to interfere with the employees' freedom of choice.

Union or Employer Interfering Conduct. Conduct that interferes with employee free choice is:

- Threats of loss of jobs or benefits by an employer or a union to influence the votes or union activities of employees;

- A grant of benefits or promise to grant benefits to influence the votes or union activities of employees;

- An employer firing employees to discourage or encourage their union activities, or a union causing an employer to take such action;

- An employer or a union making campaign speeches to assembled groups of employees on company time within the 24-hour period prior to the election;

- The incitement of racial or religious prejudice by inflammatory campaign appeals made by either an employer or a union;

- Threats or the use of physical force or violence against employees by an employer or a union to influence their votes; or

- The occurrence of extensive violence or trouble or widespread fear of job losses that prevents the holding of a fair election, whether caused by an employer or a union.

Employer Interfering or Coercing Conduct. Employer conduct that interferes with, restrains, or coerces employees in the exercise of their rights under the NLRA includes:

- Threatening employees with loss of jobs or benefits if they should join or vote for a union;

- Threatening to close down the plant if a union should be organized in it;

- Questioning employees about their union activities or membership in such circumstances that will tend to restrain or coerce the employees;

- Spying on union gatherings or pretending to spy;

- Granting wage increases deliberately timed to discourage employees from forming or joining a union; or

- Providing financial support to a union either by direct payments or indirect financial aid (excluding situations where the employer permits employees to confer with the union regarding grievances or other union business during working hours without loss of pay).

Employer's Illegal Discrimination. Employer conduct that illegally discriminates against employees includes:

- Discharging employees because they urged other employees to join a union;

- Demoting employees because they circulated a union petition among other employees asking the employer for an increase in pay;

- Discontinuing an operation at one plant and discharging the employees involved followed by opening the same operation at another plant with new employees because the employees at the first plant joined a union; or

- Refusing to hire qualified applicants for jobs because they belong to a union.

Duty of Successor Employers

An employer who purchases or in other ways acquires a business may be obligated to recognize and bargain with the union representing the employees before the ownership was changed. Generally, these responsibilities exist if the operations of this *successor employer* remain substantially the same based on these factors:

- The number of employees remaining with the business;

- The similarity of the operations and the products produced before and after the ownership is changed;

- The procedures used by the new owner to integrate the business into any existing business the new owner may have; and,

- The nature of the bargaining relationship and agreement between the union and the old employer.

These are some *violations of the duty of successor employers:*

- Not meeting with the union representatives because employees are striking;

- Not furnishing the union representatives with cost and other data pertaining to any group insurance plan covering the employees;

- Announcing a wage increase without consulting the union representatives; and,

- Failing to bargain about the effects of a decision to close a plant.[17]

Union Membership

Union membership in the U.S. has remained relatively constant in the past five years, both in total number and as a percent of all workers. What gains have been made in membership are occurring among government workers. The trends in membership for the past several years are shown in Exhibit 35-1.

Exhibit 35-1
Total & Government Worker
Union Membership, 1997-2007

Year	Total Members		Government Union Members	
	Number	% All Workers	Number	% All Workers
1997	16.1 million	14.1	6.7 million	37.2
1998	16.2 million	13.9	6.9 million	37.5
1999	16.5 million	13.9	7.1 million	37.3
2000	16.3 million	13.9	7.1 million	37.5
2001	16.3 million	13.5	7.1 million	37.4
2002	16.1 million	13.2	7.3 million	37.5
2003	15.8 million	12.9	7.3 million	37.2
2004	15.4 million	12.5	7.2 million	36.4
2005	15.7 million	12.4	7.4 million	36.5
2006	15.4 million	12.0	7.4 million	36.2
2007	15.7 million	12.1	7.5 million	35.9

Source: 2008 U.S. Department of Labor

Reasons for Decline in Union Membership

In 1983, 20.1 percent of U.S. workers were union members. Since then, union membership has declined, although in the past several years, it has remained constant. Actually, there are multiple reasons for the membership loss, such as an increase in management initiatives to oppose unions, loss of jobs in unionized industries due to imports, and fluctuations in the business cycle.

---

[17] National Labor Relations Board, *A Guide to Basic Law and Procedures Under the National Labor Relations Act*, 1997, p. 38.

Increasing Management Opposition to Unions

There is a growing number of firms that specialize in helping employers remain nonunion. Among the assistance given by these consultants is explaining the employment conditions and the type of management policies and procedures that compel employees to seek union representation. Techniques to help counter unionism include providing employees with fair pay and benefits and conducting regular compensation studies to ensure the company remains competitive with the market. Another method is to install review procedures that provide employees with an avenue to appeal disciplinary actions and grievances. Some consultants tell employers to work harder to meet employee needs for security (both psychological and physical security), recognition, and achievement. Employers are told that employees have concerns about their supervisors and other conditions of employment. To identify these concerns, management must regularly communicate with employees.

Unions are responding to these consultants in various ways. First, they are publicizing those firms engaged in "antiunion" consulting, particularly if they are not complying with the disclosure requirements of Section 203(b) of the LMRDA discussed in an earlier section of this chapter. In addition, union representatives are, unknown to the consultants, attending consultants' training seminars to learn first-hand the antiunion techniques that are taught. Finally, unions are conducting training sessions for their organizers using the same techniques used by the consultants.

Fluctuations in the Business Cycle

During the past several years, the U.S. economy has been in an unprecedented period of growth and prosperity. Workers have little difficulty obtaining employment. Furthermore, employers are doing more to retain workers because of the competition for labor. As long as this trend continues, the prospect does not look good for unions to reverse the downward trend in membership.

Jobs Lost Through Imports

In the past ten years, the U.S. has continued to incur large trade imbalances. Each imported product, such as a car or ton of steel, sold in the U.S. and not compensated for by a reciprocal sale of an American good in another country, will eventually result in lost jobs. This scenario explains what is happening in the United States. These lost jobs are occurring in those industries which have traditionally been among the heaviest organized.

Increases in Jobs in Relatively Non-unionized States

Job growth in the U.S. is primarily occurring in those states, such as Texas and Florida, that have "right-to-work" laws and are among the lowest in the percent of labor force unionized. Employers have been shifting their operations from the more heavily unionized northern and eastern states to those in the Sunbelt in which unions are far less prevalent. As this job exodus continues, unions can expect to lose some members.

International Decline in Union Membership

The decline in U.S. unionism may be part of a worldwide movement. The International Labor Organization (ILO), a union group with member organizations in 150 countries, issued a report citing the international decline and stagnation in union membership and stated some groups within the ILO believe unionism has entered a period of continued decline in membership.

Other Causes

Among the other causes for a decline in union membership is the growth among jobs in the service industries, which, except for government employees, are typically more difficult to organize. Another reason is the addition of federal and state laws that provide protections for workers, which once were among the key roles of unions.

CHAPTER 36
COLLECTIVE BARGAINING

Chapter Highlights
- Learn the process of collective bargaining
- Study the provisions that exist in collective bargaining agreements
- Examine the types of bargaining arrangements

Introduction

HR professionals who are responsible for collective bargaining play a major role in the economic direction of the organizations in which they are employed. Understanding and practicing the dynamics of the collective bargaining process is both intriguing and challenging.

Collective bargaining is the process through which employees in an appropriate bargaining unit use their union representatives to deal with their employers in setting wages, benefits, hours of work, and other conditions and terms of employment.

The collective bargaining sessions in which the representatives of the union and the employer meet to discuss proposals for a labor-management contract are called *negotiations*. A *contract* is the final product of all the bargaining proposals that have been agreed upon by both sides. Sometimes, as in this book, the term *agreement* is used synonymously with the term contract. In this chapter, collective bargaining is discussed from the management viewpoint, although in some chapter sections, union strategies are also discussed.

Collective Bargaining: The Parties and Geography

Typically, collective bargaining is negotiated between one employer and one union. However, there are also other combinations of employers and unions. Before the employer and the union can insist or even mutually agree to bargain on any basis, including the arrangement of one union and one employer, the National Labor Relations Board (NLRB) must decide if the bargaining unit is an *appropriate one*.

As discussed in Chapter 35, the NLRB considers a number of factors in deciding upon an appropriate bargaining unit. Among these factors is the desire of the employees and the employers for a particular bargaining arrangement.

In some situations either unions, employers, or both request approval of a bargaining unit other than the traditional one employer/one union relationship. The request may be for a multiemployer, multiunion, or multiplant unit. The NLRB considers several factors in deciding upon these combined bargaining units. Some of these factors are whether the parties have consented to group bargaining and whether the parties have a history of such bargaining.

In multiplant bargaining situations, the NLRB looks at other factors in addition to the two above. These other factors include the amount of centralization of management, the movement of employees among plants, the amount of production integration among plants, the location of plants, the similarities in job tasks and job specifications of employees in different plants, and the uniformity of personnel policies among the plants.

Multiunion Bargaining

Multiunion bargaining is more than one union simultaneously negotiating an agreement with one employer. Another term for this type of bargaining is *coordinated bargaining*. An example of this arrangement in the private sector is the Coordinated Bargaining Committee of General Electric and Westinghouse Unions (CBC). The CBC negotiates a separate agreement with both General Electric and Westinghouse. The eleven unions (with abbreviated titles) in the CBC are the Electrical Workers, Flint Glass Workers, Plumbers, Steelworkers, Auto Workers, Allied Industrial Workers, Machinists, Carpenters, Sheet Metal Workers, Firemen and Oilers, and the Teamsters. Coalition bargaining also exists in the public sector.

Multiemployer Bargaining

Multiemployer bargaining is more than one employer simultaneously negotiating an agreement with one union. For example, in New York the International Ladies' Garment Workers Union negotiates an agreement with several manufacturers' associations representing employers that manufacture various types of clothing.

Multiemployer bargaining can be conducted at either the local or national level. The Garment Workers' agreement with clothing manufacturers is an example of a local agreement. Perhaps the best example of a national multiemployer agreement with one union is the National Master Freight Agreement that is negotiated by an employer association called Trucking Management Inc. and the International Brotherhood of Teamsters, Chauffeurs, Warehousemen and Helpers of American (Teamsters). In addition to the National Master Freight Agreement, there are about 30 local and area supplemental agreements. The Master agreement in conjunction with the local ones represents almost all the unionized truck drivers in the U.S. For example, the Master Agreement for local cartage covers 200,000 Teamster members, the over-the-road agreement covers 100,000 members, and the automobile transporters agreement covers 20,000 members.

Multiemployer-Multiunion Bargaining

Multiemployer-multiunion bargaining is more than one employer simultaneously conducting collective bargaining with more than one union. An example is the nine unions in New York City that comprise the Hotel and Motel Trades Council. This Council collectively bargains with the Hotel Association that represents 165 hotels in New York City. The nine unions in the Council are the Hotel Employees and Restaurant Employees, Electrical Workers, Operating Engineers, Service Employees, Firemen and Oilers, Painters, Office and Professional Employees, Upholstery Workers, and Carpenters. There are 25,000 union members represented by the Council.

National and Local Bargaining

National bargaining is negotiating an agreement covering all the operations of an employer within a specific industry. For example, the United Auto Workers' Union negotiates with Ford Motor Company on a contract covering all auto workers at plants throughout the U.S. *Multiplant bargaining* is another term used for this type of bargaining.

Local bargaining is negotiating an agreement that is restricted to the membership in one plant or locality. Sometimes, national employers will negotiate local contracts. For example, Safeway Stores negotiates local contracts with the Meatcutters' Union representing the members in a local area.

Sometimes, national bargaining is conducted on a master contract covering basic provisions, such as pay and benefits, and local bargaining is conducted on issues of local concern, including the assignment of overtime work, work scheduling, and vacation scheduling. For example, the United States Postal Service conducts national bargaining with several unions. At the conclusion of the national bargaining, local bargaining commences on those matters permitted by the national agreement.

Union and Employer Viewpoints on Multiunion and Multiemployer Bargaining

Multiunion bargaining is favored by some unions, particularly those representing unskilled workers, because of the added economic threat of a strike. For example, unskilled workers could be replaced relatively easily should a strike result, so they constitute less of an economic threat to an employer. On the other hand, the threat of skilled workers striking might cause an employer to more carefully consider their demands. Furthermore, if virtually all of an employer's workforce was engaged in a cooperative bargaining effort, the employees would have a decided economic advantage.

Another reason unions favor multiplant or national bargaining is because it conserves union resources. Conducting bargaining at many plants is much more time-consuming and uses more union resources than national or multiplant bargaining.

Finally, unions favor multiemployer bargaining because they can achieve uniform wages within a locality or an industry. This helps protect the wages and benefits for all because lower wages and benefits from one employer in a locality may motivate other employers to either more strenuously resist union demands or ask for wage cuts.

Some employers favor multiemployer bargaining because they feel it gives them greater economic strength to resist union demands. For example, a small employer may feel relatively powerless in bargaining with a large national union representative. Also, multiemployer bargaining groups can afford to hire top negotiators who have the experience, abilities, and knowledge to deal with union negotiators from the national office of a big union.

Another advantage of multiemployer bargaining is that it prevents unions from whip-sawing or using bargaining gains obtained from one employer to obtain the same gains from other employers. Finally, multiemployer bargaining generally helps all employers in the event of a strike because most, if not all, the employers in the bargaining groups are included in the strike.

Pattern Bargaining

Pattern bargaining is a collective bargaining phenomena, typically within one industry, in which a settlement with the one or two major employers in the industry becomes the "pattern" for settlements that are negotiated later with the same union and other employers.

Failure to Bargain

Typically, the failure to bargain with a union representing employees in a bargaining unit is an unfair labor practice. There are situations, however, where an employer may have a "good-faith reasonable doubt" a majority of employees desire further union representation.[1] In such situations, the employer has these options:

- Request the NLRB to conduct a representation election. This is made filing an RM petition with the NLRB. A request can be made if the employer can demonstrate a "good-faith uncertainly" the union does not have a majority of support by employees.[2] If the employees vote to have a union decertified, then the employer no longer needs to bargain with it.

- Withdraw recognition from the union upon receipt of "objective evidence that the union has lost majority support."[3] An example of such evidence might be a petition signed by a majority of employees in the respective bargaining unit in which they express a desire not to be represented by the union. In such situations, a union may still file an unfair labor practice charge with the NLRB. The NLRB's decision ostensibly will rely upon the validity of evidence supporting the employer's decision to withdraw recognition.

Obviously, the latter choice is more risky for the employer. If an unfair labor practice is filed, the employer has the burden of showing evidence a majority of employees did not favor union representation.

Steps in the Collective Bargaining Process

The steps in collective bargaining are: planning for negotiations; establishing ground rules; determining bargainable or nonbargainable subjects; preparing

---

[1] U.S. Supreme Court, *Allentown Mack Sales & Service, Inc. v. National Labor Relations Board* (1998) 83 F. 3d 1483.

[2] National Labor Relations Board, Levitz Furniture Company of the Pacific, Inc., formerly Levitz Furniture Company of Northern California, Inc. d/

b/a Levitz *and* United Food and Commercial Workers Union, Local 101, United Food and Commercial Workers International Union, AFL-CIO, Case 20-CA-26596 (March 29, 2001).

[3] Ibid.

proposals and counterproposals; resolving impasses; and finalizing the contract or agreement.

Negotiations Planning

Negotiations planning is the process of getting ready for contract negotiations. This planning must be extremely comprehensive, since it includes the preparation of strategy and tactics for virtually every contingency that may occur during contract negotiations.

The *negotiations plan* is a written description of important information arranged in these six categories:

1. Background;
2. Contingency plans;
3. Management negotiating personnel;
4. Negotiating philosophy;
5. Settlement effects; and
6. Negotiations communications.

Each of these categories is discussed below.

Background

The background part of the negotiations plan sets forth the contract expiration date and explains how important these negotiations are to organization goals. A typical background clause might read, "This agreement covers employees who represent 85 percent of the company's product output." In addition, a compensation summary statement is included to show how the company's wages for each job compare with other company plants and with the area labor market. Any noticeable differences are highlighted for possible action either by the union or management. For example, union proposals would be expected if group life insurance benefits are considerably below the amount of coverage provided by employers in other plants in the area. Labor market information is obtained by conducting a labor market compensation survey. Chapter 25 explains that one purpose of labor market compensation surveys is to obtain information for negotiations planning.

Other background information includes a description of the union management climate in the plant. The union negotiating team members are described, including how they conducted themselves in past negotiations and their current relations with management. Union membership numbers and percentages of the workforce are also shown. The dates of and reasons for strikes in the past ten years are noted. Demographic data on the workforce is categorized and analyzed to determine any items that may motivate union proposals in specific areas. The plant turnover rates for various jobs and area unemployment rates are shown for the past several years. This background information, in conjunction with the area wage and benefit surveys, can help determine which jobs may be out of line with the labor market and could be targeted for action by either management or union proposals.

Important issues to employees are discovered by conducting informal interviews with them. The interview results are categorized and analyzed to reveal areas that union demands may seek to improve. Sometimes, the interview surveys show that employees do not understand various provisions in the health benefits plan. If this condition exists, management may decide to explain those provisions in a special communication release, such as a memorandum or a brief training session.

Another section of the background portion in the negotiations plan shows past and future projections of both national and local economic data, such as figures on the Consumer Price Index, unemployment rates, and indicators of economic activity. Union proposals may be based upon past sales and/or production figures, so data is also included showing the actual and projected sales, production, and employment levels.

Finally, the background portion should contain information obtained by contacting other plants of the same or other firms that have recently concluded negotiations with the union, to determine the union proposals that were made and what resulted. Activities of the national office of the union should also be identified, such as changes in negotiating strategies. Any changes in either the local or national union operations should also be noted, including an increase in dues.

Contingency Plans

This section of the negotiations plan defines management intentions in the event of a strike. It explains that a strike is not wanted and would be detrimental to employee and company interests. The plan includes a statement of the purpose of contingency plans and a complete detailed description of the actions that may be taken if a strike should develop. Sample clauses include:

General instructions;

Meeting customer needs;

Shutdown procedures;

Personnel assignments in all functions;

Plant security and police protection;

Picket line procedures;

Media and employee communication; and

Fire protection.

The contingency plan section also includes an appendix with exhibits of letters to nonunion salaried employees and striking employees informing them of their employment status and their rights to various benefits. The contingency plan also contains this information:

Wildcat strike procedures;

After strike procedures;

Supervisor guidelines;

Names, addresses, job titles, and telephone numbers of personnel; and

Letters to vendors.

Management Negotiating Personnel

This section names the management negotiating team members, explains their authority delegations, and describes who is responsible for resolving impasses.

Negotiating Philosophy

The management's negotiating philosophy is outlined, stating its intent to use good faith bargaining and careful consideration of both union proposals and management positions to them. Plans for the actual conduct of negotiations are included, covering expected union demands, preparation of counterproposals, mandatory and discretionary bargaining subjects, and legal aspects. General bargaining tactics are explained, such as off-the-record discussions and resolutions with union representatives, rewording proposal language to favor the company's position, and trade-offs or a quid pro quo approach to reaching agreements on individual proposals.

Settlement Effects

The settlement effects portion of the negotiations plan includes estimates of the economic effects of various proposals. These estimations include both direct and indirect costs. Probable union proposals are examined in conjunction with the wage and benefit surveys that were conducted. Management positions are stated for every economic subject that is expected to arise during negotiations. The extent of the chief spokesperson's authority is specifically defined so the management negotiating team is fully aware of its bargaining limits.

This section also addresses noneconomic subjects that are either in the current contract or may be proposed by the union. This information is obtained from a careful review of the existing contract to determine any provisions that need to be either changed or eliminated. The decision to change is based upon reviews of existing contract provisions that have been subject to misinterpretation at the expense of the company. Also, grievance files can be used to find language problems in the contract. Finally, discussing the contract with supervisors can help identify various provisions that inhibit their ability to manage and/or in other ways impede the efficiency of the company. After the problems are identified, proposals are prepared for presentation during actual negotiations.

A final item in the settlement section is the proposed duration of the contract. This should include a historical review of the length of past contracts. In addition, both management's position and the union's, if known, should be clearly stated.

Negotiations Communications

An essential part of contract negotiations is keeping all employees informed of progress in the negotiations. This section of the negotiations plan describes how this communication will be accomplished. One national firm uses a free hotline number that employees can call from anywhere in the U.S. to check on the status of the negotiations for the master contract during bargaining at the national level. Regular timely releases to employees throughout the organization will help develop credibility for management's positions. This process also aids final contract ratification because employees are informed of the various proposals and counterproposals made throughout the negotiations.

Establishing Ground Rules

Negotiation ground rules are the agreed-upon procedures to be followed by both union and management representatives during the period of negotiations. Some of the items typically covered in ground rules are designating where negotiations will be held, the days and hours of negotiating sessions, exchanging the names of negotiation team members, and how the final contract will be prepared. Ground rules can also be important in limiting the time length of bargaining sessions and constraining the discussion between the negotiating parties by requiring that it be channeled through the chief spokesperson. Without this constraint, negotiating sessions can be unruly with persons from each negotiating team speaking at the same time.

The ground rules also are sometimes used to explain how subcommittees will be used to research proposals. Where subcommittees are used, the ground rules usually explain that issues decided by the subcommittees must still be approved by both chief spokespersons. Ground rules may explain procedures for handling tentative agreements on selected items, such as making copies of them for distribution to the parties. Ground rules also usually explain how *caucuses* may be used and the permissible length of time for caucusing. A caucus is a private meeting of one side's negotiating team to resolve a collective bargaining issue. Sometimes, delays or postponement of negotiating sessions are required. The ground rules define the procedure to follow when that happens.

Bargaining Subjects

Subjects may be either bargainable or nonbargainable. Furthermore, bargaining subjects are either mandatory or permissive.

Mandatory Bargaining Subjects

Mandatory bargaining subjects are those subjects that employers and unions must bargain on if either side makes proposals on them. Mandatory bargaining subjects include: employee benefit plans, such as retirement and insurance; wages; the hours of work; union security clauses, unless they are prohibited by state laws enacted under Section 14(b) of the National Labor Relations Act; grievance procedures; seniority provisions; and procedures involving employee discipline, discharge, layoff, and recall. The fact that it is mandatory to bargain on a subject does not mean employers must concede to union demands or even reach an agreement. The only requirement is that employers demonstrate good faith in bargaining on the subjects. Good faith and other aspects of bargaining are discussed later in this chapter.

Permissive Bargaining Subjects

Permissive bargaining subjects are those subjects on which management or labor is not required to bargain. Permissive issues concern subjects that are usually grouped together under the heading of "management rights." Among the items defined as management rights are the business structure, products or services to be produced, plant or business locations, and the methods, means, and processes of production. Other permissive bargaining subjects included company-wide bargaining and interest arbitration. Interest arbitration is covered later in this chapter.

Nonbargainable Subjects

These are the two types of *nonbargainable subjects.* First, there are those subjects that must be provided in an agreement simply upon the request of a party. For example, a union recognition clause is nonbargainable, since it must be contained in an agreement if the union requests it. This clause simply states that management recognizes the union as the bargaining representative for the em-ployees defined in the bargaining unit. Other nonbargainable subjects are those prohibited by the NLRA. For example, a union membership requirement clause would be illegal if the state in which the bargaining is conducted has enacted a law prohibiting such a requirement under Section 14(b) of the NLRA.

Preparing Proposals and Counterproposals

A *proposal* is an initial demand made by either party. A *counterproposal* is a response by either party to a proposal.

Bargaining Approaches

Positional Bargaining

Positional bargaining is an ineffective collective bargaining strategy in which repeated impasses occur, due to the positions one or both sides take in an effort to win a concession.

Principled Bargaining

Principled bargaining is an effective collective bargaining strategy with the objective of achieving an agreement through the resolution of problems.

Distributive Bargaining

In *distributive bargaining*, a gain for one side will result in a loss for the other.

Integrative Bargaining

Integrative bargaining is a creative approach to bargaining that can result in mutual benefits to both sides.

Good Faith Bargaining

Good faith bargaining is conducting negotiations at reasonable times, in reasonable places, to confer in good faith about wages, hours, and other terms or conditions of employment, and to put into writing any agreement reached if requested by either party. The NLRA requires both employee and employer representatives to engage in good faith bargaining, but does not compel either party to agree to a proposal by the other, nor does it require either party to make a concession to the other.

Bad Faith Bargaining

Bad faith bargaining involves such tactics as stalling, taking an inflexible position on union proposals, and failing to give the union information that it is legally entitled to receive. Other evidence of bad faith bargaining is changing positions on a proposal or counterproposal once an agreement has been reached and offering counterproposals on the same item that are progressively more severe than the previous ones that were rejected by the union.

There are various remedies for employers and unions that engage in bad faith bargaining. The NLRB can issue cease and desist orders against either part guilty of bad faith bargaining. In addition, the NLRB can obtain court injunctions to enforce its orders.

Surface Bargaining

Surface bargaining is conducting negotiations without a serious intent to reach an agreement. An example is offering either proposals or counterproposals, but not making sincere efforts to adjust any differences. For example, a union may propose this item for filling job vacancies based upon seniority:

> *Job Posting. All vacancies within the bargaining unit shall be posted for seven calendar days. At the end of this period, the vacancies shall be filled by the employee in the bargaining unit with the most seniority.*

The management counterproposal could be:

> *Job Posting. All vacancies within the bargaining unit will be filled by procedures set by management.*

If management repeatedly fails to make any further efforts to reconcile the difference between its counterproposal and the union proposal, there would be evidence of surface bargaining. To prevent union accusations of surface bargaining, management could offer counterproposals that would give some consideration to seniority. For example, management could modify its counterproposal to read:

> *Job Posting. All vacancies within the bargaining unit will be filled by procedures set by management. Where management deems it is appropriate, employee seniority will be considered.*

This is a counterproposal that is even more consistent with the one proposed by the union:

> *Job Posting. All vacancies within the bargaining unit shall be posted for seven calendar days, where management determines it is appropriate. At the end of period, if the job is posted, the vacancy shall be filled by the qualified employee in the bargaining unit who has the most seniority. Management will solely determine the qualifications of applicants.*

These variations of management counterproposals demonstrate the wide latitude that exists in negotiations. Knowing the limits of that latitude and purposively negotiating within them is what separates a hard, but good faith, bargainer from a surface or bad faith bargainer.

Other examples of surface bargaining include refusing to negotiate at a time of day or at a place that is reasonable. For example, one employer demanded that negotiations be conducted at the company's home office, which was several thousand miles from the plant involved in the negotiations.

Hard Bargaining

Hard bargaining is lawful, since it shows good faith efforts to reach a settlement on issues within the context of accepted management practices. Hard, but good faith, bargaining results in the settlement of a number of bargaining issues through negotiations. Another example of hard bargaining is the preparation of multiple counterproposals in response to a union demand and showing flexibility and a willingness to reach agreement on contested items. Hard, but fair, bargaining can mean an unwillingness to compromise on issues of major economic importance to the firm. In other words, a hard bargainer can be expected to be resolute on some key issues while showing flexibility and a desire to reach agreement on others.

The essential difference between hard bargaining and surface bargaining is one of intent. The hard bargainer wants to reach an agreement, and his or her behavior demonstrates this objective through a flexible, give-and-take attitude on most issues, while remaining resolute on some key items. The surface bargainer demonstrates an unwillingness to concede even minor points. By adopting a take-it-or-leave-it attitude, the surface bargainer exhibits an intent to prevent agreement.

Bargaining Skills

Properly preparing proposals and counterproposals requires creativity, superior skills in written communication, and a practical command of semantics. Another important preparation consideration is understanding words that show degree differences between antonyms. For example, there are many words that describe different temperature levels between *cold* and *hot*, including *cool* and *warm.* Such words as *shall, will,* or *must* can be tempered with *should* or *may.* As illustrated in the job posting examples, there are numerous variations of job posting conditions between the two extremes of "all job vacancies shall be posted" and "job vacancies will not be posted." Negotiating between those two extremes involves the intelligent and thoughtful use of language.

Contract Provisions

Following are some of the more common types of provisions found in union-management agreements.

Parties to the Agreement

This provision defines the names of both the union and the employer.

Union Recognition

This is a nonbargainable clause if the union wants it in the contract. It shows the union is recognized by management, defines the bargaining unit, and sometimes lists those groups excluded from the bargaining unit.

Nondiscrimination Clause

This provision indicates that the parties to the agreement will not discriminate against employees for such reasons as race, color, religion, sex, national origin, age, handicap (or disability), or veteran status.

Management Rights

These clauses vary, but they typically state that management has the right to determine the methods, means, and technology of producing and distributing the good or service produced. Sometimes, a management rights clause contains a listing of various rights, including the right to determine what product or service to produce and how jobs will be established.

Union Security

Union security clauses may be unlawful, except for prehire agreements in the construction industry, if the state has a right-to-work law as provided for by Section 14(b) of the NLRA. These security clauses, where lawful, help ensure the union of a regular source of membership. The various types of union security provisions, such as the union shop and agency shop, are discussed in Chapter 35.

Checkoff

The *checkoff* is an agreement that management will withhold union dues from members' paychecks and remit them in a lump sum to the union. This provision relieves the union of a considerable administrative burden.

Term of the Agreement

This provision explains when the agreement takes effect and the date when it terminates. The typical period for most agreements is three years. Sometimes, on contracts extending beyond one year, there also is a clause in this section of the contract that gives either party the right to notify the other party that they want to change some provision of the contract. Normally this notification must be made within a certain period, such as 30 or 60 days before the contract's anniversary date.

Wages

This provision explains the wage rates for all the jobs covered by the agreement. In addition, the contract also shows any negotiated wage increases. Usually these increases are given by either a percentage of or the dollar amount of the increase. Usually, the date the increases take effect is also provided.

Cost of Living Adjustments

Cost of living adjustments, referred to as COLA clauses, stipulate how pay will be raised based upon increases in the Consumer Price Index (CPI). COLAs are stated as so many cents per hour increase for each percentage (or fraction of a percent) of increase in the CPI.

Other Pay

Other pay provisions cover overtime pay, holiday pay, hazardous duty pay, and shift differential pay.

Supplemental Unemployment Pay

Some unions have a supplemental unemployment benefit (SUB) for employees who become unemployed through no fault of their own, such as a layoff. The amount of the benefit depends upon the employee's wage and length of service.

Health Insurance

Sometimes, the employees' health benefits plan is included in the contract. In other cases, where the benefits are more extensive, the contract may refer to the health benefits plan and explain that the provisions are contained in a separate booklet.

Pension Retirement

Typically, the retirement benefits section states whether the plan is contributory and explains the benefits that are provided.

Vacations

Vacations are usually provided based upon the employee's length of service. The longer the period of service, the more vacation days provided, up to a stated maximum.

Leaves of Absence

Leaves of absence are granted for military service and personal reasons, such as maternity. The Family and Medical Leave Act has had a significant impact upon leave for illness and maternity or paternity reasons.

Hours of Work

Work hours usually define the hours of each shift.

Seniority

Seniority is a major section in the contract because it is a cornerstone of unionism. For example, unions attempt to obtain preferred job assignment awards based upon seniority. This provision clarifies which jobs will be filled by seniority and how the jobs will be posted and awarded. Unions also attempt to gain concessions from employers to require layoffs to be in reverse order of seniority. Other union demands for seniority-based preferences include the choice of whether to work overtime and vacation scheduling.

Safety and Health

Some contracts provide for safety and health committees. Typically, each union signatory to the contract is permitted one member on the committee. The committee usually meets on a regular basis, such as quarterly, to discuss safety and health matters. This topic is covered more extensively in Chapter 31.

Subcontracting

To reduce the costs of production, some companies subcontract work if it can be done at a lower cost and if the workmanship is equal or better than work performed in-house. Some unions attempt to control this practice (which is known as *outsourcing*) by negotiating contract provisions constraining management's latitude in making subcontracting decisions. In some cases, these clauses are stringent and require that management not subcontract work if the means, equipment, and personnel are available in-house. In other cases, the clauses provide management with the flexibility of subcontracting to protect the economic viability of the business. Generally, employers view subcontracting clauses as a constraint upon their ability to manage their businesses.

Grievance Procedure

Grievance procedures are pursued by unions in an attempt to protect employees by ensuring that disciplinary actions, such as suspensions and discharges, will be reviewed, which may prevent a disciplined employee from unfair treatment.

No-Strike Clauses

No-strike clauses are typically placed in a contract along with a no-lockout concession from the employer. These provisions are only for the life of the contract, so strikes may occur once the contract terminates; for example, when unresolved impasses occur during the negotiation of a new agreement. Nevertheless, no-strike clauses provide some security for employers that the union will not sanction a strike and, should one occur, that the union will not condone the strikers' actions. Some no-strike clauses contain a provision permitting the employer to discipline union members who violate the no-strike pledge.

Supervisors' Working

Unions attempt to protect their members' work by negotiating provisions restricting supervisors from performing work reserved for union members. Usually, these clauses do not prohibit supervisors from performing such work, rather they provide for the contingency by restricting it to emergency situations. Some contracts even define what an *emergency situation* is, such as an "unplanned and unforeseen event that is not expected to recur." Besides emergency situations, some contracts permit supervisors to perform union member tasks in conjunction with instructing employees or when necessary for the supervisor to learn how various jobs are performed.

Bulletin Boards

There are several variations on contract language involving bulletin board usage. In some contracts, unions are assigned specific bulletin boards for their exclusive use. However, management retains the right to ensure only suitable material is posted on them. In other situations, unions are permitted use of general bulletin boards to post union material, such as meeting dates. In this case, all items for posting must usually first be approved by a designated management representative.

Employee Assistance Programs

Some contracts provide for the establishment of employee assistance programs to treat employees who are suffering from problems such as alcoholism and alcohol abuse, drug abuse, mental and emotional problems, and family problems.

Impasses

An *impasse* is the failure to reach an agreement on a bargaining proposal. A lawful impasse is one that results from good faith bargaining on a mandatory bargaining subject. An impasse cannot legally exist if either party has failed to bargain in good faith.

There are two types of unlawful impasses. The first is an impasse resulting from either party's insistence on negotiating a proposal that is either a permissive or a prohibited subject for bargaining. The second unlawful type of impasse is one that results from a party's refusal to bargain, without sufficient reason.

Minor impasses may not impede the progress of negotiations, but may simply be set aside while the parties continue to negotiate on other issues. However, there are times when the issue is one of major importance, and the party that proposed the item may feel negotiations cannot proceed on other subjects until the impasse is settled.

Depending upon the circumstances, different procedures are used to settle an impasse that threatens to prevent the parties from negotiating a new contract. For example, the Federal Mediation and Conciliation Service offers its services to the parties if they are subject to the NLRA. The National Mediation Board becomes involved in impasses that occur among unions and rail and air carriers. Finally, the Federal Service Impasses Panel and the Federal Mediation and Conciliation Service are involved in settling impasses among management and unions in federal agencies. Under both the NLRA and the Railway Labor Act, neither party to an impasse is required to accept the efforts and/or the settlement proposals offered by the mediators.

Another way of settling an impasse is through *arbitration. Interest arbitration* is the type of arbitration used in settling impasses occurring in negotiating a new contract agreement. Interest arbitration is found in the public sector, but is virtually never seen in the private sector because of management's apprehensions concerning the effects of an arbitrator's decisions on the economic viability of the business. Arbitration is discussed more fully later in this chapter.

In the federal sector, the Federal Labor Relations Authority (FLRA) has the authority to resolve issues involving the negotiation of subjects presented during collective bargaining, such as whether midterm collective bargaining may be required.[4]

Secondary Boycotts

Unions also use secondary boycotts as a tactic for settling impasses. These boycotts are discussed in Chapter 35.

Work Stoppage

Another way of settling major impasses is for one or both parties to engage in a *work stoppage*. A work stoppage is either a strike or a lockout. A *lockout* is when management prevents employees in the bargaining unit from returning to

---

[4] See *Equal Employment Opportunity Commission v. Waffle House, Inc.* (2002) in the Appendix.

work by locking the premises, thereby refusing them access to the business. A *strike* is a concerted effort by employees in a bargaining unit not to return to work. The objectives of both lockouts and strikes are to compel the other party to accept its opposition's terms. As a practical matter, virtually all work stoppages result from strikes.

Exhibit 36-1 shows the trend toward a declining use of work stoppages in the U.S. There are various reasons for this. First, employers have resisted union demands for concessions that place the business at an economic disadvantage should a strike result. Increasing competition mandates that employers be more cost conscious. To remain cost-competitive, employers have demonstrated they will risk a strike. Another reason strikes are used less frequently is union members' fears of replacement if they strike.

For these and other reasons, unions are selectively using the strike weapon. For example, if profits are high, as was the case in the early 1980s in the auto industry, the union will strike. Also, in coalition bargaining situations in which several unions are bargaining with an employer association, the unions will strike those employers that the unions feel are unfairly causing impasses. Two other items that have resulted in strikes in recent years are significant reductions in health benefit plans and subcontracting work.

Unemployment Compensation. In most states, unemployment benefits are only permitted if the business continues functioning with striker replacement workers and/or supervisory personnel because the strike would not have resulted in a "curtailment of work" or a "stoppage of work," which are the conditions that typically must prevail for benefits to be denied to strikers. If the business is essentially stopped due to the strike, strikers are not entitled to benefits.

Legality. The U.S. Supreme Court has ruled that a *sit-down* strike, when employees simply stay at the place of work and refuse to work, is not protected by the NLRA. Unorganized workers may legally engage in concerted activities under the NLRA, such as strikes. A *wildcat* strike is one that occurs in spite of a no-strike clause in the labor-management agreement. A strike that violates a no-strike provision is not protected by the NLRA, and the striking employees may be discharged or otherwise disciplined, unless the strike is called to protest certain unfair labor practices of the employer. Not all refusals to work are considered strikes and do not violate no-strike provisions. For example, a walk-out by employees due to conditions that are abnormally dangerous to health, such as a defective ventilation system in a spray-painting shop, has been held not to violate a no-strike provision.

Exhibit 36-1
Strikes Idling 1,000 or More
Workers, 1989-2007

Year	Number of Strikes
1989	51
1990	44
1991	40
1992	35
1993	35
1994	45
1995	31
1996	37
1997	27
1998	34
1999	17
2000	39
2001	29
2002	19
2003	14
2004	17
2005	22
2006	23
2007	21

Source: U.S. Department of Labor

Misconduct During Strike. Examples of serious misconduct that will cause employees to lose their rights to reinstatement are physically blocking persons from entering or leaving a struck plant, threatening violence against nonstriking employees, and attacking management representatives.

Lawful Strikes. Employees who strike for a lawful purpose fall into two classes: economic strikers, and unfair labor practice strikers. Both classes continue as employees, but unfair labor practice strikers have greater rights of reinstatement to their jobs.

Strikers' Rights in Economic Strikes. Strikers who strike to obtain some economic concession, such as higher wages, shorter hours, or better working conditions, are called *economic strikers*. These strikers:

- Retain their status as employees and may not be discharged, but may be replaced.

- If the employer has hired bona fide permanent replacements who are filling the jobs of the economic strikers when the strikers apply to go back to work, they are not entitled to reinstatement at that time. However, if the strikers do not obtain regular and substantially equivalent employment, they are entitled to be recalled to jobs for which they are qualified when openings in such jobs occur if they or their bargaining representative have made an unconditional request for their reinstatement.

- Strikers who have been replaced by temporary replacement workers, however, have the right to be immediately reinstated after making an unconditional offer to return to work.

Strikers' Rights in Unfair Labor Practice Strikes. Workers who strike for reasons of unfair labor practices are entitled to immediate reinstatement. These strikers can be neither discharged nor permanently replaced. When the strike ends, the strikers, if they have not engaged in serious misconduct, are entitled to have their jobs back even if employees hired to do their work have to be discharged. Strikers who were poor performers can be denied reinstatement for that reason. Reinstated strikers are not entitled to a restoration of their seniority.

Returning to the Bargaining Table

A more peaceful way of settling impasses is for either party to request that the other return to the bargaining table. There are often compelling reasons for both sides to settle an impasse. For example, during a lawful impasse management has the discretion of implementing changes that are within the confines of its proposals before the impasse. If management and the union are deadlocked on management's proposal to implement a two-tier wage system, management could unilaterally proceed with the system while it is in impasse. Management is constrained in such situations from implementing a change that is better (from management's perspective) than the proposal or counterproposal given to the union.

Arbitration

Arbitration is the process of using a third party to settle disputes. In most cases, the NLRB defers to arbitration awards if:

- The arbitration proceedings were fair;

- The parties in the dispute agreed to accept the arbitrator's decision;

- The award is not "clearly repugnant to the purposes and policies of the NLRA;" and

- The arbitrator considered and ruled on any unfair labor practice issue.

Among the issues in which the NLRB does not defer to arbitration are unfair labor practice complaints involving union restraint or coercion of employees and claimed discrimination for filing charges with the NLRB.

Arbitration awards are generally enforceable in court. In addition, except in unusual situations, such as evidence of the corruption or misconduct of the arbitrator, a judge may not review the merits of an arbitration case.

The two major types of arbitration are: (1) arbitration of disputes under an existing agreement; and (2) interest arbitration.

Arbitration Under an Existing Agreement

The three main situations involving arbitration under an existing agreement involve interpretations of contract provisions, grievances, and compulsory arbitration under the Federal Arbitration Act.

Interpretations of Contract Provisions. Disputes between management and the union may arise over the interpretation of a contract provision. For example, management and the union may interpret this seniority provision differently:

> SENIORITY-AWARDING POSITIONS. *Vacant positions shall be awarded on the basis of senior qualified.*

Management may interpret the term "senior qualified" to mean the employee with the longest period of service who meets the *job specifications* for the position. The union on the other hand, may more broadly interpret the word "qualified" to mean only that an employee must be in the bargaining unit in which the vacancy exists. The two sides may be unable to resolve the differences in their interpretations of the provision. In such situations, some contracts provide for the selection of an arbitrator to settle the dispute.

Grievance Arbitration. The second major use of arbitration in existing contracts involves grievances. A *grievance* is any employee dissatisfaction, due to a work situation that is beyond the employee's control and that management has the means to correct. Usually, grievances are prompted by a disciplinary action the disciplined employee believes is either unnecessary or too severe. All grievance procedures do not necessarily include arbitration, but when it is included, it is the last step in the procedure. The typical steps in the grievance process are:

1. The employee should discuss the grievance with his or her supervisor.

2. If the grievance is not resolved, the grievance should be put in writing and submitted it to the plant manager or his or her designee.

3. If the grievance is not resolved at that level, it should be presented to the top HR person in the firm for a decision.

4. If not resolved, the union may submit the grievance to arbitration.

Grievance arbitration differs from legal proceedings. For example, in analyzing a case, an arbitrator is not limited to the specific provisions in a contract. In fact, the arbitrator is permitted considerable latitude in making decisions and evidence does not necessarily have to conform to legal requirements.

Compulsory Arbitration Under the Federal Arbitration Act. Recent developments involving compulsory arbitration under the provisions of the Federal Arbitration Act have significantly impacted workers' rights in both the unionized and non-unionized settings. On occasion, disputes, controversies, and the like arise at work which motivate affected workers to seek legal remedies through courts, even when they have access to grievance procedures. Legal expenses in these situations can be considerable for employers. To avoid incurring these costs, some employers institute procedures requiring employees to sign agreements to submit to compulsory arbitration any disputes, including those involving allegations of federal law violations, such as the Fair Labor Standards Act, Title VII of the Civil Rights Act, and the Age Discrimination in Employment Act.

In the case, *Circuit City Stores, Inc. v. Adams,* the U.S. Supreme Court held that employees, who have claims, disputes, and controversies due to their employment, must submit them to arbitration, if they have signed documents, such as employment applications, in which they previously agreed to such an arrangement.[5] These agreements to arbitrate do not preclude suits filed by the Equal Employment Opportunity Commission for charges filed by individuals alleging discrimination.[6]

Selecting Arbitrators

Arbitrators are selected through a variety of methods. First, an arbitrator may be permanently designated by the parties. Another alternative is for the parties to designate a permanent panel of arbitrators who alternate arbitrating grievances. Another method is for the parties to secure the services of a temporary arbitrator who is selected to arbitrate a case.

Permanent Arbitrators. Permanent arbitrators are sometimes preferable to temporary ones for several reasons. First, they are generally selected upon their record, that is, they have a proven record of impartiality and good judgment. Second, permanent arbitrators become knowledgeable of the various contract provisions, which saves them time in preparing to hear a case and in making decisions. This time savings translates into money saved, since arbitration can be very expensive.

Third, neither the union nor management has to research the backgrounds and prior awards of permanent arbitrators each time they are selected to hear a case, since information was already gathered when the arbitrator was originally selected. However, this research is required each time a temporary arbitrator is selected. Substantial time is involved in such investigations because they normally include reviewing the awards in past cases and contacting the parties who used the arbitrator to get an evaluation of the arbitrator's effectiveness. Finally, using permanent arbitrators substantially reduces the unknown possibilities in arbitration.

For example, in one situation, union and management representatives selected a temporary arbitrator to hear a disciplinary grievance. Representatives from both sides conducted some preliminary research on the arbitrator, but they were totally unprepared for the bizarre behavior the arbitrator exhibited throughout the hearing. This behavior included continually interrupting witnesses and prolonged speeches by the arbitrator on matters unrelated to the grievance. Finally, neither management nor the union was prepared for the arbitrator's bill for services rendered which was twice the amount normally paid. Since the contract required both sides to share in arbitration expenses, they had equal liability. Both sides protested the bill to the arbitrator who eventually reduced it.

---

[5] *Federal Employees v. Department of the Interior,* 132 F.3d 157 (SCt, Docket No. 97-1184). Also see *Federal Employees v. Department of the Interior* in Appendix 1.

[6] CCH HUMAN RESOURCES MANAGEMENT, *Ideas and Trends in Personnel* (April 4, 2001), p. 1.

Secure Names. When temporary arbitrators are used, the customary procedure is to secure a list of names, usually from the American Arbitration Association or the FMCS. Generally, this list has from five to seven names, and the two parties to the agreement alternately strike names. The last remaining name arbitrates the case. The basis for striking names is research information on the various arbitrators. Each side naturally wants an arbitrator who will be more favorably inclined toward its position, so the research includes determining each arbitrator's track record in similar cases.

Expense. Grievance arbitration can be expensive. In general, an arbitrator is permitted time to prepare for the grievance hearing. This time is used to review the grievance file, analyze any contract provisions involved in the grievance, and get ready for the hearing. The grievance hearing typically requires part of a day. The arbitrator is also usually allowed one or two days after the hearing to review the contentions of both sides and make a final decision. The total bill, including the arbitrator's services and expenses, may be $2,000 or more. Nearly all contracts require that management and the union share the expense.

Tripartite Panel of Arbitrators

On some occasions, both the union and management are opposed to a single arbitrator deciding the outcome of a grievance or impasse. In these cases, an alternative is to use a panel. Two arbitrators are selected for the panel, one each by the union and management. Those two arbitrators then select a third member, who is presumed to be an impartial person. Sometimes, other arrangements are used to select the panel. Regardless of the method used, the purpose of the process is to select a panel that both sides will view as fair.

Expedited Arbitration

Some contracts provide for *expedited arbitration* in grievance arbitrations to both reduce the cost of and to speed the process of reaching decisions. Expedited arbitration is a shortened version of regular arbitration allowing the arbitrator to handle up to three different grievance cases in one day. Sometimes, the procedures require the arbitrator to make a *bench decision* immediately after the union and management have presented their sides of the case. More typically, the arbitrator is given 48 hours to render a written decision.

Some contracts, such as the one between the U.S. Postal Service and postal unions, limit expedited arbitration to less serious grievances, as in cases that involve employee discipline, up to and including suspensions of 14 days.

Final Offer Arbitration

Typically in arbitration, an arbitrator hears opening arguments/statements from both sides, asks questions of the parties, listens to closing arguments/statements from each side and then makes a decision. If there is a major difference in the parties' positions, the arbitrator may make a decision which represents somewhat of a compromise. This compromise decision may either be unacceptable to both parties or acceptable to one party and not the other. In a third possible scenario, the compromise decision is acceptable to both parties. In *final offer arbitration* both sides are instructed to place their final offer before the arbitrator. Some of the doubt about the outcome is eliminated in *final offer arbitration* since the arbitrator, instead of reaching an independent decision, selects one of the final positions. Presumably, this approach motivates each side to make a final offer that will most likely be accepted by the arbitrator.

Prevalence of Arbitration for Disputes in Existing Agreements

All private and public sector employers that are subject to federal labor relations laws, such as the National Labor Relations Act, the Railway Labor Act, Title VII of the Civil Service Reform Act, and the Postal Reorganization Act, are required to negotiate on the subject of the arbitration of disputes in existing agreements if either side proposes arbitration. This requirement does not mean that an agreement has to be reached, but simply that the parties must bargain in good faith.

Interest Arbitration

Interest arbitration clauses require that disputes involved in negotiating a new contract be submitted to arbitration. For example, union and management negotiators may be unable to reconcile their differences over a contract proposal, such as the amount of pay increases to be included in the new contract. The union proposal might be for an eight percent pay increase but management's counterproposal might be four percent. If a mediator failed to settle the impasse, a work stoppage could result. To prevent that from happening, the dispute may be settled through interest arbitration.

Prevalence of Interest Arbitration

Employers in the private sector are not required to negotiate interest arbitration clauses. Consequently, interest arbitration rarely occurs among unions and private employers. However, all federal agencies covered by the Title VII of the Civil Service Reform Act and the U.S. Postal Service are required to submit national level collective bargaining impasses to interest arbitration. Impasses in agencies covered by the Civil Service Reform Act receive mediation assistance from the Federal Mediation and Conciliation Service or other third-party mediation requested by the parties. If these efforts are unsuccessful, either party may request assistance from the Federal Service Impasses Panel. This panel can settle the impasse, recommend a settlement, or direct the parties to use arbitration. The parties may not voluntarily use arbitration without the Impasses Panel's concurrence.

Different interest arbitration procedures apply to the U.S. Postal Service. Impasses occurring in national level negotiations are mediated by the Federal Mediation and Conciliation Service (FMCS). If these efforts fail, the impasse is subjected to compulsory and binding arbitration. This procedure involves the Director of the FMCS naming three persons to a factfinding panel. The panel has about 45 days to investigate the impasse and make a report. At its discretion, the panel may make a recommendation for settling the dispute. If this effort fails to produce an agreement, a three-member arbitration panel settles the impasse.

CHAPTER 37
EMPLOYEE RELATIONS

Chapter Highlights
- Understand the scope of employee relations
- Examine the dimensions of adversarial and cooperative labor relations
- Review progressive and positive discipline
- Learn employee communication methods

Introduction

Perhaps no activity of HR is so dichotomous as employee relations. This HR activity represents some of the most positive aspects of HR, such as employee communications, and some of the most aversive aspects, namely discipline and discharge.

Employee relations is the HR activity concerned with employee discipline and communication.

Adversarial v. Cooperative Employee Relations

Unfortunately, adversarial relationships too often exist between management and employees where cooperative ones would accomplish more with less strife and counterproductive behavior. Exhibit 37-1 shows some of the main distinctions in these two approaches to employee relations.

Exhibit 37-1
*Distinctions in Adversarial and Cooperative
Employee Relations*

Area/Relationship	Adversarial	Cooperative
Organization Climate	Distrust and fear	Trusting and sharing
Employee Responsibility	Coercion	Voluntarism
Teamwork	We—them	Us
Supervisor-Employee Ego States	Parent—child	Adult—adult
Discipline	Organizational punishment	Self-discipline

Organizational Climate

The *organizational climate* is the environment resulting from the prevailing management philosophy and actions. In the adversarial organization, employees distrust management because of past and present management actions. For example, in the past, management may have said things that turned out not to be true. In one company, employees took substantial wage cuts because management said they were necessary to keep the business from closing. Later, employees read in the newspapers that the business had one of the most profitable years in its history and the top executives were receiving substantial profit-sharing bonuses. This type of behavior causes employee distrust.

The type of communication in an organization has a big impact upon relationships between management and employees. In an adversarial relationship, the information flow is one way from the top. Employees have little input and are told only what management feels they need to know.

An extensive sharing of information and ideas characterizes a cooperative relationship. Employers do things, such as establish quality circles and suggestion programs, to provide a formal avenue for obtaining employee ideas. Employees recognize their responsibility to find better ways of accomplishing work, and they are rewarded for them through various pay incentives.

Hallmarks of firms with cooperative employee relationships are the socialization efforts made to orient new employees in the values, beliefs, and customs of the corporate culture. This socialization might include a rigorous selection process in which recruits are shown the good and bad points about the company, so that they can judge whether their qualifications and personality fit the company's needs. This self-selection process helps ensure person-job congruence. The socialization process might also include job assignments and responsibilities that challenge new employees openly to question their personal values and beliefs and compare them to those of the organization. Other aspects of socialization include assigning employees to role models, rewarding performance with pay and other incentives, and continually stressing those characteristics of the company, such as quality and dependability, that make it distinctive.

Adversarial management believes employees shirk responsibility, and it uses homilies, such as, "Employees do what is inspected, not what is expected." Jobs are structured so that employees cannot evade their responsibilities and any attempts at evasion are swiftly punished. Supervisors are taught to supervise employees closely to ensure jobs are properly performed. This philosophy affects the fundamental way things are done. For example, production inspectors are used to catch defects and errors instead of teaching employees to build quality into a product.

Cooperative management cultivates voluntarism. Coercion is unnecessary, since employees voluntarily accept responsibility for their own performance. Also, employees understand that they must correct any errors they make. For example, employees at Lincoln Electric Company understand the importance of product quality, and they know they must use their own time to correct any defects detected after they certify that a product meets quality standards.

Teamwork

In an adversarial environment, there is a constant tug-of-war between employees and management. This environment causes employees to choose sides in an "us versus them" fashion. Sometimes, the feelings of hostility are so intense that the term "industrial warfare" accurately describes the state of employee-management relations. Among the indices of this warfare are backlogs of grievances, many cases pending for punishment, and charges of discrimination filed with state and federal agencies.

"Us" is the word that best describes a cooperative relationship between management and labor. Employees know the goals and objectives of the company and they are pulling in the same direction to help achieve them. Management accepts employees as full partners in the business. Gordon E. Forward, president of the highly successful Chaparral Steel Company in Midlothian, Texas, believes this partnership is best exemplified by a "classless society" in the working environment where all employees, for example, are included in the firm's profit-sharing plan.[1]

Supervisor-Employee Ego States

The three ego states are adult, parent, and child. At various times people exhibit these states. For example, at play, the child's ego is more evident. Directing others' behavior is characteristic of the parent state. An example of the adult ego is accepting responsibility for one's own behavior.

In the adversarial environment, the supervisor assumes a parental role and treats employees as children, such as checking behind them to make sure they have accomplished their assigned tasks. This parent-child relationship inhibits personality growth and prevents employees from maturing as responsible adults. People react to the manner in which they are treated, so that it is no surprise that employees tend to behave in childish ways when they are treated like children.

Discipline

Management in an adversarial environment stresses organizational punishment as the principal method of achieving employee discipline. As with the benevolent parent who spanks an errant child, the parental manager punishes the deficient employee. Employers use the term progressive discipline, explained in detail later in the chapter, to describe the process of administering more severe punishment for more serious deficiencies and for less serious ones that are repeated. The word *progressive,* however, does not mean advanced or enlightened; it simply means the use of increasingly harsher punishment.

Cooperative management uses progressive discipline, but only if necessary. Instead, management relies upon methods, such as positive reinforcement and job structuring, to develop employee self-discipline. In addition, instead of progressive discipline, some companies are using a new method, called *positive discipline*, in helping shape employee behavior.

Discipline

Discipline is employee learning that promotes self-control, dedication, and orderly conduct. In relation to employees in the U.S., discipline is generally used in a restricted sense to mean punishment. Consequently, the written procedures used to punish employees for job deficiencies are called *disciplinary procedures.* *Punishment* is the process of either administering an unpleasant stimulus, such as

---

[1] Bylinsky, G., "America's Best Managed Factories," *Fortune* (May 28, 1984), p. 17.

a warning letter or a suspension, or withholding a reward, such as not granting a scheduled pay increase because of an employee's job deficiencies. Punishment is only one form of discipline; other forms are positive reinforcement, including commendations and praise, and human resources development.

Sources of Employee Discipline

Exhibit 37-2 shows three sources of employee discipline.

Exhibit 37-2
Three Sources of Employee Discipline

Self	Group	Employer
Maturation	Norms	Human resource development
Goals	Status	Performance appraisal
Needs	Roles	Rewards
		Punishment

Self

The best type of discipline is that which is exercised through self-control. Self-discipline is generally achieved through maturation. As people mature, they learn to accept responsibility for their actions. This learning process includes following the examples set by role models, including parents and teachers. Peoples' goals and needs, such as a need for recognition, also influence their self-discipline. Employers may help employees meet these needs through various methods, including relatively simple ones; for instance, giving them credit for articles they produce. One manufacturer has employees who perform the final inspection on a product insert a slip of paper with this information:

> *Your satisfaction has been our objective in producing this stapler. We know it will give you good service. I personally was responsible for the final inspection. /s/Ashley Graff*

Group

Employee work groups influence members' behavior through the establishment of norms, assignment of roles, and by conferring status. *Norms* are standards of employee behavior to which members are expected to adhere. These standards may include how much an employee is expected to produce, how the employee is expected to behave on the job, and whether an employee is supposed to cooperate with management. The more cohesive the work group—the degree to which employees associate with the group and seek acceptance from it—the more the group can influence an employee's work role perceptions. Sometimes, group influence can cause employees to behave in ways contrary to the best interests of a firm. Unions can have an especially powerful influence on employee behavior, both good and bad. For example, 13 percent of the top executives in 282 of the largest companies in the U.S. stated that they believed union influence reduced employee loyalty to their employer.

Employer

Exhibit 37-2 shows how employers influence employee discipline through human resource development, performance appraisal, rewards, and punishment.

Human Resource Development (HRD). As stated above, HRD is essential to employee discipline because it is the HRM activity completely committed to employee learning. HRD helps prevent employee deficiencies by teaching employees both how to perform their job tasks and the job conduct and attendance standards that they are expected to meet. HRD is covered in Chapter 33.

Performance Appraisal. An essential aspect of performance appraisal is establishing expected standards of behavior for each performance variable. In Chapter 29 there are selected examples of desirable and undesirable job behaviors in five major performance variables. Performance expectations are communicated to employees and their performance is appraised through the appraisal system. The employee's performance is either rewarded or punished as the circumstances warrant.

Rewards. Employees receive intrinsic and extrinsic rewards from their job performance. Extrinsic rewards discipline employee performance through positive reinforcement. Merit pay systems reward employees for overall job performance in attendance, conduct, productivity, safety, and work quality. Employees who observe management equitably basing such rewards upon performance are motivated to perform better. General pay increases and those based upon length of service do not instill self-discipline in job performance because there is no link between those rewards and performance outcomes.

Performance-based pay systems, particularly those based upon individual contributions, such as piece-rate systems, have a great influence upon employee self-discipline because they are directly linked to performance. As noted in Chapter 30, pay can be linked to various aspects of individual employee performance, such as attendance, productivity, safety, job knowledge, job skills, and work quality.

Punishment. Punishment (discipline) is another alternative employers use in disciplining employees. It should be remembered that the word discipline is the one employers invariably use to mean punishment. For example, progressive discipline is the term used for the increased severity of punishment for instances of repeated deficiencies and for those of a more serious nature. In this book, the word discipline is used in two ways. First, it is used in the broad sense as it was defined earlier in this chapter section, as employee learning that promotes self-control. The word is also used here, as it commonly is among U.S. managers, to mean the implementation of punishment.

Punishment Procedures

The effective use of punishment mandates following some orderly procedures. First, most organizations establish a list of expected behaviors. These behaviors include such variables as attendance and conduct. More typically, employers prepare tables of punishment for various levels of deficiencies. Exhibit 37-3 is an example of a progressive discipline (punishment) table.

Exhibit 37-3
Progressive Discipline (Punishment) Table

Level of Deficiency	None	One	Two	Three
		Number of Prior Deficiencies		
I	Written Reprimand	1-14 Day Suspension	15-30 Day Suspension	Discharge
II	1-14 Day Suspension	15-30 Day Suspension	Discharge	
III	15-30 Day Suspension	Discharge		
IV	Discharge			

To get some idea of the types of deficiencies at each level, an example is shown in Exhibit 37-4 for each of five performance variables. Sometimes, it is difficult to discern the differences separating the deficiencies at each level. *Seriousness* is one criterion used in assigning a deficiency to a level. In addition, *intent* is also important, particularly in deficiencies resulting in an immediate discharge. Intent can be hard to prove in some cases but administering employee punishment does not require an employer to meet legal conditions, such as "proof beyond a reasonable doubt". For example, arbitrators only look for *substantial evidence* in deciding whether the punishment is warranted in a specific case.

A second part of punishment procedures involves educating employees to follow the rules. Usually, this step is accomplished by disseminating the procedures in the employee handbook and regularly publishing various provisions in the employee newsletter and other communication media. The rules and provisions disseminated most frequently relate to those deficiencies occurring often, such as absenteeism.

Work Rules

Some areas in which employers frequently implement discipline is in the violation of work rules as shown in Exhibit 37.4. A National Labor Relations Board decision sheds some light on the legality of such rules on several subjects that sometimes are controversial, namely, procedures for complaining about terms and conditions of employment, fraternization with co-workers and customers' employees, and conducting solicitation while in uniform. On these subjects, the NLRB made these decisions:

- A rule that prohibits employees from complaining about their terms and conditions of employee is a violation of the NLRB. The employer's rules stated:

  While on duty you must follow the chain of command and report only to your immediate supervisor. If you are not satisfied with your supervisor's response, you may request a meeting with your supervisor and his or her supervisor. If you become dissatisfied with any other aspect of your employment you may write the Manager in Charge or any member of management. Written complaints will be acknowledged by letter. All complaints will receive prompt attention. Do not register complaints with any representatives of the client.

- The NLRB also found the solicitation while in uniform rule to be a violation of the NLRA. The rule stated:

Solicitation and distribution of literature not pertaining to officially assigned duties is prohibited at all times while on duty or in uniform, and any known or suspected violation of this order is to be reported to your immediate supervisor immediately.

- • The NLRB did not find the fraternization rule to be a violation of the NLRA. This rule stated:

While on duty you must NOT . . . fraternize on duty or off duty, date or become overly friendly with the client's employees or with co-employees.[2]

[2] NLRB, *Guardsmark, LLC and Service Employees International Union, Local 24/7*, Cases 20-CA-31495-1 and 20-CA-3153-1 (June 7, 2005).

Exhibit 37-4

Examples of Four Levels of Deficiencies for Five Performance Variables

Level of Deficiency	Attendance	Conduct	Performance Variable			
			Productivity	Safety	Work Quality
I	Tardiness	Refusal to work overtime	Failure to complete assigned tasks	Failure to report accident	Excessive errors
II	Failure to report to work as scheduled	Doing personal work on company time	Stopping work before lunch period/end of shift	Smoking in prohibited area	Failure to properly repair rejected products
III	Failure to submit doctor's statement for sick leave absences when on restricted sick leave	Fighting with co-workers	Failure to meet production standards at least 80 percent of the time within a 6 month period	Negligent acts that could result in death or serious injury	Negligently performs tasks that cause product recalls or complaints
IV	Leaving company premises while on company time	Theft of property from company, co-workers or customers	Deliberately withholding production	Purposely trying to cause an accident	Intentionally wasting material or causing defects in products

Administering Punishment

The effective use of punishment requires supervisors to follow several steps discussed below.

Understand the Rules and Performance Criteria

Consistent application of rules and other performance criteria among supervisors requires them to have a uniform understanding of these criteria. To obtain this understanding, supervisors typically receive extensive human resource development (HRD) aimed at learning the rules and other criteria and how to interpret them. For example, the author was conducting a performance appraisal HRD session with a group of higher level managers in one organization. The session included setting criteria for performance variables. There was a considerable difference of opinion among the managers concerning several criteria, such as punctuality. One manager felt even one tardiness was inexcusable. Another manager felt one tardiness each week, as long as the employee was not later than 10 minutes, was permissible. This example shows the difficulty in getting managers to understand and uniformly agree on specific criteria. HRD can help control that problem.

HRD also usually includes simulations, such as role-playing sessions, to give supervisors the interpersonal abilities in such areas as oral communication, stress tolerance, and sensitivity to deal successfully with deficient employees.

Set Criteria

The process of meting out punishment is in part related to employee performance appraisal. For example, employees need to be informed of performance standards, so that they can perform according to those expectations. Naturally, employees do not need to be told not to steal, but there are many performance criteria, such as expected levels of production and work quality, that can be quantified and explained to employees.

Uniformly Enforce Rules

Uniformly enforcing rules and other performance standards helps prevent problems, including grievances and discrimination complaints. When an *apparent* deficiency or rules violation occurs, supervisors should promptly take action. The word "apparent" is emphasized because the actual situation may not be fully understood until the facts are known, including the employee's explanation. Prompt action shows employees that standards are important and that attention is paid to them. The important point is not to overlook an incident and expect it to go away; it may, but the greater likelihood is it will recur.

Get the Facts

Two important parts of meting out punishment are determining and analyzing the facts and choosing the appropriate level of punishment based upon those facts. An employee who is punished may disagree with the type of punishment administered, but the facts used to make that decision should not be disputed.

The best type of facts are documental ones, such as timecard entries that show tardiness or written evidence of errors. Supervisors also should prepare written descriptions of what occurred, if they witnessed an event.

An indispensable part of fact-gathering is obtaining the employee's opinion of what happened. Generally, disciplinary action should not be taken without giving the employee an opportunity to offer this explanation. The explanation, if any is given, should be in writing, should specifically address the alleged deficiency, and should be signed by the employee.

Requests for these written responses are usually made during fact-finding interviews with the employee in which allegations are presented first to give the employee a clear understanding of the facts, as understood by management. The employee is then given the opportunity to give any response to the allegations or the facts so management can determine what disciplinary action, if any, should be imposed. Prior to or during the conduct of these interviews, the employee may request to be accompanied and/or represented by a union representative or co-worker. Employers must honor these requests, which are sometimes referred to as "*Weingarten* rights."[3]

In a June 2004 decision, the NLRB reversed an earlier decision of the Board and decided that the Weingarten rights only applied to union employees. This decision conflicted with a decision of the D.C. Circuit Court of Appeals ruling that upheld the previous Board's decision extending the rights to nonunion employees.[4]

Take Prompt and Consistent Action

Punishment, as with other methods of behavior modification, is most effective when it is promptly administered. Prolonged waiting causes employee apprehension and other problems because people forget important facts. Delay also is associated with indecisiveness that causes employees to question whether management is serious about requiring employees to meet performance standards.

Employers can be reasonably "tough" with employees provided they are consistent in meting out punishment. Inconsistency causes feelings of unfairness that can result in charges of discrimination.

Help Employees

In all types of punishment except discharge, the supervisor's intent should be to help the employee improve. Unfortunately, in every organization there is a small percentage of employees, probably less than one percent, who just seem unable or unwilling to improve. These individuals frustrate even the most patient and tolerant supervisor. These employees generally fit one or more of these categories: they have profound personal problems, such as a late stage

---

[3] The representation rights for unionized employees are outlined in a U.S. Supreme Court case (see *NLRB v. Weingarten* in Appendix 1). These rights were also extended to nonunionized employees in a U.S. Court of Appeals case (see *Epilepsy Foundation of Northeast Ohio v. NLRB* in Appendix 1).

[4] Business Legal Reports, "NLRB Limits Weingarten Rights to Unionized Workplaces," in *HR.BLR.com* (June 21, 2004). See also NLRB Decision and Order, *IBM Corporation and Kenneth Paul Schult, Robert William Bannon, and Steven Parsley* (June 9, 2004).

alcoholic; they are improperly placed, in which case the job is either too demanding and they are unable to adequately perform the tasks, or they are overqualified and they are bored to the point of exasperation; or they have a physical or mental disability or condition, such as an uncorrected vision problem that prevents them from performing adequately. Every effort should be made to diagnose these problems and help the employee. Sometimes, though, even the best help is to no avail, leaving an employer with no alternative but to discharge the employee.

Types of Punishment

Punishment is administered both informally and formally.

Informal Punishment

Informal punishment is for very minor deficiencies or infractions, is administered orally, and may or may not result in the supervisor making a written record. Two common forms of informal punishment are counseling and oral reprimand.

Counseling

Counseling is the process of discussing a deficiency with an employee and attempting to advise the individual how to improve. This punishment is for the most minor deficiencies, which are usually unintentional and are not expected to recur.

Oral Reprimand

Oral reprimand is a more severe form of informal punishment in which the supervisor emphatically directs the employee's attention to deficiencies by showing him or her the specific personnel procedures or performance criteria involved, stating precisely what improvement is needed, and outlining other punishment that may be administered if improvement is not made. Even though an oral reprimand is a stern action, supervisors should exhibit a helpful and concerned nonverbal posture during the reprimand.

Formal Punishment

The five types of formal punishment are written reprimand, suspension, demotion, withholding a pay increase, and discharge.

Written Reprimand

Written reprimand is a written notification addressed to the employee outlining specifically what deficiency occurred and what performance criteria or procedure is involved. The purposes of the written reprimand include impressing upon an employee the seriousness of a situation. Oral punishment can be severe, but when it is put in written form, it has more impact. Another purpose of the written reprimand is to produce a written record for future reference if improvement is not made. A *letter of warning* is another term often used synonymously with written reprimand. Exhibit 37-5 is a sample of a written reprimand.

Exhibit 37-5
Example of a Written Reprimand

Mr. Jim Brown

3208 Fox Chase Drive

Anytown, State

Dear Mr. Brown:

This is a written reprimand for your failure to report for work as scheduled.

On October 22 you were scheduled to report for work at 8:30 a.m. You did not report for work that day and your absence was not excused. The reason you gave for not reporting was that you forgot to read the schedule and did not know you were supposed to work on October 22. Your reason is not acceptable, since you were absent on both July 30 and August 21, even though you were scheduled to work both days. I orally warned you after each of those absences that you are required to read the schedule and report as scheduled. I also explained to you that your unscheduled absences require me to call in other employees on overtime and prevents our shift from meeting production schedules.

This reprimand is intended to impress upon you the seriousness of your not reporting to work. Future instances of unscheduled and unexcused absences will result in more severe disciplinary actions, including suspension, withholding of a pay increase, and discharge.

A copy of this letter will be placed in both your personnel file and in your performance appraisal review file. The copy in your personnel file will be used as an element of your past record in deciding what action to take within the next year from the date of this reprimand, should you incur any additional performance deficiencies. At the end of the one-year period, this reprimand will be destroyed if no other formal punishment has been taken against you. The copy in your performance appraisal file will be considered, along with your performance in other areas, in appraising you for your merit pay increase.

I sincerely hope in the future you will report for work as scheduled. I am ready to help you with any problem you may have that could be causing your unscheduled absences. Your production team needs your contribution. You are an asset to us, so please make an extra effort to check the schedule and report as you are scheduled. I am confident you can do it.

Sincerely,

Jeanie Young

Supervisor

Exhibit 37-5 contains several important components that should be placed in a written reprimand. First, it shows the specific deficiency and states when it occurred and other facts about it. Second, it contains other past deficiencies in which either formal or informal punishment was administered. A reference would be made to past informal discipline if there is a record of when it occurred. Third, the letter explains how the deficiency adversely affects the organization; that is, it points out the reason for the procedure or the performance variable involved. Fourth, information is provided explaining what disposition will be made of the reprimand and the effect it will have on future personnel decisions involving the employee. Finally, the reprimand contains an offer to assist the employee in preventing a recurrence of the deficiency along with some words of encouragement.

Suspension

Suspension is placing an employee into a non-pay status, due to more serious and/or repeated deficiencies. Layoff is also placing an employee in a non-pay status, but it is used in situations where there is not enough work available rather than for performance deficiencies. Some organizations use the term *disciplinary layoff* for layoffs used for punishment purposes. Suspensions may range from one to 30 days. Suspensions beyond 30 days are rare. Suspensions are actually short-term discharges, since the period in which an employee is suspended is unpaid and not counted for retirement or for vacation credit.

Demotion

A *demotion* is a personnel action in which an employee is placed in a job at a salary range lower than the one he or she currently is in. Demotions can either be voluntary or involuntary. Among the voluntary reasons an employee may request a demotion include wanting to be relieved of the stress or the travel requirements of a job. Sometimes, supervisors request demotions to return to their former nonsupervisory jobs because they dislike supervisory tasks and responsibilities. Involuntary demotions are caused by either a reduction-in-force or the need for punishment. Organizations reduce employment levels for such reasons as a sales slump or discontinuance of a product line. In these cases, an employee will sometimes be demoted to another job to avert layoff.

Some employers do not agree with using a demotion as punishment. They believe an employee who is demoted as punishment for deficiencies may harbor a grudge or have bad feelings against the company. Consequently, these employers feel that if an employee is so deficient or has committed such a serious infraction that a suspension will not suffice, the person should be discharged in lieu of demotion. On the other hand, a demotion may be the responsible way of handling a long-term employee whose performance is unsatisfactory because he or she has not been able to adjust to the increasing demands of a changing job. The use of a demotion in this situation is based upon the realization that jobs change and in the process the tasks may become so demanding that an incumbent may no longer be able to adequately handle them. In this case, job deficiencies in productivity and work quality may be justifiable reasons for demotion in lieu of a discharge.

Withholding Pay Increase

Withholding a pay increase is usually the result of an unsatisfactory performance rating. For example, in merit pay systems, such as those used for most federal jobs, there is a progression of steps within each pay grade. Advancement to the next higher pay step is conditional upon an employee's "satisfactory" performance during the requisite waiting period between step increases.

Some HRM professionals feel withholding a pay increase is too severe. They feel that it adversely affects an employee's pay in the long term, since it not only delays an immediate increase but also extends the waiting period for subsequent pay increases. For example, most procedures provide for a minimum withholding period, such as three months, after a decision is made not to grant an increase. During this period, the employee attempts to bring his or her performance up to expectations, so that the pay increase can be granted. As noted above, this three-month postponement extends the waiting period for the pay increase and similarly delays all future increases. The cumulative effect of these delays upon an employee's income over his or her entire career can be significant.

Critics of using withholding pay increases as punishment are particularly opposed to them when they have not been preceded by reprimands and warnings, so that employees will understand the seriousness of their deficiencies and infractions.

On the other hand, there are advantages to withholding pay increases when, as with other forms of punishment, they are used consistently and all employees understand how they are used. Chapter 26 discusses the important effects of pay upon employee behavior. For example, there is little incentive to pay systems that reward all employees equally regardless of the contribution. Such systems are perceived as inequitable by employees, cause dissatisfactions, and can adversely affect the performance of superior employees.

Discharge

A *discharge* is terminating an employee's employment due to deficiencies. Discharges are reserved for only the most serious deficiencies and in cases where employees do not improve after repeated efforts are made to correct their behavior through less serious forms of punishment, such as reprimands, suspensions, and demotions.

Discharges should be handled very carefully because they can have a profound impact upon an employee. For example, discharged employees who felt they were mistreated have sabotaged equipment, committed arson, and even murdered co-workers and their supervisors. One employee, who thought he was fired when his supervisor told him to leave the business, murdered a co-worker. Often deficient employees are troubled by such problems as substance abuse, marriage and family problems, and legal or financial difficulties. These employees may be unable to cope with a discharge, and they seek vengeance against their employer or other person in the organization who they feel is responsible for the action.

Two types of discharges that are not right and may be illegal are:

- *Constructive discharge*, which occurs when an employer makes conditions so bad for an employee that he or she resigns. This is a type of involuntary separation.

- *Retaliatory discharge*, which occurs when an employee is discharged by an employer in retaliation for something, such as reporting a safety hazard.

Advance Notice of Proposed Punishment

For serious punishment, such as suspensions, demotions, and discharges, there is merit to formally offering the employee an opportunity to reply to the alleged deficiency or infraction *before* a final decision is made. Appeal procedures, such as grievance systems, give employees the opportunity to have a punishment reviewed; however, these reviews are made *after* a decision is made and/or implemented. Exhibit 37-6 is a notice of a proposed suspension.

This notice contains several provisions demonstrating fairness and consideration. First, the notice period of 30 days gives the employee advance warning. Second, the employee is given an opportunity to respond to the allegations, and to use a representative in making such responses. Third, the allegations are specific, factual, and in sufficient detail, so that the employee can take issue with them in preparing a defense or explaining any mitigating circumstances. Fourth, the letter explains where and when the disciplinary file will be available for the employee's review. Fifth, the notice states the worst action the employee can expect, which in this case is a 15-day suspension. Finally, the employee is informed that consideration will be given to elements of his past punishment record, specifically, the written reprimand he previously received.

Consumer Credit Protection Act

The *Consumer Credit Protection Act* applies to wage garnishments, which are defined as any legal procedure through which some portion of a person's disposable earnings must be withheld by an employer for payment of a debt. Disposable earnings is the portion left after legally required deductions, such as federal and state taxes, Social Security and legally required retirement systems. Not deducted from earnings in calculating disposable earnings are payments for voluntary wage assignments, union dues and the related.

a. Applies to everyone who receives personal earnings, such as wages, commissions, bonuses and other income (typically, tips are not considered earnings under the Act).

b. No employee can be discharged for a single garnishment or multiple garnishments resulting from a single indebtedness.

c. The amount of wages that can be garnished is the lesser of 25 percent of the employees' disposable earnings or the amount of such earnings that exceed 30 times the minimum federal wage.

EXAMPLE: If Bill's disposable earnings in a week are $154.50 ($5.15 x 30) there can be no garnishment.

EXAMPLE: Jim's disposable earnings in a week are $210. In this week, 25 percent of these disposable earnings may be garnished ($210 x 25% = $52.50). Jim would be paid $157.50 after deduction for the garnishment.

d. The maximum amount of disposable income that can be withheld is higher for garnishments for child support and alimony. If the individual is supporting a second family, the limit is 50 percent, otherwise, the limit is 60 percent. An additional 5 percent is permitted to either of these maximums if there are child support arrearages over 12 weeks old.[5]

e. These restrictions do not apply to bankruptcy proceedings, to debts for state or federal taxes, and to wage settlements where workers voluntarily agree for their employers to give specific amounts of their earnings to a creditor or creditors.

See Chapter 7 for additional information on this law.

---

[5] Information obtained from U.S. Department of Labor, *Fact Sheet #30: The Federal Wage Garnishment Law, Consumer Credit Protection Act's Title 3*, October 18, 2005.

Exhibit 37-6
Example of Punishment Proposal for Serious or Repeated Deficiencies

Mr. Jim Brown

3208 Fox Chase Drive

Anytown, State

Dear Mr. Brown:

This is notice that 30 days from the date of this letter I am proposing to suspend you for not more than 15 calendar days for this deficiency:

On November 29 and 30, you did not report for work although you were scheduled on both days. When Supervisor Herb Brown asked you why you had not reported for work, you said you got confused when you read the schedule. This explanation is not acceptable.

You have the opportunity to reply to this proposed suspension in person or in writing, or both. You also have the right to be accompanied by a representative of your choice, if you so desire. Any such reply will be made to me. I can be reached at 257-6053 between the hours of 8:00 a.m.-5:00 p.m. You may contact me if you wish to review the file in this proposed action. You have seven days after receipt of this letter to make a reply.

If the allegations in this current deficiency are factual, the length of the suspension will include a consideration of the written reprimand you received for your unscheduled absence on October 22. You are assured, however, that any reply you make will be carefully considered, since the purpose of this proposal is to give you such an opportunity and to explain the action that is being proposed.

Sincerely,

Cheryl Ball

Manager, Human Resources

Appeal Procedures

The notice of proposed punishment shown in Exhibit 37-6 is intended to give an employee the opportunity to formally respond to a proposed action *before* it is taken. Many employers also realize the merit in providing appeal procedures in which a punishment decision can be reviewed by one or more parties other than the person who made the original decision.

Procedural and Merit Review

Approximately 75 percent of U.S. employees do not have access to a process where the procedures and/or the merit of more serious punishment, such as written warning letters or suspensions, can be reviewed. *Procedural reviews* determine if the stated procedures were followed. For example, an organization may have procedures requiring that an employee be given a specified period of time, such as 10 days to prepare his or her response to an allegation before the punishment is administered. A procedural review includes identifying this and other required procedures and determining if they were followed. *Merit* review procedures determine the appropriateness or the "just cause" of the punishment administered based upon the deficiency. This issue is discussed later in the chapter.

Review Procedures

Some private sector employers realize employees are attracted to unions because of the job protection they provide through such measures as grievance procedures and seniority provisions. A few such employers have adopted review procedures in which employees can appeal punishment or personnel actions, such as not receiving a promotion or a pay increase. The typical procedure is similar to the grievance procedure discussed in Chapter 36. Generally, an employee first discusses the grievance with the immediate supervisor or other person who took the action initiating the grievance. If this level does not resolve the grievance, the employee can put the grievance in writing and submit it to the plant manager.

In some cases, there is a third-level appeal to the top personnel professional in the organization. The final level usually is a hearing committee of three persons. The three persons are selected in this manner: the employee picks a representative; the manager, who is the other principal in the case, such as the supervisor who is punishing the employee for a deficiency, also selects a representative to the hearing committee; and those two representatives jointly select the third person, who also serves as chairperson. This grievance hearing committee schedules a hearing in which both sides (the grievant and the manager) present their viewpoints. The hearing committee makes a decision that is binding on the organization.

The procedures used by hearing committees generally consist of opening statements by each side; case presentation, including witnesses and documented evidence; cross-examination of witnesses of the other side; and a closing statement. In some organizations; transcripts of testimony are recorded; in these instances, a hearing officer is used in lieu of a grievance committee, evidence is usually presented under oath and the hearing assumes a more legalistic structure.

Peer Review

There are many variations of the hearing or review procedures discussed above. Some organizations use *peer review* procedures. This consists of a peer review board composed of three persons: two members are peers of the grievant, and the third member is a manager. The peer representatives are randomly selected from all the employees in the company who are in the same type of work as the grievant and are in the same or higher pay grade level. The management representative is also randomly selected from all managers in the company who are at least at the general manager level. The board considers only the written record of the grievance and makes a decision.

Compulsory Arbitration Under the Federal Arbitration Act

To avoid potential legal complications arising from the work environment, including those caused by the administration of discipline, some employers have instituted procedures requiring employees to sign agreements to submit any disputes to compulsory arbitration. In the case, *Circuit City Stores, Inc., v. Adams,* the U.S. Supreme Court held that such arrangements are legal.[6] These agreements are generally thought as favoring the employer since they preclude employees from accessing federal courts, even for allegations of discrimination under applicable federal laws. However, the procedures also offer protection to employees in the event of capricious and arbitrary actions of employees. These agreements to arbitrate do not preclude suits filed by the Equal Employment Opportunity Commission based on charges of discrimination from employees.[7]

Progressive v. Positive Discipline

As discussed previously in this chapter, progressive discipline (punishment) is widely used in the U.S., and is the principal method employers use to discipline employees. In spite of the popularity of progressive discipline, there are some serious problems with it.

First, it emphasizes procedures instead of people by training supervisors in the manner of punishing employees rather than the human considerations of employee discipline. Consequently, punishment often only addresses the observable result, that is the deficiency, and ignores the real problem, such as substance abuse, that may be contributing to the problem. Another problem with progressive discipline is that it treats employees as children. The supervisor functions in a parental role and punishes the employee in the manner of a parent punishing an errant child. Third, in progressive discipline the employee is a passive party in the decision making process; the supervisor observes the deficiency, considers any mitigation, makes a decision, informs the employee, and implements the decision. Finally, progressive discipline is best characterized by confrontation and conflict. The supervisor confronts the employee with the deficiency and then, usually, a tug-of-war begins from the conflict caused by the employee's resistance to the punishment received from the supervisor. These conflicts can generate considerable hostility and ill-feelings, which is one reason why supervisors dislike progressive disciplinary procedures and, thus, avoid using them to the detriment of the organization.

Positive Discipline

Positive discipline is the process of treating deficient employees as adults in improving their performance, and in some cases, providing a decision making leave for them to determine whether they will make a commitment to meet their job responsibilities within the company or they should seek employment elsewhere.

---

[6] CCH Human Resources Management, *Ideas and Trends in Personnel* (April 4, 2001), p. 1.

[7] See *Equal Employment Opportunity Commission v. Waffle House, Inc.*(2002) in the Appendix.

Exhibit 37-7
Distinctions in Progressive and Positive Discipline

Area/Type	Progressive Discipline	Positive Discipline
Type Discipline	Punishment	Self-discipline
Emphasis	Procedures	People
Ego States	Parent/child	Adult/adult
Decision-maker	Supervisor	Employee
Setting	Confront/conflict	Confront/cooperate

Distinctions in Progressive and Positive Discipline

There are major distinctions between progressive discipline and positive discipline. First, as noted in Table 37-3, progressive discipline is punishment, but positive discipline is not.

In positive discipline, employees are sent "reminders" and not warnings or reprimands. Warnings and reprimands fit the definition of punishment because they are unpleasant stimuli, but reminders are not. Also, employees are suspended without pay in progressive discipline but in positive discipline employees are given a day's leave with pay. The purpose of the day is for the employee to conduct a self-assessment, evaluate his or her job responsibilities, and make a decision whether to meet those responsibilities or seek employment elsewhere. Also, in all cases except discharges, the deficient employee makes a commitment of the action he or she intends to take to correct the deficiency. This commitment is an action plan for the future and thus helps shape self-discipline.

Positive discipline emphasizes people and not procedures, since it stresses humane treatment. Also, positive discipline focuses on the person's *problem* and not on the *person*, by helping the employee determine what is causing the deficiency and what can be done about it.

Positive discipline treats employees as adults and assumes they will accept responsibility for their behavior. This aids personality development and helps people mature. As a result of this adult orientation, the decision making in disciplinary cases shifts from the supervisor to the employee. The employee makes decisions concerning the steps to be taken to improve. Finally, cooperation, not conflict, results when a supervisor confronts a deficient employee because the person knows that he or she will have an opportunity to make a commitment to improve.

Positive discipline obviously cannot be used in all cases, for example, serious employee crimes mandate immediate discharge. Also, a very small percentage of employees may be either emotionally unable or too immature to make adult commitments and stick to them.

Employment-At-Will

Most employees in the United States are employed under a historical common-law rule that they can be discharged "for any reason or for no reason at all." These employees thus depend upon the good-will of their employers for continued employment. This doctrine is known as employment-at-will, meaning an employee is employed subject to the will of the employer.

Some observers feel employment-at-will is a two-way street. Employees work at their own will, that is, they are free to quit when they want and employers can also discharge employees as they see fit. Employees who are employed under these conditions may depend upon the goodwill of their employers for continued employment, that is, they will not be discharged for capricious and arbitrary reasons but rather only for justifiable causes.

Percent of Employees Affected

Approximately 75 percent of employees are at-will employees. The approximately 25 percent who are not at-will employees are shown in Exhibit 37-8 and described below.

Exhibit 37-8

U.S. Workers Not-Employed-At-Will, 2007

Category of Workers	Not Employed-At-Will	
	Number (millions)	% of All Employed Workers
Private Sector Represented by Unions[1]	8,870	8.2%
Federal, State and Local Government Workers	21,053	19.3%
Total	29,923	27.5%

[1]Workers in bargaining units represented by unions. Includes workers who are either union or non union members in such units.

Source: U.S. Department of Labor Statistics, 2007.

Federal, State and Local Government Workers

Individuals employed by federal, state and local governments, typically have the right to appeal a discharge and have it reviewed by an impartial third person (or board) to ensure it is for merit. In addition, procedures often exist giving these employees advanced notices of a proposed discharge. These procedures usually provide opportunities for employees to respond to the proposed discharge before it can be occur. Typically, the final authority in such procedures is a merit review board or a board of appeals. A very small percentage of government employees, who have "excepted appointments" or serve at the pleasure of a political appointee, may be employed-at-will and thus cannot appeal a discharge under a merit procedure.

The data in Exhibit 37-8 implies that all government employees are not employed-at-will. That is not correct. While most government employees are not employed-at-will, some are. For example, most governments, including those at the local, state and federal level, require new employees to successfully complete a probationary or trial period before they are eligible to access any grievance or appeal procedures available to career employees. Under these circumstances the employees are employed-at-will since their employment can be terminated for virtually any reason or no reason at all. In another situation an employee of a state agency filed suit against the agency, her supervisor and a co-worker alleging she was laid-off for "arbitrary, vindictive, and malicious reasons." The agency in response to state-wide budget cuts implemented a re-organization in which the employee, after declining a demotion to another position, was laid-off. In response to the suit, an appeals court ruled against her. In affirming the decision of the appeals court, the U. S. Supreme Court stated:

> "Recognition of a claim that the State (Oregon Department of Agriculture) treated an employee differently from others for a bad reason, or for no reason at all, is simply contrary to the at-will concept. The Constitution does not require repudiating that familiar doctrine."[8]

Union or Non-Union Members in Bargaining Units

Workers who are either *union or non-union members* of bargaining units represented by a union are *not* "at will" employees[9] because among other considerations, they have access to a grievance process, typically culminating in arbitration. Among other dissatisfactions which can be grieved are allegations a discharge was capricious and arbitrary and not for just cause.

Other Workers

In addition to government workers and those represented by unions, there are other employees who may have access to procedures protecting them in the event of discharge and thus could be considered as not employed-at-will. These individuals are employed by private employers who provide workers with protection, similar to grievance procedures, for such reasons as:

- To provide a fair means for employees to adjust their grievances.
- To ensure discharges are for just cause.
- To avoid lawsuits.
- To provide an alternative to employees who may otherwise file claims with federal/state agencies for violations of employment laws.

Peer Review Panel. There are several variations of such procedures including a *peer review panel* in which an employee who has a dispute with management, selects a representative to serve on the panel, management selects a second person and those two select a third person. The three persons investigate the dispute and make a recommendation to the employer, which sometimes is binding.

Alternative Dispute Resolution Procedure. Employers may also provide *alternative dispute resolution* procedures for employees to seek redress of any wrongs they experienced. *Alternative dispute resolution* (ADR) is any process or procedure, other than an adjudication by a presiding judge, in which a neutral third party (or parties) participates/participate to assist in the resolution of issues in controversy using various methods.[10] These are some of the major ADR methods:

---

[8] For more information see *Engquist v. Oregon Department of Agriculture et al.* (2008) in Appendix 1.

[9] National Labor Relations Board, *Can the NLRB Provide Assistance to You*, October 9, 1998.

[10] Public Law 105-315, October 30, 1998, *Alternative Dispute Resolution Act of 1998*.

- *Early neutral evaluation* usually involves attorneys from both sides of a dispute presenting their case before an impartial third-party who has expertise on the issue. This hearing, which is conducted in the early phase of a dispute, is informal and is not a legal proceeding. The neutral party renders a judgment which the parties can use to make a settlement but a settlement is not required. The process helps both sides understand issues more clearly.

- *Mediation* "is intervention by a neutral third party in a dispute or negotiation with the purpose of assisting the parties to the dispute in voluntarily reaching their own settlement. A mediator may make suggestions, and even (make) procedural or substantive recommendations" in helping the parties reach an agreement.[11] Mediators do not decide the outcome of the dispute, that is up to the parties involved. The job of the mediator is to use his/her competencies in getting the parties to reach an agreement.

- *Arbitration*, as noted in Chapter 36, is the process of using a third party to settle disputes. "It is generally defined as the submission of disputes to one or more impartial persons for final and binding determination. It can be the final step in a workplace program that includes other dispute resolution methods."[12] *Arbitration* can be either *pre-dispute* (the parties agree to use arbitration prior to any dispute) or *post-dispute* (the parties agree to use arbitration after a dispute occurs. *Arbitration* can also be *non-binding* (the parties are not bound by the arbitrator's decision) or *binding* (the parties are bound by the outcome).[13]

Compulsory Arbitration Under the Federal Arbitration Act. To avoid potential legal complications arising from the work environment, including those caused by the administration of discipline, some employers have instituted procedures requiring employees to sign agreements to submit any disputes to compulsory arbitration. In the case, *Circuit City Stores, Inc. v. Adams*, the U.S. Supreme Court held that such arrangements are legal.[14] These agreements are generally thought as favoring the employer since they preclude employees from accessing federal courts, even for allegations of discrimination under applicable federal laws, however, they do not bar suits filed by the Equal Employment Opportunity Commission for charges filed by individuals alleging discrimination.[15] The procedures do offer protection to employees in the event of employers' capricious and arbitrary actions, including discharges.

Constraints Upon Employment-At-Will

The four constraints upon employment-at-will are:

- Legal prohibitions;
- Implied employment contracts;

---

[11] Federal Mediation and Conciliation Service, *Customers First*, 2001.

[12] American Arbitration Association, *Resolving Employment Disputes - A Practical Guide*, 2000.

[13] Ibid.

[14] CCH, *Human Resources Management, Ideas and Trends in Personnel* (April 4, 2001), p. 1.

[15] See *Equal Employment Opportunity Commission v. Waffle House, Inc.* (2002) in the Appendix.

- Public policy exceptions; and
- The covenant of good faith and fair dealing.

Legal Prohibitions

Employers are prohibited from discharges for such reasons as these:

- To deny employees the right to organize and bargain collectively (protects employees covered by the Railway Labor Act and the National Labor Relations Act);
- An action based upon race, color, religion, sex, or national origin (Title VII of the Civil Rights Act of 1964), age (Age Discrimination in Employment Act of 1967), disability (Americans with Disability Act of 1990 or Rehabilitation Act of 1973 for contractors with federal contracts of $2,500 or more), Vietnam veterans and certain other groups of veterans (Vietnam Era Veterans Readjustment Act of 1974); or
- For filing a complaint involving minimum wages or overtime pay (Fair Labor Standards Act).
- For a garnishment resulting from a single indebtedness (Consumer Credit Protection Act).
- For exercising their rights under the Occupational Safety and Health Act, the Vietnam Era Veterans Readjustment Act, the Employee Polygraph Protection Act, the federal jurors protection law, and environmental laws like the Clean Air Act.[16]

State laws also provide protection from unfair employment discharges under a variety of circumstances, such as filing workers' compensation claims, advising authorities of an employer's activity that is illegal, serving on a jury, responding to a subpoena, and testifying in an official judicial process.[17]

These and other federal and state laws have specific provisions protecting employees from discharges, due to either discrimination or for exercising their legal rights.

Implied Employment Contracts

Employers' rights to capriciously discharge employees without cause may be constrained by company policy manuals and more specifically by written contracts outlining periods of guaranteed employment. For example, school systems often use written contracts guaranteeing employment to teachers for a specific period, usually a year. In addition, some employers have personnel policies published in employee handbooks stipulating the grounds for discharge. These policies usually have an implied promise of employment in which discharges will only result for just cause. For example, in *Woolly v. Hoffmann-LaRoche, Inc.*, the New Jersey Supreme Court ruled that an employee handbook contained an implied promise of employment because it stated that discharges would only be taken for just cause. The court said employers with such policy statements must modify them by including a provision in a prominent place in

---

[16] CCH Human Resources Management, *Personnel Practices*, ¶ 2862.   [17] *Ibid.*

the handbook or manual stating the employer retains the right to discharge an employee whether or not there is just cause.[18]

Public Policy Issues

Discharges can violate established public policies if they were motivated by either an employee action protected by law or by an employee's refusal to obey an employer's demand to violate a law. For example, in one case two employees, both stockholders, were discharged for not obeying their employer's demand to vote for a merger. The Virginia Supreme Court found the employer's action was in conflict with state law that gives employees who are also stockholders voting rights with freedom from "duress and intimidation" from employers.

Good Faith and Fair Dealing

The concept of "good faith and fair dealing" has not found much favor among the various state courts. Those courts that have considered the concept apparently see it as an extension of contract law, in which the parties to a contract are expected to deal fairly with each other. From this perspective, good faith and fair dealing would mean employers would be expected to maintain an equitable employment relationship with their employees, such as honoring past practices to discipline or discharge employees only for just cause.

Personal Communication

"What you are speaks so loudly I cannot hear what you are saying."

This saying tells us that deeds speak more loudly than words. Consequently, a fancy "employee communications program" is no substitute for the daily practice of sound human resources management. Mary Parker Follett, an eminent management philosopher, said that employee cooperation depends upon communication because employers cannot realistically expect employees to wholeheartedly cooperate with them if a meaningful and continuing dialogue does not exist.

Communication Process

The first step in the communication process is illustrated in Exhibit 37-9. In this step, the sender has an idea that he or she wants to transmit. Next, the sender decides how to best "package" or encode the idea. Encoding includes a consideration of such things as whether the idea should be transmitted orally or in writing, the communication means to use, and the choice of language. The third step is the actual transmission of the message. The receiver receives the message, decodes or interprets the message that was sent, and takes action. The responsibility rests with the sender to stimulate the receiver to take the desired action. In short, if the receiver fails to either understand the message or to take action desired by the sender, the sender did not effectively communicate the message.

---

[18] CCH Human Resources Management, *Employment Relations*, ¶ 478.

Exhibit 37-9

The Communication Process

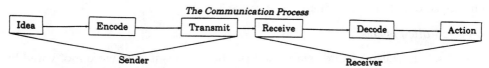

| Idea |—| Encode |—| Transmit |—| Receive |—| Decode |—| Action |

Sender   Receiver

Effective Communication

The five determinants of effective communication are language skills, appearance of the sender in personal oral communication, appearance of the messages in written communication, environmental conditions, and the ability of the sender to appeal to the receiver's needs.

Language Skills

There is nothing mysterious about effective language skills. Senders must understand basic rules of grammar.

Appearance of the Sender

After a day of interviewing at a prestigious university, a corporate recruiter was overheard remarking to a colleague, "You should have seen a guy I interviewed this afternoon—an MBA with Beta Gamma Sigma (business honors fraternity) credentials dressed in a suit he must have got from a public welfare agency." Snobbishness? Perhaps, but our appearance communicates things about us that can be incorrectly perceived. "Clothes make the man (and the woman)" is an old expression with timeless value. Grooming is equally as important as one's attire. Effective communicators are attentive to every detail in their personal appearance.

Nonverbal behavior is another aspect of appearance in communication. A. Mehrabian, an expert in communication, says only seven percent of what is accomplished in oral communications results from *what was said*, whereas 35 percent is due to *how it was said* and 55 percent results from how the sender *looked while saying it.*[19] Eye contact, firm handshake, facial expression, hand gesturing, body posture and positioning, and other nonverbal aspects are important in communication.

Appearance of Written Communication

Symmetry and neatness can be of equal importance to how a message is written. For example, errors illustrate carelessness and indifference. Receivers often evaluate the thought and validity of a written communication by the care given to its presentation.

Environmental Conditions

Environmental conditions are the physical surroundings in which the communication occurs. Lighting, noise, temperature, seating accommodations, number of participants in a room, distance among and between senders and receivers, and interior decorations are the more significant environmental conditions influ-

---

[19] Mehrabian, A. "Communicating Without Words," *Psychology Today* (September 1968), p. 53.

encing some types of communication. For example, selection interviews should be conducted in a private setting with no distractions, such as telephone calls. The counseling of employees troubled by alcoholism or family problems should be conducted in a private setting away from their workplace, so that their wishes for anonymity are assured. Also, rooms used for training purposes should be environmentally designed to facilitate the particular learning method that is used.

Appealing to the Receiver's Needs

A key principle of communication is filling the receiver's needs. For example, what needs does a company recruiter have? The need to find qualified applicants? Yes, but recruiters must recruit applicants who will reflect well upon them, such as people who will fit in with the company's culture and thus have similar values and beliefs. Identifying the receiver's needs helps the sender determine what he or she should do in preparing for the communication process. For example, an interviewee should research a prospective employer to learn such things as the products, sales, operating characteristics, competition, and market potential. In addition, the interviewee should learn about the company's culture, the unwritten standards of personal attire, beliefs, and mottos. This knowledge helps an applicant determine if his or her career needs and beliefs generally meet those of the employer. If so, the applicant is better prepared to communicate to the recruiter why he or she should be selected.

Top salespeople find a client's need and fill it. Great communicators identify their listeners' needs and fill them. Identifying another's needs requires sensitivity or the ability to empathically experience what another person is experiencing by seeing, hearing, feeling, smelling, and tasting things through that other person's senses. People follow different paths in life; to get some idea of what they have experienced, it is necessary to walk a few miles in their shoes. Communication obstacles are caused by the preoccupation with our own needs and concerns, such as the recent college graduate who only recognized his personal need to get a job he deeply wanted but didn't get because he failed to recognize the needs of the employment interviewer.

Employee Communication Methods

Employers use varied methods in communicating with employees.

Employee Handbooks

An employee handbook explains most of a company's major HRM policies and procedures, as well as the employee benefits provided by the company. A typical table of contents of an employee handbook would include most of these items:

Letter of welcome signed by the chief executive officer;

Equal employment opportunity clause;

Probationary period requirement;

Performance appraisal procedures;

Work schedules;

Employee benefit provisions;

Policy on nepotism;

Code of conduct;

Career planning system;

Promotion policy;

Resignations;

Lay-offs;

Personnel records;

Outside employment;

Personnel rules;

Safety rules; and

Disciplinary (punishment) procedure.

Due to court decisions involving the effects of handbook procedures on employment-at-will, employers are advised to conduct annual reviews of all provisions in their handbooks to ensure they reflect the current thinking of management.

Employee Newsletters

An employee newsletter can be an excellent means of communicating with employees. To increase their effectiveness, newsletters should have written editorial goals outlining the general purposes they are expected to accomplish. These are some other subjects to consider in establishing a newsletter:

- Frequency of publication;
- Whether it will be published internally or externally;
- What the budget will be;
- Who will be responsible for it;
- What sections or regular features will be used; and
- How stories will be submitted and who will approve them.

These are some of the standard features in most company newsletters:

- Presentations of safety, production, and suggestion awards;
- Employee of the month photos and background sketch;
- Comment by the plant manager or other top official;
- Question and answer section dealing with company matters, such as new products or employee benefits;
- Employee fitness and wellness programming;
- Feature stories of a new HRM program or new product; and
- Human interest stories about a company employee.

A good way to generate employee interest in a newly contemplated newsletter, or to regenerate interest in one already in existence, is to have an employee contest to select a name (or a new name for an existing newsletter) for the newsletter. An ad hoc employee committee could be selected to pick the winner who would receive a prize for his or her efforts.

Quality Circles

Quality circles (QC) are groups of employees who voluntarily meet on company time to discuss topics, such as production problems, and make suggestions to correct them. A typical circle consists of about eight employees and one facilitator, usually a supervisor. One other higher level supervisor or administrator serves on either a full- or part-time basis as the coordinator. The facilitator's tasks include chairing a circle and helping the circle members identify problems and solutions. The coordinator, as the title suggests, coordinates the activities among all the circles functioning within a plant. The coordinator also trains, advises, and assists facilitators.

Individual circle members volunteer to serve in a circle. Members are trained in basic industrial engineering techniques, such as flowcharting, to help them learn how to logically analyze work processes and identify problems. Other training given to circle members includes decision making methods and creativity techniques, such as brainstorming. In most organizations, circle members can receive credit for their adopted ideas by submitting them through the organization's suggestion program; credit can include cash awards based upon the benefit savings generated by the idea. Group awards are given when other circle members contribute to an adopted idea.

Suggestion Programs

Employee suggestion programs have been operating in the U.S. since the 1800s. The National Cash Register Company is credited with starting the first one in 1896. An *employee suggestion program* is a formal program to solicit, evaluate, implement, and reward employees for their ideas to improve the organization. Today, the word "system" is used in the place of "program" to recognize the communication linkages and the interdependencies between employee suggestions and all other aspects of an organization. Each of the concepts (solicit, evaluate, implement, and reward) are important for a suggestion system to function the way it should.

Soliciting Suggestions

Suggestion systems are established on the premise that employees are partners in the success of an organization accomplishing its goals. Employers must instill that philosophy in employees and supervisors— merely establishing a suggestion system will not ensure employee participation. Publicity is important, such as photographs and news stories of suggestion awards in the employee newsletter. Some companies, such as the Lincoln Electric Company, also include employee suggestion participation as a variable in performance appraisal.

Another important way of soliciting suggestions is to include suggestion participation in pay incentives. There are two ways this can be done. First, suggestion system participation can be included with other variables, such as productivity, in determining an employee's share under profit-sharing plans. Another use of incentives is to pay employees for their ideas.

What is a good rate of suggestion participation? The answer to that question depends upon the country. In the U.S., a 100 percent participation rate is considered very good. This rate means that on the average one suggestion is received annually from each employee. The key word is "average," since some employees never submit suggestions while others make multiple submissions. The average U.S. firm receives about one suggestion for each seven employees. In Japan, the rate is 50-60 times higher than it is in the U.S. This extremely high rate is indicative of the importance Japanese management places upon employee ideas. Employees in Japan are taught it is their duty as partners in the business to find ways of increasing efficiency.

Evaluating Suggestions

Fair evaluations are the cornerstone of a suggestion system. Employees submit suggestions if they feel their ideas are fairly evaluated and they are given credit for them. To ensure credit is given, each idea is acknowledged as soon as it is received. Normally all ideas are submitted on a form designed for that purpose. The idea is sent to a central place, usually in the HRM department, where it is recorded and an acknowledgment is sent to the suggester. The idea is sent to an evaluator, who is usually the person most knowledgeable in the area. Sometimes, opinions are obtained from several evaluators. "Approvals" are those ideas considered worthy of adoption. Carefully handling "disapprovals," that is those ideas not adoptable, is important to prevent discouraging the suggester from submitting future ideas. The best suggestion systems usually write specially prepared letters explaining why an idea was disapproved. All ideas have advantages and disadvantages and a disapproval results when the disadvantages outweigh the advantages. Employees understand why an idea was not adopted when this direct approach is used, provided the letter is factual. In addition, the suggester can be invited to rethink the idea in an attempt to correct the disadvantages that prevented the idea from adoption.

Implementation

Most adoptable ideas are implemented immediately. Occasionally, the utility of some ideas may be questionable. In these cases, one of two approaches is generally used. First, the idea may be used in a pilot project or on a trial basis. These trials help managers determine if an idea is worth complete implementation. Trials can also be used to identify any "bugs" that need correcting. Of equal importance, trials demonstrate management's sincerity in wanting to implement employee ideas. Another approach used in implementing ideas is to modify them. Many times the basic idea in a suggestion is worthy, but it needs some modification before it can be adopted.

A typical adoption rate is about 25 percent. This rate generally applies regardless of the suggestion submission rate.

Rewards

There are both tangible and intangible benefits from adoptable ideas. The tangible benefits include productivity increases and reductions in scrap or rejects. Sometimes, adopting an idea may require a cost expenditure. The net benefits are total savings minus any costs incurred. Rewards are based upon the net savings. The amount of cash awards vary, but a typical figure is 10 percent of the first year's savings. Some companies have a maximum figure for cash awards, such as $10,000. Other companies do not have ceilings.

Some companies do not give cash awards for suggestions. Instead, they give prizes or, as in the case of the Lincoln Electric Company, they use employee suggestion activity, including the amount of savings generated, in appraising each employees' performance. Depending upon the company, this information is used in computing employees' profit-sharing bonuses or merit pay increases.

The intangible benefit savings resulting from suggestions are the benefits in which the savings cannot be calculated, such as eliminating an unsafe condition that has never caused an accident. Usually, a scale is used to categorize intangible benefits as *minor*, *major*, or *extraordinary*. Each category has a definition of the type of benefits it includes and examples of suggestions.

Most forms used in suggestion systems include a statement to be signed by the employee assigning all rights to the employer. This is done to protect the employer from employees' claims to future benefits obtained from their ideas.

Employee Involvement or Communication Committees

A few companies use communication committees as one method of communicating with employees. Committee representatives consist of both managers and employees. Employee representatives are selected by their peers through annual elections. Meetings are held monthly and minutes are kept of the business transacted; the minutes are posted on employee bulletin boards. The purposes of such committees include discussing employee problems and identifying problems effecting company efficiency.

Due to the *Electromation* decision,[20] employers need to avoid actions that might lead to the conclusion that they are dominating committee actions. Electromation was the firm that established an employee participation committee that the National Labor Relations Board (NLRB) ruled was a labor organization and, thus, in violation of the National Labor Relations Act. The NLRB said that the committee was dominated by management, the only purpose of the committee was to address conditions of employment, and the committee was supported by management.

To avoid the problems experienced by Electromation, employee involvement committees should represent the employer rather than employees. For example, in a 2001 case (*Crown Cork & Seal Company, Inc. and Martin Rodriquez*), the National Labor Relations Board found that seven employee committees organized by the employer were "management" since they performed management functions and thus were not labor organizations and not in violation of the National Labor Relations Act. Committees should be used as communication instruments to address business operational problems, such as production issues or quality of work, rather than employees' concerns, including dissatisfactions

---

[20] 1992-3 CCH NLRB ¶17,609, 128 LC ¶11,181 (7th Cir. 1994).

with pay methods, etc. The operation of the committee should be stopped if a union organizing campaign is initiated. Furthermore, discussions in committee meetings should not concern any bargainable issues, and discussions on any issue should stop if a committee representative, union representative, or other party believes the issue deals with a bargainable subject.

Personal Contacts

The top executives in some companies have the operating philosophy of communicating directly with employees. This communication enables the executives to get firsthand knowledge about problems and conditions at work. A direct contact by the chief executive may intimidate some managers and employees, but the benefits outweigh the disadvantages. Employees appreciate the opportunity of talking directly with the top manager. Direct contacts also help build the image of a company team as employees see, meet, and discuss problems with their top manager. Finally, direct contacts, in which the visits are unannounced, help prevent the executive from receiving incorrect information from his or her staff. Some staff members erroneously believe the boss should be told what he or she wants to hear. Direct contacts help put things in the proper perspective.

Eliminating Architectural Barriers to Communication

Walls and partitions can impede the flow of communication. "The open-door policy" is a myth if a secretary or other functionary blocks the entrance to it. Some companies don't worry about such a policy because they have eliminated the interior walls in the business, so that there is no door to open or close.

Organization Development

Organization development (OD) is a generic term encompassing a number of intervention methods to increase organizational efficiency. The OD process varies among practitioners, but it generally includes a need determination phase in which areas are identified where various methods in HRM could be used to increase an organization's effectiveness. The need determination phase generally includes an analysis of organizational goals, strategies, and accomplishments. Exhibit 37-10 shows the relationship of selected OD strategies to an organizational goal, objective, and accomplishment. Some techniques used in organization development are action research, sensing, team building, visioning, survey feedback, sensitivity training, grid training, and quality of work-life initiatives.

Exhibit 37-10
A Selected Example of the Relationship of Organization Development (OD)
Strategies to Goals, Objectives and Results

Goal	Objective	Results	Suggested OD Strategies
Product Quality	Reduce error rate 5%	Error rate unchanged	1. Implement quality circle
			2. Employee training in product quality

Goal	Objective	Results	Suggested OD Strategies
			3. Include error rate in performance appraisal
			4. Install pay incentives on error rates

Action Research

Action research is an approach used in organization development involving interaction, typically between higher level management and employees, in which a problem or issue is diagnosed, often through group meetings, and interventions or improvements are defined, implemented, and evaluated.[21] Several steps are used in the process:

- *Diagnosis* of the problem or area in which improvement is needed. This phase would focus on the objective of the intervention, such as to increase organizational efficiency, to improve employee communication, or to increase the level of trust among employees within the organization.

- *Action planning* to develop solutions to the problem or alternatives to improve the areas identified.

- *Implementation* of the solutions or alternatives.

- *Evaluation* of the intervention(s) to measure results and whether any additional alternatives should be considered.

Usually a facilitator or other third party assists in the process. Action research can be used in either a tactical situation to address a short-term problem, such as responding to customer complaints about shipping errors, or in a long-term context to develop strategies for the accomplishment of goals, such as to increase market share.

Sensing

Sensing is an approach used to improve communication between management and employees in which groups of employees meet with management, typically higher levels of management, to exchange ideas. Sometimes the meetings are to inform employees about various topics, such as organizational performance, areas in which employee ideas are needed, and trends in competitor actions. Meetings may also have the objective of obtaining employee input. The term implies that the meetings are intended to permit both employees and managers to *sense* various issues important to each other and thereby improve communication, trust, and other characteristics requisite for organizational efficiency.

Team Building

Team building is an approach used to improve the communication and performance of employees within the same department or among employees in

---

[21] Mosely, D.C., Pietri, P.H., and Megginson, L.C. *Management: Leadership in Action* (New York: HarperCollins, 1996), pp. 432-33.

different departments. Contrary to the use of the word "team" in the term *team building,* it is not the same as a *team structure* form of organizational structuring described in Chapter 10. *Team building,* as defined above, is intended to aid the teamwork of employees so the organization functions more smoothly. In *team structures,* employees are structured into teams. In a team building project, the employees may be organized in any of the various types of structures, such as functional, team, or matrix.

The team building could be initiated through several approaches.

- The team building could be initiated by a facilitator individually interviewing the employees who will be involved[22] and asking them questions, such as "What issues are preventing you from more effectively accomplishing your work?" A positive question might be "What is an example of how other employees help you get your job done?"

- Team building can also be initiated through group meetings with employees in which various techniques like brainstorming and the nominal group method[23] are used to identify both strengths and weaknesses affecting teamwork among employees.

Once the issues are identified, solutions are proposed and discussed and action plans are formulated. Rather than a one-shot approach, team building is more effective when additional sessions are conducted to follow up on other issues and in which team members can evaluate the effectiveness of the implementation of previously-defined action plans.

Visioning

Visioning is the process of determining an image of how an organization should look and function. It is important for employees at all levels of the organization to share a common vision for the organization's mission, goals, purposes, markets, and culture so their efforts will be united. Through special information and training sessions employees can acquire this common vision.

Survey Feedback

Survey feedback is a process of using a written questionnaire to obtain employee ideas about organizational issues. The ideas are then summarized and communicated back to the employees.

Sensitivity Training

Sensitivity training involves groups of employees who meet together, often away from the work site, with the goal of increasing "the participant's insight into his or her own behavior and the behavior of others by encouraging an open expression of feelings in the trainer-guided" setting.[24] This training is also call *T-groups* (in which the "T" means "training"). French recommends that participa-

---

[22] French, W.L. *Human Resources Management* (Boston: Houghton Mifflin Company, 1998), p. 579.

[23] The *nominal group* method involves a group of people who give their ideas on a subject. Each person in turn either makes a contribution or says "I pass." After two rounds of "I pass" by all partici-

pants, ideas on the subject are assumed to be exhausted. The method is sometimes used in forecasting trends and is covered in Chapter 7.

[24] Dessler, G. *Managing Organizations* (Orlando, Florida: Dryden Press, 1995), p. 621.

tion be voluntary and that participants neither work in the same location nor have a "reporting relationship."[25] He also recommends that the groups be facilitated by a professional due to the potential stress caused by participants revealing their personal feelings and potentially sensitive individual characteristics.

Grid Training

Grid training involves the use of the Blake and Mouton "managerial grid," briefly discussed in Chapter 1.[26] Grid training assists managers in analyzing their personal attitudes and values. Scales ranging from 1 to 9 on an X and a Y axis are used to measure relative concerns for production and people, respectively. A 1,9 is a high concern for people and a low concern for production. A 9,1 is a high concern for production and a low concern for people. A person who is a 9,9 has a high concern for people and a high concern for production. The developmental aspects of grid training include motivating individuals to reshape their behavior.

Quality of Work Life

Quality of work life (QWL) is a generic term for a number of initiatives designed to increase organizational efficiency by improving the conditions in employees' work lives. OD interventions include all strategies to improve efficiency; QWL encompasses only those affecting employees' work lives. Examples of QWL strategies are forms of job restructuring, including job enrichment, and other job scheduling methods, including flextime.

One QWL strategy specifically dedicated to employee cooperation and communication is feedback sessions in which employees are kept regularly informed of organizational operating data, such as productivity and profitability, through daily bulletin board postings and weekly meetings with employees. This feedback is also sometimes tailored to meet employee group needs, such as establishing friendly informal competition between employee work groups on different shifts or in different operations. The competition can be on various topics, including productivity, number of suggestions submitted, or error rates. The winning groups are usually awarded nominal prizes. Changing the subjects in the competition introduces some variety and helps maintain employee interest. The operating data feedback sessions are sometimes given by the plant manager or other manager above the initial supervisory level. Usually, question and answer sessions follow the presentation.

Exit Interviews

An *exit interview* is an interview with an employee who has submitted a resignation to obtain information about management, personnel policies, compensation, and other matters to determine if they contributed to the employee's decision to leave. Exit interviews can be either structured or unstructured, although as with other types of interviews, structured ones are best if the objectives are clearly defined and questions are constructed to achieve them.

[25] French, p. 323.

[26] Blake, R.R. and Mouton, J.S., *The Managerial Grid* (Houston, TX: Gulf Publishing Co., 1964).

There are two main problems with exit interviews. First, departing employees may not tell the real reasons for their resignations because of the prospect the information may reflect unfavorably upon someone, such as their supervisor, who might seek retribution. This retaliation could take the form of furnishing unsatisfactory references to future employers. Also, the employee may be contemplating reemployment with the firm and he or she might fear the chances of this would be diminished if he or she appeared disgruntled. A basic principle of employee attitude/opinion surveys is protection of the employee's confidentiality to guard against the fear of reprisals. The same fears exist with exit interviews, so that similar precautions should be taken if dependable information is expected.

Another problem with exit interviews is that an employee may want to "settle a score" with a supervisor or even with the company. This is most applicable in cases where employees are leaving because they feel they were "wronged" when they were denied a promotion, misled about something, or treated unfairly in some other way. Information in these cases may be so biased and deliberately slanted that it not only would be valueless, but it could motivate unnecessary and incorrect actions. In sum, the purpose of exit interviews is to obtain information useful for decisionmaking purposes. However, it takes remarkable interviewing skills, including considerable intuition and insight, to decide what information is valid and useful.

Whistleblowing

Whistleblowing involves employee disclosures of illegal or improper organizational behavior. Whistleblowing covers many conditions ranging from reports by employees who were instructed to violate laws to complaints of improper accounting methods that overstate company profitability. All states, except Arkansas have at least one law providing some manner of protection for a whistleblower.[27] There are also several federal laws protecting whistleblowers. The Occupational Safety and Health Act provides protection against employers who discriminate or punish employees who report violations of OSHA standards. The Whistleblower Protection Act of 1989 protects federal employees who report fraud and waste in the federal government from retaliation by the agencies that employ them.

In some cases, legal safeguards either fail to protect employees or the protection is too late. Some whistleblowers who are victims of employer reprisals become frustrated by the slow bureaucratic procedures of governmental agencies and go to court to obtain punitive damages.

Ombudsman

Some companies internalize the handling of employee grievances and whistleblowing by establishing appeal systems headed by individuals who report to a top executive.

---

[27] CCH, HUMAN RESOURCES MANAGEMENT, *Personnel*, ¶ 3058.

An *ombudsman* is a person who is hired to investigate and resolve employee complaints and grievances. The ombudsman concept began in Sweden to investigate citizen complaints against the government. The idea travelled to the U.S. in the early 1970s and has expanded to include both public and private organizations.

Hotlines

Hotlines in employee communications, as distinguished from a hot-line number that sometimes serves as the crisis intervention component of employee assistance programs (EAP), is a toll-free number employees can call to voice their opinions about organizational matters. The calls can be made from any telephone, so that employee confidentiality and even anonymity are assured. Some telephone lines are staffed 24 hours a day. Employees are encouraged to use the number to report any matter, such as wrongdoing, illegal activity, or just a dissatisfaction about something. The call is taken and, depending upon its nature, the information is given to the appropriate decisionmaker. Reports of illegal or improper activities are usually given to the internal auditor or general counsel.

There are other varieties of hotlines. Some are the outreach component of the organization's ombudsman.

Other Communication Methods

Many HRM activities provide opportunities for employee communication. For example, some organizations use job evaluation committees composed of employees in various functions of the organization to aid the process of identifying benchmark jobs and conducting job evaluations. Safety and health committees help management in communicating safety and health concerns to employees and provide a channel for employees to communicate with management. The organization and role of safety and health committees are discussed in Chapter 31.

Performance appraisal systems are primarily a communication method of informing employees of the performance variables and performance criteria. Performance appraisal communication is two-way. Management tracks employee performance in various performance variables and compares it to the criteria. The communication flow loops back to the employee as management's perceptions are fed back to the employee. Some appraisal systems, particularly management by objectives, are designed with self-monitoring feedback, so that employees are continually aware of their progress.

Downsizing, Layoffs, and Plant Closure Communication

Some employers do not inform employees in advance about plans for downsizing, layoffs, and plant closures for such reasons as the real or imagined effect the actions may have on employee motivation and turnover. Also, some employers, in their haste to cut costs, have offered severance arrangements to employees, conditional upon them waiving their legal rights, without giving them sufficient opportunity to consider their options. These types of problems resulted in two federal laws protecting workers' rights.

Worker Adjustment and Retraining Notification Act (WARNA)

WARNA applies to firms with 100 or more full-time employees (part-time workers are not included). These firms are required to give 60 days advance notice of a mass layoff or plant closing to these three groups:

- Either all employees affected by a contemplated mass layoff or plant closing or to the representative of such employees, if there is one;
- The state dislocated worker unit; and
- The chief elected official of the local political unit in which the layoff or closing will occur.

The 60-day notice period may be reduced if:

1. The employer was attempting to secure financing which would have prevented either the layoff or the closing, and the advance notice would have precluded the employer from obtaining financing;
2. If business conditions prevent the employer from giving the advance notice; and
3. If a natural disaster occurred that caused the layoff or closure.

A plant closure is defined as the permanent or temporary closure of one employment site or one or more facilities or operating units in a single site during a 30-day period in which 50 or more full-time employees lose their employment. A *mass layoff is* defined as the loss of employment within a 30-day period at a single site of either: (1) at least 33 percent of the full-time workforce and at least 50 full-time persons, or (2) 500 full-time employees. *Loss of employment* includes layoffs exceeding six months in duration and reductions in the hours of work of more than 50 percent during each month in a six-month period; not included are: (1) employees who resign, retire, or are separated for just cause, and (2) employees who are offered employment without a six-month break in an area that is either at a reasonable commuting distance or at any distance if the offer is accepted.

Employers who fail to give the required notice are liable for back pay and benefits for each day of the required notice period. Under certain circumstances, civil penalties of $500 per day for each day of the required notification period may be assessed for failing to contact the local elected chief executive.

Older Workers Benefit Protection Act (OWBPA)

The OWBPA prohibits employees who are 40 and over from waiving their rights under the Age Discrimination in Employment Act of 1967, such as the right to file a charge of discrimination as part of an agreement between an employee and the employer, unless certain conditions are met. These are the general conditions that a waiver must meet:

- It is written in such a way that the average person to whom the waiver would apply can understand it.
- It includes a listing of the specific rights a person has under the ADEA.
- The employee does not waive any rights that may exist after the date of the waiver.

- The waiver is in exchange for anything of value beyond that which the employee is already entitled.
- The employee is advised in writing to consult with an attorney prior to executing the waiver.
- The employee is given 45 days to consider the waiver and the terms of the agreement if an incentive is offered or other termination program is offered to a class of employees. Otherwise, a 21-day consideration period is required.
- The employee is given seven days to revoke the waiver agreement after he or she has signed it.
- If an incentive or other termination program is offered, the employer must inform the employees at the beginning of the 45-day notice period of:
  a. the class of persons covered by the program, the eligibility terms, and the time limits; and
  b. the job titles and ages of those persons who are eligible or selected for the program and those who were not eligible or selected.

CHAPTER 38

INTERNATIONAL HUMAN RESOURCES MANAGEMENT

Chapter Highlights
- Review the qualifications for expatriates to be successful in international assignments
- Examine the methods for selecting expatriates
- Analyze the reasons expatriates fail in international assignments
- Learn how to prevent expatriate failures
- Review the methods of compensating expatriates

Introduction

As U.S. firms expand so rapidly into international markets, there simply are not enough applicants to meet the demand. The problem is so severe that even short assignments of six months cannot be filled without extraordinary effort.[1] Recruiting, compensating, and retaining employees in international jobs pose significant challenges for international human resources managers.

International human resource management is the performance of HRM activities to obtain and maintain an effective workforce in the foreign operations of a United States firm.

This chapter is structured differently from the other chapters in this book which emphasize a particular HRM activity. International HR is not a distinct HRM activity; it involves the performance of all HRM activities in the foreign operation of a United States firm.

Legal Environment

There are many differences in the political, social and economic systems among countries in the world. Operating within this dynamic environment is a constant challenge to international firms. U.S. firms must comply with some federal laws in their international operation. Later in this chapter there is a discussion of some of these laws. In addition to complying with applicable U.S. law, these firms must also with the laws in the countries in which they function. These laws cover many human resources functions such as labor relations, employee benefits and employee relations. Furthermore, many of the laws differ

---

[1] Lublin, Joann S., "Companies Send Intrepid Retirees to Work Abroad," *The Wall Street Journal* (March 2, 1998).

not only with those in the U.S. but also among other countries. These laws also change and require considerable planning to comply with them.

Example: Workplace Smoking in England

An example of a sweeping change was a law invoked in England in 2007 prohibiting smoking in all enclosed and "substantially enclosed" workplaces, including work vehicles occupied by more than one person. The law also prohibits rooms and indoor areas especially established to accommodate smokers. All smoking must be outside. There are monetary penalties for noncompliance ranging from a fine of £200 for failing to display no-smoking signs to a maximum of £2500 for managers who fail to prevent smoking in a no-smoking area.

Definitions

Employees who work in international assignments are referred to in distinct terms:

- *Expatriate.* An *expatriate* is a citizen of one country who is employed by a company with headquarters in that same country, but is working in a foreign assignment. Example: A U.S. citizen working in France for a U.S. firm. *Expatriation* is the process of preparing a person to leave on an international assignment.

- *Repatriate.* A *repatriate* is a person who is returning from an international assignment. *Repatriation* is the process of preparing a person to return from an international assignment.

- *Inpatriate.* An *inpatriate* is a citizen of a country who is on an assignment to the corporate office of a firm located in another country. Example: A citizen of Germany who is employed by a U.S. company in Germany and the person is given a work assignment in the U.S.

- *Host country national.* A *host country national* is a citizen of a country employed in a branch or plant of a company that is located in his or her country but is headquartered in another country. Example: A citizen of Italy working in Italy for a U.S. firm.

- *Third country national.* A *third country national* is a citizen of one country who is employed in another country by a firm that is headquartered in still a different country. Example: A citizen of Greece working in Spain for a U.S. firm.

In 2004, U.S. non-bank multinational companies (MNC) had 29.6 million employees worldwide of which 72 percent or 21.3 million were employed in the U. S. This figure represents approximately 20 percent of total private sector employment in the U. S. The remaining 8.3 million were employed abroad by foreign affiliates with majority ownership. From 2000 to 2005, the number of employees in U.S. MNCs declined from 32 million to 29.6 million. During the same period, the U.S. parent share of these employees declined from 74.5 percent to 72 percent.[2]

Distinctions in International and Multinational Firms

Some experts in the field of international business distinguish *international* firms from *multinational* firms.

Political Involvement

The main distinction in the two terms involve a firm's political involvement in the host country and the autonomy of local management to manage the foreign business operation.

Multinational firms tend to be more involved in the political affairs of the host country. In addition, they delegate less authority to local managers, including expatriates working abroad. Several ramifications may result from these two strategies. First, political involvement may result in the business association with unpopular political interests. This is risky, since it can result in the expropriation of business property in the event the firm is linked to those political interests on the losing end of a revolution or election. Another potentially serious consequence of political involvement is the increased risk of sabotage and acts of terrorism, such as kidnapping expatriate managers and using them for prisoner exchange or ransoms. While these same events can occur with international firms, the probability is less.

Centralized Control

Multinational firms also retain centralized control of foreign operations. The top expatriate executive in a *multinational* foreign operation functions in the same way a branch manager does in the United States. For example, if the operation is a chemical production facility, the top executive is only responsible for production; other decisions affecting raw material procurement, marketing strategies, and product distribution are made in the home office. Top managers in foreign plants of *international* firms, however, operate more like chief executive officers in the United States. Thus, they make virtually every decision affecting the foreign operation.

HR Management Impact

The distinctions in international and multinational firms affect human resource management. For example, if labor relations policy is directed from the United States corporate office, local management in the foreign operation is restricted in the number of options for resolving a labor dispute. This may result even if local management has a better understanding of the situation and how to resolve it. Centralized control usually results in local managers deferring judgment and referring matters to the central office. Eventually, this can impede communication, increase costs, and reduce efficiency. The advantages of centralized control are maintaining uniformity in policy application and maximizing

---

[2] U. S. Department of Commerce, *News Release: Summary Estimates for Multinational Companies: Employment, Sales, and Capital Expenditures for 2004.*

overall corporate objectives. For example, if labor rates are too high in a plant in one country, the corporate office can move it to another country where wages are lower. Obviously, the strategic planning in such situations requires centralized control.

Despite the distinctions in the two terms, most people either use *multinational* as the generic word for business operations in another country or they use *multinational* and *international* interchangeably. In this chapter, we will follow the latter practice.

Expanding Importance of International HRM

The demand for human resources, as with other factors of production, is a *derived* demand. This means that the demand for human resources, as with other factors of production used to produce goods and services, is derived from the consumer demand for those goods and services. Accordingly, the demand for international human resources is due in part to the expanding international market for goods and services.

Another reason for the increasing importance of international HRM is shifts in world population, as the proportion of the world in more developed countries declines and as changes occur in the proportions of the less developed countries, as shown in the following Tables 38-1 and 38-2.

Table 38-1
World Population
More and Less Developed Countries, 1996-2025

	1996	2010	2025
World	5,771,000 (100%)	6,974,000 (100%)	8,193,000 (100%)
More developed countries	1,171,000 (20.0%)	1,231,000 (17.7%)	1,268,000 (15.5%)
Less developed countries	4,600,000 (80.0%)	5,743,000 (82.3%)	6,925,000 (84.5%)

Source: Population Reference Bureau (Ed.): World Population Data Sheet 1996, Washington, D.C., 1996.

Table 38-2
Population in Less Developed Countries, 1996-2025

	1996	2010	2025
Total	4,600,000 (100.0%)	5,743,000 (100.0%)	6,925,000 (100.0%)
Africa	732,000 (15.9%)	1,039,000 (18.1%)	1,462,000 (21.1%)
Latin America	486,000 (10.6%)	584,000 (10.2%)	678,000 (9.8%)
Asia	3,375,000 (73.4%)	4,110,000 (71.6%)	4,772,000 (68.9%)

Source: Population Reference Bureau (Ed.): World Population Data Sheet 1996, Washington, D.C., 1996.

The World Federation of Personnel Management Associations

In 1976, the World Federation of Personnel Management Associations (Federation) was formed by representatives from the European Association for Personnel Management, the Interamerican Federation of Personnel Administration, and the Society for Human Resource Management (SHRM). In 1980, these groups were joined by the Asian Pacific Federation of Personnel Associations. The Federation now consists of 150,000 members representing 60 personnel organizations throughout the world. The Federation has five objectives:

- To improve the quality and effectiveness of professional personnel management and the enhancement of its role in all employing organizations, both public and private;

- To stimulate and assist in the establishment and development of regional and national personnel management associations in those parts of the world where a continental or regional association does not yet exist;

- To create and maintain contacts with all its member associations as well as with other organizations which have some activity in the same or similar field;

- To support (and represent, if requested) personnel management associations in their contacts with world organizations, such as ILO, UNESCO, UNO, etc.; and

- To undertake appropriate research activities which will further a broader understanding of personnel issues worldwide.[3]

The Federation provides a variety of mutual assistance efforts to accomplish these objectives. Federation meetings, for example, give members an opportunity for professional development of both domestic and expatriate human resource managers. Interchange meetings of representatives from various countries typically cover a wide range of topics, such as labor relations, human resource mobility, productivity, work quality, benefits, and executive compensation.

In response to the importance of international personnel management, SHRM organized an international chapter, the Society for Human Resource Management International (SHRM/I). The goals of SHRM/I are "to improve the international competence of SHRM (and World Federation of Personnel Management Associations) members and to raise the standards of their performance in all phases of personnel administration."[4] Among the principles of SHRM/I are:

- Equal treatment and recognition of the dignity of all people;

- Recognition of the human resource responsibilities at local, national, and international levels; and

- Promotion of international understanding that creates a positive influence on employee performance, personnel professionalism, and world peace.

International Terrorism

Terrorist acts against U.S. businesses and innocent U.S. citizens and others residing within the U.S., as well as U.S. expatriates working abroad, are a major concern. The attacks on the World Trade Center and the Pentagon on September 11, 2001 and the U.S. and other countries response to it (both militarily and otherwise) dramatically reshaped how the U.S. and many other countries will deal with terrorism.

Terrorists have engaged in kidnaping expatriates, particularly top level experts. Once an expatriate is kidnaped, there are few options available since the local police are usually powerless. Also, foreign governments are often more concerned with capturing the terrorists because they fear ransom payments will be used to purchase weapons. The U.S. State Department is of limited value because the agency believes paying ransoms only encourages more terrorism. In the end, companies often must resort to their own means of dealing with terrorism. Usually this means dealing directly with the terrorists or hiring specialists to do it for them.

Domestic terrorism and other industrial security matters are covered in Chapter 32. Terrorist acts against U.S. businesses and U.S. expatriates are a major concern in international HRM. Among the countries in which such acts have

---

[3] *Welcome to the WFPMA*, World Federation of Personnel Management Associations (February 1998).

[4] SHRM/I, *Fact Sheet* (Alexandria, Va: Society for Human Resource Management).

occurred are Argentina, Mexico, Ethiopia, Columbia, West Germany, El Salvador, Chile, Guatemala, and Iran.

Causes of Terrorism

The causes of terrorism are complex. Oftentimes a particular act of terrorism may stem from incidents in the distant past. Other acts of terrorism may result from recent events. For example, the Iraq war was a major cause of terrorism occurring in that country after the invasion.

Definitions of Terrorism

There are several definitions of terrorism. One of the most widely used definitions is contained in the *Code of Federal Regulations* and states:

- Terrorism is ". . . the unlawful use of force and violence against person or property to intimidate or coerce a government, the civilian population, or any segment thereof, in furtherance of political or social objectives."

Another widely used definition contained in *Title 22 of the U.S. Code* states:

- Terrorism is the "premeditated, politically motivated violence perpetrated against noncombatant targets by subnational groups or clandestine agents."

The terms "politically motivated" and "noncombatant" are subject to interpretation. The National Counterterrorism Center (NCTC) in the U.S. Department of State defines these terms rather specifically in tracking incidents of terrorism.

- *Politically Motivated*. According to the NCTC an act is "politically motivated" and thus terrorism, if it was a life-threatening attack or kidnapping perpetrated by specific organizations listed by the NCTC. More generally, acts are considered politically motivated if they are directed towards government/diplomatic officials or buildings.

- *Noncombatant*. Noncombatants are civilians, civilian police and military property outside of war zones. Combatants are military, paramilitary, militia and police that are under military command.

There are both general and specific reasons for terrorism.

General Causes

General reasons include deteriorating economic conditions prompted by debt repayments of developing countries, such as Mexico and Brazil. In order to make the debt payments, which are adversely affected by high interest rates in the U.S., foreign countries must obtain funds by reducing public subsidies to citizens and raising taxes. In addition, the foreign governments borrow more money, increasing the inflationary rate in the domestic economy. The total effect of these actions is a declining standard of living, poverty, and hunger. Inevitably, frustration and despair make U.S. companies in these countries the convenient target for aggression. Political turmoil, such as the kind that has occurred in Guatemala, Argentina, and El Salvador, also may result in terrorism against U.S. firms and expatriate personnel.

Religious, political, and cultural differences are another general reason for terrorism. There are about 85 established groups promoting terrorism for one or more of these reasons. Spain's separatists are driven by national causes; some, such as the Shiite Moslems, are religious fanatics exploited by politicians; and others are extremist ideologues, including neo-Nazis or the French organization, Action Directe.[5]

Specific Causes

Companies may be targeted for terrorism as the result of controversial actions, such as causing pollution or health hazards, or appearing to condone human rights violations. A potentially dangerous situation occurred in Guatemala when a union attempted to organize Coca-Cola employees. The organizing dispute between management and labor resulted in the deaths of several union organizers. Eventually, employees took possession of the plant and refused entry to everyone. Coca-Cola officials in the U.S. forced the Guatemalan franchise owner to sell his franchise, but subsequent owners were also unable to resolve the dispute.

Extent of Terrorism

The NCTC is the most comprehensive source of data on terrorism. As noted above, the NCTC definition of terrorism does not include combatant losses. Consequently, the enormous costs in the suffering and deaths of military personnel and the destruction of the Iraq infrastructure caused by the war are not included in the following data since they were the result of "combat."

During 2007, approximately 14,000 terrorist attacks occurred in various countries resulting in over 22,000 deaths. The number of attacks were about the same as in 2006, but the number of deaths increased nine percent or about 1,800. Eighty-seven percent of the attacks occurred in the Near East and South Asia. Forty-three percent of the attacks occurred in Iraq accounting for approximately 13,600 fatalities, which was 60 percent of the worldwide total. As fighting in Afghanistan increased in 2007 the number of attacks grew by 16 percent over 2006. Conversely, the number of attacks fell by 42 percent in the Western Hemisphere. Declines in attacks also occurred in Europe and Eurasia by eight percent and in South Asia by about seven percent. Overall, the number injured during terrorist attacks increased 15 percent.[6]

The wars in Afghanistan and Iraq were the major causes of non-terrorist (military) and terrorist (noncombatant) deaths, disabilities and destruction.

Preventive Measures

Some preventive measures that companies employ to stop terrorism include using armed guards and armored cars. Another precaution is for expatriates to vary their schedules and travel routes. Managers also use aliases and their travel plans are kept secret, even within the company, in the event the terrorist organization has spies employed there. As a precaution in the event of kidnap-

---

[5] Copeland, Lennie, "Terrorism: The Mouse That Roars," *Personnel Administrator* (September 1987), p. 71.

[6] National Counterterrorism Center, 2007 Report on Terrorism (30 April 2008), p. 9.

ing, expatriates are photographed, fingerprinted, and even voice-printed. In addition, they are taught how to behave as a hostage, namely to be docile.[7]

One expert believes another way to combat terrorism is for a company to conduct business in such a way that people within the community perceive it as a valuable resource. This approach will develop a climate of public opinion and support that will help insulate the company from potential acts of terrorism. In addition, people will develop loyalty to the company and help protect it by alerting officials about terrorist plans. This approach is also encouraged to prevent domestic acts of terrorism within the U.S.[8] In addition to company practices, perhaps the biggest disincentive to international terrorism is "no tolerance" policies of the world community.

The Iraq war added a significant new dimension to the discussion of preventing terrorism. While acts of war are often offered as preventing or attacking terrorism, the opposite is also true: war appreciably causes instability and increases world terrorism.

Recruitment and Selection

Legal Requirements

Expatriates

Generally, the Americans with Disabilities Act, the Age Discrimination in Employment Act, and Title VII apply to U.S. citizens who are employed in a different country for U.S. firms. Noncompliance with these laws is permissible if compliance would conflict with the laws of the respective country.[9] An employer incorporated or based in the U.S. is considered to be a U.S. employer based upon the relevance of these factors:

- the principal location of the firm's business;

- the nationality of dominant shareholders and/or those holding voting control; and,

- the nationality and location of management (the officers and directors of the firm).

In some cases, the issue may arise whether the laws would apply because of a question of an American employer's control over the foreign operation. In such situations, control of the operation is determined through an analysis of these factors:

- the amount of interrelationship in the domestic and foreign operations;

- the extent to which the two operations, that is, the foreign and the American, have common management;

- the focus of control in labor relations; and

---

[7] n.a., "Concerns Unable to Avert Kidnappings— Find Freeing Hostages a Tricky Affair," *The Wall Street Journal* (December 2, 1983), p. 14.

[8] Lacy, D., "Terrorism on the Home Front," *Personnel Administrator* (April 1983), p. 26.

[9] CCH HUMAN RESOURCES MANAGEMENT, *Equal Employment Opportunity*, ¶ 230.

- the extent of common ownership or financial control by the American firm.[10]

The federal laws that do not apply to foreign operations of American firms are the Fair Standards Labor Act, the Equal Pay Act, the Rehabilitation Act, and the Vietnam Era Veterans' Readjustment Act. In addition, Executive Order 11246 does not apply. The Fair Labor Standards Act has a somewhat quirky application since the law applies to U.S. citizens who perform some work in the United States during their work week, such as an employee who works three days in a work week in a plant in Canada and works the other two days for the same employer in a plant in Maine.[11]

Foreign firms with operations in the United States generally are required to comply with U.S. equal employment opportunity laws. Exemptions are permitted under "Friendship, Commerce and Navigation" treaties negotiated between the United States and other countries. Typically, however, the treaties have very specific applications. Firms from Japan, Greece, and Korea have run afoul of equal employment opportunity laws in venturing too far from treaties negotiated between their countries and the United States.[12]

Nonimmigrant Visas

Nonimmigrant visas are issued to persons who wish to work temporarily in the U. S. There are a number of procedures that prospective employers must follow before such persons can be employed, such as filing petitions (Petition for Immigrant Worker), consenting to pay the prevailing wage for the work to be performed, paying fees to the U.S. Government, and having documents available for public review concerning the employment of foreign workers. Immigrants must apply for visas, which based on type, may be subject to quotas and time limitations. These are the major categories of nonimmigrant visas for those seeking temporary employment in the U.S.:

- H-1B includes fashion models of distinction and those in specialties requiring theoretical and practical application of specialized knowledge and a baccalaureate degree or the equivalent in specific fields, such as the sciences, medicine and health care, education, biotechnology, and business. Limited to 65,000 visas per year. These categories are exempt from the 65,000 cap.

  H-1B Employer Exemptions:

  ☐ Nonimmigrants who are either employed or have an offer of employment from institutions of higher education or a related nonprofit entity.

  ☐ Also exempt are those employed or will be employed by a nonprofit research organization or a governmental research institutition.

  H-1B Advanced Degree Exemption. The H-1B Visa Reform Act of 2004 annually permits 20,000 visas exempt from the cap for foreign workers with at least a Master's degree from U.S. academic institutions H-1B1

---

[10] Ibid.
[11] Ibid.

[12] For a full discussion of this subject, see CCH HUMAN RESOURCES MANAGEMENT, *Equal Employment Opportunity*, ¶ 230.

Exemption. Exempt from the 65,000 are nationals from Chile or Singapore who will be employed in a specialty occupation (defined as a position that requires theoretical and practical application of a body of specialized knowledge.) Individuals must have at least a bachelor's (or the equivalent) in the specific specialty. The combined statutory limit is 6,800 per year: 1,400 visas are set aside annually for nationals of Chile and 5,400 for nationals of Singapore.[13]

- H-2A applies to temporary or seasonal agricultural workers.

- H-2B applies to temporary or seasonal nonagricultural workers. Limited to 66,000 visas per year.

- H-3 applies to trainees (other than medical or academic) and those receiving practical training in the education of handicapped children. Limited to 50 visas per year.

- L applies to managerial, executive or other employees of U. S. firms who have specialized knowledge and who, within the past three years, have been employed abroad continuously for one year by the same U. S. employer.

- O-1 applies to persons with extraordinary ability in the sciences, arts, education, business, or athletics, or extraordinary achievements in the motion picture and television field.

- O-2 applies to persons assisting O-1 aliens in an artistic or athletic performance for a specific event or performance.

- P-1 applies to athletes or members of an entertainment group that are internationally recognized. Limited to 25,000 visas per year.

- P-2 applies to artists or entertainers performing under a reciprocal exchange program.

- P-3 applies to artists or entertainers performing under a culturally unique program. Subject to the visa limitations under P-1.

- Q-1 applies to participants in an international cultural exchange program for the purpose of providing practical training, employment and the sharing of the history, culture, and traditions of the alien's home country.[14]

With the exception of Q-1, spouses and unmarried minor children of persons admitted under the above classifications are not subject to the visa limitations, however, they may not be employed in the U. S.

Laws affecting international trade

The Foreign Corrupt Practices Act of 1977 forbids U.S. firms from making payments to foreign officials that are illegal or questionable. Corruption and bribery are major hindrances to fair international competition and economic progress. The U.S. Commerce Department estimates that $80 billion are paid by

---

[13] U.S. Citizenship and Immigration Services, *Cap Count for H-1B and H-2B Workers for Fiscal Year, 2009* (July 29, 2008), pp. 1 & 2.

[14] U.S. Department of State, *Temporary Workers* (June 2007).

foreign firms to officials in other countries. To help prevent this problem, the Organization for Economic Cooperation and Development developed a convention to criminalize bribery, which was signed by 34 countries in December 1997.

The Trade Adjustment Assistance (TAA) program and the North American Free Trade Agreement (NAFTA) provide assistance to individuals who become unemployed, due to foreign imports (TAA) or imports from Mexico or Canada (NAFTA-TAA), to return to *suitable employment*. *Suitable employment* is defined as work of a substantially equal or higher skill level than the person's past adversely-affected employment, which pays not less than 80 percent of the employee's previous employment. The benefits provided by these programs include training, trade adjustment allowances, job search allowances, relocation allowances, subsistence allowance (while in training), transportation allowance (while in training) and reemployment services. Persons who do not meet all the requirements for benefits under either TAA or NAFTA may qualify for assistance through Title III of the Job Training Partnership Act.

Offshoring

For many years, manufacturing jobs in the U.S., particularly in textiles, leather goods, apparel, and auto parts and other semi-skilled types of work have been sent abroad to countries where labor costs were lower and labor laws were lax. More recently, white collar jobs have been experiencing the same trend. The skill levels of these jobs range from relatively unskilled, such as telemarketing to highly skilled work, such as information technology. Call center staffing, for example answering consumer questions about products, is a particular type of work which has been targeted for increasing outsourcing to other countries. This trend is predicted to continue into the future as employers lower costs in response to both foreign and domestic competition.

Outsourcing was the term used in the past to define the process of moving jobs from one firm to another, principally to reduce costs. However, there are other reasons for outsourcing, such as the following:

- Focus on the core business objectives,
- Increase or improve service delivery,
- Conserve organizational resources,
- Reduce taxes, and
- Avoid state laws, such as New York's minimum wage law.

Originally, outsourcing was largely a domestic process, however, as it became internationalized by moving jobs from one country, such as the U.S., to another country like India, the term *outsourcing* became outmoded because while the process was essentially the same and some of the reasons were the same, there were other more dominant motives motivating the movement of jobs to another country such as these:

- An abundant (and sometimes better educated in the case of India) workforce available at dramatically lower wages,
- Less restrictive national laws involving the environment and employee safety, and

- Typically either no labor unions or unions with virtually no influence.

Offshoring is the term used to describe the process of moving jobs from one country to another to either gain a competitive advantage and/or to accomplish one or more of the objectives noted above. Depending upon the circumstances, there are several variations of *offshoring*. The terms for these variations are *multishoring, nearshoring,* and *twoshoring* and these are the definitions[15]:

- *Multishoring* is the process of sending different types of jobs to different countries depending upon how well the above objectives are met,

- *Nearshoring* is *offshoring* in which the work is sent to nearby or even contiguous countries, such as U.S. firms sending work to firms in Mexico,

- *Twoshoring* is the process in which a firm performs some work in its home country and other work in another country.

Firms use these variations depending upon how well they meet their objectives. For example, a firm may elect to use a *nearshoring* arrangement if they want the work relocated to another country, where government regulations are less restrictive, but still want it close by for transportation purposes.

Offshoring work may be reversed, that is the work is returned to the firm's home country, depending upon the same circumstances motivating the original decision to send it to another country. For example, several decades ago the U.S. auto industry *offshored* some auto parts manufacturing to Japan. Later, as labor costs in Japan increased to the extent the work could be performed at a lower cost in the U.S., the process was reversed and some of the work returned to the U.S. This is known as *reverse offshoring* and is defined as a process in which countries that had been the recipient of jobs being sent from another country have instead had the process reversed with the jobs being sent back to the previous country.

The actual number of jobs that may be subject to *offshoring* ranges from 3 to 14 million. The latter figure represents about 11 percent of U.S. employment levels in 2001.[16] The actual number that is offshored will undoubtedly depend upon a number of factors, including public policy deliberations.

Groups of Employees Sent Abroad

Typically, multinational U.S. firms send abroad either highly skilled technical personnel or executives.

Recruitment Sources

The typical recruitment sources for skilled personnel are present employees of the firm, retired employees, and employees of service and equipment vendors. Usually, skilled personnel are assigned to assist in the start-up of a new facility and/or the training of host country nationals.

Executive recruitment sources include search firms specializing in placing executives in foreign assignments. The customary source of executive talent,

[15] McFedries, Paul, *The Word Spy,* September 22, 2004.

[16] Society for Human Resource Management, "Offshoring," in *Workplace Visions* (No. 2, 2004, p. 5).

even for companies that are new entrants into foreign countries, is existing management personnel. Managers recruited within the firm, however, generally do not have any international experience. Recruiting managers from the foreign operations of other domestic firms is also an option.

Another source of executive talent is the growing cadre of international executives who have experience working for a number of firms in different countries. The unification of the European Economic Community has led firms to selecting what has been referred to as the "Euro-manager." Persons in this group are knowledgeable in many diverse cultures and with the ability to organize management teams of people with diverse backgrounds.[17]

Multinational firms select host country nationals for management jobs for these reasons:

- The high failure rates of expatriate placements;
- The expense of sending expatriate executives abroad;
- To gain greater acceptance of the communities in which they function; and
- Host country nationals generally have superior knowledge of the language, customs, and economic conditions in their countries.

Expatriate Failure Rates

Approximately one-fourth of expatriates fail in their overseas assignments because they perform unsatisfactorily and/or leave the assignment prematurely.[18] Studies indicate that four out of five failures are due to personal adjustment problems. This is the order of importance for these failures:

- Spouse's problems in adapting;
- Expatriate's problems in adapting;
- Other family problems;
- Expatriate's maturity and inability to assume greater responsibilities;
- Technical incompetence; and
- Expatriate's lack of desire to work abroad.[19]

Two actions are necessary to correct these problems and to ensure that capable candidates are selected for overseas work. The first procedure entails defining those job specifications necessary for successful job performance and using valid selection methods to measure applicant qualifications. The second is properly orienting applicants and their family members to ensure they are adequately prepared for the assignment. One expert refers to these two phases as the "selection/orientation continuum" and adds a third phase, repatriation, to complete the cycle.[20]

---

[17] Hagerty, B., "Firms in Europe Try to Find Executives Who Can Cross Borders in a Single Bound," *The Wall Street Journal* (January 25, 1991), p. B-1.

[18] Conway, M.A., "Reducing Expatriate Failure Rates," *Personnel Administrator* (July 1984), p. 31.

[19] Rehfuss, J., "Management Development and the Selection of Overseas Executives," *Personnel Administrator* (July 1982), p. 41.

[20] Conway, "Reducing Expatriate Failure Rates," p. 37.

Adequate preparation can make a significant difference in the adjustment and performance of managers in international assignments. Because of the extensive preparation that Japanese firms give their executives, less than 10 percent of them fail when assigned to an international position.[21]

Unfortunately, U.S. firms generally do not adequately prepare expatriates. For example, 82 percent of 320 executives sent to Pacific Basin and Western European assignments were not briefed on the "management practices in their host countries, and 78 percent weren't even provided factual information on their destinations." Furthermore, 85 percent were not given language training. Also, 90 percent of the spouses and family members of the expatriates received neither training nor briefings on the country to which they were assigned.[22]

Determining the Job Specifications

The process of determining job specifications for foreign jobs is similar to the one used for domestic jobs. The first step is conducting a job analysis. The difficulty of this analysis is dependent upon the job's location. For example, a job in a Canadian or Mexican plant may be no more difficult to analyze than that for a domestic plant.

The next step is writing a job description and setting job specifications. Foreign jobs, as with domestic ones, require incumbents to possess job-related training, education, experience, and knowledge. Sometimes, these requirements will be the same for identical jobs located in the U.S. Typically, however, there are differences in job specifications for foreign assignments. The area with the biggest difference is *skills requirements* because of the importance of personal skills in the ability to adapt to and work in a foreign assignment.

Skills Requirements

Some of the skills related to the successful job performance of expatriates are adaptability, communication, perseverance, patience, initiative, stress tolerance, sincerity, cultural empathy, motivation, foreign language ability, and the desire and ability to live in a foreign culture. Some of these skills are interdependent. For example, *adaptability* is related to the ability to live in a foreign culture. Foreign countries often have different customs and methods, and a person must be able to cope with them. *Communication skills* are related to the skill of acquiring a working knowledge of a foreign language. For example, one study of multinational executives found that 43 percent of the expatriate managers spoke the language of the host country.[23]

Adaptability and *stress tolerance* are related to a knowledge or ability to communicate in the foreign environment. *Patience* and *perseverance* are useful skills in dealing with conditions that cannot be changed while simultaneously working to maintain productivity and efficiency. For example, family member responsibilities are very important in extended families in some third world countries. To meet this responsibility, various family members will temporarily

[21] Patterson, T.D., "The Global Manager," *World* (1990), p. 12.
[22] *Ibid.*

[23] Baker, J.C., "Foreign Language and Predeparture Training in U.S. Multinational Firms," *Personnel Administrator* (July 1984), p. 72.

leave their village and work in a plant until they have saved enough to sustain the family for a certain period. When enough money is saved, the employee will quit and return to his village and another family member will seek a job when more funds are needed. Expatriate managers must have patience to tolerate these practices.

Sincerity is a skill that requires no elaboration. Host country nationals will forgive unintentional *faux pas* if an expatriate is sincerely trying to do the proper thing. Unfortunately, Americans often have the reputation, whether deservedly or not, of committing social blunders. The deciding factor in these cases is whether an omission was sincerely in error.

Life in a foreign assignment is trying. Host country nationals have different standards of proper job performance. *Stress* is inevitable in such situations. Daily life outside work is similarly stressful. For example, language barriers can create stress when ordering a meal in a restaurant. *Cultural empathy* is related to both the skill and desire to live in a foreign country. These characteristics are evident in an expatriate's *sensitivity to* and *understanding* of foreign customs. An additional dimension of these skills is the enjoyment experienced in both learning and observing these customs. Expatriates who are sensitive to cultural differences and enjoy observing them have a greater desire to work in foreign assignments. The relative importance of different skills is not known precisely. Apparently, *cultural empathy* is close to the top of the list, but different foreign assignments may require different skills.

Technical Competence

Technical competence is another job specification frequently mentioned in selecting personnel for overseas assignments. Apparently, such competence is important to some extent in all foreign jobs. However, it is most important in those that require either troubleshooting or expertise in a specific field.[24]

Preventing Inpatriate Failures

The same care that is used in preparing expatriates for foreign assignments should also be followed in preparing inpatriates for assignment to the U.S. Inpatriates and their family members also can experience culture shock. They may also have difficulties with language barriers. Inpatriates and their family members may need assistance in opening bank accounts, obtaining driver licenses, and renting or purchasing a home.

Selection Process

Selecting applicants for foreign assignments is both similar to and different from selection processes used in domestic jobs. These are the main differences:

- Considering the spouse and other family members in selection decisions;
- Physical conditions of the spouse and family members;

---

[24] For differing points of view on the importance of technical competence, see Willis, H.L., "Selection for Employment in Developing Countries," *Person-* *nel Administrator* (July 1984), p. 54, and Rehfuss, "Management Development," p. 39.

- The importance of the applicant's physical examination and the phase of the selection process in which it is conducted;

- The importance of past domestic performance appraisal results;

- Testing for foreign language skills; and

- Measuring skills unique to a foreign assignment.

Consider Spouse and Family

Among the top reasons for expatriates' failures in foreign assignments are spouses' problems in adapting to the foreign culture and other family problems. For example, a study of 34 multinational firms found that a foreign assignment was hardest on the spouse, which resulted in increased stress on the expatriate.[25] To some extent, spousal and family adjustment problems are also present in domestic relocations when an employee is transferred or promoted to a job in another community. The adjustment problems are more significant, however, in relocations to a foreign country. In domestic relocations, spouses and family members can visit friends and relatives in the previous community; the cost of this travel is prohibitive in relocations to foreign countries. For these and other reasons, the adaptation skills of living in a foreign culture and the desires of spouses and family members to live in a foreign country must be considered in selecting employees for foreign assignments.

Obviously, it is not economical to select an employee for overseas work without first determining if the spouse and family members want to go abroad and will be able to adapt. There are several ways of obtaining this information. First, videotaped interviews can be conducted of spouses and family members living abroad. These interviews should frankly explain, in the family members' own words, what it is like to live in a foreign country. The interviews should include both the advantages and disadvantages of overseas living. Where possible, the taping may include various family members engaging in customary daily events, such as a shopping trip or going to school. Another approach used to help family members decide about living in a foreign country is a personal discussion with family members who have recently returned from a foreign country.

The dual-career family is a special problem in making overseas selections. A survey of 46 U.S. multinational firms found that in making employee selection decisions, the firms fail to effectively meet the needs of dual-career couples. The authors of the study contend that to facilitate the employment of individuals in dual-career marriages, some accommodations are needed to assist the spouse in securing employment in the location where the international job placement is occurring.[26]

---

[25] "Labor Letter," *The Wall Street Journal* (June 19, 1984), p. 1.

[26] Handler, Charles A., Lane, Irving M., and Maher, Michael, "Human Resource Planning in Multinational Corporations," *Human Resource Management Journal* (March 1997), pp. 67-79.

Physical Condition of Spouse and Family Members

A health screening of the spouse and family members is advisable to determine if a health problem exists that would either preclude relocation or would be aggravated by a relocation. Sometimes, even minor health conditions are not treatable in a foreign country because qualified health professionals are not available.

Physical Examination of the Applicant

A physical examination is rarely required for internal placements, such as promotions in either domestic or international assignments. Typically, physical examinations are not required for new hires in either domestic or international assignments, except where job conditions mandate them, such as fire fighters and airline pilots. Furthermore, for domestic assignments, the health of the employee's or applicant's children and spouse is not a concern. However, for international assignments health conditions, may be a concern if the medical facilities are not available to treat the condition. Employers cannot use either the spouse's or the children's health status in making selection decisions. Employers would be remiss in failing to advise a potential expatriate on the inadvisability of accepting an assignment to a location where medical resources would not be available to treat a condition. The ultimate decision concerning such matters, of course, remains with the applicant. Some employers do make special arrangements for medical treatments, such as compensating employees or their family members for travel to locations where health professionals are available.

If medical examinations are required for expatriates, the provisions of the Americans with Disabilities Act must be followed. According to this Act, the medical examination cannot be required until after an initial offer of employment has been extended. In addition, the medical examination must be required for all persons who are initially selected for the job in question.

Employers sending employees abroad also require that they have the necessary vaccinations recommended by the World Health Organization.

Past Performance in Domestic Assignments

In Chapter 16, practitioners are advised of the danger in relying too heavily on past job success in making promotions. The reason is simple; successful performance in a lower-level job is not necessarily a predictor of success in a higher-level one. This logic also applies to foreign assignments. First, two different domestic jobs, as with different domestic and foreign jobs, have different job specifications, so performing well in one is not necessarily a predictor of performing well in the other. Second, foreign assignments require different skills, such as cultural empathy, so superior performance in a domestic assignment may not necessarily be a predictor of success in a foreign job. Despite these distinctions, most employers highly value past records of domestic job performance in making foreign assignments.

Testing for Foreign Language Skills

Foreign language skills are a job specification unique to international jobs. Sometimes, bilingual skills are required in domestic jobs in which the employee will deal with ethnic groups. The foreign assignment, however, requires the employee and family members to use the foreign language outside of the workplace as well. Paradoxically, foreign language education in U.S. schools is decreasing as the need for such skills in the business world is increasing. In one study, 36 percent of the executives of multinational firms stated they believed knowledge of foreign languages is important in overseas assignments.[27] These skills can be acquired either before or after selections are made. In either case, some testing is necessary; for example, testing is required to measure an applicant's foreign language knowledge, if such knowledge is a requirement for selection. It also is appropriate to make a selection conditional upon passing a foreign language course if applicants are expected to learn a language once they have been tentatively selected.

Interpersonal Skills

Selection procedures used for overseas assignments must include tests that measure both interpersonal skills, such as sensitivity and oral communication, and skills unique to foreign assignments, including cultural empathy. This means special test exercises must be constructed to measure these skills. For example, exercises that place a candidate in the same foreign country setting as the assignment can be used. The scenario could include background information on local customs and worker traits. The candidates may be given role-playing assignments dealing with actual situations that have occurred in the past.

Other Selection Methods

In addition to the methods discussed above, there are other conventional methods of selecting expatriate personnel. These methods include tests, the job application, assessment centers, and verifications.

Overseas Assignment Inventory

The *Overseas Assignment Inventory* (OAI), a self-response questionnaire, was developed by Michael Tucker of Tucker International LLC. The test is used in selecting candidates for international assignments and in other applications, such as placement, counseling, workforce planning, and career development. For several of the applications, particularly selection, placement, and counseling, the OAI is administered to both the candidate and the spouse since, as noted earlier, the major reasons expatriate assignments fail are employee and spouse cultural maladjustments and other family problems.

Among the dimensions measured by the OAI are *Motivation* (defined as "reasons for wanting an international assignment"), *Expectations* (defined as "positive or negative anticipation regarding life in a different country"), *Open-Mindedness* (defined as "receptivity to the ideas and ways of other nationalities") and *Spouse Communication* (defined as the "level and quality of communication between couples"). The scores for each person are compared to a normative base to obtain a profile of cross-cultural adaptability which assists management in

[27] Baker, J.C., "Foreign Language and Predeparture Training in U.S. Multinational Firms," *Personnel Administratior* (July 1984), p. 72.

assessing both candidates and their spouses. Tucker has conducted extensive research, beginning in the early 1970s, in validating the OAI in both civilian and government settings. Included in the private sector research is validity and reliability data on more than 4,500 employees and spouses considered for assignments in 60 countries.

Applications

An application is used to measure experience and education required by the job specifications. The application can also require applicants to list the names of references who can attest to the applicant's job-related skills, including stress tolerance, sensitivity, communication, adaptability, initiative, motivation, and perseverance.

Interviews

Structured interviews are used to measure applicants' oral communication skills. They also can be used to measure applicants' foreign language proficiency if the interviewer is conversant in the language. *Content* valid questioning should be used in the interview in which the interviewee is placed in roles of actual or simulated situations. The applicant should be asked to explain the appropriate responses. This interview technique would permit the applicant to demonstrate skills in such areas as stress tolerance, initiative, motivation, adaptability, and cultural empathy. The interview is also effective in measuring the applicant's technical competence. Some firms also interview the spouse and family members to determine their ability to adjust in the foreign country.

Assessment Centers

Assessment centers (AC) are particularly suited for selecting personnel for foreign assignments because the day's exercises can be structured to simulate the foreign country, including the country's customs and language. The midday meal could consist of typical food items served in the foreign country. ACs impart considerable realism in the selection process, which helps assessors measure those skills critically important for successful adjustment abroad. The realism also helps participants decide if they are suited for the job.

Verifications

Information collected in the selection process can be verified with such sources as previous employers, supervisors, and educational institutions. Sources could also be used to verify interpersonal skills and technical competence.

Orientation

One expert suggests three orientation phases in foreign assignments; each one includes the applicant, spouse, and family members.[28] Phase 1 is a two-day briefing on the culture, the specific assignment, and relocation arrangements. This phase is actually part of the selection process, since both the applicant and family members are assessed. In addition, the applicant and the family members are emphatically assured they can, without prejudice, decline further consideration. Phase 2 is a two- or three-day predeparture orientation that reemphasizes

---

[28] Conway, "Reducing Expatriate," p. 37.

the points covered in the Phase 1 orientation. Language fundamentals are covered and travel arrangements are finalized. Phase 3 is an orientation that begins when the newly selected expatriate, spouse, and other family members are met upon arrival in the foreign country. Typically, the arrival orientation is conducted by a "sponsor" who is a company employee. The sponsor gives several days of personal assistance as the family adjusts to the new environment.

Training

Some multinational firms use the term "orientation" to explain the process of informing a newly selected expatriate about a foreign culture and assignment. Other firms use the term "training" to describe the process. The following section describes such a program designed for corporate personnel and their families:

Day One

8:30 a.m.	Welcome and Introductions Overview of Cross-Cultural Training (Quotations Analysis and Training Philosophy)
8:45	Orientation to Program Goals and Schedule
9:00	Presentation of Program Objectives "Profile of Successful Intercultural Adjustment"
9:15	Role Model Analysis: Visualizing the Position in the Foreign Country
10:00	Everyday Life and Managing a Household in the Foreign Country
11:00	Foreign Language Training: Unit 1: Introduction, Pronunciation, Beginning Words and Phrases
12:00	Lunch
1:30	Visual Presentation of the Foreign Country
2:30	Area Studies I: Historical and Geographical Background of the Foreign Country
3:30	Area Studies II: Current Events and Issues of the Foreign Country
5:00	End of Day One

Homework: Cross-Cultural Analysis—Individual Work

Day Two

8:30 a.m.	Cross-Cultural Analysis Exercise
10:00	Break
10:30	Non-Verbal Communication: Observation Exercise and Discussion
12:00	Lunch
1:30	Separate Seminars:
	"Women's World in the Foreign Country"
	"Doing Business in the Foreign Country"
3:30	Break
4:00	Focus on the Expatriate Spouse: VTR—"A Portable Life" and Discussion
5:00	Dinner at Ethnic Restaurant (Optional)
7:00	Foreign Language Training: Unit 2: Greetings, Introduction, Leave Taking, and Courtesies
9:00	End of Day Two

Day Three

8:30 a.m.	Cross-Cultural Stress and Shock (Causes, Symptoms, and Cures)
10:00	Foreign Language Training: Unit 3: Money Transactions
12:00	Lunch
1:00	Foreign Language Training: Unit 2 (continued)
4:00	Free Study Time

(Due to the intensity of the week-long program, everyone is given time off at the conclusion of Day Three. In some cases, this includes giving a cocktail party. The purpose is to give the participants an opportunity for some emotional release).

Day Four

8:30 a.m.	Critical Incidents Exercise—Individual work
9:00	Critical Incidents Exercise
11:00	Exercise: "Role Playing in Social and Business Settings"
12:00	Lunch
1:00	Foreign Language Training: Unit 4: Getting Around and Asking Directions
3:30	Foreign Language Training: Unit 4 (Continued)
4:30	End of Day Four

Day Five

8:30 a.m.	Foreign Language Training: Unit 4 (Continued)
10:30	Foreign Language Training: Unit 5: Preparation of Food and Ordering Meals
12:00	Lunch
1:30	Exercise on Family Support for Cross-Cultural Stress
3:00	Break
3:30	Foreign Language Training: Unit 5: (Continued)
5:00	Dinner
7:00	Foreign Language Training Unit 6: Shopping
9:00	End of Day Five

Day Six

8:30 a.m.	Foreign Language Training: Unit 6: (Continued)
10:30	Foreign Language Training: Unit 7: On-the-Job Communication
12:00	Lunch
1:30	Foreign Language Training: Review and Summary
3:30	Program Wrap-Up and Participant Evaluation Certificates of Completion Awarded
4:00	End of Program

Note: This schedule is flexible and may be modified slightly during the program, due to the availability of resource people and/or the needs and interests of the participants.

Training Commitment

Some firms' training and developmental activities are directed toward a long-term commitment of giving multinational work experience to executives. The philosophy behind these commitments is the belief that foreign assignments develop such skills as maturity and flexibility and give executives experience in international competition. The ultimate objective in such developmental programs is to develop a cadre of experienced multinational managers.

Career Planning

Career planning is necessary for the international training of managers to be successful. Managers who desire foreign assignments can be identified and their strengths and developmental needs assessed. Developmental efforts can proceed while the manager works in domestic assignments. For example, language training can be given if the manager is weak in language skills. Some firms pay for such training anytime an executive desires it.

Human Resource Planning

Human resource planning for international staffing requires the establishment of strategic goals in various international operations, such as management succession planning. Both human resource needs and supplies must be identified. Developmental efforts can be initiated where shortages are apparent.

Planning for Women in International Management

According to one survey, 74 percent of international firms had women expatriates, but women represented only about five percent of all U.S. expatriate managers.[29] While this is a small percentage of total expatriate employment, women have made enormous progress in foreign employment in the past 10 years. To increase the number of women employed abroad, one author recommends:

- Contrary to common belief, expatriate females will not experience prejudice in foreign assignments. In fact, they probably will be treated better than they are in the United States. Also, these expatriates will be viewed as foreigners and not as local women.

- Females make a strong contribution in foreign assignments, so that considering them for overseas jobs will expand the pool of qualified applicants.

- Female and male expatriates should be treated equally. If females are given inferior assignments or fewer perquisites than males, it will be interpreted that the organization believes that females are less competent or not expected to perform equally with males.

- Finally, females, have spouses and other family members to consider in making decisions, in the same way as males. Consequently, females should be given the same consideration, and the firm should work with them in making appropriate foreign assignments.[30]

Compensation

Sending a U.S. expatriate to a foreign assignment is a costly process. Three major objectives in international compensation programs are:

- Induce personnel to seek employment in another country;

- Maintain as closely as possible the expatriate's and his or her family's standard of living; and

- Facilitate the expatriate's return to his or her home country or to a new assignment in still another foreign country.

Induce Personnel to Seek Employment

To motivate personnel to seek foreign assignments requires that pay supplements and other forms of compensation be used for hardship conditions that occur in working abroad, such as adjusting to an adverse climate, living away from family and friends, or adapting to a foreign culture and different language.

---

[29] Solomon, J., "Women, Minorities and Foreign Postings," *The Wall Street Journal* (June 2, 1989), p. B-1.

[30] Adler, Nancy J., "Women in International Management: Where Are They?" *California Management Review* (Summer 1984), pp. 78-89.

Money is one reason for applicants seeking foreign assignments. Up to $82,400 in total compensation earned abroad is not subject to federal taxation.[31] To qualify for tax exclusion benefits a person must have a tax home in a foreign country or countries throughout a period of *bona fide foreign residence* or *physical presence* and meet one of these requirements:

- A *bona fide foreign resident* for an uninterrupted period that includes a complete tax year, OR

- A U.S. resident alien who is a citizen or national of a country with which the U.S. has an income tax treaty and is a bona fide resident of a foreign country or countries for an entire tax year, OR

- A U.S. citizen or U.S. resident alien who is *physically present* in a foreign country or countries for at least 330 full days in any period of 12 consecutive months.[32]

However, most international firms implement strategies to insure that these tax advantages do not prevent them from meeting the objective of providing the expatriate with a standard of living which is equivalent to that enjoyed in the U.S. or the expatriate's home country. That is, if the tax benefits are too liberal, the expatriates' standard of living would become considerably higher than it would be in his or her home country.

Tax Equalization and Tax Reduction

International firms use either *tax equalization* or *tax reduction* policies for employees on international assignments.

Tax Equalization. To adjust for any differences in tax laws among various countries, most international firms use a policy known as *tax equalization*. *Tax equalization* is a policy in which the expatriate pays the same amount of tax on income as would be paid in the U.S. If the tax is higher in the country to which the expatriate is assigned, the firm will pay the extra amount. If the tax is lower, the employer subtracts from the expatriate's compensation the difference between what the expatriate would pay in the U.S. and the lower amount. The firm retains the differential.

Tax Reduction. The other type of tax policy is known as *tax reduction*. *Tax reduction* is a tax policy that permits expatriates to gain from the differences in income taxes in the U.S. and the foreign country to which they are assigned or adjusts the compensation of expatriates, so that they experience no loss in income as a result of the net effect of income taxes, both foreign and U.S.

The problem with a tax reduction policy is that it fails to account for the three principles described under the compensation policy. The principal advantage to tax reduction is that employees more readily accept the notion that the firm will protect them from suffering any losses in real income, due to the net effects of income taxation while permitting them to realize any gains that may result.

---

[31] The $82,400 amount is adjusted for inflation.

[32] Internal Revenue Service, Publication 593, *Tax Highlights for U.S. Citizens and Residents Going Abroad.*

Maintain Standard of Living

Maintaining the expatriate's standard of living is a prime objective of international compensation management. The standard of living to be maintained includes both the expatriate and family members who accompanied the expatriate abroad. To accomplish this objective may require such compensation programs as assistance for the schooling of children, special arrangements for medical care, cost of living adjustments, and housing subsidies.

"Balance Sheet Approach" . Compensating employees in international assignments is costly. Consequently, employers take various measures to insure such assignments will be successful, that is employees will perform successfully and will not terminate the assignment prematurely. Careful attention to selecting, training, and orienting employees and their family members help prevent failures. In addition, the design of compensation plans are important.

The *balance sheet approach*, which is the compensation approach used by most firms, insures that employees in international assignments maintain the same standard of living they had in their home environments.[33] This objective is accomplished by using a worksheet (*"balance sheet"*) to record any additions or subtractions in employees' compensation for differences in costs of major expense items in the home and international environments. Exhibit 38-1 is a hypothetical worksheet that could be used for this purpose. Costs for the categories of goods and services would be provided by different sources depending upon the category. For example, home country housing costs would be based upon the employee's current housing expenses. Taxation rates would be those existing in the home country and the country of the international assignment. The costs of some categories, such as transportation, would be provided by international consulting firms. The firm in the illustration, ABC International, Inc., uses the *tax equalization* method of taxation.

In the final analysis, an employee's annual compensation would be adjusted based on the final calculation of the differences in costs. As shown in the worksheet illustration, this final calculated income would be increased by a *foreign service premium* and depending upon the location, a *hardship allowance*.

---

[33] Wilson, Leslie, E. The balance sheet approach to expatriate compensation: still with us after all these years. *Relocation Journal & Real Estate News* (December 2000).

Exhibit 38-1
Balance Sheet Approach to Expatriate Compensation
Hypothetical Worksheet

ABC International Inc.
International Assignment Compensation Worksheet

_____ _____ _____
(Employee)   (Home Location)   (International Location)

This worksheet is used to calculate any cost differences in the home and international locations of key goods and services and taxation and to determine the employee's rate of pay.

Goods and Services	Location and ($) Cost		Home (minus) International	
	(1) Home	(2) International	(3) If (-) Add $	(4) If (+) Deduct $
Housing				
Food				
Clothing				
Transportation				
Personal				
Medical care				
Dependent education				
Taxes (State)				
Taxes (Federal)				
Taxes (Local/property)				
Sales taxes				
Other				
Column 3 and Column 4 totals				
Net effect on annual compensation (Column 3 minus Column 4)				
+ Relocation Incentive				
+ Hardship Premium				
+ Present Pay				
= Pay in International Assignment				

Facilitate Repatriation/Reassignment

If the foreign compensation package is excessive, an expatriate can suffer financial problems upon repatriation or reassignment to another foreign country. For example, if an expatriate's total compensation in a foreign assignment is such that his or her standard of living is too high relative to what it would be in the home country or in another country to which the person is assigned, the person and/or his or her family members could experience real difficulty in adjusting to the repatriation/reassignment. Among surveyed U.S. expatriates, two of the four top concerns about repatriation were housing affordability and the cost of living.[34]

Types of Compensation

The main compensation items for expatriates involve base pay, cost-of-living adjustments, housing allowance, home leave, education for dependents, and premium pay. The U.S. Department of State indexes the living costs abroad, quarters allowances, hardship differentials, and danger pay allowances. That agency uses the indexes to compensate U.S. government civilian employees for costs and hardships related to assignments abroad. The information, published quarterly, is also used by many business firms and other private organizations to assist in establishing private compensation systems.

Base Pay

Base pay is normally related to a pay range in the home country and is adjusted for local conditions.

Cost-of-Living Adjustments

The purpose of *cost-of-living* adjustments is to prevent an erosion of an expatriate's buying power if inflation occurs in the foreign country. To achieve this objective, the expatriate's salary is increased at the same rate as the overall increase in prices. When price levels decline, downward adjustments are made in salaries. *Currency exchange rates* also influence an expatriate's buying power. Adjustments must be made for the fluctuating value of the U.S. dollar, since the expatriate's salary is based upon U.S. currency. Exchange rates fluctuate depending upon such factors as the world economy and the international balance of payments.

Housing Assistance

Housing assistance usually is provided in one of two ways. The first is free company-owned housing. The second, and more common approach, is a housing allowance that is either the difference in housing costs in the two countries or is based upon an established percentage of base salary. Housing assistance is computed for single persons and two-person families. Employees with larger families living with them receive supplements ranging from 10 to 30 percent (depending upon the number of persons) of the two-person allowance.

Premium Pay

Premium pay is offered as an incentive to compensate employees for working abroad. Premiums typically range from 10 to 50 percent of base pay depending upon such considerations as the inconvenience of an assignment's location. In addition, a hardship allowance is granted in some locations. These hardship allowances range from a five percent increase in base pay for Athens to a 25 percent increase for Sarajevo. In addition, in some locations expatriates may

---

[34] "Coming Home," *The Wall Street Journal* (November 16, 1987), p. 33.

receive "danger pay," such as an additional 25 percent in base pay for countries, including Iraq, Lebanon, and Somalia.

Home Leave

Home leave, generally consisting of four weeks, is granted to expatriates and their families every year or every other year. The leave typically includes paid round-trip airline fares.

Educational Assistance

Educational assistance for dependents varies based upon conditions in the foreign country. Assistance is not given if local schooling is deemed adequate. A variety of benefits are provided where substandard conditions exist. The employer may operate a school in the foreign country. Other options include paying for dependents' educational expenses, including room and board, to attend schools in the United States, or providing a stipend for attendance at private schools in either the U.S. or the foreign country.

Employee and Union Relations

Employee relations is the HRM activity concerned with employee discipline and communication. *Union relations* is the HRM activity concerning the recognition of unions and the process of engaging in collective bargaining with them. International HRM differs somewhat in the way both employee relations and union relations are handled in the home country. Some foreign countries, particularly those in Europe, give unions the right to participate in company management.

In Sweden, for example, unions are permitted to choose two members of a company's board of directors. In addition, Swedish unions participate in operating management decisions through work councils.

In Germany, unions have management authority through codetermination which gives unions membership on boards of directors. In German steel and coal industries, unions select five members, stockholders select five members, and those ten select an eleventh member. Outside the steel and coal industries, the number of union members on boards of directors depends upon the company's size. Unions have one-third of the membership in companies with 500 to 2,000 employees and have equal representation with stockholders in companies with 2,000 or more employees. German unions also have a role in operating management in the steel and coal industries because they have the authority to approve the chairmanship of the management board that makes daily management decisions. These and other characteristics of labor and union relations in foreign countries, such as labor political parties, are some of the challenges of international human resource management.

Employee relations, particularly in communication matters, appear more difficult in multinational U.S. firms in which decisions on foreign operations are made in the U.S. A number of workers in Holland, for example, lost their jobs when a U.S. firm moved part of the operation to Scotland. Workers were afraid further cutbacks would take place and they wanted to talk to a company representative. A spokesman for the employees said efforts would not be successful to prevent further cutbacks in Holland "because we'll never get to the man who makes the decisions. It's just one man, I think, and he's in America."[35]

Sometimes, multinational firms do not inform even the top manager in a foreign operation about pending plans. This operating characteristic is neither shared by international U.S. firms nor multinational firms located outside the U.S. For example, Japanese management is distinctively different; a survey of Japanese-owned plants in Great Britain found there is considerable information-sharing among managers and employees.[36]

Evidence also suggests that Japanese management generally tends to conform to the HRM customs of the foreign country and only gradually introduces changes characteristic of "Japanese personnel management." This approach is considerably different from a minority of U.S. multinational firms. For example, one U.S. manufacturer was taken to court for failure to follow a law requiring union consultation before moving operations to another country.[37]

Union relations strategies in foreign operations vary among U.S. multinational firms. In the auto industry, on the one hand, there is a great deal of similarity in union relations regarding plants in the U.S. and Canada. On the other hand, in Europe there are a number of differences. There, critics contend, some multinational firm managements in the U.S. play unions against each other to bargain for lower wages and other concessions. This policy is successful because unions generally are confined to one country and want to protect their members' interests.

Multinational companies, however, are not constrained by national boundaries. Some unions have set up groups composed of union officials from different European countries. The purpose of the groups is to meet, exchange information, and try to build strategies to deal with multinational management. The groups generally are not successful because not all unions meet; those that do meet, do not fully cooperate because they fear exchanging information that may provide clues another union may use to gain an advantage in dealing with management. Some unions in different countries have requested meetings with multinational management, but such offers are declined. European Common Market countries, excluding Britain, have considered requiring multinational firms to follow formal procedures in communicating plans to employees. U.S. firms oppose the plan because they do not want to disclose proprietary information and they fear the procedure may lead to "transnational bargaining."[38]

Collective bargaining does exist in some countries, particularly European ones. In some cases, the bargaining is similar to the type conducted in the U.S., but there are some differences. For example, in some European countries, such as Belgium, employee benefits are prescribed by law. In other countries, including

---

[35] Newman, B., "Border Dispute: Single Country Unions of Europe Try to Cope with Multinationals," *The Wall Street Journal* (November 30, 1983), p. 16.

[36] White, M. and Trevor, M., *Under Japanese Management: The Experience of British Workers* (London: Heinemann Educational Books, Ltd., 1983), p. 48.

[37] Newman, "Border Dispute," p. 16.

[38] *Ibid.*

some in South America, unions are not protected by law. This situation provides little union bargaining power.

Repatriation

Repatriation back into the home country may be accompanied by problems with family finances, personal adjustment, corporate adjustment, job boredom, and career disillusionment. Family financial problems are precipitated by reduced real income when overseas compensation is eliminated. Some expatriates take a job abroad with the goal of saving money. For a while they may make some progress, but eventually savings are spent on trips and other purposes. The ultimate expense is buying an expensive foreign car because "they are cheaper abroad."

Personal adjustment problems are due to the normal stress people experience when they relocate, whether domestically or from abroad. Corporate adjustment is more difficult and problems may surface if a job is not waiting for the repatriate. Sometimes, repatriates are placed in a "holding status" until a suitable vacancy is found. In other situations, repatriates are placed in boring, or less challenging, jobs than the ones they were employed in abroad.

The top concern among expatriate U.S. managers was their career future upon repatriation. The second major concern was the location of the new assignment after repatriation.[39] There is considerable evidence for the existence of these concerns. A survey of personnel managers in 56 international firms located in the U.S. found that 56 percent of the managers believed a foreign assignment either hurt or was insignificant to a person's career advancement, 47 percent said expatriates are not promised jobs upon return to the U.S., 65 percent said the firm's career planning is not integrated with foreign employment experience, 45 percent said they had problems assigning repatriates to domestic jobs, and 80 percent said their firm's repatriation policies were not adequate to meet the needs of repatriates.[40]

Career planning can help prevent repatriation problems by offering long-term planning that ensures a suitable vacancy is available for the repatriate. In addition, repatriates should be considered as corporate assets, and their advice should be sought in international business planning. Returning repatriates can also be used to help select, orient, and train other employees for foreign assignments. Some experts believe the changes that repatriates experience in returning from an assignment are greater than those they experienced leaving the U.S. A re-entry program that includes career planning can help in the returning transition.

---

[39] "Coming Home," *The Wall Street Journal*, p. 33.

[40] O'Boyle, T.F., "Little Benefit to Careers Seen in Foreign Stints," *The Wall Street Journal* (December 11, 1989), p. B-1.

Appendix 1

Significant Judicial Decisions

Aetna Health Inc., FKA Aetna U.S. Healthcare Inc. et al., v. Davila (2004). A group of individuals (respondents) sued Aetna Health Care, Inc. (Aetna) under the Texas Health Care Liability Act (THCLA) for refusing to cover some health services. The respondents alleged these refusals "...were a violation of an HMO's duty 'to exercise ordinary care' under the THCLA." The respondents further alleged they as individuals were injured by the HMO's failure to provide these services. Aetna (the petitioner) argued the charges alleged by the respondents were covered by the Employee Retirement Income Security Act (ERISA) and thus preempted the THCLA. The U.S. Supreme Court concluded the respondents sued because of Aetna's failure to provide benefits. A remedy for this failure is provided under § 502(a) (1)(B) of ERISA and therefore a claim should have been made under this provision. The Court further concluded ERISA preempts state law for these types of claims.

Albermarle Paper Company v. Moody (1975). The Court held that it was illegal to validate a selection method using performance appraisal results if a job analysis had not been conducted. If an appraisal system is used for administrative purposes, like promotions, discipline, and pay increases, then a job analysis must be conducted to ensure the performance criteria are job-related.

Albertsons, Inc. v. Kirkingburg (1999). Kirkingburg has amblyopia, which is an uncorrectable condition, causing him to have 20/200 vision in one eye and, thus, effectively resulting in monocular vision. He was hired as a truck driver, after a physician erroneously concluded that he met the Department of Transportation's (DOT) vision requirements. When the error was discovered, he was told he had to get a waiver from the DOT requirements. Prior to receiving the waiver, he was fired for failing to meet the physical requirements. Later, he received the waiver, but the firm would not rehire him. He filed suit, claiming a violation of the ADA. In reviewing the case, the Court noted that the waiver program was an experiment by the DOT to determine whether the physical requirements should be changed, and the employer was not obligated to participate in it. The Court ruled that the employer was required to comply with the DOT standards. In conclusion, the Court cited testimony indicating that Kirkingburg had adapted to the condition and, thus, monocularity in his situation was not a disability under the ADA.

Alden et al v. Maine (1999). The Court ruled that states have sovereign immunity from private suits for their failure to adhere to the provisions of the Fair Labor Standards Act of 1938. Several parole officers employed by the state of Maine filed suit in state court for the failure of the state to pay overtime in accordance with the FLSA; the Supreme Court held that the state of Maine is immune from such suits.

Alexander v. Gardner-Denver Co. (1974). Alexander, who was an African American, filed a grievance under the collective bargaining agreement, which contained an arbitration clause, that his discharge from employment was based upon race and thus in violation of Title VII of the Civil Rights Act. Prior to the arbitration hearing, Alexander also filed a charge of discrimination with the Colorado Civil Rights Commission but the Commission referred the charge to the Equal Employment Opportunity Commission (EEOC). The arbitrator ruled that the discharge was for cause and the EEOC determined that there was not a reasonable cause to believe the discharge was in violation of Title VII. Subsequent to these decisions, Alexander filed a petition in federal district court alleging the discharge was racially motivated in violation of Title VII. The district court concluded Alexander was bound by the prior arbitration award and had no right to sue under Title VII. A federal appeals court affirmed the decision. The U.S. Supreme Court reversed the decision, holding that an employee could proceed with a Title VII lawsuit even though the union to which he belonged had agreed in a collective bargaining agreement to submit discrimination disputes to arbitration.

Ansonia Board of Education v. Philbrook (1988). The Court ruled that an employer who has provided a means of reasonably accommodating an employee's religious needs has met its requirements and does not have to meet the employee's preferred means of accommodation.

Anthony Ash et al. v. Tyson Foods, Inc. (2006). The U.S. Supreme Court held that the term "boy" may be evidence of racial animus depending upon the context, historical usage, custom and the speaker's inflection and tone of voice and does not need to modified by the words "black" or "white." The Court also held that it is not necessary to establish a pretext of discrimination only when the differences in applicant' qualifications are ". . . so apparent as virtually to jump off the page and slap you in the face." Rather, a pretext of discrimination could be established through such measures as the qualifications of the plaintiff were such that no reasonable person with impartial judgment would not have selected the candidate or a reasonable employer would have found the plaintiff significantly better qualified for the position.

Arbaugh v. Y&H Corp. DBA The Moonlight Café (2006). The U.S. Supreme Court held that the 15-employee requirement does not circumscribe federal-court subject matter jurisdiction under Title VII. Arbaugh filed a claim in federal court of sexual harassment under Title VII. A jury returned a verdict for Arbaugh in the amount of $40,000. Two weeks after the trial court entered judgment for Arbaugh, Y&H claimed it did not have 15 employees and therefore Title VII did not apply to it and the federal court did not have jurisdiction. The U.S. Supreme Court ruled federal courts do have subject-matter jurisdiction (on Title VII issues, such as claims of sexual harassment) and that the 15-employee requirement related to the "substantive adequacy of Arbaugh's Title VII claim . . . could not be raised" after the close of the trial in which the merits of the case were heard.

Arizona Governing Committee for Tax Deferred Annuity and Deferred Compensation Plans v. Norris (1983). The Court ruled that the state's retirement plan, which offered gender-based annuities at retirement, is a violation of Title VII.

Barnes, in Her Official Capacity as Member of the Board of Police Commissioners of Kansas City, Missouri, et al. v. Gorman (2002). Gorman, who is a paraplegic, was seriously injured in a Police van in which he was being transported after being arrested. He sued claiming a violation of both § 202 of the Americans with Disability Act and § 504 of the Rehabilitation Act because the van was not adequately equipped to transport people with disabilities. He was awarded both compensatory and punitive damages by a lower court, which was affirmed by an appeals court. The U.S. Supreme Court, reversed the awarding of punitive damages, deciding that form of relief is not permissible for private suits filed under either § 202 of the Americans with Disability Act or § 504 of the Rehabilitation Act.

Barnhart, Commissioner of Social Security v. Thomas (2003): Barnhart, who was an elevator operator who lost her job when it was abolished. She applied for Social Security disability benefits and SSI claiming she was unable to do the work as an elevator operator because there were not a sufficient number of those jobs in the national economy. She was denied benefits because the Administrative Law Judge who reviewed her application concluded she is able to be an elevator operator even if there are not sufficient opportunities in the national economy. In reviewing the case, the U.S. Supreme Court noted the requirements for disability benefits were such that the physical or mental impairment must be of such severity that the applicant "...is not only unable to do his previous work but cannot, considering his age, education, and work experience, engage in any other kind of substantial gainful work which exists in the national economy." The Court concluded that Thomas failed to show she was unable to perform either her previous occupation or any other gainful work which exists in the national economy and for which she was qualified.

Black & Decker Disability Plan v. Nord (2003): Nord applied for disability benefits under his employer's plan, providing as evidence of his disability, statements from his personal physician and an orthopedist indicating he had back disease and chronic pain which prevented him from working. Nord's application was denied since the Plan's administrator referred Nord to a neurologist who stated with pain medication, Nord could perform sedentary work. The Court of Appeals decided that the "treating physician rule" should have been followed in the case which requires administrators to offer specific reasons based upon substantial evidence when the opinions of treating physicians are rejected. Upon review, the U.S. Supreme Court decided the "treating physician rule" was originally established by Courts of Appeal to facilitate the process of reviewing disability applications under the Social Security Act. The Court said a uniform procedure for reviewing disability applications under that Act was understandable since it was a mandatory program with specific benefits. On the contrary, the Court concluded, disability programs under private employer plans are varied and necessitate flexibility in their administration. The decision in Nord's case was vacated and remanded.

Board of Trustees of the University of Alabama et al. v. Garrett et al. (2001). Garrett and another respondent named Ash sought money damages under the Americans with Disabilities Act (ADA) for employment discrimination based upon disability by two State of Alabama agencies (the University of Alabama in Garrett's case and the Alabama Department of Youth Services in Ash's case). The

Court held that the ADA exceeds Congress' authority to abrogate States' immunity under the Eleventh Amendment; therefore, state employees cannot use the ADA to collect money damages for allegations of discrimination.

Bragdon v. Abbott (1998). The Court ruled that HIV infection is a disability covered under the Americans with Disabilities Act.

Brito v. Zia (1978). The Court held the employer's appraisal system was illegal because standardized scoring was not used. *Standardized* means that among the personnel in the organization there is commonality in appraisal system definitions, units of measurement, performance criteria and interpretations of performance. Without some standardization, appraisers independently select the variables to use in appraising employees. Experience also shows that without standards, supervisors use individualized systems of weights for different variables. Standards will help control these, and other problems, like supervisors applying differing definitions to different performance variables.

Burlington Industries v. Ellerth (1998). The Court held, in this sexual harassment claim, that an employer can be held liable for the actions of supervisors, even though the harassed employee does not report the harassment, the firm has a policy against sexual harassment, and the employee does not suffer any adverse employment consequences. In the decision, the Court noted the same two affirmative defenses that the employer can use, which were outlined in *Farragher v. Boca Raton* (1998). See *Farragher v. Boca Raton.*

Burlington Northern & Santa Fe Railway Co. v. White (2006). White, a female forklift operator filed a charge of sexual harassment with her employer. As a result, her supervisor was disciplined but she was moved from her forklift operator assignment to a "standard track laborer" position. She then filed a complaint with the EEOC alleging the reassignment was in retaliation for her filing the original charge with her employer. Subsequently, she was charged with insubordination and suspended without pay. Later, her employer determined she was not insubordinate, reinstated her and reimbursed her for the 37 days she had been suspended. Nevertheless, the suspension was the cause of another complaint of retaliation. After exhausting administrative remedies, White filed suit in federal court. The U.S. Supreme Court agreed with lower appeal court findings that a plaintiff must show that the retaliation action was sufficient to have "dissuaded a reasonable worker" from making a charge of discrimination. The Court ruled the suspension action was of such a magnitude even if an employee had been awarded back pay for the period of suspension.

Central Laborers' Pension Fund v. Heinz et al. (2004). Heinz was a construction worker when he retired under an early retirement option which paid him the same annuity that he would have received at normal retirement age. The plan stipulated the payments would cease if he engaged in "disqualified employment" which was restricted to being employed as a construction worker. Heinz got a job as a supervisor in the construction industry. Later, in 1998, the Plan expanded the definition of "disqualified employment" to include any job in the construction industry. Heinz would not agree to leave his supervisor's job so the Plan stopped his benefits. He sued claiming the Plan's action was a violation of the "anti-cutback" rule of the Employee Retirement Income Security Act (ERISA) which prohibits retirement plan changes which would result in reducing the accrued benefits of participants. In a unanimous decision, the Court decided the Plan had violated this ERISA rule.

Chamber of Commerce of the United States of America et al. v. Brown, Attorney General of California, et al. (2008). California Govt. Code Ann. §§ 16645.2(a), 16645.7(a) prohibits "employers that receive state grants or more than $10,000 in state program funds per year from using the funds 'to assist, promote, or deter union organizing.'" Some organizations, including the Chamber of Commerce of the United States of America, sued to prevent the enforcement of the above provisions because they are pre-empted by the National Labor Relations Act (NLRA) in that they inhibit free debate in union organizing. The U.S. Supreme Court ruled the provisions are pre-empted by the NLRA.

Chevron U. S. A. Inc. v. Echazabal (2002). Echazabal was employed by an independent contractor who performed work for Chevron. He had a liver condition which was worsened by exposures to toxins at the refinery. Chevron requested the contractor to reassign Echazabal to work where he would not be exposed to the toxins. He applied to work for Chevron but the firm would not hire him. The contractor laid him off since Chevron refused to hire him. Echazabal filed suit claiming Chevron's actions were in violation of the Americans with Disabilities (ADA). Chevron defended its actions relying upon an Equal Employment Opportunity Commission (EEOC) regulation in which an employer's employment decision-making could consider whether an employee's condition posed a threat to himself/herself. The U.S. Supreme Court agreed the ADA permits the EEOC's regulation.

Christensen et al. v. Harris County et al. (2000). The Court held that states and their political subdivisions can compel employees to use compensatory time, in lieu of overtime payments, under the Fair Labor Standards Act.

Circuit City Stores, Inc. v. Adams (2001). In this case the Court held that employees who have claims, disputes, and controversies due to their employment must submit them to arbitration, if they have signed documents, such as employment applications, in which they previously agreed to such an arrangement.

City of Los Angeles Department of Water and Power v. Manhart (1978). The Court held that the contributory retirement plan involved in the case could not require women to make higher contributions than men in order to receive the same annuity payment upon retirement. The Court reached this conclusion even though the Department's pension plan was based on mortality tables and its own experience showed that female employees had greater longevity than male employees and that the cost of a pension for the average female retiree was greater than for the average male retiree because more monthly payments had to be made to the female.

City of Richmond v. J.A. Croson Co. (1989). The Court held that the City's requirement was illegal in requiring prime contractors to award city construction subcontracts of at least 30 percent of the dollar amount of each contract to one or more "Minority Business Enterprises." The Court said that since the plan was not justified by a compelling city interest, the 30 percent set-aside was not narrowly tailored to accomplish a remedial purpose and because the City had no prior history of discrimination in awarding contracts.

Clackamas Gastroenterology Associates, P.C. v. Wells (2003). Wells filed suit against Clackamas Gastroenterology Associates, P.C. (employer), alleging it violated the Americans with Disabilities Act of 1990 (ADA) when she was terminated from employment. The employer responded it did not have 15 employees and therefore was not covered by the ADA. This contention focused upon whether four physican-shareholders who were owners should be counted as employees to reach the required number of 15 employees. The U.S. Supreme Court decided the six criteria defined in the EEOC's guidelines should be considered in determining whether a shareholder director is an employee. The case was remanded for a consideration of these criteria in evidence of record. (Note: Briefly, these are the six criteria:

- Can the firm hire/fire the individual or set rules/regulations for the person to follow;
- To what extent, if at all, does the firm supervise the person's work;
- To whom, if anyone, does the person report within the firm;
- To what extent does the person influence the firm;
- What are the firm's and the person's intentions, such as agreements or contracts specifying whether the person is an employee; and,
- To what extent, if at all, does the person share in the firm's profits, losses and liabilities. (Richard C. Sarhaddi, "Shareholders as "employees" versus "employers" affect outcome of anti-discrimination cases," in *Healthcare Compliance Letter* (Commerce Clearing House: September 29, 2003, p. 8)).

Cleveland v. Policy Management Systems Corp. et al. (1999). The Court held that receiving disability payments from Social Security does not prevent a person from seeking coverage as a person with a disability who is employable, with reasonable accommodation, under the Americans with Disabilities Act.

Communication Workers v. Beck (1988). The Communication Workers of America (CWA) represented employees of the American Telephone and Telegraph Company and several of its subsidiaries as their exclusive bargaining representative. The collective bargaining agreement contained an agency shop provision, which required employees who did not become union members to pay "agency fees" to the CWA in the same amounts as dues paid by union members. The agency shop provision required that employees who did not wish to join the union and failed to pay the agency fees could be discharged from employment. Twenty employees who did not join the union filed suit in federal court, contending that any fees collected from them that were beyond that necessary to finance collective bargaining activities were illegal. The activities that the employees contended were illegal included organizing the employees of other employers, lobbying for labor legislation, and participating in social, charitable, and political events. The Court ruled in favor of the employees, deciding that the National Labor Relations Act permits unions to assess only those fees and dues that are necessary to perform the duties as exclusive bargaining representative in dealing with employers on labor-management issues.

Connecticut v. Teal (1982). Teal, who is black, along with other black employees, were temporarily promoted to the position of supervisor at a Connecticut state agency but subsequently failed a test for permanent promotion. The pass rate for the test was 54 percent for black candidates, which was 68 percent of the passing rate for white candidates. Teal and the black co-workers who failed the test filed suit, alleging discrimination under Title VII because the employer made passing the test as an unconditional qualification for consideration for promotion. Before the trial commenced, the state agency made promotions from the eligibility list and 22.9 percent of the black candidates were selected for promotion, compared to 13.5 percent for white candidates. The agency contended that this "bottom-line" result, which resulted in more favorable treatment for black candidates, was a full defense to the charge of discrimination. The Court held that simply treating one group more favorably than another can never be used as a defense in discrimination cases, if the practice in question discriminates against some members of a group. The Court added that any selection method that produces such results must measure skills related to the job.

County of Washington v. Gunther (1981). The Court held that claims of sex-based pay discrimination under Title VII can be broader than those under the Equal Pay Act since it covers all forms of disparate treatment resulting from sex discrimination. See a discussion of the *Bennett Amendment* in Chapter 26.

Davenport et al. v. Washington Education Association (2007). The Washington Education Association had an agency shop agreement with Washington State authorizing the union to levy union dues against non-union employees who are represented in collective bargaining by the union. The First Amendment prohibits public sector unions from using non-members fees for non-representational purposes, if they object to such usage. State voters made an additional requirement by approving an initiative requiring the union to obtain the nonmembers' consent before using their fees for election-related (as opposed to representational) purposes. Instead of obtaining this consent, the union semi-annually sent nonmembers packets explaining their rights (called "*Hudson* packets") to object to dues usage for election-related activities. The union held the dues in escrow until the time limit for filing objections had expired. Several nonmembers filed lawsuits claiming the *Hudson* packet process did not involve the affirmative authorizations required by the Washington law. The U.S. Supreme Court decided in favor of the nonmembers stating the Washington law was constitutional as applied to public (as opposed to private sector) unions.

Desert Palace, Inc., dba Caesars Palace Hotel & Casino v. Costa (2003): Costa was the employer's only female warehouse worker and heavy equipment operator who had peer and management problems, disciplinary actions imposed against her and her employment terminated. She filed suit alleging sex discrimination. In his instructions to the jury the District Court said Costa would be entitled to damages if a preponderance of the evidence showed sex as a motivating factor for the employer's treatment of Costa, even if legal reasons were also involved unless the employer could show by a preponderance of the evidence that the same employment decisions would have been made absent gender from the decision process. The employer said these instructions were incorrect because they did not require Costa to show "direct evidence" of discrimination. The U.S. Supreme Court ruled that direct evidence is not required in mixed motive cases.

Dothard v. Rawlinson (1977). In this case the Court ruled on two issues. One involved the imposition of height and weight requirements for certain jobs, particularly the job of prison guard. The other issue involved imposing a gender requirement as a bonafide occupational qualification. The first issue involved a female applicant for the job of Correctional Counselor (Prison Guard) in an Alabama correctional institution. A female applicant (Rawlinson) was rejected for the job because she failed to meet the 120-pound minimum weight requirement. The State of Alabama contended that the weight requirement, together with a height requirement of 5 feet 2 inches, were necessary because they were associated with a candidate's strength, which in turn is an essential physical requirement for satisfactory job performance. The Court held that the State of Alabama failed to show the requirements were job related, and since the requirements would only exclude 1 percent of mailes but would exclude over 40 percent of the female population, they were unlawful. Regarding the second issue, the Court held sex can be used as a basis for employment decisions due to business necessity, where justified. The Alabama Correctional System was upheld in its practice of hiring only males as correctional officers in all-male institutions. The state's reason was some inmates were sex offenders and female correctional officers could precipitate inmate violence.

Edelman v. Lynchburg College (2002). Edelman was denied tenure at Lynchburg College and he faxed a letter, claiming discrimination (based on gender, national origin and religion) with the Equal Employment Opportunity Commission (EEOC). The EEOC sent him a Form 5, Charge of Discrimination, and advised him to file the charge within the 300-day deadline. Edelman returned the Form 5 but 313 days after he was denied tenure. The case moved to a federal court that held Edelman failed to meet the 300-day deadline. The U.S. Supreme Court disagreed and remanded it to the lower court.

Engquist v. Oregon Department of Agriculture et al. (2008). In 1992 Engquist was employed as an international food standard specialist for the Oregon Department of Agriculture. She had repeated difficulties with another employee and her supervisor sent that employee for anger management courses. In 2001, a manager was named to manage the whole unit, including her former supervisor. The manager told a customer he intended to get rid of Engquist and her former supervisor. Later in the year, due to budget cuts, the manager eliminated the former supervisor's position. In January 2002, Engquist was informed by the manager that due to a reorganization, her position was being eliminated. Engquist was covered by a collective bargaining agreement giving her the right to either "bump" someone employed at her same pay grade or accept a demotion. She was laid-off when she was found unqualified for the position at her same level and she declined to accept a demotion. She filed suit against the agency, the manager and the co-worker with whom she had the past difficulties. In her suit she alleged she was laid-off for "arbitrary, vindictive, and malicious reasons." In response to the suit, an appeals court ruled against her. In affirming the decision of the appeals court, the U. S. Supreme Court stated:

> "Recognition of a claim that the State (Oregon Department of Agriculture) treated an employee differently from others for a bad reason, or for no reason at all, is simply contrary to the at-will concept. The Constitution does not require repudiating that familiar doctrine."

Epilepsy Foundation of Northeast Ohio v. NLRB (2001). In this U.S. Court of Appeals case, the *"Weingarten* rights" (see *NLRB v. Weingarten, Inc.* in this Appendix) were broadened to include nonunionized employees. On some occasions, nonunionized employees may request to be accompanied by co-workers during fact-finding or other types of interviews involving the prospective administration of discipline. In this case, a supervisor of Epilepsy Foundation of Northeast Ohio, asked an employee to attend a meeting to discuss his "insubordinate behavior." The supervisor denied a request by the employee to have a co-worker present to determine if discipline should be imposed. The employee did not attend the meeting and was discharged. An unfair labor practice was filed with the National Labor Relations Board (NLRB). The NLRB upheld the unfair labor practice charge and ordered the employee reinstated. The Court of Appeals concurred in the unfair labor practices charge but stated the NLRB could not apply it retroactively.

Equal Employment Opportunity Commission v. Waffle House, Inc. (2002). Eric Baker worked for Waffle House where he signed an agreement requiring all work-related disputes to be settled by binding arbitration. He had a seizure at work and was fired. He filed a discrimination charge with the Equal Employment Opportunity Commission (EEOC). The EEOC filed suit alleging discrimination based upon disability and sought backpay, reinstatement, and compensatory and punitive damages because Waffle House acted with malice and reckless indifference. Waffle House contended the agreement to arbitrate, as allowed by the Federal Arbitration Act, should compel the matter to be arbitrated and stay the EEOC's suit. The U.S. Supreme Court disagreed claiming an arbitration agreement does not bar the EEOC from pursuing court action.

Espinoza v. Farah Mfg. Co. (1972). The Court held that non-citizens of the United States are entitled to protection under Title VII and, furthermore, that a requirement of U.S. citizenship may violate Title VII if it is intended to discriminate or results in discrimination based upon national origin.

Faragher v. City of Boca Raton (1998). The Court held that an employer is liable for hostile environment sexual harassment by a supervisor who has immediate authority over an employee. If no tangible employment action results from the harassment, such as discipline or discharge of the employee, the employer can present an "affirmative defense" by showing that: (1) the employer exercised reasonable care to prevent and correct the harassment, and (2) the harassed employee unreasonably failed to take advantage of any opportunities provided by the employer to prevent or correct the harassment. An anti-harassment policy, including a complaint procedure, is not always required for this defense, but such a policy could be presented as evidence of an employer's good-faith effort to prevent and correct such harassment under the first defense above. Normally, evidence that the harassed employee failed to use any complaint procedure provided by the employer would satisfy the employer's affirmative defense under (2), above. These two affirmative defenses cannot be used by employers if the supervisor's harassment results in a tangible employment action, such as a discharge, demotion, or discipline.

Federal Employees v. Department of the Interior (1999). The Court held that the Federal Service Labor-Management Relations Statute gives the Federal Labor Relations Authority (FLRA) the responsibility of resolving issues involving collective bargaining among unions and federal agencies. The specific issue in question was whether midterm negotiations were permissible under the statute. The Court ruled that this issue was best decided by the FLRA, the agency that was empowered by the statute to resolve such issues.

Garcetti et al. v.Ceballos (2006). Ceballos, a supervising deputy district attorney for the Los Angeles County District Attorney's Office believed errors were made in a search warrant but his recommendations to have the case dismissed were rejected. Later, he was called by the defense to explain his opinions about the warrant. Subsequently, he was reassigned to another position and to a different court and denied a promotion. He filed a grievance but it was denied. He then filed suit in federal court alleging the First and Fourteenth Amendments were violated, in that his right to protected free speech was denied. The U.S. Supreme Court held that public employees who make statements "pursuant to their official duties," are not speaking as private citizens and thus are not protected under the First Amendment.

Geissal v. Moore Medical Corp. (1998). The Court held that Geissal, who was terminated from employment by Moore Medical Corp., was eligible for COBRA benefits from Moore Medical Corp., even though he was covered as a dependent under his wife's medical expense benefits plan at her place of employment prior to his termination of employment at Moore Medical Corp.

General Dynamics Land Systems, Inc. v. Cline et al. (2004): A collective bargaining agreement between General Dynamics and a union contained a clause providing for the continuation of health benefits to subsequent retirees who were still employed and at least 50 but would not provide such retiree benefits to current employees who were under 50. A group of employees who were 40 but under 50 filed suit alleging the collective bargaining agreement violated the Age Discrimination in Employment Act of 1967 (ADEA) since it discriminated against workers in the age group 40 to 50. The U.S. Supreme Court decided the agreement did not violate the ADEA since nothing in the law prevents an employer from favoring an older worker in preference to a younger one.

General Electric Co. v. Gilbert (1977). The Court ruled that because the word "gender" was not used to exclude anyone from benefit eligibility, the employer's disability benefit plan did not violate Title VII because of its failure to cover pregnancy-related disabilities. The Court did acknowledge, however, that only women can become pregnant. See Chapter 12 for a fuller discussion of employer-provided disability benefits for pregnancy-related conditions.

Gilmer v. Interstate/Johnson Lane (1991). The Court ruled that Gilmer, a securities representative whose registration application contained an agreement to arbitrate any controversy arising from employment, was bound by the agreement. His employment was terminated at age 62 and he filed with the Equal Employment Opportunity Commission a charge of discrimination in violation of the Age Discrimination in Employment Act (ADEA). The Court held that an ADEA claim can be subject to compulsory arbitration.

Griggs v. Duke Power Co. (1971). The Court held that a high school diploma requirement and the use of a test are artificial, arbitrary, and unnecessary barriers to employment on the basis of race, in the absence of intent to discriminate, if they do not demonstrate a reasonable measure of relationship to job performance.

Harris v. Forklift Systems, Inc. (1993). The Court defined a *hostile work environment* as one in which a reasonable person would conclude that the workplace is permeated with "discriminatory intimidation, ridicule, and insult," that is "sufficiently severe or pervasive to alter the conditions of the victim's employment and create an abusive working environment." A *hostile environment* is one in which the comments, conduct and other aspects of the work atmosphere are such that the victim perceives them to be hostile or abusive and a "reasonable person" would also find them to be hostile. Some of the factors that could be considered in deciding whether an environment was "hostile" would be the severity, duration, and frequency of the abuse.

Hoffman Plastic Compounds, Inc. v. National Labor Relations Board(2002). Jose Castro was hired by Hoffman after he presented documentation he was legally employable in the U.S. Later Castro and other workers were laid off after they supported a union organizing campaign at the plant where they worked. The National Labor Relations Board (NLRB) determined the layoffs were a violation of the National Labor Relations Act (NLRA) and ordered reinstatement and other relief to Castro and the other workers. During a hearing on the matter, it was revealed that Castro was not legally employable in the U.S. The Hearing Officer found the provisions of the Immigration Reform and Control Act (IRCA) were violated and Castro was not entitled to recovery. Nevertheless, the NLRB contended workers' rights under the NLRA were available to undocumented workers the same as other workers. The U.S. Supreme Court disagreed stating a violation of the IRCA precluded the NLRB from awarding relief to undocumented workers.

IBP, Inc. v. Alvarez, individually and on behalf of all others similarly situated, et al. (2005). The Court held that employees must be compensated under the FLSA for the time to doff specialized protective gear, walk to their work locations and commence working. At the end of the day, the employees must also be compensated for the time required to walk to the location where the gear is doffed, as well as the time required to actually doff it.

International Union, United Automobile, Aerospace & Agricultural Implement Workers of America, UAW v. Johnson Controls, Inc. (1991). The employer had a policy excluding any women of child-bearing age from employment in jobs in which exposure to lead exceeded the OSHA standard for blood levels that could be harmful to employees who planned to have children. The Court held that the policy was discriminatory, based upon gender.

Johnson v. Transportation Agency (1987). The Court held that an affirmative action plan to select women for the job of dispatcher was permissible since it was part of a case-by-case approach, to effect the gradual improvement in the representation of minorities and women in the Agency's labor force. The Court noted that none of the 238 positions in the Skilled Craft Worker job classifications, which included the Dispatcher job, was filled by a female. Both Diane Joyce, who was selected for the job, and Johnson, a male, were considered by the Agency as well qualified for the job.

Kentucky Association of Health Plans, Inc. et al.v. Miller, Commissioner, Kentucky Department of Insurance (2003): Health maintenance organizations (HMOs) provide services to individuals, such as employees of client firms, through exclusive arrangements with selected physicians, hospitals and other providers. Kentucky enacted two laws prohibiting health insurers from discriminating against any health care provider who was willing to meet the terms and conditions of the insurers' plans ("any willing provider") in return for providing services to the plans. The laws also prohibited discrimination against any chiropractor from serving as a primary care provider, in those plans offering chiropractic services, if a chiropractor was willing to meet the conditions and terms designated by the insurance plan provider. The Kentucky Association of Health Plans, Inc., et al. (Health Plans) filed suit against the State of Kentucky arguing that the Kentucky laws were illegal since they dealt with employee health benefit plans and thus were preempted by the Employee Retirement Income Security Act (ERISA). The U.S. Supreme Court ruled the laws were specifically directed toward the regulation of insurance and thus were not preempted by ERISA.

Kimel et al. v. Florida Board of Regents et al. (2000). This decision involved three cases. One case involved two associate professors in the College of Business at the University of Montevallo, a state institution. The professors contended that an evaluation system used by the college had a disparate impact upon older faculty members. They also alleged the university retaliated against them for filing charges of discrimination with the Equal Employment Opportunity Commission. They sought back pay, promotions to full professor and compensatory and punitive damages. The second case involved professors and other employees of Florida State University and Florida International University. This group contended that the state of Florida discriminated against them because the Florida Board of Regents refused to require the two universities to allocate funds to provide previously agreed upon market adjustments to the salaries of eligible employees. The employees contended this failure had a disparate impact upon the base pay of older workers who had more years of service. The third case involved an employee of the Florida Department of Corrections. The employee contended the Department failed to promote him because of his age and because he had filed grievances concerning the alleged discrimination. The Court held that, although Congress clearly intended to abrogate states' immunity from charges of discrimination filed under the Age Discrimination in Employment Act, such abrogation "exceeded Congress' authority under the Fourteen Amendment." All three cases were thus denied.

Kolstad v. American Dental Association (1999). The Court held that a showing of egregious misconduct is not necessary for awarding punitive damages under Title VII. For such damages, it is only necessary to show that an employer acted with malice and reckless indifference.

LaRue v. DeWolff, Boberg & Associates, Inc. (2008). LaRue, who was a participant in a defined contribution plan, alleged the plan administrator failed to exercise fiduciary responsibility by not following investment instructions resulting in a $150,000 loss in LaRue's plan. The District and the Appellant Court ruled LaRue was not entitled to recovery since remedies are only available for entire plans not individuals under the Employee Retirement Income Security Act (ERISA). The U. S. Supreme Court ruled that remedies are not available for individuals enrolled in defined benefit plans unless administrator misconduct adversely affected all employees covered by the plan. Conversely, the Court ruled LaRue's case involved a defined contribution plan and remedies are available under the ERISA if an administrator's actions adversely affected an individual employee.

Ledbetter v. Goodyear Tire & Rubber Co. (2007). An employee (Ledbetter) alleged gender discrimination in that she was paid considerably less than men employed in the same job. She contended the differential in pay occurred from pay decisions based upon unfair performance appraisals in past years. Ledbetter did not charge discrimination within 180 days of any of the performance appraisals. Instead, after the time periods had expired, she alleged that several supervisors in the past had given her poor evaluations based on her sex, resulting in her being paid less than her male counterparts. The Court held that allegations of discrimination under Title VII must be filed within 180 days of the discrete act of discrimination. If this time limitation is not met, a person cannot allege discrimination based on the effects of the alleged discriminatory acts.

Marquez v. Screen Actors Guild, Inc., et al. (1998). The Court held that a union (Screen Actors Guild) security clause did not violate previous court decisions because it did not state that:

(1) An employee can satisfy the membership condition merely by paying the union an amount equal to its initiation fees and dues (see *NLRB v. General Motors Corp.*); and

(2) The fees and dues cannot be required, over the objections of nonmembers, for activities that are not germane to collective bargaining, grievance adjustment, or contract administration (see *Communication Workers v. Beck*).

Martin v. Wilks; Personnel Board of Jefferson County, Alabama v. Wilks; and *Arrington v. Wilks* (1989). The Court held that a group of fire fighters could challenge a court-ordered quota plan because they were not a party to the original suit.

McDonnell Douglas Corp. v. Green (1973). The Court set up this three-stage procedure for handling a bias claim under Title VII:

First, the individual must present evidence supporting his/her claim. This can be done (for example, in a denial of hiring situation) by showing that:

(1) The individual belongs to a protected group;

(2) The individual was qualified to perform the job for which the employer sought applicants;

(3) The individual was rejected, despite the qualifications; and,

(4) The position remained open and the employer continued to seek applications from persons having the same qualifications as the rejected individual.

Second; at this stage, the accused employer must come forward with explanations for the apparent discriminatory treatment of the complainant.

Third; at this final stage, after all the explanations have been presented, the individual complainant must be able to show that the reason(s) given by the employer for rejecting him/her are merely pretexts to cover a discriminatory motive.

Meacham et al., v. Knolls Atomic Power Laboratory, aka Kapl, Inc., et al. (2008). Knolls, a contractor for the federal government was ordered to reduce its number of employees. An insufficient number of employees elected to receive an incentive package to leave voluntarily, so Knolls instituted a lay-off plan in which employees would be appraised on their "performance," "flexibility," "critical skills," and points for years of service. Based on the appraisals, 30 of the 31 employees who were laid-off were at least 40 years old. Meacham and some others, who were at least 40 years old and laid-off, filed a disparate impact suit under the Age Discrimination in Employment Act. They used the results of an analysis conducted by a statistics expert to show that there was a statistically significant inverse relationship between the appraisals and age. The expert also found that the relationship was strongest with "flexibility" and "criticality" which were the two factors in which the evaluators had the most discretion. The U.S. Supreme Court ruled that Knolls had the burden of production and persuasion for its "reasonable factors other than age" (RFOA) affirmative defense to the disparate impact suit. In essence, the decision meant Knolls must show there is a reasonable relationship between the factors used in making the lay-offs and the lay-off decisions.

Meritor Savings Bank v. Vinson (1986). The Court held that a claim of hostile environment sexual harassment is a form of sex discrimination which is illegal under Title VII.

Metropolitan Life Insurance Co. et al. v. Glenn (2008). Metropolitan Life Insurance Company (MetLife) is the administrator and insurer for Sear, Roebuck and Company's long-term disability insurance plan. In fulfilling the dual roles of administrator and insurer, respectively, MetLife determines the validity of employee' claims and then pays benefits to employees with valid claims. Sears' employee Glenn claimed disability benefits after she was diagnosed with a heart disorder and MetLife granted her 24 months of benefits. With MetLife's encouragement, Glenn applied for and received Social Security disability benefits after the agency determined she could not do any work. After conducting a review of her case MetLife concluded Glenn could perform sedentary work and denied her claim for further disability benefits. Glenn filed suit under the Employee Retirement Income Security Act. Her claim was denied by the District Court but upon review, the 6th Circuit Court of Appeals (Court of Appeals) concluded MetLife's decision was procedurally unreasonable since it suggested she pursue a disability claim with Social Security, but then failed to accept its finding. The Court of Appeals also observed that MetLife had several conflicting medical reports relevant to Glenn's application for benefits, but used the one favoring benefits denial. Furthermore, MetLife had failed to "provide its independent vocational and medical experts with all of the relevant information" in Glenn's case. In its decision granting benefits to Glenn, the Court of Appeals "considered it a conflict of interest that MetLife both determined an employee's eligibility for benefits and paid the benefits out of it own pocket." The U.S. Supreme Court affirmed the Appeal Court's decision. In its opinion the Court said a potential conflict of interest exists when a benefits administrator both determines the validity of a claim and pays benefits on it. Whether the conflict is fairly resolved depends upon the administrator's actions, which in this case were unreasonable.

Murphy v. United Parcel Service (1999). Murphy was a mechanic who was required to drive commercial vehicles. He had high blood pressure, which was controllable with medication; however, his blood pressure exceeded the requirements of the Department of Transportation (DOT), so his employer discharged him. Murphy filed suit under the Americans with Disabilities Act (ADA). The Court held that Murphy's condition was not a disability under the ADA simply because he could not meet the physical requirements of the DOT, which were necessary for this particular job. The Court also noted testimony indicating that he could be employed as a mechanic in other jobs.

National Labor Relations Board v. General Motors (1963). The Court ruled that, in states where it is not prohibited by state law, employers must bargain with the duly certified union regarding a proposal for the establishment of an *agency shop*. An *agency shop* is an arrangement in which employees are not required to join or be members of a union but they must pay an initiation fee and dues to the union in order to remain employed. The Court also ruled that employees employed under a *union shop* arrangement will satisfy the requirements of the arrangement if they pay the initiation fee and dues to the union, even if they choose not to belong to the union or otherwise support or "join" the union. As typically defined, a *union shop* is a union security arrangement in which continued employment is conditional upon the employee becoming a member of the union representing the employees in the bargaining unit.

National Railroad Passenger Corporation v. Morgan(2002). Morgan filed suit against the National Railroad Passenger Corporation (Amtrak) alleging discrimination, retaliation, and a racially hostile work environment. Some of the incidents

Morgan alleged occurred within the 300-day deadline and others predated the 300-day period. Amtrak contended it could not be held responsible for the acts occurring prior to the 300-day deadline. The U.S. Supreme Court held that charges alleging a hostile work environment are not time barred if they are part of an unlawful practice in which at least one act falls within the 300-day deadline.

Nevada Department of Human Resources et al., v. Hibbs et al (2003). The Court decided that state employees may recover money damages in federal courts if a state fails to meet the provisions of the Family and Medical Leave Act of 1993.

National Labor Relations Board v. Kentucky River Community Care, Inc., et al (2001). In a recognition case involving a residential care facility, the NLRB determined that registered nurses in the facility were not supervisors because rather than using independent judgment as required by the above definition, they exercised, ". . . ordinary professional or technical judgment in directing less-skilled employees . . ." The Court held that the NLRA does not differentiate in different kinds of independent judgment so the NLRB erred in determining that the registered nurses' use of "professional" judgment was not independent judgment.

NLRB v. Town & Country Electric, Inc. (1995). The Court ruled that it was illegal for Town & Country Electric, Inc., a nonunion employer, to refuse to hire job applicants who were union members even if the union pays the workers (sometimes referred to as *salts* or *salting agents*) to help it organize the firm's employees. In the same case, the Court found that it was illegal for the firm to fire one union applicant who was hired and then fired after a few days on the job.

NLRB v. Weingarten, Inc. (1975). Leura Collins, an employee of Weingarten, upon being "interrogated" by the store manager and a Loss Prevention Specialist, about an allegation that she only paid $1 for chicken that sold for $2.98 and about receiving free lunches, repeatedly requested that her union representative be present during the interrogation. Her requests were denied and she was ultimately absolved of any wrongdoing. Collins reported the interrogation's details to union representatives of the Retail Clerks Union, a union representing Collins and other sales personnel at the company. The union filed an unfair labor practice with the National Labor Relations Board (NLRB). The NLRB held the employer had committed an unfair labor practice in denying Collins' request for a union representative to be present during her interrogation and issued a cease-and-desist order. The Court of Appeals refused to enforce the order. The U.S. Supreme Court held that Weingarten violated section 8 (a) (1) the National Labor Relations Act by refusing Collins' request for union representation because in so doing she was denied her right to "engage in . . . concerted activities for . . . mutual aid or protection . . . ."

O'Connor v. Consolidated Coin Caterers Corp. (1996). The Court held that a person who is in the protected age group of 40 or over does not have to have been replaced by someone under 40 for a *prima facie* case of discrimination to exist.

Oncale v. Sundowner Offshore Services, Inc. (1998). The Court held that same-sex sexual harassment is covered under Title VII.

Oubre v. Entergy (1998). The Court ruled that, although Oubre signed a release from the provisions of the Age Discrimination in Employment Act (ADEA) in return for severance pay installments, the release was not valid, since the employer failed to comply with the provisions of the Older Workers Benefit Protection Act (OWBPA). The provisions that the employer failed to follow were: (1) the time limits (45 days) for Oubre to consider the offer were not given, (2) she was not given the requisite amount of time (seven days) to withdraw her acceptance of the offer, and (3) the release did not make specific reference to claims under the ADEA. Oubre spent the $6,258 that she received for signing the release, but the Court held she did not have to reimburse the employer for the funds, since most discharged employees likely would have spent any monies received and would be unable to repay them. This reality, the Court concluded, might tempt employers to risk noncompliance with the OWBPA's waiver provisions by knowing that it would be difficult for such employees to repay the employers and, thus, effectively motivate the employees not to seek remedies under the Act. The Court also remanded the case to the lower court to consider Oubre's charges of discrimination under the ADEA.

Patterson v. McLean Credit Union (1989). The Court upheld its previous ruling in *Runyon v. McCrary* that § 1981 is restricted in application to racial discrimination in the making and enforcement of private contracts. Therefore a claim for racial harassment relating to conditions of employment is not actionable under this statute and declined to submit that part of the case to the jury.

Pollard v. E.I. du Pont de Nemours & Co. (2001). The Court held that front pay is not an aspect of compensatory damages and therefore is not subject to the damages cap.

Price Waterhouse v. Hopkins (1989). The Court held that Hopkins, who was neither offered nor denied partnership in the firm, but instead her candidacy was delayed for one year was discriminated against on the basis of sex because it was based upon comments made by partners resulting from sex stereotyping. An employer who permits discriminatory motives to be involved in an employment decision must prove that it would have made the same decision in the absence of the discrimination.

Quon v. Arch Wireless Operating Co., Incorporated, a Delaware corporation; City of Ontario, a municipal corporation; Lloyd Scharf, individually and as Chief of Ontario Police Department; Ontario Police Department; Debbie Glenn, individually and as a Sergeant of Ontario Police Department (2008). This case that was decided by the Ninth Circuit Court of Appeals involved the use of 20 two-way city-owned pagers furnished in "late 2001 or early 2002" to City of Ontario (California) employees, including Sergeant Jeff Quon in the Police Department. The City had a policy stating "the use of City-owned computers and all associated equipment, software, programs, networks, Internet, e-mail and other systems operating on these computers is limited to City of Ontario related business. The use of these tools for personal benefit is a significant violation of City of Ontario Policy." In

2000, before they received the pagers, Quon and another plaintiff in the case, signed a form acknowledging they had "read and fully understand the City of Ontario's Computer Usage, Internet and E-mail policy." This acknowledgment including the statement, "the City of Ontario reserves the right to monitor and log all network activity including e-mail and Internet use, with or without notice . . . and that users should have no expectation of privacy or confidentiality when using these resources." This policy did not specifically include pagers, but on April 18, 2002, Lieutenant Duke, who was in charge of pager use, stated in a meeting in which Quon was in attendance that pager use was considered as e-mail in the policy. Each employee was assigned a monthly allotment of 25,000 characters. Duke stated to avoid being audited, employees must reimburse the City for any overage. Quon went over the allotment for several months and on each occasion paid for the overages. On these occasions, no audits were conducted. In August 2002, Quon and another officer exceeded the allotment. Instead of informing the officers of the overage, Duke stated in a meeting that he was tired of being a bill collector, whereupon the Chief of Police asked Duke to determine if the overages were work-related (ostensibly requiring an increase in the monthly allotment) or were due to personal use. Duke obtained transcripts of the employee's transmissions, that including Quon's. The City used Arch Wireless to receive and transmit pager messages which included archiving a copy of the message. An employee of Arch Wireless stated she would only deliver messages to the contact on the account, the City of Ontario, and not the user who was Quon. Duke audited the messages and sent them to the Chief and Quon's supervisor who read and referred them to Internal Affairs for an investigation. A sergeant in Internal Affairs issued a memorandum stating that Quon exceeded his (allotment) by 15,158 characters. "Many of (the) messages were personal in nature and were often sexually explicit." Quon and three others who received his pager messages sued Arch Wireless, the City, the Police Department, the Chief of Police, and a Sergeant in the Police Department. The unanimous ruling of the Court was the message search was a violation of the Fourth Amendment and "California constitutional privacy rights because (the plaintiffs-appellants) had a reasonable expectation of privacy in the content of the text messages and the search was unreasonable in scope." The Court ruled only the Chief had qualified immunity, but "the Appellants' Stored Communications Act claim against Arch Wireless and the claims against the City, the (Police) Department and (the sergeant) under the Fourth Amendment and (the) California Constitution" could proceed.

Ragsdale et al. v. Wolverine World Wide, Inc. (2002). Ragsdale was granted 30 days of medical leave by her employer, Wolverine World Wide, Inc. but the company failed to tell her the leave would count toward her 12-week entitlement under the Family and Medical Leave Act. She requested the additional 12 weeks of leave under the Act but the firm would not grant it. She filed suit claiming a Labor Department regulation requires an employer to inform an employee if any type of leave would count toward the 12-week entitlement. The U.S. Supreme Court held if employers have more generous leave policies than that required by the FLMA, then they are not in violation for not granting leave in accordance with the Act simply because they failed to follow notice requirements.

Raytheon Co. v. Hernandez (2003): Hernandez was forced to resign after testing positive for cocaine and admitting to violating the employer's conduct work rules. Two years later he applied for reemployment and submitted a letter from his pastor attesting to his regular church attendance and another letter from an Alcoholics Anonymous (AA) counselor attesting to Hernandez' regular attendance at AA meetings and his recovery. Hernandez' request for reemployment was denied. The employer's representative who made the denial decision said it was due to the firm's policy of not rehiring former employees who were terminated for violating work conduct rules and furthermore, when the decision was made she had no knowledge Hernandez was a former drug addict. The U.S. Supreme Court decided the case involved an allegation of disparate treatment and the employer satisfied the requirements of *McDonnell Douglas* by showing Hernandez' request for reemployment was denied based on a legitimate employment decision.

Regents of the University of California v. Bakke (1978). The Court held in this Title VI case that Bakke, who applied for admission to the Medical School of the University of California at Davis in both 1973 and 1974, was excluded from entrance into Medical School on the basis of his race. In 1973 and 1974, Baake scored 468 out of 500 and 549 out of 600, respectively, on an admission test. In neither year was he selected for admission, but other applicants selected through a special program for minority applicants, who had significantly lower scores than Baakes,' were admitted.

Reeves v. Sanderson Plumbing Products, Inc. (2000). The Court held that a plaintiff's prima facie case of discrimination based upon age, as outlined in *McDonnell Douglas v. Green*, which contains sufficient evidence to reject an employer's nondiscriminatory explanation for discharging an employee, may be adequate for a jury to find an employer liable for intentional discrimination under the Age Discrimination in Employment Act.

Reno, Attorney General, et al. v. Condon, Attorney General of South Carolina, et al. (2000). The State of South Carolina, like a number of other states, released information (including person's name, address, telephone number, vehicle description, Social Security number, medical information, and photograph) about drivers and automobile owners to various individuals, including businesses. Some states sold this information to individuals and businesses and received significant amounts of revenue from the sales. In response to this use, Congress enacted the Driver's Privacy Protection Act of 1994 (DPPA), which restricted states' ability to disclose a driver's personal information without the individual's consent. The State of South Carolina filed suit, alleging that the law (DPPA) violates the Tenth and Eleventh Amendments to the Constitution. The Supreme Court held that the law was proper and did not violate the Constitution.

Rush Prudential HMO, Inc. v. Moran et al. (2002). Rush is an HMO providing medical services covered by the Employee Retirement Income Security Act (ERISA). Moran was covered by the Rush Prudential HMO (Rush). She requested surgery by an unaffiliated specialist but was denied by Rush as "medically unnecessary." She then requested an independent medical review which is provided by Illinois state law, the state in which she lived. Rush refused her request so Moran went to state court for relief. The state court ordered the review which concluded the surgery was needed but Rush denied the claim. Meanwhile, Moran had the surgery and amended her suit to seek reimbursement. Rush had the suit moved to federal court, claiming ERISA preempted the Illinois law. The federal District Court denied her claim but the Appeals court reversed. The U.S. Supreme Court ruled that ERISA does not preempt Illinois state law (the Illinois HMO Act).

Smith et al., v. City of Jackson, Mississippi, et al. (2005). The Court held that under the Age Discrimination in Employment Act, recovery was permitted under disparate impact cases comparable to that permitted under the Civil Rights Act of 1964 except that the apparent offending practice could be justified based on reasonable factors other than age. In this case, the City of Jackson gave pay raises which resulted in higher raises to younger police officers compared to most officers over 40 years of age. The City's rationale for this action was an attempt to bring the starting salaries of police officers and dispatchers up to the regional average. The Court determined that this purpose was a reasonable justification for the action which had a disproportionately adverse effect upon officers over 40 years of age.

Sutton et al. v. United Air Lines (1999). This case involved twin sisters, who had severe myopia but, with corrective lenses, both were able to function identically with individuals who did not have the condition. Both sisters were employed as pilots by a regional airline. They applied for jobs as airline pilots for a major commercial airline, but they were rejected because they did not meet the airline's minimum uncorrected vision requirement. The sisters filed suit under the Americans with Disabilities Act, (ADA) claiming that the Act prohibits employers from discriminating against individuals on the basis of their disabilities. The Court ruled that the provisions of the ADA did not apply because the position for which they applied was a single job. There were other jobs for which they did meet the requirements; thus, their condition did not substantially limit their finding employment.

Swierkiewicz v. Sorema N.A. (2002). Swierkiewicz, who is a 53 year-old person from Hungary, filed suit alleging he had been fired because of his national origin (a violation of Title VII) and his age (a violation of the Age Discrimination in Employment Act). Both the District Court and the Appeals Court dismissed his suit because he failed to show a prima facie case of discrimination as outlined in *McDonnell Douglas Corp. v. Green*. The U.S. Supreme Court reversed, stating in its opinion *McDonnell Douglas* is an evidentiary standard. To plead a case of discrimination only requires "a short and plain statement of the claim showing that the pleader is entitled to relief."

Tennessee v. Lane et al. (2004). A group of paraplegics (respondents) alleged a violation of the Americans with Disabilities Act of 1990 (ADA) on the basis of being denied physical access to courts in Tennessee and a number of counties. In *Board of Trustees of Univ. of Ala. v. Garrett*, the U.S. Supreme Court decided that the Eleventh Amendment prohibited private money damage suits against states for violations of Title I of the ADA. The Sixth Circuit later decided that the respondents' claim was a violation of Title II of the ADA because physical barriers were a denial of due process. The U.S. Supreme Court affirmed the decision in concluding that a denial of access to courts was a violation of Title II of the ADA and was a "valid exercise of Congress' authority under §5 of the Fourteenth Amendment..."

Toyota Motor Manufacturing, Kentucky, Inc. v. Williams (2002). Williams, an employee of Toyota Motor Manufacturing, had carpal tunnel syndrome which prevented her from performing all the tasks required by her assembly line job. She claimed this condition was a disability as defined by the Americans with Disability Act (ADA) and therefore asked her employer (Toyota) to accommodate her disability. Her employer did not make such an accommodation so she filed suit in federal court. The District Court did not support her claim but the Court of Appeals did. The U.S. Supreme Court, reversed the Appeals Court and ruled her condition was not a disability under the ADA because it did not substantially limit a "major life activity." **See also** *Sutton et al. V. United Air Lines* (1999) and *Albertsons, Inc. v. Kirkingburg* (1999).

United Steelworkers of America, AFL-CIO-CLC v. Weber (1979). The Court held that a plan was legal which selected trainees to fill craft jobs on the basis of seniority with the provision that at least 50 percent of the trainees were to be black until the percentage of black skilled craft workers in the plant approximated the percentage of blacks in the local labor force. The plan was legal because it was an affirmative action plan voluntarily adopted by private parties (meaning the Union and the employer) to eliminate traditional patterns of racial segregation.

US Airways, Inc. v. Barnett (2002). Barnett was a cargo handler for US Airways, who hurt his back on the job. To accommodate his physical condition, he was reassigned to a job in the mail room. The mail room job was subject to bidding under the company's bidding system and a senior qualified employee was later awarded the job. The company denied Barnett's request to accommodate his disability by permitting him to remain in the mail room job. Barnett filed suit under the Americans with Disabilities claiming the company failed to accommodate his disability by keeping in a job that he, a person with a disability, could do with reasonable accommodation. The U.S. Supreme Court ruled that placing Barnett in the job would conflict with the seniority system and therefore is unreasonable and constitutes an "undue hardship" to the employer. The Court stated plaintiffs have the burden of showing that seniority systems had been violated in the past or why special circumstances warrant making an exception to such systems.

Ward's Cove Packing Co., Inc. v. Antonio (1989). Ward's Cove Packing Company is a salmon cannery in Alaska. The two types of work in the cannery were "unskilled jobs" on the cannery lines that were mostly filled by non-white employees and the generally higher paying skilled positions that were predominately filled by white employees. Antonio and other workers in the unskilled jobs claimed they were victims of illegal discrimination because whites held a larger percentage of skilled jobs and non-whites had a higher percentage of unskilled jobs. In their suit, the workers produced evidence of neither the numbers of whites and non-whites who had applied for skilled jobs nor the selection methods used that disproportionately screened-out non-white applicants for those jobs. The Court ruled that a *prima facie* case of disparate impact job discrimination cannot be supported on the mere fact that non-whites compared to whites have a disproportionately smaller percentage of preferred jobs and a larger percentage of less preferred jobs. In such situations, those alleging discrimination must show the disproportionate statistics are due to one or more selection practices and evidence of the significant disparate impact each practice has on the employment of whites and non-whites.

Walters v. Metropolitan Educational Enterprises, Inc. (1997). In this case, the Court reviewed the requirement under Title VII of the Civil Rights Act of 1964 that an employer must have an employment relationship with 15 or more individuals for each working day in 20 or more weeks during the year in question. The Court decided that the phrase "for each working day" means that an employee is counted as an employee for each working day, starting on the day that the employment relationship begins and ending on the last day of the employment relationship. The Court held that, following this definition, employees should be counted, whether or not they are actually performing work for or being paid by the employer on any particular day.

Washington v. Davis (1976). The Court held that a written personnel test (named Test 21) that measured verbal skill was a useful indicator of training school performance (thus precluding the need to show validation in terms of job performance) for police officers in the District of Columbia, particularly because the job requires special abilities to communicate orally and in writing.

Watson v. Fort Worth Bank & Trust (1988). Fort Worth Bank & Trust used subjective judgments of white supervisors in selecting white applicants for four promotions and rejecting Watson, who was black. The Court ruled that subjective or other discretionary systems of promotion can be subjected to disparate impact analysis. In so ruling, the Court rejected the contention that subjective or discretionary systems for promotion can only be analyzed under the disparate treatment concept of discrimination.

Wright v. Universal Maritime Service Corp. (1998). The Court ruled that Wright, who was a longshoreman covered by a collective bargaining agreement, was not barred by the agreement in pursuing in federal court his claim of employment discrimination based upon a violation of the Americans with Disabilities Act. The Court determined the agreement did not contain a clear and unmistakable waiver of employee rights to pursue allegations of discrimination through the federal judiciary.

Appendix 2

SAMPLE HARASSMENT-FREE POLICY STATEMENT

I. Purpose

The purpose of this policy statement is to formally acknowledge that harassment, based upon national origin, race, color, religion, sex, disability, age, and veteran status, will not be tolerated.

Harassment can be prevented, but, if it does occur, it can be stopped. The key to prevention is for people to understand what harassment is, learn how their personal attitudes may make them prone to engage in it and understand that they must change those attitudes if they want to continue their association with our firm.

All employees are responsible for maintaining an harassment-free work environment and reporting any violations of this policy.

II. Employee Coverage

All employees are entitled to humane treatment and to perform their work, regardless of location, whether on the employer's premises or elsewhere, free from harassment.

III. Source of Harassment

All work-related harassment is prohibited, regardless of the source. Thus, employees, contract personnel, customers, and all third parties are prohibited from harassing employees.

IV. Contract Personnel, Customers, and Third Parties

All personnel who come into contact with employees during their work performance are expected to comply with this policy. This provision applies regardless of whether the contact is performed on the employer's premises or elsewhere.

V. Harassment-Free Assurance Procedure

A detailed procedure, called the *Harassment-Free Assurance Procedure*, has been implemented for employees to use in reporting any work-related harassment that they experience. *All* employees are encouraged to use that procedure to both prevent and stop harassment.

VI. Performance Appraisal

The annual performance appraisal system will include an evaluation of each employee's conduct in complying with this policy. Any instance of harassment by an employee will be considered in such decisions as pay increases, promotions, and career development that may affect the employee. Furthermore, employees who engage in harassment will be subject to disciplinary action, including discharge from employment.

VII. Harassment Awareness Training

All employees will receive training concerning their roles and responsibilities in maintaining an harassment-free work environment.

VIII. Audit Procedure

Audits will conducted periodically to ensure that this policy is followed.

IX. Violations

Prompt action will be taken against any person who violates this policy. Employees may be subjected to immediate disciplinary action, including discharge, for engaging in harassment.

Managers are responsible for both preventing and stopping harassment. Due to the pernicious nature of harassment, managers will be held to an overall higher standard of responsibility for their personal conduct. In addition, they will be held responsible for the conduct of employees assigned to them. This responsibility extends beyond conduct that they have knowledge of to include conduct that they *should have known about*.

Contractors that do business with our firm may have their contracts severed if their employees do not adhere to this policy.

Customers who violate this policy may be denied access to the business or have their contracts severed and/or not renewed.

Civil lawsuits may be pursued in aggravated harassment cases.

X. Policy Implementation Responsibilities

All employees are expected to comply with this policy. However, management personnel must assume extraordinary responsibility to ensure that both the spirit and intent of the policy are met.

The Vice President of Human Resources Management is functionally responsible for the implementation and the overall enforcement of the policy.

Appendix 3

SAMPLE HARASSMENT-FREE ASSURANCE PROCEDURE

I. Harassment is Prohibited

Harassment on the basis of national origin, race, color, religion, sex, disability, age, or veteran status is not permitted anywhere or in any place connected with the work environment. In addition to the actual workplace, the work environment includes parking lots, lunchrooms, any location in which an employee is performing assigned duties, and any facilities either owned or under contract to the employer. Harassment is prohibited, whether caused by peers, supervisors, other employees, customers or other third parties, or any person employed in any capacity by the employer or performing work for the employer, whether on the employer's premises or not.

II. Emphasis on Prevention

Every effort has been made to ensure employees are not harassed. Specific actions that have been taken to prevent harassment include:

A. Issuance of a formal policy statement prohibiting harassment;

B. Training of all employees;

C. Requiring all contractors and others who perform work for the employer, whether on the employer's premises or not, to abide-by the policy; and

D. Training management personnel not to tolerate harassment by customers or other third parties, whether on the employer's or the customer's premises or in another location.

III. Harassment Complaint Procedure

The steps outlined in (II) above hopefully will be sufficient to prevent harassment. Should harassment occur, however, employees are *expected* to report it. The following procedure will be used in vigorously resolving all complaints of harassment.

A. Any employee who believes he or she has been harassed on the basis of national origin, race, color, religion, sex, disability, age, or veteran status may either personally, or through a representative of his or her choosing, file a complaint with the Employee Relations Department either in person or in writing.

B. Any employee who desires information about whether specific conduct constitutes harassment should contact the Employee Relations Department in person, via the telephone [(800) 664-2727 (NOHARAS)], or by mail.

C. All complaints should be filed as soon as possible after an instance of harassment occurs, since the ensuing investigation typically prevents a repetition of the harassment and increases the likelihood of a prompt and just solution. Furthermore, if too much time has elapsed since the harassment occurred, some of the principals and corroborating witnesses involved in a complaint may have left the firm, or for some other reason cannot be located. For all these reasons, harassment complaints should be filed promptly.

D. All complaints of harassment shall be in writing and signed by the person or persons [hereafter called "complainant(s)"].

E. The information to be furnished in the complaint shall include this:

1. The name, work location, address, and telephone number of each complainant;

2. The name of each person who is alleged to have perpetrated the harassment (hereafter called "alleged harasser");

3. The work location of the alleged harasser, if an employee of either the firm or a contractor, or the location where the harassment occurred, if the alleged harasser was either a customer or other third party; and

4. A description of the harassment, including what happened, the date(s) when the event(s) occurred, and the place(s) where the event(s) occurred.

F. The identity of the complainant(s) shall be kept confidential except to the extent necessary to carry out the purpose of this procedure, including the conducting of any investigation.

G. No employee who files a complaint of harassment and/or any person who testifies, assists, or participates in any manner in any phase of the investigation of a complaint or who cooperates in any mediation or conciliation efforts to resolve a complaint will be intimidated, threatened, coerced, or subjected to any retaliation.

1. Any person who violates this provision will be subjected to the following actions:

a. Employees, including supervisors, will be subject to immediate disciplinary action, including discharge;

b. Contract personnel will have their contracts severed; and

c. Customers will be denied access to the business or contracts severed and/or not renewed.

2. Civil lawsuits may be pursued in aggravated harassment cases.

H. Upon receipt of the complaint, the Employee Relations Department will assign an individual (hereafter called the "Investigator") to investigate the complaint. Investigators have exceptional interpersonal abilities and are specifically trained to conduct investigations in a humane manner with particular sensitivity to any trauma that the complainant may have experienced.

I. Employees, contract personnel, customers, and other third parties are expected to cooperate with the Investigator in obtaining the facts in the complaint.

J. The role of the Investigator is to:

1. Secure the facts in the complaint through interviews and other means;

2. Make a finding of facts;

3. Mediate a settlement, where the facts warrant; and

4. Make recommendations for necessary action, including disciplinary action that should be taken, contracts terminated, or remedial relief that should be granted.

K. The Investigator has the authority to:

1. Interview and obtain written statements from the parties involved in the complaint, including any witnesses;

2. Secure the cooperation of employees, contract personnel, customers, and any other third parties in obtaining information related to the complaint;

3. Contact and interview a reasonable number of persons, including employees and others, to help confirm or refute the allegations;

4. Prepare a finding of facts in the complaint;

5. Hold conferences to settle, simplify, or fix the issues in a complaint or to consider other matters that may aid in the expeditious disposition of the complaint;

6. Require parties to state their positions with respect to the complaint;

7. Fix time limits for the submission of any evidence that is necessary to ascertain the facts in the case;

8. Make recommendations for the disposition of the case, including any management action that should be taken against any employee, contractor, customer, or third party; and

9. Conduct exit interviews.

L. Investigators shall conduct fair, speedy, and effective reviews of complaints.

M. Upon completion of the on-site review (and an off-site review, if one is necessary), including securing information from all the parties involved in the complaint, the Investigator shall schedule exit conference(s) with the principals (either separately or together, as the Investigator shall decide is most appropriate) to accomplish the following objectives:

1. Review the findings of the investigation;

2. Obtain any exceptions, corrections, or additions that the parties request to make to the findings;

3. Explain the significance of the findings; and

4. Propose a settlement to the complaint, if the Investigator determines it is appropriate.

N. The Investigator shall provide a written report to the Vice President of Human Resources who will make the final decision in the case. The Investigator's report will contain a findings of fact, including information obtained in the investigation and the exit conference and a proposed settlement of the complaint.

O. The Investigator will send copies of the written report to the complainant and the alleged harasser.

1. Both parties have 15 days after they receive the Investigator's report to appeal any or all parts of it to the Vice President of Human Resources.

2. The Vice President of Human Resources will consider any information provided in an appeal, if there is one, in making a final decision.

3. At the conclusion of the 15-day appeal period, the Vice President of Human Resources will make a final decision that will be immediately implemented.

4. The Vice President of Human Resources may decide that:

   a. Employees, including supervisors, may be subjected to immediate disciplinary action, including discharge;

   b. Contract personnel may have their contracts severed; and

   c. Customers may be denied access to the business or contracts severed and/or not renewed.

5. Civil lawsuits may be pursued in aggravated harassment cases.

Appendix 4

FORMS — FAMILY AND MEDICAL LEAVE ACT

Certification of Health Care Provider for
Employee's Serious Health Condition
(Family and Medical Leave Act)

U.S. Department of Labor
Employment Standards Administration
Wage and Hour Division

OMB Control Number: 1215-0181
Expires: 12/31/2011

SECTION I: For Completion by the EMPLOYER

INSTRUCTIONS to the EMPLOYER: The Family and Medical Leave Act (FMLA) provides that an employer may require an employee seeking FMLA protections because of a need for leave due to a serious health condition to submit a medical certification issued by the employee's health care provider. Please complete Section I before giving this form to your employee. Your response is voluntary. While you are not required to use this form, you may not ask the employee to provide more information than allowed under the FMLA regulations, 29 C.F.R. §§ 825.306-825.308. Employers must generally maintain records and documents relating to medical certifications, recertifications, or medical histories of employees created for FMLA purposes as confidential medical records in separate files/records from the usual personnel files and in accordance with 29 C.F.R. § 1630.14(c)(1), if the Americans with Disabilities Act applies.

Employer name and contact: _____

Employee's job title: _____ Regular work schedule: _____

Employee's essential job functions: _____

_____

Check if job description is attached: _____

SECTION II: For Completion by the EMPLOYEE

INSTRUCTIONS to the EMPLOYEE: Please complete Section II before giving this form to your medical provider. The FMLA permits an employer to require that you submit a timely, complete, and sufficient medical certification to support a request for FMLA leave due to your own serious health condition. If requested by your employer, your response is required to obtain or retain the benefit of FMLA protections. 29 U.S.C. §§ 2613, 2614(c)(3). Failure to provide a complete and sufficient medical certification may result in a denial of your FMLA request. 20 C.F.R. § 825.313. Your employer must give you at least 15 calendar days to return this form. 29 C.F.R. § 825.305(b).

Your name: _____
         First   Middle   Last

SECTION III: For Completion by the HEALTH CARE PROVIDER

INSTRUCTIONS to the HEALTH CARE PROVIDER: Your patient has requested leave under the FMLA. Answer, fully and completely, all applicable parts. Several questions seek a response as to the frequency or duration of a condition, treatment, etc. Your answer should be your best estimate based upon your medical knowledge, experience, and examination of the patient. Be as specific as you can; terms such as "lifetime," "unknown," or "indeterminate" may not be sufficient to determine FMLA coverage. Limit your responses to the condition for which the employee is seeking leave. Please be sure to sign the form on the last page.

Provider's name and business address: _____

Type of practice / Medical specialty: _____

Telephone: (_____) _____ Fax:(_____) _____

PART A: MEDICAL FACTS

1. Approximate date condition commenced: _____

Probable duration of condition: _____

Mark below as applicable:
Was the patient admitted for an overnight stay in a hospital, hospice, or residential medical care facility?
___No ___Yes. If so, dates of admission:

_____

Date(s) you treated the patient for condition:

_____

Will the patient need to have treatment visits at least twice per year due to the condition? ___No ___ Yes.

Was medication, other than over-the-counter medication, prescribed? ___No ___Yes.

Was the patient referred to other health care provider(s) for evaluation or treatment (e.g., physical therapist)?
____No ____Yes. If so, state the nature of such treatments and expected duration of treatment:

_____

2. Is the medical condition pregnancy? ___No ___Yes. If so, expected delivery date: _____

3. Use the information provided by the employer in Section I to answer this question. If the employer fails to provide a list of the employee's essential functions or a job description, answer these questions based upon the employee's own description of his/her job functions.

Is the employee unable to perform any of his/her job functions due to the condition: ____ No ____ Yes.

If so, identify the job functions the employee is unable to perform:

_____

4. Describe other relevant medical facts, if any, related to the condition for which the employee seeks leave (such medical facts may include symptoms, diagnosis, or any regimen of continuing treatment such as the use of specialized equipment):

_____

_____

_____

_____

_____

_____

_____

_____

PART B: AMOUNT OF LEAVE NEEDED

5. Will the employee be incapacitated for a single continuous period of time due to his/her medical condition, including any time for treatment and recovery? ___No ___Yes.

   If so, estimate the beginning and ending dates for the period of incapacity: _____

6. Will the employee need to attend follow-up treatment appointments or work part-time or on a reduced schedule because of the employee's medical condition? ___No ___Yes.

   If so, are the treatments or the reduced number of hours of work medically necessary? ___No ___Yes.

   Estimate treatment schedule, if any, including the dates of any scheduled appointments and the time required for each appointment, including any recovery period:

   _____

   Estimate the part-time or reduced work schedule the employee needs, if any:

   _____ hour(s) per day; _____ days per week from _____ through _____

7. Will the condition cause episodic flare-ups periodically preventing the employee from performing his/her job functions? ____No ____Yes.

   Is it medically necessary for the employee to be absent from work during the flare-ups? ____ No ____ Yes. If so, explain:

   _____

   _____

   Based upon the patient's medical history and your knowledge of the medical condition, estimate the frequency of flare-ups and the duration of related incapacity that the patient may have over the next 6 months (e.g., 1 episode every 3 months lasting 1-2 days):

   Frequency: _____ times per _____ week(s) _____ month(s)

   Duration: _____ hours or ___ day(s) per episode

ADDITIONAL INFORMATION: IDENTIFY QUESTION NUMBER WITH YOUR ADDITIONAL ANSWER.

_____
_____
_____
_____
_____

_____
_____
_____
_____
_____
_____
_____
_____
_____
_____
_____
_____
_____
_____
_____
_____
_____
_____
_____
_____
_____

Signature of Health Care Provider   **Date**

Certification of Health Care Provider for
Family Member's Serious Health Condition
(Family and Medical Leave Act)

U.S. Department of Labor
Employment Standards Administration
Wage and Hour Division

OMB Control Number: 1215-0181
Expires: 12/31/2011

SECTION I: For Completion by the EMPLOYER

INSTRUCTIONS to the EMPLOYER: The Family and Medical Leave Act (FMLA) provides that an employer may require an employee seeking FMLA protections because of a need for leave to care for a covered family member with a serious health condition to submit a medical certification issued by the health care provider of the covered family member. Please complete Section I before giving this form to your employee. Your response is voluntary. While you are not required to use this form, you may not ask the employee to provide more information than allowed under the FMLA regulations, 29 C.F.R. §§ 825.306-825.308. Employers must generally maintain records and documents relating to medical certifications, recertifications, or medical histories of employees' family members, created for FMLA purposes as confidential medical records in separate files/records from the usual personnel files and in accordance with 29 C.F.R. § 1630.14(c)(1), if the Americans with Disabilities Act applies.

Employer name and contact: _____

SECTION II: For Completion by the EMPLOYEE

INSTRUCTIONS to the EMPLOYEE: Please complete Section II before giving this form to your family member or his/her medical provider. The FMLA permits an employer to require that you submit a timely, complete, and sufficient medical certification to support a request for FMLA leave to care for a covered family member with a serious health condition. If requested by your employer, your response is required to obtain or retain the benefit of FMLA protections. 29 U.S.C. §§ 2613, 2614(c)(3). Failure to provide a complete and sufficient medical certification may result in a denial of your FMLA request. 29 C.F.R. § 825.313. Your employer must give you at least 15 calendar days to return this form to your employer. 29 C.F.R. § 825.305.

Your name: _____
          First   Middle   Last

Name of family member for whom you will provide care: _____
                                First   Middle   Last
Relationship of family member to you: _____

    If family member is your son or daughter, date of birth:_____

Describe care you will provide to your family member and estimate leave needed to provide care:

_____

_____

_____

_____   _____

Employee Signature   Date

SECTION III: For Completion by the HEALTH CARE PROVIDER

INSTRUCTIONS to the HEALTH CARE PROVIDER: The employee listed above has requested leave under the FMLA to care for your patient. Answer, fully and completely, all applicable parts below. Several questions seek a response as to the frequency or duration of a condition, treatment, etc. Your answer should be your best estimate based upon your medical knowledge, experience, and examination of the patient. Be as specific as you can; terms such as "lifetime," "unknown," or "indeterminate" may not be sufficient to determine FMLA coverage. Limit your responses to the condition for which the patient needs leave. Page 3 provides space for additional information, should you need it. Please be sure to sign the form on the last page.

Provider's name and business address:_____

Type of practice / Medical specialty: _____

Telephone: (_____)_____ Fax:(_____)_____

PART A: MEDICAL FACTS

1. Approximate date condition commenced: _____

   Probable duration of condition: _____

   Was the patient admitted for an overnight stay in a hospital, hospice, or residential medical care facility?
   ___No ___Yes. If so, dates of admission: _____

   Date(s) you treated the patient for condition: _____

   Was medication, other than over-the-counter medication, prescribed? ___No ___Yes.

   Will the patient need to have treatment visits at least twice per year due to the condition? ___No ___Yes

   Was the patient referred to other health care provider(s) for evaluation or treatment (e.g., physical therapist)?
   ____ No ____Yes. If so, state the nature of such treatments and expected duration of treatment:

   _____

   _____

2. Is the medical condition pregnancy? ___No ___Yes. If so, expected delivery date: _____

3. Describe other relevant medical facts, if any, related to the condition for which the patient needs care (such medical facts may include symptoms, diagnosis, or any regimen of continuing treatment such as the use of specialized equipment):

   _____

   _____

   _____

   _____

4. Will the patient be incapacitated for a single continuous period of time, including any time for treatment and recovery? ___No ___Yes.

   Estimate the beginning and ending dates for the period of incapacity: _____

   During this time, will the patient need care? __ No __ Yes.

   Explain the care needed by the patient and why such care is medically necessary:

   _____

   _____

   _____

   _____

   _____

5. Will the patient require follow-up treatments, including any time for recovery? ___No ___Yes.

   Estimate treatment schedule, if any, including the dates of any scheduled appointments and the time required for each appointment, including any recovery period:

   _____

   Explain the care needed by the patient, and why such care is medically necessary: _____

   _____

6. Will the patient require care on an intermittent or reduced schedule basis, including any time for recovery? __ No __ Yes.

   Estimate the hours the patient needs care on an intermittent basis, if any:

   _____ hour(s) per day; _____ days per week   from _____ through _____

   Explain the care needed by the patient, and why such care is medically necessary:

   _____

   _____

   _____

   _____

7. Will the condition cause episodic flare-ups periodically preventing the patient from participating in normal daily activities? _____ No _____ Yes.

Based upon the patient's medical history and your knowledge of the medical condition, estimate the frequency of flare-ups and the duration of related incapacity that the patient may have over the next 6 months (e.g., 1 episode every 3 months lasting 1-2 days):

Frequency: _____ times per _____ week(s) _____ month(s)

Duration: _____ hours or ___ day(s) per episode

Does the patient need care during these flare-ups? _____ No _____ Yes.

Explain the care needed by the patient, and why such care is medically necessary: _____

_____

_____

_____

_____

ADDITIONAL INFORMATION: IDENTIFY QUESTION NUMBER WITH YOUR ADDITIONAL ANSWER.

_____

_____

_____

_____

_____

_____

Signature of Health Care Provider   **Date**

**Notice of Eligibility and Rights &
Responsibilities
(Family and Medical Leave Act)**

U.S. Department of Labor
Employment Standards Administration
Wage and Hour Division

≡WHD★
U.S. Wage and Hour Division

OMB Control Number: 1215-0181
Expires: 12/31/2011

In general, to be eligible an employee must have worked for an employer for at least 12 months, have worked at least 1,250 hours in the 12 months preceding the leave, and work at a site with at least 50 employees within 75 miles. While use of this form by employers is optional, a fully completed Form WH-381 provides employees with the information required by 29 C.F.R. § 825.300(b), which must be provided within five business days of the employee notifying the employer of the need for FMLA leave. Part B provides employees with information regarding their rights and responsibilities for taking FMLA leave, as required by 29 C.F.R. § 825.300(b), (c).

[Part A – NOTICE OF ELIGIBILITY]

TO: _____
　　　Employee

FROM: _____
　　　Employer Representative

DATE: _____

On _____, you informed us that you needed leave beginning on _____ for:

_____ The birth of a child, or placement of a child with you for adoption or foster care;

_____ Your own serious health condition;

_____ Because you are needed to care for your _____ spouse; _____child; _____ parent due to his/her serious health condition.

_____ Because of a qualifying exigency arising out of the fact that your _____ spouse; _____son or daughter; _____ parent is on active duty or call to active duty status in support of a contingency operation as a member of the National Guard or Reserves.

_____ Because you are the _____ spouse; _____son or daughter; _____ parent; _____ next of kin of a covered servicemember with a serious injury or illness.

This Notice is to inform you that you:

_____ Are eligible for FMLA leave (See Part B below for Rights and Responsibilities)

_____ Are **not** eligible for FMLA leave, because (only one reason need be checked, although you may not be eligible for other reasons):

　　_____ You have not met the FMLA's 12-month length of service requirement. As of the first date of requested leave, you will have worked approximately ___ months towards this requirement.
　　_____ You have not met the FMLA's 1,250-hours-worked requirement.
　　_____ You do not work and/or report to a site with 50 or more employees within 75-miles.

If you have any questions, contact _____ or view the FMLA poster located in

_____.

[PART B-RIGHTS AND RESPONSIBILITIES FOR TAKING FMLA LEAVE]

As explained in Part A, you meet the eligibility requirements for taking FMLA leave and still have FMLA leave available in the applicable 12-month period. **However, in order for us to determine whether your absence qualifies as FMLA leave, you must return the following information to us by** _____. (If a certification is requested, employers must allow at least 15 calendar days from receipt of this notice; additional time may be required in some circumstances.) If sufficient information is not provided in a timely manner, your leave may be denied.

_____ Sufficient certification to support your request for FMLA leave. A certification form that sets forth the information necessary to support your request _____**is**/_____ **is not** enclosed.

_____ Sufficient documentation to establish the required relationship between you and your family member.

_____ Other information needed: _____

_____

_____

_____ No additional information requested

　　　CONTINUED ON NEXT PAGE　　　Form WH-381 Revised January 2009

1090   Appendix 4

If your leave does qualify as FMLA leave you will have the following **responsibilities** while on FMLA leave (only checked blanks apply):

_____   Contact _____ at _____ to make arrangements to continue to make your share of the premium payments on your health insurance to maintain health benefits while you are on leave. You have a minimum 30-day (or, indicate longer period, if applicable) grace period in which to make premium payments. If payment is not made timely, your group health insurance may be cancelled, provided we notify you in writing at least 15 days before the date that your health coverage will lapse, or, at our option, we may pay your share of the premiums during FMLA leave, and recover these payments from you upon your return to work.

_____   You will be required to use your available paid _____ **sick,** _____ **vacation,** and/or _____ **other leave** during your FMLA absence. This means that you will receive your paid leave and the leave will also be considered protected FMLA leave and counted against your FMLA leave entitlement.

_____   Due to your status within the company, you are considered a "key employee" as defined in the FMLA. As a "key employee," restoration to employment may be denied following FMLA leave on the grounds that such restoration will cause substantial and grievous economic injury to us. We ___ **have**/ ____ **have not** determined that restoring you to employment at the conclusion of FMLA leave will cause substantial and grievous economic harm to us.

_____   While on leave you will be required to furnish us with periodic reports of your status and intent to return to work every _____. (Indicate interval of periodic reports, as appropriate for the particular leave situation).

If the circumstances of your leave change, and you are able to return to work earlier than the date indicated on the reverse side of this form, you will be required to notify us at least two workdays prior to the date you intend to report for work.

If your leave does qualify as FMLA leave you will have the following **rights** while on FMLA leave:

- You have a right under the FMLA for up to 12 weeks of unpaid leave in a 12-month period calculated as:

     _____   the calendar year (January – December).

     _____   a fixed leave year based on _____.

     _____   the 12-month period measured forward from the date of your first FMLA leave usage.

     _____   a "rolling" 12-month period measured backward from the date of any FMLA leave usage.

- You have a right under the FMLA for up to 26 weeks of unpaid leave in a single 12-month period to care for a covered servicemember with a serious injury or illness. This single 12-month period commenced on _____.
- Your health benefits must be maintained during any period of unpaid leave under the same conditions as if you continued to work.
- You must be reinstated to the same or an equivalent job with the same pay, benefits, and terms and conditions of employment on your return from FMLA-protected leave. (If your leave extends beyond the end of your FMLA entitlement, you do not have return rights under FMLA.)
- If you do not return to work following FMLA leave for a reason other than: 1) the continuation, recurrence, or onset of a serious health condition which would entitle you to FMLA leave; 2) the continuation, recurrence, or onset of a covered servicemember's serious injury or illness which would entitle you to FMLA leave; or 3) other circumstances beyond your control, you may be required to reimburse us for our share of health insurance premiums paid on your behalf during your FMLA leave.
- If we have not informed you above that you must use accrued paid leave while taking your unpaid FMLA leave entitlement, you have the right to have ____ **sick,** ____ **vacation,** and/or ___ **other leave** run concurrently with your unpaid leave entitlement, provided you meet any applicable requirements of the leave policy. Applicable conditions related to the substitution of paid leave are referenced or set forth below. If you do not meet the requirements for taking paid leave, you remain entitled to take unpaid FMLA leave.

     ____ For a copy of conditions applicable to sick/vacation/other leave usage please refer to _____ available at: _____.

     ____ Applicable conditions for use of paid leave: _____

_____

_____

_____

_____

Once we obtain the information from you as specified above, we will inform you, within 5 business days, whether your leave will be designated as FMLA leave and count towards your FMLA leave entitlement. If you have any questions, please do not hesitate to contact:

_____ at _____.

PAPERWORK REDUCTION ACT NOTICE AND PUBLIC BURDEN STATEMENT

It is mandatory for employers to provide employees with notice of their eligibility for FMLA protection and their rights and responsibilities. 29 U.S.C. § 2617; 29 C.F.R. § 825.300(b), (c). It is mandatory for employers to retain a copy of this disclosure in their records for three years. 29 U.S.C. § 2616; 29 C.F.R. § 825.500. Persons are not required to respond to this collection of information unless it displays a currently valid OMB control number. The Department of Labor estimates that it will take an average of 10 minutes for respondents to complete this collection of information, including the time for reviewing instructions, searching existing data sources, gathering and maintaining the data needed, and completing and reviewing the collection of information. If you have any comments regarding this burden estimate or any other aspect of this collection information, including suggestions for reducing this burden, send them to the Administrator, Wage and Hour Division, U.S. Department of Labor, Room S-3502, 200 Constitution Ave., NW, Washington, DC 20210. **DO NOT SEND THE COMPLETED FORM TO THE WAGE AND HOUR DIVISION.**

Designation Notice
(Family and Medical Leave Act)

U.S. Department of Labor
Employment Standards Administration
Wage and Hour Division

U.S. Wage and Hour Division
OMB Control Number: 1215-0181
Expires: 12/31/2011

Leave covered under the Family and Medical Leave Act (FMLA) must be designated as FMLA-protected and the employer must inform the employee of the amount of leave that will be counted against the employee's FMLA leave entitlement. In order to determine whether leave is covered under the FMLA, the employer may request that the leave be supported by a certification. If the certification is incomplete or insufficient, the employer must state in writing what additional information is necessary to make the certification complete and sufficient. While use of this form by employers is optional, a fully completed Form WH-382 provides an easy method of providing employees with the written information required by 29 C.F.R. §§ 825.300(c), 825.301, and 825.305(c).

To: _____

Date: _____

We have reviewed your request for leave under the FMLA and any supporting documentation that you have provided.
We received your most recent information on _____ and decided:

_____ **Your FMLA leave request is approved. All leave taken for this reason will be designated as FMLA leave.**

The FMLA requires that you notify us as soon as practicable if dates of scheduled leave change or are extended, or were initially unknown. Based on the information you have provided to date, we are providing the following information about the amount of time that will be counted against your leave entitlement:

_____ Provided there is no deviation from your anticipated leave schedule, the following number of hours, days, or weeks will be counted against your leave entitlement: _____

_____ Because the leave you will need will be unscheduled, it is not possible to provide the hours, days, or weeks that will be counted against your FMLA entitlement at this time. You have the right to request this information once in a 30-day period (if leave was taken in the 30-day period).

Please be advised (check if applicable):
_____ You have requested to use paid leave during your FMLA leave. Any paid leave taken for this reason will count against your FMLA leave entitlement.

_____ We are requiring you to substitute or use paid leave during your FMLA leave.

_____ You will be required to present a fitness-for-duty certificate to be restored to employment. If such certification is not timely received, your return to work may be delayed until certification is provided. A list of the essential functions of your position ___ **is** ___ **is not** attached. If attached, the fitness-for-duty certification must address your ability to perform these functions.

_____ **Additional information is needed to determine if your FMLA leave request can be approved:**

_____ The certification you have provided is not complete and sufficient to determine whether the FMLA applies to your leave request. You must provide the following information no later than _____, unless it is not
            (Provide at least seven calendar days)
practicable under the particular circumstances despite your diligent good faith efforts, or your leave may be denied.

_____
(Specify information needed to make the certification complete and sufficient)
_____

_____ We are exercising our right to have you obtain a second or third opinion medical certification at our expense, and we will provide further details at a later time.

_____ Your FMLA Leave request is Not Approved.
_____ The FMLA does not apply to your leave request.
_____ You have exhausted your FMLA leave entitlement in the applicable 12-month period.

Form WH-382 January 2009

Certification of Qualifying Exigency For Military Family Leave (Family and Medical Leave Act)

U.S. Department of Labor
Employment Standards Administration
Wage and Hour Division

U.S. Wage and Hour Division

OMB Control Number: 1215-0181
Expires: 12/31/2011

SECTION I: For Completion by the EMPLOYER

INSTRUCTIONS to the EMPLOYER: The Family and Medical Leave Act (FMLA) provides that an employer may require an employee seeking FMLA leave due to a qualifying exigency to submit a certification. Please complete Section I before giving this form to your employee. Your response is voluntary, and while you are not required to use this form, you may not ask the employee to provide more information than allowed under the FMLA regulations, 29 C.F.R. § 825.309.

Employer name: _____

Contact Information: _____

SECTION II: For Completion by the EMPLOYEE

INSTRUCTIONS to the EMPLOYEE: Please complete Section II fully and completely. The FMLA permits an employer to require that you submit a timely, complete, and sufficient certification to support a request for FMLA leave due to a qualifying exigency. Several questions in this section seek a response as to the frequency or duration of the qualifying exigency. Be as specific as you can; terms such as "unknown," or "indeterminate" may not be sufficient to determine FMLA coverage. Your response is required to obtain a benefit. 29 C.F.R. § 825.310. While you are not required to provide this information, failure to do so may result in a denial of your request for FMLA leave. Your employer must give you at least 15 calendar days to return this form to your employer.

Your Name: _____
          First   Middle   Last

Name of covered military member on active duty or call to active duty status in support of a contingency operation:

_____
          First   Middle   Last

Relationship of covered military member to you: _____

Period of covered military member's active duty: _____

A complete and sufficient certification to support a request for FMLA leave due to a qualifying exigency includes written documentation confirming a covered military member's active duty or call to active duty status in support of a contingency operation. Please check one of the following:

_____ A copy of the covered military member's active duty orders is attached.

_____ Other documentation from the military certifying that the covered military member is on active duty (or has been notified of an impending call to active duty) in support of a contingency operation is attached.

_____ I have previously provided my employer with sufficient written documentation confirming the covered military member's active duty or call to active duty status in support of a contingency operation.

1. Describe the reason you are requesting FMLA leave due to a qualifying exigency (including the specific reason you are requesting leave):

    _____

    _____

    _____

    _____

    _____

    _____

    _____

2. A complete and sufficient certification to support a request for FMLA leave due to a qualifying exigency includes any available written documentation which supports the need for leave; such documentation may include a copy of a meeting announcement for informational briefings sponsored by the military, a document confirming an appointment with a counselor or school official, or a copy of a bill for services for the handling of legal or financial affairs. Available written documentation supporting this request for leave is attached. __ Yes __ No __ None Available

PART B: AMOUNT OF LEAVE NEEDED

1. Approximate date exigency commenced: _____

    Probable duration of exigency: _____

2. Will you need to be absent from work for a single continuous period of time due to the qualifying exigency? ___No ___Yes.

    If so, estimate the beginning and ending dates for the period of absence:

    _____.

3. Will you need to be absent from work periodically to address this qualifying exigency? ___No ___Yes.

    Estimate schedule of leave, including the dates of any scheduled meetings or appointments:_____

    _____

    _____

    Estimate the frequency and duration of each appointment, meeting, or leave event, including any travel time (i.e., 1 deployment-related meeting every month lasting 4 hours):

    Frequency: _____ times per _____ week(s) _____ month(s)

    Duration: _____ hours ___ day(s) per event.

1094   Appendix 4

PART C:

If leave is requested to meet with a third party (such as to arrange for childcare, to attend counseling, to attend meetings with school or childcare providers, to make financial or legal arrangements, to act as the covered military member's representative before a federal, state, or local agency for purposes of obtaining, arranging or appealing military service benefits, or to attend any event sponsored by the military or military service organizations), a complete and sufficient certification includes the name, address, and appropriate contact information of the individual or entity with whom you are meeting (i.e., either the telephone or fax number or email address of the individual or entity). This information may be used by your employer to verify that the information contained on this form is accurate.

Name of Individual: _____ Title: _____

Organization: _____

Address: _____

Telephone: (_____) _____ Fax: (_____) _____

Email: _____

Describe nature of meeting: _____

_____

_____

_____

_____

_____

_____

_____

_____

PART D:

I certify that the information I provided above is true and correct.

_____   _____
Signature of Employee   Date

PAPERWORK REDUCTION ACT NOTICE AND PUBLIC BURDEN STATEMENT
If submitted, it is mandatory for employers to retain a copy of this disclosure in their records for three years. 29 U.S.C. § 2616; 29 C.F.R. § 825.500. Persons are not required to respond to this collection of information unless it displays a currently valid OMB control number. The Department of Labor estimates that it will take an average of 20 minutes for respondents to complete this collection of information, including the time for reviewing instructions, searching existing data sources, gathering and maintaining the data needed, and completing and reviewing the collection of information. If you have any comments regarding this burden estimate or any other aspect of this collection information, including suggestions for reducing this burden, send them to the Administrator, Wage and Hour Division, U.S. Department of Labor, Room S-3502, 200 Constitution AV, NW, Washington, DC 20210. **DO NOT SEND THE COMPLETED FORM TO THE WAGE AND HOUR DIVISION; RETURN IT TO THE EMPLOYER.**

Certification for Serious Injury or
Illness of Covered Servicemember - -
for Military Family Leave (Family and
Medical Leave Act)

U.S. Department of Labor
Employment Standards Administration
Wage and Hour Division

OMB Control Number: 1215-0181
Expires: 12/31/2011

Notice to the EMPLOYER **INSTRUCTIONS to the EMPLOYER:** The Family and Medical Leave Act
(FMLA) provides that an employer may require an employee seeking FMLA leave due to a serious injury or illness
of a covered servicemember to submit a certification providing sufficient facts to support the request for leave.
Your response is voluntary. While you are not required to use this form, you may not ask the employee to provide
more information than allowed under the FMLA regulations, 29 C.F.R. § 825.310. Employers must generally
maintain records and documents relating to medical certifications, recertifications, or medical histories of
employees or employees' family members, created for FMLA purposes as confidential medical records in separate
files/records from the usual personnel files and in accordance with 29 C.F.R. § 1630.14(c)(1), if the Americans with
Disabilities Act applies.

**SECTION I: For Completion by the EMPLOYEE and/or the COVERED SERVICEMEMBER for whom
the Employee Is Requesting Leave** **INSTRUCTIONS to the EMPLOYEE or COVERED
SERVICEMEMBER:** Please complete Section I before having Section II completed. The FMLA permits an
employer to require that an employee submit a timely, complete, and sufficient certification to support a request for
FMLA leave due to a serious injury or illness of a covered servicemember. If requested by the employer, your
response is required to obtain or retain the benefit of FMLA-protected leave. 29 U.S.C. §§ 2613, 2614(c)(3).
Failure to do so may result in a denial of an employee's FMLA request. 29 C.F.R. § 825.310(f). The employer
must give an employee at least 15 calendar days to return this form to the employer.

**SECTION II: For Completion by a UNITED STATES DEPARTMENT OF DEFENSE ("DOD") HEALTH
CARE PROVIDER or a HEALTH CARE PROVIDER who is either: (1) a United States Department of
Veterans Affairs ("VA") health care provider; (2) a DOD TRICARE network authorized private health care
provider; or (3) a DOD non-network TRICARE authorized private health care provider** **INSTRUCTIONS
to the HEALTH CARE PROVIDER:** The employee listed on Page 2 has requested leave under the FMLA to
care for a family member who is a member of the Regular Armed Forces, the National Guard, or the Reserves who
is undergoing medical treatment, recuperation, or therapy, is otherwise in outpatient status, or is otherwise on the
temporary disability retired list for a serious injury or illness. For purposes of FMLA leave, a serious injury or
illness is one that was incurred in the line of duty on active duty that may render the servicemember medically unfit
to perform the duties of his or her office, grade, rank, or rating.

A complete and sufficient certification to support a request for FMLA leave due to a covered servicemember's
serious injury or illness includes written documentation confirming that the covered servicemember's injury or
illness was incurred in the line of duty on active duty and that the covered servicemember is undergoing treatment
for such injury or illness by a health care provider listed above. Answer, fully and completely, all applicable parts.
Several questions seek a response as to the frequency or duration of a condition, treatment, etc. Your answer
should be your best estimate based upon your medical knowledge, experience, and examination of the patient. Be
as specific as you can; terms such as "lifetime," "unknown," or "indeterminate" may not be sufficient to determine
FMLA coverage. Limit your responses to the condition for which the employee is seeking leave.

Certification for Serious Injury or Illness
of Covered Servicemember - - for
Military Family Leave (Family and
Medical Leave Act)

U.S. Department of Labor
Employment Standards Administration
Wage and Hour Division

SECTION I: For Completion by the EMPLOYEE and/or the COVERED SERVICEMEMBER for whom the Employee Is Requesting Leave: (This section must be completed first before any of the below sections can be completed by a health care provider.)

Part A: EMPLOYEE INFORMATION

Name and Address of Employer (this is the employer of the employee requesting leave to care for covered servicemember):

_____

Name of Employee Requesting Leave to Care for Covered Servicemember:

_____

        First   Middle   Last

Name of Covered Servicemember (for whom employee is requesting leave to care):

_____

        First   Middle   Last

Relationship of Employee to Covered Servicemember Requesting Leave to Care:
☐ Spouse ☐ Parent ☐ Son ☐ Daughter ☐ Next of Kin

Part B: COVERED SERVICEMEMBER INFORMATION

(1)   Is the Covered Servicemember a Current Member of the Regular Armed Forces, the National Guard or
        Reserves? ___Yes ___No

        If yes, please provide the covered servicemember's military branch, rank and unit currently assigned to:

        _____

        Is the covered servicemember assigned to a military medical treatment facility as an outpatient or to a unit
        established for the purpose of providing command and control of members of the Armed Forces receiving
        medical care as outpatients (such as a medical hold or warrior transition unit)? ___Yes ___No If yes, please
        provide the name of the medical treatment facility or unit: _____

(2)   Is the Covered Servicemember on the Temporary Disability Retired List (TDRL)? ___Yes ___No

Part C: CARE TO BE PROVIDED TO THE COVERED SERVICEMEMBER

Describe the Care to Be Provided to the Covered Servicemember and an Estimate of the Leave Needed to Provide
the Care:

_____

_____

SECTION II: For Completion by a United States Department of Defense ("DOD") Health Care Provider or a Health Care Provider who is either: (1) a United States Department of Veterans Affairs ("VA") health care provider; (2) a DOD TRICARE network authorized private health care provider; or (3) a DOD non-network TRICARE authorized private health care provider. If you are unable to make certain of the **military-related determinations contained below in Part B, you are permitted to rely upon determinations from an authorized DOD representative (such as a DOD recovery care coordinator).** (Please ensure that Section I above has been completed before completing this section.) Please be sure to sign the form on the last page.

Part A: HEALTH CARE PROVIDER INFORMATION
Health Care Provider's Name and Business Address:

_____

Type of Practice/Medical Specialty: _____

Please state whether you are either: (1) a DOD health care provider; (2) a VA health care provider; (3) a DOD TRICARE network authorized private health care provider; or (4) a DOD non-network TRICARE authorized private health care provider: _____

Telephone: (   ) _____ Fax: (   ) _____ Email: _____

PART B: MEDICAL STATUS

(1) Covered Servicemember's medical condition is classified as (Check One of the Appropriate Boxes):

    ☐ **(VSI) Very Seriously Ill/Injured** – Illness/Injury is of such a severity that life is imminently endangered. Family members are requested at bedside immediately. (Please note this is an internal DOD casualty assistance designation used by DOD healthcare providers.)

    ☐ **(SI) Seriously Ill/Injured** – Illness/injury is of such severity that there is cause for immediate concern, but there is no imminent danger to life. Family members are requested at bedside. (Please note this is an internal DOD casualty assistance designation used by DOD healthcare providers.)

    ☐ **OTHER Ill/Injured** – a serious injury or illness that may render the servicemember medically unfit to perform the duties of the member's office, grade, rank, or rating.

    ☐ **NONE OF THE ABOVE** (Note to Employee: If this box is checked, you may still be eligible to take leave to care for a covered family member with a "serious health condition" under § 825.113 of the FMLA. If such leave is requested, you may be required to complete DOL FORM WH-380 or an employer-provided form seeking the same information.)

(2) Was the condition for which the Covered Service member is being treated incurred in line of duty on active duty in the armed forces? _____ Yes _____ No

(3) Approximate date condition commenced: _____

(4) Probable duration of condition and/or need for care: _____

(5) Is the covered servicemember undergoing medical treatment, recuperation, or therapy? _____Yes ___No. If yes, please describe medical treatment, recuperation or therapy:

1098   **Appendix 4**

(1) Will the covered servicemember need care for a single continuous period of time, including any time for treatment and recovery? ___ Yes ___ No
      If yes, estimate the beginning and ending dates for this period of time: _____

(2) Will the covered servicemember require periodic follow-up treatment appointments?
      ___ Yes ___ No If yes, estimate the treatment schedule: _____

(3) Is there a medical necessity for the covered servicemember to have periodic care for these follow-up treatment appointments? ____Yes _____No

(4) Is there a medical necessity for the covered servicemember to have periodic care for other than scheduled follow-up treatment appointments (e.g., episodic flare-ups of medical condition)? ____Yes ____No If yes, please estimate the frequency and duration of the periodic care:

_____

_____

Signature of Health Care Provider: _____ **Date:** _____

PAPERWORK REDUCTION ACT NOTICE AND PUBLIC BURDEN STATEMENT

If submitted, it is mandatory for employers to retain a copy of this disclosure in their records for three years, in accordance with 29 U.S.C. § 2616; 29 C.F.R. § 825.500. Persons are not required to respond to this collection of information unless it displays a currently valid OMB control number. The Department of Labor estimates that it will take an average of 20 minutes for respondents to complete this collection of information, including the time for reviewing instructions, searching existing data sources, gathering and maintaining the data needed, and completing and reviewing the collection of information. If you have any comments regarding this burden estimate or any other aspect of this collection information, including suggestions for reducing this burden, send them to the Administrator, Wage and Hour Division, U.S. Department of Labor, Room S-3502, 200 Constitution AV, NW, Washington, DC 20210. **DO NOT SEND THE COMPLETED FORM TO THE WAGE AND HOUR DIVISION; RETURN IT TO THE PATIENT.**

EMPLOYEE RIGHTS AND RESPONSIBILITIES
UNDER THE FAMILY AND MEDICAL LEAVE ACT

Basic Leave Entitlement

FMLA requires covered employers to provide up to 12 weeks of unpaid, job-protected leave to eligible employees for the following reasons:

- For incapacity due to pregnancy, prenatal medical care or child birth;
- To care for the employee's child after birth, or placement for adoption or foster care;
- To care for the employee's spouse, son or daughter, or parent, who has a serious health condition; or
- For a serious health condition that makes the employee unable to perform the employee's job.

Military Family Leave Entitlements

Eligible employees with a spouse, son, daughter, or parent on active duty or call to active duty status in the National Guard or Reserves in support of a contingency operation may use their 12-week leave entitlement to address certain qualifying exigencies. Qualifying exigencies may include attending certain military events, arranging for alternative childcare, addressing certain financial and legal arrangements, attending certain counseling sessions, and attending post-deployment reintegration briefings.

FMLA also includes a special leave entitlement that permits eligible employees to take up to 26 weeks of leave to care for a covered servicemember during a single 12-month period. A covered servicemember is a current member of the Armed Forces, including a member of the National Guard or Reserves, who has a serious injury or illness incurred in the line of duty on active duty that may render the servicemember medically unfit to perform his or her duties for which the servicemember is undergoing medical treatment, recuperation, or therapy; or is in outpatient status; or is on the temporary disability retired list.

Benefits and Protections

During FMLA leave, the employer must maintain the employee's health coverage under any "group health plan" on the same terms as if the employee had continued to work. Upon return from FMLA leave, most employees must be restored to their original or equivalent positions with equivalent pay, benefits, and other employment terms.

Use of FMLA leave cannot result in the loss of any employment benefit that accrued prior to the start of an employee's leave.

Eligibility Requirements

Employees are eligible if they have worked for a covered employer for at least one year, for 1,250 hours over the previous 12 months, and if at least 50 employees are employed by the employer within 75 miles.

Definition of Serious Health Condition

A serious health condition is an illness, injury, impairment, or physical or mental condition that involves either an overnight stay in a medical care facility, or continuing treatment by a health care provider for a condition that either prevents the employee from performing the functions of the employee's job, or prevents the qualified family member from participating in school or other daily activities.

Subject to certain conditions, the continuing treatment requirement may be met by a period of incapacity of more than 3 consecutive calendar days combined with at least two visits to a health care provider or one visit and a regimen of continuing treatment, or incapacity due to pregnancy, or incapacity due to a chronic condition. Other conditions may meet the definition of continuing treatment.

Use of Leave

An employee does not need to use this leave entitlement in one block. Leave can be taken intermittently or on a reduced leave schedule when medically necessary. Employees must make reasonable efforts to schedule leave for planned medical treatment so as not to unduly disrupt the employer's operations. Leave due to qualifying exigencies may also be taken on an intermittent basis.

Substitution of Paid Leave for Unpaid Leave

Employees may choose or employers may require use of accrued paid leave while taking FMLA leave. In order to use paid leave for FMLA leave, employees must comply with the employer's normal paid leave policies.

Employee Responsibilities

Employees must provide 30 days advance notice of the need to take FMLA leave when the need is foreseeable. When 30 days notice is not possible, the employee must provide notice as soon as practicable and generally must comply with an employer's normal call-in procedures.

Employees must provide sufficient information for the employer to determine if the leave may qualify for FMLA protection and the anticipated timing and duration of the leave. Sufficient information may include that the employee is unable to perform job functions, the family member is unable to perform daily activities, the need for hospitalization or continuing treatment by a health care provider, or circumstances supporting the need for military family leave. Employees also must inform the employer if the requested leave is for a reason for which FMLA leave was previously taken or certified. Employees also may be required to provide a certification and periodic recertification supporting the need for leave.

Employer Responsibilities

Covered employers must inform employees requesting leave whether they are eligible under FMLA. If they are, the notice must specify any additional information required as well as the employees' rights and responsibilities. If they are not eligible, the employer must provide a reason for the ineligibility.

Covered employers must inform employees if leave will be designated as FMLA-protected and the amount of leave counted against the employee's leave entitlement. If the employer determines that the leave is not FMLA-protected, the employer must notify the employee.

Unlawful Acts by Employers

FMLA makes it unlawful for any employer to:

- Interfere with, restrain, or deny the exercise of any right provided under FMLA;
- Discharge or discriminate against any person for opposing any practice made unlawful by FMLA or for involvement in any proceeding under or relating to FMLA.

Enforcement

An employee may file a complaint with the U.S. Department of Labor or may bring a private lawsuit against an employer.

FMLA does not affect any Federal or State law prohibiting discrimination, or supersede any State or local law or collective bargaining agreement which provides greater family or medical leave rights.

FMLA section 109 (29 U.S.C. § 2619) requires FMLA covered employers to post the text of this notice. Regulations 29 C.F.R. § 825.300(a) may require additional disclosures.

For additional information:
1-866-4US-WAGE (1-866-487-9243) TTY: 1-877-889-5627
WWW.WAGEHOUR.DOL.GOV

U.S. Wage and Hour Division

U.S. Department of Labor | Employment Standards Administration | Wage and Hour Division   WHD Publication 1420 Revised January 2009

GLOSSARY

Ability: Variously defined as the demonstrated capacity to do something or a present competence to perform an observable behavior or a behavior which results in an observable product.

Accident: An unexpected and undesirable occurrence that may result in a property damage and/or an occupational injury.

Accident cause: According to the Occupational Safety and Health Administration, any behavior, condition, or act, whether due to negligence or otherwise, without which an accident would not have occurred. The three causes of accidents are **basic, direct**, and **indirect. Basic causes** of accidents are poor management practices, personal factors, and environmental factors. **Direct causes** of accidents are the unplanned release of energy and/or hazardous material. **Indirect causes** of accidents are the unsafe acts and unsafe conditions in the worksite. See **Failure source.**

Accident investigation: A study of an accident to assess the causes and the failure source(s).

ACES: An acronym for Additional Compensable Elements used in the Hay Guide Chart-Profile Method of job evaluation.

Achievement test: A test that measures the extent of a person's knowledge or competence within a field. See **Test.**

Adverse selection: The tendency of persons who have a greater chance of a claim to seek insurance coverage.

Affirmative action: The planning and implementing of strategies to select applicants from groups who have traditionally experienced employment discrimination. See **Goals, Good faith efforts, Quotas,** and **Reverse discrimination.**

Age Discrimination in Employment Act of 1967: A federal law covering employers who employ 20 or more employees, that prohibits discrimination against persons 40 or more years of age; also covered are employment agencies, labor unions, companies of foreign businesses located in the U.S. and state and local governments.

Agency shop: An arrangement in which employees are not required to join a union but they must pay an initiation fee and dues to a union in order to remain employed. See **Closed shop, Maintenance of Membership, Open shop,** and **Union shop.**

Aggravated assault: An attack, typically with a weapon or other means, on a person by another to cause severe bodily injury.

Albermarle Paper Company v. Moody: A Supreme Court case which concluded that it was incorrect to validate a selection method using performance appraisal results if a job analysis had not been conducted.

Alternation ranking method: A variation of the *straight ranking* method of performance appraisal in which the appraiser alternates the ranking by starting with the best employee and the worst employee.

American Federal of Labor and Congress of Industrial organizations (AFL-CIO): A national organization composed of approximately 90 national unions that provides overall direction to the union movement in the U.S. See **National union and Local union.**

Americans with Disabilities Act: A federal law that prohibits certain employers from discriminating against the disabled and requires them to make reasonable accommodation in the employment of the disabled. See **Reasonable accommodation.**

Andragogy: The science of how adults learn.

Applicant: According to the Uniform Guidelines on Employee Selection Procedures an applicant is defined as " . . . . a person who has indicated an interest in being considered for hiring, promotion, or other employment opportunities. This interest might be expressed by completing an application form, or might be expressed orally, depending upon the employer's practice."[1] Persons who voluntarily either formally or informally withdraw from selection consideration are not applicants and should not be included in any adverse impact calculations. However, records of all persons, including those who voluntarily withdraw should be retained.[2] See *Internet Applicant* in the Topical Index.

Apprenticeship: A human resource development method in which employees, called apprentices, enter into agreements with employers, in which tasks are performed at below market wage rates in return for on-the-job training by journeyman employees within the craft.

Appropriate bargaining unit: A determination, made by the National Labor Relations Board, after considering such factors as duties, job specifications, and working conditions, concerning which group of employees shall bargain separately with management.

Aptitude: According to the Department of Labor method of job analysis, one of the eleven specific capacities or abilities required of an individual in order to facilitate the learning of some task or job duty.

Aptitude test: A test that measures a person's innate or acquired capacities to learn an occupation. See **Test.**

Arbitration: The process of using a third party to settle disputes between labor and management. See **Grievance arbitration** and **Interest arbitration.**

Arbitrator: A person who settles disputes involving grievances (1) under an existing collective bargaining agreement or (2) in negotiating a new agreement. See **Arbitration, Expedited arbitration, Grievance arbitration,** and **Interest arbitration.**

Arizona Governing Committee v. Norris: A U.S. Supreme Court decision that the retirement plan involved could not offer a choice of sex-based annuities at retirement.

---

[1] *Uniform Guidelines on Employee Selection Procedures,* "Employee Selection Guidelines (Questions and Answers), Question 15," August 25, 1978.
[2] Ibid.

Arson: Attempting to burn, or willfully burning, whether an attempt to defraud is present or not, a house, building, or other property.

Assessment center: A selection method in which participants engage in multiple exercises, some of which are simulations, and their performance is appraised by trained assessors. Also used to identify the human resources development needs of participants.

Assignment: A provision in life insurance in which all or part of the ownership rights of a policy are transferred from one party to another.

Attendance: A generic term that includes punctuality, consistency in reporting for work, sick leave/days usage, and emergency or other unscheduled absences.

Attitude: An individual's inclination toward something. Opinion is an expression of a person's attitude. See **Employee attitude survey**.

Audit: The process of verifying human resources management (HRM) accomplishments, such as a general audit of all HRM activities. Specific audits focus on selected HRM activities. As used in job analysis, a method of ensuring the accuracy of information being collected; see **Desk audit and Office audit**. As used in safety and health, a method of verifying the safety and health conditions in an organization; see **Safety audit**. As used in equal employment opportunity, a method of determining if EEO laws and executive orders are being observed.

Authority: The delegated right to use the organization's resources to accomplish goals; See **Functional authority, Line authority,** and **Staff authority**.

Authorization card: See **Card solicitation**.

Automobile allowance: Assistance given to employees, such as expatriates, in securing and operating an automobile.

Bad faith bargaining: The posture in collective bargaining of engaging in such tactics as stalling, taking an inflexible position on proposals, changing positions once an agreement has been reached, failing to give the union information that it is legally entitled to and offering counterproposals on the same item that are progressively more severe than the previous ones which were rejected; illegal under the National Labor Relations Act.

Balancing account: A reserve, used in the Rucker plan, composed of about one-third of the monthly earned bonuses, to offset any "bad" months in which bonuses are not earned. See **Rucker plan.**

Bargaining table: A figurative term denoting the process of exchanging proposals and counterproposals in collective bargaining.

Bargaining unit: See **Appropriate bargaining unit.**

Basic cause: See **Accident cause.**

Basic checklist method: A method of performance appraisal in which the appraiser reviews a list of statements indicating various levels of favorable and unfavorable performance and checks those descriptive of the employee.

Behavioral interview: A type of employment interview in which questions about job requirements are posed to applicants and they are asked to explain situations in their past where they have had experience dealing with them.

Behavioral observation scale: A method of performance appraisal which is similar to the behaviorally anchored rating scales method, but the frequency of behavior is also shown.

Behavioral modeling: A human resources development method in which participants attempt to replicate either the behavior or the procedure of an expert who "models" or demonstrates the proper way a task should be performed.

Behaviorally anchored rating scales: A modification of graphic rating scales, in which different scale values in performance areas are "anchored" in explanations or illustrations of behavior.

Behaviorism: The theory that human behavior is the result of learning (1) through conditioned and/or unconditioned stimuli and (2) reinforcement.

Beliefs: The expectations and opinions that members of organizations acquire as they become acclimated to an organization.

Bench decision: An arbitrator's decision made immediately after the parties in the arbitration have concluded their case presentations. See **Arbitration.**

Benchmark job: A job used to determine the evaluation of other jobs in a job evaluation system. See **Key job.**

Benefit integration: The process of considering, in the design of a benefit plan, mandatory or voluntary plan provisions that provide the same or similar coverage. See **Coordination of benefits.**

Benefits fair: A method of communicating employee benefit information to employees over a period of one or more days during which the representatives of the benefit plans and the benefits office of the employer are available, in one location, in festively-decorated booths that resemble a fair atmosphere, to discuss their plans with employees.

Biographical information blank: An application blank in which different responses to biographical information have different values which are tallied and considered in making employment decisions.

Biometrics: A term for the use of statistics to analyze biological information.

Boards of inquiry: Established by the Federal Mediation and Conciliation Service, under the Labor Management Relations Act, to investigate the areas in disputes in the health care industry between management and labor and to make recommendations to settle them.

Bona fide occupational qualification: Defined in the Age Discrimination in Employment Act as "a qualification reasonably necessary to the normal operation of the particular business."

Bonus: A generic term used to describe cash payments in pay for performance plans; see **Performance objectives bonus.**

Bonus pool: The amount of funds available for distribution to employees through a pay for performance plan.

Bottom line: As discussed in *Connecticut v. Teal,* an employment test that has a discriminatory impact upon one group, even though the "bottom-line" result was proportionately more members received favorable treatment, is illegal unless it is job-related. In effect, the Court rejects the "bottom-line defense" and makes clear that fair employment laws protect the individual who is a victim of discrimination regardless of the total effect of a selection process.

Brito v. Zia: A Supreme Court case in which an employer's appraisal system was ruled unfair because standardized scoring was not used.

Broad-banding: Including several pay grades or job classes into one grade or class. Also sometimes called *banding* or *career banding* (when the broad-banding is used for career progression purposes).

Business agent: A paid employee, usually full-time, who manages the affairs of a union.

Business necessity: Justifying a selection method or procedure on the basis that it is necessary for the reasonable operation of the firm. Sometimes used synonymously with bona fide occupational qualification. See **Bona fide occupational qualification.**

Cafeteria plan: See **Flexible benefit plan.**

CAP Index Vulnerability Analysis: A computer model that uses crime data by census tract to predict the occurrence of crime at any given site.

Card solicitation: The process of union organizers securing the signatures of employees on cards that either (1) clearly states the signer selects the union as his or her representative (Single purpose authorization cards) or (2) designate the union as the employee's bargaining agent and also contain a statement requesting the National Labor Relations Board to hold an election (Double purpose authorization card). Thirty percent of the employees in an appropriate bargaining unit must sign a card before an election will be held.

CareerOneStop: A Web site that offers career resources and workforce information to job seekers, students, businesses, and workforce professionals to foster talent development.

Career planning: The HRM activity concerned with the process of assisting employees in defining their career interests and in preparing for career changes through human resources development.

Case method: A human resources development method in which actual or fictional written situations are used and trainees apply their knowledge applicable to the subject(s) in the case.

Case study: A research project conducted within an organization in which an effort is made through a case analysis to determine the relationship between a dependent and an independent variable. See **Research methods.**

Caucus: In collective bargaining contract negotiations, a private meeting of one side's negotiating team to resolve a collective bargaining issue or similar subject.

Causal research: A research method used to determine the causes of desired and undesired events. See **Research methods.**

Census of Fatal Occupational Injuries: A federally conducted survey of all work-related injuries, including work-related homicides and suicides.

Central tendency: A perceptual error in which appraisers or interviewers rate individuals in the middle of an appraisal instrument rather than using the most appropriate scale values.

Certification: The process through which unions become certified by the National Labor Relations Board as the exclusive bargaining agent for a group of employees. To be certified a union must receive a majority of the votes cast in the election.

Charge-back: A deduction from an employee's pay for a previously paid commission which was voided by a sale not being consummated.

Checklist: A generic method of job analysis consisting of a written form containing statements about job tasks which employees read and indicate whether they perform them; some checklists also have spaces for employees to check how much time is spent performing the task, the importance of the task in relation to other tasks and whether the employee was expected to know how to perform the task when hired. Sometimes used synonymously with the term job inventory. For check list performance appraisal systems, see **Basic checklist, Forced-choice checklist,** and **Weighted checklist.**

Checkoff: A provision in a collective bargaining agreement in which management agrees to withhold union dues from members' paychecks and then remit them in a lump sum to the union.

Citation: A document issued by the Occupational Safety and Health Administration for violations of OSHA standards and regulations. See **Inspection and Violation.**

Citizen: In the Immigration Reform and Control Act, defined as a citizen or national of the U.S. See **Intending citizen.**

City of Los Angeles, Department of Water and Power v. Manhart: A U.S. Supreme Court decision that the contributory plan in the case could not require women to make higher contributions than men in order to receive the same annuity payment upon retirement.

Civil Rights Act of 1866: A federal law that gives all persons certain rights, such as to sue; prohibits disparate treatment, by private employers, unions, employment agencies and public agencies, in employment discrimination on the basis of race, color or national origin; compensatory awards for discrimination, punitive awards if malice is shown.

Civil Rights Act of 1871: A federal law that prohibits employment discrimination based upon state law, use, or custom that infringes upon rights granted by federal law; covers age, national origin, race and sex discrimination; compensatory awards for discrimination, punitive awards if injuries are shown.

Civil Rights Act of 1964—Title VI: A federal law that prohibits employment discrimination, on the basis of national origin, race, or color, involving federally financed programs and activities; funds cut-off and equitable and compensatory relief if discrimination is shown.

Civil Rights Act of 1964—Title VII: A federal law that prohibits employment discrimination on the basis of national origin, race, color, religion and sex by employers, apprenticeship programs, employment agencies and labor unions with 15 employees/members who are engaged in any phase of interstate commerce; attorney fees, back pay, reinstatement or hiring if discrimination is shown.

Classification: The process of grouping similar or like positions into classes with the same pay grade, the same or similar job task descriptions and the same or similar job specifications. Sometimes used synonymously with job classification or position classification.

Closed panel: Requirement that employees must use one of the plan's selection of staff attorneys in a prepaid legal services plan. See **Open panel.**

Closed shop: An arrangement in which applicants for employment must be members of the union representing the employees; typically illegal except for prehire agreements in the construction industry. See **Agency shop, Maintenance of membership, Prehire agreement,** and **Union shop.**

Coaching: A human resources development method in which knowledgeable persons assist employees in either adjusting to a job environment or learning how to perform job tasks.

COBRA: See **Consolidated Omnibus Budget Reconciliation Act.**

CODAP: An acronym for Comprehensive Occupational Data Analysis Programs. An inventory or checklist instrument developed and used by the U.S. Air Force in conducting job analysis.

Coefficient of correlation: A statistical measurement of the strength (the size of the coefficient of correlation) and the direction (whether positive or negative, that is direct or inverse, respectively) of the relationship between two variables.

Coefficient of determination: A statistical measurement that indicates how much variation in one variable is attributable to another.

Cognition: The mental process of knowing that incorporates various personal characteristics, such as experience and judgment. See **Cognitive psychology.**

Cognitive psychology: The theory of human behavior that stresses the importance of the needs, wants, beliefs and understanding of people as the major causes of behavior.

Cohort: The group of persons who will be the subjects in a research study. For example, the cohort in a test validation study would be the persons who are given a selection method, such as a test, to determine whether it is a good predictor of job performance.

Coinsurance: The sharing of expenses between the insurer and the insured.

COLA: See **Cost of living increase.**

Collective bargaining: The process through which employees in an appropriate bargaining unit use their union representatives to deal with their employer in setting wages, benefits, hours of work, and other conditions and terms of employment. See **Negotiations.**

Commerce: As defined in the Fair Labor Standards Act, means any trade, commerce, transportation, transmission, or communication among the states or between any state and any place outside of it. See **Enterprise coverage** and **Individual employee coverage.**

Commission: A pay incentive that is based upon a percentage of the selling price of a product or service. See **Graduated commission, Multiple-tiered commission,** and **Straight commission.**

Commission-splitting: Dividing an earned commission among more than one sales personnel for their efforts in either assisting in the sale or fulfilling the role of a broker.

Communication committee: A committee typically composed of both managers and employees who meet on a regular schedule to discuss employee problems and to identify problems effecting organizational efficiency.

Comparable worth: The concept of paying members of both sexes equally for dissimilar jobs having the same relative worth (comparable worth) to an employer.

Compa-ratio: The relationship of an employee's pay to the midpoint of the employee's pay grade; computed by dividing the employee's pay by the midpoint of the pay range.

Compensable factor: A characteristic used to compare jobs in job evaluation.

Compensation: The process of *directly* and *indirectly* rewarding employees, on a current or deferred basis, for their performance of assigned tasks.

Compensation survey: An instrument used to obtain compensation policies, procedures, programs and data from employers. *Market pay* surveys are used to obtain such information that solely relates to pay.

Competency: An observable, measurable pattern of skills, knowledge, abilities, behaviors, and other characteristics that an individual needs to perform work roles or occupational functions successfully. Two of the principal categories of competencies are **general competencies** and **technical competencies**.

Competency-based job dimensions: A contemporary approach to job descriptions, including job specifications and assessment methods to measure the existence of those competencies in job applicants. See **Competency**.

Competency-based pay: A method of rewarding employees for the number of competencies they possess, such as the different mix of customers they can handle at a satisfactory level of performance without receiving complaints.

Competency-based performance appraisal: A method of performance appraisal in which the employees' competencies, exhibited in job performance, form the basis for the appraisal.

Comprehensive major medical coverage: Medical coverage that pays for a broad range of services and a substantial portion of catastrophic illness, subject to a coinsurance provision.

Compulsory arbitration: An arrangement in which the parties in a dispute agree to settle it through the use of an impartial third party. In *Circuit City Stores, Inc. v. Adams,* the U.S. Supreme Court held that employees who have claims, disputes, and controversies due to their employment must submit them to arbitration, if they have signed documents, such as employment applications, in which they previously agreed to such an arrangement. These arrangements are provided by the Federal Arbitration Act. Compulsory arbitration is also mandated under certain conditions for collective bargaining impasses involving federal agencies and the U.S. Postal Service.

Computer gaming: The use of computers to simulate work life situations, used in such HRM activities as selection and human resources development.

Computer interview: An employment interview in which the interviewee uses a computer keyboard or touchscreen to respond to a set of questions in a computer file pertaining to a specific job. Usually used for preliminary employment screening.

Conciliation: The process of a mediator or other third party encouraging the disputing parties to continue bargaining. See **Federal Mediation and Conciliation Service,** and **Mediation.**

Concurrent validation: A validity study which uses current employees as the subjects.

Consolidated Omnibus Budget Reconciliation Act of 1985: As amended by the Tax Reform Act of **1986** and the Omnibus Budget Reconciliation Act of 1986, a federal law that requires employers with at least 20 employees to offer continued medical expense coverage, under certain circumstances, to employees and/or their dependents, if they want to take a federal tax deduction for the expense of offering the medical expense plan; sometimes referred to as *COBRA.*

Construct: A human characteristic, such as leadership or intelligence. See **Construct validation.**

Construct validation: The process of demonstrating the degree to which a selection method measures human characteristics in candidates which are determined to be important for successful job performance.

Consumer Price Index: A monthly report issued by the U.S. Department of Labor of the changes in prices of seven groups of items. The two surveys are *The CPI for All Urban Consumers,* which measures the purchases of four-fifths of U.S. consumers and *The Revised CPI for Urban Wage Earners and Clerical Workers,* which measures the purchases of about 50 percent of U.S. consumers.

Content validation: The process of demonstrating that the content of a selection method is representative of important aspects of job performance, such as producing products, providing services, or displaying behaviors important in the job.

Contingent compensation: A term used for pay plans that are *contingent* upon the employee meeting specific objectives.

Continuous reinforcement: Reinforcing a behavior each time it occurs.

Contract: The final product of all collective bargaining proposals that have been agreed upon by both parties. Sometimes synonymously used with the term *agreement.*

Contrast effect: The tendency of a rater, such as an interviewer, to evaluate a person too high or too low, because other persons evaluated earlier were, respectively, significantly inferior or superior.

Contributory plan: An employee benefit plan in which employee contributions are required for participation in the plan.

Convenience Store Security Act: A 1990 State of Florida law which mandates all local governments to enact ordinances if they had a theft or robbery at a convenience store operating between 10:00 p.m. and 5:00 a.m. which resulted in serious injury, death or sexual battery of an employee.

Coordination of benefits: A provision in insurance plans regarding the manner in which benefits will be paid in the event the insured is covered by more than one plan. Also see **Benefits integration.**

Correlation study: A research method in which an attempt is made to determine if there are correlations between one or more dependent variables and an independent variable. See **Research methods.**

Corridor deductible: A deductible that must be satisfied by the major medical plan; the term is derived from the fact that it is a "corridor" of expenses incurred between where the basic plan coverage ends and the major medical coverage begins. See **Deductible.**

Cost containment: See **Employee benefit cost containment.**

Cost of living increase: A pay increase granted in response to changes in the Consumer Price Index or other measure of inflation; sometimes referred to in collective bargaining agreements as COLA clauses.

Counseling: Basic, technical, and in some cases, professional assistance given by skilled and knowledgeable individuals who are professionally qualified, if that level of service is rendered. In punishment, *counseling* is the process of discussing a deficiency with an employee and attempting to advise the individual how to improve. See **Discipline** and **Punishment.**

Counterproposal: See **Proposal.**

Covenant of good faith and fair dealing: See **Good faith and fair dealing.**

Craft union: A union composed of members within a skill or trade, such as the United Brotherhood of Electrical Workers. See **Industrial union** and **White-collar union.**

Credit report: A report used in making an employment decision that involves either a person's credit, character, reputation or style of living (known as a *consumer credit report*) or a full or partial report from interviews with people who know the person (known as an *investigative consumer report*).

Criterion-related validation: The process of demonstrating through empirical data that a selection method significantly correlates with job performance criteria. See **Coefficient of correlation.**

Critical incidents method: A method of performance appraisal involving the recording of significantly good and bad incidents that occur during the appraisal period.

Cultural noise: The tendency of job applicants being interviewed for a job to give answers or behave in ways he or she believes the interviewer wants to see or hear.

Cumulative trauma disorder: An illness, such as tendinitis and carpal tunnel syndrome, resulting from quick repetitive movements of the wrist and lower arm. Also called repetitive motion injury.

Currency exchange adjustment: Adjusting the pay of expatriates to account for any changes in the international exchange rates of currency.

Current Population Survey: A monthly household survey conducted by the Census Bureau which obtains a variety of information including data on earnings.

Currently insured: As applied to Social Security, a worker must have a minimum of 6 quarters of coverage that were earned in the most recent 13-quarter period.

Customs: The part of grganization culture that involves the institutionalized expressions, habits, and ways of accomplishing things. See **Organization culture.**

Data: As used in the Department of Labor method of job analysis, the seven levels of information, knowledge and conceptions, including such intangible objects as numbers, words, symbols, ideas, concepts and oral verbalization, obtained through observation, investigation, interpretation, visualization, and mental creation.

Davis-Bacon Act of 1931: A federal law requiring federal contractors who have federal or federally financed contracts for the construction, alteration or repair of public buildings or public works to (1) pay wages that are at least equal to those prevailing in the area and (2) provide employee benefits equivalent to the prevailing ones.

Decertification: The process through which unions lose their status as the exclusive representative of a group of employees. A union is decertified if a majority of those employees voting in the decertification election so vote.

Deductible: The amount of covered medical expenses that must be paid by the insured before he or she begins receiving benefits from the plan. See **Corridor deductible, Integrated deductible,** and **Initial deductible.**

Deductive hypothesis: An hypothesis that is an assumed explanation of a situation derived from general theories that are based upon research and other factual evidence. Also **see Inductive hypothesis.**

Defamation suit: A suit filed by a former employee charging an ex-employer with furnishing malicious or deliberately false or misleading information about the employee. See **Failure to disclose.**

Deferred pay plan: A pay plan principally used for executives in which earned pay is postponed to a later date, generally to retirement, to lower the tax liability.

Deferred profit-sharing plan: A profit-sharing plan that defers tax-sheltered contributions for retirement income.

Defined benefit plan: A retirement plan which specifies the amount of benefit the employee will receive upon retirement.

Defined contribution plan: A retirement plan which specifies the amount the employer will contribute to the plan on behalf of each participant.

Delphi method: A forecasting method in which a panel of experts independently review a number of subjects and estimate the likelihood of their occurrence.

Demotion: A personnel action in which an employee is placed in a job at a salary range lower than the one he or she currently is in due to job structuring changes, job evaluation, or failure to perform at acceptable levels of performance. See **Discipline, Job evaluation, Job structuring, Performance appraisal,** and **Punishment.**

Department of Labor method: A specific method of job analysis that includes procedures for classifying and recording job information.

Depth interview: A type of interview in which an applicant's qualifications are thoroughly examined in selected areas.

Desk audit: See **Office audit.**

Diary: As used in job analysis, a structured sheet on which employees list their daily tasks in chronological sequence as they are performed throughout the workday, showing the beginning and ending times and other related task information.

Dictionary of Occupational Titles: A reference source containing information on over 12,000 jobs; the reference code used in this dictionary is based on nine digits.

Differential validity: A selection procedure has differential validity when the members of one group, such as a single sex, race, or the related, obtain lower scores than the members of another group and the differences in the scores of the groups are reflected in differences in job performance. The *Uniform Guidelines on Employee Selection Procedures* contain the term "selection procedure fairness" in lieu of differential validity. See **Fairness.**

Direct cause: See **Accident Cause.**

Direct compensation: All current and deferred monetary payments that are made for either the amount of time worked, such as the number of hours, or for some measure of performance, such as the number of units produced.

Disabled: A person who has a physical or mental impairment which substantially limits one or more of such person's major life activities, has a record of such an impairment, or is regarded as having such an impairment. Referred to as **"Handicapped"** in the Rehabilitation Act.

Discharge: Termination of employment due to performance deficiencies. See **Discipline** and **Punishment.**

Discipline: Employee learning that promotes self-control, dedication and orderly conduct; sometimes used synonymously with punishment. See **Punishment.**

Discrimination: There are two definitions of *employment discrimination:* (1) intentionally treating a person less well in an employment decision because of the individual's national origin, race, color, religion, sex, disability, age, citizenship or veteran's status; and (2) using employment practices, although fair in form and applied in a nondiscriminatory manner, nevertheless have an adverse impact upon individuals because of their national origin, race, color, religion, sex, disability, age, citizenship or veteran's status.

Disparate impact: A type of discrimination in which an employment practice, though fair in form and applied in a nondiscriminatory manner, operates to discriminate against members of protected groups. Also called **Disparate effect** or **Adverse impact.** See **Four-fifths rule.**

Disparate treatment: A type of discrimination in which one individual or group is treated less well by an employment decision than another individual or group on the basis of race, skin coloring, sex, age, religion, national origin, handicap (or disability), veteran's status or alien status.

Dispute resolution procedure: An internal or external procedure for employees to use in resolving job dissatisfactions which are beyond their control to resolve and for which management has the means and authority to correct. See **Grievance procedure** and **Mediation.**

Diversity management: The process of motivating employees, who have diverse backgrounds, to increase their interpersonal communication and cooperation to unify their efforts so the organization can optimize its goals.

Doctrine of contributory negligence: A common law defense that prohibits claims against an employer for work-related illness or injury if the employee's negligence in any manner contributed to the illness or injury.

Doctrine of the assumption of risk: A common law defense against employee claims against the employer for injury or illness based upon the assumption that more dangerous jobs have a higher wage and thus workers assume any risks associated with them.

Downsizing: An employer initiative to reduce costs through such actions as work reorganization and layoffs.

Drop safe: A fixed security container, mounted in a building or vehicle that has a slot in which excess cash is periodically deposited and which cannot be opened by an employee on duty.

Driver's Privacy Protection Act of 1994: A federal law regulating the release and use of certain personal information from state motor vehicle records. Among the permissible uses are businesses that are verifying the accuracy of personal information submitted by the individual. In certain situations defined in the law, written consent of the individual to whom the information applies is required.

Drug: Defined in the Rehabilitation Act as "a controlled substance, as defined in schedules I through V of section 202 of the Controlled Substances Act."

Drug-Free Workplace Act: A federal law requiring persons with federal contracts of $100,000 or more to provide a drug-free workplace by taking specific actions, such as establishing a drug-free awareness program for employees.

Dual career marriage: A marriage in which both spouses are employed or are seeking employment.

Dual-career ladder: An arrangement, sometimes also called a *dual-career track*, in which employees, who typically are employed in professional, technical or scientific fields, are given the opportunity of pursuing their careers either within their field (profession, technology or science) or through management jobs. The purpose of the arrangement is to motivate highly qualified employees to remain with the firm, in lieu of seeking career opportunities elsewhere. Employees who elect not to pursue management tracks are given the opportunity of acquiring more specialized knowledge within their fields.

Dues: periodic payments, usually monthly, that a union member pays to support the union.

Education: Formal or informal conceptual learning that does not have a specific occupation objective but is needed to satisfactorily perform the tasks in a job. See **General educational development.**

Educational assistance: Compensation provided by multinational firms to assist expatriates in educating their children.

Effect evaluation: A type of evaluation used to evaluate human resources management programs, such as a human resources development program, in which the participants indicate any benefit they received. Also see **Process evaluation.**

Elasticity: A concept in economics that is used to explain the responsiveness of demand and/or supply of a product to the price of it.

Election: As used in National Labor Relations Board representation elections, a secret ballot vote in which employees in an appropriate bargaining unit decide whether they want to be represented by a union. See **Appropriate bargaining unit, Card solicitation, Certification,** and **Decertification.**

Element: The smallest unit of work without separately defining single motions or thought processes.

Employability: Defined in the Rehabilitation Act as "a determination that, with the provision of vocational rehabilitation services, the individual is likely to enter or retain, as a primary objective, full-time employment, and when appropriate, part-time employment, consistent with the capacities or abilities of the individual in the competitive labor market or any other vocational outcome the Secretary may determine consistent with this Act."

Employee assistance program: Programs operated either in-house or by external consortia or contractors to prevent employee problems and treat and rehabilitate troubled employees.

Employee attitude survey: A formal method of measuring employee attitudes concerning selected items. See **Attitude.**

Employee benefit cost containment: A generic term for a host of employer initiatives to control employee benefit costs.

Employee Involvement Association: A non-profit organization of private and public sector members who share a common interest in, and a dedication to, employee suggestion systems and other forms of employee involvement. Address is 10565 Lee Highway, Suite 104, Fairfax, VA 22030-3135. (703) 383-1010. Email: eia@washingtongroupinc.com.

Employee leasing: An employment arrangement in which employees are hired by a leasing company and then leased to the employer.

Employee opinion survey: See **Employee attitude survey.**

Employee pay compression: The condition of having too small a spread in the pay of an employee who is better qualified or deserves to be paid more compared to another employee.

Employee Polygraph Protection Act: A federal law that prohibits employers from using a polygraph for employment purposes except in specific situations.

Employee relations: The HRM activity concerned with the process of disciplining and communicating with employees.

Employee Retirement Income Security Act of 1974: A federal law covering all employers engaged in commerce or in industries involving commerce; the Act's provisions include employer retirement plans and other types of benefit plans.

Employee stock ownership plan (ESOP): An arrangement whereby the employees in a company are given various amounts, up to 100 percent, of ownership in a company through the issuance of stock.

Employee stock purchase plan: A stock option that permits employees to purchase stock at a reduced price and to sell it and receive preferential tax treatment, provided certain conditions are satisfied.

Employee suggestion program: See **Suggestion program.**

Employee welfare benefit plan: A term used in the Employee Retirement Income Security Act to refer to any plan or benefit provided by employers or employee organizations, or both, to employees and/or their dependents; synonymous with *employee benefits, indirect compensation,* and *fringe benefits.*

Employment-at-will: An historic common-law principle in the U.S. that employees can be discharged from employment for any reason or no reason at all. Four constraints upon this principle are: (1) legal prohibitions, (2) implied employment contracts, (3) public policy ex ceptions, and (4) the covenant of good faith and fair dealing. See **Good faith and fair dealing** and **Implied employment contract.**

Employment Cost Index: A quarterly report issued by the U.S. Department of Labor that measures the change in the cost of labor, free from the influence of employment shifts among occupations and industries. Measures changes for total compensation (wages, salaries, and employer costs for employee benefits).

Enterprise: As defined in the Fair Labor Standards Act, means activities controlled by one or more persons who have a business purpose.

Enterprise coverage: Coverage under the Fair Labor Standards Act of all employees of an employer who is engaged in interstate or foreign commerce or is engaged in the production of goods for interstate or foreign commerce. Also see **Individual employee coverage.**

Environmental condition: According to the Department of Labor method of job analysis, one of seven physical surroundings in which a job is performed.

Equal employment opportunity: The HRM activity concerned with the equal treatment of people in all HRM activities from recruiting to retirement.

Equal Employment Opportunity Commission: A federal agency responsible for enforcing certain laws, particularly Title VII of the Civil Rights Act of 1964, the Age Discrimination in Employment Act, Americans with Disabilities Act, and the Equal Pay Act.

Equal Pay Act: An amendment to the Fair Labor Standards Act requiring equal pay for both sexes for the performance of substantially the same job tasks within the same establishment.

Equilibrium point: A principle in economics in which the price per unit of quantity demanded of a product and the supply of it are the same.

Equilibrium wage: A principle in economics in which the wage for both the supply and demand of labor is the same.

Equipment: As used in the Department of Labor method of job analysis, devices which generate power, communicate signals or have an effect upon material through the application of light, heat, electricity, steam, chemicals, or atmospheric pressure.

Equity: The perceived fairness of the intrinsic and extrinsic rewards that employees receive in exchange for their performance of job tasks.

Equivalent forms reliability: A method of reliability measurement involving the correlation of scores on two different but equivalent versions of the same selection method. See **Reliability.**

Ergonomics: The study of human factors in production in order to create and adapt equipment and other technology to more effectively accommodate human needs and abilities.

Essay method: A performance appraisal method that involves the writing of narrative descriptions of employee performance.

Excess benefit plan: A pay plan typically reserved for executive personnel that provides pay in excess of the maximum allowable under qualified plans by the Internal Revenue Service; also referred to as *supplemental executive retirement plan.*

Exclusions: Conditions which are not covered under an insurance policy.

Exclusive recognition: A type of union recognition under Title VII of the Civil Service Reform Act accorded to those unions that receive a majority vote of the employees in an appropriate bargaining unit. See **National consultation** and **Title VII of the Civil Service Reform Act.**

Executive Order 11246: An executive order covering contractors with the federal government who have contracts exceeding $10,000 that prohibits employment discrimination on the basis of national origin, race, color, religion and sex; also requires affirmative action, including written affirmative action plans and on-site affirmative actions reviews for designated employers.

Executive personnel: Personnel who are employed in the top jobs in each of the functional areas of an organization up to and including the chief executive officer.

Exempt employee: An employee who is exempt from the provisions of the Fair Labor Standards Act.

Exit interview: An interview with an employee, who is resigning from an organization to obtain information about management, personnel policies, compensation, and other matters to determine if they contributed to the employee's decision to leave.

Expatriate: A citizen of one country who is employed by a company with headquarters in that same country, but is working in a foreign assignment.

Expatriation: The process of preparing a person for a foreign country assignment.

Expectancy: The probability of a first-level outcome ranging from 0 to 1. See **Expectancy theory.**

Expectancy theory: The cognitive theory of human behavior that conceptualizes the internal through processes that cause or actuate human behavior. See **Cognitive theory.**

Expedited arbitration: A shortened version of regular arbitrations in which the arbitrator may handle up to three different grievance cases in one day. See **Arbitration.**

Experience: The past performance of job tasks in either a paid or unpaid setting and on either a formal or informal basis.

Experiment: A research method in which the researcher has some control over the variables and uses a randomization method in selecting subjects for the study. In a *laboratory experiment* the researcher has more control over the variables than in a *field experiment.* See **Research methods.**

External environment: The aspect of the planning environment of strategic planning that includes the economic, social and political conditions.

External equity: The degree to which an organization's compensation program is consistent with the program rewards employees relative to their contributions compared to the rewards received for similar contributions by employees of other employers in the labor market.

Extinction: The behaviorism concept of not administering a stimulus in response to a given behavior.

Extrinsic rewards: The tangible compensatory and noncompensatory rewards that employees receive which are external to the job itself and are granted as a condition of employment and in recognition of task performance. See **Intrinsic rewards.**

Factor Evaluation System: A job evaluation method used by the U.S. Office of Personnel Management to evaluate non supervisory jobs in pay grades GS-1 through GS-15. Also known as the *Primary Standard.*

Factor method: A method of job evaluation consisting of subdividing the individual compensable factors of a job, assigning monetary values to those factors through a comparison process with the compensable factor values of "key" jobs and then tallying those values to determine the total monetary worth of the job.

Factor value scale: A scale of even monetary increments showing the monetary values of each compensable factor for jobs, particularly key or benchmark jobs. Also called a *factor wage comparison scale.*

Failure source: A source of an accident. The six sources are: *human failure* which includes physical, mental and physiological deficiencies; *technical data failure* which results from errors and omissions in instructions and operating data; *organizational failure* which is a deficiency of management in providing instructions, planning and training; *material failure* which is the physical or chemical breakdown of any material or component; *design failure* which is a deficiency in the design of a structure or component; and, *natural failure* which is an act of nature.

Failure to disclose: A term used to explain the unwillingness of former employers to reveal information, to future employers, about employees who left their employ.

Fair Labor Standards Act: A federal law covering: (1) minimum wages, (2) overtime pay, (3) child labor restrictions and (4) equal pay for equal work for both sexes.

Fairness: As defined in the *Uniform Guidelines on Employee Selection Procedures,* an employment test is fair "when members of one race, sex, or ethnic group characteristically obtain lower scores on a selection procedure than members of another group, and differences in scores (are) reflected in differences in a measure of job performance." See **Differential validity.**

Federal Arbitration Act of 1927: The Federal Arbitration Act (FAA) was enacted to require judicial enforcement of arbitration agreements. In a 2001 decision, the U.S. Supreme Court held that employees who have claims, disputes, and controversies due to their employment must submit them to arbitration, if they have signed agreements, such as employment applications, in which they previously agreed to such an arrangement. See **Compulsory arbitration.**

Federal Mediation and Conciliation Service: A federal agency created by the Labor Management Relations Act, with such functions as the responsibility of facilitating the resolution of disputes between employers and unions in collective bargaining. See **Boards of Inquiry, Conciliation,** and **Mediation.**

Fellow-servant rule: A common law defense against worker claims for an occupational illness or injury that precludes receiving any damages from an employer if the illness or injury was caused by the actions of a fellow employee.

Field audit: An auditing method used in job analysis which is performed by observing an employee at work and comparing the information that is obtained with that furnished orally and/or in writing by the employee and/or the supervisor.

First-dollar coverage: A provision in major medical plans that covers all expenses, beginning with the first dollar of charges for certain expenses, such as hospital room and board.

First impression: The tendency of a person to be unduly influenced by his or her first impression of another person.

Flag statement: A statement representing a grouping of tasks related to the same topic.

Flexible benefit plan: A plan that allows employees to choose between two or more types of benefit plans. Sometimes called *cafeteria plan.*

Flexible spending account: A plan that provides funds from employers and/or employee pretax pay to be used for expenses not covered in an employee benefit plan.

Flextime: An employee scheduling method with a core of hours when all employees must be present in each work day, combined with a one to two hour flexible period before and after the core in which employees may vary their work schedule.

Forced-choice checklist method: A variation of the checklist method of performance appraisal in which the appraiser is required to check statements, which represent various levels of performance but are randomly assigned into groups of four to six, are most and/or least like an employee. See **Checklist method.**

Forced-distribution method: A ranking method of performance appraisal in which appraisers are required to appraise employees in the same proportions as a normal population distribution.

Foreign service premium: An additional amount of pay to compensate employees for working abroad.

Formative evaluation: A type of evaluation administered during a course or training program to gauge participants'/trainees' progress. Examples of formative assessment methods are pop quizzes, short exercises, class discussions of topics, or student presentations of subject matter. Trainers/facilitators use student/participant performance on these formative measures of learning to evaluate progress being made toward learning objectives. From this evaluation any adjustments can be made, for example, in the manner in which training materials are being presented. See **Summative evaluation.**

Four-fifths rule: A rule of thumb measure in which adverse impact exists when the selection rate for protected group members is less than four-fifths of the rate for the non protected group.

401(a) plan: A savings plan in which contributions are made in after-tax dollars.

401(k) plan: A salary reduction form of retirement plan, in which contributions are made in before-tax dollars, as authorized by Section 401(k) of the Internal Revenue Code.

403(b) plan: A type of savings plan for employees in tax-exempt organizations. Also referred to as *tax-sheltered annuities* or *tax deferred annuities.*

Fringe benefits: A synonym for *employee benefits* or *indirect compensation* or *perquisites.* Historically, the term meant all employee benefits, excluding direct pay supplements; this definition is the one used in federal laws, such as the Service Contract Act.

Fully insured: As defined by Social Security, a worker who has the lesser of: (1) 40 quarters of coverage; or (2) one quarter of coverage for each year that has elapsed since 1950 (or the year the worker became age 21, if later) *through* the year *before* the worker becomes 62, or becomes disabled—but not less than 6 quarters of coverage.

Functional authority: The right to determine how delegated tasks within a function will be handled throughout an organization.

Functional job analysis: A method developed by Sidney A. Fine, in defining job tasks using: (1) a verb (worker function), (2) the immediate object of the verb (data, people and things) and (3) an infinitive phrase consisting of an infinitive (the work field) and the object of the infinitive (the Materials, Products, Subject Matter, and Services).

Gainsharing: Pay incentives that share gains among employees based upon some bottom-line measure of performance. The earliest use of the term was by F.A. Halsey in 1891.

Garnishment: A legal process through which an employee's earnings may be withheld for payment of a debt, such as for failing to make payments as required on a loan, or for the payment of a financial obligation, such as failing to pay child support obligations.

General Aptitude Test Battery (GATB): A test battery administered by the U.S. Department of Labor through the various state employment service agencies used by employers to fill a variety of jobs.

General duty provision: A provision in the Occupational Safety and Health Act that requires employers to "furnish to each of his employees employment and a place of employment which are free from recognized hazards that are causing or are likely to cause death or serious physical harm to his employees."

General Educational Development (GED): As used in the Department of Labor method of job analysis, the formal and informal education that does not have a specific occupational goal and is not vocationally-oriented.

General evaluation set: The tendency of raters to rate people in the same way, such as too harshly, too lenient or in the middle.

General pay increase: A pay increase granted to all employees through either a hump-sum payment or more typically, a percentage increase in the base salary; also called *across-the-board increase*.

Genetic test: A test which identifies genes that cause diseases and addictive behaviors.

Give-backs: A term used to describe either cuts in or the elimination of employee compensation programs.

Glass ceiling: A term used to describe artificial barriers which keep women and minorities from moving up into mid- and upper level management positions.

Goal: A statement defining the long-term plans in which organization resources should be expended in order that the organization's mission can be accomplished. In affirmative action, a goal does not mean preferential treatment or a quota.

Gold circle: Giving an employee a merit pay increase above the maximum of the range to reward performance. See **Green circle, Red circle,** and **Silver circle.**

Golden handcuffs: Variously defined as: (1) an employer-imposed condition requiring an executive to defer some direct compensation to a later date with the further requirement that the amount will be forfeited should the executive leave the organization before that date; or (2) any compensation plan, such as a bonus for exceptional performance or a perquisite like the exclusive use of a company-owned airplane, which is used as an incentive to keep an executive employed with a firm.

Golden parachute: Special compensation provided to executives in the event of a hostile takeover by another firm.

Good faith and fair dealing: A concept which has had little success in state courts, that employers would be expected to maintain an equitable employment relationship with their employees, such as honoring past practices to discipline (punish) or discharge employees only for just cause. See **Employment-at-will.**

Good faith bargaining: The process of conducting collective bargaining at reasonable times, in reasonable places, exchanging proposals and counterproposals between union and management representatives who have the authority to make decisions, and demonstrating through actions an attempt to reconcile the differences in positions on most subjects.

Good faith efforts: A term used in affirmative action to describe the establishment and implementation of plans to recruit members of protected groups who are under represented in a workplace; goals are examples of good faith efforts, quotas are not. See **Goals** and **Quotas.**

Graduated commission: A pay incentive with increased percentage rates for successively higher sales volumes.

Graphic rating scales: A method of performance appraisal in which different levels of performance are denoted by a numerical value on a scale.

Graphology: The analysis of handwriting traits, such as writing pressure and slant, to determine human characteristics.

Green-circle: Paying an employee at a lower rate of pay than the minimum of the pay range for his or her job; opposite of *red-circle*. See **Gold circle, Red circle, and Silver circle.**

Grievance: Any dissatisfaction arising out of the work environment which is beyond the employee's control and for which management has the means and authority to correct.

Grievance arbitration: The process of a third party settling a dispute involving an existing collective bargaining agreement. See **Arbitrator** and **Interest arbitration.**

Ground rules: In collective bargaining, the agreed-upon procedures to be followed by both union and management representatives during the period of negotiations.

Group deferred annuity: A retirement plan in which the employer purchases, from an insurance company, incremental paid-up retirement annuities for employees after specified periods of time, such as each year.

Group interview: A type of employment interview in which two or more persons simultaneously interview an applicant. Also called a *panel interview.*

Group pay incentives: Deferred or immediate pay incentives in which a designated group of employees share the results.

Guide for Occupational Exploration: A companion volume to both the *Dictionary of Occupational Titles* and the *Selected Characteristics of Occupations Defined in the Dictionary of Occupational Titles,* that helps individuals assess themselves to determine for what jobs they are suited and to help vocational counselors assist individuals in career planning.

Halo effect: The tendency of raters to permit one characteristic to unduly influence their total opinion about a person in either a positive (positive halo) or negative (negative halo) manner. See **Horn effect.**

Handbilling: The distribution of union materials to employees as part of a union recognition campaign.

Handicapped: A term used in the Rehabilitation Act, synonymous with **"disabled"** in the Americans with Disabilities Act. See **Disabled.**

Harassment: Intimidating, hostile, or abusive behavior toward a person or persons in an employment-related setting because of national origin, race, color, religion, sex, disability, age, citizenship or veteran's status. *Intimating* behavior is, for example, threatening to cause trouble for an employee of the opposite sex if he or she does not agree to an overture of a sexual nature. *Hostile* behavior is, for example, giving unreasonable assignments to older workers to make them quit. Finally, an example of *abusive* behavior is ridiculing a person because of his or her religion. See **Sexual harassment.**

Hard bargaining: The process in collective bargaining of demonstrating good faith in attempting to reach agreement on various proposals while remaining resolute or unwilling to compromise on key issues.

Hardship allowance: An additional amount of pay to compensate employees for the hardships involved in working in a foreign assignment.

Hay Guide Chart-Profile Method: A method of job evaluation developed from the early work of Edward N. Hay.

Hazard communication standard: A standard issued by the Occupational Safety and Health Administration requiring employers to prepare a written hazard communication program that lists the hazardous chemicals used and explains the way in which: (1) hazardous chemicals will be labeled, (2) material safety data sheets will be prepared, (3) employees will be trained, (4) employees will be informed of hazards and chemicals, and (5) other employers at multi-employer work sites will be informed of hazards. The standard also requires employers to take the actions outlined in the plan.

Hazardous duty pay: Extra pay for performing hazardous tasks.

Hazardous occupations: Those 17 occupations, such as coal mining, in which according to the Fair Labor Standards Act, children under 18 years of age cannot be employed.

Health: The absence of illness or disease.

Health care institution: As defined in the National Labor Relations Act, "any hospital, convalescent hospital, health maintenance organization, health clinic, nursing home, extended care facility, or other institution devoted to the care of sick, infirm, or aged persons.

Health hazard exposure: A biological, chemical, ergonomic, or physical condition in a workplace that may cause an occupational illness, disability or death. See **Occupational illness.**

Health insurance cooperative: Cooperatives that purchase medical expense benefit services from providers for a group of employers.

Health Insurance Portability and Accountability Act: A law which among other provisions established health care portability provisions to facilitate employees changing jobs.

Health maintenance organization: An organization that provides preventive medical service either through its own medical staff or a system of service providers under contract who agree to an established schedule of fees.

Highly compensated employee: An employee who meets one or more specific criteria, such as owns at least 5 percent of the business, as defined by the Tax Reform Act of 1986. See **Nondiscrimination tests.**

Hold-harmless agreement: A statement signed by a person accepting any risk involved in a situation and agreeing not to hold another party responsible for a peril.

Home leave: Annual or biennial trips to their home countries provided by multinational firms to their expatriates.

Homework: A job scheduling method in which employees with either part-time or full-time jobs perform some or all of their work at home.

Homicide: Intentionally killing another person or killing a person while committing another crime.

Honesty test: An instrument intended to measure applicants' inclinations to steal from an employer or to cause trouble at work. Also sometimes called **Integrity test.**

Horn effect: The tendency of interviewers to rate a person low in all categories based upon one negative characteristic.

Hospice care: A program of care for terminally ill patients who have a life expectancy of six months or less.

Host country national: A citizen of a country who is employed in a branch or plant of a company that is located in that person's country but the company's headquarters is in another country.

Hostile environment sexual harassment: See **Sexual harassment.**

Hot cargo contract: An agreement between a company and union that the company will not handle a product or do business with another company in an effort to achieve a union objective.

Hotlines: A toll-free telephone number employees can call to voice their opinions about organizational matters. In employee assistance programs, hotlines are used to provide immediate information to help employees who need assistance.

Hourly: A term often used, and sometimes incorrectly, to describe those employees who are covered by the overtime provisions of the Fair Labor Standards Act. See **Salaried.**

Household furnishings allowance: Assistance given by international firms to expatriates in obtaining household furnishings.

Housing allowance: Assistance provided to expatriates in renting/selling their domestic residence and/or securing housing in the foreign assignment.

Human Resource Certification Institute: A non-profit organization established in 1975 to accredit HR professionals; the organization offers the Professional in Human Resources and the Senior Professional in Human Resources designations. Address is 606 North Washington Street, Alexandria, VA 22314.

Human resources development: The HR activity concerned with preparing employees to maximize both their utility to the organization and their job satisfaction.

Human resources development process: The process of determining human resources development (HRD) needs, setting objectives, defining criteria, selecting HRD methods, implementing the HRD, and evaluating the effects of the HRD.

Human resources systems: Software programs to aid HR planning, decision-making and reporting.

Human resources management: The function of an organization that assists organizations in achieving goals by obtaining and maintaining effective employees.

Human resources management activity: Separate area of HRM consisting of similar or related tasks, such as job analysis or performance appraisal.

Human resources planning: The HRM activity concerned with the application of the management function of planning to human resources and encompasses various techniques and systems to ensure that HRM activities are effectively performed and meet goals.

Hybrid: Pension or retirement plans, such as *percentage-of-contribution* and *cash account pension* plans, that resemble both defined benefit and defined contribution plans. They resemble defined contribution plans because the employer agrees to contribute a certain percentage of the employees' pay to fund a retirement plan; they resemble a defined benefit plan because the employer agrees to provide a certain level of benefits. Another term for a hybrid is *cash balance plan*. Hybrids are classified by the IRS as defined benefit plans because a certain level of benefits is promised by the employer.

Immigration Reform and Control Act: A federal law designed to stem the flow of illegal immigrants into the U.S., provide a means for certain aliens who were unauthorized to be in the U.S. to obtain legal status, and to prevent discrimination against persons because of their national origin or citizenship status. Enforcement of the law is a shared responsibility of the Wage and Hour Division of the U.S. Department of Labor, the Immigration and Naturalization Service, and the U.S. Department of Justice.

Impasse: The failure to reach an agreement on a proposal in collective bargaining contract negotiations. A lawful impasse is one that results from good faith bargaining on a mandatory bargaining subject. An unlawful impasse is one that either (1) results from either party's insistence on negotiating a proposal that is either a permissive or a prohibited subject or (2) results from a party's refusal to bargain without sufficient reason. See **Good faith bargaining, Mandatory bargaining subject, Permissive bargaining subject,** and **Proposal.**

Implicit personality theory: The tendency of raters to make erroneous conclusions (implications) about a person's undemonstrated qualifications or characteristics based upon evident ones.

Implied employment contract: A statement in an employer's handbook and in other documents, such as policy manuals, that employees shall not be discharged or disciplined (punished) without good cause. See **Employment-at-will.**

Improshare: An acronym for *Im* proved *Pro* ductivity through *Shar* ing. A type of gainsharing plan in which productivity gains in saved workhours are shared with employees.

In-basket exercise: An exercise used for such purposes as selection or human resources development, in which participants handle a work basket of events representative or those encountered on a job they are either seeking or are being trained for.

Incentive stock option: A stock option which an employer grants to an employee, typically an executive, for the purpose of either motivating the employee's behavior toward the accomplishment of certain objectives or of meeting certain requirements, such as fulfilling an employment contract. See **Stock option.**

Indirect cause: See **Accident cause**.

Indirect compensation: Current and deferred non monetary rewards employees receive as a condition of their employment; also referred to as *employee benefits, fringe benefits,* or *perquisites.*

Individual employee coverage: Coverage under the Fair Labor Standards Act of employees who in any work week are engaged in interstate or foreign commerce or are engaged in the production of goods for interstate or foreign commerce. Also see **Enterprise coverage.**

Inductive hypothesis: A general conclusion made from independent observations. Also see **Deductive hypothesis.**

Industrial union: A union that represents virtually all the workers within a specific industry, like the United Auto Workers. See **Craft union** and **White-collar union.**

Initial deductible: The simplest type of deductible most commonly found in comprehensive medical plans in which the insured must satisfy a deductible amount before any benefits are paid by the plan. See **Deductible.**

Initiation fee: A one-time payment required for becoming a member of a union.

Inpatriate: A citizen of a country, who is on an assignment to the corporate office of the firm in which the person is employed, which is located in another country.

Inspection: A review of a workplace by the Occupational Safety and Health Administration (OSHA) to determine if an employer is complying with OSHA standards and regulations. The priority in inspections is: (1) imminent danger, (2) catastrophes and fatal accidents, (3) employee complaints, (4) programmed high-hazard inspections, and (5) reinspections. See **Citation, Occupational Safety and Health Administration,** and **Violation.**

Instrumentality: The probability of a second-level outcome that can range from -1 to 1. See **Expectancy theory.**

Integrated deductible: An earlier form of deductible used in major medical plans in which covered expenses under the basic plan could be used to satisfy the deductible under the major medical plan. See **Deductible.**

Integration: See **Benefit integration.**

Integrity test: See **Honesty test.**

Intending citizen: An alien who is lawfully admitted to the U.S. for permanent residence, is granted the status of an alien lawfully admitted for temporary residence, is admitted as a refugee, or is granted asylum, and who evidences an intention to become a citizen of the U.S. through completing a declaration of intention to become a citizen. See **Immigration Reform** and **Control Act.**

Interest: According to the Department of Labor method of job analysis, one of 12 interests a person should possess for selected jobs to be satisfied in a job and to prevent absenteeism and turnover.

Interest arbitration: The process in which a third party, such as an arbitrator, settles a dispute involving the negotiation of a new collective bargaining agreement. See **Arbitration** and **Grievance arbitration.**

Interest inventory: Nominally a test but more of a self-assessment of a person's interests. See **Test.**

Intermittent reinforcement: Reinforcing behavior on other than a continuous basis. See **Interval reinforcement** and **Ratio reinforcement.**

Internal environment: The planning environment in strategic planning that includes the organization culture, the organization's financial condition, and the workforce's characteristics. See **Organization culture** and **Workforce characteristics.**

Internal equity: Is the degree to which an organization's compensation program rewards employees relative to their contributions within the organization.

International HRM: The performance of all HRM activities in recruiting and maintaining an effective workforce in the foreign operations of an international firm.

Internship/traineeship: A human resources development method in which the interns/trainees are rotated through a series of planned job assignments to prepare them for higher level responsibilities.

Interval reinforcement: Reinforcing behavior based on a time frequency, such as daily or weekly. See **Behaviorism** and **Schedules of reinforcement.**

Interval scale: A type of scale used in research in which the value for each successive interval is equal such as on a Fahrenheit thermometer. See **Nominal scale, Ordinal scale,** and **Ratio scale.**

Interview: See **Behavioral interview, Computer interview, Depth interview, Group interview, Nondirective interview, Patterned interview, Situational interview, Stress interview,** and **Video interview.**

Intrinsic rewards: Rewards employees personally experience from within their psyche as a result of performing their job tasks. See **Extrinsic rewards.**

Job: A collect of tasks grouped together in a formal assignment with a unique title; sometimes used synonymously with the term *position.*

Job analysis: The systematic process of obtaining, analyzing, and interpreting valid information about jobs for various purposes, such as to aid management decision-making in activities like designing selection procedures.

Job class: A group of jobs which are similar or the same in: (1) the kind or subject area of work, (2) the difficulties and responsibilities in job tasks and (3) the job specifications. Used synonymously with *class* or *class of positions*.

Job description: A one to three page written explanation of the significant aspects of a job; other terms used for job description are *class description, class specification* and *position description*.

Job evaluation: The process of applying carefully defined compensable factors to job tasks to determine the relative worth of jobs with the goal of achieving internal pay equity among them.

Job enlargement: Broadening a job by including tasks from other jobs.

Job enrichment: Assigning employees more complex and varied tasks of a more responsible nature. Five parts of job enrichment are task variety, task identity, task significance, task autonomy and feedback.

Job fair: An aggregation of employers assembled in one location to recruit applicants for many different jobs.

Job instruction method: A human resource development method in which written instructions for operating a machine or following a procedure are listed in a series of successive steps.

Job rotation: Assigning employees to different job assignments to reduce boredom and eliminate fatigue caused by performing repetitious job tasks. Also used in human resources development to give employees experience in performing different job tasks.

Job sharing: A method of job scheduling in which two employees share a full-time job.

Job specifications: The knowledge, skills, abilities, education, experience, training and other qualifications that a person must possess to satisfactorily perform the tasks in a job.

Job structuring: The part of the organizing function of management concerned with the formal and informal process of assigning tasks to jobs and delegating authority to accomplish them.

Key job: A job used to guide evaluators in making job evaluation decisions. Sometimes used synonymously with *benchmark job*.

Knowledge: A body of information applied directly to the performance of a task or function.

Labor dispute: As defined in the National Labor Relations Act, "any controversy concerning terms, tenure or conditions of employment, or concerning the association or representation of persons in negotiating, fixing, maintaining, changing, or seeking to arrange terms or conditions of employment, regardless of whether the disputants stand in the proximate relation of employer and employee."

Labor Management Relations Act of 1947: Also known as the Taft-Hartley Act, amended the National Labor Relations Act, including providing the right for states to prohibit the union shop under certain conditions; also created the Federal Mediation and Conciliation Service.

Labor-Management Reporting and Disclosure Act of 1959: Required the reporting and disclosure of union financial records and administrative acts, to prevent union officials from failing to fulfill their proper roles and to provide for the orderly conduct of union elections.

Labor organization: As defined by the National Labor Relations Act, "any organization of any kind, or any agency or employee representation committee or plan, in which employees participate and which exists for the purpose, in whole or in part, of dealing with employers concerning grievances, labor disputes, wages, rates of pay, hours of employment, or conditions of work." In addition to the above, the Labor-Management Reporting and Disclosure Act includes, "any conference, general committee, joint or system board, or joint council so engaged which is subordinate to a national or international labor organization, other than a state or local central body." See **Union.**

Labor relations consultant: As defined in the Labor-Management Reporting and Disclosure Act, "any person who, for compensation, advises or represents an employer, employer organization, or labor organization concerning employee organizing, concerted activities, or collective bargaining activities."

Late Night Retail Workers' Crime Protection Law: A 1990 State of Washington law which requires various actions by employers of certain retail firms who conduct business between 11:00 p.m. and 6:00 a.m.

Law of demand: The principle of economics that the demand for a commodity varies inversely with the price of it.

Law of effect: The behaviorism concept that people learn and repeat acts that are reinforced and rewarded and avoid acts associated with unpleasant stimuli or punishment.

Law of supply: The principle of economics that the supply of a commodity varies directly with the price of it.

Lay-off: Placing an employee in a non-pay status due to lack of work.

Leaderless group situations: A method used for such purposes as selection or human resources development, in which a group of individuals engage in an exercise or assume roles in a simulated work situation or discuss a topic and their performance is observed and recorded by trained observers.

Learning: The act of employees acquiring the knowledge, skills and abilities through education, training and experience. *Cognitive learning* is learning facts, data, and methods. *Noncognitive learning* is acquiring behavioral abilities such as leadership and creativity. *Psychomotor learning* is acquiring competence to operate equipment or to perform tasks in which objects are manipulated. See **Education, Experience,** and **Human resources development.**

Leisure counseling: The process of helping people meet their leisure needs, such as autonomy and creativity, in nonworklife and worklife.

Lie detector: As defined by the Employee Polygraph Protection Act (EPPA), a device that includes "a polygraph, deceptograph, voice stress analyzer, psychological stress evaluator, or any other similar device (whether mechanical or electrical) that is used, or the results of which are used, for the purpose of rendering a diagnostic opinion regarding the honesty or dishonesty of an individual." Prohibited in employment situations by the EPPA (except the polygraph can be used in narrowly-defined situations). See **Employee Polygraph Protection Act** and **Polygraph.**

Likert scale: Also referred to as **Likert-type scale,** is an interval scale typically with from five to seven points, in which the respondent indicates relative amounts of agreement or disagreement with a statement. See **Interval scale.**

Line authority: The right to use organization resources in managing subordinate employees in the accomplishment of organizational goals.

Linear careerist: A person who has career ambitions focusing on an orderly progression of promotions within an occupation. Also see **Steady state careerist, Spiral careerist,** and **Transition careerist.**

Literature review: A research method in which the research of others is investigated by reading pertinent articles in periodicals, books, monographs, government documents, industry reports and similar work. See **Research methods.**

Living wage theory: A theory of wages developed by Australian Justice Higgins in which the level of wages was sufficient to meet the "normal means of the average employee regarded as a human being in a civilized community."

Local bargaining: Negotiating an agreement that is restricted to the membership in one plant or locality.

Local union: One of approximately 60,000 unions in the U.S., most of which are affiliated with national unions, that operate in a local geographical area. Craft locals typically have members that are employed by a number of different employers. Industrial locals, tend to be restricted to the employees of single employer. See **Craft union, Industrial union, National union,** and **White-collar union.**

Lockout: See **Work stoppage.**

Long-term compensation plan: A pay plan typically reserved for management or executive personnel which is based upon the performance of a firm in one or more areas over a period of four or more years.

Loss of employment: Defined in the Worker Adjustment and Retraining Notification Act, as including layoffs exceeding six months in duration and reductions in the hours of work of more than 50 percent during each month in a six-month period. See **Worker Adjustment** and **Retraining Notification Act.**

Machines: As used in the Department of Labor method of job analysis, are mechanical devices with a framework or an arrangement of fastened parts that are designed to apply a force to do work on or move materials or to process data.

Machines, Tools, Equipment and Word Aids (MTEWA): The classification of items in the Department of Labor method of job analysis used in *Worker functions.* See **Worker functions.**

Maintenance of membership: A union security arrangement in which employees who are either union members when a union-management contract is accepted by both parties, or join the union after the contract is accepted, must remain union members during the life of the contract. See **Agency shop, Closed shop, Prehire agreement,** and **Union shop.**

Major medical coverage: See **Comprehensive major medical coverage** and **Supplemental major medical coverage.**

Malice: A condition which prompts a person to do a wrongful act willfully, that is, on purpose, to the injury of another. In employment discrimination, an act is maliciously done if prompted or accompanied by ill will either toward the injured person individually or toward all persons in one or more groups of which the injured person is a member.

Management by objectives: A performance appraisal method with subordinate-supervisor interaction and various degrees of mutual decision-making in establishing task priority, preparing performance crite ria and objectives, defining operational strategies, monitoring progress, and evaluating results on a scheduled review date.

Management rights clause: A clause in collective bargaining agreements which typically states that management has the right to determine the methods, means and technology of producing and distributing the good or service produced.

Mandatory bargaining subject: A subject, such as pay rates and group insurance, that employers and unions must bargain on if either side makes proposals on it.

Manual dexterity test: A test that measures a person's motor functions, such as reaction time, quickness of arm movements, multi-limb coordination, and finger dexterity. See **Test.**

Mass layoff: As defined in the Worker Adjustment and Retraining Notification Act, the loss of employment within a 30 day period at a single site of either: (1) at least 33 percent of the full-time workforce and at least 50 full-time persons or (2) 500 full-time employees. See **Worker Adjustment** and **Retraining Notification Act.**

Materials, Products, Subject Matter and Services: The three areas into which 55 major occupational areas are grouped in the Department of Labor method of job analysis.

Maturity curve: A method of paying professionals for the amount of time or experience they have within their respective professions.

Mediation: A process in which compromises and solutions are offered to the parties in a collective bargaining dispute by a mediator or other third party. See **Conciliation, Federal Mediation,** and **Conciliation Service.**

Medical expense allowance/assistance: Assistance given to expatriates and their dependents in securing medical assistance in situations in which medical care is inadequate or not available in the foreign country.

Medicare: The hospital and supplementary medical insurance component of Social Security.

Member: Also "member in good standing," as defined in the Labor-Management Reporting and Disclosure Act, "when used in reference to a labor organization, includes any person who has fulfilled the requirements for membership in such organization, and who neither has voluntarily withdrawn from membership nor has been expelled or suspended from membership after appropriate proceedings consistent with lawful provisions of the constitution and bylaws of such organization."

Mental ability test: A test that measures a person's ability to reason, perceive relationships, understand numerical properties, and solve quantitative problems. See **Test.**

Mental Health Parity Act: A law that requires employers, who provide mental health coverage, to have the same lifetime or annual limits for mental and physical conditions.

Mental revolution: See **Object lesson.**

Mentoring: A human resources development method, in which employees are formally or informally assigned to highly qualified persons for the purposes of acquiring learning; similar to coaching, except the mentor-mentee relationship frequently is more personal and involved. See **Coaching.**

Merit budget: That portion of a compensation budget containing the funds for merit pay increases.

Merit pay: A generic term for pay incentives that reward job performance through some overall measure of job performance.

Methods verbs: As used in the Department of Labor method of job analysis, verbs which are used to denote the specific ways of performing work.

Midlife career counseling: The process of assisting employees with the physical, social, and psychological adjustments of midlife affecting both worklife and nonworklife.

Mission: A statement in strategic planning that defines the basic purpose for which the organization exists.

Money wages: A term used in economics to denote the amount of money, either through cash, check or other spendable form that is received in payment by an employee from an employer in exchange for services performed.

Monster.com: An Internet-accessible job search computer database.

Motives: characteristics unique to the individual causing the person to commit an act. Some times the motive is immediately evident. Other times, the motive for a behavior is so obscure the reason for an act cannot be determined.

Moving expense assistance: Compensation provided to domestic employees and expatriates in moving to a different assignment.

Multiemployer bargaining: More than one employer simultaneously negotiating an agreement with one union.

Multiemployer-multiunion bargaining: More than one employer simultaneously conducting collective bargaining with more than one union.

Multinational firm: A generic term for a firm with business operations in more than one country; often used synonymously with *international firm.*

Multiplant bargaining: See **National bargaining.**

Multiple-tiered commission: Similar to a graduated commission, except the higher rate of commissions are paid for all sales above a certain level; see **Graduated commission.**

Multiunion bargaining: More than one union simultaneously negotiating an agreement with one employer. Another term for this arrangement is *coordinated bargaining.*

National Committee on Pay Equity: An organization working to eliminate sex- and race-based wage discrimination and to achieve pay equity. Address: National Committee on Pay Equity, c/o AFT, 555 New Jersey Avenue NW, Washington, DC 20001-2029.

National consultation: The right, under Title VII of the Civil Service Reform Act, of federal employee unions with memberships that constitute a "substantial number" of employees in an agency to be notified of proposals involving substantial changes in personnel matters affecting its members and be given the opportunity to comment on the proposals and suggest changes in personnel policies. See **Title VII of the Civil Service Reform Act** and **Exclusive recognition.**

National Crime Victimization Survey: An annual federally-conducted survey of over 100,000 individuals age 12 or older in which information is obtained about violent acts, including those occurring while the person was either on duty or working.

National Institute for Occupational Safety and Health (NIOSH): An agency within the U.S. Department of Health and Human Services created by the Occupational Safety and Health Act to conduct research, experiments, and demonstrations relating to occupational safety and health and to conduct, directly or by grants or contracts, education programs to provide an adequate supply of qualified personnel to carry out the purposes of the Act and information programs on the importance and proper use of safety and health equipment.

National Labor Relations Act of 1935: A federal law giving employees the right to self-organize, form or assist labor organizations, bargain collectively through representatives of their own choosing, engage in other concerted activities and refrain from any or all such activities except for requiring membership in a labor organization as a condition of employment.

National Labor Relations Board: A board whose general function is to oversee implementation of the National Labor Relations Act.

National origin: Defined by the U.S. Equal Employment Opportunity Commission (EEOC) as including but not limited to, an individual's or his or her ancestor's, place of origin; or because an individual has the physical, cultural or linguistic characteristics of a national origin or group. EEOC includes both religion and national origin under the word ethnic.

National union: One of approximately 175 unions, that typically include all union members in the U.S., that operate autonomously and provide services to their member local unions. See **Local union.**

Negative reinforcement: The administration of an unpleasant stimulus with the intention of inducing a person to perform a desired act and avoid or not do an undesired one.

Negligent hiring: The potential liability of an employer for the actions of an employee who was selected for employment without adequately determining the person's qualifications and background characteristics for the job.

Negligent retention: The prospective liability an employer faces by retaining employees, who the employer knows or should have known, are not qualified to perform their job tasks or have mental or physical conditions or propensities that result in them being a hazard to themselves or others.

Negotiations: The collective bargaining sessions in which the representatives of the union and the employer meet to discuss proposals for a labor/management agreement.

Negotiations planning: The process of preparing for contract negotiations in collective bargaining.

Newborns' and Mothers' Health Protection Act: This law does not permit group health plans to restrict postpartum hospital stays to less than 48 hours for a normal delivery and 96 hours for a caesarean section.

Nominal scale: A type of scale used in research in which numbers are simply labels and have no other properties, such as indicating the magnitude of something. See **Interval scale, Ordinal scale,** and **Ratio scale.**

Nonbargainable subject: In collective bargaining, either: (1) a subject that must be provided in an agreement simply upon the request of a party, such as a union recognition clause, or (2) a subject that is prohibited by the National Labor Relations Act, such as a union membership requirement in a state with a right-to-work law.

Non-compete agreements: A contract between a firm and a current or prospective employee that restricts the employee, should he or she leave the firm, from competing with it.

Noncontributory plan: An employee benefit plan that does not require employee contributions.

Nondirective interview: A type of interview, which is based upon the principles of nondirective counseling, predicated on the theory that an applicant will assist the interviewer in determining if the person is qualified for a job if he or she understands what the job specifications are.

Nondiscrimination tests: Eligibility and benefit tests required by the Tax Reform Act of 1986 to prevent an employee benefit plan from discriminating in favor of the *highly compensated employees*. See **Qualification standards** and **Highly compensated employee.**

Nonexempt employee: An employee who is covered by the provisions of the Fair Labor Standards Act.

Nonqualified or nonstatutory stock option: A stock option that does not qualify for preferential tax treatment. See **Stock option.**

Nonverbal bias: The tendency of raters', such as employment interviewers, to be influenced by applicants' dress or personal appearance.

Objective: A short-term plan, such as those in Management by Objectives (MBO) method of performance appraisal, that is pursued to aid in goal accomplishment.

Object lesson: In F.W. Taylor's Scientific Management incentive pay plan, what each worker experienced when he or she discovered the rewards were greater under the system. *Mental revolution* is a summation of the object lessons of many employees.

Occupation Information Network (O*NET): A database system that collects, organizes, describes, and disseminates data on occupational characteristics and worker attributes.

Occupational illness: Any abnormal condition or disorder other than one caused by an occupational injury, resulting from a biological, chemical, ergonomic or physical health hazard.

Occupational injury: An injury resulting from either a work accident or an exposure in a single incident in the workplace.

Occupational Safety and Health Act (OSH Act): A federal law that applies to all employers with one or more employees that is intended in the terms of the Act "To assure safe and healthful working conditions for working men and women; by authorizing enforcement of the standards developed under the Act; by assisting and encouraging the States in their efforts to assure safe and healthful working conditions; by providing for research, information, education, and training in the field of occupational safety and health; and for other purposes."

Occupational Safety and Health Administration (OSHA): An agency within the U.S. Department of Labor created by the Occupational Safety and Health Act to carry "... out the adjudicatory functions under the Act."

Occupational Safety and Health Review Commission: An independent agency of the U.S. government. The Commission's only function is to resolve disputes that result from inspections carried out under the OSH Act. The Commission is composed of three members who are appointed by the President of the U.S. for six-year terms. The Commission employs Administrative Law Judges, who hear cases filed by employers disagreeing with some part of an OSHA citation.

Employers may contest a citation by filing a *Notice of Contest* within 15 working days of receiving a citation notice and a proposed penalty.

Office audit: A type of audit used in job analysis which is performed by the auditor (usually a job analyst) in his or her office reviewing information obtained from the job analysis to determine if all requested information was furnished and checking for discrepancies in written statements made by supervisors and employees.

Office of Federal Contract Compliance Programs: An office within the Employment Standards Administration of the U.S. Department of Labor that is responsible for enforcing the regulations requiring Federal contractors to take affirmative action and to eliminate discrimination from the workplace, and to obtain redress for victims of discrimination, particularly for such laws as the Vietnam Era Veterans Readjustment Act and the Rehabilitation Act and executive orders, such as Executive Order 11375.

Older Workers Benefit Protection Act: A federal law requiring employers with 20 or more employees to meet certain conditions if agreements are offered to employees in return for waiving their rights to file a charge of age discrimination; the law also permits employers to reduce the benefits in a bona fide employee benefit plan, based upon age, if they can prove cost considerations warrant it and so long as the employer makes the same expenditures for employee benefits for employees of all ages.

Ombudsman: A person who is hired to investigate and resolve employee complaints and grievances.

One-year renewable term insurance: Life insurance that provides protection for terms of one year.

Open panel: The option of employees to choose their own attorney in a prepaid legal services plan. See **Closed panel.**

Open shop: As the term implies, a place of work that has an "open shop" does not require union membership as a condition of employment.

Operating budget: The planned operational expenditures of an organization for it to accomplish desired goals; see **Base-line budget** and **Zero-base budget.**

Opportunity cost: A cost concept used in economics, which is not reflected in a firm's accounting methods, which is the benefit that could result from one alternative that an employer forgoes by deciding to invest resources in another one.

Ordinal scale: A type of scale used in research in which the values designate the ranking or ordering of the variable. See **Interval scale, Nominal scale,** and **Ratio scale.**

Ordinary life insurance: Insurance that provides coverage in the form of level premium permanent life insurance with premiums and coverage allocated between term and permanent portions.

Organization: A group of people working in a formal structure towards goal accomplishment.

Organization culture: The institutionalized customs, beliefs, rules, values, and philosophies in an organization.

Organization development: A generic term encompassing a number of intervention methods to increase organizational efficiency. See **Teambuilding** and **Quality of worklife.**

Organization function: A grouping of work, in an organization, in which the jobs are clearly distinguishable from others.

Outplacement: The process of ending a person's employment in one organization and assisting him or her in securing a position in another one.

Outstanding performance award: A one-time pay incentive awarded for some measure of outstanding performance.

Overinsured: The condition of being insured beyond the financial loss that is expected to occur in a particular situation.

Overseas Assignment Inventory (OAI): A self-response questionnaire, developed by Moran, Stahl and Boyer, used in selecting individuals for international assignments, to determine the cross-cultural adaptability of potential expatriates and their spouses.

Paid-up insurance: Life insurance that provides coverage consisting of a combination of annually increasing units of single-premium paid-up whole life insurance with cash value plus decreasing units of one-year renewable term insurance.

Pair comparison method: A performance appraisal method in which all employees are paired with each other and compared by the appraiser using a global measure of performance.

Panel interview: See **Group interview**.

Pattern bargaining: The situation in collective bargaining in which the provision(s) in an agreement negotiated with one or a few employers in an industry becomes the "pattern" for settlements that are negotiated later with the same union and other employers.

Patterned interview: An interview in which the interviewer uses a set of specific questions, the answers to which are presumed to be relevant to job performance.

Pay administration: The HRM activity concerned with the preparation and administration of equitable methods of paying employees.

Pay compression: The narrowing of pay differences for reasons other than what sound pay administration would require. See **Employee pay compression, Pay grade compression** and **Pay range compression.**

Pay disclosure: The concept involving various aspects of disclosing employee pay.

Pay equity: The concept involving the equitable treatment of members of both sexes in pay administration.

Pay for knowledge: A compensation method that pays employees for the number of different jobs or the number of different types of tasks that they are capable of performing.

Pay for performance: See **Pay incentive.**

Pay grade: A number that corresponds to a specific pay range, usually with minimum and maximum dollar amounts; also, a single plateau in a pay structure that is established to properly compensate one or more jobs in an organization. Also called a *pay grade number.*

Pay grade compression: The condition of having too small a differential in the pay of higher pay grades compared to the lower ones.

Pay grade "creep": The tendency to increase the upper dollar limits of some pay grades without changing others.

Pay grade table: The pay grade levels and the corresponding pay ranges for all pay grades in the same job evaluation system. Also called a *pay structure.*

Pay incentive: A form of direct compensation using an immediate and/or a deferred monetary payment that is based upon some measure of individual or group performance.

Pay range: The minimum and maximum dollar amounts in each pay grade.

Pay range compression: Having too small a differential in the pay ranges of higher pay grades compared to those in the lower grades.

Pay structure: See **Pay grade table.**

Pedagogy: The science of how children learn.

Pension: See **Retirement plan.**

Pension Benefit Guaranty Corporation: A federal agency established by the Employee Retirement Income Security Act to manage the program that insures retirement programs so workers are protected in the event that a plan fails.

People: As used in the Department of Labor method of job analysis, the *Worker Function* concerned with human beings *and* animals dealt with on an individual basis as if they were human.

Performance appraisal: The HRM activity concerned with the process of establishing written performance criteria, communicating those criteria to employees and informing employees how well they are performing in relation to them.

Performance objectives bonus: An executive bonus plan that is an annual cash payment for performance that exceeds set performance objectives.

Performance shares: An executive compensation plan in which pay incentives in the form of bonuses, stock options or a combination of the two, are given for the accomplishment of specific long-term goals.

Performance test: A test that measures a person's performance manipulating something, such as a piece of equipment. See **Test.**

Permissive bargaining subject: In collective bargaining, a subject, such as retirees' benefits, on which management and labor are not required to bargain.

Perquisites: Variously defined as: (1) special benefits exclusively given to executive-level management, (2) any indirect compensation which has a monetary benefit, or (3) used synonymously with the terms *indirect compensation* or *employee benefits*.

Personal benefits statement: A specially constructed form that is typically sent to all employees annually to advise them of the status of their employee benefit plan with the firm.

Petition: A document filed with the National Labor Relations Board by a union or employee for a representation proceeding, such as a certification of representation or decertification of representation.

Phantom stock option: A pay incentive with the appearance of a stock option in which a stipulated number of fictitious shares of stock, which are based upon the value of actual stock, are given to an executive.

Philosophy: The part of organization culture that concerns the prevalent management attitude towards growth, human resource contributions to organizational success, profitability, customer service, and social responsibility.

Physical demands: According to the Department of Labor method of job analysis, one of six physical job requirements a person must meet to satisfactorily perform the tasks in a job.

Plant closure: As defined in the Worker Adjustment and Retraining Notification Act, the permanent or temporary closure of one employment site or one or more facilities or operating units in a single site during a 30 day period in which 50 or more full-time employees lose their employment. See **Worker Adjustment and Retraining Notification Act.**

Piecework: A pay incentive method based upon the number of units of production.

Point method: A method of job evaluation that assigns points to different levels of various compensable factors and subfactors.

Point of service health care plan: A type of health care plan that requires members to select a primary care physician who gives authorization for the members to see specialists.

Policy: A broad general guideline, usually in writing.

Polygraph: As defined by the Employee Polygraph Protection Act, "an instrument that (a) records continuously, visually, permanently, and simultaneously changes in cardiovascular, respiratory, and electrodermal patterns as minimum instrumentation standards and (b) is used, or the results of which are used, for the purpose of rendering a diagnostic opinion regarding the honesty or dishonesty of an individual." For employment use see **Employee Polygraph Protection Act.**

Portability: The ability to move the vested rights in an retirement or savings plan from one employer to another.

Portal-to-Portal Act: A federal law covering the compensability of preliminary or postliminary activities that are incidental to the principal work activities.

Position: One or more assignments, whether filled by employees or left vacant, for each job.

Position Analysis Questionnaire: A 194-item structured checklist for use in conducting a job analysis with nonmanagerial and nonprofessional jobs.

Position questionnaire: A generic instrument used in job analysis to collect written information about a job encompassing a range of topics such as description of work, equipment used in the job, contacts with other persons, instructions used in the performance of tasks, types of errors occurring on the job and the responsibility for them, supervisory responsibilities, qualifications necessary to satisfactorily perform the job tasks and the tasks that are subject to review by others.

Positive discipline: The process of treating deficient employees as adults in improving their performance, and in some cases, providing a decision-making leave for them to determine whether they will make a commitment to meet their job responsibilities within the company or should seek employment elsewhere.

Positive reinforcement: The process of rewarding a desired behavior.

Postal Reorganization Act of 1970: A federal law that gave employees of the U.S. Postal Service the right to organize and bargain collectively with postal service management.

Preadmission certification: The process of an insured person and/or his or her personal physician obtaining authorization (or certification) prior to being hospitalized for non emergency medical treatment.

Preadmission testing: Administering required medical tests for the purpose of diagnosing a person's physical problems before being admitted to a hospital.

Predetermination of benefits provision: A provision in the dental coverage of medical expense plans whereby the insurer reviews the proposed dental procedures and costs of services before the employee receives treatment; the dentist completes a claim form and the insurer advises both the dentist and the employee how much it will pay of the proposed cost and/or suggest other services.

Predictive validation: A validity study in which job applicants are used as the subjects.

Preexisting condition: An illness or injury for which a person received medical treatment during a specified prior period of time.

Preferred provider organization: A system of participating providers of services that contract with employers to provide medical services for their employees at a negotiated fee.

Pregnancy Discrimination Act of 1978: An amendment to Title VII of the Civil Rights Act of 1964 that requires covered employers to treat pregnancy the same as any other disability in: (1) providing employee benefits, and (2) in granting leaves of absences.

Prehire agreement: A union security provision, legal only in the construction industry, that gives hiring preferences to union members and permits construction unions to make agreements with employers requiring them to notify the union when employment opportunities exist and to give the union an opportunity to refer qualified applicants for such employment. See **Agency shop, Closed shop, Maintenance of membership.**

Primary Standard: See **Factor evaluation system.**

Probationary period: A set period of time, typically from six months to one year, in which a newly selected employee can be terminated without recourse to internal grievance or other appeal procedures.

Procedure: A detailed instruction for the daily administration of a policy.

Process evaluation: A type of evaluation, used to evaluate human resource management programs, such as a human resource development program, in which participants evaluate the process involved in the program, such as the instructor's manner of presentation. Also see **Effect evaluation.**

Professional and Managerial Position Questionnaire: A 98-item job analysis instrument used in analyzing managerial and professional jobs.

Professional employee: As defined in the National Labor Relations Act, "(a) any employee engaged in work (i) predominantly intellectual and varied in character as opposed to routine mental, manual, mechanical, or physical work; (ii) involving the consistent exercise of discretion and judgment in its performance; (iii) of such a character that the output produced or the result accomplished cannot be standardized in relation to a given period of time; (iv) requiring knowledge of an advanced type in a field of science or learning customarily acquired by a prolonged course of specialized intellectual instruction and study in an institution of higher learning or a hospital, as distinguished from a general academic education or from an apprenticeship or from training in the performance of routine mental, manual, or physical process; *or* (b) any employee who (i) has completed the courses of specialized intellectual instruction and study described in clause (iv) of paragraph (a), and (ii) is performing related work under the supervision of a professional person to qualify himself to become a professional employee as defined in paragraph (a)."

Professional and scientific personnel: Those employees whose tasks involve the performance of specialized work within a function that requires varying degrees of vocational preparation ranging from technical training and experience to professional postgraduate education. See **Professional employee.**

Profiling: The process of determining the percent relationship of each of the three compensable factors to the total evaluation of the job; used in the Hay Guide Chart-Profile method of job evaluation.

Profit sharing: The process of paying employees sums of money, on either a current or deferred basis, which is in addition to their regular pay; the payments are made on some predetermined percentage of the company's profits.

Profit sharing plan: An *immediate* plan makes cash disbursements from a company's profits, usually on a semi-annual or annual basis; a *deferred* plan makes payments at a later date, typically when the employee retires.

Progressive discipline: The application of more stringent types of punishment to employees for their repeated instances of deficiencies or for those of a more serious nature.

Promotion: A personnel placement from a position in one job to a position in another job of a higher pay grade.

Proposal: An initial demand by either a union or management representative in collective bargaining contract negotiations. A counterproposal is a response to the proposal made by the opposite side.

Protagonist: A person who commits workplace violence because of his or her dissatisfaction or disagreement with the mission of an organization.

Protected group: Those groups protected from discrimination under federal law or executive order.

Punishment: The behaviorism concept, involving: (1) administering an unpleasant stimulus, or (2) withholding a reward.

Punitive: See **Sanction.**

Qualification standards: Specific standards, such as a plan must be in writing, which are required by the Tax Reform Act of 1986, in order for an employee benefit plan to qualify for favorable tax treatment. See **Nondiscrimination tests.**

Qualified plan: A retirement plan that is qualified under Internal Revenue regulations and thus receives tax benefits favorable to both the employer and employees.

Qualifying event: An event which qualifies employees and/or their dependents to continued health benefits coverage under their employers' health benefits plan. See **Consolidated Omnibus Budget Reconciliation Act of 1985.**

Quality circle: A group of employees who voluntarily meets on company time to discuss various topics such as production problems and suggestions to eliminate them.

Quality of worklife: A generic term that includes various management initiatives to improve organizational efficiency and increase employee job satisfaction.

Quid pro quo sexual harassment: See **Sexual harassment.**

Quota: A number or proportion of jobs that are arbitrarily assigned to groups of individuals.

Race: The five racial categories on federal agency forms are American Indian or Alaska Native, Asian, Black or African American, Native Hawaiian or Other Pacific Islander, and White. "Hispanic or Latino" is the only ethnicity category.

Railway Labor Act of 1926: Provides the right of railroad and air carrier employees to organize and bargain collectively; permits agreements between carriers and unions to establish a union shop and dues check-off, established a National Mediation Board and provides a procedure for arbitrating disputes.

Ratio reinforcement: Reinforcing a behavior each *time* it occurs. See **Behaviorism** and **Schedules of reinforcement.**

Ratio scale: A type of scale used in research in which the interval values are equal in the measurement method being used and the variable being measured. See **Interval scale, Nominal scale,** and **Ordinal scale.**

Real wages: A term used in economics to denote the amount of goods and services that can be bought with money wages. Real wages take into account any changes in value of money wages and the changes in the prices of goods and services.

Reasonable accommodation: A change in the employment application process, in the work environment or in the manner of providing the benefits of employment that would enable a qualified individual with a disability to enjoy equal employment opportunities.

Recruitment: The HRM activity concerned with developing sources of qualified applicants.

Red-circle: Paying an employee more than the maximum of the pay range for his or her job; the opposite of *green-circle.* See **Gold circle, Green circle,** and **Silver circle.**

Red flag items: Items on an employment application, such as gaps in years of employment, which warrant further scrutiny.

Reference: A person listed by a job applicant who can furnish pertinent information about the applicant's qualifications.

Rehabilitation Act: A federal law that prohibits discrimination in the employment of the handicapped by employers with federal contracts of $10,000 or more; also requires reasonable accommodation in the employment of the handicapped by such employers. See **Reasonable accommodation.**

Reinforcement: The process of recognizing and responding to behavior so desired acts will be learned and repeated, and undesirable ones will not.

Reliability: A property of an HRM instrument, like a test or job evaluation system, to produce consistent results in repeated measurements.

Religion: In equal employment opportunity law, includes religious beliefs, observances, and practices involving moral or ethical definitions as to what is right or wrong and which are sincerely held with the strength of traditional religious views.

Relocation counseling: The process of assisting employees in the economic, social, and psychological adjustments required by job relocation.

Remedy: A nonpunitive form of relief, such as back pay and restoration of other rights that were improperly denied due to illegal discrimination. See **Sanction.**

Repatriate: A person who is returning to his or her home country from employment in another country.

Repatriation: The process of preparing a person to return to his or her home country from an assignment in another country.

Report-in pay: The amount of pay that employees receive for reporting for work as scheduled, even if there is no work available.

Representative: As defined in the National Labor Relations Act, "any individual or labor organization."

Research: The investigation of a subject to determine facts and theories and/or to find practical ways to apply facts and theories.

Research methods: The methods used in conducting research. See **Case study, Causal research, Correlation study, Experiment** and **Literature review.**

Restricted stock plan: A type of deferred compensation in which an employer gives stock to an executive that is subject or "restricted" to the executive meeting certain conditions. See **Stock option.**

Retirement counseling: The process of assisting employees in preparing for the financial, psychological and social problems resulting from the transition from working to retirement.

Retirement plan: A generic term for a benefit plan that provides income for employees upon reaching an age at which they no longer desire to work or are unable to work; sometimes synonymously used with the term *pension.*

Return-to-work agreement: An agreement between an employer and employee, who is a drug abuser, in which the employee agrees to certain stipulations, such as regularly attending counseling sessions and submitting to drug testing, in return for continued employment.

Reverse discrimination: A term used to describe the use of quotas in employment decisions, typically to remedy past discrimination.

Right-to-work law: A term used to describe state laws enacted under Section 14(b) of the National Labor Relations Act which states the right to enact laws that permitted employees (except for prehire agreements in the construction industry) to individually decide if they wanted to join a union that represented their employer's workforce. See **Labor-Management Relations Act,** and **Union security.**

Robbery: Placing a victim in a state of fear or using force or threat of force to attempt to take or to take something of value in a personal confrontation with the victim.

Role: The behavior expected from someone because of his or her social position.

Role conflict: Internal conflict within a person caused by assuming different roles. **Intraperson role conflict** results when a person's expected role is incompatible with his or her values or beliefs. **Intrarole conflict** occurs when members of a role set differ on how a person's role should be performed. **Interrole conflict** is caused by people fulfilling multiple roles.

Role set: The people with whom a person regularly interacts in assuming a particular role.

Roth IRA: A nondeductible individual retirement account in which the tax advantages are "backloaded" and interest and dividends are tax-free.

Rucker formula: This gain sharing formula used in the Rucker plan—(net sales value of current production minus the costs for materials, supplies and services consumed) divided by the total employment costs of the employee population in the plan, including wages, salaries payroll taxes and all benefits.

Rucker plan: A gain sharing plan developed in 1933 by Allen Rucker, which includes a consideration of the "value added by manufacture." See **Value added by manufacture** and **Rucker formula.**

Rule: A written or unwritten standard to which employees are expected to conform.

Safety: The process of providing working conditions and requiring work act to prevent occupational accidents.

Safety audit: A comprehensive evaluation of an organization's entire safety and health program.

Safety inspection: A periodic evaluation of various departments or operational units to determine if any unsafe or unhealthy conditions exist and whether safety and health procedures are being followed.

Salary: Direct compensation paid on a regular time interval without a consideration of any specific units of output; sometimes used to distinguish employees (salaried) who are not covered by a collective bargaining agreement or in some cases, are exempt from the overtime provisions of the Fair Labor Standards Act. Also called *base salary* or *base pay.*

Salary continuation plan: A short-term disability plan that continues an employee's full salary for short periods of time, typically ranging up to a year; sometimes also called *sick leave.*

Salt: A union member or person who may be paid by a union to obain employment with a nonunion employer for the purpose of helping to organize the firm's employees. Also referred to as *salting agent.* In *NLRB v. Town & Country Electric, Inc.* (1995), the U.S. Supreme Court found the arrangement to be legal.

Sanction: A penalty imposed on an employer who fails to meet legal requirements of antidiscrimination laws. The two types are *compensatory* and *punitive*

Savings or thrift plans: A benefit plan in which employee contributions, up to a stipulated amount, are matched up to 100 percent by the employer.

Scanlon plan: A gain sharing plan developed by Joseph N. Scanlon that shares with employees any gains resulting to the organization from a reduction in payroll costs as a percentage of the value of production.

Scanlon ratio: The gain sharing ratio used in the Scanlon plan to share gains with employees; determined by dividing labor costs by the sales value of production.

Schedules of reinforcement: The frequency and other means of using the various reinforcement alternatives espoused by behaviorism. See *Behaviorism.*

Scientific personnel: See **Professional and Scientific Personnel.**

Second-injury funds: Funds that reimburse employers for the differences between the total compensation benefits and the partial compensation benefits that would have been paid had an employee not been previously disabled while working for another employer.

Secondary boycott: A generic term, that includes *secondary picketing*, for an activity, such as threats and refusing to work, directed at a secondary employer to induce the employer to take action that pressures the primary employer to concede to a union demand.

Secondary picketing: Picketing an employer's (Company A or secondary employer) premises because the employer does business with another employer (Company B or primary employer) with which the union in question has a labor problem; may be legal or illegal depending upon the circumstances.

Security: The domestic and international protection of an organization's assets, its employees and the property of employees on the employers' premises

Selected Characteristics of Occupations Defined in the Dictionary of Occupational Titles: A supplementary volume to the Directory of Occupational Titles (DOT) that provides information about the physical demands, environmental conditions, mathematical and language development training and specific vocational preparation for jobs listed in the DOT.

Selection: The HRM activity concerned with choosing people for jobs, positions or assignments after comparing their qualifications with the job specifications.

Selection method: One technique used to guide management in making selection decisions.

Selection procedure: Defined in the *Uniform Guidelines On Employee Selection Procedures* as any measure, combination of measures, or procedures used as a basis for any employment decision. This definition combines both selection method and selection process. See **Selection method** and **Selection process.**

Selection process: The arrangement of selection procedures used in choosing people for positions or assignments.

Selection ratio: A measure of applicant quality, computed by dividing the number of new hires for a period for a particular job by the number of qualified applicants for the job during the same period.

Self-funding: A system of employee benefits coverage in which the employer pays benefit claims directly from the employer's own assets.

Semantic differential scale: A type of interval scale used in research in which the numerical scale represents opposites in adjectives describing an attitude object. See **Interval scale.**

Sensory test: A test that measures a person's hearing or vision. See **Test.**

Service Contract Act of 1965: A federal law requiring contractors or subcontractors, who have contracts that exceed $2,500 for providing services to the federal government, to pay wages and provide benefits that are at least equal to those prevailing in the area.

Settlement option: An alternative method of paying the proceeds from an insurance policy, that is given to the beneficiary, in the event of the death of the insured.

Severance pay: Pay that an employee receives upon termination from employment with the organization due to job abolishment or any reason other than a resignation or being discharged for cause.

Sex: In employment discrimination, refers to male and female and not a person's preference for sexual relations.

Sex-based compensation equity: The equitable treatment of members of both sexes in all aspects of compensation.

Sex-based pay equity: The equitable treatment of members of both sexes in all aspects of pay administration.

Sexual harassment: The two types of sexual harassment are *hostile environment sexual harassment* and *quid pro quo sexual harassment*. *Hostile environment sexual harassment* is unwelcome sexual advances or sexually-based conduct which: (1) creates an intimidating, hostile, or offensive work environment, or (2) unreasonably interferes with an employee's work. *Quid pro quo sexual harassment* is requests for sexual favors, and other physical or other types of conduct of a sexual nature when: (1) submission to such conduct is made either explicitly or implicitly a term or condition of an individual's employment, or (2) submission to or rejection of such conduct by an individual is used as the basis for employment decisions affecting the person.

Shift differential: An addition to the base rate for work performed on a shift other than the day shift.

Sign-on bonus: A lump-sum cash payment used as an inducement in recruiting employees with specialized qualifications who are short in supply.

Silver circle: Paying an employee above the maximum of the pay range as a reward for superseniority or long tenure. See **Gold circle, Green circle,** and **Red circle.**

Simple assault: An attack, in which a weapon is not used, in which the victim is not seriously injured.

Simulation: A generic form of human resources development encompassing a number of worklife situations used in leaderless group situations, competitive group exercises, in-basket exercises, computer gaming and role-playing. Also used in selection procedures. See **Computer gaming, Human resources development, In-basket, Leaderless group situation,** and **Roleplaying.**

Situational interview: A type of employment interview in which questions about job situations are posed to applicants and they are asked to explain how they would respond.

Skill: In job specifications, typically defined as performance in accordance with a standard or a present observable competence to perform a learned psychomotor act; in job evaluation may include such areas as experience, training, education, and ability.

Skill-based pay: A method of rewarding employees for the number of skills they possess, such as carpentry skills, electrician skills, or plumbing skills.

Society for Human Resource Management: An organization dedicated to objectives for the advancement of the profession of human resources management. Address: 606 N. Washington St., Alexandria, VA 22314.

Society for Human Resource Management/International: The international chapter of the Society for Human Resource Management with the goals of aiding the standards of performance in all phases of international personnel administration.

Specific Vocational Preparation: As defined by the Department of Labor method of job analysis, the amount of training needed to learn the techniques, acquire the knowledge, and develop the facility to satisfactorily perform the tasks in a job.

Spiral careerist: A person who envisions his or her career as a movement among different occupations. See also **Linear careerist, Steady state careerist,** and **Transition careerist.**

Split-half reliability method: A method of reliability measurement accomplished by dividing a test in half and correlating responses (typically the even-numbered items correlated with the odd-numbered ones). See **Reliability.**

Staff authority: The right to use organization resources in advising others concerning how particular tasks can be accomplished.

Staffing firm: A firm that recruits and employs individuals who are then assigned to client firms who wholly or partially control their working conditions. Includes temporary employment agencies, contract employment firms, facilities staffing firms, and leasing or payrolling firms.

Stages of recovery: The progression of steps from shock to acceptance which victims experience in recovering from a traumatic event.

Standard value hours: The number of hours in the Improshare plan allotted to produce a set amount of output. Determined by multiplying the number of units of output of a product by the work hour standard. See **Improshare** and **Work hour standard.**

Steady state careerist: A person who has career interests that emphasize increased competency in the existing job, recognition of the value of the tasks being performed and the maintenance of employment. Also see **Linear careerist, Spiral careerist,** and **Transition careerist.**

Stereotyping: The tendency of people to make conclusions about others based upon some particular characteristic, such as their race or age.

Stock appreciation rights: A type of option typically reserved for executives, which gives the executive the "right" to any appreciation in the value of a stipulated number of shares of stock at the end of a certain period of time. See **Stock option.**

Stock Option: An agreement by an employer to sell an employee, usually an executive or manager, a certain number of shares of stock at a designed price within a specified period of time. See **Nonqualified or nonstatutory stock option, Restricted stock plan, Incentive stock option, Stock appreciation rights, Performance shares, Phantom Stock,** and **Employee stock purchase plan.**

Stop limit: A provision in major medical plans that pays 100 percent of all covered expenses after a specified dollar amount of out-of-pocket expenses have been paid by the insured.

Straight commission: A pay incentive with a fixed percentage of the sales price of the product/service that is sold.

Straight ranking method: A performance appraisal system characterized by the systematic ordering of employees from best to worst, based upon some single global statement of performance.

Strategic planning: The process of defining market strategies and developing production systems and an organizational structure to accomplish the strategies within an internal and external environment. Included in the process are defining mission statements, goals, objectives, and policies.

Strategy: A long-run plan to achieve a goal.

Stress: A nonspecific bodily reaction to a stimulus.

Stress interview: A type of interview in which stress is induced in the process to determine how the applicant will respond to it.

Strike: See **Work stoppage.**

Succession planning: The process of identifying and developing candidates to fill the key jobs in an organization.

Suggestion program: A formal program to solicit, evaluate, implement, and reward employees for their ideas to improve the organization.

Summative evaluation: A type of evaluation usually conducted at the conclusion of a course, training program, or independent module of a program or course, which provides a summary account of a student's/participant's learning. Examples of summative assessment methods include final examinations, student's/participant's assessments of learning accomplishments, or operation/ maintenance of equipment which was the subject of the training. See **Formative evaluation.**

Supervisor: As defined in the National Labor Relations Act, "any individual having authority, in the interest of the employer, to hire, transfer, suspend, lay off, recall, promote, discharge, assign, reward, or discipline other employees, or responsibly to direct them or to adjust their grievances, or effectively to recommend such action, if in connection with the foregoing the exercise of such authority is not of a merely routine or clerical nature, but requires the use of independent judgment."

Supplemental major medical coverage: Medical coverage that pays for a broad range of services and a substantial portion of catastrophic illness and which is coordinated with basic medical coverage.

Supplemental unemployment benefits: Payments made to employees, which are in addition to any unemployment compensation, for either temporary or permanent discontinuance of employment for causes beyond an employee's control.

Surface bargaining: Conducting collective bargaining without a serious intent to reach an agreement.

Survivor income benefit insurance: Insurance that provides a death benefit in the form of a monthly income to the beneficiary.

Suspension: Placing an employee in a non-pay status due to more serious and/ or repeated deficiencies in job performance.

Tactical planning: Short-term planning, including both proactive and reactive planning necessary to meet long-term organizational goals.

Tarasoff case: A judicial ruling which found that professional counselors are expected to report threats of imminent physical violence made by clients toward other persons or themselves.

Task: A comprehensive part of a job; comprised of one or more elements. See **Element.**

Tax equalization: The corporate taxation policy toward expatriates with the goal of adjusting their compensation so they pay neither more nor less income taxes than they would in their home country.

Tax reduction: The corporate taxation policy that depending upon the country involved: (1) permits expatriates to gain from the differences in income taxes in their home countries and the country to which they are assigned, or (2) adjusts the compensation of expatriates so they experience no loss in income as a result of the net effect of income taxes, both foreign and their home country.

Taylor Differential Piece-Rate Plan: A pay incentive plan developed by Frederick W. Taylor which was composed of two piece-rates; a low rate for work that was less than standard and a high one for all work above it.

Team-building: The process of using facilitators to guide ad hoc teams of employees in addressing organizational goals and problems.

Temperament: According to the Department of Labor method of job analysis, one of the eleven personal characteristics a job requires a person to possess in order that the tasks in a job can be satisfactorily performed.

Terrorism: is ". . . the unlawful use of force and violence against person or property to intimidate or coerce a government, the civilian population, or any segment thereof, in furtherance of political or social objectives" (Code of Federal Regulations). Another widely used definition contained in Title 22 of the U. S. Code defines terrorism as the "premeditated, politically motivated violence perpetrated against noncombatant targets by subnational groups or clandestine agents."

Test: A generic word encompassing a systematic method of measuring a person's qualifications through pencil and paper instruments, oral questions, the performance of exercises and the manipulation of objects.

Test fairness: See **Fairness.**

Test-retest measure of reliability: A method of reliability measurement in which the same selection method is administered more than once and the scores are correlated. See **Reliability.**

The International Foundation of Employee Benefit Plans: A nonprofit educational association with the goals of exchanging informa tion and educating people who manage employee benefit plans or work with them; the organization offers the Certified Employee Benefit Specialist designation. Address is 18700 West Bluemound Road, P.O. Box 69, Brookfield, WI 53008-0069.

The World Federation of Personnel Management Associations: An organization formed by representatives from the European Association for Personnel Management, the Interamerican Federation of Personnel Administration, and the Society for Human Resource Management for the purpose of achieving stated objectives.

Things: As used in the Department of Labor method of job analysis, the Worker Function which deals with living objects such as substances or materials, machines, tools, equipment and products.

Third-country national: A citizen of one country who is employed in another country by a firm that is headquartered in still a different country.

Time-span of discretion: A job evaluation method developed by Eliott Jaques in which the worth of a job is determined by the amount of time during which an employee can perform the job tasks without requiring supervision.

360° appraisal: A method of performance appraisal in which input is obtained from each significant public with which the employee interacts, such as customers, peers, and supervisors.

Title VII of the Civil Rights Act of 1964: A federal law covering employers with 15 or more employees and who are engaged in interstate commerce, that prohibits discrimination on the basis of national origin, race, color, religion and sex; also covered are employment agencies and unions.

Title VII of the Civil Service Reform Act: A federal law covering federal employees other than those in the U.S. Postal Service, the Tennessee Valley Authority, the Foreign Service of the United States and certain investigative agencies; deals with various issues concerning recognition of unions, determining bargaining units, and defining unfair labor practices.

Tools: As used in the Department of Labor method of job analysis, the implements which are manipulated to do work or move materials.

Total compensation: Concept of employers including both the direct and indirect aspects of compensation in compensation planning.

Training: Formal or informal learning necessary for the performance of specific job tasks; See **Specific vocational preparation.**

Transitional careerist: A person who sees his or her career as movements among different organizations in either the same or different occupations. Also see **Linear careerist, Spiral careerist,** and **Steady state careerist.**

Tripartite arbitration: An arrangement in resolving labor-management disputes in which one arbitrator is selected to a panel by the union and one by management. Those two arbitrators then select a third member, who is presumed to be an impartial person. Sometimes, other arrangements are used to select the panel. Regardless of the method used, the purpose of the process is to select a panel that both sides will view as fair.

Two-tier compensation plans: pay plans that provide one level of compensation for existing employees and a lower level of compensation for newly hired employees.

Unemployment compensation: A mandatory employee benefit plan that provides weekly cash benefits to qualified workers during periods of involuntary unemployment.

Unfair labor practice: An employer or union practice specified in the National Labor Relations Act which is prohibited.

Uniform Guidelines on Employee Selection Procedures: A set of guidelines released in 1978 by the U.S. Equal Employment Opportunity Commission to assist employers, labor organizations, employment agencies, and licensing and certification boards in complying with the requirements of Federal law prohibiting discriminatory employment practices.

Uniformed Services Employment and Reemployment Rights Act of 1994: A federal law that prohibits discrimination against a person who is a member of, applies to be a member of, performs, has performed, applies to perform, or has an obligation to perform service in a U.S. uniformed service.

Union: An organization of employees who have some common interests, like collectively bargaining with their employer over the terms and conditions of employment. Used synonymously with labor organization. See **Craft union, Industrial union, Local union, National union,** and **White-collar union.**

Union recognition: The process through which unions become certified or decertified to represent a group of employees.

Union security: A provision in union contracts, unless prohibited by a state right-to-work law, that helps ensure the union of a regular source of membership. See **Agency shop, Closed shop, Maintenance of membership, Prehire agreement, Right-to-work law,** and **Union shop.**

Union shop: A union security arrangement in which continued employment is conditional upon the employee becoming a member of the union representing the employer's workforce in that type of work. In *NLRB v. General Motors* (1963), the U.S. Supreme ruled that those workers who were employed under a *union shop* arrangement satisfied the requirements of the arrangement if they paid the initiation fee and dues to the union, even if they chose not to belong to the union or otherwise support or "join" the union. See **Agency shop, Closed shop, Maintenance of membership,** and **Prehire agreement.**

Unit benefit trusteed or insured plan: A retirement plan that provides retirement benefits based upon the accumulation of units of retirement credits earned from years of service or the amount of earnings or a combination of the two.

Usual, customary and reasonable charges: The pre-determined schedule of fees that are typically paid under a surgical expense plan.

Utilities allowance: Additional pay given to expatriates to compensate them for any added utilities expenses incurred in a foreign assignment.

Valence: values that people assign to different outcomes that may be either positive or negative. See **Expectancy theory.**

Validity: The property that an HRM instrument or method has if it accurately measures the dimension which it purports to measure. See **Construct validity, Content validity, Criterion-related validity,** and **Differential validity.**

Value: The component of organization culture that is an opinion based upon such judgments as the relative worth of different intrinsic and extrinsic rewards.

Value added: More precisely, the term "value added by manufacture," is used in economics for the value that is added to a product through manufacture.

Vandalism: Willful destruction of real or personal property.

Variable: The object of research. *Dependent variable* is one that is influenced by one or more independent variables. *Independent variable* is one that influences a dependent variable. *Moderating variable* is one that influences or "moderates" the effect of an independent variable upon a dependent one.

Verification: A selection method used to check the accuracy of information furnished by job applicants.

Vestibule training: A human resource development method in which simulated training consoles, or less often actual equipment, is placed in rooms (like vestibules) away from the work area, and used to train operators.

Vesting: A participant's nonforfeitable right to benefits upon termination of employment or upon reaching the normal retirement age.

Video interview: A type of employment interview that is conducted live through video-conferencing, often involving a panel of interviewers.

Vietnam Era Veterans Readjustment Assistance Act of 1974: A federal law that: (1) prohibits discrimination against veterans and (2) requires affirmative action in the employment of veterans by federal contractors with contracts of $100,000 or more; remedies include withholding contract payments, terminating contracts, barring future contracts, and paying back pay and granting employment.

Wage and Hour Division: A division of the Employment Standards Division of the U.S. Department of Labor that is responsible for enforcing such laws as the Fair Labor Standards Act, Davis-Bacon and Related Acts, Walsh-Healey Public Contracts Act, McNamara-O'hara Service Contract Act, and the Employee Polygraph Protection Act.

Wages: The term typically used to describe payments to workers for shorter time periods, such as hourly.

Wages Fund Theory: A theory developed by John Stuart Mill (1806-1873), supposing that the real wage of workers depends upon both the magnitude of the fund, that is the amount of capital set aside to pay workers, and the number of workers who are employed.

Waiting period: The length of time in a disability benefit plan, after the onset of a disability before benefit payments begin.

Waiver of premium: A provision in life insurance policies for the continuation of the policy if the employee becomes disabled.

Walsh-Healey Act of 1938: A federal law requiring adherence to (1) selected provisions of the Fair Labor Standards Act and (2) certain decisions of the Occupational Safety and Health Administration, by contractors, manufacturers and dealers who furnish the federal government with supplies, materials, articles and equipment in which the contract exceeds $10,000.

Weighted application blank: A type of employment application form in which answers to the various questions have different values depending upon the response. See **Biographical information blank.**

Weighted checklist method: A variation of the checklist method of performance appraisal in which weights are assigned to various levels of favorable and unfavorable performance.

Weighted graphic rating scales: A graphic rating scales method of performance appraisal in which the different performance variables are weighted differently. See **Graphic rating scales.**

Wellness: The state of personal, mental, and physical well-being as a result of employer and employee commitment to complete human health in both nonworklife and worklife.

Wellness program: A program designed to achieve personal mental and physical well being as a result of employer and employee commitment to complete human health in both nonworklife and worklife.

Whistleblowing: A term for employee disclosures of illegal or improper acts within an organization.

White-collar union: A generic term for a union of workers in such fields as clerical workers or teachers, like the American Federal of Teachers. See **Craft union** and **Industrial union.**

Win-back sales commission: A sales commission that focuses on regaining sales from former customers who are presently buying from a competitor.

Work aids: As defined in the Department of Labor method of job analysis, the miscellaneous items necessary for the accomplishment of work but that do not fit the definition of *Machines, Tools,* or *Equipment.*

Work fields: As used in the Department of Labor method of job analysis, the 100 classifications into which all work is categorized.

Work hour standard: The average number of hours or fraction of an hour which are/is necessary to produce one unit of output over a base period in the Improshare plan. See **Improshare.**

Work Hours and Safety Standards Act of 1962: A federal law that requires contractors who have contracts for work that is partly or wholly financed by the federal government to pay overtime for hours in excess of 40 per week; such employers are prohibited from requiring employees to work in conditions that are unsanitary, hazardous, or dangerous to their health.

Work Performed: The category in the Department of Labor method of job analysis consisting of: (1) Worker Functions, (2) Work Fields and (3) Materials, Products, Subject Matter and Services.

Work sample: An exercise used for such purposes as selection or human resources development, in which participants perform job tasks representative of either a job they are seeking or one for which they are being trained. See **Content validity** and **Work simulation.**

Work sampling: A statistical sampling method used to collect information on various aspects of a job, in which the work day is divided into equal time intervals and then random samples, at various times of the day, are made of the tasks being performed by employees in the sample.

Work simulation: An exercise used for such purposes as selection or human resources development, in which participants perform tasks that simulate the tasks and conditions of a job they are either seeking or are being trained to perform. See **Content validity** and **Work sample.**

Work stoppage: A cessation of work caused by either a **strike** or **lockout.** A **strike** is a concerted effort by employees in a bargaining unit not to return to work. A **lockout** is a tactic by management to prevent employees from returning to work by locking the premises and refusing them access to the business.

Worker Adjustment and Retraining Notification Act: A federal law that applies to firms with 100 or more full-time employees, requiring that advance notification be given in the event of a plant closing or a mass layoff to (1) all employees or their representative, if there is one, (2) the State dislocated worker unit under Title III of the Job Training Partnership Act and (3) the chief elected official in the locally affected political unit. See **Loss of employment, Mass layoff,** and **Plant closure.**

Worker functions: As used in the Department of Labor method of job analysis, the three essential functions that relate to (1) data, (2) people and (3) things, that exist in all jobs.

Worker traits: According to the Department of Labor method of job analysis, the requirements made upon workers in order for them to perform their jobs in a satisfactory manner, synonymous with *job specifications.*

Workers' Compensation: A compulsory employee benefit that provides medical care, monthly income replacement, and rehabilitation services to workers for job-related injuries or sickness as well as income benefits to survivors of workers whose death is job-related.

Workforce characteristics: Part of the internal planning environment that are: (1) human capital of the organization (such as training and education), (2) personal attributes (such as creativity and motivation), and (3) demographics (like race, sex, and age).

Workplace violence: Conduct in the workplace against employers and employees committed by persons who either have an employment- related connection with the establishment or are outsiders. Such violence includes: (1) physical acts against personal or employer property; (2) verbal threats or profanation, or vicious statements which are meant to harm or cause a hostile environment; (3) written threats, profanation, vicious cartoons or notes, and other written conduct of intense distortion which is meant to threaten or create a hostile environment; or (4) visual acts which are threatening or intended to convey injury or hostility.

WorldatWork A non-profit organization of HRM professionals whose job tasks entail the design, implementation, and management of compensation; the organization offers the Certified Compensation Professional designation. Address is P.O. Box 1176, Scottsdale, AZ 85252.

Zero-base budget: A financial plan in which all expenditures must be justified; as opposed to *base-line budget*.

Zipper clause: A clause in collective bargaining agreements that stipulates that the parties agree that no item absent from the existing agreement will be a subject for midterm bargaining; that is, it cannot be part of the bargaining until negotiations are reopened upon the expiration date of the current agreement.

TOPICAL INDEX